The Traveler's Handbook

Edited by
Miranda Haines

Assistant Editor
Sarah Thorowgood

The Globe Pequot Press

Old Saybrook, Connecticut

This completely revised and enlarged edition first published in 1997.

Library of Congress Cataloging-in-Publication Data
The traveller's handbook. -- 7th ed./edited by Miranda Haines: assistant editor, Sarah Thorowgood.
p. cm.
Rev. ed. of: The traveler's handbook, 6th ed. 1994.
"A Wexas publication."
Includes bibliographical references and index.
ISBN 0-7627-0145-5
1. Travel I Haines, Miranda. II. Thorowgood, Sarah. III. Traveler's handbook.
G151.T7.2 1997
910'.2'02--dc21   97-29544 CIP

Every effort has been made to ensure that the facts in this Handbook are accurate. However, travellers should still obtain advice from consulates, airines etc. about current travel and visa requirements and conditions before travelling. The editors and publishers cannot accept responsibility for any loss, injury or inconvenience, however caused.

ISBN 0-7627-0145-5

Cover designed by Wylie Design Co., London

Seventh edition/first printing

Printed and bound in Great Britain by
Clays Ltd., Bungay, Suffolk.

CONTENTS

GETTING THERE BY AIR
Chapter 4

GETTING THERE BY ROAD
Chapter 5

GETTING THERE BY OTHER MEANS
Chapter 6

GREAT JOURNEYS OVERLAND
Chapter 7

PAPERWORK AND MONEY
Chapter 8

A PLACE TO STAY
Chapter 9

A BASIC GUIDE TO HEALTH
Chapter 10

EQUIPPING FOR A TRIP
Chapter 11

COMMUNICATIONS
Chapter 12

WHEN THINGS GO WRONG
Chapter 13

TRAVEL WRITING, FILM AND PHOTOGRAPHY
Chapter 14

AND FINALLY...
Chapter 15

DIRECTORY

GETTING THERE BY AIR
Section 4

GETTING THERE BY ROAD
Section 5

GETTING THERE BY OTHER MEANS
Section 6

GREAT JOURNEYS OVERLAND
Section 7

PAPERWORK AND MONEY
Section 8

A PLACE TO STAY
Section 9

A BASIC GUIDE TO HEALTH
Section 10

EQUIPPING FOR A TRIP
Section 11

COMMUNICATIONS
Section 12

WHEN THINGS GO WRONG
Section 13

TRAVEL WRITING, FILM AND PHOTOGRAPHY
Section 14

AND FINALLY...
Section 15

AROUND THE WORLD

Foreword by Michael Palin

"Is there anywhere you haven't been?" This is the most common question I am asked when the subject of travel comes up. I usually reply 'Scunthorpe'. It is easier than saying most of the world. And it's equally true. The trouble is that people think I have been everywhere because they have seen me going everywhere on television. And most of us tend to believe what we see on television. Well, of course I have been around a bit. Seventy-one countries at the last count. But travel is much more than just country-spotting. It's much more than a series of ticks on a check list.

Paradoxically, the more I travel in the world the less of the world I feel I have seen. Travel is a constantly frustrating business. It is like studying a catalogue of fine clothes or a good menu. It opens up a world of tantalising choices. The more I know about a place the more I want to go there, and the more I go there the more I want to know about it. I can never walk through a strange city or town without wishing I had taken this turning instead of that or eaten at this restaurant instead of that or walked up one hill instead of another. It's the nature of the beast. It is also what makes travelling such a total, all-pervading, limitless pleasure. Unlike many of life's other enjoyments, travel does not have to be specific, nor does it even have to have a defined aim or purpose or end product. You can say you want to see the world, but you never will. No-one can.

But the number of little worlds to see is more than enough to keep you happy. Coming across a procession of twenty foot high wooden effigies of saints being carried through the streets of Cuzco, getting lost in the Alhambra in Granada and finding your way back by the lights on the Alhambra Hill, lying on the rim of the Victoria Falls watching what happens to a thousand tons of water when it plunges over a three hundred foot precipice, seeing a woman combing her child's hair beside the Perfume River at Hue. All these were happy unplanned accidents.

Good travel should be distracting and diverting, constantly offering prospects and experiences and alternatives and temptations. If you are not prepared every now and then to be taken somewhere you never expected, then you might as well not set out.

The Traveller's Handbook offers all sorts of delights and all sorts of information essential to the enjoyment of these delights. I know of no single volume which manages to pack so much travel advice between two covers, and still weigh the same as a water-bottle. No-one can tell you everything about travel – you must make your own adventure – but no-one will tell you more than the vast array of the wise and well-informed who have contributed to this bulging travel bible.

Michael Palin, London, March 1997

INTRODUCTION

"Reminds me of my safari in Africa ... somebody forgot the corkscrew and for several days we had to live on nothing but food and water." W.C. Fields

The Traveller's Handbook is for every type of travel venture into every kind of situation: should you decide to ride a camel, hitchhike, make a video-diary or go overland by truck – it's all in here! Or should anyone: get abducted; pick the wrong hotel; put their foot in it; eat the wrong kind of chicken; loose their appetite; turn yellow; catch malaria; climb too high; contract HIV; Bilharzia (we could go on) – then this is the ultimate "how-to" guide written by *the* experts in their field.

On the brighter side, there are articles for student, business, independent and elderly travellers, with new pieces about Gourmet Travel, Gay Travel, Diplomatic Travel, Travelling in Style and Festivals. And all the most usual (and unusual) questions are answered: What will the weather be like? What sort of equipment is needed? How high is that city? Who publishes the best books? Guide or Porter?

The book is divided into two sections: the first is a collection of "how-to-do-it" articles and, the second, a Directory, that is laden with useful names and addresses relating to specific types of travel. For example, if you wish to be a Green Traveller, read article on page 80, and then turn to page 707 of the Directory for the relevant organisations and contacts. For the first time, the articles are cross-referenced to the Directory (which includes email and web site addresses) to make it more user-friendly. Other new articles include: The Polar Traveller (written and faxed from an Antarctic hut); The World Impact of Tourism; The Musical Traveller; Surviving a Kidnap and to take us into the future, The Cyberspace Traveller.

Bon voyage into the millennium!

Miranda Haines and Sarah Thorowgood

WHERE AND WHEN
Chapter 1

PLACES IN VOGUE

by Miranda Haines

When the Halifax building society floated on the stockmarket, all the share-holders who cashed their shares worth an average of £2,300, said that over-seas holidays were top of their shopping list (then came electrical goods). Gone are the days when gleaming fridges, cars and televisions were luxury items. Now that these domestic trappings are a given, the holiday has become an ulti-mate status symbol for the millenium. And, naturally, it cannot be just any-where.

Today, it is the growing number of independent travellers, rather than the fashionable elite, who trailblaze to the most secluded and beautiful beaches only to abandon them at the drop of a Prada rucksack and hop off to the latest "in" hotspot. Then come the tour operators following quickly in their wake to kick-start development for tourists on a larger scale and at much cheaper prices. Take the beautiful people's summer playground of the 1920s and 1930s, the French Riviera in the south of France, and see what a sprawling mess of devel-opment it is 60 years on, or, more recently, Thailand.

Low prices have never dictated the Mecca of the fashionable traveller and so places in vogue tend to be expensive far-flung pockets of the globe. However, now that there is such significance attached to travel for the majority rather than a tiny minority, it is all the more important to remember that destinations are victims to the vagaries of fashion and "the good times" are never here to stay.

When Time magazine proclaimed London the most happening city in the world in February 1997, with its mixture of designers, food, clubs, art and Brit pop, it could only have been good news for the economy. There is little doubt that tourism is the future promise for wealth in the millennium. There will be 702 million international arrivals, in the year 2000, according to the World Tourism Organisation and by the year 2010 international arrivals will reach 1.6 billion. A comparitively paltry number, 592 million people, arrived into airports world-wide in 1996, which begs the question: Are there enough exotic locations left to pander to this insatiable vogue for travel, when Thailand, Bali, and Greenland have come and gone?

Trendsetting by the travelling elite is, of course, nothing new, as history relates. George IV made Brighton the place to go for the summer, whereas in the sixties hippies went east, overland to India and Nepal, where drugs, free love and eastern religion became their bent. Searching for their "inner selves" became "in" while being proverbially "out of it". Both places, in turn, have naturally become commonplace and are covered in tourists' debris; high-rise blocks, high prices, environmental destruction and a humdrum that detracts from what made the locations special in the first place.

And as the vogue for travel makes the world a global village, discrepencies in cultures become increasingly marked. While villagers in Karnatica, India continue to converse in Sanskrit, their kids surf the net. The old and new are colliding at such a speed that the world seems, not only a smaller place, but more worryingly, a less mysterious one.

Without the mystery, what still remains à la mode? Now that new-age travel is quite passé, and that eastern spiritualism is "out", it is Danger that is de rigeur. From Colombia to Cambodia there is a new adrenalin junkie generation of independent travellers who are stamping defiantly around guerrilla-infested forests and drug-ridden zones, in search of the ultimate "adventure holiday" while their parents take luxury package tours or gentle jaunts around Europe. With kidnapping and hijacking on the increase the danger is real (read chapters Surviving a Kidnap and Surviving a Hijack if you don't believe me), but the more this new generation of travellers can shock their parents (the hippies) the trendier they must be.

Naturally, if someone else has been there, then it is already too late. Take Vietnam which has all the credentials of a chic nineties destination; newly accessible, steeped in history, literary heroes, exotic and adventurous. Well, I got there a year after the government adopted the doi moi (open door) policy and although I saw the conical islands of Halong Bay, the vendors of freshly baked baguettes in Hanoi and the lush Mekong Delta in the south, already I was too late in the eyes of most travel snobs. Nowhere appears safe from our insatiable desire to be there first – not even planet Mars.

However, it is not just the independent travellers that summon places into vogue. Films, books, photographers, pop-stars, art, all pave the way. Hollywood's present love affair with Chinese occupied Tibet has made it top of any respectable adventurer's list; Martin Scorsese's Kundun; Jean-Jacques Annaud's Seven Years in Tibet; and Bertolucci's Little Buddha starring Keanu Reaves, simply put an outsider's gloss on a serious political situation. Ironically, the travellers that flock to the Dalai Lama's ex-residence, the Potala Palace in Lhasa, as a result of Hollywood's fashionable cry "Free Tibet", are in fact invariably filling the coffers of the Chinese government. Fashionable travel is inevitably politically incorrect.

So where to now? Since suntans are so eighties, naturally the coolest places to go are white. Two travel books set in Antarctica, Sara Wheeler's Terra Incognita and Jenny Diski's Skating to Antarctica set out to prove that there is more to life than a beach. The world's greatest remaining wilderness had 3,000 people visit the continent in 1991. Four years later numbers had jumped to 10,000. This year (1997) 15,000 tourists are expected to take the "penguin trail". Reports of the Brit pop stars, Oasis and Blur, in Iceland for fishing and vodka holidays, is a notable change in style from Mick Jagger's favourite spot, the Caribbean island of Mustique (which is run as a company).

Now that everyone wishes to escape the work-induced stress of our frenetic lives, this "need" for travel in the wake of the fashionable will dictate the tidal waves of more and more places destined to be in vogue. One tip: if you have not booked somewhere for the millennium (chartered a plane to Mexico, booked a castle in Morocco or a trek to the Lost City in Colombia) then you may be forced to stay home and toast the new era from your own hearth. How old-fashioned!

MORAL DILEMMAS OF TRAVEL

by George Monbiot

The main tourist hotel in Dili, the capital of East Timor, is also an army intelligence headquarters. Until recently, East Timorese political prisoners were tortured by Indonesian soldiers in the basement. Uniformed men are dispatched from its rooms to oversee the execution of dissidents.

Yet the Indonesian government is encouraging tourists to visit East Timor and stay in the hotel. Having killed one third of the occupied country's population, having destroyed the people's homes, their crops and their livelihoods, having invented torture techniques that would make the Gestapo wince, the government has managed to achieve a semblance of normality. The East Timorese are, most of the time, too frightened to protest in public. The rebels still holding out against the government are confined to the remotest places. Bringing tourists into East Timor serves both to assure the rest of the world that nothing is amiss and to legitimise the island's illegal occupation.

So should tourists do as the Indonesian government suggests, and visit East Timor? One's immediate response would be no. But the ethics of tourism, here and elsewhere, are complex: the arguments for going may be as compelling as those for staying away.

Tourists visiting East Timor, or any other country subject to the brutal whims of an intractable dictatorship, can swiftly become accessories to inhumanity. The hotel in Dili, for example, is owned by army officers: everyone who pays for a room there puts money straight into the soldiers' pockets. The ignorance in which most tourists are cocooned is infectious: when they go home and tell their family and friends that the beaches were great or the food was disgusting but say nothing about what is happening there, subtly, unwittingly, they help to blot out the efforts of people trying to draw attention to the atrocities.

On the other hand, for the first fifteen years of its occupation, East Timor languished in obscurity. The government could act without constraint, as there were few investigative journalists and human rights workers. The island was visited only by absurd processions of "independent observers" who, neither independent nor observant, were steered around the trouble spots by government minders, and concluded that the place was as peaceful as it appeared to be. The presence of tourists may impose restraints on the government's treatment of the population. It provides a cover under which investigators can work. East Timor becomes, to the outside world, a place, rather than just a name.

The dilemma, of course, is not confined to East Timor. Indonesia is one of scores of tourist destinations in which gross abuses of human rights take place. There is probably not a country in the world for which a reasonable argument for a boycott could not be made. The publishing company Lonely Planet is not producing a guide to Norway, on account of its continued harvest of the minke whales. Both Europeans (pointing to our discharges of pollution), and North Americans, (citing our continued presence in Northern Ireland), have called for a tourist boycott of Great Britain. The argument for a boycott of countries already subject to public scrutiny appears to be less clouded than the argument for a boycott of countries left out of the public eye.

At first sight, it would seem that a distinction can be drawn between the ethics of organised tours and the ethics of independent travel. Organised tour operators ensure that their customers are insulated from the unexpected. Nothing is supposed to happen which is not scheduled to happen. Tourists are kept away from trouble spots and seldom interact with anyone, other than those who serve or sell to them. Backpackers, on the other hand, claim to seek out the unexpected. In theory, they are more likely to stumble across atrocities, or meet people who can tell them what is happening. Yet the question is complicated by a further factor, for tourism is not just a means by which oppression can be either masked or exposed. Tourism itself can become an instrument of destruction.

In June 1993 the Burmese town of Pagan was emptied of its inhabitants. The State Law and Order Restoration Council, which intends to make Pagan one of the principal destinations for Visit Myanmar Year (1995) decided to spare tourists the inconvenience and unsightliness of human beings. The townspeople, whose ancestors built the very attraction the tourists will visit, were forcibly evacuated and their homes destroyed. There was no compensation.

Such clearances are a common component of national tourist industries. All over South East Asia, farms, forests, villages, even suburbs, have been destroyed to make way for golf courses. Slums are razed for fear of offending visitors. In many parts of Africa, conservation is used to justify the creation of new parks and reserves for tourism. Their inhabitants are excluded from the lands they have possessed for centuries, re-entering, in Kenya, on pain of death.

It is not just the people's land but also their culture which is expropriated for tourism by unscrupulous governments. During the 1980's, the longhouses of the Asmat people of Irian Jaya, in Indonesia, were destroyed and their traditional ceremonies were proscribed. In 1991, the government launched Visit Indonesia Year. Realising that tourists want to see how the country's ethnic peoples lived, it instructed the Asmat to rebuild their longhouses and perform ceremonies for the tourists. If they refused, they were beaten or imprisoned. Those who assumed that this meant they could once more start worshipping their ancestors were sadly mistaken: if they performed any ceremonies for their own purposes, they were, again, beaten or imprisoned.

While these are extreme examples, tourism is, wherever it occurs, an extractive industry. It extracts the differences between our land and culture and those of the nations we visit, until they scarcely exist. Remote and romantic beaches become mundane resorts. Remote and remarkable people tailor their culture to suit those who pay for it, until, in the words of the Maasai man, "We have ceased to be what we are; we are becoming what we seem." The exotic, of course, is illusory: as we approach it, it disappears. Tourism, therefore, will never be sated, even when it has penetrated the remotest parts of the world.

While organised tours may be most directly responsible for the muffling of diversity, it is the backpackers who blaze the trail they follow. An independent traveller's destination becomes a mainstream resort within a few years. Indeed, as travel becomes easier and tourists more adventurous, the distinction between the two groups is breaking down: hundreds of tour companies organise journeys which mimic those of independent travellers. Neither category —if they can be categorised — is blameless.

None of the ethical questions tourism raises can be easily answered. Tour organisers have justified their work to me on the grounds that it is a "cultural exchange". Yet what I have seen of their activities suggests that no cultural exchange is taking place. While the visitors get culture, their hosts, if they are lucky, get money. As identity is rooted in place, the tourists have little to offer.

Other people claim that tourism breaks down the barriers between our lives and those of the people we visit. Yet, in most cases, tourists remain firmly behind barriers —be they the windows of a coach, the walls of a hotel or the lens of a camera. In many parts of the world, tourism has compounded misunderstanding and hostility: the Egyptian fundamentalists threatening to blow up hotels and the Oxford householders turning their hoses on open-topped buses doubtless have sympathisers all over the world.

Tourism, we are told, brings wealth to local people. All I have seen suggests the opposite—that tourism makes a very few people extremely rich, while impoverishing the majority, who lose their land, their resources and their sense of self and make, if anything, a tiny amount of money.

Even the oldest maxim of all, that travel broadens the mind, is questionable. Tourists are the aristocracy of the New World Order. They are pampered and protected wherever they go, they are treated with deference and never corrected. Indeed, tour companies do their best to provide what the tourists expect the country can reasonably provide. For most tourists, the only surprises will be unpleasant ones, when the reality of the countries they visit pricks the bubble in which they travel. Then the shock of discovery, rather than assuaging fear, tends to enhance it: millions of people return home more convinced that foreigners are dirty, deceitful and dangerous than they were when they left.

Yet it is travelling that shapes many of those who become the social reformers, the human rights activists, the environmental campaigners and investigative journalists without whom every nation on earth would have succumbed to barren dictatorship. These are among the few for whom travel does broaden the mind, for whom exposure to injustice abroad may lift the veil from injustice at home, for whom the conditions suffered by the oppressed of the world, once seen, cannot be tolerated. While they number as tens among the millions, their enlightenment surely means that tourism, for all its monstrosities, cannot be wholly condemned.

COUNTRIES IN CONFLICT

by Andrew Duncan

With the end of the cold war and the break-up of the Soviet Union it might be thought that the world would be a safer place. Unfortunately this is not so and there are now more places which are unsafe to visit than ever before.

The possibility of a third world war starting in Europe between the forces of the communist world and the Western Alliance, NATO, which would probably have escalated into all-out nuclear war, has disappeared and although such a war was always unlikely, had it started the results would have been catastrophic.

For that reason both the super-powers, who invariably took sides in any minor third world conflict or civil war so as to embarrass each other and to vie for influence, also made sure that these conflicts did not get out of hand, preventing a direct confrontation between them. So now that the US no longer wishes to be a world policeman and Russia is unable to be one even in its own sphere of influence, the result is that conflicts are less influenced by outsider powers and so are more vicious and bloody than before. For a time the United Nations, finding it easier to get Security Resolutions passed where once they would have been vetoed either by the US or USSR, embarked on a record number of peace-keeping missions some of which were spectacularly unsuccessful.

Another result of the end of the cold war and the collapse of communism has been the rise in nationalism and religious extremism which reignited many long-standing disputes which communism had kept firmly under control. It is true that the number of wars between states has significantly fallen but sadly the instances of civil war, or situations short of full-scale civil war but where violence can erupt without warning or terrorism can be expected, have dramatically increased. All these situations are included in the global review that follows.

Countries do not become automatically safe just because a cease-fire has been arranged, nor even when this is converted into a peace settlement. For many years after fighting stops the land will still be littered with unexploded bombs and other munitions. Far worse, vast areas are usually highly dangerous to enter because of the thousands of anti-personnel mines left by the contestants, more often than not without any warning signs. There is also often a residue of armed men who can find no other way of life than that of violent crime.

Terrorist attacks are often aimed at achieving publicity and, as terrorists choose soft targets, these often include tourists and the facilities frequented by them.

Poverty often leads to crime and there are a number of countries where the crime rate, particularly that of violent crime, make them unsafe for holiday maker as opposed to business men who are unlikely to leave the centre of major towns. Because a country is mentioned here does not necessarily mean that all travel is unsafe, but Foreign Office and local security advice should be sought and followed whether it involves staying in at night or not visiting specific areas at all.

Europe

Europe is now more dangerous than ever before. Long-standing terrorist campaigns are being waged in Northern Ireland (and to a lesser extent in the UK) by the Irish Republican Army, and in Spain by the Basque separatists, ETA (Euskadi ta Askatasuna), and there are outbreaks elsewhere by dissident groups such as Algerian Islamists and Turkish Kurds seeking international publicity (a bomb in a foreign capital is often worth two at home). But these are low risk dangers with incidents at long intervals and should not deter tourists so long as local advice is heeded.

Although the fighting has been stopped in Bosnia-Herzegovina and Croatia the ancient hatreds remain. Freedom of movement is meant to be available throughout Bosnia but there are many check points and the Serbian entity (Republika Srpska) is virtually independent. Many mines still have to be lifted. Croat/Muslim differences still result in violence in Mostar and the situation around Brcko, whose control is disputed, is tense. The East Slavonia area of Croatia is still under UN control. A new Balkan conflict erupted in February 1997 when the population of Albania rebelled and looted military arms depots and other stores. A state of anarchy exists and most foreigners have been evacuated. There are fears that the violence might spread beyond Albania's borders and could involve the Albanian populations in Macedonia and the Kosovo region of Serbia.

An uneasy peace exists in the Russian Caucasus and in the former Soviet Republics of the Transcaucasus. The Russians have withdrawn their troops from Chechenya but violence could break out at any time as the various guerrilla leaders compete for power and influence. Fortunately the war did not spill over into neighbouring republics, nor have any of the other Caucasian Republics followed the Chechen example of breaking away from the Russian Federation, but this still could take place. There are many uncleared mines. To the south of the Caucasian Mountains the civil wars in Georgia have abated but the causes are not yet cured and Russian peace keeping troops are deployed along the border of Abkhazia at the north-eastern end of the country. The area of South Ossetia should also be avoided. Nor has the quarrel between Armenia and Azerbaijan over the Armenian populated enclave of Nagorno-Karabakh in Azerbaijan been solved. There is no fighting but there has been no agreement on deploying a peace keeping force (though all the plans for one have been completed by the OSCE) and Armenia still occupies a corridor of Azerbaijan land linking it with Nagorno Karabakh.

In Turkey the Kurdish uprising in the east and south-east of the country continues but at a lower intensity than before. There is still a very large military presence and clashes still regularly occur. The Kurdish Worker's Party (PKK) maintains camps across the border in Syria, Iraq, Iran and, more recently, in Armenia; from time to time the Turkish Army carries out large scale raids to destroy these.

Northern Africa

There is still no solution to the long standing problem of the Western Sahara, which was annexed by Morocco, and has been the scene of many years' fighting between the Moroccan Army and Polisario guerrillas based in Algeria. No progress has been made on holding a UN monitored referendum on the region's future. Though there is little violence at present, travel to the Western Sahara is still not recommended. The Algerian-Moroccan border is closed.

In Algeria the vicious struggle between the military government and the Islamic Salvation Front (FIS) continues, with reports of FIS massacres of civilians coming in virtually every week from all parts of the country. Army operations cause large-scale casualties too; 163 Islamic militants were reported killed in a period of four or five days in February 1997. The capital Algiers experiences car-bomb attacks regularly.

There is still a UN ban on air-travel to Libya (because of the refusal to hand over those suspected of causing the Lockerbie air disaster) and any travel to the Libyan border with Chad is still not recommended despite agreement over ownership of the Aouzou strip being reached in 1994.

Western and Central Africa

This is now probably the most conflict-torn region in the world. A number of long-standing conflicts appear to be slowly coming to an end, others are going full blast and there are more potential trouble spots waiting to erupt. The Angolan civil war seems virtually over but it will be some years before it will be safe to travel there. There have been small cease-fire violations, banditry is rife, and there are many uncleared mines. The civil war could well reignite. Likewise, in Liberia the level of violence has decreased substantially but full peace appears to elude the several parties to the conflict there, and it still remains a dangerous place.

After several periods of attempted genocide and enormous refugee flows, both Burundi and Rwanda are beginning to settle down, but it remains very unwise to visit these countries. The civil war in Rwanda which was continued amongst the many thousands of refugees, including the perpetrators of genocide who fled to Zaire, so affected that country's Tutsi population, who live mainly in the eastern province of Kivu, that they began their own revolution against Mobuto's corrupt regime. So far the rebels have taken control of nearly one third of the country; the army appears unwilling to fight and has taken the opportunity to indulge in widespread looting.

In Sierra Leone the little heard of civil war appeared to come to an end after five years when the government and the rebels of the Revolutionary United Front reached agreement. The implementation of the accord is not progressing well and violence has broken out again in various parts of the country. No agreement has been reached on a peace keeping force which the UN has offered. The Central African Republic has experienced three army revolts in the last twelve months; the latest in January 1997 was put down by French troops who have now handed over to an all African force. In Chad, lawless soldiers and other armed factions make it still dangerous to visit the Aouzoo strip, the border with Sudan and around Lake Chad.

East Africa and the Horn of Africa

In southern Sudan, the civil war continues and spreads as the mainly Christian Sudan People's Liberation Army has for the first time received active backing from Muslim opposition groups. A new front has been opened by Colonel Garang's forces in south-east Sudan close to the border with Ethiopia; both

Ethiopia and Eritrea deny Sudanese government claims that they are taking part in the offensive which has made significant gains and is threatening the important dam and hydro-electric station at Damazin.

Eritrea is in dispute with Yemen over the ownership of the Hanish Islands; Eritrea seized Greater Hanish in December 1996 while Yemen still holds the Lesser Hanish and Az-Zuqur. Both the islands and the shoreline opposite them are therefore sensitive areas. Large numbers of mines remain to be cleared on the Eritrean mainland. Both the Ethiopian and Eritrean border areas with Sudan should be avoided. Areas of Djibouti are closed to visitors and the border areas adjoining Eritrea and Ethiopia should be avoided.

Somalia still remains ungoverned and at the mercy of the feuding "warlords". Peace talks in Addis Ababa, which had been boycotted by the Hab Gedir clan who control southern Mogadishu, broke down in December. The cease-fire agreed to in October collapsed as fighting broke out in Mogadishu, causing over 300 deaths and many more wounded.

The northern part of Uganda is still controlled by two separate rebel groups: the Christian fundamentalist Lord's Resistance Army and the West Nile Bank Front (WBNF). The WBNF is mainly composed of former soldiers who wish to see the return of Idi Amin and who are mainly Muslims. The Ugandan army has made some progress against the guerrillas but cannot gain control of the region. The WBNF receives aid from Sudan. Avoid Gulu, Kitgum, Moyo, and Arua in the north and the south Rwenzori Mountains.

Southern Africa

This appears to be one area in the world where there are currently no civil wars. The main worry for travellers must be the high rate of violent crime in South Africa. Although the civil war in Mozambique ended in 1992, the UN peace-keeping force withdrew, and demobilisation of forces was completed, the country suffers from uncleared mines and high levels of armed robbery.

Middle East

The wave of suicide bombings just before the Israeli election in May 1996 led to the Likud coalition under the leadership of Benjamin Netanyahu which in its turn has brought the peace-process with the Palestinians to a halt. The start of construction work for a Jewish housing estate on a stony hill between Jerusalem and Bethlehem in March 1997 brought another suicide bomber to Tel Aviv, and caused repeated clashes between Palestinians and Israeli troops in the West Bank. Nevertheless Israel is as safe a place to visit as, say, London or Paris, both of which suffered bomb attacks during 1996. Travel to the West Bank and Gaza Strip is another matter and should not be attempted without local up to date advice and then not in a car with Israeli number plates. Parts of Lebanon are still unsafe to travel to. The south of the country is a battle ground between the Iranian backed Hezbollah movement and the Israeli Army and its allies in the South Lebanese Army. The Beka'a Valley in the east of the country is used by Hezbollah for its base-camps and training schools and tends to be the target of Israeli retaliatory air raids.

The civil war of 1994 in Yemen is over but there are continuing instances of the kidnapping of tourists; seven were released in mid-March 1997 while four more were taken at the end of that month. In Egypt, the campaign of terrorist attacks aimed at tourists by Islamist extremist groups appears to be over after a heavy-handed government crackdown; the extremists are not totally eliminated as the assassination attempt on President Mubarrak in Ethiopia and the bomb exploded at the Egyptian Embassy in Islamabad in 1995 shows, but tourists are far less at risk than before. The governorate of Minya is unsafe to visit.

Few are likely to want to holiday in Iraq and it would certainly be unwise to travel in the Kurdish populated north where there has been fighting between the two main rival groups, and where, close to the border, the Turkish army and air force mount raids against Turkish Kurd rebels.

Central Asia and the Indian Subcontinent

In early 1995 a new actor appeared on the Afghanistan civil war scene. Known as Taliban, it was originally composed primarily of Islamic students studying at Madressas in northern Pakistan and southern, Pushtun populated, Afghanistan. Initially supported and armed by Pakistan, and it is reported, in their first attacks even by Pakistani artillery. Taliban swiftly took control of Kandahar and the south and east of the country. In September 1996 Taliban took the already war-torn capital, Kabul, and instituted a strictly Islamic regime which imposed Sharia law with its harsh punishments. Since then fighting has continued north and west of Kabul but Taliban has gained little more territory. Control of Afghanistan is seen by many regional powers as opening the gates to Central Asia and its undeveloped natural assets. Taliban is therefore backed by Pakistan and Saudi Arabia while the northern, Uzbek and Tajik, Afghans are supported by Russia and Iran. Civil war can be expected to continue for some time.

In Tajikistan there is talk of peace but this has not yet materialised. It is estimated that more than 30,000 have died as a result of the civil war since 1992, despite the presence of 25,000 Russian troops. The government is weak, with the many rebel leaders doing as they please. Most recently the United Nations and other aid workers have been the target of kidnappers.

In India, Jammu and Kashmir there are still frequent clashes between the government and terrorists. Four tourists kidnapped in August 1995 remain held by their captors. North-east India is a disturbed region and travel permits are required to visit Arunachal Predesh, Manipur, Mizoram, Nagaland and Sikkim where separatist movements are active. There have also been separatist attacks by Bodo dissidents in Assam who blew up a train, killing 33, in January 1997 and another group, the United Liberation Front for Assam who blew up the crude-oil pipeline a week earlier.

The security situation in Karachi is much improved. In 1995 and 1996 there were serious outbreaks of communal violence caused by Urdu speaking Muslims who had migrated there from India after the 1947 partition, but the problem is not yet resolved. Elsewhere in Pakistan the areas bordering Afghanistan, India, Iran and the Kashmir line of control should be avoided. The Sri Lankan civil war is entering its thirteenth year with no apparent let up in the intensity of fighting between government troops and the Tamil Tiger separatists. The north and east of the country is a battlefield and terrorist attacks take place from time to time elsewhere, mainly in Colombo.

South East Asia

The Myanmar (Burma) regime, the State Law and Order Restoration Council, is widely condemned for its human rights record. The military junta enforces its control with torture, execution, forced labour and relocation of ethnic minority groups. The main areas of dissident activity and military operations are along the eastern border with China and the southern border with Laos and Thailand. Internally there have been disturbances recently in Mandalay, Moulmein, Monywa, Prome, Tougoo, and Sagaing.

In Cambodia the Khmer Rouge still maintains its guerilla war, despite large-scale defections to the government and the government's recent agreement to pardon Ieng Sary (considered to be second in command to Pol Pot and sentenced to death in his absence) in return for his joining peace talks. The Khmer Rouge still control large areas of the country adjoining Thailand and there are still even larger areas covered by uncleared mines. In Laos it is still unsafe to visit Xiang Khouang Province and the Vietnamese border area owing to mines left over from the Vietnam war and the Ho Chi Min trail.

Indonesia is still fighting two separatist wars. One is in East Timor, the former Portuguese colony which Indonesia invaded over twenty years ago, and the other is against the Free Papua Movement in Irian Jaya. Both these areas are dangerous to visit. Political dissent in Indonesia often turns quickly to violence to which the military respond with tough measures. There have also been inter-ethnic clashes in West Kalimantan.

Papua New Guinea has been unable to defeat the rebellion on the Island of Bougainville and more recently, in March 1997, a major split between the army authorities and the government occured when the latter hired a group of mercenaries for operations in Bougainville without consulting the military leadership. Looting and rioting resulted.

Some insurgency continues in the Philippines. North and South Luzon and western Minandao and the islands to its south west are affected.

Central and South America

As the various civil wars in Central America come slowly to a close their violence is being replaced by that of violent it appears that by the many unemployed former soldiers and former opposition fighters who are still in possession of weapons. El Salvador, Guatemala, Guyana, Honduras, Mexico and Nicaragua, and Colombia in South America are all listed as unsafe for visitors by the Foreign Office. In Honduras it is important to avoid the border areas with Nicaragua and El Salvador. Colombian terrorists have been reported as operating as much as 100 kilometres inside Panama.

Some parts of the interior of Peru still suffer from terrorist activity but more generally the situation is much improved. The Peru/Ecuador border dispute is over but some tourists have been kidnapped in the area. Colombia is still the scene of fierce fighting between government troops and para-military forces and left wing guerillas. The para-military groups, who employ brutal methods, are gaining some political power. In the first nine months of 1996 19,685 people were killed in Colombia; the para-militaries are said to be responsible for 59 per cent of the deaths, the army and police for eight per cent and the guerillas for 33 per cent.

The Outlook

Travelling in any of the countries mentioned above obviously carries risks. The risks are not worth taking in those countries which the Foreign and Commonwealth advise against visiting.

In many of the countries described the main centres are relatively, if not entirely, safe to visit. Here, as in many countries not mentioned, the problem is violent crime rather than war. It all depends where you go and when, and this can only decided just before you travel. "Discretion is the better part of valour" is just as true for travelling as it is for war-fighting. So take and follow advice.

The most up to date advice for travellers is provided by the Foreign and Commonwealth Office which maintains a Travel Advice Unit (tel: 0171 238 4503/4). Their advice is available on BBC Channel 2 CEEFAX page 470. Their advice includes not just the dangers of war but of crime, health, floods and volcanic eruptions.

THE WORLD IMPACT OF TOURISM

by Crispin Tickell

The only problem about tourism is the other tourists. We see yet another boat load in motorised canoes in the wide waters of the Amazon; yet more louts demanding lager and chips in Mediterranean villages; yet another tourist procession between endangered species in the Galapagos Islands; yet more feet along ever widening trails exposing mountain rocks; yet another cruise liner pouring people like an ant army onto white Caribbean beaches or even whiter Antarctica; yet more Landrover tracks across the African savanna. We love tourism and we hate it.

The problem is relatively new. As with the industrial revolution some 250 years ago, it was the British who started it. In the early days travel abroad was the preserve of the rich, who did it to enlarge their education and enjoy exotic pleasures. With the new wealth generated by business and industry, it moved rapidly down the social scale. While the Duke of Wellington was against railways because they gave the lower orders ideas above their station, Thomas Cook organised the first rail excursion from Leicester to Loughborough for a shilling. But it was only in the lifetime of present generations that tourism became the world's biggest industry with all the impacts and consequences of industrial development: the generation of wealth and employment, the opening of minds to new horizons, the pleasures of new ways of life, the impact on the environment, consumption of natural resources, production of wastes and pollutants, and not least effects on the cultural attitudes of all in contact with it.

It is worth looking at some of the figures. Tourism accounts for six per cent of world gross national product, thirteen per cent of consumer spending, and provides up to ten per cent of total employment. All this arises from the eight per cent of the world's population which travels. Some 80 per cent of tourists come from just twenty countries. In 1995 there were over five million tourists in the world, and this figure could double in the next fifteen years. Some countries have become dependent on tourism for the good health of their economies: they range from Egypt, Spain, Jamaica, and Kenya to the islands of the Caribbean and the Pacific. Some of the environment in such countries has been radically changed as a result.

There has been a substantial diversion of resources to tourist use. This is particularly important in countries short of water. Some figures produced by the United Nations Food and Agriculture Organisation illustrate the problem. 15,000 cubic metres of water can irrigate one hectare of high yielding modern rice; support 100 nomads and 450 cattle for three years; maintain 100 rural families for three years and 100 urban families for two years; or meet the needs of 100 guests in a tourist hotel for 55 days. The cost of meeting tourist needs, whether in terms of clearing land for golf courses, building major works of infrastructure, producing specialised foods, disposing of wastes and pollution and the rest, are immeasurably large. The cultural impact is also beyond measurement. I remember my shock when as an Oxford don I was the subject of tourist curiosity with flashbulbs. For once I was at one with the Matabele guide or the Amazonian Indian (who reasonably charge for having their photographs taken). Like seeing television or hearing radio programmes from another world, tourists generate unrealisable expectations and consequent frustration in others.

Yet the right to travel has become an icon of liberty, especially for those under oppressive regimes. So it should be. But rights carry obligations, and if tourism is not to be like the Indian god Kali, the creator of wealth and at the same time the destroyer of what generated it, we need to see how tourism can be brought into balance, particularly in relation to its impact on the environment.

What can we do? I believe that the first requirement in this as in so many other environmental matters, is to establish true costs, and make sure that they are met. It has been well said that markets are marvellous at fixing prices, but incapable of recognising costs. Recently a brave attempt has been made to establish the true costs of the natural services – ranging from the fertility of the soil to its ability to absorb wastes within the natural ecosystem of which humans are a tiny part – and, although the results were approximate, they are very interesting: the average works out at about $33 trillion a year while the world's gross national product is around $18 trillion a year. A good example is the price of coal. In no country does it include the cost of the effects of burning it, whether on human health, on buildings or on the chemistry of the atmosphere.

It is not easy to establish environmental costs. The last Chancellor of the Exchequer justified a continuing increase in petrol prices on environmental grounds, and the new land fill tax falls in the same category. As for tourism, there can be no question that tourists should in one way or another bear the cost of the effects of their actions.

A particular perversion is the lack of any tax on aviation fuel. It has become cheaper to convey people as well as materials by air than to use other means of transport, with effects throughout the economy. Air traffic contributes carbon to the atmosphere. It makes up eleven per cent of total transport fuel emissions, and some three per cent of the emissions which can be attributed to human activity. 60 per cent of air travel is now tourist related.

Another perversion is that very little of the wealth generated by tourism goes to the people who live on the spot. This means that local communities increasingly resent tourism, and in sensitive environmental areas have little incentive to protect and conserve them. If local people are to identify themselves with the good health of their own environment, then they must see most of the return from it. Individual tourists could make a big difference by spending their foreign currency on goods and services bought directly from the local communities.

At present most fees charged for admission to national parks or other areas of conservation, are derisory. They scarcely cover the most elementary requirements of conservation. In a way tourists rent other people's environments for brief periods, and should be ready to pay a fair price for them. This in turn requires stronger local control. Nothing is more important than control of numbers. This can be done relatively easily in such isolated places as the Galapagos Islands, Machu Picchu in Peru, or Bhutan in the Himalayas, but control elsewhere, notably in our own Lake District or the Scottish highlands has been non-existent or ineffective. Many feel that the natural environment should come for free without realising that nothing is for free, above all the impact on the natural world. The Earthwatch programme in Zimbabwe over the last four years is a good demonstration of what can be done. Yet the threat to the natural world continues to increase almost everywhere, and something like a fifth of the world's rich biological diversity could be lost in the next 20 years unless coordinated action is taken to conserve it.

I think that the tourist industry is already well aware of these problems. So far there are few signs that they are being taken as seriously as they deserve So long as the philosophy is primarily commercial, with the usual stuff about competitive markets, economic growth and promotion of mass movements of people, things are not likely to change, whatever the gloss put on them. True environmental costing has to enter in at all points.

Just as the industrial revolution did much good but created multiple problems for the good health of our planet, so its product, tourism, risks doing likewise. Indeed it is already doing so, and things could get much worse before they get better. There is a simple principle we should always bear in mind: do not kill the goose that lays the golden eggs.

WHEN TO GO

by Jill Crawshaw

"You should have been here last week/month/year!" is the knee-jerk reaction I've come to expect–and dread–in every season of the year, somewhere around the globe. When I spent a large chunk of January turning rusty on the Costa del Sol, it was "freak weather"; when I had to flee south of Marrakech in December as torrential floods had wiped out several roads, part of the railway line and hundreds of mud brick houses. It was unbelievable they claimed.

Then there were the winter wash-outs in Tahiti, or the time I spent during an

Australian summer being cling-filmed in dust by the Willy-Willies – the violent tropical storms that can hit the north coast. Sure, Downunder is *the* place to escape our winter, but only fairly low Downunder. Even Melbourne's climate can change as much as four times in a day, and Sydney is regularly dowsed, while summer monsoons can bring down rainfall in buckets during the hot and steamy Barrier Reef holiday playgrounds.

To be a really slick traveller who knows that you should avoid Mal in June, Mali in August and Mah in December, you would need to carry around the weather charts at the back of this guide, but there are a few rough and ready rules that have helped me decide whether to pack my bikini and beach mat or brolly and thermals.

For a start, any temperatures above 80 degrees Fahrenheit in humid Turkish bath zones, 85 degrees Fahrenheit in dry climes, preclude too much exploration and activity for most, while anything below 65 degrees means lots of walk-abouts and sightseeing but no beach.

The sad sight of winter holidaymakers huddled over Trivial Pursuits in all too many rainswept and deserted Mediterranean resorts has taught me to distrust the Med winter weather. Sizzling or drizzling, it's always a gamble and there's a particular cloud that arrives in Southern Europe around the third week in October (a month later in Cyprus, Lebanon, North Africa and other Southern Med resorts) sending a message to warn beach dwellers that their number is up.

Cold statistics reveal that Gibraltar or Haifa have nearly twice as much rainfall as London in January, which in turn is dryer than the Algarve, Monaco and even Cyprus and Malta, as well as Istanbul in February.

Even in that so-called winter sun Mecca Tenerife (the same latitude as Delhi and parts of Florida), a daily cloud arrives at 2 p.m. on the lush northern resort of Puerto Cruz, while on the other side of the island the sun shines evenly all day on the bare slopes and concrete jungle of Playa de las Americas – which is why the north is lush, and the south barren. Eilat too, Israel's winter offering can be grey and grizzling in January, though at least you can get away from it by exploring its technicolour wonders below sea level.

But if it's winter sunshine you are after, you have to head as far south as Luxor, with the cheapest guaranteed hot stuff in Gambia, followed by Goa and the Kenyan coast. Alas, the Caribbean is at its most pricey and exclusive during our winter.

Wherever you are travelling in desert conditions, you'll find surprisingly large diurnal variations with cool, even cold snaps at night and at dawn. But, on and around the equator you'll need to over-dose on anti-perspirant as it is nearly always hot and humid and there are so few seasonal variations that you find yourself dreaming wistfully of spring flowers in the Lake District, the autumn wine harvest in Provence or the Fall in New England. And just to remind you of the vagaries of weather, *The Times* carried a picture of New England under deep snow at the beginning of April this year.

From trial and error in the tropics, I've at least learned that December to February are the most tolerable months to tackle Bangkok, but that in the same months it is so steamy and wet in Singapore you can't ever get your smalls dry unless you have a hotel room with air conditioning.

Weather in the Far East generally can present tricky problems, even within the same or neighbouring countries. Backpackers who have boned up their weather charts will know that the May rains signal the end of the tourist season in Phuket and they must migrate to Koh Samui, moving on from there to Bali for their fun in July, August and September. Similarly Malaysia and even relatively small islands such as Sri Lanka have considerable climatic variations – bi-annual heavy rainfalls often happen at night, but winds can make the sea rough and dangerous for bathing during the day. Equally in both countries, where you can move from steamy lowlands to cool highlands in a few hours, you need to pack sweaters for evenings alongside your sun-hat for midday.

In Africa, the rains, long and short, fall somewhere throughout the year; from December to February in Zimbabwe and Southern Africa, March to May in Kenya and Tanzania; May to August in Cape Town. From November to February, just when holidaymakers are being lured to the Seychelles and Mauritius by the eternal sunshine on the glossy brochure covers, these Indian Ocean playgrounds are getting their biggest annual soaking – whereas they are both ideal escapes in our summer months, when the Med resorts have become blowsy with tourists.

East Africa's safari season is during the dry months from December to April, when the grasses are low for better game spotting, and the animals will seek out and congregate around water-holes rather than dispersing through the bush. But even here, alas, the rains don't always watch the calendar, and timing can often be a matter of luck. It took me several false starts before I caught the beginning of the migration in Serengeti – but the brief moments before dawn waiting for the sun to rise over the flat endless plains, surrounded by the shadowy silhouettes of millions of wildebeest on their starting blocks, are heart-stopping memories that will last a lifetime.

Even if you get your timing wrong, there are other compensations; some countries are almost reborn with changes of weather, none more so than Africa. Unexpected early rains in Botswana once turned my dry and dusty campsite into a Garden of Eden overnight as we awoke to *The Jungle Book* fantasy of monkeys chattering in the trees, impala playing in the bush and dragonflies and butterflies dazzling us with their pirouettes.

I witnessed one of the driest places on earth, parts of the Namib desert transformed almost into an Irish meadow by rain after several years of drought, so heaven knows what the unique species that adapted to this burning environment must have made of it. The desert onyx has developed a brain irrigated by a special network of veins that enables it to withstand fiery temperatures, while the dune beetle does handstands each morning to let droplets of Atlantic fog roll down its mouth. More soberly in such communities, you learn to realise that the weather is a matter of death or life.

Moving across from Africa to the Atlantic, anyone who believes that America's weather is a breeze may be in for some shocks. The wettest place I've been is Hawaii where I was stuck for days waiting for a helicopter trip to photograph the volcanoes, of which I got no glimpse. The hottest I've felt was in the humid concrete canyons of New York, though body temperatures plummeted to sub-Arctic levels in the icy air conditioning of the Big Apple's restaurants, hotels and even cabs.

It was Mark Twain who said "The coldest winter I ever spent was summer in

San Francisco". British holidaymakers should take note of this before they flock in droves to Florida when it's almost guaranteed to be humid and wet, the mosquitoes are at their most bloodthirsty in the Everglades, and there's a real likelihood of hurricanes as well.

After twenty years of travelling from Alaska to Zanzibar, writing hundreds of travel articles and answering thousands of questions on radio and television phone-ins, I've learned to identify the hardy perennials: "How much?", "What are the beaches like?"; "Is it safe and can you drink the water in...?".

I opine on a few general rules, pull out statistics and weather charts, and then get myself off the hook with warnings that little complications like the meltemi, the mistral or the sirocco winds can make a mockery of the most reliable Mediterranean temperature statistics; that you can get a deep suntan north of the Arctic Circle, or catch pneumonia in the desert – in other words, that the world's weather can be astonishingly unpredictable.

What would we have to talk about if it wasn't?

For more information see the World-wide Weather Guide in the Directory p.649

CLIMATE AND TRAVEL
by Gilbert Schwartz

Well, maybe there isn't much you can do to guarantee good weather but you can do some things to help minimise disappointment.

Be sure to do your homework. Look up reference books on the subject and use them to help select the most favourable times and travel locations. Remember, when interpreting climate information, some statistics are necessary but they could sometimes be misleading. Look for comparisons. Especially compare the prospective location with an area at home or with which you are familiar. For example, San Francisco, California, has a temperature range for July from a maximum average of 18°C to a minimum of 12°C with no precipitation. This becomes more meaningful when it is compared to New York City which has a range of 29°C to 20°C and, on average, eleven days during the month have rain of 0.25cm or more. So, in spite of the fact that California has a reputation for being warm and sunny, if you're planning a trip to San Francisco in the summer, don't forget to take a sweater! The average temperatures are cold and the winds are a brisk 17.5kmph, windier even than Chicago, the "windy city".

Sources
Up-to-date weather conditions and forecasts may be obtained from various sources. A current weather map, which is based on information furnished by government as well as private weather services, is the main way of getting a general picture of weather patterns over a large area. These weather maps show conditions around the country at ground level. Elements which are of particular interest to travellers and may be shown on the map include temperature, pressure changes, wind speed and direction, cloud type, current weather, and precip-

itation.

Of course, the weather information and projected forecasts must be interpreted. You may do well to alter your itinerary and stay clear of areas that project undesirable or threatening weather conditions. Especially keep alert for severe weather conditions such as storms, heavy rains, etc. For example, you should remember when travelling in mountainous regions that flash floods can strike with little or no warning. Distant rain may be channelled into gullies and ravines, turning a quiet stream-side campsite into a rampaging torrent within minutes. Incidentally, there is excellent literature available through the US Government Printing Office prepared by the National Weather Service. The information includes advice on staying safe during lightning, flash floods, hurricanes and tornadoes. Publications containing summaries and other weather data are also available. Write to Superintendent of Documents, US Government Printing Office, Washington DC 20420, for a list of publications. In the UK, information on overseas climate and weather is obtainable by telephoning Weathercall International or the WEXAS Weatherline, see Directory for details (page 658).

Basic Elements

After you have had an opportunity to review reference materials on climate and sources for weather forecasts, you should become acquainted with the meaning of some basic weather elements and learn how they may affect your travel preparations. Perhaps the most crucial weather element is temperature which is a good indicator of body comfort. The ideal air temperature is around 27°C. Temperatures generally decrease at higher latitudes and at higher elevations, on average by around 1.7°C for every 300m increase in elevation up to 9000m.

Wind, which is air in motion, is another important weather element. Winds are caused by pressure gradients, the difference in pressure between two locations. Air moves from an area of high pressure toward an area of low pressure. The greater the pressure gradient, the faster the wind. Sea breezes form when cool high pressure air flows from the water onshore to the low pressure area created by warm air over the land. On a clear, hot summer day, the sea breeze will begin mid-morning and can blow inland as far as 16 km at wind speeds of 16 to 24kmph. In the evening, the process is reversed. An offshore land breeze blows at a more gentle speed, usually about half the speed of the daytime onshore wind.

A somewhat similar situation occurs in the mountains and valleys. During the daytime, the valley floor and sides and the air above them warm up considerably. This air is less dense than the colder air higher up so it rises along the slopes, creating a "valley wind". In the summer, the southern slopes receive more sun, and heat up more which results in valley winds that are stronger than their north slope cousins. At night, the process is reversed and down-slope, "mountain winds" result from the cold air above the mountain tops draining down into the valley.

Winds are also affected by such factors as synoptic (large area) pressure differences and by day-night effects. The sun produces maximum wind speeds, while at night winds near the ground are usually weak or absent. Wind speed is also influenced by how rough the ground is. Over smooth water surfaces, the wind speed increases very rapidly with increasing altitude and reaches a peak speed at a height of about 180m. Over rough terrain, the wind speed increases more gradually with increasing altitude and does not reach its peak until about 450m.

Comfort

As we all know, wind, temperature and humidity have a bearing on our comfort. To indicate how combinations of these elements affect the weather we experience, two indices should be understood: wind chill factor and temperature/humidity comfort index.

The wind chill factor is the cooling effect on the body of any combination of wind and temperature. It accounts for the rate at which our exposed skin loses heat under differing wind-temperature conditions. In a wind of 32kmph, –4°C will feel like –19°C. This effect is called "wind chill", the measure of cold one feels regardless of the temperature. Chill increases as the temperature drops and winds get stronger–up to about 72kmph, beyond which there is little increase. Thus at 12°C, increasing the wind from 0 to 8kmph reduces temperature by only two degrees, but a change in wind speed from 64 to 72kmph reduces it only 0.5°C.

The wind may not always be caused naturally. For example, someone skiing into the wind may receive quite a chill. If one is moving into the wind, the speed of travel is added to the wind speed; thus if the wind is blowing at 16kmph and one's speed is 24kmph into the wind, the actual air movement against the body is 40kmph. At –9°C this air speed gives a wind chill equivalent to –30°C. This is easily cold enough for exposed parts of the body to sustain frostbite.

A combination of warm temperatures *and* humidity also has a significant bearing on our comfort, particularly in warmer climates when the higher the relative humidity, the less comfortable we are. This is a result of the corresponding decrease in the rate at which moisture can evaporate from the skin's surface. Since the cooling of the air next to the skin by the evaporation of perspiration is what causes a cooling sensation, a day with 70 per cent relative humidity and 27°C temperature is far less comfortable than one with 25 per cent humidity and 43°C temperature. The THI was developed in order to measure this relative comfort. But remember, where there is low humidity and a high temperature, your comfort can mislead you, for though you feel safe, you may be in danger of burning.

Layman's Forecast

Lacking the sophisticated instruments and sources for weather data, you may still be able to project your own forecasts. Become familiar with basic weather elements such as pressure signs, clouds, wind changes, etc. Learn how these indicators change before the weather does. A layman should beware of the climate statistics he sees in many tourist brochures. The climate will almost always be more severe than is evident from the quoted rainfall, temperature and sunshine figures.

All-important humidity figures are usually not given (Bali might be empty of tourists half the year if they were), and temperature figures may be averages over day and night, and well below (or above) actual normal maximum (or minimum) temperatures. Or they may represent averages recorded at 0600 or 1800 hours because these figures will look most attractive to visitors.

Something else you will not find easily is water temperature. Winter sun holidays are now extremely popular. A lot of people do not realise, however, that although the daytime air temperatures may be in the low 20's (°C), water temperatures may only be about 5 to 15°C and swimming without a wet-suit impossible. The sea takes longer to warm up than the land each summer. Conversely it takes longer to cool down in the autumn. Reckon on a lag between sea and land temperatures of about one and a half months. In Tunisia, the sea is a lot cooler in March than in October. But, by March air and land temperatures are already rising with the beginning of summer. They will reach their highest point in June/July, but the sea will take until August/September to be fully warmed up.

In winter, comfortably warm water is almost a certainty in the tropics, but more doubtful in the subtropics, and you should study year-round water temperatures. You may just decide to go in summer instead, even though it will probably cost more. In short, warm air and warm water don't always go together.

Familiarity with climate information, whether you rely on primary or secondary sources, will go a long way towards permitting you to get the most out of your next trip.

See the World-wide Weather Guide p.649 and Guide to Rainy Seasons, p.659

A GUIDE TO SEASONAL TRAVEL

by Paul Pratt and Melissa Shales

Africa

North: The climate here varies widely from the warm and pleasant greenery of a Mediterranean climate in the coastal regions to the arid heat of the deep Sahara. Rains on the coast usually fall between September and May and are heavy but not prolonged. It can get cool enough for snow to settle in the mountainous areas, but temperatures will not usually fall below freezing, even in winter. In summer, temperatures are high (up to around 40°C) but bearable.

The Sahara, on the other hand, is extreme, with maximum summer temperatures of around 50°C and minimum winter temperatures of around 3°C. The temperature can fall extremely rapidly, with freezing nights following blisteringly hot days. What little, if any, rain there is can fall at any time of the year. The desert is also prone to strong winds and dust storms.

West: At no time is the climate in West Africa likely to be comfortable, although some areas and times of the year are worse than others. The coastal areas are extremely wet and humid, with up to 2500mm of rain falling in two rainy seasons (May and June and then again in October). In the north there is considerably less rain, with only one wet period between June and September. However, the humidity is still high, only lessened by the arrival of the *harmattan*, a hot, dry and dusty north-easterly wind which blows from the Sahara.

Temperatures remain high and relatively even throughout the year.

East: Although much of this area is on or near the equator, little of it has an "equatorial" climate. The lowlands of Djibouti in the extreme east have a very low, uncertain rainfall, creating near-desert conditions plagued by severe droughts. Further down the coast, the high lowland temperatures are moderated by constant sea breezes. The temperatures inland are brought down by high altitude plateaux and mountain ranges to about the level found in Britain at the height of summer. Temperatures are reasonably stable all year round although the Kenya highlands have a cooler, cloudy "winter" from June to September. There are rainy seasons in most areas in April and May and for a couple of months between July and November, depending on the latitude.

South: The whole area from Angola, Zambia and Malawi southwards tends to be fairly pleasant and healthy, although there are major variations from the Mediterranean climate of Cape Province with its mild winters and warm, sunny summers, to the semi-desert sprawl of the Kalahari and the relatively wet areas of Swaziland, inland Mozambique and the Zimbabwe highlands to the east. In the more northern areas, there is a definite summer rainy season from December to March when the temperatures are highest. On the south coast, there is usually some rain all year round. The west coast, with little rain, has cloud and fog due to the cold Benguela current which also helps keep down the temperature. The best times of the year to visit are April, May and September when the weather is fine but not too hot or humid.

North America

Almost half of Canada and most of Alaska in the north is beyond the Arctic Circle and suffers from the desperately harsh weather associated with this latitude. The ground is tundra and rarely melts for more than a couple of feet and even though summer temperatures are often surprisingly high, the summers are short-lived. Snow and frost are possible at any time of the year, while the northern areas have permanent snow cover. The coast is ice bound for most of the year.

The whole centre of the continent is prone to severe and very changeable weather, as the low-lying land of the Great Plains and the Canadian Prairies offers no resistance to sweeping winds that tear across the continent both from the Gulf and the Arctic. The east is fairly wet but the west has very little rain, resulting in desert and semi-desert country in the south.

Winter temperatures in the north can go as low as –40°C and can be very low even in the south, with strong winds and blizzards. In the north, winter is long-lived. Summers are sunny and often scorchingly hot.

In general, the coastal areas of North America are far kinder than the centre of the continent. The Pacific coast is blocked by the Rockies from the sweeping winds, and in the Vancouver area the climate is similar to that of the UK. Sea breezes keep it cool further south.

Seasons change fairly gradually on the east coast, but the northerly areas still suffer from the extremes of temperature which give New York its fabled humid heatwaves and winter temperatures. New York, in spite of being far further north, is often much hotter than San Francisco. The Newfoundland area has heavy fog and icebergs for shipping to contend with. Florida and the Gulf States to the south have a tropical climate, with warm weather all year round, and winter sun and summer thunderstorms. This is the area most likely to be affected by hurricanes and tornadoes, although cyclones are possible throughout the country.

Mexico and Central America

The best time to visit this area is during the dry season (winter) from November to April. However, the mountains and the plains facing the Caribbean have heavy rainfall throughout the year, which is usually worst from September to February. The mountains and plains facing the Pacific have negligible rainfall from December to April.

Central and northern Mexico tend to have a longer dry season and the wet season is seldom troublesome to the traveller as it usually rains only between 4pm and 5pm. The temperature is affected by the altitude. The unpleasant combination of excessive heat and humidity at the height of the wet season should be avoided, if possible, at the lower altitudes.

South America

The climatic conditions of the South American continent are determined to a great extent by the trade winds which, if they originate in high pressure areas, are not necessarily carriers of moisture. With a few regional exceptions, rain in South America is confined to the summer months, both north and south of the Equator. The exceptions are: (i) South Brazil and the eastern coast of Argentina and Uruguay: (ii) the southern Chilean coastal winter rainfall region: (iii) the coastal area of northeast Brazil.

The highest rainfall in South America is recorded in the Amazon basin, the coast lands of Guyana and Suriname, the coastlines of Colombia, Ecuador and southwest Chile. Altitude determines temperature, especially in the Andean countries near to the equator: hot – up to 1000m; temperate – 1000 to 2000m; cold – above 2000m.

Argentina: The winter months, June to October, are the best time for visiting Argentina. Buenos Aires can be oppressively hot and humid from mid–December to the end of February. Climate ranges from the sub-tropical north to sub-antarctic in Tierra del Fuego.

Brazil: The dry season runs from May to October apart from the Amazon Basin and the Recife area which have a tropical rainy season from April to July.

Bolivia: Heavy rainfall on the high western plateau from May to November. Rains in all seasons to the eastern part of the country.

Chile: Just over the border from Bolivia, one of the driest deserts in the world faces the Pacific coast.

Ecuador: Dry seasons from June to October. The coast is very hot and wet, especially during the period December to May. The mountain roads can be very dangerous during the wet season owing to landslides. .

Paraguay: The best time for a visit is from May to October when it is relatively dry. The heaviest rainfall is from December to March, at which time it is most likely to be oppressively hot and humid.

Peru: During the colder months, June to November, little rainfall but damp on the coast, high humidity and fog. From December to May, travel through the mountains can be hazardous owing to heavy rain which may result in landslides, causing road blockage and long delays.

Paraguay: The best time for a visit is from May to October when it is relatively dry. The heaviest rainfall is from December to March, at which time it is most likely to be oppressively hot and humid.

The Far East and Southeast Asia

Hong Kong: Subtropical climate; hot, humid and wet summer with a cool, but generally dry winter. Typhoon season is usually from July to August. The autumn, which lasts from late September to early December, is the best time for visiting as the temperature and humidity will have fallen and there are many clear, sunny days. Macao has a similar climate but the summers are a little more bearable on account of the greater exposure to sea breezes. There is also an abundance of trees for shelter during the hot summer.

Japan: Japan lies in the northern temperate zone. Spring and autumn are the best times for a visit. With the exception of Hokkaido, the large cities are extremely hot in summer. Hokkaido is very cold in winter. Seasonal vacation periods, especially school holidays, should be avoided if one is going to enjoy visiting temples, palaces and the like in relative comfort.

Korea: Located in the northern temperate zone, with spring and autumn the best times for touring. The deep blue skies of late September/October and early November, along with the warm sunny days and cool evenings, are among Korea's most beautiful natural assets. Though it tends to be rather windy, spring is also a very pleasant time for a Korean visit. There is a short but pronounced wet season starting towards the end of June and lasting into early August. Over 50 per cent of the year's rain falls during this period and it is usually very hot and humid.

Malaysia: There are no marked wet or dry seasons in Malaysia. October to January is the wettest period on the east coast, October/November on the west coast. Sabah has an equable tropical climate; October and April/May are usually the best times for a visit. Sarawak is seldom uncomfortably hot but is apt to be extremely wet. Typhoons are almost unknown in East Malaysia.

Thailand: Hot, tropical climate with high humidity. Best time for touring is from November to February. March to May is extremely hot and the wet season arrives with the southwest monsoon during June and lasts until October.

Singapore: Like Malaysia, Singapore has no pronounced wet or dry season.

The even, constant heat is mitigated by sea breezes. The frequent rain showers have a negligible cooling effect.

The Philippines: The Philippines have a similar climate to Thailand. The best time to travel in the islands is during the dry season, November to March. March to May is usually dry and extremely hot. The southwest monsoon brings the rain from May to November. The islands north of Samar through Luzon are prone to be affected by typhoons during the period July to September. The Visayas Islands, Mindanao and Palawan, are affected to a lesser degree by the southwest monsoon and it is still possible to travel comfortably during the wet season south of Samar Island – long sunny periods are usually interspersed with heavy rain showers.

Indian Subcontinent

Sri Lanka: The southwest monsoon brings rain from May to August in Colombo and in the southwest generally, while the northeast monsoon determines the rainy season from November to February in the northeast. The most popular time for a visit is during the northern hemisphere's winter.

India: The climate of south India is similar to that of Southeast Asia: warm and humid. The southwest monsoon brings the rainy season to most parts of India, starting in the southwest and spreading north and east from mid-May through June. Assam has an extremely heavy rainfall during monsoon seasons. Generally speaking, the period from November to April is the best time to visit. From April until the start of the southwest monsoon, the northern Indian plains are extremely hot, though the northern hill stations provide a pleasant alternative until the start of the monsoon rains. These places usually have a severe winter.

Nepal: March is pleasant, when all the rhododendrons are in bloom. The monsoon rains begin in April.

Middle East

A large proportion of this area is desert – flat, low-lying land with virtually no rain and some of the hottest temperatures on earth. Humidity is high along the coast and travellers should beware of heat exhaustion and even heat stroke. What little rain there is falls between November and March. To the north, in Iran and Iraq, the desert gives way to the great steppes, prone to extremes of heat and cold, with rain in winter and spring.

Melting snow from the surrounding mountains causes spectacular floods from March to May. The climate is considerably more pleasant in the Mediterranean areas with long, hot, sunny summers and mild, wet winters. The coast is humid, but even this is tempered by steady sea breezes. The only really unpleasant aspect of the climate here is the hot, dry and dusty desert wind which blows at the beginning and end of summer.

Europe

Only in the far north and those areas a long way from the sea does the climate in Europe get to be extreme. In northern Scandinavia and some of the inland eastern countries such as Bulgaria, there are long, bitterly cold winters with heavy snow and, at times, arctic temperatures. In western Europe, the snow tends to settle only for a few days at a time. In Britain, the Benelux countries and Germany, winter is characterised chiefly by continuous cloud cover, with rain or sleet. In the Alps, heavy snow showers tend to alternate with brilliant sunshine, offering ideal conditions for winter sports. There are four distinct seasons, and while good weather cannot be guaranteed during any of them, all are worth seeing. Summer is generally short, and the temperature varies widely from one year to the next, climbing at times to match that on the Mediterranean. For sun worshippers, the Mediterranean is probably the ideal location, hot for much of the year but rarely too hot or humid to be unbearable. Rain falls in short, sharp bursts, unlike the continuous drizzle to be found further north. Winter is mild and snow rare.

Australasia

Australia: For such a vast land mass, there are few variations in the weather here. A crescent-shaped rain belt follows the coast to provide a habitable stretch around the enormous semi-desert "outback". The Snowy Mountains in the east do, as their name suggests, have significant snowfalls, although even here it does not lie long. The east is the wettest part of the country owing to trade winds which blow off the Pacific. The rainfall pattern varies throughout the country: the north and northeast have definite summer rains between November and April; the south and west have winter rains; while in the east and southeast the rains fall year-round. Tropical cyclones with high winds and torrential rain occur fairly frequently in the northeast and northwest. Tasmania, further south and more mountainous, has a temperate climate similar to Britain's.

New Zealand: Although at a different latitude, the great expanse of water around New Zealand gives it a maritime climate similar to Britain's. The far north has a sub-tropical climate with mild winters and warm, humid summers. There are year-round snow fields in the south, and snow falls on most areas in winter. Although the weather is changeable, there is a surprising amount of sunshine, making this country ideal for most outdoor activities. The best time to visit is from December to March, at the height of summer.

Papua New Guinea: The climate here is a fairly standard tropical one–hot and wet all year, although the time and amount of the rains are greatly influenced by the high mountains that run the length of the country. The rains are heavy, but not continuous. While the coast tends to be humid, the highlands are pleasant.

Also see the World-wide Weather Guide in the Directory, p. 649, Guide to Rainy Seasons p.659 and Selected Sea Temperatures p.662 of the Directory

FESTIVALS

by Jeremy Atiyah

Can't wait for Christmas? Why not instead go out into the world for your festivals? There is always something going on somewhere. Visiting festivals is not only a way of crashing other people's parties, it is also a way to see local people at their best and take great photos. If you don't lose your camera in the melée, that is.

Humans have been cluttering the calendar with special dates since the dawn of history. Some of these have never stopped; other new ones started up yesterday. Some are a fantastic spectacle; others offer nothing to see. If you are going half way round the world to see one, make sure you have got the dates right.

Not that you need go far of course. Every country in the world, perhaps every city, contains its own local festivals, and Britain is no exception. Annual examples here include the explosive Guy Fawke's Night on November 5, as well as curiosities such as the three-hundred year old Shrovetide football match in Ashbourne, Derbyshire, in February.

World-wide however, the origins of the oldest festivals revolve round agricultural rites, marking seasonal changes like the beginning of spring or the coming of the rains. Such festivals tend to follow the lunar calendar (lunar cycles were easier to count), which means that tourists have to check their calendars carefully. Given common agricultural origins, it is no coincidence that the end of winter is marked almost simultaneously in both Europe and China by two of the world's largest festivals.

Carnival, which takes place on the days leading up to Ash Wednesday, 40 days before Easter, is a mad party throughout the Catholic world. *Fat Tuesday* (24 February 1998) or *Mardi Gras* is the climactic finale of these celebrations. In Europe, Mardi Gras is celebrated in all Catholic countries, but perhaps most famously in Venice, where harlequins and incognito strangers in chalk white masks stalk the streets. Fantastically ostentatious fancy dress balls are also held in Vienna at this time, while in the German city of Cologne, women run around cutting off men's ties.

Mardi Gras in the Americas is even more outrageous. In New Orleans bizarrely dressed parades march to the accompaniment of an insane amount of bead-flinging, flambeaux-carrying, chanting and boozing. But even this is nothing compared to what goes down in Rio de Janeiro, probably the single most famous street party in the world, where the emphasis is heavily on transvestism, erotic costumes, scantily clad dancers and alcohol. Finally Sydney's *Gay and Lesbian Mardi Gras* parade (which actually falls a couple of weeks into Lent) is the latest spin-off from the Carnival scene.

By contrast to which, the end-of-winter festival at the other end of the Euroasian landmass–*Chinese New Year* (28 January 1998, 15 February 1999)–is altogether low key. Instead of street parties, this is a time for families to come together, the main consequence of which is closed restaurants and horribly crowded train stations. From the traveller's point of view, it is a time to avoid China. You will see more by hanging around for the lion-dance festivities in London's China Town.

Other festivals with ancient roots are to be found all over Asia. *No Ruz*, the Iranian new year marking the spring equinox, provides travellers with a fascinating glimpse into the ancient heart of Iran; apart from feasting, one age-old custom is for everyone to join in leaping over street bonfires. The symbolism of this comes straight from the pre-Islamic fire-worshipping cult of Zoroaster.

Hindu and Buddhist communities, in countries such as India, Nepal, Thailand and the Indonesian island of Bali, retain traces of ancient cults in virtually every town and village, to the extent that travellers need hardly consult their calendars to be sure of running into colourful festivities.

India is the country with the oldest recorded surviving festivals. In the north particularly, the beginning of spring is marked by a major festival, *Holi*, the Festival of Colour (full moon in late February/early March 1997), during which people bombard each other with water and paint. In Bombay, the holiday *Ganesh Chaturthi*, is dedicated to the Hindu god Ganesh, (late August/early September), and sees huge processions carrying images of the god to immerse in the sea. The whole country in fact gets through a lot of rampant celebrations at the end of the monsoons, ostensibly commemorating events from the great Hindu epic *Ramayana.*

In contrast to these ancient ceremonies, the holidays associated with the world's monotheistic religions represent attempts to modernise ancient festivals, to tie them into an up-to-date framework. It is not, for example, coincidental that Christmas falls at the time of the winter equinox, and Easter at the spring equinox. This almost certainly reflects ancient Mediterranean beliefs in a god who is born at the coming of the winter rains, only to die again at the beginning of the summer heat.

Interesting though the myths may be, for the traveller *Christmas* is rarely more than a family affair outside Bethlehem and the Vatican in Rome where huge crowds congregate to hear the Pope lead mass. *Easter* is a better time to travel: Southern Spain above all celebrates *Semana Santa* (Holy Week) in flamboyant style, especially in the Andalucian city of Seville, where colossal processions of hooded, masked figures take place with figures of the Virgin Mary and Jesus being carted around in tow (5–12 April 1998). Greek Easter, which follows some weeks later, is likewise an excellent time to be in Greece.

Islamic festivals are widely observed in the religious sense but are not exactly occasions for tourist gawping. *Eid El Fitr* (the breaking of the fast after the holy month of Ramadan) and *Eid El Adha* are big family occasions, though if you happen to be in an Islamic country at this time you may be invited to banquets involving the slaughter of fresh goats.

The biggest Shi'ite festival is *Ashura*, to commemorate the martyrdom of the Shi'ite hero Hussein, killed in the battle of Kerbala in 680AD. This is an occasion for mourning and grief rather than celebration, with young men competing to flagellate themselves more bloodily than the next. This can be seen in Iran and parts of Iraq and Lebanon though tourists may not feel very welcome.

Jewish holidays are notable for their extreme frequency, and again, where travellers are concerned, these might not be the best times to actually visit Israel. Several of the holidays, notably *Yom Kippur* and *Sukkot,* involve varying degrees of abstinence and self-purification. *Purim*, on the other hand, (February/March) is an occasion for outright revelry and it's the only chance you'll have to get drunk with orthodox Jews.

Moving away from ancient myths and religions, it is perhaps refreshing at the dawn of the 21st century to realise that festivals are not exclusively rooted in the remote past. In truth, most of us spend more time celebrating secular festivals than religious ones.

National holidays can be exciting occasions anywhere. *Independence Day*, the USA's birthday bash on July 4 is a great time to be around, with fireworks, music and large crowds gathering in towns and cities. France's *Bastille Day,* just ten days later on July 14, is another patriotic extravaganza.

The secular holiday that comes nearer than any other to being a truly world holiday is January 1. Huge crowds at places as diverse as the Vatican, Time Square, Trafalgar Square, the Brandeburg Gate, Sydney Harbour (to name but a few) spiritually unite for heavy drinking and singing of *Auld Lang Syne,* Robert Burn's song composed to mark Scotland's own *Hogmanay*.

But the modern world's real contribution to the festival lies in the great sporting events of the 20th century: the football *World Cup* and above all the *Olympic Games*, two four-yearly events for which virtually the entire world comes to a standstill. Being able to attend either event in person is the equivalent – perhaps of what a religious pilgrimage would have been in another age. Political occasions – the American elections spring to mind, can also make pretty good jamborees. If you are able to travel, it really can be Christmas every day.

See Public Holidays p.664 the Directory

Further Reading: *Wild Planet: 1001 Extraordinary Events for the Inspired Traveler* by Tom Clynes (Invisible Ink Press)

Further Browsing on the internet see Festival Finder: http://www.festivalfinder.com ∎

FINDING OUT MORE
Chapter 2

BACKGROUND READING

by Miranda Haines

It is advisable to do some background reading before embarking on a trip. But what a boring phrase! Homework before a holiday? Especially when the problem with all research and travel literature is that there is so much bad stuff to sift through and avoid. There is nothing worse than buying a book about climbing the Himalayas in Tibet because you are planning to do the same when the book is so dull and uninspiring that it puts you off the whole venture. Or reading an alarmist guidebook that lists the numerous health hazards and imminent dangers that you will encounter, that suddenly you would rather stay home – which isn't really the point.

Quite often it is considered better to buy travel books (guides or novels) for reading on arrival or even once back on home ground in order to re-live the experience and luxuriate in new-found knowledge. That way, one's time is more one's own, to make discoveries, laze about or find hidden pleasure without a prescribed agenda.

But then how could you have really seen Vietnamese life, as you sipped a Tiger beer in Hanoi, if you hadn't read *The Quiet American* by Graham Green? Or understood the workings of Colombia's cocaine economy and underworld, without the skills of another veteran journalist, Charles Nichol, in his book, *The Fruit Palace*? These stories, like all great travel books, describe the history of the place – so often lost over to the modern world and demands of tourism – the natural beauty, the people and culture with the addition of a cracking good story weaved around their observations. You don't get that from a guide book. Or at least not many guide books provide travel literature as a guide to the countries and their people. (John Murray's literary guides and Traveller's Literary Companions are exceptions.)

No doubt the proliferation of travel books are a sign of a larger and more affluent travelling nation. But perhaps we don't need them nearly as much as we are led to believe? There is an excellent well-worn oral tradition that is often overlooked. Word of mouth can be a particularly useful method to obtain precise advice from friends who have already been to a place that you are interested in and who have addresses and hot tips of their favourite spots to visit. And more importantly, those to avoid. After all, they are more likely to have similar expectations as you than the anonymous person who wrote the guidebook. It is good to remember that information profered by personal recommendation is often more valuable than the written word. Also, guidebooks are inevitably out of date by the time they reach the shelves, hotels change management, roads are built or bridges closed and the prices have almost always risen since publication. This is an easy fact to forget before leaving. As a general rule, I always cost out my trip and then add 20 per cent for inflation and contingency, which is generally sufficient for the rise in prices and any emergency measures that inevitably befall the independent traveller. A hot shower, for example, might be the only solution to guard one's sanity, even if it does cost an extra £10.

Another danger of guidebooks is that they limit the scope of your experience rather than aid it. If the suggested "things to do and see" are followed religiously then not only do you bump into every other person who has bought the same guide (usually the same nationality as yourself) but hidden marvels are easily missed. If the traveller always follows a beaten track – in fear of missing the cheapest eat or best ruin, then meeting locals, and finding good local cuisine at local prices becomes an exotic one-off experience rather than the norm. (If you want to meet French people then use the Routard Guides, for Americans, Australians and English use the Lonely Planet series.)

Douglas Schatz, managing director of the specialist travel book shop Stanford's, believes that the quality of travel books is no more scattered than the rest of the publishing industry. The reason for the proliferation of travel books goes back to the boom of the eighties he says. "The great travel writers like Chatwin, Theroux, Thubron and O'Hanlin led the way and there was an economic boom in independent travel. So publishers thought that this was the place to be, which meant that everybody and anybody got published. Even those who had never written a thing. Inevitably their journeys were justified by some superficial label, such as: first-to do something, an anniversary, travel by horse, canoe, camel, whatever. But when the recession came, the market was forced to re-think and we saw a return to proven names."

Schatz believes that Britain has the strongest tradition of travel writing in the world and that it is easy to take this for granted. The genre is a culturally established one that has allowed many quality travel writers to flourish today; William Dalrymple, Katie Hickman, Rory McClean, Philip Marsden and Dervla Murphy, to name a few.

An obvious pleasure of reading travel books is that they allow one to travel anywhere (Patagonia or the deeply fashionable Antarctica if you like) while not moving from the comfort of the home. Of course, they can be an equally fulfilling read and perhaps a different experience, depending on where you are when you read them. Yet, there is no substitute for actually visiting a place in person. No one can describe a smell, or feeling as finely as your own senses do – and Middlemarch is just as good a read on a beach in Thailand as it is in the rolling countryside of Lincolnshire. Using your own methods of finding out more and not following the rules and advice given too strictly will ensure a more individual and thoughtful way to travel. Carry a compass and map on a bus journey and the lay of the land will be put into a marvelous perspective. The journey will become one that can be translated from the two dimensional to the three.

For Recommended Reading see p.689 of the Directory

USING TOURIST BOARDS

by Caroline Brandenburger

Tourist boards range in type – from the glossy office in a smart city boulevard run by a fleet of well-groomed staff, to a dingy cubby hole in a backstreet, manned by one forlorn assistant and a cat.

A glance at the annual report of the English Tourist Board reveals a huge, multi-million pound operation involving marketing strategies, development activity and local initiatives. Now that tourism occupies such a significant place in the revenue of so many countries, clearly the role of the tourist board has undergone a radical change.

All this leaves the consumer in some confusion as to what they should expect from a tourist board. What exactly is a tourist board meant to do? Just who is a national tourist board really serving? Officially they represent the tourist industry of that country, while at the same time providing helpful and accurate information to the would-be visitor, whether it be maps, accommodation brochures, lists of sites of cultural and historical interest, information on facilities for the elderly or disabled, special events, or transport. As the founding statute of the English Tourist Board puts it, the main functions are "To promote England as a destination", and "To encourage the provision and improvement of tourist facilities and amenities within England".

But do these noble intentions get put into practice? The frustrated consumer who has spent an afternoon trying fruitlessly to get through on the telephone will say that the tourist board is merely an ineffective mouthpiece of the tourist industry. *Condé Nast Traveler* magazine conducted a survey in America in which they wrote to the tourist boards of 30 different countries. In their letters, they asked for eight points to be answered, including details of facilities for disabled people. They then monitored how long it took to get replies and how many of those eight points were covered in the replies. Mexico did not reply at all, Argentina took the longest at 96 days, Australia came third with a 33-day delay and India was the quickest, responding in just four days. However, only three countries managed to respond to the eight queries: Germany, Great Britain and Switzerland. Brazil and Thailand tackled just one point, and most tourist boards approached only managed to make a stab at five or six of the queries.

Similarly in London, we tried to telephone eleven offices. The French Tourist Board was consistently engaged, as were those for Thailand and the US. While the Australians provided an answer machine, they did not return our call.

What, then, do tourist boards have to say for themselves? Leslie Agius, former director of the Malta National Tourist Office in London, and past chairman of the ANTOR (Association of National Tourist Office Representatives in the United Kingdom) is frank: "The functions of a national tourist board are various. Some of them may not be immediately apparent to the consumer." But he elaborates: "The most time-consuming task is answering letters. People want to know what facilities there are for, say, the disabled, and we provide that information. The Spanish and French get mail by the sackful every day. On a normal day, we get 200 inquiries, they get 2000. If people complain they don't answer the phone, it's because it's not physically possible."

When Mr Agius listed all the other functions and responsibilities of the tourist board, it seems hardly surprising that travellers do not always get the service they might wish for. There are only so many hours in the day – even for tourist offices. Being the public relations board for an entire country is a large part of it: "We try to get as much publicity as possible, organise press trips, fashion shoots, getting television coverage. It may not be obvious publicity – Jersey used *Bergerac*, Malta used *Howard's Way* and *Antiques Roadshow*. Then there's advertising – we spend a hell of a lot of money advertising in this country. We spend time meeting with the advertising people, the creative people, the graphics people, deciding where to spend money. We bring out brochures – I detected a lot of people from Britain going to Malta on their honeymoon, so we've brought out a brochure on honeymoons. We're in constant discussion with travel agents and tour operators and we take some tour operators to Malta so they can see for themselves exactly what is on offer."

So how can the consumer get the very best from the tourist board of the country they intend to visit? Leslie Agius says adamantly, "The best thing is to write in. Whoever is at the receiving end will have a chance to reflect, think about what you want. If you ring, they are hurried, pressured by other calls. In your letter, be as clear as possible, so that the person at the other end can help as much as possible."

A spokesman for the Association for British Travel Agents gave similar advice for the independent traveller hoping to use the tourist board machinery successfully:

1. Write rather than ring – the lines are often blocked by children ringing up for help with their school projects. Or go in to the office in person. They're usually fairly centrally placed.

2. Be as specific as you can in your request. If, for example, birdwatching is your interest, most tourist boards will at least come up with some sort of relevant literature or contacts for you to pursue when you arrive in your destination.

3. Be realistic about what you expect from them. They can give you advice and information but they won't book your holiday for you. One information seeker rang the English Tourist Board in London and asked how long it would take to cook a leg of lamb. "We're the *tourist board*," was the rather puzzled response. "Yes," said the caller, "I'm a tourist."

Foreign Tourist Boards in the UK (including websites) are listed on p.700

A GUIDE TO GUIDES

by Tim Ellerby and Roland Butler

A guide book is one of the most essential pieces of packing and selecting a good one can make all the difference to a trip. Whether it is scholarly coverage of the religious history of the local monasteries, a means of finding a quick alternative to the dive of a hotel you were recommended before you left home, or detailed information about trekking routes on some of the world's highest mountains, you may well be glad of a guide book's services on the road.

The explosion in guide book publishing that took place in the eighties has had two positive consequences for the consumer: firstly it is now hard to find anywhere that isn't covered by at least one guide book; even the Nordic islands of Spitsbergen have a guide now (courtesy of Bradt Publications). More often than not you will be faced with a choice of at least two or three guides, often each one quite different. The second result of this explosion is the increasing availability of specialised guides for far flung destinations where previously there might only have been one basic comprehensive guide. As well as the budget guide and the cultural guide there are now trekking guides, rail guides, off-road guides, on-road guides, architectural guides, gay guides, women's guides – the list could go on but all you, the consumer, need to know is that with a little careful selection you can find the guide that best suits your itinerary and your interest.

The following survey aims to introduce some of the main players in guide book publishing and highlight the differences between them in style and content or where certain guides are considered better than others. Ultimately, however, you would be best advised to go to a specialist map and travel bookshop and spend some time comparing the guides.

General Guides for the Independent Traveller

There are a number of companies who produce comprehensive guides for travel in almost any region or country in the world. These guides all abound with practical information and usually have good coverage of the history, politics and culture of a place. While they have a lot of common features, each one is laid out differently and each publisher can be stronger in different parts of the world or put slightly more emphasis on this or that aspect of travel.

Lonely Planet is one of the most well known publishers with well over 100 titles in their core *Travel Survival Kit* series. Lonely Planet started in 1973 when Tony and Maureen Wheeler published their guide to *South East Asia on the Cheap* (based on their own experiences of travelling across South East Asia). Lonely Planet have two main series of guides: the *Travel Survival Kits*, each of which covers a single country or region and their *Shoestring Guides* covering whole continents, which are intended more specifically for budget travellers who are likely to be passing through several countries on the same trip. Originally Lonely Planet mainly covered long haul destinations outside Europe. Their coverage of Australia is second to none and their central Asia Guide is highly respected. Now the range covers most countries of the world. Lonely Planet also publishes a series of special Trekking Guides and City Guides as well as pocket phrasebooks for languages such as Tibetan, Indonesian and Quechua. All Lonely Planets are produced in a practical size for the rucksack, with durable bindings that will stand up to the rigours of the road and are updated every two to three years.

Although Lonely Planet dominate the world market, **Rough Guides** are thought to be similar to the Lonely Planet guides and in Europe they are equally popular with young travellers and students. Rough Guides tend to favour the low-priced options and give more space to off-the-beaten-track sights and accommodation then their rivals Lonely Planet. The first, *Rough Guide to Greece*, was written in 1982 by a group of English university graduates who saw the need for candid contemporary travel guides. Although originally strongest in Europe, and still thought to be so by some, Rough Guides, who recently published their 100th guide, now have almost as many countries covered as Lonely Planet. Rough Guides also produce some excellent City Guides.

Bradt Guides are a good alternative to the big two described above. Hilary Bradt, the founder of this imprint, pioneered the publishing of off-the-beaten-track guides, and now Bradt Publications are responsible for some exceptionally practical guidebooks for destinations in Europe and across the world. Bradt was the first guide book publisher to cover places like Cuba and pride itself "in providing a greater and often more considered insight into the history and people of a country".

In the 1990's the well respected and long established Trade and Travel Handbooks underwent a make-over and became **Footprint Handbooks**. For the better part of this century, *The Trade and Travel Handbook to the South Americas* has been a bible for independent travellers to that continent. Footprint Handbooks hope to take the Trade and Travel reputation and comprehensive style to many more destinations, with handbooks to individual countries and regions as well as continental handbooks. The new handbooks have the same trade mark hard covers and "bible" paper as the originals, making them both highly durable and very compact. An interesting feature of the Footprint Handbooks is that their continent Handbooks are published annually, which in some cases can make them the most up to date Guides available. The main selling point of the Footprint Handbooks is the sheer volume of information within their covers; there is no candid selection of places to eat and sleep, just straight lists of places according to Budget. Also, no town or village is left out no matter how obscure or dull a place might be they also provide above average information on the politics, history and economics of a country or region.

Moon Handbooks are an American Publisher who are strongest in the US, where they have a guidebook for each state, and also for destinations in South-East Asia, particuarly Indonesia and Bali. Their Hong Kong guide comes highly recommended and their *Tibet Pilgrimage Guide* is easily the largest single guide book we have on Tibet. These guides are packed with detailed and reliable research on all practical aspects of independent travel, and are enhanced by line maps, drawings and comprehensive, descriptive introductions.

On a Budget

Whilst all of the books mentioned so far cater for any independent traveller who is seeking value for money, there are three series of guides designed specifically for travellers on a very small budget.

The **Let's Go Guides** and **Berkeley Guides** are written and researched annually by teams of students from Harvard and Berkeley Universities respectively, and they contain all of the up-to-date, practical advice required to live cheaply on the road. There are many tales of travellers tearing out sections of the enormous *Let's Go Europe* when used, and passing the much needed extracts on to other travellers.

Vacation Work guides tackle the problem of being on a budget in a different way – instead of scrimping and saving before you go you can actually earn as you go. Their guides to working and travelling abroad are packed with ideas. Vacation Work also publishes a growing series of *Travellers' Survival Kits* which, not to be confused with Lonely Planet's TSKs, are aimed more directly at budget travellers and are an ideal accompaniment to their Working books or as guides on their own. Their guide to Cuba is one of the best.

Specialised Guides

These guides principally cover trekking and backpacking, but there are also guides to travelling by road and rail and guides for people specifically travelling to see wildlife.

Two publishers already mentioned, Lonely Planet and Bradt Publications, produce some very fine specialised guides. Lonely Planet are rapidly expanding their range of trekking guides; Spain, Australia, Karakoram, Greece, Alaska and the Himalayas are just some of their current titles. Extensive sections on travelling in the country or region and specific advice for the trekker are followed by chapters detailing a wide variety of treks in a given area, day to day descriptions of each trek are given and the treks are shown on special trekking maps. Some of the first Bradt Guides were Hiking Guides and Hilary Bradt, the company's founder, has written many of their South American Guides. Some other areas that Bradt are strong on are the Eastern European countries and Africa. Each have sketched maps accompanied by specific advice and route descriptions. Bradt Publications also publish a number of guides to travelling by rail and by road, in Europe, Asia, North America, South America and Africa, as well as some impressive wildlife guides to Antarctica and Madagascar.

There are two specialist publishers that deserve a mention: **Cicerone** and **Trail Blazer**. Without a doubt Cicerone Press, who are a long established company, highly respected among walkers, have one of the most impressive ranges of trekking guides covering almost every walking region in Europe as well as some for the more common trekking destinations across the world. Trail Blazer are a relatively new company who produce an excellent range of trekking guides for the Himalayas as well as rail guides to Siberia and Canada. Each of these publishers' books are usually pocket sized with maps, illustrations and general advice sections geared specifically towards the kind of travel the books describe.

Cultural and Luxury Guides

Not everyone travels with a rucksack and not everyone travels independently. If you want more information about the history and culture of a place and less about the basics like where to stay and how to get about, then there are many guide series that will provide you with just this balance of information.

In this category there are two extremes: highly illustrated and highly wordy. Insight Guides are of the illustrated extreme, although there are plenty of words too, with hundreds of pictures showing all aspects of a country's geography, culture and people. They are accompanied by magazine-style articles, often by famous authors, and chapters on each region. Following a similar format there are **Insiders Guides** and the slightly smaller **Nelles Guides**. Again in the illustrated category but deserving of their own mention are **Odyssey Guides'**

Introductions to the World. These are stylishly designed with quality photographs and maps, written by authors with extensive local experience and include extracts of celebrated travel writing.

With a distinctive format of their own there are the **Eyewitness Guides** by Dorling Kindersley and the **Everyman Guides**. Both series have a very modern look where text mixes delightfully with drawings, diagrams and photographs. Eyewitness Guides cover cities and regions of culture mainly in Europe, but there are a few titles for North America and Australia. Each guide has a general introduction section followed by some history of the city or region. 3-D street elevation maps then lead you to all the cultural features of an area. Everyman Guides, though similar in appearance, are quite different in content, concentrating more on the background history and culture, with sections on art and wildlife as well. They also cover more far flung destinations in Asia, North Africa and Central America.

There are three highly respected scholarly guides series offering unparalleled detail and intelligent comment on the art, architecture, history and culture of a place: **Blue Guides, Pallas Guides,** and **Companion Guides.** The Blue Guides are long established and are justly renowned for their comprehensive treatment of their subject. Although they are said by some to be rather dry to read, they are said by others to be the last intelligent word on many European locations. There rigorous detail has also been applied to such places as Mexico, China and Thailand. Pallas Guides are fewer in number but are really out on their own in terms of writing style and content. Generally considered more readable than the Blue Guides, and with impressive colour and black and white photography, they are an ideal accompaniment to your travels. Companion Guides, like the Blue Guides, are a well respected and established series containing lots of historical and cultural information, practical advice and maps, but written more in the style of a travel narrative, making these guides easy and enjoyable to read.

For travellers visiting North America exclusively there are the **Smithsonian Guides**. These are quality illustrated guides that come highly recommended and are available to cover cities, states and regions. The writing is very good as are the photographs. There are two series one exploring the man-made history of a region and one concentrating on the natural history. There is no practical information in these books but they are ideal reference guides and are excellent for reminiscing after your trip is over.

The Automobile Association are responsible for a great many guide series. The **AA Explorer** series are large colourful guides which mix information about the sights with historical and cultural information and also walking tours. A good selection of hotels, restaurants and other practical information can be found at the back of each book. A number of European cities are covered as well as countries and popular holiday regions across the world. The AA also publish the AA Essential Guides which are smaller then the explorers and lack the cultural and historical coverage. In conjunction with Thomas Cook, AA publish the **Thomas Cook Travellers**. There are over 50 titles in the range, Singapore, Berlin, New Zealand and San Francisco to name just a few. The guides are compact and ideal for a short visit. They cover walking tours, sights, and have very good sections on where to eat, shop and go for a night out.

Less concerned with luxury travel but certainly with excellent cultural coverage are **Cadogan Guides** and **Discovery Guides**. Cadogan Guides are elegantly designed, have lively and literate texts, and useful, practical recommendations appropriate for both the independent traveller and luxury tourist alike. Discovery Guides contain more photographs and slightly less cultural information than Cadogan.

Finally a company called **Windrush** publish some excellent historical guides in a series called *Traveller's History*. These are well written guides offering extensive chronological coverage of a country's history with maps and illustrations. The guides mostly cover European locations but Windrush are preparing guides for more far-flung destinations as I write.

Touring Guides

Touring Guides are aimed at the more affluent traveller. As well as detailing the sights, they provide a wide and varied selection of places to eat and stay, and their recommendations, while always promising value for money, are designed to provide the traveller with a high quality rather then budget experience.

Famous enough to be identified simply by colour, the **Michelin** *Red* and *Green Guides* are an excellent choice for a tour of Europe. The Red Guides provide an incomparable reference to the hotels and restaurants of Europe, with location maps, information on facilities and prices, and of course their famous symbols of recommendation. They are updated annually and, once you master their language, they are hugely informative. There are basic listings of principal tourist sights in the Red Michelin guides, but more substantial touring information is found in the series of Green Michelin tourist guides. These contain introductions to the history and art of an area, followed by a detailed alphabetical survey of places of interest. Their distinctive, tall format, the many maps, the star classification of sights and the clear layout make them easy to use. One of the most impressive features of both the Red and Green Michelin guides is that they are cross-referenced in detail to each other and to the full range of Michelin maps.

Outside Europe, one of the giants of guide book publishing, with over 100 titles in their list, is the **Fodor's Guides** series. As conceived by their eponymous American founder, Eugene Fodor, the guides are distinctive for being updated annually. They now cover much of the globe, though the majority are for countries and cities in the western world. Often accused of sanitising travel, Fodor's guides are in fact a useful and dependable source. They maintain a good balance between their description of sights and the practical information on transport, money, accommodation and restaurants (with recommendations) that cover a range of budgets. Travel may be less of an adventure with Fodor's but is also less likely to go wrong.

Fodors also publish the **Mobil Travel Guides** which are similar in layout to the Michelin Green Guides but cover the main regions of North America. The guides are annually updated, with road maps and city plans followed by varied selections of above average hotels and restaurants and suggestions of things to do and see in each town in the region.

Another series of guide books which, like Fodor's, originates in America and bears the name of its founder and editorial master, is Arthur **Frommer's**

Guides. These cover countries and cities world-wide with an emphasis on Europe. While they are not budget guides, they concentrate on finding value for money. Their lack of detail on sights and culture is more than compensated for by their descriptive assessments of hotels, restaurants and nightlife.

Probably the most recognisable name in travel guide books lives on in the new generation of **AA/ Baedeker Guides**. Reissued in a practical pocket size, the guides contain a comprehensive gazetteer of places to visit, along with a fold-out map stored in their plastic cover. There are only minimal listings of practical information but the Baedekers are clear, general-purpose tourist guides.

Pocket Guides

Pocket Guides are ideal for people on a brief visit and it is surprising how much information can be squeezed into them. **Berlitz** publish some of the smallest, with basic information on the sights, photographs and some practical advice. Competing with Berlitz are the **Globetrotter Travel Guides** and the **Michelin in your pocket guides**. The Globetrotter guides tackle each destination in sections, giving details on shopping, eating and sights as well as some brief historical information. The Michelin Guides have maps, background information, A-Z listings of facilities and a good section which clearly lists the sights that "must be seen" making them ideal for a short stay.

Still pocket size but with more of a mini-guide book look are the **AA Essential Guides** which offer more substantial texts. The **Insight Pocket Guides** are similar but more striking in style and incredibly good value for money with fold out maps included in nearly every one. One more advantage of the Insight Guides is the itineraries they offer, which are always varied and interesting. For example their *Kathmandu Guide* has details of biking tours around the city.

Literary Guides

Literary guides act as an optional extra if you don't mind carrying them with you. They can give a wonderfully illuminating insight into a place. Equally they can prepare you before the trip, or remind you vividly after the event. The best are published by **John Murray**, who have covered Greece, India, Egypt, Rome and Florence amongst others, with a delightful compendium of extracts from writers great and unknown. Other series to look out for are **Travellers' Tales**, by Bond, a series covering Brazil, Italy, Nepal and Japan amongst others and the *Travellers' Literary Companions*, by **In Print**.

City Guides

If you are going to be spending most of your time in just one city or are just going for a short break then you should consider a city guide. Even if you are planning to explore the surrounding countryside, a lot of the popular excursions will be covered in a city guide.

All the main publishers produce city guides and it would be impossible to list them all. But there are three city guide series that particuarly stand out. **Time**

Out city guides are laid out in a similar way to their magazine listings and their candid comments rarely fall short of the mark. **Access Guides** are clearly laid out guides that tackle a city according to area, a map of the area is followed by colour coded listings (red for restaurants, blue for hotels etc.). **AA-City Packs** are slim pocket-sized volumes that come with a fold out map, as well as the usual information there are itineraries, walks and a "top 25" list of sights.

Of the publishers already mentioned, Lonely Planet's city guides are particularly appealing as their slim format is ideal for putting in your pocket. Comprehensive listings are accompanied by colour photographs and the covers fold out to reveal excellent maps. Rough Guides are also of note as their city guides are well established and have excellent sections on history and listings that often extend beyond those of both Lonely Planet and Time Out.

Women's Travel

With the demise of Virago press there are few country-specific guides for women travelling alone or with other women. Rough Guides however publish a book called *More Women Travel* which covers over sixty countries and offers advice for women travelling in the form of first hand accounts by women. These accounts are supported by practical advice and some addresses. It is worth noting that most of the main guidebooks now have sections covering specific advice women may require when travelling in a country.

Travelling with Children

Lonely Planet produce a very popular general guide to travelling with children and Frommers produce some guides to travelling with children in the US, such as their *New York with Kids* book.

Gay Guides

Spartacus are the obvious guides to mention with a World-wide Guide as well as some guides for specific countries such as Britain and Spain. These guides are generally regarded as good, comprehensive guides with lists of the bars, clubs, cruising areas, hotels, cafés, and restaurants all accompanied by good maps and background information about the gay scene. **Scene** *Gay Guides* is another series which covers such destinations as Berlin, Thailand and New York. Each Scene Guide has an introduction to the gay scene, a section on the do's and don'ts and listings of the bars and clubs. If you are travelling to San Francisco one publication that would be impossible not to mention is *Betty and Pansy's Severe Queer Review of San Francisco*. Also, it is worth noting that a lot of the main travel guides, the Time Out and Rough Guides, in particular, each have very strong sections for gay travellers.

This survey is inevitably incomplete due to the proliferation of guide books mushrooming fast. So when possible, visit a specialist travel bookseller where you will find the widest range of choice, and possibly even some expert advice.

The list of Recommended Reading on p.689 of the Directory will tell you which guide books are available for different countries world-wide

CHOOSING MAPS

by Tim Ellerby and Roland Butler

In all the hustle and bustle of planning foreign travel it is easy to forget that good mapping of the area you are to visit can be just as useful as a guide book and under some circumstances may even help to get you out of serious trouble. Maps are also an extremely concentrated source of information which can be inexpensive and light to carry. However, perhaps the most important point to make about maps is that with a little application they can take you far beyond your guide book or even local knowledge in pursuit of the unknown and undiscovered.

Having said this, one reason that people do not naturally purchase maps is that they are unsure of how to select and use them. I hope that the following comments will help those who have no previous knowledge to feel confident enough to select the right map and make good use of it. Finally, the serious international traveller should recognise the value of mapping as an aid to advanced planning and that where possible you should purchase your maps in advance because local sources can be surprisingly difficult to locate and unreliable.

The Components of a Map

The purpose of a map is to provide information about the area covered so that the user can either locate any feature shown or visualise what it would be like to be there so that journeys can be planned or imagined. This information is presented in two ways, through the use of a quoted scale and by employing standard symbols to represent commonly occurring features.

The scale of the map is an indication of how much detail the map contains. Large scale maps have the most detail while smaller scale maps contain less detail but usually show a wider area, giving a more general picture of the land. The biggest source of confusion with scale arises because the maps referred to as small scale have the highest numbers, i.e.: 1:7,500,000. To find out which scale is right for you please read the section *The Choice of Scale*.

The symbols on the map also need a little explaining as they are in effect the cartographer's shorthand. This shorthand is "decoded" by the use of the map key which tabulates all the feature codes and tells you what each one represents. It is also important to realise that whilst location of any feature is accurately portrayed the actual feature itself is purely diagrammatic and not to scale. As an example, roads on motoring maps appear to be far wider than they really are in order to give the maximum clarity and allow junctions and other features to be usefully displayed.

One other consideration regarding both the scale of the map and the symbols used is that there is inevitably a degree of selection of the information that the map attempts to portray so that the map does not become completely cluttered and consequently unreadable. In practice this means that some features will be omitted from the map, something to consider when selecting a map. The decision about what is shown on any given map or series of maps is determined by the cartographer and publisher and is often as much a matter of tradition and style as it is convention or rule.

The Choice of Scale

If we now move on to some specific map scales we can quickly build up an idea of the sorts of maps to use for a given purpose. Most national surveys were originally based on the scale of 1:50,000 and the British Ordnance Survey was no exception. At this scale it is obvious that a series of maps is needed to cover an area the size of Britain and so a grid is used to relate map sheets of equal size to the areas that they cover and to each other. Such grids can be referred to at the map shop or sometimes are available to take away so that you can work on your requirement at home. The 1:50,000 scale is ideal for cycling and slow detailed motoring within a limited area and can also be used by walkers although it is not really ideal. At this scale you will see all the towns, villages and hamlets in a given area together with all roads, tracks, lanes and rights of way. Other features will depend on the style and type of mapping. For walking purposes a map scale of 1:25,000 is ideal where you will see in much more detail all the landmarks and features of the area right down to the field boundaries in some cases. When we move into the urban environment where the number and density of features is very high, scales of 1:10,000, 1:15,000 and 1:20,000 are frequently used and these will allow you to see individual street names and specific building locations. At the other end of the spectrum map scales of 1:100,000 and 1:250,000 (Quarter Million) or even 1:500,000 (Half Million) are regularly used for long-distance motoring and regional touring where the emphasis is on relating one major feature or area to another.

Having established the uses of scale and the importance of symbols on a given map it is helpful to look at the types of map which are generally available so that other criteria for selection can be established.

Types of Map

For the purposes of the traveller, most maps will be either *Topographic* or *Thematic* or possibly a combination of the two. Topographic maps show the general nature of the country, the physical features, the type of terrain, the location of watercourses, forests, marshes, foreshore features and all roads, railways and other lines of communication, and any other significant features be they man-made or natural. In general this type of mapping will have contours (lines connecting points of equal elevation) to indicate the physical relief and as such tends to be a survey map of the Ordnance Survey type.

Thematic maps can be very different. The most common thematic maps a traveller will encounter are tourist maps and trekking maps of various kinds. Tourist maps tend to suppress and simplify a lot of the geographical features and show only the main roads or established walks and the main points of interest to tourists, such as viewing points, guest houses and picnic spots, museums or beaches, at the expense of comprehensive road layouts, minor villages and physical relief. Trekking maps show the route of a trek overlaid on a landscape that has been simplified to show only the recognisable features for the trekker, such as ridges, rivers rocks and settlements. As trekking routes are often well established such maps are usually adequate and enough to stop you getting lost. However, if you are venturing off the beaten "trek" then you would be advised to take a detailed survey map with you, if you can get one.

This then leaves you with a choice to make in selecting the right map for the job you have in mind. In general a combination of themes or themes plus topography is what the traveller will be looking for and many combine major tourist attractions, communications networks and some physical relief.

Having decided what is the best scale and what features you want the map to show, you are now ready to compare your criteria with what is available.

Choosing a Map

Whilst there is no doubt that many maps are sold each year purely on the basis of their appearance there are a number of points which should be given priority over simply whether it looks nice or not.

First and foremost a map is a graphic representation of information, so it is important to establish how accurate that information might be. This can be established in a number of ways but it is fair to say that the publication date is one of the most useful indicators because, assuming that an area continues to develop, then the older the map the more information will be missing. Again, as an indicator this rule need not be taken to extremes as some elements of the map only change very slowly, such as relief, and so if your primary purpose is walking it might not be so critical. In urban and semi-urban areas rates of change to road networks and buildings can be extremely fast, so here you need to be much more critical. Needless to say most map producers are sensitive to such relative rates of change and will revise their urban mapping much more frequently than rural and wilderness coverage. It is also a great mistake to assume that levels of mapping and rates of updating are equal the world over; they are not and so you may have to accept the best available which could date back to the 1960's for some areas. Likewise, with scale by no means all areas of the world are mapped at 1:50,000 so again you may be forced to accept a smaller scale than you would ideally choose. The important factor in all of this is that you find a source for your map purchase which can offer reliable advice and explain all the current options available to you.

Unfortunately it is not possible to detail all the main map producers throughout the world and give an appraisal of their relative merits, but I will give a general overview by area and highlight the sorts of problems you may encounter in trying to obtain maps.

World-wide

There are, remarkably, some topographic map series that cover the whole world. At Stanfords we stock maps called *Air Navigation Charts*. These are available at either 1:1,000,000 or 1:500,000. Although this does not immediately sound that impressive, for some places these are the best and largest scale maps available and should be remembered if there is nothing else. One particuarly interesting result of the changes in Russia has been the recent availability of Russian Military Survey maps. The scales of Russian Survey maps vary from place to place, the most common being 1:200,000, but 1:500,000, 1:100,000, 1:50,000 and urban areas mapped at 1:10,000 are also available for some places. They are all in Russian, usually have to be ordered and supply can be patchy but like the Air Navigation Charts, if normal commercial mapping is unavailable then these may be your only option.

Europe

There have always been a lot of maps available for the countries of Europe and with the opening up of the former Eastern European countries the task of listing the maps available for each country is enormous. For the motorway traveller and general route planning, it is hard to beat the maps produced by Michelin, Geocenter and Kummerley and Frey. Bartholomew also produce some good maps, although some can look very dated. For want of a better way of listing the more detailed maps I shall start in the west and work along the Mediterranean coast to Turkey and then start northwards.

Portugal and Spain are mapped by their respective military and civilian agencies with survey mapping at 1:25,000, 1:50,000, and 1:100,000. Mapping for Spain is also available at the additional scales of 1:200,000, 1:400,000 and 1:800,000. Other maps worth considering are the Editorial Alpina series which covers the Pyrenees and other mountainous regions at a good walking scale, and a series of provincial maps at 1:200,000 from MOPT. Michelin and Geocenter also produce reliable general mapping for Spain and Portugal. City plans can be obtained mainly from Falk, Almax and Geocenter.

France is extremely well provided for by its national survey IGN France which produces maps at 1:25,000, 1:100,000 and 1:250,000 (but no longer 1:50,000) plus many special sheets. Of particular interest to mountain walkers are the IGN Top 25 series, the Didier et Richard series and Edition Randonnées Pyrenéennes which are over-printed with the GR routes. There is a Town-plan series published by Blay.

Italy presents some problems to the map user as its national survey is in a rather sorry state and while supply is possible, many sheets remain unpublished. Consequently you will have to rely on the commercially produced maps where, fortunately, there is good coverage from a variety of sources. TCI (Touring Club Italiano), the Italian equivalent of the AA, provides excellent road maps at 1:200,000 alongside the ubiquitous Michelin at a scale of 1:400,000. Town plans from FMB, Falk and Hallwag are readily available and the walker is more than adequately catered for by Kompass, IGC, Edizioni Multigraphic, Mapgraphic Bozen and Tabacco at a variety of suitable scales.

Slovenia, Albania and all the countries along the east coast of the Adriatic are all best covered at the moment by Russian Survey maps at 1:200,000 and then by Freytag & Berndt maps. There are good maps available of the Julian Alps published by F&B as well as general series of sheets at 1:100,000 for the Croatian coast.

Greek mapping is hampered by the Greek government, who will not sell survey information of a scale greater than 1:200,000 and then only in the form of an out-of-date provincial series at inflated prices. The result is that you have to rely on the more general mapping of the commercial companies such as F&B who produce a good series at scales between 1:250,000 and 1:400,000. For the Greek islands the detailed mapping on the market is the standard tourist series produced by Toubi, although these are very basic. A little relief is offered by the Greek Alpine Club who have published a number of detailed contour maps of the main mountain regions based on the "unavailable" 1:50,000 survey. Unfortunately these maps are not all they might be and they certainly should be used with caution. Soon to be available is a series of maps at a scale of 1:100,000 for Crete published by Harms Verlag.

Finally, at the eastern end of the Mediterranean, Cyprus is covered at 1:200,000 by maps published by Mairs and Turkey is covered at 1:200,000 by Russian Survey and by Ryborsch maps at 1:500,000. Switzerland is mapped by the Swiss National Survey and these maps are generally regarded to be exemplary in the accuracy and clarity of their mapping. Produced at the scales 1:100,000, 1:50,000 and 1:25,000, the maps are a joy to use. Special editions are available with ski routes and walking trails. Again, general road maps are published by Michelin and a good series of townplans from Orell Fussli is also available.

Austria's national survey is a reliable source of mapping but excellent coverage is given by Kompass, F&B and Alpenvereinskarte for the walking and skiing areas. Germany is well-served by its national survey with the standard scales available – 1:25,000 being the largest. For the mountain walker Kompass maps are excellent. More general coverage is provided by Mairs at a scale of 1:200,000 and Michelin at 1:400,000 and good town and city plans are published by ADAC, Falk (although their method of folding may take a little getting used to) and RV Verlag.

The Benelux countries are well-covered by their national surveys but good cycling maps for the Netherlands at a scale of 1:100,000 are provided by ANWB. General motoring mapping is again Michelin and town plans are published by Falk, although this time many of the sheets are folded conventionally.

Further east towards the Czech and Slovak Republics, Poland and Hungary, the locally produced maps for the Czech and Slovak republics are available, at 1:50,000, 1:100,000, and 1:200,000. The Tatra mountain, between Slovakia and Poland, are very well covered at 1:50,000 in 3 sheets by F&B. The rest of Poland is covered by Polish Survey maps at 1:25,000, 1:50,000 and 1:100,000. The walking areas of Poland are reasonably covered by the publisher PPWK who also produce town plans. Hungary has a series of tourist maps at a scale of 1:30,000 and 1:20,000 for many of the popular areas.

Once again Russian Survey come to the rescue in Romania, Belarus, Ukraine, Bulgaria and Macedonia with coverage at 1:200,000 scale. In the far north, the Scandinavian countries all have their own national surveys producing high quality topographical mapping at the standard scales which can be complimented by general coverage produced by commercial publishers.

North America

Survey mapping is available for the United States and Alaska; however it is not of the highest quality. Perhaps considering the vast area covered this is understandable. Scales available range from 1:25,000 through 1:100,000 up to 1:500,000 and a number of special sheets are also produced for more popular areas. Help is at hand, however, if you are travelling to any of the National Park areas in the form of the excellent Trails Illustrated maps. Printed on waterproof, tear-resistant paper and based on USGS mapping they are aimed specifically at the back-packer and explorer. If you are visiting a city there are very good maps produced by Rand McNally and Gousha and a company called Mapeasy produce some popular hand-drawn maps that include some tourist information as well. For the road user, the ubiquitous Rand McNally and Gousha are essential and whilst they may appear crude compared to survey mapping they are surprisingly useable. Other commercial map publishers such as Hildebrand and K&F produce some state and regional maps. Finally, with a land mass the size of the United States it is worth considering looking at State atlases produced by Delorme.

Canada has the Canadian National Survey and this is the main source of detailed information, readily available at scales of 1:250,000 and 1:50,000. Special sheets are produced for some of the national parks which include tourist information. General motoring coverage is available from Allmaps and Mapart together with good city plans again from Mapart.

Central America Mexico and the Caribbean

Survey information for this group of countries is naturally harder to obtain but the patient purchaser should be able to obtain mapping for the majority of popular destinations. Good general mapping comes from ITM. Mapping for Belize at 1:50,000 is available from the Ordnance Survey International (OSI) (formerly the Directorate of Overseas Survey) which is the overseas division of the Ordnance Survey. In Mexico the local cartographers Guia Roji produce good road maps of the individual states and some survey maps can be ordered. Of the remaining countries, survey mapping is available for Costa Rica and Panama, but not so readily for anywhere else. There are many high quality general maps, however. The Caribbean islands are well provided for by IGN France who produce some excellent detailed maps scaled for walking and general use. National Geographic produce a good display map of the whole region and some other good maps are available from K&F, Bartholomew and Hilderbrand. Also the TPC charts mentioned in the *World-wide* section can be good if nothing else is available.

South America

The good news with regard to the South American countries is that survey information is generally available for most of the countries including Argentina, Bolivia, Brazil, Chile, Colombia, Ecuador and Peru, though it may be significantly out-of-date and very expensive. You should also anticipate a considerable wait if your retailer does not have what you want in stock. Also good large scale maps of places of interest are available from the South American Explorers Club and Treaty Oak. Commercial mapping of note comes from ITM, Bartholomew together with a myriad of locally produced city street plans and motoring maps. Again if you become completely stuck Air Navigation Charts may be of some use.

Africa

The African continent presents many problems to the traveller wishing to purchase maps and it is useful to know something of the colonial history of the countries you are visiting when you set out to locate survey information. In general some ex-British colonies will still have mapping available from the OIS. Ex-French colonies are covered by IGN-France, and sometimes this can be the only mapping available, although often at no greater scale then 1:1,000,000! Some African countries have their own survey including Algeria, Ghana, Gambia, Madagascar, Malawi and Namibia, but as with South America you should be prepared for long waits. South Africa has an excellent survey department producing maps of a high quality. The rest of Africa is more of a problem and availability will vary with the current political climate and you will have to rely on either general commercially produced maps or Air Navigation Charts.

Middle East

In such areas of turmoil and conflict, survey mapping is inevitably restricted and at present Israel is the only country selling to the general public. Fortunately there is an excellent series of maps produced by GeoProjects which covers most of the Middle Eastern states. If more detail is required then you will have to rely on Air Navigation Charts as suggested above. Other commercial products worthy of note are produced by F&B, Bartholomew, Geocenter and K&F.

Indian Sub-Continent

Despite an immense amount of travel interest in India and its neighbours, there is very little in the way of survey mapping available to the general public and even then only by battling with a huge bureaucracy. As a result, a number of publishers have produced very good maps for the walking and trekking areas of northern India, Pakistan and Nepal. Nelles (Schneider) produce a wonderful series of contour maps covering East and Central Nepal. Mandala, imported directly from Nepal are a series of dye-line contour trekking maps which give good overall detail of the main trekking areas of Nepal. Leomann produce a series of sketched trekking maps which cover virtually all the accessible parts of the Indian Himalaya and the Karakoram. Some specific sheets are available for Everest and its national park. A good series of locally produced regional and city maps are available from TT Maps. Nelles produce excellent regional relief mapping of the whole of India and Pakistan. Finally; a reprint of the AMS/U502 series at 1:250,000 is available only from Stanfords, these cover the Himalayas and Karakoram region and will serve to fill in the gaps.

Coverage for Sri Lanka and Afghanistan is also difficult and Nelles or Geocenter would be a good choice here. Once again, Air Navigation Charts may be worth considering for more remote, less popular regions.

China, Japan and Korea

The only survey maps of China or Korea that can be obtained are Russian Survey maps and these are available at various scales. Nelles produce some good maps of the different regions of China and individual province and city maps are available but often only with Chinese or Korean text. Japan however does have excellent survey mapping but it is only available with Japanese text and can be time consuming and expensive to obtain.

South East Asia, Indonesia, Malaysia, Papua New Guinea, the Philippines and the Pacific Islands

This vast area again poses many problems to the traveller who wishes to purchase accurate, detailed mapping but there are a few notable exceptions. Survey mapping in Thailand, the Philippines and Papua New Guinea is generally available although again you may have to wait some time for delivery and coverage may not yet be complete. Other individual islands with a colonial history or which still owe their allegiance to European countries may be mapped by their country of government. Failing all else then Nelles, Bartholomew and Geocenter may come to the rescue again or, of course, Air Navigation Charts.

Australia and New Zealand

Excellent survey mapping is available for Australia and New Zealand and there is a good selection of comercial mapping too. The only problem with Australia is identifying the maps you require from the vast grids that cover the country. Good general maps come from Bartholomew and the Australian publishers UBD, state maps come from UBD and town atlases come from Gregorys who publish state maps. New Zealand Survey maps are published under the brand name Infomaps and these range from walking scale up to route planning scale maps of the whole country. As well as the Infomaps, there are good maps from Hildebrand and, again, Bartholomew.

As a final plea please remember that no shop however large could hold stock of all maps currently available, so if you are venturing off into the unknown and you need to rely on a map please make sure that you order your maps well in advance. Some foreign survey departments can take from six months to two years to respond, so give your retailer as much notice as possible otherwise you may be disappointed.

TRAVELLING ALONE

By Nicholas Barnard

The noise and movement of an elderly Land Rover negotiating a footpath within dense bush was no foil to the impact of the tales of swamp life I was being subjected to. "Of course, you realise that the crocodiles are the least of your worries," the great white pot-bellied hunter paused, wrenched the wheel this way and that, before continuing with great deliberation, "no, the crocodiles will have what is left of you after the hippo have chewed up your dug-out." The "Hip-po", previously a happy word of the nursery and cartoon, was instantly dismembered by his accent to create a clear onomatopoeic vision of a wobbly dug-out snapping in the jaws of the snarling leander. Turning to look at me in the bright moonlight, my congenial host shared with me a calabash of pertinent information. "As for the snakes for which this part of Africa is famous – don't worry, there may be a snake bite kit in the back, but if there is, what use will it be to you? Moments after most snake bites you will be completely paralysed and the polers will be standing around watching you die, for none speak or read a word of English."

By the time we reached fishing camp near the Angolan border at dawn, I believed that I had come to terms with the prospect of travelling alone for at least eight days in such taciturn company; but dying alone in their presence was an untenable thought. To endure that journey down the Okavango to the Kalahari was an early and rigorous introduction to the art of travelling alone, to the condition of being able to survive alone.

Between the concept of travelling alone and the reality of the journey, there exists a gulf that will be bridged by painful as well as pleasing experience. From country to country and culture to culture, the act of travelling alone exposes the myths and expectations of a singular path. No manner of preparation and solitariness will disguise the fact that, from leaving a homeland, one is inescapably foreign and obtrusive. How the citizens of each culture will react to this small-time intrusion will make or break the experience of travelling alone. The solitary habit may help the desire to achieve inconspicuousness or it may increase the attention received: within one land one may know just how lonely a journey may be in the close company of others and yet again, how intrusive a train compartment of strangers may prove. Dependent upon the age and sex of the would-be loner, the choice of destination certainly needs careful thought.

Travelling alone enjoys a different status within the varied regions of the world. Successful solitude may be found in the most unlikely destinations or modes of transport. Without exception, it is very difficult to travel alone outside Europe and North America. Consider how easy it is to take a railway or a bus journey across Europe in delicious isolation from the friendliness of the companions of the carriage. To ignore a possible foreigner is acceptable in those parts – in Southern Asia it is unthinkable. If you want isolation from the land and its people when travelling the Subcontinent, take the First Class air conditioned wagon or the Air India flight. There you will be forced to endure the foppish company of the politician, the government official or the corporation executive. I take the clamour of second-class reserved and share the ever-proffered tiffin with the broad-beamed smiles of the families in my compartment – and even answer all the questions I am able concerning the greatness of Tottenham Hotspur, Ian Botham and Mrs Thatcher. Indeed, I have come to relish, to look forward to these casteless ceremonies of intimate hospitality so alien to my first desire to be alone – despite seeking to be that sentinel of isolation with my open and over-thumbed leaden volume of social history I never fail to pack, never finish and always discard at a faraway hotel for a more appreciative reader.

The obtrusiveness of being foreign has, seemingly, considerable demerits. Escaping to the Omayid mosque from the demographic froth of the most wonderful Damascine bazaar, I passed through a gate to behold for the first time that temple of temples to monoaetheism. Bewitched, I entered the cathedral-lofty prayer hall and sat near the tomb of John the Baptist (for reassurance, I suppose) and observed the interplay of women and children, men and boys at prayer and at play. The all-pervading sense of tranquillity was an unparalleled experience and it was wise to have drunk so deeply, so rapidly, for my peace was to be cast aside by the introduction of a student of agriculture eager to exercise his World

Service English. It was not the interruption that was so galling, but the fact that he was so charming, so genial and good – characteristics that precluded any beastly dismissiveness on my part. As ever, so gentle a meeting converted solitude to a shared and unforgettable experience of being led with gusto to the hidden tombs, chapels and by-ways of ancient Damascus.

Being foreign and a woman alone in certain cultures is an unenviable circumstance. Certain countries are simply not enjoyable to visit for the single woman, whether for the mis-match of the religious, cultural and social mores with our own. Chittagong, like so many conurbations of Muslims the world over, is not a forum for the proselytising of worthy feminine liberal sentiments. The paucity of any kind of foreigners draws undesirable companionship, as mosquitoes to the ear. Boarding a bus I was approached by an English girl and her train of admirers. After so long in the company of well-wrapped women I was as shocked and confused by the state of her lack of clothing as the gathered young Bangladeshis. The crowd was divided in sentiment – from the full-scale stoning party to lascivious indulgence – and I was delighted when the bus pulled out of the station. I had to ask about her dress and I should have known that I was wasting my time. Fixing me with a stare that took my eyes permanently away from her partly-dressed bodice, she stated her view with a certain clarity: "Of course I realise what I should wear. These people simply will have to learn." I forfeited my 45p all-night bus ride and got off before the perimeter of the city.

The personal qualities needed for successful solitary travel are multifarious. Sitting at this desk to map out the requisite facets of character, I wrote: "Foresight, diligence, flexibility and humour." With a smile I scribbled over these worthy notions and thought of my most memorable expeditions. Many of my journeys were undertaken in a parlous mental condition, for from the experience of travel I was seeking solutions. It is this balance of being able to allow the outside world to influence one's inward-beseeching world that makes a solitary expedition worthwhile. Take a reserve of worthy notions and a good health insurance policy, for there is nothing more miserable and frightening than to be ill or damaged on the road alone.

What I appreciate about travelling alone are the extremes of experience so often encountered. The sense of solitude in a tropical land will be acutely felt in the early evening after eating – when the darkness falls like a shutter and the hours before sleep are many. A bright-beamed small torch is essential, for the lighting in inexpensive hotels is never unfailingly diabolical. The slim volumes of my favourite poets are dog-eared from browsing and memorising, and a capacious hip flask of fine whisky is always a soothing companion. By contrast, one may be transported without warning from a cycle of long evenings of quiet thoughtfulness to a night of wayward indulgence. The invasion of my private oceanside guest house in Cochin by a group of exuberant and friendly New Zealanders resulted in days of parties that became nights with new-found companions, complete with the exhausting surfeit of conversation.

Without companions the pace and direction of travel may vary to one's will. About to depart for the Amazon, I sat within a Quito hotel eating a silent breakfast, seeking not to overhear the siren conversations in English amidst the guttural clutter of the local Spanish. From such precocious eavesdropping, I gleaned an introduction to a Galapagos ornithological enthusiast. His vision was an immediate inspiration: "You haff walked a jungle before?", he swung the questions with the directness of a large Swedish wood axe, "Well, you haff seen enough. Go to the Galapagos. If you like wildlife and most important, the birds, then there is no decision!" So inspired I ditched an elaborate and painstakingly calculated schedule of buses and aeroplanes and flew west to the Pacific. He was right, there is no decision.

If you had no notion of writing a journal, the action of travel in would-be solitude is the finest inspiration. Not only is there so much more time and space for the quiet dissemination and recording of days past, but the act of mute concentration over a pen and paper will deter all but the most callous interloper of personal privacy.

Whereas the lack of company may be a boon for privacy and quietitude, the security of companionship is often sorely missed. That the urban centres of the world are hotbeds of energetic and endemic crime is obvious. The need for vigilance when alone is a source of debilitating fear for many and so it is best to avoid taking a visible array of baggage that may create so much desire. I feel safest travelling light and take less and less each journey, looking to pack what is worthless to both parties or (as necessary with a camera, travellers' cheques and cash) securely covered by a reliable traveller's insurance policy.

No manner of personal privations, however, will dampen my enthusiasm for the act of travelling alone. The diverse range of memories I carry from such journeys are legion. From anguish to exhilaration, fulfilment to the most intense and destructive frustration that only alien bureaucracy will create, I may recall the extremes of experience with a shudder of a smile. It is ironic that what makes this practice of attempted solitude so consuming and addictive is the participation of others. Leaving home without a companion is an excellent beginning, for without a partner or friends one may be a susceptible witness to the openness of the human condition that is simple friendship. Of the greatest pleasures of travel, the new-found and often sweetly ephemeral companionship of others is my source of guiding inspiration and steadfast joy.

CHOOSING TRAVELLING COMPANIONS

by Nigel Winser

"*I would say that this matter of relationships between members... can be more important than the achievement of the stated objective, be it crossing a desert or an ocean, the exploration of a jungle or the ascent of a mountain peak*" John Hunt.

"Bill always takes his boots off inside the tent and Ben has yet to cook a decent meal... yackety yack, moan, moan." A familiar and typical cry, triggered by lack of privacy and repetitive food. Add to the melting pot such problems as financial mismanagement, change of itinerary, ill health and a stolen rucksack, and you may realise that you have not given as much thought to the choice of your travelling companions as you should.

While the fire remains hot there is little you can do about it, so it is worth thinking about before you depart. All travelling groups will have storms, so don't kid yourself that they won't happen to you. But perhaps you can weather them without breaking up the party.

I am not concerned here with choosing specialist members of a scientific team for an expedition. That is up to the leader of the group. The more specialised the positions, the more specific the qualifications required. My own experience is with more formal expeditions, but any travellers, from those on a budget package to overlanders, will run up against many of the same problems, and should be able to learn from the techniques used by countless expeditions around the world.

Expedition leaders are fortunate to be able to draw on the experiences of many past ventures as well as long-term projects in Antarctica where all nations have studied personnel selection and interview techniques in detail. It is lucky we all don't have to go through such interviews because you and I probably wouldn't make it.

Common Sense

In theory, choosing your companions is common sense. You are looking for good-humoured individuals who, by their understanding and agreement of the objectives, form a close bond and so create a functional and cohesive team. It also helps if you like each other.

People go on journeys to satisfy ambitions, however disparate. The more you understand everyone else's ambitions, the better you will be at assessing the bonds that maintain the group. But it is not that easy. A common problem arises when, for instance, en route you require someone to do a job such as repair a vehicle. Suddenly your good friend has to be moulded into a mechanic, a role for which he or she may or may not be fit. The other solution is to have in your party a mechanic whom you have never met but who has to be moulded into a "good friend". If any virtues were to be singled out to aid your decision, high tolerance and adaptability would be two.

So, with no fixed guidelines, how can you begin to choose your companions? The single factor most likely to upset the group on a journey will be that an individual does not satisfy his or her own reasons for going. Fellow members of the party will be directly or indirectly blamed for preventing such satisfaction.

Travelling itself acts as a catalyst to any dispute and provocations and pressures may build up to intolerable levels. Any bonds that have formed will be stretched to the limit as individuals continually reassess their expectations.

It is assumed that differing personality traits are to blame here. While there are, of course, exceptions, I do not believe that personality clashes are sufficient to account for groups breaking up. I see them as symptoms of disorder within the group, and a lack of cohesion owing to ill-matched objectives – the original cause. It is worth mentioning here that the "organisation" of the trip will come under fire whenever difficulties arise; and while no one wants to lose the freedom of individual travel, the machinery of group travel (shared kitty, agreed itinerary, overall responsibility) should be well oiled.

Practical Tips

From a practical point of view, you may like to consider the following tips, which apply as much to two hitchhikers as to a full-blown expedition:

1. Get to know one another before you go. If necessary, go to the pub together and get slightly pickled, then see if you can get on just as well in the morning.

2. Discuss openly with all members of the group the overall objectives of the trip and see how many members of the group disagree. Are all members of the group going to be satisfied with the plans as they stand?

3. Discuss openly the leader's (or the main organiser's, if there is one) motivation in wanting to undertake this particular journey. Is he or she using the trip to further selfish ambitions? If these are made clear beforehand so much the better, particularly if the others are not connected with the hidden objective.

4. Discuss and plan to solve the problems which will certainly crop up. The regular ones are poor health, stolen goods, accidents, insurance, itinerary. If everyone knows where they stand before the chips are down, the chance of remaining a group improve.

5. If possible, have the team working together before departure, particularly if there has been an allocation of duties. To know where you fit in is important.

6. If there is to be any form of hierarchy, it must be established before leaving and not enforced en route. If everyone can be made to feel that he or she is an integral part of the group and the group's interdependence, you will all stay together throughout the journey and have a rewarding and enjoyable experience.

A list of Agencies for Single Travellers who wish to find companions can be found on p.705 of the Directory ■

SPECIALIST TRAVEL
Chapter 3

THE CONCERNED TRAVELLER

by Professor David Bellamy

Nomads travel in order to make a living from harsh landscapes, conquerors and business people to search for power and resources, holiday-makers to escape the monotony of the workplace. Adventurers, backpackers and grand tourers travel because they have to. Theirs is the quest for knowledge, a quest to be worldly-wise.

It is somewhat awe-inspiring to realise that many areas which were marked as terra incognita on the maps of my youth are now stopovers on regular tour itineraries. So much so that the two-edged sword of tourism now hangs heavily over every aspect of the heritage of this world.

If it had not been for the spotlight which has been turned onto these special regions by grand tourers, past and present, the threat, to coin a phrase, of Costa-Brava-Isation would not be there. Yet it is equally true to say that without those spotlights of interest and concern, much of their heritage could have been lost through apathy and ignorance.

Whatever regrets we weavers of travellers' tales may have, I believe the die is now cast. Tourism is the world's fastest growing industry and the only hope for much of our heritage, both natural and people-made, lies within the wise use of its tourist potential.

A row of toilets at base camp Everest or the import of food to service the tourists of Bali don't make for confidence in the sustainability of the industry unless either the tourist industry grows up and shoulders all its responsibilities or the expectation of all travellers sinks to the current norm of home entertainment: a diet of soaps and game shows.

Fortunately, there are some bright lights at the end of the tunnel. At one end are well appointed and run establishments like South Africa's *Sun City*. There, a fun oasis has been created out of what was degraded veldt. Many thousands of local jobs have been created and an adjacent area has been restocked with game both big and small. It packs them in, corralling them where they can do little harm to local culture. The only real negative effect is the use of fossil fuel and too much water, but living up to its name, it could become solar-powered and water wise. At the other end of the spectrum of caring holidays are groups like Earthwatch and Coral Cay Conservation where customers pay to be trained and then work hard in scientific research. Furthermore, a recent study of caravan parks, not usually renowned for their eco-friendliness, revealed that some had already taken up the challenge and were putting their houses into green order, caring not only for their customers but for the local community, wildlife and wider environment.

Unfortunately there is also much bad news, but that is where you all come in, for there is an immense amount of work to be done. Attitudes are changing, but is it fast enough with 1.3 billion Chinese about to be industrialised? Ten per cent of them with passports would put 130 million people on the road. If all of them decided that they must visit the English Lakes in their travelling lifetime, that would mean an extra 2.6 million visitors a year. Could they be accommodated? The answer from the industry is yes. But at what cost the Wordsworth's Open Air University?

One thing the whole industry must do, and fast, is realise that its success depends on other people's resources, landscapes and lifestyles, so they must help pay for their upkeep. They must help create local jobs, pay for local infrastructure, give more than they get. If they don't, the resource will eventually collapse.

WEXAS is of course special amongst the tour operators, setting a high standard for getting away from it all. So its members must shoulder their share of that responsibility.

As you lap up the challenge of pushing back the bounds of your personally unknown lands and discovering these pearls of heritage for yourselves, remember they are only there thanks to the natural living systems on which we all depend.

You are the ambassadors of everything that the concerned traveller should be. Set the golden example. Respect local customs and buy only local craft goods made from sustainable resources and always put as much as you can into the local economy. Be careful where you put your tripod and your feet. Flowers have power you know. Leave only ripples of good will and if you see an operator disobeying national or local rules, refuse his services.

Thank you for caring.

See p.707 of the directory for Environmental associations tour operators

THE GREEN TRAVELLER

by Matthew Brace

First a definition. The term 'ecotourism', a buzz word for the 1990s, is used to describe anything from deep green forest lodges which operate in harmony with the environment, to hotels that trample acres of precious forest and then name their rooms after the rare birds which used to live there.

A better term, which the pressure group Tourism Concern use, is 'sustainable tourism'. Tourism by its very nature is rarely wholly ecologically friendly. Even if one sailed on a home-made driftwood raft to a holiday island, dropped no litter, killed only time and left only footprints (to quote the wise, if often used, phrase) there would still have been some impact on the environment.

However, it is possible to explore this wonderful planet while dramatically reducing your effect on its ecosystems and, in some cases, actively help by contributing tourist money to fund conservation programmes. No self-respecting independent traveller with a passion for the environment should leave home without the will to seek out the most ecological way to travel.

What is needed is respect. Respect for a rainforest's beauty, respect for a tribal people's beliefs and customs, respect for nature. A little more respect, say, than a company currently offering people the chance to shoot pellets of washable, luminous, pink paint at the noble elephants of Zimbabwe. It is marketed as an "eco-safari" and just in case the elephant takes offence, a hunter is on hand to shoot it with a real bullet.

So when you step out on your trip, take time to check that, among the sun cream and guidebooks you are carrying with you, you have spared a thought for why the destination attracted you in the first place and what effect you will make.

Why Should We Care?

Increasing numbers of people are travelling to farther and farther flung destinations. One exotic destination that is gaining huge popularity for its wildlife and beauty is the tiny Central American nation of Costa Rica. Its position – a bridge between North and South America – means it is blessed with some of the most diverse flora and fauna on Earth. But all is not well in the forests. In 1980, Costa Rica had just 3,000 international visitors. By 1992 that figure had jumped to 64,000 and two years later to 750,000. Tourism brought in US$700m in 1996 – 30 per cent of total exports and 8.5 per cent of GNP.

The country is now at a crossroads in terms of tourism development. Biological reserves like Monteverde face the problem of balancing their sensitive eco-systems with the rivers of tourists that come to marvel at them. The former president of Costa Rica, Rodrigo Carazo, is very much aware of the problem but sees this as a positive opportunity to reduce deforestation, "It is about selling one tree a million times through tourism, rather than once through timber logging." However, until recently, Costa Rica has also had one of the highest deforestation rates in the world. Due mainly to agricultural demands for cattle ranching land and timber production, the amount of forested land shrank dramatically from 72 per cent in the late 1950s to just 26 per cent in 1985. It is predicted that by the year 2000 all forests outside protected areas will be flattened and a significant chunk of the world's natural heritage will have been lost.

The world's more popular tourist honey-pots are also under intense threat. According to United Nations predictions, visitors to the Mediterranean could total 760 million by 2025, adding to a resident population of 150 million and putting great strain on the local environment by increasing the amount of sewage discharged into the sea which is endangering the animals and plants that live in it.

Coral reefs are the most endangered of all the world's ecosystems (more so even than rainforests) and yet only recently have conservation projects begun in earnest to protect them from tourists breaking off coral accidentally or intentionally for mantelpiece ornaments back home.

Programmes for Change

on paper ...

Ecotourism has burgeoned to such an extent that an international agency has been set up to monitor its growth. Five years ago in Washington DC, the Ecotourism Society (TES) was established to influence the direction of eco-tourism worldwide and to balance the needs of conservation with those of the multi-million pound/dollar travel industry.

and in action ...

TES's major projects include visitor management in the Galapagos Islands – a rapidly growing tourist destination with a fragile ecosystem – park-user fees in Costa Rica, guidelines and monitoring programmes for nature tour operators with sustainable planning and design recommendations.

Although the governments of Australia, Brazil, Mexico and Malaysia have all formulated national ecotourism projects, local communities are also taking a stand, most notably in Indonesia, Belize, Costa Rica, Ecuador and Nepal, and making a success of smaller projects which have had positive results for local residents. Regional and national ecotourism associations have been formed in eighteen countries to work on policy and planning issues.

An independent green audit of ecotourism, completed by the travel writer Anne Becher who lives in the capital San Jose, found that only 50 per cent of the hotels in Costa Rica (highlighted in this chapter because of its progressive action on sustainable tourism), she visited are actually practising sustainable tourism. She concedes that the government cannot be expected to protect all the ecologically important areas but stresses that ecotourism encourages private land owners to protect their own area.

Some Simple Steps for Sustainable Travel

Do your homework. Choose your destination with care. Read up and find out the current issues of environmental contention. Ecotourism is the flavour of the month for travel agents and tour operators. However, several are far from green and are merely using the phenomenon of green travel as a device to sell more holidays. Tourism Concern has some useful questions to ask your travel agent before you go.

* can you assure me that the hotels you use do not diminish the supply of water to local people for domestic, animal or agricultural use?
* is adequate provision made for the disposal of sewage and waste without damaging the local environment?
* can you assure me that the hotels are not built on sacred sites or burial grounds?
* are any of the hotels you use owned or managed by local residents?
* can you assure me that the tourism developments you are offering have not deprived people of their homes or livelihoods?
* are you working with Tourism Concern or any human rights organisations to work out how to deal with these issues?

They may not have the answers at their fingertips but give them time to check. And Tourism Concern urges independent travellers to write and tell them what they say (see p. 709 of the Directory for their address).

And When in Paradise?

Professor David Bellamy, the renowned conservationist, believes certain rules must be adhered to if tourism is to function in harmony with the environment:
* visitor numbers must be limited
* at least 50 per cent of all profits should go back to the local community
* accommodation should be built on land already altered
* alternative resources of energy and renewable local resources must be used where possible
* local travel should be by foot or boat with the use of internal combustion engines kept to a minimum.

"If that sounds boring," says the great professor, "then please stay away. If you demand more, many people and their resources will not stand a chance of reaching the next millennium. I sincerely believe that this is both their and our last chance."

Take Bellamy at his word and add a few more sustainable travelling tips to your list. Also use public transport whenever possible to save fuel. If public transport is not available, get together with other sustainable travellers you meet along the way and hire a minibus (it will save you money too). Bicycle hire can be very cheap, and can offer you access to areas that you will not be able to reach by motor vehicle. Don't drop litter (not long ago piles of pink toilet paper were reported in the foothills of the Himalayas).

When walking through eco-sensitive areas such as national parks keep to the trails. Not only will this help to preserve the beauty of these areas but it might also save you from a close encounter with a territorially defensive snake.

THE INDEPENDENT TRAVELLER

by Dervla Murphy

Question: *When is a freak not a freak?*
Answer: *When she feels normal*

I was in my late forties before the realisation came, very, very slowly, starting as a ridiculous-seeming suspicion that gradually crystallised into an exasperated certainty. Many people think of me as a freak.

By middle age one should be well aware of one's public image, given a way of life that makes such an accessory unavoidable. But if what an individual does *feels* normal, and if people are decently reticent about analysing you to your face, it's quite understandable that for decades you see only your self image, vastly as it may differ from the false public image meanwhile gaining credibility.

The freakish thing is, of course, not me, but the modern world – from which I, like millions of other normal folk, need to escape at intervals. Those of us born with the wandering instinct, and not caught in a job trap, can practise the most effective form of escapism: a move back in time, to one of the few regions where it is still possible to live simply, at our ancestors' pace. To describe this as returning to reality would be absurd; for us the modern world is reality. However, escapist travelling does allow a return to what we are genetically fitted to cope with, as we are not fitted to cope with the freakishly hectic, technological present.

Hence the notorious 'pressures', parallelling our marvellous conveniences. We have reduced physical effort to the minimum; everything is 'labour-saving' – transport, communications, entertainment, heating, cooking, cleaning, dressing, marketing, even writing (they tell me) if one uses a repulsive-sounding thing called a 'word processor.' Yet the effort of coming to terms with this effortless world is too much for many of us. So we get ulcers, have nervous breakdowns, take to uppers and/or downers, gamble on the stock exchange – or travel, seriously, for several months at a stretch.

Today's serious travellers are often frustrated explorers who would like to have been born at least 150 years earlier. Now there is nowhere left for individuals to explore, though there may be a few untouched corners (in Amazonia?) accessible only to expeditions. But the modern hi-tech expedition, with its two-way radios and helicopters on call for emergencies, naturally has no appeal for escapist travellers. Among themselves, these lament that their traditional, simple journeys have come to seem – by a cruel twist of the technological spiral – paradoxically artificial. A century ago, travellers who took off into the unknown had to be completely isolated from their own world for months or years on end. Now such isolation is a deliberately-chosen luxury and to that extent, phoney. Had I died of gangrene in the Himalayas or Simiens or Andes, that would have been my own fault (no two-way radio) rather than a sad misfortune.

So the escapist traveller is, in one sense, playing a game. But only in one sense, because the actual journey is for real in a way that the modern expedition, with its carefully prearranged links to home and safety, is not. Whatever happens, you can't chicken out: you are where you've chosen to be and must take the consequences.

Here some confusion arises about courage. There is a temperamental aspect to this issue: optimism versus pessimism – is a bottle half empty or half full? Why should your appendix burst or your bones break abroad rather than at home? Optimists don't believe in disasters until they happen. Therefore they are not fearful and have no occasion to display courage. Nothing puts my hackles up faster than being told I'm brave. This is nonsense – albeit significant nonsense. Where is our effortless civilisation at when physical exertion, enjoyed in remote places, is repeatedly mistaken for bravery?

Genuine travellers, far from being brave, are ultra-cautious. That is an essential component of their survival mechanism and one of the dividing lines between them and foolhardy limelight-seekers. Before they start they sus out all foreseeable hazards and either change their route, should these hazards seem excessive and the risk silly, or prepare themselves to cope with reasonable hazards. Thus what looks to outsiders like a daring journey is in fact a safe toddle – unless you have bad luck, which you could have at home. Six times I've broken my ribs; the last time was at home, falling off a ladder. The other times were in

Afghanistan, Nepal, Ethiopia, Peru and Madagascar. You could say I have an unhappy karmic relationship with my ribs.

Recently I was asked, "Why is independent travel seen as so much more of an intellectual challenge? And what does it take to cope with it?" That flumoxed me. I have been an escapist traveller for more than 40 years without its ever occurring to me that I was meeting an intellectual challenge. A stamina challenge, usually; an emotional challenge, sometimes; a spiritual challenge, occasionally. But an intellectual challenge? I don't see it. Unless by *intellectual* one means that slight exertion of the grey cells required to equip oneself more or less suitably for the country in view. Yet surely that is a matter of common sense, rather than intellect?

Granted, equipping oneself includes a certain amount of reading; but this, in a literate society, scarcely amounts to an intellectual challenge. I refer only to reading history, not to any sort of heavy sociological or political research – unless of course you happen to fancy that sort of thing, in which case it will obviously add an extra dimension to your journey. Otherwise, for the average traveller, enough of current politics will be revealed en route, should politics be important to the locals; and in those few happy regions where domestic politics don't matter, you can forget about them. But to travel through any country in ignorance of its history seems to me a waste of time. You can't then understand the *why* of anything or anyone. With this view some travellers violently disagree, arguing that all preliminary reading should be avoided, that each new country should be visited in a state of innocence and experienced purely subjectively. The mind on arrival should be a blank page, awaiting one's own vivid personal impressions, to be cherished ever after as authentic and unique. Why burden yourself in advance with loads of irrelevancies about the past and piles of other people's prejudiced interpretations of the present? On that last point I concur; travellers rarely read travel books – unless they have to review them.

Reverting to this odd concept of an intellectual challenge: is the adaptability required of travellers sometimes mistaken for an intellectual feat? That seems unlikely because we're back to temperament: some people slot in easily everywhere. If travellers saw the need to adapt as an intellectual challenge they probably wouldn't slot in anywhere, except perhaps on some pretentious radio show.

Maybe the overcoming of language barriers is seen as an intellectual challenge? Yet there could scarcely be anything less intellectual than urgently saying 'P–sssss!' when you must get fast to the nearest earth closet – or at least out of the *tukul*, which has been locked up for the night. The basic need of human beings – sleeping, eating, drinking, peeing – are so basic that they can easily be understood; all our bladders function in exactly the same way. The language barrier unnecessarily inhibits many who otherwise would seek out and relish remote regions. On the practical level, it is of no consequence. I can state this with total assurance, having travelled on four continents using only English and those courtesy phrases of Tibetan, Amharic, Quechua or whatever, that you happen to pick up as you go along. Even on the emotional level, it is not as formidable as it may seem; the human features – especially the eyes – are wonderfully eloquent. In our own society, the extent to which we wordlessly communicate goes unnoticed. In Far Flungery, where nobody within 200 miles speaks a syllable of any European language, one becomes very aware of the range of moods and subtle feelings that may be conveyed visually rather than aurally. However, on the exchange-of-ideas level the barrier is, quite simply, insuperable. Therefore scholar-travellers – people like Freya Stark, Patrick Leigh Fermor, Colin Thubron – consider the learning of Arabic or Albanian or Russian or Mandarin to be as essential as buying a map. And there you have what seems to me (linguistically inept as I am) a bona fide intellectual challenge.

As a label, 'the independent traveller' puzzles me. It verges on tautology; travellers, being inherently independent, don't need the adjective to distinguish them from those unfortunate victims of the tourist industry who, because of sun-starvation on our islands, are happy to be herded annually towards a hot spot where tea and chips are guaranteed and there is no danger of meeting the natives.

I can, however, see that holiday-makers (the category in between travellers and tourists) may validly be divided into 'dependent' and 'independent.' The former, though liking to make their own plans, contentedly follow beaten tracks and book their B&Bs in advance. The latter are often travellers *manqué* for whom unpredictability gives savour to their journey: setting off at dawn with no idea of where one will be by dusk, or who with or what eating. Only a lack of *time* or money prevents them from reaching travellers' territory and usually time is their problem. Travelling can be done on quite a short shoestring, and often must be so done for the excellent reason that the traveller's theatre of operations offers few consumer goods.

Independent holiday-makers are in general much more tolerant and sociable than travellers, whose escapist compulsion causes them to feel their day has been ruined if they glimpse just one other solitary trekker in the far distance, and who break out in spots if they come upon even a vestigial trace of tourism. But that last nightmare contingency is unlikely; the paths of travellers rarely converge, unless one finds oneself within a few miles of somewhere like Machu Picchu and it seems "stupid not to see it." Incidentally, Machu Picchu provided me with my most grisly travel memory – an American helicopter landing amidst the ruins and spewing forth a squeal of excited women whose paunchy menfolk were intent only on photographing them beside the mournful resident llamas. My timing was wrong; you have to get to Machu Picchu at dawn, as I did later.

The past decade or so has seen the emergence of another, hybrid category: youngsters who spend a year or more wandering around the world in a holiday-making spirit, occasionally taking temporary jobs. Some gain enormously from this experience but many seem to cover too much ground too quickly, sampling everywhere and becoming familiar with nowhere. They have been from Alaska to Adelaide, Berlin to Bali, Calcutta to Cuzco, Lhasa to London. They tend to wander in couples or small packs, swapping yarns about the benefits – or otherwise – of staying here, doing that, buying this. They make a considerable impact where they happen to perch for a week or so, often bringing with them standards (sometimes too low) and expectations (sometimes too high) which unsettle their local contemporaries.

Of course one rejoices that the young are free to roam as never before, yet such rapid 'round-the-worlding' is, for many, more confusing than enlightening. It would be good if this fashion soon changed, if the young became more discriminating, allowing themselves time to travel seriously in a limited area that they had chosen because of its particular appeal to them, as individuals.

THE PACKAGED TRAVELLER
by Hilary Bradt

In 1841 Thomas Cook advertised that he had arranged a special train to take a group of temperance workers from Leicester to Loughborough for a meeting some 10 miles away. From this humble beginning has grown a giant tourist industry which has helped the balance of payments in countries all over the world as well as enabling almost everyone to have a taste of 'abroad.' Experienced travellers often scorn package holidays as appealing to the 'If it's Tuesday, this must be Belgium' mentality, without realising how much time and money can be saved and how much seen by joining a tour. And now that package tours have expanded into special interest and activity holidays a new world, previously impenetrable to all but the most determined individual, has opened up for the adventurous person in search of the safely exotic.

The key to successful packaged travel is to choose the right tour operator. This is less important for short haul holidays where your local travel agent will have sufficient information to steer you towards an appropriate company, but for long-haul trips, or special interest holidays it is essential that you have access to the brochures of a range of specialist tour operators. This is not always easy: good companies are not necessarily the big ones that can afford to advertise widely. You will need to shop around. In Britain, companies such as WEXAS or Trailfinders offer good, wide-ranging advice, but try to go to the travel shows *Independent Travellers World* and *Destinations* where you can visit the stands of specialist tour operators. Articles in the travel pages of newspapers and in special interest magazines are always accompanied by advertising from relevant tour operators and the internet now provides listings. Bear in mind, however, that none of these will be impartial – most companies listed in publications or on the internet will have paid for the privilege.

Do your preparatory brochure reading carefully. If you choose a trip to Madagascar in the cyclone season, that's not your tour operator's fault. Nor can he be held responsible for the inefficiencies that are inherent in Third World travel. An honest guide book will warn you of the negative aspects of the countries you are interested in and, likewise, a brochure is more likely to be taken seriously if the picture painted is not too rosy.

Long Haul

To many people these days, travel means long-haul destinations. For the packaged traveller such trips will generally either come into the category of *Special Interest*, (see next section) or trans-continental journeys in converted trucks lasting several weeks or even months. Dodge three-ton trucks, completely stripped and rebuilt to suit the needs of each company, are the vehicles preferred, being rugged enough to cope with the varied terrain and conditions found on a trans-continental journey. Nights are spent in tents or simple rest houses, and most overlanders cook their own meals on a rota system and eat occasionally in local restaurants.

With the Middle-East still too unstable to offer a reliable route to Kathmandu, this formerly popular overland route has been replaced by the trans-Africa journey which usually begins or ends in Cape Town. South America is almost as popular.

These are rugged trips and a great test of psychological fortitude as well as physical endurance. Being with the same group of people for several months in often trying conditions can be a strain on even the most sociable traveller, so if you suspect your patience may snap after a few weeks, don't try it. A long overland trip can, however, be a bargain in terms of daily expenditure.

Choose your overland company with care. Some have temptingly low prices but unscrupulous employees, like the driver I met in Africa: after dropping his group to do some sightseeing, he drove away and sold the truck! No doubt a rare occurrence but you are safer if you use a reputable company or go through an organisation which has long experience of dealing with overland companies.

For many people this is the trip of a lifetime, and much care must be taken to find both the route and the operator which suites you best. You get what you pay for: at the lower end of the market you may have inexperienced drivers who do not know the route, uncomfortable or unreliable vehicles, but a general feeling of adventure and camaraderie. The more expensive trips will be offered by well-established companies who know what they are doing, who have equipped their vehicles with an eye on comfort and maximum viewing and who will deal calmly and competently with border hassles.

Special Interest

Many companies specialise in activity holidays or adventure travel, which is the fastest growing area of the travel industry, and their brochures show a range of trips, from hang-gliding in Nepal to weaving in Ecuador, trekking in Africa or taking part in conservation projects or archaeological digs. Activity holidays appeal most to professional people in their 30s-50s, probably because they are the most expensive form of package holiday (three weeks trekking in the Himalayas can cost £2,000 or more, excluding the airfare). Most trips are graded to indicate the degree of fitness required, but companies point out that even the lowest graded tours are designed for active people and the fitter you are, the more you will enjoy the trip. Many of the companies involved in organising these tours have age barriers (usually no children and sometimes an upper limit of as little as 45) and others will ask anyone over a certain age to provide a medical certificate.

These tours often involve an impressive amount of organisation; providing transport to remote areas, porters or pack animals to carry the luggage, doctors to attend the sick, instructors, interpreters, guides and experts of all sorts. No wonder they are expensive. Carefully planned to give the feeling of adventure without the danger, they enable people to see and experience aspects of a country or culture they could not experience on their own.

Whatever your interest, there will be a holiday to suit you. The best source of information will be the specialised magazines: if you are a horse rider, the numerous horsey magazines will have advertisements for an impressive number of riding holidays all over the world. If you like to watch birds or study wildlife, there are plenty of magazines to guide you in the right direction. If your interest is in the country itself, subscribe to the travel magazines.

Don't make price the main consideration when comparing brochures. If this is going to be the trip of your life, an extra £100 is not going to make much difference. Check whether the price quoted includes the airfare. In Britain it often does, but American companies usually quote the land costs only. Don't hesitate to contact the company and ask for names of clients who have been on the trip you are interested in. A successful company will have no qualms about putting you in touch with such people.

Once you have signed up and paid your deposit, the company should send you equipment and reading lists, medical information and so on. If you are dealing with a travel agency rather than the company running the tour, make sure you receive these and take time to read them carefully. It is inconvenient and often impossible to shop for special items once you are there.

THE EXPEDITION TRAVELLER

by Shane Winser

For many, independent travel is a daunting task, and the prospect of joining a group with a pre-determined objective is attractive. Others may feel that they wish to contribute to the peoples or environment in which they travel. The options open to such individuals are enormous: from adventure holidays to community work and scientific fieldwork overseas. The better-known and well-established groups can be found in specialist directories. It may be more difficult to get to know of smaller and/or newly-emerging groups. Almost all will require some sort of financial contribution. Don't be afraid to ask questions either about the organisation itself or what your contribution covers. Try and get a feel for the organisation, and if you are not happy with its overall aims or the attitudes of the people who run it, don't sign up.

There are many tour operators in Britain and abroad offering adventurous holidays which can be ideal for somebody who wants an unusual holiday. Naturally you pay to join one of these, but the preparation and responsibilities are correspondingly few. For example, the **WEXAS Discoverers** brochure has many such trips; others are advertised in the outdoor magazines and the national press. The useful *Adventure Holidays* (Vacation Work Publications, 9 Park End Street, Oxford OX1 1HJ, tel: 01865-241978) lists holidays by the type of sport or activity. In addition there are many informal groups which set out on adventurous overland journeys. Publications such as *Time Out* and the travel magazines are useful for finding out about these. However, you should beware that the informal group you team up with is not just trying to fund a holiday for themselves. However tempting the trip sounds, don't join up if you don't like or trust the people you are going to have to travel with.

Adventure holidays and genuine expeditions differ in many ways. A scientific expedition will be expected to add to human knowledge, to 'discover' something new. Those joining expeditions will usually be expected to give up considerable time to help with preparations, be whole-heartedly committed to the project's overall aim and objectives, and be capable of working as a skilled member of the team. And that is to say nothing of the efforts required to raise the necessary funds for the expedition.

In Britain, the Royal Geographical Society is the principal organisation concerned with carrying out scientific expeditions overseas. Through the work of its **Expedition Advisory Centre**, the society provides information, advice and training to 500 or so groups each year – groups which carry out scientific, adventurous and youth projects abroad. For those who have a clear idea of what they want to do and have already formed themselves into groups, the centre has a number of important services including the annual *Planning a Small Expedition* seminar and the *Expedition Planners' Handbook and Directory*.

Many of the groups helped by the centre are from schools and universities, as the principle of outdoor adventure and challenge is widely accepted as an important training ground both for young people and potential managers alike. As a result a number of charitable and commercial organisations now offer expeditions to people of a wide age range. The Expedition Advisory Centre publishes a directory of these entitled *Joining an Expedition*. The directory includes advice on choosing an appropriate project and ideas for raising funds to join projects. Individuals with special skills to offer – doctors, nurses, mechanics, scientists – may be invited to join the register of personnel available for expeditions which is maintained by the centre and used by expedition organisers to recruit skilled individuals.

Two of the longest established expeditionary bodies include the **Brathay Exploration Group** (Brathay Hall, Ambleside, Cumbria LA22 0HP, tel: 015394-33942) which sends out several expeditions each year both in the UK and abroad, with members tending to be between the ages of 17 and 25. The **British Schools Exploring Society** (BSES), (1 Kensington Gore, London SW7 2AR, tel: 0171-591 3141) organises six week-long expeditions for 17 to 20-year-olds during the summer holidays and six month-long expeditions for those in their 'gap' year between school and university. BSES has always had a strong scientific component to its work and provides useful training for those hoping to go and organise their own expedition.

With public concern for the environment now widespread, a number of other organisations offer a chance to carry out useful fieldwork overseas. Among them are the **British Trust for Conservation Volunteers** (36 St Mary's Street, Wallingford, Oxfordshire OX10 OEU, tel: 01491-839766) which has links with many similar organisations in Europe; the **Field Studies Council Overseas Expeditions** (Montford Bridge, Shrewsbury SY4 1HW, tel: 01743-850164); **Frontier** (77 Leonard Street, London EC2A 4QS, tel: 0171-613 2422) runs conservation programmes in Tanzania, Uganda and Vietnam; **Trekforce Expeditions** (134 Buckingham Palace Road, London SW1W 9SA, tel: 0171-824 8890) organises six-week projects in the remote tropical forests of Indonesia and the **Coral Cay Conservation Programme** (The Ivy Works, 154 Clapham Park Road, London SW4 7DE, tel: 0171-498 6248) which recruits qualified divers to help monitor the reefs in a marine reserve off the coast of Belize.

Raleigh International (27 Parsons Green Lane, London SW6 4HZ, tel: 0171-371 8585) regularly recruits 17-25 year olds to take part in demanding community projects and conservation programmes lasting up to 12 weeks.

For budding archaeologists, **Archaeology Abroad** (31-34 Gordon Square, London WC1H 0PY, tel: 0171-387 7050 ext 4750) helps directors of overseas excavations find suitable personnel through its bulletins.

Earthwatch Europe (Belsyre Court, 57 Woodstock Road, Oxford OX2 6HU, tel: 01865-311600) matches paying volunteers with scientists who need their help to study threatened habitats, save endangered species and document our changing environmental heritage. Volunteers do not need to have any special skills to join expeditions and anyone aged 16 to 75 may apply once they have become members (£25 annual subscription including a bi–monthly club magazine). Their short two to three-week expeditions cost from £415 (plus travel expenses) and include full board and field expenses.

Those with medical skills to offer might like to contact **Health Projects Abroad** (PO Box 24, Bakewell, Derbyshire DE45 1ZW, tel: 01629-440051) who publish a useful booklet, the **HPA Guide to Voluntary Nursing Overseas** and recruits unskilled volunteers for health-related projects in Tanzania. The **International Health Exchange** (8-10 Dryden Street, London WC2E 9NA, tel: 0171-836 5833) publishes job vacancies, runs training courses and maintains a register of health care professionals wanting to work in developing countries.

It is possible to travel in a group and never make contact with the people of the countries you pass through. **The Experiment in International Living** (287 Worcester Road, Malvern, Worcs. WR14 1AB, tel: 01684-562577) arranges home-stay programmes for both individuals and groups. **The Commonwealth Youth Exchange Council** (CYEC, 7 Lion Yard, Tremadoc Road, SW4 7NQ, tel: 0171-498 6151) promotes contact between groups of young people of the Commonwealth by funding visits by groups from Britain to an overseas Commonwealth country or vice versa. In order to attract Council funding, the programme must be useful in its own right and involve contact between visitors and hosts, preferably including joint activities. The aim is 'to provide meaningful contact and better understanding between Commonwealth young people' and if possible should lead to a continuing two-way link. Visits must be arranged through an established organisation and led by a responsible person. Two-thirds of each group must consist of people aged between 15 and 25 years.

Those wishing to work or study abroad without necessarily joining an expedition should consult **The Central Bureau** (10 Spring Gardens, London SW1A 2BN, tel: 0171-389 4004) whose publications are extremely useful. The Bureau, which also has offices in Edinburgh and Belfast, has details of jobs, study opportunities, youth organisations and holidays in some 60 countries. *A Year Off* (CRAC Publications, Hobsons Press (Cambridge) Ltd, Bateman Street, Cambridge CB2 1LZ, tel: 01223-354551) provides information about voluntary service, work camps and summer projects, paid work, au pair work, study courses, scholarships and travel, adventure and expeditions. Aimed at people with time to spare between school and higher education, it discusses the pros and cons of using that year in this special way, giving the views of both students and career experts.

Study Abroad, (UNESCO, 7 Place de Fontenoy, Paris 75007, France and available from HMSO, PO Box 276, London SW8 5DT, tel: 0171-873 9090), describes some 2600 opportunities for post-secondary study in all academic and professional fields and lists details of scholarships, assistantships, travel grants and other forms of financial assistance available.

Vacation Work Publications (9 Park End Street, Oxford OX1 1HJ, tel: 01865-241978) publishes many guides and directories for those seeking permanent jobs or summer jobs abroad, unusual travel opportunities, voluntary work and working travel. Often travel for its own sake seems insufficient for those who wish to provide practical help for locals in the country they are to visit.

If you feel that you have both the time and the specialist skills needed to be a volunteer, you should probably start by reading two very helpful directories: *Volunteer Work* (Central Bureau) and/or *The International Directory of Voluntary Work* (Vacation Work). Both books give an outline of the organisations who are willing and able to accept volunteer workers on overseas projects and the skill and commitment required of the volunteer.

At this stage you should be aware that the majority of host countries who welcome volunteers usually require skilled personnel such as nurses, teachers, agronomists and civil engineers. They may be unable to pay even your airfares (although many provide board and lodging) and you may be expected to help for at least one or two years. Remember that during that time you probably won't be travelling but will be based in a poor urban community or remote rural village.

If you feel that you are suitably qualified and have the emotional maturity to be a volunteer you may like to discuss your hopes and ambitions to serve with someone who has already been one. You can contact an ex-volunteer through their own organisation: **Returned Volunteer Action** (1 Amwell Street, London EC1R 1UL, tel: 0171-278 0804) which maintains a register of volunteers who have served on projects in many different areas of the world. They may even be able to direct you personally to an organisation which is appropriate to both your and their needs. Their information pack *Thinking About Volunteering* is very frank about some of the problems you may face before and after you have been a volunteer. The organisation produces a full range of publications so call for more details.

Finding the right organisation to suit you can take time, so don't expect to leave next week. The four main agencies who send out volunteers from the UK as part of the British Government's Overseas Aid Programme are: **The International Co-operation for Development (ICD)**, **Skillshare Africa**, **United Nations Association International Service (UNAIS)** and **Voluntary Service Overseas (VSO)**. Over 400 volunteers go abroad each year through these organisations, all are over 21 with professional work experience.

If you wish to apply to work for an international aid organisation then the Appointments Officer, Room AH303, Department for Internatonal Development, Abercrombie House, Eaglesham Road, East Kilbride, Glasgow G75 8EA (tel: 01355-844000) can provide you with a booklet *Why Not Serve Overseas?*

For further information about expeditionary organisations on p.710 of the Directory

THE YOUNG PERSONS' EXPEDITION LEADER

by Peter Drake

It may be fun, it may be stimulating and it may be exciting but it will not be a holiday in the traditional sense of the word. My advice would be to accept that free place as an expedition leader for a group of young people with caution! I can still remember checking every passport in a party in Kenya before setting off to the airport on our way home. On arrival at the airport we had checked in at least half of the party's baggage before I found out that one of the expedition members had repacked his passport in his hold luggage. I had to ask for all the luggage to be returned so we could find the offending passport. It took over 45 minutes and the other travellers on the flight were not amused!

When you take a party abroad you have two responsibilities: firstly to your members and their parents and secondly to the other travelling public. How often have you had a pleasant trip on a boat or train or to a place of interest spoiled by a group of young people who seem to be totally out of control? After enquiry you invariably find out that those 'in charge' are ensconced in the bar or doing anything rather than being in charge.

Decide on a membership policy for the party and stick to it. If you are going to climb a mountain, one of your criteria will need to be a level of personal fitness, or if you are going to do a field study trip, an interest in the subject will be required. Taking people who do not share the main party's interest will inevitably cause disruptions. If you want to take a multi-disciplinary party away, organise different interest teams that can operate alongside each other, whilst working to their own aims as well.

Leaders who are appointed must understand that their first consideration should be the aims of the party and the welfare of the young people. There is nothing wrong with having your own agenda or aims but these must be secondary to the main party aims.

Once you have selected your party, send each member and leader a letter with the dates, cost, any ground rules and the objectives of the trip. It is a good policy to include a return slip that has to be signed by the parents or guardians to show that they understand and accept the content.

As a party organiser and leader, the first concern is communication both before and during the trip. Before the trip it is a good idea to get everybody together for at least a weekend and a session at the beginning or end of this weekend should include a time for parents, so they can ask questions and meet the leaders of the party. Like all communications, it is a good idea to present this information in written form as well. Some people have short term memories and this provides you with back up should anything go wrong later.

If your party consists of more than 14 or 15 people, it is worth breaking it down into smaller groups or teams with a leader looking after each team. It is also wise to make sure you have both males and females in your leadership team if your membership is mixed. The problem of blossoming romances in a mixed party should not be enhanced out of proportion but, if they should happen, remember you are responsible to the young people's parents. I have found that by having a word with the couple and explaining that if their behaviour is "over the top" it can be embarrassing to all those around them, any difficulties usually diminish.

During the planning stage it is a good idea to send out a form asking if any member of the party is a vegetarian or cannot eat any kind of food on medical or religious grounds. Send out medical forms as well – it is vital that you know of any special medical requirements that a member of your group may have. If in doubt about a member's physical abilities, ask their GP whether or not the member is physically capable of carrying out the aims of the trip. You will also have to inform all members of the party if they will need any vaccinations or if they are required to take other medication such as anti-malaria tablets. Equally, you will need a policy if someone in your party refuses to have the recommended vaccinations or medication. If you are taking a large party to the third world try to recruit a doctor to the leader team. It will take a great weight off your mind.

Before you leave, make sure you have three passport pictures of every member of the expedition and a photocopy of their passport so that if they do lose it (usually on Sundays when no photographers are open) you will be armed with a photocopy and photos which will speed up the issuing of an emergency passport from the High Commission or Embassy. I also send a list of all the members' names and our itinerary to the British Embassy if I am taking a party to a third world country.

It is also a good idea to take with you a number of photocopies of the full list of party members as you may be asked for these if you want special rates for entry to game parks or other tourist attractions. I also carry several photocopies of all important documents and airline tickets and spread these among the other so that if someone has their bags stolen, not all the vital documents are lost together.

If you are to have a base in your country of operation, try and find a friend who will let you use their company safe for valuables not needed during your visit. If you do this, give each person an envelope. Once they have put their valuables in, let them seal it themselves so there can be no arguments about what was put in the safe at the end of the visit. If you are travelling on a ferry, consider hiring a day cabin for luggage and as a base where anybody can return to if they have a problem. Some airports also offer rooms for stop-overs. This is worth considering as an option if you have to stop for more than two hours.

When travelling as a group, discipline is important and I have found that by splitting the party up and giving each leader a small group of the main party this makes for better control. Make sure all members of the party are aware of any local rules of etiquette or laws that may be different to those in their homeland. Taking pictures in airports and train stations can be illegal in some countries. Members of the party wearing shorts or not wearing a shirt may be offensive. You may find it useful during the training period before you depart to put special emphasis on introducing the expedition members to the culture of the country. If you can find someone from the country in question to talk about the differences and customs, this will be really beneficial.

It will help to have a home contact or agent who can keep parents informed of your progress and help you sort out any problems you may have. This person should not be related to anybody in the party so that if they have to sort out the repatriation of an injured person, or worse, a body, there will be less emotional involvement for them. They should be fully briefed on all your plans and have full details of everybody in the party.

There are many local and national organisations that exist to help young people's expeditions go abroad but one, The Young Explorers Trust, acts as an umbrella body and runs courses and seminars for leaders of young people's expeditions and offers an expedition screening service to groups of a pre-University age. Full details can be obtained by writing to The Young Explorers Trust c/o The Royal Geographical Society, 1 Kensington Gore, London, SW7 2AR tel: 0171-591 3000.

For further useful addresses, see p.710 of the Directory

THE ADVENTURE TRAVELLER

by Steve Watkins

What is an Adventure?

Have you ever dreamt of cycling around the world, kayaking down the Amazon, hiking the length of the Himalayas or even roller blading across Australia? If you have, then you are an adventurer at heart.

Adventure travel is tough to define. For some, it is dancing with death and danger in war zones, while for others it is backpacking around Greece. Turning to the dictionary for enlightenment, an adventure is deemed "an enterprise of hazard or risk" and an adventurer "one who hazards or attempts extraordinary enterprises". Again, to those involved, both the above examples could fit the descriptions, despite backpacking in Greece being less extraordinary in statistical terms. Having previously worked in the outdoor equipment industry selling gear to people heading off on similar trips, I can vouch for the fact that both the backpacker and the war junkie approach their travels with an equal amount of excitement and trepidation. So what exactly turns a traveller into an adventure traveller?

The New Adventurers

With all corners of the world becoming ever more accessible, there are few new "epic" adventures left to do. The poles have been well and truly conquered, to the point where it is now a case of finding the small print differences between the methods of getting there. Mount Everest has had over forty people on its summit in just one day and the Amazon is criss-crossed with the roads of mining and logging companies. Lets face it, there are very few places left where you have a guarantee of being the only traveller. Instead, adventure has become a more subtle and, I believe, equally fascinating version of the more blatant exploits of Scott, Hillary et al.

At its core lies the magic of inspiration and a willingness to be daring. As a youngster, I vividly recall my father telling me about my globetrotting uncle driving a little bubble car across the deserts of Libya, and how he had only just made it after the car's alternator failed. What an adventure, I remember thinking;

my head filled with Lawrence of Arabia style images. I was inspired. Years later, in 1988, I got a phone call from a university friend. "What are you up to this summer? Pete and I are going to cycle from Sicily to London. Are you coming?". My uncle's escapade sprang to mind and I said yes before it had even registered where Sicily was. My first adventure was born. I hadn't ridden a bike for ten years, nor did I own one, yet I had agreed to sit on a saddle for over two thousand miles. Naïveté and impulsive behaviour are surprisingly strong attributes when it comes to finding adventure.

I remember little about that first, manic, three week ride, other than flashing white lines, Graham's back tyre and having our "big adventure" put firmly in its place by an eighty-five year old English lady we met at Pompeii. On telling her, with puffed out chests, of our intentions to ride over the Alps, the lady retorted "Ooooh, that will be nice. I pedalled over the St. Bernard Pass (the highest in the Alps) on a Sturmey Archer three-speed when I was seventeen". A valuable lesson in humility for adventurers on ego trips! I reminisced for months afterwards and, with the adventure bug deeply embedded, I soon said yes to a bigger, more scary adventure – a year long ride through the Americas with three friends.

Plan It, Don't Kill It

Planning a trip down to the finest detail can kill it dead. The planning sessions for the Americas trip consisted of several pints of Guinness and lots of finger waving at a map of the world. This was, I'm sure, in stark contrast to the planning two guys I had met previously in Scandinavia had undertaken. On a three week Scanrail explorer trip, they had every connection time for every train they were going to catch and were hell bent on getting it right. By all means prepare equipment and finances well and thoroughly research the location but to hone a route plan can blinker you. Pick an area, get a rough idea of direction and then let it happen, because many of the best adventures are ones that are stumbled upon during a trip: when a local person asks you to follow him, when you are momentarily lost or when an alternative to the beaten track presents itself. Without resorting to utter recklessness, these impromptu situations, with a small amount of luck and a dose of self-confidence, can unfold into a memorable adventure.

During the Americas journey, we rode down the spine of the Andes. In Ecuador, at the small town of Alausi, we encountered a rail crossing. A quick peep at the guidebook revealed that the line ran to Cuenca, our destination, and was acclaimed as one of the world's great engineering feats. We had no idea what it would be like on bikes, but figured that it might just be a fun diversion from the Pan-American highway that we had got to know so well. Equally, it could have turned into an unrideable nightmare. We went for it and had one of the great riding experiences of our lives. The track rollercoasted through the mountains and steep-sided valleys, traversed spindly, wooden bridges and often left us riding either over the bumpy sleepers or on a terrifying, narrow path with vertical drops off the edge. We even came close to getting run over by the only train to run the route that day. It was indeed an adventure from the top drawer, but it wouldn't have happened if we had stayed only with the known.

Independent Endeavours

The very essence of adventure travel means that it is an independent endeavour. Despite claims to the contrary by most adventure travel tour operators, the crucial elements of risk and the unexpected are minimised, or removed, by organised tours. They may make you feel that your life is on the line when you are hanging out with lions in the Serengeti, but the reality is that you are probably safer than being at home. Itineraries are usually inflexible and many of the local people met along the way are regular hosts who wouldn't dream of ripping you off. These trips are exciting but not truly adventurous. However, if the operator gets you to sign a contract that relinquishes them from blame for any accidents due to the dangerous nature of their tour, then you could still be in for an adventure.

One such trip is run by a local agency in Antigua, Guatemala's beautiful, colonial city. Pacaya volcano has been active for over a decade and climbing it is relatively easy. Indeed, the agency takes tens of people up it every day. It is not until the ground is shaking beneath you and the molten bombs are landing within spitting distance of your vantage point, that the significance of the piece of paper they ask you to sign before leaving sinks in. A friend of mine got too close and lost the strap of his camera bag to a lump of red-hot lava, that he had abandoned when fleeing from the crater rim. Despite being there with thirty other people on an organised tour, it was most definitely an adventure.

Types of Adventures

There are many modes of transport available for the adventurer and a significant number of alternative sports that, having become more popular in recent years, are now easy ways to meet the demand for the adrenalin buzz of an adventure within a more limited timescale. Here are some examples, so control those fears of the unknown and go hang out on life's outer edges for a while.

Cycling

"He who forbade departure except on the thinnest of wheels, is in league with an everlasting roundness", wrote Giacometti in his poem *The Charioteer*. Travelling by bicycle can certainly provide a feeling of spiritual well-being, but it rarely reaches such enlightened heights on a two thousand metre hillclimb when the sweat is stinging your eyes and your thighs are burning like they've been injected with wintergreen. However, bike travel is addictive. Once you've tasted the freedom to travel when and where you like, covering reasonable distances, yet being able to stop if the whim takes you, it is difficult to accept the restrictions of other forms of getting around. Personally, I think the greatest benefit bestowed on bikers is never, or only rarely, having to deal with officialdom at train and bus stations. Get on your bike and say goodbye to the queues. Mountain bikes have revolutionised the two-wheeled scene, offering the opportunity to travel on routes that would destroy road bikes.

Hiking

If you want to get away into real wilderness, then there is only one choice of transport. Hiking. Some of the most remote and least visited places on Earth lie in mountainous regions. Whilst it is difficult to cover large distances when you have to carry all your gear and food on your back, getting more than a day or two away from civilisation can be the nearest you can get to experiencing the isolation felt by Scott et al on their epic adventures. The dangers of climbing mountains, however, should not be underestimated. Make sure that you can navigate properly, especially in low visibility, take sufficient clothing, equipment, food and water to survive a night out in the open (even if the weather looks great when you set out) and tell someone where you are heading and roughly how long it will take. A major appeal of hiking is that you don't have to travel to far off places to have an adventure. Sure, it would be nice to pop over to the Himalaya a few times a year, but a rewarding sense of adventure can be found in a weekend in the UK, particularly in Scotland.

Ski Touring

When winter bites, it puts paid to many adventurous opportunities, but, at the same time, creates others. For the adventure traveller, ski touring offers the best opportunity to satisfy that need to challenge our comfortable daily lives during the coldest months. Faster than hiking but slower than cycling, ski touring not only allows you the chance to soak up superb scenic treats, but it can also do wonders for your fitness. It is a total body workout, with the professional racers being amongst the fittest athletes in the world. Apart from the usual ski resort areas, such as the Alps and the Pyrenees, ski touring is also strong in Scandinavia, Iceland and eastern Europe. Many ski tourers have converted from downhill skiing, having realised that just zooming down slopes all day can narrow your horizons. And of course, there are no impatient lift queues to join either and the downhill slopes encountered whilst touring can be every bit as exciting as their lift-served counterparts, but with an added sense of adventure.

Paragliding

For those who find having their feet on the ground slightly mundane, paragliding is the ultimate way to fly. Little can match the adventurous feel of only having a thin seat between you and a few thousand feet drop to the ground. It is like a cross between parachuting, gliding and hot air ballooning, where you soar on thermal air ridges using a rectangular parachute canopy that allows you to control both direction and speed. It is possible to stay in the air for several hours if the desire takes you: definitely a sport where expert guidance is needed to get started. Paragliding has been successfully combined with other mountain sports, such as mountaineering, where people climb to the top and then fly back down.

Kayaking/White Water Rafting

Probably the wildest way of travelling is to kayak or raft down a frothing river edged by vertical rock faces. If you have ever stared into a washing machine and wondered what it is like to be in there, then rafting is the nearest you will come to finding out. Rafting can take you along some of the world's most awesome stretches of water, such as the Blue Nile in Ethiopia, the Sun Kosi river in Nepal and the Zambesi in Zimbabwe. Requiring little training to get started, rafting rewards you with a thrilling adventure and the satisfaction of working in a team.

Scuba Diving

Many people are unaware of the incredible world that exists beneath the sea. I remember the shock of first donning a snorkel and mask and poking my head just centimetres below the surface of the Indian Ocean. It was like finding out that I had a long lost brother or sister and I couldn't wait to find out more about it. Whilst snorkelling is a great way to see the bright colours of the coral reefs and the plethora of rainbow coloured fish that live on them, it is frustrating to have to continually resurface for air. Scuba diving doesn't just solve that problem, it adds a completely different dimension to the experience. To effortlessly move around under water for up to an hour or so, swimming amongst shoals of colour and maybe even seeing larger species, such as dolphins, rays or sharks, is possibly the most relaxing, refreshing adventure sport available. It is essential to take a recognised course, such as those offered by PADI or NAUI, to learn how to use the equipment, the standard methods of communicating underwater and how to deal with emergencies. Once you are qualified, which can take as little as three days, you are free to roam the world in search of the big blue.

Rock Climbing

Few activities require the level of concentration and ability necessary to subdue the body's natural reaction to danger than rock climbing. Even when you are securely tied to a rope that will stop you from falling far, a tricky move has fear welling up inside you. By controlling those fears and directing that energy into your fingers and feet, it is possible to scale rockfaces that, from the ground, seem to have no holds. One of the reasons behind the burgeoning popularity of climbing is that it doesn't matter how experienced you are, there is always a climb that can challenge you to push beyond your own boundaries. It is essential to receive proper training in the techniques and ropework required, as the consequences can be dire if mistakes are made. There are many indoor climbing gyms, as well as outdoor centres, around the country that offer courses.

Additional Information for Adventurers

by Paul Vickers

Sources of Information

Talk to like-minded people. It's often inspiring and first-hand information is always the most interesting and up-to-date. If you are unsure of quite what to do or how to do it, other adventurers' stories and advice are most encouraging and supportive. *The Independent Traveller* seminars organised yearly at the Royal Geographical Society are inspirational events devoted to talks, slideshows, films and informal discussion by recently returned adventure travellers. The Globetrotters Club is also a good place to meet fellow travellers and swap ideas and the club's specialist newsletter is full of useful information.

Self-sufficiency and Independence

If you are going to be off the beaten track, you have to be as self-sufficient as possible, capable of maintaining yourself, your animals and your equipment. Familiarise yourself thoroughly with your equipment, know how to dismantle and reassemble everything before you set out, and carry your own repair and tool kit. Ensure you know what to do in the case of illness or an accident and check your medical kit is comprehensive (how many water-purifying tablets or painkillers might you need?) Always be prepared for the worst. What protection do you require for the weather conditions you could experience? Crossing the Thar desert of Rajasthan by bicycle I needed a dozen litres of water each day, two days' supply was the absolute maximum I could carry and it was boiling hot by the time I came to drink it.

Equipment

He who travels light, travels far. The adventure traveller must travel light as it is he himself who must transport all his equipment. The more you carry, the more encumbered and slow you are. Lightness equals flexibility, enabling you to change your plan, route or mode of transport instantly without problems. Pack your gear three times, ruthlessly pruning out items each time or you'll find yourself leaving a trail of abandoned, expensive equipment across the globe. Carry the absolute minimum that you can safely get away with. I prefer to buy extra clothing when it gets cold and sell it or give it away as it gets warmer – infinitely preferable to carrying it hundreds of miles on the off-chance of needing it again later.

Horses, Camels and Yaks

Animals take a fair bit of handling and you need some experience. Remember they cover less ground than is generally imagined, especially when heavily laden and over long distances (approximately twice a man's daily walking distance, and half a day's cycling distance). For average cross-country rates, count on 40 kilometres a day for a horse. Yaks are slower and can't be taken below 10,000 feet altitude. Camels do need to drink!

Ballooning and Microlighting

Balloons have flown over mountain ranges and across oceans, microlights across Africa and from the UK all the way down under to Australia. They are highly specialised forms of adventure travel and require a lot of planning and preparation in advance, but they do enable man to fly independently.

Adventure travel is primarily a question of independence, determination and confidence. Anyone with an adventurous spirit can do it. The sense of achievement and self-confidence that come from it are quite immeasurable and greatly outweigh the relatively small amount of pain that goes with an enormous degree of pleasure. Don't hesitate, pack this book in your rucksack and go – you will never look back!

For adventure and sporting organisations and tour operators see p.712

Further Reading: *The Action Guide to the UK* (Harvill) is an excellent directory of the best 300 Outdoor/Adventure Sports in the UK. There are 32 categories covering all orthodox sports as well we cheese rolling and gut banging for both beginners and advanced sportsmen.

THE SKIER

by Arnie Wilson

Unless they are rich or retired or both, most skiers only manage a week or two each year in which to hone or re-acquire their skills. Because of this, it is vital (although not always possible) to select the most appropriate resort for their needs.

Apart from the annual dilemma of whether the snow will be late arriving – in other words, there is never any guarantee of sufficient snow at Christmas or even New Year – France, Switzerland and Austria are usually a safe bet. Italy has been an even better bet in the last two winters because of the weak lira and the unusually good snowfalls.

North America – once you have paid your air-fare across the Atlantic – is extremely good value, with the exception of the lift pass, which is usually more expensive than its European counterparts. But snow – with intensive snowmaking – is virtually guaranteed, and the cost of living, particularly eating out, is considerably lower than Europe. In Canada, prices are generally even cheaper, and you have the advantage of non-stop flights to Calgary. At present there are non-stop commercial flights to the American Rockies, although charter flights come and go.

Apart from the obvious – good snow – what does a skier want from a holiday? There are many considerations. Good nightlife? Cheap drinks? A pretty village? Great scenery? Good food? Slopes that are easy to get to? Good children's facilities? Friendly locals? Close to the airport? All of these, if that were possible. Or at least a good cross-section. But the chances are, the more of these elements you can combine, the more expensive the holiday will be.

Zermatt, in Switzerland, for example, is certainly not cheap. But it has a great deal going for it: the majestic Matterhorn, more mountain restaurants than any other resort in Europe, and some excellent skiing. It is not, however, easy to get to.

The French resort of Flaine, on the other hand, is close to Geneva, has some good skiing, excellent children's facilities, but would be a good candidate to win the prize in the architectural "carbuncle of the Alps" competition should the Prince of Wales ever arrange one.

Austria probably has more charm, pretty ski villages and excellent hotels than anywhere in Europe, but tends to have resorts at lower altitude so in a bad snow year, conditions can be more critical than in France or Switzerland, particularly in places like Kitzbühel and Saalbach-Hinterglemm.

If you are going to take the trouble – and the time – to cross the Atlantic, there is no point in going just for a week. The high altitude in Colorado may take its toll for a day of two, and by the time you feel you have adjusted to this and the jet lag, you may be two or three days into your holiday. In theory, the longer you stay in North America, the cheaper it gets.

If you want a short, sharp, brilliant skiing break, try weekend skiing – in Chamonix, for example. If you can afford the time to go for a week, go somewhere reasonably pretty with plenty to do apart from skiing: try Zermatt, St. Anton (Austria), St. Martin-de-Belleville (linked with France's vast Trois Vallées) or Cortina (Italian Dolomites).

In America, go for the places with some real history plus good skiing: Aspen, Telluride or Breckenridge (all Colorado).

Whatever you do, ski somewhere. Even if it's Scotland – or the Snowdome at Tamworth, near Birmingham.

THE POLAR TRAVELLER

by Ranulph Fiennes

There is a Danish word *polarhullar*, meaning "a yearning for the Polar regions" which grips the soul of a traveller so that nowhere else will ever again satisfy his appetite for the essence of "over there and beyond". A victim of polarhullar will forever be drawn back to the very extremities of Earth.

Antarctica is expensive and difficult to reach which is why, blocked by the roughest seas in the world, nobody penetrated its fastness, until, only 90 years ago, Scott, Amundsen and Shackleton struggled over the Ross Ice Shelf and onto the vast inland plateau, while the Arctic Ocean, peopled by Eskimos who for centuries have survived along its coastlines, is infinitely more accessible to travellers. Sledgers who cross Greenland, the Canadian north and Svalbard, often describe themselves as polar travellers, using the Arctic Circle as their yardstick. Thus, there are a great many more veterans of the Arctic than of Antarctica.

Travel in the remote polar reaches of the Arctic Ocean itself and the high plateaux of Antarctica demands careful preparation and constant wariness due to unpredictable weather and local hazards which can rapidly prove lethal. On the other hand, during the summer season, polar travel can be easy and almost temperate on windless days and away from problem areas. I have travelled to both poles without suffering unduly from the cold, yet I lost part of a toe from frost bite during a weekend army exercise in Norfolk. A need for wariness is not a uniquely polar prerogative.

A brief history of previous polar travellers in Antarctica would have to start in AD650 when, according to the legends of Polynesian Rarotonga, their chief Uite headed south in a war canoe until the ocean was covered with "white powder and great white rocks rose into the sky".

Soon after the discovery of America by Columbus and Cape Horn by Drake, Britain annexed Australia (1616). Then in 1700 astronomer Halley reached South Georgia and by 1774 Captain Cook had sailed south of the Antarctic circle. He then circumnavigated Antarctica without ever sighting land. Nobody over-wintered on the continent until the British Norwegian Southern Cross expedition of 1900 which preceded the "heroic age" of the Pole racers, made famous by the deaths of all Scott's team soon after Amundsen reached the South Pole in 1911. In 1914 Shackleton attempted to traverse Antarctica. He failed, but in 1958 the crossing was successfully achieved by the team led by Dr Vivian Fuchs and Sir Edmund Hillary.

A full resumé of Arctic travel that stretched over three centuries would fill many pages. Ships' captains from America and Britain vied with each other throughout the 19th century to find a "north-west passage". Entire expeditions disappeared in a mist of rumoured mutiny, murder and cannibalism.

The urge to be the first to the North Pole ended early this century with mutually disputed claims by two Americans, Peary and Cook. Both were later accused of fudging their records and the first proven journey to the North Pole was that of Ralph Plaisted, an American preacher, in 1968, a year before Britain's Wally Herbert completed the first surface crossing of the Arctic Ocean via the pole.

The achievement of linking up expeditions north and south into a circumpolar journey encircling the earth was proposed by Charles de Brosses, an 18th century French geographer, and finally executed by the Transglobe Expedition (1979-1982). This expedition's ice group, myself and Charles Burton, travelled from Greenwich across Antarctica and the Arctic Ocean, then back to Greenwich. We became the first people to reach both poles by surface travel and to circumnavigate Earth on its polar axis.

In 1993 with Mike Stroud, I crossed the Antarctic continent unsupported which was the longest unsupported polar journey in history. This took nearly 100 days, but, a year later, various types of wind-powered kites and parawings emerged which enabled Antarctica to be crossed with far less effort in a mere 50 days. Now it is possible to traverse both Antarctica and the Arctic Ocean with no "outside" support but harnessing the wind with lightweight sails.

A sledger using modern kites can pick up and harness winds from over 180 degrees. Until 1994 the great journeys of Shackleton and his successors utilised crude sails which could only run before a directly following wind. Should Mike and I have described our 1993 expedition, or Shackleton's in this time, as 'unsupported', when we harnessed the wind, albeit in a minimal way? Should I, in 1996, have used a vastly improved modern kite gadget and still have called my journey "unsupported"? It is a question of definition, for there is after all no polar version of the International Olympic Committee.

In 1993 Mike Stroud and I suffered considerable physical damage crossing the Antarctic continent by manhaul and minimal use of sails which could only use following winds. Our sledge loads, each in excess of 480lbs, required brute force to shift and ten miles a day was a fair average manhaul stint costing a daily deficit of 8000 calories leading to slow starvation.

In 1996, again towing a load of nigh on 500lbs, I deployed a 10lb kite and managed up to 120 miles a day with minimal physical effort and correspondingly less calorific expenditure. My sledge load could be halved in terms of fuel and food. What had previously proved remarkably difficult was now comparatively simple.

Polar travel has been truly revolutionised by such wind devices. It is now possible to cross Antarctica in under two months. Of course the element of luck can still play tricks. Broken equipment, unusually bad weather, sudden illness and well hidden crevasses can yet prevent a successful outcome but at least the reality of polar travel is now within the grasp of the many, not just the few.

My instructions for this section of the Handbook are to provide practical information and this would be difficult without lists. These are the result of a dozen polar journeys in many regions and with differing purposes. I have spent more days and nights out on the Arctic pack and Antarctic plateau than anyone alive but my kit lists and general tips are by no means infallible. They will not prevent you falling into the sea or an ice crack. You may still become hypothermic, snow blind, lost or eaten by a polar bear but I hope they will at least help you get started as a polar traveller of reasonable competence.

First of all read available literature by previous travellers in the area of your chosen trip. Study the annexes at the rear of expedition books. Lists of sponsors and manufacturers are often quoted and can save you time.

Then apply, perhaps through the Royal Geographical Society's Expedition Advisory Office, for information on expeditions currently planning to go into your area of interest. It will help if you have a skill to offer (cook, communications, photographer, mechanic etc.).

Go on other people's trips to Greenland, Svalbard, Iceland, Norway, anywhere with snow and ice, to gain experience before progressing to the deep South or North and to leading your own projects, eventually to and across the Poles if that strikes your fancy. Here are some guidelines. Feel free to ignore or alter wherever you can garner more appropriate advice elsewhere.

Equipment

Clothing

The heavier the weight you tow when manhauling with no wind support, the more difficult the selection of clothing, as you will sweat, despite the cold, when working and various parts of your body, especially feet and crutch will suffer if your clothing choice is not excellent.

• Fleece jacket with hood
• Ventile outer trousers with braces and long length anorak (baggy)
• Down duvet jacket with hood attached (for periods when not manhauling)
• Wick-away underwear (long sleeves and legs)
• Meraklon headover
• Duofold Balaclava with mouth hole
• Separate lip protector mouthpiece with elastic to hold in place
• Ski goggles and ski glacier glasses with nose-protecting felt pad glued in place
• 1pr thick wool socks
• 1pr thin Helly Hansen socks
• 1pr vapour barrier socks
• 1pr Dachstein mitts
• 1pr Northern Outfitters heavy gauntlets
• 1 peaked cap with kepi-style and under neck-strap
• 1pr thin working gloves
• Footwear as advised by polar travellers of your acquaintance (or from their books!), there are too many alternatives to be specific here. Correct fitting boots are of great importance
• For polar work when using snow machines, skis or dogs, shops specialising in the relevant sports gear will be able to advise you best.

General items

• Geodetic dome tents are best (2 or 3 man) but beware of the elastic holding the poles together. When cold, it loses elasticity so, if you have room on a sledge keep as many of the pole sections permanently taped together as possible. Black tents make the most of the sun's heat and can be seen nearly as well as fluorescent colours.

• Sledge harness and traces (solid traces are best for crevassed areas). In the Arctic Ocean pack ice your sledge should be 'amphibious'.

• Skis, skins, ski sticks and relevant spares. (Make sure your ski bindings mate well with your boots.)

• With your sleeping bag and tent, use stuff sacs that don't need too much effort to squeeze in.

• MSR (Mountain Safety Research) cooker. Coleman fuel is best in extreme cold. (Be sure to get a secure fitting fixed to the lid of the box you carry your cook gear in.) Clip the MSR fuel bottle into it firmly before priming. You need a firm base. Take a spare MSR and bag of spares, especially a pricker.

• Brush to clear snow: Hard bristles

• Insulated mug and spoon. Set of cooking pots and pot holder

• Zippo lighter and spare flints. Use Coleman fuel

• Spare lighter

• Silva (balanced) compass and spare compass

• Reliable watch and spare

• Optional: a light rucksack

• Optional: Windsail kit and spares in bag

• 2 ice screws. 1pr jumars with loops

• Ice axe

• 50ft length of para cord

• 100ft of thinnest relevant climbing rope

• Optional – Foldaway snow shovel

• Karabiners

• Karrimat

• Sleeping bag with inner (and optional outer) vapour barriers

• Pee bottle (Nalgene or Rubbermaid)

• PLB (Personal Locator Beacon) and spare lithium battery

• GPS (Global Positioning System) and spare lithium battery

• Optional – HF radio and ancillaries

• Video and still camera kit. Polythene bags to avoid misting up

• Steel thermos

• Rations of high calorie, low weight make-up. Be-well Nutrition are best for extreme polar work. Pack as for a 24 hour day per tent.

• Personal bag. This may contain; small adjustable spanner; pin-nose pliers; dental floss; needles; thin cord; Superglue; wire; diary and pencil; Velcro; charts and maps; Swiss Army knife (all needed implements); spare underwear (optional)

• Medical kit – this should include all that polar travellers advise, from snow-blindness relief to morphine. Oil of cloves for tooth pain, Anusol, Canestan powder, Bonjela gel, Immodium, Convatech anti-blister plasters are all liable to be needed. Don't forget lip cream, hand cream, penicillin and Ibrufen anti-inflammation pills.

• Remember that insurance, fully comprehensive and including possible Search and Rescue costs is often mandatory and always sensible.

• In Antarctica the best air charter company Adventure Network International, will give you all the necessary advice on every side of your expedition. In the Canadian Arctic, Bradley First Air are the best (based from Resolute Bay, NWT). Remember that your cargo will cost a great deal at both ends. (In Antarctica, count on US$30 per lb above your basic allowance to get you there from Chile.)

Final Advice

Don't go to the Arctic or Antarctica to do difficult journeys with folk you don't know about. They should be reliable, easy-going and experienced. You can get to both poles by paying expert guides to help you there. Some are to be avoided. Others like Pen Hadow are excellent. All are expensive. Pay more and an aircraft will take you all the way to either Pole and allow you an hour or two there, before whisking you back to warmer climes.

Never leave litter nor harm life in any form while you are there. The Everest climbers have polluted their grail. Keep our Poles clean.

Plan with great care and never rely on gizmos working, PLB's and GPS's for instance, or count on immediate rescue since storms can keep search 'planes away for days, even weeks, so play safe.

If you aim to join the weirdos' section by bicycling across Ellesmereland or "collecting" different poles (geomagnetic, magnospheric, lesser accessibility etc.) then plan accordingly. For example, if you intend doing the South pole on a pogo-stick, don't forget lots of low-temperature grease and your haemorrhoids cream. Have fun and stay cool.

For polar travel organisations and tour operators see p.715 of the Directory

THE STUDENT TRAVELLER

by Nick Hanna and Greg Brookes

If you are a student traveller you can take advantage of a comprehensive range of special discounts – both at home and abroad – which enable you to go almost anywhere in the world on the cheap. To qualify for reduced fares to most destinations you need an International Student Identity Card (ISIC) which is obtainable from local student travel offices (£5.00) or by post from ISIC Mail Order, Bleaklow House, Howard Town Mills, Mill Street, Glossop SK13 8PT. All full time students are eligible; postal applications should include proof of student status, a passport photo, full name, date of birth, nationality, address and a cheque or postal order for £5.50 payable to ISIC Mail Order. The ISIC card is issued by the Copenhagen-based International Student Travel Confederation (ISTC) who publish a booklet called *The ISIC World Travel Handbook* detailing student discounts worldwide. The ISIC card is recognised all over the world and allows holders reduced rates at many art galleries, museums and other places of cultural and educational interest, as well as reductions on local transport, restaurants and much more.

The Council of Europe Cultural Identity Card (BP431/R6, F-67006 Strasbourg, France, tel: 33-88 41 20 33) is available free to postgraduate students, teachers, and a few other categories. It gives reduced or free admission to places of cultural interest in the Vatican and all member countries of the Council of Europe (but not in the country of issue, and only when produced with a passport). The card cannot be used by those travelling for commercial reasons. For application forms and more information, write to the Central Bureau for Educational Visits and Exchange (CBEVE).

There are also a number of travel discount schemes that are not dependent upon student status, although most of these are nevertheless youth schemes for which you cease to be eligible once you reach the age of between 24 and 26. The Federation of International Youth Travel Organisations (FIYTO, Bredgade 25H, 1260 Copenhagen, Denmark, tel: 45-3333 9600) is made up of over 200 organisations in 50 countries throughout the world which specialise in youth travel. A "Go 25"membership card entitles you to a range of concessions similar, although not identical, to those given by ISIC and costs £6. The card is available to everyone under the age of 26, and is issued with a handbook listing all the concession entitlements. Another similar card is the Under 26 European Youth Card.

Accommodation

If you don't fancy spending your travels under canvas, try ISIC's *The World Travel Handbook* for details of accommodation discounts. Another good source of information will be the International Youth Hostel Federation which has more than 5000 hostels worldwide. Their directory has now been split into two books, Europe and the Mediterranean and Africa, America, Asia and Oceania. Both are available from any good bookshop and cost £6.99 each.

Slightly more expensive but better equipped, the Young Men's and Young Women's Christian Association hostels are another option for student travellers. The YMCA Directory (available for £5, or £5.50 if purchased from abroad, from the National Council of YMCAs, 640 Forest Road, London E17 3DZ tel: 0181-520 5599) lists all worldwide YMCA hostels. For the women's version, The World YWCA Directory (£6 includes postage) for travels to Europe, Pack for Europe (£1.50 plus 25p postage) contact YWCA (Clarendon House, 52 Cornmarket Street, Oxford OX1 3EJ, tel: 01865-726110).

With a little initiative, you may be able to negotiate use of student accommodation during vacation time. In West Germany, students can use university catering facilities (Mensas) which are decent, reasonably priced and open all year round. Student accommodation is only available during local university vacations. Most of the student and independent travel agencies can also now book you budget accommodation worldwide in hostels and 1,2 and 3 star hotels.

Travel Discounts

Cheap rail travel is now dependent chiefly upon age and is generally open to everyone under the age of 26. In order to cover the 26 countries and a wider target market, Inter-Rail is now available on a zonal basis – from £189 for a 15 day

1 zone pass to £279 for a month long Global pass as well as entitling you to discounts on P&O and Sealink (see Chapter 7, *Inter-Rail through Europe* and rail information in Section 6 of the directory p.793).

Eurotrain (52 Grosvenor Gardens, London SW1W 0AG, tel: 0171-730 3402) offer low prices to young travellers heading for Europe. If you are under 26 you can take advantage of a selection of European routings (including Eastern Europe) which allow stopovers and two-month ticket validity from as little as £39 to Amsterdam, for example, and include your sea crossing to the continent.

Student and youth discounts are also available for those travelling by coach. It pays to compare prices carefully between coach and rail because although coaches are normally considerably cheaper, sometimes the difference can be small and trains are obviously preferable in terms of speed and comfort. Apart from these exceptions, coaches are generally substantially cheaper than trains. Eurolines (52 Grosvenor Gardens, London SW1W 0AG, tel: 0171-730 8235) runs a daily service to Amsterdam and Paris as well as services to over 400 destinations in Europe. A four or five-journey bus pass, lasting one month costs from £159.

Within Britain, National Express (The Coach Travel Centre, 4 Vicarage, Edgebaston, Birmingham, B15 3ES tel: 0990-808080) gives students a 33 per cent reduction on all standard fares on production of the Young Person's Coach Card (£8).

Valuable discounts are also available for air travel. Student and youth discount flights are operated by the major student travel organisations under the umbrella of the Student Air Travel Association. Most of the flights are generally open to ISIC card holders under 30 (some have different age restrictions) together with their spouses and dependent children travelling on the same flight or to young persons with a valid Under 26 card. Again, The Student Traveller is a useful source of information, listing Student Travel Offices (STOs) around the world.

Travel Offices

Student travel offices are a good source of information for just about every kind of discount: there are nearly 100 of them in Britain, one for every campus or university town. Staff are often themselves seasoned travellers and can be a mine of information of budget travel in foreign countries. But check out your High Street travel agent as well, and compare prices before making a final decision.

Campus Travel (head office: 52 Grosvenor Gardens, London SW1W 0AF, tel: Europe 0171-730 3402; North America 0171-730 2101; Worldwide 0171-730 8111) is the UK's largest student travel agency with 46 branches nationwide, six of which are in London. Council Travel, the US's largest student travel agent is based in San Francisco and has 50 branches across the States, for more information contact it at Ground Floor, 530 Bush Street, San Francisco, CA 94108, tel: 415-421 3473.

Another source of information on student travel discounts is *The Guide*, produced annually by STA Travel (to obtain a free copy contact STA Travel, 74 Old Brompton Road, London SW7, tel: 0171-581 1022). Although they started out life as Student Travel Australia, the services offered by STA now cover both hemispheres. They have four offices in London and others throughout

Australia, South East Asia, the Far East and the USA.

Working and Studying Abroad

There are several very good references for students who wish to work abroad such as Working Holidays published by the Central Bureau for Education Visits and Exchanges, and a very useful series of books from Vacation Work publications.

North America is a favourite destination for students who want a working holiday. The British Universities North America Club (BUNAC) is a non-profit making organisation that exists to give students the chance to get to the States. They've got four programmes in the USA and Canada, one in Australia and one in Jamaica, offering a wide choice of jobs and locations and BUNAC gets you that vital work permit for all of them.

The general work and travel programme Work America, allows you a visa so that you can take virtually any summer job you find yourself; the airfare has to be paid in advance – they suggest that bank managers will usually oblige with a loan. Places are limited so it's vital that the lengthy application process is started early. Applicants must be at least 19 and have experience of working with groups of children. Hundreds of opportunities can also be found in BUNAC's *Job Directory*.

If you enjoy the company of children, then they have a BUNACAMP programme which places students in summer camps as counsellors. These are also open to gap-year students and non-students. The round trip ticket is paid for and you get full board and lodging plus pocket money. Students with specialist skills (music, sports, arts or science) are preferred, but, more importantly, you must be able to deal with children.

Another deal that provides you with airfares full board and lodging and a job is KAMP, the kitchen and maintenance programme. Contact BUNAC at 16 Bowling Green Lane, London EC1 0BD (tel: 0171-251 3472).

Camp America (37 Queen's Gate, London, SW7 5HR, tel: 0171-581 7373) provides similar facilities with a free flight, free board and work permit all as part of the package.

There is also GAP Activity Projects (Ltd) tel: 01734-594914 who organise voluntary work overseas (usually 6 month placements) for school-leavers who are between school and further training. It has projects in 33 countries around the world for young volunteers, who assist with the teaching of English, and help in schools generally. Volunteers are also needed for social work, caring, conservation and outward bound.

To study abroad you must first be sure you can cope adequately with the local language. Organisations such as the Central Bureau and the British Council should be able to help as should the Cultural Attaché at the relevant embassy. If possible, ask someone who has just returned for details about local conditions.

Grants

Ask your university, college, higher education department or local authority if they have any special trust funds for student travel. If it has, it won't be much but every little helps. Two handbooks on grants are *The Directory of Grant*

Making Trusts and *The Grants Register*. Both are expensive but should be in your student or, possibly, your local library. The library noticeboard is also a good place to look for details of bursaries or exchange scholarships which could well lead to a year's studying or travelling upon graduation.

For student travel organisations see p.716 of the Directory

THE EXPATRIATE TRAVELLER
by Doris Dow

Nowadays governments, large organisations and big companies all compete for the expertise and skills they require. More and more people leave their own country to live and work abroad. These expatriates go off with high hopes and expectations but in spite of increased earning power, some are disappointed and frustrated and return home for good. Others adapt well to the challenge of a new life and continue in the expatriate scene for many years, finding it difficult to repatriate.

Contracts
It is important that the terms of the contract are understood and signed by the employer and the employee; if the contract is in another language, a reliable translation should be obtained before signing on the dotted line. Contracts should set out the terms and conditions of employment, including minimum length of contract, working hours and overtime, remuneration, allowances for/provision of accommodation, car, education, medical and dental cover, leave and terminal gratuities/bonuses, dismissal clauses and compassionate leave arrangements.

Many jobs abroad offer what seem to be on paper very large salaries, but the attitude of employers, their willingness to accept responsibility and to offer support when necessary are often worth more than money. **Expats International** (29 Lacon Road, East Dulwich, London SE29 9HE, tel: 0181-299 4986) is an association for expatriates which not only has a large job advertisement section in its magazine, but will advise on contracts and finance.

Documentation
Before departure, visas, work permits, driving licences, health regulations and other documentation must be attended to. Getting the necessary visas from embassies can entail many visits and long waits, but the first lessons of an aspiring expatriate are quickly learned – the acquisition of tolerance, patience, perseverance and good humour. For those working for a large company or international organisation, the documentation is usually done for them.

Preparations for the Move
Time spent doing some 'homework' on the country you are going to, its lifestyles, traditions and customs is very worthwhile. Mental preparation is just

as important as the practical plans – working and living in a country is quite a different experience from a holiday visit.

Search libraries and bookshops for travel books and up-to-date guides. For Commonwealth countries, there are excellent permanent exhibitions at the Commonwealth Institute, Kensington High Street, London, as well as an excellent bookshop. Embassies should also be helpful on specific information on currency, import regulations etc., as well as giving advice on what not to import. Other valuable sources of information are: **Corona Worldwide** (35 Belgrave Square, London SW1X 8QB, tel: 0171-610 4407) whose *Notes for Newcomers* series features over 100 countries (£3.50 and £5 per set plus postage) and gives practical details on what to take, education, leisure activities and health etc. **Employment Conditions Abroad** (Anchor House, 15 Britten Street, London SW3 3TY, tel: 0171–351 5000) is also another useful source of information.

Finance

Arrangements should be made to continue National Health Insurance contributions, as these are an extremely good investment. All financial aspects of the move should be studied and arranged before departure – tax clearance, financial regulations and exchange controls in your country of destination, investments etc. There are firms and consultancies specialising in this field e.g. **The Fry Group** (Crescent House, Crescent Road, Worthing, West Sussex BN11 1RN tel: 01903-231545).

Despatch and Arrival of Effects

There are many international firms who specialise in overseas removals. For those who have to make their own arrangements, it is advisable to approach more than one firm for an estimate. When travelling by air, include as many basic essentials as possible in the accompanying luggage so that you are self-sufficient for the first few days (include a few paperbacks to get through lengthy waits and sleepless nights due to jetlag).

Always ensure that personal luggage is locked and insured. Many people find airfreight the quickest, easiest and safest way of consigning goods. Lists of all contents should be available for customs clearance, shipping agents, insurance etc., and two copies of these lists should always be retained. Baggage allowances are usually generous and first entry into a country generally permits duty-free import of personal and household effects.

In many countries there is a ready sale for second-hand possessions at the end of a contract, often at advantageous prices, so it is worthwhile making full use of the allowance. There are only a few instances where what is imported must be taken away again in its entirety. Heavier items for sea freight should be crated and listed – translation into the appropriate language can often hasten customs clearance. Hiring a good local agent who knows the ropes can also be a good investment. Realistic insurance of all effects is essential.

Arrival at Destination

If possible, arrange to be met at the airport, and/or have a contact telephone number. Make sure that hotel accommodation has been booked and keep all receipts for later reimbursement. Salary may be delayed so try to have some travellers' cheques to cover this eventuality. A long journey and the shock of new climatic conditions can be depressing until you are acclimatised, so use your common sense and allow yourself time to adjust. Be prepared for long delays at customs and immigration control – patience and good humour will pay dividends here. Don't judge the country by its officialdom! Do not exchange money except through official channels.

Housing

It is unlikely that permanent accommodation will be available immediately, necessitating a few day's or even week's stay in a hotel. Make use of this freedom to get acquainted with local sources of supply etc. To many expatriates, disappointment can begin with housing and furniture, which often does not match up to expectations. Reserve judgement at the beginning, because what may seem a drawback can turn out to be an advantage. There is a big difference in standards between local and expatriate employers, and there is no firm basis for comparison. In oil-rich states, it may well be that expatriate housing is much humbler than that of the nationals. On the other hand, accommodation may be very luxurious and spacious. The less fortunate expatriate should refrain from envious comparisons and, with careful thought and inexpensive ingenuity, make the best of what comes along. Work camps/compounds and high rise flats are all very real challenges to the good homemaker.

Medical Care

Primary medical care is sometimes much better than one might expect, easily contacted and near at hand. Further care may be available but, if not, serious cases are flown out for emergency or specialist treatment. Large organisations often have their own hospitals, clinics and doctors. Government contracts usually provide free medical facilities. It is always wise to have a good dental check-up before departure from home. Anybody needing medication on a regular basis should take a good supply to last until an alternative source is established.

Education

Very young children are often well catered for by play groups and nursery schools. For older children there are international schools, company schools, and private or state schools. These vary considerably, but given a good school and parents who take advantage of all there is to offer in the locality, a child will make a good start. There is often a waiting list and information about schools should be obtained and an early approach made for enrolment well ahead of departure. For those going to outlying areas, it may be necessary to consider correspondence courses, e.g. **World-Wide Education Service** (St. George's House, 14-17 Wells Street, London W1P 3FP, tel: 0171-637 2644).

Many contracts provide for boarding school in the UK and regular holiday visits to parents. As the older child might well lack stimulation and local schooling might be inadequate, early consideration should be given to choosing a boarding school. It is a hard decision to take, but the partings at the end of the holidays are compensated for by the pleasure with which children look forward to travelling out to their parents at the end of term. In some expatriate communities, special events are laid on for the children, they feel special having a home overseas and the experience of travelling alone can make them more responsible, confident and resourceful. Corona Worldwide also provides an escort service from airport to school trains etc. Children are often used as an excuse for the wife to return home, but for children at boarding school, it can be more important for them to feel that they have a solid family base than to have Mum on the doorstep.

Marriage

The move should be talked over very carefully as it can have a profound effect on a marriage. For busy working parents and weary commuters, expatriate life can be an opportunity to spend more time together as a family, and if both partners are keen, the novelty of the strange environment can be a rewarding experience. I would advise against married men taking single person's contracts or splitting the partnership for long periods of time, as it places too great a strain on communication. Starting again could help rebuild a shaky marriage, but it could also split it apart if an unwilling person is ripped away from everything familiar. So think before you move.

Single Men and Women

Single (or unaccompanied) men often live in camps which are isolated. They have frequent short leaves, and money to spend. A special interest – sport or hobby – gives them a chance to form stable friendships and does away with propping up the bar for company in their spare time. A single woman usually has to establish a home as well as tackling the job. However, the job, with a real and worthwhile challenge, gives her an advantage over many wives who often find themselves at sea with nothing to do but keep house. A single woman is generally in great demand in a lively social whirl, but this needs to be handled with great care. She is often an object of great interest to the local population who find it difficult to understand that she has no man to tell her what to do, and may receive many offers of marriage because of this.

Wives

While women are generally expected to be supportive of their husbands as they come to terms with a new job, it should also be remembered that they too need support and encouragement as they establish a new home, meet new people and adapt to a different lifestyle. At all times, the rules and regulations and laws of a country must be obeyed. Western women often find the new cultures and traditions difficult to embrace and inhibiting, e.g. in a Muslim country, and it is essential to prepare for this. One-day briefing courses for men and women, *Living Overseas*, are run by Corona Worldwide to counsel on adaptation to a new lifestyle and provide an opportunity to meet someone with current knowledge of their future country of residence. These courses are held at regular intervals, or on request, and cost £100 per person or £150 per couple. A telephone briefing costs £20.

Many women give up careers or interesting part-time jobs to accompany their husbands overseas, and in a number of places, there is no opportunity for them to get a job. Work permits can often be obtained in the teaching or medical professions but not always near to where the husband is posted. If your husband is with a big company, it might be worth asking them about jobs, or otherwise considering the possibilities of working on your own or doing voluntary work.

Careful planning and preparation for the use of leisure time (whether it is a result of having no outside employment or enjoying greater freedom from household duties thanks to servants) is essential to counteract boredom and initial loneliness. There are many hobbies and interests to be resurrected or embarked upon. Join groups with local knowledge e.g. archeological, historical, wildlife, photographic, amateur dramatics etc. Involvement in the local scene through clubs and organisations helps understanding and leads to more tolerant attitudes towards cultural differences. Learning the language or taking a correspondence course are just two possible alternatives for the wife determined to make the most of her stay in another country.

There may be a lack of facilities and the posting may entail putting up with a number of uncongenial conditions, but there are so many other rewards to compensate. Expatriates are on the whole friendlier and less inhibited than in their home environment. In hot climates, the sun and outdoor pursuits can often make people seem more attractive and relaxed. Social life is also important because with the exception of when in big cities, you will frequently have to entertain yourselves. This often provides scope for great ingenuity and many find latent and surprising talents hitherto undeveloped.

In what is often a male-orientated society, it is important for the wife to cultivate her own interests, making sure of an independent identity, rather than identifying too much with her husband's job and position. And with servants, there is more time to experiment, as she is no longer saddled with the day-to-day chores involved in running the house.

Servants

The availability of domestic help brings an easier lifestyle and is recommended for hot and humid climates where your energy will be easily sapped. Many people are diffident about employing servants and don't know how to cope with them. With an initial trial period and the advice of someone who speaks the language and has kept a servant for some time, it is possible for a good relationship to be formed. Settle for a few qualities or skills suitable for the family's needs and be tolerant about other shortcomings. Establish what is wanted and agree time off. A servant who is respected becomes part of the extended family.

Lifestyle

Wherever possible try to respect local customs and laws of behaviour and dress, and be prepared for what might appear odd or rude behaviour. Cultural differences can lead to all sorts of misunderstandings, so reserve judgement, take advice from happily established residents and concentrate first on personal relations. Forget efficiency and don't expect things to happen in a hurry. Polite conversation and courtesy are priorities – sincere interest, tolerance and a joke work wonders. Beware of criticising before you have attempted to understand a situation.

Security

Security can be a problem, but common sense measures, security guards and alarm systems are used in greater or lesser degree according to local hazards. Wilful violence is rare. It is possible for the expatriate to get caught up in political reprisals, but this is fortunately very rare indeed. It is wise to register with the Consular Section of your Embassy or High Commission so they know where to find you in cases of emergency – don't wait until trouble arises as communications can be difficult.

Summary

The expatriate can suffer considerable privation through lack of consumer goods and a low standard of living, or can be handsomely rewarded with higher standards of housing and a hectic social life as well as a worthwhile job. The challenge of helping a country to develop can be very stimulating and even addictive (whatever the conditions encountered) which is why so many expatriates return overseas again and again. Friendships made abroad are often more binding and congenial, through shared experiences, than those made at home, and valuable experience in a job often leads to promotion. The tolerance and understanding of other races and cultures learned through the expatriate experience of shorter or longer duration means that life will forever afterwards be enriched.

See p. 720 of the Directory for organisations offering assistance to expatriates

THE DIPLOMATIC TRAVELLER

by David Hannay

The diplomat travels not just because he enjoys travel, although it is as well that he should do so since he is fated to spend much of his professional life on the road, but because it is an essential part of his job. He travels to and from his posts abroad, he travels around the countries to which he is posted and, even when he is based in London, he tends to be caught up in the constant round of international meetings of which the web of modern diplomacy is composed. It all sounds pretty glamorous but, like so many other forms of modern business travel, it can easily become exceedingly humdrum if you let it. Similar airports, with similar flight delays, similar hotel rooms in impersonal international chains, and similar meeting rooms are not the stuff of which romantic travel experiences are made. The modern diplomat who wants to enjoy and benefit from his travel is going to have to work at it, not just sit back and have it ordered up by the travel section in the Foreign Office or his embassy.

Diplomatic travel begins with the journey to your posting, which can be extremely banal if you are heading for a western European capital or merely crossing the Atlantic, or potentially a bit more interesting if you are going further afield. Of course it will still be a far cry from the journey described so delightfully by Lady Macartney in *An English Lady in Chinese Turkestan* when she set off in the nineteenth century with her husband, the British Consul General in Kashgar: they travelled on the newly completed Russian railway system to Tashkent and then covered the final leg of their journey by riding hundreds of miles over the Pamirs to reach their destination.

One personal rule I did try to stick to was always initially to travel to your post over-land. This made for some very interesting experiences, particularly driving out to Tehran in 1960 – which involved some circuitous avoidance of East European Communist countries, then out of bounds to mere travellers – and through Eastern Turkey and Western Iran where a hard-top road was a rarity.

My system finally broke down after 25 years, when I was sent first to Washington and then New York, but I did manage a kind of revenge by returning on retirement from the latter via a long land journey through China and Central Asia. The object of going by land to your post is not mere whimsy, it is to try and arrive for the first time with some idea of what the country and its people look like and live like, and it is something you are unlikely to achieve on the road between the airport and the embassy.

Once you are in your posting, the opportunities for travel are greater, but again they need to be carefully planned. It is all too easy to get trapped into the bureaucratic grind of modern diplomacy – a far greater pitfall than the fabled cocktail party circuit, now largely a thing of the past – producing paper for the slave-drivers at home and missing the opportunities to get to know the complexities and attractions of the country you are in, not just its government. Once again it is a good deal less easy than it used to be to take off for a few weeks or even months into the wild blue yonder as Sir Fitzroy Maclean chronicled in *Eastern Approaches*, a record of his travels in the Soviet Union in the 1930s, or as Hugh Carless did when he accompanied Eric Newby on *A Short Walk in the Hindu Kush* in the 1950s. Nor are there many opportunities such as I had in Afghanistan between 1961 and 1963 when I was grandly titled the "Oriental Secretary" and managed to persuade my ambassador that I was more use to him on the road than in the office. It seems odd to think that we used to camp in the Panjshir Valley or catch trout at Bamyan in the shadow of the 160 foot high statues of Buddha, where now the various factions of Afghanistan's eternal civil war are slugging it out. It is almost equally odd to think that, as a Persian language student, I was encouraged, i.e. paid, to travel around southern Iran, on the condition that I went by public transport, which meant bus if I was lucky and the back of a lorry if I was not. It brings home the reality of the fact that war and instability are as often rapidly closing off places for the diplomat to travel to just as technological advances are opening them up. But political developments are not always obstacles, as is demonstrated by the scope now for travel in China where not so long ago it was hard to get permission to go outside Beijing.

It would be nice if the diplomat only had to plan his own travel but it is not so. One of his more demanding and thankless tasks is to act on occasion as a cross between a travel agent and a courier. A spell as a private secretary comes the way of many and that is when such qualities as improvisation and endurance are put to the test. It is not just a question of getting your boss to the right place at the right time, it is a matter of getting there in the right frame of mind, often a good deal less easy. I worked for four years for Christopher Soames when he was a European Commissioner, during which we travelled pretty widely. One of his main characteristics was not simply to insist on absolute punctuality, reasonable enough when catching aeroplanes or calling on Prime Ministers, but also to avoid ever arriving anywhere more than thirty seconds ahead of the appointed time. The second part of the equation caused his private secretaries a good deal of anxiety, particularly when travelling in Asia and Latin America, or trying to calculate in advance the density of traffic between the airport in, say, Paris or Rome and the Foreign ministry. His other principal characteristic as a traveller was to insist that, if he was to go sightseeing – and he was not averse to that – then there had to be a three-star restaurant handy in which to recuperate. Travel as a private secretary is not on the whole life-enhancing, though it can provide a good deal of amusement, particularly in retrospect.

The most daunting challenge for the diplomat as traveller is to make something of those one day stands which involve rushing from airport to meeting room, endless tours of the table, which have nothing to do with travel, and then a rush back to the airport – which is now the general form of modern diplomatic life. It is not easy to do. The frequency of airline flights makes it hard to convince one's employers that one simply had to travel the night before. The tendency of all international meetings to conform to a Parkinsonian law, which ensures that they last slightly longer than the time available for them to complete their work, is another complication. Nevertheless the really determined diplomatic traveller, whether his tastes be cultural, artistic or merely gastronomic, can usually manage to squeeze in the odd visit to a cathedral, an exhibition or a restaurant if he is sufficiently ruthless. Just occasionally the country caters for the travelling propensities of their guests by arranging the meetings in surroundings of beauty and interest; more often, unfortunately, they calculate that you will get more work out of people if you prevent their surroundings from being too attractive. Certainly, of the many meetings of the European Council I attended while I was dealing with the European Union, a great deal more fell into the latter rather than the former category. It took a hardy spirit, when Mrs Thatcher was leading the British delegation, to slip away, say, to that fascinating modern museum in Stuttgart.

But of course the diplomatic traveller is not limited to professional travel, important a part of his life though that may be. If he is really bitten by the bug and if he can persuade his long-suffering family to share his passion, a lifetime of diplomacy provides some ideal jumping-off points for wider travel. Brussels may not be exciting in itself but it is a remarkably good base from which to travel the European continent. New York is quite exciting for a traveller but so is the possibility of using it as a base for visiting the furthest corners of Latin America. There are few better ways to spend a tedious afternoon in one of those subterranean meeting rooms at the United Nations than in planning how to get from Machu Picchu across Lake Titicaca to Bolivia (the answer: take the train from Cuzco to the lake and hydrofoil across it).

So do 35 years or so of diplomacy dull the taste for travel? In my own case apparently not. The list of places still to be visited and *vaut le detour* in M. Michelin's inimitable phrase, seems if anything to grow longer. A willingness to rough it has certainly diminished, but so, fortunately, has the need to do so. The real challenge is to resist successfully what one could call the homogenisation of travel, the tendency to sell travel as Macdonalds sell hamburgers. The diplomatic travellers should be in the vanguard of consumer resistance to any such tendency.

THE WORKING TRAVELLER

by Susan Griffith

Camels, trains and sailing boats have their peculiar advantages as means of travelling to the far corners of the globe. But there may be times when you will decide to stop for a rest, or choose to absorb the atmosphere in one setting. Working is one way of getting inside a foreign culture, though the kind of job you find will determine the stratum of society which you will experience. The traveller who spends a few weeks picking olives for a Cretan farmer will get a very different insight from the traveller who looks after the children of a wealthy Athenian businessman. Yet both will have the chance to participate temporarily in the life of a culture rather than merely to observe.

Financial considerations are usually the traveller's immediate impetus to look for work. To postpone having to cash the last travellers' cheque, many begin to look around for ways of prolonging their trip. They may find paid work (though few of the jobs which travellers undertake will make them rich) or they may decide to volunteer their labour in exchange for a bed and food – by planting trees on a Lesotho work camp or digging for Biblical remains in Israel.

While the sole ambition of some is to extend their travels, others go abroad specifically in search of highly-paid jobs. This is easier for people with acknowledged qualifications such as nurses and agronomists, divers and pipe–fitters who often do find better-paid opportunities abroad than they would at home. A few might even have their future career prospects in view when they go abroad to teach English as a foreign language or drive a combine harvester. But the majority are trying to put off or escape from career decisions.

Even the unskilled can find jobs which pay high wages. The high minimum wage in Denmark, for example, means that a chambermaid or a strawberry picker can earn enough in a short time to fund long periods of travel. In Japan, the demand for university graduates (of any subject) willing to give English lessons is so great that many foreigners earn an average of US$30 an hour and work as many hours as their stamina will allow. Some Japanese language schools even pay the airfares of teachers whom they recruit abroad. Similarly American organisations pay the airfares of thousands of young people who go to the US each summer to instruct and care for children staying on summer camps (although in this case the advanced airfare is subtracted from the counsellor's total wage which is modest even at the outset). Paid fares are a rarity no matter what job you find. One very helpful organisation is **Vacation Work** (9 Park End Street, Oxford OX1 1HJ, Tel: 01865 241978) who have a huge amount of experience and information.

Seasonal Work

Jobs which are seasonal in nature are those which travellers are most likely to find. Unemployment statistics barely concern themselves with this large and important sector of the economy. In times of recession the number of temporary jobs available may even increase since employers are less eager to expand their regular staff but will need extra help at busy times.

The two categories of employment which appeal most to travellers (and least to a stable working population) are agriculture and tourism. Many farmers from the south of France to the north of Tasmania (with the notable exception of the developing world) cannot bring in their harvests without assistance from outside their vicinity. Similarly, the tourist trade in many areas could not survive without a short term injection of seasonal labour.

These economic facts may provide little consolation to the hopeful job-seeker who finds that all the hotels in town are already staffed by local students or that all the fruit is traditionally picked by itinerant Mexicans or Moroccans. Nevertheless, farmers and hotel/restaurant managers remain the best potential sources of employment. It should be noted that work in rural areas normally permits more genuine contact with natives of the country than jobs in tourist resorts where you could find yourself dealing mainly with your fellow countrymen.

It is not easy to look up "domestic", "au pair" or "live-in" positions in the Yellow Pages. But young women (mainly, but not only, women) who desire the security of a family placement and who may also wish to learn a European language, often choose to work with children for little money. Such positions can be found on the spot or in advance through a relevant agency, notice board or by means of an advertisement.

Volunteering

It would be wrong, of course, to assume that the love (or shortage) of money is at the root of all decisions to work abroad. Paid work in developing nations is available only exceptionally, and yet many arrange to live for next to nothing by doing something positive. For example, enterprising travellers visiting everywhere from Poland to Thailand have been welcomed into the homes of locals who are eager to share long-term hospitality in exchange for informal lessons in English. More structured voluntary opportunities exist worldwide and there are many charities and organisations which can introduce you to interesting projects such as helping a local Indian settlement to build a community centre in Northern Canada, establishing an organic farm near a tribal longhouse in Sarawak or helping in Mother Theresa's Home for Dying Destitutes in Calcutta. There is also the possibility of aid work. With the world continuing to be an unstable place, many war zones or natural disasters areas need aid workers. It is worth contacting the personnel department at the **British Red Cross** tel: 0171-235 5454, or other charities such as **Oxfam** tel: 01865-311311, **Voluntary Services Overseas** tel: 0181-780 2266, and **Save the Children,** (two years overseas experience in a developing country is required) tel: 0171-

703 5400. Be warned, this kind of work can be very emotionally challenging, do not undertake it lightly.

Many such organisations require more than a traveller's curiosity about a country; they require a strong wish to become involved in a specific project and, in many cases, an ideological commitment. The fact that few of them can offer any travel or even living expenses deters the uncommitted.

Planning in Advance

Some travellers are fortunate enough to fix up a job in advance. This means that they can be reasonably assured of an immediate income once they have arrived. The traveller who sets off without a pre-arranged job has less security, and should take sufficient reserves in case his or her job search fails. In the course of my research, I have met many examples of the fearless traveller who is prepared to arrive in Marseilles, Mexico City or even New York with a few dollars and no guaranteed job prospects. They have remained confident that it will be possible to work their way out of their penury. In most cases they have done just that, though not without experiencing a few moments of panic and desperation. It goes without saying that this situation is best avoided, for it may result in your being forced to take an undesirable job with exploitative conditions, or to go into debt to the folks back home.

There are many organisations, both public and private, charitable and commercial, student and general, which can offer advice and practical assistance to those who wish to fix up a job before leaving home (see p.721 in Section 3 of the Directory for a starting point). Some accept a tiny handful of individuals who satisfy stringent requirements; others such as the organisations which recruit voluntary staff for scientific expeditions, accept anyone who is willing to pay the required fee. School and university careers counsellors are often a good source of information, as are newspaper advertisements and the specialist literature.

The work schemes and official exchanges which do exist require a large measure of advance planning. It is not unusual for an application deadline to be six to nine months before the starting date of the scheme.

Red Tape

One of the possible advantages of fixing up a job well in advance is that you then have a chance of obtaining the appropriate work permit. Almost every country of the world has legislation to prohibit foreigners from taking jobs from nationals (although citizens of EC countries can work freely throughout the post-1992 Community). Furthermore, few countries – apart from the newly-welcoming Eastern European countries – will process visas unless applications are lodged outside the country. For example, teachers of EFL (English as a Foreign Language) can usually sort out their visas or at least set the wheels in motion before arrival in Korea, Turkey, Indonesia, Morocco or wherever. This is one area of employment in which governments are relatively generous since locals are not being deprived of jobs.

The support of an employer is virtually always a pre-requisite for conducting a job hunt at a distance. Assuming you are not eligible for one of the special holiday job visas (available in Australia, the US, Canada, Norway, Finland, etc.), the ideal arrangement may be to travel to your chosen destination on a tourist visa, persuade an employer to hire you and then leave the country to apply for a work permit. This method has the significant advantage of making it possible for employers to interview you and for you to see the potential work situation at first hand before committing yourself.

Yet it has to be admitted that temporary jobs like cherry-picking and hamburger-making will never qualify you for a work permit. This problem bedevils working travellers and inevitably weakens their position if things go wrong. Sometimes the only recourse which travellers have if they find themselves being exploited is to leave and look for something more congenial. 'Easy come easy go' becomes the motto of many travellers who pick up casual work along their route.

Improving your Chances

A number of specific steps will improve your chances either of being accepted on an organised work scheme or of convincing an employer in person of your superiority to the competition. For example, before leaving home you might take a short course in teaching English as a foreign language, cooking, word processing or sailing – all skills which are marketable around the world. If you are very serious, you might learn (or improve) a foreign language or you might simply undertake to get fit.

Contacts, however remote, can be valuable allies. Everyone has ways of developing links with people abroad, even if he or she is not lucky enough to have friends and family scattered around the world. Pen friends, fellow members of travel clubs and foreign students or visitors met in your home town might be able to help you find your feet in a foreign country. Try and publicise your plans as widely as possible since the more people there are aware of your willingness to work, the better the chance of a lead. Once you actually embark, you will be grateful for any extra preparation you have made.

Even if you set off without an address book full of contacts, it is not difficult to meet people along the way. Your fellow travellers are undoubtedly the best source of information on job prospects. Youth hostels can be a gold mine for the job seeker; there may even be jobs advertised on the notice board. Any local you meet is a potential source of help, whether a driver who gives you a lift while hitchhiking or members of a local club which interests you, such as cycling or jazz. The expatriate community might also be willing to help, and can be met in certain bars, at the English-speaking church, at the Embassy library, etc.

Of course, not all jobs are found by word-of-mouth or through contacts. Local English language newspapers like the *Anglo-Portugese News* or the *Bangkok Post* may carry job advertisements appropriate to your situation, or may be a good publication for placing an advert. The most effective method is to walk in and ask. You may have to exaggerate the amount of experience you have had and to display a little more bravado than comes naturally to you.

Persistence, optimism and resilience are essential for such a venture, since on occasion it may be necessary to pester 40 restaurant managers before one will offer you a job as dishwasher, or to visit the offices of an employment agency on many consecutive days before your eagerness will be rewarded. With such determination, it is indeed possible to work your way around the world.

For organisations for the working traveller see p.721 of the Directory

TEACHING ENGLISH ABROAD

by Sarah Thorowgood

There is no doubt about it, teaching English is one of the easiest ways of prolonging your travels once you have run out of cash. You may be confined to one area for longer than you anticipated and you may have to suffer the indignity of singing along to *If You're Happy and You Know it, Clap Your Hands* with a classroom full of bemused Nepalese teenagers, but you can earn enough money to live on, and increasingly, given the demand for English teachers, save as well.

Life in the Global Village has produced an almost an unlimited demand for English teachers the world over. It seems, also, that there is no limit to the demand for TEFL* qualifications amongst a whole new generation of school and university leavers wishing to spend some time abroad soaking up different cultures before getting a 'real' life and job.

What a happy marriage this would appear to be, not least for the TEFL institutes. Many, but fortunately not all, English language institutes worldwide insist that their teachers are holders of a TEFL certificate of some kind and teaching English abroad is very much the domain of the TEFL graduate these days. There is no shortage of schools in which to gain this hallowed qualification (see Section 12 of the Directory at the back of this book) but it will set you back anything from £200–£1500. All is not quite as rosy as it was a few years ago, however. These days, even TEFL holders are having a job finding work in Europe because the competition is so massive.

The greatest demand for English teachers is in old Eastern-Bloc countries, Poland and Romania especially and in south-east Asia in places where the ability to speak English is the key to an effective tourist industry and business, such as Thailand, Nepal, South Korea, Vietnam and Taiwan. Other countries, like Japan, have a big demand for English teachers too, mainly in schools. Those who join the JET scheme become employees of the Japanese government and can earn as much as £21,000 a year with 15-20 days holiday and a return air ticket. Taiwan and South Korea are fast catching up with Japan as the hot-spots for English teachers because demand still seems to be out-weighing the supply and the pay is on a level with Japan.

Finding a Job

There are two different approaches to this. Many people feel much happier sorting something out before they go away. Others are quite prepared to just wander off in to the blue and see what happens when they get to where they want to be. Both methods have their pitfalls and advantages.

---

* *See end of the article for further explanation of TEFL-type courses.*

In arranging a job in advance, you are at a disadvantage because it is so much harder to put your personality over, and so inevitably, you will find that there are more rejections than acceptances sitting on your doormat every morning. Also, if you do get offered a job, you will not have the opportunity to check out your working conditions until you have reached your destination. This can be one of the most dispiriting experiences for the English teacher abroad. However, if you do prefer this approach then it may be useful to get in touch with a new organisation called English Contacts Abroad (PO Box 126, Oxford, OX2 6UB). This provides a network of contacts for English language teachers but they do charge a £48 administration fee. Susan Griffith's mine of information *Teaching English Abroad* (Vacation Work) is also an invaluable source. Other than contacting language institutes in the country you wish to visit on a speculative basis, you might try the Education section of *The Guardian* on Tuesdays and the *Times Educational Supplement* on Fridays. There are also a number of agencies that you can sign up with, so look in the *Yellow Pages* and also Section 12 of the directory. It is also, of course, possible to find work teaching for voluntary organisations, so look under *Voluntary* in Section 3 of the Directory or at your library.

For those who want to job hunt on the spot, the key word is appearance. This is arguably much more important than qualifications, but even kitted out in your Gucci suit you should be ready to tramp round for days on end suffering rejections. It goes without saying that any qualifications you do have should be highlighted and exaggerated to maximum effect. The appearance of your CV is just as important as your own. A useful first port of call should be the British Council if you are in a capital city. They will be able to provide you with a list of language schools and may have more up-to-date information about job vacancies. Failing that, *Yellow Pages* will come in handy. Make sure you know the words for "English Language Institute" in whatever language necessary. It will almost certainly take some time to get work, and this is one of the main disadvantages of on-the-hoof job hunting; you will need to have sufficient funds as well as optimism to keep you going until something eventually does turn up.

There are, however, ways in which you can minimise the pain of rejection. Timing is crucial and the best time to start looking is at the beginning of the academic year in September. This is the main recruiting time for most language schools, and the time when a lot of potential English students start to think about getting round to putting their noses to the grind-stone. Needless to say, the summer months are just about the worst time to look for work.

Where to look is also an important factor. Major cities are probably a good bet to start off with but might not necessarily be the best places to find work. Tourist areas may well have a large supply of aspiring English speakers, so be prepared to be flexible as to your location or do your research well before you leave. It is also worth noting that you might have more luck approaching businesses and business schools rather than language schools, although most of them do recruit teachers through agencies and schools.

The life of the private English tutor can be exceedingly cushy, as Christopher Isherwood so enchantingly relates in *Goodbye to Berlin*, but it entails working up a large and loyal clientele and this you can only do over a long period of time. Start by posting adverts on college and university notice boards or chatting up people in university bars – as with any form of self-employment, success in this freelance field is dependent upon boundless energy, flexibility and initiative as well as a nice Gucci suit!

The Beginner's Guide to TEFL

There are two certificate courses offered in the UK, the Cambridge/RSA (CELTA) and the Trinity College, London (TESOL). Below is a brief explanation of the numerous acromyms used:

TEFL= Teaching English as a Foreign Languge (used where English will be needed for business or tourism, but where English has no official status.)

TESL= Teaching English as a Second Language (used mainly in multi-cultural societies such as USA or UK where immigrants need to speak the language on a daily basis.)

TESOL= Teaching English to Speakers of Other Languages (covers both of above and also used in a more official capacity by the Trinity College Course.)

TEFLA= Teaching English as a Foreign Language to Adults

CELTA= Certificate in English Language Teaching to Adults Covers TEFL and TESL and used in official capacity by the Cambridge RSA course.

Further Reading: *Teaching English Abroad: Talk Your Way Around the World* **by Susan Griffith (Vacation Work Publications)**
Teach Abroad **(Central Bureau, British Council)**
How to Become a Teacher of English as a Foreign Language **(leaflet produced by the British Council)**
See p.889 of the Directory for more useful contacts, TEFL centres, agencies and further reading.

THE BUSINESS TRAVELLER

by David Churchill and Sarah Thorowgood

The post-recession executive is a very different traveller from the free-spending international jetsetter of the late 1980s. The Gulf War and bitter recession has produced a marked shift in both corporate and individual attitude towards travelling on business. Gone are the hedonistic days when business travellers would only fly in business or first class, stay in five-star luxury hotels (and probably in a suite as well) and treat their charge card as a golden key to having a good time at somebody else's expense.

Tight budgets during the recession meant that travelling on business increasingly had to be justified; no longer a perk, it is seen as a crucial part of the marketing mix to win and keep new business. Those travellers who were given the go-ahead to travel during lean times also had to get used to flying at the back of the 'plane and staying in hotels that had fewer stars than they were used to.

Even though the economic position has eased, companies are still keeping a tight rein on travel costs. According to American Express, which regularly monitors corporate spending on business travel, the total spent in 1996 by US companies on business travel and related expenses reached a record high of $156 billion, up from $150 billion in the previous year. While this is the highest figure recorded by Amex, in real terms corporate expenditure in this area is still only at the level of the mid-1980s. According to the same survey, by far the highest priority in travel management is cost containment, with 90 per cent of US multi-nationals having a formal, written travel policy and 78 per cent of companies nationwide requiring employees to take the lowest available airfare.

Significantly, the responsibility for managing business travel within companies has shifted from *ad hoc* arrangements, usually involving secretaries or as a part-time job for the personnel manager, to the responsibility of travel managers who are increasingly used to making hard-headed buying decisions and under ever greater pressure from their superiors to cut travel budgets. This can make it even more difficult for the individual executive, who has to actually travel to do business on the company's behalf, to arrive in good enough shape to perform at his or her best.

Not surprisingly, suppliers of business travel – notably the airlines, hotels and car rental companies and the business travel agents who manage the travel – are all seeking to woo the business traveller as never before. The frequent flyer scheme pioneered by US airlines and now a feature of virtually all international carriers have, for example, been emulated by the leading international hotel chains which now offer similar programmes for frequent guests. American Express has entered the fray as well with its Membership Miles scheme, giving both airline and hotel points according to how much its charge card is used.

But some of these schemes to woo the business traveller have more than a hint of desperation about them and may, in fact, have overlooked the fact that the psychological profile of the frequent business traveller in the mid 1980s has changed.

For many executives, the joy of travelling at someone else's expense is beginning to pall as a result of the increased amount of time spent travelling by executives – 27 per cent of total employees now as opposed to 21 per cent in 1994. What business travellers worry about most when away from their offices is their lack of control: within their organisation their status is fixed and taken for granted; away from their office, they feel threatened by a lack of recognition and their inability to shape and control events.

These travellers, therefore, are less concerned with the in-flight pampering that features so heavily in airline advertising and are more interested in getting to their destinations on time. This is particularly important on shorter European flights, where even a slight delay can mean missed appointments. Surveys of executive travellers show that the airline schedule and punctuality record are among the most important factors when choosing an airline, not the quality of catering or calibre of airlines business lounges.

Yet it is simply because the airlines have so little effective control over departure and arrival times, due to such vagaries as the weather and intransigence of some air traffic controllers, that they spend millions on such 'gimmicks' as, for example, British Airways's new arrivals lounge at Heathrow's Terminal Four, which provides showers and changing rooms for some arriving business class passengers. As worthwhile as it may be to freshen up on arrival, most business passengers would prefer to be guaranteed of their arrival time instead.

The psychological change in post-recession business travellers, moreover, extends to a reluctance to be away from home and family. An Official Airlines Guide survey of nearly 1,000 frequent flyers found that two-thirds gave as their motivation for travel not their work or careers but helping to provide a better life for their families left behind. "Although travelling on long trips, often with extensive itineraries, their hearts remain at home," the survey suggested.

Hyatt Hotels, in a survey of over 300 regular European business travellers, also found that many preferred to spend more time in their hotel rooms when abroad. The highest accolade they could give a hotel was that it "felt just like home". When asked what extra feature they would like to see in hotel rooms of the future, the top answer was a microwave oven: one participant said that his ideal, even in a hotel while on business would be "to cook beans on toast in my room and be zonked out in front of the television."

It is hardly surprising, therefore, that one of the fastest-growing areas of the hotel business across Europe – it is already big business in the US – are apartment hotels which provide limited catering facilities and more space than average. In 1994, London saw the opening of what was claimed to be the first purpose-built apartment hotel in the capital aimed at business travellers: the Orion City apartment hotel, close to the Barbican. Each of the 129 studios and apartments has a kitchenette and there are laundry and business facilities within the hotel building. French hotel group Orion already has similar apartment hotels in Paris and Brussels and plans to open new ones in several other European cities, including Lisbon, Prague, Barcelona and Berlin.

Getting a better deal from business travel, therefore, is increasingly the name of the game. So what should the savvy business traveller look out for?

Most attention is now being focused on how to achieve a seamless, efficient service at lowest cost. One sound approach is to make use of a specialist business travel agency, such as the majors (Amex, Thomas Cook, Carlson Wagonlit and Hogg Robinson) or one of the many independent agencies which concentrate on business travel. Most are members of the Guild of Business Travel Agents (tel: 0171-222 2744) and have access to consolidated air fares and special deals on hotels and car rental.

An alternative for individual business travellers is the WEXAS Gold Card membership which provides a range of special services and other benefits for the business traveller who does not have – or want to use – a travel agency.

In theory a specialist business travel agency should always be able to get you the best deal but, in practice, poorly informed staff and mistakes with ticketing and bookings do occur. Two pieces of advice: if you find a good travel agent (preferably an individual within an agency) then stick with them; and remember that the best travel agent is likely to be yourself. While an agent may be able to obtain a corporate hotel rate for you and your company, you may be able to negotiate a better deal directly with a hotel. Depending on the season and availability, a hotel may quote you a better rate than they will offer all year round as a corporate rate.

A good travel agent should also be able to help you with add-on benefits, such as higher grade room or suite and a free breakfast with newspaper. Most hotels are seeking to woo business travellers onto the higher-priced concierge, or club, floors which usually offer complimentary drinks and snacks, are often open all day, and sometimes provide business services. It may be worth paying extra for a room on a club floor if such benefits are important to you.

But no matter how efficient the travel agent, the biggest hassle for business travellers undoubtedly comes on ground at the airport. An increasing number of airlines (but not British Airways) offer their business and first class passengers a limousine transfer included in the price of their ticket.

For those taking their car to the airport, there are a number of valet parking services available – at a price, unfortunately – but convenient for the last-minute traveller in a rush. Some airlines also allow telephone check-in on the way to the airport, but usually only if there is no hand luggage. BA, for example, has introduced such a service for Concorde passengers and those using its domestic shuttles.

Another tip for Gatwick-bound travellers to avoid check-in queues at the airport is to use the check-in facility at Victoria Station for those using the train. If arriving at Heathrow by Underground with just hand luggage, there is a special check-in desk at Terminal Four as soon as you come off the escalator.

The most useful development at both Gatwick and Heathrow has been the Fast-Track system, whereby business class passengers are processed through customs and security via a special channel and thus avoid the queues laden with leisure travellers. The Fast-Track system also provides for speedier access to currency booths and duty free and steps are being taken to extend it to other areas of the airport, including car parking.

Technological advances in ticketing and checking-in will also smooth the way of the business traveller at the airport. Although electronic ticketing has been around for a while in the US, in Europe it is just starting to realise its potential. For business travellers with hand luggage only, checking-in with certain airlines, such as British Airways, Lufthansa and EasyJet, can, we are assured, take as little time as it takes to withdraw money from a cash-point machine.

Heathrow business travellers have also been able to benefit from the fierce competition between major airlines, which has seen them develop increasingly opulent lounges. These range from Virgin Atlantic's 'Clubhouse', complete with miniature train that delivers drinks in the bar, to BA's hotel-style lounges on three floors. Both United and American Airlines have also opened new lounges at the airport.

Increasingly, it is on the ground that most efforts are being made to improve service for the business traveller, although the service and comfort in-flight is also continually being upgraded. The key development in long-haul has been the steady erosion of first class cabins, replaced by bigger seats and an improved service in business class. Airlines such as Continental, Air Canada and Northwest have abandoned their first class cabins and price structure, but retained almost equivalent-sized seats for an upgraded business class. This follows the pattern established by Richard Branson's Virgin Atlantic airline, which first introduced the concept of first-class style seats and service at regular business class prices.

Another significant in-flight development has been the introduction of personal video screens which enable a greater range and choice of programming. In addition, most airlines are experimenting with on-board telephone and fax facilities, although these are still some way from being routinely offered on all flights.

For many regular travellers, however, the most important development in recent years has been the growth of frequent flyer schemes. These originated in the US but have now spread to European airlines. The evidence is mixed about how important these are in the choice of airline and fewer than a third of allocated mileage points are actually taken up. Increasingly, there is concern that such schemes only give a benefit to the individual traveller and not to his or her company, even though it is the company that pays for the flight. While the tax authorities in Britain have so far decided to stay out of the issue of whether frequent flyer programmes are a taxable benefit, the European Commission is looking at the whole subject and may decide to introduce a European-wide ban on them.

Whether or not such schemes are a passing fad – or finally prove too expensive for the airlines to operate – there seems little doubt that the executive traveller will continue to be wooed for his or, increasingly her, business. But, according to surveys of regular travellers, it is a pity that they do not really enjoy the experience as much as they might – business travel, by its very nature, is different from other types of travel in that the traveller is travelling to make money rather than for pleasure.

For business travel agents see p.722 of the Directory

THE LUXURY TRAVELLER

by Caroline Brandenburger

The notion of luxury has become one of abused and relative value in recent years (*luxury* loo paper, *luxury* shortbread) but there still remain a few absolutes – many of them to be found in the area of travel. You may choose to travel luxuriously simply because you enjoy luxury or because you feel the rigours of the backpacking trip are beyond you. Sometimes you may combine the two – there is nothing more wonderful than to sink gratefully into the arms of comfort when life has been rather spartan.

Cruising

Cruising can be an exceptionally luxurious way to travel. **The Cruise Advisory Service** (35 Blue Boar Row, Salisbury, Wiltshire SP1 1DA, tel: 01722-335505) is an organisation without affiliation to any shipping companies and can provide you with unbiased advice. The advisory service will supply you with a general information pack and, based on its own independent surveys, will give ratings out of ten for the services of different cruise lines (cabin comfort, food etc). Once you have decided what you want, they will also handle your booking.

One unfailingly popular liner is, of course, the QE2 which journeys regularly from Southampton to New York, as well as following a number of other world-wide routings. Although one of the world's largest passenger ships, the QE2 provides one crew member for every two passengers. The crew will endeavour (within reason!) to satisfy your every whim, whether it be breakfast in bed or a private cocktail party in your stateroom. Facilities range from a designer label-strewn shopping mall to a theatre, four swimming pools, a health club, seven bars and two dance halls.

Nonetheless, the Cruise Advisory Service only rates the QE2 as a Four Star liner (the top rating is Five Star de Luxe). Few companies still provide unadulterated Five Star luxury, but the last surviving cruise companies which do include the Royal Viking Line, Cunard (Sea Goddess 1 and 2), the Seabourn Line, Crystal Cruises and the new Silversea Cruises. Ships like these carry far fewer passengers, and tend to rely on what is now considered old–fashioned attention to detail and service – as well as sumptuously comfortable suites in place of cabins.

Seriously luxurious liners will boast an endless variety of entertainments (multi-gyms, beauty salons, casinos, formal dinners) to keep passengers happy. With Seabourn you can find yourself dining at the Captain's table or al fresco on deck, you can pump iron in the fitness centre or languish in your suite watching videos. Renaissance promises you expert lectures on the local cultures you'll encounter when you put into shore, and after lolling in the ship's library you can luxuriate in the jacuzzi.

Preparations for a Royal Viking cruise may include a shopping spree at Harvey Nichols whose Complimentary Personal Shopping Service offers discounts to Royal Viking passengers cruising for longer than a set period. On board, you'll find herbal massages, tennis and clay-pigeon shooting.

Rail

Whether our impression of luxury train travel has been formed by Agatha Christie's Murder on the Orient Express, or Queen Victoria's blue, velvet-lined personal carriage (now in the London Transport Museum) the reality we generally find is far removed. However, there are a few (and, surprisingly, increasing) opportunities to experience something rather more sumptuous than the Intercity 125 and Traveller's Fare.

A journey on the Venice Simplon **Orient Express** is one way to indulge yourself. The service was discontinued at the end of the 1970s but when two of the carriages came up for sale at Sotheby's in Monte Carlo, they were bought by James Sherwood, President of Sea Containers. He then tracked down more of the carriages, in various states of disrepair and decay, and had them lavishly restored. The wooden panelled interiors and elaborate marquetry now set the scene for the journey from London to Venice (with the option for side trips on the local railway service to cities such as Innsbruck and Cologne). En route you are waited on by gloved attendants, quaff champagne, consume exquisite multiple course meals, and sleep in plush, exquisitely comfortable cabins. If you are feeling slightly less flush, take a day trip! These run to a variety of destinations, ranging from Leeds Castle in Kent, to Bath, Bristol, Chatsworth and Canterbury.

If you are travelling between Cape Town and Pretoria (or vice-versa), as a luxury junkie you can do little better than to ride the **Blue Train**. Cited by experts as the very last of the authentic great trains (it is still part of the national rail system, rather than owned by a private company) it runs for 1600km, during May, June and July only. You travel in a train that is carpeted, air conditioned and boasting well-appointed suites and couchettes, and you will eat splendidly in a dining car which looks out onto the intensely dramatic terrain that characterises the journey There is also the possibility of a "steam safari" with **Rovos Rail**, which runs a luxury train through 1000km of the Eastern Transvaal, including a night in a private game reserve. Meanwhile in Zimbabwe, there is the **Zambezi Special**, which runs from Bulawayo to Victoria Falls, through wildlife areas and great forests.

The **Indian-Pacific** travels the huge distance of 4348 km between Sydney and Perth, via Adelaide, and bridges the two oceans of its name. Passing through varied sections of Australian scenery – mountains, wheat fields and rocky plains – you will sip Australian wine in the lounge car to the accompaniment of live music.

"The Palace on Wheels", as the **Rajasthan Express** has been called, is a collection of carriages dating from 1898 to 1937, built to the luxurious specifications of Rajasthan's maharajahs. The train is pulled alternately by diesel engine and steam and begins in Delhi for a seven-day tour of the princely region of Rajasthan. You travel in the regal splendour of velvet-upholstered compartments appointed with brass fittings and eat a choice of Indian or European cuisine while being kept cool under the dining car's numerous spinning fans. Cox and Kings Ltd operate trips which include a stay in Delhi.

In 1992 the Venice Simplon Orient Express extended its network further East with the launch of the **Eastern & Oriental Express**. Travelling from Singapore to Bangkok, the 1243-mile journey takes 42 hours. The carriages, originally built for the New Zealand train, Silver Fern, are decorated with traditional wood carvings, silks and batiks. While local musicians play in the dining cars, fortune tellers predict your future and hostesses, who later act as guides, explain the cultural traditions of the region.

Air Travel

If time is a factor in your travel plans but you still want to travel with the maximum comfort, you have two options. If you're going to New York, you can travel by **Concorde**. (Anywhere else in the world, pick a good airline and travel business class or first if your budget will stretch that far.) Concorde is not only swift (you arrive five minutes after you leave!) and cuts down the jet lag, but has other advantages too. With its plush grey interior, iced bottles of Mumm champagne and gentleman's club ambience, you can strike deals with captains of industry (Lord Weidenfeld, the publisher, says seven minutes of 'meaningful conversation' on Concorde always does the trick) and star spot at the same time.

As to the best airlines, opinions vary. Different companies attract fans for different reasons. If you are travelling first class, Air France and Cathay Pacific score on the gastronomic front, while Lufthansa's efficiency is superlative and British Airways' attentiveness refreshing. However, Philippine Airways have rather trounced the competition in one respect by introducing full-length beds in their first class cabins – this really does soften the blow of long-haul trips.

Hotels

The Oriental in Bangkok is probably one of the world's best known luxury hotels. Certainly the grandest in Bangkok, it overlooks the Chao Phyra River and is a combination of old colonial and plush new marbled extensions. The Oriental has traditionally been a stopping place for royalty, politicians, artists, and numerous writers ranging from Joseph Conrad to Noel Coward and Graham Greene. The hotel's 394 exotically-appointed rooms, decorated with bowls of fresh orchids, are served by over 1000 members of staff.

Venice's **Cipriani** is utterly redolent of luxury. Those who have seen *Death in Venice* will remember the hero's arrival at the Cipriani by launch, and this is exactly how guests still arrive today. Apart from its extraordinary three-acre site on the Giudecca Island, beautiful gardens and the only swimming pool and tennis court in central Venice, the Cipriani is remarkable for the elegance of its rooms, Venetian glass chandeliers and Empire sofas. At the same time, you can gorge yourself on exquisite pasta and luscious cakes which are made every day by a busy teams of chefs.

The Four Seasons in Hamburg is unusual for having remained a private hotel, and is without doubt the best hotel in Germany. Renowned for its genuine, country–house ambience, it boasts luxuriant wooden panelling, tapestries and excellent antiques offset against impeccable service.

The **Oberoi** in New Delhi is the city's most modern hotel. With its polished, granite lobby, lush gardens and rooms decorated in subtle, eye-soothing colours, you can eat the best French food as well as indigenous cuisine.

London's newest, most lavish hotel is **The Lanesborough** at Hyde Park Corner. With more silk swags per square inch than one might think possible, it is utterly sumptuous and larger-than-life. Hard to believe it used to be St.George's Hospital: the budget per room for the interior decor was rumoured to be £2 million.

Villas

Luxury villas can be very pleasantly self-indulgent places to stay. Whether in Greece, Portugal or the Caribbean, they can provide you with not only excellent accommodation, but also staff to cook and clean for you, private swimming pools, and the use of a jeep and power boat. **Bears House** in Barbados, for example, comes with a butler, cook, laundress, maid and gardener, four bedrooms with bathrooms en suite, and a huge private pool. Two excellent companies who can help you to find sumptuous villas to stay in are **CV Travel** (43 Cadogan St., London, SW3 2PR, tel: 0171-581 0851) and **Magic of Italy** (227 Shepherd's Bush Road, London, W6 7AS, tel: 0171-533 8888). If you really want to spend time luxuriously and also in seclusion, then an island may be the answer. Mauritius, the Caribbean and the Seychelles all have islands for hire. **Abercrombie & Kent** (tel: 0171-730 9600) can organise this ultimate archipelagic experience for you.

Safaris

The very best safaris are generally to be found in East Africa – Kenya and Tanzania. While other countries, such as Zimbabwe and Botswana, offer luxury safaris, they tend to mean staying in lodges rather than tents. **Safari Consultants** (Orchard House, Upper Road, Little Conard, Sudbury, Suffolk, CO10 0NZ, tel: 01787-228494) are able to organise a tailor-made safari to suit your inclinations and requirements. Luxury in the context of a safari, say Safari Consultants, is a maximum of four people per vehicle, large, walk-in tents with proper beds, wash basins, en suite toilets and hot showers, and about fourteen staff (excluding guides) to care for eight guests (providing constant iced drinks and three or four-course meals). In other words, every moment that is not spent observing the wildlife is as pampered as they can possibly make it!

For luxury travel agents see p.722 of the Directory

THE GOURMET TRAVELLER

by Paul Wade

As a child I was lucky. My family roamed Europe during the holidays, spending time in what were then exotic spots: Dubrovnik in former Yugoslavia, Rapallo in Italy and Salzburg in Austria. My memories are of scorched, rocky shores, pavement cafés, hulking castles and ... food. Post-war Britain was still strictly a "meat and two veg" country, with powdered eggs and stock cubes in every pantry. Like a jangling alarm clock, the Mediterranean flavours of fresh tomatoes and giant water melons woke up my taste buds. Slurping spaghetti splashed with purple squid sauce and munching a properly prepared Schnitzel ensured they would never go back to sleep.

Ever since this awakening food has been an integral part of any trip, whether for a day out in the nearby English countryside or for weeks to the distant pueblos of Mexico. With my wife, who shares the same enthusiasm, I pore over guide books searching for the elusive tip that might send us to a restaurant where we can eat what the locals regard as traditional dishes. Our aim is to add taste and smell to the other three senses that are more acute when on holiday.

Guided Tours

Sadly, most guide books concentrate on museums and mosques, shopping and beaches, with food little more than an after-thought. How often is the list of "best places to eat" merely a roll call of the poshest French restaurants in town – whether you are in Chicago or the Caribbean, Munich or Manchester. These are lists for business executives, keen to impress clients with the size of their tips and their knowledge of over-priced wines. But how can you say you understand

Catalonia if you have not attended a *cocotada* in Valls, an onion barbecue, washed down with the local black wine? How can you boast that you "know" the USA if you have not put on a bib and tucked into a lobster in Maine or made a pilgrimage to the birthplace of the hamburger or the pizza?

By eating what we rate as the best rice in the world (in Iran), the best grass-fed beef (in Argentina), the most delicious oysters (straight from the squeaky-clean waters off Tasmania), we have rounded off our experience of those countries. We also have the bonus of meeting the people. Interest in good food overcomes any language or cultural barrier. The fastest way to get into conversation with locals is to ask about their specialities.

Word Play

Before I forget, let's be clear about what I mean by that much over-used word: "gourmet". Too often, along with "connoisseur" and "bon viveur", it screams snob. It also screams "expensive". But in my dictionary a gourmet is "a judge of good fare", and in my experience, real "gourmet travellers" don't need a gold credit card. Sure, once in a while, it is fun to splurge but it is just as educational to seek out local produce that is prepared with care, where freshness is rated higher than fashion and flavour is more important than fancy frills. That is why our holiday highlights include just as many simple meals as complex creations. The mountain taberna in Spain where we enjoyed thick pork chops, drizzled with lemon juice and grilled quickly over vine roots, is in no guide book that I know – and never will be. The old lady near Cortina d'Ampezzo in Italy who used to open up her house for dinner on two nights a week died several years ago, but we will always remember her, holding a vast copper pan and whipping up the most sensual warm zabaglione we have ever eaten. The texture and flavour of a pink-fleshed giant trout, freshly-hooked and hot-smoked on the shore of New Zealand's Lake Taupo is forever etched on our gastro-memory.

Star Signs

The problem is how to find these honest-to-goodness local dishes. Let's start with France, a country where food is so important that great chefs commit suicide if they lose a Michelin rosette. The famous red guide, with its mind-boggling array of wing dings, may be the bible of gastronomy, but it lacks the Bible's poetry and description. Back in the 1970s, we added the more outspoken, idiosyncratic *Gault Millau* guide to our library. Founded by a couple of journalists who focused on new French cooking and dared to praise innovation, this big yellow guide has rarely let us down. Years later, when the trendy wave of nouvelle cuisine and its descendants threatened to eradicate France's traditional regional dishes, Gault Millau introduced their *Lauriers du Terroir* awards. This laurel wreath symbol signifies restaurants offering dishes that Gran'mère would have been proud of, often with portions to match. These helped us to find unusual sweet wines in the Loire Valley, black radishes in Albi and *mouclade* (mussels in cream) on the Ile de Ré. Michelin has taken up the challenge, introducing a grinning Michelin man to point out value-for-money restaurants where food rather than formality is the priority.

These renowned guides are reliable in France but less trusty beyond the borders. The Michelin guide for Britain is notorious for praising French chefs and French-style restaurants. This is no Anglophobia; other neighbours suffer from similar chauvinism. When we are asked to choose our gastronomic heaven, we usually sigh and dream of the Engadine Valley in Graubunden, in western Switzerland. Look up five of our memorable hotel-restaurants in the Michelin guide to Switzerland, however, and the symbols tell you that they are pleasant and quiet, have terraces, exceptional views and let in dogs. What they do not and cannot tell you is that this valley is a foodie enclave, with five of our favourite chefs working within minutes of one another, conjuring up some of the best nosh in the universe.

Empire Building

A few years ago, we were in Montreal reporting on Christmas in this most Francophile city. Everyone we talked to recommended "authentic" French restaurants. These turned out to be run by expatriate Frenchmen serving up food that was considered haute cuisine thirty years ago. It was a classic example of the emperor's new clothes. Yet, right in the city, talented young Quebecois chefs were, and still are, following the French rules on techniques and use of strictly local ingredients, yet producing totally individual results that we rated 10 on the foodies' Richter scale.

It is not fair to expect such a momentous meal every night. We are just as happy with simple, clean flavours and honest dishes. Even that, however, can be difficult to find. Take the Caribbean, where the demands of the American tourist have stifled local ambition in the kitchen and swamped supermarkets with foodstuffs processed in the USA. On some small islands, it is impossible to buy locally-caught fish or locally-raised fruit and vegetables. Food has been replaced by T-shirts and baskets in the market, and restaurants serve American hamburgers, Italian veal piccata and New Orleans blackened shrimp.

When we were on the relatively unspoiled island of St John in the US Virgin Islands, we searched in vain for true Caribbean cuisine. We even tried lunch with the taxi drivers and road builders, but heavy stews and gristly pigs' trotters defeated us in the tropical heat. The best meals we had were cooked in a tiny restaurant by an American with a Thai mother. He knew how to wheedle chickens and vegetables from the islanders' own back yards and his use of spices contributed to the sense of place that is important when in another country.

The English Disease

Although the "think local" campaign has won the hearts and minds of many chefs, another food phenomenon has swept through other kitchens. This is the "United Nations" attitude to cooking, where ingredients from anywhere in the world are combined, with results veering between triumph and disaster. It has taken hold, in the main, in countries where English is the common language. Perhaps that's because, for example, in the USA and Australia, much of the food used to echo Britain: plain and hearty home cooking that rarely translated successfully on to the restaurant plate.

As in the UK, chefs in these countries are now so eclectic that critics try to wedge them into pigeon holes so that readers have some idea of what to expect:

"Floribbean" for Miami chefs who draw on Florida and the Caribbean for inspiration; "Pacific Rim" for the mixing and matching of, say, Asian spices with Peruvian purple potatoes and low-cholesterol kangaroo meat. Perhaps these novelties will eventually become classics in their own right. Perhaps not.

In trendy cities such as New York and London, "new" has come to mean "good", whilst "newest" is equated with "best". Restaurants open every week but the star chef who stood at the stove when the first diners came through the door may be on to another project after a few months, leaving a deputy to maintain his and the restaurant's reputation. What was tantalising yesterday may be tired today.

Tried and Tested

Consistency: that is the problem. In countries like France and Italy, where restaurants are often family enterprises going back decades, the secret of success is to do the same thing well, day after day, year after year. Not so long ago, deep in the countryside of southern France, we ate in the same restaurant that Elizabeth David had immortalised 30 years before. We ordered the same chicken dish (roasted, with mushrooms stuffed under the skin) that she had enjoyed. The owners saw no reason to change a winning formula, which appealed equally to guests old and new.

Cultural Cringe

So how do you find a "good place to eat"? The restaurants we like least are those that advertise most. We avoid anywhere that sells its charms in an airline magazine or on a card at the airport. To avoid ending up in a culinary ghetto with other foreigners, we rarely take advice at hotels unless the concierge seems particularly in tune with our tastes. Unfortunately, tourism is such a rampant industry that standardisation in hotels and restaurants is not only commonplace, but even embraced by local people as a sign of new-found sophistication.

What Australians refer to so vividly as "cultural cringe" is a major handicap when it comes to food. Why should anyone have to imitate European-style restaurants to gain gastronomic credibility? Italian restaurants in Africa, Greek restaurants in South America, pseudo-French bistros in Japan may offer an alternative for the inhabitants but are sheer torture for us.

Heard it on the Grapevine

The way we dig out good restaurants is by talking to people in the trade. If we like the look of a bakery or delicatessen, a butcher or fishmonger, we go inside and chat. Wine and cheese makers are usually a good bet, since they supply the better restaurants. Once two agree on their favourite spot, off we go.

We not only keep our eyes and ears open, we keep our noses sniffing. We watch where locals head when offices close. We listen for the happy hum of contented eating. We track down the source of delicious smells. Then, we order the daily special, even though we may have no idea what it is. When, in a suburb of Buenos Aires, the waiter announced that the dish of the day was *mondongo*, I chose it, only to discover that it was what I hate most: tripe. My sole consolation was that it was cheap and that I had expanded my vocabulary by one word. In Tasmania recently we came across a "bush restaurant", part of a growing trend to utilise indigenous produce, as opposed to plants and vegetables introduced by the Europeans. Here, bunya nuts, native limes and rosella petals flavour dishes ranging from crocodile and sweet potato spring rolls to wattle grubs. Although these may not be recipes to replicate at home, they certainly provide the raw ingredients for travellers tales.

Of course, you don't have to go to such extremes of geography and gastronomy. Europe may seem old hat since we are all part of the EU, but familiarity need not breed contempt. After all, with barely a wave of a passport, we can order mouth-watering meals in 15 different countries, each with dozens of regional cuisines. Travel only broadens the mind when you meet and talk to people. You don't get into discussions of pop music or politics while touring a castle or cathedral. You don't expect to argue about education or the environment while bronzing on a beach. Understanding another culture comes more easily with a glass in one hand and a fork in the other. Years ago, in a bar in Madrid, we ordered some tapas, including *pulpo*. The Spaniard next to us was incredulous: "Do you really want pulpo? Do you know what it is? Do you like it?" When we answered "Si" to each question, he grinned his approval and quipped, "you cannot be English if you like octopus." It was the beginning of a long and enjoyable evening.

For gourmet tour operators see p.731 of the Directory

THE VEGETARIAN TRAVELLER

by Andrew Sangar

What does a vegetarian do when invited by a smiling, rough-and-ready truck-driver in Eastern Turkey to join his family for dinner in a small village at the end of a long dusty track?

In many ways, limitations on what you eat, what you do and where you will go are anathema to the traveller. An open mind and a willingness to adapt make a much better approach. However, we all carry a few ethical ideas in our mental rucksack, and some of these principles are worth keeping. After all, we preserve our own moral standards when at home – even if the "locals" don't agree with us – so it's reasonable to do the same when abroad.

For vegetarians, this isn't easy. It's not just the food, but attitudes. In most parts of the world, vegetarians are regarded as mere harmless foreign lunatics. Certain countries do have vegetarians of their own: they generally have either opted to give up meat for health reasons, or they are enjoined to do so on religious grounds. Some in Europe (mainly Holland and Germany) have a political commitment to avoiding meat because of the waste of resources which it entails. Few outside the Anglo-Saxon world have any sympathy with the notion (or have even come across it) that wantonly killing animals is actually wrong. Indeed, if they were to hear it, most would fiercely oppose the idea.

A problem arises when your morality is totally at odds with that of the people around you – especially when your views are seen as a Western luxury or as an absurd ethnocentricity.

Culture and circumstances impose a diet which is right for a given people. So it can sometimes be wise (if all you want is food and no arguments) to offer the most acceptable explanation for your own vegetarianism. Among friends, this may not be necessary. In everyday encounters, however, you'll get the best out of people if you can either claim to be "on a diet", possibly under medical supervision, or dress up personal ethics as part of some religious persuasion. Above all, *don't try to persuade people that they too should give up meat*.

On the road it's essential to be flexible. Even meat-eating travellers may be faced with food (sheep's eyes, for example) which they find hard to swallow. My approach is simply to avoid meat and fish as much as possible. Usually it *is* possible, and with no greater hardship than a rather monotonous diet at times.

In Greece, for example, a vegetarian must be happy with lots of delicious *horiatiki* salad, fresh bread and oily vegetables; or in France, some marvellous four-course meals in which the main dish is always omelette; or in a dozen other countries, meals consisting entirely of snacks or a succession of starters. Some countries are easier than others. In Italy where pasta usually comes before the main course, it usually is the main course for vegetarians. Mercifully, Italy is one of those places where nobody bats an eyelid at such eccentricities, and pasta comes in a score of different forms with a dozen different meatless sauces. Meatless pizzas are everywhere, and many Italian cheeses, such as gorgonzola, are made commercially without animal rennet.

In north west Europe, eating habits are decidedly meaty, or fishy (especially in Scandinavia). But there are so many vegetarians that almost all cities and a good number of provincial towns have eating places catering for meat-free consumers. Holland and Germany, like Britain, have thousands of such establishments. Further east in Europe, there's a different problem – a lack of anything much to eat *except* meat (accompanied by potatoes and cabbages, and followed by lard-rich sticky cakes). This is not invariably the case. Czechoslovakia, or at least Prague, seems now to enjoy an abundance of produce of all kinds.

One of the best parts of the world for vegetarian travellers is the Middle East. Israel, above all, is a land of meat-free snacks and meals. All sorts of cultural reasons account for this. Many Jews are vegetarian, but in any case Jewish dietary laws prohibit the mixing of meat and milk within six hours of each other. This has led to a proliferation of "dairy" restaurants in which nothing on the menu (not even the cheese) contains any meat products. Note though that dairy restaurants do serve fish.

Israelis particularly like salads, even for breakfast, eaten with yoghurt-like milk products. More salad at lunch time or in the evening is accompanied by fried, meat-free items such as *falafel* (like meatballs made of chickpeas), *blintzes* (filled rolled pancakes), *latkes* (fried grated potato) and *borekas* (little filled savoury pastries). Some of these have been brought from Eastern Europe, others are native Middle Eastern dishes, reflecting the differing origins of the refugees who make up Israel's population.

In neighbouring Arab countries (not the Maghreb, though), and in Turkey, several of the same delicious snacky dishes can be found. A traditional Arab *mezze* (a meal consisting of many small items served all at once) can be made of such dishes, although in the Islamic world it is hard indeed to get anyone to accept that you truly don't want any meat.

That's not particular to Islam. In much of fervently Christian South America, meat is the be-all and end-all of cookery. While I was in Brazil, a crisis involving farmers led to meat shortages which actually sparked off riots – even though nothing else was in short supply. There I managed happily mainly on salads, fruit and bread. North America has followed a similar path, despite closer historic links with north west Europe. True, there is a glossy American magazine called *Vegetarian Times*, and hundreds of "veggie" eateries on the hip West Coast (some Canadian cities with even stronger British ties have vegetarian restaurants), but on the whole North America is hooked on meat, and the only alternative seems to be a cheese sandwich.

It's perhaps reminiscent of holidaymakers who go abroad loaded with the familiar foods of home, but don't be too proud to put some emergency rations in your luggage. I have staved off hunger on countless occasions – and in every continent – with a small bag of muesli, mixed with milk powder. It can be turned into a nourishing, tasty and filling snack just by adding water. If there's milk, yoghurt or fruit juice on hand, so much the better.

The one country where vegetarianism is really normal, and meat-eaters in the minority is India. Hindus are supposed to steer clear of all meat (including eggs) but yoghurt is eaten in abundance. Most Hindu eating places at the poorer end of the scale are completely vegetarian, as are the smarter (but entirely un-Western) Brahmin restaurants. Travellers tend to find themselves in a different class of establishment, quasi-European in a dignified, old fashioned way, as if the days of Raj were still not quite forgotten. Railway stations, for example, usually have a good dining room divided into meat and vegetarian sections. Many hotels do likewise. Moslem or Christian regions, say Kashmir or Goa, are less reliable. But similarly, beyond India, pockets of Hinduism provide resources throughout southeast Asia.

The places where vegetarianism is best known, and often quite well catered for, tend to be those countries formerly under British influence. Australia – which also benefits from Middle Eastern and Indian immigration – is an obvious example. And it's not for patriotic reasons that I commend British Airways to vegetarian travellers. They are more aware of what vegetarians want and more serious about providing it than just about any other of their competitors. When booking, you can opt for lacto-vegetarian, vegan or Oriental vegetarian in-flight meals. Other airlines capable of providing (rather than just promising to provide) a decent meatless meal include Air India, El Al and Swissair.

But to return to earth. I accepted the Turkish truckdriver's invitation. A goat was slaughtered and served, with no accompaniment but bread. I picked reluctantly at the meat, hoping no one would notice. While we men ate and the women peeked from the kitchen door, the severed head of the animal gazed at us horribly from the end of the table. Rough drinks were poured and we toasted mutual understanding.

See p.731 of the Directory for vegetarian associations world-wide.

THE GAY TRAVELLER
by Tony Leonard

When did gay tourism begin? Was it in 1895, when the trial of Oscar Wilde sent every society homosexual scrambling en masse to the Continent to escape a similar fate? Or were the ancient Spartan warrior-lovers the first great gaggle of queens to hit foreign climes for one hell of a party? The Grand Tour of Europe must surely have held sensual, as well as cultural delights for a "sensitive" young man of the 18th century. And Morocco had its fair share of theatrical ex-pats long before Joe Orton so elegantly chronicled his little escapades in Marrakech.

San Francisco first became a Boystown (and consequently a Gay Mecca) after World War II, when discharged sailors discovered they could have far more fun sticking together than they would back with their folks in Nowheresville, Illinois. The package tour found the clones of the Seventies charting all the major trade routes that would be well trampled to this day. They pitched camp, founding colonies that would become the staple destination of gay tourism for two and a half decades and counting.

In the US, affluent New York "A-gays" have decamped each summer to Fire Island. There they have created an alternative homosexual high society where social status permeates the rituals and traditions that have become as unchanging as anything the British class system has created.

Europe's gay hot-spots have always been rather more egalitarian, based around hedonism rather than social standing. The sun, sex and sangria of Sitges provide an opportunity for men whose everyday lives are constrained by heterosexual conventions to let rip in an atmosphere of mutual abandon. As our heterosexual counterparts discovered the delights of Torremelinos and Majorca, so gay men have made their annual pilgrimages to Sitges, Mykanos, Gran Canaria, etc., to do much the same, revelling in the sort of atmosphere epitomised by the package tours of Club 18-30.

Gay travel companies have been among the most successful of gay businesses, building primarily on a portfolio of conventional package tours to friendly resorts in Europe and North America. The most important qualification to becoming a gay resort was the perceived liberalism of its inhabitants. Pretty soon, an area builds up an infrastructure of gay bars, clubs and hotels and the colonisation is complete.

For the gay holiday-makers of the last few decades, there is safety in numbers. For most, a gay lifestyle was something they were only able to experience on occasion, be it once a week, once a month or even once a year. No surprise then, that they should wish to holiday almost exclusively in the company of other gay men, away from the bigotry and petty prejudices of everyday life. And no surprise that they should make the most of a scene that they have little access to for fifty weeks in a year.

But Joe and Joel Average have started to become rather more adventurous of late. The last few years have seen a surge in confidence amongst the gay community, matched by a greater recognition and acceptance from the wider population. As we recognise the diversity of our community, more and more highly specialised gay travel operators have sprung up to cater for every conceivable destination and activity.

For the physically active traveller, there are adventure holidays aplenty, from canyoneering and mountain biking in the wilds of Utah, discovering Aboriginal culture in the Australian Outback, white-water rafting, scuba diving, whale watching, mountaineering, skiing, snowboarding, trekking through the Amazon, the sky's the limit. Or rather it isn't; there are hang-gliding and ballooning trips. And you can be sure, when the first travel agents start sending people into space, one of them will be a gay operator.

More sedentary occupations include painting, cookery, art history and music. Self development on a Greek island or group bonding on a Turkish yacht, or perhaps a spa getaway in Iceland, the choice seems limitless. All of these holidays are being marketed directly to gay men and lesbians, by gay or gay friendly companies. Straight friends may come along, but only in the company of a responsible homosexual.

The development of the gay travel market can be directly ascribed to the concept of the Pink Pound. This came about in the late eighties with the realisation that gay people have a greater disposable income than their straight counterparts, because of their lack of dependants. This, combined with the fact that in gay couples, both members of a household unit are likely to be in full-time work, has made the gay sector a dream consumer group for marketeers of all persuasions.

Research in the US has since suggested that gay men are four times more likely to hold a current passport than heterosexual men and have a greater propensity for travel. In Britain, a survey of *Gay Times* readers found that 76 per cent take holidays abroad at least once a year and that 34 per cent travel at least twice a year.

How representative of the gay population as a whole these figures are, is open to debate, but the response to such data has been phenomenal. Major international companies have suddenly become interested in courting this previously shunned group. BA and United Airlines are competing against each other in their rush to sell gay holidays and destinations, while Virgin, who got there first, have since pulled out claiming the market isn't big enough to be viable.

And this new-found interest isn't confined to companies. Cities, states and even countries are bending over backwards to attract and accommodate the gay visitor. Sydney's Mardi Gras brings millions of dollars into the city in tourist generated revenue, a fact that the city is eager to exploit and expand on. Florida's Tourist Board had long targeted the gay visitor, as has Amsterdam. Hawaii, since its change in legislation, now promotes itself as the gay wedding capital. Politics are not entirely market driven, however. A government-produced leaflet aimed at attracting gay visitors to Spain was recently withdrawn after a change of administration.

Gay travel trade shows now take place regularly in London and throughout the US, and workshops and seminars on selling the gay consumer are legion. While specialised companies thrive, the traditional gay holiday firms have grown substantially, and are combing the globe to find new gay destinations. Prague has joined Amsterdam as an ideal location for a weekend break, while

Mexico is being tauted as the next big thing.

Exclusively gay resorts and developments are being created, where people can stay and never see a heterosexual during their entire visit. Man Friday is one such location encompassing ten acres of exquisitely manicured lawns, gardens and rainforest along Fiji's Coral Coast, where guests stay in "traditional" thatched huts.

The Desert Tropics Inn in Las Vegas, a city not noted for its tolerance, is an all male, clothing optional, complex which the management aim to expand with the addition of an all-gay casino in the near future. Even Disney has got in on the act with the Annual Gay Day at Walt's Magic Kingdom.

Of course, all this activity needs media to cover it. The numerous gay travel guides on the market have now been joined by a monthly magazine called *Our World*, a travel journal for lesbians and gays, focusing on a different part of the world in every issue.

Electronic media has become extremely important to all this. The internet has played a major role in the development of the more specialised companies, giving gay people the world over immediate access to the smallest operators.

This has made it particularly easy to find the gay holiday of your choice. IGTA, the International Gay Travel Association, is the network of the travel industry businesses and professionals involved in the gay travel market. From a group of 25 when it formed in 1983, it has grown into an organisation with over 1,200 members, and is the ideal starting point in the search for the perfect holiday.

Another excellent site is *Q-Net*, created by the publishers of the Ferrari Guides. Here you can look up holidays by destination, activity, operator or date that you wish to travel. If you can't find something that appeals here, perhaps you're better off staying at home.

The gay community has come a long way in the last few decades, and increasingly, that journey is becoming measurable in airmiles. Please note, I've concentrated exclusively on gay men in this article, because the lesbian market is a rather different, although equally vibrant, area. It's too soon to tell whether the market can sustain such exploitation and consequently, whether the intervention of the mainstream companies will continue. Current opinion is optimistic, but corporate attention can be fickle, and if they don't make their quotas, they may well go the way of Virgin. In the meantime, the gay traveller can bask in all the attention and rest assured in the knowledge that he faces a choice that, for the first time, is second to none.

For further information see p.723 of the Directory.

THE RETREAT TRAVELLER

by Stafford Whiteaker

"Going on retreat" is the alternative holiday that is winning new converts by the thousands across Europe and in the United States. It is a way of recharging your inner resources and getting some peace and quiet in a hectic and demanding world. It is a chance to get away from it all, to think things through, and to reflect on your life and the relationships in it. Monasteries and convents can also provide cheap and safe overnight accommodation, especially if you are a student or under thirty. All this yearning for peace has resulted in the biggest growth in retreats in Europe since the Middle Ages – and America is not far behind – where several million people go on retreat *every* weekend. So the choice is wide ranging on both sides of the Atlantic.

Who goes on Retreats?

You do not have to be religious or a Christian or Buddhist to go on a retreat even if you go to a monastery. People of all faiths and those of none go on a retreat. You do not have to know about alternative healing or adhere to any particular life-style to go to a New Age Centre. At a retreat you will meet people of all ages and from every kind of background – student, housewives, grandparents, business people, the rich and the poor.

What is a Retreat?

A retreat is simply a deliberate attempt to step outside your ordinary life and relationships and take time to reflect, rest and be still. It is a concentrated time in which to experience yourself and think about your relations to others and, if you are fortunate, to feel a sense of the eternal. There is a wide choice from Christian and Buddhist places to New Age and Yoga Centres. Whether you go to a traditional monastery or to a workshop on North American Indian spirituality, the end result should be the same – self-discovery and a new view of life. A retreat may last from a day to many months, but for most people a long weekend is the most suitable length of stay.

Almost all places of retreat are Christian, Buddhist or New Age based. The use of a particular approach in the form of spiritual exercises are common. These incorporate every form of examination of conscience, meditation, contemplation, and vocal and mental prayer. Such activities are designed to make the spirit – rather like a body in physical training to become fit – ready and able to get rid of spiritual flab.

In this way for Christians, the spirit may become open to love and to the discovery of God's will. The aim of Buddhism is to show us how to develop our capacity for awareness, love and energy to the point where we become "enlightened" or fully awake to reality. Other religious traditions might say it is to bring consciousness of the unity of all creation and of the eternal. These are enormous goals – but then, why not? Unlike the mind and body, the spirit goes forth with unlimited prospects.

The New Age movement is a collection of many ideas and practices aimed at personal growth. These ranges from alternative healing practices, reincarnation, environmental concern, telepathy, occultism to spiritism. However, many of the New Age ideas, techniques and approaches spring from well-established traditions of healing, self-help and self-discovery.

Different Kinds of Retreats

Retreats divide into two major groups – private retreats in which you go alone as an individual and group retreats which often have a theme and cover a particular topic or approach to spirituality and healing. Many of these are in the form of week or weekend workshops. Some are especially designed to help you unwind. Others are individually structured around a particular system of spiritual exercises, such as those of St Ignatius or based on some defined form of meditation such as *Vipassana*.

The Traditional Retreat

Traditional weekend retreats are the most popular and likely to run along the following lines if you are to be part of a group. You arrive on Friday evening, settle down in your room, meet the retreat leader and the others. After supper there may be a short discussion about the weekend activities. Then you might go for a walk in the garden or rest. Early to bed is the usual rule but not necessarily early to rise. From the first night, you cease doing much talking unless it is when you gather together for a group discussion, a talk, to learn healing or other aids to well-being, or for prayer or meditation. On Sunday there may be a religious ceremony of some sort, such as Mass if you are in a Catholic monastery. If you go alone and not as part of a group, there will be time to walk, read and just rest. It is all simple, easy and peaceful.

Theme and Activity Retreats

These offer a wide range of courses and study that combine body and spiritual awareness. The methods used spring from alternative healing practices, group psychology, or are based on rediscovering traditional religious forms of creating spiritual awareness. You enter an activity, such as painting or dance, through which you may gather your feelings, senses and intuition together into a greater awareness of yourself, of others, and of life as part of the cosmic creation. There are a great number of ways to explore this form of retreat. Some are ancient arts and others very much of our own time. Yoga retreats employ body and breathing exercises to achieve greater physical and mental stillness as an aid to meditation and contemplation. Embroidery, calligraphy, and painting retreats focus on awakening personal creativity. Nature and prayer retreats help you to see things freshly, appreciating colour, shape and texture to heighten your awareness of creation at work all around you.

Healing and Renewal Retreats

Ancient and modern techniques are drawn upon to help achieve this goal in a healing retreat. These may range from discovering the child within you to flotation sessions, nutritional therapy, holistic massage and aromatherapy. The established churches have regained their awareness of this almost lost aspect of their faith. Now inner healing and healing of the physical body through prayer and the laying on of hands have become prominent features of many Christian ministries.

Renewal Retreats

A renewal retreat is usually Christian and is seeking to find a new awareness of the presence of Christ, a deeper experience of the Holy Spirit, and a clearer understanding for the committed Christian of his or her mission in the Church.

Taking the Family or Going Just for the Day

For those places that have suitable facilities, a whole family may experience going on retreat together – even the family dog may be welcomed in some places. These retreats need to be well-planned and worked out so that each member of the family from the youngest to the oldest has a real chance to benefit from the experience. Buddhist centres and monasteries often have children's *Dahampasala* which is a school study session held each Sunday. Some convents offer creche facilities for Mother and Baby day retreats. Many places have camping facilities or a family annex.

Meditation Retreats

These are for the study and practice of meditation from the beginner level to the advanced practitioner. It is a way of opening yourself to an inner level of well-being. There are many kinds of approaches to meditation from the various Buddhist traditions to those of the Christian and Hindu faiths as well as non-religious ones.

The Experience of Silence

The most ancient retreat of all is the one of contemplation and solitude. Here you live for a few days in that great school of silence in which the legendary hermits and saints of old sought God and made all else unimportant. Silence and stillness are very great challenges in this age of diversion and aggression. Even after a few hours of stillness, an inner consciousness arises and those bound up in busy lives are often surprised at the feelings which surface. This kind of retreat is best done in a monastery or convent where the atmosphere is very peaceful.

Going on Retreat

Once you decide to go, select a place which strikes you as interesting and in an area you want to visit. Most places have a brochure or list of activities which includes charges. Write, giving the dates you would like to stay with an alternative, and making it clear whether you are a man or a woman, for some facilities are single gender. You need not declare your faith or lack of it or your age. Enclose a stamped, self-addressed envelope.

How Much Does it Cost?

Retreat costs normally include room and food. They vary little from country to country and are modest by any standard. For example, in Spain expect to pay from 800 to 1,800 pesetas. In Britain the range is £15 to £30 a day per person. Weekends cost between £35 and £125. Many Christian and Buddhist retreat houses refuse to put a price on your stay and will ask only for a donation. Expect most courses and workshop to cost about the same as similar type programmes at colleges or craft centres. If you are a student, over 60, or unwaged, there is usually a special lower rate. In New Age centres where healing therapies and special counselling are on offer, expect to pay a going commercial rate for accommodation, treatments and courses. Such charges can range from £55 a day to over £300 for the weekend plus costs of specific individual treatments. Some places offer camping or caravan facilities or a room with a common kitchen for DIY eating.

Food

Vegetarians and special diets are often catered for in Britain and the United States if you give advance notice. The food in other countries is apt to reflect the national diet and include meat. Self-catering facilities often exist in retreat guesthouses and this is one way around diet problems

A Bed for the Night

The traditional hospitality of monasteries and convents across Europe remains. If you are young and have little money, knock on the door and say so – you are likely to find warm hospitality, a meal, and a bed for the night. A bit of gardening or cleaning is usually welcomed as a way of repaying such hospitality, bearing in mind that most of these religious communities are poor themselves. Many continental monasteries do not have rooms for women nor convents rooms for men.

Further information: *The Good Retreat Guide* by Stafford Whitaker (Rider £11.99) lists over 300 places in Britain, Ireland, France and Spain; **National Retreat Association**, 256 Bermondsey Street, London, SE1 3UJ (tel: 0171-357 7736); **The Buddhist Society**, 58 Eccleston Square, London SW1 1PH (tel: 0171-834 5858 2pm-6pm); Spanish tourist offices can provide a short list of places in that country. In Italy you can expect to find a place of retreat almost anywhere. French monasteries and convents have made a real effort to cater for the growing numbers who want to go on retreat and many more produce excellent colour brochures. For other countries you will probably need to contact a religious organisation, such as the Catholic church.

THE HONEYMOON TRAVELLER

by Lucy Hone

A honeymoon is that ultimate of holidays which we all hope to take at some stage in our lives. At an average cost of around £3,000 it will probably be the most expensive trip you've ever been on and should be your perfect holiday, with memories to cherish for years to come. What a dreadful shame then that so many couples get it so horribly wrong. In my research for *The Good Honeymoon Guide* I have come across scores of honeymoon couples with disappointing tales to tell: couples lured by discount deals to the Caribbean in August only to find themselves caught in a hurricane; couples promised wonderful ocean views but given a room overlooking an adjacent building site; and the surprise sailing honeymoon booked by a groom who didn't know his spouse was prone to sea-sickness. Any seasoned traveller will tell you that the obstacles encountered while travelling are all part of the adventure, but for honeymooners such problems are nothing short of an intergalactic disaster. The Honeymoon Traveller is unlike any other kind of traveller: billed as the holiday of a lifetime, the pressure is on to enjoy every minute. As a result couples regard their honeymoon totally differently to any "normal" trip. Many couples have travelled extensively before their marriage, seeking out imaginative and far flung destinations for in-depth exploration, but the moment the ring slips upon the finger all that changes: independent travellers who have for years lived and slept by their Lonely Planet bibles suddenly find themselves looking through brochures full of what they would normally refer to as "boring beach holidays". When it comes to booking a honeymoon, couples always seem to play it safe, which usually translates into them all trooping off to the same old, trusted haunts. They flock in droves towards the reliable and idyllic islands of the Indian Ocean and the Caribbean: Mauritius, the Maldives, the Seychelles, St Lucia, Antigua and Barbados all appear regularly in the honeymoon Top Ten. If you are booking a honeymoon you'll know that this is largely because newly-weds want to be assured of that essential honeymoon ingredient: a romantic hotel with a bedroom to die for.

For many couples this is their first opportunity to stay in a luxurious hotel with all the trimmings, allowing them to revel in the glorious excesses of the hotel's room service, swim-up bars and Jacuzzis. However, an all too common mistake is made by couples who dream of simply lazing around on the beach for two weeks on their honeymoon, and actually end up feeling bored and frustrated if there's nothing to do. Check with the hotel or travel agent exactly what leisure facilities and cultural diversions are available should you get bored of the bedroom or the beach lounger!

Similarly, those planning an active honeymoon, with plenty of touring, sightseeing, and adventure activities, should take care to build in plenty of time for rest and relaxation: spend a few days lying on the beach or holed up in a mountain hideaway before you hit the trail. If you do decide on a really alternative destination remember you don't have to dash around and see every single highlight of that country in your two weeks. Many tour operators, particularly the specialist ones who are so enthusiastic about their countries, tend to push people into doing too much: don't feel afraid to say no to some sightseeing and spend the day relaxing on your own instead.

Flights are also a big consideration when booking a honeymoon, as couples tend to be pretty exhausted after the wedding and may not necessarily feel like hours cooped up on an aeroplane. Don't think that romantic has to necessarily mean distant. It doesn't. Having said that, if you've absolutely set your heart on a country and a hotel that is thousands of miles away, why not take the plunge – there is also that wonderful trick called sleeping pills enabling you to while away the hours effortlessly.

Alternative Honeymoon Destinations

If you want to avoid the crowd there is a comforting number of alternative destinations offering culture, eco-tourism, or adventure, as well as some really wonderful hotels where you can recharge your batteries and get into some serious honeymoon indulgence along the way. There's hardly a corner of the world now that doesn't boast some kind of superb hotel, making less traditional honeymoon destinations such as Costa Rica, Indonesia, Morocco, Borneo, Chile, Tanzania, India, Thailand, Brazil and Egypt all realistic contenders for your dream trip.

Keep an open mind when selecting your destination. Many couples have looked aghast at the suggestion of India or Costa Rica, but have been readily convinced by the news that they would be staying in luxury palace hotels if they chose India or hand-crafted luxury lodges set deep in the heart of the rainforest in Costa Rica.

The one golden rule of honeymoons is not to go somewhere that one of you has been to before – especially not with an ex, as there's nothing more tedious than being given a blow by blow account of a holiday they enjoyed, or even didn't enjoy, with someone else.

Who Should Book the Honeymoon?

The first thing to do once you get engaged is to decide who is going to book the honeymoon. Although most couples now choose to plan this important holiday together, there are those who still believe in the tradition that it's a man's job. As one husband to be recently said to me: "Melissa is sorting out everything else, I just want to have something that I can say is totally and utterly all mine. She hasn't got a clue where we're going, but as soon as I saw it (in a brochure) I knew it was just perfect for the two of us and am having such a great time planning it all in secret." Surprise honeymoons are great. They are romantic, dreamy, exciting and thrilling, as long as you both feel that way. So before you take the ball off into your own court, do check that your other half is genuinely happy to go ahead with the plan. And check again a week or two before the wedding, and once more a day or two before the big day, that they are still happy to hang in there until the departure lounge. Bear in mind that many people also find it difficult to get excited about a holiday they cannot visualise.

If you are booking a surprise the key is to really think about your other half and decide, honestly, what you think they would want. Don't book a trekking holiday in northern Thailand if all your fiancée wants to do is lie on the beach.

Perhaps the best trick is to plan a two-centre honeymoon with something for you both, say a few days on the beach at either end and a few days in the middle for your trekking, white-water rafting, canoeing, diving, looking around ancient temples or safari. Talk to her about the fundamentals – hot or cold – and the things that she wants to avoid – injections, spiders, or a long flight.

Before you Go

Some countries require proof of citizenship or visas, so make sure you check with your travel agent or the tourist commission that you've got everything you BOTH need as soon as you book, as it can take weeks or even months to get through the bureaucracy.

If you're plane tickets and your passport are under different names, take your wedding certificate along to the airport with you, or better still arrange for your passport changed into your married name by sending it off three months before you are due to leave.

Consult your doctor about inoculations and anti-malaria pills: some countries require certificates of vaccinations and will not permit you to enter without one.

Lastly, whatever you decide it's essential to get straight on with your booking, as the best rooms, the best views and the best deals always go first. Also, don't forget to stock up on all necessary prescriptions (including contraceptives!), try to leave these in their original bottles and keep a copy of the prescription to satisfy curious customs officials.

See p.726 of the Directory for a list of Recommended Travel Agents

THE WOMAN TRAVELLER

by Isabella Tree

"The art of travelling is learning to behave like a chameleon".   So said a woman friend of mine on her second year around the world and I don't believe a truer word was ever spoken. Blending into the background is not only a prerequisite to understanding and observing a different culture, it also keeps you out of trouble.

Indecent Exposure

For women in particular, how you behave and especially how you dress can be construed as camouflage or an open invitation; it can make you one of the crowd or a moving target. This may be an unfair state of affairs but it's a fact of life and in someone else's country one is in no position to rail against it.

Call it ignorance or misdirected feminism, but, many women make the mistake of travelling in a "no compromise" frame of mind. They wear shorts and bra tops in Marrakech and Istanbul, G-strings in Goa and Phuket, and nothing at all in the Mediterranean. I know and you know that this does not mean they are "loose women", but it does show a distinct lack of respect for local custom and the sensitivities of the men, and women, of the country.

Dress is the first line of defence and the most immediate symbol of respect. If you get that wrong you are starting your travels with a glaring disadvantage.

Of course codes of dress differ wildly from country to country. In Southern Africa and part of the Indian subcontinent short sleeves and hemlines not far below the knee are fully respectable. In Iran and strict Muslim countries, the body must be totally covered, usually by a black *chador* which drapes you completely from head to foot. A woman not wearing a veil risks flogging or imprisonment, although as a foreigner you are likely to be let off with a caution and forced to cover up.

There are legally enforced dress codes at home as well, though they're so familiar we may take them for granted. But it serves to show that though conventions may differ, they are universal. In London, or Paris or New York, you would be a fool for walking the street topless, let alone racing across a cricket pitch, and not expecting to be arrested. In rainforest tribal communities from Sumatra to the Amazon, on the other hand, bare breasts are *de rigeur.*

A culture's standard of dress has a lot to do with what parts of the body are considered sensuous or provocative. In China the feet are still thought erotic, while in many countries direct eye contact can be as promiscuous as the offer of a spare key to your hotel room. In Papua New Guinea you can bare your breast to the world, but your thighs must be covered at all times. Not only that, but the space between your legs is so sexually suggestive that trousers can be as much of a turn-on as wearing nothing at all.

It pays to be prepared for the dress sense of your destination before you head off for a pre-holiday splurge in the high street, but clearly this is not always possible. As a general rule it can be said that tight and skimpy clothes are inappropriate for most countries outside Europe and the States, and that generous, loose-fitting clothes are not only more comfortable to travel in, but less controversial.

If you don't want to wear dresses and skirts, you can't do better for propriety's sake, especially in tropical heat, than the kind of cool, cotton pyjamas worn by Chinese or Kashmiri women, or a Moroccan *jalaba.* However, in places like Burma, Thailand and Vietnam, particularly in the cities, this may be too casual. Asian women take a great deal of trouble with their appearance however poor their background, and while torn jeans and a tattered T-shirt may seem relaxed and inoffensive to the Westerner, it can seem dirty and disrespectful in Bangkok or Singapore.

If conventions are strict on the street they are doubly so in places of worship. I once met a French woman who had been stoned in Turkey – one of the most relaxed of the Muslim countries, for being dressed inappropriately in a mosque. In Greece you may be provided with frumpy, elasticated skirts to hide your trousers or miniskirt when entering an Orthodox Church. You may even be asked to cover your head. Never enter even a remote chapel on a beach in anything else than full daily dress. You may get away with it, but the distress you will cause a worshipper who stumbles on you wearing a bikini in the crypt is indefensible. In all these cases, a simple length of wrap-around cotton, like an Indian lungi or a sarong, or an African kanga or kakoi, is a handy extra to have.

The Hands-off Approach

Perhaps the most persistent and aggravating problem a woman has to deal with, particularly if she is travelling alone, is male harassment. Satellite TV and black market videos have a lot to answer for. In Third World countries Madonna and Sam Fox are seen as the archetypal western woman; while the steamier side of Swedish exports, now providing a boom business for the black market in Asia, gives the impression that American or European women have an indiscriminate and insatiable appetite for sex. Black western women fare even worse than blondes because they are considered "exotic".

The sad truth is that you can be dressed modestly and impeccably on a bus in Lima or Tangiers and still feel a hand on your bum. Ironically it is often in Catholic or Muslim countries, where impropriety is most despised, that local men feel they can take liberties with foreigners. Most self-defence experts advise; "Never create a 1:1 confrontation". "Get your hands off my bum, you filthy expletive" can exacerbate the situation or even incite a violent response. The best solution is to make a scene and enlist the support of other passengers. "Did you see what that man did to me?" creates a sense of moral outrage and people, when directly appealed to, will be more eager to leap to your defence. The same attitude that implies that Western women are "loose", can work as an effective antidote to harassment when the groper, having been sprung, is hounded out of the bus and given a going-over by the other male passengers.

In general, the first rule of self-defence, is awareness. Be alert, listen to the advice of locals and fellow travellers, develop a street sense and try not to be in the wrong place at the wrong time. Good judgement is every traveller's personal responsibility and the chances are, if you find yourself alone, late at night and being pursued up a dark alley, that you could have avoided being there in the first place.

It is politically incorrect nowadays to suggest that women should ever play a "passive" role, or – heaven forbid – that they could court disaster. But avoidance and weak-minded submissiveness are two completely different things, and the distinction is one that is crucial to survival, especially in foreign countries where the threat is an unknown quantity.

A woman is rarely a physical match for a man. And even if she is a black-belt in the martial arts, it would be unwise to launch into front kicks and elbow strikes if the man confronting her is just after money. Hand over the wallet and have done with it. Your pursuer may be armed, crazy or drunk and there is no need ever to find out if it can be avoided.

Most confrontational scenarios must be played by ear to a great extent, but there are a few universal rules: Don't turn a scary situation into a dangerous one if you can help it. Don't panic, don't show fear and don't allow the person accosting you to get the upper hand. Try to gain the psychological advantage by throwing him off his balance. In most cases a man who is attempting to intimidate a woman believes himself invulnerable and a strong show of resistance will unnerve him enough to make him back down. Never be persuaded to try and resolve the situation by moving to another place, like a car, a hotel room or someone else's house.

If you do find yourself in a dangerous, enclosed situation, try to anticipate the aggressor's next move and plan ahead for it. You may only get one chance to defend yourself – the earlier the better – and you won't want to miss it. As the innocent one in confrontation you have the advantage of surprise, but if you are forced to strike back physically, make sure it is a crippling blow that gives you a chance to escape. The last thing you want is to provoke a more serious physical attack. As one London-based martial arts master recommends: "There is only one thing better than a kick in the balls – and that's two kicks in the balls."

If you are worried about your ability to gauge dangerous situations and to defend yourself if they get out of hand, a few classes in the basic strategies of awareness and self-defence before you travel can boost your confidence immeasurably.

Warm Receptions

Stay alert and these "worse case scenarios" should never arise. I've travelled most of my life, some of it on my own, and though I'm certainly no Kate Adie, I've been caught up in anti-British demonstrations in Peru, tear-gassed in Czechoslovakia and Papua New Guinea, been ambushed by tribal warriors in Indonesia, and never had a hand laid on me in earnest.

Appreciation of the dangers should never stop you from sharing in the action, or making friends. One of the great advantages of being a woman is that men and women find you more approachable. Sometimes the offers of hospitality and kindness can be overwhelming. And any woman who has travelled with a child or a baby can regale you with stories of such warmth and tenderness that it melts the heart and restores all your faith in human nature. These are the moments one travels for and that stay with you for ever.

Contraception and Feminine Hygiene

Contraception is often difficult to come by abroad and should be acquired before you leave home. Time changes should be taken into consideration if you take a low dosage contraceptive pill. Stomach upsets and diarrhoea may also reduce or neutralise the effectiveness of oral contraception.

Condoms are not as freely available, especially to women, as they should be, and packets that you do find in clinics or chemists in areas off the beaten track may be past their sell-by-date and the rubber may break or corrode. Always take condoms with you, however remote the possibility of sex. AIDS and other sexually-transmitted diseases are, thanks to the ease and popularity of travel, a universal threat.

Women should be aware that the physical stress of travel, jet-lag and time difference can all upset the biological clock and throw even the most regular period out of kilter. Sanitary towels and tampons are also often difficult to buy abroad, especially in the Third World. A form of Tampax, with plastic or cardboard applicator, is perhaps the most hygienic and convenient to take with you, as on some occasions you may find it difficult to find clean water and soap to wash your hands. If you do prefer to take the more discreet-sized tampons without applicators, carry a sachet of disinfectant wipes to clean your hands which will guard against the transmission of germs.

Be sensitive about cultural attitudes to menstruation. In some places, especially tribal areas, men are really frightened of the powers a woman has when she is menstruating. Some cultures believe it is contaminating, and will not allow you to touch or even walk near their food. Of course, they need never know, but be careful to dispose of sanitary towels and tampons in this situation.

In brief conclusion, don't be a loud tourist, keep an open mind, stay cool and be wise, and travelling, especially if you are a woman, will be a fulfilling and exciting adventure.

See p.727 of the Directory for a list of Women's Travel Associations
Further Reading: *More Women Travel* **(Rough Guide)**

TRAVELLING WITH CHILDREN

by Rupert and Jan Grey

The difference between travelling with children and travelling without is not unlike crossing the Sahara on foot as opposed to in a Land Rover: you go much slower, it is much harder work, but it is (arguably) much more fun. Given the choice, we always take ours with us for they open doors that were previously closed. Parenthood is an international condition and the barriers erected by race and language fall away in the presence of children. Of equal importance for the travelling parent is the opportunity to experience, with and through their children, the newness of their world, their innocence and their instinctive fear of the unknown. The reactions of children are not yet blunted by the passage of years and the compromises of adulthood, and a journey to the jungles of the equator or the forests of the north can be one of discovery, between, as well as by parent and child.

Children require explanations, and their passion for knowledge is as infectious as their imagination is vivid. The dark recesses of a cave in the heart of Borneo were, for ours, the home of dragons and crocodiles, long since mourned by conservationists, which lurked in the darkening shadows over the river. The reality of adulthood suddenly became rather boring. So, of course, is changing nappies. In many parts of the world the locals will regard you with amazement; they will probably have never seen disposable nappies and for children over six months they regard them as superfluous in any event. Nappies, clothes, children's games and books are items which suddenly become indispensable, and the notion of travelling light becomes a part of your past along with many other aspects of pre-children life.

Preparation

Eric Shipton, so he said, used to plan his expeditions on the back of an envelope. Not with children, he didn't. Detailed organisation and preparation is not an optional extra. It is vital. What you take will depend on the age and individual requirements of your children. If they have a passion for pure wool Habitat ducks, as our eldest daughter did the first time we took her to Malaysia at the age of two and a half, take it. Take a second one just in case the first one gets lost. It will probably be your most crucial item of equipment.

Your choice of clothes will of necessity be dictated by the climate; cotton clothes with long legs and sleeves are best for the tropics, and for fair-skinned children a sun hat (also made of cotton) is essential – particularly if travelling on water.

While children generally adapt to heat better than adults, the younger ones are much more vulnerable to cold. Warm clothing should be in layers and easily washable, and if you put children still in nappies into ski suits you will need the patience of Job.

No less important than choosing the right equipment is packing it in the right way. There will be a '*rucksack that is only opened at night* '(all things necessary for sleeping), the '*rucksack that you have beside you at all times*'(which has a few nappies, drinks, a couple of children's books games, the teddy, guide books etc.) a '*rucksack just for nappies*', a '*rucksack just for toys*', a '*rucksack just for clothes*' and to give them a sense of participation, one little tiny rucksack for each of the children containing a couple of nappies a piece (it is bound to get lost).

As important as sorting out your equipment is preparing the children. This calls for a lot of topical reading and storytelling spread over several weeks or months before departure. The object of the exercise here is twofold: firstly to instill a sense of adventure and anticipation, and secondly as a sort of advance warning that life is going to be very different. If you are about to expose your children to a radically different culture, and extreme of climate, fly them through eight different time zones into a world of extraordinary insects, holes in the ground for lavatories and a completely unfamiliar diet, it is an advance warning that they will need. You won't, for you will probably have already been there. The demands on your children will be far greater than on you.

The children should help in the preparations. Erect the mosquito nets for them to play in, let them pack and unpack the rucksacks, read them the story of how the elephant got his trunk (Kipling) or show them pictures of how the Eskimo catch their fish, and tell them all about aeroplanes.

Flights

There are only two classes of air travel: with children and without. The former is a nightmare and the latter (in relative terms) nirvana.There are airlines that go out of their way to cater for children and those who merely tolerate them. This is a field all of its own. Bear three rules in mind: do not rely on the airline to supply nappies; the best seats are behind the bulkhead between the aisles, and book them well in advance along with the cradle that hitches to the bulkhead (the children may not like it but it is useful for stowing toys and books). Give them a boiled sweet before each descent and take-off and if they want to run about the aircraft let them. They can't fall off, they can't get lost and they might make some friends. If they cause mayhem, it is easy to pretend they're not yours.

In the Field

Tired children are grumpy, and the grump-factor escalates in direct proportion to the number of time-zones you cross. The longer you allow for their sleeping patterns to get back to normal the better, particularly if, like ours, they are not too good at going to bed in the first place. If travelling to Southeast Asia, for example, find somewhere peaceful to spend a three or four-day adjustment period in one place before engaging in any major adventures.

The usual routine for independent travellers who have a month at their chosen destination is to see as much as possible. This does not work with children. Whatever plans you fancy by way of an itinerary, the most critical ingredient is flexibility. The yardstick of a successful journey is no longer the scaling of a mountain, the descent of a river, or a visit to the Taj Mahal. It is ensuring that laughter predominates over tears, that children get enough sleep, don't get too bored for too long and eat food they find edible with reasonable regularity. The Taj Mahal will leave them completely unmoved, but the goldfish (or whatever lives in those fountains that appear in the foreground of all the photographs of the Taj) will keep them going for hours.

It is no good thinking that your children ought, for the good of their cultural souls, learn to enjoy chowmien or boiled monkey's testicles. You will have plenty of problems without inviting arguments over food, so keep packets of dried mince and Safeway's noodles in the *rucksack that you have beside you at all times*. A little bit of what they fancy will do them good, and more to the point, what does them good does you better.

This principle, indeed, governs the whole journey and it is not one that is easy to contend with for fathers who are accustomed to seeing their children in the evenings and at weekends, nor for parents who have developed an efficient pre-children system for surviving and enjoying life on the road. Forget the stories about local babysitters; they might be on hand in Marbella but they are pretty scarce in Borneo. Even if you found someone you could trust, the children already have enough novelties to contend with.

The trick, as with all expeditions, is to select targets that will motivate the expedition members and build your plan around them. A two or three-day river journey, for example, is excellent value for children of almost any age; a dug-out canoe, a little bit of slightly exciting white water, a log cabin or longhouse, a couple of fishing rods, the prospect of sighting a crocodile or a bear and a camp-fire under the stars are all good ingredients for success.

Sightseeing should not be on the agenda at all. If parents must go to a museum, select it with reference to the running-around space. Driving long distances will only be a success if done for one day at a time and punctuated regularly with diversions, the excitement of which can be built up as the journey progresses.

Disasters

There will be several of these, even for the most circumspect and cautious of parents. The first one to avoid is losing your child at the airport, particularly at Terminal 3, Heathrow. We managed this very successfully when Katherine was two and a half. She was there, and then all of a sudden, she was not. Thirty minutes later, after public announcements and private panics, she appeared through the legs of the crowd bearing a plate of chocolate cakes. She seemed quite unmoved by the experience. We both vowed that this would be our last international journey with children.

The second disaster, which is less easy to avoid, is illness. This happened to Katherine within about four hours of the first disaster. She developed tonsillitis on the plane, which was then grounded in Abu Dhabi on the grounds that she had a contagious disease and there being no doctor available to suggest otherwise. We were not popular with the other 373 passengers on board.

The acquisition of a little basic knowledge, i.e. when to worry and get moving fast, and when to hold a hand and mutter sweet nothings, is the best that a parent can do. Aside from bellyache, your children are not more likely to be ill in Singapore or the Sahara than in Brighton or Benidorm. (A helpful book is *Travellers' Health; How to stay healthy abroad*, by Richard Dawood, published by OUP £7.99).

The third disaster is injury. As a general guideline, the louder they scream, the more likely they are to be all right. A bit of sticking plaster and a lot of cuddles usually suffice to mend the wound, and an exhaustive supply of both is recommended. Katherine, on this occasion aged four and a half, disappeared through the split-bamboo floor of a longhouse in Borneo in front of our very eyes. Directly below were the longhouse pigs. Her howls of protest, which were sweet music to us, put the pigs into a panic instead, and the subsequent rescue programme was further hampered by the fact that we were both stark naked, being engaged at the time in having what passes in longhouses for a bath. Equanimity was eventually restored by a combination of *Thomas the Tank Engine*, an unlimited supply of cuddles and quite a few bits of elastoplast. The following practical tips may help to avoid or mitigate these disasters:

1. If your child knows his/her name and address you are less likely to lose him/her permanently.

2. Watch out for monsoon drains. In the wet season, your child may be swept away and drowned, and in the dry season there are things in them that it would be better that your child did not eat or roll in.

3. Small children freeze more quickly than large children, so watch them carefully when the temperature drops.

4. Children dehydrate much more quickly than adults. Watch their level of fluid intake, particularly on long flights, in hot climates and, most of all, if they contract a fever or any illness that involves diarrhoea or vomiting. Get him/her to take water mixed with sugar and a little salt. The juice of an orange will make it more palatable.

5. If your child contracts a temperature over 103F find a doctor fast. If you are in a foreign capital, the British Embassy will help. Members of the expatriate community are often a good source of information about good doctors.

6. Select your medicine bag carefully before you go, preferably in consultation with your family doctor.

7. Children do not like malaria tablets. They will be more palatable if buried in a piece of fruit and nut chocolate with the aid of a penknife (thus disguising the pill as a nut). Even then, watch them carefully. Our youngest, aged one and three quarters when we took her to Borneo, used to tuck them in her cheek and spit them out anything up to an hour later when we were not looking. The other trick was to feed them to the nearest dog. We must have left a trail of malaria-free dogs behind us on our progress around Asia!

8. Sun cream is a vital commodity.

Hotels

Travelling with children is a great deal more strenuous than travelling without them. This is partly because children are an exhausting business anyway, but mainly because the routine of home life, which provides a measure of defence for beleaguered parents, is banished by the unpredictability of life on the road. This is where hotels come in: expensive ones – the sort that have a laundry service, room service, clean bathrooms for grubby children and a bar for distressed parents. A swimming pool with reclining chairs in the shade for Mum and Dad to take it in turns to sleep is an added bonus.

It may sound extravagant, but this is money well spent. It is only in this kind of circumstance that parents on holiday with their children have a chance to find some peace and even a little time on their own.

Age of Children

There are no rules about this. The best time to start, from the children's point of view, is when they start to enjoy the world about them. There is not much point before they can walk, and better still to wait until they are out of nappies, at least during the day. At the other end of the scale, when they reach their mid–teens they will be thinking in terms of becoming independent travellers themselves, so you have about twelve to fourteen years to show them the world. No time to waste.

Further Reading: *Travel with Children* (**Lonely Planet**)

THE PREGNANT TRAVELLER

by Dr Richard Dawood

Paradoxically, some of the hazards of travel during pregnancy have increased in recent years. This is partly due to the continuing spread of drug-resistant malaria, and also arises from the fact that countries with poor medical care have become increasingly accessible to the adventurous traveller.

Good ante-natal care has brought about a dramatic reduction in the complications of pregnancy, and travel has become almost too easy – it is often taken for granted. Perhaps the first hazard that the pregnant woman faces is a psychological one; pregnancy is not the ideal time for adventurous travel, but there is a widespread belief that travel to any country should be possible and that the fact of pregnancy should not be allowed to get in the way.

The early weeks of pregnancy are an important time to be at one's home base. It is necessary to begin planning ante-natal care, and to arrange routine blood tests and ultrasound scans. Morning sickness is common, and as a result many women have no particular interest in travel at this stage. Early pregnancy is also a time when miscarriage is relatively more common. Travel itself does not increase the risk of miscarriage, but the consequences in a country where medical facilities are poor could be serious. If bleeding is severe, blood transfusion may be necessary. In many poor countries the risk of AIDS from unscreened blood transfusions is high, and facilities for surgery (including supplies of sterile medical instruments) may be difficult to obtain. Poor medical treatment may have serious consequences for future pregnancies.

Towards the later stages of pregnancy, premature delivery becomes a possibility. It is not generally feasible to predict which pregnancies are at risk. Survival of a premature baby depends upon immediate access to sophisticated neonatal intensive care facilities, and the greater the prematurity the more important this becomes. Even when such facilities are available they may be extremely expensive, and the cost of neonatal intensive care may not be covered by travel insurance. Severely premature babies may not be able to travel for several weeks, adding further to the cost. Facilities for skilled medical care during delivery, surgical facilities and access to adequate blood transfusion facilities may again be a problem.

Aeroplanes do not make good delivery suites, and while air travel does not in itself induce labour, long flights should be avoided during late pregnancy; in any case, most airlines do not accept passengers beyond the 32nd week of pregnancy.

Chief Hazards

Two direct hazards of travel deserve mention. The first is the fact that there is an increased tendency for blood to clot in the veins of the legs: deep vein thrombosis. This tendency is accentuated by dehydration and prolonged immobility, both of which are common during long air journeys. The preventive measures are simple; drink plenty of fluids, stand up and walk around the aircraft cabin at least every two hours during a flight. The same applies to travel by road; take a rest and stretch your legs at least every one to two hours on a long journey.

The second hazard has received much attention over the last two years and relates to exposure to radiation. It has long been known that exposure to cosmic radiation at normal flying altitudes (35,000 feet) is more than 100 times greater than at ground level. There has been increasing concern about the effect of low–dose radiation and calculations show that it is possible for frequent flyers to build up a significant radiation exposure. Solar flares – bursts of energy on the surface of the sun – account for periodic increases in such exposure, and occur in unpredictable patterns. The radiation exposure for a return trip between London and New York is roughly equivalent to the exposure from a single chest x-ray (0.1 milliSievert); a return flight between London and Los Angeles would clock up 0.16 mSv. Calculations on the extent of harm associated with radiation exposure are generally based on exposure to much larger doses – for example such as occurred at Hiroshima.

It is difficult to be sure how such results extrapolate to lower doses and it is conceivable that low doses may be relatively more harmful. It is also difficult to document the effects, and to know whether subtle changes such as differences in intelligence or minor defects can be attributed to such exposure rather than nature.

For this reason, it has been suggested that pregnant women should avoid unnecessary long distance flights during the early, most vulnerable stages of pregnancy. Because Concorde flies at higher altitudes, radiation exposure might be expected to be higher; this is balanced by the shorter flying time, and overall exposure is generally reduced.

Vaccinations involving a live virus should be avoided during pregnancy: these include the oral polio vaccine, and the vaccines for measles, rubella and yellow fever. If a yellow fever vaccination certificate is necessary for travel, a medical certificate should be able to circumvent the requirement. Protection against polio can be provided using a killed, injectable vaccine. Vaccines that commonly cause a fever, such as Diphtheria and the injectable typhoid vaccine should be avoided during pregnancy and the BCG vaccine should not be given.

Drug-resistant malaria continues to spread, and there are now relatively few parts of the world where chloroquine and paludrine – the two safest drugs for use in pregnancy – provide reliable protection. Mefloquine (Lariam) is a newer antimalarial drug that is now widely used for travellers to resistant areas, but there are parts of the world – especially in the region of the Thai/Cambodian border – where resistance to mefloquine is common. Mefloquine has not been in use long enough for a clear picture to have emerged regarding its safety for use in pregnancy; there is certainly no clear evidence of a risk, but caution is still advisable, especially during early pregnancy.

The particular problem with malaria in pregnancy – particularly in women visiting malarial areas as compared with local inhabitants – is that malaria attacks tend to be considerably more severe. There is a high risk of death or of losing the baby. Chloroquine and Paludrine are considered safe during pregnancy. Insect repellents and other anti–insect measures (mosquito netting, suitable clothing, insecticide sprays, etc.) should also be used assiduously to reduce the number of mosquito bites. However, there is a strong case to be made for avoiding all unnecessary travel to malarial areas during pregnancy – particularly to areas with drug resistant malaria.

Other tropical or infectious diseases tend to affect pregnancy only indirectly, such as causing dehydration or a high fever, both of which put the foetus at risk. Great care should be taken to avoid diseases such as Dengue fever (by use of anti-insect measures) and to observe careful food and water hygiene measures.

If travel during pregnancy is considered essential, it is important to find out as much as possible about local medical care – names and addresses of doctors, hospitals, and facilities for neonatal intensive care should anything go wrong. It is also important to take particular care to insure adequate insurance cover for both mother and child.

Experts consider that the most suitable time for an overseas trip during pregnancy – provided that there have been no complications or other problems – is after the majority of the ante-natal tests have been completed and the main risks of miscarriage are over, but before the foetus becomes viable and would need neonatal intensive care facilities if born prematurely. This period lies between the 18th and 24th week of pregnancy, though high risk countries should definitely be avoided throughout the pregnancy.

THE OLDER TRAVELLER

by Cathy Braithwaite

A rough orange dirt track in the scorching Maasai Mara. In a small van, five travel journalists – the young and intrepid type – clutch their seats, knuckles white, jaws set, staring straight ahead, hating every minute of the bouncy, five–hour journey.

"These roads are just too bumpy, too uncomfortable. This is ridiculous – you can't possibly call this a holiday," complains one just as another van carrying two elderly but beaming tourists bounces by.

Lesson one: remember journalists have tender bottoms and mature travellers can be a darn sight more adventurous! In fact, these days, senior citizens think nothing of tackling the most demanding challenges, and relish new experiences at an age when they have the time and money. And this is the essence of the growing market for older travellers: time and money.

The retired can travel when and for as long as they choose. No jobs to groaningly return to; no children to force through school gates. You can break the journey up into manageable sections, pausing for periods of rest when necessary.

This is good news for any travel operator or airline. It's hardly a problem to sell travel in the high season but it's a different story off-peak, which is when the buying power of older travellers really comes into its own.

The benefits of off-peak travel are many and varied: you can holiday when temperatures are kinder (avoiding the searing heat), when there are fewer crowds, lower prices and beaming smiles from travel industry staff delighted by your off-peak business.

All you, the traveller, have to do is decide is where, how and when to go. There need not even by a "why". Your horizons are impressive and while your age may prove a restriction with some operators and car hire companies (usually for travellers aged over 65), you will doubtless be spoilt for choice.

Whether you are a fit older person who can happily cope with a two-week camp and trek holiday in the Himalayas, or if a lack of stamina precludes a two–month tour of Australia's outback or a six-month journey around the world, if you recognise your limitations and are realistic about your expectations, it is possible to make travel in retirement safe and exhilarating.

Destinations

Today even the most remote corners of the world are accessible and it is tempting to embark on the most unusual and exciting journey you can find. First establish what you seek from your holiday. Then weigh up your own ability to cope. Don't fool yourself; there is no shame in admitting that a whirlwind tour of six South American countries in 30 days would be too much for you. It is far worse to arrive at the start of what would be the experience of a lifetime, only to realise your holiday has turned into a test of endurance. The maxim "different strokes for different folks" is never more applicable than in the context of older people and travel. What to one person is tame and unadventurous is to another the most daring project they've ever contemplated. But whether you are the type who would take out a mortgage to buy the latest walking boots, or you follow the "have time table, will travel" school of travelling, building your own itinerary maximises your choice. You can choose how to travel, when and where to overnight, whether or not to spend a couple of days at a stopover, and you can make the whole experience as demanding or relaxed as you wish.

Preparation

While it is romantic and inspiring to think of intrepid 85-year-olds throwing more knickers than shirts into a bag and wandering wherever the whim leads, life is so much easier if you take a few basic precautions.

Explore visa requirements and apply as much in advance as possible. Passport regulations can also differ. If you suffer from a medical condition, make sure the destination you visit easily meets your needs. Also invest in insurance which will cover all eventualities including the cost of repatriation. Not all insurance policies include this, so do check. You may need to shop around for a policy that will cover a traveller of advancing years but they do exist!

See your doctor well before you embark on your trip. He'll be able to advise and arrange vaccinations and will ensure you are prescribed for any regular medicinal needs during your time overseas. Doctors can normally only prescribe a limited quantity under the NHS but your GP may be able to make an exception or advise you of what is available at your intended destination/s. The countries you visit may also impose restrictions on certain medicinal drugs and it is always a good idea to carry notification of any significant medical condition you suffer from.

Health

The older you are, the longer it takes to recover from an illness or broken bone. So it is common sense to preclude predicaments such as being stuck in a Nepalese hospital with a leg in plaster because you were convinced you could imitate that mountain goat – and failed. Assess your level of fitness before you decide where to travel.

Up-to-date information on the health problems of the country you plan to visit is available from clinics across the UK. Contact the **British Airways Travel Clinics** on 01276-685 040 for your nearest clinic, or try the **Medical Advisory Service for Travellers Abroad** (MASTA) on 0171-631 4408. It is also sensible to have a full medical check-up before you leave.

For a free copy of the Department of Health leaflet *The Traveller's Guide to Health* (ref T4) see your doctor, travel agent, local post office or call 0800-555 777. Remember, you will not enjoy your holiday if you are constantly tired. And if you feel tired, rest. Pushing yourself to the limit all day every day, will only cause the excitement of being in a new place and witnessing a different culture to pall.

Services for Older People

There are now a number of travel companies which provide holidays specifically for older travellers. Most offer packages but there is an increasing demand for holidays which combine the advantages of package deals (easy travel arrangements, the support of large organisations should you need help) with independence once you reach your destination.

A number of specialist operators now cater for older travellers. Forty years ago **Saga** pioneered holidays exclusively for over-60s, long before anyone else realised the market potential. The company has since moved on a continent or two from UK seaside hotel holidays. Saga includes travel insurance in the cost of all overseas travel and also offers a free visa service.

Other companies offering package holidays tailored to the needs of older people include Thomson's *Young at Heart*, Cosmos' *Golden Times*, Enterprise's *Leisurely Days*.

Practicalities

No matter how dauntless you are, nothing makes for a grouchier traveller than the lack of life's little comforts. So take small inflatable cushions to rest that weary head, cartons of drink to quench that thirst when you are nowhere near civilisation, use luggage with wheels or spread the load over a couple of soft-pack bags.

And if you're the type who would consider the ultimate travel experience ruined by a lack of milk, let alone tea, check that in the destination of your choice they also appreciate such basics!

See p.729 of the Directory for list of tour operators specialising in holidays for the older traveller.

THE DIABETIC TRAVELLER

by Robin Perlstein

Holidays and travel should be something to look forward, but it is important to plan ahead – even more so if you have diabetes and you want your journey (and blood sugars) to run smoothly.

Vaccination

Some countries do insist on certain immunisations for visitors, so it is wise to check in advance what (if any) vaccinations are required. There are no vaccinations contra–indicated because you have diabetes but be aware that some may affect blood sugar level control in the hours or days following.

Identification and Customs

It is sensible to wear some form of identification bracelet/necklace indicating you are diabetic – especially if taking insulin. It is wise to have a letter from your doctor stating you have diabetes and its mode of treatment or a British Diabetic Association photo identification card. This is very important if you are taken ill while away or if you have any problems going through Customs.

However, it is not essential to declare insulin/medicines/ syringes, as these are personal medical requirements.

Insurance

The cost and availability of medical services differs from country to country. Some countries have a reciprocal health care agreement with the UK and so emergency medical treatment is free or available at a reduced cost. Many countries provide no free medical services and all treatment and medical supplies must be paid for. This can be very costly and it is vital you take out adequate medical insurance.

Insurance policies that will reimburse you if you need to be flown home in an emergency are also advisable, and ensure that holiday insurance packages do not exclude pre–existing illnesses such as diabetes.

Illness

Being ill is unpleasant and can spoil a holiday especially if you are unwell in a country where foods are different and hygiene standards dubious. Knowing what to do regarding your medication and food intake is essential and so discuss this with your diabetes nurse specialist before you leave. Find out about anti-diarrhoea medication and motion sickness tablets as well as basic food hygiene. Having the name and address of the local Diabetes Association may also be of assistance if you are taken ill.

Medical Supplies

It is very important to take enough medical supplies (insulin, syringes etc.) so that valuable time and money is not wasted. For some items, your GP can only write a prescription for three months and so if you are holidaying for an extended period of time, consulting a doctor in the place you are visiting may be necessary. Many insulins and/or oral hypoglycaemics available in the UK are available in other countries. The manufacturers of most products can also give an idea of worldwide availability. Having the generic and brand name of medication is helpful as brand names often differ in other countries.

Remember that in some countries in Europe, 40 or 80 units per ml strength insulin is still used rather than U100. If you have to use U40 insulin the simplest thing to do is ask for U40 syringes at the same time. If U100 syringes are used for U40 insulin much *less* insulin will be taken than needed, and conversely if U100 insulin is used with U40 syringes *too much* insulin will be taken.

If you have any concerns about your pending travel, you should see your Diabetes Nurse Specialist before you travel. Blood glucose control should be reviewed as well as general health, and a rough plan may need to be mapped if you are crossing time zones.

On the Journey

Whether travelling by train, plane or automobile, you should take food with you in case of delays or extensions to journey times. Include quick-acting carbohydrates such as sugar and glucose tablets and the longer-acting variety: biscuits, fruit, sandwiches, etc. If you are prone to travel sickness, you may also need to take motion sickness tablets prior to your journey.

If driving, remember you should test blood sugars before getting into the car, and eat regularly. Testing blood sugars every two hours over long journeys to avoid hypoglycaemia is essential (if on sulphonylureas or insulin).

Long periods of sitting relatively motionless may lead to a rise in blood sugars. It is preferable to have sugars running a little high than low, as hypos can be very dangerous when driving and very embarrassing and inconvenient when on buses and trains. Remember though that you may be quite active at the beginning and end of a trip, i.e. when rushing to get to the station, packing the car and lifting luggage.

Airline and shipping companies are usually helpful about arranging for special diets and will provide information on meal times. Most travellers find they can manage on the standard meals provided, especially if carrying extra food for emergencies.

Packing for the Trip

Insulin should be packed in your hand luggage, as flying altitudes can cause baggage in the hold to freeze; what is more, checked luggage might be lost or delayed. It is wise to have all essential items such as your insulin, blood glucose meter, etc. kept close or at least split between yourself and a travelling companion.

Insulin Storage

Remember that extremes of temperature (hot or cold) can lead to a drop in activity of insulin rendering it less effective. At home, most insulin is probably kept in the refrigerator and can be stored in this way for up to two years or more (depending on the expiry date). Keeping the vials of insulin out of the refrigerator will not automatically mean it is unusable: insulin activity will remain stable for about one month at 25°C (normal room temperature). So long as temperatures are not extreme, the activity of the insulin should not be altered.

If there are no refrigerators available while travelling, vials should be kept in a cool, dark place avoiding hot spots such as the glove box or back shelf of the car. There are a number of insulin carriers available which have a frozen water container acting as a coolant. Freezer facilities must be available to make use of these and vials must not be in contact with the frozen blocks.

Alternatives include placing the insulin in a plastic sandwich box to keep it cool. Wide-necked vacuum flasks and polystyrene containers are a useful and cheaper option. If you are concerned that the activity of the insulin may have been affected, check its appearance: short acting insulins should remain clear, while longer acting insulins should appear cloudy, but with no odd pieces or lumps present.

Climate

Take sensible precautions in extremes of temperatures such as using a good sunscreen and maintaining a high fluid intake in hot climates; conversely, in cooler weather wear warm socks and comfortable shoes to protect your feet. Remember also that some blood glucose test strips will over-read in very warm climates, and under-read in colder climates.

Activity

Generally, holidaymakers are more active than normal, taking long walks, trying out new sports etc. Alternatively some might do less, missing out on usual daily activities and taking time to lie on the beach and relax. It is important that blood sugars are regularly monitored and recorded as this information will prove useful for future travel.

Food

Remember that a holiday is a time to sample new and different foods. Many people are daunted by the prospect of selecting from menus and eating food they are unaccustomed to while travelling. Yet, food in most places consists of the same basic ingredients: fruit, vegetables, meats and usually plentiful supplies of starchy foods such as rice, potatoes, bread and pastas.

An increase in the amount of alcohol consumed is a common occurrence while on holiday but remember it can lower blood sugars if taking certain tablets or insulin. Therefore, it is wise to eat when drinking or even wiser to drink lower or no alcohol alternatives. Remember to drink plenty of water, but if unsure of the purity of the local water supply, drink bottled water only.

Holiday Check-list

- Ensure you have had all the required vaccinations
- Diabetic ID Card and Doctor's letter
- Adequate travel insurance (which does not exclude diabetes) is imperative
- Make sure you have thought about how to deal with becoming ill while away
- The name of the local Diabetes Association if travelling to a foreign country
- Take sufficient supplies (approximately twice as much as required normally) of: Insulin, syringes, oral hypoglycaemic agents (generic and trade name), blood glucose meter and spare batteries, testing strips, lancets, needle clipper, any other medication, glucose gel, glucose tablets/sweets, Glucagon, tissues and longer-acting carbohydrate foods (biscuits/bread/fruit)
- Useful foreign phrases
- Currency of the country being visited (to purchase food/drinks on arrival).
- Insulin storage containers – if you feel the climate/circumstances warrant it
- Pack a good sunscreen and comfortable socks and shoes for walking
- Record Book

For more information contact the **British Diabetic Association** (10 Queen Anne Street, London W1M 0BD, tel: 0171-323 1531). The BDA produces general travel information for diabetics as well as information specific to certain countries.

See p.730 of the Directory for more helpful names and addresses

THE DISABLED TRAVELLER

by Quentin Crewe

My doctor, when a patient asks whether it is wise for him or her to travel, nearly always says, "Yes, it will do you good".

He takes the view that, unless it is obviously impossible or plainly dangerous any patient who wants to go will be happier going. Only twice in his long career has he lost a patient. He still reckons that it was a good way for them to go and they might just have well died if they had stayed at home.

This is the principle I have always worked on. I live my life in a wheelchair, as I have muscular dystrophy, but I have been round the world many times. I have been blown up by a land mine in Mauritania, nearly drowned in Niger, robbed by bandits in Brazil, lost in the Saudi Arabian desert, embraced by a snake in Kenya, threatened by a bear in India, but I am still here, as John Major has been known to say.

Disability takes many forms. What is true for one person does not necessarily apply to the next one, but my hope is that as many disabled people as possible will, as it were, have a go. They will have many agreeable surprises. Who for instance would guess that Bogota is one of the best cities in the world for wheelchairs, almost every pavement carefully ramped. It is a pleasure to wander around, but I would carry a little mugging money with you.

Obviously, the easiest way to travel is by car and I must admit that most of my major journeys have been by road, including 24,000 miles round South America in a Toyota Landcruiser, which involved 1000 miles floating down the Amazon river for five days and nights on a barge, sleeping on the deck, under some lorries.

Crossing to the Continent will presumably be easier when the Eurotunnel is working, but the ferries are helpful. I have found that, if I ask politely and firmly enough, the captains of hovercrafts will let me stay in the car for the crossing. This might be nerve-wracking for claustrophobics, though they do give one a life-jacket.

Air is my next preferred method of travel. This has improved immensely in the last few years. On the whole, I do not warn anyone of my situation when I buy a ticket, taking the view that disabled people should be able to do things on the spur of the moment, like everyone else. I just turn up at the airport and leave it to them. I have found that if one goes to a travel agent and alerts them, they create problems and ask for doctor's certificates to say one is fit to travel.

I have seldom had trouble. Once some years ago in Tunis, I was asked to sign an indemnity saying that if there were a crash and I impeded someone's escape I would be liable. It seemed a reasonable chance to take. Forgetting my own rules, not long ago in India I went myself into the airline office. They asked for a doctor's certificate. There was a doctor in the same street. For a few rupees, he wrote a certificate to my dictation.

In more remote places, the airport may not have one of those narrow chairs for getting disabled people to their seats and up and down aircraft steps. On the other hand, in remote places, there are usually strong, helpful people ready and eager to carry you on and off the plane. If this could hurt you, it is worth checking beforehand. I have often been carried off upside down with all my change falling out of my pocket to the delight of the helpers. If you are flying with your own chair it is important to make sure they have put it in the hold. Taking off from Beirut once, I looked out of the window to see my chair sitting abandoned on the runway.

A major drawback to air travel is the impossibility of getting to the toilets. Fortunately air travel is de-hydrating and it is amazing what, with the help of a friend, can be achieved discreetly, by a man at least, under a rug, as I dare say members of the 'mile high club' would testify. Otherwise a G.P. could give advice about incontinence aids.

Before arrival, it is essential to check that the pilot has radioed ahead to ask for help to be ready at your destination.

Rail travel in Britain used to mean a chilly ride in the guard's van. British Rail have changed all that, but unlike the airlines it is well to warn them ahead, especially when there is a question of taking a seat out to make room for your chair.

Additional Information for Disabled Travellers

by Carey Ogilvie

The world has become so accessible in the last twenty years or so, that no one blinks an eye lid if, on the spur of the moment, you go to France for the weekend. The ease with which we are able to travel the world improves annually. With more people travelling, the industry fights for our custom, airlines negotiate new routes, operators offer more and more irresistible deals and with the abundance of guide books and information, the world is our oyster. However it has not been the same for disabled travellers. Although there are numerous organisations and charities which have offered help and advice, it is only recently that the attitude has changed within the tourist industry. As with most changes in any industry, it has been market forced. There are 14 million disabled persons in Europe.

Success as a disabled traveller often depends on attitude of mind and great things can be achieved, though you may not always find that the system works for you. Still, these are some organisations that are around to help you (an ever increasing number).

The two most useful contacts other than **RADAR** are **Tripscope** (mentioned later) and the **Holiday Care Service** (2nd Floor, Imperial Buildings, Victoria Road, Horley, Surrey, RH6 7PZ, tel: 01293 774535). The latter has been instrumental in the changes of attitude within the industry. Holiday Care Service is a registered charity, and was established in 1981, since then it has been going from strength to strength. Three years ago with Judith Chalmers, their Vice Chairman, they set up the Holiday Care Awards to encourage a better reception for disabled travellers, to recognise companies that offer superior facilities and to raise the profile of disabled travel. Holiday Care Service publishes fourteen regional guides on accommodation which are accessible for the wheelchair user, all of which can be booked through them at discounted prices.

Cars

Travelling by car is probably the easiest way of travelling, especially if it's your own car. Discounts abound with many of the ferry companies giving concessions: contact the **Disabled Motorist Federation** (tel: 01743-761889) or the **Disabled Drivers' Motor Club** (tel: 01832-734724). The **Disabled Drivers' Association** is also worth contacting for advice and information (tel: 01508-489449). For those who want to have the freedom of travelling in their own vehicle, but don't own one, help is at hand. **Wheelchair Travel Ltd**, based in Guildford (tel: 01483-233640) has five adapted mini-buses which can be hired either on a self-drive basis or with a driver. All can carry wheelchair users and are fitted with tail-lifts for easy access, perfect for the family holiday. **Hertz** have adapted cars available for hire in most international cities: contact Hertz (UK) Ltd, Radnor House, 1272 London Road, Norbury, London SW16 (tel: 0181-679 1777)

Buses and Trains

Although this is improving, public transport for the disabled passenger can depend on a sense of humour and a great deal of patience. However there is a wealth of advice and help on offer. Perhaps the most informative is **Tripscope**, The Courtyard, Evelyn Road, London W4 5JL (tel: 0181-994 9294). The service is free, and although they are not a travel agent and therefore can not arrange your bookings, their suggestions pave the way. **The Department of Transport** publish a guide called "Door to Door", this is also useful for the initial planning.

London Transport are slowly getting their act together. Although wheelchairs are no longer banned from the Underground, the tube is still inaccessible, unlike the Metro in Amsterdam. However, London can still be crossed without lining the pocket of a black cab. **The Unit of Disabled Passengers** set up by London Transport in 1984, publish a series of leaflets detailing facilities available, (tel: 0171-918 3312). Stationlink offers an hourly shuttle service linking all the mainline railway stations, this is free to holders of the British Rail Disabled Persons Card, but can take hours to get from one station to another —not ideal. Airbus routes between Heathrow and Central London are equipped with hydraulic lifts.

As for British Rail, it is improving but is a long way from being perfect. I am afraid there are still those stations that, if you are in a wheelchair and on the wrong platform, it seems to be tough luck. However they do have a leaflet "British Rail and Disabled Travellers" giving general advice and information and, if given advance warning, will try to do everything to make your journey more pleasant. They also issue the "Disabled Persons Railcard" which can entitle you to at least a third off all rail travel.

In Europe there is also room for improvement, with the exception of the new Eurostar trains. In some countries, there can be the problem of higher trains and lower platforms, not very user-friendly. It is therefore advisable to contact the UK offices of the relevant railways. Norway leads the way in Europe with specially adapted coaches for wheelchair users, with hydraulic lifts and accessible toilets. Advance ticket purchase is necessary though, contact: **Scandinavian Travel Service**, Bergham Mews, London W14 0HN (tel: 0171-559 6666).

As with trains anywhere in the world check on the width of the corridors, most I am afraid are too narrow for the standard wheelchair.

Flying

There are two schools of thought on this one. Do you alert the airline and find out all you can about the facilities at the airport, or like Quentin Crewe do you turn up and let them do the organising? If you prefer to do the former, *Care in the Air*, published by the **Air Transport Users Council** (ATUC) gives general advice for disabled air passengers. It is available from ATUC, 5th Floor, 103 Kingsway, London WC2B 6QX (tel: 0171-242 3882. **The Disabled Living Foundation,** 380-384 Harrow Road, London W9 2HU (tel: 0171-289 6111) produce a booklet in conjuction with British Airways called *Flying High* (£2.50 including P&P), this practical guide takes the reader through the flight from booking to returning home.

Organised Tours

There are numerous companies organising tours for disabled travellers, some are mixed ability tours, others solely for the handicapped, some are charities and others work on a commercial basis. The opportunities, however, are end-less. One of the most inspiring charities is **Across,** who organise tours and pil-grimages for the severely disabled in their Jumbulances. They started in 1972 with a transit van to Lourdes, they now have ten Jumbulances and as well as weekly trips to Lourdes, they also organise tours to parts of Europe and the Holy Land. For more information contact **Across Trust**, Bridge House, 70/72 Bridge Road, East Molesey, Surrey KT8 9HF (tel: 0181-783 1355).

For the more active and adventurous, **Project Phoenix Trust**, 68 Rochfords, Coffee Hall, Milton Keynes MK6 5DJ (tel: 01908-678038) is a non-profit organisation running visits overseas. These tours involve a lot of activity and are probably best suited to energetic and strong disabled people.

For those who are bored with this world, there is a club that can show you another ... Going Down is a diving club run by Leon Golding. He teaches diving to mixed ability groups in this country and then organises diving expeditions to the Red Sea, Canaries and various destinations in the Mediterranean. He can be contacted at 46 Hill Drive, Hove, Sussex BN3 6QL (tel: 01273-566616). Another sporting holiday on offer is skiing. As they say at the Uphill Ski Club, "Why shouldn't you have a wheel chair at the top of a mountain?". The club was founded over eighteen years ago and is committed to providing winter sporting activities for people with a wide range of disabilities including, CP, spinabifida, epilepsy, learning difficulties, head injuries and sensory handi-caps. The enjoyment and the morale boost felt by the skiers is illustrated by their letters, "I hope that more disabled people will, in the future, be able to experience the exhilaration that we were lucky enough to feel". For further information contact 12 Park Crescent, London W1N 4EQ (tel: 0171-636 1989).

Useful Books

With more and more disabled people travelling, that ever present market force has produced a new wealth of information. However some of the most informative guides have been around for years, for example **RADAR** publishes 2 books annually, *Holidays in the British Isles* and *Holidays and Travel Abroad*. As is to be expected they are a mine of information: being totally independent, they are unbiased in their advice. Both the RAC and AA publish their own guides, both are informative and packed full with useful names and addresses. One of the most encouraging books is *Nothing Ventured* edited by Alison Walsh, it was published in 1991, but is still available in most good bookshops. The book is a collection of tales by disabled travellers all over the world. Not only is the book inspiring but at the end of each country are useful travel notes. A second edition is in the pipeline. Alison Walsh has been an inspiration to many, she has written an excellent booklet to accompany the BBC Holiday Programme, which is a must for any disabled traveller, to obtain a copy, send a large self-addressed envelope with a 43p stamp to Disabled Traveller, PO Box 7, London W3 6XJ.

New books include the *Smooth Ride Guides*, the first edition on Australia and New Zealand was published in April 1994, the second on the USA is hitting the bookshops in March 1995.

As Alison Walsh writes "There is no such thing as a holiday which is unsuitable for disabled people: everything depends on the degree of disability and the attitude of the traveller..."

See p.732 of the Directory for more useful names and addresses

THE MUSICAL TRAVELLER

by Sarah Thorowgood

The troubadours who played at the courts of 12th and 13th century southern French lords were certainly not the first itinerant, travelling musicians, but over the years, they have done a lot for the image. Music and travel are as closely linked as religion and travel: just as millions of Muslims make the pilgrimage to Mecca, so do music lovers from all over the world brave the mud and crowds of Glastonbury in Somerset every summer or what has been described as the 'aesthetic overload' of the *Maggio Musicale* festival in Florence. The importance of music as a cultural window for the alien traveller is undeniable, whether it be through wandering round India with a guitar strapped to the back, picking up a buck or two along the way, or through hunting out music festivals and concerts worldwide from the pre-freeze Athabascan Indian gatherings in Alaska to the sweltering Cajun revelries of New Orleans.

As with all great vocal music, the songs of the troubadours entertained principally through their lyrical reflection and satire of the complicated politics of Occitania (now southern France). Today, travellers can draw on traditional, local music wherever they go, either to give them a more rounded view of where they are or to provide them with a starting point. This is the beauty of music – when conventional means of communication break down, music always manages to transcend this barrier. It is not necessary to be capable of reading the whole of *Don Quixote* in the original script to understand the warmth and passion of the Andalucians when attending one of the many Flamenco *ferias* held throughout the region. Through dance in particular, music becomes a universal language for those who cannot communicate in words. As for the musicians, jamming with others from around the globe, must surely be the easiest way to find common ground and express ideas and, in the words of Carl Jefferson, founder of the Concord Jazz Festival in California, "Music is the true Esperanto".

Busking It

Musical travellers come in many guises, perhaps the most obvious being the busker-traveller, the closest relation of the troubadour. Anyone travelling alone with a guitar will not take long to make friends whether he heads rather predictably for Kathmandu or really takes up the challenge and goes to Andalucia, where he will be in competition with some of the greatest Flamenco guitar players in the world. Busking in Europe can be a lucrative business if one finds the right spot – but this is a big 'if'. The best way to find out is to watch, and more importantly ask, other buskers. You may find a certain degree of protectiveness over pitches, but they are an easy-going breed who will usually be more than happy to have someone new to talk to and even jam with. Generally speaking there are organised rotas for the most sought-after tourist areas of cities and you definitely will not make those promised friends if you do not recognise and respect it. Another sure way to alienate yourself is to 'set up your stall' too near someone else's. It is also worth remembering that busking, as unlicensed street trading, is illegal in most countries, and you should expect to be 'moved on' every now and then. It can, like any illegal, and therefore officially uncontrolled, activity also get you into hot water with the more unsavoury side of street life as this example of a busker's experiences in Taipei (taken from Susan Griffith's *Work Your Way Around the World*) shows:
"Things were fine until strange red graffiti appeared overnight near the spot where I stood. A man who 'represented' some people (gangsters?, market traders?) told me to stop, or something might 'happen' to me."

The main problem with busking, or attraction, depending on how you see the world, is that it will never be a cut and dried enterprise and the only advice that one can give is somewhat obvious. The best way to learn is from the experience of others if you have never done it before and even this will generally turn out to be wildly dissimilar from your own experience once you have braved the streets. One friend of mine made a fortune waving a tambourine around enthusiastically, if inexpertly, to the strains of Beatles' tunes in Tokyo, whereas another more musically inclined friend told me that he had not seen a single busker in Japan in the two whole years that he lived there. Perhaps, on reflection, this explains the rather bizarre phenomenon of being able to earn a 'fortune' merely by thumping out a dubiously-tuned rendition of *Love Me Do* – the Japanese are obviously starved of quality buskers, so there may well be a niche in the market here for the more enterprising musician!

There are a few points, however, that might stand you in good stead.

1. Learn to play an instrument – unless you are of the busking school of thought that sees greater financial potential in being paid to go away.

2. The best places to busk in are tourist areas – places where there are a high proportion of people with itching palms who cannot wait to throw their money away. It is no good, I am reliably informed, busking on the outskirts of Addis Ababa!

3. Remember the visual side of busking. It is much easier to command people's attention if you look as attractive or, failing that, as ridiculous as possible. Puppets dangling on the end of your guitar and silly costumes attract the attention of children, who can be very good at spending their parents' money.

4. The best money spinners are the old favourites, as the Beatles' popularity in Japan shows. If you have the nerve, or are desperate enough, finding a convenient terrace restaurant and serenading the occupants can prove highly lucrative if you go round with a hat after your set and look suitably impoverished.

The Music Festival Junkie

Music festivals worldwide are so numerous and varied that being "spoilt for choice" seems like an understatement. Selectivity is the key and having an ear to the ground to seek out the unheard of gems that are waiting to be discovered. Most good guide books will list all the important festivals of the country or area that they cover, but if you need a bit more information or if you want to choose your destination by virtue of the festivals on offer, one of the best sources of information is the internet (see end of article). For those lesser mortals who are not on-line, you could do a lot worse than picking up a copy of Tom Clynes's book *Wild Planet* (Invisible Ink Press). This lists festivals in countries all over the world from the Australian Bush Music Festival in New South Wales, where the emphasis seems to be on didjeridooing and beer brewing to the great Salzburg classical music festival which takes over the "Musical Capital of Europe" for six weeks in July and August. Here "superlatives abound" – unsurprisingly, considering that the tickets will set you back more that $300.

On this note, there is something to be said for getting crushed by a crowd of 100,000 people at Glastonbury and paying £70 for the privilege, whilst listening to big name bands, but many music festivals cost nothing or very little. The Copenhagen Jazz Festival, which invades the city for ten days in July, is one of 400 or so jazz festivals in Europe every summer, but unlike so many "terribly serious" jazz events, this is reputedly special for its informality and spontaneity. Even better is the fact that of the 130-odd concerts, 80 per cent of them are free. On the other hand, the Newport Jazz Festival, Rhode Island ($108 for the weekend), made famous by the film *High Society*, and credited with launching the careers of such legends as Count Basie and Duke Ellington to name but a few, is undoubtedly a very different and more sober affair, given the gravitas behind its reputation, but then, where better to listen to jazz than its birthplace? The lesson here is that although money may guarantee excellent performers, it will generally be at the expense of the atmosphere.

There is certainly no danger of lack of atmosphere in Trinidad at Carnival time and no better way to witness the colour of this diverse Caribbean island.

Dubbed the "sexiest carnival in the world", here you will dragged, kicking and screaming through the streets by a tide of calypso-crazed revellers. The steel drum, invented in Trinidad after World War II, is a powerful force here which erupts once a year at carnival time in the form of the *Extempo* competitions, where the competitors have to sing improvised calypso songs to random subjects pulled out of a hat, every street corner of Port of Spain is wired up to the lamp posts with immense sound systems and at the semi-final stage the remaining contestants heap melodious rhyming insults on each other to the roars of the crowd.

But what exactly is it that makes a music festival great? According to Tom Clynes, it is a mixture of many things – all difficult to put your finger on. Aside from excellent performers, place is a big consideration, "a backdrop of snow-capped peaks or stunning urban skyline" can make all the difference. But perhaps the most important factor is a sense of community and spontaneity. Festivals that turn into all-night parties, where local food is served in abundance and where the spectators can become participants will probably create the longest memories.

Music Tourism

For those who prefer to don a more sedate image of a musical traveller, how about checking out a specialist tour operator? There are several tour operators who organise musical tours, mainly in Europe and North America. Classical music lovers in particular seem to be catered for by ACE Study Tours (see Directory for details). Why not take a trip round Italy visiting Verdi's birthplace near Piacenza, the church where he was Christened and learned to play the organ and take in a whole variety of concerts culminating in a performance of *La Traviata* in the Teatro Carlo Felice in Genoa. Alternatively, you could travel with Festival Tours and get the inside story on the New Orleans jazz scene. This is a company set up by the wife of the local jazz musician, thus ensuring plenty of insider muso-gossip.

For the armchair traveller, there is always the option of getting the world to come to you. "World Music" festivals are very much on the increase both in Europe and The States. WOMAD (World of Music Arts and Dance) which takes place on the Reading Festival site in Berkshire, in the UK, has everything from the depths of Africa, the heights of Asia and the edges of South America. Whatever takes your fancy, whether it be the Bang on a Can post-minimalist, experimental music festival in Manhattan, where cutting edge musicians congregate from all over the world, or Gregorian chanting in Wroclaw, Poland, music can bring your travels to life with a greater richness than you might think possible. Who knows, you may well end up being serenaded by Mongolian throat singers?

See p.724 of the directory for musical tour operators
Further Reading: *Music Festivals from Bach to Blues* (**Invisible Ink Press**)
Wild Planet (**Invisible Ink Press**)
The Opera Lover's Guide to Europe (**Robson Books**)
Festival Finder **http://www.festivalfinder.com** ■

GETTING THERE BY AIR
Chapter 4

THE FUTURE OF AIR TRAVEL

by Simon Beeching

In early 1984 a "new low price" for a Round-the-World airfare of £1250 was announced by British Airways/Air New Zealand. Suddenly jet travel not only made foreign holidays affordable for mass tourism to the Mediterranean, but the falling price of airfares also opened up new distant horizons for everyday travel. Now, in the late 1990s the price of a similar ticket has fallen to as low as £700, with a generation of students already having grown up with the concept of taking a "year out" before university to see the world on just such a ticket.

IATA figures for 1996 show a total of just under 400 million air passengers world-wide and project that this will increase by seven per cent a year to over 520 million by the year 2010. Growth in North America and Europe will be relatively slower with a huge growth predicted in the emerging economies of the Far East.

Such a rapid increase in air travel world-wide for both leisure and business purposes has seen travel grow rapidly from "luxury goods" status to become the biggest industry in the world, ahead of even the oil industry. With such massive economic considerations at stake, the industry is rapidly expanding its interests globally with airlines extending their route networks world-wide. Even British Airways has taken the decision to throw off its "national carrier" image and take on an image of "World Airways" through new ownership or marketing alliances with other airlines around the world and a new livery promoting its multi-national interests.

Travel retailing and tour operating have also become global businesses. American Express has taken the top world travel agency slot after its purchase of Thomas Cook Business Travel and the UK based Airtours has become the world's largest airtour operator following the acquisition of similar companies in Scandinavia, Canada and North America.

Naturally, such huge growth will also precipitate huge change. Larger aircraft will be needed to ease congestion at airports, whilst modern technology will continue to make aircraft quieter. The environmental lobby will also step up its efforts to minimise the impact of tourism on historic monuments, coastlines and the bio-diversity and cultural heritage of host countries (as well as the ozone layer).

One worrying factor for the continuing growth of international travel, however, is the gradual realisation of governments that the travel industry is not only an important service industry in its own right – contributing a lion's share of the economy in many emerging countries – but is also an easy taxation target. Airport, departure and service taxes are escalating everywhere, as exemplified by the recent introduction of APD (Air Passenger Duty) in the UK (it was to be doubled in November 1997), as well as a vastly increased insurance premium tax on travel insurance. Such local taxes already contribute as much as ten per cent to the price of an air ticket and recent trends indicate that this figure is set to increase still further.

The technological revolution is also bound to have a significant impact on the way air travel is booked and administrated. There is no doubt that the ability to buy travel products electronically from the home or the office will pave the way for a significant increase in "home shopping" for travel. Electronic ticketing and boarding passes (ATB's) and Smart Cards are also likely to make the whole process of booking/paying/checking-in and boarding much more streamlined. It is possible that all you will have to do in the future is hold up your plastic Smart Card to various sensors, on which your bank details for payment, itinerary, frequent flyer points, meal preferences etc. are encrypted – in order to pay for and walk straight through the airport to your seat on the aircraft. Indeed this technology will finally tackle one of the major frustrations of air travel: waiting in line.

Fast-track check-in, airport lounges and even beds and massages in the air and shower suites on arrival are already provided in order to make travel as hassle free and comfortable as possible. Further investment in additional comforts are bound to continue apace as airlines fight for business.

Who knows what additional boundaries air travel has yet to cross in the 21st century? NASA has already announced that it is seriously considering defraying the cost of a new generation of Shuttle flights by taking fare-paying passengers into space; and aircraft significantly faster than Concorde, flying at much higher altitudes, have already been designed, if not yet cleared for take-off. Or perhaps the explosive growth of air travel will be seen as only a twentieth century phenomenon, curtailed in the following century by environmental constraints and by the fact that modern video conferencing techniques will make travel less necessary. Furthermore with the future possibility of being surrounded by 3-D holograms of a place, with the sights, smells and sounds, you may simply choose to book virtual trips to far-flung places, without leaving home at all.

Air Transport Associations p.737, Airports World-wide p.755 Airport/departure Taxes p.760 Airpasses p.762 of the Directory

IN CONTROL OF AVIATION

by Philip Ray and Annie Redmile

The world of air travel is littered with the initials of the official bodies which on the face of it control virtually every aspect of flying – ICAO, IATA, FAA, CAA etc. It could well be asked why this particular branch of economic activity should be singled out for special treatment by governments. After all, the international shipping industry is not subject to nearly the same constraints, and a virtually free market exists. But when the governments of the world met in Chicago in 1944 to prepare the way for the post-war pattern of civil aviation, they agreed the fundamental principle, now enshrined in international law, that each nation has sovereignty over its own airspace.

This means that any government has the power to grant or refuse permission for the airline of another country to overfly its territory, to make a technical stop – to refuel, for instance – or to pick up and set down fare-paying passengers. By extension of this principle, governments also lay down the conditions under which foreign airlines may pick up traffic (for instance, by agreeing the routes which can be served, imposing the routes which can be served, imposing restrictions on capacity or approving the fares that can be charged). In practice, all these questions are resolved between governments on a bilateral basis in air service agreements (ASAs) which are subject to termination by either side after giving notice. The best-known ASA is the Bermuda Agreement which governs air services between the UK and the USA.

Regulation

Nevertheless, every government in the world also exercises regulatory control over its own airline industry to a greater or lesser extent. Perhaps the strongest argument in favour of this is the uncontroversial need to supervise safety standards. Otherwise, it is argued, airlines might cut corners in order to save costs. The main area of current debate and controversy is the extent to which regulatory bodies should exercise control over the airlines in terms of the allocation of routes, the entry of new carriers into the market, and the fares charged.

The USA pioneered complete deregulation in 1978, allowing its airlines to open up new routes or move into markets already served by other carriers without having to seek approval. Their fares, similarly, are not subject to control. Australia followed suit and liberalised its domestic services in 1990. Canada has also gone almost the whole hog towards complete deregulation. In the UK, the opening up of new domestic routes and the setting of fares have both been liberalised, but limitations on the opening of new services at Heathrow have meant that complete deregulation has so far proved impractical.

Long running talks – unresolved at the time of writing (July 1997), have been taking place between the UK and US. Britain would like freedom for its airlines to operate beyond major gateway airports in America. The Americans want greater access to Heathrow.

In 1997 the European Union completed the lengthy task of liberalising its air routes – extending the freedom of European carriers to operate anywhere within the EU's borders to domestic services. This enables a UK arline, for example, to operate a stand alone operation in another country, carrying fare paying passengers, say, between Frankfurt and Munich.

With liberalisation out of the way, some in Brussels argued that the EU should negotiate aviation issues with outside governments as a single entity – but there was certain to be fierce resistance to the idea from member states.

There is also freedom now to set fares but the authorities do have a right to withdraw a fare if they judge it to be unreasonably high or harshly competitive or predatory to the extent that some carriers could be driven out of business as a result.

Most European countries have one major international flag carrier dominating their scheduled airline network service. The world's airlines suffered huge losses in the early nineties and many of Europe's airlines fared particularly badly. This led to a number of "state-owned" airlines going to Brussels in an attempt to get approval for "state-aid" to be awarded. This issue remains highly contentious with a firm body of opinion maintaining that such sponsorship does nothing to encourage fair competition.

Independent airlines such as British Midland and Virgin Atlantic have done much to introduce competition on certain routes and the result has been lower fares to those destinations. However the fatal TWA crash in Florida recently has also raised some vital questions about the safety implications of very low cost carriers in a completely deregulated market.

At the heart of the debate is the balance that has to be struck between the need always to give the consumer good value and the equally strong requirement to maintain a strong, healthy airline industry. Regulation in such a world-wide industry is still clearly an essential element and a more detailed look at some of the organisations and bodies responsible for it may be helpful.

International Civil Aviation Organisation (ICAO): ICAO is not exactly a household name, and its activities are rarely publicised in the lay press, but it plays an important behind-the-scenes role in laying down standards and controlling the legal framework for international civil aviation. It is based in Montreal and was set up following the Chicago Convention of 1944 which laid the foundations of the international air transport system as we know it today. It is made up of representatives of some 150 governments and its controlling bodies are the Assembly, which normally meets every three years, and the Council, which controls its day-to-day activities.

The organisation also lays down standards for air navigation, air traffic control, technical requirements and safety and security procedures. It was also responsible for concluding international agreements on the action needed to deter aircraft hijackings. ICAO works closely with the United Nations and controls assistance development programmes in Third World countries under the UN Development Programme.

ICAO came into the headlines when it investigated the shooting down of the Korean Airlines Boeing 747 in September 1983. Its report was inconclusive but it led to the calling of an extraordinary session of the Assembly in 1984 which agreed an amendment to the Chicago Convention, for the first time embodying in international law a specific ban on the use of weapons against civil aircraft. On the economic front, ICAO monitors the finances and traffic patterns of the world's airlines and issues research reports from time to time.

International Air Transport Association (IATA): IATA is the trade association which represents more than 98 per cent of the scheduled airline system which carries 825,000 passengers and 25,000 tonnes of freight ever day. Some 140,000 of those passengers on any one day are interlining – in other words using the service of one or more airlines on one trip on one ticket.

IATA provides a range of services to its members including the essential

IATA Clearing House and bank settlement plan which makes the international sale and use of airline tickets possible.

Traditionally, IATA airlines used to meet in regular traffic conferences to set fares for the coming season so that all fares within, say, Europe, would be increased by a given percentage. Nowadays the system is much more flexible and airlines increasingly file new fares on a unilateral or bilateral basis without any intervention by IATA. However, the association still comes into its own in emergencies such as the Gulf crisis in autumn 1990, when it agreed special across-the-board fare increases to take account of the increased cost of aviation fuel and higher insurance premiums.

Many of IATA's activities are carried out behind the scenes. While ICAO has been agreeing standards at an international level on technical matters like air safety procedures, meteorological services, engineering and so on, it has had to lean heavily on the advice of the airlines via IATA. From the passenger's point of view, the greatest benefit has come from agreements between IATA members on a standard form of airline ticket which enables the passenger to travel round the world with, for example, six different airlines and make only one payment which is then apportioned between the carriers by the IATA Clearing House. It is also IATA which lays down the consumer protection standards for the travel agencies which it appoints to sell international air tickets.

The association has also been active in campaigning against government–imposed increases in user charges (which are ultimately reflected in higher fares) and in fighting for the elimination of airport red tape by encouraging Customs and Immigration authorities to improve the traveller's lot with innovations like the red/green channel system. In 1990 IATA launched an international campaign to create awareness of the problems of congested airports and airspace and to rally public support for government action. This campaign, organised by the Air Transport Action Group (ATAG), has gathered momentum and achieved some success. The work carried out by ATAG continues to be relevant as congestion in the air and on the ground constrains the development of service which in turn inhibits consumer choice.

US Department of Transportation (DoT): With the disbanding of the US Civil Aeronautics Board (CAB) in 1985 and the implementation of complete deregulation, the Federal Department of Transportation's powers are limited. Its most important role is to define and implement policy on international aviation, including the selection of American airlines to operate on specific routes. It also co-operates with the State Department on the negotiation of bilateral air-service agreements with other countries. With the assistance of the Department of Justice, it administers the anti-trust laws with the aim of ensuring that carriers do not reach any restrictive agreements behind the scenes, as well as being responsible for approving or disallowing airline mergers.

US National Transportation Safety Board: Independent body that will investigate air crashes.

Federal Aviation Administration (FAA): Not affected by the demise of the CAB, the FAA deals mostly with airport management, air traffic control, air safety and technical matters. Despite their complete economic freedom, all US airlines still have to conform with FAA safety standards.

Canadian National Transportation Agency (CNTA): Transport policy in Canada went through its biggest period of reform for twenty years as a result of the National Transportation Act which was passed by the Canadian Parliament in 1987. The old Canadian Transport Commission was replaced by a new body, the National Transportation Agency, which operates at arm's length from the Ministry of Transport and whose brief includes not only airlines but also railways, shipping, pipelines and so on.

The new regime also ushered in a virtually complete deregulation of the domestic aviation scene so that airlines are now free to open new routes and introduce new fares without needing approval. However, services in the far north of Canada are still regulated because of the public-service need of maintaining regular air communications in this sparsely-populated area.

The Ministry of External Affairs is responsible for issues of international relations in civil aviation in conjunction with the Ministry of Transport and the National Transportation Agency. Air safety standards and the investigation of air accidents are the responsibility of an autonomous body, the Canadian Transport Accident Investigation and Safety Board, whose brief also covers other methods of transport.

UK Department of Transport (DTp): Control of civil aviation in the UK has shuttled between one ministry and another over the years but now appears to be fairly securely housed in the Department of Transport, which also controls shipping, railways and road construction.

DTp is also responsible for laying down overall policy on the airline industry and airports, usually after consultation with the CAA (see below). The Secretary of State also considers appeals against CAA decisions on new route licences and at one time overruled the authority only rarely. Under the Thatcher Conservative government, however, Transport Secretaries tended to intervene rather more and allow appeals when they felt the CAA was being over-cautious about allowing increased competition.

DTp also handles the international relations aspects of civil aviation and regulates the foreign activities of foreign airlines in the UK in the same way that the CAA controls British carriers. Legally the Transport Secretary has to approve fares charged by foreign airlines, although in practice this vetting is carried out mainly by the CAA.

The Department has powers under the Airports Act 1986 to control airport charges and lay down rules for the distribution of traffic between UK airports, again with advice from the CAA. The investigation of aircraft accidents is carried out by the Air Accident Investigation Branch, staffed by an internationally respected team of inspectors who are independent of political control but work in close liaison with the CAA.

Civil Aviation Authority (CAA): Airline regulatory bodies are usually an integral part of a government ministry but the CAA is unusual in being only an agency of government which operates at arm's length from whichever government is in power. It functions under guidelines laid down by Parliament in the Civil Aviation Act and Airports Act, but this is a fairly loose framework which gives it considerable freedom to develop its own policies without ministers breathing down its neck. At the same time, the authority is an important source of advice to the government on aviation matters, including airport policy and consumer protection.

Broadly, the CAA's role combines those of America's FAA and the former CAB. It has a particularly important function in the monitoring of safety standards – notably in the licensing of airports and aircrew and in the approval and inspection of airlines' operational procedures.The Authority invested millions of pounds in new facilities to handle the growth in air travel, the benefits of such an investment have already been felt. Average air-traffic control delays at six major UK airports (Heathrow, Gatwick, Stansted, Birmingham, Manchester and Luton) fell from 27 minutes in 1989 to twelve minutes in 1993, though in 1996 they crept up again to fourteen minutes. (This is an average for flights which were actually held-up – not for all delayed flights.)

The CAA's economic regulatory functions have changed to a degree since the introduction of the "third package" of liberalisation measured in Europe (see section on Regulation). It is seldom required to approve or disapprove fares but it still monitors the financial integrity of both the UK's airlines and the leading package tour operators which use air services. The UK airline scene is particularly dynamic, so the Authority often has the difficult task of choosing between two or three applicants for a particular route. The CAA's powers do not extend to foreign airlines which come under the control of the DTp, but the CAA is usually represented in bilateral negotiations on air routes with foreign governments.

Under the 1986 Airports Act, the CAA acquired the important role of regulating charges at the larger airports. Airport operators now have to apply to the CAA for permission to levy charges and the Authority has power to impose conditions so as to ensure that there are no abuses of a monopoly position. Airport charges are also subject to regular review by the Monopolies and Mergers Commission (MMC).

The Authority has a general advisory role to the Government on matters such as noise restrictions, the siting of airports or drafting of rules on the distribution of traffic between airports. It also has the job of enforcing any such rules once they are agreed by government.

UK Office of Fair Trading (OFT): The OFT, a semi-autonomous agency of the Government, acquired new powers relating to civil aviation in 1985 as a backup to the licensing role of the CAA. The Director General of Fair Trading can now investigate and refer to the Monopolies and Mergers Commission any alledgedly anti-competitive practices on international charter flights. He can also ask the Commission to investigate potential monopolies on domestic flights or on international charters. The Secretary of State for Trade and Industry has the power to make monopoly references to the MMC on air transport generally, including international scheduled services.

Australian Department of Transport and Communications: Civil aviation in Australia comes under the control of the Department of Transport and Communications. Domestic services were deregulated in October 1990, ending the so-called two-airline policy which had existed since 1947. Under this policy the domestic trunk routes were restricted to the privately-owned Ansett and State-owned Australian Airlines (formerly TAA). Deregulation has led to the removal of controls on pricing and entry to the domestic market, although the regime on international services is still fairly rigid. Qantas, the Australian international flag carrier, is not allowed to handle domestic traffic, although it can carry its own international passengers who make stopovers within Australia. Australia's domestic carrier is now allowed limited access to an international network.

New Zealand Ministry of Transport (MoT): Air transport in New Zealand, excluding air traffic services, is controlled by the Ministry of Transport, which administers the Civil Aviation Act 1990. Air traffic services are now administered by an autonomous, state-owned enterprise, the Airways Corporation. The licensing of international services is undertaken by the Minister of Transport, according to criteria set out in the International Air Services Licensing Act 1947. The Air Services Licensing Authority, which formerly licensed domestic services, was abolished in 1990.

In 1985 the New Zealand Government issued a policy statement rejecting the whole issue of civil aviation deregulation. Instead, it declared its priority as being the creation of an environment for aviation which would maximise the economic benefits to the country, including a concern for tourism as well as for broader foreign policy considerations.

This broad view has led to some liberalisation, including permission for the Australian airline Ansett to set up a domestic airline in New Zealand (Ansett New Zealand). The Government has said that it will review its 1985 policy statement in due course.

AVIATION SAFETY

by David Learmount

It is easy to say that flying is safe; but safe compared with what? Fear of flying is only partly rational, which makes it difficult to persuade the afflicted with the unfeeling logic of statistics. Even when nervous fliers are provided with a comparison which brings the truth of flight safety into easy perspective, the ultimate hurdle is man's innate fear of falling from heights. The latter has never been reduced – let alone eliminated – by pointing out that people don't often fall to their death.

Those frightened of flying will hardly have been reassured by a grim procession of disasters in 1996, among them the TWA crash off Long Island, New York. Worse, the detailed courses of that particular accident may never be known. The likelihood of solving similar mysteries in future looks sure to be increased by the recent decision of the US safety authorities to demand that all airliners carry more sophisticated flight data recorders, the "black box".

Despite 1996's sad sequence of events, flight safety should be put in statistical perspective. During 1993 the world's air travellers made just over 1.3 billion flights. It was an average year for flight safety compared with the last ten years: there were 33 fatal accidents to civil airliners of all kinds, including the domestic short-hop propeller-powered type. The world total of airline deaths – including statistics from what used to be the Soviet Union – was 1,020.

Given the world average, a traveller would have to take 1.25 million flights and travel about 1.25 billion airborne kilometres before facing his or her statistical end. If that means very little to you, read on for your perspective. If it sounds horrifyingly dangerous, read on to discover how you can improve your chances enormously by knowing how to be selective about airline safety.

In the average fatal accident more than half the people on board survive. It has also been shown that frequent air travellers have a better chance of surviving accidents than occasional travellers: this is assumed to be because they know the aeroplane better, panic less, and so can get out faster.

Since you will probably be one of those who survives any accident your flight has, taken the emergency procedures briefing seriously. This is not paranoid, it's pure sense. Look at where all the exits are relative to you and imagine finding your way to them in the dark. Count the seat rows to them if it helps. Read the emergency cards carefully, study the brace position, have your seat belt *firmly* fastened at take-off and landing. Look with particular care at the diagram showing how to open the exit doors, and imagine opening them yourself in the dark. Having done all this, sit back and enjoy your flight.

Airlines specialise in delivering travellers long distances fast and safely. Risk does not increase with distance on an airline flight, whereas it increases almost directly in proportion to distance travelled in a car. According to statistics there is no country in the world where the average car driver could expect to survive 1.25 million journeys if each trip was 1,000km, which is the safety-level offered to airline passengers.

Multiple car journeys of 1000km may sound irrelevant, but the statistics could mean something to the traveller who is considering driving from, say, London to the Cote d'Azur by car: if the purpose is to enjoy the countryside and the local cuisine en route, then drive; if it is to avoid flying for perceived safety reasons, your mathematics is flawed; if you are driving because of an irrational fear of flying, then enjoy the route and good luck.

The world airline safety average, however, is a very rough guide indeed because of enormous regional variations. Actual safety depends heavily on what nationality the airline is,whether the flight is domestic or international, where the flight is taking place, whether the aircraft is jet- or propeller-powered, and what the prevailing weather is like at take-off and landing

The world's most statistically safe flight would be with an Australian airline, on an international flight to an American destination in summer (American summer), using a jet aircraft. More about regional variations later. Conversely, the least safe would be a domestic flight in a country with a "Third-World" economy (specific details later) in a propeller-driven aeroplane (particularly if the propeller is driven by a piston engine rather than a turbine), in bad weather.

Air travellers at the planning stage sometimes ask whether there is an airline safety league table. Surely, they say, the safe airlines will publicise their achievement, proudly laying claim to their place in the league? In fact, even the safest carriers do not dare to. Airline fatal accidents are so rare that even a single fatal disaster could make the top-of-the-league carrier disappear from the top twenty – and what might that do to the clientele's loyalty? Beside which, the airlines know that high places in league tables do not eliminate basic fear of flying.

How would a league table be drawn up? Should it take into account accidents since flying began? ... since jets took over? ... during the last ten or twenty years? Should the accidents taken into account be those in which someone died, or in which everyone on board died, or include also those incidents in which people were injured? And where does the league table put a brand new airline? It is unproven, inexperienced, but has not had an accident yet, so could lay claim to a place high in the league.

These difficulties of definition are among the reasons why airlines themselves steer clear of selling safety. But above all, selling safety clearly implies that there is something to worry about in the first place. Since the airlines, quite reasonably, believe there is not, they do not discuss the matter with the public. Coach companies are not expected to do so, neither are the railways, so why should the airlines?

Probably the best indicator of the safety of any form of travel – if it were possible to get the information – is the size of the operator's insurance premium. If someone has offered you a lift in a car and you want to know how safe a driver he is, ask how much he pays for his motor insurance. The higher it is, the more likely you are to die. Airlines are the same.

It is the plain truth that Third World airlines, and carriers from developing economies generally pay the highest premiums. The Third World airline market does not, it is true, have the same bargaining power with the insurance underwriters that, for example, the US airlines do. But in the end, it is simply accident rates which determine the rate of the premiums. In the USA, airlines will face annual premiums less than 0.5 per cent of the value of their aeroplanes, whereas some carriers from Africa and South America will pay more than three per cent.

Airlines can be crudely graded for air safety by the continent in which they are based: North American airlines as a whole are the most consistently safe; the Middle East has an excellent record for a long time now; western European airlines come third with a high level of safety; Asia, the Indian subcontinent and South East Asia has a mixture of adequate and bad with patches of good; South and Central America are very poor (though better than their road safety); and finally African airlines score lowest for safety, with a few exceptionally good airlines among the bad records.

The disparity is enormous: a South American or African airline is more than ten times as likely to have an accident involving fatalities than a North American, Middle Eastern or Western European one. As for where the accident is most likely to happen, the continents are ranged in the same order but the disparity widens still further, with Africa topping the league by far – at present. Finally the majority of accidents happen to domestic airlines – international carriers have a better record on average.

As for the exceptional nations, Australia is the safest along with the USA and the Middle Eastern nations, and competing for bottom marks are India, China, Korea, Colombia, and Russia.

The safest airline in the world is Australia's Qantas, which has not harmed a soul since the days of wood-and-fabric biplanes in 1937 when it was known by its original name, Queensland and Northern Territories Air Services. But just to show how misleading – even unfair – an airline league table could be, Qantas, with its half-century perfect record, would not be at the top of a ten-year table chart because it is a relatively small airline. Bigger US or European carriers which had a clear record during the last ten years (even though they might have had a fatal accident in the preceding decade) would be higher in the league table than Qantas because they would have operated more accident-free flights in the period under review.

In December 1990, the US magazine *Newsday* carried out an airline safety survey of 140 carriers between 1969 and 1990 using some unusual premises in its calculations. Nevertheless the results again confirmed the well-established truths that the airlines of the world's richer nations tend to have the best records.

Newsday's method was to take not just fatal events against number of flights, but the on-board survival rate in the accidents. This made Swissair safest in the list of those airlines which, during the 22-year period, had had at least one fatal accident. With a single crash in 2,036,000 flights and a 91 per cent survival rate in that event, *Newsday* gives the odds of dying on Swissair at 1 in 22,623,000.

It is statistically extremely shaky to forecast Swissair passengers' (or any other airline passengers') safety in that detail on the basis of a single event in 22 years. It is more accurate simply to say that Swissair is a very safe airline. In that same period the following international airlines had not had any fatal accidents: Qantas, Ansett (Australia), Aer Lingus, Austrian Airlines, Air Madagascar, Air UK, Braathens (Norway), Cathay Pacific (Hong Kong), Finnair, Malaysian Airlines, Sabena (Belgium) and Singapore International.

The biggest safety improvement in aviation's history came with the introduction of jets and turbo-prop engines because the turbines which form the core of both engine types are far more reliable than piston engines. So safety climbed steadily during the late 1950s and in the 1960s as piston-power gradually left the scene. Strangely, there was another upward hike from the Seventies to the Eighties, the reason for which was less clear. But during the last ten years, flight safety, having reached a high level, seems almost to have frozen.

The industry itself is becoming more concerned with "human factors". Pilot error has always played a part in some two-thirds of all serious accidents, so now that aircraft technology has become progressively more refined and less likely to fail with disastrous results, the experts are looking for ways of making pilots safer. Aviation psychologists are studying pilot behaviour on the flight deck, communication between pilots, and the way they handle today's modern, computerised cockpits.

There is some concern that aircrews will begin to feel superfluous in an environment which does all their tactical thinking and flying for them. The pilots' attitude to the task has to be totally different from the way it once was: once the job was to fly the aeroplane; now it is to manage the flight in a progressively more complex and crowded environment. The British Civil Aviation Authority leads the world in the "human factors" field now, demanding of pilots that they take an examination in task-related behavioural psychology as a part of their commercial pilot's licence-qualifying procedure. The intention is that they are more aware of the kinds of human mistakes their environment can lead them to make.

Obviously there is a search for the reasons why airlines from economically poorer, less sophisticated nations have less good safety records. There is good evidence that they are more likely to cut corners on maintenance and safety regulations than airlines from richer nations – often because government supervision of standards is less stringent. But the accidents themselves are, as in the richer nations, more often caused by pilot error than by aircraft engine, systems or structural failure.

Given the higher Third World accident rates, the implication is that training is less good, or the pilots' attitude towards their job is different, or both. In the end, psychologists have concluded it is largely a cultural matter.

What is it about the Australian culture that makes its airlines so safe? First, discipline is accepted as the basis of cockpit behaviour. Also authority, while respected by Australians, is not put on a pedestal by them – meaning in this context that if the captain makes a mistake the co-pilot will challenge him. There have been many serious accidents in airline history which could have been prevented if the pilot had challenged the captain's actions. For example the Japanese are a disciplined race and meticulous in their attention to technical detail; but culturally it is difficult for a subordinate to challenge authority and this cost Japan Air Lines a fatal accident in 1982.

There are new threats to safety emerging which are modifying the world's safety map. The most dramatic are in the nations of Commonwealth of Independent States, or the former USSR. Although the constituent nations have decided to retain the concept of a central aviation authority for setting and policing standards, the evidence is that it is still a shaky, embryo structure which is paid little respect by the member nations.

All the CIS nations are pledged to maintain International Civil Aviation Organisation standards in their airline operation, and their intent seems genuine. Intentions are not proving good enough, however, with accident rates in the CIS soaring in the early 1990s compared with rates in the late1980s.

Apart from the CIS's shaky infrastructure, the domestic part of Aeroflot has been dismantled and its role taken by both national airlines of the new independent states and by hundreds of private regional carriers using old Aeroflot equipment. Aircraft are frequently overloaded with people and goods, and safety regulations are breached as a matter of course. It is actually surprising, given the amount of flying that goes on in this massive area, that serious accidents are still fairly rare. Most of the time the rule-breakers get away with their shortcuts.

Aeroflot International, meanwhile maintains an acceptably high safety standard.

In China, with its weird capitalist/communist industrial structure giving it the world's fastest growing economy by far, the civil air transport industry is struggling to keep up an expansion which will provide for the exploding domestic demand. The result is that a safety record which was poor anyway has become worse. China's airlines have the youngest national aircraft fleet in the world, almost all western-built, but pilots cannot be trained fast enough, so average experience levels are going down; the same is true of air traffic controllers and technicians, and meanwhile the airports are becoming inadequate for the task.

Eventually, by putting huge resources into training and infrastructure needs, China will cope with this phenomenal airline expansion and improve its safety standards, but it is not possible to forecast when that will be.

On a smaller scale similar truths apply to other fast-growing economies on the Pacific Rim. Korean airlines are low in the safety league, as are Taiwan's.

India, never above the average, has been positively poor over the last few years. As with everything about India, there does not seem to be a simple reason for the low score, but it has been consistent for a long time now. The country's civil aviation authorities are now clamping down hard on operating standards, so perhaps things can be expected to improve.

Central and South American airlines show safety well below the world average, with Colombia the continent's worst. Its international airline, Avianca, has a poor record by international standards, and its domestic operations, faced with difficult terrain, unpredictable weather among the mountains, and a network of ground navigation aids which have been shown sometimes to be either badly maintained or damaged by terrorists, not surprisingly show a relatively high accident rate.

When considering these "below average" airlines as a mode of transport in their home countries, the alternative surface transport should be approached critically too. In a country where a cash-strapped economy and a *laissez-faire* culture lets an airline's standards drop, perhaps the same is true of the infrastructure which is supposed to preserve national road and rail safety. It may be true that the national air transport system, while it does not compare well with American or European airline safety standards, is still a relatively safe form of transport in absolute terms. Remember the very high standards with which it is being compared.

Finally, airline and airport security has become very much a part of air travel world-wide. In some parts of the world it is peremptory, but that is often because the perceived risk is low. Lockerbie jolted the airline world into a realisation that the subject of airborne terrorism was a serious one, and airlines and countries at risk usually have an adequate security system now. Hijacking is relatively rare now, but it tends to go in cycles. It will come back again. Meanwhile most hijackings today are not the protest type, but usually amateur efforts by people looking for escape and political asylum. They almost invariably fail.

The only workable advice to passengers afraid of this threat is to decide which airlines are the targets of the active terrorist groups, then to travel with airlines which are not. However, the passengers who take that choice should bear in mind that if they cause the threatened airline's business visibly to suffer they have handed the terrorist his victory, encouraging further terrorism.

UNDERSTANDING AIRFARES

by Philip Ray and Debbie Warne

The world of airline tariffs is an incredibly complex one, but given the help of a well-trained airline reservations clerk or travel agent you can make some substantial savings on your travel by using the various loopholes and legitimate discounts which the system provides.

There are so many permutations of possible fares that, as any travel agent handling complicated itineraries for business executives will tell you, six different airlines will quote six different fares for a particular trip.

To generalise, full-rate First Class and Business Class fares have shown a steady increase over the years but the cost of some promotional discounted fares has been held down, if not actually reduced. And quite apart from the vast range of "official" fares there are also the special deals offered through the "bucket shops" – these agents sell cheap seats often without the security of being bonded.

On major international routes like London-New York, some 30 different fares are available depending on the airline you fly with, the time of the year and even, in some cases, the day of the week.

On other routes to the US (London to Los Angeles, for example), it can sometimes be cheaper to take an indirect flight and change at a US airport like New York. Here are the main types of fare available:

First Class

Completely flexible fares; reservations can be changed to an alternative departure date or to another airline. No cancellation charges. Valid one year. For each destination there is an allocated mileage allowance. On a journey such as London to Sydney, you could have stops in Rome, Bangkok and Singapore as it is within the mileage permitted to Sydney. You can exceed this mileage allowance by up to 25 per cent by paying a surcharge. This comes in increments of five per cent. For example, a journey London-Paris-Frankfurt would incur a ten per cent surcharge. Concorde fares are based on the normal First-Class fare plus a supplement of about 30 per cent.

Holders of first-class tickets qualify for the full range of "perks", including a generous free baggage allowance (usually 40 kilos) and in some cases free ground transport, special lounges, sleeper seats with plenty of leg-room, lavish in-flight cuisine and VIP treatment both on the ground and in the air.

Business First Class

Fully flexible fares in a cabin which, as the name suggests, combines first and business sections. The idea has been introduced by airlines such as Continental Air Canada.

Business Class/ Full Economy Class

Completely flexible fare with same concessions for mileage deviations as First Class (see above). Business class, which is marketed under a variety of brand names like *Club World*, *Le Club* or *Ambassador Class*, usually offers an enhanced standard of in-flight service and more comfortable seating but sometimes involves a premium of between five and twenty per cent on the normal economy fare. Special facilities like executive lounges, free baggage allowance of up to 32 kilos and dedicated check-in desks are provided for Business Class passengers. Some airlines have now merged their First and Business Class service into one class, for example, Continental Airlines – Business First. Passengers are offered First Class Service at the Business Class fare.

Point-to-point Economy and Business class

Applies mainly to travel between UK and US (and on some routes to the Far East and southern Africa) and, as the name implies, is valid only for travel between the two points shown on the ticket, i.e. no stop-overs are allowed. This means that no mileage deviation is permitted, nor can the ticket be used for connecting flights with another airline. A similar fare within Europe, known as the Eurobudget, is available at a discount on the full fare but is subject to a cancellation charge of up to 50 per cent.

APEX/SUPER APEX

Stands for *Advance Purchase Excursion*. It has become the airlines' main method of official discounting and is normally available only on a round-trip basis, except to the Far East where one-way Apex fares are available. Must be booked and paid for some time in advance, ranging from seven days to one month depending on destination, and usually a minimum stay abroad is required. No stopovers are permitted and there are cancellation and amendment fees which vary with the destination. Reductions on some long-haul routes can be as high as 60 per cent off the normal full fare.

PEX/SUPER PEX

Stands for *Public Excursion* fare and is similar to Apex, except that there is no restrictive advance-purchase requirement. In Europe your stay must include a Saturday at the destination. World-wide the minimum stay ranges from seven days to two weeks. There is a penalty of up to 50 per cent for cancellation.

Excursion Fares

Available on many long-haul routes, with restrictions on minimum and maximum length of stay. Normally for round-trip travel only but with fewer restrictions than Apex or Pex – for example, flights can be changed. Typical saving on the full economy fare is between 25 and 30 per cent.

Spouse Fares

Apply on routes throughout Europe and some long-haul, for example South Africa. If one partner pays the full Business Class or Club Class fare, the other partner can travel at a 50 per cent discount. Tickets to Europe have a maximum validity of one month. No stopovers are permitted and husband and wife must travel together on both the outbound and inbound journeys.

Child and Infant Fares

An infant under two years of age accompanied by an adult and not occupying a separate seat is carried at ten per cent of the adult fare. Any additional infants under two years of age occupying a separate seat and accompanying the same adult (and any children aged two to eleven inclusive) are carried at half the adult fare. Some fares, do not carry these reductions – for example, many Apex fares allow only a one-third discount for children and certain promotional fares allow no reduction at all.

Student Fares

Provided the necessary forms are completed, bona fide students are entitled to a reduction of 25 per cent off the full fare. Students must be aged between 22 and under 31. Student fares are not available on the North Atlantic routes and are becoming less widely used elsewhere because so many other fares like Apex offer bigger reductions.

Youth Fares

Available for travel on many routes inside Europe for young people between the ages of 12 and 25. The reduction is 25 per cent off the full fare but, again, a cheaper fare like Apex or Pex is usually available.

Round-the-World Fares (RTW)

An ingenious method of keeping down your travel costs is the Round-the-World fare offered by combinations of airlines. The first sector of your itinerary usually has to be booked about three weeks in advance and the routing specified, but after that you can reserve your flights as you go along. You usually have to make a minimum number of stopovers and you are not allowed to "backtrack". The minimum stay is fourteen days and maximum stay from six months to twelve months. You can even buy a First Class or Business Class RTW ticket with some airlines which undercuts the normal economy fare.

Advance Booking Charters

Advance-booking charters (ABCs) still exist across the Atlantic, mainly during the peak summer season, although there are fewer flights nowadays because of the wide variety of attractive fares available on scheduled services. The rules for ABCs are similar to those governing the scheduled airlines' Apex fares. You have to book at least 21 days in advance and you must be away at least seven days. On flights to the US, charters can sometimes provide worthwhile savings on the normal scheduled fares but to Canada charter fares are usually at or about the Super Apex level. Charter services operate from a number of provincial points, which makes them more convenient for many people than scheduled flights.

Charters

Within Europe, there is a well-organised network of charter flights which can give savings of up to 70 per cent off the normal IATA fare. These flights operate not only to top Mediterranean sunspots but also to cities like Geneva and Munich and – following liberalisation within the EU – are no longer subject to frustrating rules demanding, for example, they could be sold only with accommodation. Charters can be booked up to the time of departure but return dates may not be so flexible as on scheduled flights. For instance, you may be able to return only seven days or fourteen days after the outward journey.

Scheduled Consolidation Fares

These are charter-priced seats sold for travel on scheduled flights. They are usually intended to be the basis of inclusive packages but often end up as flight-only tickets sold through bucket shops. These fares are administered by "consolidators", as they are known in the trade. Their role is to take advantage of special rates for group bookings by making commitments for large blocks of seats which they then make available to travel agents on an individual basis.

Airpasses

Special airpasses are available in a number of countries which enable you to make big savings on domestic travel. Some of the best value is to be had in the US, where all the major airlines offer airpass deals giving virtually unlimited travel on their networks, although you are frequently allowed to make only one stopover per city and there is a ceiling on the number of stopovers you can make. You may be restricted from flying at busy periods. Airpasses have to be bought before arrival in the US. To qualify for some of the best deals you have to travel to the US on a particular airline's trans-Atlantic services. The best plan is to find out which airline has the network which conforms most closely to your preferred itinerary.

A number of other countries with well-developed air services including Australia, Brazil, the Caribbean, India, New Zealand and Thailand also offer airpass schemes.

CHOOSING AN AIRLINE

by Philip Ray and Annie Redmile

Airlines spend huge amounts on advertising to tell us about their exotic in-flight cuisine, their glamorous stewardesses and their swish new aircraft. But surveys conducted regularly among frequent travellers – particularly among those who have to fly on business – tell us that all these "service" factors are not terribly important when it comes to choosing an airline.

What does count, however, is a particular airline's punctuality record. When Lufthansa did some market research a few years ago, it discovered that punctuality was the most important criterion demanded by business travellers, being mentioned by 98 per cent of the respondents. Close behind were favourable departure times, mentioned by 97 per cent, while separate check-in was demanded by only 78 per cent and a good choice of newspapers by no more than 44 per cent.

Another survey among readers of the Swedish business journal *Svensk Export* produced similar results. Asked to put a priority on the service features which they regarded as most crucial when choosing an airline, 92 per cent cited departure times and 87 per cent regarded punctuality as "very important". It seems, therefore, that a lot of airline advertising probably does no more than reinforce a choice which the consumer has already made.

Going Direct

Most people prefer a flight which involves few, if any, changes where possible. This can restrict choice of airline as these services are often offered only by carriers such as British Airways and the other national airlines or the US majors.

But the scene is changing and with a choice, for example, of three mainstream London airports alone – Heathrow, Gatwick and Stansted – and London City and London Luton added for good measure, choice is greater than it has ever been. Added to that the increasing number of direct services from airport like Manchester and Birmingham and the traveller is getting a much better deal.

One of the best ways of researching your choice is through the ABC World Airways Guide (or AOAG in the US and some other parts of the world), or the BAA Airport timetable. One possible trap today for unwary travellers is the proliferation of "code-sharing" deals between airlines. The same flight number does not necessarily mean the same aircraft or even the same airline any more and so it pays to check carefully.

Choice of Airports

London's two airports, Heathrow and Gatwick, have direct flights to such a range of busiest destinations that there is generally no need to fly to a continental airport and change flights there. Passengers living away from the South East may be lucky enough to have access to one of the growing number of direct services from their local airport – particularly Manchester and Birmingham which have expanded their international services considerably. If this is not the case then the alternatives include taking a flight to an airport in mainland Europe – and KLM has done much to encourage this approach, over Schiphol – or to London.

Airline Standards

There are hundred of airlines to choose from in the world but it is fair to say that there are those who adopt less rigorous safety standards and maintenance procedures than the major international carriers. Some domestic airlines in South America for instance have pretty poor safety records. There has been growing concern in the aviation industry that the explosion of growth in China's airline industry has affected standards and the profileration of airlines that now operate in the former Soviet Union cause question marks to be placed over a number of carriers where formerly there was only Aeroflot to cause concern.

A number of these airlines compete on price but it can be advisable to pay more and enjoy better comfort and more reliability.

The standards of on-board service offered by carriers from the Far East are probably the highest in the world (service is not a dirty word in Asia) but to generalise, it is probably true to say that the most efficient in terms of punctuality and operational integrity are those of Europe and North America. British Airways, for instance, has had a lot of criticism over the years but it is generally regarded as a world leader in setting high operational and technical standards. Now that its punctuality and service have been vastly improved, it is a force to be reckoned with. Other highly regarded airlines include Virgin Atlantic,

Swissair, SAS, Lufthansa, KLM and Japan Air Lines and Emirates.

Many passengers may be worried about terrorist attacks or hijackings after the events of recent years, although the chances of being involved in an accident of this kind are statistically remote. The most sensible advice is to make a mental note of any airlines or airports which appear to be particularly vulnerable and avoid them. Airlines serving the Middle East are not necessarily bad risks. Israel's national airline, El Al, probably has the most rigorous security standards of any carrier and it was thanks to its own security staff at Heathrow that a catastrophic mid-air bomb explosion was avoided in 1986.

Some Third World Airlines which excel in in-flight service may not be so good on the ground. When travelling in Third World countries, never attempt to make your reservation by phone but visit the airline's office and get them to validate your ticket in front of you. Always check and double–check your reservation – some airlines in out-of-the-way parts of the world do not have computerised reservation systems and mistakes are frequently made.

No-frills airlines

The network of charter flights both inside and outside Europe is wider than many people imagine. On international routes within Europe, charters account for more than half the market in terms of passenger kilometres. Most charter flights within Europe carry passengers going on conventional package tours but more and more flights are taking passengers on a "seat only" basis. The mid-1990s saw the spread of the no-frills airline from America to Europe. Carriers such as UK-based EasyJet and Ireland's Ryanair followed the example of Southwest Airlines in the US, offering very low, point to point fares with minimal cabin service. Typically, these airlines do not offer in-flight meals other than nibbles and charge for drinks. They do not always sell tickets through travel agents. If you buy their cheapest deals and miss, or are forced to cancel the flight, you may have to pay all over again or fork out a hefty penalty. EasyJet offers its lowest fares on a first come, first served basis with prices rising in pre-ordained increments as the jumps as seats at the cheaper rates sell out. Though it is not invariably so, these airlines often fly from airports other than the main hubs of major carriers.

Charters

There is a wide choice of charter flights across the North Atlantic year round, mostly to Florida but also to lesser destinations. In the winter of 1997 they were due to be launched between London and Ottawa, for example. Upward pressure on scheduled fares, as planes fly fuller, looks likely to encourage other, similar services. Recent years have seen a proliferation of fly drive deals, often tadvertised on Teletext, with basic prices well under £100 for travellers prepared to book at the last minute. But take care. These very low prices often more than double when you have added obligatory insurance and collision damage waiver for the rental car.

And following South Africa's all-race elections and return to international grace, winter charters also operate to Johannesburg and Cape Town.

Extras and Specials

For many scheduled flights it's possible to request certain special meals such as kosher or vegetarian, and to put in seat requests – for example, window, aisle, smoking or non-smoking etc. If travelling on a long-haul flight, it's a good idea to advise the airline of your contact phone number, so that you can be informed on the day of your departure if there is a major delay.

VIP treatment can take the form of better handling on the ground. An airline representative will smooth you through all the hassles of check-in and will escort you to the airline's own VIP lounge. The cabin crew will be informed of your presence and will make every effort to ensure that your flight is a comfortable and enjoyable one. Airlines normally grant VIP treatment to senior government officials and commercially important customers. Some airlines will allow you to use their VIP lounges if you have paid the First Class or full Economy Class fare and your travel agent has cleared this facility with the airline's sales department beforehand.

Other airlines insist that you must be a member of their executive club or "frequent traveller" club before they grant you admittance, while some carriers merely charge an annual membership fee which allows you to use their executive lounge whether or not you're actually flying with them. But don't expect VIP treatment if you're travelling at a discount rate.

Alternative Flights

It is also possible to travel as a courier for a much reduced fare. The courier "responsibility" tends only to be for one half of the journey and so it is an inexpensive way to get to your destination with just a little work to do on the way.

See p.738 of Directory for lists of airline head offices world-wide and in the UK

DISCOUNTS AND DEALS

by Philip Ray and Annie Redmile

The high level of airfares is always fair game as a topic of conversation when frequent travellers get together. It is an even more popular topic for politicians who appear to believe, probably erroneously, that cheap fares are a good vote-catcher. Some fares are certainly high, but it is still possible to fly to most parts of the world for considerably less than the full standard fare, given the assistance of a professional travel agent.

The key word when it comes to the difference between high fares and low fares is "flexibility". If you are prepared to be flexible as to the day or time of year when you want to travel and let the airline slot you onto a flight which it knows is likely to have empty seats, you can nearly always find a cheap fare. But this may well mean you have to buy your ticket either several weeks in advance or at the very last minute on a standby basis. Frequently your stay at the destination must include at least one Saturday night – a frequently-criticised requirement which is imposed by airlines to minimise the risk of business travellers trading down from the normal full fare to the cheap rate (on the theory that few business people want to spend a Saturday night away from home). And with most cheap fares, once you have booked your flight, you can usually switch to an alternative service only on payment of a fairly hefty cancellation penalty.

The other side of the flexibility coin is that if you want complete freedom to change or cancel your flight without penalty, you have to pay for the privilege, which means, in practice, the expensive full fare.

Economics

The economics of the wide gap which exists between the highest fare and the lowest are not quite so crazy as might appear at first sight. If business travellers want the flexibility to change or cancel their reservations at short notice, seats will often be empty because the airline has been unable to re–sell them, and the cost of flying that seat still has to be paid for. The price of a fully flexible ticket also has to take account of the "no-show" factor – those passengers who have a confirmed reservation but do not turn up at the airport and fail to notify the airline that they want to cancel their flight.

So there is an implicit bargain between the airline and the passenger when it comes to a cheap fare. The airline offers a discount in return for a commitment from the passenger (underpinned by a financial penalty) that he or she will actually use that seat.

The most innovative fare concept of recent years was devised by the now sadly defunct British Caledonian. Under its "Timeflyer" system, the fare was based purely on the time of departure, so that the passenger who wanted to fly at peak times paid the highest fare and anyone who was prepared to travel at a less popular time qualified for the cheaper rate. This system was blocked by some foreign governments but it still survives to the extent that many ultra-cheap fares publicised by airlines are available only on a limited number of off-peak flights.

A similar system operates in some countries on domestic routes, notably in Sweden where SAS and Linjeflyg offer big reductions on off-peak flights throughout the year – and even on peak-time services during the summer when few business executives are flying.

Flexibility

Many business travellers can probably be more flexible about their air-travel schedules and can still save quite a lot of money, provided that they don't mind travelling at the back of the aircraft with the masses.

For example, if you are planning to attend a conference, the date of which is known a long time in advance, you can frequently buy an Apex fare at anything up to half the cost of the full fare. But always bear in mind those heavy financial penalties if you suddenly decide to cancel or change your flight.

Business travellers will also find that it is often worth looking around for a package trip, like those offered by specialist tour operators to tie in with a trade fair. Some travel agencies and tour operators also offer attractive packages to business destinations which provide not only the airfare but also hotel accommodation for a total price which is often less than the normal Business Class fare.

Needless to say, this type of package does not offer the flexibility of the full-fare ticket and you will probably not be able to change your flight if your business schedule overruns.

If you are planning an extensive tour within a region such as North America, the Far East or Australia, it is well worth investigating the many airpasses available. For instance issued by US and Canadian domestic airlines which offer multi-coupon or unlimited travel over their networks for a given period (although there are usually some restrictions on routing). For travel to the USA, there are also some remarkably good-value deals on fly-drive trips, with car hire being charged at only nominal rates in many cases.

Some of the best deals for business travellers are to be found in the round-the-world fares offered by a number of airlines which can enable you to plan a complicated itinerary at a knockdown rate.

Frequent-Flyer Programmes

In the competitive world of aviation, where the frequent traveller is king – or queen – "loyalty programmes" as the "frequent-flyer" programmes are classified have become the norm. Passengers collect points or benefits each time they fly with a particular carrier and they redeem them for a free ticket for a partner or for some other benefit.

There was a time that fear of the various tax authorities view on such schemes prevented most airlines outside of the US from offering frequent flyer programme. If they were to offer a scheme it was heavily disguised and travellers had to have a US address.

Competition has forced a more open approach and nearly all airlines have their own schemed today or link in to another carrier's and the loose hotel chains are also now following suit.

There are specialist magazines aimed at frequent travellers such as *Executive Travel* or *Business Traveller* magazine in the UK – which list all the latest offer on airfares, deals and frequent flyer programmes.

Bucket Shops

The best-known source of discounted air tickets is the so-called "bucket shop", a phrase which was first coined at a travel industry conference in the early 1970s to denote an outlet specialising in the sale of air tickets at an "illegal" discount. Such is the power of the media that the term – which was derived from shady activities in the 19th century US stock market – is now universally understood. The term consolidator is more frequently used now as the term gains legitimacy as a result of lighter regulatory control.

Back in the early 1970s, the world of bucket shops was a pretty sleazy one, based on back rooms in Chinese supermarkets, or in flyblown first–floor offices in Soho. One or two of the early entrepreneurs actually ended up in prison and some of the cheap tickets which found their way into the market place had, in fact, been stolen. One bucket shop which traded as a "reunion club" ended up owing more than £620,000 to thousands of people who had been saving up to visit relatives abroad, not to mention another £614,000 owed to airlines. The owner of this club was eventually jailed for trading with intent to defraud. He knew that the "club" could not meet its liabilities and yet he continued to trade for almost a year.

Failures still do occur occasionally but the aura of backstreet sleaze has virtually disappeared. Outlets are being opened in the High Streets of provincial cities by respected companies with long experience of the travel business, and most of the household names in retail travel are now able to supply discounted tickets. At one time the Association of British Travel Agents (ABTA) officially banned its members from offering "illegally" discounted airfares, but dropped this rule when the restrictive-practices legislation began to bite on the travel business. Nowadays many "bucket shops" are members of ABTA and all discounted scheduled airfares are now covered by the CAA's consumer-protection machinery. This makes it less likely that the consumer will be left out of pocket if a "bucket shop" goes bust as repayment will be due from a bond.

The CAA recently tighted its protection rules futher, requiring all consolidators to be covered by bonds unless they yhand over tickets on the spot, immediately after receiving payment. The agent must print details of bonding and an Air Travel Organisers LIcence (ATOL) number on its documents. Consumers can check the validity of the ATOL by calling the CAA.

It is worth taking a closer look at the discounting phenomenon and at what makes it "illegal", if indeed it is. It is an economic fact of life that, on average, the world's scheduled airlines fill only two-thirds of their seats, so there is a very powerful inducement to fill the remaining one-third by any means possible. Assuming that overheads have been covered by the two-thirds paying "normal" fares (although this is not necessarily a valid assumption), anything earned from one extra passenger means a bigger profit or a smaller loss – provided that they can earn some valuable hard currency.

The "illegality" of discounting stems from the internationally agreed convention that governments can approve airlines using their airspace, and most countries have provision in their legislation which makes the sale of tickets illegal at other than the officially-approved rates. In the UK the legal position is not quite so clear cut. British airlines are regulated by the Civil Aviation Authority and there is specific legislation which lays down heavy penalties against discounting. Foreign airlines are separately controlled by the Department of Transport and, depending on whether there is a specific provision on tariffs in their permits, they may or not be liable to be brought before the courts for discounting.

There is a third class of airline – the so-called "offline carrier" – which does not actually operate services into the UK but which maintains sales offices here. These airlines can, quite legally, do whatever they want in terms of discounting, because there is no law that can catch them.

All this is somewhat academic because no British government has ever tried to enforce the law, which suggests that perhaps it is time for it to be repealed. The CAA, too, has rarely refused to sanction a new low fare filed by an airline (although it could intervene if it felt the fare was "predatory" – in other words, designed to put a competitor out of business). However, the authority has frequently refused applications by airlines to increase their full-price fares.

The Passenger's Viewpoint

The risk of losing money at a bucket shop has been reduced drastically by tighter consumer protection rules. Even the danger than an agency could go under, leaving you scrambling for an alternative deal, should not be exaggerated.

Only a tiny proportion of bucket shop clients suffer financial loss in any year, and there are plenty of satisfied customers who have managed to make substantial savings on their trip. Perhaps word-of-mouth recommendation from a friend is a good way to find a reliable outlet for a discount fare deal and in recent years the strengthening of consumer protection legislation means that any outlet displaying the ABTA and ATOL symbols is a pretty safe bet.

It is a good sign if a bucket shop has been established for some time in good premises with a street-level office. If possible you should make a personal visit to assess the knowledge of the staff rather than just relying on a telephone call. Ask as many questions as possible and find out any likely snags such as a protracted stopover en route in an unattractive part of the world; and make sure you know which airline you're flying with.

It is a good indication of a bucket shop's reliability if it holds an Access or Visa appointment because the card firms check the financial integrity of their appointed outlets very thoroughly. Use of a credit card also gives you added security because, under the Consumer Credit Act, the card company becomes liable for provision of the service you have bought in the event of the retailer's failure. It is also a good sign if the office is a member of the Association of British Travel Agents (look for the ABTA sticker on the door) or licensed by IATA (the International Air Transport Association) because you are then protected by the association's financial safeguards.

READING AN AIRLINE TICKET

By Philip Ray and Alex McWhirter

An airline ticket is really a legal contract which specifies and restricts the services that passengers may expect and when they may expect them. On each ticket, the duties and liabilities of both passenger and airline are clearly stated – whether it is a scheduled or a charter flight – and each passenger must be in possession of a ticket for the journey to be undertaken. The Warsaw Convention limits the liability of most airlines in cases of injury or death involving a passenger and also for baggage loss or damage. This agreement is usually explained on the inside cover of the ticket or on a summary inserted in a loose-leaf form.

The format of tickets issued by IATA-appointed travel agents in the UK and a number of other countries has been changed to conform with the requirements of the so-called Bank Settlement Plan (BSP). Instead of having to keep a stock of tickets for each airline with which they deal, agents now have one common stock of "neutral" tickets, but a special plate is slotted into the ticket validator at the time of issue to indicate which airline is issuing the ticket. The whole BSP operation is essentially aimed at simplifying accounting procedures for both travel agents and airlines. Tickets issued direct by airlines still carry the normal identification.

Flight coupons contain a fare construction box which, on a multi-sector itinerary, indicates how the fare is to be apportioned among the different carriers. Cities are denoted by their three-letter codes, eg LHR is London Heathrow, ROM is Rome, CPH is Copenhagen, LAX is Los Angeles and so on. The fare construction may be shown in FCUs (Fare Construction Units), a universal "currency" in which fares are frequently expressed. The amount in FCUs is converted into the currency of the country of issue which is shown in the fare box in the left-hand corner. The British pound sterling is shown as UKL so as to distinguish it from other sterling currencies. Where local taxes are to be paid these are also shown, and the final amount to be paid is shown in the total box.

At the bottom of the right-hand side is the "Form of Payment" box. If you pay for the ticket by cash, it will either be left blank or the word "cash" will be written in. If it is paid by cheque, the word "cheque" or abbreviation "chq" will be used. If the ticket is bought with a credit card, the letters "CC" will be written followed by the name of the issuing company, the card number and its expiry date. If you have an account with the travel agent the clerk will write "Non ref", which means that no refund can be obtained except through the issuing office.

In the "Baggage" section of the ticket, only the "Allow" column is completed by the agent. This shows the free baggage allowance to which you are entitled. The number of pieces, checked and unchecked weights are completed when the passenger checks in. "PC" indicates that the piece concept is in operation, as it is on flights to and from North America. There are validity boxes immediately above the cities on your itinerary. These "not valid before" and "not valid after" entries relate to promotional fares with minimum/maximum stay requirements and the relevant dates will be shown here. If you have a full-fare ticket where there is no minimum-stay requirement and the maximum is one year, these boxes are frequently left blank.

Immediately to the right of the itinerary there is a column headed "Fare/Class basis". The letters most commonly inserted are "F" for First Class, "C" for Business Class, or "Y" for Economy Class. The "Y" will often be followed by other letters to describe the fare, especially if it is a promotional type. For example, "YH" would mean a high season fare, "YZ" a youth fare, "YLAP" a low season Apex, "YE" Excursion etc.

Under the "Carrier" box is the space for the carrier code, e.g. LH for Lufthansa or BA for British Airways. However, the airline industry has now run out of possible combinations of two-letter codes, and three-letter codes are gradually being introduced. Next follows the flight number and class of travel on that particular flight. Most international flight numbers consist of three figures but for UK domestic flights four figures are frequently used. The date is written as, for example, 04 JUN and not as 4th June, while the time is shown on the basis of the 24-hour clock, eg 14.30 hrs is written instead of 2.30 pm. (The twelve hour clock is still used for domestic travel within the USA).

In the "Status" box the letters "OK" must be written if you have a confirmed flight. "RQ" if the flight has been requested but not yet confirmed, and "WL" if the flight has been wait-listed. If you haven't decided when you want to travel, the word "OPEN" is written, spread out across the flight number, date, time and status boxes. Infants, who travel for a ten per cent fare on international journeys, are not entitled to a seat or baggage allowance so that the reservations entry will be marked "No seat" and the allowance marked "nil". Your ticket is valid for travel only when date-stamped with a travel agency or airline validator which is completed with the clerk's signature or initials.

For Airport City Codes see p.750 of the Directory
For Airline Two Letter Codes see p.748 of the Directory

THE TRAVELLER'S PROTECTION

by David Richardson

The travel industry has an enviable record in protecting customers' money, but when the system breaks down there are inevitably heartbreak stories in the media and the image of the travel industry suffers. This was common-place twenty years ago before financial safeguards were put in place, but it can still happen today. The vast majority of travellers either continue their arrangements or get their money back if their travel organiser goes bust, but that will be of little comfort if you're one of the unlucky ones.

Package Holidays

The package holiday customer enjoys the highest level of financial protection, and it's well worth choosing a package rather than making your own arrangements if you're in the least worried about losing your money. And don't forget, "package holiday" doesn't mean a chartered flight and a week on the beach in Benidorm. Tour operators are increasingly targeting the independent traveller, and many people trekking in the Himalayas or scuba-diving on the Great Barrier Reef are also on a package.

When Air Europe collapsed in 1991, the traveller who had simply booked his or her own scheduled flight almost certainly lost the money. But the person booking the same flight as part of a package holiday was fully protected through arrangements made by tour operators, who have been regulated and licensed since the early 1970s. New regulations implemented in 1993, as a result of European Community (now European Union) legislation, have widened the gap still further between the cosseted package customer and the independent traveller.

The situation with package holidays by air is straightforward, and the same is true for charter flight passengers buying a seat-only deal rather than a package. All tour operators must have an Air Travel Organiser's Licence (ATOL) issued by the Civil Aviation Authority (CAA), and to get one they must satisfy the CAA that they are financially secure, providing a bond that will be used to reimburse or repatriate customers if they collapse. If the bond proves insufficient, the CAA draws on the Air Travel Trust Fund which was set up by a levy on all package holidays back in the 1970s.

The ATOL system is virtually fail-safe as regards package holidays by air departing from the UK, and now has been extended to cover packages using scheduled as well as charter flights. This includes most discounted scheduled air seats sold as "seat-only's" or as part of a tailor-made itinery for the independant traveller. Some companies advertise themselves as "agents for ATOL holders", and that might be worth checking out with the CAA. If so the ATOL holder must take responsibility for travellers if the agent fails.

The situation regarding package holidays by surface transport is much more complex. Until recently, tour operators using coach or rail transport, cruises or ferries, were not obliged to offer financial protection. Many opted to do so through various trade associations, but this was purely voluntary. But in January 1993 the British government adopted the EC directive on package travel, which introduces a wide range of consumer protection measures including the requirement for all package organisers to protect money. This was no great innovation in the UK, because of the ATOL system and the large number of tour operators providing bonds through trade associations. In some other EU countries, however, public protection lagged far behind the UK. But what may have seemed a good idea to the Eurocrats and MEPs gathered together in Brussels may cause the UK traveller a lot of confusion and give him a false sense of security.

The regulations affect all package travel arrangements sold in the UK, not just for travel to EU countries but world-wide – including holidays taken in the UK itself, incidentally. It is generally considered that the EU wanted to protect the traditional package holiday customer, but in fact the legislation goes much further. Many areas are poorly defined and the British Government has not made things any clearer.

First of all, what is a package? According to the regulation, it is a combination of any two of three elements – transport; accommodation; or other tourist services making up a significant element of a package. The latter is open to interpretation, but could include a theatre ticket, riding lessons, or golf, for example. Even a country hotel in England, including a fishing licence in its weekend rates, could be deemed to be selling a package, with the need to protect any money paid in advance.

This goes far beyond the idea of a traditional holiday package. The British government, when the regulations were debated in Parliament, admitted to having no idea how many package organisers there might be in the UK – its "educated guess" was between 10,000 and 20,000, when the total number of tour operators belonging to trade associations is less than 1,000. Many of the organisers are coach operators, who are considered to be package travel organisers even if all they do is a one-night trip to Blackpool. Others include social clubs, societies and even individuals, such as the local vicar leading an annual pilgrimage to the Holy Land. "Occasional" organisers of package travel are exempt from the regulations, but "occasional" will be defined if and when a case comes to court.

Also unresolved, at the time of writing, was the role of the travel agent in putting together packages. If you ask a travel agent to put together a flight and hotel, it could well be that he will have to provide protection as a package organiser even if the arrangements are not sold at an inclusive price. But business travel packages may not be affected, as most business travellers are on credit and do not pay until their return.

Not surprisingly, the regulations are causing grief in the travel industry and among many other organisations and individuals who had no idea they were considered package travel organisers. But what is causing even more grief, among established tour operators, is that there is no effective way of policing the regulations. A gaping consumer protection loophole is still there.

Organisers of packages using air travel must have an ATOL – that is straightforward. But the past government balked at creating a parallel licensing authority for surface travel operators. They are required to provide evidence to travellers that their money is protected, in one of three ways. Either they can provide a bond, possibly to a trade association which has reserve funds in place; they can insure against the risk of financial failure; or they can place customers' money in a trust account, and not touch it until travel has been completed.

Travellers taking a package by surface transport should look for some evidence that their money is protected – but the only policing authority is local trading standards officers, who by their own admission lack the resources and expertise to do it properly. It is now a criminal offence to operate packages without protecting customers' money, but although the maximum fine is £5,000 the first case to come to court resulted in a fine of only £250. The unlucky traveller caught up in a collapse could try to sue the directors – but if the company has gone bust, the kitty will probably be empty.

Role of the Trade Associations

The weakness of the new legislation means trade associations continue to have a strong role in protecting travellers' money – especially the Association of British Travel Agents (ABTA), the only one with a strong public profile. Surveys show that the public identify strongly with ABTA because their money is safe, and that remains true although its role is changing.

Your money is still 100 per cent safe if you book with an ABTA tour operator, as ABTA has never reneged on its promise to re-pay customers booking a package holiday with a failed member. This is because ABTA requires all its 600 tour operators to be bonded, either with the CAA through ATOL, or through ABTA itself in the case of surface travel operators. In both cases, back-up funds are in place if bonds prove insufficient.

ABTA will not accept insurance against possible failure, or trust funds, as a substitute for bonding – as allowed by the government for non-ABTA members. It points out that insurance against failure is of no help to travellers stranded abroad after a collapse, while trust accounts are open to abuse. If solicitors can run off with money placed in trust accounts – costing the Law Society millions – then so can travel companies.

ABTA is going through major changes, but its consumer promise remains intact. Before the new regulations it acted as a quasi-licensing authority, and tour operators had to join up if they wanted to sell through ABTA's 7,000 travel agents. But it is no longer a closed shop, and tour operators and agents can leave ABTA if they wish. When dealing with a non-ABTA company, the onus is on the traveller to ensure his money is safe – and if in doubt, contact your local authority trading standards officers for advice.

ABTA will also protect your money if a member travel agent goes bust, whatever kind of travel arrangement you have bought. If you already have your tickets then normally you will be able to continue, but if not then ABTA will reimburse you. This applies to independent travel as well as packages but only when the agent, rather than the travel provider, is the one who goes bust.

Other trade associations also bond their members to protect public money, although it is the CAA such as AITO (the Association of Independent Tour Operators) which licenses all air packages. These are the Association of Independent Tour Operators, the Bus and Coach Council's Bonded Coach Holidays scheme, the Passenger Shipping Association (Cruises) and the Federation of Tour Operators, formerly known as Tour Operators Study Group. But remember, protection only applies to packages, and not a simple ferry crossing or express coach ticket for example.

The Independent Traveller

If you book independently rather than a package (depending on the definition of a package which might one day emerge!), your money is much more at risk. But in reality, there are few occasions when a failure will leave you out of pocket.

The main area of risk is scheduled airlines, bringing us back to the Air Europe collapse of 1991. Despite the outcry that followed, neither the British government nor the EU in Brussels have made any moves yet to protect scheduled airline passengers' money, much to the outrage of the tour operators and travel agents who were bonded up to the hilt. Another British air-line, Dan-Air, came within a whisker of going bust in 1992 before British Airways picked up the pieces.

The risks are definitely increasing as airlines all over the world go private, free of government control but also of government support. Several US airlines are technically bankrupt, but continue to operate under US bankruptcy laws. New private airlines are starting all the time, while new state airlines in the former Soviet Union look particularly unstable.

The British Government has failed to act on a CAA proposal for a levy, partly because it would involve only British airlines' passengers and British Airways objected. As little as £1 added to ticket costs for even a short period would soon build up a substantial protection fund, but there seems no likelihood of this happening in the short-term.

But the risk of a scheduled airline collapsing is small enough for most travellers to accept, and the same is true for ferries and scheduled coach companies who may often help out the passenger if a rival collapses. Car rental companies pose a slightly greater risk, while the position of a private railway company that collapses holding customers' money is unknown – a point to consider as British Rail is privatised. And although hotels go into liquidation all the time, they are nearly always kept open to keep some money coming in.

There sale of discounted scheduled air tickets was a grey area for a long time, but the CAA has now cracked down, requiring agents offering them to be covered by ATOLSs (Air Travel Organisers' Licences) unless they hand over ticket on the spot – immdiately they receive payment. More recently it acted to make them accept responsibility when an airline goes bust. It gives them three options: they can offer insurance against the possibility of a scheduled airline failure – either free or by charging a premium on top of the fare. They may sign a formal guarantee that they will accept responsibility for customers if an airline goes under, re-booking them on alternative flights. Or they can opt to do neither. But if they *do* opt out, they must warn customers in all their paperwork and promotional material – and in suitably large print – that they part with money at their own risk. Independent travel arrangements are further safeguarded if you book through an ATOL bonded agent.

Another way of safeguarding your money is to pay by credit card, which is getting increasingly popular and is much more convenient if booking direct with travel suppliers in foreign countries, who may not even be subject to package travel regulations. Credit card companies are to some extent governed by the Consumer Credit Act to ensure that the service paid for is provided but that, like all legislation, is open to interpretation.

The waters are muddied by the fact that there are now about 40 organisations in the UK issuing credit cards, and their attitude towards refunds may vary. If in doubt ask your bank, building society or whatever, especially for an expensive travel purchase.

Some banks see this as an opportunity to boost card usage, such as Barclays which since 1992 has guaranteed to protect anyone buying a flight or holiday in the UK with Barclaycard, for transactions of over £100 with a ceiling of £30,000. But Barclays accepts no legal liability, and is looking to the travel industry to take primary responsibility.

Credit card companies tell customers to seek refunds from the CAA or ABTA in the first instance, but for non-packaged arrangements there are no bonds in place.

There are probably enough scenarios in this chapter to make even the most resolute traveller wonder if his money is safe, but in general the travel industry's record is good. If you pay in advance for a carpet, a cooker or almost any other consumer goods and the company goes bust, there is no equivalent to the CAA or ABTA to turn to.

But the travel industry is, after all, selling dreams. A ruined holiday is more serious than not getting the carpet you wanted, and the sooner all travel arrangements are fully protected, the better.

MAKING CLAIMS AGAINST AN AIRLINE

by Alex McWhirter and Annie Redmile

You have only to read the correspondence columns in the specialist business travel magazines each month to see what a fashionable occupation it is to complain about airline services. Some people seem to enjoy writing letters of complaint so much that they make a profession of it. They complain at the slightest hiccup and write long letters detailing every flaw, claiming huge sums in compensation and threatening legal action if it is not forthcoming by return.

But the fact is that no matter how much their inefficiency costs you in time, trouble, missed meetings, lost deals and overnight hotel bills, the airlines in many cases are not obliged to pay you anything. They are covered for most eventualities by their *Conditions of Carriage* which are printed on the inside cover of the ticket. However, this is not to say that in an increasingly competitive environment the more enlightened airlines do not take their customers' attitudes seriously. Some airline chief executives take a personal interest in passenger complaints and have frequent "purges" when they insist on seeing every letter of complaint that comes in on a particular day.

If you have a complaint against an airline which you cannot resolve satisfactorily it is worth contacting the Air Transport Users' Committee (5th Floor, Kingsway House, 103 Kingsway, London WC2B 6QX tel: 0171-242 3882 or fax: 0171-931 4132). The committee is funded and appointed by the Civil Aviation Authority but operates completely independently and, indeed, has frequently been known to criticise some of the authority's decisions. The committee has only a small secretariat and is not really geared up to handle a large volume of complaints, but it has had some success in securing ex gratia payments for passengers who have been inconvenienced in some way.

All the same, the committee likes to receive passenger complaints because it is a useful way of bringing to light some serious problems which can lead to high-level pressure being brought to bear on the airline or airlines involved. Some of the subjects dealt with by the committee in 1990 included European and domestic airfares, passenger safety, the pressure on airport and airspace capacity, overbooking, and baggage problems.

Procedure

Here are some tips which may make complaining to an airline more effective:

1. The first person to write to is the Customer Relations Manager. You can write to the Chairman if it makes you feel better but it makes little difference – unless that happens to be the day that the Chairman decides to have his "purge". If you've made your booking through a travel agency, send it a copy of the letter and if the agency does a fair amount of business with that carrier (especially if it is a foreign airline) it is a good idea to ask it to take up the complaint for you.
2. Keep your letter brief, simple, calm and to the point. Remember also to give the date, flight number, location and route where the incident took place. All these details seem obvious but it's amazing how many people omit them.
3. Keep all ticket stubs, baggage claims and anything else you may have from the flight involved. You may have to produce them if the airline requires substantiation of your complaint.
4. If you have no success after all this, write to the Air Transport Users' Council. Send it copies of all the correspondence you've had with the airline and let it take the matter from there.

Lost Luggage

Most frequent travellers will at some time have experienced that sinking feeling when the carousel stops going round and their baggage is not on it. The first thing to do if your luggage does not appear is to check with an airline official in the baggage claim area. It could be that your baggage is of a non–standard shape – a heavy rucksack, for example – which cannot be handled easily on the conveyor belt and it will be brought to the claim area by hand. But if your baggage really has not arrived on the same flight as yourself you will have to complete a

Property Irregularity Report (PIR) which will give a description of the baggage, a list of its contents and the address to which it should be forwarded.

It is sometimes worth hanging around at the airport for an hour or two because there is always the chance that your baggage may arrive on the next flight. This sometimes happens if you have had to make a tight flight connection and your baggage hasn't quite made it, although the current strict security requirements mean that normally a passenger and his or her baggage must travel on the same flight. But if there is only one flight a day there is no point in waiting and the airline will forward the baggage to you at its expense. In this case, ask the airline for an allowance to enable you to buy the basic necessities for an overnight stay – nightwear, toiletries and underwear for example.

If your baggage never arrives at all, you should make a claim against the airline within 21 days. Airlines' liability for lost luggage is limited by international agreement and the level of compensation is based on the weight of your baggage, which explains why it is filled in on your ticket by the check-in clerk. The maximum rate of compensation at present is US$20 per kilo for checked baggage and US$400 per passenger for unchecked baggage, unless a higher value is declared in advance and additional charges are paid.

The same procedure applies to baggage which you find to be damaged when you claim it. The damage should be reported immediately to an airline official and, again, you will have to fill in a PIR form which you should follow up with a formal claim against the airline.

Overbooking

Losing one's baggage may be the ultimate nightmare in air travel but the phenomenon of "bumping" must run it a close second. Bumping occurs when you arrive at the airport with a confirmed ticket, only to be told that there is no seat for you because the flight is overbooked. Most airlines overbook their flights deliberately because they know that there will always be a few passengers who make a booking and then don't turn up ("no shows" in airline jargon). On some busy routes like Brussels to London on a Friday evening, some business travellers book themselves on four or five different flights, so that there is a horrendous no-show problem and the airlines can, perhaps, be forgiven for overbooking.

The use of computers has enabled airlines to work out their overbooking factors quite scientifically, but just occasionally things don't quite work out and a few confirmed passengers have to be "bumped".

If you are unlucky enough to be bumped or "denied boarding", to adopt the airline jargon, you will probably be entitled to compensation. A few years ago the Association of European Airlines (AEA) adopted a voluntary compensation scheme based on a 50 per cent refund of the one-way fare on the sector involved, but early in 1991 the European Community agreed new rules which put compensation on a statutory basis. The rules lay down that passengers with a confirmed reservation "bumped" at an EC airport should receive 150 ecu (about £200) for a short-haul flight or 300 ecu (about £400) for a flight of more than 3500km (2170 miles). These amounts are halved if the passenger can get on an alternative flight within two or four hours respectively. In addition passengers have the right to full reimbursement of their ticket for any part of their journey not undertaken, and can claim legitimate expenses.

In 1997 the EC was reviewing these rules. Consumer groups had complained that compensation should cover the whole journey – and not just the sector on which the overbooking occurs. They note that a passenger flying to the Far East via Amsterdam, who is bumped off the first leg of the journey, might be held up for only an hour or so getting to Schiphol. But a missed connection could result in a much longer delay getting to Asia.

Compensation for Delays

Whatever the Conditions of Carriage may say, airlines generally take a sympathetic view if flight delays cause passengers to miss connections, possibly entailing overnight hotel accommodation. Our own experience is that most of the better-known scheduled carriers will pull out all the stops to ensure that passengers are quickly re-booked on alternative flights and they will normally pick up the tab for hotel accommodation and the cost of sending messages to advise friends or contacts of the revised arrival time.

The position is not so clear cut when it comes to charter airlines because the extent of their generosity usually depends on whatever arrangement they have with the charterer. But a number of British tour operators have devised delay protection plans which are usually included as part of the normal holiday insurance. Thomson Holidays, for instance, will normally provide meals or overnight accommodation in the event of long flight delays, and if the outbound flight is delayed for more than twelve hours, passengers have the right to cancel their holiday and receive a full refund. If they decide to continue their holiday they receive compensation up to a maximum of £60, in addition to any meals or accommodation which may have been provided. Compensation is also paid on a similar scale if the return flight is delayed.

Injury or Death

Airline liability for death or injury to passengers was originally laid down by the Warsaw Convention signed in 1929. The basic principal was that the infant airline industry could have been crippled if it had been forced by the courts to pay massive amounts of compensation to passengers or their relatives for death or injury in the event of an accident.

The trade-off was that the airlines undertook to pay compensation up to a set ceiling irrespective of whether negligence on their part was proved. The limit was set at 250,000 French gold francs, an obsolete currency which is nevertheless still used to this day as the official unit of compensation, and converted into local currencies. ∎

GETTING THERE BY ROAD
Chapter 5

OVERLAND BY TRUCK, VAN OR 4 X 4

by Jack Jackson

Travelling overland in your own vehicle gives you an independence and freedom to go where you like and when you like that no other form of travel can ever hope to match. It also provides a familiar bolt hole away from the milling crowds and the alienation one tends to feel in a different culture. The vehicle may seem expensive to start with and can involve you in mountains of bureaucracy, but considering the cost of transport and accommodation, it becomes realistic, particularly when you can escape the bed bugs and dirt that often accompany cheaper accommodation.

Which Vehicle?

The choice of vehicle will be a compromise between what can be afforded, what can best handle the terrain to be encountered, and whether spares, fuel, food and water have to be carried, or are readily available en route.

Short-wheelbase Land Rovers or Toyota Land Cruisers, Range Rovers and Land Rover Discoverys are ideal in the Ténéré Sand Sea, but are impossible to sleep full length in without the tailgate open and all the fuel, stores and water removed. Moreover, they are heavy on fuel. After a while one may long for the convenience and comfort of a Volkswagen Kombi, or similar sized panel van!

For a protracted transcontinental or round-the-world journey, you need to consider what sacrifices have to be made to have the advantages of the more cramped vehicles, including the length of time you expect to be on the road, and the degree of home comforts you will want along the way.

Where tracks are narrow, overhung and subject to landslides, as in outlying mountainous regions such as the Karakorum, then the only usable vehicles are the smallest, lightweight four-wheel drives, e.g. the soft-topped Short-wheelbase Land Rovers or Land Cruisers and the smaller Jeeps. These vehicles also give the best performance when traversing soft sand and steep dunes, but their small payload and fuel carrying capacity restrict them to short journeys.

If you do not plan to encounter soft sand, mud or snow and your payload is mostly people who, when necessary, can get out and push, then you really only require a two-wheel drive vehicle, provided that it has enough strength and ground clearance.

Avoid large American-style conversions. They have lots of room and home comforts like showers, toilets, microwave ovens and storage space; but their large size, fuel consumption, high weight, low ground clearance, poor traction, and terrible approach and departure angles, make them unsuitable for any journey off the asphalt road.

If costs were no problem and all spares were to be carried, the ideal vehicle would be an all-wheel drive with a payload of one tonne, evenly distributed between all wheels. A short-wheelbase, forward control, high ground clearance, large wheels and tyres, good power to weight ratio and reasonable fuel consumption. The vehicles best fitting this specification are the Mercedes Unimogs, the Pinzgauers, the Fiat PC65 and PC75 models and the Land Rover Military 101" one tonne. These are specialist vehicles for best cross country performance and are often soft topped to keep the centre of gravity low. However, the costs involved in buying, running and shipping such vehicles, would deter all but the very wealthy.

Considering price, availability of spares and working life, the most commonly used vehicles are the long-wheelbase Land Rovers, the smaller Mercedes Unimogs and the Bedford M type trucks. For two-wheel drive vehicles, the VW Kombi and the smaller Mercedes Panel Vans are the most popular. These are big enough to live in and carry food, water, spares, cooking stoves, beds, clothes, extra fuel and sand ladders. They also remain economical to run, small enough to negotiate narrow bush tracks and light enough to make digging out less frequent and easier.

These vehicles will carry two people in comfort, more if camping or using other accommodation overnight.

A high roof vehicle is convenient to stand up in and provides extra storage, but is more expensive on ferries. It also offers increased wind resistance, thus pushing up fuel consumption and making the engine work harder and run hotter. This shortens engine life and increases the risk of mechanical failure.

Trucks

Where heavier payloads are envisaged, such as in Africa where you will often have to carry large quantities of fuel, the most popular four-wheel drive vehicles are the Bedford M type trucks and Mercedes Unimogs. Bedford Trucks are cheap, simple and in some parts crude. They have good cross-country performance when handled sensibly and slowly, but are too heavy in soft sand. They go wrong and bits fall off, but repairs can usually be improvised, and used spares are readily available.

Bedford M type trucks, are best bought ex UK military, as are their spare parts.

Ex-NATO Mercedes Unimogs are near to perfect for heavy overland or expedition work. Their cross-country performance is exceptional, and their portal axles give them extra ground clearance, though this also makes them easier to turn over. It is almost impossible to get them stuck in sand, though they will stick in mud. Ex-NATO Unimogs usually have relatively small petrol engines, so you need to use the gearbox well, but fuel consumption is good. The standard six-speed, one range gearbox can be altered to a four-speed, two range gearbox, which is useful in sand. Four wheel drive can be engaged at any speed without declutching. Differential locks are standard. The chassis is cleverly arranged to give good weight distribution over all four wheels at almost any angle, but causes a bad ride over corrugations.

Mechanically, the Unimog is over-complicated. It doesn't go wrong often, but when it does, it is difficult to work on and often requires special tools. Later models have the clutch set to one side of the transmission, instead of in line with it, making it much easier to change.

Unimogs are best bought from NATO forces in Germany. Spares must be carried with you. Diesel Unimogs are usually ex-agricultural or building contractor and are therefore less well maintained than military vehicles and may have rust problems.

Land Rovers

Despite some weaknesses, Land Rovers are the most durable four-wheel drive small vehicles on the market. Their spartan comforts are their main attributes! Most of their recent challengers are too softly sprung and have too many car-type comforts, to be reliable in difficult cross-country terrain. Spare parts are readily available world-wide and they are easy to work on with most parts bolt-ed on. The older Series III leaf sprung models, are more durable than the newer "Defender" models and leaf springs are easier to get repaired in the Third World. The aluminium alloy body does not rust, so the inevitable bent body panel can be hammered back into rough shape and then forgotten. You don't have to be Hercules to change a wheel.

The short-wheelbase Land Rover is usually avoided because of its small load-carrying capacity; but in off- road use, particularly on sand dunes, it has a distinct advantage over the long-wheelbase models. Hard-top models are best for protection against thieves and safer when rolled, unless you have had a roll cage fitted.

When considering long-wheelbase models, it is best to avoid the six cylinder petrol engine models, including the one ton and forward control. All cost more to buy, give more than the normal amount of trouble, are harder to find spares for and recoup less on resale.

The six cylinder engine uses more fuel and more engine oil than the four cylinder engine and the carburettor does not like dust or dirty fuel, which means that it often requires stripping and cleaning twice a day in very dusty areas. The electrical fuel pump gives trouble. The forward control turns over easily and, as with the Series IIA Land Rovers, rear half shafts break if the driver is at all heavy footed.

The four cylinder models are underpowered, but the increased power of the six cylinder does not compensate for its disadvantages.

The 109" V8 Land Rover has permanent four-wheel drive, with a lockable central differential. It is an excellent vehicle, but very costly on fuel.

The Land Rover 90 and 110, now renamed "Defender", are designed for speed, economy and comfort on the newer, improved roads in Africa and Asia. Built on a strengthened Range Rover type chassis and suspension, with permanent four-wheel drive and centre differential lock, stronger gearbox, disc brakes on the front and better doors all around, the vehicle is a vast improvement on earlier models. It is ideal for lightweight safari or personnel carrier use, but for heavy expedition work the coil springs should be uprated or fitted with air-bag type helper springs.

In European Union Countries, outside of the UK, twelve seat Land Rovers should be fitted with a Tachometer and come under bus regulations.

Range Rovers and Land Rover Discoverys are not spacious enough, nor have the load carrying capacity for long journeys.

Any hard top or station wagon Land Rover, is suitable for a long trip. If you buy a new Land Rover in a wet climate, run it for a few months before setting off on a trip. This allows the wet weather to get at the many nuts and bolts that keep the body together. If these bolts corrode in a bit, it will save you a lot of time later. If you take a brand new Land Rover into a hot climate, you will regularly have to tighten loose nuts and bolts, particularly those around the roof and windscreen.

Early Land Rover diesel engines were not renowned for their reliability. The newer five bearing crankshaft diesel engines are better, but still underpowered. Land Rover Ltd still refuse to believe that the Third World requires a large, trouble-free diesel engine, and it is sometimes sensible to fit another engine such as the Isuzu 3.9 litre or the Perkins 4,154.

With the new Tdi, Turbo Diesel engines, Land Rover appear to have fixed the problems of their earlier turbo diesel and owners rave about their good fuel economy. The GRP camshaft timing belt is now 50 per cent wider but still a problem in hot dusty climates, though to be fair to Land Rover many modern vehicles have engines fitted with this type of belt and suffer the same problems.

Stretched 127/130 versions of Land Rovers are available, including crew cab versions, but fitted with the four cylinder diesel engine they are underpowered. Modern Land Rovers do not have double skinned roofs, so a loaded or covered roof rack is useful, to keep the vehicle cooler in sunny climates.

Other 4 x 4's

The latest Land Rover's superb axle articulation and lightweight body give it a distinct advantage in mud, snow and soft sand. If these are not likely to be encountered, then the leaf sprung Toyota Land Cruisers are comfortable and reliable, though heavier on fuel. Many Toyota models have large overhanging front bumpers, rear steps and running boards, which negate off road performance. The latest coil sprung Toyota Land Cruisers are less reliable. Nissan Patrols lack off-road agility and, as with American four-wheel drives, their large engines are heavy on fuel.

Despite its Paris/Dakar successes, the Mitsubishi Shogun (called Montero in the USA and Pajero elsewhere), has not proved reliable in continuous Third World use. The Isuzu Trooper is not well designed for true off-road work. Suzukis are just too small. Spares for Japanese vehicles can be a problem to obtain, anywhere in the world.

As with Range Rovers, Mercedes Benz Geländewagons, have poor load carrying capacity and their high costs limit their appeal. Several of the latest four-wheel drive vehicles are of monocoque construction, without a strong chassis; together with the Suzuki Vitara, Toyota RAV4 and the new baby Land Rover they are not suitable for overland or expedition use.

Four-wheel drive versions are available, of most popular pick-up trucks. Those most common in Africa are based on the Peugeot 504 and the Toyota Hilux. The Synchro version of the Volkswagen Kombi has an advanced fluid-coupling four-wheel drive system but poor ground clearance.

Two-Wheel Drives

The Volkswagen Kombi is in use in almost every country outside the Soviet Bloc and China. Anyone who has travelled overland through Africa, Asia, the Americas, or around Australia will notice that the VW Kombi is still a popular independent traveller's overland vehicle. Its ability to survive misuse (up to a point), and carry heavy loads over rough terrain economically, while providing the privacy of a mobile home, are some of the factors that make it so popular.

The Kombi has a one tonne payload and far more living space than a long-wheelbase Land Rover or Land Cruiser. It lacks the four-wheel drive capability, but partly makes up for this with robust independent suspension, good ground clearance and engine weight over the driven wheels. With experience and astute driving, a Kombi can be taken to places that will amaze some four- wheel drive vehicle drivers. The notorious 25km "sea of sand" between In Guezzam and Assamaka, in the Sahara, has ensnared many a poorly driven 4X4, while a Kombi has stormed through unscathed! With the use of lengths of chicken wire fencing, as sand ladders, plus some helpful pushing, a Kombi can get through quite soft sand.

The second most popular two-wheel drive vehicle for overlanders is the smaller Mercedes, diesel engined, panel van, which is very reliable. All of the stronger rear-wheel drive panel vans are suitable for overland use and most are available with a four-wheel drive conversion, at a price. Avoid vehicles that have only front-wheel drive; when loaded at the rear, they often lose traction, even on wet grass in a campsite.

Petrol versus Diesel

Weight for weight, petrol engines have more power than diesel engines, but for hard usage in Third World areas, they have several disadvantages. In hot countries there is a considerable risk of fire and the constant problem of vapour lock, which is at its worst on steep climbs, or on long climbs at altitude. Dust, which often contains iron, gets into and shorts out the distributor. High tension leads break down and if much river crossing has to be done, water in the electrics causes more trouble. A further problem is that high-octane fuel is not usually available and low-octane fuel will soon damage a sophisticated engine. However, petrol engines are more easily repaired by less experienced mechanics.

Avoid any engine with an electronic engine management system. These are not normally repairable if faulty and a flat battery can cause problems with some of these.

Diesel fuel is messy, smelly and attacks many forms of rubber but it does not have the fire risk of petrol and outside of most of Europe is usually about one third of the price of petrol. It also tends to be more available, as it is used by trucks and tractors.

Diesel engines are heavier and more expensive to buy, but are generally more reliable and require less maintenance. An advantage is that extra torque is available at low engine revolutions. This allows a higher gear in the rough, which improves fuel consumption, this means less weight of fuel needs to be carried for a section without fuel supplies – improving fuel consumption still further. There is also no electrical ignition to malfunction where there is a lot of dust or water. Against this is the fact that diesel engines are noisier and lack the acceleration of petrol engines, which can be tiring on a long journey.

A second filter in the fuel line is essential to protect the injection pump from bad fuel and a water sedimentor is useful, but needs to be well protected from stones and knocks.

Some Japanese diesel vehicles have 24 volt electrical systems.

Tyres

Long-distance travellers have to cover several different types of terrain, which makes it difficult to choose just one set of tyres suitable for the whole route. Unless you expect to spend most of your time in mud or snow, avoid the aggressive tread, so-called cross-country or all-terrain tyres. These have large open cleated treads that are excellent in mud or snow, but on sand they tear away the firmer surface crust, putting the vehicle into the softer sand underneath. Open treads tear up quickly on mixed ground with sharp stones and rocks.

If you expect to spend a lot of time in soft sand, you will require high flotation tyres with little tread pattern. These compress the sand, causing the least disturbance to the firmer surface crust. Today's standard for such work is the Michelin XS, which has just enough tread pattern to be also usable on dry roads but can slide about on wet roads or ice. The XS is a soft flexible radial tyre, ideal for low pressure use but easily cut up on sharp stones.

As most travellers cover mixed ground, they require a general truck type tyre. These have a closed tread with enough tyre width and lugs on the outside of the tread, to be good mixed country tyres, although obviously not as good in mud or soft sand. Such tyres when fitted with snow chains, are better than any all-terrain tyre for snow or mud use and, if of radial construction, can be run soft to improve their flotation on sand. The best tyre in this category is the Michelin XZY series.

Radial or Cross Ply, Tubed or Tubeless

Radial tyres are more flexible, and have less heat build-up when run soft, than cross-ply tyres. They also have less rolling resistance, thus improving fuel consumption. For heavy expedition work, Michelin steel braced radials last longer. With radial tyres you must use the correct inner tubes, preferably by the same manufacturer. Radial and cross-ply tyres should never be mixed.

Radial tyres "set" in use, so when changed around to even out tyre wear, they should preferably be kept on the same side of the vehicle. A further advantage of radials is that they are easier to remove from the wheel rim with tyre levers, when you get a puncture away from help.

Most radial tyres have soft side walls that are easily torn on sharp stones, so if you have to drive over such stones, try to use the centre of the tyre, where the tread is thickest.

For soft sand use, radial tyres can be run at 40 per cent pressure at speeds below ten miles an hour and 75 per cent pressure for mixed terrain below twenty miles per hour. Remember to reinflate to full pressure when you return to firm ground.

Tubeless tyres are totally impracticable for off-road work, so always use tubed tyres and carry several spare inner tubes.

A vehicle travelling alone in difficult terrain should carry at least one extra spare tyre, as well as the one on the spare wheel. Several vehicles travelling together can get by with only the tyres on the spare wheels so long as they all have the same size and type of tyres for full interchangeability.

Wide Tyres

There is a tendency for "posers", to fit wide tyres. Such tyres are useful in soft sand and deep snow, but in other situations they negate performance. Worse still, on asphalt roads, hard top pistes or ice, they lower the weight per unit area (= grip), of the tyre on the road, leading to slipping and skidding.

Wheels and tyres that are larger than the vehicle manufacturers recommend can damage wheel bearings and cause problems with steering and braking

Never mix tyres of different sizes on four-wheel drive vehicles.

Roof Racks

These need to be strong to be of any use. Many of those on the market are flimsy and will soon break up on badly corrugated pistes. Weight for weight, tubular section is stronger than box section and it should be heavily galvanized.

To extend a roof rack to put jerry cans of water or fuel over or even beyond the windscreen is lunacy. The long-wheelbase Land Rover for instance, is designed so that most of the weight is carried over the rear wheels. The maximum extra weight allowed for the front axle is the spare wheel and a winch. It does not take much more than this to break the front springs or distort the axle. Forward visibility is restricted when going downhill with extended roof racks. Full-length roof racks can be fitted safely, but must be carefully loaded, remember that Land Rover recommend a total roof weight of not more than 90kg. A good full-length roof rack will weigh almost that on its own!

Expect damage to the bodywork and reinforce likely points of stress, in particular the corners of the windscreen. Good roof rack designs will have their supports positioned in line with the vehicle's main body supports, and will have fittings along the back of the vehicle to prevent the roof racks from juddering forward on corrugations. Without these fittings, holes will be worn in the roof.

Modern Land Rovers have aluminium roof channels so roof racks fitted to these vehicles require additional supports to the bulkhead at the front and the lower body at the rear.

Nylon or Terylene rope is best for tying down baggage. Hemp rope deteriorates quickly in the sun and holds grit, which is hard on your hands. Rubber roof rack straps are useful, but those sold in Europe soon crack up in the sun. You can use circular strips cut from old inner tubes and add metal hooks to make your own straps. These will stand up to the constant sunlight without breaking. Ratchet straps should not be over-tightened.

In deserts, if one doesn't have a motor caravan, sleeping on the roof rack can be a pleasant way of avoiding spiders and scorpions. Fitting a full-length roof rack with plywood, makes it more comfortable as well as keeping the vehicle cool in the sun. Special folding tents for roof racks are available, at a price.

Conversions

An elevating roof or fibreglass "pop-top" motor caravan conversion has advantages over a fixed roof van. It is lower on the move, can sleep extra people up-top, e.g. children, provide extra headroom while camped and insulates well in tropical heat. Some better designed fibreglass pop-tops do not collect condensation, even when you cook inside them. Some of the disadvantages are that they can be easier to break into, they look more conspicuous and more inviting to thieves than a plain top and they have to be retracted before a driver, disturbed in the night, can depart in a hurry.

In some vans, the hole cut in the roof weakens the structure of the vehicle. Driving on very bad tracks can cause cracks and structural failures in the body and chassis; failures that would not normally occur if the vehicle spent its life in Europe. Vans should have roof-mounted support plates added along the elevating roof, to give torsional support.

A demountable caravan fitted to four-wheel drive pick-up trucks such as the Land Rover, Land Cruiser or Toyota Hi-Lux, could provide a lot more room and comfort, but demountables are not generally robust enough to stand up to the off-road conditions of an overland journey. They also add considerably to the height and width of the vehicle and are more expensive than a proper conversion. Moreover you cannot walk through from the cab to the living compartment.

Furnishing and Fittings

Camper conversions should have fittings made of marine plywood rather than hardboard, it is stronger, more durable and not prone to disintegration when hot or wet. If your vehicle is finally destined for the US, it must satisfy US Department of Transport and State regulations for the basic vehicle and the conversion. The same applies to motor caravans destined permanently for Australia, where equally strict Australian Design Rules, apply to both the vehicle and the conversion.

Most water filtration systems, e.g. Katadyn, are portable and many wall-mounted models can be fitted to a vehicle. On many motor caravans, the water tank and even gas cylinders, are mounted beneath the floor, where they are most vulnerable off-road.

Front-opening vents or window quarterlights in the front doors are appreciated in warm climates, as are a pair of fans built in for extra ventilation. However, window quarterlights are attractive to thieves. Fresh air is essential when sleeping inside a vehicle in tropical climates and a roof vent is just not enough to create an adequate draught. Equip open windows with mosquito netting and strong wire mesh.

On a long transcontinental journey, one will normally have to do without a refrigerator. (It is often preferable to use the space and weight for more fundamental items like jerry cans or spare parts). However, if you are carrying large quantities of film or medicines, one could consider a lightweight dry- operating, thermoelectric "Peltier-Effect" refrigerator by Koolatron Industries, but fit a larger capacity alternator and spare battery, with a split charge system.

Stone-guards for lights are very useful, but you need a design that allows you to clean the mud off the lights without removing them, (water hoses do not usually exist off the beaten track), and they should not be fitted with self tapping screws. Such designs are difficult to find.

Air horns should be located away from mud, e.g. on the roof or within the bodywork, where they can be operated by a floor mounted switch. An isolator may be located on the dashboard, to prevent accidental operation of the horn.

For sunny countries, paint chrome windscreen wipers, wing mirrors and any wing steps matt black, to stop dangerous reflections from the sun and have fresh windscreen wiper rubber blades, for when you return to wet climates.

A good, powerful spotlight fitted on the rear of the roof rack will be invaluable when reversing and will also provide enough light for pitching tents. Normal reversing lights will be of no use. Bull Bars, better named Nudge Bars, are usually more trouble than they are worth, may invalidate your insurance and damage the body or chassis if struck with any force. The EU wishes to ban them in the near future.

Paperwork

As well as the obvious requirement for passports, visas and personal insurance, you will require: vehicle insurance for the whole journey, the Vehicle Registration Document, a letter of permission to drive the vehicle if you are not the owner, each of the two types of International Driving Licenses (these vary in the languages of translation) and a Carnet de Passage for the vehicle. Have photocopies of all of these documents and spare passport size photographs. Some countries will insist that you also buy local insurance but this will only cover the bare minimum of Third Party Insurance.

The Carnet de Passage acts as a passport for the vehicle and is intended to stop you selling it; it will be your largest single expense and is obtainable through the AA or RAC by depositing a bond or taking out insurance. A few countries will note the vehicle in your passport instead of requiring a Carnet de Passage.

All important paperwork is best kept in a strongbox that is fixed directly to the vehicle chassis.

Finally, whatever type of vehicle you take and however you equip it, you should aim to be as self-sufficient as possible. You should have food to last for weeks not days, and the tools, spare parts and personal ability to maintain your vehicle and keep it going. Without these, and in spite of the occasional genuinely kind person, you will be conned and exploited to the extent that the journey will be a major ordeal. With adequate care and preparation, your overland journey will be an experience of a lifetime.

For motoring organisations world-wide see p.765 of the Directory
For driving requirements world-wide see p.776 of the Directory

OVERLAND BY MOTORBIKE

by Ted Simon

It seems pointless to argue the merits of motorcycles as against other kinds of vehicles. Everyone knows more or less what the motorcycle can do, and attitudes to it generally are quite sharply defined. The majority is against it, and so much the better for those of us who recognise its advantages. Who wants to be part of a herd? Let me just say that I am writing here for people who think of travelling through the broad open spaces of Africa and Latin America, or across the great Asian land mass.

Here then are some points in favour of the motorcycle for the few who care to consider them. In my view, it is the most versatile vehicle there is for moving through strange countries at a reasonable pace, for experiencing changing conditions and meeting people in remote places.

It can cover immense distances and will take you where cars can hardly go. It is easily and cheaply freighted across lakes and oceans, and it can usually be trucked out of trouble without too much difficulty, where a car might anchor you to the spot for weeks.

Sit Up and Take Notice

In return, the bike demands the highest levels of awareness from its rider. You need not be an expert, but you must be enthusiastic and keep all your wits about you. It is an unforgiving vehicle which does not suffer fools at all. As well as the more obvious hazards of pot holes, maniacal truck drivers and stray animals, there are the less tangible perils like dehydration, hypothermia and plain mental fatigue to recognise and avoid.

The bike, then, poses a real challenge to its rider, and it may seem on the verge of masochism to accept it, but my argument is that by choosing to travel in a way that demands top physical and mental performance you equip yourself to benefit a thousand times more from what comes your way, enabling you quite soon to brush aside the discomforts that plague lazier travellers.

You absolutely must sit up and take notice to survive at all. The weather and temperature are critical factors; the moods and customs of the people affect you vitally; you are vulnerable and sensitive to everything around you; and you learn fast. You build up resistances faster too, your instincts are sharper and truer, and you adjust more readily to changes in the climate, both physical and social. Here endeth the eulogy upon the bike.

One's Company

I travelled alone almost all the way around the world, but most people prefer to travel in company. As a machine the motorcycle is obviously at its best used by one person, and it is my opinion that you learn faster and get the maximum feedback on your own, but I know that for many such loneliness would be unthinkable. Even so, you need to be very clear about your reasons for choosing to travel in company. If it is only for security then my advice is to forget it. Groups of nervous travellers chattering together in some outlandish tongue spread waves of paranoia much faster than a single weary rider struggling to make contact in the local language. A motorcycle will attract attention in most places. The problem is to turn that interest to good account. In some countries (Brazil, for example) a motorcycle is a symbol of playboy wealth, and an invitation to thieves. In parts of Africa and the Andes, it is still an unfamiliar and disturbing object. Whether the attention it attracts works for the rider or against him depends on his own awareness of others and the positive energy he can generate towards his environment.

It is very important in poor countries not to flaunt wealth and superiority. All machinery has this effect anyway, but it can be much reduced by a suitable layer of dirt and a muted exhaust system. I avoided having too much glittering chrome and electric paintwork, and I regarded most modern leathers and motorcycle gear as a real handicap. I wore an open face helmet for four years, and when I stopped among people, I always took it off to make sure they saw me as a real person.

Don't ...

Finally a few things I learned not to do. Don't ride without arms, knees and eyes covered and watch out for bee swarms, unless you use a screen, which I did not. Don't carry a gun or any offensive weapon unless you want to invite violence. Do not allow yourself to be hustled into starting off anywhere until you're ready; something is bound to go wrong or get lost. Do not let helpful people entice you into following their cars at ridiculous speeds over dirt roads and potholes. They have no idea what bikes can do. Always set your own pace and get used to the pleasures of easy riding. Resist the habit of thinking that you must get to the next big city before nightfall. You miss everything that's good along the way and, in any case, the cities are the least interesting places. Don't expect things to go to plan, and don't worry when they don't. Perhaps the hardest truth to appreciate when starting a long journey is that the mishaps and unexpected problems always lead to the best discoveries and the most memorable experiences. And if things insist on going too smoothly, you can always try running out of petrol on purpose.

THE ART OF MOTORCYCLE MAINTENANCE

by Chris Scott

Setting off by motorbike is a bold but easy decision to make. However, be under no illusions as to the monumental preparation required and the sacrifices needed for two-wheeled life on the road. The chief amongst these is a bike's limited ability to carry little more than essentials. Documentation for bikes is identical to cars and one should always carry copies; (see p. 776 of the Directory). The cost of a carnet is one good reason not to take an expensive bike; the fact that a long journey will annihilate its resale value is another. Cheap bikes, well prepared, are the best way to go.

From the UK popular itineraries are across Africa to Cape Town or across Europe and western Asia to India and beyond. Both routes are frequently undertaken by bikers; Africa, with its unavoidable desert and jungle is harder, a challenge of arduous terrain and tedious borders. Before undertaking these big trips consider taking an exploratory run, to Morocco for example, to see how your bike will perform. Much can be learned on a test run, above all the shock of how well your bike handles when fully loaded on dirt roads. Allow at least a year for preparation and earning the money to pay for it as well as your trip. Trans-Africa will cost about £4,000 plus your bike, India and back about £5,000 and round the world around £10,000, depending on your route and resistance to temptations. Shipping is cheap, slow and unnecessarily complicated; air freight is much more efficient and reliable. Leave some money at home with a reliable friend, or a credit card number with a friendly bike shop, this way vital items can be quickly despatched with just one call.

Choosing a Bike

For Africa a four-stroke, single cylinder trail bike of around 600cc is best. For the main overland route to India any road bike will do, in this case a big comfortable shaft driven tourer makes a lot of sense. Road bikes will limit your ability to explore off the highway and are exhausting when you have to detour off road, but they are a better option for passengers. Whatever bike you choose, consider these factors along with the total rolling weight once loaded:

1. lightness
2. economy
3. comfort
4. mechanical simplicity
5. agility
6. reliability
7. robustness

By far the most popular bike is Yamaha's XT600Z or ZE Ténéré; pre-1989 models are best, being simpler, lighter and more economical. BMWs are also famously popular, but stick to the old 'Boxer-engined' models from 800-1000cc, or the F650 Funduro. Suzuki DRs (especially the 350) and bigger Honda XLs are also good, particularly the XL650R, but avoid XRs, Yamaha TTs and other enduro-type bikes not built for the rigours of long distance touring. Women or short-legged men might find lower-seated 350s easier to manage, though BMW singles as well as '97 Suzuki DR650s have suspension and/or seat lowering options. Avoid electric start only bikes; BMW twins can have kick starts fitted. KTM's new LC4 'Adventure' certainly looks built for tough overlanding, but costs £7,000.

Bike Modifications and Tyres

Any bike you buy which already has a big tank (i.e. at least 4.5 gallons/20 litres) is a big expense solved. Jerry cans are awkward to carry but may be essential for a desert crossing. Water cooled engines offer unnecessary complication but oil coolers for hot climates are a useful addition. Other tips are a bigger foot plate on your side stand to support the bike on soft ground, 'Barkbuster' handlebar lever protectors and security bolts (rim locks) on wheel rims. Use only top quality 'o' ring chain (DID or Regina) with wheel sprockets (the manufacturers' originals are often the best). You are inviting trouble using cheap transmission and rolling components. DID, Excel or Akront rims laced with heavy duty spokes are a good precaution for rough roads and heavy loads. Paper element in-line fuel filters are another wise modification, and if you don't trust foreign motor oil, change it every 2,000 miles. Replace cosmetic, plastic 'sump guards' with proper alloy bash plates. Carry a tool for every fitting on your bike plus duct tape, wire and glue. Modern bikes (especially the ones recommended) are incredibly reliable and so spares are up to you, but at least carry heavy duty inner tubes, control leavers and anything else that is likely to wear out or break before you can replace it.

Tyre choice is always a quandary. To cross Africa, run down to the Sahara on any old tyre and then fit Michelin Deserts, extremely tough desert racing knob-blies which will last well beyond the mud bath of Zaire with barely a puncture. Less expensive though not quite as tough are Pirelli MT21s, an excellent road/dirt compromise. In sand or mud knobbly tyres make the difference between constant slithering and prangs or sure-footed fun. Across Asia or round the world on roads, pick the longest wearing rubber you can buy. Tubeless radial tyres are relatively new to overlanding but apparently last long and can be easily repaired on the wheel with plugs and glue, plus a pump or carbon dioxide cartridges. Even then, you must be completely at ease with tyre removal and repairs; the most common cause of breakdown unless you choose to buy an Enfield Bullet in India. In this case, go for the 350cc model and expect to meet many roadside mechanics. One overlander described her Bullet as "always sick but never terminal".

Luggage and Clothing

Overloading is the most common mistake, but something to avoid if your bike is to be manageable off the road. Every biking overlander ends up giving stuff away or sending it back. Although German bikers love their huge aluminium boxes, the only advantage of this system is security and neatness. Soft throwover panniers in either tough woven nylon (such as Oxford Baggage's 'Lifetime' range), ex-army canvas bags or rucksacks, or simply home-made leather are lighter, cheaper, crashable, repairable and not prone to fracture or inflict painful injury. They will not be water, dust or theft proof, but if you keep your baggage nice and dirty no one will want to go near it. Small tank bags are also very handy for valuables but Krauser or Givi-type boxes will eventually break on your average Afro-Asian road.

Bare in mind that widely loaded bikes use more fuel, and in all cases, pack heavy weights low and towards the centre of the bike. Bulky, light items like sleeping bags can be carried high, even over the headlight, but tools are best stored in an old ammo box or pouch attached to the bash plate. Carry fuel in steel Jerry cans, they also make useful bike props, stools and are resellable anywhere. Above all, *think light:* non-bike stuff can be replenished or replaced on the way and might even become a cherished souvenir.

Your choice of clothing is limited only by its usefulness and durability. You will only wear one jacket so make it one that protects you from the rain, wind, stones and crashes. Natural fibres are light and comfy, leather can be heavy and hot and takes ages to dry. PVC ponchos are cheap and very versatile. Top quality touring jackets, such as those produced by Hein Gericke are expensive, but are light, robust and functional. The merits of breathable fabrics like Gore-Tex are dubious on a bike, but lots of big, secure pockets are very useful; use your jacket like a wallet or safe and never lose sight of it. Helmet choice is personal, but open faces make you appear more human to strangers. Always wear goggles or use a visor. Stout footwear will protect your vulnerable legs; proper motocross boots are best for off-road trips, otherwise ex-army boots will last.

Life on the Road

Pull over from the roadside and camp out of sight of passing vehicles. Never ride at night or miss a chance to fill up with fuel and water. Be aware of you and your bike's limitations when driving off-road, especially in the early days when you have yet to learn the benefits of less baggage. Even if you are a loner, you will find yourself delighted to team up with other overlanders when faced with remote or dangerous sections such as the Sahara or Baluchistan. The longer you travel, the lighter and more refined your equipment becomes.

Resist the temptation to ride and ride and ride. Whatever your stated goal, it's the people you will meet on the road that will provide the longest memories, both good or, if they are in uniform, sometimes bad. Traditionally capricious border guards are generally easy on bikers, recognising that two-wheel overlanding is no air-conditioned picnic. Nevertheless, approach borders as if you are going to be there for days. Bribes are usually small and clearly prompted, unless you are in trouble. If there is one common piece of advice most overlanding motorbikers come back with it is this: plan well but trust your ingenuity, everything works out all right in the end.

HIRING A CAR

by Paul Melly and Edwina Townsend

First hire your car.... Yes, there are a lot of countries where it is a big advantage to have your own personal transport, especially if you must keep to a tight work schedule or have bulky luggage. Yes, it is relatively easy to book anything from a Fiesta to a limousine for a fair number of the world's destinations, including some which are surprisingly off-beat. Yes, it can be very expensive – and certainly will be if the pre-departure homework is neglected. One journalist acquaintance who thought he knew what travelling was about, managed to burn up over £100 with a day and a half's car hire in Brittany by the time he'd paid all the extras.

The key rule is: don't just read the small print, work out what it actually adds up to. For example, a mileage charge really can rack up the cost, especially if you haven't measured in advance quite how far you will be travelling.

It's no use, after the event, holding a lifelong grievance against the big car hire companies. By and large they do fairly well in providing a comprehensive and reliable service in a wide range of countries, if at a price.

Travelling Cheaply

If you want a better deal, you must expect to work for it and be prepared to tramp the back streets looking for a local outfit that is halfway trustworthy – but remember you only get what you pay for! It costs Hertz, Avis, Europcar, Budget and Alamo and the rest a hefty investment to provide that easy-to-book, uniform service across national frontiers and linguistic boundaries. Centralised, computer-based reservation networks don't come free.

If you really want to keep the cost down, perhaps public transport is worth a fresh thought. Shared, long-distance taxis or minibuses are surprisingly fast and cheap in many parts of the Third World and you may have an easier time with police, army or Customs road checks which have a habit of springing up every few kilometres in some countries. If it's not you who is driving, then it's not you, foreign and unfamiliar with the local situations, who has to judge whether it is correct paperwork or a small bribe that is required. Quite apart from the ethical dilemma, there is the practical one: having to pay back-handers is bad, offering them when they are not expected is worse and can get you into far more trouble.

However, it would be stupid to allow such worries to discourage travellers from doing the adventurous thing, and hiring a car can give you the freedom to go where you want at your own pace, stopping in small villages or at scenic viewpoints when it suits you.

The big car hire firms give thorough coverage over much of the developed world and quite a number of tourist and/or business destinations in other regions. But they certainly do not have outlets everywhere and there are many places where you will have to rely on local advice in finding a reliable rental outfit. Advance reservation may well be impossible. In this case, if your time is tight, ask friendly officials in the country's embassy in your home country for suggestions. Most will have a telephone directory for their capital city at least, even if it is a little out of date.

For a few pounds, you can then ring to book in advance, or just to check availability – easier, of course, if the country is on direct dialling. This could well be more effective than asking a small High Street travel agent used to selling Mediterranean package tours to try and arrange something for you. It is also worth contacting agencies which specialise in a particular region of the world.

For most places, it is still definitely worth considering the big hire companies. In recent years they have developed a good range of lower price services to complement the plusher options for those with fat expense accounts. Thanks both to the recession and the growing interest which small firms are taking in foreign markets, there are plenty of businessmen who cannot afford to travel five star all the time.

And, though you may be abroad for work, very often you can, with forethought, make use of the special packages designed for tourists. Not only are these cheaper, but they also have the advantage of simplicity, being tailored to the needs of leisure visitors who are either not used to or do not want to be bothered with organising everything for themselves.

Meanwhile, if you are going on holiday, there is something to be learnt from those who have to travel for work, or from their companies. Clearly, big firms have buying power in the car hire market which a private individual does not, but they also pick up a lot of experience.

Here are some useful tips suggested by the travel manager of one multi-national company: read the small print, get your insurance, avoid mileage payments and large cars, and watch out for the chance to save money on the pre-booked deal.

Price, in particular, takes some calculation because of the extras which are hard to evaluate exactly. Car hire is sometimes offered per mile or per kilometre, but it is best to go for an unlimited mileage deal, even if the base price is slightly higher. While you cannot be sure how much petrol you will use or how much you will pay for it, at least the local currency cost of hiring the car for, say, six days is fixed.

Legalities

Car hire forms always include some reference to CDW (Collision Damage Waiver) and PAI (Personal Accident Insurance) additional to the cost of renting the vehicle. A customer can be held responsible for a share of loss or damage to the hire vehicle, regardless of who is at fault. But if you accept the CDW clause and pay the daily charge for it, the rental company waives this liability to the financial level advised which varies from country to country and in the US from state to state, provided the customer sticks within the conditions of the hire agreement.

Clearly if you rent a car, you must be insured against damaging it, and, more importantly, any other people or vehicles. But accepting the CDW option can prove an expensive form of protection so explore other possibilities first. For instance, your own personal car insurance at home may provide cover, or you may be able to built it into your general travel insurance policy by paying a supplement.

It is particularly important for those contemplating hiring a car in the USA to remember that the CDW charge which is included in the prepayment includes only the bare minimum amount of cover required by the laws of that state. You will more than likely be asked to top-up this cover but check first what it will cost you and what you are paying for.

Again with PAI you will find that most travel insurance policies sold here in the UK include medical expenses and hospital costs. Therefore, before accepting to pay for PAI as an additional extra with the car hire company, check your travel insurance policy as you may be putting yourself to unnecessary extra expense.

Another legal aspect it is vital to check, is whether the hire agreement allows you to drive where you want. This may seem an irrelevant point to make for anyone restricting themselves to a European city for instance, but important if you are visiting a country where you wish to go off the beaten track and drive on unmade roads. The conditions imposed by the car hire companies may insist you stick to metalled roads that may severely limit your freedom. Alternatively if driving off-road is allowed you may find an additional supplement is charged.

Driving Conditions

Perhaps this is the place to warn that roads in many countries make quite a change from Britain's consistent, if occasionally pot-holed or contra-flowed, tarmac. Clearly a good map, if you can buy one, is indispensable. But it is unlikely to give you the up-to-date or seasonal information you really need before setting out.

Many highways are just dirt or gravel and can become almost impassable at rainy times of year. If they are major trading routes this can be made even worse as huge trucks lurch through the mud cutting deep wheel ruts which fill with water. Maps will not always show the state of the roads, or what they are made of. Of course, in the dry season, such routes may be dusty, but they become much easier to use. In some areas, where the vegetation is fairly stunted, lack of tarmac can make it quite hard to follow the road.

Nor do these warnings go for tropical countries alone: the famed Alaska Hiway from Dawson Creek in Canada through to Fairbanks is largely gravel surfaced. And many minor roads in Canada turn into muddy bogs, with cars sinking up to their axles in black gumbo when it rains. The worst time of year can be the spring thaw – just when a European visitor might be expecting conditions to get easier!

Meanwhile, if you are likely to drive through mountains, including the relatively domesticated Alps and Pyrenees, make sure your car is equipped with snow tyres or chains, and you know how to them. The Alps may be crossed by motorways and tunnels, but that does not stop winter blizzards. Nor does it stop the local police from making spot checks – and spot fines – on roads where chains or snow tires are obligatory (normally indicated by a sign as you enter the relevant stretch). This advice applies particularly to people who go on business in winter to cities near the mountains and decide to hire a car and pop up the hill for a day's skiing – your tyres may feel OK in downtown Turin, but it's not so sure you'll still feel confident on the nineteenth hairpin bend up to the ski resort, with no room to turn round.

You should also check for road construction projects, especially in the Third World where massive foreign aid spending can make it happen very suddenly on a huge scale. This may sometimes cause a mess, but it can also mean a new hard-top road existed where there was only a mud-track before, opening up fresh areas for relatively easy exploration with a normal hired saloon car. On the other hand, there can be surprising gaps in otherwise fairly good networks.

The basic rule is: before you do something unusual, tell the car hire outlet where you picked up the vehicle and signed it out. And if you should have an accident or break down, telephone the hire firm before paying for expensive repairs. Otherwise you may not be reimbursed. The firm may want to make its own arrangements.

What Car?

Deciding what size of car to hire is one of the simplest questions. The main companies use fairly standard makes with which you will be familiar at home, although it is probably safe to say that you are rather more likely to get Japanese makes in Asia, French in West Africa and, not surprisingly, American in the US.

But when working out costs, don't forget that larger vehicles are also thirstier.

You should remember this especially when booking in advance – sometimes the rental deal will stipulate that if the car of your choice is not available then the agency will provide one in a higher category for no extra charge. In other words, if you reserve a small car and then turn up to find it isn't there, you may end up with one that uses more petrol – which could be an expensive penalty if you are hiring it for a long trip but the car will probably be more comfortable.

Nor should petrol bills be forgotten when you return the vehicle. Most agreements stipulate that the car is provided with a tankful of petrol and returned also with a full tank. Check that it is full before you take it out and make the final fill-up yourself. This way you will probably pay less than the charges made by the hire company as a refuelling charge is usually added by them to the cost of the petrol itself.

Booking a car in advance is usually worth considering, not only for peace of mind but because you may be able to take advantage of one of the many inclusive deals offered by the major car hire companies. You can choose to either prepay before leaving home in exchange for a prepaid voucher, or alternatively book at a guaranteed rate in the currency of the country you are visiting. These rates can include not only unlimited mileage but also CDW (Collision Damage Waiver), PAI (Personal Accident Insurance) and tax on the completed transaction. This leaves you just the petrol to pay for and any optional extras you may agree to take locally. Bear in mind that these inclusive rates are often for a minimum of a three day rental.

The incidence of extra mandatory charges, which can only be paid locally, is becoming more frequent. For instance there are an increasing number of countries where either a fixed fee, or a percentage of the rental is charged by the local authority for vehicles rented at airport locations. This is passed on to the hirer by the car hire companies. Also, in some US States, Florida immediately springs to mind, there is now a mandatory extra tax levied of approximately $2 per day in addition to the standard charges. In other words, beware of the extras.

If you are not sure whether to rent or not, why not take a prepaid voucher with you for any number of days. Once you are on the spot you can therefore weigh up the possible alternative form of transport and decided whether or not to use it. Most prepaid vouchers, if unused and returned to the outlet where you bought them, will be refunded in full. However, this is not always the case so check before buying. Also be aware that partially used vouchers are often not refundable.

Last of all, but equally important, a deposit is always required by car hire companies at the beginning of any rental. In most cases an imprint of your credit or charge card will suffice. However, you may find that a car rental company may refuse to hire you the car if you cannot produce a credit card. Alternatively, though it is unusual, you may be required to pay the deposit in cash or travellers's cheques.

When you arrive abroad it is always worthwhile asking for tips about reliable local car hire firms; hotel porters are usually a good source of information. Also once at the hire company, before revealing you have a prepaid voucher , why not check if they have any local special offers. Providing your bank balance will stand the cost of the voucher until you return home, and you have sufficient funds to pay again locally, this could be yet another way of making extra savings.

The big groups claim to offer the same level of service, whether it be one of their own offices or a franchise. While you will invariably be provided with the best available wherever you are renting, remember that in some countries new vehicles are scarcer than hen's teeth; the road conditions leave much to be desired and the standards of driving are not quite what you expected to find!

One option for cutting costs and red tape if you are staying somewhere for a lengthy period, or regularly visit the same destination, can be leasing. This is normally provided for conventional business car fleets, but you may find that if you, or a group of people, regularly need a car in one place, a lease could be cheaper. It is also simple because the deal can include repairs and service.

Safety

Of course, the bottom line when you hire a car is safety. Does the vehicle work and can you trust it? Unless you are a natural, or at least a good amateur, mechanic, there isn't much chance of really assessing whether the car is roadworthy. But one can make a few simple checks which are at least a pointer as to how well it's maintained.

Try the steering and test out the brakes by driving a few feet in the hire shop forecourt, and of course listen for any faults in the first mile or two. Have a look at the tyre treads to see if they are still fairly deep and test the lights. If you are in tropical country check the air-conditioning, if any, and in any very cold territory, such as Canada between October and April, be sure it is winterised. Just because the first snow of autumn hasn't survived in the city centre doesn't mean it has melted in the surrounding countryside and suburbs too. Make sure that any faults such as bumps or scratches are detailed on the hire form before you take the car out. Otherwise you could find yourself held liable when you return.

It is also a good idea to make sure you are allowed to use the car where you want to. Tell the hire firm if you plan to cross national or state borders, just to make sure the insurance cover extends across the frontier. And remember that while many discount rental deals allow you to drop the car off where you want in the country where you collected it, there is usually a surcharge for leaving it at one of the company's offices in a completely different country.

Getting the right paperwork is also vital. Take photocopies of all hire agreements, insurance etc., as well as such basics as an International Driving Permit (see *Documentation for the International Motorist* at the end of this chapter). And remember that in many countries travellers are expected to register with the local police on arrival in a town and stop at police posts by the roadside.

When it comes to frontiers, if the border is closed for the night, you will have to wait until morning to cross, even if there is no physical barrier in your way. Otherwise you could have problems when you come to leave and your passport lacks the proper entry stamps. Probably the only reliable way to check whether you're allowed across is to ask the drivers of local bush taxis which may have pulled in to wait for dawn. In the end, when it comes to officialdom, patience and politeness are probably more important than anything else.

For a list of major car rental companies see p.771 of the Directory

SHIPPING A VEHICLE
by Tania Brown and Keith Kimber

To find the best shipping for your vehicle you must know who sails to your destination. Most people begin by looking through the Yellow Pages and contacting shipping agents, but this will never give you a complete list of all the ships using the port. The secret is to locate the industry paper that serves the port and get the latest copy. They appear under a variety of names like *Shipping Times*, *Shipping Schedules* and some less obvious publications such as *The Bulletin* in Panama. Start by asking for them at shipping offices. Most are published weekly and contain a goldmine of information. Listings indicate destinations and arrival/departure dates for all ships in port along with pier and berth numbers that tell you exactly where the ships are located. Also indicated are the shipping line, its local agent and types of cargo carried. The same information is given for ships at sea scheduled to arrive, and there's a directory of agents' telephone numbers and addresses. In some countries this information appears as a weekly supplement to a regular newspaper.

Contact the agents that list sailings to your destination and compare freight costs (always based on volume). The basic freight rate always has three surcharges which are as follows: fluctuating fuel costs; a currency adjustment factor to compensate for exchanging rates; and wharfage charges. Make sure these are included in any quotes you receive. At times the bunker surcharge or currency adjustment factor can be negative values, and represent a discount.

Unconventional Channels

Don't only follow conventional channels. The paper will list unscheduled ships using the port mission boats, training ships, all kinds of 'oddball' one-off vessels that might take you on board. They won't have agents at the ports so you'll have to contact the Captain direct. Where port security is minimal and/or corrupt, enter the docks and speak to the Captain personally. Any visual material like photos and maps of your journey are invaluable as an introduction. One good photo can jump the language and cultural barriers and get him interested enough to talk to you. If port security is strict, there is another way. When a ship docks it is immediately connected to a telephone line. Each berth has a different telephone number. In Sydney, for example, the numbers are listed in the telephone directory. Consult your shipping journal for the ship's berth, look up the number and you can speak directly to the ship. If the numbers aren't in the 'phone book, ask at the Shipping and Port Manager's office.

Write to the Captain with your visual material and a covering letter explaining what you are doing and where you want to go. Follow it up two days later to receive his reply. That way he can see what you are doing and you get a chance to speak to him on the 'phone. If he's amenable, ask for a working passage or free shipping for your vehicle, but be prepared to follow up with a realistic offer of payment if his interest starts to wane. If you work your passage as we did, your vehicle is taken free. But we've also received offers from regular shipping lines to take our vehicle unaccompanied to various parts of the world. For this approach the Operations Manager or General Manager of the shipping line or its agent. Again, write and interest them in what you are doing. If you are on an expedition, you can generate publicity for them – point this out. If not, don't worry. Offer to give a talk and slide show for the staff in return for free shipping, plus any number of large colour photographs they can use for advertising showing the company logo on your vehicle as you tackle the next desert or jungle. The way you approach them is really more important than what you offer in return. Don't forget, people in poor countries can't always understand the desire for hard travelling and a frugal lifestyle but some dramatic photos of your journey can work wonders.

Packing your Vehicle

Your next concern is how the vehicle will travel. Try to avoid crating it if you can. Crating is expensive and involves a lot of back-breaking work. Even in countries where labour is cheap, timber is costly. It's also inconvenient – you can't drive your vehicle to the ship when it's in a crate. If you must crate, visit an import agent to try and obtain a ready-made crate the right size. Un-crated, the vehicle can go 'break-bulk,' roll-on/roll-off or containerised. Containerised is the best. The vehicle is protected from theft and the elements, and can't be damaged during loading or unloading – and you can leave all your luggage inside. 'Roll-on/roll-off' services are very convenient. The vehicle is driven onto the ship and stored below deck – just like a regular car ferry. But these only operate on certain routes and your luggage shouldn't be left in the vehicle. 'Break-bulk' means it is carried as it is, either in the ship's hold or on deck surrounded by all the other break-bulk cargo. Countries with weak economies may insist you pay for your freight in US dollars. It's advisable to carry enough US dollars (rather than pounds) for this purpose.

A forwarding agent can do all the paperwork for you although it's cheaper to do it yourself. The best way is to team up with a 'hustler' who works for a forwarding agent. These young lads spend all day pushing paperwork through the system. They know where to find port trust offices, the wharf storekeeper's office, main Customs building, port Customs building, etc., buildings and offices that are usually spaced far and wide across the city. They know how to persuade Customs officers to inspect the vehicle and wharf officers to certify documents. Better still, they know what sort of 'tips' are expected down the line. I've always found them friendly, helpful types, with great sympathy towards anyone on the same side of the counter as themselves pitted against the officials! They've never objected to my tagging along to push my own paperwork through the system. In return, I buy them cold drinks and a good meal each day we're together, and give a few dollars to thank them for their help at the end.

Be well prepared to do your own paperwork. Take a dozen sheets of carbon paper, a handful of paper clips (there will be a lot of copies), a good ball point pen, some large envelopes and a pocketful of small denomination notes in the local currency. Commit your passport number, engine and chassis number, vehicle weight and local address to memory so you can double check details as the officials type them out (this is also good practice for any overland traveller when crossing land borders). Remember if a single digit is incorrect in the serial numbers you will not be entitled to your own vehicle at your destination. People *have* lost their vehicles this way. I also carry a small 'John Bull' type india rubber kit to make up my own rubber stamps. It saves hours filling out forms – especially if you are doing a number of vehicles. It's normal practice to have to buy the forms you use for a nominal sum – either at the port or a stationer's in town. In Western countries the paperwork is often simplified and it's quite easy to do it yourself.

Clean the vehicle thoroughly before shipping (especially under the mudguards where dirt collects) to avoid the cost of it being quarantined or fumigated on arrival. Smear exposed deck cargo with grease or paint it with diesel oil. Grease the disc brakes as well. Don't worry, they will work afterwards. On a motorcycle, remove wing mirrors, the screen and indicators.

Cars should be lashed on deck with chains and bottle screws, not rope which will fray and stretch. If only rope is available look for nylon rope which won't stretch when it gets wet. Motorcycles should be off the centre-stand, wheels chocked front and back and tied to a post using wooden spacers. Look ahead and be prepared to take your own rope. On the *MV Chidambaram* in India we ended up using the guy ropes from our tent and every webbing strap we had to tie our motorcycle securely. Don't leave a vehicle unaccompanied at the dock. Paper work can usually be done two days before sailing, then the vehicle is inspected, cleared by Customs and loaded on board the day it sails. In Third World countries, insist on being allowed to supervise loading. Use rope slings, don't let them use a net. Sling a rope through the back wheel and under the steering head. A car should be lifted using pairs of boards or poles chained together under the wheels. If the correct tackle is unavailable, drive the car into an empty container so it can be lifted on board. If the vehicle must be left on the dockside and loaded in your absence, don't leave any luggage inside, don't leave the key with anyone and lash it to a wooden pallet so they can forklift it to the ship and winch it on board. Most importantly of all, don't leave the country before you've seen the vehicle off, in case they don't load it for some reason.

Meet the ship on arrival and confirm your cargo will be unloaded. When we arrived in Malaysia, they told us our bike was destined to continue to Singapore. We had an awful time convincing them they were wrong! The vehicle will then be held in Customs until you complete the paperwork to release it. Insist that it must go inside a locked shed. There may be a nominal storage charge but often the first three days are free. Be prepared to be philosophical about accepting some minor damage. Put any dents down to adventure!

Air Freight

Motorcyclists can consider airfreight as a viable alternative to shipping. Over short distances, it is often cheaper and sometimes may be the only way of getting somewhere – inland, for example. In a passenger aircraft, the motorcycle lies on its side in the cargo hold, so construct a set of crash bars to support it without damage. It must fly completely dry: no fuel, engine oil, brake fluid, coolant, battery acid or air in the tyres. People worry their battery will be ruined by draining the acid. I've drained mine many times and once left it dry for more than two weeks without any ill effects. It doesn't even lose any charge. But don't use it before refilling with acid! And don't plug the breather hole or the whole thing will explode. A wad of cotton wool over the hole will soak up any acid drops and allow it to breathe. Freight charges are based on weight.

Special Notes

Depending on the political situation in Sri Lanka you can sail to Talaimannar by ferry from Rameshwaram Island, India. Vehicles and passengers cross the Pamban Channel by train from Mandapam, the last stop on the mainland. There is no road bridge. Motorcycles are lifted into the goods carriage, cars go on a low loader which costs extra. The ferry moors a quarter of a mile off shore and is loaded by 'lighters' – small wooden boats. Cars go on a flat raft or two lighters tied together, a hair-raising experience. Paperwork takes a full day.

I have met people who have been obliged to spend US$1500 on anti-pollution devices for their cars arriving in California to comply with state laws. This doesn't apply to everyone, but if in doubt, ship to one of the other 49 states. From personal experience, Columbus Shipping Lines take excellent care of vehicles, keeping them regularly washed down with fresh water to reduce the effects of the salty sea air.

On entering Panama, you have to specify where the vehicle will be shipped from. If undecided, specify 'Colon.' When you've organised your shipping, visit the Customs head office at Ancon to make any changes. International motorcyclists in Panama shipping round the Darien Gap can contact the Road Knights Motorcycle Club at Albrook US Air Force Base for advice, use of workshops, and up to two weeks' free accommodation. It will be cheaper to ship cars to Ecuador than Colombia.

Finally, shipping really isn't all that bad. Things always go smoother and quicker than you think and there are always people who will help you out. If you encounter just a quarter of the problems mentioned here you've had an unusually bad trip!

For car ferry operators from the UK see p.774 of the Directory

OFF-ROAD DRIVING

by Jack Jackson

Off-road driving challenges the traveller in a completely new way and techniques vary with the ability and weight of the vehicle, as well as with the driver. Some vehicles have greater capabilities than many drivers can handle and there may often be more than one way of solving a particular problem.

Alert but restrained driving is essential. A light foot, and low gears in four-wheel drive, will usually get vehicles through difficult situations. Sometimes sheer speed may be better, but if you lose control at speed, you could suffer damage or injury. Careful driving saves time, money and effort. Careless driving breaks chassis, springs, half shafts and burns out clutches.

Before driving off-road, look under your vehicle and note the position of its lowest points: exhaust pipes, towing plates, springs, axles, differentials, transfer box and gearbox. These will often be lower than expected and the differentials are usually off-centre. Remember their clearance and position when traversing obstacles. Do not hook your thumbs around the steering wheel, the sudden twist of it when a front wheel hits a stone or rut can easily break them.

Have number plates and lights above bumper level to avoid damage and have strong towing eyes.

Always travel at a sensible speed, watching for problems ahead. If you are on a track where it is possible that another vehicle may come the other way, have a passenger keep a lookout further ahead, while you concentrate on negotiating difficulties.

Travel only at speeds that allow you to stop easily within the limit of clear vision. Travel slowly to the brows of humps or sharp bends; there may be large boulders, holes, or steep drops beyond them.

Apart from soft sand and snow, most situations where four-wheel drive is needed, also require low-range for better traction, torque and control. They will normally also require you to stop and inspect the route on foot first, so you can engage low-range before starting off again.

With permanent four-wheel drive systems, remember to engage lock before entering difficult situations.

On soft sand it is useful to be able to engage low-range on the move. On some vehicles this requires practice at double-declutching. For most situations, first gear low-range is too low and you might spin the wheels; use second or third gear, except over large rocks.

Before descending any steep incline, check that the vehicle is still in gear in both the main gearbox and the transfer box.

When descending steep loose or muddy inclines there is a high chance of skidding. Use second gear, low-range engine braking in four-wheel drive with any centre differential locked in. With automatic transmission use first gear plus left foot braking, and use the accelerator to keep the wheels moving. Depress the accelerator gently, when correcting a skid.

All braking on loose surfaces or corrugations should be Cadence braking, i.e. several short pumps, unless you have ABS brakes. In really loose situations turn ABS systems off.

If you have been in four-wheel drive on a hard surface, when you change back into two-wheel drive or, for permanent four-wheel drive systems, you unlock the centre differential lock, you might find this change and the steering difficult due to wind-up between the axles. This scrubs tyres and can damage the drive train. If you are lightly loaded, free it by driving backwards while swinging the steering wheel from side to side. If you are heavily loaded, you will have to free it by jacking up one front wheel clear of the ground; keep clear of the wheel, which may spin violently.

Make use of the rhythm of the suspension, touch the brakes lightly as you approach the crest of a hump and release them as you pass over it; this stops the vehicle from flying. When you come to a sharp dip, ditch, or rut, cross it at an angle, so that only one wheel at a time drops into it. Steer the wheels towards and over the terrain's high points to maintain maximum ground clearance.

Do not drive on the outside edge of tracks with a steep drop, they may be undermined by water and collapse under the weight.

Ground Inspection

Keep an eye on previous vehicle tracks, they will indicate trouble spots that you might be able to avoid.

If you cannot see the route or obstacles clearly from the driving seat, get a passenger to stand in a safe place where he or she can see the problem clearly and direct you. Arrange a clear system of hand signals with the person beforehand, vocal directions can be drowned by engine noise. Only delegate one person to do this, more than one becomes confusing.

You may have to build up a route, putting stones or sand ladders across drainage ditches, or weak bridges, chipping away high corners, or levering aside large boulders. If you have to rebuild a track or fill in a hole completely, do so from above, rolling boulders down instead of wasting energy lifting them from below. Where possible bind them together by mixing with tree branches or bushes.

If you cannot avoid a rock, drive over it square on with a tyre, which is more resilient and more easily repaired than your chassis. To traverse large boulders, use first gear low-range and crawl over, using the engine for both drive and braking. Avoid slipping the clutch or touching the brakes.

On loose surfaces, do not change gear while going up or downhill, you can lose traction.

Always change to a lower gear before you reach problems, to remain in control. If you lose traction going uphill, swing the steering wheel from side to side –you may get a fresh bite and make the top. If you fail going up a steep hill, change quickly into reverse, make sure you are in four-wheel drive with the centre differential locked if you have one and use the engine as a brake to back down the same way you came up. Do not try to turn round or go down on the brakes.

Be prepared to stop quickly on the top of a steep hill, the way down the other side may be at a different angle.

Do not tackle steep hills diagonally, if you lose traction and slip sideways, you may turn over. Only cross slopes if it is absolutely necessary. If you must do so, take the least possible angle and make any turns quickly.

Pistes/Dirt Tracks

Except on soft sand use two-wheel drive, this gives more positive steering and avoids transmission wind-up. Tyres should be at correct pressures.

Watch out for stones thrown up by other vehicles, never overtake when you cannot see through the dust of the vehicle ahead, and use the horn to warn vehicles that you are about to overtake. Culverts do not always extend to the full width of dirt roads, watch out for these when overtaking.

Avoid driving at night; potholes, culverts, broken-down trucks, bullock carts and people are difficult to see and many trucks drive at speed without lights and then blind you with full beam when spotting you. Many countries have unlit chains and logs across roads at night, as checkpoints.

Bull Dust

Bull dust hangs in the air, obscuring vision. When travelling downwind you have to stop often to let it clear. If you cannot see to overtake, drop back and wait until the piste changes direction so that the wind blows the dust to one side, providing clear vision.

Corrugations

Corrugations give an effect similar to sitting on a pneumatic drill to both vehicles and their occupants.

Light vehicles may 'smooth out' the bumps by achieving enough speed to skim over the tops. Going fast over corrugations increases tyre temperatures, causing more punctures. Softly sprung vehicles can go faster, more comfortably but often blow tyres and turn over. With minimal area of tyre in contact with the ground at any time, braking should be light cadence and any turns of the steering wheel should be gentle. Short-wheelbase vehicles often become unstable on corrugations.

Radial tyres give a more comfortable ride, but do not lower the tyre pressures – there are usually sharp stones and soft tyres run hotter.

Avoid travelling beside the corrugations, other vehicles will have tried that before and given up – hence the corrugations, take it steady and be patient.

Corrugations find weaknesses in the suspension and electrical cable insulation. Coil springs dislodge, leaf springs break, shock absorbers fail and electrical shorts cause vehicle fires, a battery isolator is essential.

Except on sand, with long-wheelbase vehicles do not use four-wheel drive on corrugations. The rear axle supports most of the load and has the strongest differential, in four-wheel drive, snatch loads could damage the front differential or half-shafts.

Ruts/Gullies

Where possible, straddle ruts with the wheels on each side. If they are unavoidable, there will be points where the lowest parts under your vehicle may ground. Where these occur, try to remove the problem or fill in the ruts with stones or brushwood, Continually grounding differentials causes drain plugs that are not recessed to come undone and drop out.

Ruts negate steering. Even in four-wheel drive, turning the steering wheel has little effect on the vehicle's direction of travel. Check regularly out of the driver's window to ensure that the front wheels point straight ahead, otherwise, if they find some traction or the side of the rut is broken away, the vehicle may suddenly veer off the track.

If you are stuck in a rut on firm ground, try rocking out by quickly shifting from first to reverse gear. Do not try this on sand or mud, you will sink in deeper. If this fails, jack up the offending wheel and fill in the rut with stones or logs. A high-lift jack makes this easier and can, with care, also be used to shunt the vehicle sideways out of the rut.

Larger ridges or ditches should be crossed at an angle in four-wheel drive. Ditches can be bridged or ramps built up to ridges with supported sand ladders. Ditches can be filled in with logs or stones, clear them again afterwards to avoid local flooding.

Deserts and Sand

Deserts are not all impassable sand dunes. Quite large dunes are passable and most deserts have larger areas of stone than sand.

Avoid travelling in the late afternoon when low sun makes it is difficult to spot sudden changes in dune strata, many accidents occur as vehicles fly off the end of steep drops.

On firm sand, two-wheel drive or with modern Land Rovers the centre differential locked-out gives more positive steering, avoids transmission wind-up and allows higher speeds.

Watch out for any changes in surface colour. If the surface you are driving on is firm and the surface colour remains the same, then the going is likely to be the same. If the colour changes, you should be prepared for possible softer sand. Moving sand dunes and dry river beds produce the most difficult soft sand.

The key to soft sand is flotation and steady momentum; any abrupt changes in speed or direction can break through the firmer surface crust, putting the wheels into the softer sand below. Use as high a gear as is possible to avoid wheelspin. Speed up as you approach a soft section and try to maintain an even speed and a straight line across it. If you find yourself sticking, press down gently on the accelerator. If you have to change down, do so smoothly.

Do not travel in other vehicles' tracks, the crust has already been broken and your vehicle's chassis will be that much lower and therefore nearer to sticking, to start with. Keeping your eye on other people's tracks will warn you of soft sections, but do not follow them for navigation, they may be 50 years old.

In general, flat sand with pebbles or grass on its surface, or obvious wind-blown corrugations, will support a vehicle. If in doubt, get out and walk the section first. Stamp your feet, if you get a firm footprint then it should support your vehicle; but if you get a vague oval, then it is too soft. If the soft section is short, you can make a track with sand ladders. Long sections require low tyre pressures and low-range four-wheel drive. Bedford trucks will not handle soft sand, without the assistance of perforated plates and lots of human pushing power.

Dry river beds can be very soft and difficult to get out of. Drift sand will always be soft. If you wish to stop voluntarily on soft sand, find a place on top of a rise, preferably pointing downhill and roll to a stop without using the brakes and breaking the crust.

Most vehicles have too much weight on the rear wheels when loaded. These wheels often break through and dig in, leaving the front wheels spinning uselessly on the surface. A couple of passengers sitting on the bonnet can help for short bad sections; but you must not overload the front continuously or you will damage the front axle.

Most deserts freeze overnight in winter making the surface crust firmer. Even if not frozen, there will be dew in the surface crust, making it firmest around dawn, this is the time to tackle dunes and the softest sections.

Sand dunes require high-flotation sand tyres. You need speed to get up a dune, but you must be able to stop on top, as there may be a steep drop on the other side. Dunes are best climbed where the angle is least, so known routes, in opposing directions, are often some distance apart to make use of the easiest angles.

When descending steep dunes, use second gear low-range and drive straight down, applying some accelerator to control any slipping and retain steering control. If the vehicle noses in, use third gear low-range with your left foot on the brake and enough accelerator to keep the wheels moving.

The bottom of the well between dunes and the leeward faces of dunes have the softest sand.

Never use aggressive-tread tyres on sand. Only a small percentage of desert sand is really soft, use tyres at normal pressures so that you can travel at comfortable speeds on the firm sections and make full use of speed where you have room on soft sections, only lower tyre pressures where necessary.

If you have to sit out a sandstorm, turn the rear of the vehicle to face the wind and cover all windows, to prevent them becoming etched by sand.

Getting Unstuck in Sand

Once you are stuck in sand, do not spin the wheels or try to rock out, you will sink deeper and may damage the transmission. First off-load the passengers and with them pushing, try to reverse out in low-range. The torque on the propeller shafts tends to tilt the front and rear axles in opposite directions relative to the chassis. So, if you have not dug in too deep, when you engage reverse, you tend to tilt the axles in the opposite direction to the direction involved when you got stuck, thus getting traction on the wheels that lost it before. If you stopped soon enough in the first instance, then this technique will get you out. If it does not, then the only answer is to start digging and use sand ladders.

It is tempting to do only half of the digging required, but this usually fails and you finish up working twice as hard in the end. Self-recovery with a winch does not work well either. Sand deserts do not abound with trees and burying the spare wheel or several stakes deep enough to winch you out, is just as hard as digging out the vehicle. Another vehicle on firm ground with a winch or tow rope can help, but you must dig out the stuck vehicle first.

Long-handled shovels are required to get under the differentials, folding tools are useless. Reconnoitre the area and decide whether the vehicle must come out forwards or backwards. Dig the sand clear of all points that are touching it. Dig the wheels clear and then dig a sloping ramp from all wheels to the surface, in the intended direction of travel.

Lay down sand ladders in the ramps, rear wheels only if things are not bad, all four wheels if things are bad. Push the ends of the ladders under the wheels as far as possible, so that they do not shoot out. A high-lift jack helps here. Mark their position in the sand with upright shovels, they often disappear in use and can be hard to find later. Then, with only the driver in the vehicle and all passengers pushing, the vehicle should come out using low-range four-wheel drive.

Very fit passengers can dig up the sand ladders quickly and keep placing them under the wheels of the moving vehicle. Sometimes, when a ladder is not properly under a rear wheel when a vehicle first mounts it, it can tip up and damage a body panel or exhaust pipe; so an agile person has to keep a foot on the free end to keep it down. Remember to move QUICKLY once the ladder settles, or you'll get run over!! Some sand ladder designs are articulated in the centre, or sectional and tied together, to correct this problem. Do not tie the ladders to the rear of the vehicle, in the hope of towing them, they may cause you to bog down again.

Driving the vehicle out backwards is usually the shortest way to reach firm ground, but you will still have to get across or around the bad section. Once out, the driver should not stop before reaching firm ground. The passengers may then have a long, hot walk, carrying sand ladders and shovels, so also carry bottles of water. With a large convoy, a ramp of several ladders can be laid down on bad sections.

Vehicles of one tonne or under need only carry sand ladders, just long enough to fit comfortably between the wheelbase. One vehicle alone should carry four; but vehicles in convoy only require two each, as they can help each other out. Heavier vehicles require perforated steel or aluminium alloy plate.

Sand ladders and perforated plates bend in use. You can straighten them out by laying them on hard ground with the ends on the ground and the bend in the air and driving over them.

Beaches

Where a beach is the only route, wait for low tide. Beaches are usually firm enough for vehicles between high tide mark and four metres from the sea itself, where there is likely to be an undertow. Beware of the incoming tide, which is often faster than you envisaged and can cut off your exit. Where there are large puddles or streaming water on a sea beach, beware of quicksand.

Salt Flats (Sebkhas, Chotts)

These behave like quicksand. You sink quickly and if you cannot be towed out quickly, it can be permanent! In areas known for their salt flats, stick to the track and convoy with other four-wheel drive vehicles. If you are unlucky enough to hit one, try to drive back to firm ground in a wide arc. Do not stop and try to reverse out.

Mud

Mud problems are not only off-road but on main pistes after rain. Many routes immediately south of the Sahara and in Southeast Asia become almost impassable for months during their wet seasons.

If mud is heavy with clay, even ultra-aggressive tread tyres clog up. The answer is normal tyres fitted with heavy-duty snow chains.

Winches are useful among trees, but unless you are operating regularly in these conditions the extra weight and cost of these plus ground anchors are rarely worth it. More important is to adapt your vehicle to accept a high-lift jack without it slipping. Fit small sections of angle iron or tube longitudinally to front bumpers and rear chassis or longer pieces transversely with suitable notches cut out, to stop jacks slipping. Adaptors are available for fitting high-lift jacks to late model Land Rover jacking sockets and Toyota Land Cruiser bumpers.

Choose the firmest ground, avoid boulders and tree roots. If necessary engineer a route, dig channels to drain away water and dig away high points that could be awkward to climb or may cause the vehicle to lean or slip sideways.

If the track slopes sideways over a drop, level it out, if the area freezes overnight or the water is fed by glacier meltwater then the route will be easier at dawn.

Momentum in four-wheel drive, using as high a gear as possible is the key to getting through mud, but there may be unseen problems beneath it. If there are existing tracks or ruts that are not deep enough to ground your transmission, then use them. Otherwise, slog through, avoiding sudden changes in speed or direction.

If you get 'high centred', either jack up one side of the vehicle and build up the ground under the wheels or shunt the vehicle to one side using a high-lift jack. If you have lost traction, but the vehicle chassis is not grounded, locked up drum brakes on wheels that have them, 'heeling' and 'toeing' or left foot braking if you have automatic transmission, are alternatives, to stop wheels spinning and divert traction to wheels that have grip.

When seriously stuck, digging out is heavy work and leaves the vehicle with a rise to climb. Jack up the vehicle and fill in under the wheels with stones, logs, brushwood and even spare wheels.

Perforated plate, placed upside down, i.e. rough side up, will give more grip to the wheels but sand ladders become slippery.

Trying to tow a stuck vehicle out if the towing vehicle is also on mud usually fails. If the stuck vehicle is of similar size to the rescue vehicle, snatch-tow, Kinetic Energy Rope Recovery using the correct KERR ropes, is the most effective solution but you must thoroughly understand the technique and its dangers.

When you return to paved road, clear as much mud as possible off the wheels and propeller shafts, the extra weight will put them out of balance and cause damage. Drive steadily for ten minutes to clear the tyre treads, or you could skid.

Crossing Water

If a Turbocharger is fitted, allow it to cool before entering water.

The latest vehicles may have catalytic converters, in rough terrain these break up and cold water destroys hot catalysts. For Third World use, remove the unit to avoid an expensive replacement on returning to the European Union. If you cannot do this or will be wading in Europe, fit a raised exhaust outlet. Any serious wading in cold water can damage catalysts.

Coat petrol engine ignition components with silicone sealant, including any breather holes in the bottom of the distributor; clear these breather holes as soon as possible after the crossing. Silicone sealant is preferable to grease, which melts in hot climates and runs onto electrical contacts.

On Land Rover vehicles fit the clutch bell housing wading plug and where supplied, the camshaft drive belt housing wading plug. These plug the holes that drain any leaking oil to prevent it getting onto the camshaft timing belt or clutch driven plate. They should be removed after wading, not necessarily immediately, but within a few days.

For regular wading, leave these plugs fitted, but remove them weekly, allow any oil to drain out and then replace them.

Late vehicles should have remote axle breather tubes, venting above the engine; check their condition regularly. Older vehicles may have Poppet valves; check that these are clean and in working order. Hot axles fitted with poppet valves, if stuck in water for any length of time, will produce a vacuum on cooling and suck water in through oil seals. Poppet valve systems are easily converted to remote breather tubes.

Inspect water on foot first. In warm climates avoid wading in bare feet, in slow-flowing water there may be Schistosomiasis (Bilharzia). In Africa, going about in bare feet is asking for worm and tick infections. Waders are more sensible than Wellington boots, there may be unseen deeper sections. Use a shovel or staff to prod for depth, boulders or soft sections.

Choose a sensible angle into the water and out on the other side. You may flood your engine if the angle in is too steep and may not be able to get up the other side if the angle is too difficult.

If the river bed is soft, lower the tyre pressures. Fast-flowing rivers will be faster and deeper, with more difficult entry and exit, where they narrow. If possible choose a wider section. Moving or stagnant water with an unbroken surface may be deep and is more likely to have a silt bottom, that vehicles could sink into. Moving water with a rippling or broken surface usually denotes a stony bottom, will be shallower and clear of silt; this is easier to cross. If there are dry patches, you can break up your crossing into stages.

Rivers fed by glaciers or melting snow will be at their slowest and lowest level at dawn.

If the water will reach above bumper level, fix a waterproof sheet across the front of the vehicle to help create an efficient bow wave. If a waterproof sheet is not available, consider crossing the water in reverse.

If the water will come above the fan, remove the fan belt to cut down the spray onto ignition components. This is important with nylon or aluminium fan blades, which may flex and damage the radiator core and essential if you decide to wade in reverse or have to back out. Only remove a fan belt for short periods, the water pump no longer operates.

If the water will come above the floor, raise any articles that could be damaged by it. The vehicle may float slightly, therefore losing traction, have the rear door open and all baggage lashed down.

Vehicles in convoy should cross one at a time. On deep crossings the rear of a vehicle and its chassis take in water, which pours out on climbing the far bank, making this slippery and more difficult for following vehicles. Later vehicles should try alternative exits or allow time for the exit to drain and dry out.

Cross difficult water in second gear, low-range four-wheel drive, with any centre differential locked in and avoid changing gear while in the water.

Keep engine speed high enough for the exhaust pressure to stop the back pressure of the water from stalling the engine. It is worth adjusting the engine tick over speed to a faster setting.

Forward speed should be high enough to create a small bow wave. The trough created behind this bow wave keeps the engine bay and side doors in shallower water, lessening any spray over the engine. A fast walking pace is about right; if spray comes over the bonnet you are going too fast.

In deep water you will require first gear, to push the wave of water ahead of the vehicle. If you stall in the water, remove the sparking plugs or injectors and try driving out in bottom gear low-range on the starter motor. This works over short distances.

If the bow wave cannot be maintained and there is a chance of the water being deep enough to reach the air intake, SWITCH OFF BEFORE THE ENGINE STOPS. This is essential with a diesel engine. Water does not compress, so catastrophic damage can occur.

If fast-moving water is above bumper height, keep the vehicle at 45° to the direction of flow. The full force of water at 90° to the body will force the vehicle downstream and negate steering. On easy crossings, keep the brakes dry by keeping your left foot lightly on the brake pedal. Once out of the water, dry out the brakes by driving for a few minutes this way. Disc brakes are self-cleaning, but drum brakes fill up with water and sediment; clean these regularly and don't forget the transmission brake.

If a petrol engine stalls or misfires, spraying WD-40 over all ignition components may get it firing again; if not, dry them all out thoroughly.

River Bed – Flash Floods

Although you may be in a river bed under a cloudless sky, heavy rain elsewhere can cause a flash flood that envelopes you. Most flash floods are seasonal, but freaks can occur at any time. Always be prepared and never camp overnight in a river bed.

Where a river bed has to be used in the rainy season, while driving upstream, watch out for possible flood-water. When driving downstream, have a passenger monitor the route behind you while your own attention is on the terrain ahead.

Make mental notes of any places where you can quickly get up the bank out of danger. If you encounter flood-water coming down, get up the nearest bank. If this is not possible, drive quickly downstream to the first available escape route.

Third World Ferries

Third World ferries should be embarked and disembarked in four-wheel drive with any centre differential locked in. This ensures that you do not push the ferry away from the bank, leaving your vehicle in the water.

Weak Bridges

Inspect local bridges before using them. If there are signs that local vehicles cross the river instead of the bridge, then that is the safest way to go. If in doubt and the bridge cannot be avoided, unload the vehicle and cross slowly in four-wheel drive, with only the driver in the vehicle.

Snow and Ice

Snow is deceptive because it does not always conform with the terrain it covers. On roads or tracks, keep to the middle to avoid sliding into ditches or culverts at the side. Drive slowly in four-wheel drive, in as high a gear as is possible and avoid any sudden changes in speed or direction. Use the engine for braking.

Snow chains should be either on all four wheels, or on the rear wheels only. Having chains on the front wheels only, will cause a spin if you touch the brakes going downhill.

With vehicles that have large axle articulation, some designs of snow chains could sever the brake hoses, so check with your vehicle manufacturer before buying snow chains.

If the vehicle is empty, put some weight over the rear axle.

If you drive into a drift, you will have to dig out and it is easier to come out backwards. Off-road driving in snow will be easier at night, or in the early morning, when the snow is firmest and the mud below it frozen. As with sand, on really deep snow, high-flotation tyres are an advantage. If they are fitted with chains, they should be at the correct pressures, not at low pressure, or the chain swill damage them.

If you skid or spin, do not touch the brakes; depress the clutch, then, with all four wheels rolling free, you will regain control. Areas subject to wind or shade may have black ice.

In very cold conditions, if you have a diesel engine, dilute the diesel fuel with one part of petrol to fifteen parts of diesel, to stop it freezing up (use one to ten for Arctic temperatures). This is illegal in the UK and could damage modern high speed diesel engines, but is often necessary in the Third World.

Convoy Driving

Vehicles in convoy should be well spread out, so that each has room to manoeuvre, does not travel in another vehicle's dust and has room to stop on firm ground should one or more vehicles get stuck. Adopt the system where any vehicle which gets stuck, or requires help, has its headlights switched onto mainbeam. This is particularly important in desert situations. All drivers should keep an eye out for headlights in their mirrors, as these can usually be seen when the vehicle cannot.

The last vehicle should have a good mechanic and a good spare wheel and tyre, to cover breakdowns.

Keep to the allotted convoy order to avoid confusion and unnecessary searches. The convoy leader should stop at regular intervals, to check that all is well with the other vehicles.

For a list of specialist vehicle conversion and off-road vehicle companies see p.783 of the Directory

RUNNING REPAIRS

by Jack Jackson

Before you depart on an overland journey, use your vehicle for several months, to run in any new parts properly. This will enable you to find any weaknesses and become acquainted with its handling and maintenance. Give it a thorough overhaul before leaving. If you fit any extras, make sure that they are as strong as the original vehicle. For precise navigation, you should know how accurate your odometer is, for the tyres fitted. Larger tyres, e.g. sand tyres, will have a longer rolling circumference.

Once in the field, check the chassis, springs, spring shackles and bushes, steering, bodywork, exhaust and tyres, every evening when you stop for the day. Every morning, when it is cool, check engine oil, battery electrolyte, tyre pressures and cooling water, and fill the fuel tank. Check transmission oils and hydraulic fluids at least every third day. In dusty areas, keep breather vents clear, on the axles, gearbox, and the fuel tank filler cap. Keep an eye on electrical cables for worn insulation, which could lead to a fire.

Fit a battery isolation switch. It could save your vehicle in a fire and is an excellent anti-theft device. New models of these will allow enough power through, to run any necessary clocks and memory systems, when disconnected.

Make sure that you carry and use the correct oils and fluids in all systems. Deionising water crystals are easier to carry than distilled water, for batteries. Remember to lubricate door hinges, door locks, padlocks etc., and remember that in many deserts you need antifreeze in the engine for night temperatures.

Brush all parts clear of sand or dust before working on them. When working under a vehicle, have a groundsheet to lie on and keep things clean, wear goggles to keep dirt out of your eyes. A small vice-fitted to a strong part of the vehicle, will aid many repairs. In scrub or insect country you will need to brush down the radiator mesh regularly.

Maintenance

By using several identical vehicles travelling in convoy, you can minimise the weight of spares and tyres to be carried. The idea of using one large vehicle to carry fuel etc., accompanying several smaller, more agile vehicles, does not work out well in practice. The larger vehicle will often be heavily bogged down and the smaller vehicles will have difficulty towing it out, often damaging their drive train in the process. Also, the vast difference in general journey speed and the extra spares needed cause many problems, unless you are to have a static base camp.

Overloading is the largest single cause of broken-down vehicles and the easiest to avoid. Calculate your payload against the manufacturer's recommendation for the vehicle. Water is 1kg per litre, fuel roughly 0.8kg per litre, plus the weight of the container. Concentrate on the essentials and cut back on the luxuries. It could make all the difference between success and failure.

For rough terrain, trailers are not advisable. They get stuck in sand, slip into ditches and overturn on bad tracks. Powered trailers have been known to overturn the prime vehicle. On corrugated tracks, trailer contents soon become so battered as to be unrecognisable. Trailers are impossible to manhandle in sand or mud and make life difficult if you have to turn around in an awkward situation. They also reduce the efficiency of the front wheels driving and put extra strain on the rear axle.

If you must take a trailer, make sure that it has the same wheels and tyres as the towing vehicle, that the hitch is the strong NATO type and that the wiring loom is fixed above the chassis, where it will be protected.

Overturned Vehicles

Short-wheelbase vehicles have a habit of breaking away or spinning on bends and corrugations, often turning over in the process. So drive these vehicles with extra care. Given the nature of the terrain they cover, overturned vehicles are not unusual on expeditions. Normally it happens at such a slow speed that no one is injured, nor even windows broken. First make sure the engine is stopped and battery disconnected. Check for human injury, then completely unload the vehicle. Once unloaded, vehicles can usually be righted easily using manpower, though a second vehicle or winch can make things easier, in the right conditions. Once the vehicle is righted, check for damage, sort out all oil levels and spilt battery acid and then turn the engine over several times with the sparking plugs or injectors removed to clear the bores of oil above the pistons.

CAUTION:
STAND WELL CLEAR OF THE SIDE OF THE ENGINE THAT HOUSES THE SPARKING PLUG SOCKETS OR INJECTOR PORTS AND ANY POINT IN LINE WITH INJECTOR HIGH PRESSURE PIPE OUTLETS. Fluids will eject from these at pressure high enough to penetrate skin or blind. Replace the sparking plugs or injectors and run the engine as normal.

Drowned Vehicles

Make sure that the occupants are safe, otherwise rescue them first, then recover the vehicle to safe ground, where it will not obstruct other traffic. Empty the vehicle and allow it and all electrical components to drain and dry out. Check for water and silt in drum brakes, all oils and fluids, the air filter and the air inlet system, clear and clean as necessary. Water is heavier than oil, it sinks to the lowest point and can be drained at the drain plugs. If oil looks milky, it will have been emulsified by moving parts, wait several hours, drain off any free water and replace with new oils as soon as is possible.

Drowned Engines

With diesel engines, change the fuel filter and clean the sedimentor if fitted. Remove the sparking plugs or injectors and turn the engine over in short bursts with the starter motor. (NOTE THE CAUTION UNDER *Overturned Vehicles* ABOVE.) Continue until there is no sign of water in the cylinders. If there is sediment, strip the engine down. Refit all components and run the engine till warm, check for problems, especially for shorting out of electrical components, these could cause a fire. Stop the engine and recheck fuel filters for water and drain or clean as necessary.

When you reach civilisation, have the vehicle hosed out with freshwater and replace all oils and fluids with new ones. With diesel engines fully service the injector pump and injectors. If the vehicle drowned in sea water, have the complete wiring loom replaced and all electrical connections cleaned or you will be plagued by minor electrical problems for evermore.

Punctures

Punctures are the most common problem in off-road travel. Rear wheel punctures often destroy the inner tube, so several spare inner tubes should be carried. Wherever possible, I prefer to repair punctures with a known good tube and get the punctured tube vulcanised properly, when I next visit a larger town. However, you should always carry a repair kit, in case you use all your inner tubes. Hot patch repair kits do not work well enough on the truck type inner tubes, that are used in four-wheel drive vehicle tyres.

Michelin radial tyres have the advantage that their beads almost fall off the wheel rim when flat. If you cannot break a bead, try driving over it or using a jack and the weight of the vehicle. If the wheel has the rim on one side wider than the other, remove the tyre over the narrowest side, starting with both beads in the well of the wheel. Narrow tyre levers are more efficient than wide ones. Sweep out all sand and grit, file off any sharp burrs on the wheel and put everything back together on a groundsheet, to stop any sand or grit getting in to cause further punctures.

When refitting the tyre, use liquid soap and water or bead lubricant and a Schrader valve tool to hold the inner tube valve in place. Start and finish refitting the tyre, by the valve. Pump the tyre up enough to refit the bead on the rim, then let it down again to release any twists in the inner tube. Then pump the tyre up again to rear tyre pressure. If the wheel has to be fitted on the front later, it is easy to let out some air.

Foot pumps have a short life in sand and are hard work. If your vehicle does not already have a compressor, then use a sparking plug socket fitting pump if you have a petrol engine, or a 12 volt electric compressor, which can be used with either petrol or diesel engines. Keep all pumps clear of sand. When using electric compressors, keep the engine running at charging speed.

Damaged steel braced radial tyres often have a sharp end of wire internally, causing further punctures. These should be cut down as short as is possible and the tyre then gaitered, using thicker truck inner tubes. The edges of the gaiter should be bevelled and the tyre must be at full pressure to stop the gaiter moving about. On paved roads, gaitered tyres behave like a buckled wheel, so they are dangerous. Most truck tyres including Michelin XZY, can be re-cut when worn and these re-cuts are useful to use in areas of sharp stones or Acacia thorns, where tyres damage easily. These re-cuts are not legal on light vehicles in the U.K.

Wheel braces get overworked in off-road use, so also have a good socket or ring spanner available, to fit the wheel nuts.

In soft sand, use a strong one-foot-square metal or wooden plate under the jack, when jacking up the vehicle. Two jacks, preferably including a high-lift jack, are often necessary in off-road conditions.

With a hot wheel after a puncture, you may need an extension tube on the wheel brace, to undo the wheel nuts; but do not retighten them this way or you will cause damage.

If your vehicle spare wheel is stored under the chassis, it can be very difficult to get out, when you have a puncture off-road. Store it inside the vehicle or on the roof.

Fuel Problems

Bad fuel is common; extra fuel filters are useful and essential for diesel engines. The main problems are water and sediment. When things get bad, it is quicker long term to drain the fuel tank, decant the fuel and clean it out. Always keep the wire mesh filter in the fuel filler in place. Do not let the fuel tank level fall too low, as this will produce water and sediment in the fuel lines. With a diesel engine, you may then have to bleed the system. If fuelling up from 40 gallon drums, give them time to settle and leave the bottom inch, which will often be water and grit.

If you have petrol in jerry cans in a hot, dry climate, always earth them to discharge any static electricity, before opening and earth the vehicle before touching jerry cans to the fuel filler pipe. Fuel starvation is often caused by dust blocking the breather hole in the fuel tank filler cap.

Electric fuel pumps are unreliable; carry a complete spare. For mechanical fuel pumps, carry a reconditioning kit. In hot countries or in low gear at altitude, mechanical fuel pumps on petrol engines often get hot and cause vapour lock. Wrap the pump in bandages and pour water onto it to cool it. If this is a constant problem, fit a plastic pipe from the windscreen washer system, to the bandaged fuel pump and squirt it regularly.

Low pressure fuel pipes can be repaired using epoxy resin adhesives, bound by self-vulcanising rubber tape. High-pressure injector pipes must be brazed or completely replaced. Carry spares of these and spare injectors. Diesel engine problems are usually fuel or water, you should know how to bleed the system correctly. If this fails to correct the problem, check all fuel pipes and joints, fuel pump and filter seals, for leaks. Hairline cracks in the high pressure injector pipes are hardest to find. Fuel tank leaks repair best with glass reinforced plastic kits.

Electrical Problems

These are a constant problem with petrol engines. Carry a spare distributor cap, rotor arm, sparking plugs, points, condenser and coil; all tend to break up or short out in hot countries. Replace modern high tension leads with the older copper wire type and carry a spare set. Keep a constant check on sparking plugs and contact breaker points. If you are losing power, first check the gap and wear on the points. Spray all ignition components with Silicone sealant to keep out dust and water.

Keep battery connections tight, clean and greased. Replace battery slip-on connections, with clamp-on types. Keep battery plates covered with electrolyte, top up only with distilled water or deionised water. Batteries are best checked with a battery hydrometer. There are special instruments for checking the modern sealed-for-life batteries.

Alternators and batteries should be disconnected before performing any electrical arc welding on the vehicle. Never run the engine with the alternator or battery disconnected. Alternators are not as reliable as they should be. If the diodes are separate, carry spares, if not, carry a complete spare alternator. On some vehicles the red charging warning light on the dashboard is part of the circuit, so carry spare bulbs for all lights. Make sure you carry spare fuses and fan belts.

Regularly check that batteries are well clamped down and that electrical wires are not frayed, or passing over any sharp edges. The risk of electrical fire due to shorting, is very high on rough tracks.

Cold Weather

Arctic temperatures are a very specialist situation. Vehicles are stored overnight in heated hangars. When in the field, engines are either left running or else have an electric engine heater, which is plugged into a mains' power supply. Oils are either specialist or diluted to the makers' recommendations. Petrol is the preferred fuel for lighter vehicles, but for heavier uses, diesel vehicles have heaters built into the fuel system and the fuel is diluted with petrol. All fuel is scrupulously inspected for water before being used. Batteries must be in tip-top condition, as they lose efficiency when cold.

General Problems and Improvisations

Steering locks are best removed; if not, leave the key in them permanently in dusty areas. A spare set of keys should be hidden safely, somewhere under the body or chassis.

When replacing wheel hub bearing oil seals, also replace the metal mating piece.

Wire hose clips are best replaced with flat metal Jubilee type clips. Carry spare hoses, although these can be repaired in an emergency with self-vulcanising rubber tape. Heater hoses can be sealed off with a sparking plug.

Bad radiator leaks can be sealed with epoxy resin or glass reinforced plastic. For small leaks, add some Radweld, porridge, or raw egg, to the radiator water. Always use a torque wrench on aluminium cylinder heads or other aluminium components.

In sand, always work on a groundsheet and don't put parts down in the sand. In sand storms, make a protected working area around the vehicle, using groundsheets. If possible, park the vehicle rear on, to the wind and cover all windows to prevent them being etched by the sand.

Clean the threads of nuts and bolts with a wire brush, before trying to remove them.

If you get wheel shimmy on returning to paved roads, first check for mud, buckled wheels, gaitered tyres and loose wheel bearings. If it is none of these, check the swivel pins, which can usually be dampened by removing shims.

Carry any spare parts containing rubber well away from heat, including the sun's heat on the bodywork.

If you cannot get into gear, first check for stones caught up in the linkage.

If you use jerry cans, carry spare rubber seals. Always carry water in light-proof polypropylene cans, to stop the growth of algae. (Available ex-military in the U.K.)

Lengths of strong chain with long bolts, plus wood or tyre levers can be used as splints on broken chassis parts, axles or leaf springs. If you do not have a differential lock and need one in an emergency, you can lock the spinning wheel if it has a drum brake, by tightening up the brake adjuster cam, but only use this system for a few metres at a time.

For emergency fuel tanks, use a jerry can on the roof, with a hose connected to the fuel lift pump. Drive slowly and never let the can get lower than half full.

If one vehicle in convoy has a defunct charging system, swap that vehicle's battery every 100 kilometres.

For repair work at night, or camp illumination, small fluorescent lights have the least drain on the battery.

If the engine is overheating, it will cool down quickest, going downhill in gear, using the running engine as a brake. If you stop with a hot engine then, unless it is showing signs of seizure, keep the engine ticking over fast; this will cool it down quicker and more evenly than if you stop it. If you switch off an overheating engine, you are likely to get a warped cylinder head.

Make sure that there are not any pin holes in the rubber connecting hose, between the air filter and the engine inlet manifold.

If you have a partially seized six cylinder engine, remove the piston and connecting rod involved, disconnect the sparking plug and high tension lead (or the injector if diesel). Close the valves by removing the push rods, or rocker arms if overhead cam. If diesel, feed the fuel from the disconnected fuel injector pipe, to a safe place away from the heat of the engine, and drive slowly. If you have a hole in the block, seal it with any sheet metal plus glass reinforced plastic and self-tapping screws to keep out dust or sand.

In an emergency, you can run a diesel engine on kerosene (paraffin) or domestic heating oil, by adding one part of engine oil to 100 parts of the fuel, to lubricate the injector pump. In hot climates, diesel engine crankcase oils are good for use in petrol engines; but petrol engine crankcase oils should not be used for diesel engines.

Bent track rods should be hammered back as straight as possible, to minimise tyre scrubbing and the possibility of a roll.

With four-wheel drive vehicles, if you break a rear half-shaft, you can continue in two-wheel drive, by removing both rear half-shafts and putting the vehicle into four-wheel drive. If the front or rear differential is broken, remove both of the half-shafts on that axle and the propeller shaft concerned and engage four-wheel drive. If a permanent four-wheel drive jams in the centre differential lock position, remove the front propeller shaft and drive on slowly.

Temporary drain or filler plugs can be whittled from wood and sealed in with epoxy resin.

Silicone RTV compound can be used for most gaskets, other than cylinder head gaskets. Silicone RTV compound or PTFE tape is useful when putting together leaking fuel line connections.

Paper gaskets can be reused if smeared with grease.

If you develop a hydraulic brake fluid leak and do not have enough spare fluid, travel on slowly, using the engine as a brake. If the leak is really bad, you can disconnect a metal pipe upstream of the leak, bend it over and hammer the end flat, or fit an old pipe to which this has already been done. Rubber hoses can be clamped, using a round bar to minimise damage. If you have a dual system, then the brakes will still work as normal, but if not, you will have uneven braking on only three wheels. If you lose your clutch, you can still change gear, by adjusting the engine speed, as with double-declutching. It is best to start the engine with the gearbox already in second gear.

Four wheel drive vehicles are high off the ground and it is often easier to work on the engine if you put the spare wheel on the ground and stand on it. If your bonnet can be hinged right back, tie it back so that the wind does not drop it onto your head.

Steering relays that do not have a filler hole can be topped up by removing two opposite top cover bolts and filling through one of the holes until oil comes out of the other.

If you burst an oil gauge pressure pipe, remove the 'T' piece, remove the electric pressure sender from it and screw this back into the block. You will then still have the electric low pressure warning light.

For a mortorist's check-list see p.783 of the Directory

BUYING AND SELLING A CAR ABROAD

by Paul Melly

Who wants to get rid of a car in Jakarta? Well, if you've just spent seventeen weeks driving all the way from London, there's a fair chance that a 'plane, at seventeen hours, will seem much the most attractive mode of travel back home. Either way, if you do sell a car or camper van, make sure that anybody who could be affected knows what you've done. Whether you think you still own the vehicle is merely the first stage. The important thing is to be certain that the authorities, both where you bought it and where you sell it, understand the position. What you have to tell them partly depends on where you bought the vehicle and what its status is.

Buying

Traditionally, the favoured market-place for those planning long overland trips, especially Australians and New Zealanders, is a car park near Waterloo Station and the Festival Hall on the South Bank of the Thames in London. On Fridays, Saturdays and Sundays, this is busy with travellers haggling over battered camper vans, many of them various conversions of VW Kombis.

Prices can range from several hundred to several thousand pounds but real bargains are becoming fewer, as dealers begin to muscle in on the market. Many vehicles are actually registered on the continent, with some of the cheapest coming from the Netherlands. Provided the car is not kept in the UK for more than twelve months at a stretch (unlikely if you are buying it specially for a trip) you do not need to incur the costs of UK registration.

However, many of those sold at Waterloo have already done a huge mileage and, although there may be nothing obviously wrong with them, vital parts can be almost worn out, landing you with hefty repair bills soon afterwards.

A more reliable option can be the normal second-hand market: classified adverts, car auctions and so on. *Complete Car Auction* magazine gives information on sales all over the UK together with guideline prices. Of course, a vehicle bought this way will probably be registered in the UK.

Obviously, tyres, brakes and suspension should be checked wherever you buy. But, if a long trip is planned through countries where spares will be hard to get, it is worthwhile investing in a professional mechanical check of the vehicle, and the AA, among others, offer this service. After all, even if the seller does provide some kind of guarantee, you're going to have difficulty enforcing it in Kurdistan or Mizoram.

Insurance

Before leaving, it is also essential, if you can, to get full details of the vehicle registration rules for any country you could be passing through. These are often available from tourist offices or embassies. Insurance cover providing for at least local vehicle recovery is also a good idea. If you should have an accident or breakdown and decide to abandon the car altogether, there is much less chance of slipping away unnoticed with your battered suitcases than in the days before computers made police and governments across the world more inquisitive, or at least more efficient at being inquisitive.

Insurance can be expensive, but it probably won't be as expensive as the fine or recovery fee you may end up having to pay a foreign government embassy for leaving them to clear away what was left of your camper van.

The AA and RAC have co-operation deals with their European counterparts, but once you've crossed the Bosphorous, Mediterranean or South Atlantic, you will probably have to turn to someone offering world-wide cover such as Europ Assistance (Perrymount Road, Haywards Heath, West Sussex, UK, tel: 0181-680 1234).

When you come to sell at the other end, immediately contact the insurers to cancel the balance of insurance time remaining, for which you should get a rebate.

Before leaving you should take two photocopies of all your motoring documents proving insurance registration, ownership, road tax, and if applicable, MOT, together with your passport. You should keep the originals with you, keep one copy in a locked compartment in the vehicle and deposit one copy with the bank or a PO Box number at home where it can be checked out if necessary. This should help you to prove ownership if the police in any country or the insurance authorities require it.

The papers will also be useful when it comes to selling the car – showing that you own it and are therefore entitled to sell.

Selling

When you sell, it is vital to make sure that the transaction is recorded in the presence of a witness who can be easily contacted later if necessary. Motoring journalist Brian Charig recalls the case of the American student who found a garage willing to buy his camper van in India. In this instance the customer asked the manager of the hotel where the student had just paid his bill with an American Express Card (which is traceable) to witness the deal formally. They wanted to be protected in case something went wrong.

Written proof of sale is a safeguard against someone else committing a motoring offence, or even using the car for a serious crime, after you have sold it. You can demonstrate to the local police that it was nothing to do with you. In fact, it is best to tell the police anyway when you sell the car.

One final point: when you sell your car you hope to keep, or spend, all the money you are paid for it, so it is vital to make sure the Contract of Sale stipulates that the local buyer will meet the cost of all taxes, import duties or other official fees involved. When a foreigner sells a vehicle to a local, that normally constitutes an import, so be certain that the price you agree is net of all customs dues, sales, tax etc. And before you leave home, check (anonymously) with the embassy of the country where you plan to sell as to how the deal will be viewed by officials. If they record the fact that you bring in a car on your passport or entry document, the people checking you out at the airport Customs or Passport Control may well want to know what you have done with it.

There are one or two legal ways to beat the import duties, which can be as much as 400 per cent of the value of the vehicle. If you have owned the car for at least a year, plan to own it for another two, and if it is the first you have imported into that country, you can normally take it in duty free. If the buyer is remaining in the country, they could leave it in your name for the required two years. Only do this, however, if you know the buyer well enough, either personally or by repute, to ensure that they are trustworthy. Or you can legally sell it in the zone between two borders, although this would mean the buyer would have to have access to free passage of a fairly large sum of money across the borders. Or you can sell it to another traveller, diplomat or foreign resident who is, for whatever reason, not bound by local laws. But you may well find that in many countries, such as Zimbabwe, while foreign currency is in desperately short supply, there is no shortage of local currency, and buyers will be queuing, even with the high price demanded by the duties, for vehicles such as Land Rovers in a good state of repair.

Using the Money

A further factor to bear in mind, which could influence your choice of country to sell in, is currency status and regulations. Many, but by no means all, Third World countries have a currency which is not internationally exchangeable and a large number of these have controls on what you can take out in both local money and foreign exchange.

So ideally choose a country which has an internationally convertible currency, such as the Singapore Dollar, or the CFA (African franc, underwritten by the Bank of France). That way, if you do take out the payment for the car, you will be able to change it into money you can spend at home such as sterling or dollars. Or you may even be able to buy western currency in a local bank.

If you cannot plan to land up in a hard currency nation, find out what the local exchange control rules are. Otherwise you may find that you cannot take money out in either cash or traveller's cheques, local or foreign currency. Many countries are so short of hard currency they must restrict its use to buying essential imports, and these are unlikely to include fifth-hand cars from foreign tourists. Even some countries which do have a convertible currency restrict what funds can be taken abroad.

The simplest answer is to check before you leave what you can buy with the local money – food, souvenirs, and often hotel accommodation, sometimes even air tickets – and spend your takings on the spot. The problem is to guess how much you may be paid for the car. But then, interesting travel is never without its complications.

PS. The career of the amateur currency smuggler is a hazardous one, especially if you aren't much good at telling lies. And customs officers have a talent for mental arithmetic designed to catch you out as you try to persuade them you lived in their country for a week on £3.

MOTOR MANUFACTURERS' CONCESSIONAIRES AND AGENTS

by Colin McElduff

Motor manufacturers have concessionaires and agents throughout the world who are responsible for the importation of vehicles, availability of services and spares etc. Once you have decided on the vehicle to use, you should approach its manufacturer for a list of their representatives in the countries you are visiting so that you are able to evaluate its spares potential.

Today, motor manufacturers are constantly reviewing their viability in terms of production and sales. The effect on universal availability of spares is, however, long term, so the transcontinental motorist derives little immediate benefit. Nevertheless, there is the possibility that the spares of one manufacturer's vehicles will be suitable for another and a careful study of the subject is always worthwhile.

Whatever you do, choose a vehicle with a good spares potential, for it is inevitable that you will be faced with a breakdown at some stage of your journey. Be prepared by finding out your vehicle's weak points and use this as a basis for choosing spares to be taken with you, for you must not rely too much on being able to obtain them en route. When it comes to the crunch, the factors determining spares availability may be divided into three: the assumed, the known, and the unknown. It is unwise to assume that because you have a list of the vehicle's concessionaires and agents, the spares you require will be readily available. They never are, for some of the countries you are visiting may have broken off old ties and now no longer enjoy the expertise and use of equipment so provided in the past. This is often the case in Third World countries. Sometimes the cause of shortages may be the country's balance of payments problems, at other times, just downright political instability.

A great deal is known and can be used to get round the problem of no spares, however, such as using parts designed for another vehicle. To reiterate, check out the manufacturer of your vehicle and obtain a family tree of its affiliations, so that you will have some idea where to direct your search should the need arise. For example, vehicles produced by Vauxhall and Opel have parts common to each other, as also do Ford (UK) and Taunus (Germany) together with Saab, whose V4 engine is used in some Ford models. Rover and BMW now have an affiliation. Because of the intricate spider's web representing connections between manufacturers, it would be confusing to expand on this here, but look into it for your own vehicle.

As always, the unknown is legion, but when in doubt, apply logic. Ask yourself how a local would approach your situation where, for instance, there is little hope of obtaining that urgently needed spare part. The answer? He will cannibalise, and is an expert in doing so. The 'bush' mechanic exists by virtue of his resourcefulness and his ability to adapt under any conditions. He may not know what a concessionaire is, but he does know, as John Steele Gordon puts it in *Overlanding*, how to make the "radiator hose of a 1953 Chevrolet serve as an exhaust pipe for a 1973 Volkswagen and vice versa".

DOCUMENTATION FOR THE INTERNATIONAL MOTORIST
by Colin McElduff

The following advice is directed principally towards motorists from the UK and should be used as a general guide only, as each and every case produces its own requirements dependent on the countries concerned and the circumstances and regulations prevailing at the time.

As many travellers neglect documentation – some of which should be obtained well in advance of departure – list all that is known to be relevant to your trip and make enquiries as to the remainder. I have included only those documents specifically related to vehicles. For most overland trips you will need the following:

1. Driving Licence
2. Insurance – Third Party and/or:
3. International Motor Insurance Certificate (Green Card)
4. International Registration Distinguishing Sign (GB, etc)
5. Vehicle Registration Certificate. Depending on your country of departure and those through which you will be travelling, you may additionally need your birth certificate, extra passport photographs and:
6. Bail Bond
7. *Carnet* ATA
8. *Carnet Camping*
9. *Carnet de Passages en Douane*
10. Letter of Authority to use borrowed, hired or leased vehicle
11. VE103 – Hired/Leased Vehicle Certificate
12. International Certificate for Motor Vehicles
13. International Driving Permit (IDP)
14. Motoring Organisation Membership Card
15. Petrol Coupons

Driving Licence

Most countries will allow you to drive for six months on your national driving licence. After this you must have an IDP or take a local test. In Italy a translation of the visitor's National Driving Licence is required if the National Licence is the older UK all green colour licence. This may be obtained from motoring organisations. Motorists in possession of an IDP do not require a translation. It is probably also useful to have a translation if travelling in Arab countries. In some countries car-hire companies require an IDP to be produced.

Third Party Insurance

This is essential to cover claims relating to death of or bodily injury to third parties as a result of the vehicle's use. When travelling in countries outside the scope of the 'Green Card' – which is generally outside Europe – Third Party insurance should be taken out at the first opportunity on entering the country.

International Motor Insurance Certificate (Green Card)

Whilst a Green Card is technically no longer necessary in EC countries, it is extremely unwise to visit these countries without it as it remains readily acceptable as evidence of insurance to enable a driver to benefit from international claim-handling facilities. In any case, a Green Card is required in all European countries outside the EC. It should be obtained from the insurance company that is currently insuring your vehicle.

International Registration Distinguishing Sign

This sign is mandatory and should be of the country in which your vehicle is registered, thus identifying your registration plates.

Vehicle Registration Certificate

This is an essential document to take. However, further proof of ownership or authority to use the vehicle may sometimes be required.

Bail Bond

For visitors to Spain, it was always a wise precaution to obtain a Spanish Bail Bond from the vehicle insurers since the driver involved in an accident could have been required to lodge a deposit with the local Spanish Court and failure to meet that demand could result in imprisonment for the driver and detention of the vehicle until funds became available. Now that Spain is in the EC, this requirement is no longer technically applicable, but many insurers will still issue a Bail Bond at nil cost for anybody who wants to play doubly safe.

Carnet ATA

This is a customs document valid for twelve months, which facilitates the entry without payment of customs duties, etc., on professional equipment, goods for internal exhibition and commercial samples, temporarily imported into certain countries – a list of which may be obtained from the London Chamber of Commerce and Industry (33 Queen Street, London, EC4R 1AP, tel: 0171-248 4444) or through one of their many offices throughout the UK.

Carnet Camping

An international document jointly produced by the three international organisations dealing with camping and caravanning – the Fédération Internationale de l'Automobile, the Fédération Internationale de Camping et Caravanning and the Alliance Internationale de Tourisme. It serves as an identity document and facilitates entry to sites under the wing of these organisations sometimes at – reduced rates. In addition, the document provides personal accident cover up to a specified sum for those names on it. You should approach a motoring organisation for this document.

Carnet de Passages en Douane

This is an internationally recognised customs document. If acceptable to a country, it will entitle the holder to import temporarily a vehicle, caravan, trailer, boat, etc., without the need to deposit the appropriate customs duties and taxes. The issuing authority of the *carnet* is made directly responsible for the payment of customs duties and taxes if the *carnet* is not discharged correctly, i.e. if the owner violates another country's customs regulations by selling the vehicle illegally. Consequently, any substantial payment will be recovered from the *carnet* holder under the terms of the signed issuing agreement.

Motoring organisations are issuing authorities and will provide issue documents upon receipt of a bank guarantee, cash deposit or an insurance indemnity from an agreed firm of brokers to cover any liability. The sum required is determined by the motoring organisation, taking into consideration the countries the vehicle will enter (destinations are declared when the application for the *carnet* is made).

Normally the amount of the bond required as security is related to the maximum import duty on motor vehicles required in the countries to be visited, which can be as high as 400 per cent of the UK value of the vehicle.

In the case of a bank guarantee, you need to have collateral with the issuing bank or funds sufficient to cover the amount required to be guaranteed. These funds cannot be withdrawn until the bank's guarantee is surrendered by the motoring organisation. This is done when the *carnet* is returned correctly discharged. The procedure is for the bank manager to provide a letter of indemnity to the motoring organisation, normally the motoring organisation's specially printed documents.

If you have insufficient funds or security to cover the bond, you may pay an insurance premium (the AA and the RAC have their own nominated insurance companies with which they have carnet indemnity agreements) and the company will act as guarantor. There are certain points to watch, however. The car must usually be registered in the country where the *carnet* is issued. In some cases (at the discretion of the issuing club or association) being a citizen of the country where the *carnet* is issued as an alternative – even though the car has been registered elsewhere. In all cases, membership of the issuing club is a requirement.

A *carnet* is required for most long transcontinental journeys and should be obtained regardless of the fact that some of the countries on the itinerary do not require it. To be without one where it *is* required usually means being turned back if you have insufficient funds to cover the customs deposit for entry.

A *carnet de passages en douane* is valid for twelve months from the date of issue and may be extended beyond the expiry date by applying to the motoring organisation in the country you are visiting at the point of expiry. The name of the motoring organisation is shown in the front cover of the *carnet*. An extension should be noted on every page and not just inside the cover in order to avoid difficulties at border checks. When a new *carnet* is required, the application must be made to the original issuing authority. *Carnets* are issued with five, eleven or 25 pages, depending on the number of countries to be visited, and a nominal fee is charged accordingly to cover administration. Each page contains an entry voucher (*volet d'entrée*), exit voucher (*volet de sortie*) and a counter-foil (*souche*). When the vehicle leaves the country, the customs officer endorses the exit part of the counterfoil and detaches the appropriate exit voucher, thus discharging the *carnet*. If you have not taken care to have this done, the validity of the *carnet* may be suspended until this is rectified.

Certificate of Authority for Borrowed or Hired Vehicle

This is required when a vehicle is borrowed or hired and should bear the signature of the owner. This must be the same as on the Registration Certificate which must also be taken. A motoring organisation will provide a 'Vehicle on Hire/Loan' certificate, VE103.

International Certification for Motor Vehicles

In countries where the British Vehicle Registration Certificate is not accepted, this document is required and is issued by a motoring organisation.

International Driving Permit

An IDP is required by the driver of a vehicle in countries that do not accept the national driving licence of the visiting motorist. It is issued on request by motoring organisations for a small fee and is valid for twelve months from the date of issue. An IDP can only be issued in the country of the applicant's national driving licence.

Motoring Organisation Membership Card

Most countries have a motoring organisation which is a member of the Alliance Internationale de Tourisme (AIT) or the Federation Internationale de l'Automobile (FIA) and provides certain reciprocal membership privileges to members of other motoring organisations.

Petrol Coupons

These are issued to visiting motorists in some countries either to promote tourism or where there are restrictions on the residents' use of petrol. Motoring organisations can advise which countries issue petrol coupons.

For Driving Requirements World-wide see p.776 of the Directory
For a list of international vehicle licence plates see p.772 of the Directory ■

GETTING THERE BY OTHER MEANS
Chapter 6

THE TWO-WHEELED TRAVELLER

by Nicholas Crane

Ever since John Foster Fraser and his buddies Lun and Lowe pedalled around the world in the 1890s, the bicycle has been a popular choice of vehicle for the discerning traveller. It is the most efficient human-powered land vehicle and it is clean, green and healthy.

The standard bicycle is also inexpensive, simple and reliable. Its basic form is similar the world over, with its fundamental parts as available in downtown Manhattan as they are in Douala. With the exception of remote settlements reachable only by foot, most of the world's population are acquainted with the bike. It can never be as symbolic of wealth as a motor vehicle and neither is a bike-rider alienated from his or her surroundings by metal and glass. It's a humble vehicle. It is approachable and it is benign. Bird song and scents are as much a constant companion as voices and faces.

Cycling is slow enough to keep you in touch with life; fast enough to bring daily changes. A fit rider ought to be able to manage an average of 80 to 100 kilometres a day. Pedalling puts you part way between pedestrians and motor cars: a bike can manage a daily distance four times that of a walker and a third that of a car.

Bikes can be carried in 'planes, trains, boats and cars, on bus roofs, taxi boots; parked in hotel bedrooms and left-luggage stores. They can be carried by hand and taken apart.

But isn't cycling hard work? Sometimes, but for every uphill or head-wind there's a descent or tailwind that's as fun as flying. What happens when it rains? You get wet or stop in a bar. How many punctures do you get? On my last ride (5200 kilometres), two. How do you survive with so little luggage? It's leaving behind the clutter of everyday life that makes bike touring so fun.

Where to Go

If you are unsure of your stamina, choose somewhere mild such as East Anglia or northern France for your first trip. Beware of being tricked by the map: it's not always the places with the highest mountains that are the most tiring to ride. Scotland where the roads often follow valley bottoms, is a lot easier than Devon where the roads hurry up and down at ferocious angles. The Fens, Holland and Ganges Delta may be as flat as a pancake but it's this flatness which allows the wind to blow unchecked – exhilarating if it's going your way, but if it isn't …

You may already have a clear idea of where you would like to ride. Hilliness, prevailing winds, temperature, rainfall, whether the roads are surfaced or dirt, are all factors worth quantifying before you leave. Then you must fit the route with the places of interest and accommodation. There may be duller sections of your route which you would like to skip; if so you need to find out in advance whether you can have your bike transported on buses or trains.

You do not have to be an athlete, or even able to run up three flights of stairs without collapsing, to ride a bicycle. It is a rhythmic, low-stress form of exercise. Riding to work or school, or regularly during evenings and weekends, will build a healthy foundation of fitness. If you have never toured before, try a day ride from home (40 kilometres maximum), or a weekend ride.

Once you know how many miles you can comfortably ride in a day, you can plan your tour route. *Always* allow for the first couple of days to be "easy": set yourself distances which you know you can finish comfortably and this will allow you to adjust to the climate and the extra exercise. It will also let your bike and luggage "settle in".

Main roads must be avoided. This means investing in some good maps. As a rule scales of 1:200,000 will show all minor roads. For safe cycling on rough tracks, you'll need maps of 1:50,000 or 1:25,000. Stanfords (12-14 Long Acre, London WC2E 9LP, tel: 0171–240 3611) are the best supplier of cycling-scale maps.

The type of accommodation you decide upon affects the amount of luggage you carry, and the money you spend. Camping provides the greatest flexibility but also the greatest weight of luggage. With (or without) a tent you can stay in all manner of places. Farmers will often consent to the use of a field-corner, and in wilderness areas you camp where you choose (leave nothing; take nothing). With two of you, you can share the weight of the tent, cooking gear and so on. If you are using youth hostels, bed-and-breakfast or hotels, you can travel very lightly but your route is fixed by available accommodation.

"Wild camping", where you simply unroll your sleeping bag beneath the stars on a patch of unused land, is free and allows you to carry a minimum of camping gear. Always be careful to check the ownership of the land and bear in mind that you have no "security" beyond your own ability to be inconspicuous.

The best source of information on the geography of cycle-travel is the **Cyclists' Touring Club** (to join, contact the CTC at Cotterell House, 69 Meadrow, Godalming, Surrey GU7 3HS, tel: 01483-417217).

The Bike and Clothing

Unlike the purchase of a motorised expedition vehicle, the bicycle need cost no more than a good camera or backpack. Neither need it be an exotic mix of the latest aluminium alloys and hi–tech tyres. John Foster Fraser covered 19,237 miles through seventeen countries on a heavy steel roadster fitted with leather bags. Unlike bike frames made from steel, those constructed using carbon-fibre, titanium or even aluminium alloys will be beyond the skills of local blacksmiths to repair. Destinations are achieved through the urge to make the journey, rather than through the colour of the bike frame.

Given the determination to succeed, virtually any type of bicycle will do. The author Christa Gausden made her first journey, from the Mediterranean to the English Channel, on a single-speed shopping bike. My early tours across Europe were made on the heavy ten-speed I had used for riding to school. Spending time and money on your bike does however increase your comfort and the bike's reliability.

For road riding the most comfortable machine is a lightweight 10- or 12-speed touring bike. Gear ratios in the UK and USA are measured somewhat quaintly, in inches – the given figure representing the size of wheel which it would have been necessary to fit to a Penny Farthing to achieve the same effect. *Richard's New Bicycle Book* (and various others) contains detailed gear ratio tables. For normal touring, the lowest gear should be around 30 to 35 inches; the highest, 80 to 90 inches. With these ratios a fit rider ought to be able to pedal over the Pyrenees, while the top gear is high enough to make the most of tail winds.

Good quality wheels and tyres are important. If you can afford it, have some wheels built by a professional wheel-builder, asking him to use top quality pre-stretched spokes and the best hubs and rims. For continental touring it's handiest if the rims are of the size to take the metric 700 C tyres. Some rims will take a variety of tyre widths, allowing your one set of wheels to be shod either with fast, light, road tyres, or with heavier tyres for rough surfaces. Buy the best tyres you can afford. Quality tyres can be expected to run for 8,000 kilometres on a loaded bike ridden over mixed road surfaces.

"Drop" handlebars are more versatile than "uprights", providing your hands with several different positions and distributing your weight between your arms and backside. Drops also permit for riding in the "crouch" position – useful for fast riding, or pedalling into head-winds. Drop handlebars come in different widths; ideally they should match the span of your shoulders. The saddle is very much a question of personal preference; try several before deciding. (Note that you should fit a wide "mattress" saddle if you have upright handlebars, as most of your weight will be on your backside.) Solid leather saddles need treatment with leather oils then "breaking in" – sometimes a long and painful process but one which results in a seat moulded to your own shape. Also very comfortable are the padded suede saddles which require no breaking in. Since they never change shape, be sure this sort of saddle is a perfect fit before you buy. Steer clear of plastic-topped saddles.

It is very important that your bike frame is the correct size for you. There are several different methods of computing this, but a rough rule of thumb is to subtract 25 centimetres from your inside leg measurement. You should be able to stand, both feet flat on the ground, with at least three centimetres between the top tube and your crotch. The frame angles should be between 71° and 73°. The strongest and lightest bike frames are commonly made from Reynolds tubing, most usually of the "531" specification (look for the label). On lighter models it may be "double-butted". An option for those with bigger purses is to have a bike frame built to your own specifications and size. Many of the top frame-builders advertise in the magazine *Cycling Weekly* and in *Cycle Touring and Campaigning*, the magazine of the Cyclists's Touring Club.

Generally speaking, the more you spend on your brakes and pedals, the stronger and smoother they will be. Pedals should be as wide as your feet (note that some Italian models are designed for slim continental feet rather than the flat-footed Britisher). Toe-clips and straps increase pedalling efficiency.

Luggage should be carried in panniers attached to a rigid, triangulated carrier which cannot sway. Normally, rear panniers should be sufficient. If you need more capacity, use a low-riding set of front pannier carriers (such as the Blackburn model) and/or a small handlebar bag. Lightweight items, such as a sleeping bag, can be carried on top of the rear carrier if necessary. The guiding rule is to keep weight as low down and as close to the centre of the bike as possible. Never carry anything on your back.

Clothing chosen carefully will keep you warm and dry in temperate climates; cool and comfortable in the heat. Choose items on the "layer" principle: each piece of clothing should function on its own, or fit when worn with all the others. The top layers should be wind-proof, and in cold or wet lands, waterproof too. Goretex is ideal. Close-fitting clothes are more comfortable, don't flap as you ride, and can't get caught in the wheels and chainset. In bright conditions a peaked hat or beret makes life more comfortable, and cycling gloves (with padded palms) will cushion your hands from road vibration. Cleated cycling shoes, as worn by racers, are impossible to walk in and not worth taking; choose shoes with stiff soles (i.e. not tennis shoes) which will spread the pressure from the pedals, and which are good for walking too. Specially designed touring shoes can be bought at the bigger bike shops.

The Touring Department of the CTC publish technical information sheets on equipping bike and rider.

Mountain Bikes

If you're planning to venture off the beaten track, on rough roads and tracks, a mountain bike will provide strength and reliability. Mountain bikes evolved in California from hybrid *clunkers* during the '70s, first arriving in Britain *en masse* in 1982. Since then, mountain bikes have become lighter, swifter and stronger. For tarmac riding, a mountain bike is still heavier, harder work and slower than a lightweight touring bike. The mountain bike's fatter tyres create greater rolling resistance and the upright riding position offers greater wind resistance. The additional weight requires more pedalling effort on hills but on dirt roads and trails mountain bikes are in their element: easy to control, with excellent traction and superb resistance to vibration, knocks and crashes.

Mountain bikes generally come with 18 to 21 gears, with a bottom gear of around 25 inches. (In practice five or so of these gears are always unusable because of the sharp angle which the chain is forced to make when it is running on the largest front chainring and smallest rear sprocket – and vice versa). Mountain bike brakes are generally more powerful than those on road bikes and their heavy-duty ribbed tyres are virtually puncture proof. Lighter tyres with smoother tread patterns and higher pressures can be fitted for road-riding. For sheer toughness, a mountain bike is impossible to beat, but you pay for this toughness by pedalling more weight in a less efficient riding position.

Buying Secondhand

Buying secondhand can save a lot of money – if you know what to look for.

Touring bikes and mountain bikes are advertised regularly in the classified columns of the bi-monthly magazine of the CTC, the monthly cycling magazines, and in *Cycling Weekly*. Before buying, check that the frame is straight, first by sight, and then by (carefully!) riding no-hands. If the bike seems to veer repeatedly to one side, the frame or forks are bent. Spin the wheels and check they are true. Wobble all the rotating parts; if there is a lot of "play", the bearings may be worn. Above all, only buy from somebody you feel is honest.

On the Road

The greatest hazard is other traffic. Always keep to your side of the road, watching and listening for approaching vehicles. In Asia and Africa, buses and trucks travel at breakneck speeds and expect all to move from their path. Look out too for carts and cows, sheep, people, pot holes and ruts – all of which can appear without warning.

Dogs deserve a special mention. Being chased up-hill by a mad dog is the cyclist's nightmare. I've always found the safest escape to be speed, and have yet to be bitten. If you are going to ride in countries known to have rabies, consider being vaccinated before departure. It goes without saying that you should check with your GP that you have the full quota of inoculations (including tetanus) suited for your touring area.

Security need not be a problem if you obey certain rules. Unless you are going to live with your bike day and night, you need a strong lock. Always lock your bike to an immovable object, with the lock passing round the frame and rear wheel. For added security, the front wheel can be removed and locked also. Before buying, check that the lock of your choice is big enough for the job. Note that quick-release hubs increase the chance of the wheels being stolen. Always lock your bike in a public place, and if you're in a cafe or bar, keep it in sight. In most Third World countries, it is quite acceptable to take bicycles into hotel bedrooms; elsewhere, the management can usually be persuaded to provide a safe lock-up.

The CTC sells travel insurance and bicycle insurance policies.

Expedition Cycling

Bikes have been ridden, carried and dragged in some ridiculous places: across the Darien Gap, through the Sahara and up Kilimanjaro. They have been pedalled round the world, many times. And they have been used as a sympathetic means of transport into remote, little-visited corners of the globe. The step up from holiday touring in Europe to prolonged rides to the back-of-beyond requires sensible planning. Choice of bicycle and equipment will have great bearing on the style of the ride. If you want to be as inconspicuous as possible, the best machine will be a local black roadster. Such a bike will probably need constant attention, but pays off handsomely in its lack of western pretension. I once pedalled across the African Rift Valley on a bike hired from a street market in Nairobi; the bike fell apart and had to be welded and then rebuilt, but the ride was one of the most enjoyable I've ever had.

For serious journeys defined by a set goal and a time limit, you need a well-prepared, mechanically perfect machine. If much of the riding is on dirt roads, a mountainbike may well be the best bet. If you can keep your weight down, a lightweight road-bike will handle any road surface too. On the *Journey to the Centre of the Earth* bike ride across Asia with my cousin Richard, our road bikes weighed 10kg each, and our total luggage came to 8kg each. We carried one set of clothes, waterproofs and a sleeping bag each, picking up food and water along the way. Our route included a crossing of the Himalayas, and then a south to north traverse of the Tibetan Plateau and Gobi Desert. Objectivity obliges me to note that I've seldom come across other cyclists travelling this light; most voicing the opinion that they'd rather carry their cooking stove, pans, food, tent, and extra clothes.

The Expeditionary Advisory Centre (whose home is at the Royal Geographical Society, 1 Kensington Gore, London SW7 2AR, tel; 0171-591 3000) publish an excellent manual called *Bicycle Expeditions*, the new edition having been revised by a man who pedalled across Russia.

Spares

Lightness gives you speed. One spare tyre and one spare inner tube, and a few spokes are the basic spares. Rear tyres wear faster than front ones, so switch them round when they are part worn. For rides of over 5000 kilometres, in dry or gritty conditions, a replacement chain will be necessary too. In "clean" conditions a good-quality, regularly lubricated chain will last twice that distance. The tool kit should include a puncture repair kit, appropriate Allen keys, chain-link remover, freewheel block remover, small adjustable wrench and cone–spanners for the wheel-hubs. Oil, grease and heavy tools can be obtained from garages and truck drivers along the route.

Saving weight saves energy. Look critically at your equipment, and have some fun cutting off all unnecessary zips, buckles, straps, labels. Discard superfluous clothing and knick-knacks. Make sure there are not unnecessary pieces of metal on the bike (such as wheel guides on the brakes).

It is useful to know what the absolute maximum is that you can ride in one day, should an emergency arise. On a loaded bike ridden on tarmac when fully fit, this could be as much as 200 to 300 kilometres, but it will vary from person to person. With a constant air-flow over the body, and steady exertion, a cyclist loses body moisture rapidly – particularly in hot climates where it's possible to become seriously dehydrated unless you drink sufficient liquid. You need a minimum of one litre carrying capacity on the bike; whether you double or treble this figure depends on how far from habitation you are straying. In monsoon Asia I've drunk up to thirteen litres a day.

You may have surmised from all this that there are as many different ways of making an enjoyable bicycle journey as there are stars in the sky. I've yet to meet two cyclists who could agree on what equipment to carry.

I have already mentioned *Richard's New Bicycle Book*, which is published by Pan, and which has for years provided the answers to all those oily technical questions. Richard Ballantine has now produced a more specific work, called *Richard's Bicycle Repair Manual*, published by Dorling Kindersley.

For Cycling Associations and Tour Operators see p.787 of the Directory

HITCHHIKING
by Simon Calder

Why hitch? Hitchhiking as an art, or science, is almost as old as the motor car. Originally the concept was largely synonymous with hiking. You started walking, and if a car came along you put out your hand; mostly you ended up hiking the whole way. From this casually optimistic pursuit, hitching has evolved into a fast, comfortable form of travel in some parts of the world. Elsewhere it remains one big adventure.

Hitching has many virtues. It is the most environmentally-sound form of motorised transport, since the hitcher occupies an otherwise empty space. Socially it can be rewarding, enabling you – indeed obliging you – to talk to people whom you would not normally meet. Financially it is highly advantageous: hitching allows you to travel from A to B for free or next-to-nothing, whether A is Aberdeen or Auckland, and B is Birmingham or Bucharest.

Yet standing for hours at a dismal road junction with the rain trickling morosely down your neck as heartless motorists stream past, is guaranteed to make you question the wisdom of trying to thumb a ride. And placing yourself entirely in the hands of a complete stranger can be harrowing. Some travellers dislike the degree of dependence upon others that hitchhiking engenders. Hitchhiking can also be enormously lonely. Expect the elation of getting the ideal lift to be tempered with stretches of solitude and frustration and bear in mind that motorists rarely give lifts out of pure philanthropy. Your role may be to keep a truck driver awake with inane conversation, to provide a free English lesson or to act as a sounding board for a life history. But no two rides are ever the same. Techniques and conventions of hitchhiking vary considerably around the world, most notably the divergence between fast, money-saving hitching in the West and the slower and more chaotic practices of lift-giving in less developed countries.

The West and the Developed World

In Europe, North America and Australasia, hitching can be an almost mechanically precise way of travelling. The main criteria are safety and speed. To enable a motorist to decide whether or not to pick you up, he or she must be able to see you and stop safely. The driver must evaluate whether he or she can help you, and if you would enhance the journey. Make yourself as attractive as possible by looking casual, but clean. Hitching in a suit raises driver's suspicions (normal dress for an average hitcher being denim). Looking as though you've been on the road for a year without a wash is equally counter-productive. So freshen up, choose a suitable stretch of road, smile and extend your arm. The actual gesture is a source of possible strife. In most parts of Europe and North America, the raised thumb is understood to be an innocent gesture indicating that a lift is needed. Elsewhere it represents one of the greatest insults imaginable. A vague wave in the general direction of the traffic is safest.

Never accept a lift with anyone who is drunk, high or otherwise gives you cause for concern (e.g. by squealing to a halt in a cloud of burning rubber after crossing six lanes of traffic to pick you up). Turning down a ride is easier said than done, especially if you have been waiting for six hours on a French autoroute and night is falling, but try to resist the temptation to jump into a van full of dubious characters. If you find out too late that you've accepted a dodgy ride, feign sickness and ask to be let out. It sometimes works.

Some offers should be turned down simply because they are not going far enough. Hitching right through Germany from the Dutch border to the Polish frontier can be done in a day, but it is best achieved by using discrimination in your choice of lifts. Refuse a ride which would take you only 20km to the next town. By hopping from one autobahn service area to another, you can cover ground phenomenally quickly.

All kinds of gimmicks can help you get rides more easily. The most effective device is a destination sign. Road systems in developed countries are often so complex that a single road may lead to several different directions. The only commonly enforced law on hitching is the one forbidding hitching on motorways, freeways or autopistas. By using a sign you minimise the risk that the driver who stops will want to drop you at an all-motorway junction such as those on London's M25 or the Boulevard Peripherique in Paris. Make your destination request as modest or as bold as you wish – from London you could inscribe your sign "Dover" or "Dar Es Salaam", but always add "Please".

Sophisticated hitchers concentrate their attention on specific cars. The real expert can spot a Belgian number plate at 100 metres. He or she will refuse lifts in trucks (too slow), and home in on the single male driver, who is easily the most likely provider of a lift. So good is the hitching in Germany that if you vowed to accept only lifts in Mercedes, you would still get around happily. Neighbouring France, in contrast, is hell for hitchers, as is much of southern Europe and Scandinavia.

Hitchers fare well in the newly liberated nations of eastern Europe, especially Poland. It has a Social Autostop Committee – effectively a ministry for hitchhiking – which provides incentives for motorists to pick up hitchers.

Having taken Lou Reed and Jack Kerouac's advice, and hitchhiked across the USA, I would hesitate to recommend the experience to anyone. While the chances of being picked up by an oddball or religious fanatic in Europe are tiny, in the States almost every lift-giving motorist is weird and not necessarily friendly. New Zealand could not be more different nor less threatening: if you need a place to stay, just start hitching around nightfall, and a friendly Kiwi will almost certainly offer you a ride and a room. In Australia, the hitcher is the object of greater abuse than anywhere else, with insults (and worse) hurled from car windows alarmingly often.

One exception to the hitching lore of the developed world is Japan. Western hitchhikers are picked up, usually very quickly, by one of the extremely considerate local drivers. In the absence of any other information, he or she will assume that you want to go to the nearest railway station. But upon learning that your final destination is hundreds of miles away in, say, Kyoto, the driver may feel duty bound to take you all the way there.

Japan is one place where women can feel comfortable hitching alone. The conventional wisdom is that women should never hitch alone. Single women hitchhikers are all too often victims of male violence. Nevertheless, women continue to hitch alone, and get around without problem; some maintain that safety is largely a question of attitude: if you are assertive and uncompromising, you survive.

If "real" hitching does not appeal, ride-sharing agencies exist in many countries. The idea is simply that travellers share expenses, and often the driving, and pay a small fee to the agency that arranges the introduction. Be warned, however, that there is no guarantee that a driver you contact in advance will not turn out to be a psychopath or a drunk as you hurtle through the Rocky Mountains or central Australia.

The concept of hitching can be extended to boats and 'planes. Hitching on water can involve anything from a jaunt along a canal in Europe to a two-month voyage to deliver a yacht from the Canary Islands to Florida. And in countries where private flying is popular, rides on light aircraft have been successfully procured.

Less-developed Countries

At the other extreme are the dusty highways of Nigeria or Nicaragua. In the Third World, the rules on hitching are suspended. Almost any vehicle is a possible lift-provider, and virtually every pedestrian is a potential hitchhiker. Amid such good-natured anarchy, hitching is tremendous fun.

You have to accept any form of transport from a horse and trap upwards. To make the most of opportunities, it helps to be adept at riding side-saddle on a tractor engine, or pillion on a moped for one.

Purists who regard paying for petrol as contrary to the ideals of hitchhiking, and dismiss the idea of asking a driver for a ride as capitulation, can expect a miserable time in the Third World. Definitions of what constitutes a bus or a taxi, a truck or a private car, are blurred. Sometimes the only way to reach a place is by hitching, and local motorists may exploit their monopoly position accordingly.

El Salvador's transport system has been devastated. Everyone hitches, and you are expected to pay the equivalent of the fare on the [notional] bus. The same applies in large swathes of Latin America, Africa and south Asia. Unless you have insurmountable moral objections or a serious cash-flow crisis, you should always offer something for a ride. More often than you might expect, the ride will cost nothing more than a smile. In Indonesia, for example, the Western hitchhiker is a curiosity, to be taken [temporarily] home and paraded in front of friends and relations as an exotic souvenir. You too can become an instant celebrity.

Cuba has massive transport problems, some of which are solved by an intriguing form of mass hitch-hiking. Little old ladies and large young louts join forces to persuade passing trucks to stop, or pile into a Lada saloon driven by a grumbling member of the bourgeoisie.

In such places hitching is at its simplest and most effective. Thumbing a ride enables you to see corners of the world which might otherwise remain hidden, and to meet people whom you would surely pass by. And, in the final analysis, there are worse ways to travel than being chauffeur-driven.

For further information on Hitchhiking Associations see p.788 of the Directory

OVERLAND BY PUBLIC TRANSPORT

by Chris Parrott

It's not everyone who has the resources to plan, equip and insure a full-scale Range Rover expedition across one of the less developed continents, although it's the sort of thing we all dream about. One possible answer is to travel with an overland company, but here the drawback is that you can neither choose your travelling companions nor your itinerary. You can, however, do it all more cheaply on your own, by public transport. Generally speaking, wherever overland companies take their trucks, public transport goes too. And often public transport goes where overland companies cannot: over the snow-bound Andes to Ushuaia in Tierra del Fuego, across Siberia to the Pacific.

Of course, Damascus to Aleppo is not quite the same as getting on a coach to Washington DC at the New York Greyhound Terminal, nor does "First Class" imply in Bolivia quite what it does on the 18.43 from Paddington to Reading.

A Schedule of Surprises

The Damascus to Aleppo bus is an ancient Mercedes welded together from the remains of past generations of Damascus/Aleppo buses, and propelled in equal proportions by a fuming diesel engine, the Will of Allah, and the passengers (from behind). It makes unscheduled stops while the driver visits his grandmother in Homs, when the driver's friend visits the Post Office in the middle of nowhere, and when the whole bus answers the call of nature – the women squatting on the left, and the men standing on the right (the French normally display more cool at moments like this).

First Class in Bolivia means hard, upright seats, already full of people and chickens spilling over from Second Class; whimpering children; no heating, even in high passes at night in winter; passageways blocked by shapeless bundles and festering cheeses; impromptu Customs searches at 4am; and toilets negotiable only by those equipped with Wellingtons and a farmyard upbringing. Trains rarely arrive or depart on time, and the author has experienced a delay of 26 hours on a journey (ostensibly) of eight hours. But these trains are nothing if not interesting.

The secret of the cheapness of this means of travelling lies in the fact that it is *public,* and therefore the principal means by which the public of a country moves from place to place. It follows that if the standard of living of the majority of people is low, so will the cost of public transport be low. A twenty-hour bus ride from Lima to Arequipa in Southern Peru can cost as little as $20; a twenty-hour bus ride in Brazil from Rio de Janeiro to the Paraguayan border costs about $40; whilst a twenty-hour bus ride through France or Germany would cost twice as much. It all depends on the ability of the local population to pay. Of course there are disadvantages to travel by public transport:

1. Photography is difficult at 70mph, and though most drivers will stop occasionally, they have their schedules to keep to.
2. You may find that all transport over a certain route is fully booked for the week ahead, or there is a transport strike.

3. You may find that your seat has been sold twice. In circumstances like this, tempers fray and people begin to speak too quickly for your few words of the local language to be of much use.

Efficiency of reservation arrangements varies from one part of the world to the next. The following may serve as a general guide to travelling in the undeveloped parts of the world.

Booking

Whenever you arrive in a place, try and find out about transport and how far ahead it is booked up. It may be, for example, that you want to stay in Ankara for three days, and that it's usually necessary to book a passage four days in advance to get to Iskenderun. If you book on the day you arrive, you have only one extra day to wait; if you book on the day you intended leaving, you have four days to kill. This is a basic rule and applies to all methods of transport.

Routing

Try to be as flexible as possible about your routing and means of transport. There are at least six ways to get from La Paz in Bolivia to Rio de Janeiro in Brazil. Check all possible routes before making a final decision.

Timing

Don't try and plan your itinerary down to the nearest day – nothing is ever that reliable in the less developed world (or the developed world for that matter). You should allow a ten to twenty per cent delay factor if, for example, you have to be at a certain point at a certain time to catch your plane home.

Possessions

Baggage is often snatched at terminals. Be sure, if you are not travelling within sight of your bags, that they have the correct destination clearly marked, and that they do actually get loaded. Breakfast in New York, dinner in London, baggage in Tokyo happens all too often. Arriving or leaving early in the morning or late at night you are particularly vulnerable to thieves. This is the time when you must be most on your guard. Never leave anything valuable on a bus while you have a quick drink, not even if the driver says the bus door will be locked.

Borders

Prices rise dramatically whenever your route crosses a national frontier. Usually it's cheaper to take a bus as far as the frontier, walk across and then continue your journey by the local transport in the new country. "International" services are always more expensive, whether airlines, buses, trains or boats. (The author recalls that a donkey ride to the Mexican frontier cost him twenty pesos but to have crossed the international bridge as far as the Belize Immigration Office, an extra 40 metres, would have increased the cost to 40 pesos).

Fare and Medium

Each particular medium of transport has its own special features. Trains are generally slower than buses, and the seats may be of wood. There is often no restriction on the number of seats sold, and delays are long and frequent.

However, slow trains make photography easier, and the journeys are usually more pleasant than on buses if not too crowded. It's often worth going to the station a couple of days before you're due to depart and watching to see what happens. It will tell you whether you need to turn up two hours early to be sure of a seat.

Buses reflect the sort of terrain they cross. If the roads are paved and well maintained, the buses are usually modern and in fair condition. If the journey involves unmade mountain roads, your bus and journey are not going to be very comfortable.

If you are travelling through bandit country – or a country where political stability conforms to the Third World stereotype – the company may be a consolation when the whole bus is stopped and robbed by bandits or searched by transit police (robbed too, some say). If you're in your own vehicle or hitchhiking, it is somehow far more demoralising. You probably lose the same things or have your Tampax broken in half by over-zealous soldiers in search of drugs, but it affects you less if you're just part of a coach load.

Urban Transport

One of London's biggest failures has been its inability to provide a cheap mass transit system within the city. Other Western industrialised capitals seem to have managed it to a greater or lesser extent, but the Third World has really got the problem licked – for the locals at least. Most urban dwellers in the Third World own no car; they have to travel by public transport – by train, rickshaw, underground and so on.

The networks are labyrinthine in their complexity, the services are frequent and the fares cheap. Everyone uses the system. Which generates which, I don't know, but it works. The problem is that there is rarely any information available for the traveller. He or she is meant to go by taxi or limousine. Buy yourself a city map, jump on a bus and explore. It's a great way of seeing the city cheaply with no censorship, and spending next to nothing in the process.

Boats

This, if you're lucky, could mean an ocean-going yacht that takes passengers as crew between, say, St. Lucia and Barbados, a cement boat from Rhodes to Turkey, or an Amazon river steamer. With a little help from your wallet, most captains can be persuaded to accept passengers. A good rule is to take your own food supply for the duration of the trip and a hammock if there is no official accommodation.

Cargo boats ply the rivers Amazon in Brazil, the Congo and Ubangi in the Democratic Republic of Congo, the Niger in Mali, the White Nile in the Sudan, the river Gambia and Ecuador's river Guaya, where an all-night crossing costs next to nothing.

'Planes

In areas where 'planes are the only means of communication, they are often very cheap or even free. Flying across the Gulf of Aden to Djibouti, for example, costs as little as sailing. A good trick is to enquire about privately owned 'planes at mission schools (in Africa) or at aeroclubs. Someone who is going "up country" may be only too pleased to have your company.

Similarly, in parts of South America, the Air Forces of several countries have cheap scheduled flights to less accessible areas, though, of course, one must be prepared for canvas seats and grass runways.

TRAVEL BY TRAIN

by Keith Strickland

"I have seldom heard a train go by and not wished I was on it," wrote Paul Theroux at the start of *The Great Railway Bazaar*, his account of a train journey from London to Tokyo. Commuters on the London Underground or the New York subway might not share this sentiment, but trains are more than just a means of getting from A to B.

At one extreme, they give the traveller an insight into the everyday life of the countries they serve. To see and experience India away from the main tourist attractions, there is no better way than to take the train. Railway stations themselves are a microcosm of Indian life. The homeless and beggars may spend their whole time cooking, drinking, washing and sleeping on platforms. Then there are the tradesmen – *chai-wallahs*, book-sellers, stall-holders – and, of course, the crowds.

At the other end of the spectrum, the traveller can enjoy five-star luxury on wheels. South Africa's Blue Train from Cape Town to Johannesburg has gold-tinted windows, haute cuisine and en suite accommodation.

You can take a train for a one-off trip, or you can spend your whole holiday on one. Sometimes there is no alternative form of transport – unless you are a mountain climber, the only way of ascending the Jungfrau in Switzerland is rail.

Wherever you want to go, some planning is essential. In parts of the world, trains run much less frequently than in the UK. The famous line through the Khyber Pass in Pakistan used to have only one a week. If you missed it, you would have to wait seven days for the next! (Unfortunately, this meagre service is "temporarily" suspended). Even in the USA passenger trains are much scarcer than we British are used to.

The most comprehensive guides to train times are *Thomas Cook's European Timetable* and *Overseas Timetable* (available from Thomas Cook Publications, PO Box 227, Peterborough PE3 6SB). The latter includes road services and shipping as well as railways. Both concentrate on major routes. For minor lines, one must consult local timetables. The best known is *Newman's Indian Bradshaw* which contains every passenger train on the 35,000 miles of India's rail network.

Sometimes, there is no way of getting advance information. In parts of South America, the timetable consists of nothing more sophisticated than a handwritten poster at the local station.

Tickets

Three things need to be said:

1. No railway administration likes ticketless travellers. You may get away without paying in places like India, especially if you enjoy riding on the carriage roof, but in many countries fines are stiff. The same goes for riding first class with a second class ticket.

2. Train travel can be incredibly cheap, particularly in the Third World. If you want relative comfort and space, use first class accommodation (if it's available) – you won't have to raise a mortgage.

3. Rover tickets offering unlimited travel within a geographical area are real value for money. Lovers of India know of the Indrail pass. Students and those under 26 years of age have long enjoyed cheap travel in Europe, and there is an all–European rail pass for the over-26s. Major travel companies will have details. So will British Rail's international travel centre at Victoria Station, London, (tel: 0990 848 848) but the efficiency of its telephone service leaves much to be desired. See also Section 6 of the Directory in the back of this book.

Luggage

Travel light. It's amazing when looking at pictures of Victorian travellers to see the massive trunks they took with them. What did they pack? The station porter may be a rare species in Britain but flourishes elsewhere – at a price. Even so, a mass of luggage is an encumbrance on a train. Pack essentials only. Choose according to the length of the journey and the climate of the country.

Security

Petty theft is a fact of life almost everywhere. Unattended luggage is easy game. Remember that in the Third World the value of a camera may equate to several months' average wage. Keep money and other valuables on you. If you have to leave baggage, make sure it is locked and try to chain it to some immovable object such as the luggage rack. Also make sure you have adequate insurance.

Food

On long train journeys, find out in advance if food and drink are likely to be available. On-board catering should be indicated in the timetable, though standards and prices vary enormously. South African dining cars offer superb food and wine at modest prices. France is disappointing: food on the high-speed TGV is a no more than average aircraft-style meal. Catering on the Trans-Siberian Express is, by most people's accounts, hardly bearable.

Don't overlook the possibility of station restaurants, but in the Third World, western stomachs should be wary of platform vendors. Their wares look colourful but can have devastating effects. Treat local drinks with caution. Peru has its own version of Coke – green Inca Cola – as nauseating to look at as to drink. *Chai* (sweet milky tea) is the safest drink in India. Every station has its *chai-wallah*.

Health

The first item in my personal medical kit is a bottle of eye drops – essential for countries where trains are still pulled by steam engines. Sooner, rather than later, the inevitable smuts will be acquired! Other than this, there are no special health hazards associated with trains. But a long journey is not the best way to pass the time if you are unlucky enough to be ill, and on-board toilet facilities are pretty primitive in many places. So it's important to take the health precautions necessary for the country you are visiting.

Sleeping

There's no experience quite like sleeping on a train. Again, if you plan to do this, plan ahead. Find out from the timetable if sleeping facilities are available, and if so, what they are. There may be a sleeping compartment with fresh sheets, its own loo, and an attendant. Couchettes are popular in some countries (beware, the sexes are not always segregated). In India and Pakistan, sleeping accommodation means a bed-roll spread out on an ordinary compartment seat.

Whatever the facilities, a supplementary fee and advance reservation are almost always essential, though greasing the palm of the conductor often works wonders in countries where backhanders are a way of life. In the Indian sub-continent, the more important stations have retiring rooms where a bed can be rented for the night.

Class of Travel

How to travel: First or Second Class? Express or slow train? By day or by night? The answers depend on the time and money you have at your disposal, and on the aims of the journey. Do you want to be cosseted from the outside and pampered with luxury? Do you prefer to mix with local people? It's entirely up to you; the choice is enormous. But remember one golden rule: the more comfort you want, the more you'll have to pay, and the greater will be the likelihood of having to make reservations in advance of your journey. Conversely, second class travel is cheaper, does not need to be booked ahead, but will inevitably be more crowded. Incidentally, some countries have more than two classes. India has six, though you won't necessarily find them all on the same train.

Suggested Routes

Starting at the top of the market, the **Blue Train** has already been mentioned. In the same class is the **Orient Express** from London to Venice. Can there be a more romantic way to arrive than by this train of restored luxury carriages? In India, the **Rajasthan Express** or "Palace on Wheels" takes a week on its circuit of Rajasthan. Guests live and sleep in carriages which once belonged to princes. (See also *The Luxury Traveller* in Chapter 3.)

These trains are designed specifically for the tourist trade. But the long-distance train survives in every day use in many parts of the world. **The Trans Siberian Express** runs daily from Moscow eastwards to the Pacific Coast. One can still cross the USA by rail, though not as one continuous journey. Trains travel vast distances in both India and China. The **Indian–Pacific** traverses the complete width of Australia, from Sydney to Perth. And there is no better way of getting to the Victoria Falls than by the overnight train from Bulawayo with its teak-panelled sleeping cars.

From an engineering point of view, the most remarkable line is the **Central**

Railway of Peru. From Lima, loops and zig-zags take the tracks to 15,500 feet above sea level – the highest point in the world reached by a passenger train. The conductor dispenses oxygen to those in need!

There are not many railwayless countries, and the possibilities for train travel are limitless. Don't just stick to the well-known routes. Branch out and see what you discover. The most memorable journey is often the least expected. Tucked away in a remote, mountainous region of Peru are the towns of Huancayo and Huancavelica. The train takes all day to go from one to the other, stops everywhere and is full of people going to market with their produce and livestock. There are tunnels, steep gradients, river gorges and all the while the Andes form a stunning backdrop. This is a humble line and an extraordinary and exhilarating experience.

Special Interests

To many, railways are a hobby; some would say an addiction. Every aspect of railway history and operation has been studied in great detail; but it is the steam locomotive which commands the most devotion. Steam has an atmosphere all of its own. One can see it, hear it, smell it and taste it. Steam buffs travel the world to experience its thrill.

China is the enthusiasts' mecca. With cheap labour and plentiful coal supplies, China was still building steam engines in the late 1980s, and there are probably 10,000 at work on the country's railways. Next comes **India**. Most mainline trains are now diesel or electric hauled, but steam locos can be found all over the sub-continent.

Elsewhere the number of countries where steam is in everyday use is dwindling fast. **Poland** and the former **East Germany** are the only European ones. Further afield are **Zimbabwe**, **Pakistan** and parts of **South America**.

There is a compensating increase in museum and preserved railways, but to the purist these are no substitute for the real thing: he or she wants to search out every last steam location, however remote or obscure. Visits to places like Cuba or Vietnam are best made in organised groups. For a list of specialist rail travel operators see p.792 of the Directory.

Reading Material

Trains are places for meeting people. You will rarely be on your own. It is only in England that strangers never converse. Nevertheless, make sure you put a good book in your luggage. Every journey has a dull moment.

Books about railways are legion. Fodor's *Railways of the World* provides a general introduction. Of books on rail travel in individual countries, the best is *India by Rail* published by Bradt. There is also *France by Rail*, by Simon Vickers and *Italy by Rail*, by Tim Jepson (both published by Hodder & Stoughton). Paul Theroux's *The Great Railway Bazaar* remains the most readable account of one man's journey. Even my own *Steam Railways around the World* (Alan Sutton Publishing) may be worth looking out for.

Above all, buy a timetable. It is a mine of information. My Pakistan Railways timetable tells me the cost of a bed in the retiring rooms at Karachi; breakfast on the Shalimar Express consists of "a choice of two eggs, two toasts with butter and jam, pot of tea", and I can find out the colour of staff uniforms in station tea-rooms. If I want to take a rickshaw with me as part of my luggage, it will be deemed to weigh 150kg and charged accordingly. And I duly note the solemn warning: "Passengers are requested in their own interest not to light or allow any other passenger to light any oil stove or any other type of fire in the passenger carriages as this practice is not only fraught with dangerous consequences but is also a penal offence under the Railways Act."

And look at the names of the trains. Whose imagination fails to be stirred by the *Frontier Mail*, the *Himalayan Queen*, or the *Assam Mail*? Trains are not some sort of travel capsule. They seem natural – a part of the landscape almost. They certainly reflect the characteristics and atmosphere of the countries and communities through which they run, in a way air travel, cruise ships or air-conditioned road coaches can never do.

Flanders and Swann put it rather differently in one of their songs: "If God had meant us to fly, he would never have given us railways."

*See p.791 of the Directory for more world-wide rail information including a list of rail passes world-wide and also **Inter-rail Through Europe** in Chapter 7, p336.*

SAILING

by Robin Knox-Johnston

Sailing beneath a full moon across a calm tropical sea towards some romantic destination is a wonderful dream, but to make it become a reality requires careful preparation, or the dream can turn into a nightmare.

The boat you choose should be a solid, robust cruiser. There is no point in buying a modern racing yacht as it will have been designed to be sailed by a large crew of specialists and will need weekly maintenance. The ideal boat for a good cruise should be simple, with a large carrying capacity, and easy to maintain. Bear in mind that it is not always easy to find good mechanics or materials abroad, and most repairs and maintenance will probably be done by the crew.

It is important to get to know the boat well before sailing so that you will know how she will respond in various sea states and weather conditions. This also enables one to make out a proper check list for the stores and spares that will need to be carried. For example, there is no point taking a spare engine, but the right fuel and oil filters, and perhaps a spare alternator, are advisable. Try and standardise things as much as possible. If the same size of rope can be used for a number of purposes, then a spare coil of that rope might well cover nearly all your renewal requirements.

Electronics

There is a huge array of modern equipment available and these "goodies" can be tempting. It pays to keep the requirement to a minimum to reduce expense and complexity. Small boat radars are now quite cheap and can be used for navigation as well as keeping a look-out in fog. The Decca Navigation system is due to be extended, but the date is as yet unspecified. However, the new Global Positioning System (GPS) is now in service and, about the same price as Loran or Decca, does now give very accurate positions with a world-wide coverage. There is a world-wide system of Radio Direction Beacons and a receiver for these stations is not that expensive although the range is not great. All these "Black Boxes" are only aids to navigation however, and the knowledge of how to use a sextant and work out a position from the reading is essential.

Radio communications are now everywhere and are important for the boat's safety. Short range, Very High Frequency (VHF), is in use world-wide for port operations and for communications between ships at sea. It is best to buy a good, multi-channel set and make sure that the aerial is at the top of the mast as the range is not much greater than the line of sight, so the higher the aerial, the better. For long range communications, there is a world-wide maritime communications network using Single Side Band in the medium and high frequency bands. There are now easy-to-operate SSB sets at quite reasonable prices – with patience I have managed to contact the UK from the Caribbean with only 150 watts of output.

Before sailing it is advisable to study the Radio Telephone procedure andtake the operator's examination which is organised in Britain by the Royal Yachting Association. The Admiralty publishes lists of frequencies for all Radio Communications and Direction Finding stations world-wide. An alternative is to qualify as an Amateur Radio Operator or "ham". There are hundreds of thousands of enthusiastic hams all over the world and an increasing number of special maritime networks which will arrange regular schedules if requested.

Meteorology plays an important part in any voyage and the rudiments of weather systems, and how they are going to affect the weather on the chosen route, is essential knowledge for anyone making any voyage. Weather forecasts are broadcast by most nations but it is possible to buy a weatherfax machine which prints out the weather picture for a selected area and costs about the same as an SSB radio set.

The Crew

The choice of crew will ultimately decide the success or otherwise of the venture. They must be congenial, enthusiastic and good work sharers. Nothing destroys morale on board a boat more quickly than one person who moans or shirks their share of shipboard duties. Ideally the crew should have previous sailing experience so that they know what to expect, and it is well worth while going for a short shakedown sail with the intended crew to see if they can cope and get on well. Never take too many people, it cramps the living quarters and usually means there is not enough work to keep everyone busy. A small but busy crew usually creates a happy purposeful team.

Beware of picking up crew who ask for passage somewhere at the last minute. For a start, you will not know their background and you will only find out how good or bad they are once you get to sea, which is too late. In many countries, the Skipper of the boat is responsible for the crew, and you can find that when you reach your destination immigration will not allow the marine "hitchhiker" ashore unless they have the fare or ticket out of the country to their home. If you do take people on like this, make sure that they have money or a ticket and I recommend that you take the money as security until they are landed. I once got caught out in Durban with a hitchhiker who told me I would have to give him the airfare back to the US. However, he "accidentally" fell into the harbour, and when he put his pile of dollars out to dry, we took the amount required for his fare. Never hesitate to send crew home if they do not fit in with the remainder. The cost will seem small in comparison to a miserable voyage.

Provisions

Always stock up for the longest possible time the voyage might take, plus ten per cent extra. The system that I use for calculating the food requirement is to work out a week's worth of daily menus for one person. I then multiply this figure by the number of weeks the voyage should take plus the extra, and multiply that figure by the number of crew on board.

Always take as much fresh food as you can. Root vegetables will last at least a month if kept well aired and dry, greens last about a week. Citrus fruit will last a month. Eggs, if sealed with wax or Vaseline, will last a couple of months. Meat and fish should not be trusted beyond a day or two unless smoked, depending on the temperature. Flour, rice and other dry stores will last a long time if kept in a dry, sealed container.

The rest of the provisions will have to be canned, which are of good quality in Europe, the US, South Africa, Australia and New Zealand, but not so reliable elsewhere. Code all the cans with paint, then tear off the labels and cover the whole tin with varnish as protection against salt water corrosion and stow securely in a dry place on-board. Freeze-dried food is excellent, but you will have to take extra water if you do use it.

When taking water on board, first check that it is fresh and pure. If in doubt, add Chloride or Lime to the water tanks in the recommended proportions. Very good fresh water can be obtained from rain showers. The most effective method is to top up the main boom, so that the sail "bags" and the water will flow down to the boom and along the gooseneck where it can be caught in a bucket. There are a number of de-salination plants on the market. If the budget allows this could be worthwhile in case the water tanks go foul and rain water is hard to come by.

Safety

The safety equipment should be up to the Offshore Racing Council's minimum standards. Ensure that the life raft has been serviced before sailing, and that everyone on board knows how to use their life-jackets and safety harnesses. A number of direction-finding and recovery systems have been developed recently for picking up anyone who falls overside, and this drill should be practised before the start of the voyage. A 406Mhz EPIRB Distress Beacon is essential and make sure it is properly registered with its relevant authority.

Paperwork and Officialdom

Before setting out on a long voyage, make sure that someone at home, such as a member of the family or your solicitor, knows your crew list, their addresses and your intended programme – and keep them updated from each port. Make sure your bank knows what you are planning, and that there are enough funds in your account for emergencies. It is better to arrange to draw money at banks en route rather than carry large sums on board.

It is always wise to register the boat. Not only is this proof of ownership and nationality, but it also means that your boat comes under the umbrella of certain international maritime agreements.

A Certificate of Competence as a Yachtmaster is advisable. Some countries (e.g. Germany) are starting to insist on them. The crew must have their passports with them, plus required visas for countries such as the USA, Australia and India. More countries are demanding visas these days and it is advisable to check with the embassies or consulates for details. You should also check the health requirements and make sure that the crew have the various up-to-date inoculation or vaccination certificates. It is always advisable to have tetanus jabs.

Finally, before setting out, obtain a Clearance Certificate from Customs. You may not need it at your destination, but if you run into difficult officials, it will be helpful.

On arrival at your destination, always fly your national flag and the flag of the country you have reached on the starboard rigging and the quarantine flag (Q). If the Customs and Immigration do not visit the boat on arrival, only the Skipper need go ashore to find them and report, taking the Registration Certificate, Port Clearance, crew passports and any other relevant papers.

Smuggling and Piracy

Smuggling is a serious offence and the boat may be confiscated if smuggled items are found on board, even if the Skipper knows nothing about the offending items. There are certain areas where smuggling and piracy have become common and, of course, it is largely in the same areas that law enforcement is poor. The worst areas are the Western Caribbean, the North Coast of South America, the Red Sea and the Far East. There have also been a number of attacks on yachts off the Brazilian coast. The best protection is a crew of fairly tough-looking individuals, but a firearm is a good persuader. Never allow other boats to come alongside at sea unless you know the people on board, and if a suspicious boat approaches, let them see that you have a large crew and a gun. Call on VHF Channel 16, as this might alert other boats, and if the approaching vessel is official, they are probably listening to that channel. When in a strange port, it is a good rule never to allow anyone on board unless you know them or they have an official identity card.

If you do carry a firearm, make sure you obtain a licence for it. Murphy's Law says that if you carry a rifle, you will never have to use it – it is what the law says if you don't carry one that causes concern!

For Sailing Associations and Holiday Operators see p.797 of the Directory
*See also **Safety and Survival at Sea** by Robin Knox-Johnston in Chapter 13, p.537*

RIVER TRAVEL

by John and Julie Batchelor

Wherever you want to go in the world, the chances are that you can get there by river. Indeed, the more remote your destination, the more likely it will be that the only way of getting there, without taking to the air, will be by river. This is particularly true of tropical regions where, throughout the history of exploration, rivers have been the key that has opened the door to the interior. It is still the case that for those who really want to penetrate deep into a country, to learn about a place and its peoples through direct contact, the best way to do so is by water. River travel splits neatly into three categories: public transport, private hire and your own transport.

Public Transport

Wherever there is a large navigable river, whether it be in Africa, South America, Asia or even Europe, you will find some form of river transport. This can range from a luxury floating hotel on the Nile to a dug-out canoe in the forests of Africa and South America. And between these extremes, all over the world there can be found the basic work-a-day ferries which ply between villages and towns carrying every conceivable type of commodity and quite often an unbelievably large number of people.

Let's start by examining travel on an everyday ferry. First you must buy your ticket. The usual method is to turn up at the waterfront, find out which boat is going in your direction and then locate the agent's office. With luck, this will be a simple matter, but on occasion even finding out where to purchase your ticket can be an endless problem. Don't be put off. Just turn up at your boat, go on board and find someone, preferably someone in authority, to take your money. You'll have no difficulty doing this, so long as you do not embarrass people by asking for receipts.

Board the boat as early as possible. It is probable that it will be extremely crowded, so if you are a deck passenger you will need to stake out your corner of the deck and defend it against all comers. Make sure of your sleeping arrangements immediately. In South America this will mean getting your hammock in place, in Africa and the Far East making sure you have enough space to spread out your sleeping mat. Take care about your positioning. If you are on a trip lasting a number of days do not place yourself near the one and only toilet on board. By the end of the journey the location of this facility will be obvious to anyone with a sense of smell. Keep away from the air outlet from the engine room unless you have a particular liking for being asphyxiated by diesel fumes. If rain is expected, make sure you are under cover. On most boats a tarpaulin shelter is rigged up over the central area. Try to get a spot near the middle as those at the edges tend to get wet. Even if rain is unlikely it is still a good idea to find shade from the sun. For those unused to it, sitting in the tropical sun all day can be unpleasant and dangerous.

Go equipped. There may be some facilities for food and drink on board, but in practice this will probably only mean warm beer and unidentified local specialities which you might prefer not to have to live on. Assume there will be nothing.

Take everything you need for the whole journey, plus a couple of days just in case. On the Zaire river, for instance, it is quite common for boats to get stuck on sand banks for days on end. And don't forget the insects. The lights of the boat are sure to attract an interesting collection of wildlife during the tropical night, so take a mosquito net.

Occasionally, for those with money, there may be cabins, but don't expect too much of these. If there is supposed to be water, it will be only intermittent at best, and there certainly won't be a plug. The facilities will be very basic and you are almost certain to have the company of hordes of cockroaches who will take particular delight in sampling your food and exploring your belongings. Occupying a cabin on a multi-class boat also marks you out as "rich" and thus subject to attention from the less desirable of your fellow passengers. Lock your cabin door and do not leave your window open at night. In order to do this you will also have to go equipped with a length of chain and padlock. On most boats the advantages of a cabin are minimal.

Longer journeys, especially on African rivers, tend to be one long party. Huge quantities of beer are drunk and very loud music plays through the night. It is quite likely that you will be looked on as a guest and expected to take an active part in the festivities. It's a good way of making friends, but don't expect a restful time.

Given these few common-sense precautions, you will have a rewarding trip. By the time you have reached your destination you will have many new friends and will have learned a few essential words of the local language, all of which make your stay more pleasant and your journey easier.

Private Hire

In order to progress further up the river from the section navigable by larger boats, you will have to look around for transport to hire. This may be a small motor boat, but is more likely to be a dug-out canoe with an outboard motor. When negotiating for this sort of transport, local knowledge is everything: who's reliable and who owns a reliable boat or canoe. With luck, your new-found friends from the first stage of your journey will advise you and take care of the negotiations over price. This is by far the best option. Failing that, it is a question of your own judgement. What you are looking for is a well-equipped boat and a teetotal crew. In all probability such an ideal combination doesn't exist – at least we have never found it. So we are back to common sense.

Look at the boat before coming to any agreement. If possible try to have a test run just to make sure the motor works. Try to establish that the boatman knows the area you want to go to. If he already smells of drink at ten in the morning, he may not be the most reliable man around. This last point could be important. If you are returning the same way, you will need to arrange for your boatman to pick you up again at a particular time and place. The chances of this happening if he is likely to disappear on an extended drunken binge once he has your money is remote in the extreme. Take your time over the return arrangements. Make sure that everyone knows and understands the place, the day and the time that they are required to meet you. Don't forget that not everyone can read or tell the time. If you have friends in the place, get them to check that the boatman leaves when planned. Agree on the price to be paid before you go and do not pay anything until you arrive at the destination. If the part of the deal is that you provide the fuel, buy it yourself and hand it over only when everyone and everything is ready for departure. Establish clearly what the food and drink arrangements are as you may be expected to feed the crew.

Once you are on your way, it is a question again of common sense. Take ready-prepared food. Protect yourself from the sun and your equipment from rain and spray. If you are travelling by dug-out canoe, it will be a long uncomfortable trip with little opportunity for stretching your legs. Make sure you have something to sit on, preferably something soft, but don't forget that the bottom of the canoe will soon be full of water.

Once you have arrived at your destination, make sure that you are in the right place before letting the boat go. If the boatman is coming back for you, go over all the arrangements one more time. Do not pay in advance for the return if you can possibly avoid it. If the boatman has the money, there is little incentive for him to keep his side of the bargain. If absolutely necessary, give just enough to cover the cost of the fuel.

Own Transport

After exhausting the possibilities of public transport and hire, you must make your own way to the remote head-waters of your river. You may have brought your own equipment, which will probably be an inflatable with outboard motor or a canoe. If you have got this far, we can assume that you know all about the requirements of your own equipment. Both inflatables and rigid kayaks are bulky items to transport over thousands of miles so you might consider a collapsible canoe which you assemble once you have reached this part of the trip. We have not used them personally but have heard very good reports of them in use under very rigorous conditions.

Your chances of finding fuel for the outboard motor on the remote head-waters of almost any river in the world are negligible. Take all you need with you. Your chances of finding food and hospitality will depend on the part of the world you are exploring. In South America, you are unlikely to find any villages and the only people you may meet are nomadic Indians who, given present circumstances, could be hostile. You will have to be totally self-sufficient. In Africa the situation is quite different. Virtually anywhere that you can reach with your boat will have a village or fishing encampment of some description. The villagers will show you hospitality and in all probability you will be able to buy fresh vegetables, fruit and fish from the people. Take basic supplies and enough for emergencies but expect to be able to supplement this with local produce.

Another alternative could be to buy a local canoe, although this option is fraught with dangers. Without knowing anything about mechanics, buying a second-hand canoe is as tricky as buying a second-hand car. You can easily be fobbed off with a dud. We know of a number of people who have paddled off proudly in their new canoe only to sink steadily below the surface as water seeped in through cracks and patches. This is usually a fairly slow process so that by the time you realise your error you are too far away from the village to do anything about it. A word or two about dug-out canoes: these are simply hollowed-out tree trunks and come in all sizes. The stability of the canoe depends on the expertise of the man who made it. They are usually heavy, difficult to propel in a straight line, prone to capsize, uncomfortable and extremely hard work. The larger ones can weigh over a ton which makes it almost impossible for a small group to take one out of the water for repairs. Paddling dug-outs is best left to the experts. Only if you are desperate – and going downstream – should you entertain the idea.

Travel Etiquette

When travelling in remote areas anywhere in the world, it should always be remembered that you are the guest. You are the one who must adjust to local circumstances and take great pains not to offend the customs and traditions of the people you are visiting. To refuse hospitality will almost always cause offence. Remember that you are the odd one out and that it is natural for your hosts to be inquisitive and fascinated by everything you do. However tired or irritable you may be, you have chosen to put yourself in this position and it is your job to accept close examination with good grace. Before travelling do take the trouble to research both the area you intend to visit and its people. Try to have some idea of what is expected of you before you go to a village. If you are offered food and accommodation, accept it. Do not be squeamish about eating what is offered. After all, the local people have survived on whatever it is, so it is unlikely to do you very much damage.

No two trips are ever the same, thank goodness! The advice we have tried to give is nothing more than common sense. If you apply this to whatever you are doing, you will not go far wrong. Just remember that what may be impossible today can be achieved tomorrow… or the next day. Don't be in a hurry. There is so much to be enjoyed. Take your time… and good luck!

CRUISING

by Tony Peisley

More than four million cruise holidays are now taken every year, most of them by North Americans, but recently, the British have overtaken the Germans to become second in the cruising league.

The key word is "holiday", because ocean-going travel is almost exclusively about leisurely travel for its own sake. Not a race from A to B with the destination the object of the trip, rather than simply one of its highlights.

The jumbo jet put paid to liner travel. The first jet crossed the Atlantic in 1959 and by the mid-1970s the jumbos had become the only way to cross as far as most travellers were concerned. All of the major transatlantic liners bar the QE2 were put out of business and it was the same story on other popular seagoing journeys from the UK to Australia, South Africa and the Middle East.

Some liners (and cruise lines) couldn't or wouldn't adapt to changing times and they disappeared from the scene. Others just changed tack and decided to slow down the journey, add ports of call, and return to base every week or fortnight. Although there were "cruises" like this in the Mediterranean as far back as the 1930s, it was in the Caribbean in the 1970s that cruising holidays really came into their own.

The Caribbean is still the world's most popular destination and it is the cruise lines' competitive pricing of Caribbean cruise packages that has done most to stimulate renewed interest in cruises among British passengers. But the range of cruise destinations has never been wider and new places are being added to itineraries all the time.

There are lots of different cruises and lots of different cruise ships, but certain rules do apply when booking a cruise, any cruise:

1. Make sure you're getting good advice. Many travel agents know little about cruising and some will book you a ship that you won't enjoy, rather than own up to their lack of knowledge.

2. If you are a first-time cruiser, ask about cruises designed for "new-comers". Several lines, including P&O, Cunard, and Royal Viking Line, now offer these. On such cruises, first-timers will have their own dedicated check-in desk to take the hassle out of what can seem a confusing embarkation procedure to the uninitiated: welcome gifts (champagne, flowers, chocolate etc.) in the cabins; designated tables in the on-board restaurant exclusive to first-time passengers; and either simplified tipping procedures or no tipping at all.

3. If you are travelling with children, ask about the facilities on board. On some ships there is far more done to entertain children than on others. Some positively discourage children from their cruises while others have sophisticated entertainment programmes just for children, with designated "hosts" or "counsellors" to organise them on board and also at ports of call. This is particularly true of lines in the Caribbean during the traditional summer holiday months. Princess Cruises have good children's programmes, while Norwegian Cruise Line have just revamped theirs following a deal with Universal Studios that means there will be film stars and shows on board. A good choice for families is Premier, and the world's biggest cruise liners, Carnival.

4. It is the same story if you are disabled or intend cruising with somebody who is: some lines/ships are very much better than others, although, as so many new ships are being built these days, there has been much more chance to incorporate more facilities for disabled passengers in new ships than to convert older ships built at a time when the interests of the disabled were very low on anyone's priority list. Some common sense is also required here on the part of the disabled passenger and his/her companions. There is no point in not telling the whole truth about the level of disability, as ship's staff are much better able to cope when fully advised of any walking or other problems in advance. Also, however well-equipped the ship and helpful the staff, they can only have a limited effect on the on-shore part of the holiday. If there are severe walking difficulties, then enjoyment of a cruise to, say, the Galapagos is going to be limited as much of it is to be gained from clambering in and out of small boats and yomping across rocks and other unfriendly terrain.

5. If you are not a good sailor (or think you won't be), there are various remedies, including wrist-bands or patches to wear behind the ear, which you can either get from your doctor or chemist before you go, or from the ship's doctor (it's usually cheaper ashore). But it does make sense to choose a larger ship (above 20,000-ton for sure, and above 35,000-ton for preference). And try to stick to an area that isn't prone to bad weather, i.e. the Caribbean rather than the Canaries in winter, and never the Atlantic at any time of the year. The vast majority of ships now have stabilisers, so opt for one of those. But stabilisers cannot make a force ten into a flat-calm, therefore be advised! Cabins on higher decks are usually more expensive, those on lower decks (especially amidships) give the smoothest ride.

Outside of these general guidelines of what to look for when it comes to booking a cruise, choosing one to suit comes down to personal taste, and this is where a few cruise myths need to be debunked.

The first is that only old people go on cruises or that the average age of cruise passengers is deceased! Some cruises – usually the very expensive or the very long (three weeks plus) – do attract mainly people in the 55 to 75 age bracket, as they are the passengers with the most disposable time and income. But, overall, the average age is nearer 40. It is below 30 on short cruises from Florida to the Bahamas, and in the mid-30s for one-week Caribbean cruises, which are the most popular of all cruises at the moment. Discos and health spas are now as important a part of a ship's attractions as the more traditional cruising entertainments: bingo, cabaret, and deck sports.

This leads us to another myth: that cruise ships are just like floating holiday camps. They never really were: British camps had to ensure their guests were organised every minute of the day to take their minds off the often indifferent weather and poor quality food and accommodation they were enduring; while ships, with one or two dishonourable exceptions, were usually better appointed and cruised where the sun shone. The simple difference has always been that there has never been any feeling that passengers *must* join in the many cruise ship on-board activities to enjoy themselves or to make an "atmosphere". Many people just find a corner, read a book, sunbathe, swim in the pool and wouldn't dream of joining the dancing, bridge, aerobic or macramé classes that run through a typical day on board. They are just as typical and made just as welcome as the joiners-in.

Perhaps the most enduring myth, though, can be blamed on all those old Somerset Maugham cruise tales which told of the rich and/or snobbish old fogeys permanently in DJs and evening dresses. Round-the-clock formality disappeared when one-class ships replaced two- and three-class liners. Only the QE2 still has a first and second class and then only on its transatlantic runs.

The norm nowadays is for ships to have a couple of formal days during the week (for Captain's welcome and farewell dinners). On those evenings, depending on the ship (rule of thumb: the more expensive, the more formal) some passengers will wear black tie, while others will simply wear suits and smart dresses. For the rest of the cruise, jacket and tie or just shirt and slacks for the men, and anything other than swim-suits or shorts for the women, is in order for dinner. During the day, casual wear (designer or otherwise) is de rigueur with most ships offering on-board buffet breakfasts and lunches, as well as the slightly more formal dining room affairs.

The quality of food will, of course, depend on the ship – you get what you pay for – but the quantity is assured. However, in these more health conscious days, late night snacks have replaced the gargantuan midnight buffet on some (but not all) ships. There are also usually low calorie alternatives to the main menus. Unfortunately the food faddism that has gone hand-in-hand with health-awareness has led to much blander-tasting food being the norm on cruise ships, particularly in the Caribbean, where the majority of passengers are American.

On the other hand, while Americans are not fazed at all by the cruise tradition of tipping cabin stewards and table waiters at the end of the cruise, the British have never taken to it – so much so that one line, Cunard, has adopted a separate system on its Caribbean ships whereby the American passengers tip as normal, but the British pay theirs as part of the cruise price. One or two other lines have a no-tipping policy for all their passengers, but still the majority have retained tipping. The recommended levels vary according to the cost of the cruise, but an average would be £2.50 per passenger, per day for each of the cabin steward and the table waiter and £1.50 per day for the busboy.

It is, though, one of the definite attractions of a cruise that there are very few extras once the brochure price has been paid: just those tips, drinks on board (watch out for ships where service charges are automatically added to drinks' bills and make sure you don't tip twice!), and shore excursions. All the entertainment on board is included, except casino bets.

Most ships also operate a signing system so that bills can be paid (by credit card usually) at the end of the cruise. Shore excursions can also be paid for by credit card, so there is no need to take wads of money or travellers' cheques in most cases. Those that you do take should be in the on-board currency, usually dollars or sterling but check with your agent or in the brochure.

With a dozen or so new ships being built every year the general standard of on-board accommodation and public facilities has come on in leaps and bounds during the past three or four years. A typical cabin on a medium-priced ship will have its own colour TV, individually-controlled air-conditioning, direct-dial telephone, as well as its own bathroom with shower/wc.

The larger ships now have entire shopping malls or decks on board, while some of the smaller ones have their own watersports marina extendible from the stern.

There is also good news for people who don't like flying: a resurgence in demand for cruises that leave and return to British ports.

Most companies selling Caribbean cruises package them with a week in Florida, and there are some good deals (from Costa Line, for one) where a week's room in Florida and a week's car hire only costs an extra £100 or so on the price of the cruise. Prices are also being kept down by lines using charter instead of scheduled flights. Cunard is doing this for cruises out of San Juan and Fort Lauderdale.

Another interesting development is the return of the sailing ships. Windstar started it with its sail-assisted ships offering high-priced cruises in the South Pacific, Caribbean and Mediterranean; Club Med followed suit with a larger but similar style ship at a more middle-range price for passengers, combining it with a week ashore at a Club Med village. And from 1991 a fully-fledged sailing ship cruise was on offer from new line Star Clippers with its authentic tall ships.

The major cruise destinations are the Caribbean, Mediterranean, Alaska, the Baltic/Scandinavia, the Far East, the Mexican Riviera (including Acapulco), and South America, in that order. There are also cruises that transit the Panama

Canal between the Caribbean and the US West Coast.

So-called adventure or expedition cruise lines are also increasingly popular – and adventurous. Destinations include the North West Passage and Antarctica. These are usually small ships with even smaller inflatable boats which can take passengers right amongst the ice floes and wildlife.

In mainstream cruising, ship sizes vary considerably from small, yacht-like ships carrying 100 passengers to huge, mini-city ships carrying upwards of 2000 passengers. The on-board differences are fairly obvious but, in brief, if you are looking for masses of entertainment, shops, and potential new friends, choose the leviathans; if peace and quiet, personal service, and top-class food are the criteria, small is beautiful. A couple of final tips on choosing the right cruise:

1. Travel agents displaying the PSARA sign, belong to the Passenger Shipping Association Retail Agent training scheme. This means that at least some of the staff have taken courses specifically designed to increase their knowledge of ships and cruising.
2. *The Berlitz Complete Handbook to Cruising* by Douglas Ward, which is up–dated every couple of years, has plenty of information on different ships.

For Cruise Lines and Operators see p.791 of the Directory

TRAVEL BY CARGO SHIP: ABROAD AND ABOARD

by Hugo Verlomme

Why, in this age of jet-plane commuting, would one travel by freighter? Surely it must be a boring, wet, lonely, and above all, terribly slow way to go?

In fact this is exactly why travel by cargo ship is such a pleasure. If you want to go on holiday then a cruise liner, which is a floating luxury hotel that rarely "goes" anywhere, is for you. If you want to really travel the seas then freighters are the genuine experience. Etymologically, "to travel" means "to follow a path", and not simply "to arrive". Robert Louis Stevenson understood the nature of leisurely travel when he wrote: "To travel hopefully is a better thing than to arrive."

I have indeed noticed that some of my most vivid memories were related to unexpected events happening in the course of travel. At sea it could be the tail of a typhoon in the China Sea, whales in the St Lawrence river, and more importantly, encounters with people, officers, crew members from various countries, or fellow travellers – some of whom became my friends.

Being on the move for days and days on the rolling hills of the ocean has been described as "the royal way". As we walk, drive, fly, over land, we forget that our blue planet is composed of 71 per cent oceans. Why limit our travelling to 29 per cent of the globe?

"But isn't the sea always the same?" I have been asked many times...He who hasn't seen the changing colours of water, the British Channel's ochres, the Atlantic's ultramarine, the Mediterranean's lapis lazuli, the Caribbean's turquoise or the deep Pacific's indigo, might think so. The sea is an incredible, changing scenery full of surprises for those who keep their eyes open: islands, storms, calms, squalls, dolphins and whales, fishes and birds, icebergs and atolls. Freighters are privileged platforms to observe seas and skies, human activity and the sea and animal life.

Not so long ago, liners were the regular way to reach any destination "overseas". These were glorious times when microcosms of society crossed the oceans, mixing together families and loners, travellers and businessmen, migrants and adventurers. Today's liners are exclusively dedicated to the holiday cruising industry, which is booming. I remember with nostalgia enchanting Atlantic crossings aboard a Polish liner, one of the last "Transatlantic", the Stefan Batory, who did her last crossing in 1988.

In order to travel by sea there remains only one possibility: freighters. Many people believe that embarking on a cargo ship means sleeping in a small cheap cabin, and maybe giving a hand on deck or in the kitchen to pay the fare. The good old times when famous writers like Joseph Conrad, Blaise Cendrars, Malcolm Lowry or Jack Kerouac were travelling (and working) on freighters, are gone. The romantic old beaten tramp patched with rust, as in Alvaro Mutis's novels, has been replaced with armadas of modern container ships, some of them so wide they cannot go through Panama Canal anymore.

Tramps, Ro-Ros, Reefers...

To grasp the array of possibilities in today's merchant navy, just try to guess what percentage of the world trade is transported in ships: 98 per cent! This leaves a meagre two per cent for trucks, trains, planes.

The amount of cargo that can be piled aboard a ship is such that the maritime route remains the major axis of the world's economy. Among the 40,000 or more freighters plying the seas, only a few carry passengers. The available space rarely exceeds twelve people. Sometimes there might be only one passenger on board.

Many different kinds of freighters welcome passengers, from luxurious to more modest, weathered ships. Containers have radically changed the picture: they can hold anything from objects large and small to liquids, perishable goods or dangerous chemicals. Because these boxes are standard the world over, they are loaded with machinery, direct from truck or train; the process is so fast that container ships often do not spend a whole day in their ports of call, to the great disappointment of passengers who wish to go ashore.

For longer stops one might prefer bulk carriers, which take longer to load, remaining several days in harbour. I once received a postcard from a friend who was delighted because his ship – a Polish bulk carrier on her way to Chile – was delayed for days in the Belgian harbour of Antwerp: heavy rain prevented the loading of sacks of grain that could not get wet. My friend took the opportunity to visit the city and its surroundings, using the ship as a floating hotel moored in the famous harbour.

Container ships, bulk carriers, good old ocean tramps (that take no definite route and may change their port of call mid-route if there is a better cargo to pick up somewhere else), ro-ros (from "roll on/roll off") loaded with cars... each ship is a different experience. Real fans of cargo ship travel like tramps particularly, for the unpredictability and hence added adventure of the route.

If you board a refrigerated container ship, like those carrying fruit between Europe and the Caribbean, you will find yourself on the most luxurious of freighters. Painted white, these so-called "reefers" are the modern version of the "banana boats": fast top of the range vessels. A steward will take care of you, and in your cabin, you will find your own fridge, a VCR, a coffee machine, with meals and services of a high standard. Now if you leave on a cargo-liner, like the one that sails from Great Britain to South Africa via the Canary Islands and St. Helena, you will experience a warm atmosphere, a happy, but only too rare, marriage between freighters and liners, carrying over a hundred passengers as well as cargo – and mail (St Helena island has no airport).

Onboard

Modern technology, computers and satellite communication systems have greatly reduced crews and incidentally allowed for spare cabins. The amount of officers doesn't exceed four people on small ships, the rest of the crew (usually from poorer countries, especially the Philippine Islands) assuming work on deck, in the engine room, and general maintenance.

Cabins opened to passengers are usually officers' cabins, which means spacious accommodation (much more than on cruise liners), wide port holes, private bathroom and shower and the best location on the ship's higher decks. Meals are taken in the same room and on the same schedules as officers. Of course, meals and food vary greatly, according to the standard of the ship, its nationality, as well as the cook's country of origin. Travelling on a Chinese cargo-liner between Singapore and Hong Kong I was introduced to jellyfish soup for breakfast. Later, boarding a French banana boat from Guadeloupe, meals were served by a maitre d' who proposed wine bottled by the shipping company itself. Most of the time, however, passengers are served Western food, unless they want to try some spicy, exotic food from a Kenyan or a Philippino cook.

One must remember that freighters are first of all work places. Passengers should not infringe on ship's life. I was told by a German captain of an indelicate passenger who almost triggered a mutiny by telling the crew that their wages were much too low.

Onboard freighters, passengers are expected to be self-sufficient as far as entertainment is concerned. Before you leave for an ocean voyage, make sure you take your own "food for thought". Time and quietness are one of the main luxuries on a ship. This is the perfect time to do things you have always wanted to do but never had the leisure for. Books are ideal companions. Some travellers make the best of lengthy voyages to finally get into the complete works of Proust or Dostoievski. Others take along drawing or painting material, or recorded music. Some artists, painters, writers and poets travel by cargo ship to practise their art without the intrusion from the outside world.

People travelling by sea range from the retired (a frequent occurrence), to young adventurers wishing to savour every mile of their journey. Facilities are shared with officers. It is not rare to find a swimming pool (filled with ocean water), a sauna, a small gymnasium, a table tennis table, a bar, a video lounge, aboard freighters. Since VCRs have become very common on merchant ships, videos are popular among sailors and make a good gift.

So now, to answer the expected question: "But how much does all this cost?" First, do not try to compare sea-fares and air-fares, because you spend days, weeks, aboard these comfortable sailing hotels, with room, board and facilities included, as well as getting to faraway and exotic destinations. The average fare is around $100 per day, which, considering what you get, is moderate. Of course prices vary from one ship to another, as well as according to the time of year.

Cargo Travelling Revival

Back in 1992 I wrote a guide on how to travel by cargo ship, because so many people were asking me how to do it. While doing research for this guide – the first of its kind – I encountered scepticism (including from professionals from the merchant navy): "You'll hardly find a few freighters accepting passengers; not even enough to fill a book. Those times are over", I was told many times. But the opposite proved to be true. *Travel by Cargo Ship* has been published in French, English, German and Italian. It is now possible to sail to most major harbours throughout the world. Travel agencies specialising in freighters are growing and blooming on all continents, and every day more and more people are discovering the joys of ocean crossings. There are fans who travel at least once a year by freighter, for the sheer pleasure of being on a ship, no matter where it goes. The trend is undoubtedly established. In Paris, a "Cargo Club" meets on the first Wednesday of every month in a small bookshop on the Ile Sainte-Louis, with each time more old salts coming back from distant oceans, or dreamers eager to hear stories and gather tips before their departure.

But do not travel by freighter if you have a problem with not departing or arriving on schedule: at sea, as well as in harbours, all kinds of delays can happen, from weather to red-tape, but some consider this an added charm, a sprinkle of the unexpected. Sometimes, the very port of call is changed at the last moment (this being particularly true of tramps).

Within shipping companies themselves, things are subject to change: ships change hands, names and flags, new routes are opened, others are closed. My advice: if you are looking for a particular itinerary and are told that no ship is going there, be stubborn. Faxes and telephones can create miracles. Remember also that public demand does shape the future.

Travelling by cargo ship is here to stay and we can hope to see more and more space for passengers on freighters, big and small, but also on liners, or even scientific ships: the brand new French oceanographic vessel *Marion Dufresne II*, fully equipped with labs, drilling equipment and helicopters, was designed to accommodate (wealthy) passengers wishing to sail in southern seas to the Kerguelen islands, near Antarctica.

If you have never tried sea travel, you could do a trial run of a few days, with several ports of call, such as in the Baltic sea or the Mediterranean. If you are seeking the ultimate freighter experience, you could embark on a round-the-world voyage through the Pacific islands, a trip almost three months long. And who knows, tomorrow silent cargo-liners, propelled by wind power, will perhaps sail the seas, carrying freight and a happy bunch of passengers?

For a list of cargo shipping companies see p.790 of the Directory

TRAVEL BY CAMEL

by René Dee

In this mechanised and industrial epoch, the camel does not seem to be an obvious choice of travelling companion when sophisticated cross-country vehicles exist for the toughest of terrains. Add to this the stockpile of derisory and mocking myths, truths and sayings about the camel and one is forced to ask the question: why use camels at all?

Purely as a means of getting from A to B when time is the most important factor, the camel should not even be considered. As a means of transport for scientific groups who wish to carry out useful research in the field, the camel is limiting. It can be awkward and risky transporting delicate equipment and specimens. However, for the individual, small group and expedition wishing to see the desert as it should be seen, the camel is an unrivalled means of transport.

Go Safely in the Desert

From my own personal point of view, the primary reason must be that, unlike any motorised vehicle, camels allow you to integrate completely with the desert and the people within it – something it is impossible to do at 80 kmph enclosed in a "tin can". A vehicle in the desert can be like a prison cell and the constant noise of the engine tends to blur all sense of the solitude, vastness and deafening quiet which is so intrinsic to the experience.

Travel by camel allows the entire pace of life to slow down from a racy 80kmph to a steady 6.5kmph, enabling you to unwind, take in and visually appreciate the overall magnificence and individual details of your surroundings. Secondly, camels do, of course, have the ability to reach certain areas inaccessible to vehicles, especially through rocky and narrow mountain passes, although camels are not always happy on this terrain and extreme care has to be taken to ensure they do not slip or twist a leg. They are as sensitive as they appear insensitive.

Thirdly, in practical terms, they cause far fewer problems where maintenance, breakdown and repairs are concerned. No bulky spares or expensive mechanical equipment are needed to carry out repairs. Camels do not need a great deal of fuel and can exist adequately (given that they are not burdened with excessively heavy loads) for five to ten days without water. Camels go on and on and on and on until they die; and then one has the option of eating them, altogether far better-tasting than a Michelin tyre.

Lastly, camels *must* be far more cost effective if you compare them directly with vehicles, although this depends on whether your intended expedition/journey already includes a motorised section. If you fly direct to your departure point, or as near as possible to it, you will incur none of the heavy costs related to transporting a vehicle, not to mention the cost of buying it. If the camel trek is to be an integral portion of a motorised journey, then the cost saving will not apply as, of course, hire fees for camels and guides will be additional.

In many ways, combining these two forms of travel is ideal and a very good way of highlighting my primary point in favour of transport by camel. If you do decide on this combination, make sure you schedule the camel journey for the very end of your expedition and that the return leg by vehicle is either minimal or purely functional for I can guarantee that after a period of ten days or more travelling slowly and gently through the desert by camel, your vehicle will take on the characteristics of a rocket ship and all sense of freedom, enquiry and interest will be dulled to the extreme. An overwhelming sense of disillusion and disinterest will prevail. Previously exciting sights, desert towns and Arab civilisation, will pall after such intense involvement with the desert, its people and its lifestyle.

First Steps

For the individual or group organiser wanting to get off the beaten track by camel, the first real problem is to find them and to gather every bit of information possible about who owns them. Are they for hire, for how much, what equipment/stores/provisions are included (if any) and, lastly, what are the guides/owners capable of and are they willing to accompany you? It is not much good arriving at Tamanrasset, Timbouctou or Tindoug without knowing some, if not all, of the answers to these questions. Good pre-departure research is vital but the problem is that 90 per cent of the information won't be found from any tourist office, embassy, library or travel agent. Particularly if you're considering a major journey exclusively by camel, you'll probably have to undertake a preliminary fact-finding recce to your proposed departure point to establish contacts among camel owners and guides. It may well be that camels and/or reliable guides do not exist in the area where you wish to carry out your expedition.

I would suggest, therefore, that you start first with a reliable source of information such as the Royal Geographical Society, which has expedition reports and advice which can be used as a primary source of reference including names and addresses to write to for up-to-date information about the area that interests you. Up-to-date information is without doubt the key to it all. Very often this can be gleaned from the commercial overland companies whose drivers are passing through your area of interest regularly and may even have had personal experience of the journey you intend to make.

Equally important is the fact that in the course of their travels, they build up an impressive collection of contacts who could well help in the final goal of finding suitable guides, smoothing over formalities and getting introductions to local officials, etc. Most overland travel companies are very approachable so long as you appreciate that their time is restricted and that their business is selling travel and not running an advisory service.

In all the best Red Indian stories, the guide is the all-knowing, all-seeing person in whom total faith is put. However, as various people have discovered to their cost, this is not always such a good idea. Many so-called guides know very little of the desert and its ways. How then to find someone who really does know the route/area, has a sense of desert lore and who preferably owns his best

camel? I can only reiterate that the best way to do this is through personal recommendation.

Having found him, put your faith in him, let him choose your camels and
make sure that your relationship remains as amicable as possible. You will be
living together for many days in conditions which are familiar to him but alien
to you, and you need his support. Arrogance does not fit into desert travel, especially from a *nasrani*. Mutual respect and a good rapport are essential.

Pack up your Troubles

Once you've managed to establish all this and you're actually out there, what
are the do's, don'ts and logistics of travel by camel? Most individuals and expeditions (scientifically orientated or not) will want, I imagine, to incorporate a
camel trek within an existing vehicle-led expedition, so I am really talking only
of short-range treks of around ten to fifteen days' duration, and up to 400km. If
this is so, you will need relatively little equipment and stores, and it is essential
that this is kept to a minimum. Remember that the more equipment you take, the
more camels you will need, which will require more guides, which means more
cost, more pasture and water, longer delays in loading, unloading, cooking and
setting up camp and a longer wait in the morning while the camels are being
rounded up after a night of pasturing.

Be prepared also for a very swift deterioration of equipment. In a vehicle you
can at least keep possessions clean and safe to a degree, but packing kit onto a
camel denies any form of protection, especially since it is not unknown for
camels to stumble and fall or to roll you over suddenly and ignominiously if
something is not to their liking, such as a slipped load or uncomfortable saddle.
My advice is to pack all your belongings in a seaman's kit-bag which can be
roped onto the camel's side easily, is pliable, hard-wearing and, because it is
soft and not angular, doesn't threaten to rub a hole in the camel's side or back-
bone. (I have seen a badly-placed baggage saddle wear a hole the size of a man's
fist into an animal's back.)

If rectangular aluminium boxes containing cameras or other delicate equipment are being carried, make sure that they are well roped on the top of the
camel and that there is sufficient padding underneath so as not to cause friction.
Moreover, you'll always have to take your shoes off while riding because over a
period of hours, let alone days, you could wear out the protective hair on the
camel's neck and eventually cause open sores.

Water should be carried around in goat-skin guerbas and twenty-litre round
metal bidons which can again be roped up easily and hung either side of the baggage camel under protective covers. Take plenty of rope for tying on equipment,
saddles etc., and keep one length of fifteen metres intact for using at wells where
there may be no facilities for hauling up water. Don't take any sophisticated
tents either; they will probably be ruined within days and anyway are just not
necessary.

I have always used a piece of cotton cloth approximately six metres square,
which, with two poles for support front and rear and with sand or boulders at the
sides and corner, makes a very good overnight shelter for half a dozen people.
Night in the desert can be extremely cold, particularly in the winter but the

makeshift "tent" has a more important role during the day when it provides shelter for the essential two-hour lunch stop and rest.

The Day's Schedule

Your daily itinerary and schedule should be geared to the practical implications of travelling by camel. That is to say that each night's stop will, where possible, be in an area where pasture is to be found for the camels to graze. Although one can take along grain and dried dates for camels to eat, normal grazing is also vital. The camels are unloaded and hobbled (two front legs are tied closely together) but you will find they can wander as much as three or four kilometres overnight and there is only one way to fetch them: on foot. Binoculars are extremely useful as spotting camels over such a distance can be a nightmare. They may be hidden behind dunes and not come into view for some time.

Other useful equipment includes goggles for protection in sandstorms, prescription sunglasses and, of course, sun cream. Above all, take comfortable and hard-wearing footwear for it is almost certain that you will walk at least half the way once you have become fully acclimatised. I would suggest that you take Spanish felt boots or something similar, which are cheap, very light, give ankle support over uneven terrain and are durable and very comfortable.

The one disadvantage of boots by day is that your feet will get very hot, but it's a far better choice than battered, blistered and lacerated feet when one has to keep up with the camel's steady 6.5kmph. Nomads wear sandals, but if you take a close look at a nomad's foot you will see that it is not dissimilar to the sandal itself, i.e. as hard and tough as leather. Your's resembles a baby's bottom by comparison, so it is essential that you get some heavy walking practice in before hand with the boots/shoes/sandals you intend to wear. If your journey is likely to be a long one, then you could possibly try sandals, as there will be time for the inevitable wearing-in process with blisters, as well as stubbed toes and feet spiked by the lethal acacia thorn.

For clothing, I personally wear a local, free-flowing robe like the *gandoura*, local pantaloons and *cheche*, a three metre length of cotton cloth which can be tied round the head and/or face and neck for protection against the sun. You can also use it as a rope, fly whisk and face protector in sandstorms. In the bitter cold nights and early mornings of winter desert travel, go to bed with it wrapped around your neck, face and head to keep warm.

If local clothing embarrasses and inhibits you, stick to loose cotton shirts and trousers. Forget your tight jeans and bring loose-fitting cotton underwear. Anything nylon and tight-fitting next to the skin will result in chafing and sores. Do, however, also take some warm clothing and blankets, including socks and jumpers. As soon as the sun sets in the desert, the temperature drops dramatically. Catching cold in the desert is unbearable. Colds are extremely common and spread like wildfire. Take a good down sleeping bag and a groundsheet.

Your sleeping bag and blankets can also serve as padding for certain types of camel saddle. In the Western Sahara you will find the Mauritanian butterfly variety, which envelops you on four sides. You're liable to slide back and forth uncomfortably and get blisters unless you pad the saddle. The Tuareg saddle is commonly used in the Algerian Sahara. This is a more traditional saddle with a fierce-looking forward pommel which threatens man's very manhood should you be thrown forward against it. In Saudi Arabia, female camels are ridden and seating positions are taken up behind the dromedary's single hump rather than on or forward of it.

Culture Shock

Never travel alone in the desert, without even a guide. Ideal group size would be seven group members, one group leader, three guides, eleven riding camels and three baggage camels. The individual traveller should take at least one guide with him and three or four camels.

Be prepared for a mind-blowing sequence of mental experience, especially if you are not accustomed to the alien environment, company and pace, which can lead to introspection, uncertainty and even paranoia. Travel by camel with nomad guides is the complete reversal of our normal lifestyle.

Therefore it is as important to be mentally prepared for this culture shock as it is to be physically prepared. Make no mistake, travel by camel is hard, physically uncompromising and mentally torturing at times. But a *Meharee* satisfactorily accomplished will alter your concept of life and its overall values, and the desert's hold over you will never loosen.

TRAVEL BY PACK ANIMAL

by Roger Chapman

The donkey is the most desirable beast of burden for the novice and remains the favourite of the more experienced camper – if only because the donkey carries all the traveller's equipment, leaving them free to enjoy the countryside unburdened. Although small and gentle, the donkey is strong and dependable; no pack animal excels him for sure-footedness or matches his character. He makes the ideal companion for children old enough to travel into the mountains or hills, and for the adult who prefers to travel at a pace slow enough to appreciate the scenery, wildlife and wilderness that no vehicle can reach.

The rock climber, hunter, fisherman, scientist or artist who has too much gear to carry into the mountains may prefer to take the larger and faster mule, but if they are sensible, they will practice first on the smaller and more patient donkey. The principles of pack-animal management are the same, but the mule is stronger, more likely to kick or bite if provoked, and requires firmer handling than the donkey. The advantage of a mule is obvious. Whereas a donkey can only carry about 50kgs (100lbs), the mule, if expertly packed, can carry a payload of 100kgs (200lbs). Although both are good for fifteen miles a day on reasonable trails, the donkeys will have to be led on foot, whereas mules, which can travel at a good speed, require everyone to be mounted, unless their handlers are fast hikers.

Planning

To determine the number of donkeys needed before an expedition or holiday, the approximate pack load must be calculated. The stock requirement for a ten-day trip can be calculated by dividing the number of people by two, but taking the higher whole number if the split does not work evenly. Thus, a family of five would take three donkeys. It is difficult to control more than ten donkeys on the trail, so don't use them with a party of twenty or more unless certain individuals are prepared to carry large packs to reduce the number of animals. Mules are usually led by a single hiker or are tied in groups of not more than five animals led by a man on horseback. This is the "string" of mules often mentioned in Westerns; each lead rope passes through the left-hand breech ring of preceding animal's harness and is then tied around the animal's neck with a bow-line. One or more horses are usually sent out with the pack mules because mules respect and stick close to these "chaperones".

Whichever method you decide to use, don't prepare a detailed itinerary before your journey; wait and see how you get on during the first few days, when you should attempt no more than eight to ten miles (12 to 16kms) a day. Later you will be able to average 12 to 15 miles (20 to 24kms), but you should not count on doing more than 15 miles (24kms) a day although it is possible, with early starts and a lighter load, if you really have to.

Campers who use pack animals seldom restrict themselves to the equipment list of a backpacker. There is no need to do so, but before preparing elaborate menus and extensive wardrobes, you would do well to consider the price of hiring a pack animal. The more elaborate, heavy equipment, the more donkeys or mules there are to hire, load, unload, groom and find pasture for. In selecting your personal equipment you have more freedom – a "Karrimat", or a larger tent instead of the small "Basha" – but it should not exceed 12kgs (924lbs) and should be packed into several of those small cylindrical soft bags or a seaman's kit-bag. You can take your sleeping bag as a separate bundle and take a small knapsack for those personal items such as spare sweaters, camera, first aid kit and snacks required during the day. But there are some special items you will require if you are not hiring an efficient guide and handler: repair kit for broken pack saddles and extra straps for mending harnesses. An essential item is a 100lbs spring scale for balancing the sacks or panniers before you load them on the pack animals in the morning. Remember too that each donkey/mule will be hired out with a halter, lead rope, tow "sacks", a pack cover, and a 30ft pack rope. In addition, there will be pickets and shackle straps, curry combs, froghooks, canvas buckets, tools and possibly ointment or powders to heal saddle sores.

Animal Handling

The art of handling pack animals is not a difficult one but unfortunately you cannot learn it entirely from a book. With surprisingly little experience in this field, the novice soon becomes an expert packer, confident that he can handle any situation which may arise on the trail and, above all, that he has learnt the uncertain science of getting the pack animal to do what he wants it to do. The donkey is more responsive than the mule and is quick to return friendship, especially if he knows he is being well packed, well fed and well rested. The mule tends to be more truculent, angry and resentful until he knows who is in charge. Therefore, an attitude of firmness and consideration towards the animal is paramount.

Perhaps the easiest way to learn the techniques of handling pack animals is to look at a typical day and consider the problems as they arise:

Collecting in the morning: Pack animals can either be let loose, hobbled or picketed during the night. The latter is preferable as even a mule which has its front legs hobbled can wander for miles during the night searching for suitable grass. If the animal is picketed, unloosen the strap around the fetlock which is attached to the picket rope and lead him back to the campsite by the halter. If the animals are loose, you may have to allow a good half hour or so to catch them. Collect the gentle ones first, returning later for the recalcitrant animals. Approach each cautiously, talking to him and offering a palmful of oats before grabbing the halter.

Tying up and grooming: Even the gentlest pack animal will need to be tied up to a tree or post before packing. The rope should be tied with a clove hitch at about waist height. Keep the rope short, otherwise the animal will walk round and round the tree as you follow with the saddle. It also prevents him stepping on or tripping over the rope. It is advisable to keep the animals well apart, but not too far from your pile of packed sacks or panniers.

Often, donkeys in particular, will have a roll during the night, so they require a good work-over with the brush or curry comb to remove dust or caked mud. Most animals enjoy this, but you musn't forget that one end can bite and the other end can give a mighty kick. Personally, I spend some time stroking the animal around the head and ears, talking to him before I attempt to groom him. Ears are very good indicators of mood. If the ears are upright he is alert and apprehensive, so a few words and strokes will give him confidence; soon the ears will relax and lie back. If the ears turn and stretch right back along his neck, then there is a good chance you are in for trouble. The first time he nips, thump him in the ribs and swear at him. He will soon learn that you do not appreciate this kind of gesture.

Your main reason for grooming is to remove caked dirt which may cause sores once the animal is loaded. Remove this dirt with a brush and clean rag and, if there is an open wound, apply an antiseptic ointment or sprinkle on boric acid powder which will help dry it up. Finally, check each hoof quickly to see that no stone or twig has lodged in the soft pad. Lean against the animal, then warn him by tapping the leg all the way down the flank, past the knee to the fetlock, before lifting the hoof; otherwise you will never succeed. If there is a stone lodged between the shoe and the hoof, prise it out with a frog hook.

Saddling and loading: Animals are used to being loaded from the left or near side. First you fold the saddle blanket, place it far forward then slide it back into position along the animal's back so that the hair lies smooth. Check that it hangs evenly on both sides, sufficient to protect the flanks from the loaded sacks. Stand behind the mule or donkey – but not too close – and check it before you proceed further. Pick up the pack saddle (two moulded pieces of wood jointed by two cross-trees) and place it on the saddle blanket so it fits in the hollows behind the withers. Tie up the breast strap and rear strap before tying the girth tight. Two people will be required to load the equipment in the soft canvas sacks onto the saddle pack, but it is essential to weigh the sacks before you place them on the cross-trees; they should be within two kgs of each other. If the saddle is straight, but one sack is lower than the other, correct the length of the ear loops.

On the trail: Morning is the best time to travel, so you must hit the trail early, preferably before 7am. At a steady two kms an hour, you will be able to cover the majority of the day's journey by the time the sun is at its hottest. This will allow you to spend a good three hours' rest-halt at midday before setting off once more for a final couple of hours before searching for a camp-site. Avoid late camps, so start looking by 4pm.

During the first few days you may have some trouble getting your donkeys or mules to move close together and at a steady pace. One man should walk behind each animal if they are being led and if there are any hold ups, he can apply a few swipes of a willow switch to the hind-quarters. It is a waste of time to shout at the animals or threaten them constantly as it only makes them distrustful and skittish. The notorious stubbornness of the mule or donkey is usually the result of bad handling in the past. Sometimes, it is a result of fear or fatigue, but occasionally it is sheer cussedness or an attempt to see how much he can get away with. The only occasion when I could not get a mule moving was travelling across some snow patches in the mountains of Kashmir. Eventually, after losing my temper and lashing him with a switch, I persuaded him to move slowly across the icy surface and disappear into a snow hole. It took my companion and me three hours to unload him, pull him out and calm him down before we could re-pack. I learned a good lesson from my lack of awareness of the innate intelligence of the mule.

Understanding: There is no problem with unpacking which can be done quickly and efficiently. Just remember to place all the equipment neatly together so it is not mixed up. Keep individual saddles, sacks and harnesses close enough together to cover with the waterproof cover in case of rain. Once unloaded, the donkeys can be groomed, watered and led off to the pasture area where they are to be picketed for the night.

Not long ago, I took my wife and two young daughters on a 120-mile journey across the Cevennes mountains in south-east France. We followed Robert Louis Stevenson's routes which he described in his charming little book *Travels With a Donkey*. We took three donkeys – two as pack animals and one for the children to take turns in riding – on a trail which had not changed much over the past hundred years. It made an ideal holiday, and we returned tanned, fitter, enchanted by the French countryside and aware that it was the character of our brave little donkeys which had made our enjoyment complete.

The speed with which the children mastered the technique of pack animal management was encouraging because it allowed us to complete our self-imposed task with enough time to explore the wilder parts of the mountains and enjoy the countryside at the leisurely pace of our four-footed companions. We also took a hundred flies from one side of the Cevennes to the other, but that is another story.

TRAVEL BY HORSE

by Robin Hanbury-Tenison

If the terrain is suitable, then riding a horse is the ultimate method of travel. Of course, in extreme desert conditions, or in very mountainous country, camels, donkeys or mules may be more appropriate. The previous two sections, by René Dee and Roger Chapman describe these methods clearly and they also give a great deal of excellent practical advice which is equally applicable to horses and which should be read by anyone planning a long-distance ride. This is especially the case if the decision is to take a pack animal or animals, since the care of these is as important as that of the animal you are riding yourself.

But for me the prime purpose of riding is the freedom which it can give to experience fully the sounds, smells and sights of the landscape through which I am passing; to divert on the spur of the moment so as to meet local people or look closer at interesting things; to break the tedium of constant travel by a short gallop or a longer canter in the open air, surely the closest man or woman can come to flying without wings.

One way to achieve this freedom is to have a back-up vehicle carrying food for both horses and riders, spare clothes, kit and all the paraphernalia of modern life such as film, paperwork and presents. Often it may not be necessary to meet up with the support team more than once or twice a week, since it is perfectly possible to carry in saddle-bags enough equipment to survive for a few days without overloading your horse. In this way an individual, couple or group can live simply, camping in the open or in farm buildings. If a rendezvous is pre-arranged, the worries of where to stop for the night, whether there will be grazing for the horses and what sort of accommodation and meal awaits at the end of a long day in the saddle is removed.

Fussing about this can easily spoil the whole enjoyment of the travel itself and it is well worth considering carefully in advance whether sacrificing the ultimate vagabondage of depending solely on equestrian transport for the serenity of mechanical support is worth it. It does, however, involve a certain amount of expense, although this may be less in the long run than being at the mercy of whatever transport is available locally in an emergency, and most significantly, as with ballooning, it depends on having someone who is prepared to do the driving and make the arrangements.

The alternative is to use time instead of money and resolutely to escape from a fixed itinerary and desire to cover a pre-determined distance each day. This is quite hard to do, since we all tend today to think in terms of programmes and time seems to be an increasingly scarce commodity.

Where to Go

After half a lifetime spent on other types of exploratory travel through tropical rainforests and deserts, I came to long distance riding more by accident than design. My wife and I needed some new horses for rounding up sheep and cattle on our farm on Bodmin Moor in Cornwall and we bought two young geldings in the Camargue where the legendary white herds run free in the marshes. Riding them home across France we discovered that the footpaths are also bridle-paths and there is an excellent and well-marked network of *sentiers de grande ran-donnée*. Thanks to this we were able to avoid most roads and instead ride across country. It was an idyllic and addictive experience during which we rode some 1000 miles in seven weeks. Leaving the horses to graze each night in grassy fields, for which we were never allowed to pay, we either camped beside them or stayed in remote country inns so far off the beaten track that the prices were as small as the meals were delicious. This was an unexpected bonus of riding: the need to arrange accommodation around a daily travelling distance of no more than 30 miles or so – and that, in as straight a line as possible, took us to villages which did not appear on even quite detailed maps but where the culinary standards were as high as only the French will insist on everywhere.

Later, we were to ride 1000 miles along the Great Wall of China. There we had to buy and sell three different pairs of horses and my suspicions were confirmed that horse dealers the world over tend to be rogues. We were luckier with our mounts on similar subsequent rides in New Zealand and Spain, but with horses nothing is certain and it is essential to be constantly on guard for the unexpected. However, this only serves to sharpen the senses and when something really wonderful happens, like reaching a wide, sandy beach on the coast, riding the horses bareback out into huge breakers and teaching them to surf, then you know it has been worthwhile.

This piece is meant to be full of practical advice and information, but I am hesitant to give it where horses are concerned. People are divided into those who are "horsey" and those who are not. The former know it all already and do not need my advice. The latter (and I include myself among them, in spite of having spent much of my life around horses) have to rely on common-sense and observation. It is, on the whole, far better to fit in with local conditions than to try and impose one's ideas too rapidly. For example, we learned to appreciate the superb comfort of the Camargue saddles which we acquired for our ride across France and we took them with us on all our subsequent rides. But in both China and Spain, I found that mine did not suit the local horse I was riding and, to preserve its back, I had to change to a local model, which was much less comfortable for me but much better for the horse.

And it is the horses' backs which should be the most constant concern of all on long-distance rides. Once a saddle sore develops it is very difficult to get rid of and prevention is far the best cure. To begin with it is wise to use a horse whose back is already hardened to saddle use. Scrupulous grooming and regular inspection of all areas where saddle or saddle-bags touch the horse is essential. Washing helps, if water is available and a sweaty back should be allowed to dry as often as possible, even if it does mean unsaddling during a fairly brief stop when one would rather be having a drink and a rest oneself. A clean, dry saddle cloth is essential (felt, cotton or wool) so find out what the horse is used to.

There are many local cures for incipient sores. I have found surgical spirit good, though it will sting if the skin is at all sore or sensitive. Three tablespoons of salt to a pint of water will help harden the skin if swabbed on in the evening, but complete rest is the best treatment. The same goes for girth galls, although these should be avoided if the girths are tightened level and a hand run downwards over the skin to smooth out any wrinkles. A sheepskin girth cover is a good idea too, as it prevents pinching. If it is absolutely essential to ride a horse with a saddle sore, the only way to prevent it getting worse is to put an old felt *numnah* under the saddle with a piece cut out so as to avoid pressure on the affected part.

It is also vital to keep checking the feet, ideally every time you rest and dismount. Stones lodge easily between the frog and the shoe and soon cause trouble if not removed. Small cuts and grazes can be spotted and treated with ointment or antiseptic spray at the same time and a hand passed quickly up and down each leg can give early warning of heat or other incipient problems. Once again the best general cure is usually to take the pressure off horse and rider by resting, if necessary for a day or two.

While putting on a new set of shoes is a skilled business which should not be attempted by the amateur, it is invaluable to have enough basic knowledge of shoeing to be able to remove a loose shoe or tighten it by replacing missing nails from a supply of new ones, which should always be carried in the saddle-bag. I have had to do this with a Swiss Army knife and a rock but it is much better to carry a pair of fencing pliers since these are essential in an emergency if your horse should get caught up in wire.

Your own footwear is also important on a long ride, since it is often necessary to walk leading your horse almost as much as you ride. Riding boots which protect your calves from rubbing on the saddle are useful, especially at the start and if you are using an English or cavalry saddle, but you must be able to walk in them. With a Western type of saddle and once your legs have settled down, it is better to wear comfortable walking shoes or trainers. Leather chaps, which can be found at most country shows, are also invaluable. The protection they give to legs both against rubbing and from passing through bushes easily outweighs the heat and sweat they may generate in a hot climate.

Choosing your Horse

As Christina Dodwell says in *A Traveller on Horseback,* a valuable horse is more likely to be stolen and what you need is "a good travelling horse.' Tschiffely, on the most famous of all long distance rides, from Buenos Aires to Washington in the 1920s, had two Argentinian ponies already fifteen and sixteen years old when he acquired them. He covered 10,000 miles in two and a half years, covering about twenty miles a day on the days he rode, but making many long stops and side trips.

Tim Severin started out on his ride to Jerusalem on a huge Ardennes Heavy Horse as used on the First Crusade. In spite of suffering from heat exhaustion it reached Turkey before being replaced with a more suitable thirteen hand local pony. The ideal horse for covering long distances in comfort is one possessing one of the various "easy' inbred gaits which lie between a walk and a trot. We were lucky enough to use "amblers' in New Zealand. These had been bred to have a two beat gait in which the legs on either side move together giving an impression a bit like the wheels of a steam engine. Once we learned to relax into the unfamiliar rhythm and roll a little from side to side with the horse, we found it wonderfully comfortable and the miles passed effortlessly and fast. However, even then we seldom averaged more than four mph (seven kmph). Unless you are setting out to break records or prove a point, the object of a long distance ride should be the journey itself not the high performance of your mount. The close relationship which develops between horse and rider is one of the bonuses of such a journey and as long as your prime concern is your horse's welfare before your own you won't go far wrong.

On a horse it is uniquely possible to let an intelligent creature do most of the thinking and all of the work, leaving you free to enjoy and absorb your surroundings. Birds are not afraid to fly near and be observed; the sounds of the countryside are not drowned by the noise of a motor or the rasping of one's own breath; and if you are lucky enough to have a congenial companion, conversation can be carried on in a relaxed and pleasant way. Notes can even be taken en route without the need to stop or the danger of an accident, especially if you carry a small portable tape recorder. This helps greatly in taking down instant impressions for future inclusion in books and articles which are surely the chief justification of pure travel. Photographic equipment can be readily to hand in saddle-bags, and much more can be carried. Above all, those you meet along the way, whether they be fellow travellers, farmers or remote tribes people, are inclined to like you and respond to your needs.

For a list of Equestrian Associations, see p. 796 of the Directory.

LONG DISTANCE WALKING
by Nicholas Crane

W e are all bipeds. We are all *experts* at walking. Legs require no skills to use or licence to operate. They're built in, cost us nothing to use and are greener than any other means of transport. Legs! Stick 'em in a couple of boots and they'll do thousands of miles without so much as a service. Marvellous things.

Legs have been a recent discovery for me. For years I've been travelling on bicycles, occasionally boats and under pressure, some kind of motorised transport. Horses are fine, but are limited to particular types of terrain. Legs are versatile. You can vary your mode of transport on a whim. Rides in trains or haycarts, buses and boats are all possible complements to a foot-journey.

At walking pace you become part of the infinitely complex matrix which is the countryside. After a while, animals and birds tend not to take flight at your approach. Strangers stop to chat, flattered that you are exploring their neighbourhood at a civilised, respectful pace. On foot you pose no threat and appear to have nothing to hide.

My life as a leg-advocate began with my decision to walk across Europe, following the mountain ranges of the continent from Cape Finisterre in Spain to the Black Sea. This 10,000-kilometre hike took me one and a half years, and was the greatest adventure of my life. I learnt a lot from that walk and I hope that the notes below will be helpful to you. I must however ask you to remember that I am a newcomer to long-distance walking (my only other hikes have been a youth hostelling trip in the Peak District with my mother, a one-week hike in Wales, and another week in the Greek mountains) and so my "tips" are based on a limited number of extremely vivid experiences, rather than a lifetime's worth of gnarly miles.

I'd like to divide this into two sections: principles and practicalities.

First, Principles

When I began my trans-European walk I made the basic mistake of being so excited that I forgot to rest. I walked for eighteen days non-stop through the sierras of northern Spain. It did not occur to me to take a break until my right leg swelled up like a balloon and reduced me to an agonised hobble. After that I made it a rule that I must stop every five to seven days for at least one day's rest. I learnt that being conscious of incipient ailments will prevent them from becoming problems. Blisters, muscle strain and back-pain can be avoided by being continually aware of how your body-as-machine is functioning.

Interestingly, the Romans, who were experts at thousand-mile marches, walked to a system of three days on, one day off, a routine which they found to be ideal for legions crossing continents. One other authority I'd like to mention is Christopher Whinney, who once walked from London to Rome and who subsequently set up the walking-holiday company Alternative Travel Group. After prolonged trial and error, Christopher found that, just like the Romans, his groups remained the most happy and cohesive if they took every fourth day as a rest day.

Ultimately, of course, you must find your own best rhythm. There is no golden mean for everyone. If you walk one day and take two off, that's fine if it's bringing the best rewards from the journey. On several occasions on my European amble, I spent a week or so in one place, or made wide detours from my planned route, and on a couple of occasions walked *backwards* to visit places I'd missed the day before. There is no magic distance which should be covered each day; a fit walker with a medium-sized pack can cover say 20 or 30 kilometres in one day with no trouble. Sometimes I've walked over 50 kilometres in one day, but as a result have been wrecked the following day.

To round off this rhythm section, I'll just add that I'm not a believer in training. If you want to try a long-distance walk, just go. Take it easy and use the first days (or weeks) to get fit.

So much for the rhythm. Now, where to go? Because walking is the slowest form of travel, you do need to choose a route which brings variety on an almost hourly basis. Either you choose a landscape which is choc-a-bloc with physical changes, or you learn to spot the interest in what to many would seem a dull landscape. An interest in flora and fauna, history, geomorphology, agricultural implements, mountain cultures ... whatever (the list is endless) will turn a walk into a fascinating treasure trail. Some landscapes hand the walker hourly interest on a plate. Rambling in mountains; following the courses of rivers; following coastlines are all "themes" which will, through the natural lie of the land, create a change of view with every hour. Also in this category is the long-distance footpath, way-marked and "themed" to provide interest, for example the pilgrims" Camiño de Santiago, across northern Spain.

The one area of essential knowledge which is required before embarking upon a long walk in wilderness areas is navigation. This means being able to use a compass accurately and in gales and mists. It also means being able to read maps and to master "dead-reckoning" – the ability to estimate how much time it will take to cover a certain compass-bearing. It is essential to know how to do this before walking in mountains.

There are some terrains, and I'm thinking of mountains in particular, which are potentially dangerous for inexperienced walkers. It is important not to be lulled into a sense of false security by believing that superior equipment is a substitute for old-fashioned savvy. Had I not spent 25 years messing about trying to climb mountains in Scottish winter white-outs, I would not have survived my trans-European wander. To walk safely in mountains, it is essential that you feel confident using a map and compass in zero visibility and gale force winds on precipitous ridges. This is unlikely ever to happen, all being well, but it is a possibility and you need to be ready to cope. This kind of knowledge can be built up over time, in the company of a more experienced companion, on, say, the hills of Wales, the Pennines, the Lake District or Scotland. The most testing ground I've ever found for navigation in mist was Dartmoor.

Saving weight has the dual benefit of making the walking less strenuous and of reducing the clutter of everyday life to a minimum of essentials. I cut my comb in half, trim the edges of maps and keep my hair short, not because these minor weight reductions are going to be noticeable individually, but because each minimalisation reminds me daily not to overload my rucksack with unnecessary stores. Carrying a half-kilo of jam unopened from one town to the next is a waste of effort. And while a shortage of water is to be avoided at all costs (dehydration is dangerous), it is worth remembering than one litre of liquid really does weigh one kilogram. It pays to think ahead, ask locals where the next spring or tap can be found rather than load up like a camel.

So, on to Practicalities

It is not worth getting obsessive about equipment, beyond the one rule of minimal weight and maximal safety. There are, however, a number of equipment items whose suitability to your needs will affect your enjoyment of the walk.

The single most important requirement is suitable footwear. The first decision to make is between running/training shoes or boots. The former do not need wearing in; are far lighter than boots and have a "softer" feel. Boots offer ankle support; a leather construction which breathes better than man-made fibres; an element of water-proofness and grippy treads for steep or uneven surfaces. Again, it is down to personal preference; when my cousins Richard and Adrian made their foot-traverse of the Himalayas in 1982, they wore running shoes; when I made my European mountain hike ten years later, I wore boots. After much experimentation I settled on the British-designed "Brasher Boot", which combines running-shoe technology with the construction of traditional leather boots. Brasher Boots are lightweight and comfortable

Footwear more than any other item of walking equipment has the power to determine whether a hike is hellish or heavenly. A perfect fit is critical. My method for selecting the correct size (taught to me by Chris Brasher, the Olympic gold medallist runner and designer of the Brasher Boot) is to push my foot forward as far as possible in the unlaced boot or shoe. There should be space to fit a finger down the gap between my own heel and the inside of the boot/shoe. Footwear which is slightly too tight is the most common cause of foot problems. No matter how good the footwear, extraneous factors such as wet weather or extreme heat can cause sores and blisters. On extended hikes, washing feet daily prevent infection. Over-long toenails collide with the front of the boot or shoe during descents and, after a period of excruciating discomfort, will turn black then fall off. During my hike I lost a total of ten toenails, to no noticeable disadvantage. They seem fairly superfluous.

Foot problems can be largely circumvented by giving these put-upon appendages considered thought at least three times a day. At the end of a day's walk, I wash my feet, even if doing so mean using precious supplies of drinking water. With practice, it is possible to wash two feet in half a litre of water, tipped in a trickle from a mug. In winter, feet can be cleaned by running very fast on snow, but the subsequent pain as they thaw is dramatic. Washing feet in the evening means that they spend the night bacteria-free in the sleeping bag, thus encouraging the healing of any sores.

In the morning I inspect each toe and every point of wear on each foot. I always pierce blisters the moment they appear, using the tip of a sewing needle, sterilised in the flame of a cigarette lighter. Blisters are more likely to appear when the skin has been softened by water-logged footwear or sweat. Morning is also the time to clip toenails, which left unattended, can wear holes in adjacent toes and abrade the ends of socks.

At midday, half-way through a day's hike, I de-boot for lunch, giving my feet the chance to bask in ultra-violet and my boots the opportunity to air. Unfortunately, this pleasurable diversion has to be forsaken if lunch is being taken in a bar or restaurant.

Toe technology is a limited field, but the one device which I have found particularly useful is the *Scholl's Toe Separator*. This is a small wedge of foam rubber which can be inserted into the gap between two quarrelling digits. For anyone prone to pronation (walking on the outside of your feet), a toe divider inserted between the two smallest toes on each foot will prevent the little toe being rolled under the ball of the foot and gradually eroded.

While I'm dealing with leg-matters, I'll briefly mention knees. After feet, these are the rambler's least reliable component. Aches (and damage) most frequently occur as a result of long descents or stumbles. I have no idea whether there is any physiological sense in this, but my own technique on long descents is to take exaggeratedly short steps, keeping my knees bent. Walking thus, the legs act like car shock-absorbers. The shorter strides also allow greater control and more precise placement of every footstep. It is easier to be thrown off balance while carrying a loaded rucksack, and the knees are frequently the weak link which hit the ground first, or which suffer violent twisting. An accident can be caused by a minor misplacement of the foot: the boot skating on a tiny, unseen pebble, or glancing off a curl of turf, or a heel skidding on a coin-sized spot of ice.

Many walkers protect their knees by using a walking aid. There are three alternatives. A conventional walking stick is the least expensive and in most mountainous areas can be bought locally. A hi-tech equivalent favoured by many Himalayan mountaineers for their multi-day treks to the foot of their climb, is the telescopic ski-stick. When not in use, the three sections retract and can be strapped to the side of the rucksack. Finally there is the combined umbrella/walking stick (see below).

After boots, the rucksack is the next most critical item of equipment. Like footwear, the rucksack should be carefully chosen to fit the wearer. A waist belt is essential, as is a chest strap. A properly-fitting rucksack divides the load between the shoulder straps and the waist-belt. Rucksacks of the same capacity can range widely in weight. In the Karrimor range for example, the 45-litre capacity ultra-light "KIMM II" model weighs only 450 grams, while the high-specification "Alpiniste 45" (also 45 litres) weighs 1,200 grams. After various experiments, I now find that it is worth carrying the extra grams to guarantee that a rucksack is comfortable. Rucksacks with non-adjustable backs are substantially lighter than the more sophisticated adjustable models. A zip compartment at the foot of the rucksack can be useful for stowing a tent, where it can be kept separate from the rest of the luggage; sensible since it will sometimes be wet.

Individual items of clothing should be chosen for their light weight, comfort and insulation properties. On my legs I usually wear poly-cotton trousers, which dry quickly and, with the "poly" for extra strength, tend to last longer than all-cotton trousers. The most comfortable walking trousers I have ever used were made from Ventile, a very fine weave of cotton, which is both windproof and has an almost silk-like feel. My shirts are always 100 per cent cotton. Here the poly element is less important since a shirt gets less of a hammering than trousers. With a rucksack semi-permanently glued to the shirt, natural fibres are easier on the skin. I favour shirts with two breast pockets for carrying my compass and money. If possible, the shirt should have double shoulders, to cope with the wear of the rucksack straps.

For summer walking I usually wear Marks and Spencer wool/nylon mix ankle socks, which are durable and which dry overnight after being washed. For extra insulation in the winter, the "Thor-Lo" brand, with their differentially-padded panels, are comfortable and warm (and expensive).

A foot-trick of which I am rather proud is my practice of carrying a spare set of "footbeds" (the insoles which fit onto the floor of the boot). When my boots get wet, I start the next day with the spare, dry pair of footbeds, thus thwarting the misery of early-morning rising damp.

I always carry an "emergency layer" such as a second fleece jacket, or a sleeping bag (which, wrapped around the torso beneath a waterproof jacket, works like a duvet). I have an "emergency rule" which is that one set of thermal underwear is kept inside my sleeping bag, which is kept inside a plastic bag, inside the rucksack. Under no circumstances are the sleeping bag or underwear allowed to get wet. This means that in a crisis I always have a complete set of warm, dry insulation.

The item I feel most particular about is my hat, which should have a brim to keep the sun (the ultra-violet is intense at higher altitudes) from the eyes and the back of the neck. French berets are virtually indestructible but cast shade on only one part of the head at a time. More suitable is the Basque beret, with its greater diameter. Best of all though is the lightweight travelling trilby, which can be rolled up like a cornet when not in use, whilst on the head, its generous brim works well as a cranial parasol. The best trilby I have found is made by

Herbert Johnson of New Bond Street, London. It should be noted that the trilby does not perform well in high wind. I always carry supplementary headwear, in the form of a very lightweight thermal balaclava. And of course my waterproof jacket (whether Ventile or Goretex) has an integral hood. Reducing heat loss from the head is one of the most efficient methods of maintaining overall body temperature.

The other item essential for head protection is a pair of sunglasses. In mountains some walkers prefer the glasses which have leather side-pieces fitted, which cut out lateral glare. Walking on snow with unprotected eyes can cause "snow-blindness", both painful and damaging to the eyes.

The only item of equipment which I duplicate is my compass. Without one of these I am lost, literally and philosophically. I use liquid-filled, Swedish-made "Silva " compasses. The "Type 3" model is carried in my breast pocket, tied by cord to the button-hole. The much smaller "Type 23" model, which weighs only 15 grams and is supplied in a modified form to the pilots' survival packs in the seats of Tornado aircraft, is kept in reserve, in my rucksack.

Without maps, long-distance walking can be erratic. Every popular mountain area in western Europe is mapped at a scale of 1:50,000 or, even better, 1:25,000. No other series however is comparable for accuracy or clarity to our own Ordnance Survey, so Britons heading overseas must prepare for a lesser quality of cartography. The best source for walking maps in Britain is Stanfords, 12-14 Long Acre, London WC2E 9LP. For hiking in Eastern Europe, the best source is the shop Fretytag & Berndt, Kohlmarkt 9, Vienna 1010, Austria and the Bundesamt fur Eich-und Vermessungswesen at Krotenthallergasse 3, Vienna 1080, who sell the old maps of the Austro-Hungarian Empire. The sense of history imparted by these beautifully-drawn maps compensates for the fact that most users will spend 90 per cent of the time completely lost. I relied on them for walking 3,000 kilometres through the Carpathians. They were invaluable.

There is an inverse relationship between the number of days you've been hiking, and the number of tent-pegs remaining to erect your nightly home. Pegs disappear in long grass, drop down rabbit holes, or get used as a tea-stirrer then left on a tree-stump. Peg loss can be reduced by reciting BBC-man Brian Hanrahan's famous Falklands quote: "I counted them all out; I counted them all back", when inserting pegs in the evening and retrieving them next morning.

I've often noticed how that red-handled talisman, the Swiss Army knife, is more treasured than it is used. At the top of the Victorinox range of penknives is the "Swiss Champ", whose 29 features (among them a hacksaw, a reamer and a ballpoint pen) would be useful for hiker who think that they might be called upon to construct a bi-plane using nothing but driftwood and the contents of their rucksack. I carry the smallest, lightest in the range, the two-bladed *Pocket Pal*. I use the larger blade for cutting food and the smaller blade for less hygienic roles such as emergency chiropody.

I would not go walking without an umbrella. Furled, it can be used for parrying dog-attacks or beating back briars. Driven spike first into the ground, it is handy for drying socks. Reversing the umbrella and holding the spike converts it into a harvesting tool for out-of-reach blackberries. In the open mode, it is both rain and snow shelter, a sun shade and during exposed picnics, a handy wind-break, My favourite umbrella was obtained when I visited the "Que Chova" (it means "What Rain!" in Calician) umbrella factory in Santiago de Compostela, one of the wettest places in Europe. The best mountaineering umbrellas are made by James Smith & Son (53 New Oxford Street, London) whose hickory-shafted model is strong enough to serve as a walking stick, and unlike the metal-shafted models, does not act as a lightening conductor when strapped to a rucksack. A good mountaineering umbrella has 8 ribs; it is fallacy that 10- and 16-rib umbrellas are tougher; the extra ribs create variable shrinkage in the umbrella's fabric, and thus encourage wear and tear.

After some experimentation, I have settled on the Parker "Vector" fountain pen, which costs less than a round of beer and is available throughout Europe (on the Continent, it is a favourite among French schoolchildren, an indication more of its durability than its writing quality). Such a pen is more suitable than a ballpoint, whose ink become treacly at low temperatures and leaks in the heat; fancy fibre-tips are expensive and have to be thrown away once they have run dry – not a very green option. In sub-zero temperatures, the conventional ink in my fountain pen will thaw from frozen after a few minutes compression under an armpit. Ten spare Parker cartridges bunched in an elastic band lasted me about 1,000 kilometres of note-making and postcard writing.

Diet is not a facet of everyday life which many long-distance walkers are likely to be able to control to any great extent. You eat what you can find (I do not carry food from home, since part of the interest of travelling is in discovering the local food). But on extended walks, dietary deficiencies can lead to a lowering of the body's defences against bugs and a reduction of its capacity to heal wounds. During my 507-day hike across Europe I lived largely on bread and sardines, bread and pork fat, and bread and jam – the staples generally available in mountain villages. During the same period I ate 1,014 tablets of Vitamin B Complex, Vitamin C and zinc. I was never ill and wounds healed within 3 or 4 days, without the use of antiseptic.

I'll round off this fairly random checklist of my tips with the thought that the best way of finding out about long-distance walking is to start with a short walk and not to stop.

For Walking Associations see p.797 of the Directory. For relevant tour operators see "Adventure and Sporting" in Section 3, p.712

THE MICROLIGHTING TRAVELLER

by Christina Dodwell

To travel long distance by microlight aircraft is sometimes harder to organise logistically than to carry out. It took me nearly three months to sort out the route and obtain the necessary permits for my four-month microlight flight through West Africa.

The most obvious essential is to fit the journey to the prevailing winds; travel is hard enough without wasting fuel in headwinds. My best advice about winds come from the **Locust Control Unit** whose London office has extensive reference windcharts. The Met. Office in Bracknell were also helpful.

The second controlling factor of the route was the terrain which had to offer plenty of open landing areas; we had no back-up ignition system. Our fuel tank size was increased to 49 litres, and we used an average of twelve litres per hour in flight. We were fortunate that Mobil sponsored us and agreed to stash sealed jerrycans for us at intervals along our route. The alternative of using a support vehicle would mean following roads.

The type of fuel at roadside petrol stations was very low octane and in remote places was contaminated by transportation in unclean containers. In the mountains of Cameroon, petrol was being sold in old Coke bottles.

When route and timing are known you should apply for flight clearances. This is done by letter/fax or telex to the CAA or relevant authority of each country en route, and in due course they should each give you a clearance number. While travelling you must put that number on all flight plans. If the country is a military state or dictatorship, you also need a Military Clearance Number. Although I had received mine for Nigeria, I was arrested on arrival because the number was not on government-headed paper. It took 24 hours to sort out.

Nowadays one can use a Clearance Agent to arrange all these details. A recommended one is Mike Gray of **Overflight International**, tel: 01682-842311. For those who wish to organise their own clearances, there is an excellent free advice and access to addresses from **AIS Briefing Services** (part of the CAA), tel: 0181-745 3447, open seven days a week. They will give all the necessary "info" on rules, regulations and how to apply. Also they sell the CAP 555 which lists the entry and exit requirements of every country. They strongly recommend that microlight pilots carry ELT (electronic locator transmitter) and navigate with GPS (global positioning system). GPS didn't exist in West Africa in my days but I am assured there is now world coverage. We did have an ELT disaster signal but a curious person pulled out its pin the day before the journey began, leaving it exhausted.

When flying in ultra inhospitable regions (as I found out mid-Sahara) one is obliged by law to have or hire a support vehicle, and the aircraft must carry fuel and water for a minimum of about five days.

In parts of Europe, the regulations against microlights have recently tightened and they are banned from certain major airports. It would be simpler to enter such a country by road with microlight in tow and assemble it there. This requires only a courtesy call as a visitor asking to fly in their airspace, plus flight plan. For all advice on procedures, contact AIS (above) and also the very helpful Department of Transport whose International Aviation Section, tel: 0171-271 5000, is run by Hugh Hopkins.

If a microlight does not have the fuel capacity to reach an international airport as the first stop, you can get permission to stop and re-fuel, and to check-in with any immigration and custom postbut remember to report to the local Chief of Police.

As to the practical side, it wasn't until we began our journey in Cameroon that we learnt our compass was calibrated to northern latitudes and unusable in the tropics, the only tropical compasses for sale were brass maritime heavies. Even the most basic things have a way of growing complicated. Luggage, camping gear, tools of lightweight aluminium, and spare parts were loaded into panniers strapped outside the cockpit, plus spare wheel and spare propeller, while water cans and oil were stowed under the seats and sleeping bags were securely tied to the trike's mast.

If things fall off, they usually get sucked into the propeller. I remember Mik Coyne saying when they threw cereal packets out of a microlight for promotional photography, the packets were drawn into the propeller and chipped it badly. Our propeller had chunks torn out of it on several occasions, usually by sticks and stones whirled up on landing and taking off. But we glued the chunks back into place, or refilled the gap with wood carved to shape. Also I had to stitch patches on the wing when it was torn by thorns. Others have trouble from thorns in tyres, for which Richard Meredith Hardy recommended putting strips of carpet between tyre and tube.

My microlight was a standard Pegasus XL, which has an all-up weight capacity of 390 kg, inclusive of trike, wing, two people and everything. When we overloaded by 30 kg we had a total engine failure at 50 ft while taking off, and we fell to the ground like a stone. But nothing broke. At normal full weight there were no adverse effects except for heavier fuel consumption (up to nineteen litres an hour in take-off) and a longer take-off and landing run. Perhaps it made us more stable in the air, though on occasions when we were tossed into negative gravity the stress was appaling and I was surprised that nothing snapped. It was a sturdy machine.

In fact the dangers were few but naturally we had a lot of narrow escapes, particularly when landing on roads with unforeseen traffic. Our worst was a steeply banked road where we landed after dark with no lights, only to find a truck with no lights driving towards us. Sandstorms were not much of a problem, you can usually jump over them. They grow bigger as they approach but you can judge the size. Our standard type was two miles wide and 2,000 ft tall. Flight rules say that when storms blow up you must land and secure your aircraft but often it would have been too dangerous to land and there was nothing to tie the wing to, so we stayed airborne. One time a storm grew so big we couldn't find its top and at 4,000ft we were being pushed backwards by the strength of the wind. Windspeed increases with height, it was futile to go higher and we decided to try flying low down in the storm; it wasn't fun.

Thermal pillars used to start bouncing off the desert by 11am. By midday they were uncomfortable. The only practical times for flight were a few hours morning and evening. If you arrive at an airport after sunset, approximately 6pm, you will be charged for landing lights which tends to be expensive.

When taking off near towns or villages with no airstrip, there is a danger of causing harm to people. In their delight the crowds go crazy and, not wanting you to leave, they dash forward to try and grab your moving wing-tips, or rush behind the propeller where a whirled up stone can kill. Sometimes it is worth asking the local police or headman to hold crowds behind the aircraft. Don't allow people to form a corridor during take-off because they will run into your path.

The horrors were equalled by the moments of pure joy; I loved the aerial perspective and being able to see how things fit together. We could pick out the shape of tombs and ancient fortresses that would be invisible from the ground, and we were free to land anywhere looked interesting. Some weirdly eroded rocks turned out to house caves with wall inscriptions and some bone fragments led to the discovery of a dinosaur skeleton. It all combines to make a memorable way to travel.

For Microlighting Associations see p. 798 of the Directory

THE MOUNTAINEERING TRAVELLER

by Chris Bonington

It doesn't matter how brilliant the adventure, how talented the team, if a vital piece of equipment is missing, or the food or fuel has run out, not only could the expedition fail to achieve its objective, but lives could be put at risk. Sound logistic planning ensures having the right supplies to achieve the objective and survive, in relative comfort and with enjoyment.

The principles are the same for any type or scale of expedition or journey, though the size of the party and the nature of the objective obviously must affect the complexity of the logistics. Since my own expertise is in mountaineering, I shall use the planning of a mountaineering expedition as my model, but the principles behind this could be transposed to almost any venture.

It is important to start by deciding exactly what the objective is to be – this might sound very obvious but it is amazing how many people become confused about precisely what they are trying to achieve and end up with a set of conflicting objectives, which in turn make it difficult, if not impossible, to prepare a workable plan. There could, for instance, be a conflict between trying to introduce a group of youngsters of different nationalities to the mountains and tackling a very difficult unclimbed peak.

Having clarified the aim, the next step is to formulate an outline plan of how to achieve it. In the case of a mountain objective the first consideration is the style of climbing proposed to tackle it. There are two approaches: alpine style – packing a rucksack at the bottom of the peak and then moving in a continuous push to the top, bivouacking or camping on the way; or siege style – establishing a series of camps up the mountain, linked by fixed rope on difficult ground. The latter inevitably demands a larger team, more gear and more complex logistics. These have to be worked out in detail, from the number of camps needed, the quality of rope to be fixed if the ground looks steep, the cooking gear needed for each tent, and then the amount of food and fuel necessary to feed the climbers and/or porters while they force the route and ferry loads.

It pays to start the calculations with a summit bid of, say, two people from a top camp of one assault tent and then work back down the mountain. As a rule of thumb, estimate a camp every five hundred metres which represents a reasonable distance for a load carry. Loads of around fifteen kilos can be carried comfortably up to seven thousand metres, but the higher you get the lighter the load should be. It is also important to allow adequate rest periods, so that the team doesn't burn itself out. Using a spread sheet on a computer makes the calculations easier and the various "what if?" scenarios can then be played out.

Planning in this detail at an early stage automatically supplies information about the size of the team needed and the kind of skills required. This will help choose a team that is not only the right size but also the right composition. This may not appear to come under the heading of logistics but it most certainly does, for without the right people to carry out the tasks in hand, the best laid plans and logistics fall apart. From this point of view, in choosing a team it is essential to have a good balance between people who are capable of taking on organisational or management roles and those with skills to attain the objective – in the case of a climbing expedition, talented climbers, or for a scientific one, people with the right scientific qualifications and knowledge. It is also important that the team is compatible, that the brilliant expert, – climber, canoeist or scientist – will work effectively for the team as a whole.

The foundations of the expedition are laid in this initial planning phase and are then built into the organisational stage in the home country when everything is being assembled. If vital items of food or equipment are left out, shipping arrangements mishandled, or perhaps most important of all, there is a shortfall in the amount of money to pay for the enterprises, it could be condemned to failure before even setting out. In this organisational phase it is important for the leader to delegate responsibility effectively, in the first instance ensuring that the right person has been given the right job, giving briefs of what is required and the deadlines to be reached and finally leaving them to get on with it, but having a reporting-back system so that if there are any critical problems, the leader can take any necessary action. This role should be one of support rather than interference.

Sound budgeting and raising sufficient funds is obviously a key task in this preparatory phase. In getting sponsorship it is also very important to be realistic over what is promised, so that not only can the promises be fulfilled but, equally important, the commitments to a sponsor do not prejudice achieving the end objective or the way the expedition is conducted.

It pays to build some slack into the schedule to allow for delays and crises. In 1970 when I went to the south face of Annapurna we sent all the expedition gear by sea, scheduled to arrive in Bombay a fortnight before we were due to reach Nepal by air. The ship carrying it broke down off Africa and was over a month late, giving us a major crisis at the very beginning of the expedition. We got round it with the help of an Army expedition going to the north side of Annapurna. They allowed us to send some gear out with their air freight and loaned us some excellent army Compo rations. This kept us going until the main gear caught up with us but it caused a lot of unnecessary worry and delay. Even today when most expeditions use air freight for their baggage, gear can be lost, delayed in customs or sent to the wrong place, so it pays to allow plenty of time, particularly for clearing customs.

When packing, keep in mind at which stage of the trip the different items of food or gear will be used and also how they are going to be carried to the base of operations. Put together all the items not needed until base camp. The gear and food for use on the approach march needs to be separate and accessible. It is best carried in lockable containers and it pays to get a set of padlocks with a uniform key so that any team member can get access to communal equipment.

It saves a lot of time and hassle if containers are kept to a weight that can be carried by local porters or pack animals and protected robustly to withstand rough treatment and exposure to the weather. It is best to distribute similar items in different loads, so that if a single box goes missing the total supply of a vital piece of equipment is not lost, all the oxygen masks, or for that matter, all the matches. The other vital task is to list everything and mark all the boxes clearly with some form of identification that gives no clue of the contents to the casual observer.

Remember that certain items cannot be sent by air. It is irresponsible and dangerous to try to smuggle such items through. Gas cylinders can be sent by cargo plane, but must be specially packed. The air freight agent can give advice on these matters.

Once at the roadhead life becomes much more simple. At last everyone is together and with luck all the gear and food is there with you. It is just a matter of keeping the porters happy – not always easy – and keeping tabs on gear and loads. To make this easier, on some expeditions, I have issued each porter with a numbered plastic disk to coincide with the number of the load and then taken a Polaroid photo of him holding his disk and load.

An approach march can be a leisured delight or a nightmare, depending on the behaviour of the porters. Very often problems with the porters are outside your control, since so much depends on the local situation, the attitude of the liaison officer and the conduct of the *naik* or overseer who might have extracted a large commission from the porters in return for employment. It is very difficult to advise on any specific reaction other than to stay cool, to listen carefully and to bargain effectively.

And then to base camp. The objective – in my case, a mountain – is in sight and some might think that this is where the real challenge begins. However, the eventual success or failure will have been strongly influenced by everything that has been done in the preparatory phase and the approach. If the expedition has been planned out in detail, all the essential gear packed away in the containers that have come straight through to base camp, is now ready for use. Provided team members are fit and relaxed and happy, they certainly have a much better chance of success, or at least of having a good try at achieving the objective and enjoying themselves at the same time.

In the case of a mountain, particularly one that is unclimbed, the first priority, having made base camp comfortable, is to make a thorough recce, to check out if the actual terrain corresponds with what pictures and maps you have managed to get hold of, and whether the plan of campaign needs changing or adjusting. A plan should always be flexible. It is possible to change and adapt it to circumstances, but it must be a well-thought out plan in the first place. On the south west face of Everest in 1975, we completed a detailed plan using a computer model back in Britain, but made frequent changes during the expedition. However, with the original plan which acted as a solid foundation, we could never have climbed the south west face as quickly and smoothly as we did.

It is all too easy, when the weather is good, to believe it will last forever. Each fine day needs to be regarded as the last one you will get on the expedition. Equally, when the weather is bad, it is also easy to slip into lethargy. It is just as important to be poised to take advantage of a clearance.

We all want to achieve success, to reach our objective, but I believe it is important to remember that the journey is as important as the final objective. The way that journey is carried out not only determines the eventual outcome, but equally important, how you are going to feel about it in the future. If the logistics are right, if everyone works well together as a team, with each individual being prepared to sacrifice personal ambition for the good of the group as a whole, being aware of the needs of others and helping where necessary, the venture has achieved complete success. Sound planning from the very beginning provides the foundations of that success.

For mountaineering associations see p.798 of the Directory
See also "Adventure and Sporting" list in Section 3, p.712 ■

GREAT JOURNEYS OVERLAND
Chapter 7

OVERLAND THROUGH AFRICA

by Warren Burton

It is no wonder that the vastness of Africa's landmass, unknown and untamed, has presented the ultimate challenge to the European for centuries. Its size was only realised by sea-faring explorers who began charting the coastlines during the 17th and 18th centuries. That it contains the world's largest desert, the longest river, represents just part of Africa's statistics. But little is really known about it, though the Great Rift Valley contains the evidence of the origins of mankind. The records of exploration undertaken by Livingstone, Burton and Speke still, today, inspire many to take on Africa's challenge.*

Crossing the Sahara to Central Africa

Hardly a year goes by without some part of Africa being considered a 'no-go' region. The Sahara is no exception and despite its usual barriers – the extremes of heat, lack of roads, closed frontiers – it is now the Sahara's own internal unrest which stands in the way. The established and rather traditional route that has been followed for some 25-30 years, is now very questionable.

In the past (and we hope these options will return), journeys either started from Morocco crossing the Atlas Mountains into Algeria, or alternatively sailing from Italy entering at Tunis. Either route takes you south on the 'Trans Sahara Highway' to the oasis towns of Ghardaia, El Golea, In Salah and finally Tamanrasset, at the base of the mighty Hoggar Massif. More adventurous overlanders, with well-equipped 4-WD vehicles and ample supplies of fuel and water, opted for the dramatic and somewhat tortuous route east via the Tassili plateau and extraordinary rock formations around Djanet. Here, found in caves, are 3000-year old rock inscriptions, records of Sahara life before the expanding sands engulfed much of its vegetation. Desert tracks marked occasionally by oil drums then lead you south to Tamanrasset and the ever-elusive 'Highway'. The Sahara has its own way of dealing with development – no sooner do the Algerian and Nigerian governments lay a few more kilometres of bitumen, than along comes a typical desert 'flash flood' which can destroy years of work in a few hours.

A less popular but practical alternative, again with a suitable vehicle (carrying long range fuel and water supplies), was to travel directly south from Bechar to Reggane, to follow the Tanzerouft route in Mali. Either way, the present

---

* *Please note that many of the countries mentioned in this article, The Democratic Republic of Congo (Zaire) in particular, are at the time of writing undergoing massive political upheaval, and Foreign Offices are advising against travel there.*

political unrest and rise of Islamic fundamentalism in Algeria renders the country unsafe and therefore these routes are unviable. Regrettably this has followed a long period of unrest in the south of the Sahara, on the frontier lands of Algeria, Niger and Mali. During 1991 and 1992 unruly factions of Tuareg, seeking autonomy and self control, set about attacking and robbing any vehicle entering the region. Several incidents led to travellers being robbed of their vehicles and belongings, with isolated reports of shootings. Alternative routes had to be found. Crossing Libya into Chad is out of the question, so all attention was focused on a route through the former Spanish Sahara (now administered by Morocco) into Mauritania. However, whilst overlanders have obtained permits from the Moroccan authorities, the Mauritanian Government have never really acknowledged this and permission to enter from Morocco is often refused.

Still, it can be done – but you are *strongly* advised to investigate this route thoroughly first. Whilst many still attempt and succeed in crossing Africa without 4-WD, it is still wise to do so, and particularly as this alternative route certainly presents some tough days of soft sand in northern Mauritania.

Carnet de Passage documents are required for your vehicle once you leave Morocco and most, if not all, countries in Africa are now very wised up to the requirements of vehicle insurance.

Visas are required to enter Mauritania and you are advised to obtain these in Europe (Bonn, Paris or Madrid) as it is reported that they are almost impossible to obtain in Rabat, Morocco. It is also best to obtain visas for Mali whilst in Europe – thus avoiding the risk of not being able to obtain them before exiting Mauritania. Most other visas can be obtained en route in neighbouring countries. Up-to-date medical advice should also be sought before departure, because health risks in Africa are ever present and especially the risks of malaria, which is now on the increase, particularly in Sub-Sahara and West Africa.

The route through Morocco should certainly go via the imperial city of Fes renowned for its huge walled Medina. Then crossing the High Atlas to Todra Gorge and the edge of the Grand Erg Occidental with its 'sea of sand dunes'. Marrakech still retains its mystic aura, and is your last 'semi-civilised' centre, before heading south to the coastal sands of the Western Sahara. Following the Atlantic coast via Layounne you arrive in Dakhla, the formal exit point from Morocco. Here at least a day of tedious paperwork and form-filling enables you to join a twice-weekly 'convoy' south to the frontier post at La Gouria. A short but tricky desert crossing brings you into Mauritania at Nouadhibou – a strange town, servicing the rail link and port which is essential to the export of the country's phosphate reserves.

Mauritania is an Islamic Republic and thus prohibits the import of alcohol, so it is wise to consume or dispose of this prior to entry. Furthermore, overland travel has only recently arrived on Mauritania's doorstep – so one should tread lightly and savour the rather timid reception you may receive, though early reports state that generally local folk are very friendly and helpful.

Formalities are slow on entry and you must obtain a '*Laissez Passe*' (permit) to travel south to Nouakchott. For the more adventurous and with the 'recommended' assistance of a local guide, try the route directly south with plenty of sand-matting. You then have to catch the low tide in order to drive the last 150 kilometres along the beach into Nouakchott. A bitumen road takes you east to Nema before joining some rough tracks south into Mali and on to Bamako.

Borders have opened with Mauritania and Senegal, so a route encompassing all of West Africa can be considered, but check for the rainy season – it can make many routes impassable.

If time permits then Mali presents a wealth of culture, history and tradition, much of which is found around Mopti and Djenne in the lands of the Songhai. A little east is the Bandiagara Escarpment, the home of the Dogon people, with their traditional lifestyle in evidence. South from here you cross into Burkina Faso (formerly Upper Volta), through Ouagadougou and on to Niger. Niamey, its capital, though offering little of interest, does provide the opportunity to obtain several visas before heading off to Nigeria. The popular route now is to Kano in northern Nigeria – time out to service vehicles and restock for Central Africa and Zaire. Then into northern Cameroon and the spectacular route through the Kapsiki Mountains.

The alternative is to head south from Ougadougou to the Ivory Coast, Ghana, Togo, Benin and southern Nigeria. This route will provide more varied insight into West Africa but will obviously add considerable time to your journey. From Nigeria you will enter Cameroon by the southern route visiting Doula and Yaounde, the capital, en route to the Central African Republic. Whilst visas are readily available to enter Gabon and the Republic of Congo, any route further south appears doubtful. Angola has reverted to a state of unrest and civil war and former Zaire, now the the Democratic Republic of Congo is still highly volatile.

Back on the traditional overland trail takes you into Central African Republic via Bouar to Bangui, the sleepy, but shifty colonial capital renowned for its French patisseries – make the most of them, you won't find too many in Zaire.

Former Zaïre to East Africa

The route east through Central Africa Republic to southern Sudan, Juba, then south to Kenya, has really been 'out of bounds' for some years now. The continuance of civil war with the North shows no let up, much to the suffering of the local Dinka and Nuer tribes people who roam these lands.

So far, and for the foreseeable future, the only route 'open' to East Africa is through Zaire. Zaire, now rather optimistically called the Democratic Republic of Congo, after struggling under President Mobutu, its ruler, for over 30 years, has a new and unstable regime led by Laurent Kabila. At the time of going to press, travel in the DRC is not recommended but this situation is not necessarily long term and this is still the best route through to East Africa. Corruption is rife, fuel and food shortages are common, and the 'roads' deteriorate by the year. Hence one is warned to go prepared with a vehicle in sound state (very little in the way of spares or assistance is available on the way). Certainly reserve food and fuel supplies are a must.

There are presently two entry points into DRC from Central Africa, both involving a ferry crossing of the rivers that form the frontiers. Entering at Zongo (across the river from Bangui) will take you southeast via Gemena to Lisala and the Zaire River. Here there may be the opportunity to board a barge or one of the river ferries travelling upstream to Kissangani (formerly Stanleyville during the colonial days of the Belgium Congo). The overland route follows north of the river via Bumba, Buta and then south to Kisangani.

Either way progress is slow. The ferries and barges constantly run aground on shifting sand bars, whereas the road will inevitably be the worse for wear especially during and after the long rainy season (July to November).

The other alternative is to travel further east in the Central African Republic, viewing the awesome Kembe Falls, en route to Bangassou. Having crossed the Mbomou River you join a 'secondary road' (more like a track) south to Bondo then to Buta – makeshift 'bridges' on this route are very suspect and should always be checked.

Into eastern DRC via the Ituri Forests and the home of the Pygmies, you arrive at a point where the option is to either cross Uganda, or to travel further south through the Virunga National Park and enter Rwanda. Here on the densely forested slopes of the Virunga volcanoes is the home of the much threatened Mountain Gorilla. Their plight was much publicised by the movie *Gorillas in the Mist*. Protection projects operated in DRC, Rwanda, and more recently Uganda, have helped to safeguard their environment and partially protect them from ever-present poachers. The projects are funded by charging a fair price to travellers wishing to hike with guides into the forest to view these wonderful gentle giants comfortable in their mountain habitat. However, Rwanda is still very unstable and should be considered out of bounds at the time of writing.

Were you to exit DRC directly into Uganda, a route taking you through Murchinson Falls National Park, you will be well rewarded. Here you are at the meeting points of the Victoria and Albert Niles, as they form the mighty White Nile and the start of its long slow route to the Mediterranean. Uganda, once the 'Jewel of Africa', has had a long road to recovery following the horrific periods of rule by Amin and Abote, which left this friendliest of countries in rack and ruin. Uganda's people offer you wonderful hospitality, definitely include it on your route.

From Kampala there are several choices of route. Either head directly into Kenya and through the rift valley and its lakes of Baringo, Naivasha and Nakuru to Nairobi. Or take the southerly route round Lake Victoria directly into Tanzania and on to Mwanza. By doing this you can then visit the game-filled plains of the Serengeti, discover the Oldovia Gorge then climb to the rim of the Ngorongoro Crater. This natural haven for wildlife can be visited by descending in a landrover, locally chartered at the park's wildlife headquarters.

From here you descend into Tanzania's rift valley, via Lake Manyara and the Masai tribelands to Arusha sitting at the base of Mt Meru. Time is well spent exploring the game reserves of Kenya, the Indian Ocean coast from Lamu to Malindi and the old Arab trading port at Mombassa. Then go south via the slopes of Kilimanjaro, Africa's highest peak where, with the support of local guides and porters, one can make a non-technical climb to its snow-capped summit of 19,000ft.

The Rift Valley to the Cape

Recent political changes in South Africa and the structured move to abolish

Apartheid, have eased travel to the south dramatically. Gone are the days of questioning border controls, intent on stalling your progress south through Tanzania, Zambia and Botswana, knowing full well that your destination was ultimately South Africa. Now very few visas are even required to travel through this section and the only real challenge is deciding on your route and preferences.

The popular journey is south via Dar es Salaam and with time out to visit the exotic spice island of Zanzibar. Here life is dramatically different to that of the mainland. Then by joining the 'Tanzam Highway' one actually enters the eastern fork of the Great Rift Valley which leads you down into Malawi to the characteristic fishing villages dotted along the shores of its beautiful lake. To Lilongwe, Malawi's peaceful capital, then entering Zambia, your choice is either to head south via Lake Kariba into Zimbabwe and Harare. Or to head for Livingstone and the thundering Victoria Falls on the frontier of Zimbabwe and Zambia. Here activities include white-water rafting, bird's eye flights over the falls and would you believe, bungy jumping off the bridge joining the frontiers.

There are many variations of routes from here to the Cape, but most now prefer crossing Botswana, including an excursion into the waterways of the Okavango Basin. The 'islands' of the delta are a haven for wildlife and birds. Then a route through the Caprivi Strip into Namibia, the unique Etosha Pans and the vast mountainous sand dunes that fall dramatically into the Atlantic. The rugged shoreline is littered with skeletons of shipwrecks for which the coastline is notorious. Sealife havens can be visited when you travel south via Walvis Bay and Luderitz. The Fish River Canyon is a must before leaving Namibia to cross the Orange River into South Africa. Several days' drive brings you to the end of an incredible journey – and Cape Town, overlooked by its distinctive Table Mountain, is an ideal place to end.

Cairo to the Cape

Regrettably with southern Sudan still a 'no go' zone, the route directly south from Egypt up the Nile to Khartoum, Kosti, Juba and into Kenya is still not possible. The little-used route from Wad Madani to the gorges of the Blue Nile into Ethiopia and Lake Tana is still not possible, the borders between Sudan and Ethiopia being still effectively closed, although there has been talk of opening up this route to overland travellers. However, Addis Ababa perched on the 'wall' of the Great Rift Valley now offers a viable route south through the lakes and desert lands bordering on Kenya. This is harsh country experiencing extreme temperatures, yet it is now at least part of an overland route which has not been possible for some twenty years.

For overland tour operators see p.799 of the Directory

AROUND SOUTH AMERICA

by Chris Parrott

'The Gringo Trail' (not to be confused with the Inca trail) is what everyone calls the most frequently travelled route through and around South America. *Gringo* is derived either from 'Green go home' in the days when the US Army used to wear green uniforms, or from *Greigo*, the Spanish word for Greek.

Despite assurances in the guide books that the term is widely used in friendly reference to anyone with a pale complexion, it is definitely not a complimentary form of address. If you need confirmation, watch how a blond Argentine reacts to being called *Gringo*.

The trail begins in whichever gateway happens to be the cheapest to fly into from Europe or the USA. Let's start in the north, in Colombia. The coast here boasts beautiful golden beaches, clear water and crystal streams cascading down from the 5800m summits of the Sierra Nevada. To the south is the big industrial port of Barranquilla and then Cartagena, an impressively fortified town dating from 1533, through which, for nearly 300 years, gold and treasures were channelled from throughout the Spanish colonies. Passing through the hot swampland and then inland up the attractive forested slopes of the Cordillera Occidental, the traveller emerges on a high plateau where Bogotá is sited, at 2620m. The Gold Museum has over 10,000 examples of pre-Columbian artefacts. An hour away are the salt mines of Zipaquira, inside which the workers carved an amazing 23m high cathedral.

South from Bogotá are the Tequendama Falls, the splendid valley of the Magdalena river and, high up on the Magdalena Gorge, the village of San Agustín. Here, hundreds of primitive stone statues representing gods of a little-known ancient Indian culture, guard the entrances to tombs. The road then loops back over high moorland to Popayan, a fine city with monasteries and cloisters in the Spanish style. The tortured landscape near here has been said to resemble "violently crumpled bedclothes." And so the road crosses into Ecuador. Just north of Quito, the equator, *La Mitad Del Mundo*, cuts the road a few hundred meters from the grand stone monument built to mark the meridian. Quito itself is at 2700m, ringed by peaks, amongst them the volcanoes of Pinchincha. It has much fine colonial architecture including, according to *The South American Handbook*, 86 churches, many of them gleaming with gold.

The Andes

Travellers then cross the Andes, passing from near-Arctic semi-tundra, through temperate forest, equatorial jungle and down to the hot total desert of the Peruvian coast, punctuated by oases of agricultural land where irrigation has distributed the melt-waters from the Andes over the littoral. Here too the ancient empires of the Chavin, Mochica, Nazca and Chimu people flourished. Ruined Chan-Chan, near Trujillo, was the Chimu capital; nearby Sechin has a large square temple, 3500 years old, incised with carvings of victorious leaders and dismembered foes.

A popular detour here is to turn inland at the fishing port of Chimbote and head for the Callejon de Huaylas. The route passes through the spectacular *Can* óon del Pato, where the road is literally drilled through the rock wall of the canyon, with 'windows' looking down to the roaring maelstrom of the Santa river below.

The Callejon de Huaylas valley runs along the foot of the Cordillera Blanca; here the 1970 earthquake buried the town of Yungay under an avalanche of mud. The towns of Caraz and Juaraz make good centres for walking and trekking in the Cordillera, and the road south across the mountains has spectacular views of the snowcapped Cordillera Blanca.

The coast near Lima is picturesque and rich in fish and birdlife, owing to the Humboldt Current. Lima itself has both shanty towns (*barrios*) and affluent suburbs, parks and fine beaches. Well worth seeing are the National Museum of Anthropology and Archaeology, the Gold Museum at Monterrico on the outskirts of town, and the Amano private museum.

South from Lima

From Lima, there are two routes south. One branches into the mountains (the pass reaches 4800m) through the zinc smelting town of La Oroya, to Huancayo. The road continues through Ayacucho and Abancay to Cuzco, and though Lima/Cuzco looks a relatively short distance on the map, it actually represents about 50 hours of continuous travel overland. The other route follows the fast coast road through the desert past the wine centre of Ica to Nazca with its vast and little-understood lines, on to Arequipa. There are several cut-off routes – from Pisco or Nazca, for example, or you can take the train in a grand circle from Arequipa to Cuzco.

One thing that is certain: any route in Peru that crosses the Andes is tortuous, time-consuming, and stunningly spectacular. Cuzco sits in a sheltered hollow at 3500m. This was the capital of the Inca Empire. Inca stonework forms the base of many of the Spanish buildings and the ancient city layout survives to this day.

Overlooking Cuzco's red roofs is the ruined fortress of Sacsahuaman. Nearby too are the ruins of Pisac and Ollantaitambo and, reached by train only, down the valley of the Urubamba (further up-stream, this is called the Vilcanota), the 'Lost City of the Incas', Machu Picchu. This magnificent ruined city site, nearly 500m above the river, was overgrown with jungle until its discovery in 1911. There are several legends which add to the mystery of the lost city. One states that after the sacking of Cuzco, the Virgins of the Sun fled to this city, whose existence was unknown to the Spanish. Others say that the Incas themselves had erased all mention of the city from their oral histories, retribution for some, now forever-censored, local uprising long before Pizarro and his men set foot in Peru.

From Cuzco, the road crosses the watershed of the Andes to the dry and dusty Altiplano, a high treeless plateau stretching from here across much of the Bolivian upland. Here lies Lake Titicaca, at 3810m the world's highest navigable lake, blazing a deep blue because of ultra-violet rays. On the floating reed islands of the lake live the Uru-Aymara Indians. Across the border in Bolivia are the ruins of Tiahuanaco, relic of an ancient race; the main feature is the carved 'Gate of the Sun'. La Paz lies in a valley just below the rim of the Altiplano, the city centre lying at approximately 3500m.

La Paz and Beyond

From La Paz, there are three possible routes, depending on the size of the circuit that you intend making:

1. Eastwards through the relatively low-lying city of Cochabamba to Santa Cruz, then on by rail to Corumba on the Brazilian border, from where you can head for São Paulo or the Iguaçu Falls. The road from Santa Cruz to Corumba and any of those from Bolivia to Paraguay are suitable for four-wheel-drive only.

2. Southwards via Cochabamba to Sucre and the mining town of Potosi to Villazón on the Argentine border and points south. NB: UK passport holders no longer need visas for Argentina.

3. Southwards to Arica in northern Chile. The roads gradually peter out over the salt pans and quicksands that stretch over this region – a region that should only be traversed in the dry season (May to November) and then with very great care. The road passes through the very beautiful Lauca National Park, and then continues (for the most part tar-sealed) through the Atacama desert, the farmlands and vineyards of central Chile to the so-called 'Little Switzerland' of mountainous southern Chile.

There is no road in Chile south of Puerto Montt, and the most usual point of crossing the border south of Santiago is that near Osorno to reach Bariloche, now a fashionable ski resort in Argentina. This route may not be passable in winter (June to October). The road from Santiago to Mendoza via Uspallata is kept open all year round, though in winter the road uses the railway tunnel and does not pass the famous Christ of the Andes statue. Travel south from Bariloche frequently takes you over unmade roads in the foothills of the Andes through the beautiful Argentine lake district to Viedma and Calafate. Here the lakes are fed by melt-waters from the Patagonian ice cap, and 'arms' of the lakes are sometimes blocked by tongues of glacial ice. The scenery around Lago Argentino, for example, is some of the most spectacular anywhere in the world. Roads here are passable at most times of year, though from June to October, four-wheel drive is advisable.

Alternatively you can combine the Pan American highway with local ferries via the island of Chiloe and the Chonchi to Chaiten ferry. You can also travel east out of Puerto Montt using the local *Balsa* or ferries crossing the numerous rivers and fjords on the way to Chaiten. The road continues down to Cochrane but ferry services stop during winter. Bear in mind that periodically, heavy rains cause landslides which end all hope of travel.

The South

It is possible to reach South America's southernmost tip, Tierra del Fuego, by ferry from near Rio Gallegos, or from Punta Arenas across the border in Chile. In winter it is impossible to cross the mountains by road to reach the small town of Ushuaia on Tierra del Fuego's south coast, but there are regular flights throughout the year from nearby Gallegos and Rio Grande.

A worthwhile excursion from Punta Arenas (Chile) is to Puerto Natales and the famous Torres del Paine National Park; a must for mountaineers, and an unforgettable experience for anyone who thinks that those etchings by early explorers always made mountains look ridiculously precipitous.

The fast, straight east coast road through temperate scrubland takes you north again via Comodoro Rivadavia, and Puerto Madryn with its Welsh-speaking colony, to Bahia Blanca and Buenos Aires. This cosmopolitan city of nearly ten million inhabitants lies on the estuary of the River Plate, a few hours by ferry from Montevideo in Uruguay.

Most travellers tend to bypass the rolling cattle-grazed plains of Uruguay in favour of the roads northwards, either through Santa Fé and Resistencia to Asunción, or direct to Iguaçu via Posadas and the Misiones province. Ferries are now almost extinct but new bridges (Ponte President Tancredo Neves between Argentina and Brazil, and the Friendship Bridge, between Brazil and Paraguay) make the journey quicker – if less interesting. There are also three bridging points across the Parana River between Buenos Aires and Asunción. The first is at Zarate; the second is the tunnel from Santa Fé to Rosario; and the third is the bridge between Resistencia and Corrientes.

There is a good fast road from Asunción to Foz do Iguaçu where the frontier is crossed by bridge. Car and passenger ferries from Foz de Iguaçu (Pôrto Meira) in Brazil to Puerto Iguaçu (or Iguassu) in Argentina, make it possible to visit these spectacular falls from both sides of the river.

Plantations of Brazil

The dense forest that once spread across Brazil from Iguaçu to Rio and beyond is gradually making way for coffee and soya bean plantations, though there is a particularly special stretch of road between Curitiba and São Paulo, since the new road follows the Serra do Mar coastal range. Carriageways are often separated by several kilometres as east-bound traffic goes around one side of a jungle-clad mountain, while westbound takes the high road.

From São Paulo there are two routes to Rio – one through Santos and Angra dos Reis along a beautiful coast road; the other the fast motorway, along the ridge of the mountains via the steel town of Volta Redonda. Rio is a focus; from here routes divide once more:

1. The north-east coast road through Salvador, Recife and Fortalaza to Belém at the mouth of the Amazon. Many travellers feel that this route, passing through the regions first settled by Portugal and her slaves four centuries ago, is the real Brazil.

2. North west via Belo Horizonte and the old mining towns of Minas Gerais province, such as Ouro Preto, Congonhas, Tiradentes and Mariana. This route leads to that oasis of modernity, that ultimate in planned cities, Brasilia.

There are several routes up to the Amazon basin from Brasilia, the fastest and easiest of which is direct to Belém via Anapolis. On this road there is a cut-off at Estreito, along the Transamazónica Highway to Altamira and Santarem.

Alternatively you can follow the newer road west to Cuiabá , and then take the Transamazónica north to Santarém. At both Belém and Santarém there are river steamers to Manaus though, for anyone with their own vehicle to ship, car ferries are few and far between. A more practical route in this instance is that to the west, to Cuiabá and Pôrta Velho, and then north along the new road via Humairá to Careiro on the south bank of the Amazon opposite Manaus. From here there are three ferries daily across to Manaus.

In the days when Brazil held a monopoly of rubber supplies, Manaus built a splendid (and recently restored) opera house for the best mezzosopranos in the world, and the rubber barons lit their cigars with 1000 *millreis* notes. Most of that glitter has faded, though edifices built of stone imported from Britain are still to be seen.

From here, riverboats ply the Rio Negro and the Rio Branco, tributaries of the Amazon, and they provide a break from overlanding and a convenient, if primitive, way of visiting remote villages. North from Manaus the authorities have 'subdued' the Indians who for years threatened white lives on the road to Boa Vista, and the route is now passable in safety.

Angel Falls

The road between Boa Vista and the gold mining town of El Dorado (Venezuela) winds through spectacularly beautiful country passing the sheer-sided 'lost world' of Mount Roraima at the junction of the three countries. Side trips can be taken to the world's highest waterfall, Angel Falls (979m), either from El Dorado or from Puerto Ordaz (now part of the new city of Ciudad Guayana).

After crossing the Orinoco, you'll soon reach Caracas, having completed almost a full circle of the continent. If you've still not seen enough, there's a route eastwards that is definitely not on the Gringo Trail. It is not possible, owing to border disputes, to cross the frontier from Venezuela to Guyana.

From Boa Vista (Brazil) however, there is a road of sorts to the frontier and a fordable river into Lethem. In the dry season, it is possible to drive all the way to Georgetown, and from there along the coast to the Corentyne River. Getting across that and into Nieuw Nickerie in Surinam will cause problems for those with their own vehicles, though there is an infrequent ferry. In fact, it is possible to drive all the way to Cayenne in French Guiana, though the road is little more than a sand track in places, and there are a number of rivers that have to be crossed by ferry.

Saint Laurent lies just over the river from Suriname, in French Guiana, and the remnants of both this penal colony and the better-known one of the Isles de Salut are beginning to prove something of a tourist attraction. Devil's Island is part of the Isles de Salut Group, but is hard to reach.

At Cayenne, the road ends, though it is possible to fly either direct to Belém at the mouth of the Amazon or to Saint Georges just across the river from the Brazilian river port of Oiapoque, from where a road runs all the way to Macapa. There are ferries to Belém from there, and that puts you back on the route southwards to Rio either along the northeastern coast, or south to Brasilia. In fact, you could just keep circling and recircling the continent in ever decreasing circles, clockwise and anticlockwise. It's a very dizzying part of the world in every respect!

THE CLASSIC OVERLAND THROUGH ASIA

by Warren Burton

The journey across Asia must still be considered the original of all overland routes. History provides us with sketchy accounts of the great overland journeys by Alexander, Hannibal, and Marco Polo. Those routes can still be taken to India and beyond, despite conflicts such as the Gulf War and continuing tribal conflict in Afghanistan. There is always a way through. The Middle East has continued to present some instability, yet there has always been a safe alternative to follow. With the revolution in Iran almost fifteen years ago, the country is no longer the bureaucratic and logistical struggle that prevailed during those few years of turmoil. Visas are available to all, except holders of USA passports, and in spite of being issued only a seven day Transit Visa, one can extend these up to 21 days with relative ease whilst in Iran. However, following the Gulf War in 1991, and despite promises to the Kurds from the Western Powers, unrest has erupted in Southeast Turkey (Turkish Kurdistan). Yet again the suppressed and isolated Kurds struggle for autonomy and the Turkish government's answer to this has been– send in the Army! So this region should most definitely be avoided.

With the continued breakup of former Yugoslavia, the most direct route to Istanbul following the E5 is not recommended. By diverting through Hungary, Romania and Bulgaria one can still arrive in Turkey (and Asia) without travelling too many more miles. Certainly you will see countries which have experienced considerable change since the breakup of the Eastern Bloc.

However the crossing of Asia remains a bureaucratic challenge, so you must go prepared with the correct vehicle documentation, most importantly a *Carnet de Passage* and your vehicle *Registration Document*, both correct in every detail – border officials can be very uncompromising. Furthermore almost all nationalities now require a visa for all countries east of Turkey. These must be obtained *before* departure as they *cannot* be issued on entry and are often not obtainable in neighbouring countries.

Istanbul East

Istanbul, where Europe meets Asia, is the perfect place to slow down, and finalise your plans and timings. The city is well serviced and although it is not the capital of Turkey, most countries on your route have diplomatic representation here. Istanbul is also an ideal meeting place for travellers heading east and you may be fortunate to meet some who have come west-bound – recent information from them is always the most up-to-date source.

The most direct route to Iran and beyond, is to travel via Ankara (the capital) then rising on to the Anatolian Plateau through Sivas, Erzincan, Erzurum to Dogubayazit (last stop in Turkey). This region has been affected recently by the Kurdish unrest, therefore you should check with local authorities before leaving Ankara. In any case, do not drive at night and stay in towns rather than camping.

The alternative longer route and by far the most rewarding is to head south from Istanbul via the Gallipoli Peninsular, crossing the Dardanelles to Canakkale. Then the choice is yours, but why not visit Troy, Bergama, Kusadasi (and Epheseus), then east to Pamukkale before crossing the mountains to the south coast. Several days can then be spent lazing on the beaches and coves of Olu Deniz, before following the dramatic coastal route from Fethiye via Kas to Antalya, Side and Anamur. This route is not only scenically spectacular but dotted with ancient Roman sites, Crusader castles and coastal villages of typical Turkish character.

Having virtually travelled the entire length of the south coast, Adana is the crossroads. South to Syria and a diversion to the Middle East (see below) or north across the Taurus Mountains to Cappadocia (and the environs of Goreme) and on north to rejoin the 'main road' at Sivas.

Diverting into the Middle East

If time and money permits, then certainly consider visiting Syria and Jordan. More recent conflicts and friction between neighbours restrict you to where you can travel, but the situation is ever changing. The Israel/Palestine peace process could well change the entire area – even Syria and Israel are at last talking to each other over conference tables.

Visas are required for both Syria and Jordan which should be obtained before you leave Europe. You do not require any other special paperwork for your vehicle, but be patient on the Syrian borders, they can be very autocratic and time-consuming.

From Adana head, south to the coastal town of Iskenderun and then cross into Syria at the Baba el Hawa border and on to Allepo, which has the largest medieval citadel in the world and the largest bazaar/*souq* in the Middle East. Further south are the water wheels at Hama, and from there to Homs and then Damascus, Syria's bustling capital. Cross the Jordanian border at Dar'a then to Amman, the capital. The city has little of interest but the site of Jerash to the north is well worth a visit.

Jordan surprises many travellers, the people (65 per cent of the population being Palestinian) are extremely friendly and hospitable, but also the country is geographically stunning and historically dramatic. A route via the Dead Sea takes you along the King's Highway from Madaba to Keraka and Petra, the hidden city of Nabateans. Several days here would not be wasted before heading south to the Aqaba on the Red Sea.

One can complete a circuit by returning to Amman along the Desert Highway and it is highly recommended to do an excursion en route to Wadi Rum, (famous in the days of Lawrence of Arabia). Take a local Bedouin guide and you will travel through some of the most spectacular desert scenery to be seen anywhere in the Middle East.

From Amman it is possible to take an excursion to the 'West Bank', but you require a special permit and you are not permitted to take your own vehicle. Fortunately, border controls between Jordan and Israel do not stamp your passport. However, on return from Jordan you must ensure that you have no evidence of Israeli goods, souvenirs etc – otherwise you will run into great difficulty attempting to re-enter Syria.

At the time of writing a route into Iraq is not advisable. Furthermore, you are still not permitted to travel overland through Saudi Arabia.

On re-entering Syria from Jordan and returning to Damascus you should consider the route northeast to the remote desert ruin of Palmyra – the Roman city built on the ancient Greek site dating back to 1000BC. Your route could then take you via Lake Assad on the Euphrates, returning via Allepo to re-enter Turkey. Again, due to the present Kurdish unrest the region east and northeast of Gaziantep and Diyarbakir is best avoided, most certainly any route around Lake Van is out of bounds.

Iran to India

The only practical entry point to Iran from Turkey is the border of Barzagan. Before entering, in order to conform with Islamic dress codes, you must, if female, equip yourself with a *chadoor,* a long loose-fitting gown that will cover your head, shoulders and conceal the distinguishing shape of your body. This must be worn in public. Furthermore, alcohol is strictly forbidden, so drink it all before the border. Having said all this, the border control, although slow, is usually very civil and again as long as everything is in order, then all should run smoothly.

The direct and most travelled route goes via Tabriz, Zanjan then south to Esfahan via Hamadan avoiding Tehran – unless of course you want to tackle the worst traffic jams in Asia. Esfahan is the cultural centre of Iran, and still houses some of the most valuable craft workshops and bazaars of the Middle East. The Shah Abbas Mosque is spectacular with the turquoise blue ceramics covering its domes and minarets.

A day's drive south to Shiraz, the garden city renowned for its hospitality, and the nearby ruin of Persepolis. This 2500-year old site was built by the Persian King, Darius the Great, only to be destroyed by Alexander the Great around 300 BC.

You now follow the old southern trade routes across Dasht-e-Lut, via Kerman and Zahedan. The way is marked with Caravansari and desert fortresses, one in particular at Bam is still very intact.

Afghanistan though very near, is definitely out of bounds to overland travel for the foreseeable future. Therefore crossing the Baluchistan desert into Pakistan is the only viable route. However, this is a very sensitive region and one should proceed with caution, avoiding any night-driving and 'camping out'. You should also avoid any form of disagreement or conflict, no matter who might be at fault. Folk are 'touchy' in this area, most are armed, so be diplomatic and you should have no problems.

The rather chaotic border post at Mijaveh/Taftan is usually straightforward and travellers are often welcome to sleep overnight at the Pakistan Customs post.

Attempts are being made to complete the construction of a bitumen road through the desert to Quetta – though it is a long process and the constant affects of drifting sand and seasonal flash floods seem to hinder progress.

Quetta is very much a frontier town and a real crossroads for traders and 'smugglers'. Whilst the town has very little architectural character, the people, who congest the streets and markets, replace what is missing – Afghani, Baluchi and Pathans all mingle in this mountain oasis to make a colourful bazaar of trade (and not all of it legal!).

Following nomad routes into the Indus river valley, Pakistan's lifeline, you head north via Multan to Lahore. However, if time and resources are still available, Northern Pakistan is a must, especially during the months (May to September).

The frontier region of west Pakistan bordering on Afghanistan is tribal and restricted. Therefore if you are going to visit the north, follow the Indus Valley via Dera Ismail Khan to Khot and then Peshawar. On reaching Peshawar you then have the choice of exploring the Northwest Frontier or taking the Grand Trunk Road – which the British built from Kabul to Calcutta.

From Peshawar the Hindu Kush and the Swat valley can be explored. Further north, Chitral and the Kalash Valleys are inhabited by the Kafirs – possible descendants of Alexander the Great. The North West Frontier is inhabited by people with cultures so established that you would never believe that time moves on.

To Islamabad from Peshawar the route crosses the Indus river overlooked by the mighty Attock Fort, then to Rawalpindi and Islamabad, Pakistan's satellite capital. From Islamabad it is possible to do another excursion, this time north to the Hunza valley and the Karakorams. Although the land border is open over the Khunjerab Pass to China and Xinjiang Province, it is only possible to do this using local public transport. The Chinese authorities still make it very difficult to obtain permission to enter with foreign-registered vehicles, though to go by public transport provides an alternative, via Kashgar and Urumqi following the ancient Silk Route through the land of Ghengis Khan to Beijing and Shanghai.

However, continuing from Islamabad, south again, into the heart of the Punjab to Lahore, with its Moghul Red Fort and Shalimar Gardens: Lahore is a bustling thriving city – to the overlander with your own vehicle, it is an ideal centre to make any repairs before entering India.

From Lahore the Grand Trunk Road takes you the short distance to the Wagah/Attari Road border with India. Here strict times of opening and 'bureaucracy personified' welcome you to India. You will very soon see and feel the change.

India and Beyond

This fascinating country of diverse culture, terrain, language and religion, with its 920 million people creating the largest democracy in the world, is predominately Hindu but still has the largest Muslim population in the world. The history and sights provide the overlander with a unique journey whether taking a direct route to Nepal or following the Grand Trunk Road to its end, at Calcutta.

The first stop into India, is the wealthy Punjab State, Amritsar – the centre of the Sikh religion. The holy shrine to their faith is the Golden Temple which welcomes visitors and pilgrims alike. Now to Delhi – from here the choice is yours!

During autumn, winter and early spring the colourful desert state of Rajasthan makes a rewarding diversion. Some head further south to Goa and its beaches or further still to the 'hill stations' of the south.

During the summer months, to avoid the heat and rain of the monsoon, the Himalayan foothills offer some respite. Simla, the Kulu valley and Darhamsala are wonderful spots to relax.

Following the overland route, one cannot miss Agra and the Taj Mahal, the highlight of any journey to India. East to Varanasi on the Ganges is one of the holiest places for the Hindu faith, with early morning cremations on the historical Ghats. Not only is Varanasi sacred to the Hindu, the Muslim faith of India also hold the city dear in their religion. Nearby, at Sarnath, is the site where Buddha gave his first sermon.

The traditional route of the past 25 years or so takes most overlanders to the Himalayan Kingdom of Nepal and to Kathmandu. Once the hidden-away capital of a relatively private kingdom, it is now the busy tourist centre servicing climbing, trekking, and rafting expeditions. Nepal will always be the welcome rest at the end of a long journey; its friendly people, scenery and climate provide a welcome contrast to finish a trip or take a break, if venturing on further.

However, for those who wish to continue, during the summer months many cross the passes of the Himalaya onto the Tibetan plateau and in through the back door of China. However, entry is still generally restricted to organised tour groups, and again it is not possible to enter with foreign-registered vehicles. The other alternative: travelling to Bangladesh and on to Myanmar is still not possible, yet times are changing – recent reports state the opening of some land borders between Myanmar (Burma) and Thailand.

There may yet be the opportunity of a complete land route to Singapore, and (with a few sea crossings) on to Sydney.

OVERLAND THROUGH SOUTHEAST ASIA

by Myfanwy Vickers

The principle of an overland trip is that it is as good to travel as to arrive. Most guidebooks will jump you from site to site, city to city, beautiful beach to ancient temple, and tell you little if anything about the stretches in between. But precisely because of this, it is here that you will find the vital heart of the country.

Overland travel, in my view, is best undertaken independently, by self-propelled means: not only do you have total freedom of movement, but your pace is adjusted to that of the life going on around you. If you travel by train, bus, jeep or any other local means, you still have the opportunity either to take a side road or to get out mid-way to do some exploring. Failing this, so-called independent travel can hover close to the tour: you meet the same people on the same route in the same places, and the mystique of the exotic somehow eludes you.

The choices available are more or less the same in every country, but part of the fun is the variety of transport on offer throughout Southeast Asia. Not only buses and trains, which may bear little resemblance to that which goes under the same name back home, but trucks and jeeps, taxis and *tuk-tuks*, *bemos* and *becaks*, rickshaws and trishaws, pony and traps. For the weary traveller, a ride around town in a bicycle rickshaw which resembles an open-air armchair on wheels, decked out with bells and bunting, is a luxury hard to beat – and this despite the constant stream of commercial invitations at your ear ("Batik?

Statues? Sarongs? My cousin's factory? Cheap rates!"). What is more, it will probably only cost you about 30p an hour.

Nevertheless, travel on public transport can be less than fun. Simply buying a ticket can be a chaotic and frustrating experience. You might be forgiven for mistaking the process for some other pursuit, like a treasure hunt or mystery tour – or even an oblique way of inflicting punishment on those foolish enough to be visiting the place. This, coupled with the principle of not setting off until the vehicle is filled to three times its capacity, can be a maddening experience for the Anglo-Saxon. Once aboard, you have not just your fellow passengers to contend with, but baskets and boxes, goats and birds (caged and uncaged), babies and elbows, airlessness, cramp, perhaps the distorted wail from an amplifier in your ear, and a permanently worrying sense that you have paid over the odds for something which is heading in the wrong direction and provides nowhere for your feet. There is, perhaps, little that is more frightening than travel in an Indonesian public bus, the cab's holy shrine swaying as it bears down, avenger-like, on yet more passengers on a bend in the road – its apparent intent to carry people off into the next world becoming, on occasion, all too grim a reality.

In such a situation, try telling yourself that it is all part of 'the experience'. Not only the ability to be assertive when necessary, but an inexhaustible sense of humour, are great assets. But with time on your hands, you can give yourself space to recover from the rigours of travelling.

Most tourists fly into Bangkok and head north to trek in Chiang Mai, proceeding south to the beaches. Avoid this trail if you can. For those of you arriving overland from India and Nepal, Thailand is a blessing for travel is easy. When I was there on a bicycle, barely a day passed without a vehicle stopping to offer me a ride; hitchhikers should not have a problem. Thailand's public transport system is increasingly modern and efficient – *and* it keeps pretty good time!

The four trunk routes of the State railway run to the north, north east, east and south; long-distance trains have sleeping cars and/or air-conditioned coaches. Slower than buses, they are safer and, as with all trains everywhere, you have the added advantage of not being pinned to your seat.

Both State and private buses are cheap and uncomfortable, and tend to be accident prone; this is not unusual in Asia and many travellers still use them. Whilst private buses are in some ways more civilised, you may find that curtains sealing off the view while a video of 'Life in Rural Thailand' blares through the bus is something of a horror. Do not accept food or drink: whole coach-loads of people have awoken from a peculiarly deep sleep to find all their belongings gone.

Reputable rental companies such as Hertz and Avis operate out of Bangkok and Chiang Mai and there is the usual panoply of taxis, *tuk-tuks* and *bemos*. Travel by motorbike or bicycle is easy, and increasingly seems the only way to see parts of the country that are not well-trodden by others. Mae Hong Son, long cut off by mountains, is being promoted as one of the last undeveloped areas for trekking, but when you learn that Thai Airways flies from Bangkok and twice daily from Chiang Mai, you begin to see why the in-between bits become almost essential. Head out to the north east, a dry plateau known as 'Isaan', meaning 'vastness', before the hordes.

Overland travel is interrupted by Myanmar (Burma): you are not allowed to enter through any of its five land borders and unless you attempt to ford a river, you are forced to take to the air. Vast areas of the country are out of bounds to visitors, and any bikes will be temporarily impounded. With the ongoing troubles, regulations have tightened up. Check on the latest before departure. With restrictions to your movements and your time (seven days) it may be that you are best advised to resort to internal flights. However, despite the machinations of the state-run Tourist Myanmar to thwart your every move, it is just feasible (if you plan your time efficiently in advance) to see the open areas within the week. If you feel anxious about fitting it all in, you could fall back on a Tourist Myanmar package.

Trains in Myanmar are cheap, but the only rail route authorised for use by tourists is the fourteen-hour Yangon (Rangoon) to Mandalay. Cheap buses run everywhere. Jeeps run randomly, leaving when they are full. Hiring is expensive, and if you stray off limits you may waste time being stopped. Bicycle trishaws and pony traps can be hired for the day – but you may end up walking some of it out of compassion. Ferries are excellent for getting around, the twelve-hour trip down the Irawaddy from Mandalay to Pagan being the one package worth doing through the official channels.

A possible itinerary (suggested by Frances Capel in the Cadogan guide) makes the most of your time and concentrates on Pagan. Take the night train from Yangon to Mandalay, explore Mandalay, fly to Pagan (boat if in season). Explore Pagan and Mount Popa, then fly to Heho; bus to Yaunghwe for boat tour of Lake Inle. Then bus to Thazi for night train to Yangon and get off two hours short of Yangon to explore Pegu in the early morning, catching a later train out.

The 13,000 islands making up the Indonesian archipelago are all slightly different when it comes to transport! Only Java and Sumatra, for example, have a railway – consult a specialist guidebook for details. Java and Bali are now well served with new roads, but getting off the beaten track in Indonesia means just that: the road may be hard to locate! Parts of the so-called Trans Sumatran highway are like a battlefield, pitted with pot-holes and scattered with boulders. Wooden bridges built for buffalo carts now take heavy goods traffic; the lorries have a system of grinding to a virtual halt at the bridge, throwing themselves into top gear, and then lurching across with engines roaring, as if taking the bridge by surprise might somehow forestall its collapse. Roads in the less developed southeastern islands, Nusa Tenggara, are even bumpier and liable to have been flooded and washed away in the rainy season (November to March). Here, outlying areas are served by an irregular public transport system, and you are better off going under your own steam.

In Kalimantan, however, dense jungle, a sparse population and a natural network of waterways make rivers the main arteries. If they are not navigable, travel is virtually impossible except by air. Take outboard motor boats, longboats, dug-outs, ferries and water taxis. In Irian Jaya, you will need a spirit of adventure and a sharp implement for cutting your way through tangled vegetation.

Whilst the Philippines boast very cheap internal flights, these get heavily booked, so be prepared for a wait. Overland travel here is quite hard work, and whilst boats are a must, bear in mind that only the luxury end will be relaxing.

Every type of tub and ferry is available; ask at the port if you get no joy in the office. Be wary of travelling in bad weather, however: safety precautions are nil and people regularly drown in shipping accidents. Unique to the Philippines is the *jeepney*, an ex-US jeep festooned with flashing lights, garishly painted cut-out characters, bells and baubles. Shout and gesticulate when you want to get out.

Although most current guide books will tell you it is not possible to travel independently overland in Indo-China, it is. However, unlike Malaysia and Singapore, where travel is self-explanatory and far from alien, these countries are only just opening up, after long periods of devastation, and there are things you need to know.

Vietnam has an extensive network of decrepit, crammed and exhausting buses. Trains are more reliable, but can average as little as fifteen kilometres an hour! Thanks to the war efforts of the Americans, the roads are not bad, and you can always hire a car with driver.

In Laos, secure yourself an inter-province pass from the Department of Commerce before doing anything else – without one you can be arrested and deported. Then investigate flights: Laos is incredibly mountainous, it has no railway, and the roads are abysmal even by Asian standards. Tortuous dirt roads will defeat you utterly between June and September (rainy season). The major towns are linked by air, and rivers form some of the country's main thoroughfares.

Tourists are forbidden to travel on buses in Cambodia and huge areas are without roads anyway. Again, ferries provide a useful service, and the railway functions despite frequent delays. For those keen to economise at any price, the front two cars of any train are free – they may act as a detonator to mines on the track… A limited number of flights on set routes are available, and others are added when there is sufficient demand.

Everything about transport in Indo-China reinforces the point I made at the outset: self-propelled means are the most effective! People are already walking and mountain biking in Indo-China; I do urge you, with undisguised bias, to try it! It is often, paradoxically, less tiring than mechanical means, and it has an uncanny way of making everything seem more wonderful. You are grateful, perhaps, for small mercies when you finally arrive. But appreciating the little things, and the everyday, is what overland travel is all about.

INTER-RAIL THROUGH EUROPE

by Max Thorowgood

Vast social and technological changes have given the twentieth century traveller unprecedented access to the remotest regions on earth. Consequently, the classical marvels which enticed eighteenth century dilettantes from the serenity of their country residences seem hidebound to the modern grand tourist. However, in their anxiety to taste the delights of the newly accesible, today's travellers too often fail to examine their more immediate cultural stimuli before thrusting themselves upon the unsuspecting objects of their wanderlust. In so doing they limit the benefit to themselves and their victims. An Inter-or Eu-Rail ticket is the cure to these ills and heir to the spirit of the Grand Tour.

In 1972 the Inter-rail ticket burst upon the scene and Britain joined the Common Market. The former event was the more genuinely pan-European in scope. The object of the International Confederation of Railways (which included, even then, the less regressive east European countries) was to promote international rail travel. It devised a system whereby a single ticket afforded the bearer one month's unlimited rail travel on the participating networks. In so doing it did much to foster European integration because the Inter-rail ticket affords an unrivalled opportunity to discover European civilisation.

Inter-rail permits the spirit of European integration and enlightenment to flourish not only because of its amazing scope, but because train travel is a wonderfully convivial means of transport, and no conveyance is so congenial as the compartments which still form the large part of European rolling stock. You can roam the train; enjoy the ride, or the people riding with you and their picnics; and when the general gaiety begins to pall, make a moderately uncomfortable bed from the compartment's sliding seats. With the exception of hitchhiking, there is no cheaper way to travel in Europe – by the time you reach Nice, your card has all but paid for itself, and the plains of Italy spread out at your feet. The grand tourist may drink deeply of the spirit of the Renaissance, whilst the connoisseur of more ephemeral pulchritude can scan a good proportion of the beaches and the costas, the rivieras and the Greek islands. Europe, from the Atlantic to the Carpathians, and from the land of the midnight sun to the flesh-pots of Morocco, is your oyster.

Eurostar is the best route out of Britain, there are bargains to be had, and you'll be able to travel at 200 miles an hour (in France). **Lesson 1:** the Inter-rail ticket only covers ordinary trains, fast trains: and couchettes are extra. The tariff varies considerably depending on the conductor so you've got to haggle, but generally France and Italy are more expensive, Germany is cheaper, and in most other countries most trains are standard. It is not normally necessary to take fast trains, but couchettes are well worth it if you are interested in sleeping – and they are cheaper than hotels.

A cursory glance at the map supplied with the ticket reveals that central Europe has the most comprehensive rail network. In Holland, Germany, Poland, the Czech Republic, Slovakia and Hungary it is quite easy to get where you are likely to want to go by train. The same is broadly true of Italy and France, though in Italy the non-supplement trains, of which there are a limited number, tend to be very busy. Switzerland has good coverage but many of the lines are privately owned and offer only a 50 per cent discount (Switzerland is expensive). Rail travel on the Iberian peninsula leaves a lot to be desired, fast trains aside. It can only be recommended to serious Hispanophiles and to those whose destination is Morocco – don't be taken in by the timetable, do take a month.

There are four ways to get to Greece: by ferry from Brindisi, in southern Italy, the ticket should get you a reduction; from Munich on the fancifully named "Hellos Express" through what used to be Yugoslavia, taking in Zagreb and Belgrade; from Venice by way of Sarajevo; and, avoiding the former Yugoslavia, by a circuitous route via Hungary, Romania, Bulgaria and Turkey which would certainly be a challenge but good if you are committed to enjoying the journey. The routes through former Yugoslavia are open again, though their condition (which was never exactly the best) is doubtful. Croatian and Slovenian railways, it seems, are independent but the rest remain under the umbrella of Jugoslav Railways. Whichever way you cut it, getting to the Big Olive is liable to be a somewhat lengthy business on crowded trains, but it is a treat when you get there.

Because the Aegean islands are such an important adjunct to Greece they are exceedingly well served by ferries from Piraeus (and other ports) for which there are Inter-rail discounts. Getting to Piraeus can be 'fun' so it may be worth getting a taxi; agree the price in advance. For your discount you will have to sleep on the deck, so avoid the bow and the waves: it will be cold but the stars will be brilliant. From the islands such as Samos you can get boats to Turkey. Visas are necessary and can be obtained for a relatively modest charge. The train from Izmir takes you to the Sea of Marmara where you will need to take another ferry to Istanbul.

Lesson 2: Although it is generally possible to buy food on trains it is invariably of low quality and high price. Pack a penknife and take on supplies before boarding anything, European platforms are not a patch on their Eastern counterparts. A good supply of comestibles can work wonders in the cut and thrust of the search for a comfortable berth.

Lesson 3: Don't worry about getting value for money from your ticket. Unless you are spectacularly unadventurous it cannot fail to pay. The new city everyday approach much vaunted by the International Rail marketing men is ultimately sterile. Cultural overload is a danger. Vary the diet – inter-railing is not the preserve of the culture vulture.

Enjoining light travel is a peculiarly fruitless exercise since aptitude for it is genetic. However, it is doubly important when it is necessary to walk along crowded narrow corridors in unstable trains carrying your luggage. It is desirable therefore, to keep the number of trips you have to take to a minimum. One trip down the corridor, fat rucksack on back, will be more than enough to make the bearer heartily unpopular.

Lesson 4: The hottest tip of all is: 'Left Luggage'. Money spent on Left Luggage is money well spent. Take a small pack for essentials, and dump your bag at the station upon arrival. The cheapest hotels are normally near the station, but that does not mean they will be easy to locate or that they will have room, so a recce without luggage is strongly recommended.

The under–26 system divides the participating networks into seven zones as follows: **A** the Republic of Ireland and Great Britain; **B** Scandinavia; **C** Germany, Switzerland, Austria and Denmark; **D** the Czech and Slovak Republics, Poland, Hungary, Bulgaria, Romania, Croatia and Serbia; **E** Benelux and France; **F** the Iberian Peninsula and Morocco; **G** Italy, Greece, Turkey, Slovenia and what remains of Yugoslavia. A global ticket costs £279 at time of going to press. Alternatively, up to three zones can be selected for reductions (one zone for fifteen days – £185; two zones for one month – £224; three zones for one month – £249). The beauty of the Inter-rail ticket is in the amazing freedom of movement it offers, that freedom is unduly restricted by the zonal system; therefore the global ticket is preferable. A ticket for those over 26 is now also available for £275, but it does not include France, Italy, Belgium or Morocco.

Such is the facility of movement offered by the Inter-rail ticket, and the myriad opportunities offered by Europe, that the prospect of recommending a route is daunting. Divide Europe, as Charlemagne did, into three (vertically): East, Middle and West. You then have roughly four different route choices – two *outside in's* and *two inside out's*. Decide upon the furthest extent of your trip, then think in terms of convection currents and proceed accordingly.

If that is too schematic, I offer an example: broadly and inside out. Folkestone to Ostend. Ostend to Munich from where you get the Hellos Express. Through the fabulous scenery of Slovenia to Zagreb, Belgrade, Skopje and eventually Thessalonika. From Thessalonika you can get access to the coast and the islands of the north Aegean. If that does not appeal, proceed through Greece to the Big Olive where cheap accomodation is readily available. See the Parthenon even if you don't like climbing hills and try the street kebabs. Take a boat to an island, explore it and do the beach thing in the enchanting waters of Poseidon (take *The Magus* by John Fowles). Then get another boat to Izmir, check that out, and move on to Istanbul, by train and boat, for a peek at the Sultan's palace from which you get the top down view on the gateway to the Orient. Say your *salaams* to the Byzantine world and proceed along the Greek coast, via Thessalonika again, to Belgrade. Get a train to Prague, suffer the hordes, and move swiftly on to Dresden, the *Florence of the Elbe*. If you have time, take it to sample the Saxenschweiz, the gorge through which the Elbe flows so adroitly. This is a short day-trip from Dresden – Konigstein can safely be recommended as a sight of interest. Also just outside Dresden is the Schloss Pilnitz which is quite lovely. Time will be short now, but don't bottle out. Go to Berlin, sample the after dark scene, then try Amsterdam for size to round things off. Return via Hoek van Holland to Harwich.

For a list of all inter-rail regulations and Rail Passes World-wide see p.793 of the Directory ■

PAPERWORK AND MONEY
Chapter 8

TRAVEL INSURANCE
by Ian Irvine

Insurance plays an important part in planning a trip abroad, but is frequently overlooked until the last minute. A "rush job" can have serious consequences when you find yourself needing to be airlifted out of the Indonesian jungle with a broken leg only to discover that your insurance doesn't cover air transportation and you will have to foot the £20,000 bill yourself. It is, therefore, essential that you obtain the correct insurance to suit the particular travel and activities to be undertaken. The vast range of choice can be daunting – different types of travel insurance are sold from numerous sources; banks, building societies, the Post Office, airlines and credit card companies, but if you are unsure of exactly what cover you need, you are best advised to seek free professional advice from an insurance broker. Make sure that you read the policy, particularly the small print and fully understand it before committing yourself.

In 1996 a major travel insurance scheme underwritten at Lloyd's of London, produced statistics showing that almost 40 per cent of claims paid related to medical expenses, 30 per cent to baggage losses and 25 per cent to cancellation claims with the most expensive claim costing £240,000 for medical expenses.

As long as the nature of travel is understood by the insurers, an inclusive policy will meet your requirements and cover the following principal risks.

Medical Expenses

This is probably the most important form of insurance, as the consequences of a medical problem may be severe – one can replace, or do without lost belongings, but one cannot replace one's health or body. Advances in medical treatment and the general availability of medical attention have increased costs considerably, and so an absolute minimum cover of £500,000 is necessary and these days most policies give higher cover. Repatriation costs are an essential part of medical insurance and under no circumstances should be limited in the policy. They can be high if a person is in a remote area and any form of complicated or specialist medical treatment is necessary. Air ambulances are regularly used to bring seriously ill travellers to the UK from Europe at costs of several thousands of pounds. When these are required for destinations further afield, inevitably prices escalate rapidly. For example, an accident in Nepal might mean a short helicopter flight to a light aircraft landing strip, followed by a light aircraft flight to an international airport, where a fully equipped medical jet could be waiting to bring the casualty back home. For severe illness, or serious accident, a medical team would need to accompany the injured person and the costs could be as high as £60,000.

Also, any good travel insurance policy must include a 24 hour emergency service, although assistance is only available if an injured person, or a hospital or embassy acting on their behalf, makes contact in the UK. Essential air evacuation anywhere in the world should be covered, but this will not include "search and rescue" expenses if someone is missing, even if there is concern for their health. Additional insurance for this can be arranged at an extra premium, dependent on location, duration and type of travel.

Private medical insurance in the UK is increasingly popular and often applies on a world-wide basis. However, it is important to note that such insurance often only insures the pure cost of direct medical treatment, and that repatriation cover is not automatic. Generally speaking, the cover is more restricted than that of a travel policy.

Personal Accident

This insurance pays a lump sum benefit if a traveller is unfortunate enough to have an accident which results in death, permanent disablement or the loss of an eye or limb. Some travellers may already have life assurance which applies on a world-wide basis and in the event of death would also pay a lump sum. For that reason, the death benefit under travel insurance is normally limited to £10,000. However, benefits for permanent disablement in a travel insurance policy may be as high as £40,000 or £50,000 and, if necessary, can be increased.

Cancellation or Curtailment

When a journey has to be cancelled or curtailed unavoidably, the cost of a deposit or payments made in advance for travel can be recovered through your insurance policy, but it is important to check that provision has been made for this. The sum insured must be adequate to cover a traveller's total costs and an amount of £3,000 is usually provided, although again, this can be increased if necessary. It is important to remember that travel costs may include car hire, accommodation, excursions and tours as well as airfares or other transportation. Cancellation of travel immediately prior to departure could mean losing everything paid for unless the correct cover is in force.

Personal Liability

If a traveller injures someone, or damages their property, they could be liable to pay compensation. Personal liability deals with such claims and should provide a cover of at least £1 million. Do note though, that this insurance DOES NOT COVER any claims arising from the use of cars or motorcycles, which must be insured separately.

Delayed Departure

Delays are increasingly common and whilst this is the airline's responsibility, travellers, particularly on economy tickets are often left to fend for themselves. If the delay lasts twelve hours or more due to strike, industrial action, bad weather or the breakdown of the aircraft, insurers will pay compensation to assist with the cost of incidental expenses. This should be no less than £25 for the first complete twelve-hour period, with subsequent enhancements for longer delays. If the delay affected travel at the point of departure to the extent that the entire trip had to be cancelled, compensation of up to £1,000 should be payable.

Personal Effects and Money

The majority of travellers take as little clothing as possible when travelling and with the increased use of credit cards and travellers' cheques, cash is usually kept to a minimum. In addition, many travellers have household policies which automatically insure their personal effects on a world-wide basis. However, when taking out cover for your personal effects it is important to make sure that their value does not exceed the provision in the policy, which should be for a minimum of £1,200. Money should be insured for at least £250.

All travel policies limit cover for valuables (defined as jewellery, gold and silver articles, watches, photographic equipment, binoculars, telescopes, personal radios, TV, HiFi equipment, computer and electronic equipment) and impose conditions regarding security. Valuables are in use throughout the year and so are normally insured under a household policy which is why travel insurers usually limit cover for valuables to, say, £250 for any one article and £350 for all articles. If valuables are worth more than this they will invariably not be covered under the travel policy.

Security for valuables is important and most insurers insist that they either be kept in hotel safes, locked bedrooms or wardrobes, or carried on the traveller's person. With this in mind, policies should be read very carefully – valuables will NOT be insured if they are not secured in a way specified by the policy. Money insurance usually covers airline tickets as well. A fairly typical limit for tickets would be £1,500, but it is important to be aware that tickets are insured for their cost price and not their replacement value. If a ticket is lost, the travel agent should be contacted, or the travel insurance claims adjuster – very often it can be arranged for tickets to be re-issued thus avoiding more expensive replacements.

Vehicle Insurance Outside Europe

Vehicle insurance in the UK is simple to arrange and can easily be extended to include Europe with a Green Card. Outside Europe, particularly in Third World countries, vehicle insurance is difficult to arrange and there is no such thing as a comprehensive policy. Insurance needs to be divided in two; third party cover to protect against claims from others and accidental damage, fire and theft cover, to protect the traveller's own vehicle. Third party cover can normally only be purchased at the borders of countries; some insist on insurance, others are indifferent. This insurance cannot be arranged in the UK.

The traveller's own vehicle can be insured for accidental damage, fire and theft risks on a world-wide basis, but specialist advice would be need to be taken from an insurance broker.

A WORD OF WARNING: Vehicle insurance in North America differs from state to state but generally speaking has very low third party limits. Compared with UK limits, they are inadequate and unless increased would expose the traveller to unnecessary risk. The limits can be increased by purchasing Top Up Liability insurance when hiring a vehicle.

Carnet Indemnity Insurance

If you intend travelling by vehicle outside Europe, you should, technically speaking, pay import duty on your vehicle every time you enter a country. This is obviously impractical and the problem can be resolved by obtaining a *Carnet de Passage* before leaving the UK. This is a multi-page document which is stamped when entering a country and stamped again when leaving the country to show that the vehicle has both been imported and exported, and as such no duty is payable.

Carnet Indemnity Insurance is arranged in conjunction with Carnet de Passage documents issued by the Automobile Association and avoids having to provide a bank guarantee and tying up funds. The AA will require a financial guarantee equivalent to the highest duty of the various countries through which travel is intended. This can be as high as three times the value of the vehicle in the UK.

Insurance premiums are normally calculated at five per cent of the indemnity figure, but if the indemnity is in excess of £25,000 a sliding scale comes into operation. The AA require a service charge of about £75 to provide the Carnet de Passage and a refundable deposit of £500. Strict instructions for the use of the Carnet de Passage are issued and it is important that these are complied with, in particular, getting the Carnet document stamped when entering and leaving any particular country.

It is important to be aware that the insurance guarantee against a Carnet only provides immediate funding if duty becomes payable. It does not absolve the responsibility of paying the duty at a later date. To avoid this, a Double Indemnity can be arranged on a separate basis. All insurances for Carnets issued by the AA can be arranged by Campbell Irvine Limited of 48 Earls Court Road, Kensington, London W8 6EJ, tel: 0171-937 6981.

Life Assurance

These policies normally grant cover on a world-wide basis and would therefore apply whilst travelling. If, however, a particularly unusual or hazardous form of travel was contemplated, it would be sensible to check with a Life Assurance company to make sure that no limitations apply.

Claims Procedure

Claims which necessitate immediate attention can be dealt with by emergency claims facilities, something made available these days by all insurance companies. This is particularly relevant for medical claims, especially those involving repatriation. However, it is important to remember that contact must be made to get the best use of emergency facilities. Routine claims can normally be dealt with at leisure or on return to the UK. Any documentation relevant to a claim needs to be kept secure, so if it has to be posted it is important to take copies.

If property is lost, Claims Loss Adjusters normally require some evidence of value. Original purchase receipts may not be available, so it will normally suffice to state when and where lost property was purchased, and how much was paid for it.

All insurance policies carry excesses which are normally deducted from the settlement figure of a claim. Travel insurance claims are usually subject to an excess which should not exceed £50 but vehicle insurance excesses tend to be higher and an amount of £250 would not be unusual. Excesses are always clearly shown on policy documents and if there are any doubts about this, the position needs to be checked before travelling rather than leaving it until a claim is made.

For Travel Insurance Specialists see p.802 of the Directory

VISAS

by Ralph Whitmarsh

The subject of visas is an everchanging scene. Not only are the rules and regulations frequently being revised, but the way the Embassies and High Commissions impart the information to the public and process the visa applications is constantly being altered, often not to the benefit of the traveller.

Such is the world today that there is a steady drift of people trying to leave their country and rebuild their lives elsewhere, either due to wars, famine or persecution. This is putting an increasing strain on the immigration policies of various governments, and the regulations dictating whether you may enter a country visa-free are always being reviewed. Whilst the situation for UK passport holders is reasonably static, there are many other nationalities resident in the UK who no doubt may read these pages, and who may be subject to a different set of rules.

The ever-increasing desire to travel and the spontaneity with which travel can be organised has little impact on the authorities who issue passports and the required visas. Some countries have closed their UK provincial consulates, thus putting an additional strain on the hard pressed London-based staff, guaranteeing long queues especially at peak travel times of the year. The Spanish, however, insist that you apply to the consulate closest to your place of residence. This all adds up to the fact that whilst you can virtually arrange a round-the-world itinerary in a matter of minutes, if your documents are not in order, you cannot travel. So some thought has to be given to the matter of your passport and the possible need to obtain visas for the countries you wish to visit.

Efficiency and Bureaucracy

The cost to a government of maintaining an Embassy or High Commission overseas is enormous, and most, if not all, are conscious of the need to reduce costs, or raise extra revenue. Some have introduced premium rate telephone lines for the public to use when wishing to make an enquiry; others have installed an automated switchboard, which is fine if you know the extension number you want. You may have to listen to a long message before reaching the information you are seeking; sometimes your question may not be answered at all. These means of imparting information to the caller enable the Embassy or High Commission to reduce the number of staff (or hopefully redeploy them to issue visas), and raise revenue from the premium rate telephone line.

It is necessary to do your research regarding visas early in your travel planning process, for, according to where you are going, your reasons for visiting a country, and your nationality, the issuing time can vary from a matter of hours to weeks. The reader must appreciate the role of the Embassy or High Commission and the staff working there. You are very much in their hands as to whether a visa is granted or not, and any Consular Official has the authority to reject an application if he or she thinks fit. If a rejection takes place, it may only require an extra supporting document such as a bank statement to resolve the matter. Beware though, the Americans and Indians actually endorse the passport when an application is rejected, whereupon a fresh application needs to be submitted, the paperwork for which has to persuade the Embassy to reverse their previous decision.

Understanding

It is necessary to appreciate that when entering an Embassy you are entering the territory of another country, and frustrating though it may be after you have spent much time in the queue, you need to be polite and tolerant with the Consular Official who, after all, is only carrying out the checks and procedures imposed by his government. You may need to remind yourself that British and US Embassies abroad may be just as daunting a place to other nationals. The opening hours are limited to enable the staff to issue the visas once the public have left the premises, but for those people residing some distance from London accessibility is difficult and can be costly if you have to stay overnight in London. Postal applications are treated as non-urgent by the authorities and your envelope may remain in the mail bag for some weeks before it is opened and dealt with by the Embassy or High Commission. It is unrealistic to expect them to spend time searching for your application amongst hundreds of others.

In addition one has to be aware of the public holidays recognised by these authorities. Not only do they close on UK public holidays but on their own as well. This obviously disrupts the issuing process and after a few days of closure, the sudden demand can be very high. Be aware of the holy month of Ramadan when appropriate Embassies change their hours of business and at the end of this period they close altogether. Be aware also of the Chinese New Year dates and other important religious festivals. See *Public Holidays World-wide* in Section 1 of the Directory.

Your Passport

Obviously, before you can leave these shores you require a ten-year passport. The MRP (machine readable passport) is available in two versions, one costing £18, and the other, with additional pages costing £27 at the time of writing. Many countries require a minimum of six months' validity remaining on the passport when you either enter or leave their territory, so first of all check your passport's date of expiry. Make sure the passport has one blank page for each visa required, as well as sufficient space for entry and exit stamps. Some Embassies will only issue a visa on a right-hand page.

Ensure your passport is signed. Again, many authorities, the Indian High Commission among them, will not grant a visa on an unsigned passport. Some Embassies grant visas, the validity of which exceeds the validity of the passport, but others restrict the visa validity to coincide with the passport expiry date.

Take great care of your passport not only when you are travelling, but also in between journeys. Keep it secure, as a UK or US passport can command a price of many hundreds of pounds on the black market.

Visa Requirements

There is much to consider here. Business or tourism? How many entries and for how long? The United States have over twenty different categories of visas reflecting different reasons for travel – but only one application form. The Saudis have four different forms covering varying reasons for travel. Non-UK-passport holders may find their application referred with a delay of about four weeks if they are not a permanent resident of the UK.

Most visas are valid from the date of issue, frequently for three months. Some, for example, Russian, are valid from the date you enter the country. In this example the entry and exit dates are clearly stated on the visa and you cannot enter Russia before, or leave after the date quoted. It is therefore necessary to plan when to apply for a visa to avoid a situation where it expires before you even arrive in the country. Other countries issue visas which may be valid for twelve months and allow multiple entries with no restrictions.

You will need to make allowances in your financial calculations for the purchase of the visas you require. The majority cost under £25, but some are granted free of charge. There are some for which you will have to pay considerably more, particularly if your reason for travel is business. The price may also vary according to your nationality and the costs are agreed between governments. To these costs must be added the charges incurred in actually getting the paperwork to the Embassy – are you going to employ the services of an agent who specialises in visa procurement, or are you going to spend a lot of your time making trips to the Embassies and waiting in queues?

Some countries, for example, Rwanda, Burundi, Mali and Mauritania, have no representation in London. Their nearest Embassy is in Paris and this fact can only add to the cost and logistics of acquiring the visa.

Many nationals have for a few years now been able to travel to the United States for a maximum of 90 days without a visa, providing they meet the criteria set down on the "waiver" form. However, if you have incurred a conviction you must declare this and apply for a visa. The Australian Working Holiday visa for those under 26 years of age is valid for thirteen months and is an attractive proposition, as a period of holiday can be combined with work in order to help finance additional travel.

Beware of an Israeli stamp in your passport should you wish to visit the Arab countries in the Gulf area. Ask the Israeli entry and exit controls to stamp a loose leaf document. A South African stamp in the passport is not the problem it used to be, as South Africa is gaining acceptability in the world.

Ready to Go?

Check your visa for accuracy and to ensure it covers you for your plans. Mistakes are frequently made due to the pressure of work loads in Embassies and even the computer-issued visas are only as accurate as those who input the data. If taking family members who are on your passport – husband or wife or children under sixteen– ensure that the visa issued covers them as well, or that a separate one has been issued. Some visa application forms, for example, India, Australia, and Egypt include space for all those included on the one passport, but some other countries require one form to be completed per person. Remember that children who have reached sixteen years of age require their own passport.

Visa Trends

In recent years we have witnessed the breakup of the USSR; the Iron Curtain has come down; Czechoslovakia has become two separate countries, and Yugoslavia has fragmentated into pieces. In South America, Argentina and Brazil do not require a visa from UK nationals, but tourists to Venezuela will require a tourist card obtainable from the airline on which you are arriving in the country (check this when booking your seat).

Although the Commonwealth of Independent States (USSR) has become more accessible, the documents required for a visa has changed little, viz, either an invitation from the company being visited, if travelling on business, or confirmation of your accommodation if travelling as a tourist. Poland, Hungary, Czech and Slovak Republics no longer require a visa from UK passport holders, but visitors to Bulgaria and Romania still need a visa. Those requiring a German visa must show the Embassy proof of medical insurance cover: an E111 from the Post Office, if you are a UK resident and registered under the National Health Service, is sufficient.

The requirements for entering France and Spain on a non-UK passport are complicated, and surprisingly Australian passport holders require a visa for both countries, although they are issued free of charge if married to an EC passport holder and the partner's passport is produced for the Embassy together with the original marriage certificate.

India is an ever-popular destination and the High Commission offer a tourist visa valid for a 30-day stay providing you arrive in India within 30 days of the issue date of the visa. At £3 it is excellent value, but do not apply by post as you will probably not receive your passport back in time. Taiwan has relaxed visa requirements for periods of stay up to fourteen days depending on nationality. Whilst still in the Far East, UK nationals can stay in Thailand for fifteen days as a tourist providing they are in possession of air tickets with confirmed bookings in and out of the country. A two-month stay is allowed in Indonesia visa-free, provided entry and exit is made through designated air and sea ports. Residing with friends and relatives during the visit is not allowed and not all nationals are permitted this 60 day stay visa-free. China requires to see a visa for all visitors, as do Vietnam and Myanmar (Burma), which are now being visited in greater numbers.

Finally, even though you have got all your visas, an immigration official has the power to deny you entry to his or her country if they so wish, and they are not obliged to state their reasons. The United States is perhaps the most formidable in this respect so it is always sensible to have an onward or return ticket with you, altogether with proof of sufficient funds to support yourself, and additional evidence that you have good reason to return to your country of residence from the USA.

For Visa Requirements World-wide for UK and US citizens see the Geographical Section of the Directory p.621
For Visa Agencies see p.801
For Passport Offices in the UK see p.802

PERMITS, REGISTRATIONS AND RESTRICTED AREAS
by Jack Jackson

Travel in the Third World used to be easy for Westerners, with few restrictions and little in the way of police checks, paperwork or permissions, to hold travellers back. Europe in those days, offered more barriers to travellers, with frequent customs and police enquiries.

Nowadays the position is reversed. In most Third World countries the hindrances to free travel grow yearly, in number and variety. Ambiguous taxes are demanded at borders and airports. The legality of these may be questionable, but the man behind the desk is all-powerful, so travellers do not have any choice. Many countries where monetary systems are unstable and which therefore have flourishing black markets, now require travellers to complete a currency declaration on entry, detailing all monies, jewellery, cameras, tape recorders. etc. This is checked on departure against bank receipts for any money changed. Some countries are very thorough in their searches of departing travellers and border officials are often corrupt.

With groups, border officials naturally try to cut down massive form-filling, by completing just one form for the group leader. This can make life very difficult later, if one person in a group wishes to change money at a bank, or wishes to leave the group, but does not have their own individual form and cannot immediately produce the group form, or the leader to vouch for him. Individual forms should always be obtained if possible.

Deliberate Delays

Some countries purposely delay the issue of permits in capital cities, so that the travellers will spend more money there. As most travellers are limited for time, a straightforward Tourist Tax would be more acceptable.

Registration

In many places the law requires that you register with the police within twenty fours hours of arrival. Often a fee is charged for this. Usually, if you are staying at a hotel, the registration is done for you by the hotel and the costs are included in your room charges; but if you are in a very small hotel, camping or staying with friends, you will either have to do it yourself, or pay someone to do it for you. As this often entails fighting through a queue of several hundred local people at the Immigration Office, with the chance that you have chosen the wrong queue anyway, *baksheesh* to a hotel employee to do it for you is a good investment.

Most of these countries also require that you register with the police in each town in which you stop. In some cases, e.g. South Sudan, you have to report to the police in every town or village through which you pass. In smaller places the registration is usually much easier.

Permission from the central government may be necessary to travel outside major cities. Usually, for this permission you go to the Ministry of the Interior, but if a Tourist Office exists, it is wise to check there first. Any expedition or trekking party will have to do this anyway. This system is not always just "red tape". If there is local strife it may be for travellers' safety.

Restricted Areas

Many countries have restricted or forbidden areas somewhere.

Much of Africa and Asia has large areas of desert or semi-desert. Restrictions on travel in these areas are formulated by governments for travellers' safety and take account of such obvious things as ensuring that travellers have good strong vehicles carrying plenty of water and fuel and are spending the nights in safe places.

Unfortunately, officials in these out-of-the-way places, tend to be the "bad boys" of their profession. Forced to live in inhospitable places, they are usually very bored and often turn to drink and drugs. When a party of Westerners suddenly turns up, they see this as a chance to show their power, get their own back for the old colonial injustices, hold travellers up for a day or more, charge them baksheesh, turn on a tape recorder and insist on a dance with each of the girls and suggest they go to bed with them. If there is a hotel locally they may hold them overnight, so as to extract a percentage from the hotel keeper.

Unfortunately, your permit from central government means nothing here. These people are a law unto themselves. Some have been known to insist on visas from nationals of a country who do not require one. This often requires that you go back to the nearest capital city, where incredulous officials may, or may not, be able to sort things out.

The police in very remote areas often arrange that you cannot get fuel to move on without their permission and to get that you have to spend a lot of money with the local tourist organisation and hotel, as well as fork out *baksheesh* to the police themselves. Local officials also have a habit of taking your government permit from you and then "losing" it. This makes life difficult both there, and with local officials later on, in other areas. It is best to carry many photocopies of the original government permission, (photocopying machines are always available in capital cities) and never hand over the original. Let officials see the original if necessary, but always give them a photocopy instead.

If you are travelling as a group, most officials and most hotels will want a group list from you. Carry enough copies of a group list made up of names, passport numbers, dates of issue of passports, dates of expiry of passports, dates of issue of visas, dates of expiry of visas, numbers of visas and occupations.

Fortunately new passports no longer quote occupations; but where these are asked for, never mention the following: photographer; journalist; writer; or member of the armed forces, unless you are travelling in such a capacity officially.

Photography Permits

Some countries, e.g. Sudan, Mali, Cameroon, require that you obtain a photography permit. These are usually only available in the capital, so overland travellers will have problems, until they can get to the capital and obtain one. As with currency declarations, officials obviously like to save work by giving one permit for a group; but it is best to get one per person. I have known several instances where big-headed students have made citizen's arrests of travellers taking photographs, who then had to spend a couple of hours at the police station, waiting for their group leader with the photo permit to be located!

Possession of a photo permit does not necessarily mean that you can take photographs! It is usually best to enquire with the local police first. In some areas where photography is forbidden, local guides may goad you on to take photographs. Beware of this situation, they are likely to blackmail you for money or other gifts by threatening to inform the police.

In theory, you should be able to find out about documents and permit requirements from the consulate in your country of origin; but for Third World countries this can never be relied on, as local officials make their own rules. Information from source books such as this one, and from up to date travellers, are your best guide.

Visas

In an effort to control illegal immigrants, Western countries now often require visas from nationals of countries that did not require them a few years ago. In a tit-for-tat response, these countries now require visas from the nationals of Western countries and often charge extortionate prices to issue them in the West. These charges often cause the numbers of tourist visitors to collapse so after a while they are lowered. Where such visas can be obtained at local airports, borders or Consulates in neighbouring countries they may be cheaper.

Before issuing visas, most countries will require at least two clear pages left in your passport and the passport to be valid for at least six months after your date of entry into the country concerned. Some countries will also require proof that you have suitable funds available and a return or onward, air ticket. Some even require onward air tickets for overland travellers. You may also require a letter of introduction from your own government, or a sponsor if on business or working.

If you are travelling overland or on an extended continuous journey, visas for later destinations may become out of date before you reach those destinations. So enquire whether or not you can get such visas, while en route.

Some Gulf countries require a certificate of "no objection". Some Third World countries may hold your passport for six weeks or more, while searching their archives for any previous records on applicants, before issuing a visa. If you have to travel somewhere else during this period, UK citizens can obtain a temporary second passport. NEVER carry both passports on the same journey!

Visas for some countries, e.g. ex-French or Belgian Colonies, may not be obtainable in the UK: it is cheaper to have visa services get these for you than to go to Paris or Brussels yourself.

Many countries still refuse to issue visas to anyone whose passport contains Israeli stamps. If you visit this country, ask the immigration officials not to stamp your passport. If your passport does contain Israeli stamps, get a new passport as soon as possible.

If for some reason you have to obtain a new passport while you are away, if your current passport contains an active visa this will have to be retained and either the current passport extended or the older passport attached to the new one. If you have the right of residence in the UK, make sure that this is clearly stated in any replacement passport.

Business passports, with their larger number of pages, can cause problems in the Third World. If you have had many visas for the same country, local immigration officers may start questioning you as to why you keep coming back.

For the Third World the standard size passport is preferable and the new type EC passport is smaller and more convenient to carry under clothing, for safety.

Do as much organisation as you can before you leave home. Carry plenty of passport size photographs and be prepared for delays, harassment, palms held out and large doses of the unexpected.

Warning

Be especially careful of crossing borders with anyone that you do not know well because if that person has a previous record or is carrying banned substances, you could also be arrested. Likewise NEVER take another person's belongings across a border.

For Working Restrictions see p.839 of the Directory

MONEY PROBLEMS — THE ILLEGAL SIDE
by Jack Jackson

It used to be common for dealers on black markets in Third World countries to offer money at three or more times the official rate. Nowadays however, most such countries have black market rates of only 10-20 per cent higher than the normal rate. Buyers should always weigh up the risk before dealing, remembering that in black market operations the traveller, just as easily as the dealer, can end up in prison.

In countries recently ravaged by war or coup d'état, black markets usually continue to thrive at good rates.

Dollar Mania

Black markets usually operate best in ports; where money can be easily smuggled out and goods back in and where, with the help of baksheesh to customs officers, nobody in government pay needs to know, or admit to knowing. However, a quasi black market is operated by expatriate technicians working in oil fields or international aid or construction programmes. Paid part of their salary in local currency, usually more than they need to live on, they are keen to get rid of some of it in exchange for US dollars, at a good rate to the buyer.

In much of Islamic Africa and the poorer Middle Eastern countries you will also find Egyptian, Sudanese, Syrian, or Palestinian teachers, employed in smaller villages, who are very keen to convert their local salary into US dollars.

Another method of dealing, common in countries where businessmen do not feel safe and cannot get their money out legally, is for businessmen or hotel owners to "lend" you funds locally, which you repay in hard currency into a relative's bank account in the West. Those who travel regularly often arrange this in advance before departure; but local businessmen will take a risk on unfamiliar travellers, if they are reasonably dressed and staying in recognised smaller hotels, because their own local currency is worthless to them.

Even in large top-quality hotels, cashiers will often take payment in hard currency at near black market rates, if the customer pays them outside of the manager's normal working hours.

Travellers should particularly avoid street dealings, as they are more likely to be short-changed, given bad notes, caught in a police "sting" operation, or robbed.

On-the-spot black market deals nowadays are always for cash and mostly for US dollars. A few countries with strong links and trade with the UK or Germany will trade in pounds sterling or Deutschmarks, but other currencies, even strong ones such as the Swiss franc or Dutch Guilder, will find few black market buyers. Deutschmarks go down well in Turkey, pounds sterling in Pakistan, India and Nepal, but elsewhere the US dollar is the prime requirement.

Normally, larger denomination notes fetch a higher rate, as they are easier to smuggle out. Avoid the older one hundred dollar bills which do not have "In God We Trust" written on them: even though they may not be forgeries, most dealers will not touch them. Also avoid English £50 notes, which may be unknown to smaller dealers.

There is no longer any problem attached to taking money out of the UK, so it is best to buy US dollars there before you leave. The old tricks with sterling travellers' cheques are no longer required!

Even for normal legal transactions many countries now insist on clean unmarked notes.

Declaration Forms

Many countries with black market problems insist on a declaration of all money and valuables on entry and check this against bank receipts on exit. Remember that you may be searched, both on entry and exit and any excess funds will be confiscated.

If you want to take in some undeclared money to use on the black market, you should understand the risks. Obviously you must change a reasonable amount of money legally at a bank and keep receipts, so that you will be able to explain what you have lived on, during your stay. You will also need these receipts if you are trying to change local currency back into hard currency, when you leave. It is usually inadvisable to try, since most countries make it very difficult for you to do this, despite their literature claiming that you can.

Local officials, who probably don't read the literature, like to remove your excess local money and keep it for themselves. The bank clerk who tells you he cannot change your money back is often in on the act. He informs the custom officials how much money you have and they, acting on his tip-off, search you as you leave.

On the plus side, allowing customs or money declaration officials to remove a reasonable amount of money from you at the point of departure often minimises further red tape.

Currency declaration forms are taken very seriously in some countries and you must have an explanation for any discrepancy. Make sure that the amount written agrees with the amount in figures. If any money which is entered on your form is stolen, get a letter giving details from the police, or you may have trouble when you wish to leave the country.

Some countries get around some of the black market by making you pay for hotels in hard currency, at the official rate.

In such hotels you can usually get away with paying for meals with black market cash, so long as you pay for it at the time. If you sign a restaurant bill to be paid for later, then you will be charged in hard currency. Corrupt hotel staff may refuse to accept cash payment in the restaurant, in which case you will be better off taking your custom to restaurants outside the hotel.

International airline tickets will always be charged for in hard currency, plus a premium ordered by IATA, to cover currency fluctuations. Hence, such tickets are much cheaper bought in Europe. Internal air tickets can usually be bought with black money, but you may have to pay a local ticketing agent to do it in his name.

Beware of black market currency quotations by normally acceptable press, such as Broadsheet Sunday papers, Newsweek and the BBC. These quote from local correspondents who have to be careful what they say.

Street Trading

Black market dealers are usually found where budget travellers are most likely to be, e.g., smaller hotels, bars and shops selling tourist items; in very small towns try the pharmacy.

In the main streets of a city or port, street traders will chase you and, assuming that you do not know the correct rate, will start with a very low rate. It is usually worth bargaining to see how high a rate you can get, then approach safer places, such as small hotels, to check the real rate. Street trading is very risky: you should never show that you have a lot of money. There is a high chance that you will be short-changed, given notes that are no longer legal tender, have money stolen from the bundle by sleight of hand, see all your money grabbed and run off with, or meet one of those dealers who has a crooked, profit-sharing partnership with the police.

In general, show only the amount of money you want to exchange and keep all other money out of sight, beneath your clothes.

Refuse any approaches to buy your passport or traveller's cheques. This kind of trading has become so common that many embassies delay issuing fresh passports to travellers who, may or may not, have genuinely lost their own. Getting traveller's cheques replaced in the third world, can take months, as can funds wired to banks or American Express offices. Never rely on receiving hard currency transferred in this way, you are likely to be forced to accept local currency.

Black market rates fluctuate with both inflation and availability. Rates will increase dramatically in the Islamic world, when the time for the annual pilgrimage to Mecca (the Hajj) approaches, and decreases rapidly when the pilgrims return, or when a lot of "up-market" travellers are in town, or a cruise ship or fleet ship is in port. Dealing out of season usually commands a better rate.

Central London banks often carry an excess of Third World currency and one of their branches may be happy to off-load a weak currency at a good rate. It is always worth checking whether this is so, before you buy; but remember that the bank notes may no longer be legal currency.

Wherever you are, always check that you have not been short-changed. Bank cashiers try this on regularly, in the Third World. Many people end up changing on the black market, just because it can take up to two hours to change money legally, in some countries.

Currently, like in the Balkans, the black markets of eastern European states and the Commonwealth of Independent States are strong. Many of them are technically bankrupt, have rampant inflation, pay their employees with unredeemable money and are changing their currencies. So you must be careful not to be given out of date banknotes. In Uzbekistan, when I legally changed US $4, I was given a wad of newly printed "Monopoly Money" 100 cm thick.

The best way to travel in countries like this, or those with high rates of inflation, is to carry a large number of small denomination US dollar bills, change a little at a time as you go along and where possible, pay for everything in US dollars, so that you do not collect worthless change. UK banks do not like holding US $1 bills, so give them plenty of warning when ordering currency and stipulate clean, unmarked notes.

Beggars

Begging is probably the world's second oldest profession. In the Muslim and Hindu world, giving a percentage of one's income to the poor is considered a legal form of paying tax. However, with the increase of mass up-market tourism, begging is becoming an increasingly popular way of making a living, not only among the obviously poor people of the Third World, but also among Western hippies and some better dressed, professional confidence tricksters, who claim to be refugees. This form of begging is now common on the London Underground.

In some countries beggars are very persistent, knowing full well that wearing you down produces results. Mere persistence may not be too hard for you to repel, but worst of all are the young children, often blind or with deformed limbs, who are guaranteed to arouse your pity.

What you may not realise, however, is that the child may have been intentionally deformed or blinded by its parents or "master", in order to make a successful beggar. The child is almost certainly encouraged by his family or ringleader to beg and may be the chief source of their income, since the child beggar can perhaps earn more in a day, than his father working in the fields or factory. Remember that a child who is out begging is necessarily missing school.

An adult with no education or experience, other than begging, tends to be less successful than a child beggar. What are his options? Crime, if he is fit, destitution if crippled. Begging is obviously easier than work, but to give money is to contribute to a vicious circle. By withholding money, you may indeed be helping to eradicate these appalling practices.

MONEY PROBLEMS — THE LEGAL SIDE
by Harry Stevens and Melissa Shales

I belong to that generation whose first real experience of foreign travel was courtesy of HMG – when European towns were teeming with black marketeers trying to prove to every young serviceman that 200 British cigarettes were really worth 200 or even 300DM. Travellers' cheques and banks hardly existed and credit cards, like ballpoint pens, had not yet been invented. Consequently, my trust in ready cash as the essential ingredient for trouble-free travelling is no doubt due to this early conditioning.

Cash is, of course, intrinsically less safe to carry than traveller's cheques, especially when these are fully refundable when lost (this is not always the case, particularly if a "finder" has cashed them in before the loss has been reported).

Nowadays, I carry all three: traveller's cheques, credit cards, and cash; but only a slim book of traveller's cheques, which I hold in reserve in case I do run out of cash – and for use in countries which do not allow you to bring in banknotes of their own currency. If travelling in Europe, it is also worth applying for a Eurocheque book and card which allows you to write cheques on the continent as you would at home. This could mean that you don't have to go to the trouble of getting foreign exchange before departure – particularly convenient for short trips. However, the cash I carry always includes a few low denomination dollar bills useful for "emergency" tips, or taxi fares in almost any country.

Small Change
There are a number of cogent reasons for equipping yourself with the currency of the country you are about to visit before you get there:

1. Even on the 'plane you may find you can make agreeable savings by paying in some currency other than sterling.

2. Immediately on arrival it may be difficult, or even impossible to change your money and in any case, you may be doubtful as to whether you are being offered a good rate of exchange.

3. Yes, the immediate problem of tipping a porter, making a phone call and paying for a taxi or airport bus must be solved long before reaching your hotel. And when you do eventually get there, this does not necessarily solve your problem as not all hotels exchange traveller's cheques for cash (and not necessarily at any time of day or night) and if they do, the vexed question of the rate of exchange arises once more.

Many countries do not allow unrestricted import or export of their currency – and in a number of countries for "unrestricted" read "nil"! – so one has to exchange traveller's cheques or hard cash on arrival (there is usually a small exchange rate advantage in favour of the cheques). In addition, if you plan to visit several countries, it is usually best not to keep bank notes of a currency no longer required on that journey (although I do hold on to small change and some low denomination notes, if there is a likelihood of a next time). Every such exchange results in a loss but the sums involved are usually not large and one can console oneself with the thought that the next taxi ride will help to recoup it. Remember to keep a record of all financial transactions, particularly in sensitive countries, as you may well be asked to account for everything before you are allowed to leave.

Nest Eggs

If you are planning to be away for a long time, and possibly travel through many countries, there is one other way to ensure that you don't have to carry too much with you and risk losing it all in some remote village. Before you leave home, set up a number of accounts along the way through banks affiliated to your own and arrange for money to be wired over to you at regular intervals. Ask the foreign section of your bank to advise you on the best way of doing this.

It is a simple-sounding operation, but as with most aspects of travel, reality is infinitely more complex, each transaction taking weeks longer than claimed and your money being misplaced en route or misfiled on arrival. The bureaucracy alone could make the whole exercise too difficult to be worthwhile, never mind the fact that you are having to place an immense amount of trust in bank staff who may be corrupt. It is probably not worthwhile unless you are planning to spend some considerable time in the country. Whatever you decide to do, don't rely on having money waiting for you – keep an emergency fund for survival while you are trying to wring your money out of them.

Even if you haven't set up accounts along the way, ask your bank for a list of affiliated banks in the countries you will be visiting. In an emergency, you can ask for money to be wired out from home to any bank, but if you can choose one that is already in contact, it should make life considerably easier. Always ask for a separate letter, telex or fax confirming that the money has been sent and specify that it should be sent to SWIFT (express).

Be careful not to wire more money than you will need into countries with tight export restrictions. No one will mind the sterling coming in, but they may well object to it leaving again, and if not careful you could find yourself with a nest egg gathering dust in a country you are never likely to visit again.

For Currency Restrictions see p.832 of the Directory ∎

A PLACE TO STAY
Chapter 9

CHOOSING THE RIGHT HOTEL

by Susan Grossman

In the old days a bed for the night used to be all a traveller would expect when he booked into a hostelry. These days most would be horrified if they weren't also offered a mini bar and satellite TV, let alone somewhere to park the car and a restaurant serving decent food. Of course, hotels vary the world over and most travellers know exactly what they want and shop around until they find it.

City Hotels

Not surprisingly, city hotels are often different from those in rural areas and holiday resorts. Given the choice, most people generally want their hotel to be within walking distance of the main sites. Since cities are noisy places, they also usually want a quiet room or at least one that is double glazed. If you haven't booked, most European cities have a tourist office that will help locate hotels with a vacancy.

Some will make a booking for you and there is usually an office in the main railway station or at the airport, though it is best to get the address from the national tourist board in London before you set off, and have enough local currency on you to pay for the phone call or booking fee that the office may charge.

Don't judge a hotel by its star rating. Every country has a different hotel rating system, so a two-star hotel in France, for example, will bear little resemblance to a similarly accredited hotel in Eastern Europe. Extra stars don't necessarily mean extra comfort either; they may simply refer to whether the hotel has a lounge, or whether you can get a cup of tea at 3am, something which may not be important to you at all.

Cheap hotels in cities tend to be near railway stations or have some other disadvantage, like being by the port or in the heart of the red light district. If you don't fancy climbing upstairs to get to your room at the top, check if the hotel has a lift; smaller hotels often don't. City hotels often don't have dining rooms, which is not necessarily a disadvantage since it is often not only cheaper but a distinct advantage to take breakfast and indeed other meals at a neighbouring cafe. In Italy, for example, a cup of *espresso* and a doughnut from a small *pasticeria* round the corner can be a much more attractive way in which to start the day than the stale coffee and plastic toast and jam on offer in the hotel dining room.

En Route

If you are driving abroad, either as a complete holiday or en route to your destination, you may well need a hotel as a stopover or a break from driving. The later in the day you leave it, the less chance you have of finding one when you want it. In towns, it is worth parking the car and walking up back streets to find a hotel, rather than relying on those on the main through routes. If you can't get into a hotel in the town of your choice, the receptionist at a hotel belonging to a chain may phone ahead for you.

In France, the en suite facilities may confuse you. The French tend to find bidets more important than toilets, which may well be down the corridor rather than in the bedroom. Towels are often wafer-thin, even in the best establishments, but certainly in the cheaper ones; it is also best to take your own soap.

Hotels Outside Europe

British travellers are often surprised at the different style of hotels world-wide, particularly those in hot climates. Hotels in the Caribbean, for example, rarely exceed three stories and accommodation is often low-lying, simple bungalows scattered in the grounds. The central area housing the sitting area and dining room may well have a roof that is open to the elements, attracting a variety of flying visitors when the lights go on in the evening. It is often important to ask whether there are mosquito nets over the windows or nets over the beds, and air conditioning certainly adds to the comfort as well as keeping insects out.

Double Beds

In the States you won't have any problem getting a double bed, you'll probably get two. On the Continent, in holiday resorts, they're pretty hard to find. It is worth looking up the word in the dictionary if you want to ask for a double bed when you book in – in Italy, for example, it is called a *lit matrimoniale*.

The Guidebooks

Hotel guidebooks, on the whole, make confusing reading. But what most readers do not appreciate is that around two-thirds of all guidebooks only include hotels that pay to be there. The ratings vary too. All sorts of intriguing and often contradictory criteria are taken into account in the overall rating, from the provision of shoe-cleaning facilities to whether the hotel can provide a cooked breakfast in bed. Some hotel guidebooks have a confusing array of symbols from which you have to pick out the facility you find most important. In England there is no statutory registration scheme and no "official" grading system. In France, all hotels have to be registered with their local *Prefecture*. If they want to be graded, it costs them nothing, but hefty increases in VAT, for higher rated hotels have meant that a large number of French four–star hotels have asked to be downgraded to three!

Hotel Chains

Hotels that belong to chains aren't all bad, but some are dreadful. The worst are owned by anonymous corporations who install piped musak, patterned carpets, plastic flowers and disinterested staff, and fill their bedrooms with disillusioned travelling businessmen. In these hotels, if you want tea, you have to make it yourself from a little kettle and sachets in the room, if you want your shoes cleaned another sachet will provide the polish. Some hotel chains are, of course, better than others, but hotels that are expensive are not necessarily any better than those that are not.

Family-owned and Run

Fewer hotels these days are family-owned and run, though in the Mediterranean you may find five generations of the same family in a typical Italian *pensione*. In Britain, many top country house hotels are family-owned and run. These properties, often inherited, would otherwise have gone to the tax man, and have been kept on as private hotels.

British Country House Hotels

In Britain country house hotels are spending thousands and often millions of pounds on adding leisure centres and sports facilities. Often open to non-residents as well as to residents of the hotel, these facilities are usually free to guests. As well as a swimming pool, many have well-equipped gymnasiums with instructors prepared to assess fitness or programme a specific range of exercises.

There are usually saunas and steam rooms too. In addition, the more up-to-date leisure centres come with a whole range of staff ready to massage and wax legs as well as offer a variety of alternative therapies from aromatherapy to reflexology. Hotels with these leisure centres need not be expensive as use of the facilities is usually free to guests (though individual treatments are often extra). Special low-cost weekend breaks are also worth enquiring about.

Travelling with Children

If you've got young children, the important criteria are the same the world over. Nevertheless, on the Continent they take a lot more kindly to young children than they do in Britain – thinking nothing of putting an extra bed into your room, providing small portions at meal times and having someone on hand willing to baby-sit.

In Britain, hoteliers generally take a dim view of children and are often keener on dogs. A significant number ban children altogether, something completely unheard of abroad. Some hotels ban children from the dining room or insist that they eat earlier than adult guests. What many fail to understand is that the average toddler does not take kindly to being left alone in a hotel bedroom while you go down to dinner.

Some hotels allow children (up to sixteen years old in some cases) to share your room for nothing. The large hotels chains, like Forte, often adopt this policy. However, this is not always as beneficial as it might sound. The bedroom in which the hotel is prepared to put another bed may be so small that you find yourselves leap-frogging over each other down to breakfast.

If you are looking for a suitable hotel for a young family, it is worth finding out a number of things before you make a booking. If you need a cot for a young baby, for example, bear in mind that on the Continent they may not have the same standards as we have in Britain. Cots provided by overseas hotels are often too dangerous to put the baby in. It is worth checking whether the gaps in the bars are too wide, or whether your healthy bouncing baby will end up in a heap on the floor.

And Finally...

The worst hotel experiences usually occur when you have arrived too late in the day to make a choice and you end up staying somewhere ghastly. As George Bernard Shaw said: "The great advantage of a hotel is that it's a refuge from home life." Sometimes home life can be infinitely more desirable.

SELF–CATERING

by Caroline Brandenburger

Self-catering need not be the chain and ball round the ankle that some might imagine. It is a particularly good idea if you're travelling with children, and it can act as a base where you only occasionally use the kitchen. You can come and go as you like, without incurring the wrath of the management, spend as much or as little time there as you want – and it can be fairly cheap.

Another advantage is the enormous range of accommodation to choose from – villa, castle, flat, log cabin, house boat – in all parts of the world. In Britain you can stay in anything from a National Trust thatched cottage set deep in a forest to a stone pineapple folly, the wing of a stately home or a seaside bungalow. In France it might be a chateau, in Italy a Tuscan farmhouse and in Spain try a villa equipped with its own private swimming pool.

Not surprisingly, the price and value for money varies enormously. Your holiday home can be private and secluded or part of a large complex of identical properties. If it's the former, you'll probably need a car, just so you can get to the nearest shops, restaurant, pub or beach. If it's the latter, there may be facilities on site, a swimming pool, a tennis court, launderette – even discos and restaurants in particularly organized self-catering complexes.

Another thing to think about if you're planning to self-cater abroad, is that food prices may be higher than you're used to, in which case you should account for this in your budget. Thomas Cook recently conducted a survey of comparative food prices in different countries, and found that, for example, eggs were more expensive in Corfu than in Britain, and tea was more than double British prices in Portugal. Wine, however, was cheaper everywhere! Nevertheless, it is worth remembering that one of the great pleasures of being abroad is buying in local markets, browsing in intriguing food shops, and sampling the different fare.

How you equip yourself is dependent on each individual property. Many are privately owned so there are no hard and fast rules, but often linen will be provided, and sometimes even microwaves, dishwashers, high chairs, cots and board games for rainy days. If the brochure is not clear and you have particular requirements, then check before you go. Don't risk spoiling your enjoyment by being bereft of that vital garlic crusher or clock radio.

To find out how you can book self-catering accommodation, both here and abroad, get in touch with the appropriate Tourist Board. If they don't actually have lists of companies operating in this field, they should certainly be able to point you in the right direction. The big shipping companies such as P&O, Sealink and Brittany Ferries offer self-catering packages, and a decent travel agent should know exactly what's available.

One of the most commonly-used sources of self-catering accommodation is private advertisements in the classified sections of national and local newspapers and magazines. If you are booking through a private individual, it is even more important that you find out exactly what facilities are on offer – both at the property and in the vicinity – and that you are very clear about terms and conditions relating to utility costs and damage.

What to Find out Before you Book

1. Accommodation: number and type of bedrooms, beds, bathrooms, living areas; cooking facilities, garage, heating, bed linen, cots.
2. How far is the property from the nearest shops, restaurants, bars, town or village? If you are in an isolated area with limited shopping facilities, prices are likely to be high.
3. How far from the beach, recreational facilities for adults and/or children, places of interest? It's all very well finding yourself an idyllically secluded cottage if you are after seclusion, but a disaster if you have teenage children chafing at the bit for the company of their peers.
4. Hazards for young children: an unfenced garden? An unattended pool or nearby pond or river, main road?
5. Hidden extras: are utilities included in the cost, is the electricity run on a metre, how is this measured, is there a deposit, what are the conditions under which you lose this deposit?
6. Is the property serviced by maids, cooks or baby-sitters?

What to Take

Trial and error has taught most of us what to take on a self-catering holiday and our shopping list will also depend on the destination – you are hardly likely to take your favourite wine to France, but you might pop a jar of Branston Pickle in your suitcase. Nevertheless, we usually manage to forget some vital article.

Even if you do arrive with some vital implement missing, the best advice is to try not to get too worked up about it. After all, this is a holiday, and the intention is not to try and transpose all your domestic habits to the Dordogne. A self-catering holiday will not necessarily offer a restful break (someone has to do the washing-up) but it can offer the privacy and flexibility which, even with the best will in the world, is sometimes lacking in a hotel holiday.

For a list of agencies that deal with self-catering see p.846 of the Directory

TIMESHARE AND HOME EXCHANGE

by Michael Furnell and Diana Hanks

The majority of people believe that timesharing is something new which has only developed over the last fifteen years or so, but in fact it is not really a new concept because as far back as the last century, villagers were time-sharing water in Cyprus where there was no piped supply.

Property timeshare is believed to have been initiated in the 1960s when certain French developers of ski apartments experienced difficulties in selling their leisure accommodation outright and decided to offer for sale the ownership of weekly or fortnightly segments at the same time each year for ever.

The idea spread to other parts of Europe, including Spain. On the Costa Blanca a British company, which was building apartments in Calpe, offered co-ownership of two-bedroomed flats in the main shopping street near the sea. Prices were as little as £250 per week's usage in the summer in perpetuity. Winter periods were even cheaper at £180 for a month, and easy terms were available on the payment of a £50 deposit with the balance payable at £4.50 per month over three years.

The Americans soon recognized this form of holiday home ownership and in the early stages converted condominiums, motels and hotels – unviable in their original form – into time-share units. Often these had rather basic facilities and it is only in recent years that developers in Florida and elsewhere have realized that top-quality homes with luxury facilities are the key to successful multi-ownership.

It was not until 1976 that timesharing was launched in Britain. The first site was in a beautiful loch-side location in the Highlands of Scotland. This was a luxury development with excellent sporting facilities and prices were set from about £5000 per week.

How it Works

The aim of timesharing is to provide luxury quality accomodation for which a once-only capital sum is paid at today's prices. Future holidays are secure without the need for hotel bills or holiday rents – just an annual sum to cover maintenance expenses and local taxes.

Timeshare is sold by several different methods at prices from as little as £2500 (low season, studio) to £22,000 and over (peak season, three bedrooms, highest quality resort) for deluxe accommodation and on-site leisure facilities.

About 920,000 European families owned timeshare in 1996. There are now over 1,410 European resorts (4,500 world-wide), over 3.5 million owners world-wide and at least 108 resorts in the UK itself. In Europe some 920,000 families are timeshare owners, of which about 317,000 live in the UK.

When a freehold is purchased, as in Scotland, the period of time which you buy is yours to use "forever", and you may let, sell, assign or leave the property to your heirs in your will. In England and Wales, the law only permits ownership for a maximum of 80 years, but in many other parts of the world, ownership in "perpetuity" is possible.

An alternative is membership of a club which grants the right to a club member to use specified accommodation in a specified property for either specified weeks in the timeshare calendar, or "floating time" in the high/medium/low season time band (choosing which weeks annually for a stated number of years is an alternative scheme). Hence the assets of the property, i.e. buildings, lands and facilities are conveyed (or leased) to custodian trustees, (often a bank or other institution) which holds the property for the benefit of the club members. The rights of all owners collectively are regulated by the Club Constitution. This legal structure works well in the UK and, with modifications, in developments overseas.

A third alternative is to buy "Points" in a timeshare club, giving you considerable flexibility to take, for example, two short breaks of less than a week's duration rather than owning a specified week or weeks in a specified timeshare resort.

The formation of a public limited company with the issue of ordinary shares which vary in price according to the season chosen for occupation and apartment size is another form of holiday ownership, although not strictly timeshare. Each share provides one week's occupancy for a set number of years, usually 20 or 25 years. The properties are then sold in the open market and the proceeds divided among the shareholders.

One company uses capital contributed by participants to purchase land and build holiday homes in various parts of Europe. Each member is entitled to holiday points which can be used for a vacation of a week or more in a chosen development at any time of year.

Another provides for the sums paid by participants to be converted into a single-premium insurance policy. Part of that premium is invested in fixed-interest securities and another portion is used to acquire properties (over 400 in about twenty locations). "Bondholders" pay a user charge to cover the maintenance cost of the property for each week's holiday taken, and are given a "points per week" basis depending on the accommodation's size, location and season chosen. Investors are permitted to encash their bonds (whose price is quoted daily in the financial press) at any time after two years. A capital sum is repaid upon death of the bondholder – the amount determined by the age at which the holder took out the insurance policy. Such bond schemes are subject to legal regulations which are not applicable to the timeshare concept.

Golden Rules

The Golden Rules to be remembered when buying a timeshare home are:

1. Purchase from a well established developer or selling agent who already has a reputation for fair dealing and offering really successful schemes.
2. The location of the property is vital, so be sure to select a well-situated development with adequate facilities and a quality atmosphere. Be sure that it appeals to the family as well as yourself so that you are all able to enjoy regular visits. If you are likely to want to resell in the future, the location will prove even more important.
3. Remember that the UK Timeshare Act 1992 and the Timeshare Regulations of 29th April 1997 provide for simply a fourteen day cooling off period for those who are in the UK when they sign a purchase agreement (the actual loca-

tion of the timeshare resort is irrelevant). The Regulations also ban the company concerned from taking any deposit from you within those fourteen days. However, the EU directive on timeshare which came into force in the Member States on 29 April 1997 provides for a minimum ten day cooling off period rather than fourteen days and some member states are allowing deposits to be taken by third parties (for example a trustee/escrow account). Some EEA Member States are behind schedule with introducing their national legislation to take account of the Directive so care needs to be taken that no assumptions are made that you will necessarily be granted the cooling off period until late 1997, when it is expected that even those furthest behind with implementation will have the relevant laws in place.

4. Check carefully the annual maintenance costs and be sure you know what they cover. Part of the yearly charges should be accumulated in a sinking fund by the management company to cover replacements, new furnishings and regular major redecorations.

5. If all the amenities promised by the sales staff are not already in existence, get a written commitment from the vendors that they will be completed, and when.

6. Ascertain the rights of owners if the builder or management company gets into financial difficulties, and ascertain if it is possible for the owners to appoint a new management company if they are not satisfied with the service of the original one. The *Constitution* and the *Management Agreement* are the two documents to show to a specialist lawyer to determine that title is safeguarded and occupation rights protected.

7. Find out about the timeshare concept and the wide variety of resorts available in Europe by reading up on the subject. Compare resorts to find the most suitable. Is it one of the two exchange networks, RCI or Interval International? Find out if the vendor owns the property, and if they do not, discover who holds the freehold and if there is any mortgage on the property. Before signing any documents check if a "cooling off" period (in which one can have a change of mind) is written into the purchase agreement: (see Point 3 above). A solicitor can check the wording of agreements relatively easily, but it will be a considerably greater task – and thus more expensive – to consider the occupation rights granted, the nature of the developer's title, details of any mortgages or encumbrances on the timeshare property, the granting of correct local planning permission, the legal structure of the scheme in the context of that country's property laws, the effects of jurisdiction, the safeguards for monies paid for an unbuilt or incomplete property and the arrangements at the termination of the period of lease.

8. Talk to an existing owner wherever possible before purchasing.

9. The experts believe that any timeshare scheme should have a minimum of ten units to be viable. If it is too small, amenities may be lacking and each owner's share of management costs may be excessive.

10. Are payments held in trust pending the issue of title documents, or a licence to use, and has a trustee been appointed to hold the master title deeds?

11. A solicitor should scrutinize the documentation and perform independent checks regarding payments held in trust pending the issue of title documents, club membership certificates and a licence to use. Is the Trustee reputable?

12. If you wish to have the flexibility to swap world-wide, the timeshare resort should be affiliated to one of the two international exchange resorts, Resort Condominiums International (RCI) or Interval International, its smaller competitor. Check any claim to affiliation.

Investment

Timesharing is not a conventional money-making investment in property, although some owners who purchased time in the earliest schemes have enjoyed substantial capital appreciation over the past ten years. Essentially, you are investing in leisure and pleasure but you cannot expect inflation-proof holidays. What you are buying is vacation accommodation at today's prices. Expenditure on travel, food and entertainment is still likely to rise in future years according to the rise of inflation.

Exchange Facilities

It was recognized long ago that after a few years, many timeshare owners may want a change of scene for annual holidays, and as a result, organisations were established to arrange exchange facilities for timesharing owners. There are exciting possibilities for owners wanting to swap their seaside apartment in, say, England's West Country, for a contemporary-style bungalow in Florida or an Andalucian *pueblo* in Spain. Today there are two major exchange organisations operating in the UK and between them they offer an immense variety of timeshare accommodation in many holiday destinations. Both had their origins in America and now have their offices in England.

RCI, the largest established exchange organisation, had 1.7 million timeshare owners registered on its exchange system at the close of 1993, and 2,600 resorts available in 70 countries world-wide. Interval International had about 500,00 members registered and over 1,200 resorts offered.

There is normally an annual membership fee payable by each family wishing to join the exchange system. The developer usually pays this for each family for the first two or three years as a purchase inducement. In addition, a modest fee (£61) is due when an exchange is successfully organised.

Orderly Growth

There is a single professional timeshare trade body in the UK, Timeshare Council (23 Buckingham Gate, London SW1E 6LB, tel: 0171-821 8845). TC has been set up to represent all legitimate interests in the industry including developers, marketers, resale companies, trustees, finance houses and exchange organisations, with an independent Executive Chairman. It also aims to monitor consumer protection issues, and the orderly growth of the industry. It gives free advice to customers of its members, and makes a small charge for conciliation where customers of non-member resorts are concerned. TC has Rules and Codes for the various classes of membership. It has lobbied the European Parliament for sensible pan-European controls to be exercised, which has culminated in the EU Timeshare Directive which came into force on 29 April 1997 providing for a minimum ten day cooling off period for all timeshare purchasers in the EEA.

An encouraging aspect for the future well-being of the timeshare industry is the active participation of well-known building firms who all have their own developments in the UK, Spain or Portugal, lending respectability to an area renowned for its appalling press and dubious operators.

In an attempt to educate the public to buy timeshare wisely, to avoid commitment without prior checks through the Trade Body or professional advisers, the UK Department of Trade and Industry has now up-dated its leaflet for prospective timeshare purchasers *The Timeshare Guide*. The new leaflet is available from the DTI or Citizen's Advice Bureaux.

Home Exchange

Many British home owners fancy the idea of exchanging their home with another family in Europe or elsewhere for a fortnight or a month, in order to enjoy a "free" holiday (apart from transport costs). Although the idea is attractive, there are many problems to be overcome unless you arrange the swap with friends. A number of relatively small organisations have been established to arrange holiday home exchanges, but few of them have been successful. A new American publication, *The Vacation Home Exchange and Hospitality Guide* (£8.95 plus £1 postage, ASAP Publications, Prospect House, Downley Road, Downley Common, High Wycombe, Bucks HP13 5XQ), is a helpful introduction to home exchange and the various organisations world-wide who can help. The Worldwide Home Exchange Club (50 Hans Crescent, London SW1X 0NA, tel: 0171-823 9937) is a subscription-based organisation which publishes directories of available properties.

Ideally, a swap should be with a like-minded family or group of a similar size, so both will feel at home, and will look after the property well. The various organisations work in two ways. Some simply publish a directory listing the property, with size, location and basic features, and leave it to the individual to make contact and iron out all the details of the arrangement. Others work more like a dating agency, visiting the property, taking down its (and your) details, together with what you are looking for, whether you are prepared to lend your car, feed cats, water plants etc. They will then cross-match you with another suitable scheme member. This obviously costs more but, from the amount of hassle saved, is probably worthwhile.

Alternatively you can advertise in a suitable publication. The journal of a university in the area you want to go to is a good idea. Academics often spend a summer attached to a foreign university, and if you're lucky there may be someone planning to come and work at whatever establishment is near you.

Whichever method you use, make sure that every eventuality has been covered and agreed in writing, that your insurance cover is full and up to date, and that neighbours or friends are primed before you leave. Put away anything you are worried about and leave detailed notes about how the washing machine works, what the rabbit eats, where the nearest transport is, and all possible numbers needed in case of an emergency. At the end of your time in someone else's home, be sure that you leave it sparkling, replace anything damaged or broken, or leave the money for them to do so, and generally behave in the way you hope they are also behaving. Some people have become hooked on home-swapping as a way of travelling, and do so at least once a year, loving the opportunity to live within a real community and meet the "natives" while away. Others, who have had more sobering experiences, swear never to try again. It is a more risky business than a normal holiday in a purpose-built hotel, but the rewards can, if you're lucky, be infinitely greater. You just have to be prepared to take the risk.

See p.849 of the Directory for useful names and addresses

ON A LIMITED BUDGET

by Pat Yale

After transport, accommodation is likely to burn the biggest hole in budget travellers' pockets. Luckily this is one area where economies can still be made. The cheapest accommodation is, of course, completely free and there's not much of it.

In a few parts of the world it's fine to sleep on the beaches. However, not only are the rules subject to unexpected change and the whim of the local police, but beach bums are deprived of necessities such as washrooms, making this an unsatisfactory way to pass more than the odd emergency night. Those with a tent may find local farmers prepared to let them use their fields and facilities but such ad hoc arrangements tend to depend on negotiating skills.

Some Indian and African Sikh temples also offer free accommodation. Don't expect luxury – one large bed may serve for any number of visitors. Nevertheless staying in a temple can be a magical experience, offering the chance to find out about the religion at the same time. Visitors must abide by prohibitions on smoking, drinking and eating on the premises, but will often be included when the post-service sweetmeats are being handed out. While there is rarely an official fee, most temples appreciate a "donation" and may keep a visitor's book indicating what is expected.

"Networking" can also result in free accommodation. Members of the Globetrotters Club (BCM Roving, London, WC1N 3XX) or of Servas (77 Elm Park Mansions, London, SW10 0AP) can sometimes stay with fellow members in other countries. Home owners can even swap their homes with others in a similar situation (see previous article).

Travellers who hitch or use public transport may also find themselves invited to stay with people they meet on the way. This can be the perfect way to find out about a place but in developing countries may mean staying in houses without running water or toilets, and where conventions, particularly concerning women, may be very different from those at home. The tradition of hospitality to strangers, especially in Muslim countries, is still strong and may mean someone going without to provide for the guest.

It pays to be aware of local customs: in some countries anything a guest admires must be given to them, in others, refusing food can cause offence. Clearly women must be especially careful about accepting offers of hospitality, particularly in Islamic countries where such offers will invariably come from men. If you think you would like to take up offers of hospitality, squeeze suitable thank-you presents into your backpack – pictures of London, British coins, malaria pills and biros often do the trick.

Organised camping is the next best option, particularly in Europe and North America where there are lots of well-equipped sites. The main snag, unless you have a vehicle, is having to carry the tent and cooking equipment. However, companies like Robert Saunders, Vango and Lichfield sell tents weighing less than three kilograms.

Camp-sites are frequently in the middle of nowhere: in developing countries you may find that by the time you've added the cost of getting to and from them to the site fee, it is cheaper to stay in a budget hotel. Staying in hostels can minimise accommodation costs while also ensuring you meet other travellers. There are more than 5000 International Youth Hostel Federation hostels and most are open to members of all ages, with priority going to younger members at busy times. Although you can usually take out temporary membership on the spot it is often cheaper to join before leaving home.

Despite their name, YMCA/YWCA hostels are not usually any more overtly religious or restrictive than other hostels. In the UK guests are still expected to work for their keep; elsewhere this custom has been quietly dropped. Many hostels now offer central heating, cooking facilities and relative privacy. However, most still close during the day, segregate the sexes and impose evening curfew. In Third World countries, some serve as long-stay accommodation for the homeless. In Europe expect noisy school parties.

If you want to stay in cheaper hotels you must normally rely on guidebooks and recommendations; travel agents and tourist offices rarely keep details of budget accommodation, although Campus Travel shops stock *Sleep Cheap* guides to popular destinations like Bangkok. If you haven't got a guidebook, the best hunting ground is likely to be near bus and railway stations (for a good night's sleep make sure you get a room at the back of the building).

In Europe the "pension" equivalents of British bed and breakfasts generally omit the breakfast. As with the more expensive hotels, some pensions are subject to tourist board inspection, ensuring reasonable standards. Travel agents usually charge for booking hotels, however cheap. Instead get the address from a telephone book in the library reference section. If possible write in the relevant language, and enclose a Post Office international reply paid coupon. If you prefer to phone but would find this difficult, British Telecom's translation service can work out cheaper than paying an agent to make your booking. To cut down communication costs, use central reservation offices for cheaper hotel chains such as Travelodge.

Finding budget accommodation in the United States can be difficult and package deals often offer excellent value. The US Tourism Administration has details of companies which can make bed and breakfast bookings. Groups of three or four people can reduce costs by sharing twin rooms which often have two double beds. Avoid unpleasant extra costs by carefully observing the latest check-out times, and never make 'phone calls from your room.

In developing countries, rooms costing only a couple of pounds a night may only be furnished with a bed and chair. Where dormitories are more popular than individual rooms, some will not accept women travellers. Even when they do, the same rooms double as children's nurseries, guaranteeing sleepless nights. Before accepting a very cheap room, check that the fan works, that the door locks properly, that the window will close and is fitted with mosquito-protection where appropriate, that there are no peep-holes in partition walls, that the walls reach right to the ceiling and that there are no tell-tale signs of bed bugs, ants or other insects. Then check the state of the toilets and the water supply (in Islamic countries the *hammams* or public baths make private baths and showers less important).

Try and pair up with someone else before booking in to avoid being charged a single supplement. Train travellers can evade accommodation costs if they're prepared to sleep sitting up in frequently crowded conditions. Within Europe you'll get a better night's sleep at a reasonable price by opting for a couchette, a sort of fold-down shelf-bed which comes much cheaper than a true sleeping berth. Bear in mind that not everyone can sleep through a train's stopping and starting and that ticket collectors often time their visits for the early hours. Outside Europe some sleeping cars offer an experience not to be missed. Nairobi to Mombasa sleepers, for example, have fold-down sinks and dining cars of near-Orient Express splendour. Their route also ensures that you wake up with the Tsavo National Park drifting past your bedroom window.

Taking a campervan or caravan with you obviously eliminates accommodation costs. However, few budget travellers can afford the initial outlay, the extra ferry fares and the high cost of petrol. Nevertheless, package deals to the United States which include a campervan offer excellent value for money.

A cautionary note on false economy. In some parts of the world, hotel prices are ludicrously low in comparison with the UK. In Udaipur (India) it's possible to stay in the usual £1-a-night pit; however, you could also stay in the fairy-tale Lake Palace Hotel, an ex-Maharajah's palace, for a fraction of what it would cost at home. Likewise in Yangon (Rangoon) you can find a cheap room or upgrade to the fading colonial Strand. With Raffles in Singapore having been resurrected in a new guise with London-style prices, it's worth snapping up the real bargains that still remain to be had.

For hostelling associations see p.849 of the Directory

HOTELS FOR BUSINESS TRAVELLERS

by Carey Ogilvie and Sue Walsh

Getting the Best Deal

The cost of accommodation and food undoubtedly eats up the biggest chunk of the business traveller's budget (some say as much as 60 per cent) and so, in these post-recession times, it should be a high priority area for most companies who send their executives abroad frequently. Seasoned business travellers have often complained about the high prices of scheduled air fares yet, paradoxically, these same people are quite willing to pay the full "rack" rate in a five star hotel, when more often than not, they could have got a much better deal for comparatively little effort. This article by no means guarantees unbeatable prices at five star hotels, but it will point you in the right direction.

Whilst airlines penalise business travellers by offering cheaper flights if you stay over a Saturday, hotels are generous to the corporate traveller, offering special rates. If you turn up at a hotel without pre-booking, you will more than likely be offered a room on the rack rate. However, if you work for a large corporation, and your company regularly sends employees to that hotel or hotel chain it is more than likely that you will have negotiated your own corporate rate. Some hotels will offer corporate rates to any bona fide business traveller, although in most cases you will have to book a number of rooms to qualify.

Travel agents, clubs and associations are able to offer corporate rates which they have negotiated on behalf of their clients. These "Corporate Rates" offer savings of between ten and fifteen per cent off the published rack tariff. The level of discount will depend on the volume of room nights the agent or company gives the hotel or hotel chain. Some hotel companies will offer agents who book a high number of clients with them a "Preferred Corporate Rate" which could represent a saving of up to 30 per cent on the rack rate. Guests staying on a preferred rate often receive added benefits as well as savings. For example, some hotels will give complimentary upgrades subject to availability at check-in. For these reasons individual business travellers and businessmen who travel to a wide variety of destinations could consider joining WEXAS travel club or Club Reserve operated by Gray Dawes Travel or IAPA (the International Airline Passengers Association). These companies negotiate discounts of between 10 per cent and 68 per cent world-wide. Such savings are greater than individual travellers or small to medium sized firms could ever hope to achieve. For example at the time of going to press WEXAS quotes a rate of £165 at the 5 star Royal Garden Hotel in London compared to the published price of £275. Visitors to Hong Kong could expect to pay HK$3050 instead of the published rate of HK$4450 at the Mandarin Oriental when booking through WEXAS.

It is worth remembering that often the best deals of all can be obtained on your behalf by the firm you are visiting. In the Gulf or Far East for example, local banks and trading houses often have financial stakes in the city's better hotels. So it is a good idea to ask them to book your room, as their influence may secure you a more competitive rate in a better room.

With budget in mind, "Off Season" rates are another option for the business traveller, whose travel is not limited to the school holidays. Many 3, 4 and 5 star hotel chains offer seasonal rates during the quieter times of year, with savings of up to 60 per cent. Some hotels will offer a flat discount and in other cases the rate will be made to look more attractive by value added benefits such as airport transfers, breakfast, free use of health club, late check-out etc. The Marco Polo Hotel group offer "Summer Saver" rates between June and September, and their packages include value-added benefits and discounts of up to 55 per cent on the regular room rates.

Some hotel companies have year round packages for individual business traveller, which they sell alongside their published and corporate rates. These package rates may not be volunteered by the hotel or the reservationist, so always ask or check with a travel agent first. Shangri-La Hotels and Resorts in the Far East, for example, currently have the "Valued Guest Programme", with benefits including a guaranteed room upgrade, round-trip limousine transfers from the airport to hotel, daily breakfast, free local calls, international calls and fax at cost, and 6pm late check-out. Inter-Continental's "Global Business Options" (which provide upgrade to suite accommodation) and Mandarin Oriental's winter and summer "Interludes" packages are also popular schemes offering value for money at present.

As with airlines, some hotels offer APEX bookings (Advance Purchase rates). Guests must be prepared to book 14 or 21 days prior to the arrival date in return for a saving of up to twenty per cent. Marriott, ITT Sheraton and Radisson SAS Hotels all offer APEX rates. Beware though, APEX bookings have very steep penalties if you amend or cancel your booking.

Which Hotel?

Location is a particularly important factor for the business traveller because invariably they will need to be near the city centre. City hotels pamper the business traveller because more businessmen and women stay in their hotels than the budget conscious tourist. However, with the gradual climb out of the recession, finding the discounted rate is harder as city hotels are running much higher occupancy levels and are therefore not as generous as they were three to five years ago.

It goes without saying that airport hotels are, on the whole, places to be avoided. They can be worthwhile, however, if you need a room for a day on a stopover, so you can have a wash and a rest, or if you need somewhere for business meetings. They are geared to short stays and odd arrival and check-out times and will be far more likely to accommodate you than the most interesting, city centre hotels. As a general hotel principle, small is beautiful. In anything under 50 rooms, more attention to detail and character are to be expected.

After location, the main factor in choosing a particular business hotel will be the facilities it offers, whether it be meeting rooms or personal computers, personalised fax machines and email in your room. Although cost is still important, more companies now in the post recession era are prepared to pay for their executive to stay in hotels with a wide range of facilities and benefits. While this is slightly more expensive, it is felt that the advantages of less stress and a more comfortable hotel stay will result in a more successful and ultimately more profitable business trip.

Another factor that has come into play in the last decade in the business executive's choice of hotel is loyalty awards. Frequent-flyer schemes were launched in the States by the major US Airlines in the early 1980's and the hotel industry inevitably followed suit. Today virtually every major hotel group has its own reward programme for frequent guests and the majority of hotel loyalty programmes have travel industry partners. For example Hyatt Hotel's loyalty programme is called Gold Passport and is linked to Alaska, Aeromexico, American, Asian Frequent Flyer, Delta, Northwest, South African Airways and USAir United airline companies, as well as Alamo, and Avis Car rental companies. These loyalty clubs have become a huge success giving the member rewards and the hotels a database of information on their guests. Marriot's Honoured Guest Rewards has 5.7 million members world-wide, Holiday Inn has 5 million world-wide, Renaissance Hotels and Resorts 1.5 million, and

Sheraton Hotel 1.2 million. Some hotel chains do not charge for joining their frequent guest programme, whilst others command a joining and annual fee. Inter Continental currently charge an enrolment fee of $100, then $25 annually thereafter. Sheraton have a current fee of $25, subject to change, while the Holiday Inn and Marriott schemes are free.

Members of the frequent-stayer schemes often receive priority booking and preferred rates and room preference is recorded. Points can be collected and redeemed for travel packages, specially selected merchandise, room upgrades, free weekend stays and even free flights. The most popular frequent-flyer scheme in the UK is the British Airways Executive Card. Air miles are awarded when members stay at the following hotels: Concorde Hotels, Hilton International, Hilton Hotels and Resorts, Hyatt Hotels and Resorts, Mandarin Oriental Hotels, Marriott Hotels and Resort, Radisson Hotels World-wide, the Ritz-Carlton Hotel Company, the Savoy Group and the Taj Group of Hotels. Therefore executives who predominantly use British Airways tend to use these hotels chains and boost their air miles.

What's in a Room?

Long gone are the days where the only amenities a business traveller would find in his or her room were a telephone and a teasmaid. Today hotels try and offer not just the home away from home but the office away from the office.

Hotels have had business centres for many years within the hotel, but more are now offering business accessories within the room itself. These can include personal computers, printers and fax machines. The Kowloon Hotel in Hong Kong has a Telecentre in each of its 736 rooms. The Telecentre is linked to the Sony TV and, like Ceefax, allows access to computerised business and leisure information including financial reports, tourist information, shopping, maps and continual updates on flight schedules. It also includes facilities such as in-house email messages, hotel bill check, video games, word processing and printouts together with personal email access and a personal fax machine.

Marriott Hotels have launched "The Room that Works" and in 1997 ITT Sheraton launched the "Smart Room" exclusively for business travellers in Europe. These guest rooms are designed not just as luxurious bedrooms but as fully functioning offices as well. Each room has a large desk, with easily accessible power outlets, a printer, fax and copier, a dual line speaker phone, and an ergonomically designed business chair as well as a large comfortable bed. Internet access can also be provided for guests.

Executive Floors

Most business hotels have an "Executive Floor" for business travellers. This is usually on the top floor of the hotel and is designed to offer privacy and a more premium service. Benefits normally include superior accommodation and additions such as private express check-in, and late check out, use of an Executive Lounge which normally offers breakfast and evening cocktails on a complimentary basis, plus complimentary use of small meeting rooms. Other advantages may include a meet and greet service at the airport, complimentary use of health facilities, express laundry and dry cleaning service. The Ritz-Carlton Millennia in Singapore presents guests staying on their Club floor with business cards printed with their name and hotel address.

Despite the rush of the average business trip and the different priorities of the business traveller, this group of travellers are in a very good position to get the most out of the hotels they use whilst away. More and more, hotels are gearing themselves towards their needs and making every effort to solicit and keep their valuable custom. The key is, of course, information, which is where the travel agent comes in, but equally, the business traveller who wishes to have value for money must be aware of the increasing amenities at his or her disposal and expect more.

For main hotel chain reservation numbers, see p.847 of the Directory
For business travel agents see p.722 of the Directory

A SAFE HOTEL STAY

by Samantha Lee and Sarah Thorowgood

One of the first recorded hotel fires took place at Kerns Hotel in Lancing, Michigan, on November 12, 1934. Thirty five people lost their lives. Just over a decade later in 1946, one of the worst fires occurred when 119 people perished – again in the States but this time in Georgia.

As recently as 1986, on New Year's Eve, 96 unfortunate souls met their maker as a result of a huge conflagration at the Hotel Dupont Plaza in Puerto Rico. After the disaster it was found that the building, upon which no expense had been spared in the luxury department, had been totally unprepared for an emergency of any description. Safety precautions were so inadequate as to be almost non-existent. The hotel had no evacuation plan and no staff training in emergency procedures. There was no smoke detection system to alert the occupant to danger, exits from the Casino were woefully sparse and the hotel boasted a number of unprotected vertical, horizontal openings.

Such a fire could never happen in Britain. Fire regulations in the UK are tight and strictly enforced but world-wide travellers would do well to remember that not all countries are quite so well-organised.

In 1989 *Which?* magazine repeated a survey into fire safety precaution in holiday hotels which they had originally carried out ten years previously. The survey revealed that little had changed in the preceding decade.

Which? reported that many hotels lacked even the most basic fire safety provisions and hoteliers displayed a frightening ignorance of, or disregard for, fire safety measures.

In Europe, Greece and Spain were singled out for particular censure with ten out of eleven hotels rated "poor"("poor" means that in a serious fire many – or all – of the hotel's occupants might not get out).

The 1977 Fire Precautions Act states that every hotel with space to sleep more than six people must have a Safety Certificate. This certificate requires that the hotel have protected escape routes, fire doors, a fire alarm system and portable fire extinguishers.

The former Trust House Forte chain made it a policy to install smoke detectors in all their hotels – both at home and abroad. As an added precaution, there is also a system whereby the Night Porter checks the hotel from top to bottom every two hours between 11pm and 7am. He carries a key which he inserts into a time clock at strategic points around the route. This "keying-in" procedure is recorded on a type which the Manager then checks the following day.

If a hotel or hotel chain has poor safety standards, some big companies such as Shell have a policy of banning them for company personnel. Wherever possible it is advisable to stay in a hotel with sound fire safety regulations but it is also important to remember that not all fires are caused by negligence. One cannot always anticipate the arsonist or indeed an incendiary bomb planted by a terrorist group. The bottom line is that like the good old Boy Scouts, it is better to take ultimate responsibility into your own hands and be prepared.

After a long and gruelling journey, searching out the nearest hotel fire exits is probably not going to be your number one priority but it should be. A few minutes "casing the joint" before you order up the G and T or slip into the pre-prandial bath, could mean the difference between life and death should the unthinkable occur.

If fire breaks out, two factors govern your chances of escape: hotel design and available fire safety equipment (extinguishers, fire doors, safety lighting, escape signs and smoke alarms).

You can't do much about hotel design at this stage but remember that smoke, rather than the fire itself, is the major killer, and that if the hotel has a large open-plan ground floor with wide unprotected stairways leading upwards, then smoke will move quickly, and easily permeate the upper reaches of the building. If there are no alternative stairways and exits from the ground floor dining rooms, bars and discos seem cramped or inadequate, you might want to lift your bags off the bed and find yourself another place to lay your weary head.

If the hotel seems to have covered these points adequately, you might move on to a few responsible measures of your own. Most people caught in a life-threatening situation for which they are not prepared will panic. With good reason, since trying to find the nearest Fire Exit when the smoke is already filtering under the door will not maximise your chances of survival. Below are a few sensible precautions which will.

On Arrival

Check the ground floor layout and identify escape routes. Read the fire emergency instructions in your room and find the fire exit, making sure that it is clear and obstruction-free (if not notify the management and complain). Walk the route counting the number of doors from your room to the exit (an aide memoire should the lighting fail or smoke obscure the view). Note the location of fire alarm call points and fire fighting equipment in the vicinity of your room. Familiarise yourself with the layout of your room and the way to the door (particularly important if you've arrived late, after a large and liberally liquid dinner). Find out what (if anything) lies outside the window and keep your valuables next to the bed for easy access. Don't smoke in bed and never ignore a fire alarm.

In Case of Fire

Report the outbreak immediately, either by phoning reception or by breaking a fire alarm. Don't attempt any fire-fighting heroics unless you are an off-duty fireman. Close the door of the room where the fire is located (to restrict the spread of flames and poisonous fumes) and use the nearest exit to leave the building but don't use the lift. Don't open any closed doors without first feeling them for heat (there may be a fire directly behind them). If your escape route is filled with smoke, keep low, on your hands and knees, where air quality and visibility will probably be better. Stay close to the wall to avoid disorientation. On leaving the hotel, report to your evacuation point so that people know you are safe and won't risk their lives unnecessarily looking for you.

If you are cut off by fire try to contact the reception and report the situation. Close the door of the room. Run the bath to soak bedding curtains, carpets etc., and block up any cracks with wet towels. Fill the wastepaper bin with water to fight any outbreak of fire in the room and go to the window to attract attention. If possible open the window to vent smoke from the room where necessary. Do not break the glass since you may have to close the window to prevent smoke from below blowing in.

Jumping from even a second floor window is not advisable and with this in mind you might like to specify in advance that you want a room on the first floor!

Security

Theft in hotels all over the world is a frequent occurence from bag snatching and pickpocketing in the lobby to full-scale theft from hotel rooms of thousands of pounds worth of jewellery. Hoteliers, not surprisingly, are reluctant to talk on the subject of security and it appears that, preferring to keep the matter quiet, they rarely take the perpetrators to court.

However, certain hotel chains are very aware of the problem and as well as installing video surveillance throughout their hotels, are training their staff accordingly. Sheraton hotels, for example, have a security policy and every staff member is trained accordingly. This highlights the importance of such things as not disclosing names and room numbers over the telephone, discretion at reception and awareness of security measures for maids whilst cleaning occupied rooms, like not leaving the door open or unblocked by a trolley.

Virginia Duncan, a travel safety consultant, recently advised readers of *Business Traveller* magazine to think of the following points when choosing their hotel:

• Do the room doors open on to a hallway or directly to the outside?
• What sort of keys system does the hotel use? Electronic card keys and metal keys with a magnetic strip are used in most western business hotels now and provide greater security as the locks can be changed after every visitor has left.
• What sort of locks do the doors have on the inside? Ideally the door should be a self-locking one with a deadbolt, peephole and security chain or bar. Also check the door frames to make sure they sturdy.
• Is there 24-hour front desk staffing?
• Never leave a room key exposed in a public place, such as on a bar table.

- Never leave valuables of any description in your hotel room. Hotel safes can generally be relied upon in western business hotels, but the same may not apply for budget hotels in many developing countries. If you must take valuables, carry them with you at all times.

As with everything, prevention is the key to good security – awareness at all times to the potential threat will make a thief's job considerably more difficult and need not make your life any harder, once it has become a force of habit.

HOSTELLING

by John Carlton, Diane Johnson and Kent Redding

Youth hostels are ideal for the budget traveller, offering an extensive network of accommodation around the world of a reasonable standard and at very affordable prices. Hostels are designed primarily for young people, but there is now no age limit and they are used by the "young at heart" of all ages. Youth hostel facilities are provided by a club run not for profit, but to help young people travel. They aim to encourage a knowledge and love of the countryside as well as an appreciation of other cultures, thereby promoting international friendship.

Each country runs its own hostels independently (usually by committees from within its membership) but the national Youth Hostel Associations of every nation are linked through the International Youth Hostel Federation. The IYHF lays down recommended standards for member associations world-wide.

Theoretically, membership of the YHA is compulsory for all travellers wishing to use the facilities, but this rule is not so stringently applied in some countries outside Europe. However, membership is worthwhile, even as a precautionary measure. In England and Wales, the annual subscription is currently £3.50 for five to seventeen-year-olds, £9.50 for eighteen and over and £19 for a family membership (two adults and all children aged under seventeen) – life membership costs £130. A similar small fee is the norm elsewhere. You can join the YHA at association offices (and sometimes at a hostel) outside your country of residence, but it usually costs more.

Facilities

As a member you can stay in any of over 5000 hostels in more than 60 countries world-wide. A youth hostel will provide a bed in a dormitory of varying size, and will normally have anything from four to 100 beds. There are toilet and washing facilities and a communal room where members can meet. In most countries, members will find facilities to cook their own food. Cooking utensils and crockery are provided, but not always cutlery. In some countries, cheap meals cooked by the warden or staff in charge are available.

One familiar feature of youth hostel life is the sheet sleeping bag – a sheet sewn into a bag with a space for a pillow. Any traveller intending to use the hostels should have one, although at some hostels there are sheets which may, or indeed, must be hired to protect the mattresses. Most hostels provide blankets and consider that these are adequately protected by the traveller's own sheet sleeping bag. In this respect, as in others, Youth Hostel customs vary from country to country.

A full list of the world's youth hostels can be obtained from information centres. Ask for the *International Handbook* (two volumes, *Europe and the Mediterranean* and *Africa, America, Asia and Australia*). As well as listing the addresses and facilities of each hostel, the handbook summarises the local regulations for age limits, youth hostel facilities for families, etc. However, all the information given is subject to correction as circumstances change during the year and, of course, prices will inevitably rise in time.

Europe

Europe (including many countries in Eastern Europe, but not Russia) is well covered by hostels and the wide variation in their characteristics reflects the local culture of each country. Hostels in the British Isles are perhaps now unique in expecting a small domestic duty from members before departure, but this does help to emphasise to members that they are part of a self-helping club. This idea is less apparent in some countries where the youth hostel is often run as a service by the local municipality (with the agreement of the National Association concerned) and relations between members and staff are strictly commercial.

The club atmosphere is also stronger in France, Holland and Greece. For "real" hostel atmosphere, try Cassis, situated in an isolated position on the hills overlooking the *calanques* of Marseilles, 30km from the city. In Germany, where the youth hostel movement started in 1909, hostels are plentiful – mostly large, well-appointed buildings, but lacking members' cooking facilities and largely devoted to school parties. Scandinavian hostels are also usually well appointed, many having family rooms, and therefore more emphasis on family hostelling.

Africa

In North Africa, there are hostels in Morocco, Tunisia, Libya, Egypt and Algeria. These too reflect the local culture. Try calling at Asne, a hostel in a Moroccan village 65km south of Marrakesh on the edge of the High Atlas mountains. Here the warden has three wives and will talk to you with great charm in French.

The Kenyan YHA has nine hostels, two of which are on the coast. One is at Malindi and another at Kanamai (about 25km north of Mombassa) in an idyllic setting amongst the coconut palms a few yards from a deserted white sandy beach. The Nairobi hostel is a meeting place for international travellers and at Nanyuki the hostel is close to one of the routes up Mount Kenya. Kitale hostel, near the Ugandan border, is part of a farm with accommodation for eight people and the one room serves as dormitory, dining and common room.

The rest of Africa is devoid of hostels until one reaches the south. At the last count, Lesotho had one hostel, Mazeru, which is well worth a visit. Local young Basutos use the property as a youth centre, so travellers have a chance to meet them.

Middle East and Asia

Israel's YHA consists of some 27 hostels – the smallest, in the heart of the old city of Jerusalem, having 70 beds. All provide meals, and many have family rooms, but the members' kitchens are poor. Orphira hostel in southern Sinai boasts superb snorkelling and diving close to hand. Syrian hostels are small and reasonably equipped and many hostellers travelling to or from India meet in Damascus. There are nineteen very well equipped hostels in Saudi Arabia, but only one or two are as yet open to women.

There is a good network in Pakistan, mostly well kept, and there are also a number of government rest houses open to hostellers, as are some schools in certain areas during school holidays. Indian hostels tend to be mainly in schools and colleges and are therefore only open for short periods of the year, although there is a large permanent hostel in Delhi. Some hostels do not provide any kind of bedding, even mattresses. Sri Lanka has several hostels including one in Kandy and one in Colombo. Here, too, government rest houses and bungalows provide alternative accommodation at a reasonable price.

The Philippines, South Korea, Malaysia and Thailand all have some hostels of which the Malaysian properties are particularly well organised. In Thailand, some hostels listed in the International Handbook appear not to exist. The two Bangkok hostels, however, certainly do. None of the six Hong Kong hostels is in the city itself. A hostel has recently been opened in New Caledonia under the auspices of the French Association.

Japan has the most extensive network of hostels outside Europe, numbering some 600. There are two kinds – Western-style with the usual bunk beds, and Japanese-style with a mattress rolled out on the floor. Television is a common feature. Several hostels are on the smaller islands of the country such as Awaji, an island in the Inland Sea. Japanese food is served in most hostels – a bowl of rice, probably served with raw egg, fish and seaweed, and eaten with chopsticks.

Australasia and America

Australia has over 100 hostels, mostly in New South Wales, Queensland and Western Australia. Distances between them are great. The smaller, more remote hostels do not have a resident warden and the key has to be collected from neighbours.

New Zealand has hostels throughout the country. They are fairly small and simple, with no meals provided, but have adequate cooking facilities. Many are in beautiful country, such as the hostel near Mount Cook.

The Canadians still give preference to those arriving on foot or by bike over motorists. They also run a number of temporary city hostels in the summer. There are not many hostels in North America, considering the size of the continent but there are a few hostels in some of the biggest cities. (In the USA, a city hostel will often turn out to be a YMCA offering rooms to YHA members at reduced rates.) The majority are found in isolated areas of scenic interest not always accessible by public transport. There are, however, chains of hostels in New England, Colorado and the Canadian Rockies. A feature of the United States hostel scene is the "Home Hostel" service where accommodation is offered to members in private houses.

In Central and South America, youth hostelling has not yet caught on seriously, although there are a few hostels in Mexico, Peru, Argentina, Chile, Brazil, Costa Rica, Uruguay and Colombia. Although in poorer countries you can find accommodation which is as cheap as the local youth hostel, members have the advantage of being able to look up an address in advance at points all over the world. They can then stay at the local branch of their own "club" finding (albeit minimal) common standards of accommodation, and be sure of meeting and exchanging experiences with fellow travellers.

See p.849 of the Directory for Hostelling Associations

CAMPING

by Anthony Smith, Jack Jackson, Melissa Shales and Martin Rosser

Travelling Light

Anthony Smith: The first real camping I ever did was on a student expedition to Persia. There I learned the principle of inessential necessities. We were travelling by truck and could therefore pile on board everything we might possibly need. The truck could transport it all and we only had the problem of sorting through the excess whenever we needed something. Later we travelled by donkey and, miraculously, the number of necessities diminished as we realised the indisputable truth that donkeys carry less than trucks. Later still, after the donkey drivers had failed to coerce higher rates of pay from very empty student pockets, we continued on foot.

Amazingly, the number of necessities decreased yet again as a bunch of humans realised they could carry far less than donkeys and much, much less than trucks. The important lesson learned was that happiness, welfare and the ability to work did not lessen one iota as the wherewithal for camping decreased in quantity. It could even have been argued that these three blessings increased as less time was spent in making and breaking camp.

This lesson had to be learned several times over. Some time later I was about to travel from Cape Town to England by motorbike. As I wished to sleep out, provide my own meals and experience a road network that was largely corrugated dirt, I found no difficulty in compiling a considerable list of necessities. We must have all made these lists (of corkscrews, tin openers, self-heating soup) and they are great fun, with a momentum that is hard to resist. "Why not a spare tin opener?" "And more medicine and another inner tube?" "Isn't it wise to take more shirts and stave off prickly heat?" Fortunately the garage that sold me the bike put a stop to such idiotic thinking. I had just strapped on a sack containing the real essentials (passport, documents, maps, money and address book) when a passing mechanic told me that any more weight would break the machine's back. (It was a modest machine.) Thus it was that I proceeded up the length of Africa without a sleeping bag, tent, groundsheet, spare petrol, oil, tools, food or even water, and never had cause for regret concerning this lack of wealth.

Indeed I blessed the freedom it gave me. I could arrive anywhere, remove my one essential sack and know that nothing, save the bike itself, could be stolen. To have possessions is to be in danger of losing them. Better by far to save the robbers their trouble and start with nothing.

Kippered Hammock

A sound tip is to do what the locals do. If they sleep out with nothing more than a blanket, it is probable that you can do likewise. If they can get by with a handful of dates at sunset, it is quite likely that you too can dispense with half a hundred-weight of dried egg, cocoa, vitamin tablets, corned beef, chocolate – and self-heating soup. To follow local practice and then try to improve on it can, however, be disastrous. Having learned the knack of sleeping in a Brazilian hammock as if it were in bed, I decided one thunderous night to bring modern technology to my aid. I covered myself with a space blanket to keep out the inevitable downpour.

Unfortunately, while I was asleep, the wretched thing slipped round beneath me and I awoke to find my body afloat in the pool of water it had collected. Being the first man to drown in a hammock is a poor way of achieving immortality. I looked over at my Indian travelling companion. Instead of fooling around with sublethal blankets, he had built a fire longitudinally beneath his hammock. Doubtless kippered by the smoke, but certainly dry, he slept the whole night through.

Planning and Adventure

One trouble with our camping notions is that we are confused by a lingering memory of childhood expeditions. I camp with my children every year, and half the fun is not quite getting it right. As all adventure is said to be bad planning, so is a memorable camping holiday in which the guys act as trip wires, the air mattress farts into nothingness and even the tent itself falls victim to the first wind above a breeze.

Adults are therefore imbued with an expectation that camping is a slightly comic caper, rich with potential mishap. Those who camp a lot, such as wildlife photographers, have got over this teething stage. They expect camping to be (almost) as smooth and straightforward a business as living in a house. They do their best to make cooking, eating, washing and sleeping no more time-consuming than it is back home. The joy of finding grass in the soup or ants in the pants wears off for them on about the second day. It is only the temporary camper, knowing he will be back in a hotel (thank God) within a week, who does not bother to set things up properly.

Surviving Natural Hazards

I like the camping set-up to be as modest as possible. I have noticed, however, though that others disagree, welcoming every kind of extra. A night spent beneath the stars that finishes with the first bright shafts of dawn is hardly punishment, but some seem to think it so, and concentrate on removing as much of the natural environment as possible.

I remember a valley in the Zagros mountains where I had to stay with some colleagues. I had thought a sleeping bag would be sufficient and placed mine in a dried-up stream which had piles of sand for additional comfort. Certain others of the party erected large tents with yet larger flysheets (however improbable rain was at that time of year). They also started up a considerable generator which bathed the area in sound and light. As electricity was not a predominant feature of those wild regions, considerable numbers of moths and other insects, idling their way between the Persian Gulf and the Caspian Sea, were astonished at such a quantity of illumination and flew down to investigate. To counter their invasion, one camper set fire to several of those insect repellent coils and the whole campsite was shrouded in noxious effluent. Over in the dried-up stream I and two fellow spirits were amazed at the camping travesty down the way. We were even more astonished when, after a peaceful night, we awoke to hear complaints that a strong wind had so flapped at the fly sheets that no-one inside the tent had achieved a wink of sleep.

The most civilised camping I have ever experienced was in the Himalayas. The season was spring and tents are then most necessary both at the lower altitudes (where it rains a lot) and at the higher ones (where it freezes quite considerably). Major refreshment is also necessary because walking in those mountains is exhausting work, being "always up", as the locals put it, "except when it's down." We slept inside sleeping bags on foam rubber within thick tents. We ate hot meals three times a day. We did very well – but we did not carry a thing. There were 36 porters for the six of us, the numbers falling as we ate into the provisions the men carried for us. I laboured up and down mighty valleys, longing for the next refreshment point and always delighted to see the ready-erected tents at each night's stopping place.

Personally, I was burdened with one camera, the smallest of notebooks and nothing more. The living conditions, as I have said, were excellent but what would they have become if I had been asked to carry everything I needed myself? It is at this point, when neither donkeys nor incredibly hardy mountain men are available, that the camper's true necessities are clarified. For myself, I am happy even to dispense with the toothbrush if I have to carry the thing all day long.

Fixing a Tent

Jack Jackson: If you aren't worried about weight, and you are not constantly on the move, you might as well make yourselves as comfortable as possible, which can mean virtually building a tented village. Large groups will find it very useful to have a mess tent where the party can all congregate during bad weather and for meals.

On hard, sunbaked ground in hot countries, pegs normally supplied with tents are of little use, so have some good, thick, strong ones made for you from 60mm iron (or use 15cm nails). As wooden mallets will not drive pegs in, carry a normal claw hammer – you can also use the claw to pull the pegs out again. In loosely-compacted snow, standard metal pegs do not have much holding power, so it is useful to make some with a larger surface area from 2.5cms angle alloy. Even this does not solve all the problems because any warmth during the day will make the pegs warm up, melt the snow around them, and pull them out causing the tent to fall down. The answer is to use very big pegs or ice axes for the two main guys fore and aft and then, for all the other guys, dig a hole about 25 cms deep, put the peg in horizontally with the guy line around its centre and compress fresh snow down hard on the peg with your boots to fill the hole.

Vango now offer a special "tent anchor" for snow and soft sand; it is not any better in snow than the method described above, but is good in soft sand. Four of these would normally be all you would carry per tent.

If you sleep without a tent, you need a mosquito net in some areas. There are several types on the market, including the ex-army nets which have the advantage of needing only one point of suspension, a camera tripod or ice axe will do for this if there is not a vehicle or tent nearby. However, commercial manufacturers have now produced lighter and more compact nets and special impregnation kits are available which enhance the effectiveness of the net.

Since tents take heavy wear, carry some strong thread and a sailmaker's needle for repairs plus some spare groundsheet material and adhesive. Tents which are to be carried by porters, on donkeys or on a vehicle roof rack are best kept in a strong kit bag or they will soon be torn. If it is not a windy area, a "space blanket" covering the reflecting side of the tent will help keep the tent cool during the day.

A Site for Sore Eyes

Melissa Shales: If a large group of you are travelling together in the more civilised parts of the world, you won't have the option of just choosing a suitable area to camp, particularly if you want to explore the towns. In many countries, or in National Parks, it is actually illegal to camp outside the official sites. These, however, are often a very good option, far cheaper and cleaner than inexpensive hotels. Some motels have camp sites attached which allow you the option of using their restaurant facilities, swimming pools etc. The Caravan Club of Great Britain (East Grinstead House, East Grinstead, West Sussex RH19 1HA, tel: 01342-326944) is a useful source of information about good sites in Europe (for tented camping as well as caravanning) and also runs various small sites around the UK. Contact the club for details about their publication *Continental Sites Guide*.

If there is an option, aim for a smaller site first. During the height of the tourist season, the larger ones tend to get very crowded, to the point where guy ropes are overlapping and you can hear the conversation in the tent next door. Some have hard stands which, while conveniently clean, are exceptionally hard unless you are travelling with the full paraphernalia of air beds etc. They also become horribly sterile areas that destroy virtually the entire ethos of camping. Avoid them if possible.

Many of the better sites will either have barbecues or special sites for fires. You will rarely be allowed to have a fire wherever you choose. The caretaker will often be able to supply wood if you ask in the morning. Check the toilets and washing facilities before you book in. Unless very small, when all you can expect is a primitive or chemical toilet and a stand-pipe, there should be showers and laundry facilities and a plentiful supply of hot water. In some countries, such as Zimbabwe, the sites will even have servants attached who will do your washing, sweep out the tent, run errands and build your fires for a small fee.

As with hotels, there are listings, and even star ratings in many places. If you want to go to what is obviously a highly rated site, visit the only one in the area, or are travelling in high season try and book first.

Camping on the Hoof

Martin Rosser: It's not the expense of campsites that I object to, but having to put up with the others that are crammed in around you. I camp to find peace and solitude, to commune with nature. How to do that on a canvas conurbation is beyond me. As for facilities, I can and do bathe in the woods and prefer it to slopping around in an overcrowded concrete shower block.

If you make the decision to camp freely, you have to decide whether to ask the landowner for permission or remain discreetly out of sight. Which you do will depend solely on the circumstances. I am aware that trespassing campers have an awesomely bad reputation, so I prefer just to get on with it quietly. Nine times out of ten I am not discovered and leave everything as it was except for a piece of flattened grass. I doubt if anyone is the wiser. If you are discovered, your best defence is the clean and tidy way you are camping, so that it can be readily seen that nothing has, is, or will be damaged. It helps if you can greet the person without guilt (I have only once received more than a general caution to take care and that once was well deserved – we had left a cooking fire unattended).

When you come to select a spot, remember to avoid all extremes. If the climate you are in is hot, seek shade; if the land is marshy, look for high, well drained ground. Don't leave selecting your sight to the last minute, stopping in late twilight and having to choose within a small area. From late afternoon on you should keep an eye open and be prepared to stop a little short of your planned destination – or backtrack a mile or so if need be. A bad night's sleep or wet and damaged gear are well worth avoiding.

The selection of a resting place that is not to be final involves experience: here I can do little more than outline the general do's and don't's. After that, bitter experience starts to take over. I rarely camp with a tent, preferring a bivi-bag, which makes my choice of spot very versatile. Generally, I select a spot protected by trees or in a sheltered dip. The patch need not be bigger than eight by four feet for me and my gear. I have even slept on substantial slopes – the record being 45°. I avoid all low-lying wetlands (and even streams in summer) because flying bloodsuckers enrage me to the point of sleeplessness. In areas I know are going to be extra bad, I try to find ground high enough to have a constant stiff breeze. This is the most sure way I have of deterring the Scottish midge or the Australian mosquito.

For those who carry tents, the rules are slightly different. The ground you are after has to be as flat and with as few rocks as possible. Take a leaf out of the London taxi driver's book who knows the exact dimensions of his cab. Just as he is able to slide his cab into the most unlikely looking gaps, you too should know where and, more importantly, where not to pitch. Sleeping in a tent, you have less to worry about on the insects front, but you should be more wary of falling branches and the like. Tents are far easier to damage than bivouac sheets, and more expensive to repair or replace. If you have the opportunity, face the tent doors eastwards. That way you don't have to get up, or even fully wake up, to watch the dawn break. For the rest, just apply common sense. Don't pitch a tent with its only door facing into a gale, and don't camp in a dry river bed when the rains are due, although it has to be said that dry river beds are very comfortable in the right season – flat floor, and plenty of firewood to hand.

The reason I prefer bivouacing is that it forces you to take greater notice of the terrain that surrounds you. You become more versatile in your camping and more ready to sleep anywhere. I have slept in derelict buildings and under bridges whilst experiencing the low life; up trees; in caves; and I once found a sea cliff with a horizontal crack running three feet high and over ten feet deep. Sleeping in there was an experience and a half as it was 60 feet above a rocky shore on which the waves crashed all night.

A friend went onto greater things and slept behind a waterfall (and once in the down turned shovel of an ancient and abandoned mechanical digger). So if there is a moral to this tale of where to camp: use your common sense; break all the rules in the boy scout manual – but sensibly; and finally, be adventurous and try new ways. Even if you carry a tent you don't have to use it.

For Camping Associations and Clubs see p.845 of the Directory ■

A BASIC GUIDE TO HEALTH
Chapter 10

HEALTH PLANNING

by Drs Nick Beeching and Sharon Welby

The most carefully planned holiday, business trip or expedition may be ruined by illness, much of which is preventable. It is logical to put as much effort into protecting your health while abroad as you have into planning your itinerary and obtaining the necessary equipment and travel papers. Unfortunately, it is not in the best commercial interests of travel companies to emphasise the possible health hazards of destinations that are being sold to potential customers: most holiday brochures limit health warnings to the minimum legal requirements, and some travel agents are woefully ignorant of the dangers of travel to more exotic climates. We have recently treated a travel agent for life–threatening malaria caught on the Kenyan coast. He had not taken malaria prophylaxis, despite the long and widespread recognition of the dangers of malaria in this area.

Happily, travellers' health problems are usually more mundane. Fatigue from overwork before a business trip or much-needed holiday, the stress of travel itself, exposure to new climates and over-indulgence in rich food, alcohol and tobacco all contribute to increased vulnerability to illness. Short-lived episodes of diarrhoea affect up to 50 per cent of travellers, and up to one fifth of tourists on some Mediterranean package holidays will have mild respiratory problems such as head colds, 'flu-like illnesses or, rarely, more severe pneumonias such as Legionnaires' disease. Sunburn or heat exhaustion are common, and accidents associated with unfamiliar sports such as skiing are an obvious hazard. The most common cause of death among expatriates is road traffic accidents – not exotic infections.

Pre-travel Health Check-list

Starting three months before you travel, consult your family doctor and specialist agencies as necessary to:

1. Obtain information about specific health problems at your destinations
2. Consider current health, medical and dental fitness for travel and current medications
3. Obtain adequate health insurance (and form E111 if travelling to an EC country)
4. Check again that health insurance is adequate

5. Plan and obtain necessary immunisations and malaria prophylaxis
6. Plan and obtain other medications and first aid items and any necessary documentation
7. Consider need for first-aid training course.

Information Sources

The depth of preparation required before travel clearly depends on the general health of the individual and on his or her destination(s). Since the last edition of this handbook in 1994 accessible information on health for travellers has improved considerably. The following sections in this chapter are only intended to provide a brief outline of steps to be considered.

Travellers to areas outside Europe, North America or Australasia are advised to invest in a copy of *Travellers' Health: How to Stay Healthy Abroad* (3rd edition OUP, £7.99) by Dr Richard Dawood – a guide which contains a wealth of information on all aspects of travel medicine. This is updated by regular features in TRAVELLER magazine (published by WEXAS), and is particularly recommended for those planning to work abroad or embarking on prolonged overland trips or expeditions in remote areas.

British travellers should obtain the booklet *Health Advice for Travellers Anywhere in the World*, prepared by the Department of Health and the Central Office of Information (booklet T5). This contains details of the documentation required for entitlement to free medical care and can be obtained from Post Offices, GP surgeries and vaccination centres or by telephoning the Health Literature Line (Freephone 0800 555 777). The leaflet is also constantly updated, on pages 460-464 of CEEFAX and on the computerised data services PRESTEL and ISTEL to which most travel agents have access.

When travelling outside Europe, it is wise to obtain information about compulsory immunisation requirements from the appropriate Embassy, Consulate or High Commission of each country that you plan to visit. However, do not expect their personnel to be able to give you general medical advice, and their information is not always as up to date as it should be.

British travellers to exotic locations should also consult their District Public Health Department or one of the centres of specific expertise listed in the Directory (Section 10) for the latest information on immunisation requirements and malaria prophylaxis. Those planning to work abroad should try and contact an employee of the company to ensure that adequate provision for medical and dental care is provided within their contract. If necessary, they should also consider taking out health insurance in addition to company policies.

Medical and Dental Health

If in any doubt about possible hazards of travel because of a pre-existing medical condition, consult your family doctor. People with heart or chest problems, recurrent blood clots in the legs or lungs, recent strokes, uncontrolled blood pressure, epilepsy, psychiatric disorders or chronic sinus or ear problems may be at risk when flying.

Late pregnancy is a contra-indication to flying, diabetics taking medication will need special advice and the disabled will have specific requirements that may need to be notified to airline and airport authorities (see article *The Disabled Traveller* in Chapter 3). People with chronic health problems or women who are obviously pregnant should ask their doctor to complete a standard airline form certifying their fitness for flying. This form should be obtained from the airline concerned.

Adequate supplies of all routinely-prescribed medications, including oral contraceptives, should also be obtained before departure. For short trips within Europe, these will be provided as NHS prescriptions. Those planning longer stays abroad should determine the availability of their medication overseas or take adequate supplies (you may need to pay for these on private prescription). It is also strongly recommended that you obtain a certificate from your doctor detailing the drugs prescribed, including the correct pharmacological name, as well as the trade name. This will be necessary to satisfy customs officials and you may need to obtain certified translations into appropriate languages. Some drugs readily obtainable in the UK are viewed with great suspicion elsewhere (codeine, for example, is considered a controlled drug in many countries, and tranquillisers such as diazepam can cause problems). Women working in Saudi Arabia should take adequate supplies of oral contraceptives and will need a certified Arabic translation of the certificate stating that the contraceptives have been prescribed for their personal use.

Those with recurring medical problems should also obtain a letter from their family doctor detailing the condition(s) – the letter can then be shown to doctors abroad if emergency treatment becomes necessary.

People with surgically implanted devices are also advised to carry a doctor's certificate to show security officials. Artificial hip replacements frequently set off metal detection security alarms at airports, as do indwelling intravenous (e.g. Portacath) central venous lines. People with cardiac pacemakers are unlikely to run into problems due to electrical interference from British or North American airport metal detectors, but should try to avoid going through them and arrange instead for a personal body check by security officials.

Expatriates taking up a contract abroad will often have to submit to a detailed medical examination as a condition of employment. Many countries insist on a negative HIV-antibody test before allowing foreigners to work. Some will not allow any known HIV-positive individual to enter the country, despite advice from the World Health Organisation (WHO) that such regulations are ineffective as a means of controlling the spread of HIV infection.

HIV-positive travellers should consult their medical specialist and local support groups about specific travel insurance problems and the advisability of travel. Individuals with specific chronic health problems such as epilepsy, diabetes or long term steroid treatment, should obtain a "Medic-alert" bracelet or similar, which is more easily located in a medical emergency than a card carried in a pocket.

Dental health is often taken for granted by British citizens who get a rude shock when faced with bills for dental work overseas. Those embarking on prolonged travel or work abroad, or planning to visit very cold areas, should have a full preventative dental check up before leaving.

Spare spectacles, contact lenses and contact lens solutions should also be obtained before travelling. If you are planning a vigorous holiday or expedition (e.g. skiing, hill-walking etc.) you will need to begin an appropriate fitness regime long before departure.

Insurance

Falling ill while abroad can be very expensive. Partial exemption from medical charges only applies in certain circumstances – primarily in EC countries. Those travelling to the EC should obtain the booklet *Health Advice for Travellers Anywhere in the World* (T5, as mentioned before). This contains the form CM1 which must be completed in order to obtain the important E111 form which you should carry with your travel documents to be eligible for benefit in all EC countries (except for UK residents on a temporary visit to Austria, Denmark, Finland, Gibraltar, the Irish Republic, Norway and Portugal which do not require form E111).

The EC will allow eligible citizens of any member country to get urgent treatment free, or at a reduced cost, during temporary stays. Continuing treatment for a pre-existing illness, e.g. asthma, high blood pressure, etc., may not fall within the definition of urgent treatment and may not attract these benefits. What is more, these arrangements do not apply if you are working or living in another EC country. In these circumstances you should write to the DSS Contributions Agency, Overseas Branch Newcastle upon Tyne, NE98 1YX seeking information on your rights to health care in another EC country.

In some EC countries (e.g. France and Belgium) you will only be covered for approximately 70 per cent of treatment and the remainder may be costly. You may also have to pay the full cost initially and then claim back the 70 per cent share. For these reasons, travellers should consider taking out private insurance to cover that part of the cost they may have to meet themselves.

Outside the EC, some countries offer emergency care either free or for a part fee only. This concession may apply only in public health hospitals and not in private clinics. It is also often necessary to show your National Health Service medical card as well as your UK passport. Details of reciprocal health agreements for all countries are listed in DSS leaflet NI38, available from local DSS offices or the DSS Overseas Branch. Specific leaflets giving details of health care in individual countries can also be obtained from the DSS Overseas Branch.

Elsewhere, the cost of consultation, medicines, treatment and hospital care must be paid by the patient. As this could be financially crippling, full health insurance is a wise precaution (see Travel Insurance article in Chapter 8 for more details). If you are taken gravely ill or severely injured in the USA, the final medical bill may seem astronomical.

Discuss the adequacy of your cover with your travel agent, especially if high technology medical care may be needed. Those working or travelling abroad for extended periods and those taking part in hazardous expeditions, should ensure that travel insurance has adequate allowance for emergency evacuation to a country with good medical facilities.

If you incur medical expenses, present your policy to the doctor and ask him/her to send the bill direct to your insurance company. Many doctors demand cash (and the level of their fees may alarm you) so keep a reserve of travellers' cheques for this purpose. Insist on a receipt and the insurance company will reimburse you on your return.

Do not expect to find the same medical standards as those of your home country during your wanderings. Some practitioners routinely include expensive drugs for the simplest of conditions; multi-vitamin therapy, intravenous injections and the inevitable suppositories may also be given unnecessarily to run up a bigger bill. Be prepared to barter diplomatically about this, to offer those drugs you are carrying for treatment if appropriate, and even to shop around for medical advice.

Immunisations

Immunisations may be necessary to prevent illnesses that are common in many countries but which are rarely encountered in Western Europe, North America or Australasia. In the UK you can get most vaccinations through a general practitioner or a specialised vaccination centre (see Directory, Section 10). Some will be free of charge, but the majority will have to be paid for privately. The exact requirements for a traveller will depend on his or her lifestyle, intended destinations and personal vaccination history, but should be considered at least two to three months before departure.

Modern immunisations are remarkably safe and well-tolerated. However, some vaccines contain traces of penicillin or neomycin and allergy to these antibiotics should be declared. Some vaccines are prepared in eggs and serious allergy to eggs will preclude some inoculations. Patients with chronic illness, particularly immune deficiency due to steroid treatment, cancer chemotherapy or HIV infection, should not receive most vaccines containing live organisms (such as oral polio vaccine), while pregnancy is also a contra-indication for several vaccines.

International regulations cover the minimum legal requirements for a few vaccinations, particularly yellow fever which has to be administered in a designated centre and recorded on a specific internationally-recognised certificate. Many countries have idiosyncratic certificate requirements – cholera vaccinations, for example – and the situation will change if an epidemic is in progress, hence the need for up-to-date information before you travel.

If in doubt about the need for International Certificates for yellow fever or cholera, it may be wise to obtain one before travel rather than being forced to accept vaccination (using needles of dubious origin and sterility) on arrival at your destination.

It is equally important that the traveller has adequate protection against infections such as hepatitis A, polio and tetanus, even though proof of this will not be required by immigration officials at your destination. All travellers should have up-to-date tetanus immunisations, and travellers outside Europe, North America and Australasia should ensure that polio immunisation is adequate. Children should have received all their childhood immunisations, and children who are going to live in the tropics should have early immunisation against tuberculosis (BCG) and hepatitis B infection.

The following list summarises information on the most commonly required vaccinations. For a guideline of requirements for each country see the Geographical Section at the beginning of the Directory. The information below is in alphabetical order.

Cholera: A profuse diarrhoeal illness which poses little risk to the majority of travellers, and which is acquired from contaminated food or water. There have recently been large epidemics in much of South America and regions of Central Africa and the Indian Subcontinent. Limited protection (about 50 per cent) is by vaccination which ideally consists of two injections at least ten days apart. New oral vaccines available in Europe may become available in the UK in the near future particularly for the high risk traveller. Some countries still insist on a cholera vaccination certificate which is only valid for six months and can be provided after one injection.

Diphtheria: Still common in many parts of the tropics although rarely a hazard for Western tourists. There have recently been epidemics in several member states of the former USSR. Most travellers will have received adequate immunisation in childhood (the 'D' in DPT), but may require a booster. Older adults may not have had the vaccine and will need a full course of three doses separated by a month each.

Hepatitis A: A water-borne virus infection that poses a significant health hazard for travellers to all parts of the tropics. The illness has an incubation period of three to six weeks and causes lethargy and jaundice which may last for several weeks. The illness is often very mild in children aged less than five, and often goes completely unnoticed in this age group, so some adults will already have immunity even if they never had jaundice.

There are two options for protection. The old-fashioned immunisation with a gammaglobulin injection just prior to travel provides reasonable protection for about three months, after which a repeat will be needed if still travelling. This is still a suitable option for the "one off" traveller going on a short trip, but supplies of gammaglobulin are erratic and time should be allowed to ensure that the immunisation is available. This option is less effective than vaccination.

Frequent travellers, or those planning to stay abroad for more than six months, should consider having the new hepatitis A vaccine. One dose of vaccine at least ten days before travelling gives good protection for at least one year. A booster dose six to twelve months later gives protection for ten years. The vaccine is expensive and frequent travellers can ask for a blood test first to see if they are already immune to hepatitis A.

Hepatitis B: A common infection in the tropics and countries bordering the Mediterranean, hepatitis B is caused by a virus that is transmitted by sex, by an infusion of contaminated blood or by sharing or reusing hypodermic needles. Hepatitis B shows similar symptoms to those of hepatitis A but sometimes is more severe and may lead to lasting liver damage. It is preventable with safe and highly effective injections given at three intervals, ideally with the second and third injections following at one and six month intervals after the first. More rapid protection can be provided by giving the third dose two months after the first, but this has to be boosted by a fourth dose at one year if protection is to last for several years.

The vaccination is recommended for health workers and those working in refugee camps and similar environments, as well as for people planning to live in the tropics for more than six months. It should also be considered by all adults who might have sexual contact with travellers (other than their regular partner) or with anyone living in areas where the infection is prevalent, and by all people who misuse intravenous drugs.

Combined Hepatitis A and B vaccine: A new combined vaccine *Twinrix* is now available which will give protection against both hepatitis A and hepatitis B. Three injections are required, the second is given one month later and the third at six months. Protection is given after the second injection and the booster dose will give further protection for five years. This vaccine is particularly useful for the frequent business traveller and the back packer who have not been previously vaccinated, the advantage being the reduction in the number of vaccinations from five to three.

Japanese encephalitis: A rare virus infection causing severe encephalitis (inflammation of the brain) primarily in rural areas of Asia, especially during the rainy season. A moderately effective vaccine is obtainable only through specialist vaccination clinics and usually restricted to those wandering off the beaten track for prolonged periods. Three injections spaced over one month provide protection at the end of the month, lasting for two years. The vaccine is associated with a low incidence of serious but treatable side-effects and is not recommended for people who have a history of "urticarial" rash ("hives").

Malaria: No vaccine available, see the article on malaria in this chapter for details about prevention.

Meningococcal meningitis: Epidemics recur in many parts of Sub-Saharan Africa (mainly in the dry season) and an epidemic which began in Nepal moved to many other countries via the 1987 Haj pilgrimage to Mecca. The Saudi Arabian authorities now require Haj pilgrims to provide certificates of vaccination against the infection, and a safe and effective vaccine against strains A and C of the organism is now available. This vaccine does not protect against strain B of the meningococcus which is the commonest strain found in the UK. The vaccine is not normally required by tourists unless travelling to an area with a current epidemic, or unless you plan to work in a region (especially in hospitals or schools) where the infection is common. One injection at least ten days before travel provides protection for three years.

Poliomyelitis (polio): This viral infection, which causes untreatable meningitis and paralysis, is still a problem in most parts of the tropics and can be prevented by vaccination. Most adults have been immunised but should receive a booster if this has not been done in the past ten years. Vaccination is usually given by mouth using a "live" polio virus variant that provides protection but does not cause illness. Patients with immune suppression can receive injections of killed organisms instead (the "Salk" vaccine).

Rabies: This virus infection of animals is found in most countries apart from the UK and Australia and New Zealand. It is untreatable once symptoms have developed. Avoid contact with all dogs or cats while abroad, or with any animal that behaves strangely. Vaccination before travel is safe but is usually reserved for those working with animals or those planning expeditions or employment in remote areas (see the following article on health problems abroad for action to be taken if bitten). Three injections over 1 month give protection for 2 years.

Smallpox: This vaccination is no longer required following the successful world-wide eradication of smallpox.

Tetanus: This severe illness can follow even minor trauma that introduces soil through the skin (e.g. thorn injuries). Vaccination effectively prevents this and a booster dose will be needed for adults who have not been immunised in the last ten years. Routine childhood immunisation did not begin in the UK until 1961 and older adults may need a full course of immunisation if they have missed out on this. However, if you have had a total of at least five tetanus vaccinations in your life, no further jabs are needed unless you have a tetanus-prone wound. Any contaminated wounds received while abroad should be cleaned and medical consultation sought concerning the need for antibiotics and additional vaccination.

Tuberculosis: Although this bacterial infection is widespread in the tropics, it does not pose a major hazard for most travellers. Most British (but not North American) adults, and children aged over thirteen, will have already been immunised against TB (BCG vaccination). Those embarking on prolonged travel or employment abroad should consult their doctor about their TB immune status. Pre-employment medical examinations usually include this.

Typhoid: This bacterial infection is acquired from contaminated food, water or milk in any area of poor sanitation outside Europe, North America or Australasia.

Typhoid vaccination is not necessary for most short-stay tourists, but should be considered by all planning prolonged or remote travel in areas of poor hygiene. The old-fashioned TAB (typhoid and paratyphoid A and B vaccine) and typhoid vaccines are no longer used, as there are now several alternatives.

The older vaccine (two injections) provides moderate protection for about three years, after which a single booster dose is required. The vaccine commonly causes a sore arm and fever, especially in those who have had the vaccine before. The side-effects may be lessened if the vaccine is given in the skin tissues (intradermal injection). A new injected vaccine (*Typhim Vi*) gives equivalent protection after one dose only and is preferred now.

The third alternative is a course of capsules containing a live vaccine strain ("Ty 21a"), taken by mouth over several days. This may appeal to those with a phobia of needles, but the course is expensive, must be taken strictly according to the manufacturer's instructions, and only provides immunity for one year after which it will need to be repeated. It cannot be taken at the same time as oral polio vaccine or any antibiotic, or within twelve hours after taking mefloquine. As with other live vaccines, it is not recommended for pregnant women.

Yellow fever: This virus infection, causing a lethal hepatitis, is transmitted by mosquitoes and is restricted to parts of Africa and South and Central America. It can be prevented by a highly effective and safe vaccine, the certificate for which is valid for ten years, starting ten days after vaccination. Vaccination and the International Certificate can only be given at World Health Organisation approved centres – in Britain this has now been extended to include many GPs.

Simple First Aid

Individual requirements vary greatly and most travellers do not need to carry enormous bags of medical supplies. This section covers a few health items that the majority of travellers should consider. Those going to malarious areas should read the advice given on malaria in this chapter, and those going to areas without ready access to medical care should read the article on health problems abroad for further suggestions for their kit bag.

First-aid training is appropriate for travellers to remote areas and those going on prolonged expeditions which might include a medical officer. As the medical needs of expeditions vary so much, an expedition kit bag list has not been included in this edition of the handbook. Expedition leaders should consult their own organisation or one of the specialist agencies for advice.

Painkillers: We always carry soluble aspirin (in foil-sealed packs) which is an excellent painkiller and reduces inflammation associated with sunburn (just be careful about the water you dissolve it in!). Aspirin should not be given to children aged less than twelve, I take paracetamol syrup for my young children. Both paracetamol and aspirin reduce fever associated with infections.

Adults who cannot tolerate aspirin because of ulcer problems, gastritis or asthma, should instead take paracetamol (not paracetamol/codeine preparations). To avoid potential embarrassment with customs officials, stronger painkillers should only be carried with evidence that they have been prescribed.

Cuts and grazes: A small supply of waterproof dressings (e.g. *Band-Aids*) is useful together with a tube of antiseptic cream such as *Savlon* – especially if travelling with children.

Sunburn: British travellers frequently underestimate the dangers of sunburn and should take particular care that children do not get burnt. Protect exposed areas from the sun, remembering the back of the neck. Sunbathing exposure times should be gradually increased and use adequate sunblock creams (waterproof if swimming), particularly at high altitude where UV light exposure is higher. Sunburn should be treated with rest, plenty of non-alcoholic drinks, and paracetamol or aspirin. Those who burn easily, may wish to take a tube of hydrocortisone cream for excessively burnt areas. (See article *Health in the Heat* in this chapter.)

Motion sickness: If liable to travel sickness, try to sleep through as much of the journey as possible and avoid reading. Avoid watching the horizon through the window and, if travelling by boat, remain on deck as much as possible.

Several types of medication give potential relief from motion sickness when taken before the start of a journey, and sufferers should experiment to find out which suits them best. Antihistamines (e.g. *Phenergan*) are popular, especially for children, but should not be taken with alcohol. Adults should not drive until all sedative effects of antihistamines have worn off. Other remedies include *Kwells* (hyoscine tablets), *Dramamine* (dimenhydrinate) and *Stugeron* (cinnarazine). *Scopoderm* patches, only available on prescription, release hyoscine through the skin for up to three days. Hyoscine taken by mouth or by skin patch causes a dry mouth and can cause sedation.

Constipation: The immobility of prolonged travel, dehydration during heat acclimatisation and reluctance to use toilets of dubious cleanliness all contribute to constipation. Drink plenty of fluids and try to eat a high fibre diet. Those who are already prone to constipation may wish to take additional laxatives or fibre substitutes (e.g. *Fybogel*).

Diarrhoea: Although this is a common problem, it is usually self-limiting and most travellers do not need to carry anti-diarrhoea medication with them (see the article *Diarrhoeal* Illness below). Diarrhoea reduces absorption of the contraceptive pill and women may wish to carry supplies of alternative contraceptives in case of this.

Female problems: Women who suffer from recurrent cystitis or vaginal thrush, should consult their doctor to obtain appropriate antibiotics to take with them. Tampons are often difficult to buy in many countries and should be bought before travelling. Periods are often irregular or may cease altogether during travel but this does not mean that you cannot become pregnant.

Insect bites: Insect bites are a nuisance in most parts of the world and also transmit a variety of infections, the most important of which is malaria. Personal insect repellents will be needed by most travellers and usually contain DEET (diethyltoluamide). Liquid formulations are the cheapest but less convenient to carry. Lotions and cream are available and sprays are the easiest to apply but are bulky to carry. Sticks of repellent are easier to carry and last the longest. All these should be applied to the skin and to clothing adjacent to exposed areas of skin, but should not be applied around the eyes, nose and mouth (take particular care with children).

DEET dissolves plastics, including carrier bags etc. so beware! An alternative to DEET containing repellents is *Mosiguard Natural*. Marketed by MASTA, this is made from a blend of eucalyptus oils and is as effective as repellents based on DEET, and is more suitable for people who are sensitive to DEET.

When abroad, try to reduce the amount of skin available to biting insects by wearing long sleeves, trousers or skirts. If a mosquito net is provided with your bed, use it. Permethrin-impregnated mosquito nets are effective and can be purchased before travel to malarious areas. "Knock-down" insecticide sprays may be needed, and mosquito coils are easy to carry. Electric buzzers (that imitate male mosquito noises) are useless and candles and repellent strips (containing citronella) are not very effective. If bitten by insects, try to avoid scratching which can introduce infection, particularly in the tropics. Eurax cream or calamine lotion can relieve local irritation, and antihistamine tablets may help those that have been bitten extensively.

Antihistamine creams should be used with caution as they can cause local reactions, and we prefer to use weak hydrocortisone cream on bites that are very irritating. Hydrocortisone cream should only be used if the skin is not obviously broken or infected. Increasing pain, redness or swelling or obvious pus suggest infection, and medical attention should be sought.

HIV prevention: Most HIV infections are acquired sexually (see article on Sex Abroad in this chapter). All adults should consider taking a supply of condoms. Travellers to countries with limited medical facilities should consider taking a supply of sterile needles and syringes so that injections required abroad are not given with re-usable needles of doubtful sterility.

Personal supplies of syringes and needles can make customs officials very suspicious, and condoms are not acceptable in some countries – particularly the Middle East and the Republic of Ireland.

To avoid problems at the border, it is worth buying these items as part of a small HIV/AIDS prevention pack which are available from most of the medical equipment suppliers listed in Section 10 of the Directory. Larger "HIV prevention packs" that may include blood product substitutes, are rarely worth carrying.

On Your Return

On returning from a long trip, most travellers will experience some euphoria and elation, as well as family reunions and the interested enquiries of friends. After this, as relaxation, and possibly jet lag set in, a period of apathy, exhaustion and weariness can follow. Recognise this and allow a few quiet days if it is feasible. There are usually many pressures at this stage, especially if equipment is to be unpacked and sorted, photographs processed, etc.

Another pressure for most people is the none too welcome thought of returning to the mundane chores involved in earning one's daily bread. If your travels have been challenging, then a couple of recovery days will probably make you work more efficiently thereafter and cope more expeditiously with the thousands of tasks which seem to need urgent attention.

After a time of excitement and adventure, some will go through a period of being restless and bored with the simple routine of home and work. They may not be aware of this temporary change in personality but their families certainly will be. Having pointed out this problem, we cannot suggest any way of overcoming it except perhaps to recommend that everyone concerned try to recognise it and be a little more tolerant than normal. This may not be a sensible time to take major decisions affecting career, family and business.

Some will be relieved to arrive in their hygienic homes after wandering in areas containing some of the world's nastiest diseases. Unfortunately, the risk of ill health is not altogether gone as you may still be incubating an illness acquired abroad – incubation for diseases such as hepatitis or malaria could take a few months or in the extreme case of rabies, a few years.

After your return, any medical symptoms or even just a feeling of debility or chronic ill health must not be ignored – medical help should be sought. Tell your physician where you have travelled (in detail), including brief stopovers. It may be that you are carrying some illness outside the spectrum normally considered. Sadly this has been known to cause mistaken diagnosis so that malaria, for example, has been labelled as influenza with occasionally fatal consequences.

Tropical worms and other parasites, enteric fevers, typhus, histoplasmosis (a fungal disease breathed in on guano, making cavers particularly vulnerable), tuberculosis, tropical virus diseases, amoebic dysentery and hepatitis may all need to be treated. For these illnesses to be successfully treated, many patients will need expert medical attention.

Routine tropical disease check ups are provided by some companies for their employees during or after postings abroad. They are not generally required by other travellers who have not been ill while abroad or after their return. People who feel that they might have acquired an exotic infection or who have received treatment for infection abroad, should ask their doctor about referral to a unit with an interest in tropical diseases. Most health regions have a suitable unit and more specialist units are listed in the Directory.

All unprotected sexual encounters while travelling carry high risks of infection with various sexually transmitted diseases in addition to HIV and hepatitis B. A post-travel check up is strongly advised, even if you have no symptoms. Your local hospital will advise about the nearest clinic – variously called genito-urinary medicine (GUM) clinics, sexually-transmitted disease (STD) clinics, sexual health clinics, VD clinics or "special" clinics. Absolute anonymity is guaranteed, and no referral is needed from your general practitioner.

After leaving malarial areas, many will feel less motivated to continue their antimalarial drugs. It is strongly recommended that these be taken for a minimum of 28 days after leaving the endemic area. Failure to do this has caused many travellers to develop malaria some weeks after they thought they were totally safe. This is more than a nuisance: it has occasionally been fatal.

Fortunately, the majority of travellers return home with nothing other than pleasant memories of an enjoyable interlude in their lives.

For a list of Vaccination and Information Centres see p.851 of the Directory
For Emergency Medical Kit Suppliers see p.853 of the Directory
For Major Hospitals World-wide see p.854 of the Directory

TRAVEL STRESS

by Hilary Bradt

The scene is familiar: a crowded bus station in some Third World country; passengers push and shove excitedly; an angry and discordant voice rings out, "But I've got a reserved seat! Look, it says number eighteen, but there's someone sitting there!" The foreigner may or may not win this battle, but ultimately he will lose the war between "what should be" (his expectations) and "what is" (their culture) – becoming yet another victim of stress.

It is ironic that this complaint, so fashionable among businessmen, should be such a problem for many travellers who believe they are escaping such pressures when they leave home. But by travelling rough, they are immediately immersing themselves in a different culture and thus subjecting themselves to a new set of psychological stresses.

The physical deprivations that are inherent in budget travel are not usually a problem. Most travellers adjust well enough to having a shower every two months, eating beans and rice every day and sleeping in dirty, lumpy beds in company with the local wildlife. These are part of the certainties of this mode of travel. It is the uncertainties that wear people down: the buses that double-book their seats, usually leaving an hour late but occasionally slipping away early; the landslide that blocks the road to the coast on the one day of the month that a boat leaves for Paradise Island; the inevitable *mañana* response; the struggle with a foreign language and foreign attitudes.

Culture Shock

It is this "foreignness" which often comes as an unexpected shock. The people are different, their customs are different, and so are their basic values and moralities. Irritatingly, these differences are most frequently exhibited by those who amble down the Third World Corridors of Power controlling the fate of travellers. But ordinary people are different too and believers in Universal Brotherhood often find this hard to accept – as do women travelling alone. Many travellers escape back to their own culture periodically by mixing with the upper classes of the countries in which they are travelling – people who were educated in Europe or America and are westernised in their outlook. Come to think of it, maybe this is why hitchhikers show so few signs of travel stress: they meet wealthier car owners and can often lapse into a childlike dependence on their hosts.

Fear and Anxiety

At least hitchhikers can alternate between blissful relaxation and sheer terror, as can other adventurous travellers. Fear, in small doses, never did anyone any harm. It seems a necessary ingredient to everyday life; consciously or unconsciously, most people seek out danger. If they don't rock climb or parachute jump, they drive too fast, refuse to give up smoking or resign from their safe jobs to travel the world. The stab of fear that travellers experience as they traverse a glacier, eye a gun-toting soldier or approach a "difficult" border is followed by a feeling of exhilaration once the perceived danger has passed.

A rush of adrenaline is OK. The hazard is the prolonged state of tension or stress, to which the body reacts in a variety of ways: irritability, headaches, inability to sleep at night and a continuous feeling of anxiety. The budget traveller is particularly at risk because money shortages provoke so many additional anxieties to the cultural stresses mentioned earlier. The day-to-day worry of running out of money is an obvious one, but there is also the fear of being robbed (no money to replace stolen items) and of becoming ill. Many travellers worry about their health anyway, but those who cannot afford a doctor, let alone a stay in hospital, can become quite obsessional. Yet these are the people who travel in a manner most likely to jeopardise their health. Since their plan is often "to travel until the money runs out", those diseases such as hepatitis with a long incubation period will manifest themselves during the trip. Chronic illnesses like amoebic dysentery undermine the health and well-being of many budget travellers, leaving them far more susceptible to psychological pressures. Even the open-endedness of their journey may cause anxiety.

Tranquillisers

Now I've convinced you that half the world's travellers are heading for a nervous breakdown rather than the nearest beach, let's see what can be done to ease the situation (apart from bringing more money). There are tranquillisers. This is how most doctors treat the symptoms of stress since they assume that the problems causing the anxiety are an unavoidable part of everyday life. Travellers should not rule them out (I've met people who consume Valium until they scarcely know who they are) but since they have chosen to be in their situation, it should be possible to eliminate some of the reasons.

They can begin by asking themselves why they decided to travel in the first place. If the answer is that it was "to get away from it all", journeying for long distances seems a bit pointless – better to hole up in a small village or island and begin the lotus-eating life. If the motive for travel is a keen interest in natural history, archaeology or people, then the problems inherent in getting to their destination are usually overridden in the excitement of arriving. However, those who find the lets and hindrances that stand between them and their goal too nerve-wracking (and the more enthusiastic they are, the more frustrated they will become) should consider relaxing their budget in favour of spending more money on transportation, etc., even if it does mean a shorter trip.

The average overlander, however, considers the journey the object and will probably find that time on the road will gradually eliminate his anxieties (like a young man I met in Ecuador: he was forever thinking about his money, but when I met him again in Bolivia, he was a changed man, relaxed and happy. "Well," he said, in answer to my question, "You remember I was always worrying about running out of money? Now I have, so I have nothing to worry about!").

If a traveller can learn the language and appreciate the differences between the countries he visits and his own, he will come a long way towards understanding and finally accepting them. His tensions and frustrations will then finally disappear.

But travellers should not expect too much of themselves. You are what you are, and a few months of travel are not going to undo the conditioning of your formative years. Know yourself, your strengths and weaknesses, and plan your trip accordingly. And if you don't know yourself at the start of a long journey, you will by the end.

CULTURE SHOCK

by Adrian Furnham

Nearly every traveller must have experienced culture shock at some time or other. Like jet lag it is an aspect of travel which is both negative and difficult to define. But what precisely is it? When and why does it occur? And, more importantly, how can we prevent it or at least cope with it?

Although the experience of culture shock has no doubt been around for centuries, it was only 25 years ago that an anthropologist called Oberg coined the term. Others have attempted to improve upon and extend the concept and have come up with alternative jargon such as "culture fatigue", "role shock" and "pervasive ambiguity".

Strain

From the writings of travellers and interviews with tourists, foreign students, migrants and refugees, psychologists have attempted to specify the exact nature of this unpleasant experience. It seems that the syndrome has six facets. Firstly, there is strain caused by the effort of making necessary psychological adaptations – speaking another language, coping with the currency, driving on the other side of the road, etc. Secondly, there is often a sense of loss and a feeling of deprivation with regard to friends, possessions and status. If you are in a place where nobody knows, loves, respects and confides in you, you may feel anonymous and deprived of your status and role in society, as well as bereft of familiar and useful objects. Thirdly, there is often a feeling of rejection – your rejection of the natives and their rejection of you. Travellers stand out by their skin, clothes, and language. Depending on the experience of the natives, they may be seen as unwanted intruders, an easy rip-off, or friends.

A fourth symptom of culture shock is confusion. Travellers can become unsure about their roles, their values, their feelings and sometimes about who they are. When a people lives by a different moral and social code from your own, interaction for even a comparatively short period can be very confusing. Once one becomes more aware of cultural differences, typical reactions of surprise, anxiety, even disgust and indignation occur. The way foreigners treat their animals, eat food, worship their god, or perform their toiletries often cause amazement and horror to naive travellers. Finally, culture shock often involves feelings of impotence due to not being able to cope with the new environment.

Little England

Observers of sojourners and long-term travellers have noted that there are usually two extreme reactions to culture shock: those who act as if they "never left home" and those who immediately "go native". The former chauvinists create "little Englands" in foreign fields, refusing to compromise their diet or dress, and like the proverbial mad dogs, insisting on going out in the midday sun. The latter reject all aspects of their own culture and enthusiastically do in Rome as the Romans do.

Most travellers, however, experience less dramatic but equally uncomfortable reactions to culture shock. These may include excessive concern over drinking water, food, dishes and bedding; fits of anger over delays and other minor frustrations; excessive fear of being cheated, robbed or injured; great concern over minor pains and interruptions; and a longing to be back at the idealised home "where you can get a good cup of tea and talk to sensible people".

But, as any seasoned traveller will know, often one begins to get used to, and even learns to like the new culture. In fact writers have suggested that people go through a number of phases when living in a new culture. Oberg, in his original writings, listed four stages: the "honeymoon" which is characterised by enchantment, fascination, enthusiasm and admiration for the new culture as well as cordial (but superficial) relationships. In this stage people are generally intrigued and euphoric. Many tourists never stay long enough to move out of the honeymoon period. The second phase heralds crisis and disintegration. It is now that the traveller feels loss, isolation, loneliness and inadequacy, and tends to become depressed and withdrawn. This happens most often after two to six months of living in the new culture.

The third phase is the most problematic and involves reintegration. At this point people tend to reject the host culture, becoming opinionated and negative partly as a means of showing their self-assertion and growing self-esteem. The fourth stage of "autonomy" finds the traveller assured, relaxed, warm and empathic because he or she is socially and linguistically capable of negotiating most new and different social situations in the culture.

And finally the "independent" phase is achieved – characterised by trust, humour and the acceptance and enjoyment of social, psychological and cultural differences.

U-Curve

For obvious reasons, this independent phase is called the "U-curve" hypothesis. If you plot satisfaction and adaptation (x axis) over time (y axis), you see a high point beginning, followed by a steep decline, a period at the bottom, but then a steady climb back up. More interestingly, some researchers have shown evidence not of a U-curve but a "W-curve", i.e. once travellers return to their home country, they often undergo a similar re-acculturation, again in the shape of a U. Hence a "double U" or W-curve.

Other research has shown similar intriguing findings. Imagine, for instance, that you are going to Morocco for the first time. You are asked to describe or rate both the average Briton and the average Moroccan in terms of their humour, wealth, trustworthiness etc., both before you go and after you return. Frequently it has been found that people change their opinions of their own countrymen and women more than that of the foreigners. In other words, travel makes you look much more critically at yourself and your culture than most people think. And this self-criticism may itself be rather unhelpful.

The trouble with these stage theories is that not everyone goes through the stages. Not everyone feels like Nancy Mitford when she wrote: "I loathe abroad, nothing would induce me to live there… and, as for foreigners, they are all the same and make me sick." But I suspect Robert Morley is not far from the truth when he remarked: "The British tourist is always happy abroad so long as the natives are waiters."

Then there is also the shock of being visited. Anyone who lives in a popular tourist town soon becomes aware that it is not only the tourist but also the native who experiences culture shock. Of course, the amount and type of shock that tourists can impart to local people is an indication of a number of things, such as the relative proportion of tourists to natives, the duration of their stay, the comparative wealth and development of the two groups and the racial and ethnic prejudices of both.

Of course not everybody will experience culture shock. Older, better educated, confident and skillful adults (particularly those who speak the language) tend to adapt best. Yet there is considerable evidence that sojourners, like foreign students, voluntary workers, businessmen, diplomats and even military people become so confused and depressed that they have to be sent home at great expense. That is why many organisations attempt to lessen culture shock by a number of training techniques. The Foreign Office, the British Council and many multi-nationals do this for good reason, learning from bitter experience.

Training

For a number of reasons, information and advice in the form of lectures and pamphlets, etc., is very popular but not always very useful. The "facts" that are given are often too general to have any clear, specific application in particular circumstances. Facts emphasise the exotic and ignore the mundane (how to hail a taxi, for example). This technique also gives the impression that the culture can be easily understood; and even if facts are retained, they do not necessarily lead to accommodating behaviour.

A second technique is "isomorphic training". This is based on the theory that a major cause of cross-cultural communication problems comes from the fact that most people tend to offer different explanations for each other's behaviour. This technique introduces various episodes that end in embarrassment, misunderstanding or hostility between people from two different cultures. The trainee is then presented with four or five alternative explanations of what went wrong, all of which correspond to different attributions of the observed behaviour. Only one is correct from the perspective of the culture being learned. This is an interesting and useful technique but depends for much of its success on the relevance of the various episodes chosen.

Perhaps the most successful method is "skills training". It has been pointed out that socially inadequate or inept individuals have not mastered the social conventions of their own society. Either they are unaware of the rules and processes of everyday behaviour or, if aware of the rules, they are unable or unwilling to abide by them. They are therefore like strangers in their own land. People newly arrived in an alien culture will be in a similar position and may benefit from simple skills training.

This involves analysing everyday encounters such as buying and selling, introductions, refusal of requests. You will also observe successful culture models engaging in these acts and will practise yourself, helped in the learning process by a video tape of your efforts. This may all sound very clinical, but can be great fun and very informative.

Practical Advice

Many travellers, unless on business and with considerable company resources behind them, do not have the time or money to go on courses that prevent or minimise culture shock. They have to leap in at the deep end and hope that they can swim. But there are some simple things they can do that may well prevent the shock and improve communications.

Before departure it is important to learn as much as possible about the society you are visiting. Areas of great importance include:

Language: Not only vocabulary but polite usage; when to use higher and lower forms; and particularly how to say "yes" and "no".

Non-verbal cues: Gestures, body contact, and eye gaze patterns differ significantly from one country to another and carry very important meanings. Cues of this sort for greeting, parting, and eating are most important, and are relatively easily learnt.

Social rules: Every society develops rules that regulate behaviour so that social goals can be attained and needs satisfied. Some of the most important rules concern gifts, buying and selling, eating and drinking, time keeping and bribery and nepotism.

Social relationships: Family relationships, classes and castes, and working relationships often differ from culture to culture. The different social roles of the two sexes is perhaps the most dramatic difference between societies, and travellers should pay special attention to this.

Motivation: Being assertive, extrovert and achievement-oriented may be desirable in America and Western Europe but this is not necessarily the case elsewhere. How to present oneself, maintain face, etc., is well worth knowing.

Once you have arrived, there are a few simple steps that you can take to help reduce perplexity and understand the natives:

Choose locals for friends: Avoid only mixing with compatriots or other foreigners. Get to know the natives who can introduce you to the subtleties and nuances of the culture.

Practical social activities: Do not be put off more complex social encounters but ask for information on appropriate etiquette. People are frequently happy to help and teach genuinely interested and courteous foreigners.

Avoid "good"/"bad" or "us"/"them" comparisons: Try to establish how and why people perceive and explain the same act differently, have different expectations, etc. Social behaviour has resulted from different historical and economic conditions and may be looked at from various perspectives.

Attempt mediation: Rather than reject your or their cultural tradition, attempt to select, combine and synthesise the appropriate features of different social systems whether it is in dress, food or behaviour.

When you return, the benefits of foreign travel and the prevention of the "W-curve" may be helped by the following:

Become more self-observant: Returning home makes one realise the comparative and normative nature of one's own behaviour which was previously taken for granted. This in turn may alert one to which behaviour is culturally at odds (and, perhaps, why) – in itself helpful for all future travel.

Helping the foreigner: There is no better teaching aid than personal experience. That is why many foreign language schools send their teachers abroad not only to improve their language but to experience the difficulties their students have. Remembering this, we should perhaps be in a better position to help the hapless traveller who comes to our country.

Travel does broaden the mind (and frequently the behind), but requires some effort. Preparation, it is said, prevents a pretty poor performance and travelling in different social environments is no exception. But this preparation may require social, as well as geographic maps.

FOOD AND DRINK
by Dr Nick Beeching

Airline catering apart, one of the great pleasures of travel is the opportunity to sample new foods. Unfortunately the aphorism "Travel broadens the mind and loosens the bowels" holds true for the majority of travellers. A huge variety of micro-organisms cause diarrhoeal illness with or without vomiting, and these are usually ingested with food or water. Food may carry other health hazards – unpasteurised milk and milk products transmit brucellosis in the Middle East and parts of Africa, and raw fish and crabs harbour a number of unpleasant worm and fluke infections. Even polar explorers face hazards – the liver of carnivores such as polar bears and huskies causes human illness due to Vitamin A poisoning.

Although it is impossible to avoid infection entirely, the risk can be reduced by following some simple rules. The apparent prestige and expense of a hotel are no guide to the degree of hygiene employed in its kitchens, and the following guidelines apply equally to luxury travellers and those travelling rough.

Assurances from the local population (including long-term expatriates) that food is safe should not be taken too literally. They are likely to have developed immunity to organisms commonly present in their water supply. Sometimes it is impossible to refuse locally prepared food without causing severe offence, and invitations to village feasts will need to be dealt with diplomatically.

The major sources of external contamination of food are unclean water, dirty hands and flies. Pay scrupulous attention to personal hygiene, and only eat food with your fingers (including breads or fruit) if they have been thoroughly washed. Avoid food handled by others who you suspect may not have been so careful with their hands – and remember that in many countries toilet paper is not used.

Water

The mains water supply in many countries is contaminated with sewage, while streams, rivers, lakes and reservoirs are freely used as toilets, and for personal bathing and clothes washing. The same water may be used for washing food (especially salads and fruit) and may also be frozen to make ice cubes for drinks. Water should always be boiled or treated before drinking or use in the preparation of uncooked food (detailed advice is given in this chapter in the article *Water Purification*).

Hot tea or coffee are usually safe, as are beer and wine. Bottled water and carbonated drinks or fruit juice are not always safe, although the risk of adulteration or contamination is reduced if you keep to internationally-recognised brands. Insist on seeing the bottle (or can) before it is opened, thus confirming that the seal is tight and the drink has not been tampered with.

If you have any doubts about the cleanliness of plates and cutlery, they can be rinsed in a sterile solution such as tea or coffee, or wiped with an injection swab. If this is not feasible, leave the bottom layer of food on the plate, especially if it is served on a bed of rice. If drinking utensils appear to be contaminated, it may be preferable to drink straight from the bottle.

Food

Food that has been freshly cooked is the safest, but must be served hot. Beware of food that has been pre-cooked and kept warm for several hours, or desserts (especially those containing cream) that have been inadequately refrigerated after cooking. This includes many hotel buffets. Unpasteurised milk or cheese should be avoided, as should ice cream. Food that has been visited by flies is certain to have been contaminated by excrement and should not be eaten.

Salads and peeled fruit prepared by others may have been washed with contaminated water. In some parts of the tropics, salads may be highly contaminated by human excrement used as fertiliser. Salads and fruits are best avoided unless you can soak them in water that you know is clean. Unpeeled fruit is safe provided that you peel it yourself without contaminating the contents. "Wash it, peel it, boil it or forget it" seems to be the best advice.

Shellfish and prawns are particularly high risk foods because they act as filters, concentrating illness (they often thrive near sewage outfalls). They should only be eaten if thoroughly cooked and I recommend resisting the temptation altogether. Shellfish and prawns also concentrate biological toxins at certain times of the year, causing a different form of food poisoning. Raw fish, crustaceans and meat should always be avoided.

Hot spices and chillies do not sterilise foods, and chutneys and sauces that are left open on the table may have been visited by flies. Be cautious with chillies: they contain capsicin which is highly irritable to the bowel lining. Beware of trying to impress your hosts by matching their consumption of hot foods.

Alcohol

The temptation to over-indulge starts on the airplane, but in-flight alcohol should be taken sparingly as it increases the dehydration associated with air travel and worsens jet lag. Intoxicated airline passengers are a menace to everybody, and drinking impairs your ability to drive on arrival.

In hot countries, beware of rehydrating yourself with large volumes of alcoholic drink. Alcohol promotes the production of urine and can actually make you more dehydrated.

Excessive alcohol consumption promotes diarrhoea and prolonged abuse reduces the body's defences against infection. The deleterious social, domestic and professional hazards of prolonged alcohol abuse are well recognised problems for expatriates.

WATER PURIFICATION

by Julian McIntosh

Polluted water can at best lead to discomfort and mild illness, at worst to death, so the travelling layman needs to know not only what methods and products are available for water purification but also how to improvise a treatment system in an emergency.

Three points about advice on water treatment cause misunderstanding. Firstly, there is no need to kill or remove all the micro-organisms in water. Germs do not necessarily cause disease. Only those responsible for diseases transmitted by drinking water need be treated. And even some water-borne diseases are harmless when drunk. Legionnaires' disease, for example, is caught by breathing in droplets of water containing the bacteria, and not by drinking them.

Secondly, in theory, no normal treatment method will produce infinitely safe drinking water. There is always a chance, however small, that a germ might, by virtue of small size or resistance to chemicals or heat, survive and cause disease. But the more exacting your water treatment process, the smaller the risk – until such time as the risk is so tiny as to be discounted. The skill of the experts lies in assessing when water is, in practice, safe to drink. Unfortunately different experts set their standards at different levels.

Thirdly, beware the use of words like "pure", "disinfect" and "protection", common claims in many manufacturers' carefully written prose. Read the descriptions critically and you will find that most are not offering absolutely safe water but only a relative improvement.

Suspended Solids

If you put dirty water in a glass the suspended solids are the tiny particles that do not readily sink to the bottom. The resolution of the human eye is about one-hundredth of a millimetre, a particle half that size (five microns) is totally invisible to the naked eye and yet there can be over 10 million such particles in a litre of water without any visible trace. Suspended solids are usually materials such as decaying vegetable matter or mud and clay. Normally mud and clay contamination is harmless, but extremely fine rock particles including mica or asbestos occasionally remain in glacier water or water running through some types of clay.

Chemical Contamination

Most people will have experienced the taste of chlorine, the metallic taste of water from jerricans or the stale taste from water out of plastic containers. These tastes, and many others including those from stagnant water, are caused by minute quantities of chemicals that make the water unpleasant or even undrinkable but can easily be removed by charcoal or carbon filtration.

Microbiological Contamination

Eggs, worms, flukes, etc.: Organisms, amongst others, that lead to infections of roundworm (*Ascaris*), canine roundworm (*Toxocara canis*), guinea worm (*Dracunculus*) and bilharzia (*Schistosomiasis*). They are relatively large, although still microscopic, and can be removed by even crude forms of filtration. The very tiny black things that you sometimes see wriggling in very still water are insect larvae, not germs, and are not harmful. Practically any form of pre-treatment will remove them.

Protozoa: In this group of small, single-celled animals are the organisms that cause Giardiasis (*Giardia lamblia*), an unpleasant form of chronic diarrhoea, and amoebic dysentery (*Entamoeba histolytica*). Both of these protozoa have a cyst stage in their life cycle, during which they are inert and resistant to some forms of chemical treatment. However, they quickly become active and develop when they encounter suitable conditions such as the human digestive tract. They are sufficiently large to be separable from the water by the careful use of some types of pre-filter.

Bacteria: Very small, single-celled organisms responsible for many illnesses from cholera, salmonella, typhoid and bacillary dysentery, to the many less serious forms of diarrhoea known to travellers as Montezuma's Revenge or Delhi Belly. A healthy person would need to drink thousands of a particular bacterium to catch the disease. Luckily, the harmful bacteria transmitted by drinking contaminated water are fairly "soft" and succumb to chemical treatment – their minute size means only a very few filters can be relied upon to remove them all.

Viruses: These exceptionally small organisms live and multiply within host cells. Some viruses such as Hepatitis A and a variety of intestinal infections are transmitted through drinking water. Even the finest filters are too coarse to retain viruses. The polio and hepatitis viruses are about 50 times smaller than the pore size in even the finest ceramic filter.

Selection of a Water Supply

Whatever method of water treatment you use, it is essential to start with the best possible supply of water. Learning to assess the potential suitability of a water supply is one of the traveller's most useful skills.

Good points: Ground water, e.g. wells, boreholes, springs. Water away from or upstream of human habitation. Fast running water. Water above a sand or rock bed. Clear, colourless and odourless water.

Bad points: Water close to sources of industrial, human or animal contamination. Stagnant water. Water containing decaying vegetation. Water with odour or a scum on its surface. Discoloured or muddy water.

Wells and boreholes can be contaminated by debris and excreta falling or being washed in from the surface, so the top should be protected. A narrow wall will stop debris. A broad wall is not so effective as people will stand on it and dirt from their feet can fall in. Any wall is better than no wall at all. Fast running water is a hostile environment for the snails that support bilharzia.

Pre-treatment

If you are using water from a river, pool or lake, try to not to draw in extra dirt from the bottom or floating debris from the surface. If the source is surface water such as a lake or river, and very poor, some benefit may even be gained by digging a hole adjacent to the source. As the water seeps through, a form of pre-filtration will take place, leaving behind at least the coarsest contamination.

Pouring the water through finely woven fabrics will also remove some of the larger contamination. If you have fine, clean sand available, perhaps taken from a stream or lake bed, an improvised sand filter can be made using a tin can or similar container with a hole in the bottom. Even a (clean!) sock will do. Pour the water into the top, over the sand. Take care to disturb the surface of the sand as little as possible. Collect the water that has drained through the sand. The longer the filter used, the better the quality of the water so re-filter or discard the first water poured through. Discard the contaminated sand after use.

If you are able to store the water without disturbing it, you could also try sedimentation. Much of the dirt in water will settle out if left over a long enough period. Bilharzia flukes die after about 48 hours. The cleaner water can then be drawn off at the top. Very great care will be needed not to disturb the dirt at the bottom. Siphoning is the best method.

If the water you are using has an unpleasant taste or smell, an improvement can be achieved by using coarsely crushed wood charcoal wrapped in cloth. When the "bag" of charcoal is placed in the water or the water is run through the charcoal (like a sand filter) the organic chemicals responsible for practically all the unpleasant tastes and smells will be removed. Some colour improvement may also be noticed. The water will still not be safe to drink without further treatment but you should notice some benefit.

Treatment of a Water Supply

Boiling: Boiling at 100°C kills all the harmful organisms found in water except a few such as slow viruses and spores which are not dangerous if drunk. However, as your altitude above sea level increases, the weight of the atmosphere above you decreases, the air pressure drops, as does the temperature at which water boils. A rule of thumb for calculating this is that water boils at 1°C less for every 300 metres of altitude. Thus if you are on the summit of Kilimanjaro, at 5895m, the water will boil at only 80°C.

At temperatures below 100°C, most organisms can still be killed but it takes longer. At temperatures below 70°C, some of the harmful organisms can survive indefinitely and as the temperature continues to drop, so they will flourish.

There is one more important consideration. When water is boiling vigorously there is a lot of turbulence and all the water is at the same temperature. While water is coming to the boil, even if bubbles are rising, there is not only a marked and important difference between the temperature of the water and the temperature at a full boil but there can also be a substantial difference in temperature between water in different parts of the pan, with the result that harmful organisms may still be surviving.

To make water safe for drinking you should bring water to a full boil for at least two minutes. Boil water for one minute extra for every 300 metres above sea level. Do not cool water down with untreated water.

Filtration: The key to understanding the usefulness of a filter is ensuring you know the size of the particles that the filter will reliably separate, and the dirt load the filter can tolerate before it clogs up. If the pores in the filter are too large harmful particles can pass through. If small enough to stop harmful particles, the pores can block up quickly, preventing any more water from being filtered.

To reduce this problem, manufacturers employ ingenious means to increase the filter area, and filter in at progressively smaller stages. But even in one apparently clean litre of water there can be a hundred thousand million particles the same size or larger than bacteria. And to stop a bacterium, the filter has to take out all the other particles as well. If the filter is small (of the drinking straw type for instance) or if the water is at all visibly dirty, the filter will block in next to no time.

There are three solutions: water can be filtered first through a coarse filter to remove most of the dirt, and then again through a fine filter to remove the harmful bacteria; a re-cleanable filter can be used; or finally, only apparently clean water could be used with the filter. The use of a coarser filter is called pre-filtration. Viruses are so small they cannot be filtered out of drinking water by normal means. However, because they are normally found with their host infected cells and these are large enough to be filtered, the finest filters are also able to reduce the risk of virus infection from drinking water.

A filter collects quite a lot of miscellaneous debris on its surface and in order to prevent this providing a breeding ground for bacteria, the filter needs to be sterilised from time to time. Some are self-sterilising and need no action but others should be boiled for 20 to 30 minutes at least once every two weeks.

Where filters are described as combining a chemical treatment, this is for self-sterilisation. The chemical is in such small concentrations and in contact with water passing through the filter for such a short period that its use in improving the quality of the filtered water is negligible.

Pre-filtration: Pre-filters should remove particles larger than five to ten microns in size and be very simple to maintain. They will be more resistant to clogging since they take out only the larger particles. They will remove larger microbiological contamination including protozoal cysts, flukes and larger debris that might form a refuge for bacteria and viruses. Pre-filtration is normally adequate for washing. Further treatment is essential for safe drinking supplies.

Fine filtration: To remove all harmful bacteria from water a filter must remove all particles larger than 0.5 microns (some harmless bacteria are as small as 0.2 microns). Filters using a disposable cartridge are generally more compact and have high initial flow rates but are more expensive to operate. Alternatively there are ceramic filters that use porous ceramic "candles". These have low flow rates and are fairly heavy. Some need special care in transport to ensure they do not get cracked or chipped thus enabling untreated water to get through. Ceramic filters can be cleaned easily and are very economic in use.

Activated carbon/charcoal filters: Carbon filters remove a very wide range of chemicals from water including chlorine and iodine and can greatly improve the quality and palatability of water. But they do not kill or remove germs and may even provide an ideal breeding ground unless self-sterilising. Some filters combine carbon with other elements to make a filter that improves the taste as well as removing harmful organisms.

Chemical Treatment

There are broadly three germicidal chemicals used for drinking water treatment. For ease of use, efficiency and storage life, the active chemical is usually made up as a tablet suitable for a fixed volume of water although the heavier the contamination, the larger the dose required.

Germs can also be embedded in other matter and protected from the effects of a chemical, so where water is visibly dirty you must pre-filter first. Chlorine and iodine have no lasting germicidal effect so on no account should untreated water be added to water already treated.

Silver: Completely harmless, taste free and very long lasting effect, protecting stored water for up to six months. The sterilisation process is quite slow and it is necessary to leave water for at least two hours before use. Silver compounds are not effective against cysts of Amoeba and Giardia, so use pre-filtration first if the water is of poor quality.

Chlorine: Completely harmless, fast acting and 100 per cent effective if used correctly. A minimum of ten minutes is required before water can be used. The cysts of Amoeba and Giardia are about ten times more resistant to chlorine than bacteria but both are killed if treatment time and dose are adequate. If in doubt, we recommend that the period before use be extended to at least twenty and preferably 30 minutes.

If heavy contamination is suspected, double the dosage. Alternatively, pre-filter. Some people find the taste of chlorine unpleasant particularly if larger doses are being used. The concentration of chlorine drops quickly over several hours and more so in warm temperatures so there is very little lasting effect. Excess chlorine may be removed using Sodium Thiosulphate or carbon filters.

Iodine: Fast acting and very effective, normally taking ten minutes before water is safe to use. It has a quicker action against cysts than chlorine. Double dosage and extended treatment times or pre-filtration are still very strongly recommended if heavy contamination is suspected. Iodine is more volatile than chlorine and the lasting effect is negligible. Excess iodine may be removed by Sodium Thiosulphate or a carbon filter.

Note: Iodine can have serious, lasting physiological side effects and should not be used over an extended period. Groups particularly at risk are those with thyroid problems and the unborn foetuses of pregnant women. Thyroid problems may only become apparent when the gland is faced with excess iodine, so in the unlikely event of the use of iodine compounds being unavoidable, ask your doctor to arrange for a thyroid test beforehand – or use a good carbon filter to remove excess iodine from the water.

Rules

Order of treatment: If chemical treatment and filtration are being combined, filter first. Filtration removes organic matter which would absorb the chemical and make it less effective. If of a carbon type, the filter will also absorb the chemical leaving none for residual treatment.

In some cases, the filter may also be a source of contamination. If water is being stored prior to treatment then it is worthwhile treating chemically as soon as the water is collected and again after filtration. The first chemical dose prevents algae growing in the stored water.

Storage of water: Use separate containers for treated and untreated water, mark them accordingly and don't mix them up. If you are unable to use separate containers take particular care to sterilise the area round the filler and cap before treated water is stored or at the time treatment takes place. In any case, containers for untreated water should be sterilised every two to three weeks.

Treated water should never be contaminated with any untreated water. Treated water should never be stored in an open container. Treated water left uncovered and not used straight away should be regarded as suspect and re-treated.

SEX ABROAD

by Dr Richard Dawood

Have you talked to your doctor about sex, lately? Doctors who give pre-travel health advice are generally more inclined to launch into a discussion of the latest research into malaria, or even travellers' diarrhoea, than raise the issue of casual sex. After all, doesn't everybody already know about HIV? The truth is, however, that one important fact about HIV seems to have escaped most people's attention: HIV infection resulting from sex abroad has now overtaken every other tropical and infectious disease hazard, to become the single most frequent cause of lethal infection in travellers.

The comparison between HIV and malaria is an interesting one. Malaria's place in the pantheon of travel-related disease, and in the thoughts and fears of departing travellers and their doctors, is secure. There are approximately two thousand cases of malaria in British travellers every year, causing between ten and fifteen deaths; we agonise over each fatal case that occurs in the near certain knowledge that it could have been prevented, and we scrutinise every detail for lessons that can be learned for the future. Yet during 1996 there were 495 confirmed cases of HIV infection resulting from heterosexual sex abroad. These cases include migrants to the UK, not just travellers; but in view of the long delay before infection becomes apparent, they represent the tip of a much larger iceberg: the true rate of infection is probably twice this number. The HIV infection rate in travellers is currently one hundred times higher than fatality rate from malaria, and it is rising.

These figures mean that no fewer than 80 per cent of British HIV cases in heterosexuals are acquired abroad. So far, 85 per cent of these overseas infections have originated in Africa, but other regions are catching up: almost two thirds of the total number of infections acquired in Asia have occurred since 1993. There has also been a dramatic increase in the numbers of cases in the countries of the Soviet Union.

In developing countries world-wide, the rates of HIV infection are mounting, and the pattern of infection is also changing. HIV is increasingly a disease of the young: some 60 per cent of new infections are in people aged between 15 and 24. Young women are particularly at risk: in Uganda, for example, the rate of infection among women in the 13 to 19 age group is 20 times higher than in men, and a recent survey of pregnant teenage women in Zimbabwe found 30 per cent of them to be HIV positive. Among people of both sexes in the commercial sex industry, infection rates in many parts of the developing world approach 100 per cent.

Other sexually transmitted diseases, from gonorrhoea and syphilis to more exotic and unfamiliar diseases such as chancroid, may seem to pale into insignificance beside the risks of HIV, but they have not disappeared from the scene: STD's are now nearly as common as malaria, with more than 250 million new cases world-wide every year: each year, one in twenty adolescents world-wide contracts a sexually transmitted disease.

How have travellers responded to these growing risks? In a survey of 782 returning travellers at the Hospital for Tropical Diseases, in London, 18.6 per cent reported having sex with at least one new partner while away almost half of them with more than one partner. Another, smaller survey, found that twelve out of seventeen people who admitted to having sex with a new partner while abroad had carried condoms, but had failed to use them on account of getting very drunk. A recent Swiss study found that four per cent of Swiss visitors to Kenya had sex with local people often without using condoms, while a survey of Swedish travellers found that 28 per cent had sex with a new partner while travelling in Europe. These figures appear to reflect remarkable levels of restraint by comparison with a British survey of visitors to Torquay, where, out of 1000 people aged 16-29, 600 said that they had had sex with a new partner without a condom during their visit. (Another finding from the same study: holiday makers who were engaged to be married but had left their partners at home were more likely to report a sexual encounter than other visitors.)

Sex with fellow travellers rather than local people is not necessarily an entirely safer option since surveys have shown that many people are prepared to lie in order to have sex. One survey of young, sexually active Californians showed that 47 per cent of the men, and 60 per cent of the women, claimed that they had been lied to for the purposes of sex; 34 per cent of the men and ten per cent of the women admitted that they themselves would also be prepared to lie. twenty per cent of the men said that they would lie about having a negative HIV-antibody test, and nearly half of both men and women said that they would understate their number of previous partners. Of those who had been sexually involved with more than one person at a time, more than half said their partners did not know.

In Thailand, where the sex tourist once reigned supreme, public attitudes are only now beginning to change. Largely through the efforts of former government minister Mechay Viravaidya (widely known in his country as Mr Condom), an energetic programme of public education and condom distribution is under way. In the Philippines, a British travel agent received a sixteen-year prison sentence for organising paedophile sex tours into the country as part of a new drive by President Fidel Ramos to curb sex tourism. Such initiatives are still relatively rare in the developing world, and will have to be carefully-planned, vigorous and sustained before they will have any real impact upon the health of local people.

When Edwina Currie advised travellers to avoid temptation by taking along their partner, she at least managed to hit the headlines. Current British efforts to educate departing travellers consist of distributing soft-sell leaflets to GP waiting rooms, and an occasional poster at Heathrow. Until we can find more effective ways to increase public awareness of the problem, and to persuade travellers to avoid or reduce their exposure, HIV infection will remain the most formidable disease hazard of modern international travel.

HEALTH IN THE HEAT

by Dr Richard Dawood

Travel broadens the mind and brings untold benefits to the human spirit, but in doing so it often rains a multitude of physiological insults upon the human body. Dehydration is one of the most fundamental of these, but there have been some important recent developments in our understanding of its mechanisms and how to avoid it.

In a temperate climate, most people need a daily fluid intake of two litres of water to remain in balance. In a hot, humid climate, and with increased physical activity ten litres a day – one seventh of body weight – and sometimes more may be needed.

It takes about three weeks for people who normally live in a temperate climate to acclimatise to a hot one: for most trips by British holiday-makers, there is therefore no chance of acclimatising fully. During acclimatisation sweat glands develop the ability to produce more sweat, to respond more quickly, and to lose less salt; stomach and intestines also adapt to become better able to absorb salt and water more efficiently. Without acclimatisation, newcomers to hot climates have difficulty conserving water and salt and are at a significant risk of developing heat-related illnesses. (Excessive physical exertion increases the risk; avoid this until acclimatisation is complete.)

Acclimatisation is usually much more difficult in hot and humid climates than hot and dry ones. In humid climates, sweat does not evaporate easily and temperature and humidity tend to remain high through the night. This is a continuous stress, whereas in dry climates they both tend to fall at night, allowing the sweating mechanism to rest.

Small, thin people tend to acclimatise most easily to the heat – because their body surface area is relatively higher in relation to their volume, giving a relatively greater area from which to sweat and lose heat. Unfit, overweight people acclimatise more slowly, and do badly in the heat. People with high blood pressure and heart disease may be at risk from complications.

To remain in balance under such conditions, the body needs a greatly increased intake of salt and water. The trouble is that thirst and taste give an extremely poor indication of exactly how much is required. Many people have a reduced appetite on first arrival in a warm climate, which may reduce salt intake even further.

Deficiency of salt, water, or both, is called heat exhaustion. Lethargy, fatigue and headache are typical features, eventually leading to coma and death. Many sufferers do not even feel thirsty, and may have no idea that they are suffering from this problem. They feel "hung over". In fact, most symptoms of a typical, bad hangover are the direct result of dehydration. They feel irritable, and simply want to be left alone.

Prevention is by far the best approach. Perhaps the best method is the British Army's pre-salted water regime. Salt is added to all fluids —tea, coffee, soup, fruit juices, water. the required amount is one quarter of a level teaspoon (approximately one gram) per pint – which results in a solution that is just below the taste threshold. (Don't use salt tablets – they are poorly absorbed, irritate the stomach and may cause vomiting.) Plenty of pre-salted fluid should be the rule for anyone spending much time in the tropics.

The only reliable guide to how much you need to drink in a tropical climate is the colour of your urine. Always drink enough to ensure that it is consistently pale in colour, and don't just wait until you feel thirsty before drinking.

Heat exhaustion should not be confused with heatstroke (formerly called sunstroke). Although dehydration is almost always a factor, the main problem is a failure of the body's heat control mechanisms. Sweating diminishes and the body temperature rises, headache and delirium also occur. Prompt treatment is essential. Once the body temperature begins to rise, death may occur within four hours. The priority is to lower body temperature. Remove clothing, and cover the victim with a wet bed-sheet, while arranging transfer to hospital. There are well-documented cases of travellers who have been left in their hotel rooms to die, simply because their condition was mistaken for a drunken stupor.

Infectious diseases that cause a fever can sometimes be mistaken for heatstroke, again with potentially fatal results. Malaria and meningitis are especially important in this context because in both cases deterioration is rapid if treatment is not given.

Prickly heat is the most common heat-related skin disorder – a sweat rash occurring on the sweatier parts of the body and consisting of tiny blisters on sore, reddened, mildly inflamed skin. You can prevent it with frequent showers and by keeping the skin clean and dry. Treat with calamine lotion.

Brown without Burning

The effects of the sun on skin include sunburn, thickening and – in the longer term – drying, loss of elasticity, wrinkling, loosening, discolouration, premature ageing and skin cancer. People with fair, blond or red hair are most at risk, even after they've turned grey. Acute sunburn is a miserable way to begin a holiday. It results in a blotchy uneven tan and is all the more miserable for children whose skin is easily damaged.

If you're not bothered about a tan, cover up and use a high protection factor sunscreen. But if vanity gets the better of you, tan very slowly. The protection factor numbers on skin preparations provide a rough measure of how much longer you can stay out in the sun without burning. If your skin normally burns in strong sunlight after twenty minutes' exposure, for example, a sunscreen with a protection factor of four will allow you to stay out for four times as long (80 minutes). After that you would have to cover up; you would have had your maximum dose of sunlight and more factor four would not protect you. If you wanted to stay out in the sun for 160 minutes, you would burn if you used anything less than a protection factor of eight. Protection factor numbers refer mainly to UVB protection – protection against the rays that cause acute sunburn. Protection against UVA – the rays mainly responsible for ageing and skin cancer effects – is usually shown by means of a star rating system. Clearly, using a sunscreen that only protected against UVB rays but allowed people to spend more time in the sun, might actually increase the possibility of long term damage. Check that any product you use gives protection against both.

Apart from cosmetic acceptability and protection factor, there is, however, little else to choose between the different brands of sunscreen. Whichever brand you pick, you should re-apply it frequently, especially when swimming or sweating. Most of the leading manufacturers now produce waterproof sunscreens which are particularly useful for children.

Some parts of the body are especially vulnerable and need extra care – the face, particularly the nose and forehead, neck and ears; parts of the body that are normally covered; the tops of the collar bones, bald patches on the scalp; and feet. Avoid sunbathing in the hottest part of the day and be guided by the habits of those more accustomed to hot climates, who take a relaxing indoor siesta instead.

If you burn, calamine lotion will soothe affected areas and mild painkillers are often helpful. More extensive or severe burns should be treated with a mild antiseptic and kept clean and dry. Stay out of the sun or use a total block sunscreen until the skin has healed.

The eyes, too, can be affected by the sun. The conjunctiva and retina are sensitive to ultra-violet light and are easily damaged. Pain usually begins several hours after exposure, when the delicate cells of the conjunctiva swell and become painful and inflamed. In the long term, excessive exposure to the elements causes a "pterygium" – an unsightly yellow patch on the white of the eye that may need to be removed. Good quality sunglasses provide effective protection.

Skin Cancer and the Sun

In the last few years the number of cases of skin cancer in the UK has risen. The number of people taking holidays abroad has also risen, so the Royal College of Physicians in London commissioned a special study to determine whether or not there was a link. The results of this work have important implications for travellers: it found that the risks of skin cancer and skin damage from strong sunlight relate not just to long-term exposure, but also to the number of episodes of acute sunburn.

Skin cancers grow slowly and tend to destroy the area of skin in their immediate vicinity. Since they usually occur on exposed area – President Reagan's nose was one well-publicised site – they can inflict much cosmetic damage. Some types – melanomas especially – become able to spread through the body. The Royal College of Physicians advises examining every pigmented patch and mole on your skin as follows:

1. Does it itch, or sensation alter over it?

2. Is its diameter 1cm or more?
3. Is it increasing in size?
4. Is its border irregular in shape?
5. Does the density of black or brown colour within it vary?
6. Is the patch inflamed?
7. Is there bleeding or crusting?
If the answer is "yes" to three or more of these questions, seek medical advice. The treatment is simple if the cancer is detected at an early stage.

ALTITUDE SICKNESS

by Dr Richard Dawood

My first exposure to the effect of high altitude was in Nepal, several years ago. I was on a trek six days' journey from Kathmandu. It is a bizarre and unnerving feeling to discover that your exercise tolerance is suddenly no more than a few slow paces; that your pulse races with each step you take, and that you are obliged to stop to catch your breath every few feet, waiting for the palpitations to subside while local people of all ages – some carrying heavy loads – stop, stare, then overtake. I was a fit young medical student, but my body felt as though it belonged to the victim of some dreadful disease that I had just been studying – chronic bronchitis perhaps, emphysema or asbestosis.

I developed a hammering headache, and became more and more breathless, even at rest. I was lucky; although I didn't know it, these were important warning signs of acute mountain sickness (AMS). I decided to come down. In fact, the medical profession has a poor track record when it comes to heeding their own symptoms, and an especially poor record at high altitude. In a report on seven deaths from mountain sickness on Himalayan treks, three of the seven who died were themselves doctors.

The tragic fact about deaths from mountain sickness is that they are preventable in every case. The purpose of this article is therefore threefold: to offer some practical information about AMS, its warning signs and prevention: to discuss the merit of drugs that are sometimes suggested for prevention: and to consider other approaches to emergency treatment.

Mountain Sickness

The driving force for the absorption of oxygen through the lungs into the bloodstream is atmospheric pressure – the "weight" of the column of air that extends for ten miles or so above our heads. As we ascend, atmospheric pressure is reduced. Complex mechanisms exist to compensate for the resulting lack of oxygen: these include an increase in breathing rate and depth, and changes in the blood and tissues that increase their efficiency in carrying and using oxygen. However, the increased breathing results in reduced levels of carbon dioxide, causing the body to become more alkaline, and in turn causing numerous other physiological changes to occur, not all of which are clearly understood. The kidneys are able to compensate for changes in alkalinity and acidity, but the process of acclimatisation to high altitude can take several days – longer under conditions of low temperature and increased exercise.

AMS tends to occur within two days of exposure. It usually begins with loss of appetite, headache, nausea, vomiting and sleeplessness. This is the early, benign form. It may simply resolve, but may also progress to a more serious so-called "malignant" form. It should be regarded as an important warning.

Malignant AMS may be fatal, and it may begin with little or no warning. Pulmonary oedema develops – a build-up of fluid in the lung tissues, that further interferes with absorption of oxygen, leading to breathlessness that persists even at rest. There is also a cough, with white, pink or frothy sputum, and the lips may turn blue. A build-up of tissue may also occur in the brain – cerebral oedema. This results in headache, drowsiness, impaired co-ordination, abnormal or drunken behaviour, confusion, impaired consciousness, and coma. Progression to coma may occur quite rapidly.

Benign AMS can be handled initially by remaining at the same altitude until symptoms resolve. If they do not improve, the best treatment is prompt descent. Victims of malignant AMS need to be brought down immediately, and most sufferers need to be carried down. Experts on AMS advise that descent should not be delayed while aid is summoned, and should start even at night if possible.

Mountain sickness is most often a problem at altitudes over nine or ten thousand feet, though in some people it may occur as low as seven or eight thousand, this means that a hazard exists at many popular travel destinations. Crucial factors in determining susceptibility to AMS are speed of ascent, and the altitude at which you sleep. If possible, begin by avoiding sleeping above ten thousand feet for the first few nights. "Climb high, Sleep low," is the rule to follow. Then increase your sleeping altitude by no more than one thousand feet per day – even this may be too fast for some people to adapt to.

High on Drugs

Whilst the most important approach to treatment is descent, there is an increasing trend towards advising trekkers and climbers to consider carrying medication, two drugs for the treatment and prevention of AMS. These drugs are acetazolamide (Diamox) and dexamethasone. A third drug, nifedipine, has shown promising results, but is not usually suitable for self treatment.

Acetazolamide is a diuretic drug that increases excretion of bicarbonate by the kidney, tending to counteract the increase in alkalinity referred to above. Some experts consider that it speeds acclimatisation, while others believe that it may mask early symptoms that are not a great nuisance in themselves, but that provide useful warning signs that severe AMS may be developing. There is no consensus. I have spoken to doctors who swear by acetazolamide, and to others who are greatly troubled by such side-effects as nausea, tiredness, poor sleep, and "pins and needles" in the arms and legs. There are many cases on record of malignant AMS occurring despite the use of acetazolamide. It may, nonetheless provide some worthwhile benefit. Dexamethasone is a powerful "steroid" drug that has many actions; the most beneficial of these, as far as high altitude is concerned, is a tendency to reduce oedema. It does not affect acclimatisation, but merely alleviates some of the symptoms. It is safe for most people when taken for only short periods, but serious side-effects do occur, especially in people with diabetes. It may be useful to carry this drug for emergency use in descent.

The Gamow Bag

The best treatment for a victim of the effects of reduced oxygen pressure is, obviously, to increase the pressure. Bringing the victim down is usually the fastest and simplest way of doing this. However, a new approach also has its appeal. This is the use of a simple, portable compression chamber known as the Gamow bag. It looks like an oversized sleeping bag that can be inflated with a foot-pump. It has to be pumped continuously, to eliminate waste gases, and this can be tiring at altitude. Alternatively, a carbon dioxide extractor is available for it. A larger model capable of accommodating two people is also available.

Achievable compression is roughly equivalent to a five-thousand-foot descent, depending on your altitude. This would certainly buy time in an emergency, though there is no substitute for descent for people who are seriously ill. It has already been used with great success by expeditions to remote places where rescue is difficult. Its cost makes it suitable for groups and expeditions rather than routine treks.

In a recent case, however, one victim of AMS died while left unattended overnight in such a chamber. It is very important for people with AMS to be carefully monitored throughout the course of their illness and to be brought down if there is no rapid response to the increased pressure.

Conclusion

The best approach to AMS is prevention, and the most important measure is gradual ascent. Problems are particularly common with people on a tight time schedule, who fly in to high altitude destinations, and try to cram in the maximum amount of sights and activity into the shortest time possible. One simply cannot expect to be able to fly in to places like La Paz, Cuzco or Leh and carry on sightseeing without allowing ample time – perhaps several days – for rest and acclimatisation. Yet there are cases on record where unfit, elderly people have been booked on tours to Peru without any warning about the dangers of high altitude, and have died as a result. Mountain sickness is a preventable illness, and all travellers to high altitude regions should make sure they are fully informed about it.

MALARIA

by Drs Sharon Welby and Nick Beeching

Malaria remains rife throughout much of the tropics, and causes a huge burden in terms of illness and death for the indigenous population. It poses a significant and difficult problem for the traveller. The ever-changing pattern of drug resistance, along with concerns about side-effect of anti-malarial drugs, result in confusion regarding the selection of anti-malarial drugs. Awareness of the very real hazard of malaria and the importance of gaining accurate pre-travel advice is vital for travellers to the tropics.

Malaria is a parasitic blood infection transmitted by the bite of the female anopheline mosquito. There are four types of malaria: *Plasmodium falciparum, Plasmodium ovale, Plasmodium vivax* and *Plasmodium malariae*. P. falciparum, also known as malignant malaria, is the most serious: more than two million people living in endemic areas die as a result of it each year. In spite of persisting efforts, adequate control of malaria has not yet been achieved and there is a significant risk for travellers to most parts of the Indian Sub-continent and the Far East, Sub-Saharan Africa and parts of Central and South America. The risks in North Africa and countries in the east Mediterranean littoral and the Middle East are more variable.

The Illness

The incubation period after a mosquito bite varies from a minimum of eight to ten days up to several years. Most people who are infected by falciparum malaria develop symptoms within a couple of months, but the longest symptom-free period we have seen was over a year. The earliest symptoms are non specific and are often wrongly diagnosed as 'flu or gastroenteritis. Most people develop symptoms of fever, headache and generalised aches and pains, and about a quarter of people have pronounced vomiting and diarrhoea. It is therefore essential that travellers have an immediate blood test for malaria if they develop a fever a week after arriving in a malarious area or within a year of their return. If left untreated, patients (especially expatriates who have not been exposed to malaria before) can rapidly develop high fevers or lapse into a coma and die. Between five and fifteen people die of malaria infection in the UK each year, and many of these are due to delay in seeking medical advice.

The other three forms of malaria are rarely life-threatening but can have a more prolonged incubation period of up to two years. They cannot be distinguished from life-threatening falciparum malaria unless a blood film is examined. These three forms of malaria sometimes relapse after effective treatment of the first illness, so further drug treatment is usually required with a drug called primaquine.

Prevention

Personal protection for the traveller focuses on two main aspects, the first is to prevent being bitten by mosquitoes and the second relies on taking antimalarial drugs regularly. When a malaria-carrying mosquito bites a person, the malaria parasites travel to the liver via the blood stream and develop there without causing any signs of illness. Once the parasite is ready, it leaves the liver and attacks the red blood cells. This is the stage at which anti-malarial drugs act, by preventing the parasite from infecting blood cells and thereby preventing the symptoms of malaria from developing. It is important to keep taking antimalarials regularly while abroad, so that drug levels in the blood are sufficient to prevent disease, and to continue taking the drugs for four weeks after leaving the malarious area so that the incubation period after any potential bites is covered by the drugs.

The malaria carrying mosquitoes bite from dusk to dawn and bites can be prevented by using a combination of methods:

• Wearing shirts and trousers after dusk. Clothing can also be soaked in repellent, 30 millilitres of repellent dissolved in two hundred and fifty millilitres of water is an effective mixture.
• Sleeping in an air-conditioned or a screened room, or under a bednet (prefer-

ably one impregnated with permethrin (0.2 grams of permethrin per metre of material).

• Repelling and killing any mosquitoes which have entered the bedroom with pyrethrum sprays, mosquito coils or electrical insecticide dispensers. Electronic buzzers are not effective.

• Using repellents containing diethyltoluamide (DEET) or using the new eucalyptus based repellent *Mosiguard Natural*.

Anti-malarial Drugs

Anti-malarial drug therapy is an area fraught with difficulty. The changing pattern of drug resistance, together with possible side-effects of the drugs, have made it increasingly difficult to choose the correct regimens. With this in mind it is advisable for all travellers to obtain specialist advice prior to their trip. In Britain there are currently four main anti-malarial drugs in use: chloroquine, proguanil, mefloquine and doxycycline.

Chloroquine and Proguanil

Chloroquine and proguanil (*Paludrine*) are the oldest and most widely used. They are safe to take long-term (however, eye check-ups are recommended after three years of use) and the wealth of experience suggests that they are safe to use during pregnancy. Unfortunately there is now widespread resistance to these drugs rendering them much less effective in some parts of the world. Depending on the area to be visited, they are either taken alone or together. Travellers should start anti-malarials at least a week before travel, mainly to make sure that they do not react to the medication, continue whilst there and for at least four weeks after leaving a malarious area. The usual adult dose is chloroquine two tablets once a week together with proguanil two tablets daily (a total of sixteen tablets per week). The main side-effects of the chloroquine/proguanil combination (apart from an unpleasant taste) are nausea, stomach upsets and mouth ulcers. Chloroquine should not be taken by people who are currently suffering from epilepsy or have had epilepsy in the past, or by people who suffer from psoriasis, a common skin disorder.

Mefloquine (*Lariam*)

There has been a lot of controversy surrounding the use of mefloquine for malaria prophylaxis. Publicity in the media and conflicting medical advice have led to confusion, and subsequently some travellers are not taking any drug prophylaxis at all for countries where it is recommended. This could lead to potentially life threatening malaria infection. Every traveller needs to consider the pros and cons of mefloquine and decide if the drug is suitable for them.

Mefloquine is first choice for areas where there is widespread chloroquine resistance such as sub-Saharan Africa, the Amazonian basin and parts of South East Asia. Mefloquine is not suitable for everyone and it should not be taken by:

• women in the first 12 weeks of pregnancy, women who are breast feeding or women who might become pregnant within three months of taking the last tablet.

• people with a history of epilepsy or a strong family history of epilepsy

• people who have any mental health problems, e.g. depression, anxiety attacks

or mood disturbances
- people who are taking certain kinds of blood pressure tablets (ß blockers)
- people whose jobs depend on a high degree of co-ordination, such as airline pilots or professional divers
- It is not suitable for young children under 15 kgs (this limit may be lowered soon) or for people with severe kidney or liver problems.

Studies from Africa show that mefloquine is more effective at preventing malaria infection then a combination of chloroquine and proguanil (90 per cent compared to 60-70 per cent). Mefloquine is also convenient to take as it is a weekly dose and it is now licensed to be used for up to one year. However it is relatively expensive.

All drugs have side effects: studies have shown that mefloquine can cause problems such as dizziness, headache, insomnia, vivid dreams and depression in a few people. A recent study showed that around a quarter of those people taking mefloquine and an eighth taking chloroquine and proguanil experienced these problems. Some studies have shown that in about one in ten people the side-effects interfered with planned activities and in one in 10,000 people a severe side-effect occurred. The majority of side-effects with mefloquine start within three weeks of starting the drug and stop within three weeks of stopping. It is recommended that you start mefloquine at least two weeks before travelling so that if any side-effects should occur you can change to an alternative drug.

Doxycycline
The third alternative is an antibiotic called doxycycline (a form of tetracycline). This is particularly popular with Australian travellers but British authorities mainly recommend it for travellers to the border areas of Thailand / Myanmar (Burma) and Thailand / Cambodia as well as the western province of Cambodia, where falciparum malaria is often resistant to both chloroquine and mefloquine. Doxycycline should not be taken by pregnant women or children under the age of eight. It should be taken with liberal quantities of fluid to prevent ulceration and discomfort in the oesophagus (gullet). The main side-effect is that some people become very sensitive to the sun and become sunburnt easily (a good sun tan cream is recommended – factor 15+). Doxycycline interferes with the contraceptive pill and it is recommended that women also use barrier methods of contraception in the first 2 weeks of starting doxycycline. Women taking regular doxycycline may be prone to recurrent vaginal thrush. Balancing these side effects, doxycycline provides good anti-malarial protection and also reduces the incidence and duration of travellers' diarrhoea.

Children and Pregnant Women

Children require lower doses of antimalarials, depending on their age and weight. They soon learn to dislike both chloroquine and proguanil. Although chloroquine syrup is available proguanil is only available as tablets. The tablets can be ground up and hidden in treats (jam, sandwiches, chocolates etc.) to persuade children to take them. Pregnant women are prone to severe malaria attacks and should be advised not to travel to areas with a significant malaria risk – especially sub Saharan Africa – unless it is unavoidable, when they must take malaria prophylaxis. It is recommended that pregnant women also take folic acid (a vitamin) at the same time as proguanil.

Expatriates

Long-term expatriates are more difficult to advise. Many adopt a "macho" attitude to malaria and discontinue any malaria prophylaxis in the mistaken belief that they have developed protective immunity. Due to rapid emergence of drug resistant malaria, we believe that this is an unwise option. The best advice will be given on a personal level by your GP because all these cases will be different.

Standby Treatment

The more adventurous traveller going to places where rapid access to medical advice is not available may wish to carry a course of anti-malarial "standby" treatment. This should be taken if symptoms of possible malaria develop, but it is not a substitute for medical care, and it is important to seek medical advice and a blood film. The standby regime will depend on the drug resistance in the area which you are visiting and on which anti-malarial drugs are being taken. It is advisable to seek specialist advice. Some examples of standby medications are:

Fansidar – three tablets taken at the same time is the most convenient, but this is not suitable for people who are allergic to sulpha drugs.

Mefloquine – two tablets taken together followed by 2 tablets 12 hours later. The main problem with this dose of mefloquine is severe nausea and vomiting and the increased risk of neuropsychiatric side-effects.

Halofantrine – Until recently a third option, halofantrine (*Halfan*) was very popular for self treatment, particularly in East Africa, but side-effects of this drug affecting the heart have now been identified and we recommend that it should not be used.

Quinine – (adult dose 2 tablets 3 times a day for 3 days) and tetracycline (adult dose 1 tablet 4 times a day for 7 days) are recommended as stand by medication in areas with a lot of drug resistance.

Summary

The risk of malaria infection poses a real and significant problem for the traveller. It is essential that pre-travel advice is sought and that each traveller takes anti-mosquito bite measures and decides which anti-malarial drug regime is suitable for them. It is important to remember that no anti-malarial drug is 100 per cent effective and any illness, especially if there is fever, must lead to a blood test to exclude malaria infection. It is also important to inform the doctor that you have been to a malarious area within the preceding two years. If this advice is ignored, the diagnosis of malaria will not be considered until too late, and tragic and preventable deaths will continue to occur.

Key Points

1. Take measures to prevent mosquito bites:
> *repellents*
> *impregnated bed nets*
> *suitable clothing*

> *sleep in a screened room and use knock down insecticides, coils or electronic vapourisers*

2. Take appropriate anti-malarial drugs regularly and complete the course.
3. Remember that no prophylaxis is 100 per cent effective and in the event of any illness, especially if there is fever, seek immediate diagnosis (with a blood film) and treatment.
4. Consider carrying "standby treatment".

DIARRHOEAL ILLNESS

by Dr Nick Beeching

The world-wide distribution of traveller's diarrhoea is reflected in its many geographical synonyms – Delhi belly, the Aztec two-step, Turista, Malta dog, Rangoon runs, to name a few. Typically, the illness starts a few days after arrival at your destination and consists of diarrhoea without blood, nausea with some vomiting and perhaps a mild fever. The mainstay of treatment is adequate rehydration and rest, and the illness is usually self-limiting within a few days. Antibiotics to treat or prevent this common illness are not usually prescribed in anticipation of an infection. Exceptions to this rule are business travellers or others embarking on short trips (less than two to three weeks) for whom even a short period of illness would be disastrous, e.g. athletes attending international meetings.

The most important aspect for the treatment of diarrhoea is the replacement of fluids and salts that have been lost from the body. For most adults, non-carbonated, non-alcoholic drinks that do not contain large amounts of sugar are quite adequate. For adults with prolonged diarrhoea and for children, it is more important to use balanced weak salt solutions which contain a small amount of sugar that promotes absorption of the salts. These can be obtained in pre-packaged sachets of powder (e.g. *Dioralyte*, *Rehidrat*) that are convenient to carry and are dissolved in a fixed amount of sterile water. *Dioralyte* can also be bought in the UK as effervescent tablets.

If pre-packaged mixtures are not available, a simple rehydration solution can be prepared by adding eight level teaspoonfuls of sugar or honey and half a teaspoon of salt to one litre of water (with flavouring to tempt small children).

Nausea, which frequently accompanies diarrhoea, can usually be overcome by taking small amounts of fluid as often as possible. For small children it may be necessary to give spoonfuls of fluid every few minutes for prolonged periods. If you or your child have severe vomiting which prevents any fluids being taken, medical attention must be sought immediately.

Anti-diarrhoeal drugs are not usually recommended and should rarely be given to children. Kaopectate is safe for children aged over two years but not very effective (Kaolin and morphine should not be carried). For adults, codeine phosphate, loperamide (*Imodium* or *Arret*) or diphenoxylate (*Lomotil*) are sometimes useful. These drugs should never be given to children and should not be used for bloody or prolonged diarrhoea. They are best reserved for occasional use to prevent accidents while travelling – for example before a prolonged rural bus trip. Prolonged use of these medications may prevent your body from eliminating the diarrhoea – causing organisms and toxins which may lead to constipation.

Preparations containing clioquinol are still widely available outside the UK, where it was previously sold under the trade name *Enterovioform*. These preparations are useless and should not be taken (they have been linked with severe side effects in some parts of the world). Other than rehydration solutions or the medications discussed in this section, I do not recommend purchasing medicines for diarrhoea from pharmacies or chemists.

Prevention

Travellers who wish to prevent diarrhoea should consult their medical adviser about preventative medication (a controversial issue within the profession) before travel. Liquid bismuth preparations (not an antibiotic) are effective but huge volumes need to be carried in luggage (very messy if broken), and bismuth tablets are difficult to obtain in the UK. Various groups of antibiotics may be used, including tetracyclines (eg doxycycline), sulphur containing antibiotics (e.g. *Steptrotriad* or cotrimoxazole, *Septrin* or *Bactrim*) and quinolone agents (e.g. ciprofloxacin, norfloxacin).

Prophylactic antibiotics are not recommended for the majority of travellers because of the limited duration of effectiveness and the possibility of side effects, including, paradoxically, diarrhoea.

Self-treatment

Self-treatment with antibiotics for established diarrhoeal illness is usually inappropriate unless qualified medical attention is impossible to obtain. Travellers to remote areas may wish to carry a course of antibiotics for this eventuality. Bloody diarrhoea with abdominal pain and fever may be due to bacillary dysentery (shigella organisms) or a variety of other organisms such as campylobacter or salmonella. The most appropriate antibiotic would be a quinolone such as ciprofloxacin, or a sulphur drug such as cotrimoxazole. Prolonged bloody diarrhoea with mucus (jelly), especially without much fever, may be due to amoebic dysentery which is treated with metronidazole (*Flagyl*) or tinidazole (*Fasigyn*).

Prolonged, explosive diarrhoea with pale creamy motions may be due to giardia, a common hazard for overlanders travelling through the Indian subcontinent. This responds to metronidazole or tinidazole. These two antibiotics should not be taken at the same time as alcohol because of severe reactions between them.

If you have to treat yourself, obtain qualified medical investigation and help at the earliest opportunity. This is essential if symptoms do not settle after medication. Travellers who anticipate the need for self-treatment should take Richard Dawood's book *Travellers Health: How to Stay Healthy Abroad*. Diarrhoea may be caused by other, more severe illnesses, including typhoid and malaria, and these will need specific treatment.

HEALTH PROBLEMS ABROAD
by Dr Nick Beeching

Travellers should always seek qualified medical attention if any illness they are suffering gets worse despite their own remedies. Large hotels usually have access to doctors, typically a local family doctor or private clinic. In more remote areas, the nearest qualified help will be a rural dispensary or pharmacist, but seek advice from local expatriate groups, your consulate or embassy for details of local doctors. In large towns, university-affiliated hospitals should be used in preference to other hospitals. In remote areas, mission hospitals usually offer excellent care and often have English-speaking doctors. The International Association for Medical Assistance to Travellers (IAMAT) produces directories of English-speaking doctors and some addresses are listed in Section 10 of the Directory.

If you feel that your medical condition is deteriorating despite (or because of) local medical attention, consider travelling home or to a city or country with more advanced medical expertise – sooner rather than later.

Medication

Medicines sold in tropical pharmacies may be sub-standard. Always check the expiry date and check that medications that should have been refrigerated are not being sold on open shelves. There is a growing market in counterfeit drugs and locally-prepared substitutes are often of low potency. Stick to brand names manufactured by large international companies, even if these cost more. Insist on buying bottles that have unbroken seals and, wherever possible, purchase tablets or capsules that are individually sealed in foil or plastic wrappers. It is difficult to adulterate or substitute the contents of such packaging.

It is usually wise to avoid medications that include several active pharmacological ingredients, most of which will be ineffective and will push up the cost. Medication that is not clearly labelled with the pharmacological name as well as the brand name of ingredients is suspect (e.g. *Nivaquine* contains chloroquine).

Fevers

Fever may herald a number of exotic infections, especially when accompanied by a rash. Fever in a malarious area should be investigated by blood tests, even if you are taking antimalarials. A raised temperature is more commonly due to virus infections such as influenza, or localised bacterial infections that have obvious localising features such as middle ear infections or sinusitis (local pain), urinary tract infections (pain or blood passing water), skin infections (obvious) or chest infections including pneumonia (cough, chest pain or shortness of breath).

If medical attention is not available, the best antibiotic for amateurs is cotrimoxazole (*Bactrim* or *Septrin*) which contains a sulphur drug, and trimethoprim. This covers all the above bacterial infections as well as typhoid fever. Travellers who are allergic to sulphur drugs could use trimethoprim alone or coamoxyclav (*Augmentin*) which is a combined oral penicillin preparation.

Local Infections

Eyes: If the eyes are pink and feel gritty, wear dark glasses and put in chloromycetin ointment or drugs. Seek medical attention if relief is not rapid or if a foreign body is present in the eye.

Ears: Keep dry with a light plug of cotton wool but don't poke matches in. If there is discharge and pain, take an antibiotic.

Sinusitis: Gives a headache (feels worse on stooping), "toothache" in the upper jaw, and often a thick, snotty discharge from the nose. Inhale steam or sniff a tea brew with a towel over your head to help drainage. Decongestant drops may clear the nose if it is mildly bunged up, but true sinusitis needs an antibiotic so seek advice.

Throat: Cold dry air irritates the throat and makes it sore. Gargle with a couple of Aspirins or table salt dissolved in warm water, or suck antiseptic lozenges.

Teeth: When it is difficult to brush your teeth, chew gum. If a filling comes out, a plug of cotton wool soaked in oil of cloves eases the pain; *gutta percha*, softened in boiling water, is easily plastered into the hole as a temporary filling. Hot salt mouth-washes encourage pus to discharge from a dental abscess but an antibiotic will be needed.

Feet: Feet take a hammering so boots must fit and be comfortable. Climbing boots are rarely necessary on the approach march to a mountain; gym shoes are useful. At the first sign of rubbing put on a plaster.

Blisters: Burst with a sterile blade or needle (boiled for three minutes or hold in a flame until red hot). Remove dead skin. Cover the raw area with zinc oxide plaster and leave in place for several days to allow new skin to form.

Athlete's Foot: Can become very florid in the tropics so treat this problem before departure. The newer antifungal creams e.g. *Canesten*, are very effective and supersede antifungal dusting powders, but do not eliminate the need for sensible foot hygiene. In very moist conditions, e.g. in rain forests, on cave explorations or in small boats, lacerated feet can become a real and incapacitating problem. A silicon-based barrier cream in adequate supply is essential under these conditions.

In muddy or wet conditions, most travellers will get some skin sepsis or small wounds. Without sensible hygiene these can be disabling, especially in jungle conditions. Cuts and grazes should be washed thoroughly with soap and water or an antiseptic solution.

Large abrasions should be covered with a vaseline gauze, e.g. *Jelonet* or *Sofratulle*, then a dry gauze, and kept covered until a dry scab forms, after which they can be left exposed. Anchor dressings are useful for awkward places e.g. fingers or heels. If a cut is clean and gaping, bring the edges together with *Steristrips* in place of stitches.

Unconsciousness

The causes range from drowning to head injury, diabetes to epilepsy. Untrained laymen should merely attempt to place the victim in the coma position – lying on their side with the head lower than the chest to allow secretions, blood or vomit to drain away from the lungs. Hold the chin forward to prevent the tongue falling back and obstructing the airway. Don't try any fancy manoeuvres unless you are practised, as you may do more harm than good. *All unconscious patients, from any cause, particularly after trauma, should be placed in the coma position until they recover. This takes priority over any other first aid manoeuvre.* Fainting: lay the unconscious person down and raise the legs to return extra blood to the brain.

Injury

Nature is a wonderful healer if given adequate encouragement.

Deep wounds: Firm pressure on a wound dressing will stop most bleeding. If blood seeps through, put more dressings on top, secured with absorbent crepe bandages and keep up the pressure. Elevate the injured part if possible.

On trips to remote spots at least one member of the party should learn to put in simple sutures. This is not difficult – a friendly doctor or casualty sister can teach the essentials in ten minutes. People have practised on a piece of dog meat and on several occasions this has been put to good use. Pulling the wound edges together is all that is necessary, a neat cosmetic result is usually not important.

Burns: Superficial burns are simply skin wounds. Leave open to the air to form a dry crust under which healing goes on. If this is not possible, cover with *Melolin* dressings. Burn creams offer no magic. Deep burns must be kept scrupulously clean and treated urgently by a doctor. Give drinks freely to replace lost fluids.

Sprains: A sprained ankle ligament, usually on the outside of the joint, is a common and likely injury. With broad *Elastoplast* "stirrup strapping", walking may still be possible. Put two or three long lengths from mid-calf on the non-injured side, attach along the calf on the injured side. Follow this with circular strapping from toes to mid-calf overlapping by half on each turn. First Aid treatment of sprains and bruises is immobilisation (I), cold e.g. cold compresses (C) and elevation (E); *remember ICE*. If painful movement and swelling persist, suspect a fracture.

Fractures: Immobilise the part by splinting to a rigid structure; the arm can be strapped to the chest, both legs can be tied together. Temporary splints can be made from a rolled newspaper, an ice-axe or a branch. Pain may be agonising and is due to movement of broken bone ends on each other; full doses of strong pain killers are needed.

The aim of splinting fractures is to reduce pain and bleeding at the fracture site and thereby reduce shock. Comfort is the best criterion by which to judge the efficiency of a splint but remember that to immobilise a fracture when the victim is being carried, splints may need to be tighter than seems necessary for comfort when at rest, particularly over rough ground. Wounds at a fracture site or visible bones must be covered immediately with sterile or the cleanest material available, and if this happens, start antibiotic treatment at once. Pneumatic splints provide excellent support but may be inadequate when a victim with a broken leg has a difficult stretcher ride across rough ground. They are of no value for fractured femurs (thigh bones). If you decide to take them, get the Athletic Long Splint which fits over a climbing boot where the Standard Long Leg splint does not.

Swimming

Freshwater swimming is not advisable when crocodiles or hippopotamuses are in the vicinity. Beware of polluted water as it is almost impossible to avoid swallowing some. Never dive into water of unknown depth. Broken necks caused by careless diving are a far greater hazard to travellers than crocodiles.

Lakes, ponds, reservoirs, dams, slow streams and irrigation ditches may harbour bilharzia (schistosomiasis). This is a widespread infection in Africa, the Middle East and parts of the Far East and South America, and is a genuine hazard for swimmers. The mature human infection is a blood fluke, the eggs of which are passed out in human urine or faeces and which infect snails in the water. These in turn release minute larval forms (*cercariae*) which readily penetrate unbroken skin exposed to infected freshwater. Non-immune travellers often develop short-lived itching within a few hours of water contact, or may have no symptoms for some months when fever, bloody diarrhoea or blood in the urine may become evident. Treatment of bilharzia has improved in recent years and any traveller who has had contact with infected water should have a tropical check up, at least three months after the last exposure, in case they have undiagnosed infection.

Personal protection consists of avoiding bathing or wading in infected water whenever possible, however tempting it may appear. Local advice that the water is "safe" should usually be disregarded. Contrary to common belief, it is not safe to swim from a boat in deeper water in the middle of an infected lake. If you have to wade through streams or ditches, do so upstream of areas of human habitation and try to cover skin that is exposed. Rubber boots and wetsuits offer some protection but should be thoroughly dried after use. Skin that has been in contact with water should be dried by vigorous rubbing as soon as possible.

Water that is chlorinated is safe to drink or swim in, but be wary of private swimming pools supplied by a local stream or that have been neglected allowing colonisation by snails. Water for drinking should be filtered and allowed to stand for 48 hours if chlorine or other purification methods are not available.

Sea swimming has many hazards other than sharks. Scratches from coral easily become infected, and most waters harbour sea urchins and more venomous fish. Footwear is strongly recommended, especially when swimming on coral beaches. Avoid swimming in water that contains jellyfish, and shuffle through shallow water to warn stingrays and stonefish of your approach. Do not attempt to handle sea snakes or colourful tropical fish (particularly the "lion fish" or "zebra fish") and do not poke your hand in crevices in reefs.

The pain of most marine stings is relieved by immersion of the affected limb in hot water – as hot as the sufferer can stand. Obvious imbedded stings or spines should be removed intact, and medical attention may be needed to extract residual foreign material as this easily becomes infected. Jellyfish tentacles should be neutralised before removal by strong alcohol (e.g. gin), vinegar or sand before being *lifted* off the person, rather than being dragged across the skin. Stonefish, jellyfish and conefish stings can all lead to rapid development of shock and mouth-to-mouth resuscitation and heart massage should be continued for prolonged periods until medical aid is summoned. A tight tourniquet around the thigh or upper arm will delay absorption of venom.

Scuba divers should be sure that local instruction and equipment is adequate and should always swim with a partner. Do not fly within three hours of diving, or within 24 hours of any dive requiring a decompression stop on the way back to the surface. Travellers who anticipate scuba diving in their travels are strongly advised to have proper training before setting out.

Mammalian Bites

All mammalian bites (including human ones) are likely to become infected and medical advice should be obtained about appropriate antibiotics and tetanus immunisation. First aid measures start with immediate washing of the wound in running water for at least five minutes, scrubbing with soap or detergent, and removal of any obvious imbedded foreign material. Wiping with topical iodine, an alcohol injection swab or neat alcohol (gin or whisky will do) helps to sterilise the area. Colourful topical agents such as mercurochrome are useless. At the hospital or dispensary the wound should be further cleaned and dressed as necessary, but do not allow the wound to be sutured.

Rabies is a serious hazard throughout most of the world, including continental Europe and the USA. Domestic or wild animal contact should be avoided at all times, particularly if a normally wild animal is unusually docile or vice versa. Rabies affects a wide variety of mammals, particularly carnivores and bats. Wild dogs are a common nuisance in the tropics and should be given a wide berth.

The rabies virus is carried in the saliva of affected animals and can be transmitted to man by *any* contact of saliva with broken skin, the cornea (eye) or the lining of the nose or mouth. Even minor scratches or grazes of the skin can allow the virus through human skin after it is licked by an infected dog. Deep or multiple bites carry more risk, especially if unprovoked. Rarely, cavers in a bat-infested cave may inhale the virus.

All potentially infected exposures should be taken seriously. First aid measures above may kill the virus in the wound, but specific medical attention should be obtained immediately. If it is not available locally, break your journey to get to suitably qualified doctors, returning home if necessary. Modern rabies vaccines (such as the human diploid cell vaccine made by Merieux) are not always available in the tropics but are safer, more effective and less unpleasant than older vaccines. Depending on the apparent severity of exposure or bites, you will need a prolonged course of vaccinations and may also need specific antiserum against rabies. As the incubation period may extend to weeks or months, late post-exposure vaccination is better than none. Once symptoms develop, an unpleasant death is inevitable.

If exposure involves a domestic animal, try to ascertain from the owner whether it has been vaccinated against rabies and whether it has been behaving abnormally. Record details of how to contact the owner one week later to see if the animal remains healthy (in which case rabies is much less likely). If it is safe to do so, other animals should be captured and placed under safe observation for signs of illness, or killed for specialist examination of the brain for signs of rabies.

Local folk remedies are useless against rabies and should not be used. British doctors may not be as aware of the risks of rabies abroad as they should be, and you should insist on obtaining specialist advice on the correct course of vaccinations after possible exposure. This can be obtained from units with an interest in tropical medicine (see the Directory) or from the Central Public Health Laboratory in London (tel: 0181-200 4400).

Snakes

Snakes only attack humans if provoked and snakebite is a rare hazard for most travellers. Never handle a snake, even if it appears to be dead, and try not to corner or threaten live snakes. If you encounter a snake on the path, keep absolutely still until it moves away. Always look for snakes on paths ahead, using a torch at night. If hiking on overgrown paths, through undergrowth or sand, wear adequate boots, socks and long trousers. Snakes are often found in wood piles, crevices or under rocks and these should not be handled. Integral groundsheets and tightly closed tent flaps help to keep snakes out of tents, and make it less likely that you will roll over on a snake in your sleep (generally viewed as threatening behaviour by the snake).

Not all snakes are venomous and only a minority of bites by venomous species are accompanied by a successful injection of venom. The most important first aid for a victim is to keep calm and provide reassurance that envenomation is unlikely. Immobilise the bitten limb by splinting and rest the victim.

Do not offer alcohol. Even if venom has been injected, severe effects take several hours to develop and there should be adequate time to carry the patient to a dispensary or hospital for trained help. A tight tourniquet around the thigh or upper arm is only indicated for bites by cobras, kraits, coral snakes, sea snakes and most Australian snakes. Usually, it is best to apply a tight pressure dressing over the bite or crepe bandaging on the affected limb (which should be immobilised).

"Boys' Own" remedies such as incision of the wound to suck out the venom are harmful and should not be employed. Local sprays, cold packs, topical antiseptics and even electric shocks are equally useless.

If the snake has already been killed, place it in a bag or box and take it for identification by medical staff attending the victim. Amateur attempts to capture a snake that has been provoked may result in further bites and a good description of the snake by an unbitten comrade is preferable.

Depending on the type of snake, venom may reduce the clotting activity of the blood, causing bleeding, typically from the gums, or induce paralysis – first manifested by an inability to open the eyes properly, followed by breathing problems. Shock and kidney failure are possibilities and some venoms cause extensive damage to tissue around the bitten area. Immediate pain relief should never include Aspirin, which impairs the ability of blood to clot. All bites, with or without envenomation, carry a risk of infection.

Antivenom should never be used unless there are definite signs of envenomation, and then only with adequate medical support. Travellers should not routinely carry antivenom. Expatriates working in high-risk remote areas or expedition organisers may wish to carry a small stock of antivenom. British travellers who wish to carry antivenom should obtain specialist advice from the WHO Centre at the Liverpool School of Tropical Medicine several months before they intend to travel. Package inserts with multi-purpose antivenoms and even local advice are often incorrect.

Scorpions

Scorpion stings are far more likely to be a problem for travellers and are always very painful. Scorpions are widespread, particularly in hot dry areas. If travelling in such areas wear strong footwear and always shake out your clothes and shoes before putting them on. The pain of stings requires medical attention, which may include strong, injected pain-killers. Many species are capable of inflicting fatal stings, particularly in children, and antivenoms should be available in areas where these species are present.

Other Beasts

A myriad of other stinging and biting beasts threaten the traveller. Some spider bites can cause rapid paralysis and should be treated with a local pressure dressing or tight tourniquet until medical help is obtained. Leeches can be encouraged to drop off by applying salt, alcohol or vinegar or a lighted cigarette end. Do not pull them off, as infection may follow if parts of the mouth remain in the wound. Leeches inject an anticoagulant into the wound and local pressure may be required to reduce bleeding. If travelling in damp jungle areas through water with leeches, inspect all exposed areas regularly for leeches.

FEAR OF FLYING

by Sheila Critchley

More people fly today than ever before, yet many experienced air travellers, as well as novices, suffer anguish and apprehension at the mere thought of flying. A survey by Boeing suggested that as many as one out of seven people experience anxiety when flying and that women outnumber men two to one in these feelings of uneasiness. The crews know them as "the white-knuckle brigade".

A certain amount of concern is perhaps inevitable. The sheer size of modern jet aircraft, which appear awkward and unwieldy on the ground, makes one wonder how they will manage to get into the air – and stay there. Most of these fears are irrational and are perhaps based on the certain knowledge that as passengers, once we are in the aircraft we are powerless to control our fate (this being entirely dependent on the skill and training of the crew). These nervous travellers find little comfort in the numerous statistical compilations which show that modern air transport is many times safer than transport by car or rail.

According to Lloyds of London it is 25 times safer to travel by air than by car. A spokesman for Lloyd's Aviation Underwriting said that if you consider all the world's airlines, there are some 600 to 1000 people killed every year on average. This figure compares to an annual toll on the roads of some 55,000 in the United States, 12,000 in France and 5000 in the UK. One sardonic pilot used to announce on landing, "You've now completed the safest part of your journey. Drive carefully". (See essay on Aviation Safety, Chapter 4, Page 182)

Anxiety

Most people's fear remains just that – anxiety which gives rise to signs of stress but remains on a manageable scale. For others, however, the anxiety can become an unimaginable fear, known as *aviophobia* or fear of flying. Symptoms include feelings of panic, sweating, palpitations, depression, sleeplessness, weeping spells, and sometimes temporary paralysis. Phobias are deep seated and often require therapy to search out the root cause. Psychologists studying aviophobia suggest that in serious cases, there may be an overlap with claustrophobia (fear of confined places) and aerophobia (fear of heights).

Professional help can be obtained from specialists in behavioural psychotherapy. However, unlike other phobias which may impair a person's ability to function in society, those suffering from aviophobia may simply adopt avoidance of air travel as a means of coping. Only those whose lifestyles necessitate a great deal of foreign travel are forced into finding a solution.

One source of many people's fear of flying is simply a lack of knowledge about how an aircraft works and about which sounds are usual and to be expected. Visiting airports and observing planes taking off and landing can help overcome this problem. Reading about flying can also help (though air disaster fiction can hardly be recommended).

What to do...

Talking to other people who fly regularly can also be reassuring. Frequent air travellers are familiar with the sequence of sounds which indicates everything is proceeding normally: the dull "thonk" when the landing gear retracts on take-off; the seeming deceleration of the engines at certain speeds among other things. Since most people are familiar with the sounds in their cars and listen almost subconsciously to the changed "tones" that indicate mechanical difficulties, those aircraft passengers who are unsure about flying often feel a certain disquiet when they cannot distinguish "normal" from "abnormal" sounds in an aircraft.

Air turbulence can also be upsetting. Most modern aircraft fly above areas of severe winds (such as during thunderstorms) and pilots receive constant reports of upcoming weather conditions. Nonetheless, air currents up to 20,000 feet may buffet aircraft and the "cobblestoning" effect can be frightening even to experienced air travellers. Flight crews are aware of this problem and usually make an announcement to allay undue worries.

If you are afraid to fly, tell the stewardess when you board so that the crew can keep an eye on you. Hyperventilation is a common symptom of anxiety; the cure is to breathe slowly and deeply into a paper bag. Remember that all aircraft crew are professionals; their training is far more rigorous than, say, that required to obtain a driving license.

Emergencies

It is probably worth mentioning that the cabin crew's main responsibility is not dispensing food and drink to passengers but rather the safety of everyone on board. There is usually a minimum of one flight attendant for every 50 passengers. The briefings on emergency procedures which are given at the beginning of every flight are not routine matters: they can mean the difference between life and death and should be taken seriously. Each type of aeroplane has different positions for emergency exits, oxygen supplies and different design and positioning of life jackets. The air crews' demonstrations of emergency procedures are for the benefit of everyone on board and should be watched and listened to attentively. In an emergency situation, reaction is vital within the first fifteen seconds – there is no time to discover that you do not know where the emergency exits are situated. Learning about what to do in an emergency should reduce fear, not increase it.

Relaxation

One way of coping with fear of flying (at least in the short term) is to learn how to relax. In fact, in-flight alcohol (in sensible quantities), movies, reading material and taped music are all conducive to relaxation.

If these are not sufficient to distract you, some airlines conduct programmes for those they call "fearful flyers". These seminars consist of recorded tapes offering advice on relaxation techniques, statistical information on how safe it really is, group discussions where everyone is encouraged to discuss their fears and recorded simulations of the sounds to be expected in flight.

Familiarisation is the key concept behind all of these behaviourist therapy programmes; instruction in rhythmic deep breathing and sometimes even hypnosis can assist the person in learning to control his or her physical signs of anxiety. A graduate of one of these programmes confirmed its beneficial effects: "I enjoyed the course, especially sharing my misgivings with other people and discovering I wasn't alone with my fears. At the end of the course, we actually went up on a one-hour flight and I was able to apply all the techniques I had learned. In fact, I actually managed to enjoy the flight – something I would not have ever believed I could do."

A certain amount of anxiety about flying is to be expected. For most people, a long distance flight is not something one does every day. On the other hand, there is always a first time for everyone – even those who have chosen to make flying their career. The more you fly, the more likely you are to come to terms with your fears. Some anxiety is inevitable, but in the case of flying, the statistics are on your side.

Recommended Reading: *Taking the Fear Out of Flying* (**David and Charles**)

FLYING IN COMFORT

by Richard Harrington

Flying is physically a lot more stressful than many people realise. And there is more to the problem than time zones. Modern jet aircraft are artificially pressurised at an altitude pressure of around 1500 to 2000m. That means that when you are flying at an altitude of, say, 12,000m in a Boeing 747, the cabin pressure inside is what it would be if you were outside at a height of 1500 to 2000m above sea level. Most people live a lot closer to sea level than this, and to be rocketed almost instantly to a height of 2000m (so far as their body is concerned) takes a considerable amount of adjustment. Fortunately, the human body is a remarkably adaptable organism, and for most individuals the experience is stressful, but not fatal.

Although it might seem more practical to pressurise the cabin to sea level pressure, this is currently impossible. A modern jet with sea level cabin pressure would have to have extremely strong (and therefore heavy) outside walls to prevent the difference between inside and outside walls causing the aircraft walls to rupture in mid-flight. At present, there is no economically viable lightweight material that is strong enough to do the job. Another problem is that if there were a rupture at, say, 14,000m with an interior pressure equal to that at sea level, there would be no chance for the oxygen masks to drop in the huge sucking process that would result from the air inside the cabin emptying through the hole in the aircraft. A 2000m equivalent pressure at least gives passengers and oxygen masks a chance if this occurs.

Inside the cabin, humidifiers and fragrance disguise all the odours of large numbers of people in a confined space. On a long flight you are breathing polluted air.

Surviving the Onslaught

What can you do to help your body survive the onslaught? First you can loosen your clothing. The body swells in the thinner air of the cabin, so take off your shoes (wear loose shoes anyway, it can be agony putting tight ones back on at the end of the flight), undo your belt, tilt your seat right back, put a couple of pillows in the lumbar region of your back and one behind your neck, and whether you're trying to sleep or simply rest, cover your eyes with a pair of air travel blinkers (ask the stewardess for a pair if you haven't brought any with you).

Temperatures rise and fall notoriously inside an aircraft, so have a blanket ready over your knees in case you nod off and later find that you're freezing. When I look at all the space wasted over passengers' heads in a Boeing 747, and all those half-empty hand baggage lockers, I often wonder why aircraft manufacturers do not arrange things so that comfortable hammocks can be slung over our heads for those who want to sleep – or better still, small couchettes in tiers like those found in modern submarines. Personally, I would prefer such comfort, whatever it might do to the tidiness of the cabin interior. Though if you do not mind paying, you can actually lie down in bed both on Philippine Airlines' First Class and now also on British Airways. BA will tuck you up in a "comfort suit", with hot chocolate and biscuits to complete the experience.

On a long flight it is tempting to feel you are not getting your money's worth if you do not eat and drink everything that is going. Stop and resist the temptation – even if you're travelling in First Class and all that food and drink seems to be what most of the extra cost is about. Most people find it best to eat lightly before leaving home and little or nothing during the flights. Foods that are too rich or spicy and foods that you are unaccustomed to will do little to make you feel good in flight. Neither will alcohol. Some people claim that they travel better if they drink fizzy drinks in flight, although if inclined to indigestion, the gas can cause discomfort as it is affected by the lower pressure in the cabin. Tea and coffee are diuretics (increase urine output) and so have the undesirable effect of further dehydrating the drinker who is already in the very dry atmosphere of the cabin. Fruit juices and plain water are best.

Smoking raises the level of carbon monoxide in the blood (and, incidentally, in the atmosphere, so that non-smokers can also suffer the ill effects if seated close to smokers) and reduces the smoker's tolerance to altitude. A smoker is already effectively at 1500 to 2000m before leaving the ground, being more inclined to breathlessness and excessive dryness than the non-smoker.

Walk up and down as frequently as possible during a flight to keep your circulation in shape, and do not resist the urge to go to the loo (avoid the queues by going before meals). The time will pass more quickly, and you will feel better for it, if you get well into an unputdownable novel before leaving home and try to finish it during the flight. This trick always works better than flicking half-heartedly through an in-flight magazine.

You may try to find out how full a 'plane is before you book, or choose to fly in the low season to increase your chance of getting empty seats to stretch out on for a good sleep. If you have got a choice of seats on a 'plane, remember there is usually more leg room by the emergency exit over the wings. On the other hand, stewardesses tend to gather at the tail end of the 'plane on most airlines, so they try not to give seats there away unless asked. That means you may have more chance of ending up with empty seats next to you if you go for the two back rows (also statistically the safest place in a crash). Seats in the middle compartment over the forward part of the wing are said to give the smoothest ride; the front area of the 'plane is, however, the quietest.

You might try travelling with your own pillow, which will be a useful supplement to the postage-stamp sized pillows supplied by most airlines.

Finally, if you plan to sleep during the flight, put a "Do Not Disturb" notice by your seat and pass up the chance of another free drink or face towel every time your friendly neighbourhood stewardess comes round. You probably will not arrive at the other end raring to go, but if you have planned it wisely to arrive just before nightfall, and if you take a brisk walk before going to bed, you might just get lucky and go straight to sleep without waking up on home time two hours later.

BATTLES WITH JET LAG

by Dr Richard Dawood

The human body has in-built rhythms that organise the body function on roughly a 25-hour daily cycle. These rhythms can be influenced and adjusted to a large extent by environmental factors – the time on your wristwatch, whether it's light or dark, and changes in temperature. Rapid passage across time zones disrupts the natural rhythms, outstripping the ability of the body to readjust.

Few people who travel are unfamiliar with the resulting symptoms: general discomfort, fatigue, inability to sleep at the appropriate time, reduced concentration, impaired mental and physical performance, altered bowel habit and disrupted appetite and eating patterns – all are typical features of jet lag.

Adaptation

The body adapts to time changes at a rate of roughly one hour per day so that after a journey across eight time zones, it may take up to eight days to adjust fully to the new local time. Westward travel is, for many people, slightly better tolerated than eastward travel: westward travel results in a longer day which benefits those whose natural body rhythm is longer than a 24-hour cycle. Clearly a flight that does not cross time zones – north/south travel, for example – will not cause jet lag.

Further problems may also be experienced by those on medication that has to be carefully timed (e.g., insulin doses for diabetics require careful planning and women on low dose contraceptive pills may lose contraceptive protection when doses are missed or much delayed).

Children are often less affected by jet lag than adults; the elderly may have great difficulty. Altogether, around 70 per cent of travellers are much disturbed by the symptoms. A wide variety of solutions has been proposed for those unfortunate enough to be badly affected.

Solutions

Melatonin

Melatonin is a naturally-occurring hormone that functions in the body as a powerful internal signal of the approach of night. Melatonin is secreted by the pineal gland in the brain, in a pattern that normally follows a strict daily cycle. Melatonin secretion is suppressed by the presence of bright light.

In a number of placebo-controlled studies, small evening doses of melatonin have been shown to have a significant effect on speeding up recovery from jet lag – by about thirty per cent. Unfortunately, conducting trials on a large scale is a complicated process. The fact that melatonin is cheap and difficult to protect with patents means that pharmaceutical companies have had little commercial incentive to explore its potential in full – though they are working on melatonin analogues – synthetic substances that might have similar properties, but that could be patented.

Melatonin capsules are available in the USA as a food supplement, and sold in health food stores. It has not been approved by the FDA or by drug regulating bodies elsewhere, and the situation has become further confused by recent extravagant claims that melatonin is cure for almost everything from impotence to old age. Consequently, regulatory bodies are unhappy about its ready availability.

A recent informal survey of travel medicine practitioners attending an international conference suggested that over half of them had taken melatonin themselves, and more than 80 per cent were satisfied with the resulting benefit.

Light Exposure

Exposure to light suppresses melatonin secretion, and controlled exposure is known to alleviate jet lag. Various strategies have been proposed, some of which are difficult to understand and follow. At the simplest level, it is possible to use daylight simply as an environmental cure. More complex formulas claim to use precisely timed light and darkness to achieve dramatic jumps in "clock setting".

Researchers at Harvard have attempted to patent various regimens of light exposure, a controversial move that will be interesting to follow.

The Jet Lag Diet

Ehret and Scanlon's book, *Overcoming Jet Lag* (1983), with its "jet lag diet", was an instant best-seller – trading heavily on the claim that this was the strategy used by Ronald Reagan during his presidency. In the diet, protein and carbohydrate intake is scheduled in an attempt to enhance the synthesis of certain neurotransmitters within the brain at appropriate times. It is suggested that protein-rich meals that are high in tyrosine, when taken at breakfast and at lunchtime, increase catecholamine levels during the day, while an evening meal high in carbohydrates provides tryptophan for serotonin (and therefore melatonin) synthesis at night.

In travel medicine circles, the diet has achieved a reputation for being almost impossible to follow – and so almost impossible to disprove.

It is true, however that meal timing is an important zeitgeber – a significant factor in influencing the body clock in its adaptation to a new time zone. So, if it is not your habit to eat heavy meals in the middle of the night, don't do so when served a meal during a flight, if you are offered food at a time that is inappropriate to the time at your intended destination.

Sleeping Medication

Carefully-timed sleeping medication can help reduce the fatigue of the journey – an issue quite separate from that of jet lag. The important points are to choose a drug that is short acting and has no hangover, and to avoid alcohol while taking it. It is important only to take sleeping medication during flights that are long enough to permit at least six hours' sleep.

Widespread use of the drug Halcion during the late Eighties, taken halfway across the Atlantic, often with alcohol, resulted in an epidemic of short-term travel amnesia: travellers would develop amnesia for everything they did during the first few hours following arrival.

Sleeping medication can also reduce fatigue during adjustment to a new time zone – it can help you get some sleep when you need to rest at what – for your body – is still an inappropriate time, and it can also help you sleep through the night when you might otherwise awake inappropriately. Zopoclone is believed to cause the least sleep disturbance; the best alternative is probably Temazepam; for any drug always use the lowest dose in the recommended range.

Melatonin also has a soporific effect, and some specialists have argued that this is the only explanation for its effect on jet lag.

Aromatherapy
One range of products appears to be extremely successful – in terms of sales, anyway. It is Danielle Ryman's Awake (said to smell like a walk through a pine forest) and Asleep, available from the aromatherapy shop at London's Park Lane Hotel. Aromatherapy products are offered to passengers on a routine basis by a small number of airlines.

Vitamins
E-mergen-C is a fizzy cocktail produced by the Alacer Corporation of California, intended to give a natural boost to sufferers from post-flight exhaustion; "Having sampled it, I would say a Diet Coke at breakfast might be more beneficial to me" was the verdict of one reviewer.

Homeopathy
A much used homeopathic remedy is Arnica 6c, every six hours during a flight and the following day – it is recommended by Abercrombie and Kent, for example.

The Tudor Hotel, New York, and the Rembrandt Hotel, London both have "circadian rooms" – in which guests and their body functions can be left in peace, operating on whichever time zone meets their needs.

Concorde
Travelling supersonically cuts the transatlantic journey time down to about three hours, dramatically reducing the fatigue of the journey. It makes no difference to jet lag, however: the process of adjusting to a new time zone is still the same.

Experience
There is no doubt that over time, frequent travellers develop their own strategy, almost without thinking about it. That is one reason why formal evaluation of cures for jet lag can be so difficult – the task of unscrambling the influence of other factors is a major problem, and large numbers of travellers are necessary for scientific study.

Planning your Own Jet Lag Strategy
Whatever your approach to jet lag, here are some tips to bear in mind:
1. Flying westbound has the effect of lengthening your day. Avoid taking naps during the flight – this may prevent you from falling asleep later.
2. Avoid alcohol, tea or coffee, during and after your flight – all of them interfere with sleep.

3. During eastbound overnight flights ,such as the transatlantic "red eyes", eat only a light meal before taking off, and ask the cabin crew not to disturb you during the flight, so as to get the maximum amount of sleep possible. Consider taking a mild sleeping tablet.

4. If you can afford the luxury of time, take daytime flights where possible; although they do not necessarily help you adjust better to the time difference, these cause the least fatigue and loss of sleep, and allow you to arrive in best shape.

5. Expose yourself to cues that belong to your new time zone, as soon as you can: reset your watch, eat meals and go to bed at appropriate times, and spend plenty of time outdoors.

6. Body temperature falls naturally during the night, and a common symptom of jet lag is to feel cold during the day: try a hot bath.

7. Accept that there is bound to be some loss of performance when you first arrive in a new time zone, and plan your trip to avoid important business meetings for the first 24 hours after arrival; if you have to schedule a meeting on arrival, choose a time of day when you would normally – on home time – be most alert.

On Arrival

On arrival at your destination, it is best to stay awake until night time, without taking a nap. On the first night in the new time zone, a sleeping tablet is again useful to help initiate sleep at an unusual time.

The occasional use in this way of short-acting, mild sleeping tablets can be valuable and does no harm. Most doctors are willing to prescribe small quantities for this purpose. Possibly the best suited drug is zimovane (it has a slightly bitter taste) which is short acting and causes very little sleep disturbance.

Clearly, sleeping tablets should only be used on flights that are long enough: it is not sensible to take a tablet that will make you drowsy for eight hours, two hours into a five-hour flight. Use the lowest dose that will work, and avoid alcohol. And remember that alcohol, sleeping tablets, fatigue and jet lag do not mix well with driving: too many people stagger off aircraft after a long journey and attempt to drive when clearly in an unfit state to do so.

Whatever one's approach, however, it is important to recognise that one's performance is almost inevitably going to be reduced and it is sensible to avoid important commitments and business arrangements for at least the first 24 hours after arrival.

Postscript

The information in this chapter is technically correct in July 1997. However, traveller's healthcare and the situation regarding the safety and use of anti-malarial drugs in particular continues to change and this chapter should be read bearing this in mind. Travellers should always obtain current advice from their medical advisor. ■

EQUIPPING FOR A TRIP
Chapter 11

TRAVELLING IN STYLE

by Miranda Haines

Where to go to go, how to get there and what to see and take? Now that these questions can be answered the next is more elusive: How does one travel with style?

There is a cartoon on a greetings card, circulating in London at the moment, that shows a cratered rose-coloured Mars landscape with a small Ikea shop in the background. Underneath reads: *A recent photograph suggests that there is life-style on Mars*. This vignette appeals to most people who are aware that travel and style are not only becoming synonymous but also a national obsession. Exploration without the two-layered, multi-pocketed and superbly coloured Berghaus jacket ? Unthinkable! A fashionable dinner party without mention of a holiday, pre-booked and researched months in advance, to a place no-one has even heard of? Really *chic*.

And so travelling is not enough any more. You may go to Brighton, Bali or Boston, but the number one rule for the hip and modern traveller is Travel in Style (or frankly you might as well stay at home in shame). This weighty chapter that gives practical advice on essential items for various types of trips: best luggage; security; lightweight clothing; shoes; hats; mattresses; stoves; blankets; food stuffs and tents–to name just a few, but what no-one has dared dictate is an individual's image abroad. It is fine to read about where to go, how to get there and what to see or take, but stylish travel is a much more elusive goal and much harder to attain.

Gertrude Bell, probably the most stylish traveller of all time, explained that in travel, "there's no there, there." Her travel equipment acted as a comfort-blanket in such harsh terrain. Named the "Desert Queen" Bell was adventurer, adviser to Kings and ally of Lawrence of Arabia. As she forged across the Arabian desert (at a time when women did not go unchaperoned) Bell was decked out in the latest Parisian fashions, with a large entourage in tow to carry the silver cutlery, parasols, picnic hampers and white-laced tablecloths, that were famously part of her *modus operandi*.

More recently, Grace Kelly made an Yves St. Laurent bag so much her signature as she was pictured stepping on and off planes, out of boats, and chauffeur driven cars, that the large leather bag has been dubbed "The Grace Kelly Bag" and is still a hotly desired item for the jet-set traveller. So much so, that there is a waiting list for it in St. Laurent's shop, on Sloane Street. Another example of a stylish traveller of her time is Jackie Onnasis, who was never seen *en route* without her panda-eyed dark glasses, that made "the sunglasses look" not only an essential travel look but also a symbol of the sixties.

Fashion folk, who globe-hop constantly, often set the pace for the style-conscious traveller. The Queen of all fashion writers and perpetual traveller, Suzy Menkes, is notably seen everywhere in Issey Miyake's pleated clothes. The fabric is not only *haute couture* but also perfectly modern and practical for travel anywhere, since the dresses are made from a single piece of pleated polyester fabric that can be twisted and folded into a pocket – rather in the style of a lightweight mackintosh. Neither do Miyake's clothes need handwashing or ironing. In short Menkes sports the perfect travel attire for the stylish traveller. But why should we care?

A practical, and no doubt valuable, reason for every traveller is that looking prepared for any situation is good ammunition for the visitor, who will inevitably feel more at ease in foreign surroundings if their image is "right". Luxury travel items are arguably a more practical option now that world travellers swap between business and pleasure at the drop of a time-zone or sundowner. This is made easier by the globalisation of fashion. The baseball hat is a world accessory.

Obviously the style of locations, whether it be a B&B, castle, monastery or yacht, dictates the desired image. A holiday on the fashion designer, Valentino's £60 million, 165ft yacht, *T.M. Blue One*, (created with the help of a naval architect and hot New York interior designer, Peter Marino), requires the utmost "yachtiquette". The upholstery is changed from white, for the day, into navy blue, for the evening – usually while the guests bathe before dinner. Each bedroom has a walk-in closet, so it is advisable for guests to have enough items for the space (see *Space to Spare* page 460 "Do not stint on things that might seem frivolous before you leave, but can make an enormous difference to your morale"). A helpful list of don'ts might read: Don't: Wear clogs or stiletto heels; Wear socks with deck shoes; Apply fake tan on white cushions; Eat lettuce in a high wind.

Another practical reason for a smart image, is that it may help you get upgraded on the outbound flight and will ensure the maximum amount of respect from officials, hoteliers and fellow travellers the world over. There is also something to be said for dressing in local style–a *shalwar qamiz* in Afghanistan perhaps or a *jallabah* in Morocco–but remember that an Indian sari generally looks ridiculous on a Westerner and will invite giggles from the locals.

Whether you are the TV presenter type like Jonathan Ross who packs "plenty of hardware: an Applemac computer; a CD Walkman; classical CDs; mini TV and travel insurance–or like the wry British fashion designer, Vivienne Westwood, who packs a sense of humour before all else, ("I like wearing a safari suit for shooting tigers in")–the days of scruffy travel are over. In the past, world travellers either had smelly rucksacks and matted hair or silk stockings and Panama hats. Nowadays, it would be hard to distinguish a business traveller from a backpacker, since, it is possible to have style and stay practical.

It is worth remembering the words of an Oscar Wilde character, famous for both his art and flamboyant style, who maintained: "I never travel without my diary. One should always have something sensational to read in the train."

LUGGAGE

by Hilary Bradt

The original meaning of "luggage" is "what has to be lugged about". Lightweight materials have made lugging obsolete for sensible travellers these days, but there is a bewildering choice of containers for all your portable possessions.

What you buy in the way of luggage and what you put in it obviously depends on how and where you are travelling. If your journey is in one conveyance and you are staying put when you arrive, you can be as eccentric as the Durrell family who travelled to Corfu with "two trunks of books and a briefcase containing his clothes" (Lawrence) – and "four books on natural history, a butterfly net, a dog and a jam jar full of caterpillars all in imminent danger of turning into chrysalides" (Gerald, who described this vast logistical exercise in *My Family and Other Animals*).

If, however, you will be constantly on the move and will rarely spend more than one night in any place, your luggage must be easy to pack, transport and carry.

What to Bring

There are two important considerations to bear in mind when choosing luggage. First, weight is less of a problem than bulk. Travel light if you can, but if you can't, travel small. Second, bring whatever you need to keep you happy. It's a help to know yourself. If you can travel, like Laurie Lee, with a tent, a change of clothes, a blanket and a violin, or like Rick Berg, author of *The Art and Adventure of Travelling Cheaply* who took only a small rucksack (day pack) for his six-year sojourn, you will indeed be free. Most people however are too dependent on their customary possessions and must pack accordingly.

Suitcase or Backpack

Your choice of luggage is of the utmost importance and will probably involve making a purchase. Making do with Granny's old suitcase or Uncle John's scouting rucksack may spoil your trip.

Anyone who's had to stand in a crowded Third World bus or the London Underground wearing an external frame rucksack will know how unsuitable they can be for travelling. You take up three times more room than normal, and the possessions strapped to the outside of your pack may be out of your sight, but will certainly not be out of the minds of your fellow passengers, or out of their eyes, laps and air space. It is no wonder backpackers have a bad name. And because they do, many Third World countries are prejudiced to the extent of banning them. On arriving at the Paraguayan border some years ago I was forced to wrap my pack in a sheet sleeping bag and carry it through.

That aluminium frame is fragile, as you will soon discover when someone stands on it, and since you carry the backpack behind you, you're particularly vulnerable to thieves. Or have you ever hitch-hiked in a Mini carrying your pack on your lap? Can you honestly say you were comfortable? Leave the frame packs to the genuine backpackers they were designed for. Hitchhikers and travellers should still carry a backpack, but one with an internal frame. This small variation in design makes all the difference – the pack can be carried comfortably on your lap, it need be no wider than your body, and everything can be fitted inside. It can be checked onto a 'plane with no trouble, and carried on a porter's head or mule's back.

For the average overland traveller, the ideal solution is the combination bag and backpack. This type of luggage has become justly popular in recent years. Basically it is a sturdy bag with padded shoulder straps that can be hidden in a special zip compartment when approaching a sensitive border or when travelling by plane.

If you are joining an organised group or do not expect to carry your own luggage, you will find a duffel bag the most practical solution. Or two duffel bags since you have two hands. These soft zipped bags are strong and light and can fit into awkward spaces that preclude rigid suitcases. They fit snugly into the bottom of a canoe or the back of a bus and are easily carried by porters or pack animals. When selecting a duffel bag, choose one made from a strong material with a stout zip that can be padlocked to the side, or otherwise secured against thieves. Avoid those khaki army sausage bags with the opening at one end. The article you need will invariably be at the bottom.

Suppose you are a regular air traveller, what will be the best type of suitcase for you? Probably the conventional suitcase, and in that case, you will be well advised – as with most travel purchases – to get the best you can afford, unless you want to replace your "bargain" luggage after virtually every flight. Cheap materials do not stand up to the airline handling, which usually involves being thrown twenty feet onto a hard surface, standing on the tarmac in all weathers, and generally being flung about fairly violently. Now that some airlines have eliminated the weight allowance in favour of a limit of two pieces, neither of which must measure more than 67 inches (that's height by length by width), it's as well to buy luggage that conforms to that size. Suitcases with built-in wheels can be an advantage in the many airports which do not supply trolleys. But be careful, they can easily get snapped off or broken during the suitcase's passage, so recessed wheels are probably the best.

The traditional hard cases do tend to survive best of all, choose items made from a strong material e.g. nylon. These can go up to 1000 denier. Leather items should be scrutinised around the expanded areas: the leather should be of a uniform thickness throughout the item. Check the zip, which should not only be strong but also unobtrusive so as not to catch on clothing etc, and the stitching, which should be even and secure with no gaps or loose threads. If you have the choice, get a bag with one handle only: porters tend to toss luggage around by one handle and this can play havoc with a bag designed to be carried by two. Conveyor belts have a nasty habit of smearing luggage: darker colours stand up to this treatment more happily. Before walking away with your purchase, remember to ask about its care, especially which cleaning materials you should use.

All unnecessary appendages (straps, hangers, clips, etc.) should be removed before check-in, especially old destination labels, which can cause the case to be misdirected.

Luggage experts and even those in the airline business often recommend sticking to a carry-on bag if possible. If you can manage to cram everything in, it's preferable to submitting your case to the violence of the handling, the damage and even loss that may ensue. If not, use a carry-on bag for anything you can't do without for a few days, whether it's photos of your children, your own special sleeping tablets or the address of the friend you're going straight from the airport to visit. Not to mention "uninsurables" such as sums of money or vital papers. To fit under an aeroplane seat, a carry-on bag must measure no more than 450 x 350 x 150mm (18 x 14 x 6 ins).

As well as a carry-on bag, you are allowed the following free items: a handbag (women only – as this is in addition to the carry-on luggage, better take as big a handbag as possible to make the most of your luck), an overcoat, an umbrella or walking stick, a small camera, a pair of binoculars, infant's food for the flight, a carrying basket, an invalid's fully collapsible wheelchair, a pair of crutches, reading material in reasonable quantities and any duty free goods you have acquired since checking-in.

Some thought should be given to accessory bags. Everyone ends up with more luggage than they started because of presents, local crafts, maps etc., collected on the way, and a light foldable bag is very useful. Canvas and straw have their followers. I'm devoted to plastic bags myself and carry a good supply, even though the bottoms usually fall out or the handles tear.

Security

Choose your luggage with security in mind. Your possessions are at risk in two ways: your bag may be opened and some items removed, or the whole bag may be stolen. Most travellers have been robbed at some time or other, the most frequent occurrence being that small items simply disappear from their luggage. Make sure that your luggage can be locked. With duffel bags, this is no problem – a small padlock will secure the zip to the ring at the base of the handle. Adapt the bag yourself if necessary. Combination locks are more effective than standard padlocks as they are rarely seen in the Third World and so thieves have not learned how to pick them. They also protect the clients of those manufacturers whose products are all fitted with the same key! It is harder to lock a backpack; use your ingenuity. One effective method is to make a strong pack cover with metal rings round the edges, through which can be passed a cable lock to secure the cover round the pack. Luggage may also be slashed, but this treatment is usually reserved for handbags. Apart from buying reinforced steel cases there is little you can do about it. A strong leather strap around a suitcase may help to keep your luggage safe and will be a life saver should the clasps break.

For easy identification, try coloured tape or some other personal markings on the outside. Stick-on labels are safer than the dangling kind, as they cannot be ripped off so easily.

During my travels, I've been robbed of five small bags. I finally learned never to carry something that is easy to run off with unless it is firmly secured to my person. If you keep your most valuable possessions in the centre of a locked heavy pack or bag they are pretty safe. If you can barely carry your luggage, a thief will have the same problem.

Weight Allowances for Air Travel

On international flights, the IATA Tourist and Economy Class allowance is normally 20kgs (44lbs), for First Class 30kgs (66lbs). For transatlantic flights and some others (e.g. USA to South America), however, you can take far more luggage since the weight system has been cancelled and the only restriction is to two pieces of luggage no larger than 67 inches. Before you fly, always ask the airline about luggage allowances and ask if the same applies to the home journey. For instance, if you fly Ecuatoriana from Miami to Quito, you will fly down on the two piece system, but will be restricted to 20kgs for your return – a nasty shock for the present-laden tourist.

What to do if you have excess baggage? You could, of course, just pay the charges. If you know in advance, you could send the excess freight. Do not, under any circumstances, entrust luggage to anyone else, nor agree to carry someone's bags for them. Drugs or bombs could easily be secreted. If you are not much over the limit, don't worry. The airlines will usually give you some leeway. My record is five bags weighing a total of 70kgs transported from South America to Miami (weight limit 20kgs) and on to London (piece limit – two) without paying excess charges.

Packing

Joan Bakewell, in *The Complete Traveller*, suggests thinking of what to take under the following headings: toiletries and overnight, unders, overs, accessories, paperwork and extras. While it is true to say that everything can be classified under these headings, campers and others who must take with them the appurtenances of home will almost certainly find that the "extras" section expands dramatically over the few extras required by, say, airline passengers.

The latter should be warned that aerosol and the ink in fountain pens tend to leak in the pressurised atmosphere of an aeroplane – such items should not be packed in your suitcases but may be safe enough in your hand luggage where you can keep an eye on them. Lighter fuel is not permitted on an aircraft. Knives, even penknives, may be confiscated from your hand luggage. You are meant to get them back, but in practice this is rare.

When packing, put irregular-shaped and heavy items such as shoes at the bottom, remembering the case will be on its end while being carried topped by clothes in layers separated by sheets of plastic or tissue paper (and do not forget to fill up the shoes with soft or small items such as underwear or jewellery). Trousers, skirts and dresses, still on their hangers or folded with tissue paper between layers, go towards the top, but the topmost stratum in your case should be occupied by T-shirts, blouses and shirts, small items of clothing, and then some enveloping piece such as a dressing gown or shawl over everything. Some travellers like to keep their toilet items in different groups, which makes sense when you consider that you do not wash your hair with the same frequency as you wash your face or go out in strong sun.

Do not over pack: if you have to force the lid of your suitcase, you may bend the frame or break the hinges, with the obvious ensuing risk to the contents. Underpacking, especially in soft-sided luggage is also undesirable since the cases need to be padded out to resist tears to the outer covering.

TRAVEL CLOTHING
by Clive Tully

The whole point of travel clothing is that it is not "run of the mill". When choosing what to pack for a big trip, therefore, comfort, robustness and ease of care should be the prime considerations. The way it all fits into your luggage should a high priority too, since there is no point in packing garments which are heavy or bulky.

Ease of care is also important. Naturally the simplest way to travel lighter is to take fewer items of clothing, which means that what is taken should be as washable in a hotel handbasin as in a mountain stream. In most cases, synthetic fibres not only wash more easily, they dry more quickly too. Personally I have been a fan of the lightweight travel clothing (pioneered by Rohan) since it became available. It has the benefits of being both light and durable and while cheap alternatives tend not to have reinforcing bar tacks stitched into the ends of the zippers or securing the belt loops and zipped security pockets (impossible to pick), I still recommend this style. You might not care to try it, but yes, a pair of Rohan's best-selling Bags trousers really does fit into a Coke can!

Social

There are plenty of reasons why one should not want to draw undue attention while travelling. Inappropriate dress can cause unwanted attention when it is often preferable to blend in with the scenery – crossing borders, checking into hotels, even minding your own business waiting at railway stations. Yet often, when it comes down to it, being thin, tall and pale, I know I am going to stick out anyway. My advice is not to go over the top. Nobody expects me to wear a kilt when I go to Scotland (except perhaps for Burns Night) so dressing up in any kind of ethnic kit is likely to leave me looking pretty ridiculous.

About ten years ago, DPM (disruptive pattern material) clothing was all the rage in outdoors circles, with everything from clothing to rucksacks sporting camouflage patterns in commando styles. There were even reports of DPM-clad backpackers in the Pyrenées being shot at by the local bandits! Of course you may have to consider the way you are dressed in certain situations to avoid offending local sensibilities, or in order not to make yourself a target for muggers. There are times when common sense should also prevail. This generally means not exposing too much bare skin when it really is inappropriate (besides, see Sun Protection below), which will generally apply to women much more than men.

Having said that, western style is prevalent all over the world, and there are few big towns and cities where you will not see the likes of Coca Cola T-shirts and baseball caps. Out in the provinces, the situation may well be different. The best advice is simply to be guided by what you see around you.

The Practical Side of Clothing

If we work on a system of layered clothing, you will find you can cater for just about every kind of climate from temperate to downright cold, with only a few adjustments needed for hotter or more humid conditions.

Base layers

What you wear next to the skin is of paramount importance. How comfortable you feel, and how efficiently the layers worn on top work all comes down to wearing the right base layer. In short, the kiss of death is anything made of 100 per cent cotton. The problem with cotton is that it absorbs moisture and it takes forever to dry out. More preferable is the "wicking effect", where moisture passes through the base layer fabric so the skin stays as dry as possible, rather like a high-tech nappy. This effect is important in cold conditions, where you have layers on top, because keeping the moisture moving away from you will prevent the chills when you stop moving. And it is particularly important if your outer shell is a breathable waterproof because if cotton is worn next to the skin, you might just as well wear a bin liner rather than a £200 or £300 Gore-Tex jacket.

In warmer conditions, where the base layer may be all you are wearing on top, it helps keep you cool by wicking the moisture to the surface of the garment where it can evaporate most readily and therefore cool one down. Helly Hansen started the ball rolling years ago with polypropylene base layers, but technology has moved on considerably since then. Polyprop tends to get smelly very quickly, whilst the latest polyester fabrics epitomised by Polartec's BiPolar have anti-microbial treatments which will keep them working and smelling sweet even under the most arduous laundry-free conditions.

Mid layers

The traditional garment here is the woolly sweater, and devotees say that not only does wool absorb moisture, but it even generates a certain amount of heat when it does so. But once again, if you are wearing a high-tech breathable waterproof on top, it is not allowed it to do its job by encouraging moisture to hang about inside your little micro-climate.

The modern alternative is fleece, made from knitted polyester, napped and sheared in a wide variety of different velour finishes depending on the performance and look required by the manufacturer. As with the polyester used in base layers, it absorbs a mere one per cent of its own weight in water, and the sophisticated techniques used in its construction ensure excellent insulation for the weight of the fabric.

Fleece comes in different weights, and the most widely available weight – best suited to a broad range of temperatures – is the 200gms/sq.metre fabric epitomised by Polartec 200. The heavier weights are better for very cold conditions or inactivity in less extreme temperatures, while the lighter ones are useful for warding off the chills of a summer evening, or as an extra "thermal" layer.

On its own, fleece is not windproof. In many situations with high activity, a certain amount of air permeability can be an advantage. If windproofing is needed then you can either wear your waterproof on top, or a lightweight windproof layer made from poly/cotton or microfibre synthetic. Windproof fleeces made with a laminate sandwiched by two thin layers of fleece fabric are available, and while they do an excellent job, it is at the expense of flexibility in an overall layered clothing system.

The Legs

Cotton canvas jeans have been around for over one hundred years but while they are robust they have little else to offer. Unless you buy the stretch variety, jeans are unyielding, and if washed take forever to dry. In my opinion, they make appalling travel clothing. Get them wet in cold windy conditions, and they become downright dangerous. Water conducts heat away 26 times as efficiently as air, so cotton trousers which absorb gallons of the stuff are not good news for the legs unless you are a fan of hypothermia.

Polyester/cotton or polyester microfibre fabrics fare much better in those unexpected extremes because they dry off much quicker. Besides, most travel trousers made from these kind of fabrics look smarter, too. For trekking and mountain walking, the best performer without a doubt is Polartec Powerstretch fleece, but given that a pair of leggings made from Powerstretch will be "form-fitting", do bear in mind any social considerations when wearing them away from the mountains.

Waterproofs

The buzzword these days is "breathability". Most will have heard of Gore-Tex, the best known microporous laminate, but there are also microporous polyurethane coatings, and there are, in addition, coatings and laminates which are hydrophilic. They work by different mechanisms, but the effect is the same. Moisture vapour on the inside gets transmitted through the membrane or coating to the outside. They work best when there is the greatest difference in both temperature and humidity between the micro-climate inside your clothing, and the air outside. In other words, cold and dry conditions will see the best performance.

While there are differences in performance between fabrics, and even different versions of the same fabric, what is probably more useful is to concentrate on the design of the jacket. If the most robust waterproof is needed, you should aim for one of the laminated fabrics in a three-layer configuration. They are good performers, but not necessarily the best looking if looking for something a little more general purpose. Here the two-layer laminate with a separate lining comes into its own, in fact all but budget jackets made from polyurethane coated nylon or polyester will come with a drop-lining as well. The advantage is that they feel softer and jackets using this kind of construction generally look smarter.

The main zip needs protection from a storm flap to stop water getting through. This should be either Velcro or press stud fastened, and the inner flap slightly oversized to form a gutter so that any drips managing to infiltrate that far can run down to the bottom hem.

A good hood is essential. A walking jacket may have a fixed hood, but more are now coming with rollaway hoods which stow in the collar – simply because people want the jackets to be multifunctional. The drawcord adjuster should bring the hood snug around your face without too much fabric bunching up, and it should allow you to turn your head from side to side without your face suddenly disappearing inside the hood!

Also useful is a decent peak or visor to keep drips from running down your face. Visors made for typical hillwalking or mountaineering will tend to come with some form of stiffening – either a thin plastic strip or malleable wire. Old-fashioned designs do give a rather closed-in feel – the best ones have cutaways at the side of the face so no peripheral vision is lost- important when you are picking your way across uncertain terrain. If you really want to batten down the hatches in bad weather, look for elasticated drawcords at both waist and bottom hem as well as the hood, while cuffs need to have a good range of adjustment to allow for sealing around gloves.

Pockets are really down to one's own preference and needs. Certainly if you are navigating yourself through wild terrain, a map pocket in the proper place can save you some grief. Decent map pockets will be situated at chest height with the zipped opening beneath the main zip storm flaps, but outside the main zip itself, affording access to your map without opening up the main body of the jacket.

Insulated Clothing

If you are heading for really cold climes, or maybe you just need something warm to wear around camp if the temperature plunges to freezing or below, you might consider an insulated jacket, something filled either with polyester wadding or down. As with sleeping bags, the two forms of insulation have their pluses and minuses. Duck or goose down provides the best insulation for the weight – it is also more compressible, and it regains its loft better after compression. The big minus is that it loses its insulation value if it gets damp. Even an insulated jacket with a breathable waterproof shell can suffer from a build-up of moisture which will affect its performance. The first line of attack is to ensure not getting it wet. You can also impregnate the whole garment with a waterproofing agent which will enable the down to loft even in damp conditions.

Synthetic waddings tend to be cheaper than natural fillings, and in general they are bulkier and have a shorter lifespan, though with the huge advances being made in the technology over the last few years, this is not always the case. Their big winning point is the fact that damp does not affect the performance.

Head and Hands

The head radiates more heat per square inch of skin than any other part of the body (up to 70 per cent of the total heat loss from the body). The moment you start feeling cold it is advisable to put a hat on. A woolly hat is fine, although if you find wool next to the skin a bit irritating, there is a huge range of styles made from polyester fleece.

For maintaining any dexterity, in order to operate a camera for example, you are better off using thin liner gloves with heavier gloves or mittens on top.

Sun Protection

The rate of increase in new cases of skin cancer is alarming, and the age of onset is getting lower. We now know there is no such thing as a healthy tan, but also that we can improve our protection against the sun by wearing the right kind of clothes. Most people are unaware that while parts of the body covered by light clothing do not get tanned or burned in strong sunshine, the skin is still being damaged. UV-A rays cause tanning and burning but UV-B rays go deeper, causing more long-term damage, and they can penetrate many types of light clothing. The average cotton T-shirt has a SPF of 6-9. That drops to less than half if the T-shirt is wet.

We tend to regard lighter colours as more suitable in bright conditions because they reflect better. In fact the opposite is true. Darker colours absorb more UV and therefore provide better skin protection. The best fabrics for sun protection can still be lightweight, but are close-weave. Some travel clothing companies now quote sun protection factor ratings for their products.

As with base layers, synthetic or synthetic/natural fabrics are best. First of all, synthetic fibres can be made finer than cotton, and are therefore capable of being closer woven. Secondly, their quick-drying ability means enhanced cooling in conditions where you are likely to be sweating. A hat makes good sense, too. The head and neck are prime targets, with one third of all skin cancers occurring on the nose. A mesh-topped baseball hat or open-weave straw hat might feel good, but they do not offer sufficient protection. A hat with a 4" all-round brim is much more effective.

Footwear

What one wears on the feet can make or break any trip. So whether your preferred footwear happens to be trainers, loafers, deck shoes, brogues, walking boots, sandals or wellies, you can do yourself a big favour by making sure they fit properly, and not leaving it until just before you head off into the blue yonder to buy a new pair.

Boots

Walking boots used to be heavy unbending lumps of leather which were designed to inflict major injuries on feet until they had stomped at least one hundred miles in them. Nowadays, whilst boots may need a little period of "acclimatisation", they are designed to fit, and to be comfortable, straight out of the box. For non-demanding walking and trekking, lightweight boots such as the mega-selling Brasher Boot will be just the job, and they do not look too bad for wandering around markets either.

The main choice is between all-leather and fabric/leather boots, and within those distinctions there are models built to cater for very wide levels of usage, from general ambling on undemanding terrain to four-season mountaineering. Much of it comes down to the stiffness of the sole unit, but even a boot designed for footpath walking – with a reasonable amount of flex in the sole – should still not be able to twist too much. If it does, it will offer little support on rougher terrain, and the feet are likely to tire more quickly.

The key to ensuring a decent fit lies in making sure you have the socks you intend to wear when you are shopping for boots. Remember that you should leave space in front of your toes to allow for feet expansion, and the easiest way to do that is to slide your foot forward as far as it will go in the unlaced boot. You should then be able to slip your index finger into the space between the heel and the back of the boot. If you can move the finger about, the next size down is needed, if it is very tight – then thee next size up. Any outdoors shop worth its salt will have the means to measure feet accurately.

Shoes and Trainers
Since it is likely you will spend lots of time on your feet, it can be worth investing in a pair of closed-cell foam insoles like those that are provided as a standard in many walking boots. A good few trainers come with them too, but quite often they are fairly soft, when what you really need is something firmer. They help cushion the feet and prevent blisters.

Happy Feet
Decent socks are as much a key to foot comfort as the shoe or boot itself. Look for socks without bulky protruding seams over the toe or round the heel, and check the elastication at the top is not too tight. For walking and general travelling, loopstitch socks provide greater cushioning underneath the heel and ball of the foot, and you do not have to burden feet with the extra insulation of a full loopstitch sock – socks with the loop pile just in the strategic areas are now available.

Remember that the layer principle gives the greatest means to mix 'n' match, both in terms of performance and looks. The good backpacker keeps his load light by using items of clothing and equipment which, where possible, serve more than one purpose. So as one begins to select clothing to put into that rucksack, travel bag or suitcase, think versatility, and don't take more than you really need.

For Equipment Suppliers see p.857 of the Directory

SPACE TO SPARE

by Jack Jackson

If you have a roomy vehicle, are not worried about weight and are not constantly on the move, you might as well plan to make yourselves as comfortable as possible. Do not stint on things that might seem frivolous before you leave, but can make an enormous difference to your morale. This is particularly true if camping.

Fragile items and paperwork, which must be kept away from dust and water, are best kept in Pelican or Underwater Kinetics cases, which have silicone gasket seals. These come in many sizes, with foam inserts that you can customise to fit fragile equipment. These cases are so effective, that even if you have descended a couple of thousand feet down an escarpment, you will have to release the purge button, before you can open the case.

Cases containing clothes can be sealed with strips of foam. Good strong cases are now available in polypropylene, but are usually awkward shapes. Fibre suitcases are available in squared-off shapes that pack better, but they loose their shape if they get wet. Lashing down cleats will keep baggage in place and cut down annoying rattles.

If you plan to sleep without a tent, you will need a mosquito net in some areas. There are several types on the market, but they are not usually big enough to tuck in properly to make sure there are not any gaps. Ex-military ones have the extra advantage of needing only one point of suspension. A camera tripod or ice axe will do for this if there is not a vehicle or tent nearby.

Malaria is an increasingly serious problem, so it is worth getting a net that is already impregnated with a safe insecticide. On a long journey, carry the correct insecticide to re-impregnate the net.

If you do sleep without a tent, make a note of where the sun should rise and position yourself to be in the shade, or the sun could wake you up earlier than you would like to.

A full-length roof rack covered in plywood not only makes a good sleeping platform, but acts as a double skin, to keep the vehicle cooler in sunny conditions.

Mattresses

In cold places, you should not sleep directly on the ground, so use some form of insulation. Air beds are very comfortable and are preferred by some to foam, but they do have disadvantages. They are generally too heavy to carry unless you have a vehicle and inflating them is hard work. Thorns and sunlight all work against them and you will certainly spend a lot of time patching holes in them.

If you decide to use one, be sure it is made of rubber and not of plastic, and only pump it up half full. If you inflate it any harder you will roll around and probably fall off. Perspiration condenses against the surface of air mattresses and on cold nights you will wake up in a puddle of cold water, unless you have put a blanket or woollen jumper between yourself and the mattress.

Camp beds tend to be narrow, collapse frequently, tear holes in the groundsheet and soon break up altogether. Even worse, cold air circulates underneath the bed, since your body weight compresses the bedding. Only several layers of blankets under you will give you the insulation you need.

Open cell foam mattresses are comfortable but often too thin, so it is best to have two thicknesses or else to put a closed cell foam mattress, such as a Karrimat, on the ground and an open cell foam mattress on top of it. Open cell mattresses wear quickly, but if you make a washable cotton cover that fully encloses them, they will last for several years. Foam mattresses, being bulky, are best wrapped in strong waterproof covers during transport. One advantage of foam mattresses is that the perspiration that collects in them evaporates very quickly when aired so they are easy to keep fresh and dry. Remember to give the foam an airing every second day.

The most popular mattresses these days are self-inflating ones. As with air beds, in really cold climates you will be warmer if you put a blanket or sweater between your sleeping bag and the mattress.

Closed cell foam mats, such as Karrimat come in a 3mm thickness, suitable for putting under a groundsheet for protection against sharp stones or on ice, where otherwise the tent groundsheet could stick to the ice and be torn when trying to get it free.

On a long overland trip, you can combat changing conditions with a combination of two sleeping bags. First get a medium quality nylon covered, down sleeping bag and if you are tall, make sure it is long enough for you. This bag will be the one you use most often for medium cold nights. Secondly, get a cheap all-synthetic bag, i.e. one filled with artificial fibre. These cheap, easily washable bags are best for use alone on warmer nights and outside the down bag for very cold nights. Make sure the synthetic bag is big enough to go outside the down bag, without compressing the down bag when it is fully lofted up.

In polar and high mountain areas, the golden rule when travelling is never to be parted from your own sleeping bag, in case a blizzard or accident breaks up the party. This would hold true when travelling anywhere that is cold.

Furniture and Utensils

The aluminium chairs on the market today are covered with light cotton. This rots quickly in intense sunlight. Look around for nylon or terylene covered chairs or replace the cotton covers with your own. Full-size ammunition boxes are good for protecting kitchenware and make good seats.

When buying utensils, go for dull-grey aluminium billies. Shiny-type aluminium billies tend to crack and split with repeated knocks and vibration. Billies, pots and pans, plates, mugs, cutlery, etc. should be firmly packed inside boxes, with cloth or thin foam separating metal utensils and cutlery, or they will rub against each other and become covered in a mass of metal filings. A pressure cooker will guarantee sterile food and can double as a large billy, so if you have room, it is a good investment.

Kettles with lids are preferable to whistling kettles, which are difficult to fill from cans or streams. For melting snow and ice, it is best to use billies. Big, strong aluminium ones are best bought at the Army and Navy auctions or surplus stores. If you are flying out to the Third World, good alternatives will be readily available in local markets.

A wide range of non-breakable cups and plates are available, but you will find that soft plastic mugs leave a bad after-taste, so it is better to pay a little more and get melamine. Stick to large mugs with firm, wide bases, that will not tip over easily. Insulated mugs soon become smelly and unhygienic, because dirt and water get between the two layers and cannot be cleaned out.

Many people like metal mugs, but if you like your drinks hot you may find the handle too hot to touch, or burn your lips on the metal. Melamine mugs soon get stained with tea or coffee, but there are cleaners available, or Steradent tablets are a perfectly adequate and cheaper substitute. Heavyweight stainless steel cutlery is much more durable than aluminium for a long expedition.

For carrying water, ex-military plastic jerry cans are best, as they are light-proof and therefore algae will not grow inside them – as it does with normal plastic containers.

Stoves and Gas

The 2.7 kgs cartridge or the 4.5 gas cylinder, are the best sizes to carry. Gas is the easiest and cleanest fuel to use for cooking.

Liquid petroleum gas is usually called Calor Gas or butane gas in the UK and by various oil company names world-wide, such as Shellgas or Essogas. Though available world-wide, there are different fittings on the cylinders in different countries and these are not interchangeable. Where you use a pressure reduction valve on a low pressure appliance, there will always be a rubber tube connection. Make sure that you carry some spare lengths of the correct size rubber tubing.

Gas cylinders are heavy and re-filling can be difficult. Re-fillable Camping Gaz cylinders as supplied in Europe, are intended to be factory re-filled; but in some countries, e.g. Algeria, Morocco and Yemen, they are available with an overfill release valve, so that you can fill them yourself from a larger domestic butane gas supply. In Asia enterprising campsite managers and gas suppliers have discovered ways of filling gas cylinders from their supply. Stand well clear while they do this, as the process involves pushing down the ball valve with a nail or stone, then over-filling from a supply of higher pressure. This can cause flare-up problems when the cylinder is first used with standard cooking equipment, so if you use such a source of supply, it is advisable to release some of the pressure by opening the valve for a couple of minutes (well away from any flame), before connecting up.

Lighting any stove is always a problem in cold climates or at altitude. Local matches never work, unless you strike three together, so take a good supply of the 300 match size, called Cook's Household Matches. The best answer seems to be a butane cigarette lighter, kept in your trouser pocket, where it will be warm. Remember to carry plenty of refills.

There are many good camping gas stoves available, but when cooking for large groups outside, I prefer to use the large cast-iron gas rings used by builders to melt bitumen. These are wide, heavy and stable when very large billies are used and do not blow out in the wind. In cold areas, try to get propane gas instead of butane gas,

If gas supplies are a problem, there are good twin burner stoves that use unleaded petrol or kerosene. There are also single burner, multi-fuel stoves, that will operate on diesel fuel.

Space Blankets

Space blankets are, on the evidence, not much better than a polythene sheet or bag. Body perspiration tends to condense inside them, making the sleeping bag wet, so that the person inside gets cold. In hot or desert areas, however, used in reverse to reflect the sun, they are very good during the heat of the day to keep a tent or vehicle cool. If necessary, a plastic sheet or space blanket can be spread over a ring of boulders to make an effective bath; they are also ideal for making desert stills.

Buying

When buying equipment be especially wary of any shop that calls itself an expedition supplier, but does not stock the better brands of equipment. All the top-class equipment suppliers will give trade discounts to genuine expeditions, or group buyers such as clubs or educational establishments, and some, such as

Field and Trek and Cotswold Camping, have special contract departments for this service.

Check-list

For a party of four with no worries about travelling light:

Good compass, maps and guidebooks
Selection of plastic bags for packing, waste disposal, etc
Clingfilm and aluminium foil for food and cooking
Large bowl for washing up and washing
4 x 20 litre water cans – strong ex-military type (polypropylene)
Fire extinguisher
Large supply of paper towels, toilet paper, scouring pads, dish cloths and tea towels
Large supply of good matches in waterproof box and/or disposable lighters
Washing up liquid for dishes (also good for mechanics' greasy hands)
Frying pan
Pressure cooker
Selection of strong saucepans or billies
Kettle with lid (not whistling type, which is difficult to fill from cans or streams)
Tin opener – good heavyweight or wall type
Stainless steel cutlery
Plastic screw top jars for sugar, salt, washing powder etc. (Nalgene are the best)
1 large sharp bread knife
2 small sharp vegetable knives
Kitchen scissors
1 large serving spoon and soup ladle
Plates and/or bowls for eating
Wide base mugs, which do not tip over easily
Good twin burner for your gas supply, otherwise petrol or kerosene twin burner cooker – multi fuel stoves are available, that will work with diesel fuel
Good sleeping bag or sleeping bag combination for the climate expected, plus mattress of your choice
Mosquito nets
Combined mosquito and insect repellent spray
Battery-powered fluorescent light
4 lightweight folding chairs
Short-handled hand axe, for wood fires
Thin nylon line to use as clothes line, plus clothes pegs
Washing powder for clothes 2 separate 6-metre lengths of plastic tubing, one to fill water tank or water cans; the other for fuel cans
2 tubes of universal glue/sealant eg Bostik
Chamois leather
Sponges
6 heavy rubber "tie downs"
Water purification filters plus tablets or iodine as back-up
Phrase books/dictionaries
2 torches plus spare batteries

Ordinary scissors
Small plastic dustpan and brush
Soap, shampoo, toothpaste, towels
Medical first aid kit, plus multivitamins and rehydration salts
Elastic bands, sewing kit and safety pins
Cassette player and selection of cassettes
Selection of reading material including local book on local flora and fauna plus
AA multilingual vehicle parts guide.
Hidden strong box and money belt
Passports, visas, traveller cheques, cash, vaccination certificates, car papers,
insurance papers, UK and International driving licence, permissions to drive
letter (if you do not own the vehicle), photocopies of travel and medical insur-
ance policies and 6 spare passport photographs.

Many other things can be taken along, but most of these are personal belongings. They include: dental floss; waterproof watch; tissues (good for many other
reasons than blowing your nose); clothing, including a tie for formal occasions
that may crop up and dealing with embassies (store the tie rolled up in a jar with
a lid), dress (for that same occasion), jackets, waterproofs, gloves, swimming
costume, sweaters, parkas with hoods; moisturising cream; toothbrushes;
comb; Swiss army knife; camera; film; photographic accessories; anti-malaria
tablets and salt tablets where required; sun barrier cream; sunglasses;
medicines; spare prescription spectacles if worn; insurance papers; airmail writing paper; envelopes and pens.

*For a list of Specialist Equipment Suppliers, Photographic, Optical and
Medical, see p.859 of the Directory*

FOOD ON THE MOVE

by Ingrid Cranfield

L iving a regular life, in one place most of the time, people get to know what
foods they like and dislike and base a balanced diet on this rather than on text
book nutrition. The problem is, how do you ensure you will have good food on
the move? When travelling, you are constantly faced with new foods and it can
be easy to lose track of how you are eating, simply because your rule of thumb
menu-planning breaks down. This can lead to fatigue, a lack of energy and even
poor health.

Essentially there are two ways of coping. You can either pick up local food as
you travel, or you can take with you all your needs for the duration. Eating local
food may give you a feeling of being closer to a country's way of life, but could
also make you severely ill. Taking your own supplies is safe and very necessary
if you are going into the wilds, but how do you stop your palate becoming jaded
with endless supplies of dried food?

It is sensible to be able to recognise the constitution of all foods and to know
what is necessary to keep you well fed. A balanced diet breaks down into six
main areas: sugars, carbohydrates, fats, proteins, minerals/vitamins/salts and

water – all are necessary, some in greater quantities than others.

Sugars: Technically called simple sugars, these are the simplest form of energy-stored-as-food. Because they are simple, the body finds them easy to absorb into the bloodstream – hence the term blood sugar. From here sugars are either turned directly to energy, or are stored as glycogen. The brain is very partial to using sugars for energy and if it is forced to run on other forms of food energy it complains by making you feel tired, headachy, and generally wobbly-kneed.

Though it is important to have some sugars in your diet, try not to depend on them too much. Weight for weight they give you fewer calories than other food types. Also if you take in lots of sugars at once, the body will react by over-producing insulin because your blood sugar is too high, so that in the end your blood sugar is taken down to a lower level than before. If you feel a desperate need for instant energy, try to take sugars with other food types to prevent this happening. While travelling, it is simple enough to recognise foods with lots of sugars – they're sweet. Simple enough, too, to avoid sugar excesses, whose pitfalls are well documented in the West. In less developed areas, sugar is still something of a luxury.

Carbohydrates: Basically, carbohydrates are complex structures of simple sugars. Plants generally store energy as carbohydrate while animals store food energy as fat or glycogen. Carbohydrates have to be broken down into simple sugars by the body before they can be used as energy, so it takes longer to benefit from them after eating. Weight for weight, however, you will get three or four times more calories from carbohydrates than from sugars.

Recognising carbohydrates is simple. They are stodgy, starchy and very filling: breads in the Western world, mealies in Africa, rice in the East, etc. The majority of food energy comes from carbohydrates, so, when travelling, find the local equivalent and base a diet around it.

Fats: Next to carbohydrates, most of our energy comes from fats. Our bodies store energy as fat because it is the most efficient way to do so. Weight for weight, fats give you nearly three times the energy of carbohydrates, so they are an extremely efficient way of carrying food energy. The body can take quite a while to break down fat into a usable form – from minutes to half an hour.

Fats, of course, are fatty, oily, creamy and sometimes congeal. Foods high in fat include butter, dairy foods, etc., although there are other high fat foods that are less well known, such as egg yolk or nut kernels. Fats are necessary now and again because one reclusive vitamin is generated from a fat and, more obviously, because without these concentrated doses of energy it would take a lot longer to eat all the food you need, as with cows or elephants.

Proteins: One of the most misunderstood types of food in the West is protein. Traditionally thought of as something essential, and the more the better, the truth is that for adults very little is needed each day and bodies in the West work very hard to convert unnecessary protein into urea so that it can be flushed away.

Protein is used to build and repair bodies, so children need plenty of it, as do adults recovering from injury. Otherwise, the amount of protein needed each day is small – maybe a small egg's worth. Other than that, protein cannot be readily used for energy, and the body does not bother converting it unless it is heading for a state of starvation. Those people on a red meat diet are using very little of the protein it contains, relying on the fat content which can be up to 45 per cent. When you are wondering where protein appears in your food, bear in mind that protein is for growth, so young mammals have protein-packed milk, unhatched chicks have their own supply in the meat of an egg and to help trees off to a good start there is a healthy package of protein in nuts. Even the humble grain of wheat has a little, if it isn't processed away.

Minerals, Vitamins and Salts: All of these are essential for all-round health and fitness. Most of them cannot be stored by the body and so they should be taken regularly, preferably daily. Ten days' shortage of Vitamin C, for instance, and you feel run-down, tired and lethargic – perhaps without knowing why.

In the normal diet, most of your minerals and vitamins come from fresh fruit and vegetables. If you feel that you may not get enough fresh food, take a course of multivitamin tablets with you for the duration of your travels. They do not weigh very much and can save you lots of trouble.

If you are getting your vitamins and minerals from fresh foods, remember that they are usually tucked away just under the skin, if not in the skin itself. Polished and refined foodstuffs have lost a lot, if not all, of their vitamins, minerals and dietary fibre.

As regards salts, there is little cause for concern. It is easier to take too much than too little, and if you do err on the low side your body often tells you by craving salty foods. So do not take salt tablets. You could upset your stomach lining.

How Much?

Nutritionists have a term for the amount of food energy needed to keep a body ticking over –the basal metabolic rate. Take a man and put him in a room at ideal temperature, humidity, etc., and make sure he does no work at all except stay alive and he will use about 600kCal in a day. This is his basal metabolic rate.

Those of us who do not lie stock still in a room all day need energy over and above that basic amount, to work and to keep warm. For living and working in average conditions, our daily energy requirement rises to about 2500kCal. If you are going to be physically active (backpacking, say) in a temperate climate, your energy use will go up to around 3500kCal per day. If we do the same hard work in an extremely cold climate, our energy rate could go up to 5000kCal. To need more than this we would need to do an immense amount of work or have an incredibly fast metabolism. Sadly for women, they do not burn up nearly as much energy doing the same work as men.

A little experience will tell you whether you need a little more or a little less than the average. With this knowledge, you are ready to plan just how much food you need to take for the number of days you are travelling.

When you come to work out amounts of various foodstuffs that make up your calorie intake for the day, books for slimmers or the health conscious are invaluable. They list not only calories, but often protein and other nutritional breakdown. Sometimes, nutritional information is also given on the packet.

Eating Local Food

In developing countries, canned, powdered and dried foods are usually safe to eat, provided they are made up with purified water. Staples such as flour and cooking oils are nearly always safe.

Meat, poultry, fish and shellfish should look and smell fresh and be thoroughly cooked, though not over-cooked, as soon as possible after purchasing. They should be eaten while still hot or kept continuously refrigerated after preparation. Eggs are safe enough if reasonably fresh and thoroughly cooked.

Milk may harbour disease-producing organisms (tuberculosis, brucellosis). The "pasteurised" label in underdeveloped countries should not be depended upon. For safety, if not ideal taste, boil the milk before drinking. (Canned or powdered milk may generally be used without boiling for drinking or in cooking).

Butter and margarine are safe unless obviously rancid. Margarine's keeping qualities are better than those of butter. Cheeses, especially hard and semi-hard varieties, are normally quite safe; soft cheeses are not so reliable.

Vegetables for cooking are safe if boiled for a short time. Do check, though, that on fruit or vegetables the skin or peel is intact. Wash them thoroughly and peel them yourself if you plan to eat them raw.

Moist or cream pastries should not be eaten unless they have been continuously refrigerated. Dry baked goods, such as bread and cakes, are usually safe even without refrigeration.

Always look for food that is as fresh as possible. If you can watch livestock being killed and cooked or any other food being prepared before you eat it, so much the better. Do not be deceived by plush surroundings and glib assurances. Often the large restaurant with its questionable standard of hygiene and practice of cooking food ahead of time is a less safe bet than the wayside vendor from whom you can take food cooked on an open fire, without giving flies or another person the chance to contaminate it. Before preparing bought food, always wash your hands in water that has been chlorinated or otherwise purified.

In restaurants, the same rules apply for which foods are safe to eat. Restaurants buy their food from shops just as you would. It is wise to avoid steak tartare and other forms of raw meat in the tropics as there is a risk of tapeworm. Fruit juice is safe if pressed in front of you. Protect freshly bought meat from flies and insects with a muslin cover.

Meat that is just "on the turn" can sometimes be saved by washing it in strong salty water. If this removes the glistening appearance and sickly sweet smell, the meat is probably safe to eat. Cold or half-warmed foods may have been left standing and are therefore a risk. Boil such meats and poultry for at least ten minutes to destroy bacteria before serving. Ice-cream is especially to be avoided in all developing countries.

Rice and other grains and pulses will probably have preservatives added to them. These will need to be removed by thorough washing as they are indigestible.

Eating in developed countries is not entirely hazard-free. You should remember that the Mediterranean countries and the former USSR host typhoid (against which vaccination is recommended), and that Delhi Belly is no respecter of language and is just as likely to strike in Spain as in India. The rules for avoiding tummy trouble are much as above: stick to foods that are simple and hygienically prepared, and as close as possible to those you know and love – at least until your digestive system slowly adapts to change.

Off the Beaten Track

There is no right menu for a camping trip, because we all have slightly different tastes in food and there is an almost endless number of menu possibilities. So, what should you pack? Here are a few points you'll want to consider when choosing the right foods: weight, bulk, cost per kg.

Obviously, water-weighted, tinned foods are out. So are most perishables – especially if you are going to be lugging your pantry on your back. You will want only lightweight, long-lasting, compact food. Some of the lightest, of course, are the freeze drieds. You can buy complete freeze dried meals that are very easily prepared: just add boiling water and wait five minutes. They have their drawbacks, however. First, they are very expensive. Second, even if you do like these pre-packaged offerings, and many people do not, you can get tired of them very quickly.

A much more exciting and economical method is to buy dehydrated foods at the supermarket and combine them to create your own imaginative dinners. Dried beans, cereals, instant potato, meat bars, crackers, dry soup mixes, cocoa, pudding, gingerbread and instant cheesecake mixes are just a few of the possibilities. But do not forget to pack a few spices to make your creations possible.

Quantity and Palatability

Most people tend to work up a big appetite outdoors. About 0.9kg to 1.2kg of food per person per day is average. How much of which foods will make up that weight is up to you. You can guess pretty accurately about how much macaroni or cheese or how many pudding mixes you are likely to need.

Last, but not least, what do you like? If you do not care for instant butterscotch pudding or freeze dried stew at home, you will probably like it even less after two days on the trail. And if you have never tried something before, don't take the chance. Do your experimenting first. Don't shock your digestive system with a lot of strange or different new foods. Stick as closely as possible to what you're used to in order to avoid stomach upsets and indigestion. And make sure you pack a wide enough variety of foods to ensure you will not be subjected to five oatmeal breakfasts in a row or be locked into an inflexible plan.

Packaging your Food

After purchasing your food, the next step is to re-package it. Except for freeze dried meals or other specially-sealed foods, it is a good idea to store supplies and spices in small freezer bags. Just pour in your pudding powder, salt or gingerbread mix, drop an identifying label in, to take all the guesswork (and fun) out of it, and tie a loose knot. Taking plastic into the wilderness may offend one's sensibilities but it works well. Out in the wilds you learn just how handy these lightweight, flexible, recyclable, moisture-proof bags really are.

Preparing Great Meals

Although cooking over an open fire is great fun, many areas do not allow and cannot support campfires, so don't head off without a stove. When choosing a stove, remember that the further off the beaten track you go, the more important become size, weight and reliability. Aside from a stove, you will also need a collapsible water container, means of water purification and a heavy bag in which to store your soot-bottomed pans. You will need individual eating utensils: spoon, cup and bowl will do. Also take a few recipes with you, or learn them before you leave. You can even have such luxuries as fresh baked bread if you are prepared to make the effort. Some tips about camp cooking learned the hard way:

1. Cook on a low heat to avoid scorching
2. Taste before salting (the bouillon cubes and powdered bases often added to camp casseroles are very salty: don't overdo it by adding more)
3. Add rice, pasta, etc., to boiling water to avoid sticky or slimy textures and add a knob of butter or margarine to stop the pan from boiling over
4. Add freeze dried or dehydrated foods early on in your recipes to allow time for rehydration
5. Add powdered milk and eggs, cheese and thickeners to recipes last when heating
6. When melting snow for water, do not let the bottom of the pan go dry or it will scorch (keep packing the snow down to the bottom
7. Add extra water at high altitudes when boiling (water evaporates more rapidly as you gain altitude) and allow longer cooking times – twenty minutes at 1000m, for example, as against ten minutes at sea level.

Cleaning Up

Soap residue can make you sick. Most seasoned campers, after one experience with "soap sickness of the stomach", recommend using only a scouring pad and water. Boiling water can be used to sterilise and, if you have ignored the above advice, is good for removing the remains of your glued-on pasta or cheese dinners. Soak and then scrub.

Use these recyclable plastic bags to store leftovers and to carry away any litter. Leave the wilderness kitchen clean – and ready for your next feat of mealtime magic!

LIGHTWEIGHT EQUIPMENT

by Martin Rosser

When I first came to lightweight backpacking, I knew very little and did not bother to ask for advice. I learned from bitter experience and, interspersed with misery, very exciting it was too. The main drawback is expense. Based on trial and error, costs soon mounted to prohibitive proportions before I had what I wanted. The lesson: if you are beginning, a little advice is worth a lot. When you become more practised, then is the time for bitter experience to take over.

In this article, I intend only to cover the main purchases you will make, missing out on the way food, clothing, and any more technical sporting equipment. This leaves (in descending order of what it will probably cost you) tent or shelter, sleeping gear, rucksack, boots and cooking and eating gear.

If you are going backpacking, there are a number of objectives you will have in mind. *Weight* is usually at the top of the list: you want everything as light as possible. *Performance*: you want it to be good enough for everything you are going to put it through. *Expense*: you have to be able to afford it. These three criteria form what could be termed the eternal triangle of backpacking.

As we go on, you will see compromises arising, but one aspect of weight can be covered now. Most lightweight gear comes marked with a weight, but manufacturers being manufacturers, these are not always as accurate as they might be. Furthermore, some sleeping bags come marked with the weight of the filling only. It is easy to become confused or misled. The easiest answer is to shop for your kit armed with a spring balance (anything measuring up to fifteen lbs is sufficient if it can be read to the nearest ounce or two). If you want to know where to get a balance, ask a fisherman.

Tents and Shelters

At one time, the ridge pole was the only tent you could get, short of a marquee. Then some bright spark designed an A-pole ridge so that the pole did not come straight down the doorway. Today you can still get both these designs and the ridge pole (in the form of the Vango Force Ten) is still preferred by many as a heavy duty tent that can take a lot of punishment.

However, with the advent of flexible poles that could be shoved through sleeves, new designs became possible and new advantages arose. Such models give you plenty of headroom, something as important as ground space if you intend to live in your tent during bad weather. There are disadvantages of course. The tents are both more expensive and more fragile. To get a structurally strong flexible-pole tent, you have to go up-market to the geodesic designs, and that costs a lot of money.

After flexible poles, Gore-tex made its mark on the tent scene with single-skin tents. Reputably water tight, with built-in breathability, you get a condensation-free tent that weighs even less than regular flexible pole types. These tents also tend to employ flexible poles so the space inside is good. However, Gore-tex is a very expensive material, so as the weight goes down, the prices go up.

Single skin tents soon became available in one-man versions with only the barest skeleton of a frame. Because the material breathes, it does not matter if there is no circulation of air around it. With one hoop at the front, these tents resemble a tunnel that you have to crawl into feet first. Then the hoop was removed and the Gore-tex "bivi-bag" was born – a waterproof and fully breathable covering for your sleeping bag. These are probably the ultimate luxury in bivouacking, but the cost is again high. However, weighing in at next to nothing, these bags are well worth considering.

Last, but not least comes the humble bivouac sheet or, to use the army parlance, the "basha sheet". This 6ft by 8ft piece of PU nylon has tags around the outside so that it can be pegged down. It is the most versatile, lightweight, inexpensive and durable of all shelters so far discussed. It is limited only by the ingenuity and expertise of the user – and therein lies its fault: you need to know how to use it. But if you do not have any money, or if you can put the occasional soaking down to experience, give it a go.

So which one do you choose? Narrow the field by asking yourself these questions: how many people do you want it to sleep? How high up are you going to camp? (The higher you camp, the harsher the conditions, so the sturdier the tent you need.) Is headroom important to you? (Perhaps you want a flexible hoop design.) Do you want it to last a long time? (If so you will have to go for a heavier duty model.)

It has to be said that even if you designed the tent yourself, compromises would have to be made, so be prepared to make them when buying. However, with care and proper scrutiny of the maker's specifications, you should get something suitable.

Whatever you end up with, try to get a tent with mosquito netting on every entrance, even the vents. Rare indeed are the countries with no flying biters. The tent you end up with will probably have a super thin ground-sheet to save weight, so you might want to get some 2mm foam to use as an underlay. It will keep you surprisingly warm and will cut down on wear and tear. However, this will add to the weight and bulk of your tent system. Bear this in mind before you reject the heavier tent with the stronger ground sheet.

Sleeping Gear

Without a shadow of a doubt, the best you can sleep in is a down bag. It promotes fine dreams, is aesthetically pleasing, is lighter for any given warmth rating than any other fill and packs away smaller than any other bag, lofting up afterwards to coset you at night. Nothing else comes close to down, unless, of course, you are allergic to feathers.

Yet down has a terrible Achilles heel. If it gets wet, it is next to useless and very unpleasant to be next to. Furthermore, wet it a few times and it starts to feel very sorry for itself, losing efficiency rapidly.

If your bag is likely to get wet, steer clear of down. The alternative is a man-made fibre bag. These come in many guises but the principle is the same in all. A long, man-made fibre is hollow and thus traps air. As with down, it is the trapped air that keeps you warm. Call it Holofill, Superloft, Microsoft or whatever, the consensus of opinion is that the difference in performance is marginal. The fibres probably differ slightly to get around patents rather than to improve performance.

The advantages of artificial fibres are clear. The bags are cheaper than down, they are warmer underneath you (because they are harder to compress), they keep you warmer when wet, and they are easier to keep clean. Disadvantages? They are substantially heavier and bulkier than down, and will not last you anywhere near as long.

The compromise is clear. If you can stay out of the wet and can afford to pay more, invest in down which lasts longer, so costing the same in the long run. If you constantly get wet when camping, buy a man-made fibre bag and stick to feeling the down bags in the shops lovingly.

There is one more alternative, Buffalo Bags, made from fibre pile covered in pertex. These are unique and have their own special advantages, though the disadvantages can be stated easily: they are very heavy and bulky. Buffalo Bags are based on the layer system, making it handy to add layers for cold weather and subtract for hot. They are tough and very washable. Thanks to the pertex covering they are not easily wetted, and if they do get wet, the pile wicks away moisture and the pertex cover dries it out rapidly. The same pertex covering makes the bag very windproof. The bag is very good for those who bivouac and can be used to effect with a good down inner bag. Handle, or better still, borrow one to try before you buy.

Try the bag on in the shop, however foolish you feel, and leave your clothes on while you do so. This minimises embarrassment, and one day you might be cold enough out in the wilds to sleep fully clothed. Pull the hood of the bag tight around your face to cover the head. If you cannot do this, the bag cannot be used for any kind of cold weather. A large part of the body's heat loss is from the head. Shove your feet into the bottom of the bag and wriggle. If the bag constricts you, it is too small. Any point where you press against the bag will turn into a miserable cold spot at night. If you are a restless sleeper, make sure the bag is wide enough around the middle to contain all your squirming. If you feel like a solitary pea rattling around in an empty pod, the bag is too large and you will waste heat warming up empty space.

General good points in a bag include a box or elephant-type foot; a draw-cord at the shoulder as well as the head; and the option of a right or left handed zip so that in an emergency you can share your warmth with an extra special friend. Zips should all be well baffled to prevent loss of heat. If the sack you choose is of man-made fibre, check to see if it comes with a compression stuff sack. If it does not and you want one, this will add a few pounds to the final price.

I have deliberately ignored baffle constructions as the subject is complicated and best covered with examples to hand. Seek advice on site. Similarly with the season rating of the bag: "season" system is simple but should only be used as a rough guide. One season (summer) for very casual use in warm weather; two season (summer and spring) is a little better; three seasons should be good for winter use; and five seasons for use in severe conditions. However, simple systems like this leave room for manufacturers to fudge their claims. One man's three seasons is another man's four. Query the general reputation of the bag you fancy with as many experts as you can find. I find that "lowest temperatures" to use the bags in are next to useless: they are inevitably rated for still air, and who camps in that? As well as ignoring the massive effect of wind chill, they can also ignore the fact that some people maintain a higher body temperature at night than others.

Last but not least with sleeping gear, you would be well advised to put something under your sleeping bag; namely a "kip mat". The most widely used is the closed cell foam type which is bulky but lightweight and durable. Ignore all advice that tells you that they are all made of the same stuff and that for expensive ones you simply pay for the name – it is patently untrue. A simple test is to inflict severe damage on various types – such damage as scoring, tearing, and compressing flat. Choose one that withstands these injuries best and it will probably be the one that feels warmest when pressed between the palms. It will probably cost more, but in my experience the cheap ones are simply not worth it.

Rucksacks

With rucksacks two things are important from the outset: size and waterproofness. You have available to you any size of 'sack you want and (whatever the manufacturer may say to the contrary) none of them are waterproof. The capacity of a 'sack is measured in litres. A small day pack weighs in at about 25 litres. From there you have various sizes up to a general all round 'sack sized at 75 litres. With one of these you will be able to manage anything up to mountaineering (at a push), but you pay a price for the facility. Having 75 litres to play with you feel a terrible urge to fill up all the space, even for summer camping in the lowlands.

To restrict yourself to what you need rather than what you have room for, takes discipline. Because of this, some people prefer a 65 or even a 50-litre 'sack. Going upwards from 75 litres, there is almost no end, but the higher you go the more specialised the use; expedition travel overseas perhaps or for humping all you need up to a base camp from which you intend making sorties with smaller loads.

When you look at the vast array of rucksacks available, you will find that fashion dictates two things at present. First is the anatomical, internal frame system. External frames are fuddy duddy now, though the internal frame is not the all-round answer to carrying loads. The second (and far less valid) fashion is adjustable harnesses. If you can (and it gets harder every season) avoid these. There are more fiddly bits that can go wrong, usually at an awkward moment (mine went halfway up the ascent to a glacier), and as your back should not be due to change shape significantly for another 30 years at least you may as well save yourself some bother. Settle for a 'sack that is fixed at one size and just happens to fit you.

Something that has always been a very important asset to a rucksack is a hip belt. When walking, the hip belt transfers roughly 60 per cent of the pack weight to your legs, leaving only 40 per cent for your more delicate shoulders and back. Therefore any rucksack you buy should have a wide, sturdy, and very well padded hip belt. That thick padding should also appear at the shoulder straps. Thin bands will cut off the circulation, giving you the sensation of having two useless and heavy ropes dangling from your shoulders instead of arms.

After those important criteria, the rest more or less comes down to personal preference. If you are organised in the way you pack, a one-section rucksack is simpler and more effective. It is an advantage if your pockets can be detached, but having them fixed saves a bit of weight. Some harnesses leave more room for air to circulate between you and the 'sack. If you hate getting hot and sweaty as you walk, try for one of these.

When you buy your pack, enquire about the repair service. Well established manufacturers such as Karrimor and Berghaus give excellent service, often without charging. Some will even give a lifetime's guarantee, though I can never work out if this applies to the life of the 'sack or the life of its owner.

Boots

As far as boots are concerned, leather is still the most wonderful material going. Fabric boots have come and gone, and plastic shell boots have managed to retain only a very small part of the market. Meanwhile, leather goes from strength to strength. To spot a good leather boot is fairly simple. It is as far as possible made from one bit of leather. The stitching is double, sometimes triple. The ankle is well padded to give comfortable support. The inside of the boot is lined with soft leather, and there are no rough seams around the heel. Feet tend to blister in disapproval of poor design.

Check the weight of several different pairs. It costs you energy to clump around with a heavy weight on each foot, and you may well decide that the terrain you usually walk on is not demanding enough to require such solidness.

If you intend to use your boots with crampons, however, you will need a fairly rigid sole at least. If you intend to go front pointing you will need a boot with a steel shank in the sole. For the common walker, though, these should be avoided. The boot becomes very heavy and uncomfortable to walk in over any great distance.

Traditionally, two pairs of socks are worn with boots, and some celebrated old timers even wear more, choosing oversize boots to compensate. However, modern thinking says that boots are not as uncomfortable as they used to be and one pair of socks is quite enough. So unless you suffer terribly from cold feet, prepare to try on your boots with just one pair of thick socks. With the boots laced up, rap the heel on the floor and check to see if you can wiggle your toes freely. If you can, the boots are not too tight for you, the blood will still circulate and you should be free from the horrors of gangrene and cold toes.

Cooking and Eating

For this pleasant pastime you will need a stove, something to cook in, something to eat out of, something to eat with and (very importantly) something to carry water in.

A water container should hold about a litre and can be of any shape or design that takes your fancy. The solid plastic army types are robust but heavy. The thin aluminium ones are lighter but more fragile. One rule goes with all water bottles, though. Put anything other than water in them and they will be tainted for life.

The essential part of the "something to eat with" is a general purpose blade. This will cut up anything you want to eat into manageable portions as well as whittle sticks and slice your tongue open if you lick it once too often. Beyond this, you only need a spoon. Anything more is redundant. Save the weight by cutting down on the number of utensils you take rather than by using flimsy "camping" ones which bend the first time you use them.

For those who are into time and motion, what you eat out of is also what you cook in. Those who find this idea displeasing will know best what they want. However, when you look for a cooking/eating billy make sure of two things. Firstly, it should have a good handle (preferably one that will not get too hot to hold whilst cooking is in progress). Secondly, it must have a close-fitting lid. This too must have a handle, so it can be lifted on or off, or be used as a frying pan by those terrible people who can suffer fried eggs and bacon for breakfast.

There are many styles of billy available to choose from. I use a two pint "paint tin" type, because I like the shape and enjoy hanging it over wood fires. Others choose the rectangular army type that hold up to a litre. These fit nicely into the side pocket of a rucksack and can be filled with snack foods and brew kit.

On now to the more complex subject of stoves. The choice here is between solid fuel, liquid or gas. Solid fuel comes in blocks that resemble white cough candy. A packet fits neatly into the metal tray that you burn them in. The whole affair is little bigger than a pack of playing cards. The system is foolproof since you merely set a match to the blocks and add more for extra heat, take away for less heat. The fuel is resistant to water, though you may have trouble lighting it if it is damp. Its main drawback is that it does not produce an intense heat and so is slow to use. It also produces noxious fumes and so should not be used in an enclosed space.

Moving on to liquid stoves, your choice increases considerably. Most simple of all is the meths burner. Here you have a container into which you pour meths and then set fire to it. The more sophisticated (and expensive) sets have a wind-shield built round the container which also neatly holds the billy. Again the design is foolproof. Its advantages include a cleaning, burning flame, and quite a range of burners, from inexpensive to high-tech and costly. However, the fuel is relatively expensive and may be difficult to get hold of if you are off the beaten track. Furthermore, the rate of burn cannot be controlled. The choice is simply on or off.

Still in the liquid fuel range, there are the pressurised burners, running on either paraffin or petrol. The burner for paraffin is the well known primus stove. Though it is a relatively complicated device, compared with other stoves it can be readily mastered. Once burning, the flame is intense and efficient and can be adjusted to give various rates of heat. As a fuel, paraffin is cheap and almost universally available. The disadvantages of pressurised paraffin are that a small amount of a second fuel must be carried to prime the stove which needs some maintenance. However, primus stoves are known in most parts of the world, so spare parts should not be too much of a problem.

An alternative to pressurised paraffin is pressurised petrol. Again this type of stove is quite complicated and needs occasional maintenance. Furthermore it usually demands to be fed unleaded petrol, so buying fuel whilst travelling could present problems. Like paraffin, however, it burns hot and fast, heating quickly and efficiently. Petrol and paraffin also produce noxious fumes and both should be used in a well ventilated space.

Gas stoves are simple to use. They are relatively cheap to buy but are expensive to run. They burn cleanly and the flame can be controlled, but when pressure runs low the flame stays stubbornly and annoyingly feeble. You can usually find somewhere to buy replacement canisters, but in out of the way places the cost will be high. The little Camping Gaz canisters that are ubiquitous around Europe are difficult to find in the Third World and you are not allowed to take them on 'planes. Unlike paraffin, gas is not an everyday fuel in most places. Using gas stoves in low temperatures is inadvisable as their performance drops dramatically.

As with most areas of equipment, there is a stove to beat all stoves. It can run on any liquid fuel you care to feed it, including (apparently) vodka, should you be so inclined. It comes with an attachment that screws directly into a regular metal fuel bottle and away you go. Should you be interested in buying one, be prepared to spend a lot.

Once again, compromise is the final solution. You will generally find that pressurised paraffin is the tried and trusted stove for most formal expeditions, and is the general favourite of many. I find solid fuel a useful last resort to have available when you are travelling light and having difficulty lighting wood fires. Gas fuel is simple to use in all but extreme conditions. You pays your money and you takes your choice.

With so much wonderful equipment around it is easy to get carried away and aim for the best in everything. A large rucksack to carry a five season down bag with a Gore-tex bivi-bag, a "superstove" and a geodesic dome tent. Thankfully most people's pockets refuse to support such notions.

In reality, if you think carefully about the use to which your equipment will be put, you will often find that the best is not suitable for you and you are just as well off with something cheaper. Then, when your style of travelling or camping does demand the best, the expense becomes worthwhile and supportable. So do not end up being parboiled in a five season sleeping bag which you only ever use in summer. The money could be better spent elsewhere.

For Specialist Equipment Suppliers see p.859 of the Directory

PERSONAL FREIGHT AND UNACCOMPANIED BAGGAGE

by Paul Melly

Few people bother to think about baggage. Until, that is, they become that annoying person at the front of the airport check-in queue, searching for a credit card to pay the extortionate bill for bringing home an extra suitcase on the same plane.

The alternative – shipping separately – is often disregarded, or looked upon as the sort of thing that people did in the days when Britain had an empire – shipping luggage seems to conjure up images of gigantic Victorian trunks or battered tea chests creaking home from the Far East in the hold of a mail steamer. But it is actually worth investigating. With just a little planning, you can save a fair sum of money for relatively little delay by sending your surplus bags as freight.

The alternative is to pay the full whack for excess baggage while making a handsome contribution to airline profits. This is such a good earner it is given a separate entry in the multi-million dollar revenue graph of one Middle Eastern carrier's annual report.

Costly Limits

The reason excess baggage charges are so high is the strict limit on how much weight an airliner can carry. There is a premium on the limited reserve space. So, if you significantly exceed your individual quota as a passenger and want to take that extra bag on the same flight, you must pay dearly for the privilege. Of course, it then comes up on the luggage carousel with everything else at the end of your journey, which is more convenient but it is also very much more expensive than sending it unaccompanied by air, sea, road or rail. Advance planning can ensure that your baggage will be waiting for you on arrival.

For those caught unawares, one UK operator, the London Baggage Company (Gatwick London Air Terminal, Victoria Place, London SW1W 9SJ, tel: 0171-828 2400) is conveniently located by Victoria Station, the London check-in terminal for several airlines flying out of Gatwick.

Your local *Yellow Pages* will give details of all the various specialist companies under "Freight Forwarding and Shipping and Forwarding Agents". While the British International Freight Association (Redfern House, Browells Lane, Feltham, Middlesex TW13 7EP, tel: 0181-844 2266) publishes the *Year Book*, listing all BIFA members and their freight speciality.

Of course freight services are not only useful for those who have too much travel baggage. If you are going to work abroad, take an extended holiday, embark on a specialist expedition or even a long business trip, you may well have equipment or samples to take. And if you have just finished or are about to start a course of academic or vocational study, there could be a hefty pile of books for which your normal baggage allowance is totally inadequate.

The More You Send...

Although one, two, three or even half a dozen cases may seem a lot to you, for a specialist freight forwarder, airline or shipping company, handling hundreds of tonnes, it is peanuts. Generally, in the cargo business, the more you send the cheaper the price by weight – above a basic minimum which, unless you are sending small expensive items express, can be more than most private individuals want to send. Naturally, you can send less than the minimum, but you still have to pay that standard bottom rate because most freight companies are in business to cater for the needs of industry, not individuals.

When industry does not come up with the traffic, however, they can be glad to get what private business is around. The depressed oil market in 1986, for example, led to an economic slowdown in the Gulf and a consequent slump in export cargo to the region, but airline freight bookings out of Bahrain, Abu Dhabi and Dubai were bolstered by expatriate workers sending home their goods and chattels after their contracts expired and were not renewed.

However there are specialist outfits catering for the private individuals using their bulk buying power to get cheap rates which are then passed on to customers. They can also help with technical problems: how to pack, what you cannot send, insurance and so on.

Sending by Sea

Seafreight is little-used these days except for shipments between Europe and Australia or New Zealand where the great distances involved make it a lot cheaper than air. The time difference between air and sea freight is from seven weeks (sea) and perhaps seven to ten days (air). Air takes longer than one might expect because of red tape, the time needed for goods to clear Customs and the wait until the freight company has a bulk shipment going out.

The London Baggage Company reports that nearly all its seafreight bookings are for Australasia, with most of the remainder for New York or California. On these routes, there is enough business for freighting firms to arrange regular shipments of personal cargo but when it comes to the Third World, the traffic is more limited so the price is higher and it is often just as cheap – and more secure to use the air.

Seafreight is charged by volume rather than weight and is therefore particularly suitable for books or heavy household items; the goods can be held in the UK and then shipped out to coincide with your expected date of arrival in, for example Melbourne or Auckland.

If you want to send stuff straight away, you should remember it will wait an average of seven days before actually leaving – freight forwarders book a whole container and only send it when there is enough cargo to fill it. Shipping on some routes is regarded as high risk so insurance premiums increase – further reducing any price differential with airfreight.

Road and Rail

Within Europe, rail is a useful option, especially for Italy. There is only limited and relatively expensive airfreight capacity from London to Milan and Rome. A rail shipment to Naples from the UK may take just six to eight days. Rail has the added advantage that most stations are in the city centre so you can avoid the tiresome trek out to an airport cargo centre to collect your bags. Of course, it may well be cheaper to travel by train yourself and pay porters at each end to help you carry the cases, than to spend hundreds of pounds having items sent separately while you fly. There is normally no official limit on what baggage you are allowed to take free with you on a train.

Trucking is also an option for continental travellers. There is a huge range of haulage services and some carriers do take baggage. But prices are often comparable to airfreight and journey times are probably a day or two slower. European airfreight is a highly competitive business and can actually be cheaper than trucking if you measure size and weight carefully. There are direct routes to most destinations and delivery can normally be guaranteed the next day. However, the short distances involved mean that rail and road operators can often compete on timing as, although most flights last only a couple of hours (or less) many hours can be used up waiting for a consolidation – bulk air shipment – or, at the end of the trip, for Customs clearance.

Express services, operated by the airlines themselves or specialist companies, are growing rapidly but they are expensive and only worthwhile for high value items or those of commercial value such as scientific equipment, computer disks, spare parts or industrial samples. Normally these will offer a guarantee of least-guideline transit time.

Whatever your method of shipment, there are some practical problems to be wary of. For example, Spanish and Portuguese Customs can be finicky if items are sent by truck, and you may find yourself paying duty on some goods when they arrive even though you were first told that there would be no charge.

Into Remoter Regions

More surprising is the ease of getting stuff to quite remote, long-haul destinations. The key question is: how far is your final delivery point from the nearest international airport? Normally you, or someone representing you, will need to collect the bags at the place where they clear Customs and it is often impossible to arrange local onward shipment, at least under the umbrella of the baggage service in your home country. Delivery can sometimes be arranged within the city catchment area of the airport but that rarely extends to more than 20 or 30 kilometres away. If you are based in Europe, it is also often difficult to get detailed information about onward transport services in the Third World — whether by air, train, truck or even mule.

One option is to go to a specialist freight forwarder who has detailed knowledge of a particular region of the world and is competent to arrange for local distribution. However, as a personal customer providing a relatively small amount of business, you may not be able to get an attractive price and it could prove cheaper in the end to collect the bags from the airport yourself. There do not have to be direct flights from London, as long as your cargo can be routed to arrive in a country at the right city and pass Customs there.

You can take the bags into a country yourself across the land border but you may face more complications taking five suitcases alone through a small rural frontier post than if they arrive at the main airport under the aegis of an established freight company. Customs regulations are complex and it is vital that the status of research equipment or commercial samples is checked with Customs on arrival by the freight group's local agent.

There is no firm rule as to which places are most difficult to reach but perhaps the complications are greatest when you want to ship to a remote corner of a large Third World country, and you may well find the only reliable option is to collect the bags from the capital city yourself.

Shipping to small island destinations, such as Fiji, Norfolk Island or the Maldives, can be fairly routine, but there are also good services to some places with particularly tough reputations.

Pricing

Pricing in general has two elements: a standard service charge which covers documentation, handling and administration by the shipping agent, and a freight charge per kilo which varies according to the airline, destination and particular bulk shipment deal the agent has been able to negotiate. Storage can be arranged as can collection within the company's catchment area – sometimes free of charge. Outside this radius you will probably have to use a domestic rail or road parcel service rather than asking the agent to arrange a special collection, although a few larger companies do have regional offices.

Do's and Don't's

There are a number of important practical tips to bear in mind. A highly individual distinguishing mark on a case or carton will make it easier for you to pick out when you go to collect it from a busy warehouse or office. It is also important to mark it with your address and telephone number in the destination country so the receiving agent there can let you know when it has arrived.

If you must send really fragile items, pack them in the middle of the case and tell the freighting office. Many have full packaging facilities and will certainly let you know if they think a bag should be more securely wrapped: for some destinations they cover boxes with adhesive banding tape so that anyone can see if it has been tampered with. You should not overload a case and you should watch out for flimsy wheels or handles that could easily be broken off. The agent's packers can provide proper crates if needed. Proper packing is vital – especially if you plan to ship the luggage by road. In many countries the wet season turns cart tracks into swamps. Expeditions or development aid teams will often have to ship into remote areas with poor roads.

If you are moving abroad, do try and differentiate between household items and personal effects such as clothing or toiletry. The latter are covered by a quite strict legal definition for regulations. You may find it best to send heavy household items separately by sea.

If you have something awkwardly shaped to send, such as a bicycle, the agent is probably much more experienced in packing it safely than you will be. He also knows what the airline rules are: some carriers will not accept goods unless they are "properly" packed and that can sometimes mean banding with sticky tape.

Insurance is essential. You may find you are covered by your own travel or company policy but the agents can also provide cover specially designed for unaccompanied personal freight. Without insurance, you are only protected against provable failure by the freighting company you booked the shipment with, and only in accordance with the strict limits of their trading terms and conditions.

As with normal airline baggage, there are certain items you cannot put in the hold of a plane. This is an extraordinary hotch-potch list, but here are some of the main banned items.

1. Matches
2. Magnetised material
3. Poison weedkiller
4. Flammable liquids
5. Camping gas cylinders
6. Most aerosols
7. Car batteries
8. Glue or paint stripper

For shipment by sea or land there are also strict restrictions on dangerous goods which have to be packed specially.

If you buy things in the UK for immediate shipment abroad, you are entitled to claim back the VAT (17.5 per cent) paid on the purchase. Some freight forwarders offer a specialist service whereby you can send them the goods directly to be certified for export and thus reclaim the tax more quickly. Several other countries operate similar schemes which are worth investigating.

One key point to watch is payment. Special vouchers called "Miscellaneous Charge Orders" (MCOs), available from airlines, can be used at the traveller's convenience to pay for freight. But these are made out for that particular airline and can only be used on another if specially endorsed by the issuing airline. They can be used with some freight companies, but they could restrict the agent's ability to get you the best price if, for example, he had a cheap deal arranged on a carrier competing directly with the company which sold you the MCO. Clearly the issuing airline would probably not be prepared to endorse the MCO so that you can ship with a rival.

You should particularly avoid MCOs which specify that they can only be used for 'excess baggage' because you may then be forced to pay the full excess rate rather than the lower unaccompanied freight price. And having bothered to make all the arrangements to ship your personal freight unaccompanied and more cheaply, that would be a pity!

For a list of Freight Forwarders see p.861 of the Directory ■

COMMUNICATIONS
Chapter 12

LEARNING A LANGUAGE

by Dr Jay Kettle-Williams and Caroline Brandenburger

Whether for holiday purposes, for business reasons or simply for the sheer joy of its possibilities and new horizons, foreign-language learning is all the rage – in higher demand now than at any other time in recent years. The interest we see in foreign language acquisition across Europe owes much to the developments associated with 1992.

English and Empire

For reasons of historical accident – 19th century hegemony of the British Empire, technological advances under the banner of North American English – it is now the turn of English to be the world's *lingua franca*, the preferred medium of international communication. And those whose mother tongue is English are often lulled into a false sense of security.

But to ignore the forces of today's international developments is to ignore the fact that we now live in a multilingual society, one for which we must all be prepared.

Improved communications over recent years have expanded our vision to encompass the entire globe – the whole world has become one theatre, but now with a variety of languages. Although the full force of recent developments has yet to be appreciated, one problem stands out sharply: shortfall in foreign language competence.

New Materials

To match the increased demand for foreign languages, dozens of people these days seem to be joining the bandwagon in devising their own method or material to help people along the road to foreign language acquisition. There is a lot to choose from: Interactive Video Discs (IV) for self-paced, individual tuition which weigh in at a few thousand pounds for the hardware and about £1500 for software; accelerated-learning audio-lingual packages retailing from £10 to £100; Computer-Assisted Language Learning (CALL) packages – £15 to £100; the BBC Tutored Video Instruction (TVI) packages for the dedicated telly addict; and CD-ROM command programmes at £100 plus which enhance the CALL option and offer voice cards. Alternatively you can opt for the "executive toy" school of language learning with a pocket, computerised translator. For the future, would-be linguists can look forward to the Computer Disc-Interactive (CD-I) which, once moving graphics become the norm, will offer a highly cost-effective programme through the TV screen.

How to Learn

Private tuition: Private language schools and some LEAs have private classes. **The Institute of Linguists** (Southwark St. London SE1, tel: 0171-940 3100) can give details of private tutors or where to find out about them; also look under "Tutoring" in the Yellow Pages or the small ads in, for example, the LEA guides to courses. Cost: from £12 per hour. Intensive courses can be very expensive. **Berlitz Language School** (9-13 Grosvenor Street, London W1A 3BZ, tel: 0171-915 0909), offers short crash courses for beginners and a two-week *Total Immersion* course for people with some previous knowledge.

Prices of courses are dependent on the structure of the individual course. They also have branches in Birmingham, Leeds, Manchester and Edinburgh. Probably the most expensive programme is offered by **Stillitron** (72 New Bond Street, London W1Y 0QY, tel: 0171-493 1177). It runs an intensive ten day, non-consecutive language programme which is geared towards each person's interests and uses direct as well as audio visual methods. Languages included are French, German, Spanish, Portuguese, Italian and Arabic. The cost is £5,500 + VAT.

Correspondence courses: Offered by some colleges and listed by the **Council for the Accreditation of Correspondence Colleges** (CACC), 27 Marylebone Road, London NW1 5JS, tel: 0171-935 5391). Costs start from £100. Intensive or advanced courses can cost a lot more.

Teach yourself: Using books, cassette tapes, records, radio, video, computer, television. Books cost nothing if borrowed or you can spend up to several hundred pounds for a full programme of cassettes and learning books.

Language laboratories: Offered by LEAs (particularly in the larger polytechnics or technical colleges) and private language schools. They may be flexible, "use-the-lab-when-you-want" schemes, fixed classes or supplementary to other courses (mainly group). The style varies from simple tape recordings with headphones to computer-controlled systems with individual booths connected to a master console. In some laboratories, students can work at their own pace, recording and then listening to their own voices. In others, pace is controlled by the teacher, so a student can't play back his own tapes. A lot depends on how much supervision the teacher is able to give, and the strength of the material. Repeated drills can quickly become boring.

Full information about these methods can be obtained from the **Centre for Information on Language Teaching and Research** (CILT), 80 Bedfordbury, London WC2N 4LB, tel: 0171-379 5101. Their publication *Language Courses for Adults* is a guide to part-time and intensive study opportunities for learning languages and is especially useful.

CILT's publications catalogue contains many other guides and books you might find helpful. Their library is very informative and includes directories and lists of course materials as well as advice on the type of course to suit you, and where you can find it. Write to them, giving as many details of yourself and your needs as you can.

Which to Choose

People learn at different rates, often in different ways. Your training programme will further depend on the time you have available, your starting point, your dedication and discipline, your goals and your budget.

The old adages about horses for courses and paying for your choice hold good. Your next step should take into account the following points and considerations:

Training: Residential or non-residential; self-disciplined, partially or fully-tutored; tele-guided; individual or group study; time of the day/week?

Costs: Intensive one-to-one training costs start at about £1500 per week of residential training at home or abroad, from £1000 per non-residential week with an eight-hour day.

Intensity: Intensive (eight hours plus per day), extended or on-going? In general terms you should dedicate 80 hours to achieve a functional level or to progress from one level to another.

Design: Languages for specific purposes; ratio between the linguistic and para-linguistic (e.g. cultural/social awareness and cross-cultural briefing); initial and refresher courses; competences and grades.

Materials: Printed word/manuals; graphics; radio; audio cassettes; Tutored Video Instruction (TVI); passive video viewing; Interactive Video (IV); Compact Disc Interactive (CD-I); Computer Assisted Language Learning (CALL); CD ROM with or without voice cards.

Content: Active/reactive; encoding/decoding; one-to-one or group; role-play or contexts?

Accreditation: Professional progression; external or internal awards; identification of appropriate standards and awarding bodies?

See p.888 of the Directory for foreign language centres and institutes in the UK
See p.884 of the Directory for English language newspapers world-wide
See p.880 of the Directory for American Express travel service centres world-wide

BREAKING THE BARRIERS

by Jon Gardey

Barriers to communication off the beaten track exist just because of who you are – a visitor from another civilisation. It is necessary to show the local people that underneath the surface impression of strange clothes and foreign manners exists a fellow human being.

The first step is to approach local inhabitants as if you are their guest. You are. It is their country, their village, their hut, their lifestyle. You are a welcome, or perhaps unwelcome, intruder into their familiar daily routine. Always be aware that they may see very few faces other than those of their family or the other families in the village. Their initial impression of you is likely to be one of unease and wariness. Be reassuring. Move slowly.

If possible learn a few words of local greeting and repeat them to everyone you meet in the village. It is very important to keep smiling, carry an open face, even if you feel exactly the opposite. Hold your body in a relaxed, non-aggressive manner.

In your first encounter, try to avoid anything that might anger them or make them shy with their initial approaches to you. If they offer a hand, take it firmly, even if it is encrusted with what you might consider filth. Don't hold back or be distant, either in attitude or voice. On the other hand, coming on strong in an effort to get something from a local person will only build unnecessary barriers to communication.

Words and Pictures

Begin with words. If you are asking for directions, repeat the name of the place several times, but do *not* point in the direction you think it is, or suggest possible directions by voice. Usually the local person, in an effort to please his visitor, will nod helpfully in the direction in which you are pointing, or agree with you that, yes, Namdrung *is* that way, "If you say so." It may be in the opposite direction.

Merely say "Namdrung" and throw up your hands in a gesture that indicates a total lack of knowledge. Most local people are delighted to help someone genuinely in need, and, after a conference with their friends, will come up with a solution to your problem. When *they* point, repeat the name of the place several times more (varying the pronunciation) to check if it is the same place you want to go. It is also a good idea to repeat this whole procedure with someone else in another part of the village (and frequently along the route) to check for consistency.

In most areas it is highly likely that none of the local people will speak any language you are familiar with. Communicating with them then becomes a problem in demonstration: you must *show* them what you want, or perform your message.

If you are asking for information that is more difficult to express than simple directions, use your hands to build a picture of what you need. Pictures, in the air, on the sand, on a piece of paper, are sometimes your only means of communication and, frequently, the clearest. Use these symbols when you receive blank stares in answer to your questions. Use sound or objects that you have in your possession that are similar, or of which you would like more.

Giving and Getting

Not all of your contact with local people will be about getting something from them. Don't forget that you have a unique opportunity to bring them something from your own culture and try to make it something that will enrich theirs. Show them what it looks like with the help of postcards and magazines. Let them experience its tools. If you have a camera, let the local people, especially the children, look through the viewfinder. Put on a telephoto lens so they can get a new look at their own countryside. If you have a Polaroid camera, photograph them, and give them the print (a very popular offering but be careful, don't finish by photographing the whole village). And most important of all, become involved. Carry aspirin to cure headaches – real or imagined. If someone in the village seems to need help, say in lifting a log, offer a hand. Contribute yourself as an expression of your culture.

If you want to take photographs, be patient. Don't bring out your camera until you have established a sufficient rapport, and be as unobtrusive as possible. If anyone objects, stop. A bribe for a photograph or payment for information is justified only if the situation is unusual. A simple request for directions is no reason for a gift. If the local people do something out of the ordinary for you, reward them as you would a friend at home. The best gift you can give them is your friendship and openness. They are not performers doing an act, but ordinary people living out their lives in circumstances that seem strange to us.

I have found myself using gifts as a means of *avoiding* contact with remote people, especially children, as a way of pacifying them. I think it is better to enter and leave their lives with as much warmth as I can give, and now I leave the sweets at home. If you are camped near a village, invite some of the local people over to share your food, and try to have them sit among your party.

On some of the more travelled routes, such as Morocco, or the main trekking trails of Nepal, the local children, being used to being given sweets by passing trekkers, will swarm around for more. I suggest that you smile (always) and refuse them. Show them pictures or your favourite juggling act then give them something creative, such as pencils.

If a local event is in progress, stand back, try to get into a shadow, and watch from a distance. You will be seen and noticed, no matter what you do, but it helps to minimise your presence. If you want to get closer, edge forward slowly, observing the participants, especially the older people, for signs that you are not wanted. If they frown, retire. Respect their attempts to keep their culture and its customs as free as possible from outside influence.

The people in the remote places are still in an age before machines, and live their lives close to the earth in a comfortable routine. Where you and I come from is sophisticated, hard and alien to them. We must come into their lives as gently as possible, and when we go, leave no trace.

Officialdom

In less remote areas where the local people have had more experience of travellers, you must still observe the rule of patience, open-mindedness and respect for the lifestyle of others. But you will encounter people with more preconceived notions about foreigners – and most of those notions will be unfavourable.

In these circumstances – and indeed anywhere your safety or comfort may depend on your approach – avoid seeming to put any local person, especially a minor official, in the wrong. Appeal to his emotions, enlist his magnanimous aid, save his face at all costs. Your own calmness can calm others. If you are delayed or detained, try "giving up," reading a book, smiling. Should you be accused of some minor misdemeanour, such as "jumping" a control point, far better to admit your "mistake" than to be accused of spying – though even this is fairly standard practice in the Third World and shouldn't flap you unduly.

Wherever you go in the Third World, tones and pitches of voice will vary; "personal distance" between people conversing may be less than you are used to; attitudes and priorities will differ from your own. Accept people as they are and you can hope that with time and a gentle approach, they will accept you also.

Language

When you have the opportunity of learning or using a smattering of the local language, try to make things easier for yourself by asking questions that limit responses to what you understand and prompt responses which will add helpfully and manageably to your vocabulary. Make it clear to your listeners that your command of the language is limited. Note down what you learn and try constantly to build on what you know.

Always familiarise yourself with the cultural limitations that may restrict topics of conversation or choice of conversation partner.

Keep Your Hands to Yourself

Gestures can be a danger area. The British thumbs-up sign is an obscenity in some countries, such as Sardinia and parts of the Middle East, where it means roughly "sit on this" or "up yours." In such places (and anywhere, if in doubt) hitch a ride by waving limply with a flattened hand.

The ring sign made with thumb and forefinger is also obscene in Turkey and elsewhere. And in France it can mean "zero" i.e. worthless – the exact opposite of the meaning "OK" or "excellent" for which the British and Americans use it.

By contrast, our own obscene insult gesture, the two-finger sign, is used interchangeably in Italy with the Churchillian V-sign. Which way round you hold your fingers makes no difference – it's still understood as a friendly gesture meaning "victory" or "peace".

In Greece, as the anthropologist Desmond Morris tells us, there is another problem to do with the gesture called the *moutza*. In this, the hand is raised flat, "palm towards the victim and pushed towards him as if about to thrust an invisible custard pie in his face". To us it means simply to "go back", but to a Greek it is a hideous insult. It dates from Byzantine times, when chained prisoners were paraded through the streets and abused by having handfuls of filth from the gutter picked up by onlookers and thrust into their faces.

Though naturally the brutal practice has long since ceased, the evil meaning of *moutza* has not been forgotten.

HOW TO BE IN WITH ISLAM
by Peter Boxhall

Like any nation with an important history, the Arab people are proud of their past. Not only because of an empire which once stretched from the far reaches of China to the gates of France, or their many great philosophers, scientists, seafarers, soldiers and traders; but because they are one people, sharing a common language and culture, and following the same religion which has become an integral part of their lives and behaviour.

Language

Arabic is a difficult language for us to learn but it is a beautiful, expressive language which, in the early days of Islam, came to incorporate all the permissible culture, literature and poetry of Arab society. Small West African children sitting under *cola* trees write their Koranic lessons on wooden boards; infant Yemenis learn and chant in unison *Surahs* of the Holy Book; school competitions are held perennially in the Kingdom of Saudi Arabia and elsewhere to judge the students' memory and knowledge of their written religion.

So, as in any foreign environment, the traveller would do well to try and learn some Arabic. For without the greetings, the enquiries, the pleasantries of everyday conversation and the ability to purchase one's requirements, many of the benefits and pleasures of travel are foregone. Best, too, to learn classical (Koranic) Arabic which is understood throughout the Arabic-speaking world (although the farther one is away from the Arabian Peninsula in, for example, the Magribian countries of Morocco, Tunisia, and Algeria, the more difficult it is to comprehend the dialectal replies one receives).

Not long ago, before the advent of oil, when one travelled in the harsh environment of the Arabian Desert, the warlike, nomadic Bedu tribes would, if they saw you came in peace, greet you with *salaam alaikum* and afford you the hospitality of their tents. If "bread and salt" were offered to you, you were "on their face": inviolate, protected, a welcome guest for as long as you wished to stay. *Baiti Baitak* (my house is your house) was the sentiment expressed. This generous, hospitable principle still prevails throughout the Arab world.

Bureaucracy

Although they are subordinate to the overall sense of Arabness, each of the Arab kingdoms, emirates, sultanates and republics has its own national characteristics. In those far-off medieval days of the Arab Empire, there were no frontiers to cross, no need for passports, there was a common currency, a purer language. Today it is different. There is bureaucracy abroad in the Arab world – mostly, it can be said, a legacy of former colonial administrations. So be patient, tolerant and good-humoured about passports, visas, immunisation, currency controls and customs. And remember that many of the Arab countries emerged only recently to their present independent status and it has taken us, in the West, some hundreds of years to evolve our systems of public administration and bureaucratic procedure.

One has to remember that generally the Arab does not have the same pressing (obsessional?) sense of urgency that we do. No discourtesy is meant. Does it really matter? Tomorrow is another day and the sun will rise again and set. Neither in his bureaucratic or even everyday dealings with you does the Arab take much notice of your status, official or induced.

When I was Personal Secretary to the Governor of Jeddah, important corporation chiefs and industrialists used to visit him in his *majlis*. They were received courteously and served the traditional *qahwa*. The Arab, however, is a great democrat and even these important people had, often to their annoyance, to wait their turn. Yet on one occasion, a comparatively poor *shaiba* came straight up to His Excellency, kissed him on the shoulder and extracting a scroll from the voluminous folds of his *thobe* (the uniform dress worn by all Saudis), proceeded to read its full, eulogistic length in a high-pitched quavering voice.

To the Arab, it is of little importance to know who or what you represent; he is more interested in who you are. If he likes you, you will soon be aware of it. The sense of touch is to the Arabs a means of communication. Westerners, from colder climates, should not therefore be too reticent, distant or aloof.

Watch and listen, for example, to how the Yemenis greet each other: the long repetitious enquiries as to each other's state of health; the handshake; the finger that will sometimes curl towards the mouth, to indicate they are merely on speaking terms, casual acquaintances; sometimes to the heart, to indicate that they are intimate friends. The embrace, the kiss on both cheeks, which are mainly customary in the Near East and Magribian countries... If you allow the Arab to take you as a friend in his way, he may even invite you to his house.

Social Conventions

Baiti Baitak is the greatest courtesy. Do not, though, be critical, admiring or admonitory towards the furniture in the house. If you admire the material things, your hospitable host may feel impelled to give you the object of your admiration. Conversely, remember that if your taste in furnishing does not correspond with that of your host, don't whatever you do exaggerate how much you admire their material goods!

If it is an old-style house, you must always take your shoes off, and may be expected to sit on the floor supported by cushions. Then all manner of unfamiliar, exotic dishes may be served to you. If it is painful to plunge your fingers into a steaming mound of rice, and difficult to eat what are locally considered to be the choice pieces of meat, forget your inhibitions and thin skin, eat everything you are offered with your right hand and at least appear to enjoy it. Remember, your host is probably offering the best, sometimes the last remaining provisions in his house.

Once, in the Jordan desert, I was entertained by an important tribal sheikh in his black, goat-hair tent. An enormous platter, supported by four tribal retainers, was brought in and put in our midst. On the platter, surmounted by a mound of rice, was a whole baby camel, within that camel a sheep, within that sheep, pigeons. Bedu scarcely talk at all at a meal; it is too important, too infrequent an occasion. So we ate quickly, belching often from indigestion, with many an appreciative *Al Hamdulillah*, for it is natural to do so. When replete, rose-water was brought round for us to wash our hands and we men moved out to the cooling evening sands to drink coffee, converse and listen to stories of tribal life, while the tribal ladies, who had cooked the meal, entered the tent from the rear with the children, to complete the feast.

In some Arab countries, alcoholic drink is permitted. In others, it is definitely not. From my two years' experience in Saudi Arabia and three in Libya, I know it is actually possible to obtain whisky, for example, but it is at a price – perhaps as much as £70 a bottle which, for me at least, is too expensive an indulgence, even if it were not for the penalties for being caught.

Coffee and tea are the habitual refreshments: in Saudi Arabia, as was the custom in my municipal office, the small handle-less cups of *qushr* are poured from the straw-filled beak of a brass coffee pot. "Arabian coffee" is also famous: almost half coffee powder, half sugar. One should only drink half or two thirds, however, and if you are served a glass of cold water with it, remember that an Arab will normally drink the water first (to quench his thirst) then the coffee – so the taste of this valued beverage may continue to linger in the mouth.

In North Africa, tea is a more customary drink. Tea *nuss wa nuss* with milk, in Sudan, for example; tea in small glasses with mint in the Magrib; tea even with nuts, in Libya. Whoever was it said that the English are the world's greatest tea drinkers? Visiting the Sanussi tribe in Libya, in Cyrenaica, I once had to drink 32 glasses of tea in the course of a morning. The tea maker, as with the Arabian coffee maker, is greatly respected for his art.

Dress

In most of the Arab world, normal European-type dress is appropriate, but it should be modest in appearance. Again if, as we should do, we take notice of Arab custom, which is based in history on sound common sense, we might do well to remember that in hot, dusty conditions, the Bedu put on clothes to protect themselves against the elements, not take them off, as we Westerners do.

The question of whether one should adopt the local dress in the particularly hot, arid countries of the Arab world is probably a matter of personal preference. The *thobe* is universally worn in Saudi Arabia, the *futah* in the Yemen and South Arabia. I personally used to wear the *futah*; in Saudi Arabia, however, the Governor suggested I should wear the *thobe* but I felt inhibited from doing so, as none of the other expatriates appeared to adopt it.

Religion

The final, and perhaps most important, piece of advice I can offer to the traveller is to repeat the need to respect Islam. The majority of Arabs are Muslim, and Islam represents their religion and their way of life, as well as their guidance for moral and social behaviour.

In the same sense that Muslims are exhorted (in the Koran) to be compassionate towards the non-believer (and to widows, orphans and the sick), so too should we respect the "Faithful." Sometimes one may meet religious fanatics, openly hostile, but it is rare to do so and I can only recall, in my many years in Arab countries, one such occasion. Some schoolboys in south Algeria enquired why, if I spoke Arabic, I was not a Muslim, and, on hearing my answer, responded: "*inta timshi fi'n nar*" ("You will walk in the fires of Hell").

In some countries, you can go into mosques when prayers are not in progress, in others entry is forbidden altogether. Always ask for permission to photograph mosques and (in the stricter countries) women, old men and children.

Respect, too, the various religious occasions and that all-important month-long fast of Ramadan. My Yemeni doctors and nurses all observed Ramadan, so one year I joined them, to see exactly what an ordeal it was for them. Thereafter, my admiration for them, and for others who keep the fast, was unbounded, and I certainly do not think we should exacerbate the situation in this difficult period by smoking, eating or drinking in public.

Ahlan wa sahlan: welcome! You will hear the expression often in the Arab world, and it will be sincerely meant.

TRAVELLING IN A BUDDHIST COUNTRY

by Gill Cairns

"Dalai Lama Pic-a chur? You how much? How much you say?" Anyone who has travelled in Tibet, will have heard this constant refrain from children, accompanied by constant tugging on your shirt sleeve. A photograph of Tibet's spiritual leader, who has lived in exile since 1959, is a highly prized item in this part of the world, followed closely by "school pens, miss?" The photos of the Dalai Lama are scattered on the shrines in Buddhist temples, along with rice grains and *katha,* white offering scarves that are part of the rich panoply of offerings made by devotees who circumnambulate the shrines, with strings of *mala* beads in their hands, counting the *mantras* they repeat with intense murmurings.

In Tibet, Buddhism has been entwined with the fabric of its culture as far back as the seventh century. Today there are still practising Buddhists, men and women, lay and monk, despite the desecration brought to their temples by the Chinese occupation in the Fifties and the Cultural Revolution in the Sixties and Seventies and intensifying sinofication of the area. Others who, with the invasion of Lhasa in 1959, fled along with the Dalai Lama into exile at Dharamsala, have set up communities on the Indian side of the Himalayas, in parts of Nepal and beyond.

Buddhism originates from the teaching of Siddharthur Gautama, who was born around 2,500 years ago, the son of Suddhodana of the Sakya clan, in Lumbini on the Nepal/Indian border. Having heard that there was life beyond the confines of his luxurious palace, he went forth to seek and eventually gain "Enlightenment" and liberation from the cyclic existence of birth, death and rebirth. After his Enlightenment he was known as Buddha, which means Awakened One, and his subsequent teaching spread from India, south into Sri Lanka, then to Myanmar (Burma), Thailand, Cambodia and east into Tibet, China and Japan. While in India Buddhism was subsumed into Hinduism and then eroded by the Muslim Moguls, it has enjoyed a small but significant revival more recently, since Independence, with pockets of Buddhists, notably around Bombay and the South and in North-Eastern India near the borders with Tibet; Ladakh, which is known as Little Tibet, Sikkim, and the area around Dharamsala, where the Dalai Lama and his government in exile are based.

Today there are several schools of Buddhism. The *Theravadins,* who maintain traditional rules regarding discipline for monks and practitioners, based on the original letter of the teachings of Buddha, are found in parts of southern India, Sri Lanka, Myanmar (Burma), Thailand and Cambodia. The *Mahayana,* developed in northern India and Nepal among the lay as well as monastic population, emphasise not only the historical teachings of Buddha but also the Buddhas of the past and future and the altruistic ideal of seeking Enlightenment for the benefit of all beings (the Bodhisattva Ideal). In the 8th century Mahayana Buddhism was introduced into Tibet, where it developed a distinct flavour of its own with the beginning of *Lamaism,* in which highly spiritually developed religious teachers are revered as incarnations, or *tulkus,* of their predecessors. It is said that the current Dalai Lama, the fourteenth in the lineage, is the embodiment of the compassionate aspect of Enlightenment, which is archetypally represented in religious paintings by the Bodhisattva Avalokoteshvara, whose most common form has eleven heads and a thousand arms. A further development from the Mahayana in Tibet was the *Vajrayana* or *Tantra,* an even more devote version (not for the faint-hearted) which introduced the possibility of reaching Enlightenment in one lifetime.

Today Buddhism flourishes in pockets of Asia. In some countries, like Bhutan, it is the state religion, in others it is virtually outlawed. In some places tradition allows for people to be a Buddhist monk for a week, while in others you might not be part of a monastic order but you might very well be a sincere practitioner. All this may seem a little confusing to the Western traveller. Perhaps it is enough to say that the wearing of a robe is not the only indication that you may be travelling among Buddhists.

In Tibet, Ladakh, and the Himalayan regions, the outward expression of Buddhism is manifested not only in the richly decorated monasteries or *gompas* (places of meditation) which are often found wedged in impossibly inaccessible mountain tops, but also in the character of its people both lay and monk. It is as if all the positive emotion generated by Buddhist practice has infused its people with a remarkable cheerfulness, humour and lightness. The rugged monochrome landscape is sprinkled with intense colours that are characteristic of Buddhist devotion: brightly coloured prayer flags flutter from the golden roof tops of temples; boulders painted with Buddhist deities; the famous *mantra* of Avaolkiteshvara "Om Mani Padme Hum"; and *chortens,* stone structures containing relics built on a stack of geometrical shapes to represent the five elements of earth, fire, water, air, and ether.

Many of the *gompas,* are encircled by a pilgrim circuit, a narrow trail which devotees circle, often prostrating themselves (raising their hands above their heads, and then flinging their bodies forward to the ground, the process is then repeated until the circuit is complete). The prostration practice is said to engage the body, speech and the mind fully in devoting one's life to the Buddha and the ideal of Enlightenment.

On approaching a *gompa* you may find, built into the perimeter walls, a row of prayer wheels, which are turned in a clockwise direction – inside these brass and wooden barrels are scrolls inscribed with hundreds of *mantras*, as they are turned the *Dharma* or Buddhist teachings and prayers are sent.

When you enter a *gompa* it is customary to remove footwear and ensure that you are modestly dressed. Monks take vows of celibacy and it is therefore respectful not to wear revealing clothing. At the entrance of larger temples, white offering scarves are on sale, and these can be placed on the shrines, along with small amounts of change. The darkness of the interior of the *gompa* takes some adjusting to, so a torch is handy, for on close inspection, every inch of wall space is either painted with scenes from the life of the Buddha, Buddhist iconography, or adorned with Thangkas (wall hangings depicting particular deities, mounted on silk). It is disrespectful to touch any of the Buddhist statues *(rupas)* or these paintings. Butter lamps are lit as a prayer and often you can approach a *konyer* (chaplain) and give him money to light one for you. Buddhists make their way round the shrine room in a clockwise direction and to do otherwise is considered offensive. On leaving places of worship, Buddhists either back out, or bow gently to the shrine before turning to leave, it is courteous to do the same.

You may be lucky enough to witness a *Puja,* (devotional worship) which involves the chanting of *sutras* or scriptures, and *matras,* which are orchestrated by the occasional ringing of bells, and beating of drums, and the haunting call of strange horns fashioned from giant brilliant white conch shells. Sit quietly at the back of the gathering while the ritual is carried out. Monks at the *Puja* ceremonies sit on the ground, and care should be taken not to step over them, or pieces of text or books. During the course of the ceremony offerings are made to the shrines of the Buddhas and Bodhisattvas: incense, rice grains, yak butter lamps. At the end of the ceremony a bowl of salty butter tea may be put in front of you, this is definitely an acquired taste, however it is disrespectful to show dislike, so if you find it undrinkable, leave the bowl full without any fuss.

As a general rule, taking photographs in temples is regarded as an intrusion – the dark interior would require a flash and this interrupts the concentration of devotees. In some *gompas,* however, monks will allow photography, but normally for a fee.

Taking pictures of the Dalai Lamas into Tibet as gifts, should be viewed cautiously. Whilst they might be very much appreciated, there is no doubt that this is a politically sensitive issue. According to the Tibet Information Network, several tourists have recently had problems with the Chinese authorities. It is therefore perhaps more prudent to show pictures of the Dalai Lama in your guide book, rather than making presents of them.

One recent abhorrent development that has affronted Tibetan sensitivities is the increasing number of tourists who have shown a morbid fascination in witnessing the sky burial ritual. A sky burial involves taking a corpse to a special site on a mountainside, where it is cut into pieces and left to be eaten by birds. Following the offensive behaviour of tourists not only photographing but also videoing this ritual, Westerners have now been banned from such ceremonies in Lhasa. Although in other parts of Tibet you may still be invited, it is strongly advised to turn down the offer, as a mark of respect to the dead and their relatives.

Tibetan culture appears to be happy-go-lucky, and while that may largely be the case, it does not necessarily mean that anything goes. Politeness is a part of Tibetan culture, to the point that many are loathe to say no to requests from travellers. For example, if a woman in a short skirt asks the incumbent monk of a temple if she can go inside, he may mutter that it is rather cold inside, indicating he feels uneasy about it, but he would be unlikely to refuse her entry.

Finally for those who want to learn more about Buddhism, there are a number of centres where travellers can not only learn about the religion and meditation, but go on a meditation retreat. The Friends of the Western Buddhist Order in Kathmandu runs meditation courses and retreats which are held in Pulchowk monastery in Patan (contact PO Box 5336 Thamel, Kathmandu, Nepal). The Mt Everest Centre for Buddhist Studies at the Kopan Monastery, GPO Box 817, Kathmandu, can also be of help.

OVER THE AIRWAVES

By Steve Weinman

The magic of shortwave radio is that it can turn the homebound into travellers while keeping travellers in touch with home. Roaming the international wavebands from the comfort of an armchair is an agreeably painless – and cheap – way to travel. No visas, tickets or baggage are needed and often, because so many nations broadcast externally in English, there is no language barrier.

Some 140 stations broadcast internationally in English, and, whether you tune in to Radio Moscow, Voice of America, Deutsche Welle or HCJB The Voice Of The Andes, you will find that the world is only too willing to come to you.

Once you venture abroad, of course, especially off the beaten track, short-wave can become a lifeline. Not only does it supply you with news from home but, if your home station is BBC World Service, it might well provide more reliable news and information about those parts of the world you are visiting than will be available from local services.

This reflects the fact that so much of the world's media is government-sponsored and controlled – the listener believes all he hears at his peril. New short-wave users are confused to find a number of stations broadcasting in English which sound superficially like the BBC: this is because they model their style and delivery on that of World Service with the aim of boosting their credibility as objective global reporters.

The BBC World Service broadcasts in English 24 hours a day, every day of the year, although it will not necessarily be audible all day in the places you intend to visit. It carries news on the hour backed up by current affairs and business affairs analysis and commentary, and in between offers a rich and varied diet of sport, music, features, science, drama and light entertainment. Close to home, it can be heard on mediumwave and at times longwave, but beyond northwestern Europe and out of reach of the morning papers you'll need a shortwave receiver to keep in touch.

Shortwave Radio

So what is shortwave (also known as world band radio), and how can the traveller get the best out of it? Signals from the familiar longwave, mediumwave and FM stations on which you listen to domestic broadcasts, travel in a straight line from transmitter to receiver and so are limited not only by the strength of the signal but by the curvature of the Earth. In other words, if you venture more than about 300 miles from London, you will be over the horizon and probably unable to pick up *The Archers* on Radio 4 longwave.

Shortwave signals overcome such earthbound restrictions by proceeding from the transmitter in a series of giant hops between Earth and the ionosphere to the receiver – your radio set. The ionosphere is the Earth's natural satellite, a series of electrified layers of gas which extend hundreds of miles above the planet. As shortwave signals bounce around the world a certain amount of clarity can be lost in the process. Broadcasters compensate for this by enhancing the signal from strategically-placed relay stations.

The complication is that reception varies depending on where you are in the world, the time of year and even the time of day. In the late 20th century we have come to expect our news at the touch of a button. Shortwave listening can be like that, but often, when you are on the move, it is not. To get the most from it requires a little planning.

Because the ionosphere is created by the sun's rays, it is denser during the day than at night, and denser during the summer than in winter. Broadcasters use different shortwave frequencies depending on the time and the target area to take account of these effects, as well as interference from other stations, sunspot activity and so on.

The stations will be happy to provide you with frequency guides which set out which wavelengths to try, when and where. BBC World Service is unusual in offering a magazine, *BBC On Air,* which is able to reflect frequency changes from month to month. It also tells you when you can expect to pick up transmissions wherever you are, and provides full programme details. Most major broadcasters offer six-monthly or yearly outline schedules of programmes and frequencies. See also the list of World Service frequencies in the Directory.

For the traveller there are likely to be three main considerations in choosing a radio: budget, compactness and efficiency. Shortwave receivers can cost anywhere between £30 and £3,000, but if your priority is good quality contact with your home station rather than shortwave hobbyism, the practical price range for a portable is between £75 and £300.

The traditional analogue set has manual tuning and either a single tuning scale or a number of separated shortwave bands (as well as a combination of mediumwave, longwave and FM bands). Separating the huge spectrum of shortwave frequencies into bands makes tuning simpler as the stations are less crowded on the scale: the more bands the better.

Using the frequency guide you can navigate around the airwaves on an analogue set and pick out the desired station by turning the knob or adjusting the slider. This is not a particularly easy or precise process and now that analogue sets offer little price advantage, they are increasingly being displaced by the type of receiver which has a memory and digital display.

If you do decide to go for a low-priced analogue model you might find that, lower battery consumption apart, it proves a false economy once on the road. A digital set allows greater precision in tuning. Using preset frequencies you can cover all the possibilities in the part of the world you are visiting at the touch of a keypad.

Nowadays leading shortwave radio manufacturers like Sony and Grundig often preselect the frequencies of major shortwave stations on their sets before they leave the factory. This gets you off to a good start and you can later customise the selection as required.

Good digital sets start at around £180 and for that price you can buy one of the ultra-mini receivers which are so useful when travelling light is a consideration. These sets are no bigger than audio cassettes, so they will fit comfortably in a pocket and won't even pull it out of shape with a weight of 220g. An average compact set might weigh 600g and measure 20cm, while bigger portables weigh 1.75kg and measure 30cm. You wouldn't want to take that on a trek.

You will want at least ten memory presets; many sets carry 40-plus. Shortwave transmission can be susceptible to interference from other stations as well as an assortment of fades and spacey noises. Fortunately modern technology comes to the rescue in the shape of features like microprocessor-locked synthesised tuning, to ensure that the best possible signal is heard at all times, and automatic scanning of a selected waveband for the best signal.

Ideally the set you choose will allow close control of bandwidth (a narrow band cuts out interference, a wider one improves the audio quality and, like heads, two band-widths are better than one) and sensitivity, which enables you to maximise the signal from a weak station without increasing any surrounding noise. International broadcasters usually schedule their programmes in Greenwich Mean Time and to help you follow the guides many sets have built in dual-time clocks which can be set to both GMT and local time.

It isn't always easy to try out shortwave radio in a shop, especially if it is part of a metal-framed building. If you can, take the set outside. Listen to find out whether it is "lively" – that is, whether it picks up plenty of stations with a minimum of interference.

Once on the move you will probably not be listening in for more than an hour or two each day but bear in mind that batteries run down fast with heavy use. In some parts of the world batteries are hard to come by, so unless you want to carry a lot of spares or a charger, a world-wide mains adaptor might be a good investment.

Also worth the outlay is a portable booster aerial, because while built-in telescopic antennae are often adequate there are times when a booster can make an enormous difference to reception quality. For most purposes £220-£250 will cover the cost of a good quality compact set with adaptor and booster aerial.

A Rough Guide to Tuning

The Hertz is the standard unit of frequency (the number of waves that pass a fixed point each second), the metre is the unit of wavelength (the distance between each wave). The tuning scales of modern sets are most often marked in kiloHertz (1 kHz = 1000Hz) or megaHertz (1 MHz = 1,000,000Hz).

Shortwave stations are generally spaced out at 5kHz intervals within each waveband. Your receiver should cover at least 6 to 17MHz (49 to 16 metres) shortwave. During the day, long-range reception is better on high frequencies (15 to 21MHz) while at night lower frequencies (6 to 7MHz) are recommended. There is a transition period at dawn and dusk when 9 and 11MHz is probably best. During periods of sunspot activity higher frequencies are generally advisable.

Remember to keep any aerial, whether telescopic, booster or simply a length of insulated wire, clear of metallic obstructions and be prepared to experiment with its length and position within a room. Reception can often be improved by standing the set itself on a large metal object such as a radiator, kitchen appliance, water pipes or filing cabinet, or putting it near a window, particularly if you are in a steel-framed building.

The strongest shortwave signals arrive at a steep angle, so if the ground in front of the receiver slopes down in the direction of the transmitter the signal will be better than if the ground slopes upwards. This is worth bearing in mind if you are in a hilly area and find you are having any difficulties.

Shortwave listening does involve a certain level of commitment on the part of the listener but hundreds of millions of people around the world are clearly prepared to make that commitment. Don't be put off – when it comes down to it, all you need is a shortwave radio, a frequency guide and some ideas about how to improve the weaker signals.

And remember that you will often find yourself in an area in which your preferred station is "rebroadcast". This means that a local station, perhaps broadcasting on FM, will arrange to pick up shortwave programmes from an international broadcaster and relay them on its own wavelength, in some cases 24 hours a day. By this means you can pick up BBC World Service as clearly in, say, New Zealand as you can in Belgium.

See p.882 of the Directory for a list of World Service Frequencies world-wide

TELECOMMUNICATIONS AND THE TRAVELLER

by Stephen McClelland

There has never been a better time for the traveller to go almost anywhere and still be in touch by telecommunications. But be careful, because staying in touch conveniently could mean racking up an enormous cost. With a little thought and some elementary background knowledge, it is possible to save a huge amount of money – and still get what you want.

There are a lot of choices available, so consider what your needs actually are: business/independent pleasure travel, location, degree of mobility, voice or voice and data services including Internet access, frequent or occasional use. Making a decision about the best options depends on all of these criteria. Moreover, products and services are not necessarily identical in every country and getting a single "international" solution, usable anywhere, will probably be impossible, or extremely difficult. This article will attempt to simplify the range of international voice and data offerings now available for travellers. First of all, check if you will need a simple voice telephony via the "fixed" network, or if your travelling schedule in or between countries necessitates a mobile voice connection. Think about email and perhaps Internet access, and the degree of mobility required for this also.

Voice Telephony

It's an amazing thing that you can make a phone call to anywhere in the world. The key thing is to make it as cheaply as possible. International direct dial (IDD) enabling effective person-to-person calling is now available in almost all countries. A minority remain so underdeveloped in terms of infrastructure that they will still require some form of operator connection, but bear in mind that these are generally now only found in true war zones.

First a few basic facts. Traditionally, in spite of a huge diversity of policies, networks and charging systems, telecommunications activities around the world have been dominated by a group of (usually) government-owned Posts, Telegraph and Telephone organisations, the PTTs, and international services provided by agreements between them. The PTTs in most countries were responsible for the provision of both postal and telecommunications services, and in particular the network that provides basic communications services, the Public Switched Telecommunications Network (PSTN). But technological development and deregulation have meant that a massive change is now underway, with new services and new providers coming on stream. Because of these issues, communications are getting better and better, and it's also – believe it or not – actually getting cheaper and cheaper.

What are the basic options for calling your home or office? Assume firstly that it probably will not be worth actually signing up with a local operator for the installation of a phone wherever you happen to be (this is expensive and involves bureaucracy in many countries and most administrations could be wary about assigning facilities to travellers anyway). The more feasible options include:

IDD

IDD is theoretically available from almost any public payphone, residential phone, mobile phone or hotel phone in the world. This can be an expensive option, and may not always be available. In a number of countries such as Japan, for example, the international operators are separated from the local ones so require booked, pre-assigned or some special access arrangements. International payphones likewise in Japan are distinguished from inland ones. Additionally, watch out for hotels and other sites that simply bar international access altogether to avoid being caught with large unpaid bills from guests. Outside in the street, using a payphone means you have to work out how to pay. Unless you are flush with foreign currency, the only options are likely to be through card phones (see below).

Hotel Phones

You should recognise that many hotels probably make as much profit in absolute terms from telephony services as they do from renting rooms. Call charges are likely to be therefore extremely high. Under pressure because of unfavourable media attention recently, many have begun reducing their tariffs. The more responsible hotels notify you of the charging structure in advance, but you should always check, if you plan to make frequent calls, or arrange for people to call you instead. Note that hotels often make high fax charges too, and many charge for inbound faxes.

PTT Bureaus
These exist around the world, especially in countries where access has traditionally been poor. They provide a walk-in service for IDD, fax, and telex services at stipulated IDD rates, on a cash or sometimes credit card basis. Tourist information offices should always know where they are located.

Prepaid Cards
One of your best bets is to use some sort of card phone. There are several different types. Prepaid card phones do what they suggest; they are payphones where you must buy a card in advance of calling from a store or hotel, go to a payphone, dial a number and the card value is the payment for the call. They are convenient and have the big advantage that you know exactly what you can spend in advance, but generally speaking, cards must be bought in the country of use and are not transferable.

Credit Card Phones
These are simple variations on the basic payphone which accept credit cards as an alternative or substitute for pre-paid cards or coins. Be careful, credit card phones may well be convenient but rack up a very high charge beginning with a high standing connect charge. Unless you are desperate, they are best avoided, particularly in airports.

Collect Calling (Reverse Charging) and Home Direct Services
You should try to avoid these like the plague too and only use them where there are absolutely no alternatives: they are all incredibly expensive since they are operator connected. So-called "Home Direct" (calling sometimes "Country Direct") options seen on payphones around the world are also a form of reverse charging, differing only in the fact that you usually set up the call via an operator in your home country rather than locally.

Calling Cards
Practically every major operator in the world now issues some form of calling card. These credit card sized items basically give you a pre-assigned identity (account) number and personal identification number (PIN). In use, you call the particular operator who has assigned you the card from your location, give the identification numbers and the destination number you want, and the operator picks up your call and re-routes it to the destination. With most systems, the final bill appears in a statement from the operator or directly on your credit card, so leave a method of payment in place if you are travelling. The big advantage of the calling card is that it should be significantly cheaper than calling from hotel rooms, although there are wide variations in actual pricing. Because of this it pays to be careful or to check charges in advance with the operator. Note also that hotels have realised that their own charging is being short circuit-

ed by this method and occasionally have engaged in tactics such as charging for free-phone access from rooms (many calling cards have a freephone or low rate access for the first leg of the call into the operator to encourage users), or occasionally barring numbers altogether. Calling cards however can also give you access to all the clever services that operators have on offer. Most advanced networks have call redirection facilities for example to enable automatic transfer from one number to another, conference calling for multiple users, translation or help lines.

Callback Services

Potentially these are the cheapest of all, with savings of between 30 per cent to 80 per cent possible on many expensive IDD routes. You should seriously investigate these if you are an independent or even business traveller. Callback services have become available as a result of the wide disparities in international calling charges. Basically, a callback service offers the opportunity for a subscriber to route his or her call through a country which can provide cheaper international access (usually this is the USA), regardless of where the call actually originated or is destined. For example, if you want to call France from India, you first notify a callback provider (perhaps in the USA) and immediately hang up. The callback service (which invariably has a pre-arranged subscription with you) then calls you back in India (hence the name) but in doing so gives him or her a dialling tone enabling onward dialling to the final destination, in this case, France. The call is cheaper because of the much lower rates offered by US to India and US to France than India direct to France.

Callback services have mushroomed in popularity as a result of the obvious good deals they offer. Authorities, however, are not so sure, given that the PTTs are clearly losing substantial amounts of revenue on this basis. Some have even resorted to means legal and illegal to block callback providers or bar access to them, particularly in Argentina, Uruguay and various West African countries. China is also said to take a dim view. These tactics work for a time, causing everyone inconvenience but sooner or later the callback provider has circumvented the restrictions and the process starts again.

To be sure, callback services vary in the sophistication they can provide to you, so check the facilities. You may have to designate a particular phone you will use for the service for example. Some providers save you the money of calling them by automatically detecting the signalling coming from your phone system and working out the number you are calling from, before calling back. Your call is not technically received or connected so you are not charged for this leg of the route. Some are even equipped to circumvent hotel switchboards by using computer generated voice techniques to ask automatically to be connected to the subscriber's room. Cheap fax services may also be available. The major callback providers generally advertise in the main English language newspapers around the world (at least the sort that are likely to be read by travellers). A few unscrupulous ones exist but generally the field has a good reputation. Check the degree of your advance financial commitment – you may be asked to put down a deposit debited from your credit card for example.

Messaging Mailboxes

These might be a good option if you want to keep in touch. Voice messaging is the voice equivalent of electronic mail (see below). If the called party is unavailable, the operator system responds with a suitable message and invites the caller to leave the message in a voice mailbox; it is recorded by the network operator (often, the PTT). To listen to the message, the called party can call up the messaging system – theoretically from anywhere in the world – and listen to it. Alternatively, an answering machine may be used, although with less convenience, since it actually has to be sited somewhere and lacks the more advanced facilities that operators can provide themselves. Check on the newer types of mailbox facilities; in several countries "multimedia services" are possible which use the same facilities to store voice, fax and even email transmissions, ready for caller access, and all on the same number.

Mobile Telephony

Mobile communications is on a massive roll world-wide as investors and operators see it as one of the big commercial money spinners of modern times. It could also be a key development for the modern traveller. To get the best out of it, you need a quick tutorial in the subject. It is important to be aware that this is so-called "cellular" technology. This splits countries or areas up into "cells" up to a few miles wide. Different cells use the same radio channels, and in doing so vastly increase the network radio capacity, so millions of subscribers can be supported on the same network. Clever electronics in the system ensures that it "knows" when subscribers move around and can re-route calls accordingly.

The cellular phone, unlike other radio systems, acts in exactly the same way as a conventional fixed phone and invariably links into the PSTN at some point. In terms of making or receiving calls anywhere in the world, the systems are therefore effectively interchangeable from the point of view of numbering, etc. However, in practically every country in the world, cellular services are invariably more expensive than fixed PSTN services over the same distance (the only exception I have found is Israel where it is possible to make cheaper long distance calls by cellular). However, the key point to note is that cellular systems are being established very quickly; even large countries can be covered in a matter of months because the mobile radio systems are much easier to set up than the traditional fixed network. [NB. "Cordless" radio technology, fundamentally different to cellular technology, permits a very short range (up to 100 or 200 metres) of wireless extensions to conventional phones, but are not cellular and do not in general permit mobility or roaming.]

Now for the bad news. There is no such thing as a world standard in mobile communications, so it is not necessarily possible to take a phone from one country to another and expect it to work, termed "roaming" in the industry. The biggest offenders in this respect are the older "analogue" systems, so if you want to travel, avoid buying them, no matter how good the deal appears to be. The best bets for roaming are the new digital cellular systems now available. There are a number of incompatible standards around the world for digital cellular but the situation is eased if you know where you want to travel. The nearest thing to a world standard in digital cellular is the GSM (Global System for Mobile) technology, now available in more than 90 countries and used by nearly 200 operators. It is overwhelmingly dominant in Europe, the Middle East, South East Asia, South Africa, and Australasia. It is therefore possible for a European to travel to Australia, or a Singaporean to travel to the Middle East and without further fuss switch on his or her mobile phone and find it working immediately if coverage exists in his or her location. In all these cases, the network "knows" where the phone is when it is switched on, and manages the call routing and billing back on the subscriber's home bill appropriately. The snag is: another set of standards exists for the Americas, and a third for Japan. (China awkwardly is a mix of standards but has established a large number of GSM networks; Russia also has several in major areas but is likewise a hotch-potch.) Generally you cannot take phones between these three major areas and expect roaming availability. In some cases, operators have agreements in place where you can swap the so-called SIM cards which carry control and subscriber information for the GSM phone handset into a handset suitable for the new country. Roaming then becomes possible; you should check on this option with your service provider but do not be surprised if you cannot be accommodated.

A final note on roaming. If you travel, expect big bills if you use the digital cellular technologies. Roaming implies calls made are international calls and are given a premium price, and calls which appear "local" to you in the new country would still be treated by the network as "international".

An alternative to roaming would of course be to sign up and subscribe to the local cellular network, although this could prove time-consuming and you will be expected to agree to a contract which is likely to prove an extremely expensive commitment, although you would not have the automatic international charging associated with roaming unless you explicitly called overseas. Airport bureaux often offer cellular phones on a short term basis especially for travellers, these will be cheaper on an overall basis but incur high daily charges.

Other drawbacks of mobile networks include a lack of coverage in the most remote areas, particularly deserts and mountains where the population is too sparse to economically support a mobile system (although you may be surprised exactly how much coverage is available). Generally, the policy of deployment in any country is to give major cities and commercial centres the priority in the first wave of cellular establishment and this also includes major roads and highways (worth noting if you are in a remote location). Thereafter, deployment is to secondary centres on a planned or phased basis.

Satellite Systems

If you think satellite technology was really only for the most sophisticated travellers of all, you are in for a surprise. Over the next three years, a number of systems will be activated which will girdle the globe. The idea is to give coverage practically anywhere on the planet using hand held phones that will look like and directly compete with digital cellular technology. Costs should run again comparably with cellular systems, in the US\$1-3 per minute range. These could represent the biggest breakthrough of all for the independent traveller.

Paging

Unless you are visiting specific locations for reasonable amounts of time, paging (which should be a good answer for travellers) will probably prove to be unworkable. Paging generally offers a one way link from a caller to you. Two kinds of pagers are basically available: tone, and alphanumeric which "beep", and display short messages, respectively. Pagers are invariably cheaper to buy and use and more convenient to carry than mobile phones, hence their attraction. But international coverage and co-ordination of paging networks and services are highly fragmented. It is worth a try if you are visiting the USA (which has a number of very good services covering the entire country) or Hong Kong or Singapore (where more than a quarter of the population carry pagers), but elsewhere don't expect too much, although it may be easier to get paging service than cellular service in Russia, China and parts of Latin America. Some paging providers offer a voice messaging service with the paging which has proved useful in several markets.

Electronic Mail

The explosion of the Internet world-wide has made communications by email a much more effective tool now than ever before. Internet access also means that subscribers can navigate the World Wide Web with all its facilities. In communications terms, email properly used can give you enormous facilities at very low cost. There are many email systems now in use in the world. Strictly speaking these are separate networks, but they all invariably can "talk" to each other and to the Internet itself. Each system differs in fine detail but all email systems perform the same basic functions, in allowing computer to computer communications. The systems are complicated, but think of them as direct analogues to the postal system. Every registered email possesses an "electronic mailbox" with a unique electronic address in which messages may be stored or received or from which messages may be sent. The advantages of email are that it is nearly instantaneous and probably cheaper on a per message basis than ordinary post. Reportedly, more emails are now sent in the US than posted letters. Email is suitable for messages of almost any length although cost varies with message size and number of messages. In many cases different types of data can be transferred over the network including both text files produced by word processing and spreadsheet information (this is easiest if both the sender and receiver use the same email networks).

As a basic kit, you will need:

1. A data terminal device (the desktop, laptop or notebook-sized computer).
2. Suitable word processing and communications software with which the message may be written and formatted in a form suitable for sending, and a browser software if you want to use the World Wide Web on the Internet.
3. A modem, which converts the streams of computer data into a form suitable for transmission through the national PSTN.
4. Appropriate email registration for the country/service you are using.
5. Access to a public telephone connection e.g. by socket or phone.
6. A local printer if you want to print information.
7. Cables to connect the above (and power supplies/adaptors for the country).

The principal disadvantage with email is that you need a computer system to both send and receive it. Nor is the recipient automatically aware that he or she has a message waiting in the mailbox; regular ad hoc box interrogation is therefore necessary.

But you should note that operationally there may also be differences which are important to you when travelling. If you subscribe to one of the international on-line services which include extensive email facilities, like CompuServe, for example, you will find that the service can be accessed by dialling up a network "node" in the country you are located in. These network nodes are provided by CompuServe or a partner network and cut costs for you since connecting to them requires an inland (often local) rather than international call.

The problem is really that due to differences in technical characteristics it remains generally difficult to connect a device like a modem, specified for one country, to the PSTN or hotel room socket in another. The differences can be quite minor but infuriating: there are nearly 40 different types of phone sockets around the world, and even where physically similar, may be wired differently. The dialling system of the modem may not work or may connect incorrectly because of national technical and numbering differences. There are ways around this, but you could be unlucky and find systems or hotels which are unforgiving. That said, I have used the same laptop, modem and plug combination in hotel rooms in the UK, USA, Canada, Finland, Sweden, Singapore, Taiwan, and Hong Kong, with a payphone (equipped with a data socket) in Japan, and even flying over California (with an aircraft seat phone, again equipped with a data socket). In many cases, the plug/socket combination you will require is termed RJ-11 (widespread in the USA). For hotel rooms equipped with this (and there will often be an RJ-11 data port set into the side of the phone handset) there should not be too many problems. However, in other areas there may be difficulties. There is always a risk that hotel switchboards, more properly called "private automatic branch exchanges" (PABXs), may be incompatible with your modem and may even damage it in use. The most "difficult" travelling areas are in mainland Europe, and there may also be problems in parts of the underdeveloped world and possibly in the former colonies of the European nations. Specialists in this area are TeleAdapt (+44 181 421 4444 or World Wide Web http://www.teleadapt.com) who will probably have all the information, connectors and other hardware that you will ever need. If you continue to have real problems you may be forced to buy a modem and suitable jack in the country. Another option would be to use what is known as an "acoustic coupler" which is a modem device that fits over a conventional phone handset but requires no plug and socket connection at all, but these tend to permit low connection speeds, reducing your options. A final option – which may prove increasingly attractive in the future – is to forget about hotel room phones, jacks and sockets altogether, and use a mobile (cellular) phone for your connection. You will need a special modem unit. Remember, however, that sending data over cellular has the same limitations as voice, in that the GSM systems, for example, will only work in areas of the world that have adopted GSM as a standard, and so on. Consequently, you will have to have different modem and phone units for the Americas and Japan. Recently, Nokia have introduced the Communicator, a device allowing GSM phone and data access (including email and WWW access) in the same hand-portable unit, which could be a particularly neat option to get all of this in one package. Bear in mind that this sort of access does not permit high speed or sophisticated services at the moment, although these will undoubtedly come.

A final point on local access. You should note that if your home connection is with an Internet Service Provider rather than an online service like CompuServe, it may not have a cheap local way of getting Internet access for you if you are travelling. In this case you have several options. One would be to make international calls to your home provider every time that you wanted to connect. Another would be to register with a local Internet Service Provider and have your mail forwarded to it or mailers advised of your new address. Another would be to use services like the Global Reach Internet Connection (GRIC) which is basically an international alliance of Internet Service Providers. GRIC provides a transparency between ISPs in any two member countries. Currently, GRIC covers a hundred ISPs world-wide from the USA, Australia, Brunei, Canada, China, France, Hong Kong, Indonesia, Japan, Korea, Malaysia, Nepal, New Zealand, the Philippines, Romania, Singapore, Spain, Switzerland, Taiwan, Thailand, the UK and Venezuela. Many more are being added all the time (see http://www.gric.com).

Internet and on-line services are being expanded all the time. One innovation that could make a significant difference to travellers was launched in Summer 1997 by CompuServe: the Global Connect Card. This calling card not only functions as a standard calling card which can cut long distance phone charges but it also offers voice and fax mailboxes, and in a particular development, the service allows subscribers to access their email and have it "read" to them, by phone rather than by computer. This is possible because the CompuServe network has implemented a text-to-speech conversion system. Users may also have the email redirected to any fax machine they choose. Overall the system saves toting the computer hardware above, although it would still be required to transmit messages.

Fax Facilities

The explosion of fax machine sales over the past ten years testifies to their popularity and ease of use. Unlike most other forms of data communication, fax machines use the voice network (PSTN) exclusively. International fax format standardisation has progressed to the point where any so-called Group II/III machine in the world should be able to communicate with any other. The principal drawback is that it is by definition a paper-based service; further manipulation of fax information means that it generally has to be re-keyed. Another drawback is that, unlike telex messages, fax messages are not usually regarded as legally binding documents.

If you have a laptop computer, a modem will usually incorporate a fax facility. This will enable fax messages to be sent and received assuming that you have the appropriate software, although you would need to keep the laptop permanently on and connected to the telephone network. This set-up is therefore best for sending only occasional messages. Many email and Internet facilities do have an email-to-fax conversion option too, which is useful for sending to destinations which have fax but not email facilities. Usually, however, a dedicated fax machine is the best option. Portable fax machines (battery driven) are now available. These can be set up and used almost anywhere that there is access to a telephone point, but again watch out for the need for a variety of plugs and sockets as with email. It is also possible to connect portable faxes to cellular phone systems in some countries via an interface unit enabling a truly mobile office to be built around the phone, fax and even portable computer and email facility.

A potentially costly item will be the number of PSTN connections needed overall for equipment like faxes, computers, telephone/answering machines. Ideally, it should be one per item but since lines may take a long time to install and accrue both an installation charge and a rental charge in most countries, it may be necessary to economise. A particularly useful device now widely available is the "fax-splitter" which is directly connected to the phone socket, and determines whether incoming calls are for the fax machine or the telephone, routing them appropriately. Outgoing calls are not affected. This is only possible for direct connections to the PSTN, and not, for example, in hotel rooms.

By Disk

If you have very large amounts of text or data to send or receive, but you have a very slow or unreliable local email connection, you could try the post. This could well prove the simplest and cheapest method. You simply make a copy of the disk and send it through the post to the recipient to read on his or her computer directly. This is very effective where the data is not required speedily (use express post or courier service requiring special customs documentation and labelling for magnetic – disk – media where you do) and very large amounts of data can be shipped in this way. A state of the art optical disc would store 100Megabytes of data (a CD-ROM considerably more), roughly the equivalent of 160 good sized novels put together but would still fall into the lower charge bands for letter post. Or several could be packed into a half-kilo package, the first charge band for many international courier services. No email registration or communications facility is required. Unless you are desperate, do this or use email to send large amounts of data. Fax is expensive relatively speaking and the data may have to be rekeyed at the other end – this would take time and may introduce errors.

Internet (IP) Telephony

Communications has come full circle with the advent of Internet or IP Telephony. This basically means that the Internet system, a system meant for data, can have voice traffic sent across it. You need the hardware listed above, some appropriate software, cheap microphones and speakers and you are all set to go. The advantage if you have not worked it out: low or no cost long distance and international phone calls! The disadvantages are that voice quality is likely to be inferior to the conventional voice telephony, that pre-arrangement at both ends of the connection is necessary, and of course the called party has to have the hardware and software set up as well. These disadvantages seem slight when overall use costs roughly US$2 per hour for calls anywhere in the world are taken into account, and imply you could have the "phone" switched on almost permanently!

For a Country by Country Guide to Contacting the UK see p.863 of the Directory. For a list of International Direct Dialling Codes see p.877

THE CYBERSPACE TRAVELLER

by Miranda Haines

The original definition of the internet, in non-techie terms, is one that might have detered even the most adventurous cyber-traveller: "Someone went into the biggest library in the world, knocked over all the shelves and left the books on the floor with the lights out." However, with the help of search engines these days, like Yahoo, that travel book, air-ticket, train-timetable, map or specialist travel product – be it in Thailand or Tyneside – is much easier to track down and eventually buy. If cyber-travel works for researching destinations, learning about local time-tables, routes, health hazards, and then actually buying tickets and booking hotels and carhire, then, this has to be wonderful news for the world traveller. But does it work?

Who are the Cyberspace Travellers?

Jack Barker, editor of the UK's e-zine Travelmag: *http://www.travelmag.co.uk*, says that most people spend their time cluttering up newsgroups, where travellers may swap stories, ask questions and generally meet. However, the most useful and underused capability of the internet for travellers, he says, is that one can discover more adventurous holiday itineraries with smaller companies that cannot afford to advertise world-wide. "I wanted to do a motorcycle tour recently and I looked up where I could rent Harley Davidsons cheaply and I found a really good range of tours from Lima to Machu Pichu, from Costa Rica to northern Thailand into Laos and Burma."

But worryingly, Barker says, not only can one book the Harley Davidson tour from the other side of the world, but, also, it can be paid for by credit card. "The problem is that all you know about the company is that they have a web site. Personally, I make sure that they can take credit cards (a good sign) but the fear is that you arrive in South America at the airport with no Harley Davidson waiting and no £1000 in the bank."

Booking Holidays via the Internet

The main problem about booking a holiday on the internet is one of credibility. How are we to know that the hotel is any good? Or that it even exists, and if it does will it take more of your money once you have given them your credit card details? One British couple I met recently, who live in Turkey, booked their whole holiday via the World Wide Web and double-checked the details on Lonely Planet's web site. Although this is not as good a security as having a reputable travel agent, recommend a hotel, an airline and a carhire company that has been tried and tested and having them book for you, it certainly worked for this couple. It did, however, take considerably longer to research than a telephone call to a travel agent, who arguably gives one more choice aswell, and this is an important consideration. If you wish to speed up your search on-line, then turn off the graphics which slow things down considerably. Travel sites are heavy on images which take a long time to appear on the screen.

The time factor apart, brand recognition in the marketplace is the most powerful tool on the internet as the success of US hotel chain, Marriott, proves. Over one million visitors per month visit the Marriott site which makes it in the top five per cent of web sites in terms of visitor numbers. Perhaps more significantly Microsoft's venture into the on-line travel business, in the form of their site Expedia, now claims revenues of over $1 million per week from on-line purchases of air-travel, hotel reservations and car bookings in the US. Estimates put Expedia at the 30th largest travel agent slot in the US which is pretty impressive for an on-line service in its infancy.

Security Booking

As for security, Luke Taylor, a partner in the internet company Oyster Systems, insists that there is no longer a security scare on the internet. The real issue, he says, is one of consumer perception which will, in time, change and learn to trust the medium. "The secure encryption technology, called 'secure socket-layer technology', is sufficiently sophisticated to guarantee that credit card numbers cannot be encrypted", Taylor explains. "Why are so many people happy to give a credit card number over the telephone, which is much easier to tap into, when they are loathe to give it on the internet? It has been proven that the risk of fraud is much greater on the telephone." He has a point.

There is little doubt that travel is going to be enormous business on the internet. A TravelTech '97 report that analysed how technology is used by the travel industry for the distribution of products and services showed that on-line spending for travel products originating in the UK will be over £1 billion by the year 2002, with consumer air-flights representing the largest sector. Travel related sites are said to be the fourth most popular and lucrative sites after business, education and personal communication (excluding pornography of course).

Ed Whiting, who is product manager for EMAP's on-line site *http://www.bargainholidays.com*, suggests that anyone who purchases over the internet should check to see that the company is ABTOL and IATA bonded which goes for any travel related purchase in the UK whether it be on-line or not. *http://www.bargainholidays.com* is the internet's answer to Teletext. But the huge advantage it has over Teletext for purchasing last minute bargain flights and holidays is that it is interactive and has an unlimited amount of pages of offers, which are updated twice daily. "It is like watching the stock market because it changes all the time", explains Whiting.

EMAP is hoping, that since the UK is the bargain basement of Europe, people from, say Stockholm, will book the cheap flights from London, stop-off for a few nights in the capital, book some theatre and/or opera tickets and a hotel for those days via EMAP's service *http://www.whatson.com/stage* and continue with their onward flight to the Canary Islands, for example. Everything can be booked over the internet but at the last stage there is a telephone number so that all details can be confirmed by a person. "This is mostly for reassurance", says Whiting, "because most people like a bit of human contact somewhere along the line".

Surfing the Sites and Are They any Good?

Alan and Dolly Graham are wildlife photo-journalists who have converted to the internet as a research tool. No longer do they buy the guidebooks when they go to Ghana, or even maps of Africa. Instead, they surf the net for hours, on Saturday and Sunday, when it costs only 69p an hour. "It is the most up-to-date information that you can get", enthuses Alan Graham. "The maps of Ghana in the tourist guides are all wrong, so we print off the satellite maps. That way we can see where the rainforest really is rather than where it is supposed to be. Obviously, to see the wildlife, there must be vegetation and although the guides always publish maps that show where the elephants and hippopotamus and antelope are said to live, often the forest is simply not there."

I decided to try a bit of research, myself, for a trip to Morocco in September. I tapped in the Moroccan Tourist Board's site as a sensible starting point *http://www.znet.se/marocko/* (found from the Tourism Offices World-wide Directory at *http://www.mbnet.mb.ca/lucas/travel* – Also see page 700 of the Directory for tourist board web sites) and in the list of good Moroccan web site links I found myself interested in a page called Morocco FAQ (Frequently Asked Questions) that has been maintained, since 1992, by a certain Jey Burrows with the help of many travellers. Here, I learnt in detail how to make real Moroccan mint tea! But more importantly it answered questions such as: Will I catch anything? What customs should I follow? What are the usual scams? Is it safe? What festivals happen where and when? – all answered in detail and by varied personal accounts. This was definitely more up-to-date than many guidebooks I had found. The women's account of how to travel, in this notoriously difficult country for a women, was a lot more reassuring and informative than the usual one paragraph in the Lonely Planet guidebook.

However, the Lonely Planet Guides do have a super site themselves *http://www.lonelyplanet.com.au* and although their books are not on-line they have destination guides which give the basics about a country, city or region and they have "detours" to out of the way places. There are also "postcard" pages with tips from other travellers. The Rough Guides were the first publishers to put their excellent guidebooks on the World Wide Web (their address is *http://www.roughguides.com/*) and the well-respected Footprint Handbooks (previously Trade and Travel) have a new and innovative site worth checking out at *http://www.footprint-handbooks.co.uk.* Another two sites I find useful often are the British Foreign and Commonwealth Office travel advise unit at *http://www.fco.gove.uk/* and for information on world-wide health and the latest risks for travellers The World Health Organisation: *http//www.who.ch/*.

The most important thing to remember is that web sites change all the time; even the useful addresses listed in the Directory at the back of this book may well be out-of-date by the time you decide to visit them. Visit the WEXAS web site *http://wexas.com/travel* for an update on addresses and good travel related links and to see parts of *The Traveller's Handbook* and *Traveller* magazine on-line. Of course the best way of finding anything is to get connected and venture out there to see for yourself.

For list of travel related web sites see p728 of the Directory ■

WHEN THINGS GO WRONG
Chapter 13

AVOIDABLE HASSLES

by Tony Bush and Richard Harrington

A traveller's best friend is experience and it can take dozens of trips to build this – and the hard way. Fortunately, there are some tips that can be passed on to help the unwary before they even step on a plane.

Most people have the good sense to work out their journey time to the airport and then add a "little extra" for unforeseen delays. But is that little extra enough should something major go wrong – if the car breaks down, for instance, or there are traffic tailbacks due to roadworks or an accident?

Remember, too, to try and avoid travelling at peak periods such as Christmas, Easter and July and August when families are taking their holidays. This applies particularly to weekends, especially Saturdays.

Taxis and Taxes

Most travellers would agree that the task of dealing with taxi drivers could just about be elevated to a science. In some parts of the world overcharging alone would be a blessing. What is really disconcerting is the driver who cannons through red lights or uses part of the pavement to overtake on the inside.

And what about the fare? Without a meter, the obvious foreigner will almost certainly be overcharged. But even the sight of a rank full of taxis with meters should not raise too much hope. Meters often "break" just as you are getting in.

Two good tips for dealing with the drivers of unmetered taxis are:

1. Know a little of the local language – at least enough to be able so say "hello" "please take me to", "how much ?" and "thank you". This throws the driver a little. After all, the driver's aim is only to try and make an extra pound or two. He doesn't want to get involved in a major row at the risk of being reported to the authorities.

2. Try and have the correct amount ready to hand over. It prevents the driver pleading that he has not got sufficient change – a ruse that often succeeds, particularly when the fare is in a hurry. It also avoids "misunderstandings".

A typical misunderstanding might go like this: the traveller hands over a note worth, say, 100 blanks for a trip that he believed was going to cost him 20 blanks. However, the driver, with the note safely tucked into his pocket, tells him he was wrong, he misheard or was misinformed. In fact, the journey cost 30 blanks and 70 blanks is handed over. This leaves the passenger in an invidious position. He cannot snatch his note back and is faced instead with the indignity of having to argue about a relatively small amount (very rarely would a driver attempt to cheat on too large scale).

In most cases, the traveller will shrug his shoulders, walk away and put his loss down to experience. And this is what the driver is relying on. That is the reason he is not greedy. He knows that even the most prosperous-looking passenger would baulk at too big a reduction in his change.

The traveller should find out before or during his trip whether he will be required to pay an airport tax on departure and, if so, how much. This is normally only a token sum, but it would be frustrating to have to change a £50 travellers' cheque in order to pay it. Departure taxes are almost always payable in local currency. Occasionally an equivalent sum in US dollars will be accepted. The ideal arrangement is to work out roughly how much transport to the airport will cost, add on the airport tax, if any, and then throw in a little extra for incidentals.

Tea Oils the Wheels

If you must spread around a little "dash" to oil the palms that facilitate your progress, do so carefully after checking how to do it properly with someone who knows the ropes. You may be able, for instance, to avoid a few days in a Mexican jail for a mythical driving offence. On the other hand, you could end up in jail for trying to bribe an officer of the law – and then you might have to hand out a great deal more to get out rather than rot for months waiting for a trial.

The $1 or $5 bill tucked in the passport is the safest approach if you do decide on bribery, as you can always claim that you keep your money there for safety. But it may only be an invitation to officials to search you more thoroughly – and since all officials ask for identity papers, you could go through a lot of dollars in this way. When you think a bribe is called for, there's no need for excessive discretion. Ask how much the "fine" is or whether there is any way of obtaining faster service.

Bribes, by the way, go under an entertaining assortment of different names. "Dash" is the term in West Africa, except in Liberia, where the euphemistic expression is "cool water". *Mattabiche*, which means "tip", "corruption" or "graft", oils the wheels in Zaire. In East Africa, the Swahili word for tea, *chai*, serves the same function. *Baksheesh* is probably the best known name for the phenomenon and is widely used in the Middle East. It is a Persian word, found also in Turkish and Arabic, that originally meant a tip or gratuity, but took on the connotation of bribe when it was used of money paid by a new Sultan to his troops. *El soborno* is "payoff" in Spanish-speaking countries, except Mexico, where the word for "bite", *la mordida*, is used. In India you have the "backhander"; in Japan *wairo* or, when referring more generally to corruption *kuori kiri*, which translates lyrically as "black mist". The French refer to the "jug of wine" or *pot de vin*; the Italians use the term "little envelope", a *bustarella*, and Germans have an honestly distasteful term for a distasteful thing: *Schmiergeld* which means "lubricating money". Even here, however, exporters gloss over the matter by simply using the abbreviation "N.A.", *Nuzlich Abgabe*, which means "useful contribution".

Smiling Strangers

Beware of the "Smiling Strangers" when abroad. It is here that experience really counts as it is often extremely difficult to separate the con man from a genuinely friendly person. A favourite ploy is for him to offer his services as a guide. If he asks for cash, don't say "I would like to help, but all my money is tied up in travellers' cheques". The Smiling Stranger has heard that one before and will offer to accompany you to your hotel and wait while a cheque is cashed.

The warning about confidence tricksters also applies to some extent to street traders. Not the man who operates from a well set-up stand, but the fellow who wanders about with his arms full of bracelets or wooden carvings. He may give the souvenir hunter a good deal, but prices on the stands or in the shops should be checked first. Sometimes they will be cheaper in the latter, when, frankly, they should not even compare. After all, the wanderer does not have any overheads.

Local Courtesies

One of the biggest minefields for the unsuspecting traveller is local courtesies and customs, and most of us have our pet stories about how we have unwittingly infringed them.

It is worth knowing that you should not insult a Brazilian by talking to him in Spanish. The Brazilians are proud of the fact that they are the only nation in South America to speak Portuguese.

It's also important to understand that the Chinese, Japanese and Koreans believe in formalities before friendship and that they all gobble up business cards. Everyone should certainly realise that they must not ask a Muslim for his Christian name. And it is of passing interest that Hungarians like to do a lot of handshaking.

It is easy to become neurotic about the importance of local customs, but many Third World people today, at least in the major towns, have some understanding of Western ways and, although they do not want to see their own traditions trampled on or insulted, they don't expect all travellers to look like Lawrence of Arabia or behave like a character from The Mikado! Civility, politeness, warmth and straight dealing transcend any language and cultural barriers.

The Model Visitor

Men should wear a dark suit, white shirt, and a dark tie. Women should make sure their skirts are well below the knees, their necklines demure and their arms, if not always their heads, covered. Sometimes dark glasses are not a good idea – take them off, so your eyes can be seen. In practice, this is not much fun when the temperature is 45°C in the shade, the humidity is 100 per cent and your luggage weighs 35kg. Nevertheless, try to keep your clothes clean. If not backpacking, use a suitcase instead of a rucksack and (if male) shave and get your hair cut as close to a crew-cut as possible without looking like an astronaut. A moustache is better than a beard, but avoid both if possible. Long hair, as long as it is suitably neat, is usually more acceptable for women, who thereby look suitably feminine.

Do not try smuggling anything through customs, especially drugs. Hash and grass may be common in the countries you visit, but be careful if you buy any. A local dealer may be a police informer. Prosecutions are becoming more common and penalties increasingly severe – from ten years' hard labour to mandatory death for trafficking in "hard" drugs – and in some countries, sentences are hardly more lenient for mere possession. There's no excuse for failing to research the countries you intend to visit. Talk to people who have lived in or visited them and find out what problems you are likely to encounter. If you go prepared and adopt a sympathetic, understanding frame of mind you should be able to manage without trouble.

THEFT

by Christopher Portway and Melissa Shales

Obviously one of the most important things to keep in mind while travelling is the safety of your possessions. Do your best to minimise the chances of theft and you will run far less risk of being left destitute in a foreign country. Try and separate your funds, both in your luggage and on your person, so as to frustrate thieves and reduce losses. And before you leave home, make arrangements with a reliable person whom you can contact for help in an emergency.

American Express probably issue the most reliable and easily negotiable travellers' cheques, have the most refund points in the world and possibly hold the record for the speediest reimbursements. If you don't have plenty of plastic to keep you going for the two to three weeks it can take to get replacement cheques or new funds via the bank, take these.

Play for Sympathy

If you come face to face with your robbers then use all the skills in communication you have picked up on your travels. Try humour. At least try and get their sympathy, and always ask them to leave items which will be of no immediate value to them but are inconvenient for you to replace. They are usually after cash, and valuables which are easily converted into cash. Try to get the rest back and risk asking for enough money for a taxi fare if you feel the situation is not too tense. Acting mad can help, as can asking for help or advice. One man, when approached in Kenya, claimed to be a priest and put on such a convincing act that the robbers ended by giving him a donation!

Many thefts will be carried out (without your noticing) from your hotel room – or by pick-pockets in a crowded street. Never use a handbag that isn't zipped, and keep your hand covering the fastener at all times. They can still slit the fabric or leather, but the odds are lengthened as to their success. Never carry anything valuable in the back pocket of your trousers or the outside pocket of a jacket. Even the top inner pocket can be picked easily in a crowd. A money-belt is the most secure method of carrying valuables although even this isn't foolproof.

Never leave valuables in a hotel room, even out of sight. A good thief will know far more tricks than you and is probably likely to check under the mattress, or behind the drawers of the dressing table before searching more obvious places. As long as the hotel is fairly respectable and isn't likely to be in cahoots with local criminals, put valuables in the hotel safe, and make sure you get a proper receipt.

While on the move, never let your luggage out of your sight. Wrap the straps round your leg while sitting down (a good reason for a longer shoulder strap) so you can feel it if not see it. Lock or padlock everything. This will not deter the most hardened types, but should lessen the chance of casual pilfering. A slightly tatty case is far less inviting than brand new matching leather Gucci.

Violence

The crime of violence is usually committed with the aim of robbery. My advice in this unhappy eventuality is to offer no resistance. It is virtually certain that those who inflict their hostile attentions upon you know what they are doing and have taken into account any possible acts of self-defence on the part of their intended victim. It may hurt your pride but this way you live to tell the tale, and after all, if you're insured, the material losses will be made good by your insurance company following the submission of a police report of the incident.

In many poorer countries, it is advisable not to wear or hold anything that is too obviously expensive, especially at night. You should be particularly wary in Africa and South America. The most robbery-with-violence prone city I know is Bogota, Colombia, where in certain streets you can be 99 per cent certain of being attacked. Having had most of my worldly goods lifted off me – but not violently – in neighbouring Ecuador, I made sure I lost nothing else by walking Bogota's treacherous streets with a naked machete in my hand. This, however, is probably a little drastic and not generally advised. You could become a target for the macho element – and you could get arrested for carrying an offensive weapon.

The British exporter robbed three times – once at gunpoint – in as many days in Rio, spent his remaining week there avoiding *favelas* (shanty towns on the outskirts of the city where many thieves live) and making sure that he was in a taxi after nightfall (when local drivers start to shoot the lights for fear of being mugged if they stop). Sometimes rolled-up newspapers are thrust through quarter-lights and drivers find themselves looking at the end of a revolver or the tip of a sheath-knife.

One of the worst cities in Africa for theft is Dar Es Salaam where locals tell of Harlem-style stripping – a practice that is spreading across the continent anywhere cars or parts are in short supply. Drivers return to where they are parked to find that their wheels, and often anything else that can be removed down to the windscreen and doors, have been removed. An expert gang can pick a vehicle clean in under ten minutes.

In 1977 I walked right through Peru not knowing that the region was infested with cattle rustlers reputed to kill without mercy if they thought they'd been seen. Occasionally, ignorance can be bliss. Since then, of course, the situation in Peru has worsened, the bandits being joined by guerrillas to make the mountains decidedly unsafe.

Within urban areas, the best advice is to stay in the city centre at night. If it is imperative to move away from the lights, go by taxi and try not to go alone. And don't forget to press down the door locks when you get in. There are some countries – Egypt is a prime example – where other people just jump in if the car has to stop for any reason. Naturally, they're normally just an extra fare, but you can never be certain.

If, by mischance, you do find yourself walking along a remote, unlit road at night, at least walk in the middle of it. This will lessen the chances of being surprised by someone concealed in the shadows. And when you have to move over for a passing car, use its headlights as your "searchlight" over the next ten or twenty metres.

Protecting yourself from attack by carrying a firearm is *not* recommended. Even in those countries that do permit it, the necessary papers are difficult to come by and in countries where the law is ticklish over the subject of mercenaries, a gun of any sort could brand you as one. One traveller was arrested in Zambia just for having a bullet on him! But that is not the point. The idea that a pistol under the car seat or one's belt is protection is usually nonsense. In many countries a gun is a prize itself to a violent thief who will make every effort to procure one.

What to do Next

Consider what action you can take if you find yourself penniless in a foreign land. Report thefts to the police and obtain the necessary form for insurance purposes. You may have to insist on this and even sit down and write it out for them to sign. Whatever it takes, you musn't leave without it. It may be essential to you for onward travel.

Local custom may play a part in your success. In Lima, for instance, the police would only accept statements on paper with a special mark sold by one lady on the steps of an obscure church found with the help of a guide. They have a way of sharing in your misfortune – or sharing it out!

If there is an embassy or consulate, report to them for help. In a remote spot, you are more likely to get help from the latter. You may have to interrupt a few bridge parties, but insist it is your right to be helped. In cases of proven hardship, they will pay your fare home by (in their opinion) the most expedient route in exchange for your passport and the issue of travel papers. If your appearance suits they may also let you phone your family or bank for funds.

Have the money sent either to the embassy via the Foreign Office or to the bank's local representative with a covering letter or cable sent to you under separate cover. This will give you proof that the money has been sent when you turn up at the bank. I have met many starving people on the shiny steps of banks being denied money which is sitting there in the care of a lazy or corrupt clerk – or in the wrong file. Other countries do not always use our order of filing and letters could be filed under 'M' or 'J' for Mr John Smith. Have your communications addressed to your family name followed by initials (and titles if you feel the need).

Quite an effective, proven way of moving on to a more sophisticated place or getting home, is to 'phone your contact at home and ask him to telex or fax air tickets for a flight out. They pay at home and the airline is much more efficient than the bank. This has the additional advantage of circumventing the Mickey Mouse currency regulations which various countries impose. Algeria is a perfect example. The country insists that airfares are paid in "hard" currency, but the money transferred into the country is automatically changed into the Algerian currency as it arrives. One then has to apply to the central bank for permission to change it back (at a loss) in order to buy your air ticket. A telexed ticket can have you airborne in a couple of hours (I've done it).

Local Generosity

In desperate situations, help can be obtained from people locally. These fall into two main groups. Expatriates, who live unusually well, are often not too keen on the image that young travellers seriously trying to meet the local scene create, but once you have pierced the inevitable armour they have put up from experience, they are able to help.

They often have fax facilities at their disposal, business connections within or out of the country and friends amongst the local officialdom. Their help and experience is usually well worth having.

Next, the missionaries. From experience I would suggest you try the Roman Catholics first as the priests often come from fairly poor backgrounds themselves and have a certain empathy with empty pockets. Other denominations tend to live better but put up more resistance to helping. (I came across an American/Norwegian group in the Cameroons suffering from a crisis because the last plane had left no maple syrup). Swallow your principles or keep quiet and repay the hospitality when you can. They often need their faith in human nature boosted from time to time.

You will receive kindness from other temples, mosques and chapels and can go there if you are starving. Again, do not abuse assistance and repay it when you can.

Real desperation may bring you to selling blood and branded clothes in which you have thoughtfully chosen to travel, in exchange for cheap local goods. But local religious communities are the best bet and usually turn up an intelligent person who can give advice.

In Third World countries, being poor and going without is no big deal – you may be in the same boat as some 90 per cent of the population. A camaraderie will exist, so you will probably be able to share what little is available. It would be wrong to abuse the customs of hospitality, but on the other hand, be very careful of your hygiene, so as not to give yourself even more problems through illness.

IN TROUBLE WITH THE LAW

by Bryan Hanson

Ignorance of the law is no more of an excuse abroad than it is at home. Consideration is usually given to the traveller but this is often in direct proportion to the funds available.

Always keep calm: to show anger is often regarded as a loss of face. Be humble and do not rant and rave unless it is the last resort and you are amongst your own kind who understand. Try to insist on seeing the highest official possible. Take the names of all others you come across on the way up – this tends to lead you to someone who is senior or intelligent enough to make a decision away from the book of rules. Also, in totalitarian regimes, having your name taken is positively threatening.

Pay the Fine

If you are guilty and the offence is trivial, admit it. Do not get involved with lawyers unless you really have to. The fine will most probably be less painful on your funds than legal fees.

On the other hand, do not misinterpret the subtleties of the local system. In Nigeria, I pleaded guilty to a trivial offence without a lawyer and found myself facing the maximum sentence. If I had used one, an "agreement" fee would have been shared with the magistrate and the case dismissed on a technicality. In other words, if we had paid the small bribe initially demanded by the police, we would not have gone to court!

More serious situations bring more difficulties and you should make every effort to contact your local national representative. The cover is thinning out – "our man in Dakar", for instance, has to cover most of West Africa. A lawyer is next on the list to contact, probably followed by a priest.

It is a good idea to carry lists of government representatives in all the countries through which you intend to travel – especially if you are leaving the beaten track. Remember they work short office hours (I once had a long and very fruitless conversation with a Serbo-Croat cleaner because I expected someone to be there before ten am and after noon!). There should be a duty officer available at weekends.

Keep in Contact

Regular messages home are a good practice. Even if they are only postcards saying "Clapham Common was never like this", they narrow down the area of search should one go missing. If doubtful of the area you are travelling in, also keep in regular contact with the embassy, and give them your proposed itinerary so that if you don't show up by a certain time, they know to start looking.

The tradition of bribery is a fact of life in many countries and often reaches much further down the ladder than it does in the Western world. I find the practice distasteful and have avoided it on many occasions, only to find myself paying eventually in other ways. In retrospect, I am not sure if "interfering with these local customs" is wise. But how to go about it when all else has failed?

In Detention

Once you've been locked up and all attempts to contact officials have been denied, a more subtle approach is needed. One can only depend on locals delivering messages to the outside world or, probably more reliable, a religious representative prepared to take the risk. Sometimes it is possible to use a local lad and send him cash on delivery to the nearest embassy or consulate (even if it's over the border) with a suitably written plea.

Third World detention premises are usually primitive and provide the minimum of filthy food. You may even have to pay to feed yourself. Time has little significance, so make your means spin out. Even though money talks the world over, try not to declare your resources or you may not get any satisfaction until the last penny has been shared out among the locals. If you get stuck Prisoners Abroad is a helpful organisation: Prisoners Abroad, 78-82 Rosebery Avenue, London EC1R 4RR, tel: 0171-833 3467.

Humour and a willingness on your part to lose face can often defuse a tense and potentially awkward moment. Travelling gives you life skills in judging people and an instinctive knowledge of how to act. Use your experience to your advantage and don't let daunting lists of advice keep you quivering at home.

If you have the gall, it is often a good idea to learn the names of a few high-ranking officials and name drop blatantly. How far you carry this is up to you, but when I married off my cousin to the Minister of Justice in Turkey, he didn't mind a bit.

See p.803 of the Directory for Canadian, UK and US embassies world-wide

Additional Information

by Christopher Portway

Being something of an inquisitive journalist with a penchant for visiting those countries normal people don't, I have, over the years, developed a new hobby. Some of us collect stamps, cigarette cards, matchboxes. I collect interrogations. And the preliminary to interrogation is, of course, arrest and detention, which makes me, perhaps, a suitable person to dwell for a few moments on some of the activities that can land the innocent traveller in prison as well as the best way of handling matters arising thereof.

In some countries, there are no set rules governing what is and is not a crime. Different regimes have different ways of playing the game and it's not just cut-and-dried crimes like robbing a bank or even dealing on the black market that can put you behind bars. Perhaps a brief resumé of some of my own experiences will give you the idea and suggest means of extracting yourself from the clutches of a warped authority.

Espionage: a Multitude of Sins

It is that nasty word "espionage" that becomes a stock accusation beloved by perverted authority. Spying covers a multitude of sins and is a most conveniently vague charge for laying against anyone who sees more than is good for him (or her). It is often in Communist countries where you have to be most careful, but some states in black Africa, Central America and the Middle East are picking up the idea fast. Spying, of a sort, can be directed against you too. In my time I have been followed by minions of the secret police in Prague and Vladivostok for hours on end. Personally, I quite enjoyed the experience and led a merry dance through a series of department stores in a vain effort to shake them off. If nothing else, I gave them blisters.

In World War II, to go back a bit, I escaped from my POW camp in Poland through the unwitting courtesy of the German State Railway. The journey came to an abrupt end at Gestapo HQ in Cracow. In post-war years, the then Orient Express carried me visa-less, into Stalin-controlled communist former Czechoslovakia. That journey put me inside as a compulsory guest of the STB, the former Czech secret police. I have met minor inconveniences of a similar nature in countries like Russia, Albania, Yugoslavia and several in the Middle East but it was only in the '70s that I bumped into real trouble again – in Idi Amin's Uganda.

Interrogations à la James Bond

The venues of all my interrogations have been depressingly similar. That in Kampala, for instance, consisted of a bare, concrete-walled office containing a cheap desk, a hard-backed chair or two, a filing cabinet, a telephone and an askew photograph of Idi Amin. This consistency fitted Cracow, Prague and Kishinev, except that in Nazi days nobody would dream of an askew Fuhrer. Prague boasted an anglepoise lamp, but then Communist methods of extracting information always did border on the James Bond.

Methods of arrest or apprehension obviously vary with the circumstances. For the record, in World War II, I was handed over to the Gestapo in Cracow by a bunch of Bavarian squaddies who could find no excuse for my lobbing a brick through the window of a bakery after curfew. In Czechoslovakia I was caught crossing a railway bridge in a frontier zone and, with five burp-guns aligned to one's navel, heroics are hard to come by. In the Soviet Union it was simply a case of my being caught with my trousers down in a "soft-class" toilet and with an out-of-date visa valid only for a place where I was not. And in Uganda there was no reason at all beyond an edict from Idi that stipulated a policy of "let's-be-beastly-to-the-British!"

Keep your Answers Simple

But the latter's line of questioning was different. It wasn't so much why had I come, but why had I come for so brief a period? That and the young Ugandan law student arrested with me. Being in close confinement in a railway carriage for 24 hours, we had become travelling companions which, coupled with my suspiciously brief stay, spelt "dirty work at the cross-roads" to the Ugandan authorities. And rummaging about in our wallets and pockets, they found bits of paper on which we had scribbled our exchanged addresses. It had been the student's idea and a pretty harmless one but, abruptly, I was made aware how small inconsistencies can be blown up into a balloon of deepest suspicion. All along I maintained I hardly knew the guy. Which reminds me that the Gestapo too had an irksome habit of looking for a scapegoat amongst the local populace.

Then we came to the next hurdle. "How is it your passport indicates you are a company director and this card shows you are a journalist?" To explain that I was once a company director and had retained the title in my passport in preference to the sometimes provocative "journalist" would have only complicated matters. So I offered the white lie that I was still a company director and only a journalist in my spare time. It didn't help much.

And, you know, there comes a moment when you actually begin to believe that you are a spy or whatever it is they are trying to suggest you might be. It creeps up on some harmless answer to a question. In Kampala I felt the symptoms and resolved to keep my answers simple and remember them the second time round.

For instance: "What school did you attend?" I gave the one I was at the longest. There was no need to mention the other two.

My regimental association membership card came up for scrutiny. "What rank were you?" I was asked. "Corporal," I replied, giving the lowest rank I had held. Pride alone prevented me from saying "Private". "Which army?" came the further enquiry. I had to admit that it was British.

Every now and again I would get in a bleat about having a train to catch – more as a cornerstone of normality than a hope of catching it. And there comes a point in most interrogations when there is a lull in proceedings during which one can mount a counter-attack. The "Why-the-hell-am-I-here? What-crime- am-I-supposed-to-have-committed?" sort of thing which at least raises the morale if not the roof.

Of course, in Nazi Germany such outbursts helped little, for, in declared wartime, one's rights are minimal and the Gestapo had such disgusting methods of upholding theirs. But in the grey world of a cold war the borderline of bloody mindedness was ill-defined. At Kishinev the KGB had the impertinence to charge me a fiver a day for my incarceration in a filthy room in a frontier unit's barracks. I voiced my indignation loud and clear and eventually won a refund. In Czechoslovakia my outburst had a different effect. The interrogator was so bewildered that he raised his eyes to the ceiling long enough for me to pinch one of his pencils. And in the cell that became my home for months, a pencil was a real treasure. Now let it be said, in general, that the one demand you have the right to make is that you be put in touch with your own embassy or consulate. I once wasn't and it caused an international incident.

In another of Kampala's Police HQ interrogation rooms, all my proffered answers had to be repeated at dictation speed. It was partly a ruse, of course, to see if the second set matched the first and I was going to be damn sure it did.

I suppose one lesson I ought to have learnt from all this is to take no incriminating evidence like press cards, association membership cards, other travellers' addresses and the like. But a few red herrings do so add to the entertainment.

See p.803 of the Directory for Canadian, UK and US Embassies world-wide

SURVIVING A HIJACK

by Mike Thexton

Hijacking comes and goes as a fashion among terrorists. It is probably some-thing that most travellers will think about at some time – to some it may be a vague anxiety; to others, part of a Rambo-style daydream. Anyone who worries about it a great deal is likely to be too nervous to be a regular traveller.

The most important thing is *not* to worry about it. The whole point of terror-ism is to create a fear completely out of proportion to the risk – to get the maxi-mum effect for the minimum effort. Don't give them that victory. Think about the huge number of trouble-free flights every day. It's very unlikely to happen to you.

However, it sometimes does. It happened to me on 5 September 1986, when four Palestinian terrorists stormed a Pan Am 747 on the ground at Karachi air-port, Pakistan. Any hijacking is likely to be different (the security forces try to bolt all the stable doors, so the successful terrorist will have to do something original) but there are some points which could be useful in any such situation. Armed men ran up the steps and took over the cabins as the last passengers were boarding. Accept it that you will not react very fast in this situation, nor should you. Civilians are usually stunned by violence, or the threat of it, because it is so shocking. If you do have an opportunity to escape at this time, make sure that it is a clear and safe one – the terrorists are also very hyped-up, and are most likely to shoot you. It may be better to wait a while.

You will need to get control of yourself. If fear takes over, you will not be able to do anything useful if an opportunity presents itself. Everyone will have to fight their own battle in their own head. I started by thinking that some people usually escape hijacks, and I saw no reason why I would not be included. I admit that I took comfort from the fact that there were Americans aboard. Since Ronald Reagan had ordered the bombing of Libya, they had to be more unpopu-lar than the British – not much, but a bit more unpopular.

Make yourself inconspicuous. It is generally fatal to be memorable: if the ter-rorists single someone out, it is usually to shoot them. Don't volunteer for any-thing, even if you think you might ingratiate yourself with them. Keep your head down. Don't catch their eyes. I was wearing a red duvet jacket, which was a bad start, but I knocked my Panama hat off my head with my raised hands, and sank into the seat as far as possible.

Do what they say, within reason. I would not co-operate to the extent of join-ing them (as happened in a famous Stockholm siege), but if they say, "Hands up, no moving", do it. We all sat in silence with our hands above our heads, looking into our laps. There is a problem here. Two terrorists kept about 350 passengers completely quiet for the whole day. No one dared to look round. They could have gone away for a cup of tea and come back in half an hour, and we would still have been in our seats – no one would have looked round, for fear that a ter-rorist was standing right behind them. If you can, you want to get as much infor-mation as possible about the number of terrorists, weapons and position, but you are safer taking no risks.

The pilots escaped right at the beginning, so we were stuck on the ground – a great relief. We sat with our hands in the air for the first three hours of the siege. I was beginning to think it would really be all right when one of the flight attendants came around collecting passports. If you can avoid giving your papers in, do – they become a means of singling you out. Take any opportunity to dispose of anything which might be "incriminating" in the mind of the terrorist. Of course, if you have a wholly "terrorist-credible" nationality, it matters less, but I heard one of them venting his hatred for "all Westerners". He listed practically every nation, including the *Spanish*. I didn't think the Spanish had ever done anything to offend anyone. These people are indoctrinated.

The flight attendant knew that American passports were what the terrorists were after, so she dropped them all under the seats as she went. This was very brave and quite proper, but it promoted the British as second most unpopular nation. My passport was picked out, and I was summoned to the front of the plane. I didn't think that it would be possible to play hide-and-seek, so I went.

Controlling fear at this point is an entirely different exercise. I went from thinking, "Some people always get off", to "Someone always gets shot". Dealing with the expectation of imminent death must be very personal. I started with blind panic; I moved on to prayer, but felt very hypocritical ("Er, God, remember me? I haven't been good at keeping in touch, but could you …"); I made some promises to God in case he was listening, but only ones which I felt I could keep (and I did). What seemed to work best was to think of all my family and friends in turn, and to say goodbye to them. I thought about the mountaineering expedition I had just completed, and what a good time it had been. I settled in my mind any arguments I had with my friends so that the sun would not go down on my anger. I also determined that I was not going to die frightened – if they wanted to shoot me, I would stiffen my upper lip, shake them by the hand, and tell them to make a decent job of it. I doubt if I could have done it, but I felt better for the intention.

They kept me at the front of the plane for twelve hours or so, thinking about shooting me to emphasise some particular demand. I think it is important to retain your dignity – begging would not help, nor would offering bribes or assistance. You don't have anything they need. To them, you are simply a piece of breathing merchandise, to be traded or cashed in. If you can obtain their sympathy, or in some way turn yourself into a human being, try it – but don't speak unless spoken to, and don't irritate them. They may be trigger happy. I think that the sight of me praying, and my calm acceptance (after a while!) of my situation may have impressed them. As the day went on, it became harder for them to shoot me.

I thought about telling them that I was Irish, and a fervent supporter of the IRA, but I doubt if it would have helped. If they know enough for it to benefit you, they will also probably know enough to see through it. They asked me if I was a soldier, and I guessed that it was important to say "No". I gave "teacher" as a neutral occupation – after all, no one *admits* to being a chartered accountant. When asked later if I liked "Mogret Thotcher", I was able to give the required answer with conviction. It would be more difficult if they had asked me to say something I really disagreed with (perhaps in a statement to those outside) – it may seem safest to go along with them, and it may be extremely dangerous to do anything else. However, you may need to keep your self-respect to avoid mental collapse, and you may need to keep their respect as well. I am glad I did not have this test.

You must not raise your expectations of release. Set long horizons. Disappointment could be crushing. This was easy for me, as I was convinced I was not getting out anyway. You should ignore any information given to you by the terrorists. Remember that the authorities are the "good guys", and they will be trying hard to get you out, but they *cannot* give in – if they do, there will be another plane-load of passengers in your situation the next week, and the week after. Hostages are sometimes convinced by their captors that the authorities are being uncooperative, that it is all the authorities' fault: hold on to reality. It isn't.

Make yourself as comfortable as possible. It might be a long stay. Massage your joints, if you are allowed to. Stretch whatever you can. Clench your fingers and toes to keep the blood moving. Any movement will stop you seizing up, and will give you something to do. It can be very boring! Any exercise for the mind is also useful – you do not want to dwell on the nastier possibilities of the position. Remembering favourite pieces of writing, picturing peaceful scenes, daydreaming – all help.

Back in economy, the passengers enjoyed a slightly more relaxed atmosphere for a while. Afterwards I met two who spent the afternoon playing cards. Anything which passes the time is useful. It also helps to exchange names, addresses and messages for next-of-kin.

Take advantage of any opportunity you get to do anything which may make yourself more comfortable or safe – get a more inconspicuous seat, go to the toilet, eat or drink. You don't know whether you will get another chance for days. However, you should probably *not* take advantage of an opportunity to make yourself a hero. You will probably get killed, and will also cause the deaths of a number of others.

Movies are unrealistic. A large man with a Kalashnikov is very hard to take on with your bare hands; a man holding a grenade in his hand with the pin between his teeth *cannot* be over-powered, unless you want a posthumous medal for bravery. In case you are unsure, you can't put the pin back in once he's dropped the grenade. It *will* explode.

The most important piece of advice is to be ready to get out, if the opportunity comes. Some experienced travellers think it's "cool" to sleep through the safety announcements. It's more cool to know where the doors are, and to be sure how to open them. Think through the quickest way out, and have alternatives ready in case your exit is blocked. Think about how far down it is, and know about pulling the red handle if the chute does not come down. Remember that all this takes time, and that it will not be possible to get out of a door in the time that one of your captors has turned his back!

After twelve hours, they put me back with the rest of the passengers. The lights went out, because the generator had broken down. I could feel the tension increasing, and crouched as low as possible in my seat. For a reason which has never been established, they started shooting at random in the darkness, and throwing hand-grenades about. Some of the passengers decided that they had had enough, and opened the emergency doors. The man in the next seat told me to keep down, but I was not staying – the plane had been refuelled for an eight-hour flight. I pushed him in front of me towards one of the doors … I was out on the wing, looking for a way down … the chute had not come out automatically … I'm afraid of heights, but I jumped off the back of the wing without much hesitation (about two storeys up but still the lowest point) and ran away. Many people were hurt jumping off the wings because they had taken their shoes off to make themselves comfortable. Be ready, and move quickly.

It was a bloody event, with more than twenty dead and more than a hundred injured. I was very lucky to escape with a scratched elbow. But I was very unlucky to be hijacked in the first place – it *won't* happen to you!

SURVIVING A KIDNAP

by Daniel Start

Irian Jaya – Indonesian New Guinea – is a vast tropical wilderness of glacier-capped mountains, pristine rain forest and lowland swamps sparsely populated by tribal peoples living much as they have done for many thousands of years. It might seem an unlikely place to be taken "hostage" by "terrorists", both words being so modern in their connotation, but this is what happened to our group of twelve biologists in January 1996. It goes to show that no corner of the world is so remote and untouched that it can be assumed immune from such threats.

Closer to home is no safer. Spain and Italy, for instance, rank in the top ten of countries with most kidnappings in the world. Every country has some form of internal strife, some group that is fighting the state. Even if there is no history of kidnapping, there is no guarantee that one of these groups might not decide to take hostages as part of some crazy new strategy. However, if you are an independent traveller who stays on the beaten track and follows FCO or State Department advice closely the chances of ending up in shackles are negligible. But those people whose work, study or inquisitive nature takes them to more unusual places must do extra research.

Our group spent two years in preparation. We knew about the existence of the OPM Papuan independence movement and knew that the Indonesian military had committed atrocities in Irian Jaya. The missionaries, mining companies, governments and many other organisations that we consulted suggested there was no risk. It seemed a sensible conclusion. The atrocities were too far in the past, the current trouble spots were too far away from us and the OPM had too few supporters. We were all wrong. Resentment among a people lingers and spreads. The OPM had wide support and although they could not read or write and had only bows and arrows they were still very dangerous. It is essential to understand the history of an area; don't ever underestimate the risks and don't always believe the experts' advice, however much you want to.

When we first arrived by light aircraft at our remote village in the mountains everything seemed peaceful and trouble free. The village head men greeted us and smiled happily and for two months everything went very well. It is easy to be lulled into a false sense of security, and important to be aware that there may be other factions who see your arrival differently. In our case they numbered 200, were from the next valley and they ambushed us on 8 January 1996. We knew some of them already. Almost all of them were young men about our own age living normal Papuan lives. These are the type of people who make up most guerrilla outfits.

The ambush was a very frightening experience. The crowd had worked themselves into a frenzy and had painted bodies, head-dresses and machetes. We thought we would be killed but much of the aggressiveness was theatre and no harm was done to us. When it started to rain the mode seemed to pass, they introduced themselves as OPM rebels and we all went inside and ate lunch together.

At first we were worried that they would abuse the women (men in large phallic penis gourds can tend to look quite threatening) but none of the five women were seriously molested. One of the hostages was pregnant and greatly respected because they believed pregnant women could cast powerful curses. We made it clear that every woman was married to at least one of the men. We were also very concerned for the Indonesians – the obvious enemies of the Papuans. Thankfully the OPM had accepted that we were all there with good intentions so we were treated with respect; more like guests than prisoners.

In fact our group was seen as a gift from the Lord. White people are almost revered by the Papuans because of the work of the missionaries. In our case it was naïvely believed that we were so important and powerful that we could be traded for independence – a "free country". The child of the pregnant hostage was even thought to be the new Messiah who would lead the Papuans to victory. These interpretations helped to seal our fate. Be aware that other cultures may see things in radically different ways from us. To minimise the effect, keep visits short. It takes time for rumour and superstition to spread and even longer for people to act on it.

The first night in the village seemed quite exciting but it was so bizarre I found it difficult to take seriously. However, the next morning they said they were taking us into the forest to be hidden and I suddenly became very frightened. We packed up everything; about half a tonne of the stuff. Much of the useless equipment made good presents for people – even cameras and Walkmans were valued for their shiny components. As we were marched into the jungle I remembered the old army adage that "the longer one waits the harder it becomes to escape" and so I began to make many dare-devil plans. Thankfully I didn't attempt any but from then on I always kept a knife, compass, matches and iodine in my pocket – just in case.

At first we were sure it would all be over within days but quickly we realised the situation was very serious. For a start they said the baby – the new Messiah – had to be born on Papuan soil but it wasn't due for another six months. Our main fear though, was that the Indonesian military would come in and bomb the whole place and declare we had been murdered by the rebels. The OPM were as frightened of them as we were. Almost immediately we had common ground. First priority was to get news of our kidnap to the outside so that our embassies could stop the military wiping everyone out. As only one or two OPM men could read or write we prepared all the letters for them. They were sent out by runner to the nearest town (about one week away) but finally our short band radio was found and was used to negotiate with the missionaries. Thankfully in these first days we were able to communicate a lot of information about our situation. We also became very involved with the negotiations on the OPM's behalf and got quite carried away with our demands; thinking that we could organise both sides into compromising a little. It is tempting to think that your situation is a special case so always remember that no respectable authority will openly make concessions to terrorists.

This alliance with our captors ensured they treated us well. Many were very nervous at first and hid this with a false bravado which was fairly easy to break through. I made a concerted effort to joke and laugh with the men believing they would be less likely to kill me if they liked me. In fact we soon realised that all the OPM actively wanted to be our friends because it gave them status. We used this to our advantage by giving presents only to those who treated us well or seemed to think we should be released. It created competition and jealousy among the OPM and gave us more power.

While we also wanted the OPM to like us we had to be careful not to be too compliant. The odd refusal or confrontation made them think twice about asking us to do stupid things. As time went by we made a point of showing our frustration and unhappiness so they would not forget that they had taken innocent people prisoners.

Over the four months the conditions in the mountainous jungle were very harsh. We were moved 28 times; sometimes staying in pretty villages but more often being hidden in remote forest. Although we were never tied up and were able to wander around reasonably freely there was little chance of escape. Our captors knew we were almost totally dependent on them for food, shelter and direction.

Many of us got malaria, dysentery, tropical ulcers and infections but we had just enough basic medicines to treat ourselves. Thankfully we suffered no serious accidents and no run-ins with snakes or poisonous spiders. For me boredom and hunger were the worst things, especially when they were combined. You can only make conversation with your companions for so long. After that it is a matter of reliving old journeys, daydreaming, making plans or playing games – if you can find the material to make dice or a pack of cards. The OPM worked hard to find us what food they could (mainly sweet potatoes) but we soon learnt to appreciate anything that moved: frogs, rats, bats, tree kangaroos, weevils. More than once we got food poisoning from meat that was too old.

Food was so limited and we were so hungry that initially it was the cause of all major arguments. After a while we realised that if we could rise above our animal instincts and give a little extra rather than take a little extra the world became a much more pleasant place to be. Despite these conflicts, the entire group became very loyal to one another, like a family. However, it was a lonely time. You can't expect to find a soul mate in everyone. In a way this was good because we learnt to be strong, independent and self-supporting. This made us better able to take care of each other in a crisis. Images of family and home were very important in battling with depression and despair. Some found solace in fantasy worlds, others in prayer or meditation. Certainly we all rekindled the remnants of any faith we had once had.

The OPM promised many times to release us but not one promise was kept. There was so much conflicting news that it was tempting to attach too much significance to rumours of release. The disappointments were bitter and it took us several months before we realised that the most painless way to get through was to let go of our hopes of release. Once I had resigned myself to being there forever I began to appreciate the present more: the small things in life like a beautiful sunrise or a moment of shared laughter. I also gained comfort and enjoyment from simple habits and routines such as going to wash, collecting water or preparing food. The moment I stopped counting the hours the days seem to pass more quickly. Most important for me was understanding that the captivity wasn't wasted time, but an experience that would make me stronger and become an important part of who I was.

After about two months in captivity the Red Cross made contact. From then on we were able to receive and write letters to our families about once a fortnight. There were also medicines, books and food but soon the OPM came to enjoy the free presents so much that the Red Cross had to stop bringing in anything. This made the OPM angry but also focused their minds on the negotiations. Finally they agreed to hold a pig feast and release us on 8 May 1996 but at the last minute they refused. Perhaps they thought they should hold out for more. Maybe it was an act of angry defiance. Whatever, the next day we heard helicopters, gunfire and then a series of huge explosions (possibly blanks, but certainly powerful enough to blow down trees and start landslides).

This was the military operation we had dreaded. After an initial period of intense fear and panic we managed to think rationally. We had been told by the Red Cross that if things got nasty we should just lie down. But this was not an option as we had to get away from the house in case the military bombed it or the hard-line OPM came to get us. We heard about four helicopters circling trying to find us but the canopy was too thick. Then we heard a high pitch whine – which I now know were troopers being winched down into the forest. In hindsight probably we should have split up and hidden in the forest close by until the military found the house. Instead we made for a clearing from which we could signal but were intercepted by a group of OPM before we got there. We were taken into the mountains and for five days the military tracked us with sniffer dogs, a heat imaging camera mounted on a pilot-less drone and trackers who followed our footprints (the Papuans do not wear shoes). On the sixth day, quite unexpectedly and very calmly, our captors attacked us and executed the two Indonesian males. The rest of us were able to get away. We ran down to a river and there we found a small military patrol camped on the bank. The OPM had seen the patrol, realised everything was over and killed the Indonesians to show that they would not be beaten.

We were helicoptered out and looked after incredibly well by the Indonesian government and British Embassy but it was difficult to celebrate with the horror hanging over us. The press followed us everywhere and were such a problem that we decided to do an exclusive for one paper so that the others would leave us alone. Although we would have liked to address the political and human rights issues in a broad-sheet interview we were so confused and angry that we felt happier telling our story to a tabloid who would leave these things well alone. We chose the *Mail on Sunday* who did one big feature, treated us exceptionally well, reported very accurately and paid us enough to provide some security in the coming months of readjustment.

For a few weeks I found I was very nervous and frightened of simple things such as going outside alone. It was exhausting speaking to friends on the telephone and so instead everybody wrote. We were offered counselling by the Foreign Office but we needed to arrange it through our GPs and in the end it all seemed too much hassle and none of us bothered. I decided the best therapy was time with my family in Cornwall. Within three weeks I plucked up the courage to go and see friends in Cambridge and I was amazed at how quickly I was back in the swing of going to pubs and parties again. I felt very detached from my experiences in Irian Jaya, perhaps because they seemed so surreal. It might have been easy to pretend the whole thing never happened but I could feel the experience had changed me and I was not happy having all these unconscious emotions inside me. I decided to write a book, not only for catharsis but because I felt it was a story that needed to be told.

The book was a gruelling experience and it felt a little like a penance but the six months of writing helped me to come to terms with my anger and the guilt. When it was finished I found I had little idea what I wanted to do. But perhaps that is no bad thing. Being taken hostage teaches you that you never know what's around the corner…

See p.891 for a list of Red Cross and Red Crescent societies world-wide

THE EXECUTIVE TARGET

by Roy Carter

All over the world, in such diverse areas as Central America, or the Middle East, the level of politically-motivated violence increases almost daily. The victim's nationality – or supposed nationality – is often the sole reason for him or her being attacked. Gone forever are the days when kidnap and murder threatened only the wealthy and influential. Instead, political and religious fanatics often regard ordinary citizens as legitimate targets, and this view will become more prevalent as prominent people take ever more effective steps to protect themselves. The average traveller is much more vulnerable, but still worthy of publicity – which is generally the motive behind all terrorist action.

Measuring the Threat

Measuring the threat is difficult, if only because of conflicting definitions of what constitutes terrorist activity. Incidents involving civil aviation, however, afford a generally uncontentious barometer. In the decade to mid-1983, a fearsome total of 748 people were murdered world-wide in terrorist attacks against aircraft or airports. A similar number suffered serious injury, and the problem is by no means confined to the traditionally volatile areas of the world. Of 144 significant terrorist acts recorded against civil aviation in 1983, no less than 55 took place in Europe. Almost all the victims were innocent travellers. And it is self-evident that this single aspect of the problem represents only the tip of a much larger iceberg.

No one travelling to certain parts of the world can sensibly afford to ignore the danger. If the risk exists everywhere it naturally increases dramatically in known trouble spots. Nor is it wise to rely on the law of averages for protection. Terrorism and crime thrive on complacency and a fatalistic attitude can actually create danger. Awareness is vital, and it is surprisingly easy for any intelligent person to do the sort of homework that can pay life-saving dividends.

The first step is to understand something of the anatomy of political crime. Terrorist violence is rarely, if ever, carried out quite as randomly as it sometimes appears. Particularly in the case of kidnapping, the victim will first be observed – often for a period of days – for evidence of vulnerability.

Translating an awareness of the threat into a few simple precautions means offering a difficult target to people who want an easy one. Invariably they will look elsewhere. It is impossible to say how many lives have been saved in this way, because the threat, by its very nature, is covert, but the number is undoubtedly high. The huge majority of terrorist abductions are facilitated by the victim developing a regular pattern of behaviour, or being ignorant of the dangers in a strange country. No experienced traveller would forego vital inoculations or fail to enquire about the drinking water. Testing the political climate should be regarded as a natural extension of the same safeguards. After all, the object is the same, and the price of failure at least as high.

Of course, the most straightforward response to ominous events is simply to cancel or postpone the visit. In extremes this option should not be disregarded, but there will be occasions, especially for the business traveller, when such a drastic answer is difficult or impossible. An intelligent interest in the press and television news is a fundamental requirement in making the final decision. And sensible analysis of media reports will answer many questions about known trouble spots and help predict others. If nothing else, it will highlight areas for further study. Equally important, but easily overlooked, sound research can help put less serious situations into perspective. Unnecessary worry based on sensationalism or rumour can be a problem in itself.

Official Attitude

It is crucial to get a balanced idea of the official attitude in the country to be visited. The host government's status and its relationship with the visitor's country are always critical factors. A basically hostile or unstable government will always increase the danger to individual travellers, either directly, or by such indirect means as ineffective policing. A recent example of the former risk was seen very clearly in the imprisonment of British businessmen in both Libya and Nigeria, following diplomatic rows. The latter risk is exemplified on a regular basis in the Lebanon, Mozambique and Angola.

Finding the truth will usually involve delving below the headlines. In Britain, an approach to the Foreign Office can produce surprisingly frank answers. Next, and more obviously, an analysis of recent terrorist activity should aim to answer three essential questions: when and where it happens, what form it takes and, most importantly, whom is it directed against? The first two answers help establish precautionary measures. The third may indicate the degree of risk by revealing common factors. A series of identical abductions from motor vehicles in a particular part of the city, involving the same nationalities or professions, for example, should be augury enough for even the most sceptical observer.

Local Feeling

It is also as well to know as much as possible about feelings among the local populace, which are by no means guaranteed to be the same as those of the government. National identity, and even religion, are often viewed quite differently "on the streets", although the bias is just as likely to be favourable as not. One need not even step outside the UK to demonstrate the validity of this advice, as an Englishman on the streets of West Belfast could quickly discover. And in a country with a large Western expatriate community, for instance, any Caucasian will generally be regarded as belonging to the predominant race. Depending on the local situation, this type of mistaken identity can be dangerous or advantageous. At least one case, the March 1985 abduction of three British visitors to Beirut by anti-American Muslim extremists, resulted from a mistake in the victims' nationality.

These attacks, and others involving French and US citizens, took place outside the victims' homes, highlighting perfectly standard terrorist methods. Known reference points such as home or places of work, are always by far the most dangerous. The much-publicised kidnap and subsequent murder of former Italian premier, Aldo Moro, by the so-called Red Brigade was a notable example of this fact.

Soft Targets

Importantly, but often forgotten, this demonstrates more than a need for extra care at home and in the office. It shows equally the terrorist's need for soft targets and their reluctance to proceed beyond basic research to find them. Terrorist resources and abilities are limited and to regard them as omnipotent is both mistaken and dangerous. Sensible precautions, like varying times of arrival and departure, parking in different places – facing in different directions, watching for and reporting suspicious activity before leaving home, and entering and leaving by different doors, sound almost too simple, but they really do work. Only the most specific kind of motivation would justify continued surveillance of a clearly unpredictable and cautious target.

Company Image

In addition to this kind of general precaution, the business traveller will usually need to examine more particular issues. He will need to know how his company is perceived by various local factions. Previous threats or attacks on company employees should be studied with great care, as should incidents involving similar organisations. Where applicable, the local knowledge of expatriate colleagues will be useful, but watch for bias or over-familiarity. In the absence of any actual events, examine the company's standing in the community, especially where a conflict of interest exists between government and opposition groups. Never forget that a company will often be judged solely on the basis of its clients and associates. Always consider the status of the people you intend to visit. In these days of trade sanctions and mutually antagonistic markets, the chances are high that any association will offend someone.

Practical Action

But analysis is only a partial answer. The results must be translated into coherent action. In extreme cases, the business traveller might need special training in such areas as defensive driving, emergency communication and surveillance recognition. Many of the larger companies will provide special briefings but their failure to do so should never be taken as a sign that no danger exists. It could equally indicate a lack of awareness or a misguided decision not to cause alarm. There is nothing at all wrong with alarm if it is justified. It may even be a necessity.

Regardless of whether special training is given or not, all travellers to high-risk areas should follow certain basic rules as a matter of course. Keep friends and colleagues informed of your whereabouts and stay in company as much as possible. Use inconspicuous transport but avoid public transport in favour of taxis. If in doubt, wait for the second cab in the rank. Never take a taxi if the driver is not alone. Dress down and leave expensive accessories at home. Don't book hotels in the company's name. In all, practise being nondescript in public.

Try not to think of these rules as an inconvenience, but as a natural consequence of your stay in a strange country, like remembering to use a foreign language. Relaxing one rule might be tempting but it could be the mistake that negates all the rest. Better to extend precautions than limit them. For example, travelling regularly by the same route can undo all the good work on the home front. The kidnap and murder of German industrialist Hans-Martin Schleyer was carried out because his attackers were able to predict confidently both his route and timing. The murder in India of British diplomat Percy Norris by Middle Eastern terrorists likewise occurred along his regular route to work. Mr Norris was shot to death in the back seat of his chauffeur–driven car when it halted at traffic lights.

On the Move

Make a habit of changing places in the car if you have a driver or use a taxi now and then instead. The chances of being attacked on the move are extremely remote. It follows that road junctions, traffic signals, etc. are always more dangerous than, say, stretches of dual carriageway. A prospective attacker will study his victim's route carefully and identify vulnerable spots. If he can do so, so can you. Be aware of these danger areas and stay on the alert when negotiating them. If driving yourself, keep the car in gear and ready for a quick getaway at temporary halts. Keep sufficient space between yourself and any leading vehicles to avoid being boxed in. Routinely lock all doors and keep the windows wound up.

Last of all, remember that you stand more chance of being an accident casualty than a terrorist victim. Far from being dangerous, a little knowledge can stack the odds even higher in your favour. You'll probably never know if it passes the acid test – but you'll be in no doubt at all if it doesn't.

SAFETY AND SURVIVAL AT SEA

by Robin Knox-Johnston

A very sensible list of safety equipment to be carried on board a boat is published by the Offshore Racing Council (ORC) in their 1994/5 Special Regulations Governing Offshore Racing. The list is extensive, but because it is comprehensive, it is given below:

2 Fire extinguishers; accessible and in different places
2 Manually operated bilge pumps
2 Buckets; strong construction, fitted with lanyards
2 Anchors and cables (chain for cruising is sensible)
2 Flashlights; water resistant and capable of being used for signalling, with spare bulbs and batteries
1 Foghorn
1 Radar reflector
1 Set of International Code Flags and a code book
1 Set of emergency navigation lights
1 Storm trysail
1 Storm jib
1 Emergency tiller
1 Tool kit
1 Marine radio transmitter and receiver
1 Radio, capable of receiving weather forecasts
Life-jackets: sufficient for the whole crew
1 Buoyant heaving line at least 50 feet (16m) long
2 Life buoys or rings
1 Set of distress signals
12 Red parachute flares
4 Red hand flares
4 White hand flares
2 Orange smoke day signals
1 Life-raft of a capacity to take the whole crew, which has: a valid annual test certificate; two separate buoyancy compartments; a canopy to cover the occupants; a sea anchor and drogue; bellows or pump to maintain pressure; a signalling light; 3 hand flares; a baler repair kit; 2 paddles; a knife; emergency water and rations; a first-aid kit and manual.
In addition, it is worth carrying a portable, waterproof VHF radio and an emergency distress transmitter (E.P.I.R.B.)

Medical

The health of the crew is the Skipper's responsibility and he or she should see that the food is nourishing and sufficient, that the boat is kept clean and that the crew practise basic hygiene. A good medical kit must be carried.

There is an excellent book (published by HMSO for the British Merchant Navy) called *The Ship Captain's Medical Guide*. It is written for a ship that does not carry a doctor and includes a recommended list of medical supplies. Most doctors will supply prescriptions for antibiotics when the purpose has been explained. Two other books to recommend are *The International Medical for Ships*, published by the World Health Organisation and *First Aid at Sea*, by Douglas Justins and Colin Berry (Adlard Coles Nautical, London)

Safety on Deck

Prevention is always better than cure. Everyone on board should know their way about the deck, and know what everything is for. A good way of training is to take the boat out night sailing so that the crew get to know instinctively where everything is and what to avoid. Train the crew to squat whenever the boat lurches – it lowers the centre of gravity and makes toppling overside less likely.

In rough weather, make sure that all the crew wear their life-jackets and safety harnesses when on deck, and that they clip their harness to a strong point. If the crew have to go out from the cockpit, they should clip the harness to a wire which runs down the middle (the length of the boat) for this purpose.

Man Overboard

If someone falls overside, immediately summon the whole crew on deck and throw a lifebuoy to the person in the water. The problem is to get back and pick them up as quickly as possible, so post a look-out to keep an eye on the casualty, and the rest of the crew should assist with turning the boat around. It is worthwhile putting the boat straight in the wind, as this stops you close to the casualty, then start the engine and motor back. On one occasion in the Southern Ocean, we lost a man overside, and we ran on more than half a mile before we could get the spinnaker down. The only way we could see him when we turned round was by the sea-birds that were circling him. We got him back, after about twenty minutes, by which time he was unable to assist himself because of the cold.

In the upper latitudes, there is a real danger from hypothermia and it is vital to warm the person as quickly as possible. Strip off their wet clothing and towel them dry, then put them in a warm sleeping bag. The heat is retained better if the sleeping bag can be put into a plastic bag. If the person is very cold, it may be necessary for someone else to strip and climb into the bag with the casualty and warm them with their own body.

If the casualty is conscious, feed them hot soup or tea. Remember that it can be a nerve-shattering experience and that they may need time to get over the shock.

Abandoning the Boat

When, as a last resort, it becomes necessary to leave the boat, inflate the life-raft and pull it alongside. Put one or two of the crew on board, and, if there is time, pass over as much food, water and clothing as possible, plus the Distress Beacon. If the boat's dinghy is available, tie it to the life-raft, as it will give extra space and also help create a larger target. Only leave the boat if there is absolutely no alternative. Life-rafts are small and not particularly robust, and it is always preferable to keep the boat afloat if humanly possible.

The usual reason for abandoning a boat is that it has been holed. One method of improving its survivability is to fit it with watertight bulkheads so that its volume is roughly divided into three. This is now a rule for the BOC Challenge Around Alone Race, and means that if the boat is holed, the chances are that it will lose only one third of its buoyancy and there will still be dry, safe shelter for the crew. From the comparative safety of one of the "safe" parts of the boat, a plan can probably be made to fix the leak.

When it is necessary to abandon the boat, having got as much food and useful equipment aboard as possible, cut the painter and get clear. Then take stock of what you have, and post a look-out. Activate the Distress Beacon to alert aircraft and ships to the fact that someone is in distress.

Ration supplies from the start. The best way to do this is to avoid food for the first day, as the stomach shrinks and the body's demand for food falls. Ration water to about half a pint (quarter of a litre) a day and issue it in sips. On no account should sea water be drunk, but it can be used for washing and cooling in hot weather. Humans can last for amazingly long times without food, but they do need water. Any rain should be trapped and saved. The canopy of the life-raft can be used for this purpose, as could the dinghy if it has been taken along. Unless there is a plentiful water supply, do not eat raw fish as they are very rich in protein and ruin the liver unless the surplus can be washed out of the system. As a general rule, one volume of protein will require two volumes of water. Where water is plentiful, fish should be hunted. Most pelagic fish are edible, and quite often they will swim around a boat or dinghy out of curiosity. Inedible fish are found close to land or on reefs.

Keep movement to a minimum to conserve energy, and in cold weather, hold onto urine as long as possible to retain its heat. In hot, sunny weather, try to keep everyone in the shade. Find some mental stimulus in order to maintain morale, and remember that the crew will be looking to the skipper to set an example, so remain positive. Humans have survived for well over three months on a life-raft, but only because they had a strong will to live and were able to improvise. My book *Seamanship* (Hodder and Stoughton) may prove useful further reading.

See also **Sailing** *by Robin Knox-Johnston in Chapter 6, p.277*

SURVIVAL IN THE DESERT

by Jack Jackson

The most important thing about desert survival is to avoid the need for it in the first place! Know your vehicle's capabilities and do not overload it. Know how to maintain and repair it. Carry adequate spares and tools. Be fit yourselves and get sufficient sleep. Start your journey with 25 per cent more fuel and water than was calculated as necessary to cover extra problems such as bad terrain, leaking containers and extra time spent over repairs or sitting out a bad sandstorm.

Know accurately where your next supplies of fuel and water are. Carry plastic sheets to make desert stills; carry space blankets. Carry more than one compass and know how to navigate properly. Use magnetic compasses well away from vehicles and cameras. Do not rely exclusively on electronic Global Positioning Systems, or the batteries that power them and do not leave the piste unless you really do know what you are doing. Travel only in the local winter months. Know how correct your odometer is for the wheels and tyres fitted to the vehicle. Make notes of distances, compass bearings and obvious landmarks as you go along, so you can retrace your route easily if you have to.

Observe correct check-in and out procedures with local authorities. Preferably convoy with other vehicles. When lost, do not continue. Stop, think and, if necessary, retrace your route.

Back-up Plans

If you are a large party, you should arrange a search and rescue plan before you start out. This would include the use and recognition of radio beacons or flares for aircraft search. Many countries do not allow you to use radio communication; but if you can use them, carry modern portable satellite communications.

For most people, an air search is highly unlikely and high-flying commercial passenger aircraft overhead are unlikely to notice you whatever you do. A search, if it does come, will be along the piste or markers. Most often this will just be other vehicles travelling through being asked by the local authorities to look out for you because you have failed to check in.

Local drivers will not understand or appreciate coloured flares, so your best signal for outside help is fire. If you hear a vehicle at night, cardboard boxes or wood are quickly and easily lit, but during the day you need lots of thick black smoke. The best fuel for this is a tyre. Bury most of a tyre in the sand to control the speed at which it burns (keep it well away from and down wind of the vehicles or fuel) and start the exposed part burning with a rag soaked in either petrol or diesel fuel. As the exposed part of the tyre burns away, you can uncover more from the sand to keep it going, or cover all of it with sand if you wish to put out the fire. Avoid inhaling the sulphurous fumes. Headlights switched on and off at night can also be used while the battery still has charge.

If you are found by aircraft, the International Ground/Air Code, for wanting to be picked up, is to stand up with your arms held aloft, in an obvious "V" shape.

A Need to Survive

Once you are in a "need to survive" situation, the important things are morale and water. Concentrate on getting your vehicles moving again. This will keep you occupied and help to keep up morale. To minimise water loss, avoid manual work during the day, work at night or in the early morning. Build shade and stay under it as much as possible, keeping well covered with loose cotton clothing. "Space blankets", with the reflective side facing out make the coolest shade. Keep warm and out of the wind at night. In really hot climates, replacing lost potassium with Slow K can make a big difference to your general alertness.

Unless you are well off the piste with no chance of a search, you should stay with your vehicle. If someone must walk out, pick one or two of the strongest and most determined persons to go. They must have a compass, torch, salt, anti-diarrhoea medicine, loose, all-enveloping clothes, good footwear, good sunglasses and as much water as they can sensibly carry. In soft sand, a jerry can of water can easily be hauled along on a rope from the waist. On mixed ground, tie the jerry can to a sand ladder, one end of which is padded and tied to the waist.

Those who walk out should follow the desert nomad pattern of walking in the evening till about 2300 hours, sleep until 0400 hours, walk again till 1000 hours, then dig a shallow hollow in the sand and lie in it under a space blanket, reflective side out, until the sun has lost its heat. If they have a full moon they can walk all night. In this way, fit men would make 60 to 70 kilometres on ten litres of water – less in soft sand.

Water

In a "sit it out and survive" situation, with all manual labour kept to a minimum, food is unimportant and dehydration staves off hunger, but water is *vital*. The average consumption of water in a hot, dry climate should be eight litres a day. This can be lowered to four litres a day in a real emergency. Diarrhoea increases dehydration, so should be controlled by medicine where necessary. Salt intake should be kept up. Licking your bare arms will replace some lost salt.

Water supply should be improved by making as many desert stills as possible. To make one, dig a hole about one third of a metre deep and one metre in circumference, place a clean saucepan or billy in the centre of the hole with a two metre square plastic sheet weighted down with stones, jerry cans or tools, at the edges. Put one stone or similar object in the centre to weigh it down directly over the billy. Overnight, water vapour from the sand will evaporate and then condense on the underside of the plastic sheet. In the morning, running a finger down from the edge to the centre of the sheet will cause the condensation to run down and drip into the pan. All urine should be conserved and put into shallow containers around the central billy can. The water so collected should be boiled or sterilised before drinking.

If you have anti-freeze in your radiator, *don't* try to drink it as it is *highly poisonous*. Even if you have not put anti-freeze in the radiator yourselves, there is still likely to be some left in it from previous use, or from the factory when the vehicle was first manufactured. Radiator water should be put into the desert still in the same way as the urine and the resulting condensate should be boiled or sterilised before drinking. Water from bad or brackish wells can be made drinkable in the same way. Note, however, that solar stills can take a lot of energy to create and will yield little water in return. Until the situation is really desperate, they are probably not worth considering as a viable means of collecting water.

The minimum daily water required to maintain the body's water balance at rest, in the shade, is as follows: If the mean daily temperature is 35°C, then you will need 5.3litres per 24 hours. If 30°C, then 2.4 litres, if 25°C then 1.2 litres, if 20°C and below then 1.0 litres. It must be stressed that this is for survival. There will be a gradual kidney malfunction and possibly urinary tract infection, with women more at risk than men.

The will to live is essential. Once you give up, you will be finished. If you find people in such a situation and do not have a doctor to handle them, feed them water (to which has been added one level teaspoon of salt and two tablespoons of sugar per litre of water), a teaspoonful at a time, every few minutes for a couple of hours. It is essential to try to stabilise them in this way before trying to take them on a long tough drive to hospital. Sachets of salts for rehydration are available for your medical kit.

See also Off-Road Driving by Jack Jackson in Chapter 5, p.233

SURVIVAL IN THE JUNGLE
by Robin Hanbury-Tenison

The key to survival in the tropics is comfort. If your boots fit, your clothes don't itch, your wounds don't fester, you have enough to eat and you have the comforting presence of a local who is at home in the environment, then you are not likely to go far wrong.

Of course, jungle warfare is something else. The British, Americans and, for all I know, several other armies, have produced detailed manuals on how to survive under the most arduous conditions imaginable and with the minimum of resources. But most of us are extremely unlikely ever to find ourselves in such a situation. Even if you are unlucky enough to be caught in a guerrilla war or survive an air crash in the jungle, I believe that the following advice will be as useful as trying to remember sophisticated techniques which probably require equipment you do not have to hand anyway.

A positive will to survive is essential. The knowledge that others have travelled long distances and lived for days and even months without help or special knowledge gives confidence, while a calm appraisal of the circumstances can make them seem far less intimidating. The jungle need not be an uncomfortable place, although unfamiliarity may make it seem so. Morale is as important as ever, and comfort, both physical and mental, a vital ingredient.

Clothing and Footwear

To start with, it is usually warm, but when you are wet, especially at night, you can become very cold very quickly. It is therefore important to be prepared and always try to keep a sleeping bag and a change of clothes dry. Excellent strong, lightweight plastic bags are now available in which these items should always be packed with the top folded over and tied. These can then be placed inside your rucksack or bag so that if dropped in a river or soaked by a sudden tropical downpour – and the effect is much the same – they, at least, will be dry. I usually have three such bags, one with dry clothes, one with camera equipment, notebooks, etc., and one with food. Wet clothes should be worn. This is unpleasant for the first ten minutes in the morning, but they will soon be soaking wet with sweat and dripping in any case, and wearing them means you need carry only one change for the evening and sleeping in. It is well worth taking the time to rinse them out whenever you are in sunshine by a river so that you can dry them on hot rocks in half an hour or so. They can also be hung over the fire at night which makes them more pleasant to put on in the morning, but also tends to make them stink of wood smoke.

Always wear loose clothes in the tropics. They may not be very becoming but constant wetting and drying will tend to shrink them and rubbing makes itches and scratches far worse. Cotton is excellent but should be of good quality so that the clothes do not rot and tear too easily.

For footwear, baseball boots or plimsolls are usually adequate but for long distances good leather boots will protect your feet much better from bruising and blisters. In leech country, a shapeless cotton stocking worn between sock and shoe tied with a drawstring below the knee, outside long trousers, gives virtually complete protection. As far as I know, no one manufactures these yet, so they have to be made up specially, but they are well worth it.

Upsets and Dangers

Hygiene is important in the tropics. Small cuts can turn nasty very quickly and sometimes will not heal for a long time. The best protection is to make an effort to wash all over at least once a day if possible, at the same time looking out for any sore places, cleaning and treating them at once. On the other hand, where food and drink are concerned, it is usually not practical or polite to attempt to maintain perfectionist standards. Almost no traveller in the tropics can avoid receiving hospitality and few would wish to do so. It is often best therefore to accept that a mild stomach upset is likely – and be prepared

In real life and death conditions, there are only two essentials for survival, a knife or machete and a compass (provided you are not injured, when if possible the best thing to do is to crawl to water and wait for help). Other important items I would put in order of priority as follows:

1. A map
2. A waterproof cover, cape or large bag
3. Means of making fire, lifeboat matches or a lighter with spare flints, gas or petrol
4. A billy can
5. Tea or coffee, sugar and dried milk.

There are few tropical terrains which cannot be crossed with these, given time and determination. Man can survive a long time without food, so try to keep your food supplies simple, basic and light. Water is less of a problem in the jungle, except in limestone mountains, but a metal water container should be carried and filled whenever possible. Rivers, streams and even puddles are unlikely to be dangerously contaminated, while *rattans* and *lianas* often contain water as do some other plants whose leaves may form catchments, such as pitcher plants. It is easy to drink from these, though best to filter the liquid through cloth and avoid the "gunge" at the bottom.

Hunting and trapping are unlikely to be worth the effort to the inexperienced, although it is surprising how much can be found in streams and caught with hands. Prawns, turtles, frogs and even fish can be captured with patience and almost all are edible – and even tasty if you're hungry enough. Fruits, even ripe and being eaten by other animals are less safe while some edible-looking plants and fungi can be very poisonous and should be avoided. Don't try for the honey of wild bees unless you know what you are doing as stings can be dangerous and those of hornets even fatal.

As regards shelter, there is a clear distinction between South America and the rest of the tropical world. In the South American interior, almost everyone uses a hammock. Excellent waterproof hammocks are supplied to the Brazilian and US armies and may be obtainable commercially. Otherwise, a waterproof sheet may be stretched across a line tied between the same two trees from which the hammock is slung. Elsewhere, however, hammocks are rarely used and will tend to be a nuisance under normal conditions. Lightweight canvas stretchers through which poles may be inserted before being tied apart on a raised platform make excellent beds and once again a waterproof sheet provides shelter. Plenty of nylon cord is always useful.

Fight It or Like It

The jungle can be a frightening place at first. Loud noises, quantities of unfamiliar creepy crawlies, flying biting things and the sometimes oppressive heat can all conspire to get you down. But it can also be a very pleasant place if you decide to like it rather than fight it – and it is very seldom dangerous. Snakebite, for example, is extremely rare. During the fifteen months of the Royal Geographical Society's Mulu Expedition, in Borneo, no one was bitten, although we saw and avoided or caught and photographed many snakes and even ate some! Most things, such as thorns, ants and sandflies are more irritating than painful (taking care to treat rather than scratch usually prevents trouble).

Above all, the jungle is a fascinating place – the richest environment on earth. The best help for morale is to be interested in what is going on around you and the best guide is usually a local resident who is as at home there as most of us are in cities. Fortunately, in most parts of the world where jungles survive, there are still such people. By accepting their advice, recognising their expertise and asking them to travel with you, you may help to reinforce their self-respect in the face of often overwhelming forces which try to make them adopt a so-called "modern" way of life. At the same time, you will appreciate the jungle far more yourself – and have a far better chance of surviving in it.

SURVIVAL IN THE COLD

by Dr Mike Stroud

"The wind was blowing briskly as I stepped out of the tent, but the sun was shining and it didn't feel too bad. When I had been out earlier, briefly, answering nature's call, the air had been still, and despite it being minus 40°C it had seemed quite warm in the sunshine. I had decided to wear only a cotton windproof over underwear and fleece salopettes. It was amazing how little one needed to keep warm as long as you kept on working hard.

Ran and I took down the tent and packed up our sledges. The South Pole was only 30 kms away and with luck we would reach it within two days. It helped to have it so close. We had been going twelve hours a day for more than two months, and the effort had taken a terrible toll. It had been both mental and physical hell. It was not long after we set off that I realised my mistake. As well as only putting on a single jacket, I was wearing only thin contact gloves inside outer mitts and after an hour with the wind rising even more my hands were suffering badly and not warming up despite moving. They became so bad that Ran had to help me put on the extra mittens from my sledge, my fingers were too useless to get them on. When we set off again, I was getting generally chilled. After the long stop fighting with the gloves, I found that I could barely pull the sledge with my cold muscles. I was in trouble, and I realised I would have to stop and put my fleece jacket on as well, but to do this meant removing my outer jacket completely and once again my fingers were useless and I was unable to do up the zips. Ran was there to help again, but I had entered a vicious circle. My thinking was beginning to fade, and although I kept walking for another half-hour or so, I was never with it. It was only through Ran's description, that I know what happened next.

I had apparently begun to move very slowly and to wander from side to side. When Ran asked if I was okay, I had been unintelligible, and he had realised immediately that I must be hypothermic. He then tried to get me to help with the tent, but I just stood around doing nothing. So he put it up alone and pushed me inside. Eventually he got me in my sleeping bag and forced me to take some hot drinks. After an hour or so I recovered, but it had been another close call. Obviously we were getting vulnerable and we discussed pulling out at the Pole..."

The above is an excerpt from my book *Shadows on the Wasteland* about my crossing of Antarctica with Sir Ranulph Fiennes. Under the circumstances, it was perhaps not surprising that I became hypothermic, for cold easily creates casualties and can even kill. Yet, with the correct preparation, man can operate successfully even in the harshest of climates. The secret is to match the body's heat production – chiefly dictated by activity – with its heat losses – chiefly governed by clothing and shelter. You should aim to neither overheat nor cool down. Both can have unwelcome consequences.

An inactive adult produces about a light bulb's worth of heat (100 Watts), which is not really much to keep the whole body warm in the face of the cold, wind and rain. It is therefore generally wise to keep moving for the most of the time in cold conditions until you have either reached or created proper shelter. However, many reasons, such as getting lost or injured, may force you to halt or lie up under adverse circumstances and you are then going to need to reduce your heat losses to less than the 100 watts that you will be producing. This may be an impossibility if ill-equipped or conditions are really harsh. If you can't reduce heat losses enough, your body will cool and you will start to shiver. This can increase your resting heat production to as much as 500 watts, but even this may be inadequate and the shivering itself is uncomfortable and tiring for the muscles. If cooling still continues, you will become hypothermic and can be in great danger. It is definitely best to carry enough protection to deal with getting stuck out in the worst possible conditions you may meet.

When you are active, things are quite different. Working hard leads the body to produce as much as a good room heater – 2000 watts or even more. It is therefore more common to get too hot rather than too cold, even in the worst conditions. Initially, getting too hot may not be important, but it does lead to sweating which can ruin the insulation of your clothing by wetting it from the inside and later, when you have decreased your activity or the conditions have worsened, this wet clothing will have lost its ability to protect you properly. Sweating may also lead to dehydration which in turn will make you vulnerable to fatigue, and it is with the onset of tiredness and then slowing up, that heat production will start to fall and you will cool rapidly to become at risk from the "exhaustion/hypothermia" syndrome. Even the most experienced of people have become victims under such circumstances.

In order to match heat losses to heat production, clothing must have the flexibility to be both cool and warm. It must also be able to provide windproofing and waterproofing. Such flexibility can only be achieved by the use of layers which must be easy to put on and take off and comfortable to wear together. In all but the very coldest regions – where rain or melting snow won't occur – I would favour the use of modern synthetics in the insulation layers which tend not to degrade very much when wetted by sweat or the environment, and which also dry spectacularly quickly. If affordable, waterproofs/windproofs should be moisture vapour permeable (MVP) since these will limit the accumulation of sweat and condensation in inner garments and will allow the evaporation of some sweat which will help to keep you cool if overheating. However, it needs to be remembered that even MVP garments are only partially vapour permeable (especially in the cold when water vapour will condense or even freeze on the inner surface of the garment and will then be trapped by its waterproof qualities) and so it is always better to remove the waterproof if it is not actually raining and activity is making you too hot.

Additional flexibility when trying to maintain a comfortable body temperature can be granted by changing your head covering. In the cold, when wearing good clothing, as much as ninety per cent of your heat losses can come from your head, so by putting on or taking off a warm hat or balaclava and by adjusting a windproof hood, you can make enormous changes to your heat losses much more easily than by adjusting other garments. It is often said that if you get cold hands you should put on a hat.

Eating is also an important factor in keeping warm. Even at rest a meal will rev up your metabolism and make that 100 watt bulb glow brighter, while during exercise it will considerably increase your heat output for any given level of activity. More importantly, food also helps to sustain the supply of fuels to the muscles and this will allow you to continue working, or for that matter shivering, for longer. In addition, it will make it much less likely that you will develop a low blood sugar – a factor now thought to be important in the onset of some cases of exposure/exhaustion. Almost any food will help, but it is probably best for it to contain a fair amount of carbohydrate. Grain-based snack bars are as good as anything, but snacks based on chocolate are also excellent, even if there is a greater fat content.

When hypothermia does begin to occur in an individual, a number of changes are seen which make the diagnosis pretty easy as long as the possibility is carefully considered. Unfortunately, the person suffering from the cold is often unable to consider things properly, since he or she may not realise what is happening and often, after feeling cold, shivery and miserable initially, they may feel quite happy and even warm. It therefore goes without saying that a problem may only become evident when things have already become quite bad, and that if a victim is alone or everybody in a party becomes hypothermic simultaneously, things are very serious. The signs to watch out for are quite similar to those seen with becoming increasingly drunk. At first the victim may slur speech and begin to be unnaturally happy with the situation. This normally corresponds to a core temperature of around 35°C compared to the normal 37°C, although the actual temperature varies from individual to individual and some people feel quite unwell at 36°C. Then, as cooling continues, the victim may begin to stumble or stagger and may go on to become aggressive or confused. This often correlates with a core temperature of around 33-34°C. Eventually, at a core temperature of around 32°C, they will collapse and become unconscious, and they can go on cooling to stop breathing at around 27°C. However, their heart may not stop until core temperature is as low as 22°C and so it is vital to remember that however bad things seem, attempting rewarming and resuscitation may still work.

When someone first starts getting cold, act quickly by increasing clothing insulation, increasing activity or by seeking shelter. However, if choosing to shelter, remember that it may entail lying up in bad conditions and the loss of activity will cut heat production right down. This may have devastating results, and so the decision to go on or to seek emergency protection requires great judgement. Generally, I would recommend that if the victim is only just beginning to cool, push on if proper warm conditions are likely to be reached reasonably quickly. Hot drinks and food are also of great value and will only be helpful while the victim is conscious and cooperative. Once again, however, remember that sitting around preparing them may have adverse effects.

If the victim is worse and is actually showing signs of staggering or confusion, the situation is becoming dangerous. Obviously additional clothing, hot drinks, or seeking a course out of the wind remain of paramount importance, but the question of carrying on becomes more difficult since now it is probably better to stop if reasonable shelter is available. When going out in cold environments, you should always plan to carry some sort of windproof and waterproof bivouac protection – noting that, although tempting weight-wise, lightweight silvered survival blankets have been shown to be no more effective than a plastic sheet and definitely worse than a plastic or more rugged waterproof bag. You may of course be planning on camping anyway, in which case you need only ensure that your tent is adequate and that you have practised pitching it when the wind is up. It is no good finding out that it cannot be done with your model when you need it in emergency. Ideally, you should also be carrying a sleeping bag even if you had no plans to get trapped outside, for there is no doubt that putting a victim in a good bag, and if necessary getting in it with them, is the best course of action if you are forced to stop.

Obviously, shelter can be sought as well as carried. In an emergency it is a nice warm building that is best, but this is not normally an option. The priority then becomes getting out of the wind and wet, and any natural feature that you can get under or into the lee of is of great value. Also remember that effective shelter may often be found close in on the windward side of an object, particularly if it has a vertical side which will generate back pressure and a "dead spot" immediately in front of it. Much to many people's surprise, the shelter there may even be better than to leeward since swirling vortices of snow do not come curling round and drifting over you. In conditions with decent snow cover, compacted snow or ice can be used to create a whole range of possible shelters ranging from simple snowholes to multiple roomed camps, but really you need to have been taught how to make them and be carrying a suitable snow shovel. Reading about building such shelters cannot replace experience and before going out in really severe conditions one should have practised in safe conditions. Ideally you should have attended a proper course on winter survival such as those run by the British Mountaineering Council in Scotland or North Wales.

If a victim has cooled so much that they are unconscious, they need medical attention urgently. However, while this is sought or awaited, every measure mentioned above should be made to protect them from further cooling. As a general rule, never give up trying to protect and warm them, even if they appear to be dead. People have been successfully resuscitated many hours after they have apparently stopped breathing and you cannot rely upon being able to feel a pulse or hear their heart. It is said the hypothermia victims are "not dead until they are warm and dead", and so generally it is impossible to be sure while you are still out in the field.

I would reiterate that with the correct preparation you can operate safely and relatively comfortably in terrible conditions but doing so is an art. That art needs to be learned and it is a mixture of education, preparation and forethought. Remember that hypothermia could happen to you or one or your party even in a temperate climate and indeed, it is more likely to happen in milder wetter conditions than in the truly cold regions of the Earth.

I will finish with an anecdote that illustrates just how easy it is to be caught out, and how simple it is to remedy the situation.

"As he approached, I wondered what was wrong. He was moving slowly and seemed to be fiddling with his clothing, trying to undo the zip on the front of his sodden jacket. He was smiling and certainly looked happier than he had done fifteen minutes back but I noticed that he stumbled a couple of times despite it being pretty flat. He drew up beside me where I stood with my back to the gale.

"Jusht a moment," he said, and then after quite a pause, "I've jusht got to get thish jacket off."

His voice was slurred and I looked at him more closely. Although he smiled, there was a strange, wild expression on his face and his eyes were slightly glazed. He wasn't shivering any more but his skin was as white as marble and I noticed that he had taken his gloves off and they were nowhere to be seen. He was also swaying as he began to almost rip at his clothing, frustrated by his fruitless attempts to pull down the zip with cold fingers.

"Are you OK?" I asked, but I got no reply, only an inane black grin as he continued with his attempts to undress. The truth began to dawn on me.

"Come on," I said, grasping him by the arm and pulling him towards the edge of the ridge. "We'll go down here and drop out of the wind."

The effect was quite spectacular. As we entered the lee of the Cwm the noise and buffeting that we had endured all day ceased and the world became an almost silent place. It seemed so much warmer that as I hurried downward, I began to sweat, but for my companion who I almost dragged along beside me, the move into shelter brought a different experience. Although he too began to warm, it only brought him back towards the normal and with it he began to shiver and feel miserably cold.

I could scarcely believe what I had just witnessed. It was only September on Snowdon, yet my father had been to the edge of disaster ...”

Remember, always treat the cold with respect and never underestimate what even the UK weather can produce.

Additional Information

by Dr Richard Dawood

Colonel Jim Adam, the military physiologist until recently responsible for maintaining "combat-effectiveness" of British troops under all conditions, advises observing the following steps in the event of hypothermia:

1. Stop all activity.
2. Protect those at risk by rigging a make-shift shelter from the wind, rain and snow; lay the victim on the ground, on a ground sheet or space blanket.
3. Remove wet clothing, and insulate the victim in a sleeping bag.
4. Re-warm the victim with hot drinks, followed by hot food or high-energy snacks; unconscious victims need to be rewarmed by the body warmth of a companion.
5. Observe the victim for the cessation of breathing or pulse, and start mouth-to-mouth resuscitation or cardiac massage if necessary.
6. Send for help.
7. Insist on treating the victim as a stretcher case.

Acute Hypothermia

This is a medical emergency, and is almost always the result of falling into water colder than 5°C: the victim shivers violently, inhales water, panics, may have respiratory or cardiac arrest, and is dead from drowning in about five to fifteen minutes. Survival is more likely if the victim is wearing a life-jacket that keeps the face out of the water, and is able to keep perfectly still.

Careful first-aid is essential. Following rescue from the water, do not allow the victim to move or make any physical effort. Keep the victim horizontal or slightly head-down; protect against further heat loss, and arrange transportation immediately to a hospital so that rapid re-warming may begin. The most effective way of re-warming is a bath – at 42°C or as hot as the bare elbow can tolerate. Until normal body temperature is restored, the victim is at high risk from sudden death, partly because re-warming may actually trigger an initial further drop in body temperature: many victims of accidents at sea die after they have been removed from the water – sometimes even in hospital.

Frostbite

Localised injuries from the cold can affect the limbs of exposed skin even when core body temperature is entirely normal, when insulation is not adequate or on account of other factors such as a restricted blood supply due to clothing that is too tight. Injuries of this kind range from frostbite following freezing of the tissues of the nose, cheeks, chin, ears, fingers and feet, to more common problems like frost nips and chapping of the skin, especially of the lips, nose and hands, and often compounded by sunburn.

The best way to deal with frostbite is to take careful steps to prevent it. Ensure, particularly, that gloves, socks and footwear are suitable for the conditions and the task in hand and do not choose extreme conditions to wear any of these items for the first time. Carry a face-mask to protect from high wind and driving snow. Also carry chemical handwarmers that can be used when needed.

Impending frostbite is usually signalled by intense pain in the part at risk: this should not be ignored, and prompt re-warming is necessary. For example, hands and fingers should be slipped under the clothes and warmed in the opposite armpit. If the pain is ignored it eventually disappears: the part becomes numb, white and hard to touch – it is frozen.

Established frostbite is a serious problem that may need lengthy hospital treatment: once thawing has taken place, tissue is liable to much more extensive damage from even slight chilling. During evacuation, keep the affected part clean and dry and give pain killers and antibiotics (if available) to prevent infection. Never rub frostbite with snow or anything else, because the tissues are extremely fragile and will suffer more damage.

Some Do's and Don't's

1. Don't drink: alcohol causes peripheral vasoldilation – it increases blood flow through the skin – which can dramatically increase heat loss in extreme temperatures.

2. Don't smoke: nicotine can cause vasi-constriction – reduction in blood flow to hands, fingers and toes – increasing the likelihood of frostbite.

3. Carry high-energy carbohydrate snacks – such as glucose sweets or Mars bars.

4. Carry extra layers of clothing.

5. Carry chemical hand-warming sachets to put inside gloves and shoes in extreme conditions.

6. If you are on an expedition, or are looking after a large group, carry a special low-reading thermometer to measure body temperature: normal clinical thermometers are not adequate for detecting hypothermia. You may also be well advised to carry instruments for measuring high wind speed and estimating wind chill.

7. Anything that reduces activity such as being stranded on a chair lift, or being injured, can result in a rapid fall in body temperature; if this happens to you, try to maintain some muscular activity to generate warmth.

8. Children are at special risk. In particular, they are likely to need extra head protection (mechanical as well as against heat loss), and frost nip and frostbite can affect later growth.

9. In cold conditions it is easy to under-estimate the need to protect skin and eyes against excessive sunlight. Take extra care.

SURVIVING A SKIING ACCIDENT

by Arnie Wilson

Skiing injuries can and do happen when you least expect them, let alone when you are taking risks: there are documented cases of skiers breaking a leg as they climb down the aircraft steps before even setting foot in a ski resort.

Some years ago a producer working on a TV commercial – in which a hero clutching a box of chocolates had to out-ski an avalanche – fell over and broke her leg when she was just standing on a mountainside watching.

Not so long ago, I met a ski holiday rep who had damaged his cruciate ligament while skiing without even falling over – he just hit a bump awkwardly and tore it. And only last winter, Konrad Bartelski, Britain's most successful world cup skier ever, damaged his cruciate ligament during a race without knowing it until he crossed the finishing line. Ligaments, cartileges and tendons are the things that get hurt these days. Thanks to modern equipment, including more and more sophisticated bindings, broken legs are much rarer than they used to be. But something's got to give, and if it's not your leg, it's likely to be your cruciate.

Although advanced skiers travel at speed and are vulnerable to spinal and head injuries, surprisingly often it is the beginners who are most at risk. They tend to ski slowly, and more often than not it is the slow, sickening, twisting fall that causes the damage – not the high speed fall which catapults the skier out of his bindings. Unless of course the fall projects him or her into a rock. Which leads us to head injuries and protective helmets. Are they necessary? In Scandanavian resorts they are virtually compulsory for young children and a lot of people believe that by the end of the century or earlier, skiers should be required to wear them. Yet statistics show that remarkably few skiing accident cause head injuries. What they also show is that a frightening number of accidents on the slopes are drink-related.

Drink is freely available – and its consumption encouraged – in a host of mountain restaurants. Marco Grass, a member of the Saas Ski School in Klosters, Switzerland says: "Drinking when you are skiing is just as dangerous as when you are driving a car. You think you are in control but in reality your reactions are slow and ill-judged. Statistics relating to injuries in this major ski area of Klosters/Davos show that more and more are drink-related. And we have no reason to think this trend is only happening here".

In North America, people skiing recklessly can have their lift ticket taken away and even be arrested. In practice – unless they actually injure another skier – they often get away with it. Having monitored American skiing in almost 100 resorts right across the continent, the closest I have come to seeing an errant skier being punished was in Snowshoe, Virginia, when a member of the ski patrol leapt onto a chair to catch the culprit but lost him on the mountain.

Colin Allum, whose Fogg (as in Philleas) Travel Insurance Services specialises in skiing insurance, says: "Skiing is a high risk sport. About one person in 50 who goes skiing is liable to receive some form of medical treatment during the course of a normal winter-sports holiday. This can range from a twisted ankle or bruised shoulder to the extreme cases of serious back or head injury, or in those fortunately very remote cases, the skier is killed."

If you happen to be the first on the scene after an accident, it is important to cross two skis in the snow about ten metres up the slope from the injured skier. Don't try to move the victim, and if it is a leg injury, don't try to remove the boot: it can act as a splint. Keep the injured skier warm, but do not give him or her any alcohol. Knees are the most prone to injury, but almost no part of the human body is immune from one sort of skiing injury or another.

A broken leg or a damaged cruciate ligament are among the worst things than can happen to your legs: but it's not always the big injuries that can cause pain and curtail skiing. Some skiers – myself included – can endure endless agonies over boots. Like many other skiers, I have the wrong fundamental foot shape for most boots. (They were described as "shaped like bricks" by one expert boot fitter in Aspen.)

I remember cracking or at least bruising a rib or two when I was learning to ski in Verbier, Switzerland, and a friend of mine is always damaging hers. You can't do much with cracked ribs except perhaps strap them up, but she always continues to ski regardless. Like many skiing injuries, it is often less painful to carry on skiing than walk around or even lie down in bed. That goes for shoulders too.

In California I fell heavily on my left shoulder twice in two days and the pain affected me for months. Skiing was not a problem (except the worry of falling on it again) but lying in bed could be agony. Usually an anti-inflammatory cream and resting it will do wonders. Wearing a sling can help.

Shoulders are always a problem. They have such a sophisticated collection of moving parts that any one of them could be damaged in an accident without the others being affected. You may find you can ski yourself silly without so much as a twinge, but looking at your watch almost kills you! Still – at least I haven't torn my dreaded cruciate ligament yet. But no doubt it is only a matter of time!

Says Allum: "The advent of quick-release bindings has dramatically reduced the number of fractures – but dramatically increased the number of ligament injuries. In the days when bindings simply did not release, it was almost inevitable that a leg would be broken. Nowadays 50 per cent of what may be regarded as "serious" injuries – those which in due course will require some operative treatment – are knee ligaments injuries.

"Many accidents are caused by people skiing across the tops of protruding rocks which are seen too late. This type of accident tends to produce head injuries, because the skier is released from the bindings and propelled forward, rather on the lines of a swimmer in a start in the 100 metres Olympic swimming trials!

"Skis themselves can cause accidents if they are the wrong ski for the skier concerned, It is always important that skiers ski within their limitations, and ski a length of ski to which they are suited rather than one decided by bravado. It is much more sensible to have a happy and successful holiday skiing a 195 centimetre ski than finish up in hospital skiing a 210."

So much for the skis. But what about the skier? "There are those of us who may readily admit to being beginners even after twenty years of skiing. And there are others who will only admit to being advanced after twenty minutes," says Allum.

One good way to try to prevent injury on the slopes is to get fit before you go. Enter the Cybex machine. It sounds like something out of Dr Who, but what it actually does is check the strength of your hamstrings, quads abductors and adductors and then target any of these for strengthening with a customised programme of weight training and exercises.

Among Alan Watson's clients at the BiMAL Clinic in Hammersmith, West London is Will Carling. Says Watson: "Cybex will pinpoint any weakness in strength or symmetry."

Weather and altitude can all play their part in making a skier's life a pain. Some people can get serious altitude sickness in America, where skiing in the Rockies can mean altitudes of 11,000 or 12,000 feet or more. At such height it is not unusual to feel some effects, including headaches, nausea, breathlessness etc. These should wear off after two or three days (a good reason not to go skiing in the USA just for the week, or your holiday might be half over before you're ready to face it) but if they persist you should see a doctor. Drinking plenty of water – much more than you think you need – helps alleviate the problem. But serious altitude sickness can only be dealt with by getting the patient to a lower altitude as quickly as possible. Your doctor can prescribe tablets to lessen the impact of altitude.

As for weather: watch out for frostbite! I got my first taste of it in Colorado, skiing Breckenridge's peak 7. The trouble is you never know you've been affected unless someone tell you (it's a bit like the old B.O. adverts!). My nose went white, but I had no idea. As a damage limitation exercise, it is important to cover any frostbitten extremity and keep it warm. Experts argue over whether it is better just to cover it or knead it slightly to get the blood back in. Those against kneading say it could damage the cells while they are frozen. The consensus is just keep it warm: if you need it again, don't knead it!

Strong sunlight can be a major problem too. Always wear good protective creams even when it may seem that the sun is not coming out today. As the saying goes, you may not be able to see the sun, but the sun can see you! Even a couple of hours skiing in high altitude without protection, especially during the later months of March, April and May can cause serious sunburn and even sunstroke, because of the strong ultra-violet rays.

Much is said of the danger of skiing off piste, and it is true that without a guide, skiers leaving marked trails may cause or be caught up in avalanches and even fall into a crevasse. However skiing in a resort on a marked run is arguably just as dangerous. In fact when you compare the numbers of people on piste with those who ski off them, the chances of a collision in a resort must be just as high as falling foul of nature outside a resort. Almost ten per cent of skiers who end up in Davos hospital have been involved in collisions. And collisions nearly always cause injuries, sometimes serious ones.

As I found out in a very tragic way when my girlfriend Lucy Dicker was killed in La Grave following our successful mission to ski every day in 1994, even skiing off-piste with a guide, however, is no guarantee that no harm will come to you. Or the guide for that matter. There is a cynical saying that all the avalanche experts are dead. Tragically, there is some truth in this.

According to the rescue service SOS which operates in the Parsenn area of Davos – one of the most extensive ski areas in Europe, which also prides itself on its avalanche research centre – "Avalanches are a natural phenomenon and therefore no absolute safety from them can be guaranteed. We must emphasise that even after the most experienced judgement and safety measures have been taken, an avalanche can still break loose and run over an open and marked piste."

Always obey avalanche warning signs and stay out of high-risk areas unless a qualified high mountain guide is skiing with you. He may have specialist knowledge and will certainly not take you off-piste if there is a serious risk.

Just as experts argue over the best way of dealing with frostbite, they also have different views about how to try to survive an avalanche. There is no way of guaranteeing that you will not die, If an avalanche has your name on it, there is nothing you can do about it. There are all sorts of avalanche patterns, from powder avalanches which drown you to slab avalanches which can break every bone in your body or at least batter you senseless. You might start it yourself, or you might be engulfed in one started by another skier. Most likely it will start spontaneously and trap you in its path.

Avalanches can move frighteningly fast. You may only have a second or two to react. One possible reaction is to ski diagonally out of the avalanche's path. Another is to take your skis off and try to "swim" on the surface of the snow. If you are sucked under the surface, try to keep a pocket of air in front of you by cupping your mouth and nose with your hand. When skiing off-piste wear an avalanche transceiver, never ski alone and if possible always take a guide.

On a more optimistic note, the latest figures for skiing in the Davos/Klosters area are encouraging: in the winter of 1973/74, out of 5.5 million skiers there, there were 628 accidents. Almost two decades later, in the winter of 1992/93, the number of skiers had risen to 7.5 million, yet the number of injuries fell to 428 – a reduction of almost 32 per cent.

Ueli Frei, President of the Mountain Guides Association in Grindelwald, who specialises in helicopter skiing and regularly rescues climbers stranded on the North face of the Eiger, one of Europe's most feared peaks, says: "You have to respect the mountain. But for me there is more risk in crossing a busy street in London." Yet he admits that two of his most experienced colleagues have died in avalanches this season.

Incidentally, three per cent of injured skiers each year are those with broken thumbs. But that can happen even before you go skiing. Many people who practice on dry ski slopes sprain or break thumbs when they fall on the unforgiving plastic surface and sandwich a thumb between the slope and their body. But don't let that encourage you to give skiing the thumbs down. It's far too much fun. Just take it easy! And take care.

SURVIVING A CIVIL WAR

by Anne Sharpley

Don't take it too personally when the shooting starts. They are almost certainly not shooting at you – and if they are, it is even safer since the level of marksmanship is so low, at least in all street-shooting I have been caught up in, that you are almost invulnerable. Hollywood never comes to your aid at such moments. You would have thought that the rigorous early training we all get at the movies in both armed and unarmed fighting would have got into our reflexes. But it is all so much more muddled when it happens. Far from knowing when and where to duck, I could never make out where the fighting was coming from or which side of the wall or handy car to duck behind.

As for hand-to-hand fighting, far from the balletic, clearly defined movements of cinematic bouts, everyone gets puffed, or sick, or falls over in a shambles of misunderstood intentions. Nor is there that crack on the jaw to let you know who is being hit when. So it is even poor for spectator interest.

As a reporter, it is usually my actual work to be there and see what is happening. This means I cannot follow my own best advice, which is to get out.

Sticking around is the easy bit. It is the next stage of events, which sets in during and after the street blocks, cordons, summary arrests and general paralysis as order is imposed on a troubled area that presents the visitor with new problems.

Communications with the outside world cease, public utilities go wrong and airports close. It is this sort of scene you can guarantee will take over. So forget the bullet-proof vest you wish you had thought of and get on with the practicalities. The first and best rule is worth observing before you leave home – never pack more than you can run with. Always include a smaller, lighter bag such as an airline bag because if things get really nasty you need something handy with a shoulder strap to pick up and clear out in a hurry.

Essentials

If you are in a situation in which something is likely to happen, it is worth keeping this bag packed with essentials. Do not run about with suitcases, it cannot be done for long.

Always bring in your duty free allowances if you know things are likely to get tough. Even if you are a non-smoking, tee-totaller who hates scent, they are the stuff of which bribes and rewards for favours are made. And as banks close or the money exchange goes berserk, they may end up as your only bargaining resource. And remember that drink is a useful stimulant, as well as solace. If I have to stay up all night, I do it on regular small nips of whisky.

The next bit of advice will seem absurd at first, but you will regret having laughed if you ever get into one of those long-standing, semi-siege situations that sometimes happen when you are stuck in a hotel that either cannot or will not provide for you. Take one of those little aluminium pans with a solid fuel burner – so small it will slip into your pocket. You can boil water at the rate of quarter of a pint to one solid fuel stick, which is about the size of a cigarette. You can get the whole thing from camping shops for relatively little.

If you take a few tea bags or a small jar of instant coffee, this will not only help if you are an addict of these things, but again wins friends and allies in an hour of need. Serve it up in a tooth mug, but do not forget to put in a spoon before you pour in boiling water or you'll crack the glass.

As the water either goes off completely, or turns a threatening colour, it is just as well to have a means of making water sterile. And at the very least it provides a shave.

If things look ugly, it is a good idea to fill the bath. You can keep filling it if supplies continue, but you cannot get water at all if they really stop. Not only have you a means of keeping the toilet in a less revolting state, but you can wash yourself and keep away thirst (boil the water first, of course). I always like to carry a small box of biscuits, although this is not anything more than a psychological trick to reinforce a feeling of self-sufficiency.

If things get really hectic, nobody in a hotel wants to know about you but they get rather interested in your property. It is a great time for getting everything stolen. I came back from Prague in 1968 with scarcely a thing left. What is yours suddenly becomes theirs. So remember that overnight bag and carry it with you everywhere.

Whether you should try to look less conspicuously foreign is a moot point. War correspondents usually get themselves kitted out in a sort of quasi-military set of clothes and where there are women soldiers, as in Israel, I have too. If nothing else, it meant I could fill my taxi with girl soldiers and let them get me past the road blocks with their papers. But when I found myself in action before I had time to change, I was told later by a captured sniper that it had only been my pretty pink blouse that had saved me. He'd had me on his sights and liked the colour so he couldn't bring himself to shoot me!

However, you are much more likely to be holed up in your hotel. If things are exploding, it is as well to get whatever glass is removable down on the floor, draw curtains and blinds against window glass and drape mirrors you can't take down with blankets and towels. Glass is the biggest danger you face. Locate the fire escape and if it's remote, get yourself somewhere else to stay either in the same hotel or elsewhere.

Identity in a Crisis

It is always worth trying to pretend you are from a country they are not having a row with, although local knowledge of nationalities is always limited, so don't try Finnish or Papuan. This is for occasional use when they are running around looking for someone to duff up. Hit the right nationality and you are so popular they won't put you down. Crowds are very emotional and the least thing sends them one way or the other. In Algeria, I found I had a winning ticket by saying I was British – or English, to be more precise. I became the object of gallant attention from a group of youths who decided to accompany me as a sort of bodyguard. All very honourable and very sweet.

Women are still quite often chivalrously treated in the Middle East. I found that to get through road blocks in Algeria I could simply say I was an "English Miss" without having to hand over my passport with the damning word 'journalist" in it. What echoes it evoked, why they were so responsive, I never quite found out but I liked to think that I modestly linked up with those amazingly bossy English women, from Hester Stanhope onwards, who had been in the Middle East.

Certainly I found that Muslim sentries were unable to challenge me. I always walked straight through, looking determined. Another useful tip for visiting women in tricky situations in Muslim countries is to apply to visit the chief wife of whoever is in power. There is always a go-between who will arrange it for a sum, escort you there and help generally. As women in harems are bored out of their minds, they are usually delighted to see another woman from the outside world. If they like you, which you must make sure of (that's where the duty free scent or your best blouse or scarf come in), they will do a great deal to help. They always have more power than is generally believed.

Keep Calling

While ordinary communications often stop altogether, it is a good idea to tell your family or company to keep on telephoning you from the outside. So often, I have found it impossible to get calls out while incoming calls made it.

You can always try the journalist's old trick of getting out to the airport and picking a friendly face about to board whatever aircraft is leaving and get them to take a message.

One belief I have always had, which may not necessarily work, but always has for me, is that befriending a taxi driver can be extremely useful. They are a much maligned lot. What you do is to practice your basic physiognomy – a derided skill, but it's all you've got – and pick a driver you think you could trust. Then use him all the time, paying him over the odds, of course. Take an interest in him and his family, and you will find a friend.

A taxi driver not only knows where everything is and what is going on, but can also act as interpreter and spare hand. Explain what you are trying to do and they soon enter into the spirit of things. There was one taxi driver in Cyprus who virtually did my job for me. He was not only fearless, he was accurate too!

For Red Cross Societies World-wide see p.891 of the Directory
For Canadian, UK and US Embassies world-wide see p.803 of the Directory ■

TRAVEL WRITING, FILM AND PHOTOGRAPHY
Chapter 14

TRAVELS WITH MY CAMERA CREW

by Clive Anderson

Making TV documentaries is a great way to travel. Since I have managed occasionally to creep out of the studio and onto the road (and rail and aeroplane), for the purposes of making television programmes, I have been despatched to Hong Kong, China, Mongolia, Hawaii, Cuba, Dominica, Goa, Calcutta, Kenya, Nigeria, Beirut and a variety of bits of the United States. Not to mention Montreal and Edinburgh to cover comedy festivals and Bayeux to film a tapestry. Join the BBC, it turns out, and see the world.

Overall, I have enjoyed myself hugely and I hope some of the programmes have turned out all right as well. But there are some disadvantages. Documentary making is not one long holiday, nor even one long *Holiday Programme*, whatever viewers might suspect. Or indeed whatever I secretly hoped before I started. Sad to say, even though you might spend two weeks on location making a 40 minute film, there is precious little time to lounge around on the beach, or for "researching" local night clubs. Rather disappointingly, even relatively straightforward films seem to take endless amounts of time to shoot. And films never seem that straightforward when you are on location trying to film them. Also budgets being what they are means that filming has to start virtually from the moment the presenter arrives and continue until the minute he leaves. Even rare days timetabled as days off turn all too regularly into days catching up.

There are, of course, plenty of meals and drinks to be had with the crew, but this is a vital part of bonding together as a group and should not be seen as a pure pleasure. And if you meet up with local people as well, this must be regarded as a vital process of learning about other cultures and not just partying for the hell of it.

Time to acclimatise never seems to be allowed at all. Take Hawaii. I landed late at night on the other side of the world. Had we crossed the international date line? I literally did not know what day of the week it was. But I soon discovered I had to be up at the crack of dawn the next morning to row in a Hawaiian canoe. Several gorgeous, sun-tanned twenty-something oarsmen teamed with me: pale of skin, lacking of sleep, sleight of frame and spread of middle age. All to produce a few frames of *Hawaii 5-0* parody for the end credits. However, as the director pointed out, it could have been so much *more* if I had had the sense to fall in and start drowning on camera.

Then there is the travelling itself. As I know to my cost the modern child requires a vast amount of baggage in order to get from A to B. Cuddly toys, back packs and buggies, snack foods and nappies, plus an array of items constructed entirely from garish coloured plastic are *de rigeur*. This, however, is not a patch on a film crew. Even the most solitary looking TV journey is made by a small army of voyagers: a cameraman, a soundman, a camera assistant, a director and or a producer, and perhaps a researcher, translator or local fixer. With them come their equipment. Metal boxes full of film or video tape, metal boxes full of lights, reflectors, batteries, cameras, tripods, metal boxes full of tape recorders, tape and microphones. Metal boxes, for all I know, full of spare metal boxes.

All of these have to be dragged around airports, checked onto planes, and loaded into vans, boats and trains. On the first leg of the great railway journey across China we were worried about getting our equipment stolen, so we locked it in a soft class sleeper, while we mere humans struggled onto hard class bunks at the cheaper end of the train. Who else would give up their seats, and their beds, to their luggage? On a later leg of the same journey all the equipment travelled on to Beijing with just our Chinese speaking translator for company, while the rest of us stayed the wrong side of the barrier at Jinan station getting arrested. On a later film, the whole lot flew to the wrong island because some idiot (me, since you ask) said the wrong thing at an airport check-in. Still, in these days of high security awareness, it is nice to know that 50 or so metal boxes can still fly unaccompanied on a small passenger plane without let or hindrance!

In Lagos, Nigeria, we managed to get arrested twice in two weeks. Once for filming for several days with the full knowledge of the Ministry of Information but *without* the express permission of the secret police, and secondly for filming a roadside food stall without the permission of the local police station. It is remarkable the effect cameras have on insecure members of the security forces the world over.

Cameras do bring out the more adventurous side of some people though. The most stressful part of my normal travelling life is attempting to hail a taxi in Oxford Street. But in my documentary existence I am forever leaping onto tiny aeroplanes, dodgy helicopters, over-laden landrovers, unstable fishing boats, unconventional ferries and unpredictable horses. Needless to say, each owner, pilot, guide or driver, inspired by the presence of a camera, races, shows off and generally pushes his or her vehicle to its limit. It is as though they want them and me to die on camera, or at any rate come close to it. I know how they feel. I was fortunate enough to be given the chance to take over the controls of a small aeroplane flying over the sea between Cuba and Florida. You pull the joystick one way to go up, the other way to go down, left to go left, right to go right, in, out, in, out, shake it all about ... I was ordered to stop by the director getting seasick and squeezed in the back, "For God's sake Clive, let the real pilot take over again and let's go back to base as soon as ..." (Sound track then obscured by retching sound.)

Ah, illness. All travellers risk upset, infection and disease, but the TV presenter risks his particular bout of Delhi belly, sleeping sickness or raging fever being caught on camera for the delight of the watching millions. Indeed, when I turned to Michael Palin for advice on the point, he assured me being ill on screen is vital to maintain viewer interest. But when you feel your insides are about to become outsides, it is no fun being "Our Man in a Pale Suit" trying to conduct an interview in a steaming hot location miles away from your old friend Armitage Shanks.

This brings me to another danger. It is important that the film maker does not wind up filming someone else's film crew. With Michael Palin circling round the world in every possible direction, with every holiday destination covered by the *Holiday Programme*, or *Wish You Were Here*, with every war zone attracting crews from all over the world, with every Amazon Indian tribe apparently attached to its own resident camera crew, with every part of the natural world negotiating a series with David Attenborough, with every exotic railway journey the subject of a TV travelogue, this becomes ever more difficult.

I was once filming on the beautiful but generally little known island of Dominica in the Windward Islands. At exactly the same time Tony Robinson was on the same island making another film for the BBC. Now what are the chances of that?

But it has to be said, documentary making abroad is much less dangerous than fighting a war, less demanding than relief work, better paid than VSO, less exhausting than grape picking, more fun than a sales conference and seldom more uncomfortable than travelling on the Northern Line. In fact my only real complaint is that I am at home writing this, rather than away on another trip. Maybe next year ... .

TRAVELS WITH MY VIDEO DIARY
by Benedict Allen

Getting on the Box – and is it worth it?

It is an exciting prospect to have your travels shown on television to a potentially huge and enthusiastic audience. Thanks to the advent of comparatively cheap and light broadcast quality video cameras as well as the proliferation of television channels, this is now a real possibility. However, it is still a highly specialised field, and one strewn with ghastly difficulties.

Getting your Idea Commissioned

Let's face it, you are still not going to be granted a "TV spectacular" about your forthcoming round-the-world gypsy caravan odyssey. Because it all comes down to cost. A standard length (say 50 minute) travel programme would be budgeted at about £150,000 – this is for a three week shoot. Surprisingly, the cost of a Video Diary (a format without film crew) isn't exactly chicken feed either – here the expense lies in the editing. All this means your film proposal has to be a very bankable proposition to even be considered – you are expected to be notable in your field, or at least someone's field, and to be undertaking something that is unique, as well as fascinating. As if that weren't enough, unlike a writer or a photographer, you must be able to communicate your own feelings even under pressure – the pressure of, say, four bored moronic members of a film crew eyeing you – and be authoritative, articulate and "person-able". In short, climbing Everest – even climbing solo without oxygen up the south west face – nowadays simply isn't good enough.

Still not Put Off?

A couple of statistics: an independent TV production company would consider itself lucky if one in 25 of its programme proposals gets commissioned by the channel – this ratio might be as high as one in ten for the first rank of "independents". The process is this: whether through independents, or directly, your proposal is submitted on paper (one or two sides of A4 maximum) to a TV channel, and its merits assessed, along with other hundreds, through the long, perhaps six or nine months, selection process. Your proposal might find a slot either in a magazine programme – it might be a five minute item on Blue Peter by a teenager questing after hairy-footed gerbils in the Kalahari. Alternatively, as a full programme on one of the occasional "strands" – examples have been Channel 4's *Travels with My Camera* or the BBC's *Great River Journeys*. Of these two options, the magazines are most likely to offer the commissions – they have more slots because they are looking for five or ten minute items and will probably accept Hi-8 video quality. Although the emergence of digital Hi-8 technology will bring down the cost of foreign filming, and open other avenues, at present the only other option is boldly to ask a channel for a whole TV series – and there's fat chance of getting one of those beauties unless you already have a proven track record on telly.

Although the BBC has its own production base, and so can be approached directly with an idea, most channels – including the other two major travel programme outlets, Channel Four and (in the US) Discovery – commission from independents. One way or other, unless you are an experienced operator, with a nose for a marketable storyline, the general rule is that you need a commission, or definite expression of interest, before you set off abroad. The obvious exceptions are regional news programmes, which might welcome a "local explorer" item, or if you have potential headline material – which sadly means if you are the subject of a disaster story or are a witness to someone else's misery, as they succumb to massacre, coup or mudslide.

Behind the Camera

Before undertaking this tedious commissioning process, it is as well to consider whether dragging about camera equipment or – horror of horrors – a camera crew, is anyway quite your cup of tea. For many travellers, it suffices simply to have a visual record of the journey – on your return you might want to give a presentation to the worthy businessmen who supported your venture, or wish to use a film clip as an educational tool for the local primary school. Similarly, footage brought back on a recce trip might raise sponsorship prior to you setting out in earnest, or act as valuable briefing material for the main body of the expedition team. For these purposes, it's enough to pack into your rucksack a Hi-8 camcorder, tripod and stash of batteries.

For those who are prepared to "go the whole way", and try for that TV commission, there are obvious financial advantages. The income you are likely to accrue from the programme probably will not do more than cover the cost of a modest expedition, but television coverage can have a pleasing effect on those to whom you are indebted. This can mean commercial sponsors – though rules on product placement are now very strict outside the realm of news coverage and sport – or even politicians. Two years ago I applied to the Namibian government to walk up the Namib Desert, something never permitted before – not least because diamonds lie scattered in the sands. Armed with a TV commission, I was in a position to offer the government coverage world-wide of an exquisitely beautiful portion of their country, which I suggested would be a fillip to their tourist industry; but the master stroke turned out to be that I also persuaded the BBC to offer free broadcast of the future programme on Namibian television, which would allow Namibians to do the journey, by watching my, rather painful, progress through the sanddunes, on the TV. So, for the first time, total access was granted by the government to this very special place, while delicate chunks of the desert were still protected from the impact of tourists by the national parks. However, there was a proviso: I would be filming my progress alone, not with a camera crew. And this is where the real problems with telly begin.

The Dreadful Film Crew

There's no escaping it, but travelling with a film crew is not travelling at all. In bringing a crew, you bring a part of your world with you, and that part happens to be a circus. However hard you try, travelling becomes an act. Forget the lone caver, inching forward belly-first through slime. As likely as not, the camera man, lighting man, sound man and director have got there first. It's the same for every market scene and every mountain top soliloquy. In Kenya and Uganda, filming a BBC *Great Railway Journey*, I found myself lumbered with a crew that was ten strong, including the official government minder, two local "fixers" and two mini-bus drivers who served as roadies to ferry everyone else around, along with their kit. And here we come to the main point: keeping this show on the road costs a fortune, so before you even leave home, an hour by hour itinerary has to be worked out – worked out according to the needs of a film crew, not a traveller. "Chance encounters" are arranged, tribal dances ordered up. Effectively, the filmmaker is re-assembling the components of a journey for the enjoyment of others, not actually doing one at all. There may be many justifications for this – for me East Africa, the film crew scrambling aboard a crowded Kampala train was in itself good for a comedy sequence. But if you say you are doing your trek along the Great Wall of China for your own sake, and it just happens to be filmed, then you are deceiving yourself. The answer is that, like the very best circus act, it's little more than a stunt.

Video – The One Man Band

There is another option. Modern technology has now enabled expeditions to be filmed on video with a small, or no, additional film crew. In addition to the previous possibilities on offer from the slightly cumbersome Beta video camera is the small 8 Hi camcorder, now with digital technology, bringing the small camera well up to broadcast standard. While glossy shots and a first grade soundtrack are still best captured by a crew, these cameras and the tape they use, are cheap and robust and for the first time expeditions can be recorded comprehensively and as they unfold naturally. Thus for my three and a half month Namib trek, I simply strapped solar panels either side of the hump of Nelson (my lead camel) and with them recharged camera batteries for my little Hitachi VM-80. I was totally self sufficient with the aid of the Hi-8 and tripod recording whatever was to befall me (and camel companions) as we plodded hopefully through the dunes. In the Peruvian Amazon, a camcorder (SONY TR805) again enabled me to record a journey over an extended period. The use of video also helped me in recording the everyday life of my guides. Instead of feeling like a predatory outsider, as I'd always felt before when taking photographs of indigenous people, I was now able to involve them in the process, in this case getting the local Matses Indians to film themselves. The hundred or so hours of tape from the expedition also proved an invaluable record – from the evidence I recorded during interviews, the BBC had enough hard evidence to justify including footage of drug dealers, and even an ocelot-type cat, which rightly or wrongly, the Matses believe in the Upper Javari often exhibits aggressive behaviour to humans.

A further note of warning. Just when you are congratulating yourself on having survived the film crew, the tangles of the battery charger units, the frog march to jail, it's time to begin battling back home, in the cutting room. Your producer knows what makes "good TV", and that usually means a "comic relief" of your precious journey. That said, TV at its best gives the traveller something unique – the chance to pass on to others direct experience of different worlds. This is more than simply gratifying. Travellers must nowadays be able to justify the act of imposing themselves on foreign turf. Sharing their journey with the millions who are less privileged is one way of doing that.

MOVIES ON THE MOVE

by Dominic Boland

Simple movie making is, like simple stills photography, actually very straightforward, and once you have mastered the basic skills the potential is huge. Your resulting movies will soon start to look quite professional. Before looking at the essential techniques though, let's have a quick glance at the equipment hardware so that a decision can be made between the two movie-making formats – video or cine.

Video Equipment

Using a video camera – a camcorder – is similar to using a 35 mm SLR camera, inasmuch that "you see what you get" through the view finder. (There have been some direct vision camcorders but it's best to avoid these). You'll also find that most controls are pretty familiar. An autofocus zoom lens with manual override, plus auto exposure with some degree of manual control, are all pretty standard and of course there will be controls for the tape, which are essentially the same as for an audio tape recorder. Perhaps the biggest difference between video and stills, though, is that with video you can be up and taking pictures, and *viewing* them through the built-in monitor, within minutes of your first tentative steps. Getting the hang of using a camcorder is really simple, and as you are shooting on tape there are no processing costs and you can use the tape over and again.

When looking at camcorders, seek out one with a reasonably good zoom range, from wide angle to telephoto, but don't be too over-optimistic. A zoom range of 8mm to 64mm (equivalent to roughly 40-300mm on a 35mm SLR) will prove more than adequate for most purposes. Remember that ultra-long lenses will record every little jerk your body makes – even the thumping of your heart – making the picture jumpy. In any case, there are dozens of accessory lenses available to give extra wide or telephoto coverage, if needed at a later date.

Choice of video format these days is invariable 8mm. The tiny 8mm cassettes seem little different in appearance and size from an audio cassette but their dimensions belie their extraordinary performance, especially with the top quality Hi-8 format. Small cassettes mean small camcorders ("palmcorders" for the really tiny models) which can often be no larger than the book you're holding.

Of course, there are other formats to choose from. There are camcorders that take the full format VHS cassette (the same as used in the video cassette recorder under a television), or its more diminutive cousin the VHS-C (compact) cassette. And there are the professional U-matic and S-Beta formats. But pro-formats are extremely expensive, VHS-C format appears to be losing out, by and large, to the alternative 8mm.

Whichever format you fancy, you'll be confronted by further choices, such as hi-fi stereo sound or the top quality Hi-band, Hi-8, or S-VHS sub-formats, and there will be dozens of options such as "shutter speeds" for slow-motion effects. More confusingly, there will be talk of digital results, from image stabilisation and zoom to character generation and effects. Sadly, video jargon has gone the way of hi-fi jargon and becomes quickly impenetrable, so when you reach this stage, talk to a knowledgeable friend or read up about the subject through the various camcorder magazines and books.

Just remember that video is extremely easy to use and, of course, simple to view. The built-in viewfinder allows you to immediately see what you have just recorded, or you can plug the camcorder straight into a TV set for full-colour, big screen replay – the camcorder itself acts as the replay machine. Some TV systems abroad may only play back a mono image, or a silent one, in which case simply rely on the built-in monitor.

The major drawback to video is the initial cost of the camcorder but if you aim for a fairly basic machine you can save up to half the cost of the latest models. And remember too that hiring is a viable alternative to buying if you are looking at shooting only the occasional movie. Because the camcorder market is really booming there is also a lot of secondhand equipment available, but camcorders are electronic and electronics can go wrong, so you need to cover yourself. Until you really know what you're doing, only deal with reputable retailers if buying used equipment.

Cine is Dead?

With video seeming so good why bother with cine? The traditional reasons are: superior image quality, higher reliability and specifications, and ease of editing.

But times change and whilst film can still produce better quality than video tape, most people's movies are now viewed on television, not projection screens. (There's a huge growth of industry in converting cine to video for ease of viewing). Secondly, cine cameras, being still largely mechanical, can be more robust but camcorder manufacturers have realised the needs of travellers and produced models that are more rugged. Finally it used to be the case that if you wanted automatic fading, frame-by-frame exposure, ultra close-ups, time-lapse, sound-on-video and other such features, cine was the only real choice. Not any longer, as video can match it, and with video editing now so simple there is very little attraction to cine, especially when you add the inconvenience of actually viewing cine film.

Perhaps the final nails in the cine coffin, as far as most people are concerned, are the running costs. A cine film cartridge gives you roughly three minutes of single-use film which has to be reasonably carefully exposed and which can't be viewed until after processing. For the same price you can buy 30 minutes of top quality video tape that can be viewed straight after recording and which can be used over and over again.

However, cine is still top of the list for major documentaries and the professional 16mm form is still alive and kicking – albeit horrendously expensive. The alternative, and the most popular format for the average traveller, has been Super-8mm film which comes in pre-loaded, drop-in cassettes. There is a small but active Super-8 following, but cine cameras are becoming increasingly few and far between, the best-known makes being imported from the USA.

Film and Tape

Many video tapes, like audio tapes, are sourced from the same manufacturer. Avoid cheap extra-long play tapes. Simply keep to the best named, highest specification brand you can afford. Even so, tapes do wear out with use, particularly if you use freeze-frame when replaying. Tape wear varies with quality. A cheap tape will stretch, snap or show magnetic drop-out on the screen (white lines, dots, etc.) after ten or so showings. Top quality tape will last for over 100 showings.

Video tapes play on one side only and can be extremely susceptible to damage. Keep them as you would film; heat, moisture and dust are the main enemies, but add to this magnetic fields created by loudspeakers and electric motors. Also, take care of the cassettes themselves. Believe it or not, they contain very advanced and delicate engineering and should be stored upright in their protective sleeves.

Super 8mm film is made in both sound and silent versions. Buy film in bulk for discount and make sure it's balanced for daylight and not tungsten light. There's little choice in film sensitivities, ISO 40 being the most common, with ISO 160 also available.

Just like any 35mm transparency film, cine film exhibits the same variety of characteristics from make to make, the most popular brands being Kodak and Agfa. With the exception of Kodachrome, all other types of film incur processing charges. Processing quality varies too, so when you find a good lab stick with it.

Digital Video – or "DV" as it is known – is the lastest format to appear, and is presently revolutionising television. Its big advantages lie both in quality, and ease of editing. Images are captured as digital data, in binary code, instead of being stored as varying signals on the conventional analogue tape. Visual and aural quality is enhanced, and editing can be done by computer, even by plugging your camera directly into a laptop.

Accessories and Protection

Safety and precaution instructions come with your equipment. So read them before you use the gear. Video cameras in particular don't like extremes of heat (never point one at the sun) or cold, whilst direct contact with moisture usually results in complete failure. They can't cope with physical drops either and any sharp bang can ruin the "tracking" of the camera sufficiently to turn it into a write-off. For this reason adequate insurance cover is a must. The key to using video? Be gentle! Field repairs aren't going to be easy as both cine and video equipment rely heavily on electronic components. Don't open up a video camera. Some delicate parts can be ruined even by moisture from your fingers. But a first aid kit comprising of a set of jeweller's screwdrivers, a "puffer brush", proper camera cleaning tissues (not cloths) and a roll of gaffer tape will see you through most emergencies.

As for accessories, the Boy Scout approach of "essential, useful and luxurious" comes in here. Essential are spare batteries (at least two *spare* video battery packs – one to be recharging, one to have in the pocket when shooting), plenty of film or tape, and an intimate knowledge of the instruction book. It is also essential to check carefully the import controls of the countries you intend to visit well in advance. Video equipment, particularly, is often "confiscated". Several copies of receipts, equipment descriptions and serial numbers, to be stamped when entering and leaving countries, will be invaluable.

Useful would be a selection of ordinary photographic filters for special effects, a shoulder stock to help hold the camera steady against the body, and a customised bag to carry everything. As video batteries only last about 30 minutes between charges, another very useful accessory is a special vehicle battery adaptor cable. Many overland vehicles deliver higher than normal voltages, so you might need to have the lead regulated accordingly. Solar-powered recharges are also beginning to appear.

Sheer luxury would be a tripod, supplementary lighting, a separate audio tape recorder – and a sherpa.

Shooting Skills

Whether you're intending eventually to use cine or video camera, your first step should be to borrow or hire a video camera so that you can begin learning the techniques without spending a fortune on film.

Golden rule number one is to read the instructions thoroughly. Also, plug into a television when you can. The larger screen is an enormous help.

Golden rule number two is to practice before you head off into the wilderness. This will teach you what works and what doesn't when it comes to using all those wonderful controls at your fingertips.

A good initial training run is to watch television with the sound turned down. See how the director chops and changes not only the scenes, but the angles and viewpoint. Even a twenty second commercial demonstrates the huge variety of techniques available. Don't try to pack it all in like this yourself or your audience will start suffering eye strain, but do experiment with the following ideas.

Calling the Shots

You don't have a film crew with two or three cameras, so don't attempt the type of shoot they could. You're more like the documentary or news reporter. Remember that most of the time you won't have any control over the events you're capturing, so "storyboarding," where each shot is visualised as an illustration before the camera ever hits the action, won't be too useful. You'll learn far more from simply going and doing.

Where you do have control is over the type of shot you use and, especially with video, you should use "in camera" editing. This just means thinking ahead and trying to put the shots in some logical sequence and not a random, haphazard series of takes that will need days of later editing.

There are four main types of shot you'll find useful. The *very long shot* (or vista shot) is used to give a sense of place. It will show the setting but isn't trying to capture action.

Next is the *long shot* which will move in tighter to show a specific point of interest. It could be a group of people, a row of houses, or a general view of an activity. A *medium shot* moves in closer still. Whereas the previous shot would include head and feet, the medium shot would only show the head and shoulders of an individual. It is commonly used during dialogue.

Finally, the *close-up* excludes most extra detail; a tightly cropped head shot, an isolated detail of architecture. Practice using these shots to relate a story. Start off with straightforward sequences, then be more adventurous. For instance, cutting from a long shot of a dangerous waterfall to a medium shot of a small boat drifting down a river, and then back to the waterfall again, implies that the boat is heading toward an accident – and all without a word being said.

Camera Movements

The zoom action of the cine or video lens is a convenient way to change the focal length for each shot. You can of course zoom from one end of the lens range to the other whilst filming, but use this sparingly and gently. Constant zooming in and out of a scene ("tromboning") is very tiring for your audience.

Another very good technique to use is "panning". Start off with a couple of seconds of still scene, then slowly rotate your body at the hips keeping the camera perfectly horizontal. End the shot with another couple of seconds still shooting. A more interesting variation is to follow action whilst panning, ending on a descriptive shot. For instance, film a cyclist working his way down a busy street, past your position. Then let him ride out of shot (you stop panning) leaving the camera focused on a street sign that describes where you're filming.

"Tilting" is the same as panning but moving the camera vertically instead. Again the start and stop sequences allow the eye a resting place at either end of the shoot. Amateur films tend to include too much panning and tilting, known as "hosepiping", so as with all techniques use them only when they're applicable.

The transition from one scene to another can be accomplished in a number of ways, the simplest being the "cut". Shoot a scene, stop the film or tape movement until you reach your new location, then shoot the next take. Sounds simple, and so it is. As often, the simplest things can be the most useful. Shooting a market scene with long and medium shots, you can add plenty of close-up cuts of hands, faces and other details to add activity and excitement. You can cut into a scene like this or cut out. Medium shots of camel drivers resting and eating can cut out to atmospheric vista shots of the desert with a shimmering heat haze.

If the cut technique is too short and sharp, another transitional device is the fade. Not all cameras allow this, but the idea is to slowly darken (or indeed lighten) the scene until only a blank screen is left. The tape or film is then paused until the opening sequence of the next shot when the new scene re-emerges from a fade. Why not mix cutting and fading? Try fading out from a tranquil vista shot then cut dramatically into a noisy, bustling close-up.

As you can see, there's enormous control available to you. Add to these basics other techniques such as using filters, creative exposure control, "tracking" shots where the camera keeps alongside the subject as it moves, mixing still and moving pictures, and the exciting possibilities of video and cine seem endless. Do exercise care and caution though. Good camera technique shouldn't really be noticed – unless you have an audience of cameramen you're trying to impress!

Editing

The final act before you reveal your masterpiece to the world lies in editing, and it's arguably the single most important part of the movie-making process.

Although expensive, it is the film itself that in the past has been the major advantage that cine has had over video. Film can be easily edited using an inexpensive cutting tool and some tape or cement to splice it back together again in the chosen sequence. It is quite common to have a duplicate copy of the original made, and this is then edited first, with the final edit then being applied to the original. That way the original doesn't run the risk of becoming scratched, no matter how many times the edited pieces are reshuffled. Another advantage of film is that the whole lengths can be scanned very quickly to find a particular frame, not so convenient to do with video which often had to be copied in "real time".

A few years ago editing amateur video was fraught with problems. For a start, the tape itself couldn't be cut and pasted like cine because the electronic signal was laid down on the tape in a diagonal pattern, with the picture and sound signals often being physically apart. The best method, copying the original signal using an editing suite, was very expensive commercially and few parts of the country had editing facilities for the public to use. Instead, video makers resorted to the time consuming approach of having to physically wind and rewind the images between two tape machines, laying down out-of-sequence sections of the original onto a new tape. Fuzzy electronics "joins" were common.

Today, thanks to the advances in electronics, home editing suites which can lift the signal from the original tape, store it and place it back accurately onto a copy with almost no loss of quality are not only available but also comparatively cheap. And the massive boom in interest with video means that there are clubs and societies which allow very sophisticated equipment to be shared amongst members. Video editing is one of the growth areas so prices will eventually fall whilst specifications, like the new true digital systems, will continue to arrive.

Whether it's video or cine that you are editing you will find that a stopwatch and note pad are going to be used a great deal. Don't be too ambitious at the beginning, stick to a plan of action and be methodical. Just try to get your movies into a reasonable, understandable sequence that tell some sort of story. You will quickly realise that editing is made much simpler when you have developed a good shooting technique. If you start off with the highest quality images then the finished results will be that much better, so make sure that your cine or video camera is kept clean, that you use the best film and tapes that you can afford and pay special attention to focusing

You will quickly learn how even short sequences can be used to great effect when editing, even when relating fairly complicated storylines. You'll also learn how sound can be edited just as much as the picture, either in-camera when you are shooting or later when assembling the final sequences.

No matter which medium you decide to use, shooting moving pictures is a fascinating, highly enjoyable and ultimately addictive way of recording the world through which you travel. Don't be put off by the apparent technical nature of shooting movies. The end result will always spark off the memories, and your journeys will never be forgotten.

ADVENTURE TRAVEL PHOTOGRAPHY

by Steve Watkins

On many occasions you will hear disappointed travellers complaining that their photographs just didn't capture the spirit of their trip. They resolve to take a better camera next time or maybe even leave the camera behind. Yet, with a little thought and by following a few guidelines, any camera can take reasonable pictures if their limitations are understood and the traveller develops an eye for interesting images.

1. Equipment – "Light is Right"

Cameras

The performance gap between single lens reflex (SLR) and compact cameras has narrowed considerably in recent years. The benefits of the SLR are more important if you wish to sell your pictures afterwards. These include bigger, more accurate viewfinders for better composition, a wide selection of top quality, interchangeable lenses and more control over the camera's operation, allowing changes to apertures and shutter speeds to create dynamic images. Most modern SLR cameras also offer an intelligent program mode, or point-and-shoot mode, that can automatically adjust the settings to suit the subject matter, i.e. landscape, portrait, action. They are not foolproof but can be useful when something sudden happens and you want to snap it, like your travel buddy falling out of a dugout canoe on the Amazon. The disadvantages of these cameras are that they are bulkier and heavier than compacts, cost more and require slightly more maintenance.

Today, compact cameras offer excellent zoom lens options, high quality lenses and the higher priced ones even allow a reasonable amount of operation control. They are light, easy to tuck into a pocket or bumbag and unobtrusive in sensitive shooting situations. In short, unless you want to use your pictures for more than personal memories, compacts offer a very convenient way of getting images that capture the spirit of your trip.

Recently introduced is the Advanced Photo System (APS) format. Available in both compact and SLR specification, it provides very user-friendly features, such as choice of three print sizes, including panoramic, for each shot rather than a whole roll, automatic film loading and the ability to change rolls mid-film and to re-load it later. The latter allows the use of different film speeds with only one camera body. Being a smaller format than 35mm, it means the cameras can be smaller and lighter. Good news for travellers.

For those who choose SLR cameras, a frequent dilemma is whether to buy a totally mechanical, manual focus camera or a computerised, autofocus model. Some of the world's best travel photographers still use manual cameras, but, generally, it would be wiser for the inexperienced photographer to take an autofocus model. They still require a reasonable knowledge of photography, but should ensure that travellers produce a far greater percentage of good shots. Modern autofocus systems can accurately focus on subjects far quicker than even the most experienced shooter with a manual system. Using manual cameras as backup on particularly rough trips seems to be less important these days as computerised ones are proving themselves to be as reliable, if not more so. On my mountain biking and hiking trips, the cameras have rarely given any problems that couldn't be solved by simply using fresh batteries. Before the trip, ensure that your insurance policy covers your equipment properly. Small, single item figures can often include cameras and lenses as one item. Also, if you sell pictures, then most travel policies deem you to be a professional and will not cover any losses.

Lenses

Unless you fancy carrying around a heavy bag filled with fixed, or prime, lenses, travellers should use zoom lenses (a standard feature on most compacts). My personal favourites are a 24-85mm and a 100-300mm, though a 28-80mm and a 70-210mm would cover most situations. Wide-angle lenses, those below 50mm, give a large area of view and are great for landscapes or in tight situations, such as markets. They suffer less from camera-shake at slow shutter speeds, but can give a distorted effect around the outside and in the centre of the image. A full face portrait with a 28mm lens would make your subject's nose seem huge. Telephoto lenses, those above 50mm, are good for portrait shots and allow you to shoot from a respectable distance, with those above 100mm particularly useful for clandestine pictures. To shoot wildlife, a minimum of 300mm is needed for safari-type journeys, but most professional wildlife photographers would be using 600mm or above, but these lenses are enormous and heavy on the wallet. Teleconverters are small adaptors that magnify your biggest lens. Available in 1.4 and 2 times magnification, they are a cheap alternative to buying a big lens, but do not match the quality. They reduce the speed of the lens by one and two stops respectively, i.e. an f5.6 lens becomes f11 with a x2 converter. Telephotos can also be used creatively for flattening perspective in landscape shots. Buy the best lenses (generally those with smaller minimum F-stop numbers) you can afford, such as those made by the main manufacturers, Nikon, Minolta, Pentax and Canon, as they, rather than the camera body, make the difference. If you want to carry one lens then choose a 28-80mm, though Sigma make a compact, lightweight 28-200mm that deserves consideration.

Flash Guns

Natural light is the most appealing way of lighting a scene, but at times it is either impossible or produces shadow problems, so it's worth having a flash unit. Flash units built into the camera are okay for close work, up to about five metres, but do not light up the Grand Canyon! With an in-camera flash, make sure that it can be turned off, otherwise low light photography of distant objects becomes impossible. With SLR cameras, it is definitely worth carrying an off-camera, more powerful flash. These can provide fill-in flash to eliminate facial shadows in portraits and are ideal for lighting indoors. Make sure that the flash covers the same area as your wide-angle lens or shots will darken around the edges. And try to buy one that at least allows a degree of manual control and that has a GN rating (an indication of power) greater than 20m. A very useful accessory is a flash diffuser. Bare flash light is harsh and unflattering and should be softened. The Sto-Fen Omni Bounce (seen on most news photographers flashes) is a small, ultra-lightweight plastic cover that fits over the head of off-camera flash guns. It is quick to attach and very light, but it does reduce the power of the light output by two stops. The LumiQuest Pro-Max folds flat for storage and attaches via velcro to the head. It gives very even light and only reduces power by one stop, but it is more fiddly to attach and rather large when opened. Remember that flashes normally only work between shutter speeds of 1/60th and 1/200th second, so ensure your camera's settings are right.

Film

Certainly prints are easier to show your friends when you get back, more forgiving with exposures that aren't quite right and they are relatively cheap. However, they are almost impossible to sell for publication. Using 100 or 200 ISO rated film, such as the highly rated Fuji Super G or Kodak Gold, should suffice for most conditions and produce sharp images. For telephoto lenses it may be worth taking some ISO 400 or "pushing" ISO 200, by manually setting the ISO rating on the camera to 400 and then telling the processing lab when you get it developed. (Keep a note of film by numbering them all with labels.) Faster film has less contrast and weaker colours than slower film. Although high street processing is cheap, it is usually poor quality. Professional labs are more expensive but produce far better prints.

Transparency, or reversal film produces sharper, more colour saturated images and is essential for selling to magazines and libraries or giving lectures. Transparencies are not as convenient as prints for showing to friends, but projected onto a screen they do have more impact. Exposures must be very accurate, particularly in variable light situations. Most professional photographers use slower films, such as Fuji Velvia, ISO 50, or Kodachrome 64, but these can make it hard to hold the camera steady in low light without a tripod. There are some excellent ISO 100 films available that produce very sharp images and rich colours. Fuji Provia 100 and Fuji Sensia 100 are virtually identical (they have the same emulsions but Sensia is released before it has reached its prime, Provia is batch dated and released at optimum quality). Kodak Elite 100S is another good choice. Don't worry too much about storage problems with so-called professional films. I have never had a problem in extreme heat or cold with them, nor have I heard of any problems from other photographers. Non-professional films, such as Sensia, are supposed to be more stable though. All films requiring E6 processing have shorter archival lives (six-ten years) than films using other processes, such as Kodachrome (25 years plus).

Black and white film can produce strong travel pictures, but it requires careful processing and printing. This is expensive if you don't have access to or the inclination to use a darkroom yourself. They can be sold to magazines and newspapers, but the market is rather limited. However, they are perfect for exhibitions and it is possible to use faster speed films as the image quality is much higher than equivalent colour films.

Film Care

Don't leave film in extremely hot or cold places. In below freezing temperatures E6 transparency film becomes brittle and is prone to tearing, so warm it up before use and manually rewind it rather than allowing the motordrive to do it. It is widely believed that X-ray machines at airports damage films. Generally, this is untrue at airports in developed countries, where low dosage machines are "film-safe". However, in other countries, using older machines, you should insist on having your film checked by hand. Keep it handy in a clear plastic bag. X-rays should not be a problem for slower films up to ISO 400, but faster films, especially colour negative ones, should be hand-checked at all airports as they are more sensitive. It is better to be safe than to find out after a trip that the film was fogged. Radiation dosages build up, so the more times the film is checked by machine the greater the likelihood of damage. Don't take leftover film on subsequent trips. Always take film in your hand luggage as checked luggage scanners are ten to twenty times more powerful. A soft cool-bag, like those used for carrying cold drinks, is ideal for keeping film in when you are travelling around.

Filters

During a journey, it is not always feasible to wait for great natural light, though it is preferable. Filters can be used to enhance an image, to mimic a lighting situation that would naturally happen or to help the film to record more accurately what the eye can see. Basic filters for travel are the Skylight (neutral colour, reduces haze and protects the lens from scratches) and the Polarizer (minimises haze, saturates colours, turns hazy skies blue and cuts reflections from water or glass). The Polarizer reduces the light entering the camera by two stops and is most effective when used at 90 degrees to the sun. Autofocus cameras require a circular Polarizer. Other filters worth considering are an orange warm-up filter (adds warmth to shots taken in brighter light and for flashed portraits) and graduated neutral density/grey filters. The graduated filters are more important with transparency film as it can only record detail to around +/- two stops. The human eye can see detail in light varying up to thirteen stops. The graduated filters help to balance out bright skies and dark foregrounds, without altering the colours. Use fancy colour filters if you wish, but they do little to impress potential markets and, in my view, look terrible. There are no filters available for compact cameras.

Light Meters and Grey Cards

Although in-camera meters have reached a high level of sophistication, they all suffer from reading only reflected light. All meters are based around a standard reflectance of eighteen per cent grey, so if you have photographed a snow scene and wondered why it comes out grey, this is the answer. If your main subject is brightly coloured in a dull scene, the camera will underexpose, if it is a darker colour in a bright scene, it will overexpose, as the meter does not take colour into account. To reduce this problem, it is necessary to measure the light falling onto the subject rather than the light being reflected off it. A hand-held light-meter is the best method and prices and sizes are falling all the time. The Sekonic L308BII is tiny and reasonably priced. Another option is to buy a grey card, which can be placed near the subject and the in-camera meter used to read off it. In hurried situations or if you don't have the above, then nature lends a hand. In the northern hemisphere, a reading from the sky, 90 degrees from the sun and roughly 45 degrees up from the land, is equivalent to eighteen per cent grey, as is green grass in bright sunshine. Snow in sunshine is one to one and a half stops brighter than the standard setting. The other method is to experiment with taking readings off the back of your hand in different light situations and then adjust the camera settings to match. Caucasian skin is normally one to one and a half stops over eighteen per cent grey. Beware of sun tans changing this!

Tripods

Many of the most memorable moments on a trip are around sunrise and sunset when the light is warmer and softer. It is much easier to capture these scenes with a tripod, as it is almost impossible to hand-hold the long exposures needed with slower film. A number of mini-tripods, weighing very little, are available. They can be rested on a rock, fence or table to get the necessary height, but are not suitable for use with big lenses. Lightweight, full size tripods are okay but check that they are solid enough when the telescopic legs are extended. Stability can be increased by taking a nylon bag that you can fill with stones and hang from the centre column. Gitzo make superb, lightweight tripods, but they are rather expensive. Try to use a shutter release cable when shooting on tripods as the slightest touch on the camera can cause shake, especially with telephoto lenses. On safari, beanbags offer a versatile method of steadying yourself on car bonnets or windows, but beware of vibration if the engine is left running. Without a tripod, it is possible to build supports from stones or to place the camera on a high surface and use the self-timer. Monopods can be of some use at fast moving events, such as festivals, but they don't help in really low light.

Straps

SLR cameras can be quite heavy so a wide, well-padded shoulder strap significantly eases the burden. The best ones, such as those made by Op-Tech, are made with neoprene, which acts as a shock absorber. A very useful strap for travel and action photography is OpTech's Stabiliser. Made of neoprene, it straps around your midriff and has a hole cut into it to slide the lens through. It stops the camera swinging around, deters thieves and keeps the camera at hand for quick photography.

Camera Bags

Whether using a compact or a comprehensive SLR kit, it is essential to protect it from the elements and shocks encountered on your journey. There are padded bags of every size and description to choose from so it's a case of trying a few. Good brands include CCS, Lowe, Billingham, Heritage and Tamrac. I have found the half-moon shaped bum bags, such as the LowePro OrionAW, particularly good. The camera is easily accessible with the lid opening away from the body, and the closed bag provides a platform for changing lenses. The OrionAW also features a foldaway waterproof cover for extra protection against rain, dust and sand. Karrimor make good, handlebar-mounted camera bags for bicycles. Canvas bags, such as Billingham and Heritage, are naturally waterproof. For watersports or particularly rough trips, consider storing the gear in a solid, waterproof case. They come in plastic or metal and provide the ultimate protection, but are more cumbersome to work from. Keep some packets of silica gel in the bag for absorbing moisture.

Cleaning

Only use special lens cloths and blower brushes to remove dust from lenses and inside the camera. Check the lenses frequently and the camera every time you change a film. A tiny piece of dust in the film gate can scratch a whole film. Never touch the sensitive shutter curtains or the mirror with your hands.

Useful Accessories

A roll of duct tape is useful for all sorts of things, from sealing camera openings against fine dust to fixing broken tripod legs. A must for all camera bags. Small torches are perfect for checking camera settings in the dark or can even provide the necessary illumination for focusing in poor light. A Swiss Army knife, especially those that feature the jeweller screwdriver for tiny screws, will always be used at some stage. Cotton buds are perfect for cleaning the nooks and crannies of the camera body. A small, police-style notebook is great for recording details of pictures or grabbing addresses of people you meet. Take plenty of spare batteries for cameras, lightmeters and torches. AA size batteries are available in most countries but you will not find special lithium batteries in many places. No matter how well you know your camera, take the manual. A compass can help you get to the right place for sunrise and sunset. Lastly, take a good supply of zip-loc plastic bags, or lightweight dry bags (from kayak stores), for protecting cameras and film in wet conditions.

2. Techniques – "Little Change, Big Difference"

Composition

Using some simple guidelines (not rules because intuition and creativity are more powerful than rules ever can be) when composing images in the viewfinder can have a dramatic effect on how interesting the resulting picture is to the eye. Divide the frame into thirds both horizontally and vertically. Rather than placing the main subject in the middle of the frame, position it on one of the third intersections. Use visual lines, such as roads, rivers, fences or beaches, to draw the viewer's eye into the image by running them diagonally into the frame. Think of the image as having three levels, fore, middle and background. Try to have something interesting in each area, as it helps to create depth and gives perspective. Another dynamic shape to include is the triangle. It may consist of three points, e.g. two hands and a head or two nomads and a horse, or a triangular block of colour or light.

Angle of View

An instant way to capture a viewer's attention is to shoot from strange angles. Stand on a wall, shoot down from a hotel balcony, crouch, lie on your back or even tilt the camera 45 degrees. Whatever works with the subject. This approach can be particularly effective for capturing the dynamic nature of festivals.

Sense of Place

National Geographic photographers are superb at adding a sense of place to their pictures. Rarely, if ever, will you find a full face portrait or abstract image in their pages. Subjects are shot in their surroundings, either by using telephoto lenses to compress people into a landscape or, more often, through the creative use of wide angle lenses to include the person and the background. Not every shot needs to use this principle, but it does help people to build a better mental picture of your trip. Think like a movie director. Open with an establishing shot, a wide view of the general location, and work your way into more detailed pictures.

The Moment

The difference between a good picture and a great picture is that fleeting moment when everything comes together to create a magical image. It can be a smile, a twist of the head, a momentary splash of sunlight breaking through the clouds, the festival drummers beating in unison. It is what many photographers spend their whole life chasing, so don't expect to capture it in every image. Odds of success can be shortened by observation, anticipation and relaxation. Great shots rarely happen when you are rushing to catch a bus. For me, one of the great benefits of travel photography is that it makes me slow down and observe. By acquainting yourself with the ebb and flow of a market scene, for example, you can begin to predict the most interesting moments for your pictures. The magical moment may never come, or you may press the button just as it disappears, but at least you will leave with a better feel for the lives of the people you encounter.

Exposure

With colour print film, exposures are not so critical as the film is able to record detail across a large variation of light in a scene. Transparency films are not so forgiving, requiring very accurate exposures to within half a stop. If you rely on the camera's in-built lightmeter, it is important, with both SLR and compact cameras, to know how that meter measures the light. Many cameras take a "centre-weighted" reading, meaning that it reads the light from most parts of the viewfinder area, but it gives extra importance to the section in the middle. Compacts offer few ways of controlling this, but a good tip is to exclude any excessively bright or dark areas from the viewfinder when you partially depress the button and then recompose the picture to how you want it. Be careful that it focuses on something at the same distance as the subject. Modern SLR cameras have sophisticated metering systems that are hard to fool, including matrix metering (light is read individually from up to fourteen honeycomb segments and account is taken of which segment contains the subject), centre-weighted and spot metering (reading is taken only from a tiny circle in the centre of the viewfinder). Thoroughly learn how the camera's lightmeter works and think briefly before shooting. If a scene is fairly evenly lit then most meters should produce reasonable results. If there are excessive areas of light and shadow, stop and meter from your subject. An easy guideline is to always expose for your most important highlight.

Speeds

Shutter speed is the most important setting to get right for reasonable pictures. To freeze action, use faster shutter speeds – 1/250th or 1/500th should cover most travel situations. Faster speeds are needed for subjects moving across the lens than those moving towards it. For people shots, 1/125th should eliminate any slight movements. In low light it is necessary to set a speed that can be hand held without causing blur. A simple rule for any lens is that the slowest safe speed for hand held shots is 1/focal length of the lens, e.g. 28mm lens needs 1/30th second, 100mm lens needs 1/125th or 200mm needs 1/200th second. At slower speeds, pull your arms in tight to your body, press the camera against your forehead and exhale before pressing the button.

Apertures

The aperture (size of the hole in the lens) determines how much of the image is in focus (depth of field). Big holes (rather confusingly the lower aperture numbers on the camera, e.g. f4 or f5.6) give little depth of field. They are useful for portraits to throw the background out of focus or to concentrate the viewer's eye on your subject. Small holes, e.g. f11 and upwards, make most things in the shot appear sharp, which is great for landscapes. If your camera has a depth of field button, press it to view the effects of any given aperture.

3. Approach – "Mental Shots"

Photographs – Who Needs Them?

The first question to ask yourself before a trip is how important photographs are to you. Good images require some effort, which can alter the nature of your trip. If travelling alone, this may not be such a big deal, but it can cause friction when you are with a non-photographic companion. Few people share a photographer's enthusiasm for standing around waiting for the sun to hit the right spot in your epic landscape image. It is a question of compromise. Unless you are going to try to sell the images afterwards to pay for the trip, then it is best to just strike when you can and concentrate on enjoying the journey. If your main aim is photography, then it may be wise to travel alone and join up with other travellers when you want to socialise, or pick a partner with a similar or complementary interest, e.g. drawing or painting. You can then split up during the day and meet up again later with your pictures taken.

Planning

The best planners get the most luck. Research your destination – go to the book-shops, scan newspaper travel sections, surf the internet. Remember though, if you plan your trip down to the last detail, it will blinker you from the impromptu opportunities that always crop up on a journey. Plan, but stay open-minded. Most trips do not allow for extended stays in one place so a shortcut to improved local knowledge is to check out postcards or magazines of the area. Don't just copy them though. Try to find a different vantage point. Buy a local map, take a compass and plan your shots around the best times of day for the sunlight.

Shots in Your Head

Some of the most memorable travel pictures were conceived long before the photographer's plane touched down in the location. A useful way to pass the flight time is to think visually about where you are going. What are the important aspects that can sum up a place? Is it the beach, palm trees and a local fisher-man casting a net or an ice-encrusted climber camping on a tiny snow ledge with a background view of distant mountains? Get some picture ideas in your mind and then try to find them when you are there. Even if you don't get exactly that shot, the previsualisation will help to you to recognise strong images when they appear.

Patience

If photos are important then be prepared to spend the time trying to get them. The longer you are out on the streets or hiking in the country, the better chance you have of seeing something special. Few great travel photographs were taken sitting in a hotel room. Find an interesting scene and hang around, watching and waiting for someone to walk by or something to happen to make it into a good image. Using a modest degree of common sense, talk to as many people as you can. Many picture opportunities can arise from a chance conversation and may even get you a free meal with a family or see you whisked off to some local vantage point that isn't in the guidebook.

Head First

Imagine your overland group having to wade through a raging brown river in deep jungle. A good photograph would bring the memories flooding back when you return home. The secret to really showing how deep and dangerous the river was, would be to capture your companions, fearful faces as they resist being swept away. It's no use being the last person to cross if you want to get the picture. If there is an adventure to be photographed, be the first to do it. You then know where the best grimaces are likely to take place!

Up Early, Out Late

Travel photography is not for late-risers or early drinkers. Some of the best light is from one hour before to two hours after sunrise and from 4pm to one hour after sunset. It certainly isn't easy to crawl out of a warm bed on the off-chance that you may get a great shot of the rising sun glinting through the icicles hanging from the roof of your mountain hut, but it has to be done if you want that special image. Likewise, after a long day of walking around markets, museums and galleries, it is very tempting to slope off for an early beer instead of walking up that hill to shoot the last rays clipping the town's impressive church tower. If you want the image, you have to be there ... period.

Focus on the Bad Times

When things get tough, it is difficult to keep taking pictures, yet these events often form the defining moments of a trip. If you can have the presence of mind to get off a few quick shots when your partner is fighting blizzards on a mountain, slumped in despair after losing their passport or suffering from a vehement dose of Delhi belly, then you will treasure the shots for years to come.

Guidance Control

In many destinations, local guides are either unavoidable or useful enough to employ for your visit. However, remember that they are probably stuck in a rut of where to go, what to see and even the pace at which you should see things. All of these factors can limit the photographic opportunities at a place that you may never visit again. Take control. You are employing them and customers, wishes should always come first. If you want to go off their normal route to check out something that catches your eye, do so, but be as pleasant about it as you can. If you seriously delay them, then consider paying them more for their time, as you are reducing their chances of picking up other clients, but don't be hurried by their well honed ability to look impatient.

Respect

To really have a chance of capturing the spirit of a place on film, you have to be accepted by the local people. Show respect for their customs, private space and intelligence and you will go a long way towards getting good pictures. If you fail to realise that they have different values and refuse their offers of hospitality, then do not be surprised if your images have a distant feel too. Spend time with the people, take a genuine interest in their lives and, again using a modest amount of common sense, go with the flow when they want to take you to places. It is almost always worth it. Remember, though, that there is a fine dividing line between respect and reticence. Don't automatically assume that people don't want their picture taken. Not all places are receptive to outsiders. A good test is to learn how to say "hello" in their language and use it. Their reaction should tell you if they want you around. Another good icebreaker is to have a portable party trick. Juggling, playing an instrument, a magic trick or simply being able to pull silly faces can all help to put local people at ease.

Camera In, Camera Out

Whether to approach people with your camera out or hidden away is a personal dilemma. My favoured method is to have the camera showing at all times. By doing this, people know exactly who I am and that it is likely that I would like a photograph of them. Building a level of trust is essential and I think that suddenly pulling out a camera after a seemingly innocent conversation is too much of a shock, often resulting in the person refusing to pose for a picture. This is particularly relevant to brief meetings. If you have plenty of time, it can be worth getting to know the person well first and then introducing the camera. Try both approaches to see which works best for you.

To Ask or Not to Ask

Photographing people from a distance, possibly without their knowledge, adds a documentary feel to the image, something that many publications desire. Recreating that feel after asking permission to take the picture can, at best, be difficult. Few people have the ability to pose naturally when faced with a camera. If I do take a clandestine picture and the person gets upset, then I go over to them, shake their hand and have a joke about it. Don't sneak off with your tail between your legs. If you do ask and are confronted with a poker-faced, hands by the side pose, then shoot one frame, then, when they relax, shoot another couple. There are no hard rules though. It is a case of trusting your own judgment, something that only improves with experience of success and failure.

To Pay or Not to Pay

With increasing frequency, travellers are facing demands for payment for photographs. These can range from half-hearted appeals to your good nature to quite intimidating threats. For guidance, I normally refuse to pay for pictures. If the demand is made before I take the shot then, unless the image is so outstanding that I have to get it and there isn't a crowd, I put the camera away and walk off. This is most important with children, for it can only be damaging to their future to make them dependant on begging. If I ask the person to do something for the picture then it is reasonable to expect to pay them something for their time. With market sellers, a good way of avoiding the link between photography and payment is to buy something from their stall, which, in developing countries, is often sold at an inflated price to visitors. Both parties get what they want and retain their dignity.

Fun or Photos

Most, if not all, people are travellers first and photographers second. There is little point in going on a journey and not enjoying it because of the pressure of trying to capture the place on film. The importance of the experience will always win over the importance of a photograph.

Five Tips for Better Pictures

People Portaits

- 70-100mm lens
- big aperture (f4 or f5.6)
- focus on the eyes
- fill-flash with high sun
- shoot a dummy shot of rigid poses, then shoot again

Landscapes

- 24-35mm lens for general scenes or 200-300mm for compressed abstract
- small aperture (f16 upwards)
- include people to give sense of scale
- use a tripod for slow exposures
- put horizon on a third rather than in the middle

Wildlife

- 300-600mm lens
- big aperture for animal portraits (f5.6 or less)
- focus on eyes
- use a bean bag or tripod for low-light shots
- highest possible shutter speed (1/350th second and above)

Architecture

- with wide angle lenses, don't point the camera up too much, lines converge
- with large buildings, shoot details/abstracts
- include people to give sense of scale
- check map for best time of day for sunlight
- small apertures (f11 or above)

Festivals

- Find a high vantage point for sense of place shots
- Use slow shutter speeds and fill flash to emphasise motion
- Use wide angle lens and get in amongst the action
- shoot around the main action, e.g. crowds, drunken revellers
- take plenty of film and keep shooting

For associations for photographers see p.901 of the Directory
For photographic equipment suppliers see p.860 of the Directory

PHOTOGRAPHY BENEATH THE WAVES

by Dave Saunders

Anyone who has put on a mask and snorkel and floated over a coral garden or sunken boat will have had a glimpse of the fascinating world beneath the surface of the ocean. But we are not built to exist for long underwater and nor are most cameras. It is an alien environment with a new set of rules for the photographer.

The nice thing about underwater photography is that you can approach it at any level. It is possible to take satisfactory pictures with an ordinary land camera through the "window" of a glass-bottomed boat, or even in rock pools using a bucket or water-tight box with a glass base. If the sun is shining on the subject, the pictures will be bright and clear.

But be careful when you are near water, especially salt water. Ordinary land cameras are like cats – they just don't want to get involved with water. So if you want to take a camera underwater, you will need either a purpose-built underwater camera or a water-tight housing.

The 110 format underwater cameras are no longer made as this film size has pretty well died out. Minolta make a Weathermatic DL for use with 35mm film down to five meters. It has both a 38mm and 50mm lens with a close-up attachment used underwater to overcome diffraction. It is fully automatic and has a built-in flash.

For deeper diving, Sea & Sea produce two models of 35mm underwater camera, the Explorer and the more expensive Motormarine 2, for use down to 40 meters, both have the option of interchangeable lenses and flash.

The Nikonos is probably the underwater camera most used by the scuba divers. It is no larger than an ordinary 35mm camera, it is easy to operate and can give good results. Based on the French Calypso design, it is continually being improved. The Nikonos V has a fully-automatic exposure system, optional motordrive and automatic flash gun. There is no rangefinder for focusing, so you have to estimate focusing distances. Being a non-reflex camera, with a direct vision viewfinder, you may have problems with parallax when close to the subject. An external sportsfinder frame can be fixed to the top of the camera making viewing easier. The Nikonos V has a choice of auto or manual exposure. A bright LCD display in the viewfinder tells you the shutter speed, warns of over or under exposure and has a "flash ready" signal.

There is also the Nikonos RS, an autofocus SLR with interchangeable lenses and optional flash equipment.

The standard lens is the W-Nikkor 35mm f2.5. Also available are 15mm, 28mm and 80mm lenses. For detailed shots of coral and tame fish there are special close-up lenses or extension tubes.

Underwater Housings

Rather than investing in a whole new camera system, an alternative approach is to use an underwater housing around your land camera. In shallow water of less than 10m, flexible plastic housings provide a relatively cheap method of protecting your camera. Controls are operated through a rubber glove which is set into the case.

In deeper water, the flexible design is inappropriate as pressure increases with depth and the housing would collapse. Ikelite housings are made for 110, 35mm reflex and non-reflex and roll film cameras. These are rigid and some models can safely be taken to a depth of 100m.

The housing has controls which link into the focusing and aperture rings, as well as shutter release and film advance mechanisms. Rubber "O" ring seals produce a water-tight chamber which keeps the camera dry. To avoid flooding, the rings must be cleaned and lightly greased with silicone each time a film is changed. Metal housings are very strong and durable, but are heavy to carry and need careful attention to prevent corrosion. Plexiglass housings are much lighter and cheaper, and are available for a wider range of cameras. However, the plastic type ages more quickly and will eventually leak.

How Light Behaves

Light is refracted or bent more in water than in air. Objects underwater appear to be larger and nearer than they really are. Your eye sees the same distortion as the lens, so, with a reflex camera, you simply focus through the lens and the subsequent picture will then be in focus. The subject may be 1.5m away, but will appear closer to the eye and to the lens. However, if you then look at the focusing ring, it will set at about 1m.

Because of the way light refracts through water, the effective focal length of the lens is increased, making it more telephoto when a flat underwater porthole is used. So, in effect, a 35mm lens underwater is approximately equivalent to a 45mm lens on land. Likewise a 15mm lens is equivalent to a 20mm.

A dome-shaped porthole, on the other hand, enables light from all directions to pass through it at right angles. This eliminates the problem of refraction and the angle of view of the fitted lens is unchanged.

Lenses

Wide angle lenses are generally more useful underwater. Visibility is seldom as good above water, especially if there are numerous suspended particles. For a clear image it is important to move in close so as to reduce the amount of water between the camera and the subject. To include a whole diver in the frame when using a 35mm lens on a Nikonos, you need to be about 2m away. A wider lens, say 15mm, means you can move in much closer to the subject and thus minimise the amount of obstructing material between the camera and the subject.

Generally camera-to-subject distance should not exceed a quarter of the visibility. If the visibility is only 1.5m (as it often is in temperate seas or inland lakes), you should restrict yourself to only taking subjects up to 0.3m from the lens.

Flash

With high speed emulsions such as Ektachrome 400 (transparencies) and Kodacolour 400 (prints) it is often possible to get away without using flash, especially near the surface where it is brighter. When the sun is shining through the surface layers of water, you can obtain good results down to about 2m without flash. However, the deeper you go below the surface layers of water, the more the light is filtered out by the water. At 10m below the surface, all the red has been filtered out of the ambient light, and flash is needed to restore the absorbed colour.

In tropical waters, the guide number of the flash gun (which indicates its power) is usually reduced to about a third of the "in air" number. It is much safer to bracket your exposures, as the expense of film is nothing compared to the trouble and expense of getting into the water.

Underwater flashguns are either custom-made, or normal land units in plastic housing. Custom-made guns generally have a good wide angle performance, whereas units in housings generally have a narrow angle.

Instead of using a flash gun mounted close to the camera, place it at arm's length away, or even further, to give a better modelling light to the subject. Having two flash guns is even better and will give much greater control over lighting. With the flashgun further from the camera, fewer particles between the camera and the subject will be illuminated. If the flashgun is near the camera, the particles will be illuminated and detract from the subject.

Aiming the flash can be tricky. Although your eye and the camera lens "see" the subject to be, say, 2m away, it is actually further. As the flash must strike the subject directly in order to light it up, the unit must be aimed *behind* the apparent position of the subject.

Diving Problems

Test your equipment in the swimming pool before you take it into the sea. Plan the shots before hand. It is always better to have a good idea of what you want *before* you go into the water so you can have the right lens on the camera to do the job.

Keeping yourself stable while trying to take a picture can be a problem. Underwater you should be neutrally buoyant, such that you can hang suspended in the water without moving up and down. By breathing in you should rise slowly, and by breathing out you should sink. Wearing an adjustable buoyancy life jacket will allow you to increase or decrease your buoyancy by letting air into or out of the jacket.

Sometimes you may need to grab onto a piece of coral to steady yourself. A wetsuit will help protect you against stings and scratches. And as you will be moving around slowly when taking pictures, you will feel the cold earlier than if you were swimming energetically, and you will appreciate the warmth the suit gives you.

Near the sandy sea bed it is easy to churn up the water and disturb the sand, making the water cloudy. The secret is to keep as still as possible, and remove your fins. Restricting rapid movements also avoids scaring the more timid fish away. Taking a plastic bag of bread down with you usually guarantees plenty of potential subjects for your photography.

Good Subjects

Even with very simple equipment it is possible to record interesting effects simply by looking at what is naturally around you underwater. Rays of light burst through the water in a spectacular way and are especially photogenic when they surround a silhouette. And you can get impressive effects by catching reflections on the surface when you look up at the sky through the water.

The best pictures are usually simple and clear. Select something to photograph, such as an attractive piece of coral, then position yourself to show it off to best advantage without too many distractions in the picture.

With a little thought and planning beforehand, achieving good results underwater is quite straightforward although you should not be deterred by a high failure rate at first.

SELLING TRAVEL PHOTOGRAPHS

by John Douglas

A two-man canoe expedition up the Amazon ... a one-man trek through Afghanistan... a full-scale assault on Everest involving a party of sixty ... a student group studying the fauna and flora of a remote Pacific island.

Question: *What two features do these travellers have in common?*
Answer: *They will all be short of money and they'll all be taking at least one camera.*

The object of this article is to draw attention to the fact that these two features are not unrelated. Too few expeditions or independent travellers – whether they be on the grand scale or simply a student venture – are aware that the camera can make a substantial contribution to much-needed funds. When it is pointed out that a single picture may realise as much as £100, the hard-pressed traveller begins to see that he or she may be neglecting a very substantial source of revenue. While it is true that income from photography may not be received until some considerable time after arriving home, it can be used to pay off debts – or perhaps to finance the next excursion.

If photography is to pay, then advance planning is essential. Too often planning is no more than quick decisions regarding types of camera and the amount of film to be taken. Of course, these *are* essential questions and something might first be said about their relevance to potential markets.

Unless sponsorship and technical assistance are received, a movie camera is not worth taking. The production of a worthwhile expedition film or travelogue is such an expensive, specialised and time-consuming matter that it is best forgotten. In order to satisfy television and other markets, a film must approach near professional standards with all that implies in editing, cutting, dubbing, titling and so on, to say nothing of filming techniques. Of course, if a film unit from, for example, a regional TV network can be persuaded to send along a crew, then some of the profit, as well as a fine record of the traveller's achievements may accrue. But for the average trip this is unlikely, to say the least. By all means take along a good 8mm movie camera or video but don't think of it as a source of income.

Format and Colour

With still photography, the position is quite different. It *is* worthwhile investing in a good range of equipment (or having it on loan). It will probably be advisable to take perhaps as many as three cameras; two 35mm SLR's and a large format camera with an interchangeable back. If the latter is not available, then contrary to advice sometimes given, 35mm format is quite satisfactory for most markets (except some calendar, postcard and advertising outlets).

A common planning argument is the old "black and white versus colour" controversy. It is *not* true that mono reproduction from colour is unacceptable. Expertly produced, a large proportion of colour shots will reproduce satisfactorily in black and white. However, conversion is more expensive and difficult than starting in the right medium, and there are far more markets for mono than for colour. Although prices paid for black and white will only be some 50 to 60 per cent of those for colour, it is the larger market that makes it essential to take both sorts of film. A good plan is to take one-third fast black and white film and two-thirds colour reversal film. For formats larger than 35mm, take colour only. The reason for this imbalance is that it is easier to improve a sub–standard black and white during processing. To all intents and purposes, the quality of a colour picture is fixed once the shutter closes.

It is advisable to keep to one type of film with which you are familiar. Different colour films may reproduce with contrasting colour quality and spoil the effect of an article illustrated with a sequence of colour pictures. Colour prints *will not* sell.

Outlets

Before leaving, the travel photographer should contact possible outlets for his work. Magazines generally pay well for illustrations, especially if accompanied by an article. You can approach UK markets such as *Traveller* and *Geographical* magazine, the colour supplements of the Sunday newspapers or *Amateur Photographer*. Although they may not be able to give a firm "yes", their advice can be helpful. Specialist journals, assuming they are illustrated, may be approached if the trip is relevant, but it should be remembered that the smaller circulation of such journals yields a lower rate of payment. It can be worth advertising the journey in the hope of obtaining lucrative photographic commissions, but beware of copyright snags if the film is provided free.

Overseas magazines, such as the American *National Geographic*, often pay exceptionally high rates, but the market is tight. Much nearer home, local and national newspapers may take some pictures while the traveller is still abroad. If the picture editor is approached, he may accept some black and white pictures if they can be sent back through a UK agent. If the expedition is regionally based, local papers will usually be quite enthusiastic, but it is important to agree a reasonable fee beforehand, otherwise the payment may not cover the costs involved. Local papers may also agree to take an illustrated story on the return home, but again it is important to ensure that adequate payment will be made for the pictures published.

It is not the purpose of this article to discuss techniques of photography but before he or she leaves home, the photographer working with an expedition is well advised to seek guidance from others who have worked in the area. There can be problems with climate, customs and the like of which it is as well to be aware before starting out.

Finally, one potentially contentious point *must* be settled before the first picture is taken. This is the matter of copyright ownership and the income received from the sale of photographs. In law, copyright is vested in the owner of the film and *not* in the photographer. This can cause headaches if the traveller has had film given to him by a third party.

Universal Appeal

Once the trip has started, the travel photographer should look for two sorts of photograph. Firstly, of course, there will be those which illustrate their travels, the changing scene, human and physical. But secondly, and so easily neglected, are those pictures which have a universal appeal irrespective of their location. Such shots as sunsets, children at play, brilliant displays of flowers and so on always have a market. It is important, too, not to miss opportunities that are offered en route to the main location in which the travel photographer is to operate. Don't pack away your film while travelling to your destination. Have the camera ready on the journey.

Not unnaturally, the question "What sells?" will be asked. There is no simple answer except to say that at some time or other almost any technically good photograph may have a market. (It is, however, assumed that the photographer is able to produce high quality pictures: there is never a market for the out-of-focus, under-exposed disaster.) Statements like, "The photograph that sells best is the one that no one else has" may not seem very helpful, yet this is the truth. It is no use building a collection which simply adds to an already saturated market. For example, a traveller passing through Agra will certainly visit the Taj Mahal – and photograph that splendid building. Yet the chances of selling such a photograph on the open market are dismal. It's all been done before, from every angle in every light and mood. Perhaps a picture of the monument illuminated by a thunderstorm might be unusual enough to find a buyer but the best that can reasonably be hoped for is that the photographer will hit on a new angle or perhaps a human interest picture with the Taj as background. On the other hand, a picture of village craftsmen at work might sell well, as will anything around which a story can be woven. Landscapes have a limited market but, given exceptional conditions of light, then a good scenic picture might reap high rewards in the calendar or advertising markets. The golden rule is to know the markets well enough to foresee needs. Sometimes the least obvious subjects are suddenly in demand.

Such was the case, for example, in 1976 during the raid on Entebbe Airport by Israeli forces. My own agency, Geoslides, was able to supply television with photographs of the old section of the airport and of the Kampala hospital just when they were needed. Yet who would expect a market for such subjects? Perhaps this is just another reason for carrying plenty of film. My own experience on my travels is that I am constantly looking around for subjects. Certainly it is no use sitting back waiting for something to appear in the viewfinder. It is wise not to ignore the obvious, everyday scenes – while I was preparing this article, Geoslides were asked for a photograph of a hailstorm in our Natal collection. Bad weather photographs sell well, so you should not always wait for brilliant sunshine.

Record Keeping and Processing

One most important but easily over-looked point is the matter of record keeping. In the conditions experienced by many travellers, this will not be easy, yet it cannot be emphasised too strongly that meticulous care must be taken to ensure that every picture is fully documented. It is true that certain photographs may be identified at a later date (macro-photography of plants, for example) but no shot should be taken without some recording of at least its subject and location. It is usually best to number the films in advance and to have an identification tag on the camera which will indicate the film being exposed. A notebook can also be prepared before the traveller leaves.

With the advertising market in mind, it is helpful to make sure that good photographs are taken which include the traveller's equipment. Less obviously, there is a market for photographs of proprietary brands of food, magazines, newspapers, items of clothing and equipment and so on in exotic and unusual settings.

If the traveller is to be away for a long time, it can be important to get some of the exposed film back home. There are dangers in this procedure because of the uncertainty of postal services, but provided some care is taken – perhaps with arrangements made through embassies – then there are advantages. Apart from the obvious problem of keeping exposed film in sub-optimum conditions, some preparatory work can be carried out by the traveller's agent. Of course, if the film is sent home, it is essential that labelling and recording are foolproof.

Serious Selling

Once the travel photographer has returned home, the serious business of selling begins. Topicality is a selling point, so there is no excuse for taking even a few days off, no matter how exhausted you may feel. Processing the film is clearly the first task, followed by cataloguing and the reduction of sample black and white enlargements. No one is going to buy if the goods are badly presented, so it is worth making sure that a portfolio of high quality mono enlargements and colour transparencies is prepared with a really professional appearance. Put together a stock-list of all your photos (what countries and subjects, colour and black and white, and how many you have in each area) and circulate it around all the magazines and papers you can think of. As long as it is kept up to date, you should be able to sell one-offs for some way into the future.

The first market to tackle will be the local newspapers. Following up the advances made before you set out is very important, no matter how lukewarm the original response. It often *looks* more professional if there are both a writer and a photographer to produce a magazine article, but it should be made clear to editors that a separate fee is expected for text and illustrations. This is invariably better than a lump sum or space-payment.

A direct source of income from photography can be slide shows for which the audience is charged. These are relatively easy to organise but must be prepared with slides of maps and accompanying tape or live commentary. Incidentally, do not mix vertical and horizontal frames. It gives an untidy appearance to the show – even when the screen actually accommodates the verticals. The bigger the screen the better. If these shows are to have a wide audience, it may be necessary to put the organisation in the hands of an agent.

A photographic exhibition can provide helpful publicity but it will probably raise little or no income itself. Branch librarians are usually helpful in accommodating exhibitions and if these showings precede some other event like a lecture or slide show, they can be indirect money spinners. For an exhibition, great care should be taken in making the display as professional as possible. Again, the bigger the enlargements, the better. As far as photography is concerned, "big is beautiful," and it is worth investing in a few really giant enlargements.

Depending on the standing of the photographer, it can be a good plan to show some prints to the publicity department of the camera company or franchise agent whose equipment has been used, especially if you have made exclusive use of one company's products. The same may apply to the makers of the film that has been used.

If the traveller has not been too far off the beaten track, then travel firms may take photographs with which to illustrate brochures and posters. However, as with the calendar and postcard market, it must be pointed out that this is a specialist field, requiring not only particular sorts of photographs but pictures of a very high technical quality. This also applies to photographs used for advertising, although suggestions made earlier regarding pictures of proprietary brands leaves this door slightly wider than usual.

Whenever an original transparency or negative is sent to or left with a publisher or agent, a signature must be obtained for it, a value placed on it should it be lost or damaged (as much as £500 per original) and a record kept of its location.

Using an Agency

Lastly, when the catalogue is complete, the travel photographer will wish to put the whole of his saleable photograph collection on the market. Now a decision must be reached on the thorny issue of whether or not to use an agency. Of course, direct sales would mean an almost 100 per cent profit, while the agency sales will probably net only 50 per cent of the reproduction rights fee. But, as so often happens, it is the enlargement of the market, the professional expertise and marketing facilities of the agency which are attractive. It is worth making enquiries of a number of agencies (see the *Writers' and Artists' Year Book*) and finding a company which offers the sort of terms and assistance that satisfy the travel photographer's requirements. It is usually preferable to deal with a company which does not expect to hold the collection but simply calls for pictures when needed. This allows much greater freedom to the copyright owner as well as being a check on what is happening in the market. Some agencies offer additional services to associate photographers in the way of help with the placing of literary as well as photographic material, and in the organisation of lecture services.

It may even be better to contact an agency before leaving. For a small consultancy fee, a good agency may be able to advise on the sort of pictures which sell well and on the level of reproduction fees which should be charged. There is nothing more annoying than selling rights for £50 and then finding that the market would have stood £100. Many amateurs sell their pictures for too low a fee and others assume that there is a set price irrespective of the use to which the photographic material is put. In fact, the market for photographic reproduction is something of a jungle and it may be better to gain professional advice rather than get lost. The same applies to locating markets. It is almost impossible for the inexperienced amateur to identify likely markets for his work. There are thousands of possible outlets and a small fortune could be lost in trying to locate a buyer for a particular picture, no matter how high in quality.

An ambitious and skilled travel photographer should expect to make a substantial profit from his photography, providing an effort is made along the lines indicated. In the case of a specialised and well-publicised trip, it is not unknown for the whole of the cost of mounting the venture to be recouped from the sale of pictures. There are some simple points to remember: don't treat the camera as a toy; don't give the job of photographer to a non-specialist; don't put all those transparencies and negatives in the back of a drawer when you get home. As a money-spinner, the camera may be the most important piece of equipment the traveller carries.

For a list of associations for photographers and travel/feature editors see p.899 of the Directory

TRAVEL WRITING FOR BEGINNERS

by Sarah Gorman

The profession of travel writer seems to excite the imagination of hordes of would-be authors, judging by the quantity of unsolicited manuscripts which land heavy – and largely unwelcome – on travel editors' desks. Is it because it combines the perceived glamour of travel and journalism, or is it (for those who haven't quite got the stomach for live ammunition) simply the next best thing to being a foreign correspondent?

Whatever the motivation, there's no reason for anyone not to try their hand at a spot of travel writing. After all, most of us born in the western world within the past 50 years are reasonably experienced travellers, and all of us, in some degree or other, have been inspired/educated/horrified/delighted by our encounters overseas – there's certainly no shortage of experiences to share. You may choose to keep a diary of your trip, and you may write a piece for your Parish magazine or a copy-starved features page on the local paper. But with all due respect to these more parochial publications, the journey between this level of "journalism" and seeing yourself in print in one of the Sunday nationals is as long and as arduous as any of your own recent voyages of discovery, and the chances are that most of you reading this article will not have what it takes to finish the journey.

Sadly, travel editors do not often have the time or the heart to tell would-be contributors that they'd be "better off taking up gardening" (as one manuscript-weary editor confided). An unbroken stream of impersonal rejection letters is usually enough to discourage most embryonic Bruce Chatwins, but there are those who persevere – either through a justified belief in their their own talent or a staggering oblivion to their lack of it.

If you are one of the former (the latter, please seek help or an honest editor with time on his hands) you will need to develop a very thick skin, assuming that you have not done so already. As one freelance travel writer of many years' standing puts it: "If you are a good writer and if despite all the discouraging replies, you still persist, then you are probably the right person." If you have given up the proverbial day job in order to devote all your time to travelling and getting established within the field, you will invariably need a sympathetic bank manager – and possibly a degree in marketing. Selling yourself and your talent is an integral feature of life in the freelance lane, and as the freelancer quoted above points out "You do have to be very pushy. I hate selling pieces and I haven't yet met anyone who enjoys it."

So not only will you find travel writing a difficult field to break into, you may also discover that the lifestyle involves financial and personal sacrifices which are equally difficult – however great your talent. Yes, there are those romantic tales of amateur writers making their first submission to the *Daily Telegraph* and being welcomed with open arms. It does happen (occasionally) but not only is this the delighted amateur's *first* submission, it will more than likely be his only successful submission. Leaving aside the Colin Thubrons and Jan Morrises of the travel writing world, there are probably just a handful of travel writers who appear regularly in the travel pages of the national papers. In fact the current recession has seen a trend towards newspapers insisting that staff writers take up offers of press trips so saving the paper its contributors' costs.

The Right Stuff

Now that we've established that it is largely the talented (surprisingly, there are veteran exceptions) and the persistent who succeed, perhaps it wouldn't be too dangerous to try and define what makes a "talented" travel writer. It is safe to say that what it is not is someone who belongs to the "what I did on my holidays" school of writing – a travel writer who boasts more 'I's than a hospital cornea unit. A rambling, unstructured piece is equally unwelcome, as is a fondness for superlatives (those with an affection for "wonderful", "magnificent", "superb", etc., should join Adjectivals Anonymous before making another submission). The other side of this unbankable coin is the rather dry, flat piece which leaves the reader yawning after the first few paragraphs. An experienced editor can usually get an idea of whether an article is "possible" or "impossible" from the first sentence, so bear this in mind when you are constructing your opening paragraph – it may be the only paragraph that is read. Articles that have clearly been "cribbed" from guidebooks and which offer no fresh insight into a destination or event, also pass too frequently through a travel editor's in-tray, while material that displays no sign of research, historical or otherwise, will be very quickly rejected.

Originality of observation and expression are all. Michael Thompson-Noel, previously Travel Editor of the *Financial Times*, puts it succinctly: "Whether the destination is humdrum or exotic, it is the quality of the observation which counts." Such qualities are difficult to stage manage – either you've got the "eye" for fresh observation or you haven't. Good journalistic training (that well worn path through provincial newspapers) will help disguise this lack to a point, but an ability to avoid cliché and to invoke a more than interesting picture of your chosen destination will depend largely on your command of vocabulary and, ultimately, your personality.

Preparing for the Market

All the major national newspapers in the UK run regular travel pages (usually in the weekend supplements) while the vast majority of consumer magazines offer travel news and advice, or some kind of destination report. However, the number of specialist travel titles is limited. *Traveller* (first published by WEXAS in 1970) is one of the only surviving specialist UK title which features pure "travel" as opposed to "holiday" features. *Geographical* and *World* magazines offer some scope for travel pieces with an environmental "angle", while the north American and Far Eastern markets boast a number of specialist travel titles (see page 686 of the Directory for listing).

One thing all these publications have in common is an excess of unused travel articles. Some of them will be excellent pieces which have been "shelved" as emergency fillers or as "unsuitable in the current political climate" (you may have noticed a distinct lack of feature material on the Middle East during the Gulf crisis). Other articles will be borderline cases which an editor will hang on to until something better comes along (it generally does). And then of course there will be the untried writers' material, freshly packed in large brown envelopes, full of expectation and eager to jump the queue.

If you are lucky, some publications may offer advice on how to get to the head of this apparently endless line, and *Traveller*, rather unusually, produces written "guidelines" for contributors. However, your best preparation is simply to study the style and idiosyncrasies of the title you are targeting. And as a lady on *The Independent* features desk rather frostily put it, offering general guidelines to would-be contributors "is not our job." It is a buyer's market and the last thing a travel editor has time to do is wet-nurse you through stylistic and procedural requirements. Equally, he or she will be totally unsympathetic, and probably rather angry about wasting time on submitted material which is inappropriate – so do your homework first or you may spoil your chances for any future submissions. Another habit of greenhorn contributors which alternately amuses and invokes contempt is the phrase "First British Serial Rights" written rather pompously on the title page of a submission. Unless you are Colin Thubron and plan to syndicate your material world-wide, "FBSR" is something of a moot point.

Making a Submission

It is highly unlikely that an editor will commission you to write a piece unless you have already been published – not quite Catch-22, but almost. Therefore your first unsolicited submission is all-important (if an editor has rejected you once because he didn't like your style, he will probably look upon a second submission with some scepticism – you couldn't come up with the goods first time around so why should your next piece be any different?) Leaving aside all issues of style and ability, double-spaced, cleanly typed/word processed copy is vital. Handwritten copy is *unacceptable* (although surprisingly the odd manuscript does still slip through), and if you want to ensure your material is returned, enclose a self-addressed, stamped envelope.

The length of the piece will depend entirely on the requirements of your chosen market but as a rule of thumb, anything more than 2000 words is too long, and under 300 in danger of being terminally brief. If you are not sure, a quick call to the editor might get you an informative response. You may also like to check in advance whether or not your planned destination will be welcome or if "yet another feature" on Agra and the Taj Mahal has really had its day – at least for the next six months. Bear in mind that destinations can go through phases of being "done to death" on the travel pages (usually for reasons of fashion) and that some publications will have a policy of not repeating coverage of destinations within a certain period. You may also find that some regions are out of bounds. *Traveller*, for example, rarely features material on western Europe so a piece on the delights of the Cornish coastline, however original, will get short shrift.

The quickest way to find out if a travel editor is interested in your proposed destination is a phone call. Don't waffle on about what a wonderful trip you had, and don't treat the call like a travel writer's help line. Remember the golden rule, it is a buyer's market and anything in your behaviour which will anger, irritate or simply waste the travel editor's time will do you no favours whatsoever.

A letter detailing proposals for a selection of features is an alternative, but you will probably have to wait longer for a reply (if you get any reply at all). Make sure your letter is correctly addressed to the travel editor, and avoid over-familiar forms of address (most editors will not be impressed by letters addressed using either their first name, or that of their predecessor). A response of "yes, I would be interested to see something on hill walking in Tanzania" is not a signed and sealed contract to print whatever you submit. All the editor is telling you is that if your writing is up to scratch, and there happens to be an appropriate slot sometime in the future, yes, he may think about using your piece. This is the extent of his commitment so don't, as some rather naive contributors have been wont to do, assume that this is a definite commission. As already mentioned, editors only commission established writers whose material they know and like, and if you are reading this, it is unlikely to be you – yet!

Your next best move, once you have submitted the piece, is to forget about it. Don't badger the editor with phone calls or expect him to have read your article within a week or even four weeks of having received it. Travel editors, as has already been tirelessly pointed out, are inundated with manuscripts and don't need to be reminded that they haven't had a chance to read them all. If you would like an acknowledgement that your material has arrived safely, enclose a self-addressed, stamped postcard which can then be sent to you with little effort on the part of the editor or his staff. If you have had no reply within a period of three months, a letter requesting some kind of decision or response is reasonable, and, perhaps at a later date (deliberately indeterminate because a lot depends on the circumstances of your submission), a phone call to find out what's happening. It is at this stage that you must play a delicate balancing act between being firm about expecting a reply, and not pushing the editor so far that he says to hell with it and sends your piece to the post room as soon as he has put the phone down to an irate call from you. One thing you can be reasonably happy about, if the editor still has your piece after six months (yes, it can take that long for a decision) at least he hasn't yet said no!

You might like to submit your article to several publications but be careful about playing one off against the other, and if your material has come from a press trip, make sure that your fellow travelling journalists aren't selling a similar story to a competing publication. Two publications coming out with the similar story by different (or heaven forbid the same) journalist(s) does not a happy travel editor make.

Practical Tips on the Job

Although research is important, don't read too many guidebooks or you may find yourself, subconsciously (or otherwise) regurgitating the insight of others. Make a trip your own voyage of discovery. Talk to native inhabitants wherever possible (useful background and often the source of enlightening anecdote) and use your powers of observation to the fullest. If you can accompany your piece with a selection of photographs (colour transparencies for magazines and black and white for newspapers) so much the better, and you may find that using a camera will give you a fresh insight into your destination – alternatively don't spend your trip thinking like a travel photographer or you will miss other essential ingredients for a good travel piece.

Most professional travel writers make notes during their travels, and unless you have a photographic memory, a reporter's notebook is an important accessory. If you need to carry out a little research while you are away, contact the British Council or British Embassy/Consulate (if you are in a big city) for advice on libraries, sources of information, and so on. If you are travelling for a long period of time and want to submit material on the hoof, many branches of international hotel chains now offer business centres with secretarial and international communications facilities. Some destinations may have been the subject of international media coverage in recent years in which case you may like to check recent newspaper cuttings at the Colindale library (British Library, Newpaper Library, Colindale Avenue, London NW9 5HE, tel: 0171 412 7353).

If you have a particular theme in mind, or plan to tackle regional issues in a travel piece, you might try sending out a few letters of introduction to suitable contacts or interviewees before you go. The embassy or consulate of your intended destination may be able to help and *NewsGuides* (World Division Australia, 1 Vision Drive, Burwood East. You can of course contact the editor before you go, warning him about your intended submissions. This may help him remember you when your piece on Timbuktu arrives along with all the other hopeful articles on a grey Monday morning, but previous contact is no guarantee that he will be more interested in your work than anyone else's.

Making a Career of It

If you become so enamoured with travel writing that you plan to make it a permanent career, bear in mind the need for a *very* understanding bank manager. Unless you are of independent means, or have been organised enough to have saved for the possibility of lasting for at least six months without earning a penny, you will have to consider all your submissions as potential investments – even if they are accepted they are unlikely to pay dividends for many moons (getting money out of some newspapers and magazines is notoriously difficult). The most successful freelance journalists tend to be those who have been employed within their particular field of specialisation and who have already established a career's worth of contacts willing to buy work from them. This is less likely in the travel writing business since most travel editors operate a one man show and are less likely to give up the combined advantages of a salaried position and travel perks. Consequently most travel writers are, and always will be freelance.

Contacts, nevertheless, are very important. If you can build up a relationship with any editors who like your work and trust you to deliver the copy when you say you will, you are in a strong position for laying the foundations of a freelance career. A regular outlet in a favoured publication is ideal but don't expect to rely on this to pay the electricity bills. You may need to diversify and above all, you must learn to get as many angles out of one trip as is humanly possible – without affecting the quality of your work. You may turn your nose up at trade journals and anything that is not pure "travel" but this could be your only means of funding the time to do more personal, idiosyncratic pieces. "People come into the profession with this illusion that they are going to write delightful prose about interesting, exotic places," says one freelancer, "but in practice they are expected to produce more technical or "holiday stuff". If your idea of travel writing does not include a tour of the Manila Hilton's penthouse suite or a dawn visit to Jakarta's newest international conference centre, then strike all ideas of ever taking a press trip. If you become established on the circuit and you are invited on a press junket, you will probably discover that you and your hosts have very different ideas about what does and doesn't make for an interesting tour. You will also have to learn to find your own saleable angles on a trip where seven or eight other journalists are eagerly taking notes beside you. Also beware travel companies, tourist boards, etc., who will only offer you a trip in return for restrictions on what, when and where you publish material gleaned from a press trip, and consider that some publications including *The Independent* and *The New York Times* will not accept articles resulting from press trips or any other kind of "freebie".

Specialising in a particular continent or region may help ensure you regular work as an acknowledged expert, and if you are very familiar with a particular destination, guide book writing is a reliable, if occasionally tedious, means of plugging the commission gaps. Travel narratives are another possibility but they usually involve tales of travellers who have spent a good deal of time overseas, and unless you plan to uproot are not much use. The British Guild of Travel Writers, an association for established freelance travel writers could, prove a useful source of advice and information, and will probably get you on the mailing list for just about every travel public relations company in the UK. Wading through sackfuls of press releases is probably not the sort of thing you had in mind when dreaming about purple prose among the hill tribes of Chang Mai.

For lists of travel/feature editors and associations for journalists see p.899 of the Directory ■

AND FINALLY …
Chapter 15

WHITHER THE TRAVEL INDUSTRY?

by Roger Bray

The wakening of Albania after half a century of introversion and dictatorship provided a perfect illustration of one of tourism's fundamental dilemmas.

Here was a virgin coastline where resorts and hotels could be built in harmony with their surroundings, a blank page on which to avoid all the architectural blots which have disfigured so much of the Mediterranean landscape. Here there were no intrusive roadside billboards, hardly any restaurants, only the most rudimentary shops and, apart from the grim apartment blocks constructed during the regime of Enver Hoxha, an absence of high rise concrete. Yet here too, was a desperate lack of resources and, as an inevitable consequence of that, a political climate so volatile that it needed one spark – a nation-wide pyramid selling scandal – to explode in bloodshed.

It is a sad truth that countries with the greatest potential for the development of sustainable tourism are also those with the greatest incentives to do exactly the opposite, to build infrastructure as rapidly as possible in order to reap the benefits of an industry which brings quick economic returns. Tourism creates jobs very quickly and that can be as important to a country emerging from conflict, but with relatively ready access to funds, such as Lebanon, as it is to those which are simply grindingly poor. And it can have an impact beyond their borders, not just on their neighbours, to whom they might otherwise export instability, but on more distant countries, from which their increased wealth will allow them to import goods and services.

It is equally frustrating that such countries are potential valves through which the pressure of tourism on other, overdeveloped regions, could be reduced. The awkward fact that international tourism is a victim of its own success is no longer disputed. There is now widespread acceptance that excess of it is destroying the very things people travel to see and experience. More and more multi-storey hotels cast ever lengthening shadows over once deserted beaches. Cathedrals which were places of tranquil contemplation are jammed with sightseers. Florence, for example, is limiting the number of coaches allowed into its centre and Venice is also now forced, occasionally, to stop them crossing the causeway from the mainland. The Austrian resort of Lech will turn skiers away if more cars than it can handle come pouring over the Flexen Pass and Prague has seen such a massive invasion of visitors since the Velvet Revolution that the authorities there have even considered charging people to enter the old heart of the city.

Travel to and around the Asia-Pacific region is growing at such a terrifying rate that some observers believe it will be not much more that twenty years before domestic air traffic in China is second only to that of the United States. Some £40 billion are being spent on new or upgraded airports to cope with this growth and Shanghai alone is planning one capable of eventually handling 70 million passengers a year.

In the West, many airports are already close to saturation. BAA is ready to spend more than £1 billion on a fifth passenger terminal at London's Heathrow. Robert Crandall, the chairman of American Airlines, said once that take-off and landing slots there were so precious that they were worth some £5 million each. Aviation authorities have been spending enormous sums to expand the capability of air traffic control, the Civil Aviation Authority alone investing £750 million to increase airspace capacity in South East England by one third.

Recognising that in densely populated countries it will be difficult, not to say impossible, to build new runways, major aircraft manufacturers are discussing with the airlines means of getting more out of existing ones by developing a new generation of ultra-large aircraft which will carry more travellers in one go – perhaps eventually as many as 1000 passengers.

The impression is of an imminent Apocalypse – if not now then very shortly – and this is a feeling that has been fuelled by the Economist Intelligence Unit report which predicted that, by the turn of the century, total tourism to the Mediterranean area would have roughly doubled in a decade, from 115 million to 200 million. Picture, in your mind's eye, a package beach on the Costa del Sol in July. This Apocalyptic vision has not been dimmed by a perception that independent travel is increasing rapidly at the expense of package holidays, with the result that a new breed of tourist is reaching corners previously known only to the environmentally correct. To anyone who accepts this Malthusian view unquestioningly, the consequences are obvious. Pressure on the land and infrastructure must force up prices. Perhaps the palmy days of heap travel are numbered.

I have always believed that tourism, on balance, is more likely to educate than to reinforce prejudice and ignorance. The exclusion of people with limited budgets, not least those too young to have formed preconceptions, would be socially retrograde. Countries sending each other tourists are less likely to fight each other. Obviously there are always exceptions; not even tourism was able to prevent the crumbling cement that bound the former Balkan states together as Yugoslavia, but the general rule holds good.

So just how close is the Apocalypse? And is there still time, if not to head it off comprehensively, at least to push it far into the future? I believe there is. The notion that the planet is being overrun by tourists is greatly exaggerated and there is more world left than some might have us believe – there are even beaches where you can still be alone. It came home to me most forcibly on a recent visit to West Australia. We had parked our campervan for the night at Pardoo Station, a cattle spread off the highway from Port Headland to the remote pearl fishing port turned sunshine holiday resort of Broome. In the morning we walked across the scrub to the ocean. Kangaroos leaped away from us as we crossed the dunes. We were roughly at the southern end of a stretch of shoreline known as Eighty Mile Beach and it seemed as though you could walk that far and never encounter another human.

Not long afterwards we were sitting by a camp fire at the entrance to Windjana Gorge in the Kimberly, the last frontier of the safe world, as they like to call it, a rough expanse of country which was, until recently, inaccessible to most travellers. We had put up nylon tents in the blazing heat with little shade, plagued by flies that crawl into your eyes for moisture and cluster on your back like ripe blackberries. We had cooked over the flames, cracked beer and were feeling pretty hard bitten.

"This is nothing", snorted a fellow camper at the fireside. "This is not real wilderness. Now in Zambia ..." Some people are never satisfied, and yet, unwittingly, she had struck a telling point: everyone's tolerance of other tourists is different. Many people would agree that parts of Kenya's Masai Mara game park have been turned into something uncomfortably close to a safari park by convoys of camera-happy tourists in open-topped vehicles. For the biggest sector of the holiday market, however, even the Mara would seem a place of awesome emptiness.

The conventional sun, sea and sand holiday remains by far the most popular, representing around half those taken by the British, for example. The perception that independent travel has grown at the expense of the package does not stand up to close inspection. Figures from the UK Office of National Statistics suggest that in the fifteen years from 1980-1995, the number of Britons taking exclusive holidays increased by 144 per cent, the total travelling independently by 136 per cent.

The main reasons why major package tour operators are holding their own is that they have extended their range to cover almost every conceivable destination at all available times of year. Whilst rich independent travellers may have scorned the Caribbean in the summer major tour firms have snapped it up and where there is not enough business to justify a page in a large operator's brochure, smaller, specialist companies have prized open niches which might not have afforded them a living even a decade or two ago, successfully marketing anything from holiday homes in Asturias to rafting in Nepal.

Besides, many of those switching to independent holidays have simply depackaged the package. They are going to the same resorts but organising their own flights and car hire. The number of Britons claiming to travel on independent holidays to Spain rocketed by more than 400 per cent in the fifteen years to 1995. If one also takes into account the fact that the biggest destination for independent holiday makers is France (around 33 per cent in 1995), which attracts a very particular market, and that one of the fastest growing is the US, where there is no real language barrier, the premise that the British are suddenly striking out in significant numbers for the unknown looks somewhat shaky.

There is still time then, for countries not yet on the tourist milk run to ensure that they take due account of past mistakes and that their development is sensitively planned. In this respect India could prove an early test bed. Though it is still haunted by extreme poverty, it also has a burgeoning middle class and is experiencing a boom in investment: airlines and railways have been opened to private participation, Kerala is already established on the package trail and soon Orissa, described so brilliantly by Norman Lewis in his book *A Goddess in the*

Stones, may go the same way. Government and developers must take care not to damage India's fundamental attraction, however. It is a profoundly seductive place whose allure depends on diversity, the mystery and some would say impenetrability, of its cultures. Harm them, and you diminish the reason for travelling there.

Of course the temptation to sacrifice all to the quick buck will remain and the industry's history is littered with pious intentions, the world's coastlines scarred with the results of broken promises, but there is hope and there is breathing space. The greying of Europe's population will lift some of the urgency from coastal development because many older travellers have gentler, less intrusive demands. Over the next ten years or so, walking holidays, for example, will enjoy a significant growth.

Some Western governments have already grasped the point that it is in their own interests to encourage sustainable tourism and that in the long term allowing outside developers to ride in like white knights and gallop off, like the James gang, with the loot, could be counter productive. The European Union provides funds which are aimed specifically at helping local people in non-member countries to become stakeholders in their economies. I saw an example of this in the costal village of Qeparo, on the optimistically named Albanian Riviera. The EU's PHARE programme, provided 184,000 ECUs towards the conversion of a hilltop mansion into a guesthouse, the hope being that others would copy, laying a carpet of grassroots enterprise.

Major travel companies have also recognised the importance of taking the long term view. British Airways, for example, sponsors the world-wide Tourism for Tomorrow environmental awards. At the 1997 awards ceremony, the global accolade went to Taybet Zaman, a 19th century Jordanian village whose homes have been converted into accommodation for visitors to Petra, the ancient Nabataean "red rose city" of Burgeon's much-quoted poem. It was chosen for the way it integrates tourists with the community. Better this than some shimmering palace of a hotel, impenetrable to local people except as service staff.

The World Travel and Tourism Council, a forum for the chief executives of businesses from airlines to hotel chains, has been advising countries with nascent tourism industries on the way to create model resorts. It is self interest, of course, but it is enlightened self interest. If anyone can think of a better alternative, I would love to hear about it. In the meantime, it should be encouraged. Sustainable tourism, spreading the impact while limiting the damage, is the only way forward.

CUSTOMS

by John Rose and David Shenkin

Contrary to popular belief, customs officers do accept that most travellers are ordinary citizens going about their legitimate business and are *not* smugglers. So why is it that most travellers claim to feel nervous whenever they approach Customs, and actually feel guilty when negotiating a Green Channel?

It may be the uncertainty about the extent of allowances and precisely what is and is not permissible. The lists in the Directory on p.903 of this book should help. It may also be apprehension about the possibility of being singled out for checking – having bags emptied and even being personally searched. The modern Customs service recognises these pressures and considerable effort is made to make checks highly selective and well targeted at areas of highest risk so that the vast majority of travellers are not inconvenienced.

Today, Customs face a dramatically changing scenario, as trade barriers are dismantled, fiscal and physical frontiers are removed, journey times are reduced and ever-increasing traffic flows demand fast and efficient customs clearance.

A balance must be struck between the often conflicting demands of the free movement of travellers while at the same time protecting society. But from what? Serious threats are posed by the considerable number of prohibited and restricted items that may be either unwittingly carried by the uninformed traveller, or smuggled by and on behalf of the unscrupulous. Customs, Consulates and Ministries can give advice, often in the form of leaflets, about what can and cannot be imported. Examples which may be encountered by any traveller include the following:

Plant and animal health risks: Commercial importations are carefully controlled to prevent the spread of pests and disease, but thoughtless importation could quickly introduce an epidemic. Rabies is the most publicised threat but there are many more, including bugs and grubs which could devastate crops in a new environment. A health certificate, licence and/or quarantine is necessary for many plants and animals, and all live birds.

Endangered species: Few people bring home a wild animal from their travels. But many buy articles made from them (a skin handbag and shoes, an ivory ornament) without knowing that the species is in danger of extinction. Even trade in tourist souvenirs can threaten the most endangered species. In many countries it is illegal to cut or pick wild plants and flowers for the same reasons. They may be freely available and on sale in the country you are visiting but if you do not get a permit before you import them they are likely to be seized.

Obscene and indecent material: Changing social and cultural attitudes make this a sensitive area so check first and you will not be embarrassed.

Firearms, weapons, explosives, gas canisters: Travellers face stringent security checks before the start of their journey in an effort to separate them from even the most legitimate of these such as the sporting gun or the fisherman's knife. But on arrival at the destination their importation is likely to require a licence, and may be prohibited. Check first, or be sure to tell Customs on arrival.

Drugs: Personally-prescribed drugs and medicaments are best carried in properly labelled containers and, if they are for regular use, carry a letter from your doctor. Illicit drugs are a major and increasing concern for all Customs services and are often the principal reason for checks on travellers. Whilst the possession of very small quantities may be permissible in a few countries, their carriage across frontiers is invariably prohibited. Penalties are severe, and usually carry the risk of imprisonment.

Countries with long land frontiers may choose to exercise some controls inland but travellers through ports and airports provide a concentrated flow which enables an efficient screening and checking by Customs. Particularly in the prevention of drug trafficking, the search at the frontier enables Customs to identify and seize large commercial shipments, before they are distributed inland for sale in small, usable quantities. In addition, Customs and Police will often cooperate to monitor the delivery of a consignment to its inland destination in order to identify principals in smuggling organisations.

Many people think that drugs are found from tip-offs, and that routine checks are not necessary. That is not so. Valuable intelligence does come from co-operation between Customs and Police services around the world. But detections made in the day-to-day work of ports and airports depend on the Customs Officer's initiative and experience in assessing risks and choosing the right passenger. The overall Customs effort against drug trafficking is a mix of intelligence, information, judgement and intuition. Officers are carefully trained to observe, select, question and examine. "Profiles" are built up from instances where patterns have emerged, but they are but one tool in a large bag, and need to be constantly up-dated and refined as methods and types of courier change. Spot checks may need to be done to test out Customs' perception of risk, and that is where the innocent traveller may come under examination. Co-operation will help allay suspicion of the innocent, and full searches – including a body search – are only undertaken under strict supervision and where there are strong grounds for suspecting an offence.

Checking Travellers

An officer who stops a passenger needs information before making a decision (whether or not a full examination is needed) and so questions must be asked. The officer is looking for tell-tale signs that something is not right. The smuggler cannot be completely honest about himself and must tell lies to stand any chance of success. It is that deceit that a Customs officer is trying to see through. Travel documents, passports, questions about the purpose of the journey – all give a picture which the officer can test for credibility against what he sees and what he hears and, ultimately, what he feels. He may not get it right every time, but intelligent, intuitive assessments do result in the discovery of people attempting to smuggle.

The traveller who objects to the way he or she is dealt with at Customs should complain to a Senior Customs official at the time of the incident. In that way most complaints can be dealt with to everyone's satisfaction, and while events are fresh in everyone's mind. By all means follow up with a letter if you feel you have not got satisfaction. But a written complaint made for the first time several days after an incident is difficult to investigate and rarely produces a satisfactory outcome for the complainant.

In addition to their role in protecting society, the Customs service has a duty to collect import taxes (which can still be substantial on luxury goods, despite moves to harmonise more tax rates and remove barriers to trade). The expensive watch, silk carpet, video camera or item of jewellery can still result in a hefty tax bill on arrival home. Goods in excess of allowances must be declared to

Customs, or you risk having them confiscated, and criminal proceedings taken for smuggling. Many offences of this nature are settled between Customs and the traveller by the payment of a fine and few cases go to court. However, if you also have to buy your confiscated goods back, the overall penalty can amount to a large sum. In addition, the amount of time and effort spent by Customs dealing with such irregularities increases the opportunity for the drugs courier to get through undetected.

The business traveller can usually be relied on to know what personal allowances can be carried into each country, but a misunderstanding can occur when business goods are carried. Lap-top computers, replacement parts for equipment, parts for repair and sample prototypes can all find their way into a business traveller's baggage. Sometimes he will act only as a "courier" for another part of his company. Such items are invariably liable to some form of control as frontiers are crossed and a declaration to Customs on each occasion is the safest way – unless you have personally checked with a reliable authority and you are confident you know what you are doing.

As a general rule, do not carry packages for anyone if you are unsure what they contain. Whether it is personal or business, your freedom or even your life could be at stake if something goes wrong.

On 1 January 1993, the Single European Act heralded the free movement of goods and people within the European Community (EC). For visitors, controls on goods and the collection of taxes generally take place at the first point of entry into the Community, and subsequent travel involves only checks for prohibited and restricted goods. For travellers within the Community, personal allowances for tax paid goods have increased substantially. However, the very large differences in the price of alcoholic drink and tobacco goods within the European Community still result in some restrictions on the quantities permitted to be carried, for both health and fiscal reasons.

Since the advent of the single market, Customs' controls on EC passengers at airports and ferry ports have been improved to provide a faster and more efficient service which targets the high risk traveller, but permits the majority to move unimpeded through customs.

Make sure you are properly informed when you travel. A confident traveller will project his or her innocence and help Customs to concentrate on their own priorities, for all our good.

For customs regulations for the UK, the USA, Canada, Australia and New Zealand see p.903 of the Directory
For duty free allowances world-wide see p.909 of the Directory

SHOPPING AND DUTY FREE

by Caroline Brandenburger

Shopping should perhaps carry a government health warning. Taken to excess, it can have damaging effects – and not only on your purse. Travelling, particularly in less developed countries where prices seem so much lower, can lead to a fatal shopping addiction that one friend who lived in Hong Kong called "shopping sickness". Dazzled by items for sale that are so very different from what is available at home, by the staggering workmanship of arts and crafts, or simply the cheap pastiche of the familiar, shopping can become wholly obsessive and indiscriminate!

Nevertheless, it is possible to buy memorable souvenirs – the kind which will give you lasting pleasure, and not be discarded at the back of a cupboard soon after you arrive home.

Knowing where to go is half the battle. There are numerous shopping guides to different parts of the world but I invariably find their materialistic tone nauseating – as if the world were simply a bran tub for the sated Westerner to dip into. Recommendations are probably your best source of advice but keep your eyes peeled while you travel.

Clearly, the range of available goods will depend on where you are, as will the way in which you buy them. Bartering will be perfectly appropriate in some places – a street market in India or a stall in Mexico – while wholly inappropriate in a smart European boutique. Still, even in smart shops you may be able to negotiate on price according to whether you pay by cash or credit card.

Hardened bartering experts recommend starting at a quarter of the starting price. To most Western minds this seems cruelly low, but the argument runs that there is an instant mark-up on the price as soon as your tourist face appears on the horizon. Having said that, it is quite likely that the original price is still less than you would pay for a similar item back home (if you could get it), so half that price still represents quite a bargain. Don't get obsessional about driving a really hard bargain. Obviously you don't want to be ripped off, but equally, you don't want to screw the vendor into the ground, however much of a rascal you might think him.

If you simply can't arrive at a mutually agreed price, retire gracefully. Sometimes that's not always easy if you've been plied with mint tea or cold drinks and generally made to feel a sense of obligation. But don't get brow-beaten into buying something you don't want. My parents found themselves in an oriental antique shop in San Francisco, looking at a box for $2000. After half an hour of unusually intense and heavy selling technique on the part of the shopkeeper, they made moves to leave – without buying. At which point the shopkeeper flung himself into the corner of the shop and burst violently into tears. My parents looked on aghast as, through the tears, he explained that his business was about to go bust and he desperately needed $3000 to keep afloat. They tried to calm him, feeling quite distressed themselves, and only just emerged financially unscathed.

When you're contemplating buying something, do remember that you've got to get it home. It may be portable, in which case you can carry it yourself. Or you can pack it up and send it, parcel post, through the local post office – a process which may take as long as six or eight weeks. (See Chapter 11 for information about freight forwarding.)

If it's large and unwieldy, you'll have to investigate other ways of getting it back. Some shops may have a perfectly efficient system of sending goods to your home, whether by air or by sea, packing items free and charging only for the postage or freight. A major shop will probably use a good shipper who charges a reasonable amount, packs well, and is reliable. If you do choose to let the shop ship your goods for you, make sure you have a confirming receipt, emphasise careful packing, and check it's insured against loss or breakage. But do be careful: in some less reputable shops, the cost could be enormous, completely cancelling any discount you've just managed to negotiate.

Equally, there are horror stories of the happy shopper paying for his bolt of silk or lacquered pot, arranging for the dealer to send it home, and never seeing it again. But this can happen even if you arrange the passage yourself – things do unaccountably disappear and whether stolen or lost, you'll probably never know. On the whole, though, goods will arrive.

If you arrange the packing and shipping yourself, it may well be cheaper. But it can be a complicated process, involving working out local rules and regulations about permits, packing, materials, sizes and weights. Nevertheless, it could be worthwhile if you have several large items to send. Find out a reliable local shipper by asking in a good hotel.

Duty Free

Perhaps one of the first things to be aware of is the distinction between "duty free" and "tax free". Duty free is defined as a product free of duties and taxes, and applies to liquor and tobacco products only. It is really a historical hangover from the 17th century when excise duty was introduced on alcohol to deter people from getting drunk.

Tax free is defined as products free of taxes (i.e. VAT), which covers perfumes, cosmetics, fashion accessories, watches, jewellery, electrical and electronic goods, photographic equipment, china, crystal and other gift items.

The shops in airports are administered by airport operators, and the in-flight or on-deck outlets by the relevant airline or shipping company. The British Airports Authority (BAA), the main airport operator in Britain, apparently establishes its prices conducting regular high street surveys.

Duty free discounts vary, but tax free discounts tend to be 20 per cent. Although the price will be lower than the high street, it will still be higher than the original price of the product from the manufacturer. As a spokesman for BAA explained, "We have a policy which splits the benefit between the passenger/ purchaser and the company. It provides the passenger with a good bargain at high street prices, and also a significant source of revenue for the airport, which keeps down the price of landing charges, and therefore the fare prices. It also means we can provide new facilities. Duty free benefits all passengers, not just the ones that buy."

Nevertheless, the booming business of duty and tax free goods (earning BAA more than £150m annually) has taken a staggering blow. "1992" and the deregulation within the European Community, *in theory* has marked the end of duty free shopping since a single market inevitably means no duty free zones. BAA held the belief that the logistical problems of introducing harmonisation of prices within the EC may well mean that the existing system continues. Bringing prices in line in all the different countries, they surmised, would lead to drastic reductions in some and increases in others – potentially the source of major political conflict. For instance in Denmark, a packet of twenty cigarettes is 1.96 European Currency Units (ECUs) while in Greece it is 0.28 ECU. Any attempt by the Greek government to raise cigarette prices in a nation of heavy-smokers would do little for their ratings in the polls. As ever, the solution is compromise. Duty-free is to be phased out during the 1990's, and clearly the loss of revenue means that BAA will be concentrating heavily on its ordinary retail activities to make up the shortfall.

Tips for Travelling Shoppers

1. Duty free items are more of a bargain than tax free, because you save on excise duty as well as VAT.

2. Most airports in the UK have fairly similar duty free prices, but there are greater differences between the ferries.

3. If you want to buy perfume, it is probably best to buy it at the airport shop where it will be up to 20 per cent less than high street prices. If you buy it on the plane, there is usually only a limited range sold in small bottles.

4. Cameras also tend to be cheaper in UK airport duty free stores than in the high street (10 per cent on average), but this is not a hard and fast rule. Also bear in mind that if you are passing through some of the Middle Eastern airports, or travelling to the Far East or New York, you will probably be able to find photo-graphic equipment at even cheaper prices.

5. Duty free spirits are about 40 per cent cheaper than High Street prices for standard products, but in some European countries such as Spain you will find spirits are even cheaper.

6. When comparing prices of spirits, note different bottle sizes and alcohol strengths.

7. It is often possible to phone ahead to check what is in stock and the prices available, and the airlines (with a little persuasion) should also be able to for-ward you a price list of in-flight duty free goods.

8. *Business Traveller* magazine carries a monthly feature on world-wide duty free news and information as well as a spot price comparison between major world airports on up to four items.

9. Don't forget that your best source of information is the personal experiences of recent and regular travellers. Don't be afraid to ask for their advice: shopping is usually a major feature of most traveller's journeys and many will be happy to wax lyrical about their "bargains".

For duty free allowances worldwide see p.909 of the Directory

GUIDE OR PORTER?
by Richard Snailham

There is something timeless about the problems of travel with guides and porters. Stories in Henry Morton Stanley's late-Victorian best sellers find their echoes today, and it was instructive to learn that a recent Cambridge University Expedition to Sangay in Ecuador had the same problems that I had had on an ill-fated expedition to Sangay ten years before: the local Indians had either refused to take their mules to the agreed objective or simply defected.

Nevertheless, a local guide is often useful, sometimes indispensable. Small boys hover outside the souk in Marrakesh and we once spurned them only to become comprehensively lost in the myriad covered alleyways. Rather less useful is the young boy who tags along on the streets of a Third World city with which you might be quite well acquainted. He will get into a conversation with you and then offer to show you the principal sights. Before your tour is finished you may find you are sponsoring him through school.

Sometimes a guide is obligatory, as at a French chateau – and generally good value. Where they are not, a judgement has to be made. In wild, sparsely populated, ill-mapped country I would say a guide was essential, especially where you do not speak the prevailing language and the local people do not speak yours. In Samburu country recently, with a map that was far too large-scale, I needed our camel-handlers to steer us to the objective.

How to Get the Best

Fix your price. If a journey is involved and you require any form of transport or any great length of time, it is best to find out the cost in advance – if only to minimise the shock of the often inordinate sum asked. Guides have no meters and rarely are they governed by any regulations. A price agreed at the outset, especially if there are other guides in the offing (and thus a choice), is often substantially less than that demanded at the end. Even in Nairobi I recently fell into the trap of failing to establish the price before taking a taxi to the outer suburbs (and was still mightily stung, even after an unedifying argument at the journey's end). Before you clinch the deal, bargaining is generally possible and is often expected.

Pick the right man. Your selection of the right guide is very important. Unfortunately this often involves a snap judgement based on appearances. Women often seem to have better intuitive judgement than men, I find, and a few quick questions on the spot before departure are valuable in ensuring you have a good man. For how things can go wrong, read Geoffrey Moorhouse's *The Fearful Void*. Some unscrupulous guides lead their charges into remote regions and then refuse to conduct them back without a big bonus. Never entirely trust a guide's navigational ability. He will not usually admit to being lost, but can often become so. Try to keep a check on distance covered, note all prominent landmarks and take their bearings from identifiable points on your route and the time that you took them. Avoid questions like "Is it far?" or "Will we get there tonight?" Guides often have more inclination to please their employers than to tell the sometimes painful truth, and the answers to these two questions will invariably be "no" and "yes."

Problems with Porters

The days of mammoth expeditions with armies of porters are probably over. I was once manager and paymaster of a constantly changing team of about 130 porters in Nepal, but smaller, faster-moving assaults are now the order of the day and they normally require less manpower. The problems are otherwise the same, however, and most have been hinted at in the above section on guides. Here are a few further suggestions:

1. Be totally familiar with the local currency and its exchange rate before you embark on any negotiation.

2. Try and secure the services of a local "minder" to help firm up the local *bundobust* (useful Hindi word meaning "the logistical arrangements"). On a recent camel safari I took a young NCO from the Kenya General Service Unit who was excellent in his dealings with porters and headmen. Policemen, soldiers, students have all served me well in this role.

3. Remember that guides and porters have to have food and shelter. Who is providing this, you or they? You may have to offer advance payment and provide for their journeys home.

4. This goes for their animals too (if any). Camels often have to carry their own forage across deserts and yaks carry theirs up the last stages of the climb to the Everest base camp. Remember they always travel home faster than they travel out!

5. A head porter or *sirdar* is often a good idea if you have a large number in your party. He will be worth his extra pay.

6. Only pay a portion of the agreed fee at the outset. Keep the balance in your money belt until you get there.

7. Guides should, of course, lead but porters should take up position in the middle of your party. This prevents "disappearances" and enables you to react if a porter becomes ill or tired.

The Brighter Side

Finally, if in doubt, take a guide or porter rather than try to struggle on without them. They add colour to the whole enterprise, are generally honest and good-hearted and could well end up firm friends. It is worth while taking a few presents with you as a mark of gratitude. Some of your own kit will be much appreciated. Otherwise, penknives, folding scissors and cigarettes go down well. British Commemorative coins, postcards of HM the Queen, empty screw-top tobacco tins – even my old shirts – have proved acceptable gifts.

SPONSORSHIP

by Myfanwy Vickers

The quest for sponsorship for your trip is not a bad test of qualities that will stand you in good stead as a happy and successful traveller: grit, tenacity, enthusiasm and unflagging energy. It is also the aspect of travel most reminiscent of the job you thought you were getting away from: raising money is hard work. It generates bureaucracy and administration, photocopying and phone calls – all of which absorb your well-saved money.

But it can also be rewarding in more ways than the purely financial; indeed, the contact you will have with people during the preparations prior to the trip can be every bit as heart-warming as that which you will experience once you are launched in far-flung places. But if you are to persuade people to give you funds, you are embarking on a campaign as well as an expedition. Securing the sponsorship is not the end of the matter either, as you will have to execute the follow up, contacting donors and sponsors once again, keeping your side of the bargain, delivering the goods and saying thank you. Be realistic, and bear this in mind before you start. It is not easy; what *is* easy is to be caught up in the next stage of your own life once you're back home, having enjoyed all the backing. Don't promise more than you can deliver. You burn your boats for next time, and make it doubly difficult for everybody else who is seeking the same thing.

You can seek sponsorship from business and industry, the media, grant-giving organisations, clubs and local groups, friends and the public. The vast bulk will come from business and industry (in kind rather than cash) and in return for publicity. Some firms will offer their services, e.g. free printing, and many will offer you goods at reduced or cost price.

Remember how many appeals land on the desk of people you are targeting (Kodak receive 300 a week): they will be quick to dismiss a shoddy, ill-considered, greedy or otherwise unseductive approach. Capture their attention and command their interest from the word go. Make the package professional. Invent your own logo; do not use that of other organisations without their permission – for all your good intentions, you could end up with a court case on your hands. Each letter should be typed, addressed personally, and tailored to the individual or his company (telephone beforehand, if necessary, to get the right name). Don't duplicate round robins; canvassing indiscriminately is rarely worth the paper it is xeroxed on.

Where appropriate, an eminent patron can give an expedition authority and gravitas. A copy of a supportive letter from the patron will lend credibility to the venture, and tempt people to put their faith where others have already shown confidence.

Provide a clear outline of what you plan to do and why, enclose a route map, and a breakdown of costs. Indicate how much of the budget you are covering out of your own pocket, and stipulate what you would like, rather than issuing a general plea for anything and everything. Provide a concise profile of the team members, with any relevant experience or achievements to date. Show in your letter that you have already done considerable planning, research and preparation (which you have, of course!), and that departure is not wholly dependent on backing; sponsors are much more willing to help those with evidently serious intent who are already helping themselves. Once you have done all this, feel pleased with yourself if you get a 10 per cent response rate!

Think local when appealing to businesses, companies, equipment stockists and so on. Smaller businesses receive fewer requests and they may like to be involved. Often you will simply find greater goodwill and a more personal approach than in a rule-bound conglomerate or multinational. Can you find a connection between the business and its interests, your trip and the destination?

The greater logic you can give to any potential generosity, the better.

The main, if not the only thing that most people can offer sponsors is publicity, and securing this is not always easy. Be realistic about what you are offering, clear that you know just what the company is asking for, and certain you are able to provide the goods. Are you offering to sport a shirt with the sponsor's logo on it, and if so, is anyone going to see it except the lost ape men of Sumatra? If it is photographs you are providing, give evidence of your ability with a camera; very few people take really good shots that can be used in a national campaign. They do not happen by themselves, either – you will have to set them up, and the best ones always present themselves when you are at your most exhausted. Can you get media coverage? Only pre-paid commissions will impress firms who know how unlikely you are to make headline news otherwise. So try to sell articles to papers, magazines and colour supplements before departure, finding out what particular angles interest the editor. Any contract with film or TV will assure you immediate and abundant offers of sponsorship as there is no more powerful publicity for any product. Is there a promising audio angle? If so you could sell to radio.

If publicity en route is to be part of the deal, start setting up contacts in the country concerned: ask the embassy for advice, arm yourself with the names of the appropriate people in the media, and find ways to overcome man's innate reluctance to give some sponsor a plug at his expense! Obviously, if you can give evidence of successful marketing in the past, and ways in which other companies have benefited from your efforts, you are at an advantage.

Having said all this, many companies and suppliers have a margin for those who will not, in their opinion, achieve much publicity but who they like, quite simply, as individuals. Some also invest in what they call "good citizenship", although almost without exception this applies to field projects or research-based expeditions where a commercial company can be seen to be putting something back into the host country at the same time as raising its profile in the minds of potential new recruits. The "We're going to Tibet and we want to do some science so as to help raise funds" approach tends not to wash, and a sponsor such as Shell or the Royal Geographical Society looks for a prior degree of competence within, and commitment to, the field.

Most grant-giving organisations only provide money for specific "scientific" or investigative projects, but sift discriminatingly through libraries and specialist directories and target the few that you think likely. It may seem unpromising, but the money has to go to someone.

Finally, you can raise money by arranging your own special events – anything from a sponsored parachute jump to selling cakes at the local jumble sale. If your project has a charitable goal, give lectures to schools, colleges, clubs etc. This, however, can be time-consuming, with lots of unsuspected, hidden costs and a disproportionately small amount of money raised.

It is, naturally, easier to persuade people to give money away if you in turn are helping someone or something else. Consequently many travellers decide to raise money for charity. But what it boils down is that you personally are never going to make much out of it, and, let's face it, neither should you. A percentage of the money raised, say 10 per cent, may go to defray your costs, but any more than this is likely to lose you sympathy. You *must* contact the charity concerned for their authority before you start; a letter from them will show that you are bona fide. And open a special bank account in the name of the cause, so as to keep careful track of the money.

Contacts are not essential in this game, but anybody can unearth them and even create them. Do not be timid about approaching people, however elevated they may seem, for their potential interest and support. More often than not you will be pleasantly surprised at the response and the extent to which people will put themselves out on behalf of a project they take to. Liaise with organisations that are happy to advise, such as the extremely helpful enthusiasts at the Royal Geographical Society.

Beware, however, of danger of having the "freebie" tag attached to your efforts. Although pleasure is as valid a reason for travel as any other, people can, understandably, be quick to resent the idea that they should help finance what they see as "a jolly" on your behalf. Bring your tact and your conviction to bear with such an attitude, but don't bang your head against a brick wall: if the reaction is resentful, try elsewhere.

Perhaps the best bit of advice is: start early, like the proverbial worm catching the bird. Plan ahead! It may seem unlikely, but some firms like as much as a year's notice; in this way the project can be incorporated into their plans for the following financial year's budget. Everything takes much longer than you think, and many appeals are disappointed because the departure date is just too imminent.

Sponsorship is one of the few gentleman's contracts that still exists. When you get back, stick to your word. Do not be disappointed if, after all this, they don't make full use of the material – but give them every opportunity to do so. Most companies say that they never hear from travellers again. A thank you, a copy of a published article – all will be appreciated, and will stand you in good stead for the next time.

Throughout the whole thing, be organised and efficient; keep a record of all correspondence. Don't take rejections personally; pursue those who show interest like a limpet. Be lively and polite. They don't *have* to give you anything. But don't bury your individuality in business-like formalities; at the end of the day, it is yourself rather than a journey you are selling. Apply your own flair, and enjoy it!

THE TICKET OUT

by Ingrid Cranfield

Many countries require travellers to show a ticket out of the country before they are issued with a visa or allowed over the border. This onward ticket is normally expected to be a 'plane ticket, though sufficient evidence of the traveller's respectability and solvency can ensure that a ticket for some other means of transport will be accepted. The other alternative to an airline ticket is the purchase of travellers' cheques. Normally £600 of photocopied travellers' cheques is sufficient to demonstrate solvency. There is the option to cash in the cheques after the visa has been obtained.

Onward tickets are no problem for travellers who wish to use them, but many people, especially overlanders, want to enter a country, but have no intention of flying out. For them, it will be desirable to try and get a refund.

Some countries require that the onward ticket be shown on application for a visa, but not thereafter. The purchaser can get a visa and then cash in his ticket before actually leaving home. If you do this, it is best to buy the ticket on credit, so that no cash need change hands either on purchase or on refund.

However, countries with this pre-condition for a visa will nearly always want to see the onward ticket at the point of immigration. If the buyer does not intend to use it, he will have to obtain a refund either in the country or after leaving. For many reasons it is best, therefore, to buy direct from a large carrier with many offices in convenient places and not through a travel agency, and to pay in cash or travellers' cheques. In effect, a full fare ticket should be purchased to ensure a full refund.

Buying outside the region for travel to the Third World, you should use a hard currency which will be foreign to your destination. In many countries you will not be allowed to purchase in any but a hard currency. If you buy in one soft currency, you cannot expect to be refunded in another, and this could prove inconvenient. Some Third World authorities are anxious to prevent export of their currency and will prefer refunds to be given in hard currency. Elsewhere, they will be desperate to get their hands on your hard currency and refunds will be given in the local currency, which will generally be a soft one. If your original purchase was in hard currency, you are, at least, in a stronger position when requesting the same in exchange.

Buying in the region is usually cheaper, especially if the black market rate is favourable, except where taxes are very high. To avoid paying such taxes, buy elsewhere, or get a friend to buy you a ticket in another country and post it to you (suitably disguised). The rules on refunding tickets vary from one place and one carrier, sometimes even one office, to another. Tickets are sometimes stamped "non-refundable" (and the ink is sometimes even eradicated by unscrupulous travellers), but such tickets are, in any case, usually transferable. Refunds in the form of MCOs (Miscellaneous Charges Orders) should be accepted, as these can be used to buy an airline ticket or service. An MCO can even serve as an altered ticket and, like a ticket, can be cashed in separately.

Finally, make a note of the ticket number in case of loss; buy yourself a return or onward ticket to avoid being stranded if you're visiting a really remote destination; and do, for the airline's sake, cancel any reservation you don't intend to use.

COMING HOME

by John Blashford-Snell

Until Rula Lenska joined us on a quest in Nepal I had no idea that actors and expeditioners suffer from the same problem at the end of the show. Both tend to get "post project depression" (PPD) or "after expedition blues".

When a play ends or the filming of a series finishes, Rula explained, the cast is suddenly split up, left to find new jobs or return home for a well-earned rest. The friendships and working relationships break up, the team disappears and a different life style starts overnight. So it is with expeditioners, and, I imagine, ocean voyagers.

Dr John Davies, one of Britain's leading exploration medics, once started a lecture at the Scientific Exploration Society with the statement" "Expeditions may endanger your health." He went on to point out that for the novice, the experience can be an introduction to negative aspects of one's personality easily suppressed in normal daily life. However, with appropriate counselling and support, this can be a journey of self-discovery leading to increased confidence and a more enlightened attitude to others.

Seasoned adventurers, like experienced actors, recognise post expedition blues, the symptoms of which are similar to bereavement. This is triggered by the loss of one's new found "family" of expedition friends in a widely different culture and suddenly being cut off from the excitement on return home.

"I just can't face going back to nine to five in the Tax office," groaned an Inland Revenue Officer who had spent three months in the Gobi. Routine and mundane lifestyle aggravate the condition and for many it is cured only by involvement in another challenge. Returning explorers also face isolation from family and colleagues, who have no concept of their recent intense experience. They are often perplexed by the indifferent response to their stories and may end up silent and withdrawn. The envy and resentment of the uninitiated, who imagine that one has been on a jolly picnic or at best some self-inflicted masochism, is also common.

"Don't know what you've done to my mother," complained a son after his mum had returned from one of the Discovery Expeditions in South America, "She's awfully quiet." But meeting the lady in question at a reunion a few months later, I found her in great spirits, reliving the experience with her old pals.

John Davies, with whom I have been on many trips, advises "returnees", especially the older ones, to spend several days enquiring about the day to day problems that have occurred in their absence, before slowly beginning to recount their experiences. So, on being met by my wife as I stepped off a comfortable British Airways flight from Delhi recently, I asked, "How are those new trees in the garden coming on?" "Have you gone mad?" replied Judith, well used to a dozen tales of high adventure before we reached the car park. But perhaps I'm beyond hope!

However, there may be medical problems, as I discovered a year after a Sandhurst expedition in Ethiopia when my right leg started shaking uncontrollably whilst I was lecturing. "How strange," I thought, trying not to notice the offending limb. Two weeks later, lying racked with a fever in hospital, it was found that I had malaria, by which time I also had blurred vision and had lost twenty pounds in weight. But once diagnosed, malaria is usually fairly easily cured and the doctors knew I'd been to the tropics.

Sadly not all ailments are so quickly dealt with, as I realised after twelve months of visits to the St. Pancras Hospital for Tropical Diseases. Strange hot flushes, violent stabbing pains in my stomach, aches and itches in awkward places were making life extremely uncomfortable. "There's nothing wrong with you," boomed one of the world's leading specialists in tropical diseases, after exhaustive tests proved negative. "You young fellows imagine you've caught everything under the sun if you spend six weeks in the jungle. When I was in Burma ..." he droned on. My morale at was rock bottom and it took great courage to return to the hospital a few weeks later, after the symptoms had become almost unbearable.

As luck would have it, a charming and much more sympathetic Asian doctor was on duty and in no time he had me face down on a trolley with a flexible viewing device inserted up my rear end and my shirt over my head. "Keep him still," he beseeched as two strapping Fijian nurses pinned me down. "Oh! my goodness," exclaimed the physician. "What a fine example. Excuse me, sir, but you have a splendid parasite. It is quite unusual to see one so well developed. Would you mind if we allowed a class of medical students to see it?" Before I could even protest, I was wheeled in to a theatre full of students, many of them, I noted, looking between my legs, were extremely attractive young women. One by one they came forward, without even a titter, to peer intently up my bottom. At last I was taken away and the awful tube removed. "What now?" I asked. "Oh – just swallow these pills and you'll be as right as rain," smiled the doctor.

So it is my advice that if you feel ill after an overseas visit, go straight to your GP and say where you have been. Mark you, they might diagnose jet lag which can affect one more than most care to admit.

This handbook contains useful tips on surviving the onslaught and reducing its effects to the minimum so I'll not dwell on it. Suffice to say that when I get home I keep going until nightfall, doing simple uncomplicated things like unpacking or weeding, then I take a very mild sleeping pill and totter off to bed. With luck I can usually sleep for six hours. The important thing is to avoid stressful situations and don't make any important decisions until after your body has readjusted. In my case this is usually 24 hours. Indeed, even weeding may not be a good idea. Having stepped off a long flight from Mongolia, I pulled up all my wife's carefully planted ground cover instead of the weeds.

If I am still feeling low, I concentrate on writing my thank-you letters (if not done on the 'plane!) and amending my packing list, whilst memory of all the things I forgot to take and all unnecessary items that went with me is still fresh. Then it's down to sorting out photos, slides, videos and writing reports and articles. Next comes repairs to kit, getting cameras serviced and preparing lectures.

If you start to feel sorry for yourself, you are not really bringing the benefits of your experiences to your life at home. Indeed I expect you will find that you have changed but the world has not.

The whole point is to keep active and look forward to the next challenge, and, if you can't afford another trip, why not use your vigour and energy to help others in your area, sick children, old people or anyone who could use some voluntary assistance.

For the adventurous there are some opportunities supporting organisations like the Duke of Edinburgh's Award or Riding for the Disabled and there are dozens of environmental groups needing help. (See Section 3 of the directory for Specialist Organisations)

The great cry is, if you want to avoid PPD, keep busy. ■

Directory

WHERE AND WHEN
Section 1

GEOGRAPHICAL SECTION

Please note that all the information in this section is subject to change. The world has changed rapidly within the last few years, and will probably continue to do so. New countries have emerged, such as Eritrea, and the former Yugoslavia has split into individual republics, governments will change, and countries, such as Albania can become dangerous for the tourist within a matter of weeks. Therefore it is advisable to contact the Foreign Office on the latest up to date information. Please treat this section as a guideline only.

The Visas included in this section are applicable to Australians, Americans, British, Canadians and New Zealanders. Entry requirements can also change, especially in the CIS, therefore it is always advisable to contact the relevant embassy/consulate and check. See Section 8 for the address of the relevant embassy.

Inoculations also change, with new outbreaks of diseases, please therefore check with an immunisation centre or your doctor several months before travelling . We have also included Cholera, which is still a serious risk in many parts of the world. However the World Health Organisation stated that the immunisation against Cholera was not effective. We have not included Tetanus, because it is felt that this is an injection worth having constantly up to date. Many other injections may be needed, for example, Hepatitis A, Japanese B Encephalitis, Meningococcal Meningitis, Rabies, so please check. Where inoculations have an asterisk*, this means that the vaccine is a requirement as opposed to a recommendation.

Airlines and the average length of flights are based from London.

Countries are listed by continent alphabetically.

AFRICA

Algeria
Capital Algiers (El Djezair) **Lang** Arabic and French **Currency** Dinar = 100 centimes **Govt.** Multi-party Republic **Rel** Islam (Sunni Moslem) **Size** 2,381,741 sq km – 919,595 sq miles **Pop** 26,581,000 **GMT** + 1 **When** North of the Sahara September to May South of the Sahara October to April **Visas** Required by all (No Israeli stamps in passports) **Validity** Tourist-30 days from date of issue Business-90 days **Time to Get:** 2-3 days **Safety** High risk area, in the last three years there have been many attacks on westerners. Curfew between 23.30 and 04.00 **Inoc** Yellow Fever* if you have come from an infected area, Typhoid, Polio, Malaria, **Airlines** Air Algerie, Iberia, Swiss Air, Air France, Alitalia **Average length of flight** 2.5 hours **Food** Meaty, similar to Moroccan and Tunisian

Angola
Capital Luanda **Lang** Officially Portuguese and Bantu languages **Currency** New Kwanza = 100 lwei **Govt** Under the constitution of the Second Republic of Angola – unstable **Rel** Mostly Tribal **Size** 1,246,700 sq km – 481,354 sq miles **Pop** 1,609,000 **GMT** +1 **When** May to October – presently no travel allowed though **Visas** Required by all but no tourist visas issued at the moment **Safety** volatile situation, check with Foreign Office **Inoc** Yellow Fever*, Hepatitis A, Cholera, Typhoid, Tetanus, Polio, Malaria, Rabies **Airlines** Air France, Sabena **Average length of flight** 19.5 hours including stopovers **Food** Simple, Portuguese influence

Benin
Capital Porto Novo **Lang** French and indigenous tribal languages **Currency** CFA Franc = 100 centimes **Govt** Relatively stable democracy **Rel** Mainly tribal, christian and muslim **Size** 112,622 sq km – 43,484 sq miles **Pop** 5,215,000 **GMT** +1 **When** January to April

Visas Required by all *Validity* 15 days within 3 months of issue *Time to get* 1 day or 30 days if information has to come from Benin *Safety* Poorly lit roads make night travel hazardous. Armed robbery and muggings are on the increase *Inoc* Yellow Fever*, Cholera, Typhoid, Polio, Malaria *Airlines* Air France, Sabena, Ghana Airways *Average length of flight* 10 hours *Food* African seafood with French influence

Bophuthatswana

Capital Mmabatho *Lang* Setswana *Currency* South African Rand = 100 cents *Govt* Independent homeland of South Africa. Regional authorities elected by tribal chiefs-unstable *Rel* Christian *Size* 44 sq km – 17 sq miles *Pop* 1,800,000 *GMT* +2 *When* All year *Visas* Required by all except UK nationals *Safety* cautious travel is advised *Inoc* Yellow Fever* if arriving from an infected area, Cholera, Typhoid, Polio, Malaria. *Airlines* Via Jan Smuts Johannesburg *Food* Local food is meal based – international cuisine available.

Botswana

Capital Gaborone *Lang* English and Setswana *Currency* Pula = 100 thebes *Govt* Botswana Democratic Party is currently in power, but elections in 1994 *Rel* Tribal *Size* 582,000 sq km – 224,711 sq miles *Pop* 1,450,000 *GMT* +2 *When to go* May to September *Visas* Not required *Inoc* Malaria, Typhoid, Polio, Cholera *Airlines* British Airways, Air France *Average length of flight* 15 hours *Food* Meat, maize and potato based. Western food also available

Burkina Faso

Capital Ouagadougou *Lang* French and several indigenous *Currency* CFA Franc= 100 centimes *Govt* Presidential dictatorship *Rel* Animist *Size* 274,200 sq km – 105,870 sq miles *Pop* 9,889,000 *GMT*: GMT *When* December to March *Visas* Required by all *Validity* 3 months *Time to get* Immediately *Safety* Towns can be violent after dark, avoid unnecessary travel in rural areas *Inoc* Yellow Fever*, Cholera, Typhoid, Polio, Malaria *Airlines* Aeroflot, Air Afrique, Ethiopian, Air France, UTA *Average length of flight* 8.5 hours *Food* Rice, maize and millet based

Burundi

Capital Bujumbura *Lang* French and Kirundi *Currency* Burundi Franc = 100 centimes *Govt* Front for Democracy is currently the elected Govt led by Ndadaye, a Hutu, initiating liberal reforms *Rel* Mainly Roman Catholic *Size* 27,834 sq km – 10,747 sq miles *Pop* 6,134,000 *GMT* +2 *When* June to September *Visas*

Required by all *Validity* 30 days *Safety* Unsafe due to tribal tension and recent coup – contact Foreign Office *Inoc* Yellow Fever* if you have come from an infected area, Cholera, Typhoid, Polio, Malaria *Airlines* Sabena, Air France, Ethiopian Airlines *Average length of flight* 10 hours *Food* Basic and limited

Cameroon

Capital Yaounde *Lang* French and English *Currency* CFA centimes = 100 centimes *Govt* Biya has been President since 1982, however there is now strong opposition to him and rumours abound of fraud *Rel* Animist, Christian and Muslim *Size* 475,442 sq km – 183,569 sq miles *Pop* 11,540,000 *GMT* +1 *When* November to February *Visas* Required by all *Validity* Up to 3 months use with 3 months of issue *Time to get* 2 days by person, longer by post *Safety* Douala can be dangerous after dark *Inoc* Yellow Fever*, Cholera, Malaria, Polio, Typhoid *Airlines* Swissair, Air France, Nigeria Airways, Air Afrique *Average length of flight* 7 hours *Food* Abundance of fruit, vegetables and seafood in the south – French and Lebanese influences

Central African Republic

Capital Bangui *Lang* French and Sango *Currency* CFA Franc = 100 centimes *Govt* Although called a republic, Kolingba voids elections if he does not win *Rel* Animist *Size* 622,984 sq km – 240,535 sq miles *Pop* 2,463,616 *GMT* +1 *When* November to April, but always tropical heat *Visas* Required by all *Time to get* Normally 2 days *Safety* Volatile – contact Foreign Office. Represented only by honourary British Consulate, contact French or German Embassies in emergencies *Inoc* Yellow Fever*, Cholera, Typhoid, Polio, Malaria *Airlines* Air France, Air Afrique *Average length of flight* 9.5 hours *Food* Simple

Chad

Capital Ndjamena *Lang* French, Arabic and 50 indigenous langs. *Currency* CFA Franc = 100 centimes *Govt* Unstable single-party state, although changing and national elections are set for 1994 *Rel* Muslim or Animist *Size* 1,284,000 sq km – 495,800 sq miles *Pop* 6,214,000 *GMT* +1 *When* November to March *Visas* Required by all *Validity* Varies *Safety* Dangerous – contact High Commission in Abuja *Inoc* Yellow Fever*, Malaria, Cholera, Polio, Typhoid *Airlines* Flights via Paris, Air France *Average length of flight* 7 hours *Food* European-style in the capital, scarce elsewhere

Congo

Capital Brazzaville *Lang* French *Currency*

CFA Franc = 100 centimes *Govt* Although a multi-party democracy (since 1992) it has been a Socialist one-party state *Rel* Animist and RC *Size* 342,000 sq km – 132,047 sq miles *Pop* 1,843,421 *GMT* +1 *When* May to September *Visas* Required by all except by French + German nationals *Validity* 15 days *Time to get* immediate in person *Safety* UK nationals at risk contact Foreign Office for up to date info. *Inoc* Yellow Fever*, Malaria, Polio, Cholera, Typhoid *Airlines* Air France, BA, Swissair, Aeroflot, Air Afrique *Average length of flight* 11 hours including stopover in Paris *Food* French influence with excellent seafood on the coast

Côte d'Ivoire (Ivory Coast)

Capital Yamoussoukro *Lang* French *Currency* CFA Franc = 100 centimes *Govt* Elected President, although other parties were allowed to stand at the last election it is really a one-party state *Rel* Tribal *Size* 322,462 sq km – 124,503 sq miles *Pop* 13,695,000 *GMT* GMT *When* Mid December to mid March *Visas* Not required by UK or US nationals *Validity* 3 months *Time to get* 2 days *Safety* Generally safe but has its full share of street crime after dark *Inoc* Yellow Fever*, Cholera, Malaria, Polio, Typhoid *Airlines* Sabena, Air France *Average length of flight* 6 hours *Food* Spicy and bananas are often used in cooking

Djibouti

Capital Djibouti *Lang* Arabic and French *Currency* Djibouti Franc = 100 centimes *Govt* Multi-party elections since 1992 *Rel* Muslim and Roman Catholic *Size* 23,200 sq km – 8,959 sq miles *Pop* 519,900 *GMT* +3 *When* October to April *Visas* Required by all *Validity* 1-3 months *Time to get* 2 days *Safety* Areas in the country remain closed. Risk of banditry at night *Inoc* Yellow Fever* if arriving from an infected area, Hepatitis A, Malaria, Polio, Typhoid *Airlines* Air France *Average length of flight* 11 hours *Food* shortages

Egypt

Capital Cairo *Lang* Arabic *Currency* Egyptian Pound = 100 piastres *Govt* Democracy *Rel* Islamic *Size* 997,739 sq km – 385,229 sq miles *Pop* 57,581,000 *GMT* +2 *When* All year *Visas* Required by all *Validity* Varies *Time to get* 1-10 days *Safety* An increase of attacks on tourist by religious extremists *Inoc* Yellow Fever* if arriving from an infected area. Hepatitis A, Cholera, Malaria, Polio, Typhoid *Airlines* British Airways, Egyptair *Average length of flight* 4 hours 45 minutes *Food* Middle eastern cooking

Equatorial Guinea

Capital Malbabo *Lang* Spanish *Currency* CFA Franc = 100 centimes *Govt* Dictatorship, followed by a single party-state, reforms in place for multi-party elections within the next 2 years *Rel* Roman Catholic *Size* 28,051 sq km – 10,830 sq miles *Pop* 356,000 *GMT* +1 *When* November to March *Visas* Required by all except US nationals *Time to get* At least two months *Safety* Exercise caution. There is no British Consular presence. If in difficulties seek assistance from the French or Spanish *Inoc* Yellow Fever* if arriving from an infected area. Cholera, Hepatitis A, Malaria, Polio, Typhoid, *Airlines* Iberia via Madrid, Cameroon Airlines via Paris *Average length of flight* 11 hours excluding stopover *Food* Good seafood, but few restaurants

Eritrea

Capital Asmara *Lang* Arabic and Tigrinya *Currency* No currency of their own Ethiopian Birr and Sudanese Pound are used *Govt* Since independence from Ethiopia in 1993 it is under the control of the Eritrean People's Liberation Front and a new constitution has yet to be introduced *Rel* Orthodox and Muslim *Size* 124,000 sq km – 48,000 sq miles *Pop* 3,435,500 *GMT* +3 *When* May June, Sept, Oct *Visas* Required by all *Validity* 4 weeks from date of issue *Time to get* 1 day *Safety* Avoid Sudan border. Don't travel after dark. Register with the Consulate in Asmara if travelling outside the capital *Inoc* Yellow Fever* if arriving from an infected area, Cholera, Typhoid, Polio, Hepatitis A, Malaria *Airlines* Ethiopian Airlines *Average length of flight* 11.5 hours *Food* Italian cuisine and local spicy dishes

Ethiopia

Capital Addis Ababa *Lang* Amharic *Currency* Ethiopian Birr = 100 cents *Govt* Democratic constitution *Rel* Christian *Size* 1,251,282 sq km – 483,123 sq miles *Pop* 56,677,100 *GMT* +3 *When* May, June, Sept, Oct *Visas* Required by all *Validity* 2 months *Time to get* 2 days *Safety* Sudan and Somalia borders areas should be avoided. Don't travel after dark and register with an Embassy if travelling outside the capital by road *Inoc* Yellow Fever* if coming from an infected area, Cholera, Malaria, Polio, Typhoid *Airlines* Ethiopian Airlines, Lufthansa *Average length of flight* 10.5 hours *Food* Spicy meat and vegetable dishes served on flat spongy bread

Gabon

Capital Liberville *Lang* French *Currency* CFA Franc = 100 centimes *Govt* A multi-party constitution with rumours of fraud, previously a one-party state *Rel* Mainly Christian *Size* 267,667 sq km – 103,347 sq miles *Pop* 1,011,710 *GMT* +1 *When* May to September *Visas* Required by all *Validity* 3 months *Time to get* 2-4 weeks *Safety* Generally stable but elections cause tension – check with foreign office *Inoc* Yellow Fever*, Malaria, Polio, Cholera, Typhoid *Airlines* Air Afrique, Air France, Sabena, Swissair *Average length of flight* 10.5 hours *Food* spicy meat and vegetables

The Gambia

Capital Banjul *Lang* English *Currency* Gambian Dalasi = 100 bututs *Govt* Partly elected govt, currently held by People's Progressive Party *Rel* Muslim *Size* 11,295 sq km – 4,361 sq miles *Pop* 1,038,145 *GMT* GMT *When* Mid November to mid May *Visas* Required but not by British tourists, Australians and Canadians *Validity* 90 days *Time to get* 48 hours in person, longer by post *Safety* Calm since military coup of 1994, but check with Foreign Office *Inoc* Yellow Fever* if arriving from an infected area, Malaria, Polio, Cholera, Typhoid *Airlines* Air Gambia, Sabena *Average length of flight* 5.5 hours *Food* Spiced

Ghana

Capital Accra *Lang* English *Currency* Cedi = 100 pesewas *Govt* Although an elected govt, Ghana is partly under the control of the armed forces *Rel* Christian *Size* 238,537 sq km – 92,100 sq miles *Pop* 17,000,000 *GMT* GMT *When* August to January *Visas* Required by all *Validity* 3 months from date of issue *Time to get* 2 days *Safety* Precautions should be taken, travel after dark not recommended *Inoc* Yellow Fever*, Cholera, Malaria, Polio, Typhoid *Airlines* Ghana Airways, British Airways, KLM, Lufthansa, Aeroflot *Average length of flight* 6.5 hours *Food* Plantains used in cooking also guinea fowl and grasscutters (rodent)

Guinea Republic

Capital Conakry *Lang* French *Currency* Guinea franc = 100 centimes *Govt* Having been a socialist regime, since 1990 it is changing to democracy, multi-party elections due in 1995 *Rel* Muslim *Size* 245,857 sq km – 94,926 sq miles *Pop* 5,600,000 *GMT* GMT *When* November to April *Visas* Required by all *Time to get* 5 weeks *Safety* High levels of violent street crime. Leave valuables in secure place *Inoc* Yellow Fever* if arriving from an infected area, Malaria, Polio, Typhoid, *Airlines* Air France, Sabena, Aeroflot *Average length of flight* 9 hours *Food* Hot and spicy with rice.

Guinea-Bissau

Capital Bissau *Lang* Portuguese *Currency*

Guinea-Bissau Peso = 100 centavos *Govt* Socialist, multi-party elections due in 1994 *Rel* Animist and Muslim *Size* 36,125 sq km – 13,948 sq miles *When* December to April *Visas* Required by all *Inoc* Yellow Fever* if arriving from an infected area, Malaria, Polio, Typhoid, Yellow Fever *Airlines* TAP, Aeroflot *Average length of flight* 10 hours *Food* Rice, chicken and fish dishes

Kenya

Capital Nairobi *Lang* Swahili and English *Currency* Kenyan Shilling = 100 cents *Govt* Lead by Moi, becoming more liberal having been a one-party state *Rel* Tribal and Christian *Size* 580,356 sq km – 224,081 sq miles *Pop* 29,292,000 *GMT* +3 *When* June to September *Visas* Not required by British and Canadian citizens *Validity* Up to 3 months *Time to get* normally 24 hours *Safety* Generally safe in tourist areas, but care should be taken *Inoc* Yellow Fever* if arriving from an infected area, Malaria, Polio, Cholera, Typhoid *Airlines* British Airways, Kenyan Airways *Average length of flight* 8 hours *Food* Local food is maize based, international food available in all tourist areas

Lesotho

Capital Maseru *Lang* Sesotho and English *Currency* Loti = 100 lisente *Govt* Democracy, elections held in 1993, all seats won by the Basotho Congress Party *Rel* Christian mainly Catholic *Size* 30,355 sq km – 11,720 sq miles *Pop* 1,700,000 *GMT* +2 *When* May to September *Visas* Not required by UK *Validity* 3 or 6 months *Time to get* 1 day *Safety* Travel with caution *Inoc* Yellow Fever* if arriving from an infected area, Polio, Cholera, Typhoid *Airlines* British Airways, Air Lesotho *Average length of flight* 14 hours including stopover *Food* Lots of fresh water fish – other foods imported from South Africa

Liberia

Capital Monrovia *Lang* English *Currency* Liberian Dollar = 100 cents *Govt* Elected Govt, *Rel* Officially Christian *Size* 97,754 sq km – 37,743 *Pop* 2,700,000 *GMT* GMT *When* November to March *Visas* Required by all *Validity* 60 days from date of issue *Time to get* 1 day *Safety* The British Embassy in Liberia was closed in 1991. The Foreign Office do not advise travel. *Inoc* Yellow Fever*, Malaria, Polio, Cholera, Typhoid *Airlines* No direct flights at the time of writing *Average length of flight* 9 hours 40 minutes *Food* Rice based, local dishes include toasted termites and frog soup

Libya

Capital Tripoli *Lang* Arabic *Currency* Libyan Dinar = 1000 dirhams *Govt* Muammar al-Qathafi is the Leader of the Revolution (socialist) and holds supreme power *Rel* Sunni Muslim *Size* 1,775,500 sq km – 685,524 sq miles *Pop* 4,899,000 *GMT* +1 *When* November to February *Visas* Required by all, extremely difficult to get, apply in Paris *Safety* Avoid internal air flights. Incidence of mugging increasing. Unwise to carry cameras. Harsh penalties are imposed for the possession or use of alcohol or drugs and for criticizing the country, its leadership or religion. Register with the British Interests Section of the Italian Embassy on arrival *Inoc* Yellow Fever* if arriving from an infected area, Typhoid, Cholera, Polio, Hepatitis A *Airlines* No flights, UN embargo *Average length of flight* 6 hours *Food* Arabic food with an Italian influence

Madagascar

Capital Antananarivo *Lang* Malagasy and French *Currency* Malagasy Franc = 100 centimes *Govt* Elected government, with Albert Zafy as President *Rel* Animist and Christian *Size* 587,041 sq km – 226,658 sq miles *Pop* 12,092,157 *GMT* + 3 *When* April to October *Visas* Required by all *Validity* 30 or 90 days, valid for 6 months from date of issue *Time to get* 1 day in person, 1 week by post *Safety* Be aware of mugging danger. Register presence at the Embassy *Inoc* Yellow Fever* and Cholera* if arriving from an infected area,Typhoid, Polio, Malaria *Airlines* Air France, Air Madagascar, Aeroflot *Average length of flight* 14 hours including connection in Paris *Food* Rice based and can be very hot

Malawi

Capital Lilongwe *Lang* English *Currency* Kwacha = 100 tambala *Govt* A one-party state led by Banda, however multi-party elections have been promised for 1994, to satisfy foreign governments who have withheld aid until the regime improves its human rights record *Rel* Christian and Animist *Size* 118,484 sq km – 45,747 sq miles *Pop* 10,032,600 *GMT* +2 *When* April to October *Visas* Not required *Safety* Avoid travelling after dark, especially off the main towns *Inoc* Yellow Fever* if arriving from an infected area, Malaria, Polio, Typhoid *Airlines* British Airways direct, Air Zimbabwe, Kenya Airways, Air Malawi, South African Airways, Air France, Ethiopian Airlines *Average length of flight* 12 hours *Food* Delicious fish from Lake Malawi

Mali

Capital Bamako *Lang* French *Currency* CFA

Franc = 100 centimes *Govt* Having been a military dictatorship, multi-party elections were held in 1992, however, the existing govt is unstable due to economic unrest *Rel* Majority Muslim *Size* 1,240,192 sq km – 478,841 sq miles *Pop* 8,156,000 *GMT* GMT *When* October to February *Visas* Required by all *Validity* 1 month from date of entry *Time to get* 5 days *Safety* Many areas north of Bamako are unsafe due to clashes between Tuareg and army. *Inoc* Yellow Fever, Cholera, Malaria, Polio, Typhoid *Airlines* Air France, Sabena *Average length of flight* 11 hours *Food* Rice or millet based

Mauritania

Capital Nouakchott *Lang* Arabic and French *Currency* Mauritanian Ougiya = 5 khoums *Govt Rel* Islamic *Size* 1,030,700 sq km – 397,950 sq miles *Pop* 2,211,000 *GMT* GMT *When* November to March *Visas* Required by all *Validity* 1 month *Time to get* 3 Days *Safety* Disputes with Senegal, contact Foreign Office *Inoc* Yellow Fever, Malaria, Polio, Typhoid *Airlines* Air France, Air Afrique *Average length of flight* 7 hours *Food* Basic – lamb, goat, fish and rice

Morocco

Capital Rabat *Lang* Arabic *Currency* Moroccan Dirham = 100 centimes *Govt* Elected govt with King Hussan retaining executive power *Rel* Muslim *Size* 710,850 sq km – 274,461 sq miles *Pop* 26,023,717 *GMT* GMT *When* Apr to Oct *Visas* Not required *Safety* Safe for tourists, beware of drugs being offered though *Inoc* Polio, Typhoid *Airlines* Air France, British Airways, Alitalia, Royal Air Maroc *Average length of flight* 3 hours *Food* Meat and sweet pastry based – not suitable for vegetarians.Delicious couscous

Mozambique

Capital Maputo *Lang* Portuguese *Currency* Mozambique Metical = centavos *Govt* President holds all power. The country has been at civil war for 16 years, although there has been a recent peace agreement there is still unrest *Rel* Christian *Size* 799,380 sq km – 308,641 sq miles *Pop* 17,423,000 *GMT* +2 *When* April to September *Visas* Required by all *Validity* 1 month *Time to get* Well in advance (several months) *Safety* Not recommended for the tourist, great care should be taken at all times. *Inoc* Yellow Fever*, Cholera*, Malaria, Polio, Typhoid *Airlines* Air Zimbabwe, South African Airways, LAM *Average length of flight* 14 hours including stopover in Johannesburg *Food* Portuguese and Far Eastern influences

Namibia

Capital Windhoek *Lang* English *Currency* South African rand = 100 cents *Govt* Elected President and National Assembly *Rel* Christian majority *Size* 823,144 sq km – 317,816 sq miles *Pop* 1,500,000 *GMT* +2 *When* September to May *Visas* Not required *Validity* 3 months *Time to get* 2 days *Safety* Relatively safe *Inoc* Yellow Fever* if arriving from an infected area, Polio, Malaria, Typhoid. *Airlines* Namib Air, Air France, Lufthansa, South African Airways, Air Zimbabwe, *Average length of flight* 18 hours *Food* German influence – dried and smoked meat based

Niger

Capital Niamey *Lang* French *Currency* CFA Franc = 100 centimes *Govt* Elected, 6-party coalition *Rel* Muslim *Size* 1,267,000 sq km – 489,191 sq miles *Pop* 8,361,000 *GMT* +1 *When* Oct – May *Visas* Required but not by UK citizens *Validity* Varies *Time to get* 2 days *Safety* Potentially unstable: check with Foreign Office *Inoc* Yellow Fever*, Cholera*, Malaria, Polio, Typhoid *Airlines* Air Afrique, Air France *Average length of flight* 6 hours *Food* Rice based, couscous, can be shortages in remote areas

Nigeria

Capital Abuja *Lang* English *Currency* Naira = 100 Kobo *Govt* Unstable democracy *Rel* Islamic *Size* 923,768 sq km – 569,669 sq miles *Pop* 88,514,501 *GMT* +1 *When* Nov to April *Visas* Required by all *Time to get* 2 days *Safety* Political situation is uncertain. High incidence of street crime and business fraud. Travelling outside cities after dark is unsafe *Inoc* Cholera*, Yellow Fever*, Malaria, Polio, Typhoid *Airlines* British Airways, Nigerian Airways *Average length of flight* 7 hours 40 minutes *Food* Yams, sweet potatoes, and plantains, typically West African

Rwanda

Capital Kigali *Lang* Kinyarwanda and French. Kiswahili *Currency* Rwandese FRANC = 100 Centimes *Govt* Extremely unstable *Rel* Christian *Size* 26,338 sq km – 10,169 sq miles *Pop* 7,164,994 *GMT*+2 *When* June to December *Visas* Required by all *Validity* 3 months *Time to get* Weeks – nearest Visa office to London is Brussels *Safety* Security still unstable, police and judicial systems yet to be fully restored *Inoc* Yellow Fever*, Cholera*, Malaria, Polio, Typhoid *Airlines* Sabena, Air France, Ethiopian Airways *Average length of flight* 13 hours *Food* French and Belgian influences

São Tomé e Principe

Capital São Tomé *Lang* Portuguese *Currency* Dobra = 100 centimos *Govt* Democracy *Rel* Roman Catholic *Size* 964 sq km – 372 sq miles *Pop* 125,000 *GMT* GMT *When* June through September *Visas* Required by all *Validity* varies *Inoc* Yellow Fever* if arriving from an infected area, Cholera, Hepatitis A, Malaria, Polio, Typhoid *Airlines* Via Libreville in Gabon *Average length of flight* 10 hours *Food* Seafood and spicy

Senegal

Capital Dakar *Lang* French and Wolof *Currency* CFA Franc = 100 centimes *Govt* Elected president holds executive power, with a National Assembly responsible for legislation. The socialists have been in power since independence (1960) *Rel* Muslim *Size* 196,722 sq km – 75,955 sq miles *Pop* 8,152,000 *GMT* GMT *When* December through to May *Visas* Required by Australia and New Zealand nationals *Validity* 3 months from date of issue *Time to get* 1 day in person *Safety* Some unrest, take local advice *Inoc* Yellow Fever*, Antimarsh Fever (July and August), Cholera*, Malaria, Polio, Typhoid *Airlines* Swissair, Sabena, Iberia, Air France *Average length of flight* 6 hours and 15 minutes *Food* Regarded as one of the best in Africa, can be spicy, normally chicken or fish based

Sierra Leone

Capital Freetown *Lang* English *Currency* Leone = 100 cents *Govt* Unstable one-party state, led by 28-year old Captain Valentine Strasser, who overthrew the corrupt regime in 1992 *Rel* Animist *Size* 71,740 sq km – 27,699 sq miles *Pop* 4,509,000 *GMT* GMT *When* November to April *Visas* Required *Validity* 1 week (extendible) commencing on arrival *Time to get* 3 days normally *Safety* Dangerous, militery coup again supplanting brief democratic civilian government, contact the Foreign Office before departing *Inoc* Yellow Fever* if arriving from an infected area, Cholera*, Malaria, Polio, Typhoid *Airlines* Air France, KLM, Aeroflot, Air Gambia *Average length of flight* 6.5 hours *Food* Excellent fish, lobster and prawns

Somalia

Capital Mogadishu *Lang* Somali and Arabic *Currency* Somali Shilling = 100 cents *Govt* As the country is in a state of civil war, there is no effective central government. The military commander, General Aideed, controls the capital *Rel* Muslim *Size* 637,657 sq km – 246,201 sq miles *Pop* 7,691,000 *GMT* +3 *When* Don't *Visas* Required by all *Validity* varies *Time to get* 1 month *Safety* Very dangerous – all embassies are currently closed, fierce fighting in the capital *Inoc* Yellow Fever* if arriving from an infected area, Cholera*, Typhoid, Polio, Malaria *Airlines* Daallo Airlines, Somali Airlines *Average length of flight* 15 hours with stopovers *Food* Pork and seafood, often spiced

South Africa

Capital Pretoria *Lang* Afrikaans and English Currency Rand = 100 cents *Govt* Finally a fully democratic govt, giving all adults the vote regardless of colour *Rel* Mainly Christian *Size* 1,221,037 sq km – 471,445 sq miles including the 4 homelands (Transkei, Bophuthatswana, Ciskei and Venda) *Pop* 41,244,000 (including the homelands) *GMT* +2 *When* All year *Visas* Not required *Safety* Variable, depends on areas, take advice *Inoc* Yellow Fever* if arriving from an infected area, Cholera, Malaria, Polio, Typhoid *Airlines* British Airways, South African Airways *Average length of flight* 12 hours 50 minutes *Food* Meat based – Braais (barbecues) and stews

Sudan

Capital Khartoum *Lang* Arabic *Currency* Sudanese pound = 100 piastres *Govt* Military government – unstable *Rel* Muslim in the north, Christian and Animist in the South *Size* 2,505,813 sq km – 967,500 sq miles *Pop* 24,940,683 *GMT* +2 *When* November to March *Visas* Required *Validity* 30 days within 3 months of issue *Time to get* 1-3 weeks *Safety* Not advised to travel anywhere in the South or Ethiopian and Eritrean borders contact Foreign Office *Inoc* Yellow Fever* if arriving from an infected area, but recommended anyway, Malaria, Polio, Typhoid *Airlines* Sudan Airways, Lufthansa, Air France, KLM *Average length of flight* 8 hours *Food* Fool (bean) and dura (millet or maize) is the staple diet

Swaziland

Capital Mbabane *Lang* English and Siswati *Currency* Lilangeni *Govt* Power rests with the monarch who appoints a Prime Minister and a Cabinet, with the exception of 10 elected senators *Rel* Mainly Christian *Size* 17,363 sq km – 6,704 sq miles *Pop* 879,000 *GMT* +2 *When* April to September *Visas* Not required *Safety* generally stable but growing number of attacks on expatriates *Inoc* Yellow Fever* if arriving from an infected area, Cholera, Malaria, Polio, Typhoid *Airlines* Air Zimbabwe, *Average length of flight* 16 hours *Food* Mealie Mealie and meat stew

Tanzania

Capital Dodoma *Lang* Swahili and English *Currency* Tanzanian Shilling = 100 cents *Govt* one-party state *Rel* Mixed – Muslim, Christian and traditional *Size* 945,087 sq km – 364,900 sq miles *Pop* 30,340,000 *GMT* +3 *When* June to November *Visas* Required, UK nationals require a Visitors Pass *Time to get* 7 days *Safety* more stable now, but mugging and theft common *Inoc* Yellow Fever, Cholera, Malaria, Polio, Typhoid *Airlines* British Airways, Gulf Air, Alliance *Average length of flight* 12 hours 45 minutes *Food* Maize based with seafood and fruit

Togo

Capital Lome *Lang* French *Currency* CFA Franc = 100 centimes *Govt* One-party military state *Rel* Mainly animist and Christian *Size* 56,785 sq km – 21,925 sq miles *Pop* 3,928,000 *GMT* GMT *When* mid July – mid September *Visas* Not required by UK, Canadian and US Citizens *Validity* 30 days *Time to Get* 2 days *Safety* Quiet at the moment, but potentially unstable, be vigilant *Inoc* Yellow Fever*, Cholera, Hepatitis A, Malaria, Polio, Typhoid *Airlines* Sabena, Air France, KLM *Average length of flight* 7 hours *Food* Spicy meat, poultry and seafoods

Tunisia

Capital Tunis *Lang* Arabic *Currency* Tunisian Dinar = 1000 millimes *Govt* Multi-party state, although only certain parties are recognised *Rel* Moslim *Size* 154,000 sq km – 59,460 sq miles *Pop* 8,947,100 *GMT* +1 *When* Spring and Autumn *Visas* Not Required by Canada, UK and US citizens *Validity* Up to 4 months *Safety* Relatively safe *Inoc* Yellow Fever* if arriving from an infected area, Cholera, Polio, Typhoid *Airlines* British Airways, Tunis Air *Average length of flight* 2.5 hours *Food* Cooked with olive oil and delicately spiced

Uganda

Capital Kampala *Lang* English *Currency* Uganda Shilling = 100 cents *Govt* One-party state, with a president (Museveni) is Head of State and holds executive authority *Rel* Mainly Christian *Size* 241,139 sq km – 93,104 sq miles *Pop* 16,671,705 *GMT* +3 *When* June to October and December to March *Visas* Not Required *Validity* 3 months from date of issue *Time to get* 1 days *Safety* Armed robbery and road ambushes throughout Uganda. Do not travel at night *Inoc* Yellow Fever* if arriving from an infected area, Malaria, Polio, Typhoid, *Airlines* Kenyan Airways, British Airways, Air India *Average length of flight* 8 hours *Food* Lots of bananas, millet bread and stews

Democratic Rep. of Congo (Zaïre)

Capital Kinshasa *Lang* Officially French, many African languages used *Currency* Zaire = 100 makuta *Govt* Unstable *Rel* Christian mainly Roman Catholic *Size* 2,344,885 sq km – 905,365 sq miles *Pop* 36,672,000 *GMT* +1 and +2 depending on region *When* December to March in the North and May to October in the south *Visas* Required by all *Validity* 1, 2 or 3 months *Time to get* 2 days minimum *Safety* Check with Foreign Office,the east should be treated as a war zone *Inoc* Yellow Fever*, Cholera, Malaria, Polio, Typhoid *Airlines* Sabena and Swissair *Average length of flight* 8 hours *Food* National dish is Moambe made with meat usually chicken in a peanut and palm oil spicy sauce. Very good pink bananas and pineapples

Zambia

Capital Lusaka *Lang* English *Currency* Kwacha = 100 ngwee *Govt* Having been a one-party state, the country is now led by the Movement for Multi-party Democracy Party and the constitution is changing *Rel* Christian *Size* 752,614 sq km – 290,586 sq miles *Pop* 8,210,000 *GMT* +2 *When* May to November *Visas* Required by US and UK citizens *Validity* 3 months from date of issue *Time to get* At least 3 days *Safety* Travellers should be vigilant *Inoc* Yellow Fever* if arriving from an infected area, Cholera, Malaria, Polio, Typhoid *Airlines* British Airways, Zambia Airways *Average length of flight* 10 hours *Food* Very good fresh fish from Lake Kariba

Zimbabwe

Capital Harare *Lang* English *Currency* Zimbabwe Dollar = 100 cents *Govt* Democracy *Rel* Christian *Size* 390,759 sq km – 150,873 sq miles *Pop* 11,215,000 *GMT* +2 *When* April, May, August and September *Visas* Not required *Safety* Safe *Inoc* Yellow Fever* if arriving from an infected area, Cholera, Malaria, Polio, Typhoid *Airlines* Air Zimbabwe , British Airways *Average length of flight* 9 hours *Food* Maize and meat with relish.

NORTH AMERICA

Canada

Capital Ottawa *Lang* French and English *Currency* Canadian Dollar = 100 cents *Govt* Liberal Party *Rel* Christian majority Roman Catholic *Size* 9,970,610 sq km – 3,849,674 sq miles *Pop* 29,248,000 *GMT* from -3.5 to -8 *When* All year *Visas* Not required *Safety* Safe *Airlines* Air Canada, British Airways amongst many others *Average length of flight* Ottawa 7

hours *Food* Varied, French influences

United States of America

Capital Washington DC *Lang* English *Currency* US Dollar = 100 cents *Govt* A federal republic of states, with a stable democracy *Rel* Christian *Size* 9,372,614 sq km – 3,618,770 sq miles *Pop* 264,648,291 *GMT* -5 to -10 *When* all year *Visas* Required by Australian and New Zealanders *Validity* Varies *Time to get* Can be up to 3 weeks by post *Safety* Depends on the area, take local advice, especially in Florida *Inoc* Polio for Hawaii *Airlines* United Airlines, Continental Airlines, British Airway fly direct to Washington – many other airlines operate to other cities in the USA *Average length of flight* 8 hours *Food* Home to the fast food chains, hamburgers, french fries. Pancakes for breakfast

CENTRAL AMERICA

Anguilla (UK)

Capital The Valley *Lang* English *Currency* Eastern Caribbean Dollar (EC$) = 100 cents *Govt* Separate dependency under the British Government *Rel* Christian *Size* 91 km sq – 35 sq miles *Pop* 10,300 *GMT* -4 *When* Mid December to mid April *Visas* Not required *Safety* Safe *Airlines* LIAT,American Airlines, British Airways *Average length of flight* 12 hours including stopover in Antigua *Food* Caribbean, a variety of seafood including lobster and whelk

Antigua and Barbuda

Capital St John's *Lang* English *Currency* Eastern Caribbean Dollar (EC$) = 100 cents *Govt* Elected Parliament (Antiguan Labour Party) with British Sovereignty *Rel* Christian *Size* 440 sq km – 170 sq miles *Pop* 64,166 *GMT* -4 *When* Mid December to Mid April *Visas* Not required *Safety* Safe *Inoc* Hepatitis A, Polio, Typhoid *Airlines* British Airways, BWIA, Lufthansa *Average length of flight* 8 hours *Food* Barbecues and roasts are a speciality, along with red snapper and lobster

Aruba (The Netherlands)

Capital Oranjestad *Lang* Dutch but English and Spanish are also spoken *Currency* Aruba Florin/Guilder = 100 cents *Govt* Part of the Kingdom of the Netherlands but own Governor *Rel* Roman Catholic *Size* 193 sq km – 74.5 sq miles *Pop* 80,333 *GMT* -4 *When* All year but showers in Oct, Nov and Dec *Visas* Not required *Safety* Safe *Inoc* Yellow Fever* if having come from an infected area, Polio, Typhoid *Airlines* KLM, VIASA, British

Airways *Average length of flight* 11.5 hours *Food* Not a large variety of local food – meat or fish based. International cuisine also available

Bahamas

Capital Nassau *Lang* English *Currency* Bahamian Dollar = 100 cents *Govt* Governed by the Free National Movement party *Rel* Christian *Size* 13,939 sq km – 5,382 sq miles *Pop* 269,000 *GMT* -5 (-4 in summer) *When* Mid December to mid April *Visa* Not required *Safety* Safe *Inoc* Yellow Fever* if having come from an infected area, Polio, Typhoid *Airlines* American Airlines, Bahamasair, British Airways *Average length of flight* 9 hours *Food* Fresh fish and exotic fruit

Barbados

Capital Bridgetown *Lang* English *Currency* Barbados Dollar = 100 cents *Govt* Democratic Labour Party *Rel* Christian *Size* 430 sq km – 166 sq miles *Pop* 264,000 *GMT* -4 (-5 in summer) *When* Mid December to mid May *Visas* Not required for stays up to 90 days *Safety* Don't carry any valuables, mugging on the increase *Inoc* Yellow Fever* if having come from an infected area, Hepatitis A, Polio, Typhoid *Airlines* British Airways, BWIA *Average length of flight* 7.5 hours *Food* Mainly fish including the delicacy flying fish

Belize

Capital Belmopan *Lang* English *Currency* Belizean Dollar = 100 cents *Govt* A democracy led by the United Democratic Party *Rel* Christian – mainly Roman Catholic *Size* 22,965 sq km – 8,867 sq miles *Pop* 209,000 *GMT* -6 *When* October to May *Visas* Not required *Safety* Mugging and theft occur, but not as bad as South America *Inoc* Yellow Fever* if having come from an infected area, Typhoid, Polio, Malaria *Airlines* American Airlines, Continental *Average length of flight* 11 hours *Food* International but also Latin American and Creole

Bonaire (Netherland Antilles)

Capital Kralendjik *Lang* Dutch *Currency* Netherland Antilles Guilder or Florin = 100 cents *Govt* Part of the Netherland Antilles therefore part of the Dutch Govt, elected local council *Rel* Roman Catholic *Size* 288 sq km – 111 sq miles *Pop* 10,187 *GMT* -4 *When* Feb to June *Visas* Not required for visits of up to 14 days, issued locally for extended visits *Inoc* Yellow fever* if coming from an infected area, Typhoid, Polio *Airlines* KLM *Average length of flight* 11 hours *Food* Creole

Cayman Islands (UK)

Capital George Town *Lang* English *Currency* Cayman Island Dollar = 100 cents *Govt* A British Dependent Territory with a Governor *Rel* Christian *Size* 259 sq km – 100 sq miles *Pop* 32,000 *GMT* -5 *When* October to May *Visas* Not required *Safety* Safe *Inoc* Polio, Typhoid *Airlines* British Airways, Cayman Airways *Average length of flight* 9 hours *Food* Seafood

Costa Rica

Capital San Jose *Lang* Spanish *Currency* Costa Rican Colon = 100 centimos *Govt* A democracy: although one of the more stable govts in Central America, it suffers from some civil unrest. *Rel* Roman Catholic *Size* 51,060 sq km – 19,720 sq miles *Pop* 3,500,000 *GMT* -7 *When* Dec to Apr *Visa* Not required *Safety* Beware of tides while swimming *Inoc* Malaria, Polio, Typhoid *Airlines* KLM, Iberia, American Airlines *Average length of flight* 12 hours *Food* Rice, beans, beef, yuca, corn, nampi and chayote

Cuba

Capital Havana *Lang* Spanish *Currency* Cuban Peso = 100 centavos *Govt* Communist *Rel* Roman Catholic *Size* 110,860 sq km – 42,803 sq miles *Pop* 10,901,000 *GMT* -4 *When* Nov to April *Visas* Required by all *Validity* 6 months *Time to get* 2-3 days *Safety* Be aware of bag snatchers *Inoc* Polio, Typhoid *Airlines* Cubana, Iberia, Viasa, Aeroflot *Average length of flight* 19 hours including stopovers *Food* Continental and Cuban – fish and exotic fruit

Curaçao (Netherlands Antilles)

Capital Willemstad *Lang* Dutch *Currency* Netherlands Antilles Guilder or Florin = 100 cents *Govt* Self governing, part of the Netherlands *Rel* Christian *Size* 444 sq km – 171 sq miles *Pop* 144,097 *GMT* -4 *When* Mid December – mid April *Visas* Not required for visits up to 14 days *Inoc* Yellow Fever* if arriving from an infected area, Polio, Typhoid *Airlines* KLM, American Airlines, United Airlines *Average length of flight* 11 hours *Food* Dutch and spicy Creole

Dominica

Capital Roseau *Lang* English *Currency* East Caribbean Dollar = 100 cents *Govt* Democracy, held by the Dominican Freedom Party *Rel* Roman Catholic *Size* 750 sq km – 290 sq miles *Pop* 71,183 *GMT* -4 *When* January – May *Visas* Not required *Safety* Safe *Inoc* Yellow Fever* if arriving from an infected area, Polio, Typhoid, *Airlines* British Airways, LIAT *Average length of flight* 10 hours *Food* Creole

Dominican Republic

Capital Santo Domingo *Lang* Spanish *Currency* Dominican Republic Peso = 100 centavos *Govt* Democracy elections to be held in 1994 *Rel* Roman Catholic *Size* 48,422 sq km – 18,696 sq miles *Pop* 7,769,000 *GMT* -4 *When* December – April *Visas* Not required for up to 60 days by US, Canada, Australia, UK nationals *Inoc* Hepatitis A, Polio, Malaria, Typhoid, *Airlines* Air France, Iberia, American Airlines *Average length of flight* 11 hours including stopover *Food* Spanish influences, pork, goat and seafood are the staple diet

El Salvador

Capital San Salvador *Lang* Spanish *Currency* Colon (Peso) = 100 centavos *Govt* Unstable republic *Rel* Roman Catholic *Size* 21,721 sq km – 8,124 sq miles *Pop* 5,047,925 *GMT* -6 *When* Don't *Visas* Not required by UK or New Zealand nationals *Validity* Up to 90 days *Time to get* 10 days *Safety* Robbery and murder are not uncommon, for advice contact Embassy in San Salvador *Inoc* Yellow Fever* if arriving from an infected area, Malaria, Polio, Typhoid *Airlines* TACA International Airlines, American Airlines *Average length of flight* 10.5 hours excluding stopover in Miami *Food* International and Mexican

Grenada

Capital St Georges *Lang* English *Currency* Eastern Caribbean Dollar = 100 cents *Govt* Democracy, currently ruled by the National Democratic Congress, elections due in 1995 *Rel* Christian *Size* 334.5 sq km – 133 sq miles *Pop* 94,806 *GMT* -4 *When* January to May *Visas* Not required if staying less than 14 days *Inoc* Yellow Fever* if arriving from an infected area, Polio, Typhoid *Airlines* Caledonian Airways, American Airlines, British Airways *Average length of flight* 9 hours *Food* Seafood and vegetables

Guadeloupe

Capital Basse-Terre(admin) Pointe-a-Pitre (comm) *Lang* French *Currency* French Franc = 100 centimes *Govt* Four representatives in the French Govt *Rel* Roman Catholic *Size* 1,780 sq km – 687 sq miles *Pop* 387,034 *GMT* -4 *When* January – May *Visas* Required by Australians *Validity* Up to 3 months *Time to Get* Same day *Inoc* Yellow Fever* if arriving from an infected area, Polio, Typhoid *Airlines* Air Canada, American Airlines, Air France via Paris *Average length of flight* 12 hours 40 minutes *Food* Spicy Creole

Guatemala

Capital Guatemala City *Lang* Spanish

Currency

Currency Quetzal = 100 centavos *Govt* Democracy *Rel* Roman Catholic *Size* 108,429 sq km – 42,042 sq miles *Pop* 10,322,011 *GMT* -6 *When* October – May *Visas* Not required by UK, Canada or USA nationals if arriving by air *Validity* 90 days from date of entry *Time to get* 1 day in person *Safety* Beware of fighting between guerrillas and government soldiers *Inoc* Cholera, Yellow Fever* if arriving from an infected area, Malaria, Polio, Typhoid *Airlines* KLM, Iberia, American Airlines *Average length of flight* 8 hours *Food* Like, but not as good as, Mexican food

Haiti

Capital Port-au-Prince *Lang* French and Creole *Currency* Gourde = 100 centimes *Govt* Following a strict regime it is now extremely unstable *Rel* Roman Catholic – Voodooism is also still practised *Size* 27,750 sq km – 10,714 sq miles *Pop* 7,041,000 *GMT* -5 *When* November to March *Visas* Not required by UK US and Canada *Validity* 90 days from date of issue *Safety* political unrest – check with Foreign Office *Inoc* Yellow Fever* if arriving from an infected area, Polio, Malaria, Typhoid *Airlines* Air France, American Airlines *Average length of flight* 8 hours *Food* Creole

Honduras

Capital Tegucigalpa *Lang* Spanish *Currency* Lempira = 100 centavos *Govt* Democratic *Rel* Roman Catholic *Size* 111,888 sq km – 43,277 sq miles *Pop* 5,770,000 *GMT* -6 *When* November to April *Visas* Not required *Validity* Up to 1 month *Safety* Violence has increased, do not wear jewellery or carry large amounts of cash *Inoc* Yellow Fever* if arriving from an infected country, Malaria, Polio, Cholera, Typhoid *Airlines* Via Houston and Miami, SAHSA or American Airlines, Continental Airlines *Average length of flight* 12.5 hours *Food* Seafood and tropical fruits

Jamaica

Capital Kingston *Lang* English *Currency* Jamaican Dollar = 100 cents *Govt* Elected Labour govt *Rel* Protestant *Size* 10,991 sq km – 4,244 sq miles *Pop* 2,374,193 *GMT* -5 *When* December to April *Visas* Required by NZ *Safety* Generally safe for tourists but be vigilant, do not walk at night or use public transport *Inoc* Yellow Fever* if arriving from an infected area, Polio, Typhoid. *Airlines* British Airways direct or American Airlines via Miami, Air Canada, KLM *Average length of flight* 10 hours *Food* Fire and spice

Martinique (France)

Capital Fort-de-France *Lang* French *Currency*

French franc = 100 centimes *Govt* Overseas Department of the Republic of France sending 4 representatives to the French National Assembly *Rel* Roman Catholic *Size* 1,100 sq km – 425 sq miles *Pop* 370,800 *GMT* -4 *When* December to June *Visas* constantly changing, check with French Embassy *Inoc* Yellow Fever* if arriving from an infected area, Cholera, Polio, Typhoid *Airlines* British Airways, Air France *Average length of flight* 12 hours including stopover in Paris *Food* Creole and French cooking, delicious seafood

Mexico
Capital Mexico City *Lang* Spanish *Currency* Peso = 100 centavos *Govt* Federal republic, elected national congress, unstable due to guerrilla activity *Rel* Roman Catholic *Size* 1,958,201 sq km – 756,066 sq miles *Pop* 93,008,000 *GMT* -6 to -8 *When* October to May *Visas* Not required, but check *Safety* Central Chaipas remains tense, seek local advice *Inoc* Cholera*, Yellow Fever* if arriving from an infected area, Malaria, Polio, Typhoid. *Airlines* British Airways (direct), KLM, Air France, Lufthansa, United Airlines, Iberia, Virgin Atlantic, Mexicana. *Average length of flight* 12 hours 20 minutes *Food* Tortillas, tacos, enchiladas, chilli and guacamole

Montserrat (UK)
Capital Plymouth *Lang* English *Currency* East Caribbean Dollar = 100 cents *Govt* Led by the National Progressive party *Rel* Christian *Size* 102 sq km – 40 sq miles *Pop* 10,581 *GMT* -4 *When* January – June *Visas* Not required *Inoc* Yellow Fever* if arriving from an infected area, Cholera*, Polio, Typhoid *Airlines* British Airways, LIAT *Average length of flight* 8.5 hours *Food* A delicacy is mountain chicken (frogs' legs) – barbecues are very popular

Nicaragua
Capital Managua *Lang* Spanish *Currency* Nicaraguan Gold Cordoba = 100 centavos *Govt* Elected National Assembly – unstable *Rel* Roman Catholic *Size* 120,254 sq km – 46,430 sq miles *Pop* 4,500,000 *GMT* -6 *When* Dec – May *Visas* Not required by UK and US Nationals *Validity* 1 month *Time to get* 48 hours *Safety* political stability and safety can not be guaranteed, contact Foreign Office *Inoc* Yellow Fever* if arriving from an infected area, Malaria, Polio, Typhoid *Airlines* Iberia, Aeroflot *Average length of flight* 20 hours 30 minutes including stopovers *Food* Little variety, mainly eggs or meat, beans and rice.

Panama
Capital Panama City *Lang* Spanish *Currency* Balboa = 100 centesimos *Govt* Democracy, although unsteady due to economic difficulties *Rel* Roman Catholic *Size* 75,517 sq km – 29,157 sq miles *Pop* 2,613,586 *GMT* -5 *When* January through April *Visas* Not required by UK nationals *Validity* 30 days from date of entry *Time to get* 24 hours *Safety* Do not visit the Colombian border. Muggings have increased in tourist areas *Inoc* Yellow Fever*, Malaria, Typhoid *Airlines* KLM, American Airlines *Average length of flight* 14 hours *Food* Hot and spicy

Puerto Rico (USA)
Capital San Juan *Lang* Spanish *Currency* US Dollar = 100 cents *Govt* A Commonwealth State of the US, with an elected governor *Rel* Roman Catholic *Size* 8,959 sq km – 3,459 sq miles *Pop* 3,720,000 *GMT* -4 *When* Hot and tropical all year *Visas* The same as the USA *Safety* Beware of pickpockets *Inoc* Polio, Typhoid *Airlines* British Airways, American Airlines *Average length of flight* 8 hours *Food* Spanish based with rice and beans as the staple diet

Saba (Netherlands Antilles)
Capital The Bottom *Lang* English and Dutch *Currency* Netherlands Antilles Guilder or Florin = 100 cents *Govt* Part of the Kingdom of the Netherlands, but own Governor *Rel* Roman Catholic *Size* 13 sq km – 5 sq miles *Pop* 1,130 *GMT* -4 *When* Dec – July *Visas* Tourists allowed 14 days without visas *Inoc* Yellow Fever* if arriving from an infected area, Typhoid, Polio *Airlines* Via St Kitts *Average length of flight* 11 hours *Food* Exotic fruit and spicy meat

St Eustatius
Capital Oranjestad *Lang* English *Currency* Netherlands Antilles Guilder *Govt* Part of the Kingdom of the Netherlands, but own Governor *Rel* Protestant *Size* 21 sq km – 8 sq miles *Pop* 1,839 *GMT* -4 *When* January to June *Visas* Tourists allowed 14 days without a visa *Inoc* Yellow Fever* if arriving from an infected area, Polio, Typhoid *Airlines* Via Antigua and St Kitts *Average length of flight* 12 hours *Food* Creole – International

St Kitts and Nevis
Capital Basseterre *Lang* English *Currency* Eastern Caribbean Dollar = 100 cents *Govt* An independent state within the British Commonwealth, with an elected National Assembly, present government a coalition *Rel* Anglican *Size* 168.4 sq km – 65.1 sq miles *Pop*

44,380 *GMT* -4 *When* January to April *Visas* Not required *Inoc* Yellow Fever* if arriving from an infected area, Typhoid, Polio *Airlines* British Airways to Antigua, then LIAT *Average length of flight* 10 hours *Food* Seafood and exotic fruits, St Kitts has a reputation for good food

St Lucia

Capital Castries *Lang* English *Currency* Eastern Caribbean Dollar = 100 cents *Govt* Elected govt, presently the United Workers Party are in power *Rel* Roman Catholic *Size* 616 sq km – 238 sq miles *Pop* 139,908 *GMT* -4 *When* Jan – April *Visas* Not required *Safety* Safe *Inoc* Yellow Fever* if arriving from an infected area, Polio, Typhoid *Airlines* British Airways, BWIA *Average length of flight* 8.5 hours *Food* Creole – very good local fish

St Maarten

Capital Philipsburg *Lang* English *Currency* Netherlands Antilles Guilder or Florin = 100 cents *Govt* French and Dutch dual sovereignty *Rel* Mainly Protestant *Size* 41 sq km – 16 sq miles *Pop* 32,221 *GMT* -4 *When* January to May *Visas* Not required by tourists if staying less than 14 days *Inoc* Yellow Fever* if arriving from an infected area, Polio, Typhoid *Airline* American Airlines, Lufthansa, British Airways, LIAT *Average length of flight* 12 hours *Food* Dutch, French, English and Creole

St Vincent and Grenadines

Capital Kingstown *Lang* English *Currency* Eastern Caribbean Dollar = 100 cents *Govt* Elected Govt, with the New Democratic Party winning every single seat in the last election *Rel* Christian *Size* 344 sq km – 133 sq miles *Pop* 111,000 *GMT* -4 *When* Jan – May *Visas* Not required *Safety* Safe *Inoc* Yellow Fever* if arriving from an infected area, Polio, Typhoid *Airlines* British Airways, LAIT *Average length of flight* 9 hours *Food* Delicious seafood

Trinidad and Tobago

Capital Port of Spain *Lang* English *Currency* Trinidad and Tobago Dollar = 100 cents *Govt* democracy *Rel* Christian *Size* 5,128 sq km – 1,980 sq miles *Pop* 1,249,738 *GMT* -4 *When* December to May *Visas* Required by Australia and New Zealand *Validity* 3 months *Time to get* 2 days *Inoc* Yellow Fever* if arriving from an infected area, Polio Typhoid *Airlines* BWIA, British Airways, Caledonian Airways *Average length of flight* 10.5 hours *Food* Creole, very good seafood

Turks and Caicos (UK)

Capital Cockburn Town *Lang* English

Currency US Dollar = 100 cents *Govt* British Monarch is Head of State with an elected parliament *Rel* Roman Catholic *Size* 430 sq km – 166 sq miles *Pop* 14,000 *GMT* -5 *When* January to August *Visas* Not required *Inoc* Polio, Typhoid *Airlines* Via Nassau or Miami *Average length of flight* 13.5 hours *Food* Seafood based

Virgin Islands (UK)

Capital Road Town *Lang* English *Currency*: US Dollar = 100 cents *Govt* Internal self-govt led by Stoutt, leader of the Virgin Islands' Party, defence and foreign affairs controlled by London *Rel* Christian *Size* 153 sq km – 59 sq miles *Pop* 19,000 *GMT* -4 *When* All year *Visas* Not required *Safety* Safe *Inoc* Polio, Typhoid *Airlines* British Airways, Continental Airlines, LIAT *Average length of flight* 10 hours *Food* Bounteous seafood

Virgin Island (US)

Capital Charlotte Amalie *Lang* English *Currency* US Dollar = 100 cents *Govt* A US colony, the executive authority is vested in the elected Governor *Rel* Christian *Size* 354.8 sq km – 137 sq miles *Pop* 101,809 *GMT* -4 *When* All year *Visas* Required but not by UK, US and Canadian citizens *Safety* Safe *Inoc* Polio, Typhoid *Airlines* American Airlines *Average length of flight* 14 hours *Food* Some of the best in the Caribbean

SOUTH AMERICA

Argentina

Capital Buenos Aires *Lang* Spanish *Currency* Neuvo Peso = 100 centavos *Govt* Menem (a Peronist) is the elected President *Rel* Roman Catholic *Size* 2,766,889 sq km – 1,068,302 sq miles *Pop* 34,180,000 *GMT* -3 *When* All year round *Visas* Only required for business visits, not tourists except by Australians *Safety* beware of pickpockets, register with British Embassy on arrival *Inoc* Yellow Fever, Cholera, Malaria, Typhoid, Polio *Airlines* British Airways, Aerolineas Argentinas *Average length of flight* 18 hours *Food* Famous for their beef, the local cuisine has Basque, Spanish and Italian influences

Bolivia

Capital La Paz *Lang* Spanish *Currency* Boliviano = 100 centavos *Govt* Elected Govt, current President is Gonzalo Sanchez de Lozado *Rel* Roman Catholic *Size* 1,084,391 sq km – 424,164 sq miles *Pop* 7,237,000 *GMT* -4 *When* April – November *Visas* Required by Australians and Canadians and for business

Validity 30 days from date of entry *Time to get* 1 day *Safety* Care should be taken, theft can be rife. The cocaine growing areas should be avoided *Inoc* Yellow Fever* if coming from an infected area or going to Beni or Santa Cruz, Malaria,Typhoid, Polio *Airlines American* Airlines, Lufthansa *Average length of flight* 17 hours *Food* Hot chilli sauces – meat based

Brazil

Capital Brasilia *Lang* Portuguese *Currency* Cruzeiro = 100 centavos *Govt* Conservative – Itamar Franco as President *Rel* Roman Catholic *Size* 8,511,996 sq km – 3,286,500 sq miles *Pop* 155,822,440 *GMT* from -3 to -5 *When* The Carnival in February and any other time as the country has four different climatic regions *Visas* Required by Australians, Canadians and Americans and UK nationals on business *Validity* 90 days *Time to get* 2 days *Safety* As with all countries in South America beware of pickpockets *Inoc* Yellow Fever* if arriving from an infected area, vaccines recommended for some rural areas, Cholera, Polio, Malaria, Typhoid *Airlines* Varig, British Airways and many more *Average length of flight* 11 hours *Food* Varied, renowned for their beef

Chile

Capital Santiago *Lang* Spanish *Currency* Peso = 100 centavos *Govt* Democracy following Pinochet's dictatorship *Rel* Roman Catholic *Size* 756,626 sq km – 292,135 sq miles *Pop* 14,210,429 *GMT* -6 *When* October to April *Visas* Not required *Safety* Safe *Inoc* Polio, Typhoid *Airlines* American Airlines, British Airways, Viasa *Average length of flight* 18 hours 45 minutes *Food* Typically South American, except Conger Eel is their national dish.

Colombia

Capital Sante Fe de Bogota *Lang* Spanish *Currency* Peso *Govt* *Rel* Roman Catholic *Size* 1,141,748 sq km – 440,831 sq miles *Pop* 34,520,000 *GMT*-5 *When* December – March *Visas* Not required if staying less than 90 days – check with Embassy *Safety* Violence and kidnappping remain a serious problem. The South American Handbook recommends not to accept food, sweets or drinks from strangers, they can be drugged. *Inoc* Cholera, Malaria, Polio, Typhoid, Yellow Fever *Airlines* British Airways *Average length of flight* 13.5 hours *Food* Corn pancakes, chicken, seafood and rice, delicious avocados and exotic fruits

Ecuador

Capital Quito *Lang* Spanish *Currency* Sucre = 100 centavos *Govt* Democracy – far right *Rel*

Roman Catholic *Size* 272,045 sq km – 104,506 sq miles *Pop* 11,460,117 *GMT* -5 (Galapagos Islands -6) *When* June to October *Visas* required for business only *Safety* Ecuador is one of the safest countries in South America but still be on your guard, violent crime increasing in all areas *Inoc* Yellow Fever* if arriving from an infected area, Cholera, Malaria, Polio, Typhoid *Airlines* Lufthansa, American Airlines, Air France, Iberia, KLM *Average length of flight* 17 hours *Food* National delicacy – Guinea Pig

French Guiana (France)

Capital Cayenne *Lang* French *Currency* French franc = 100 centimes *Govt* *Rel* Roman Catholic *Size* 91,000 sq km – 35,135 sq miles *Pop* 114,808 *GMT* -3 *When* July to mid November *Visas* Subject to change *Inoc* Yellow Fever* if arriving from an infected area, Malaria, Polio, Typhoid *Airlines* Air France via Paris *Average length of flight* 11 hours *Food* Seafood – anything else is expensive

Guyana

Capital Georgetown *Lang* English *Currency* Guyana Dollar = 100 cents *Govt* Democracy *Rel* Mainly Christian – some Hindu *Size* 214,969 sq km – 83,000 sq miles *Pop* 737,947 *GMT* -3 *When* February to March and August to October *Visas* Not required *Safety* Violent crime common in Georgetown *Inoc* Yellow Fever* if arriving from an infected area, Malaria, Polio,Typhoid, Yellow Fever *Airlines* British Airways, BWIA *Average length of flight* 10 hours *Food* Indian, African and Portuguese influences

Paraguay

Capital Asuncion *Lang* Spanish and Guarani *Currency* Guarani *Govt* Having been a military regime until 1992, it is now a multi-party democracy *Rel* Roman Catholic *Size* 406,752 sq km – 157,048 sq miles *Pop* 4,642,624 *GMT* - 4 *When* June – Sept *Visas* Not required by US and UK nationals travelling as tourists for less than 90 days *Inoc* Malaria, Polio, Typhoid *Airlines* British Airways, American Airlines, Iberia *Average length of flight* 15 hours *Food* Maize based – soup very popular

Peru

Capital Lima *Lang* Spanish and Quechua *Currency* Nuevo sol = 100 centimos *Govt* stability is returning with the imprisonment of Senedro (leader of the Shining Path) and democratic elections in 1995, but terrorism is still a very real danger, viz. the situation at the Japanese embassy in Lima *Rel* Roman Catholic *Size* 1,280,000 sq km – 496,225 sq miles *Pop*

23,088,000 *GMT* -5 *When* December through April *Visas* Not required by tourists from UK, US and Canada up to 90 days *Safety* Extremely dangerous in places, especially the central highlands. Tourists in the past have been attacked by the Shining Path (the terrorist organisation) *Inoc* Cholera, Yellow Fever* if arriving from an infected area, Malaria, Typhoid, *Airlines* KLM, Lufthansa, Viasa, American Airlines, Iberia, Air France *Average length of flight* 14 hours *Food* Lots of vegetables and potatoes. In Lima ceviche (raw fish marinated in lemon juice and hot peppers) is popular

Suriname

Capital Paramaribo *Lang* Dutch *Currency* Suriname Guilder = 100 cents *Govt* Having been through various regimes and coups since independence in 1975, there now is an elected govt *Rel* Majority Christian *Size* 163,265 sq km – 63,037 sq miles *Pop* 418,000 *GMT* -3 *When* December to April *Visas* Required by all *Validity* Varies *Time to get* 1-6 weeks *Inoc* Yellow Fever* if arriving from an infected area, Cholera, Malaria, Typhoid, Yellow Fever *Airlines* KLM *Average length of flight* 10 hours *Food* Creole – Indonesian influences

Uruguay

Capital Montevideo *Lang* Spanish *Currency* Uruguayan Peso = 100 centesimos *Govt* Stable democracy *Rel* Roman Catholic *Size* 176,215 sq km – 68,037 sq miles *Pop* 3,167,000 *GMT* -3 *When* December to March *Visas* Not required by UK citizens *Time to get* 4 days *Inoc* Typhoid *Airlines* Iberia, Air France, Aerolineas Argentinas *Average length of flight* 15 hours *Food* Lots of meat, mainly beef

Venezuela

Capital Caracas *Lang* Spanish *Currency* Bolivar = 100 centimos *Govt* Now a more stable democracy *Rel* Roman Catholic *Size* 912,050 sq km – 352,144 sq km *Pop* 21,377,000 *GMT* -4 *When* January to April *Visas* Not required but issued with a Tourist Card on 'plane *Safety* Violent crime increasing in cities, register with British Embassy in Caracas *Inoc* Yellow Fever, Malaria, Polio, Typhoid *Airlines* Viasa, British Airways *Average length of flight* 12 hours *Food* Good beef, maize bread, most food delicately spiced

ASIA

Afghanistan

Capital Kabul *Lang* Pashtu and Dari, some

English spoken *Currency* Afgani (Af) = 100 puls *Govt* Taleban, the hard-line Pakistani backed Islamic movement has taken control of the capital and most of the country but still highly unstable *Rel* Islamic *Size* 652,225 sq km – 251,773 sq miles *Pop* 17,080,000 *GMT* + 4.5 *When* Summer and early Autumn – Winter can be very cold indeed in the mountains *Visas* Required by everyone but at present difficult to obtain *Safety* Dangerous at present, strict Muslim majority therefore women should not travel alone and should be totally covered, outside Kabul in tribal areas very little protection. At present politically unstable – check with Foreign Office – British and US embassies are closed in Kabul *Inoc* Yellow Fever* if arriving from an infected area, Cholera, Typhoid, Polio, Malaria, *Airlines* Ariana Afghan Airlines *Average length of flight* 11 hours including stopovers *Food* Indian style (spicy)- lots of meat especially goat

Armenia (C.I.S.)

Capital Yerevan *Lang* Armenian and Russian *Currency* Newly introduced Dram=100 luma *Govt* Levon Petrosyan is the elected President, Leader of the Armenian Pan-National Movement *Rel* Christian *Size* 29,88 sq km- 11,500 sq miles *Pop* 3,354,000 *GMT* +3 *When* June to September *Visas* Required by all *Validity* 21 days or 1 year *Time to get* Not less than 10 days before departure *Safety* Due to the political and religious unrest with Azberbaijan tourists are strongly advised not to go to any of the Trans-Causican republics although cease fire has been in place since May 1994, register with relevent embassy in Yerevan *Airlines* Via Paris, State Airlines Company of Armenia (SACA) *Food* Lamb is favoured highly, sadly though unless you eat in a private house, the food tends to be heavy and greasy, an influence of the Soviet era.

Azerbaijan (C.I.S)

Capital Baku *Lang* Azerbaijani *Currency* Manat = 100 gyapik Russian Rouble is also legal tender *Govt* Elected President and Parliament. Aliyev is currently President, a communist he was a member of the Politburo *Rel* Muslim – mainly Shia *Size* 86,600 sq km – 33,400 sq miles *Pop* 7,499,000 *GMT* + 4 *When* June to September *Visas* Required by all *Time to get* Not less than 14 days before departure *Safety* Although cease fire in place since May 1994, the western area of the country is still volatile. Street crime increasing in all cities *Inoc* Malaria *Airlines* Azerbaijan Airlines *Food* Turkish, Georgian, and central Asia influences. Plov is the most common dish consisting of rice, mutton and spices

Bahrain

Capital Manama **Lang** Arabic and English **Currency** Dinar = 1000 fils **Govt** Ruled by an Arab monarchy (no elections) **Rel** Muslim **Size** 693 sq km – 267 sq miles **Pop** 568,063 **GMT** +3 **When** December to March: rest of year very hot **Visas** Not required by UK, required by US, Australians and Canadians (no Israeli stamps in passports) **Time to get** 1 day **Safety** Safe **Inoc** Polio,Typhoid **Airlines** British Airways, Gulf Air, amongst others **Average length of flight** 6 hours **Food** Spicy and strongly flavoured – meat mainly lamb

Bangladesh

Capital Dhaka **Lang** Bengali and English **Currency** Bangladeshi Taka = 100 Poishas **Govt** Ruled by the Bangladesh National party **Rel** Muslim **Size** 147,570 sq km – 56,977 sq miles **Pop** 117,787,000 **GMT** +6 **When** November to March **Visas** Required by all-except Australians, Canadians and US nationals if staying less than 15 days **Validity** 3 months **Time to get** 1-5 working days **Safety** Safe if sensible, women should be covered **Inoc** Yellow Fever* if arriving from an infected area, Cholera, Malaria, Polio, Typhoid **Airlines** Bangladesh Airlines, British Airways **Average length of flight** 10.5 hours **Food** Spicy seafood, chicken and lamb, limited Western food

Bhutan

Capital Thimphu **Lang** Dzongkha **Currency** 1 Ngultrum = 100 chetrums **Govt** Ruled by the monarch Jigme Singye Wangchuck **Rel** Buddhist **Size** 46,500 sq km – 17,954 sq miles **Pop** 600,000 **GMT** +6 **When** October, November and April to mid-June **Visas** Required by all. Can be difficult to obtain **Validity** Visas issued on arrival however application must be sent 3 months before departure **Safety** safe **Inoc** Yellow Fever* if arriving from an infected area, Cholera, Typhoid, Polio Malaria **Airlines** Druk Air from India, Nepal or Thailand **Food** Like Nepalese food, quite spicy with Chinese influence – mainly vegetarian

Brunei

Capital Bandar Seri Begawan **Lang** Malay (English also spoken) **Currency** Brunei Dollar = 100 sen **Govt** Sultan – His Majesty Paduka Seri Baginda Sultan Haji Hassanal Bolkiah Mu'izzaddin Waddaulah (Supreme) **Rel** Mainly Sunni Muslim **Size** 5,765 sq km – 2,226 sq miles **Pop** 284,500 **GMT** +8 **When** April – September **Visas** Required by Australians (US and Canadians if more than 14 days) **Validity** 3 months **Time to get** 2 – 3 days **Inoc** Yellow Fever* if arriving from an infected area,

Cholera, Polio, Typhoid **Airlines** Royal Brunei Airlines **Average length of flight** 17 hours **Food** Abundance of fresh fish and rice – spicy Malay influence

Cambodia

Capital Phnom Penh **Lang** Khmer – Chinese and Vietnamese also spoken **Currency** Riel = 100 sen **Govt** An elected Govt with Prince Sihanouk as President still faces the threat from the Khmer Rouge, which controls large parts of the country **Rel** Buddhist **Size** 181,035 sq km – 69,898 sq miles **Pop** 9,568,000 **GMT** +7 **When** December – April **Visas** Required by all **Validity** 1 month **Time to get** Anything from 3 days to 2 weeks **Safety** Extremely unsafe, fighting and kidnapping still a serious risk, the presence of unexploded mines makes travel off the beaten track very dangerous **Inoc** Yellow Fever* if arriving from an infected area, Cholera, Malaria, Polio, Typhoid **Airlines** Thai Airways via Bangkok **Average length of flight** 11 hours **Food** Rice based, popular dishes include salted fish

China

Capital Beijing **Lang** Mandarin Chinese **Currency** 1 Yaun = 100 fen or 10 chiao **Govt** Communist, possible instability looming following the death of Deng **Rel** Buddhist **Size** 9,571,300 sq km – 3,695,500 sq miles **Pop** 1,198,500,000 **GMT** +8 **When** Any time as China is so vast there is a diversity of climate **Visas** Required **Validity** Dependent on length of stay **Time to get** Allow as much time as possible **Safety** Safe if sensible **Inoc** Yellow Fever* if arriving from an infected area, Cholera, Malaria **Airlines** British Airways, Air China **Average length of flight** 14 hours **Food** Very good in cities, basic in outlying provinces

Georgia

Capital Tbilisi **Lang** Georgian, Russian **Currency** Still using the Russian rouble, but are introducing their own currency the Lary **Govt** Elected President Eduard Schevardnadze **Rel** Christian majority **Size** 70,000 sq km – 27,000 sq miles **Pop** 5,471,000 **GMT** +4 **When** May to September **Visas** Required through the Russian embassy **Time to get** Allow 14 days **Safety** Avoid travel at night outside Tbilisi – contact Foreign Office **Airlines** Via Moscow **Food** Best food found anywhere in the former Soviet Union

Hong Kong (UK)

Capital Hong Kong **Lang** Chinese and English **Currency** Hong Kong Dollar = 100 cents **Govt** Now a Special Administrative Region of the People's Republic of China since July 1st 1997

Rel Buddhists, Christians, Confucian, Taoists and Muslims *Size* 1,076 sq km – 415 sq miles *Pop* 6,189,800 *GMT* +8 *When* October to May *Visas* Not required *Safety* Safe *Inoc* Polio, Typhoid *Airlines* Cathay Pacific, British Airways, Virgin Atlantic *Average length of flight* 13.5 hours *Food* Better Chinese food than available in China – International

India

Capital New Delhi *Lang* English *Currency* Rupee = 100 paise *Govt* Federal republic currently ruled by the Congress Party *Rel* Majority Hindu *Size* 3,287,262 sq km – 1,269,218 sq miles *Pop* 920,000,000 *GMT* +5.5 *When* All year but if June – August go to far north (Ladakh) *Visas* Required by all *Validity* 1 or 6 months from date of issue *Time to get* 2 days in person, 4-5 weeks by post *Safety* Safe if sensible. Certain areas e.g. Jammu and Kashmir, in state of unrest and should be avoided, kidnapping a serious risk *Inoc* Yellow Fever* if arriving from an infected country, Cholera, Malaria, Polio, Typhoid *Airlines* Air Canada, Air India, Thai International, British Airways *Average length of flight* 9 hours *Food* Delicious curries, suitable for vegetarians

Indonesia

Capital Jakarta *Lang* Bahasa Indonesian *Currency* Rupiah = 100 sen *Govt* Basically a military regime with Suharto as President, although there is an elected Govt *Rel* Muslim majority *Size* 1,904,569 sq km – 735,358 sq miles *Pop* 194,440,100 *GMT* +7 – +9 *When* June to September *Visas* Not required if a tourist *Safety* Petty crime attacks on foreigners has increased, also kidnap by OPM is a risk in Irian Jaya *Inoc* Yellow Fever* if having arrived from an infected area, Malaria, Polio, Typhoid *Airlines* Garuda Indonesia, British Airways, other airlines fly there using transfer connections *Average length of flight* 20 hours 20 minutes *Food* Highly spiced

Iran

Capital Tehran *Lang* Persian (Farsi) *Currency* Iranian Rial = 100 dinars *Govt* Elected President (Rafsanjani) although all other candidates are hand-picked to lose *Rel* Islamic *Size* 1,648,000 sq km – 636,296 sq miles *Pop* 59,778,000 *GMT* +3.5 *When* November to March *Visas* Required by all *Validity* Up to 3 months from date of issue *Time to get* 4 weeks *Safety* Take sensible precautions, there is a total ban on video cameras, women should be completely covered up *Inoc* Yellow Fever* if arriving from an infected area, Malaria, Polio, Typhoid *Airlines* British Airways, Iran Air *Average length of flight* 8 hours *Food* Staple

diet is rice and meat, mainly mutton

Iraq

Capital Baghdad *Lang* Arabic *Currency* Iraqi Dinar = 20 dirhams = 1000 fils *Govt* Dictatorship – Saddam Hussein, elections are meant to be held every 4 years, no elections since Saddam came to power in 1979 *Rel* Muslim both Sunni and Shi'ite *Size* 438,317 sq km – 169,235 sq miles *Pop* 17,903,000 *GMT* +3 *When* Nov – March *Visas* Issued only at the express invitation of the Iraqi govt mainly only for business purposes *Time to get* 2 weeks *Safety* The Foreign Office do not recommend any visits to Iraq – extremely dangerous *Inoc* Yellow Fever* if arriving from an infected area, Hepatitis A, Malaria, Polio, Cholera, Typhoid *Airlines* At present no aircraft allowed to land at Baghdad *Average length of flight* 6 hours *Food* Minced meat, spices and rice

Israel

Capital Jerusalem *Lang* Hebrew and Arabic *Currency* New Israel Shekel = 100 new Agorot *Govt* Elected (Labour – Rabin) *Rel* Jewish *Size* 21,946 sq km – 8,473 sq miles *Pop* 5,462,200 *GMT* +2 *When* All year (Red Sea) *Visas* Stamp issued on arrival, UK nationals require a visa *Safety* Mainly safe, but unrest in certain areas, take local advice *Inoc* Polio, Typhoid *Airlines* British Airways, El Al Israel Airlines *Average length of flight* 5 hours *Food* A combination of Oriental and European cuisine

Japan

Capital Tokyo *Lang* Japanese *Currency* Japanese Yen *Govt* Elected coalition *Rel* Shintoist and Buddhist *Size* 377,815 sq km – 145,875 sq miles *Pop* 125,200,000 *GMT* +9 *When* All year *Visas* Required by Australia *Time to get* 7 days *Safety* Safe *Inoc* Polio, Typhoid *Airlines* Aeroflot, British Airways, Virgin Atlantic, All Nippon Airway, Japan Airlines *Average length of flight* 11 hours 30 minutes *Food* Crisp vegetables and raw fish – Saké, hot rice wine

Jordan

Capital Amman *Lang* Arabic *Currency* Dinar = 1000 fils *Govt* Constitutional monarch with an elected House of Representatives *Rel* Sunni Muslim *Size* 97,740 sq km – 37,738 sq miles *Pop* 5,198,000 *GMT* +2 *When* All year – very hot in summer though *Visas* Required by all – passport must not have Israeli stamp *Validity* Normally 3 months *Time to get* 2 days if applying in person *Safety* Safe *Inoc* Yellow Fever* if arriving from an infected area, Polio, Typhoid, Cholera *Airlines* Royal Jordanian Airlines, British Airways *Average length of* *flight* 5.5 hours *Food* Arabic and European dishes

Kazakhstan
Capital Almaty *Lang* Kazakh *Currency* 1 Tenge = 100 tiyin *Govt* Elected socialist Republic *Rel* Mainly Sunni Muslim *Size* 2,717,300 sq km – 1,049,150 sq miles *Pop* 16,763,000 *GMT* +5 (+6 in summer) *When* May – Sept *Visas* Required by all (liable to change) *Validity* Varies *Time to get* Allow weeks *Safety* Increase in attacks on trains and in larger cities, travel in groups *Inoc* Typhoid, Polio *Airlines* Uzbekistan Airways, Aeroflot *Average length of flight* 8 hours via Moscow *Food* Mutton and horse-meat, Almaty is renowned for its apples

Korea (North)
Capital Pyongyang *Lang* Korean *Currency* Won = 100 jon *Govt* Communist, ruled with an iron rod by Kim Il Sung (The Great Leader), now deceased to be succeeded by his son *Rel* No official religion but some Buddhists *Size* 120,538 sq km – 46,540 sq miles *Pop* 23,483,000 *GMT* +9 *When* Spring and Autumn *Visas* Required by all and difficult to get *Time to get* 1 month *Inoc* Polio, Cholera, Typhoid *Airlines* Aeroflot, Air China *Average length of flight* 16 hours *Food* Rice and noodles based – fond of pickles

Korea (South)
Capital Seoul *Lang* Korean *Currency* Won *Govt* Elected Govt (Democratic Liberal Party) *Rel* Buddhist *Size* 99,299 sq km – 38,340 sq miles *Pop* 44,850,801 *GMT* +9 *When* Spring and Autumn *Visas* Not required if staying less than 15 days (USA) or 3 months (UK, Canada, Australia and New Zealand) and have onward ticket *Safety* Safe *Inoc* If staying more than three months AIDS certificate is required. Polio, Typhoid *Airlines* Korean Air, British Airways *Average length of flight* 12 hours *Food* Like North Korean – as many as 20 side dishes to one main course

Kuwait
Capital Kuwait City *Lang* Arabic and English *Currency* Kuwait Dinar = 1000 fils *Govt* Executive power held by the Emir, a member of the Royal Al-Sabah family, elections held in 1992 for the consultative assembly. Political parties are banned *Rel* Muslim *Size* 17,818 sq km – 6,880 sq miles *Pop* 1,575,983 *GMT* +3 *When* October to May *Visas* Required by all *Validity* 1 month from date of entry *Time to get* 24 hours *Safety* The border with Iraq should be avoided, and care should be taken in more remote spots for unexploded ordnance *Inoc*

Polio, Cholera, Typhoid *Airlines* British Airways, Kuwait Airways *Average length of flight* 6 hours *Food* International and Arab cuisine

Kyrgyzstan (C.I.S.)
Capital Bishkek *Lang* Kyrgyz *Currency* 1 som = 100 tyn *Govt* Elected President, new constitution and elections set for 1997 *Rel* Sunni Muslim *Size* 198,500 sq km – 76,640 sq miles *Pop* 4,476,400 *GMT* +5 *When* May – Sept *Visas* Required by all – liable to change *Validity* Varies *Inoc* Typhoid, Polio *Airlines* Kyrgyz Air via Moscow *Average length of flight* 8 hours excluding stopover *Food* Mutton and horse meat

Laos
Capital Vientiane *Lang* Laotian *Currency* Laotian New Kip = 100 cents *Govt* Communist regime *Rel* Hinayana (form of Buddhism), Confucianism and Animism and some Christian *Size* 236,800 sq km – 91,400 sq miles *Pop* 4,581,258 *GMT* +7 *When* Nov – April *Visas* Required by all *Validity* 7 days transit, tourist visas also available if tour booked through Laos agency *Time to get* As far in advance as possible *Inoc* Yellow Fever* if arriving from an infected area, Malaria, Polio, Cholera, Typhoid *Airlines* Thai Airways, British Airways, Loa Aviation *Average length of flight* 19 hours *Food* Similar to Thai – local dishes include rice and fermented fish

Lebanon
Capital Beirut *Lang* Arabic *Currency* Lebanese Pound = 100 piastres *Govt* Democracy elections held every 4 years *Rel* Majority Muslim but Christians also *Size* 10,452 sq km – 4,036 sq miles *Pop* 3,855,000 *GMT* +2 *When* Mid March to November *Visas* Required by all (no Israeli stamps in passport) *Validity* 2 weeks – 3 months *Time to get* 6-8 weeks *Safety* Unstable, check with Foreign Office *Inoc* Yellow Fever* if arriving from an infected area, Polio, Cholera, Typhoid *Airlines* Middle East Airlines, British Airways, Air France, Olympic Airways, Malev, Tarom, KLM *Average length of flight* 5 hours *Food* Staple diet of vegetables, rice and mutton

Macau
Capital Macau *Lang* Portuguese and Chinese *Currency* Pataca = 100 avos *Govt* A Special Territory of Portugal, headed by the Governor, however in 1999, like Hong Kong in 1997, Macau will be handed over to the Chinese *Rel* Diverse from Roman Catholic to Buddhism, Daoism and Confucianism. *Size* 18 sq km – 6.95 sq miles *Pop* 400,000 *GMT* +8 *When*

October to March *Visas* Not required *Safety* Safe *Airlines* Singapore Airlines, Korean Airlines, Malaysian Airlines via Hong Kong *Average length of flight* To Hong Kong 14 hours *Food* Spicy and combination of Chinese and Portuguese cooking

Malaysia
Capital Kuala Lumpur *Lang* Bahasa Malaysia *Currency* Ringgit = 100 sen *Govt* Elected Govt, presently the National Front Party, however some power still remains with the nine hereditary sultans who elect the Head of State *Rel* Mainly Muslim, some Buddhist *Size* 329,758 sq km – 127,320 sq miles *Pop* 20,103,000 *GMT* +8 *When* The climate varies in different regions, generally though January – March *Visas* Not required, but a Visit Pass is issued on arrival *Safety* Safe *Inoc* Yellow Fever* if arriving from an infected area, Cholera, Polio, Malaria, Typhoid *Airlines* Malaysia Airlines, British Airways *Average length of flight* 12 hours *Food* Subtly spicy

Mongolia
Capital Ulan Bator *Lang* Mongolian Khalkha *Currency* Tugrik = 100 mongos *Govt* Having been a one-party communist state, in 1992 it became a democratic parliamentary state *Rel* Buddhist Lamaism *Size* 1,565,000 sq km – 604,250 sq miles *Pop* 2,317,000 *GMT* +8 *When* May to September *Visas* Required by all *Validity* Varies *Time to get* 7 days *Safety* There is some street-crime in Ulan Bator *Inoc* Medical insurance certificate required, Polio, Typhoid *Airlines* Aeroflot *Average length of flight* 14 hours including stopovers *Food* Meat-based diet – not suitable for vegetarians. Lots of yak butter tea – an acquired taste

Myanmar (Burma)
Capital Yangon (Rangoon) *Lang* Burmese *Currency* Kyat = 100 Pyas *Govt* State Law and Order Restoration Council – dictatorship *Rel* Theravasa Buddhist *Size* 676,552 sq km – 261,218 sq miles *Pop* 41,550,000 *GMT* +6.5 *When* November to April *Visas* Required by all *Validity* 14 days within 3 months from date of issue *Time to get* 2 days *Safety* Unstable, check with Foreign Office. Tourists are required to keep to officially designated areas *Inoc* Yellow Fever* if arriving from an infected area, Cholera, Malaria, Polio, Typhoid *Airlines* Thai Airlines, Singapore Airlines, Silk Air *Average length of flight* 23 hours including stopovers in Singapore or Bangkok *Food* Rice and rice noodle based, lightly spiced curries

Nepal
Capital Kathmandu *Lang* Nepali *Currency* Nepalese Rupee = 100 paisa *Govt* Constitutional monarchy *Rel* Buddhist and Hindu *Size* 147,181 sq km – 56,827 sq miles *Pop* 19,280,081 *GMT* + 5.45 *When* October to May *Visas* Required by all *Validity* 30 days within 6 months from date of issue *Time to get* 1 day or 10 minutes at the airport on arrival *Safety* Safe *Inoc* Yellow Fever* if arriving from an infected area, Cholera, Malaria, Paratyphoid, Polio, Typhoid *Airlines* Royal Nepal Airlines, Aeroflot, PIA, Lufthansa *Average length of flight* 10 hours *Food* Rice based, mild curries

Oman
Capital Muscat *Lang* Arabic and English *Currency* Omani Rial = 1000 baiza *Govt* Ruled by Sultan Qaboos whose family have held power since the 18th century *Rel* Ibadi Muslim *Size* 300,000 sq km – 120,000 sq miles *Pop* 2,096,000 *GMT* +4 *When* August to May (still very hot though) *Visas* Required by all – will be denied if Israeli visa stamp in passport *Validity* 2 weeks within one month of issue *Time to get* 7 days *Safety* Safe *Inoc* Yellow Fever* if arriving from an infected area, Cholera, Malaria, Polio, Typhoid *Airlines* British Airways, Gulf Air *Average length of flight* 8 hours 10 minutes *Food* International

Pakistan
Capital Islamabad *Lang* Urdu and English *Currency* Pakistani Rupee = 100 paisa *Govt* Elected National Assembly *Rel* Muslim *Size* 796,095 sq km – 307,374 sq miles *Pop* 126,610,000 *GMT* +5 *When* November and March – South May, June, September, and October – North *Visas* Required by all *Validity* 3 months, must be used within six months of issue *Safety* Safe if sensible in northern areas, however central and south Pakistan are unsafe and advice should be taken *Inoc* Yellow Fever* if arriving from an infected area within six days, Cholera* Malaria, Polio, Typhoid *Airlines* British Airways, PIA – more options if flying to Karachi *Average length of flight* 8 hours *Food* Masala Curry – not as hot as India. In the North Afghan influences such as goat kebab. Lots of chapatis

Philippines
Capital Manila *Lang* Filipino *Currency* Philippine Peso = 100 centavos *Govt* The new constitution introduced in 1987 is a directly elected government *Rel* Mainly Roman Catholic *Size* 300,00 sq km – 115,831 sq miles *Pop* 67,038,000 *GMT* +8 *When* November to June *Visas* Not required by EC tourists up to 21

days *Validity* 59 days from date of entry *Time to get* 1 day *Safety* Some areas unstable, take local advice *Inoc* Yellow Fever* if arriving from an infected area, Cholera, Malaria, Polio, Typhoid *Airlines* British Airways, Philippine Airlines *Average length of flight* 18 hours *Food* A mixture of Spanish, Malay and Chinese cooking – rice is the staple food

Qatar

Capital Doha *Lang* Arabic *Currency* Qatar Riyal = 100 dirhams *Govt* Ruled by the Al-Thani family *Rel* Muslim *Size* 11,437 sq km – 4,416 sq miles *Pop* 593,000 *GMT* +3 *When* October to May *Visas* Required by all *Inoc* Yellow Fever* if arriving within 6 days from an infected area, Cholera. If staying longer than 30 days a medical test is required *Airlines* Gulf Air, Air France *Average length of flight* 7 hours 15 minutes *Food* International

Russian Federation

Capital Moscow *Lang* Russian *Currency* Rouble = 100 kopeks *Govt* Having been part of the communist Soviet bloc is now a democracy with teething problems *Rel* Russian Orthodox *Size* 17,075,400 sq km – 6,592,850 sq miles *Pop* 148,000,000 *GMT* +3 to +12 *When* May-Sept *Visas* Required by all *Validity* Varies from date of entry *Time to get* 2 weeks *Safety* Moscow and St Petersburg both have a high crime rate, take local advice, areas like Chechnia are extremely dangerous *Inoc* Typhoid, Polio *Airlines* SAS, Aeroflot *Average length of flight* 3 hours 45 minutes *Food* Salmon, caviar, borsch, on the whole however food in restaurants is not good, and there can be shortages

Saudi Arabia

Capital Riyadh *Lang* Arabic *Currency* Saudi Arabian Riyal = 100 halalah *Govt* King Fahd is an absolute monarchy, with no political parties *Rel* Sunni Muslim *Size* 2,240,000 sq km – 864,869 sq miles *Pop* 16,929,294 *GMT* +3 *When* October – April *Visas* Required *Validity* Varies *Safety* Safe *Inoc* Yellow Fever* if arriving from an infected area, Cerbero-spinal meningitis if arriving from an infected area or during the month of August (Hajj), Malaria, Polio, Typhoid *Airlines* British Airways, Saudi *Average length of flight* 6.5 hours *Food* Strongly flavoured and spicy, meat is normally lamb or chicken.

Singapore

Capital Singapore *Lang* Chinese *Currency* Singapore Dollar = 100 cents *Govt* Power lies with the elected Prime Minister, the current govt is the People's Action Party, who have held power since 1972 *Rel* Mixed – Confucian, Taoist, Buddhist, Christian Hindu and Muslim *Size* 626.4 sq km – 242 sq miles *Pop* 2,986,500 *GMT* +8 *When* February to October *Visas* Not required. Social Visit Pass issued on arrival *Safety* Safe *Inoc* Yellow Fever* if arriving from an infected area, Cholera, Polio, Typhoid *Airlines* Royal Brunei Airlines, Singapore Airlines, British Airways, Qantas *Average length of flight* 13 hours *Food* A gourmet's paradise – Chinese, Malay, every sort of dish

Sri Lanka

Capital Colombo *Lang* Sinhala, Tamil and English *Currency* Sri Lankan rupee *Govt* directly elected President and Assembly *Rel* Mainly Buddhist *Size* 64,454 sq km – 24,886 sq miles *Pop* 18,000,000 *GMT* +5.5 *When* July through Sept and Jan through March *Visas* Issued free of charge at airport to tourists *Safety* Mainly safe, take local advice, tension between Tamil Tigers and security forces, but central and south of island largely unaffected *Inoc* Yellow Fever* if arriving from an infected area, Cholera, Malaria, Polio, Typhoid *Airlines* Air Lanka *Average length of flight* 13 hours 45 minutes *Food* Spicy

Syria

Capital Damascus *Lang* Arabic, French and English *Currency* Syrian Pound = 100 piastres *Govt* Democracy *Rel* Sunni Muslim and Christian *Size* 185,180 sq km – 71,498 sq miles *Pop* 15,000,000 *GMT* +2 *When* Spring and Autumn *Visas* Required by all *Validity* 3 months *Time to get* 3-4 days *Safety* Care should be taken to behave appropriately, photography near military bases and government installations is prohibited *Inoc* Yellow Fever* if arriving from an infected area, Cholera *Airlines* Syrian Arab Airlines, Air France, Lufthansa, Cyprus Airways, Malev, Tarom, Austrian Airlines and Turkish Airlines *Average length of flight* 7.5 hours *Food* Lots of minced meat

Taiwan

Capital Taipei *Lang* Mandarin Chinese and English *Currency* New Taiwan Dollar = 100 cents *Govt* Elected National Assembly, constitutional changes scheduled for 1995 *Rel* Buddhist *Size* 36,000 sq km – 13,900 sq miles *Pop* 21,125,792 *GMT* +8 *When* November to May *Visas* Required by all *Validity* 60 days within 3 months from date of issue *Time to get* depending on visa – 48 hours *Safety* Safe *Inoc* Cholera, Yellow Fever* if arriving from an infected area, Polio, Typhoid *Airlines* EVA Airways, British Airways *Average length of flight* 20 hours *Food* Delicious seafood

Tajikistan

Capital Dushanbe *Lang* Tajik *Currency* Russian rouble *Govt* Changes to the constitution are being introduced in 1994/5, with a President as head of state, and an elected parliament *Rel* Sunni Muslim *Size* 143,100 sq km – 55,250 sq miles *Pop* 5,751,000 *GMT* +5 *When* May- Sept *Visas* Required by all *Validity* Varies *Time to get* 10 days or longer through the Russian Embassies *Safety* Terrorism a risk and there is no British mission – check with US or German Embassies before travelling *Inoc* Cholera, Malaria *Airlines* Tajik Air *Average length of flight* 6 hours *Food* Sweet food as a starter, followed by meat dishes. Excellent fruits

Thailand

Capital Bangkok *Lang* Thai *Currency* Baht = 100 satang *Govt* Constitutional monarchy, with an elected House of Representatives, large military influence and the King is regarded as a demi-god *Rel* Buddhist *Size* 513,115 sq km – 198,115 sq miles *Pop* 60,000,000 *GMT* +7 *When* November to February *Visas* Not required if a tourist and staying less than 15 days *Safety* Safe apart from border with Myanmar *Inoc* Yellow Fever* if arriving from an infected area, Cholera, Polio, Malaria, Typhoid, *Airlines* Thai Airways, Philippine Airlines, Qantas, Eva Airlines, Garuda (Indonesia), British Airways *Average length of flight* 13 hours 40 minutes *Food* Hot and spicy

Turkey

Capital Ankara *Lang* Turkish *Currency* Turkish Lira *Govt* Democratic but increasing rise of fundamentalism *Rel* Muslim *Size* 779,452 sq km – 300,948 sq miles *Pop* 61,644,000 *GMT* +2 *When* April to October *Visas* Required by UK citizens obtainable at the airport on arrival *Safety* Dangerous in the east and southern east provinces, contact the Foreign Office for advice Western and Central Turkey has seen attacks on tourists by the PKK *Inoc* Malaria, Polio, Cholera, Typhoid *Airlines* Turkish Airlines, British Airways *Average length of flight* 3 hours 45 minutes *Food* Meat based, normally lamb

Turkmenistan

Capital Ashgabat *Lang* Turkmen *Currency* 1 Manat=100 tenge *Govt* Elected govt *Rel* Sunni Muslim *Size* 488,100 sq km – 188,456 sq miles *Pop* 4,483,300 *GMT* +5 *When* Spring and Autumn *Visas* Required by all, liable to change *Validity* Varies, normally 10 days if issued at the airport *Time to get* 5 days *Inoc* Malaria *Airlines* Turkish Airlines *Average length of flight* 6 hours excluding stopover in Turkey

Food Typically Central Asian mutton and rice

United Arab Emirates

Capital Abu Dhabi *Lang* Arabic *Currency* UAE Dirham – 100 fils *Govt* The seven Emirates are each governed by the ruling family, each family is part of the Supreme Council which is the federal authority for UAE, the council appoints the President. There are no political parties *Rel* Sunni Muslim *Size* 77,700 sq km – 30,000 sq miles *Pop* 2,377,700 *GMT* +4 *When* October to May *Visas* Required but not by UK citizens *Validity* 30 days *Safety* Safe *Inoc* Malaria, Polio, Cholera, Typhoid *Airlines* British Airways, Gulf Air and Emirates *Average length of flight* 6 hours 35 minutes *Food* Salads, sheep's brains and delicious seafood

Uzbekistan

Capital Tashkent *Lang* Uzbek *Currency* Som Som being introduced in 1994 *Govt* One-party state, with Karimov as elected President *Rel* Mainly Sunni Muslim *Size* 447,400 sq km – 172,740 sq miles *Pop* 22,098,000 *GMT* +5 *When* Spring and Autumn *Visas* Required by all *Validity* Varies *Time to get* 20 days *Safety* Dress down and avoid travelling at night *Inoc* Cholera, Typhoid, Polio, Malaria, Hepatitis A *Airlines* Uzbekistan Airways *Average length of flight* 7 hours *Food* Typically Central Asian

Vietnam

Capital Hanoi *Lang* Vietnamese *Currency* New Dong = 10 hao = 100 xu *Govt* Communist *Rel* Buddhist *Size* 330,341 sq km – 127,545 sq miles *Pop* 70,982,000 *GMT* +7 *When* November to April *Visas* Required by all *Validity* 1 month *Time to get* 10 working days *Safety* Travel in some areas is dangerous, seek local advice *Inoc* Yellow Fever* if arriving from an infected area, Cholera, Typhoid, Polio, Malaria *Airlines* Aeroflot, Cathay Pacific, Thai Airways, Air France *Average length of flight* 17 hours *Food* Thai and Chinese mix

Yemen

Capital Sana'a *Lang* Arabic *Currency* Yemeni Dinar = 1000 fils *Govt* Changing constitution *Rel* Sunni Muslim *Size* 527,969 sq km – 203,850 sq miles *Pop* 14,561,330 *GMT* +3 *When* October to April *Visas* Required by all *Validity* 1 month *Commencing* Within 3 months *Safety* Security improved but still volatile areas, check with relevent embassy *Inoc* Yellow Fever* if arriving from an infected area, Cholera, Malaria, Polio, Typhoid *Airlines* British Airways, Yemen Airways *Average length of flight* 10 hours *Food* seafood, also *haradha*, and mincemeat and pepper dish

EUROPE

Albania

Capital Tirana **Lang** Albanian but Greek is also spoken **Currency** Leks **Govt** Was communist until elections in 1991, but now ruled by the Democratic Party who continue to introduce economic reforms, although at time of writing, President Berisha's hold on the country is slipping. **Rel** Previously forced atheism, now allowed to worship openly (70% Muslim) also Catholic and Orthodox **Size** 28,748 sq km – 11,100 sq miles **Pop** 3,363,000 **GMT** + 1 (+2 in summer) **When** May/June and mid September to mid October **Visas** Not required by UK, US and Canadian citizens – required by Australians **Validity** Depending on length of stay **Time to get** 4 weeks **Safety** riots bordering on civil war at time of writing, because of collapsed pyramid selling enterprises **Inoc** Cholera present, Typhoid, Polio, Hepatitis A **Airlines** MALEV, Alitalia, Tatra Air Albanian Airlines, Swiss Air **Average length of flight** 4 to 5 hours **Food** Turkish influences

Andorra

Capital Andorra La Vella **Lang** Officially Catalan, but French and Spanish also used **Currency** French Francs and Spanish Pesetas **Govt** No formal constitution – co-principality with France and the Spanish Bishop of Urgel **Rel** Roman Catholic **Size** 468 sq km – 181 sq miles **Pop** 65,227 **GMT** +1 (+2 in summer) **When** All year round (winter for skiing) **Visas** Not required for Andorra but Australians need visas for Spain and France **Safety** Safe **Airlines** Nearest airport Barcelona (Spain) **Food** Catalan omelettes, local sausages and cheese

Austria

Capital Vienna **Lang** German **Currency** Austrian Schilling = 100 Groschen **Govt** Socialist **Rel** Roman Catholic **Size** 83,859 sq km – 32,378 sq miles **Pop** 8,031,100 **GMT** +1 **When** All year **Visas** Not required **Safety** Safe **Airlines** Austria Airlines, British Airways, Air France and many more **Average length of flight** 2 hours **Food** Influenced by southeast European cuisine – various types of cured and smoked meat.

Belarus

Capital Minsk **Lang** Belarussian **Currency** Belarussian Rubel = 10 Rub; Russian roubles are also in use **Govt** Communist **Rel** Christian **Size** 207,595 sq km – 80,153 sq miles **Pop** 10,297,000 **GMT** +2 **When** May to September **Visas** Required by all **Validity** 30 days – 1 year **Time to get** 5 working days **Safety** Seek local advice **Airlines** Austrian Airlines **Average length of flight** 5 hours including stopover **Food** Vegetable based, most famous is Borsch – beetroot soup

Belgium

Capital Brussels **Lang** Flemish and French **Currency** Belgian Franc = 100 centimes **Govt** Coalition Government with a constitutional monarch – King Albert **Rel** Roman Catholic **Size** 30,519 sq km – 11,783 sq miles **Pop** 10,100,631 **GMT** +1 **When** All year **Visas** Not required **Safety** Safe **Airlines** Sabena, British Airways, British Midland, Air UK, Singapore Airlines **Average length of flight** 55 minutes **Food** Similar to French, fries and chocolate particular specialities

Bosnia-Herzegovina

Capital Sarajevo **Lang** Serb-Croat and Croat-Serb **Currency** Yugoslav Dinar = 100 paras Croatian Dinar = 100 paras **Rel** Extremely unstable **Rel** Muslim, Orthodox and Roman Catholic **Size** 51,129 sq km – 19,736 sq miles **Pop** 3,527,000 **GMT** +1 **When** All year round **Visas** Not available **Safety** Extremely dangerous – despite peace agreement, violence still a hazard **Airlines** None presently **Food** Shortages

Bulgaria

Capital Sofia **Lang** Bulgarian **Currency** Lev = 100 stotinki **Govt** Elected Govt currently the Union of Democratic Forces although under economic pressure **Rel** Eastern Orthodox Church **Size** 110,994 sq km – 42,855 sq miles **Pop** 8,427,418 **GMT** +2 **When** April – September **Visas** Required by all unless holiday booked through **Balkantourist** or a US citizen **Validity** 3 months **Time to get** 7 days **Safety** Beware of their driving habits **Airlines** Balkan Airlines **Average length of flight** 3 hours **Food** Spicy and filling

Croatia

Capital Zagreb **Lang** Croat-Serb and Serb-Croat **Currency** Croatian Dinar = 100 paras **Govt** Croatian Democratic Union is fighting to keep their lands within the former Yugoslav Republic **Rel** Roman Catholic **Size** 56,538 sq km – 21,829 sq miles **Pop** 4,779,000 **GMT** +1 **When** All year **Visas** Not required for UK nationals **Safety** Earth tremors in Southern Croatia, border areas are dangerous – consult Foreign Office **Airlines** Croatian Airlines, Swiss Air and Lufthansa **Average length of flight** 2 hours **Food** The coast is noted for its seafood

Cyprus (Southern part of the island)
Capital Nicosia *Lang* Greek *Currency* Cyprus
Pound = 100 cents *Govt* Democracy *Rel* Greek
Orthodox *Size* 9,251 sq km – 3,572 sq miles
Pop 729,800 *GMT* +2 *When* All year *Visas* Not
required *Airlines* Cyprus Airways, British
Airways *Average length of flight* 4.5 hours
Food Charcoal grills, kebabs, typical Greek
food

Czech Republic
Capital Prague *Lang* Czech *Currency* Koruna
or Crown = 100 haleru *Govt* Democratic state
Rel Christian *Size* 78,864 sq km – 30,450 sq
miles *Pop* 10,333,616 *GMT* +1 *When* May –
September *Visas* Required but not by UK
nationals *Validity* 30 days within 6 months of
date of issue *Time to get* Same day *Airlines*
CSA, British Airways *Average length of flight*
1 hour 45 minutes *Food* Austro-Hungarian
dishes – lots of pork

Denmark
Capital Copenhagen *Lang* Danish *Currency*
Danish Krone =100 ore *Govt* Democracy
currently held by the Social Democrats *Rel*
Evangelical Lutheran *Size* 43,093 sq km –
16,638 sq miles *Pop* 5,215,718 *GMT* +1 (+2 in
summer) *When* All year *Visas* Not required by
EC nationals *Safety* Safe *Airlines* British
Airways, Scandinavian Airlines, Maersk Air
amongst others. *Average length of flight* 1 hour
50 minutes *Food* Rye bread, open sandwiches
with seafood, meat or cheese – lots of pickled
herrings and of course Schnapps

Estonia
Capital Tallinn *Lang* Estonian *Currency* 1
Kroon = 100 cents *Govt* Unstable coalition
Govt *Rel* Protestant *Size* 45,226 sq km – 17,462
sq miles *Pop* 1,476,301 *GMT* +2 (+3 in
summer) *When* April – October *Visas* Not
required *Safety* Safe *Airlines* SAS *Average
length of flight* 5 hours *Food* Fish, especially
trout and herring

Finland
Capital Helsinki *Lang* Finnish *Currency*
Markka = 100 pennia *Govt* Coalition
democracy *Rel* Lutheran *Size* 338,145 sq km –
130,559 sq miles *Pop* 5,098,754 *GMT* +2
When all year *Visas* not required *Safety* Safe
Airlines Finnair, British Airways *Average
length of flight* 2 hours 55 minutes *Food*
Excellent fish – French and Russian influences

France
Capital Paris *Lang* French *Currency* Franc =
100 centimes *Govt* Democratic Republic *Rel*
Roman Catholic *Size* 543,965 sq km – 210026

sq miles *Pop* 57,903,000 *GMT* +1 *When* All
year *Visas* Required by Australians *Validity* Up
to 3 months *Time to get* 24 hours *Safety* Safe
Airlines British Airways, Air France, British
Midland, Air UK, Singapore Airlines, Cathay
Pacific *Average length of flight* 1 hour 5
minutes *Food* Garlicky and rich, good cheese

Germany
Capital Berlin *Lang* German *Currency*
Deutsche Mark = 100 Pfennigs *Govt*
Democracy *Rel* Christian *Size* 356,854 sq km –
137,817 sq miles *Pop* 81,338,093 *GMT* +1
When All year *Visas* Not required *Safety* Safe
Airlines British Airways, Lufthansa, Conti-
flug, United Airlines *Average length of flight* 1
hour 40 minutes *Food* Heavy lunches and of
course sausages (frankfurters)

Gibraltar
Capital Gibraltar *Lang* English and Spanish
Currency Pound sterling = 100 new pence *Govt*
Self-governing British Crown Colony *Rel*
Mainly Roman Catholic *Size* 6.5 sq km – 2.5 sq
miles *Pop* 28,051 *GMT* +1 *When* All year
Visas Not required *Safety* Safe *Airlines* GB
Airways *Average length of flight* 2 hours 45
minutes *Food* Offers British, French, Spanish
and Moroccan food

Greece
Capital Athens *Lang* Greek *Currency*
Drachma *Govt* Democracy *Rel* Greek Orthodox
Size 131,957 sq km – 50,949 sq miles *Pop*
10,368,600 *GMT* +2 *When* April to October
Visas Not required *Safety* Safe *Airlines*
Olympic Airways, British Airways, Virgin
Atlantic *Average length of flight* 3 hours 15
minutes *Food* Olive oil used in cooking,
delicious fish and charcoal grilled meats

Greenland
Capital Nuuk *Lang* Greenlandic (like Inuit)
Currency Danish Krone = 100 ore *Govt*
Domestic affairs dealt by the elected
Landsstyre, foreign affairs controlled by the
Danish Govt *Rel* Church of Greenland
(Protestant) *Size* 2,175,600 sq km – 840.000 sq
miles *Pop* 55,732 *GMT* -4 *When* May to
September *Visas* Not required *Safety* Safe,
beware of freezing temperatures *Airlines* Via
Denmark, Greenlandair, SAS *Average length
of flight* 5.5 hours *Food* Whale meat used
locally, but thankfully not in every restaurant,
also reindeer, musk ox, and seafood

Guernsey
Capital St Peter Port *Lang* English *Currency*
Pound Sterling = 100 pence *Govt* Internal self-
Govt. British Govt responsible for external

affairs *Rel* Church of England *Size* 65 sq km – 25 sq miles *Pop* 58,867 *GMT* GMT *When* All year *Visas* Not required *Safety* Safe *Airlines* British Airways, Air UK, Jersey European Airways, Air UK *Average length of flight* 45 minutes *Food* French and English cooking

Hungary

Capital Budapest *Lang* Hungarian *Currency* Forint = 100 filler *Govt* Formerly a soviet-style socialist state, it has since 1990 been governed by an elected coalition *Rel* Roman Catholic *Size* 93,033 sq km – 35,920 sq miles *Pop* 10,276,968 *GMT* +1 *When* Any time – winter can be very cold though *Visas* Required by Australia and NZ *Validity* 30 days within 6 months *Time to get* 2 days *Safety* Safe *Airlines* British Airways, Malev *Average length of flight* 2 hours 40 minutes *Food* Soups and stuffed vegetables

Iceland

Capital Reykjavik *Lang* Icelandic *Currency* Iceland Krona = 100 aurar *Govt* Elected coalition *Rel* Lutheran *Size* 103,000 sq km – 39,769 sq miles *Pop* 267,809 *GMT* GMT *When* All year but especially June for the summer solstice *Visas* Not required *Safety* Safe *Airlines* Icelandair *Average length of flight* 2 hours 50 minutes *Food* Fish and lamb based

Ireland (Eire)

Capital Dublin *Lang* English and Gaelic *Currency* Irish Punt = 100 pence *Govt* Elected coalition *Rel* Roman Catholic *Size* 70,283 sq km – 27,136 sq miles *Pop* 3,582,200 *GMT* GMT *When* All year *Visas* Not required *Safety* Safe *Airlines* Aer Lingus, British Midland, British Airways, Ryanair *Average length of flight* 50 minutes *Food* Irish Stew, Connemara lamb, Dublin Bay prawns, soda bread and the famous Guinness

Italy

Capital Rome *Lang* Italian *Currency* Italian Lira *Govt* Democracy *Rel* Roman Catholic *Size* 301,227 sq km – 116,324 sq miles *Pop* 57,268,578 *GMT* +1 *When* All year round *Visas* Not required *Safety* Safe *Airlines* Alitalia, British Airways, Ethiopian Airways, Philippine Airlines, Kenya Airways, Air Seychelles *Average length of flight* 2.5 hours *Food* Pasta, pizza, pepperoni, prosciutto, pesto, and swilled down with Peroni, and Prosecco

Jersey

Capital St Helier *Lang* English *Currency* Pound Sterling = 100 pence *Govt* British dependency (not part of UK) *Rel* Christian *Size* 116 sq km – 45 sq miles *Pop* 85,150 *GMT* GMT *When* All year *Visas* Not required *Safety* Safe *Airlines* British Airways, Jersey European Airways, Air UK *Average length of flight* 40 minutes *Food* English and French influences

Latvia

Capital Riga *Lang* Latvian *Currency* 1 Latvian Lat = 100 santimi *Govt* New constitution being drafted since independence *Rel* Lutheran *Size* 64,589 sq km – 24,938 sq miles *Pop* 2,529,500 *GMT* +2 *When* Apr – Oct *Visas* Not required by UK and USA citizens *Validity* 3 months *Time to get* 1 day *Safety* Safe *Inoc* Hepatitis A *Airlines* Baltic International Airlines, SAS, Lufthansa *Average length of flight* 5.5 hours *Food* Rye bread and fish and thick soups

Liechtenstein

Capital Vaduz *Lang* German *Currency* Swiss Franc = 100 centimes *Govt* Elected coalition with the Monarch being head of state *Rel* Christian – mostly Roman Catholic *Size* 160 sq km – 62 sq miles *Pop* 30,629 *GMT* +1 *When* All year *Visas* Same as Switzerland *Safety* Safe *Airlines* There is no airport in Liechtenstein, most convenient is Zurich and then a 75-mile drive. Flights to Zurich include British Airways, Swissair, Cathay Pacific Kenya Airways, Crossair *Average length of flight* To Zurich 1.5 hours *Food* Swiss and Austrian influences

Lithuania

Capital Vilnius *Lang* Lithuanian *Currency* The Litas = 100 centu *Govt* Elected Govt currently held by the ex-communist Lithuanian Democratic Labour Party *Rel* Mainly Roman Catholic *Size* 65,300 sq km – 25,212 sq miles *Pop* 3,717,700 *GMT* +2 *When* April to October *Visas* Not required for stays of up to 90 days *Validity* 90 days *Time to get* 5 days *Safety* Safe *Airlines* Lithuanian Airlines direct or SAS, Lufthansa, Austrian Airlines *Average length of flight* 4 hours *Food* Lots of pork and cabbage

Luxembourg

Capital Luxembourg-ville *Lang* German *Currency* Luxembourg franc = 100 centimes *Govt* Constitutional monarch and elected govt currently a coalition *Rel* Roman Catholic *Size* 2,586 sq km – 999 sq miles *Pop* 406,600 *GMT* +1 *When* All year *Visas* Not required *Safety* Safe *Airlines* Luxair, British Airways *Average length of flight* 1 hour *Food* French, Belgian and German influences

Macedonia (Former Yugoslav Republic of Macedonia)

Capital Skopje *Lang* Macedonian *Currency* Macedonian Denar = 100 deni – a new currency in the form of coupons *Govt* Elected assembly *Rel* Eastern Orthodox Macedonians *Size* 25,713 sq km – 9,928 sq miles *Pop* 1,936,877 *GMT* + 1 *When* Apr – Sept *Visas* Not required by UK citizens *Validity* 3 or 6 months *Time to Get* Australian and Canadian nationals can obtain visas on entry *Safety* Seek advice from the Foreign Office *Airlines* via Berlin, Copenhagen and Vienna *Food* Turkish and Greek influences

Malta

Capital Valletta *Lang* Maltese *Currency* Maltese Lira = 100 cents = 1000 mils *Govt* Elected centre-right government *Rel* Roman Catholic *Size* 316 sq km – 122 sq miles *Pop* 369,451 *GMT* +1 *When* Apr – Sept *Visas* Not required *Safety* Safe *Inoc* Yellow Fever* if arriving from an infected area *Airlines* Air Malta, Austrian Airlines, Swissair *Average length of flight* 3 hours *Food* Good simple cooking, thick vegetable soup and rabbit is the national dish

Moldova

Capital Chisinau *Lang* Romanian *Currency* Leu =100 bani *Govt* A member of the CIS, with an elected president, currently the constitution is under reform *Rel* Mostly Eastern Orthodox *Size* 33,700 sq km – 13,000 sq miles *Pop* 4,350,000 *GMT* +2 *When* May – Sept *Visas* Required by all *Validity* Varies, can be obtained at the airport *Time to get* Immediately *Safety* Seek advice from the Foreign Office before travelling *Airlines* Aeroflot, Air Moldova *Average length of flight* 6 hours *Food* Romanian influenced

Monaco

Capital Monaco-ville *Lang* French *Currency* French franc *Govt* Elected govt presently the National and Democratic Union although supreme authority rests with Prince Rainier *Rel* Roman Catholic *Size* 1.95 sq km – 0.75 sq miles *Pop* 29,972 *GMT* +1 *When* All year *Visas* Not required *Safety* Safe *Airlines* There is no airport, a helicopter links the Principality to Nice Airport *Food* French

The Netherlands

Capital Amsterdam *Lang* Dutch *Currency* Guilder = 100 cents *Govt* Constitutional monarchy *Rel* Christian *Size* 33,938 sq km – 13,104 sq miles *Pop* 15,385,000 *GMT* +1 *When* All year *Visas* Not required *Safety* Safe *Airlines* KLM, British Airways, British Midland, Air UK, Transavia Airlines *Average length of flight* 1 hour 5 minutes *Food* Prepared meats, sausages and cheese is a typical meal

Norway

Capital Oslo *Lang* Norwegian *Currency* Norwegian Krone = 100 ore *Govt* A constitutional monarch, with an elected parliament *Rel* Lutheran *Size* 323,877 sq km – 125,050 sq miles *Pop* 4,348,410 *GMT* +1 *When* May to September *Visas* Not required *Safety* Safe *Airlines* British Airways, SAS *Average length of flight* 1 hour 45 minutes *Food* Fish, cold meats and cheese. Open sandwiches are a favourite at lunchtime

Poland

Capital Warsaw *Lang* Polish *Currency* Zloty = 100 groszy *Govt* Elected parliament with Walesa as President *Rel* Roman Catholic *Size* 312,685 sq km – 120,728 sq miles *Pop* 38,609,000 *GMT* +1 *When* All year *Visas* Not required by tourists from UK and US *Validity* 6 months *Time to get* 7 days *Safety* Safe *Airlines* British Airways, LOT-Polish Airlines *Average length of flight* 2.5 hours *Food* Soups and sour cream – meat can be scarce at times – lots of cabbage and onions

Portugal

Capital Lisbon *Lang* Portuguese *Currency* Escudo = 100 centavos *Govt* Elected government- Social Democrats *Rel* Roman Catholic *Size* 92,389 sq km – 35,672 sq miles *Pop* 9,902,200 *GMT* GMT *When* March to October *Visas* Not required for tourists up to 2 months *Safety* Safe *Airlines* TAP, British Airways *Average length of flight* 2.5 hours *Food* Fish based

Romania

Capital Bucharest *Lang* Romanian *Currency* Leu = 100 bani *Govt* Having been a communist regime, now an elected govt – Democratic National Salvation Front *Rel* Romanian Orthodox and Roman Catholic *Size* 237,500 sq km – 91,699 sq miles *Pop* 22,730,622 *GMT* +2 *When* May to October *Visas* Required *Validity* 3 months from date of issue *Time to get* 7 or more days, can pay extra for urgent visas *Safety* Bag snatching on the increase, beware of bogus policemen *Inoc* Cholera, Typhoid, Polio *Airlines* Tarom, British World Airlines and Austrian Airlines, Lufthansa, Delta Airlines, Swissair, Malev *Average length of time* 3 hours *Food* Not the highlight of the country

San Marino

Capital San Marino *Lang* Italian *Currency* Italian Lira *Govt* Elected govt (Great and General Council) currently a coalition of the Christian Democrats and the Socialists *Rel* Roman Catholic *Size* 60.5 sq km – 23.4 sq miles *Pop* 25,058 *GMT* +1 *When* All year *Visas* Not required *Safety* Safe *Airlines* Nearest airport Bologna – Alitalia and British Airways *Average length of flight* 2.5 hours *Food* Italian

Slovak Republic

Capital Bratislava *Lang* Slovak *Currency* Koruna or Slovak Crown = 100 haleru *Govt* Democratic state, having split from the Czech Republic in Jan 1993 *Rel* Roman Catholic *Size* 49,035 sq km – 18,932 sq miles *Pop* 5,367,800 *GMT* +1 *When* May to September *Visas* Not required by UK and USA nationals *Validity* 30 days within 6 months of issue *Time to get* 1-2 day, have to apply in person *Safety* Relatively safe *Airlines* Czechoslovak Airlines *Average length of flight* 1 hour 45 minutes *Food* Hungarian influences but still uninspiring-mainly pork

Slovenia

Capital Ljubljana *Lang* Slovene *Currency* Slovene Tolar = 100 stotins *Govt* Multi-party democracy *Rel* Roman Catholic *Size* 20,254 sq km – 7,820 sq miles *Pop* 1,989,477 *GMT* +1 *When* May to September *Visas* Not required except by New Zealanders *Validity* 1 week – 3 months *Safety* Safe *Airlines* Adria Airways *Average length of flight* 2 hours *Food* Austrian influence

Spain

Capital Madrid *Lang* Spanish *Currency* Peseta *Govt* Democracy – socialist *Rel* Roman Catholic *Size* 504,782 sq km – 194,897 sq miles *Pop* 39,188,194 *GMT* +1 *When* All year *Visas* required by Australians *Validity* 30 days *Time to get* 1 day *Safety* Spain *Airlines* Iberia, British Airways, Viva Air *Average length of flight* 2 hours *Food* Tapas, seafood

Sweden

Capital Stockholm *Lang* Swedish *Currency* Swedish Krona = 100 ore *Govt* Democracy, currently a four-party centre-right coalition *Rel* Evangelical Lutheran *Size* 440,945 sq km – 170,250 sq miles *Pop* 8,839,000 *GMT* +1 *When* May to September *Visas* Not required *Safety* Safe *Airlines* SAS, British Airways, Transwede Airways, *Average length of flight* 2 hours 30 minutes *Food* Fish based – pickled herrings etc.

Switzerland

Capital Bern *Lang* German *Currency* Swiss Franc *Govt* Democracy *Rel* Roman catholic and Protestant *Size* 41,293 sq km – 15,943 sq miles *Pop* 7,019,019 *GMT* +1 *When* All year *Visas* Not required *Safety* Safe *Airlines* Air France, Swiss Air, British Airways *Average* 1.5 hours *Food* Delicious cheese and fondues

Ukraine

Capital Kiev *Lang* Ukrainian *Currency* Karbovanets *Govt* Elected Parliament with executive power being held by the elected President (Yuri Meshkov) *Rel* Ukrainian Orthodox *Size* 603,700 sq km – 241,200 sq miles *Pop* 51,728,400 *GMT* +2 *When* May – Sept *Visas* Required by all *Validity* 90 days from date of issue *Time to get* 3-10 days depending on type of visa *Safety* Car-jacking and mugging on the increase – be vigilant *Inoc* Diphtheria *Airlines* Air Ukraine International *Average length of flight* 3.5 hours *Food* Soups – beetroot, cabbage, mainly

United Kingdom

Capital London *Lang* English *Currency* Pound = 100 pence *Govt* Stable democracy *Rel* Church of England *Size* 242,429 sq km – 93,602 sq miles *Pop* 58,394,600 *GMT* GMT *When* Spring to Autumn *Visas* Not required *Safety* Safe *Food* Roast beef and Yorkshire pudding – steam pudding and crumbles – fish and chips

Vatican City

Capital Vatican City *Lang* Italian *Currency* Vatican Lira *Govt* Ruled by the Pope, who is elected for life, by the College of Cardinals *Rel* Roman Catholic *Size* 0.44 sq km – 0.17 sq miles *Pop* 1500 *GMT* +1 *When* All year *Visas* Not required *Safety* Extremely safe *Airlines* Alitalia, British Airways *Average length of flight* 2.5 hours *Food* Italian

Yugoslavia (Montenegro and Serbia)

Capital Belgrade *Lang* Serbo-Croat *Currency* New Yugoslav dinar = 100 paras *Govt* A Federal Republic controlled by Milosevic's Serbian Socialist Party and Bulatovic's League of Communists of Montenegro *Rel* Eastern Orthodox *Size* 102,173 sq km – 39,447 sq miles *Pop* 10,482,000 *GMT* +1 *When* May to September *Visas* Required by all *Validity* 6 months from date of issue *Time to get* 7 days by post, immediate by person *Safety* Avoid Croatian border car theft and mugging have increased register with relevant embassy *Airlines* British Airways, Swiss Air, Austrian Airlines *Food* Smoked meats, jellied pork, stuffed cabbage leaves

ATLANTIC AND INDIAN OCEAN ISLANDS

Bermuda
Capital Hamilton *Lang* English *Currency* Bermuda Dollar = 100 cents *Govt* A British colony with its own Government currently ruled by the United Bermuda Party *Rel* Christian *Size* 53 sq km – 20.6 sq miles *Pop* 59,549 *GMT* -4 *When* May to November *Visas* Not required *Safety* Safe *Airlines* British Airways, American Airlines *Average length of flight* 7 hours *Food* International and seafood in abundance

Cape Verde
Capital Cidade de Praia *Lang* Portuguese *Currency* Cape Verde Escudo = 100 centavos *Govt* Ruled by the Movimento Para Democracia who won the multi-party elections in 1991 *Rel* Roman Catholic *Size* 4,033 sq km – 1,557 sq miles *Pop* 341,491 *GMT* -1 *When* November to June *Visas* Required by all *Time to get* Can be immediate, but allow as much time as possible *Inoc* Yellow Fever* if from an infected area, Polio, Cholera, Malaria, Typhoid *Airlines* Transportes Aeros de Cabo Verde, American Airlines, TAP *Average length of flight* 7 hours *Food* Wholesome, bumper crops of exotic fruits

Comoros
Capital Moroni *Lang* French and Arabic *Currency* Comoros Franc = 100 centimes *Govt* Union of Democrats for Democracy *Rel* Muslim *Size* 1,862 sq km – 719 sq miles *Pop* 484,000 *GMT* +3 *When* May to November *Visas* Required by all *Validity* Various 45 and 90 days *Inoc* Yellow Fever*, Malaria, Polio, Typhoid *Airlines* Air France *Average length of flight* 18 hours including stopover in Paris *Food* Spicy

Falkland Islands (UK)
Capital Stanley *Lang* English *Currency* Falkland Island Pound = 100 pence *Govt* British Crown Colony *Rel* Christian *Size* 12,173 sq km – 4,700 sq miles *Pop* 2,050 *GMT* -4(-3 in winter) *When* October – May *Visas* Not required *Safety* Safe, except there are marked unexploded mines left over from the war, seek local advice. *Airlines* RAF from Brize Norton or via Santiago and Aerovias *Average length of flight* 18 hours *Food* Essentially British – good island lamb and beef, lots of fish

Maldives
Capital Malé *Lang* Dhivehi *Currency* Maldivian Rufiya = 100 laris *Govt* Elected President and 40 out of 48 members of the Majli are also elected *Rel* Sunni Muslim *Size* 298 sq km – 115 sq miles *Pop* 244,644 *GMT* +5 *When* November to April *Visas* Issued on arrival at the airport *Validity* 30 days on arrival *Safety* Safe *Inoc* Yellow Fever* if having arrived from an infected area, Cholera, Polio, Typhoid *Airlines* Air Lanka, Emirates, PIA *Average length of flight* 11 hours *Food* Spicy fish – international food also available

Mauritius
Capital Port Louis *Lang* English *Currency* Mauritian Rupee = 100 cents *Govt* A republic since 1992 *Rel* Hindu majority *Size* 2,040 sq km – 788 sq miles *Pop* 1,112,607 *GMT* +4 *When* June – November *Visas* Not required *Safety* Safe *Inoc* Yellow Fever* if arriving from an infected area *Airlines* Air Mauritius, British Airways *Average length of flight* 11.5 hours *Food* Creole and international

Reunion (France)
Capital Saint-Denis *Lang* French *Currency* French Franc = 100 centimes *Govt* An Overseas Department of the Republic of France, right-wing General Council *Rel* Roman Catholic *Size* 2,512 sq km – 970 sq miles *Pop* 642,200 *GMT* +4 *When* May to October *Visas* Subject to change *Safety* Safe *Inoc* Yellow Fever* if arriving from an infected area, Cholera* Typhoid, Polio *Airlines* Air France *Average length of flight* 14 hours 40 minutes *Food* Creole cuisine

Seychelles
Capital Victoria (Mahe) *Lang* Creole *Currency* Seychelles Rupee = 100 cents *Govt* A one-party state from 1977 (the coup) to 1992, it is now multi-party with the People's Progressive Party in power with Rene who has been president since 1977 *Rel* Roman Catholic *Size* 454 sq km – 175 sq miles *Pop* 74,000 *GMT* +4 *When* June to September *Visas* Not required *Safety* Safe *Inoc* Yellow Fever* if arriving from an infected area in Africa, Polio, Typhoid *Airlines* Somali, British Airways, Air France, Aeroflot *Average length of flight* 11.5 hours *Food* Creole – fish based, can be spicy – exotic fruits

OCEANIA

American Samoa (US)
Capital Pago Pago *Lang* Samoan and English *Currency* US Dollar *Govt* Self-government

with elected Governor *Rel* Christian *Size* 194.8 sq km – 76.1 sq miles *Pop* 53,000 *GMT* – 11 *When* Winter (theirs) May to September *Visas* Not needed if staying for less than 30 days *Safety* Safe *Inoc* Yellow Fever* if arriving form an infected area Typhoid, Polio *Airlines* Polynesian Airlines, Hawaiian Airlines *Average length of flight* 25 hours with stopovers *Food* Polynesian and American – exotic fruits

Australia
Capital Canberra *Lang* English *Currency* Australian Dollar = 100 cents *Govt* Labour Government led by Joh Howard *Rel* Christian *Size* 7,682,300 sq km – 2,966,151 sq miles *Pop* 17,657,400 *GMT* +8-+10 *When* All year round *Visas* Required *Validity* 3 months to be used within 4 years *Time to get* 1-5 day if by person or 4 weeks by post *Safety* Relatively safe *Airlines* British Airways, Qantas and many more *Average length of flight* 22 hours *Food* Beef is the most popular meat followed closely by lamb

Cook Islands (New Zealand)
Capital Avarua on the island Rarotonga *Lang* Maori, English also spoken *Currency* New Zealand Dollar = 100 cents *Govt* Self Government as a New Zealand dependency *Rel* Christian *Size* 237 sq km – 91 sq miles *Pop* 19,000 *GMT* -10 *When* May to October *Visas* Not required *Safety* Safe *Inoc* Polio, Typhoid *Airlines* Air New Zealand via Los Angeles *Average length of flight* 24 hours *Food* Copious exotic fruits and fish

Fiji
Capital Suva *Lang* Fijian and Hindi *Currency* Fijian Dollar = 100 cents *Govt* Following a period of unrest and military coups, elections were held in 1994 *Rel* Christian and Hindu *Size* 18,333 sq km – 7,078 sq miles *Pop* 797,078 *GMT* +12 *When* May to October *Visas* Not required *Safety* Safe *Inoc* Yellow Fever* if arriving from an infected area, Polio, Typhoid *Airlines* Canadian Airlines, Air New Zealand *Average length of flight* 27 hours 45 minutes *Food* Marinated steamed fish, coconuts and Indian cuisine

French Polynesia (France)
Capital Papeete (Tahiti) *Lang* Tahitian and French *Currency* French Pacific Franc = 100 centimes *Govt* Internally self-governing, with the exception of the French High Commissioner who controls not only foreign policy but also the judicial system *Rel* Christian mainly Protestant *Size* 4,167 sq km – 1,609 sq miles *Pop* 199,031 *GMT* -9 or -10 *When* March to November *Visas* Required by Australians *Time to get* 1 day *Safety* Safe *Inoc* Yellow Fever* if arriving from an infected area, Polio, Typhoid *Airlines* Air France, Air New Zealand *Average length of flight* 20 hours *Food* Fruit and fish – French influences

Guam (US)
Capital Agana *Lang* English and Chamorro *Currency* US Dollar = 100 cents *Govt* Internal self-govt *Rel* Christian *Size* 549 sq km – 212 sq miles *Pop* 146,000 *GMT* +10 *When* January, February and March *Visas* Same as USA *Safety* Safe *Inoc* Typhoid, Polio *Average length of flight* 14.5 hours *Food* Like Spanish food

Kiribati
Capital Tarawa *Lang* I-Kiribati and English *Currency* Australian Dollar – 100 cents *Govt* Directly elected President who is head of state and Govt, 36 elected govt members *Rel* Christian *Size* 861 sq km – 332 sq miles *Pop* 77,658 *GMT* +12 *When* August to November *Visas* Not required by UK (except N Ireland) New Zealand and Canadian citizens *Validity* Varies *Safety* Safe *Inoc* Yellow Fever* if arriving from an infected area, Polio, Typhoid *Airlines* Air Nauru via Sydney *Average length of flight* 30 hours excluding stopovers *Food* Lots of coconuts – canned food regarded as a luxury

Marshall Islands (US)
Capital Majuro *Lang* Marshallese *Currency* US Dollar = 100 cents *Govt* Self-governing state, with the US guidelines for foreign policy *Rel* Christian *Size* 494 sq km – 191 sq miles *Pop* 52,000 *GMT* +12 *When* December to April *Visas* Required by all except US *Validity* 90 days *Time to get* 1 week by post *Inoc* Paratyphoid, Typhoid *Food* Fish, rice and breadfruit

Micronesia, Federated States of (US) (607 islands)
Capital Pohnpei *Lang* English and Micronesian Japanese *Currency* US Dollar = 100 cents (Local residents on Yap still use giant stone money – some coins weigh up to 4.5 tons and are 12ft in diameter) *Govt* Democracy *Rel* Roman Catholic *Size* 770 sq km – 270 sq miles *Pop* 104,724 *GMT* +9 or +10 depending on island *When* January to March (less rain but still very wet) *Visas* Not required if staying less than 30 days *Safety* Safe *Inoc* Paratyphoid, Typhoid *Airlines* Air Micronesia *Average length of flight* 23 hours *Food* Fish

New Caledonia (France)
Capital Noumena *Lang* French *Currency*

648

French Pacific Franc = 100 centimes *Govt* French Overseas Territory governed by an interim constitution, with a referendum on full independence set to take place in 1998 *Rel* Christian – Roman Catholic *Size* 19,203 sq km – 7,376 sq miles *Pop* 183,000 *GMT* +11 *When* All year round *Visas* Not required if staying less than one month *Safety* Safe *Inoc* Cholera* and Yellow Fever* if arriving from an infected area, Polio, Typhoid *Airlines* Air France *Average length of flight* 26 hours *Food* French influenced

New Zealand
Capital Wellington *Lang* English *Currency* New Zealand Dollar = 100 cents *Govt* Elected Parliament, currently the National Party, the British monarch is Head of State *Rel* Christian *Size* 2270,534 sq km – 104,454 sq miles *Pop* 3,592,000 *GMT* +12 *When* All year *Visas* Not required *Safety* Safe *Airlines* British Airways, Air New Zealand, Canadian Airlines, United Airlines amongst others *Average length of flight* 30 hours *Food* Meat based – very good lamb

Northern Mariana Islands (US)
Capital Saipan *Lang* English *Currency* US Dollar = 100 cents *Govt* US Commonwealth Territory, domestically self-governing *Rel* Roman Catholic *Size* 457 sq km – 177 sq miles *Pop* 52,900 *GMT* +10 *When* January to June *Visas* Not required for visits of less than thirty days *Inoc* Paratyphoid, Typhoid *Airlines* Air Micronesia *Average length of flight* 23 hours *Food* Fish, coconuts and chicken

Papua New Guinea
Capital Port Moresby *Lang* English and Pidgin English *Currency* Kina = 100 toea *Govt* Democracy *Rel* Christian *Size* 462,840 sq km – 178,840 sq miles *Pop* 3,997,000 *GMT* +10 *When* May to November *Visas* Required by all *Validity* 2 months *Time to get* At least 2 days *Safety* Extremely dangerous – take local advice, Port Moresby has gangland violence *Inoc* Yellow Fever* if arriving from an infected area, Malaria, Polio, Typhoid *Airlines* No direct flights – Philippine Airlines, Air Nuigini or Cathay Pacific/British Airways and Air Nuigini *Average length of flight* 30 hours *Food* Lots of fruit, locals tend to eat mostly root crops. Pigs are cooked in the earth on special feast days

Samoa (Western)
Capital Apia *Lang* Samoan *Currency* Western Samoan Dollar or Tala = 100 cents *Govt* Stable democracy *Rel* Christian *Size* 2,831 sq km – 1,093 sq miles *Pop* 164,000 *GMT* -11 *When* May to October *Visas* Not required for visits up to 30 days *Safety* Safe *Inoc* Yellow Fever* if arriving from an infected area, Polio, Typhoid *Airlines* Air New Zealand (lots of stopovers), Air Pacific *Average length of flight* 26 hours *Food* Fish, pork or chicken based

Solomon Islands
Capital Honiara *Lang* English *Currency* Solomon Island Dollar = 100 cents *Govt* Multi-party democracy *Rel* Christian *Size* 27,566 sq km – 10,639 sq miles *Pop* 366,000 *GMT* +11 *When* May through September *Visas* Not required *Safety* Safe *Inoc* Yellow Fever* if arriving from an infected area, Malaria, Polio, Typhoid *Airlines* Via Brisbane: Qantas and Solomon Airlines *Average length of flight* 29 hours 45 minutes *Food* Fish based

Tonga
Capital Nuku'alofa *Lang* Tongan and English *Currency* Pa'anga = 100 seniti *Govt* The King is head of state and Government, the govt is elected *Rel* Roman Catholic *Size* 748 sq km – 289 sq miles *Pop* 98,000 *GMT* +13 *When* May to November *Visas* Not required *Safety* Safe *Inoc* Yellow Fever* if arriving from an infected area, Polio, Typhoid *Airlines* Via Australia or New Zealand *Average length of flight* 20 hours *Food* Fish, tropical fruits and salads

Tuvalu
Capital Funafuti *Lang* Tuvalaun and English *Currency* Australian Dollars and Tuvalaun Dollars = 100 cents *Govt* The British Monarch is Head of State, with an elected parliament *Rel* Protestant *Size* 26 sq km – 10 sq miles *Pop* 9,000 *GMT* + 12 *When* March to October *Visas* Required by citizens of the USA *Safety* Safe *Inoc* Yellow Fever* if arriving from an infected area, Polio, Typhoid *Airlines* Via Fiji *Average length of flight* 30 hours *Food* Fresh fish and tropical fruits

Vanuatu
Capital Port Vila *Lang* Bislama *Currency* Vatu = 100 centimes *Govt* democracy *Rel* Christian *Size* 12,190 sq km – 4,707 sq miles *Pop* 165,000 *GMT* +12 *When* May to October *Visas* Not required *Safety* Safe *Inoc* Hepatitis A, Malaria, Polio, Typhoid *Airlines* Via Australia or New Zealand *Average length of flight* 30 hours *Food* Chinese and French influences

Further Reading: *World Travel Guide 1997* **(Columbus Press)**

WORLD-WIDE WEATHER GUIDE

The information given below details temperature and humidity at major cities throughout the world:

Temperature: Average daily maximum and minimum temperatures are shade temperatures. Maximum temperatures usually occur in early afternoon, and minimum temperatures just before sunrise.

Humidity: Measured as a daily figure at one or more fixed hours daily. It is normally lowest in the early afternoon and highest just before sunrise. High humidity combined with high temperatures increases discomfort.

Precipitation: Includes all forms of moisture falling on the earth, mainly rain and snow. Average monthly.

		J	F	M	A	M	J	J	A	S	O	N	D
Accra, Ghana													
Temperature °F	Max	87	88	88	88	87	84	81	80	81	85	87	88
	Min	73	75	76	76	75	74	73	71	73	74	75	75
Temperature °C	Max	31	31	31	31	31	29	27	27	27	29	31	31
	Min	23	24	24	24	24	23	23	22	23	23	24	24
Humidity %	am	95	96	95	96	96	97	97	97	96	97	97	97
	pm	61	61	63	65	68	74	76	77	72	71	66	64
Precipitation	mm	15	33	56	81	142	178	46	15	36	64	36	23
Amsterdam, Netherlands													
Temperature °F	Max	40	42	49	56	64	70	72	71	67	57	48	42
	Min	31	31	34	40	46	51	55	55	50	44	38	33
Temperature °C	Max	4	5	10	13	18	21	22	22	19	14	9	5
	Min	-1	-1	1	4	8	11	13	13	10	7	3	1
Humidity %	am	90	90	86	79	75	75	79	82	86	90	92	91
	pm	82	76	65	61	59	59	64	65	67	72	81	85
Precipitation	mm	68	53	44	49	52	58	77	87	72	72	70	64
Athens, Greece													
Temperature °F	Max	55	57	60	68	77	86	92	92	84	75	66	58
	Min	44	44	46	52	61	68	73	73	67	60	53	47
Temperature °C	Max	13	14	16	20	25	30	33	33	29	24	19	15
	Min	6	7	8	11	16	20	23	23	19	15	12	8
Humidity %	am	77	74	71	65	60	50	47	48	58	70	78	78
	pm	62	57	54	48	47	39	34	34	42	52	61	63
Precipitation	mm	62	37	37	23	23	14	6	7	15	51	56	71
Auckland, New Zealand													
Temperature °F	Max	73	73	71	67	62	58	56	58	60	63	66	70
	Min	60	60	59	56	51	48	46	46	49	52	54	57
Temperature °C	Max	23	23	22	19	17	14	13	14	16	17	19	21
	Min	16	16	15	13	11	9	8	8	9	11	12	14
Humidity %	am	71	72	74	78	80	83	84	80	76	74	71	70
	pm	62	61	65	69	70	73	74	70	68	66	64	64
Precipitation	mm	79	94	81	97	127	137	145	117	102	102	89	79
Bahrain													
Temperature °F	Max	68	70	75	84	92	96	99	100	96	90	82	71
	Min	57	59	63	70	78	82	85	85	81	75	69	60
Temperature °C	Max	20	21	24	29	33	36	37	38	36	32	28	22
	Min	14	15	17	21	26	28	29	29	27	24	21	16
Humidity %	am	85	83	80	75	71	69	69	74	75	80	80	85
	pm	71	70	70	66	63	64	67	65	64	66	70	77
Precipitation	mm	8	18	13	8	0	0	0	0	0	0	18	18

		J	F	M	A	M	J	J	A	S	O	N	D
Bangkok, Thailand													
Temperature °F	Max	89	91	93	95	93	91	90	90	89	88	87	87
	Min	68	72	75	77	77	76	76	76	76	75	72	68
Temperature °C	Max	32	33	34	35	34	33	32	32	32	31	31	31
	Min	20	22	24	25	25	24	24	24	24	24	22	20
Humidity %	am	91	92	92	90	91	90	91	92	94	93	92	91
	pm	53	55	56	58	64	67	66	66	70	70	65	56
Precipitation	mm	8	20	36	58	198	160	160	175	305	206	66	5
Beirut, Lebanon													
Temperature °F	Max	62	63	66	72	78	83	87	89	86	81	73	65
	Min	51	51	54	58	64	69	73	74	73	69	61	55
Temperature °C	Max	17	17	19	22	26	28	31	32	30	27	23	18
	Min	11	11	12	14	18	21	23	23	23	21	16	13
Humidity %	am	72	72	72	72	69	67	66	65	64	65	67	70
	pm	70	70	69	67	64	61	58	57	57	62	61	69
Precipitation	mm	191	158	94	56	18	3	0	0	5	51	132	185
Berlin, Germany													
Temperature °F	Max	35	37	46	56	66	72	75	74	68	56	45	38
	Min	26	26	31	39	47	53	57	56	50	42	36	29
Temperature °C	Max	2	3	8	13	19	22	24	23	20	13	7	3
	Min	-3	-3	0	4	8	12	14	13	10	6	2	-1
Humidity %	am	89	89	88	84	80	80	84	88	92	93	92	91
	pm	82	78	67	60	57	58	61	61	65	73	83	86
Precipitation	mm	46	40	33	42	49	65	73	69	48	49	46	43
Bombay, India													
Temperature °F	Max	83	83	86	89	91	89	85	85	85	89	89	87
	Min	67	67	72	76	80	79	77	76	76	76	73	69
Temperature °C	Max	28	28	30	32	33	32	29	29	29	32	32	31
	Min	12	12	17	20	23	21	22	22	22	21	18	13
Humidity %	am	70	71	73	75	74	79	83	83	85	81	73	70
	pm	61	62	65	67	68	77	83	81	78	71	64	62
Precipitation	mm	2.5	2.5	2.5	0	18	485	617	340	264	64	13	2.5
Brussels, Belgium													
Temperature °F	Max	40	44	51	58	65	72	73	72	69	60	48	42
	Min	30	32	36	41	46	52	54	54	51	45	38	32
Temperature °C	Max	4	7	10	14	18	22	23	22	21	15	9	6
	Min	-1	0	2	5	8	11	12	12	11	7	3	0
Humidity %	am	92	92	91	91	90	87	91	93	94	93	93	92
	pm	86	81	74	71	65	65	68	69	69	77	85	86
Precipitation	mm	66	61	53	60	55	76	95	80	63	83	75	88
Buenos Aires, Argentina													
Temperature °F	Max	85	83	79	72	64	57	57	60	64	69	76	82
	Min	63	63	60	53	47	41	42	43	46	50	56	61
Temperature °C	Max	29	28	26	22	18	14	14	16	18	21	24	28
	Min	17	17	16	12	8	5	6	6	8	10	13	16
Humidity %	am	81	83	87	88	90	91	92	90	86	83	79	79
	pm	61	63	69	71	74	78	79	74	68	65	60	62
Precipitation	mm	79	71	109	89	76	61	56	61	79	86	84	99
Cairo, Egypt													
Temperature °F	Max	65	69	75	83	91	95	96	95	90	86	78	68
	Min	47	48	52	57	63	68	70	71	68	65	58	50
Temperature °C	Max	18	21	24	28	33	35	36	35	32	30	26	20

		J	F	M	A	M	J	J	A	S	O	N	D
Cairo continued...													
	Min	8	9	11	14	17	20	21	22	20	18	14	10
Humidity %	am	69	64	63	55	50	55	65	69	68	67	68	70
	pm	40	33	27	21	18	20	24	28	31	31	38	41
Precipitation	mm	5	5	5	3	3	0	0	0	0	0	3	5
Calcutta, India													
Temperature °F	Max	80	84	93	97	96	92	89	89	90	89	84	79
	Min	55	59	69	75	77	79	79	78	78	74	64	55
Temperature °C	Max	27	29	34	36	36	33	32	32	32	32	29	26
	Min	13	15	21	24	25	26	26	26	26	24	18	13
Humidity %	am	85	82	79	76	77	82	86	88	86	85	79	80
	pm	52	45	46	56	62	75	80	82	81	72	63	55
Precipitation	mm	10	31	36	43	140	297	325	328	252	114	20	5
Christchurch, New Zealand													
Temperature °F	Max	70	69	66	62	56	51	50	52	57	62	66	69
	Min	53	53	50	45	40	36	35	36	40	44	47	51
Temperature °C	Max	21	21	19	17	13	11	10	11	14	17	19	21
	Min	12	12	10	7	4	2	2	2	4	7	8	11
Humidity %	am	65	71	75	82	85	87	87	81	72	63	64	67
	pm	59	60	69	71	69	72	76	66	69	60	64	60
Precipitation	mm	56	43	48	48	66	66	69	48	46	43	48	56
Colombo, Sri Lanka													
Temperature °F	Max	86	87	88	88	87	85	85	85	85	85	85	85
	Min	72	72	74	76	78	77	77	77	77	75	73	72
Temperature °C	Max	30	31	31	31	31	29	29	29	29	29	29	29
	Min	22	22	23	24	26	25	25	25	25	24	23	22
Humidity %	am	73	71	71	74	78	80	79	78	76	77	77	74
	pm	67	66	66	70	76	78	77	76	75	76	75	69
Precipitation	mm	89	69	147	231	371	224	135	109	160	348	315	147
Copenhagen, Denmark													
Temperature °F	Max	36	36	41	51	61	67	71	70	64	54	45	40
	Min	28	28	31	38	46	52	57	56	51	44	38	34
Temperature °C	Max	2	2	5	10	16	19	22	21	18	12	7	4
	Min	-2	-3	-1	3	8	11	14	14	11	7	3	1
Humidity	am	88	86	85	79	70	70	74	78	83	86	88	89
	pm	85	83	78	68	59	60	62	64	69	76	83	87
Precipitation	mm	49	39	32	38	43	47	71	66	62	59	48	49
Delhi, India													
Temperature °F	Max	70	75	87	97	105	102	96	93	93	93	84	73
	Min	44	49	58	68	79	83	81	79	75	65	52	46
Temperature °C	Max	21	24	31	36	41	39	36	34	34	34	29	23
	Min	7	9	14	20	26	28	27	26	24	18	11	8
Humidity %	am	72	67	49	35	35	53	75	80	72	56	51	69
	pm	41	35	23	19	20	36	59	64	51	32	31	42
Precipitation	mm	23	18	13	8	13	74	180	173	117	10	3	10
Frankfurt, Germany													
Temperature °F	Max	38	41	51	60	69	74	77	76	69	58	47	39
	Min	29	30	35	42	49	55	58	57	52	44	38	32
Temperature °C	Max	3	5	11	16	20	23	25	24	21	14	8	4
	Min	-2	-1	2	6	9	13	15	14	11	7	3	0
Humidity %	am	86	86	84	79	78	78	81	85	89	91	89	88

		J	F	M	A	M	J	J	A	S	O	N	D
Frankfurt continued…													
	pm	77	70	57	51	50	52	53	54	60	68	77	81
Precipitation	mm	58	44	38	44	55	73	70	76	57	52	55	54

Hamilton, Bermuda

		J	F	M	A	M	J	J	A	S	O	N	D
Temperature °F	Max	68	68	68	71	76	81	85	86	84	79	74	70
	Min	58	57	57	59	64	69	73	74	72	69	63	60
Temperature °C	Max	20	20	20	22	24	27	29	30	29	26	23	21
	Min	14	14	14	15	18	21	23	23	22	21	17	16
Humidity %	am	78	76	77	78	81	82	81	79	81	79	76	77
	pm	70	69	69	70	75	74	73	69	73	72	70	70
Precipitation	mm	112	119	122	104	117	112	114	137	132	147	127	119

Harare, Zimbabwe

		J	F	M	A	M	J	J	A	S	O	N	D
Temperature °F	Max	78	78	78	78	74	70	70	74	79	83	81	79
	Min	60	60	58	55	49	44	44	47	53	58	60	60
Temperature °C	Max	26	26	26	26	23	21	21	23	26	28	27	26
	Min	16	16	14	13	9	7	7	8	12	14	16	16
Humidity %	am	74	77	75	68	60	58	56	50	43	43	56	67
	pm	57	53	52	44	37	36	33	28	26	26	43	57
Precipitation	mm	196	178	117	28	13	3	0	3	5	28	97	163

Hong Kong

		J	F	M	A	M	J	J	A	S	O	N	D
Temperature °F	Max	64	63	67	75	82	85	87	87	85	81	74	68
	Min	56	55	60	67	74	78	78	78	77	73	65	59
Temperature °C	Max	18	17	19	24	28	29	31	31	29	27	23	20
	Min	13	13	16	19	23	26	26	26	25	23	18	15
Humidity %	am	77	82	84	87	87	86	87	87	83	75	73	74
	pm	66	73	74	77	78	77	77	77	72	63	60	63
Precipitation	mm	33	46	74	137	292	394	381	367	257	114	43	31

Istanbul, Turkey

		J	F	M	A	M	J	J	A	S	O	N	D
Temperature °F	Max	46	47	51	60	69	77	82	82	76	68	59	51
	Min	37	36	38	45	53	60	65	66	61	55	48	41
Temperature °C	Max	8	9	11	16	21	25	28	28	24	20	15	11
	Min	3	2	3	7	12	16	18	19	16	13	9	5
Humidity %	am	82	82	81	81	82	79	79	79	81	83	82	82
	pm	75	72	67	62	61	58	56	55	59	64	71	74
Precipitation	mm	109	92	72	46	38	34	34	30	58	81	103	119

Jakarta, Indonesia

		J	F	M	A	M	J	J	A	S	O	N	D
Temperature °F	Max	84	84	86	87	87	87	87	87	88	87	86	85
	Min	74	74	74	75	75	74	73	73	74	74	74	74
Temperature °C	Max	29	29	30	31	31	31	31	31	31	31	30	29
	Min	23	23	23	24	24	23	23	23	23	23	23	23
Humidity %	am	95	95	94	94	94	93	92	90	90	90	92	92
	pm	75	75	73	71	69	67	64	61	62	64	68	71
Precipitation	mm	300	300	211	147	114	97	64	43	66	112	142	203

Jeddah, Saudi Arabia

		J	F	M	A	M	J	J	A	S	O	N	D
Temperature °F	Max	84	84	85	91	95	97	99	99	96	95	91	86
	Min	66	65	67	70	74	75	79	80	77	73	71	67
Temperature °C	Max	29	29	29	33	35	36	37	37	36	35	33	30
	Min	19	18	19	21	23	24	26	27	25	23	22	19
Humidity %	am	58	52	52	52	51	56	55	59	65	60	55	55
	pm	54	52	52	56	55	55	50	51	61	61	59	54
Precipitation	mm	5	0	0	0	0	0	0	0	0	0	25	31

		J	F	M	A	M	J	J	A	S	O	N	D
Jerusalem, Israel													
Temperature °F	Max	55	56	65	73	81	85	87	87	85	81	70	59
	Min	41	42	46	50	57	60	63	64	62	59	53	45
Temperature °C	Max	13	13	18	23	27	29	31	31	29	27	21	15
	Min	5	6	8	10	14	16	17	18	17	15	12	7
Humidity %	am	77	74	61	56	47	48	52	58	61	60	65	73
	pm	66	58	57	42	33	32	35	36	36	36	50	60
Precipitation	mm	132	132	64	28	3	0	0	0	0	13	71	86
Johannesburg, South Africa													
Temperature °F	Max	78	77	75	72	66	62	63	68	73	77	77	78
	Min	58	58	55	50	43	39	39	43	48	53	55	57
Temperature °C	Max	26	25	24	22	19	17	17	20	23	25	25	26
	Min	14	14	13	10	6	4	4	6	9	12	13	14
Humidity %	am	75	78	79	74	70	70	69	64	59	64	67	70
	pm	50	53	50	44	36	33	32	29	30	37	45	47
Precipitation	mm	114	109	89	38	25	8	8	8	23	56	107	125
Kathmandu, Nepal													
Temperature °F	Max	65	67	77	83	86	85	84	83	83	80	74	67
	Min	35	39	45	53	61	67	68	68	66	56	45	37
Temperature °C	Max	18	19	25	28	30	29	29	28	28	27	23	19
	Min	2	4	7	12	16	19	20	20	19	13	7	3
Humidity %	am	89	90	73	68	72	79	86	87	86	88	90	89
	pm	70	68	53	54	61	72	82	84	83	81	78	73
Precipitation	mm	15	41	23	58	122	246	373	345	155	38	8	3
Kuala Lumpur, Malaysia													
Temperature °F	Max	90	92	92	91	91	91	90	90	90	89	89	89
	Min	72	72	73	74	73	72	73	73	73	73	73	72
Temperature °C	Max	32	33	33	33	33	33	32	32	32	32	32	32
	Min	22	22	23	23	23	22	23	23	23	23	23	22
Humidity %	am	97	97	97	97	97	96	95	96	96	96	97	97
	pm	60	60	58	63	66	63	63	62	64	65	66	61
Precipitation	mm	158	201	259	292	224	130	99	163	218	249	259	191
Lagos, Nigeria													
Temperature °F	Max	88	89	89	89	87	85	83	82	83	85	88	88
	Min	74	77	78	77	76	74	74	73	74	74	75	75
Temperature °C	Max	31	32	32	32	31	29	28	28	28	29	31	31
	Min	23	25	26	25	24	23	23	23	23	23	24	24
Humidity %	am	84	83	82	81	83	87	87	85	86	86	85	86
	pm	65	69	72	72	76	80	80	76	77	76	72	68
Precipitation	mm	28	46	102	150	269	460	279	64	140	206	69	25
Lima, Peru													
Temperature °F	Max	82	83	83	80	74	68	67	66	68	71	74	78
	Min	66	67	66	63	60	58	57	56	57	58	60	62
Temperature °C	Max	28	28	28	27	23	20	19	19	20	22	23	26
	Min	19	19	19	17	16	14	14	13	14	14	16	17
Humidity %	am	93	92	92	93	95	95	94	95	94	94	93	93
	pm	69	66	64	66	76	80	77	78	76	72	71	70
Precipitation	mm	3	0	0	0	5	5	8	8	8	3	3	0
Lisbon, Portugal													
Temperature °F	Max	57	59	63	67	71	77	81	82	79	72	63	58
	Min	46	47	50	53	55	60	63	63	62	58	52	47
Temperature °C	Max	14	15	17	20	21	25	27	28	26	22	17	15

		J	F	M	A	M	J	J	A	S	O	N	D
Lisbon continued...													
	Min	8	8	10	12	13	15	17	17	17	14	11	9
Humidity %	am	85	80	78	69	68	65	62	64	70	75	81	84
	pm	71	64	64	56	57	54	48	49	54	59	68	72
Precipitation	mm	111	76	109	54	44	16	3	4	33	62	93	103
London, UK													
Temperature °F	Max	43	44	50	56	62	69	71	71	65	58	50	45
	Min	36	36	38	42	47	53	56	56	52	46	42	38
Temperature °C	Max	6	7	10	13	17	20	22	21	19	14	10	7
	Min	2	2	3	6	8	12	14	13	11	8	5	4
Humidity %	am	86	85	81	71	70	70	71	76	80	85	85	87
	pm	77	72	64	56	57	58	59	62	65	70	78	81
Precipitation	mm	54	40	37	37	46	45	57	59	49	57	64	48
Madrid, Spain													
Temperature °F	Max	47	52	59	65	70	80	87	85	77	65	55	48
	Min	35	36	41	45	50	58	63	63	57	49	42	36
Temperature °C	Max	9	11	15	18	21	27	31	30	25	19	13	9
	Min	2	2	5	7	10	15	17	17	14	10	5	2
Humidity %	am	86	83	80	74	72	66	58	62	72	81	84	86
	pm	71	62	56	49	49	41	33	35	46	58	65	70
Precipitation	mm	39	34	43	48	47	27	11	15	32	53	47	48
Manila, Philippines													
Temperature °F	Max	86	88	91	93	93	91	88	87	88	88	87	86
	Min	69	69	71	73	75	75	75	75	75	74	73	70
Temperature °C	Max	30	31	33	34	34	33	31	31	31	31	31	30
	Min	21	21	22	23	24	24	24	24	24	23	22	21
Humidity %	am	89	88	85	85	88	91	91	92	93	92	91	90
	pm	63	59	55	55	61	68	74	73	73	71	69	67
Precipitation	mm	23	13	18	33	130	254	432	422	356	193	145	66
Melbourne, Australia													
Temperature °F	Max	78	78	75	68	62	57	56	59	63	67	71	75
	Min	57	57	55	51	47	44	42	43	46	48	51	54
Temperature °C	Max	26	26	24	20	17	14	13	15	17	19	22	24
	Min	14	14	13	11	8	7	6	6	8	9	11	12
Humidity %	am	58	62	64	72	79	83	82	76	68	61	60	59
	pm	48	50	51	56	62	67	65	60	55	52	52	51
Precipitation	mm	48	46	56	58	53	53	48	48	58	66	58	58
Mexico City													
Temperature °F	Max	66	69	75	77	78	76	73	73	74	70	68	66
	Min	42	43	47	51	54	55	53	54	53	50	46	43
Temperature °C	Max	19	21	24	25	26	24	23	23	23	21	20	19
	Min	6	6	8	11	12	13	12	12	12	10	8	6
Humidity %	am	79	72	68	66	69	82	84	85	86	83	82	81
	pm	34	28	26	29	29	48	50	50	54	47	41	37
Precipitation	mm	13	5	10	20	53	119	170	152	130	51	18	8
Miami, USA													
Temperature °F	Max	74	75	78	80	84	86	88	88	87	83	78	76
	Min	61	61	64	67	71	74	76	76	75	72	66	62
Temperature °C	Max	23	24	26	27	29	30	31	31	31	28	26	24
	Min	16	16	18	19	22	23	24	24	24	22	19	17
Humidity %	am	81	82	77	73	75	75	75	76	79	80	77	82

		J	F	M	A	M	J	J	A	S	O	N	D
Miami continued...													
	pm	66	63	62	64	67	69	68	68	70	69	64	65
Precipitation	mm	71	53	64	81	173	178	155	160	203	234	71	51

Moscow, Russia

		J	F	M	A	M	J	J	A	S	O	N	D
Temperature °F	Max	15	22	32	50	66	70	73	72	61	48	35	24
	Min	3	8	18	34	46	51	55	53	45	37	26	15
Temperature °C	Max	-9	-6	0	10	19	21	23	22	16	9	2	-5
	Min	-16	-14	-8	1	8	11	13	12	7	3	-3	-10
Humidity %	am	82	82	82	73	58	62	68	74	78	81	87	85
	pm	77	66	64	54	43	47	54	55	59	67	79	83
Precipitation	mm	39	38	36	37	53	58	88	71	58	45	47	54

Nairobi, Kenya

		J	F	M	A	M	J	J	A	S	O	N	D
Temperature °F	Max	77	79	77	75	72	70	69	70	75	76	74	74
	Min	54	55	57	58	56	53	51	52	52	55	56	55
Temperature °C	Max	25	26	25	24	22	21	21	21	24	24	23	23
	Min	12	13	14	14	13	12	11	11	11	13	13	13
Humidity %	am	74	74	81	88	88	89	86	86	82	82	86	81
	pm	44	40	45	56	62	60	58	56	45	43	53	53
Precipitation	mm	38	64	125	211	158	46	15	23	31	53	109	86

Nassau, Bahamas

		J	F	M	A	M	J	J	A	S	O	N	D
Temperature °F	Max	77	77	79	81	84	87	88	89	88	85	81	79
	Min	65	64	66	69	71	74	75	76	75	73	70	67
Temperature °C	Max	25	25	26	27	29	31	31	32	31	29	27	26
	Min	18	18	19	21	22	23	24	24	24	23	21	19
Humidity %	am	84	82	81	79	79	81	80	82	84	83	83	84
	pm	64	62	64	65	65	68	69	70	73	71	68	66
Precipitation	mm	36	38	36	64	117	163	147	135	175	165	71	33

New York, USA

		J	F	M	A	M	J	J	A	S	O	N	D
Temperature °F	Max	37	38	45	57	68	77	82	80	79	69	51	41
	Min	24	24	30	42	53	60	66	66	60	49	37	29
Temperature °C	Max	3	3	7	14	20	25	28	27	26	21	11	5
	Min	-4	-4	-1	6	12	16	19	19	16	9	3	-2
Humidity %	am	72	70	70	68	70	74	77	79	79	76	75	73
	pm	60	58	55	53	54	58	58	60	61	57	60	61
Precipitation	mm	94	97	91	81	81	84	107	109	86	89	76	91

Oslo, Norway

		J	F	M	A	M	J	J	A	S	O	N	D
Temperature °F	Max	28	30	39	50	61	68	72	70	60	48	38	32
	Min	19	19	25	34	43	50	55	53	46	38	31	25
Temperature °C	Max	-2	-1	4	10	16	20	22	21	16	9	3	0
	Min	-7	-7	-4	1	6	10	13	12	8	3	-1	-4
Humidity %	am	86	84	80	75	68	69	74	79	85	88	88	87
	pm	82	74	64	57	52	55	59	61	66	72	83	85
Precipitation	mm	49	35	26	43	44	70	82	95	81	74	68	63

Ottawa, Canada

		J	F	M	A	M	J	J	A	S	O	N	D
Temperature °F	Max	21	22	33	51	66	76	81	77	68	54	39	24
	Min	3	3	16	31	44	54	58	55	48	37	26	9
Temperature °C	Max	-6	-6	1	11	19	24	27	25	20	12	4	-4
	Min	-16	-16	-9	-1	7	12	14	13	9	3	-3	-13
Humidity %	am	83	82	84	76	77	80	80	84	90	86	84	83
	pm	76	73	66	58	55	56	53	54	59	63	68	75
Precipitation	mm	74	56	71	69	64	89	86	66	81	74	76	66

		J	F	M	A	M	J	J	A	S	O	N	D
Papeete, Tahiti, French Polynesia													
Temperature °F	Max	89	89	89	89	87	86	86	86	86	87	88	88
	Min	72	72	72	72	70	69	68	68	69	70	71	72
Temperature C	Max	32	32	32	32	31	30	30	30	30	31	31	31
	Min	22	22	22	22	21	21	20	20	21	21	22	22
Humidity %	am	82	82	84	85	84	85	83	83	81	79	80	81
	pm	77	77	78	78	78	79	77	78	76	76	77	78
Precipitation	mm	252	244	429	142	102	76	53	43	53	89	150	249
Paris, France													
Temperature °F	Max	43	45	54	60	68	73	76	75	70	60	50	44
	Min	34	34	39	43	49	55	58	58	53	46	40	36
Temperature °C	Max	6	7	12	16	20	23	25	24	21	16	10	7
	Min	1	1	4	6	10	13	15	14	12	8	5	2
Humidity %	am	88	87	85	82	83	83	83	87	90	91	91	90
	pm	80	73	63	54	55	58	57	61	65	71	79	82
Precipitation	mm	56	46	35	42	57	54	59	64	55	50	51	50
Port-of-Spain, Trinidad													
Temperature °F	Max	87	88	89	90	90	89	88	88	89	89	89	88
	Min	69	68	68	69	71	71	71	71	71	71	71	69
Temperature °C	Max	31	31	32	32	32	32	31	31	32	32	32	31
	Min	21	20	20	21	22	22	22	22	22	22	22	21
Humidity %	am	89	87	85	83	84	87	88	87	87	87	89	89
	pm	68	65	63	61	63	69	71	73	73	74	76	71
Precipitation	mm	69	41	46	53	94	193	218	246	193	170	183	125
Prague, Czech Republic													
Temperature °F	Max	31	34	44	54	64	70	73	72	65	53	42	34
	Min	23	24	30	38	46	52	55	55	49	41	33	27
Temperature °C	Max	0	1	7	12	18	21	23	22	18	12	5	1
	Min	-5	-4	-1	3	8	11	13	13	9	5	1	-3
Humidity %	am	84	83	82	77	75	74	77	81	84	87	87	87
	pm	73	67	55	47	45	46	49	48	51	60	73	78
Precipitation	mm	18	18	18	27	48	54	68	55	31	33	20	21
Rio de Janeiro, Brazil													
Temperature °F	Max	84	85	83	80	77	76	75	76	75	77	79	82
	Min	73	73	72	69	66	64	63	64	65	66	68	71
Temperature °C	Max	29	29	28	27	25	24	24	24	24	25	26	28
	Min	23	23	22	21	19	18	17	18	18	19	20	22
Humidity %	am	82	84	87	87	87	87	86	84	84	83	82	82
	pm	70	71	74	73	70	69	68	66	72	72	72	72
Precipitation	mm	125	122	130	107	79	53	41	43	66	79	104	137
Rome, Italy													
Temperature °F	Max	52	55	59	66	74	82	87	86	79	71	61	55
	Min	40	42	45	50	56	63	67	67	62	55	49	44
Temperature °C	Max	11	13	15	19	23	28	30	30	26	22	16	13
	Min	5	5	7	10	13	17	20	20	17	13	9	6
Humidity %	am	85	86	83	83	77	74	70	73	83	86	87	85
	pm	68	64	56	54	54	48	42	43	50	59	66	70
Precipitation	mm	71	62	57	51	46	37	15	21	63	99	129	93
San Francisco, USA													
Temperature °F	Max	55	59	61	62	63	66	65	65	69	68	63	57
	Min	45	47	48	49	51	52	53	53	55	54	51	47
Temperature °C	Max	13	15	16	17	17	19	18	18	21	20	17	14

		J	F	M	A	M	J	J	A	S	O	N	D
San Francisco continued...												

		J	F	M	A	M	J	J	A	S	O	N	D
	Min	7	8	9	9	11	11	12	12	13	12	11	8
Humidity %	am	85	84	83	83	85	88	91	92	88	85	83	83
	pm	69	66	61	61	62	64	69	70	63	58	60	68
Precipitation	mm	119	97	79	38	18	3	0	0	8	25	64	112

Singapore

		J	F	M	A	M	J	J	A	S	O	N	D
Temperature °F	Max	86	88	88	88	89	88	88	87	87	87	87	87
	Min	73	73	75	75	75	75	75	75	75	74	74	74
Temperature °C	Max	30	31	31	31	32	31	31	31	31	31	31	31
	Min	23	23	24	24	24	24	24	24	24	23	23	23
Humidity %	am	82	77	76	77	79	79	79	78	79	79	79	82
	pm	78	71	70	74	73	73	72	72	72	72	75	78
Precipitation	mm	252	173	193	188	173	173	170	196	178	208	254	257

Stockholm, Sweden

		J	F	M	A	M	J	J	A	S	O	N	D
Temperature °F	Max	30	30	37	47	58	67	71	68	60	49	40	35
	Min	23	22	26	34	43	51	57	56	49	41	34	29
Temperature °C	Max	-1	-1	3	8	14	19	22	20	15	9	5	2
	Min	-5	-5	-4	1	6	11	14	13	9	5	1	-2
Humidity %	am	85	83	82	76	66	68	74	81	87	88	89	88
	pm	83	77	68	60	53	55	59	64	69	76	85	86
Precipitation	mm	43	30	25	31	34	45	61	76	60	48	53	48

Sydney, Australia

		J	F	M	A	M	J	J	A	S	O	N	D
Temperature °F	Max	78	78	76	71	66	61	60	63	67	71	74	77
	Min	65	65	63	58	52	48	46	48	51	56	60	63
Temperature °C	Max	26	26	24	22	19	16	16	17	19	22	23	25
	Min	18	18	17	14	11	9	8	9	11	13	16	17
Humidity %	am	68	71	73	76	77	77	76	72	67	65	65	66
	pm	64	65	65	64	63	62	60	56	55	57	60	62
Precipitation	mm	89	102	127	135	127	117	117	76	74	71	74	74

Tehran, Iran

		J	F	M	A	M	J	J	A	S	O	N	D
Temperature °F	Max	45	50	59	71	82	93	99	97	90	76	63	51
	Min	27	32	39	49	58	66	72	71	64	53	43	33
Temperature °C	Max	7	10	15	22	28	34	37	36	32	24	17	11
	Min	-3	0	4	9	14	19	22	22	18	12	6	1
Humidity %	am	77	73	61	54	55	50	51	47	49	53	63	76
	pm	75	59	39	40	47	49	41	46	49	54	66	75
Precipitation	mm	46	38	46	36	13	3	3	3	3	8	20	31

Tokyo, Japan

		J	F	M	A	M	J	J	A	S	O	N	D
Temperature °F	Max	47	48	54	63	71	76	83	86	79	69	60	52
	Min	29	31	36	46	54	63	70	72	66	55	43	33
Temperature °C	Max	8	9	12	17	22	24	28	30	26	21	16	11
	Min	-2	-1	2	8	12	17	21	22	19	13	6	1
Humidity %	am	73	71	75	81	85	89	91	92	91	88	83	77
	pm	48	48	53	59	62	68	69	66	68	64	58	51
Precipitation	mm	48	74	107	135	147	165	142	152	234	208	97	56

Vancouver, Canada

		J	F	M	A	M	J	J	A	S	O	N	D
Temperature °F	Max	41	44	50	58	64	69	74	73	65	57	48	43
	Min	32	34	37	40	46	52	54	54	49	44	39	35
Temperature °C	Max	5	7	10	14	18	21	23	23	18	14	9	6
	Min	0	1	3	4	8	11	12	12	9	7	4	2

		J	F	M	A	M	J	J	A	S	O	N	D
Vancouver continued...													
Humidity %	am	93	91	91	89	88	87	89	90	92	92	91	91
	pm	85	78	70	67	63	65	62	62	72	80	84	88
Precipitation	mm	218	147	127	84	71	64	31	43	91	147	211	224
Vienna, Austria													
Temperature °F	Max	34	38	47	58	67	73	76	75	68	56	45	37
	Min	25	28	30	42	50	56	60	59	53	44	37	30
Temperature °C	Max	1	3	8	15	19	23	25	24	20	14	7	3
	Min	-4	-3	-1	6	10	14	15	15	11	7	3	-1
Humidity %	am	81	80	78	72	74	74	74	78	83	86	84	84
	pm	72	66	57	49	52	55	54	54	56	64	74	76
Precipitation	mm	39	44	44	45	70	67	84	72	42	56	52	45
Warsaw, Poland													
Temperature °F	Max	32	32	42	53	67	73	75	73	66	55	42	35
	Min	22	21	28	37	48	54	58	56	49	41	33	28
Temperature °C	Max	0	0	6	12	20	23	24	23	19	13	6	2
	Min	-6	-6	-2	3	9	12	15	14	10	5	1	-3
Humidity %	am	90	89	90	85	80	82	86	90	92	93	93	92
	pm	84	80	70	61	56	59	63	63	64	73	83	87
Precipitation	mm	27	32	27	37	46	69	96	65	43	38	31	44
Yangon, Myanmar													
Temperature °F	Max	89	92	96	97	92	86	85	85	86	88	88	88
	Min	65	67	71	76	77	76	76	76	76	76	73	67
Temperature °C	Max	32	33	36	36	33	30	29	29	30	31	31	31
	Min	18	19	22	24	25	24	24	24	24	24	23	19
Humidity %	am	71	72	74	71	80	87	89	89	87	83	79	75
	pm	52	52	54	64	76	85	88	88	86	77	72	61
Precipitation	mm	3	5	8	51	307	480	582	528	394	180	69	10
Zurich, Switzerland													
Temperature °F	Max	36	41	51	59	67	73	76	75	69	57	45	37
	Min	26	28	34	40	47	53	56	56	51	43	35	29
Temperature °C	Max	2	5	10	15	19	23	25	24	20	14	7	3
	Min	-3	-2	1	4	8	12	14	13	11	6	2	-2
Humidity %	am	88	88	86	81	80	80	81	85	90	92	90	89
	pm	74	65	55	51	52	52	52	53	57	64	73	76
Precipitation	mm	74	69	64	76	101	129	136	124	102	77	73	64

Weather Information

London Weather Centre
Penderel House
284-286 High Holborn
London
WC1V 7HX
Public Enquiries: Tel: 0171-696 0573
Will answer all regional weather enquiries

Meteorological Office (Overseas Enquiry
Bureau)
Tel: 01344-420242 *and ask for appropriate
country*

Weather call *(Major cities)* 0891 500 +
Northern Europe 969;
Central Europe 970; Southern Europe 971;
USA 972; Far East 973

Holiday Weatherline 0891 500 +
Eastern Mediterranean 974;
Italy/Malta 977; North Africa 978; USA 979

WEXAS Weatherline 0891 770796 +
Algarve 400; Amsterdam 300; Athens 301;
Barcelona 302; Beijing 314; Brussels 303;
Brisbane 315; Canary Isles 401; etc.
See WEXAS directory of membership services

GUIDE TO RAINY SEASONS

Within each region, the destinations listed are arranged in order of decreasing latitude north of the equator, increasing latitude south of the equator. This is a reminder that at any given time of the year, opposite seasons are to be found north and south of the equator. December to February, for example, bring winter to the northern hemisphere, summer to the southern hemisphere. In the belt stretching about up to 10° north and south of the equator, the equatorial climate tends to prevail: the seasons are almost indistinguishable from each other and rain, broadly speaking, is more evenly spread throughout the year than elsewhere. But a lot depends on altitude and other features of geographical location —proximity to the seas or to mountains, and the nature of prevailing winds and currents.

The places listed are not necessarily typical of other places within the same region or country. And they represent only a minute sample globally. Total annual rainfall should always be taken into account, since the rainy season in one place may well be less wet than the dry season in another. At best, this table is a rough guide only.

³ represents a month having more than $1/_{12}$ of the annual total rainfall
◆ represents a month having less than $1/_{12}$ of the annual total rainfall
• indicates the month(s) with the highest average rainfall of the year

	Total annual rainfall (cm)	J	F	M	A	M	J	J	A	S	O	N	D	Latitude
Asia														
Istanbul, Turkey	80.5	³	³	³	◆	◆	◆	◆	◆	◆	³	³	•	41°00'N
Beijing, China	134.1	◆	◆	◆	◆	◆	³	•	•	³	◆	◆	◆	39°50'N
Seoul, Korea.	125.0	◆	◆	◆	◆	◆	³	•	•	³	◆	◆	◆	37°31'N
Tokyo, Japan	156.5	◆	◆	◆	³	³	³	³	³	•	³	◆	◆	35°45'N
Tehran, Iran	24.6	•	³	◆	³	◆	◆	◆	◆	◆	◆	◆	³	35°44'N
Osaka, Japan	133.6	◆	◆	◆	³	³	•	³	³	³	³	◆	◆	34°40'N
Kabul, Afghanistan	34.0	◆	³	•	•	◆	◆	◆	◆	◆	◆	◆	³	34°28'N
Beirut, Lebanon	89.7	•	³	³	◆	◆	◆	◆	◆	◆	◆	³	•	33°53'N
Damascus, Syria	22.4	•	◆	•	◆	◆	◆	◆	◆	◆	◆	³	³	33°30'N
Baghdad, Iraq	15.0	³	³	•	³	◆	◆	◆	◆	◆	◆	³	³	33°20'N
Nagasaki, Japan	191.8	◆	◆	◆	³	³	•	³	³	³	◆	◆	◆	32°47'N
Amman, Jordan	27.9	•	•	³	◆	◆	◆	◆	◆	◆	◆	³	³	32°00'N
Jerusalem, Israel	53.3	•	•	³	◆	◆	◆	◆	◆	◆	◆	³	³	31°47'N
Shanghai, China	113.5	◆	◆	◆	◆	◆	•	³	³	³	◆	◆	◆	31°15'N
Wuhan, China	125.7	◆	◆	◆	³	³	•	³	◆	◆	◆	◆	◆	30°32'N
Kuwait City, Kuwait	12.7	³	³	•	◆	◆	◆	◆	◆	◆	◆	³	•	29°30'N
Delhi, India	64.0	◆	◆	◆	◆	◆	³	•	•	³	◆	◆	◆	28°38'N
Kathmandu, Nepal	142.7	◆	◆	◆	◆	³	³	•	•	³	◆	◆	◆	27°45'N
Agra, India	68.1	◆	◆	◆	◆	◆	³	•	•	³	◆	◆	◆	27°17'N
Cherrapunji, India	1,079.8	◆	◆	◆	³	•	•	•	³	³	◆	◆	◆	25°17'N
Taipei, Taiwan	212.9	◆	◆	³	◆	³	³	³	•	³	◆	◆	◆	25°20'N
Karachi, Pakistan	18.3	◆	◆	◆	◆	◆	◆	•	³	◆	◆	◆	◆	24°53'N
Riyadh, Saudi Arabia	9.1	◆	³	³	•	³	◆	◆	◆	◆	◆	◆	◆	24°41'N
Guangzhou, China	164.3	◆	◆	◆	³	³	•	³	³	◆	◆	◆	◆	23°10'N
Calcutta, India	160.0	◆	◆	◆	◆	³	³	•	•	³	◆	◆	◆	22°36'N
Hong Kong	216.1	◆	◆	◆	◆	³	•	•	•	³	◆	◆	◆	22°11'N
Mandalay, Myanmar	82.8	◆	◆	◆	◆	•	◆	³	³	³	³	◆	◆	22°00'N
Jeddah, Saudi Arabia	8.1	◆	◆	◆	◆	◆	◆	◆	◆	◆	◆	•	•	21°29'N
Hanoi, Vietnam	168.1	◆	◆	◆	◆	³	³	³	•	³	◆	◆	◆	21°50'N
Bombay, India	181.4	◆	◆	◆	◆	◆	•	•	³	³	◆	◆	◆	18°55'N
Hyderabad, India	75.2	◆	◆	◆	◆	³	³	³	•	³	◆	◆	◆	17°10'N
Yangon, Myanmar	261.6	◆	◆	◆	◆	³	³	•	³	³	◆	◆	◆	16°45'N

	Total annual rainfall (cm)	J	F	M	A	M	J	J	A	S	O	N	D	Latitude
Manila, Philippines	208.5	◆	◆	◆	◆	◆	3	•	•	3	3	◆	◆	14°40'N
Bangkok, Thailand	139.7	◆	◆	◆	◆	3	3	3	3	•	3	◆	◆	13°45'N
Madras, India	127.0	◆	◆	◆	◆	◆	◆	◆	3	3	•	•	3	13°80'N
Bangalore, India	329.2	◆	◆	◆	◆	◆	•	◆	3	◆	◆	◆	◆	12°55'N
Aden, Yemen	4.8	3	◆	3	◆	◆	◆	◆	3	•	◆	◆	◆	12°50'N
Colombo, Sri Lanka	236.5	◆	◆	◆	3	◆	3	◆	◆	◆	•	•	◆	6°56'N
Sandakan, Malaysia	314.2	•	3	◆	◆	◆	◆	◆	◆	◆	•	3	◆	5°53'N
Kuala Lumpur, Malaysia	244.1	◆	◆	3	•	3	◆	◆	◆	3	3	3	◆	3°90'N
Singapore	241.3	•	◆	◆	◆	◆	◆	◆	◆	◆	3	•	•	1°17'N
Jakarta, Indonesia	179.8	•	•	3	◆	◆	◆	◆	◆	◆	◆	◆	3	6°90'S

Africa

	Total annual rainfall (cm)	J	F	M	A	M	J	J	A	S	O	N	D	Latitude
Algiers, Algeria	76.5	3	3	3	◆	◆	◆	◆	◆	◆	3	•	•	36°42'N
Tangier, Morocco	90.2	3	3	3	3	◆	◆	◆	◆	◆	◆	•	3	35°50'N
Tripoli, Libya	38.9	3	3	3	3	◆	◆	◆	◆	◆	3	3	3	32°49'N
Marrakesh, Morocco	23.9	3	3	•	3	◆	◆	◆	◆	◆	3	3	3	31°40'N
Cairo, Egypt	3.6	3	3	3	◆	◆	◆	◆	◆	◆	◆	◆	3	30°10'N
Timbuctou, Mali	24.4	◆	◆	◆	◆	◆	3	•	•	3	◆	◆	◆	16°50'N
Khartoum, Sudan	17.0	◆	◆	◆	◆	◆	◆	3	•	3	◆	◆	◆	15°31'N
Dakar, Senegal	155.4	◆	◆	◆	◆	◆	◆	3	•	3	◆	◆	◆	14°34'N
Zungeru, Nigeria	115.3	◆	◆	◆	◆	3	3	3	3	•	◆	◆	◆	9°45'N
Harar, Ethiopia	89.7	◆	◆	3	3	3	3	3	3	•	◆	◆	◆	9°20'N
Addis Ababa, Ethiopia	123.7	◆	◆	◆	◆	◆	3	•	•	3	◆	◆	◆	9°20'N
Freetown, Sierra Leone	343.4	◆	◆	◆	◆	◆	3	•	•	3	3	◆	◆	8°30'N
Lagos, Nigeria	183.6	◆	◆	◆	3	◆	◆	3	◆	◆	3	◆	◆	6°25'N
Cotonou, Benin	132.6	◆	◆	3	3	•	•	◆	◆	◆	3	◆	◆	6°20'N
Monrovia, Liberia	513.8	◆	◆	◆	◆	3	•	•	•	3	3	◆	◆	6°18'N
Accra, Ghana	72.4	◆	◆	3	3	3	◆	◆	◆	◆	3	◆	◆	5°35'N
Mongalla, Sudan	94.5	◆	◆	◆	3	3	3	◆	3	3	3	◆	◆	5°80'N
Libreville, Gabon	251.0	3	3	3	3	3	◆	◆	◆	◆	3	•	3	0°25'N
Entebbe, Uganda	150.6	◆	◆	3	•	3	◆	◆	◆	◆	◆	3	◆	0°30'N
Nairobi, Kenya	95.8	◆	◆	3	◆	3	◆	◆	◆	◆	◆	3	◆	1°20'S
Mombasa, Kenya	120.1	◆	◆	◆	3	•	3	◆	◆	◆	◆	◆	◆	4°00'S
Kinshasa, Zaire	135.4	3	3	3	3	3	◆	◆	◆	◆	3	◆	3	4°20'S
Kananga, Zaire	158.2	3	3	3	3	◆	◆	◆	◆	◆	3	◆	•	5°55'S
Lilongwe, Malawi	78.7	•	•	3	◆	◆	◆	◆	◆	◆	◆	◆	•	14°00'S
Lusaka, Zambia	83.3	•	3	3	◆	◆	◆	◆	◆	◆	◆	3	•	15°25'S
Harare, Zimbabwe	82.8	•	3	3	◆	◆	◆	◆	◆	◆	◆	3	◆	17°50'S
Tamatave, Madagascar	325.6	3	3	•	3	◆	3	3	◆	◆	◆	◆	◆	18°20'S
Beira, Mozambique	152.2	•	3	3	◆	◆	◆	◆	◆	◆	3	3	3	19°50'S
Johannesburg, SA	70.9	3	3	3	◆	◆	◆	◆	◆	◆	◆	3	•	26°10'S
Maputo, Mozambique	75.9	•	3	3	◆	◆	◆	◆	◆	◆	3	3	3	26°35'S
Cape Town, South Africa	50.8	◆	◆	◆	3	3	3	•	3	3	◆	◆	◆	35°55'S

Sub–Arctic

	Total annual rainfall (cm)	J	F	M	A	M	J	J	A	S	O	N	D	Latitude
Reykjavik, Iceland	77.2	3	◆	◆	◆	◆	◆	◆	◆	3	•	3	3	64°10ºN

Australasia and the Pacific

	Total annual rainfall (cm)	J	F	M	A	M	J	J	A	S	O	N	D	Latitude
Honolulu, HI, USA	64.3	•	3	3	◆	◆	◆	◆	◆	◆	◆	3	•	21°25'N
Tulagi, Solomon Is.	313.4	3	•	3	3	◆	◆	◆	◆	◆	◆	◆	3	9°24'S
Port Moresby, PNG	101.1	3	•	3	◆	◆	◆	◆	◆	◆	◆	◆	3	9°24'S
Manihiki, Cook Is.	248.2	•	3	◆	◆	◆	◆	◆	◆	◆	3	3	3	10°24'S
Thursday Is., Australia	171.5	•	3	3	3	◆	◆	◆	◆	◆	◆	◆	3	10°30'S
Darwin, Australia	149.1	•	3	3	◆	◆	◆	◆	◆	◆	◆	3	3	12°20'S
Apia, Western Samoa	285.2	•	3	3	3	◆	◆	◆	◆	◆	◆	3	3	13°50'S

	Total annual rainfall(cm)	J	F	M	A	M	J	J	A	S	O	N	D	Latitude
Cairns, Australia	225.3	3	3	•	3	♦	♦	♦	♦	♦	♦	♦	3	16°55'S
Tahiti, French Polynesia	162.8	•	•	3	3	♦	♦	♦	♦	♦	♦	3	•	17°45'S
Suva, Fiji	297.4	3	3	•	♦	♦	♦	♦	♦	♦	♦	♦	3	18°00'S
Perth, Australia	90.7	♦	♦	♦	♦	3	•	•	3	3	3	♦	♦	31°57'S
Sydney, Australia	118.1	♦	3	3	•	3	3	3	♦	♦	♦	♦	♦	33°53'S
Auckland, NZ	124.7	♦	♦	♦	♦	3	3	•	3	♦	♦	♦	♦	36°52'S
Melbourne, Australia	65.3	♦	♦	3	3	♦	♦	♦	♦	3	•	3	3	41°19'S
Wellington, NZ	120.4	♦	♦	♦	♦	3	3	•	3	♦	3	♦	♦	41°19'S
Christchurch, NZ	63.8	3	♦	♦	♦	3	3	•	♦	♦	♦	♦	3	43°33'S

Central America

	Total annual rainfall(cm)	J	F	M	A	M	J	J	A	S	O	N	D	Latitude
Monterey, Mexico	58.2	♦	♦	♦	♦	♦	3	3	3	•	3	♦	♦	25°40'N
Mazatlan, Mexico	84.8	♦	♦	♦	♦	♦	♦	3	3	3	♦	♦	♦	23°10'N
Havana, Cuba	122.4	♦	♦	♦	3	3	3	3	3	3	•	♦	♦	23°80'N
Merida, Mexico	92.7	♦	♦	♦	3	♦	3	3	3	3	3	♦	♦	20°50'N
Mexico City, Mexico	74.9	♦	♦	♦	♦	♦	3	•	3	3	♦	♦	♦	19°20'N
Port–au–Prince, Haiti	135.4	♦	♦	♦	3	•	♦	♦	3	3	♦	♦	♦	18°40'N
Santo Domingo, Dom. Rep.	141.7	♦	♦	♦	♦	3	3	3	3	•	3	3	♦	18°30'N
Kingston, Jamaica	80.0	♦	♦	♦	♦	3	3	♦	3	3	•	3	♦	18°00'N
Acapulco, Mexico	154.2	♦	♦	♦	♦	•	3	3	3	3	♦	♦	♦	16°51'N
Salina Cruz, Mexico	102.6	♦	♦	♦	♦	♦	3	3	•	♦	♦	♦	♦	16°10'N
Dominica, Leeward Island	197.9	♦	♦	♦	♦	3	•	3	3	3	3	♦	♦	15°20'N
Guatemala City, Guatemala	131.6	♦	♦	♦	3	•	3	3	3	3	♦	♦	♦	14°40'N
Tegucigalpa, Honduras	162.1	♦	♦	♦	♦	•	3	♦	3	3	♦	♦	♦	14°10'N
San Jose, Costa Rica	179.8	♦	♦	♦	3	3	3	3	•	•	♦	♦	♦	10°00'N
Balboa Heights, Panama	177.0	♦	♦	♦	3	3	3	3	3	•	•	♦	♦	9°00'N

South America

	Total annual rainfall(cm)	J	F	M	A	M	J	J	A	S	O	N	D	Latitude
Caracas, Venezuela	83.3	♦	♦	♦	♦	3	•	•	•	•	•	3	♦	10°30'N
Ciudad Bolivar, Venezuela	101.6	♦	♦	♦	♦	3	3	3	3	♦	3	♦	♦	8°50'N
Georgetown, Guyana	225.3	3	♦	♦	♦	3	•	3	♦	♦	♦	♦	3	6°50'N
Bogota, Colombia	105.9	♦	♦	3	3	3	♦	♦	♦	♦	•	3	♦	4°34'N
Quito, Ecuador	112.3	3	3	♦	3	♦	♦	♦	♦	♦	♦	♦	♦	0°15'S
Belem, Brazil	243.8	3	•	•	3	3	♦	♦	♦	♦	♦	♦	♦	1°20'S
Guayaquil, Ecuador	97.3	•	•	•	3	♦	♦	♦	♦	♦	♦	♦	♦	2°15'S
Manaus, Brazil	181.1	3	3	♦	♦	♦	♦	♦	♦	♦	♦	3	3	3°00'S
Recife, Brazil	161.0	♦	♦	3	3	3	♦	3	3	♦	♦	♦	♦	8°00'S
Lima, Peru	4.8	♦	♦	♦	♦	3	3	3	•	•	•	♦	♦	12°00'S
Salvador (Bahia), Brazil	190.0	♦	♦	♦	•	•	3	3	♦	♦	♦	♦	♦	13°00'S
Cuiaba, Brazil	139.5	3	3	•	♦	♦	♦	♦	♦	♦	3	3	3	15°30'S
Concepçion, Bolivia	114.3	•	3	3	♦	♦	♦	♦	♦	♦	♦	•	3	15°50'S
La Paz, Bolivia	57.4	♦	3	3	♦	♦	♦	♦	♦	♦	♦	3	3	16°20'S
Rio de Janeiro, Brazil	108.2	3	3	3	3	♦	♦	♦	♦	♦	♦	3	•	23°00'S
São Paolo, Brazil	142.8	3	3	3	3	♦	♦	♦	♦	♦	♦	3	•	23°40'S
Asunçion, Paraguay	131.6	3	3	♦	3	3	♦	♦	♦	♦	3	3	•	25°21'S
Tucuman, Argentina	97.0	♦	3	3	♦	♦	♦	♦	♦	♦	3	3	3	26°50'S
Santiago, Chile	36.1	♦	♦	♦	3	•	3	3	3	♦	♦	♦	♦	33°24'S
Buenos Aires, Argentina	95.0	♦	♦	3	3	♦	♦	♦	♦	3	3	♦	♦	34°30'S
Montevideo, Uruguay	95.0	♦	♦	•	•	3	3	♦	♦	♦	♦	♦	♦	34°50'S
Valdivia, Chile	260.1	♦	♦	♦	3	3	•	3	3	♦	♦	♦	♦	39°50'S

SELECTED SEA TEMPERATURES (°C)

	J	F	M	A	M	J	J	A	S	O	N	D
Acapulco Mexico	24	24	24	25	26	27	28	28	28	27	26	25
Agadir Morocco	17	17	18	18	19	19	22	22	22	22	21	18
Algiers Algeria	15	14	15	15	17	20	23	24	23	21	18	16
Athens Greece	14	14	14	15	18	22	24	24	23	21	19	16
Bangkok Thailand	26	27	27	28	28	28	28	28	28	27	27	27
Barcelona Spain	13	12	13	14	16	19	22	24	22	21	16	14
Cairo Egypt	15	15	18	21	24	26	27	27	26	24	21	17
Copenhagen Denmark	3	2	3	5	9	14	16	16	14	12	8	5
Corfu Greece	14	14	14	16	18	21	23	24	23	21	18	16
Dubrovnik Croatia	13	13	13	15	17	22	23	24	22	19	16	14
Faro Portugal	15	15	15	16	17	18	19	20	20	19	17	16
Hong Kong	18	18	21	24	25	27	28	28	27	26	24	21
Honolulu Hawaii, USA	24	24	24	25	26	26	27	27	27	27	26	25
Istanbul Turkey	8	8	8	11	15	20	22	23	21	19	15	11
Kingston Jamaica	26	26	26	27	27	28	29	29	28	28	27	27
Las Palmas Canary Islands	19	18	18	18	19	20	21	22	23	23	21	20
Lisbon Portugal	14	14	14	15	16	17	18	19	19	18	17	15
Los Angeles USA	14	14	15	15	16	18	19	20	19	18	17	15
Malaga Spain	15	14	14	15	17	18	21	22	21	19	17	16
Malta	15	14	15	15	18	21	24	25	24	22	19	17
Miami USA	22	23	24	25	28	30	31	32	30	28	25	23
Mombasa Kenya	27	28	28	28	28	27	25	25	27	27	27	27
Naples Italy	14	13	14	15	18	21	24	25	23	21	18	16
Nassau Bahamas	23	23	23	24	25	27	28	28	28	27	26	24
New Orleans USA	13	14	14	15	18	21	24	25	23	21	18	16
Nice France	13	12	13	14	16	20	22	23	21	19	16	14
Palma Majorca	14	13	14	15	17	21	24	25	24	21	18	15
Rio de Janeiro	25	25	26	25	24	23	22	22	22	22	23	24

Brazil												
Rome	14	13	13	14	17	21	23	24	23	20	18	15
Italy												
San Francisco	11	11	12	12	13	14	15	15	16	15	13	11
USA												
Stockholm	3	1	1	2	5	10	15	15	13	10	7	4
Sweden												
Sydney	23	24	23	20	18	18	16	17	18	19	19	21
Australia												
Tahiti	27	27	27	28	28	27	26	26	26	26	27	27
French Polynesia												
Tel Aviv	16	16	17	18	21	24	25	27	27	24	21	18
Israel												
Tenerife	19	18	18	18	19	20	21	22	23	23	21	20
Canary Islands												
Tunis	15	14	14	15	17	20	21	22	23	23	21	20
Tunisia												
Vancouver	8	7	8	9	11	13	14	14	13	12	11	10
Canada												
Venice	9	8	10	13	17	21	23	24	21	18	14	11
Italy												
Wellington	17	18	18	17	14	14	13	13	12	14	14	17
New Zealand												

SELECTED CITY ALTITUDES (M)

Amsterdam, Netherlands	5	Karachi, Pakistan	15
Asuncion, Paraguay	77	Kingston, Jamaica	8
Athens, Greece	0	La Paz, Bolivia	3720
Auckland, New Zealand	0	Lima, Peru	153
Bangkok, Thailand	12	Lisbon, Portugal	87
Beirut, Lebanon	8	Madrid, Spain	55
Bogota, Colombia	2590	Manila, Philippines	8
Bridgetown, Barbados	0	Mexico City, Mexico	2240
Brussels, Belgium	58	Montevideo, Uruguay	9
Buenos Aires, Argentina	14	Moscow, Russia	191
Calcutta, India	26	Oslo, Norway	12
Cape Town, South Africa	8	Panama City, Panama	12
Caracas, Venezuela	964	Port-au-Prince, Haiti	8
Casablanca, Morocco	49	Port-of-Spain, Trinidad	8
Cayenne, French Guiana	8	Quito, Ecuador	2819
Copenhagen, Denmark	8	Rabat, Morocco	0
Curaçao, Netherlands Antilles	0	Rio de Janeiro, Brazil	9
Damascus, Syria	213	Rome, Italy	14
Dublin, Ireland	9	St George's, Grenada	0
Frankfurt, Germany	91	St John's, Antigua	0
Geneva, Switzerland	377	Santiago, Chile	550
Glasgow, Scotland	59	Singapore	8
Guatemala City, Guatemala	1478	Stockholm, Sweden	11
Havana, Cuba	9	Suva, Fiji	0
Helsinki, Finland	8	Sydney, Australia	8
Hong Kong	8	Tegucigalpa, Honduras	975
Istanbul, Turkey	9	Tehran, Iran	1220
Jerusalem, Israel	762	Tokyo, Japan	9
Juneau, Alaska	0	Vienna, Austria	168
Kabul, Afghanistan	2219	Yangon, Myanmar	17

PUBLIC HOLIDAYS

The following is a rough guide to selected public holidays world-wide. The dates of some Religious Holidays may change from one year to another according to the Lunar Calendar.

Afghanistan	Ramadan; Jan 10 1997, New Year's Day, Iranian calendar; Apr 27, Islamic Revolution Day; May 1, Workers Day; May 18 Ashura (Martyrdom of Imam Husayn; July 18 Prophet Muhammad's Birthday; Aug 18, Independence Day; Dec 31 Start of Ramadan. Plus all Muslim festivals, dates vary from year to year.
Albania	Jan 1; Jan 11, Proclamation of the Republic; Easter; May 1; Nov 28, Independence Day; Nov 28 Liberation Day; 25 Dec Christmas Day
Algeria	Jan1; Ramadan Jan 10 1997; May 9 Islamic New Year; Jun 19; Jul 5; Jul 18; Aug 19, Prophet's Birthday; Nov 1; Nov 28; Dec 31 1997 Start of Ramadan. Plus all Muslim festival dates very year to year
Andorra	Jan 1; Jan 6; Feb/Mar Carnival; Easter; May 1; Aug 15; Sept 8, Nov 1; Christmas.
Angola	Jan 1; Feb 4; Mar 27, Victory Day; Apr 14, Youth Day; May 1, Workers Day; Aug 1, Armed Forces' Day; Sep 17, National Heroes' Day; Nov 11, Independence Day; Dec 1, Pioneers' Day; Dec 10; Dec 25, Family Day.
Anguilla	Jan 1; Easter; Whitsun; May 1; May 30 Anguilla Day; Jun 16, Queen's Birthday; Aug 8; Dec 19; Christmas.
Antigua and Barbuda	Jan 1; Easter; May 5; May 19; Whitsun; Jul 7, Caricom Day; Aug 4-5 , Carnival; Nov 1; Christmas.
Argentina	Jan 1; Easter; May 1, Labour Day; May 25, Revolution Day; Jun 9, Malvinas Day; Jun 23 Flag Day; Jul 9, Independence Day; Aug 18 San Martin's Day; Oct 13, Colombus Day; Dec 8, Immaculate Conception; Christmas.
Armenia	Jan 1; Jan 6, Armenian Christmas; Easter; Apr 25, Commemoration of 1915 Genocide; May 28, Anniversary of First Armenian Republic; Sep 21 Independence Day; Dec 7, Commemoration of 1988 Earthquake.
Australia	Jan 1; Australia Day (last Monday in Jan); Easter; Apr 25, Anzac Day; Jun 13, Queen's Birthday; Christmas.
Austria	Jan 1; Jan 6; Easter Monday; May 1, Labour Day; May 12, Ascension Day; Whit Monday; Jun 2, Corpus Christi; Aug 15; Assumption Day; Oct 26, National Day; Nov 1, All Saints Day; Dec 8, Immaculate Conception; Christmas.
Azerbaijan	Jan 1; Mar 8, International Women's Day; Mar 21-27, National Culture Week; May 28, Republic Day; Oct 9, Day of Armed Forces; Oct 18, Independence Day; Nov 17 National Renaissance Day; Dec 31 Azeri World Solidarity Day.
Bahamas	Jan 1; Easter; Whitsun; Jun 3, Labour Day Whit Monday; July 11 Independence Day; Aug 4, Emancipation Day; Oct 12, Discovery Day; Christmas.
Bahrain	Jan 1; Ramadan; Jun 10, Islamic New Year; Jun 19, Ahoura; Aug 19, Prophet's Birthday; Dec 16, National Day; Plus all other Muslim Holidays

which vary year to year.

Bangladesh Jan 1; Feb 21, National Mourning Day; Ramadan; Mar 26, Independence Day; Easter; May 1; Jun 10, Islamic New Year; Aug 19, Prophet's Birthday; Nov 7, National Revolution Day; Dec 16, Victory Day; Christmas; plus all Muslim Holidays which vary year to year.

Barbados Jan 1; Jan 21, Errol Barrow Day; Easter; Whitsun; Aug 1 Kadooment Day; Oct 7, United Nations Day; Nov 30, Independence Day; Christmas.

Belarus Jan 1; Jan 7, Russian Orthodox Christmas; Mar 8, International Women's Day; Apr 27, Belarus Popular Republic Day; May 1, Labour Day; May 9, Victory in Europe Day; Jun 27, Independence Day; Christmas.

Belgium Jan 1; Easter; May 1, Labour Day; Ascension Day; Whitsun; July 21, National Holiday; Aug 15. Assumption Day; All Saints Day; Nov 11, Armistice Day; Nov 15, King's Birthday (only for administrative and public offices, schools etc); Christmas.

Belize Jan 1; Mar 9, Baron Bliss Day; Easter; May 1, Labour Day; May 24, Commonwealth Day; Sept 10, St George's Cay Day; Sept 21, Independence Day; Oct 12, Pan American Day; Nov 19, Garifuna Settlement Day; Christmas.

Benin Jan 1; Jan 16, Martyr's Day; Ramadan; Apr 1, Youth Day; Easter; May1, Worker's Day; Ascension Day; Whitsun; Oct 26, Armed Forces Day; Nov 30, National Day; Christmas; Dec 31, Harvest Day; plus all Muslim Holidays which vary year to year.

Bermuda Jan 1; Easter; May 24, Bermuda Day; Jun 20, Queen's Birthday; Jul 28, Cup Match Day; Jul 29, Somer's Day; Sep 5, Labour Day; Nov 11, Remembrance Day; Christmas.

Bhutan Nov 11, King's Birthday; Dec 17, National Day; plus all Buddhist festivals which vary year to year.

Bolivia Jan 1; Feb, Carnival Week (preceding Lent); Holy Week (3 days preceding Easter; May 1, Labour Day; Jun 10, Corpus Christi; Aug 6, Independence Day; Nov 1, All Saints Day; Christmas.

Botswana Jan 1; Jan 2; Easter; May 12, Ascension Day; July 16, President's Day; Sep 30, Botswana Day; Christmas.

Brazil Jan 1; Carnival (3 days preceding Lent); Easter; Apr 21, Discovery of Brazil; May 1, Labour Day; Sept 7, Independence Day; Oct 12, Our Lady Aparecida; Nov 2, All Souls' Day; Nov 15, Proclamation of the Republic; Christmas.

British Virgin Islands Jan 1; Mar 6, Commonwealth Day; Easter; Whitsun; Jun 6, Queen's Official Birthday; Jul 1, Territory Day; 1st Mon, Tue, Wed in Aug; Oct 21, St Ursula's Day; Nov 14, Prince of Wales' Birthday; Christmas.

Brunei Jan 1; Chinese New Year; Ramadan; Jun 1, Royal Brunei Armed Forces Day; Jun 10, Islamic New Year; Jul 15, Sultan's Birthday; Aug 19, Prophet's Birthday; Christmas; plus all Muslim holidays which vary year to year.

Bulgaria Jan 1; Mar 3, National Day; Easter; May 1, Labour Day; May 24, Education Day; Christmas.

Burkina Faso	Jan 1; Jan 3, Anniversary of the 1966 *coup d'etat*; Ramadan; Easter; May 1, Labour Day; May 12, Ascension Day Whitsun; Aug 4, National Day; Aug 15, Assumption; Aug 19, Prophet's Birthday; Nov 1, All Saints Day; Christmas; plus all Muslim festivals that vary year to year.
Burundi	Jan 1; Easter; May 1, Labour Day; May 12, Ascension Day; Jul 1, Independence Day; Aug 15, Assumption; Sep 3, Anniversary of the Third Republic; Sep 18, Victory of UPRONA Party; Nov 1, All Saints; Christmas.
Cambodia	Jan 1; Apr, Camodian New Year; May 1; Sep, Feast of the Ancestors; Nov, Full Moon Water Festival.
Cameroon	Jan 1; Feb 11, Youth Day; Ramadan; Easter; May 1, Labour Day; May 12, Ascension Day; May 20, National Day; May 21, Festival of Sheep; Aug 15, Assumption; Dec 10, Reunification Day; Christmas.
Canada	Jan 1; Easter; May 23, Victoria Day; July 1, Canada Day; Sep 5, Labour Day; Oct Thanksgiving; Nov 11, Remembrance Day; Christmas.
Cape Verde	Jan 1; Mar 8, Women's Day; May 1, Labour Day; Jul 5, Independence Day; Aug 15, Assumption; Nov 1, All Saints; Christmas.
Cayman Islands	Jan 1, Easter;May 2, Labour Day; May 16, Discovery Day; Whitsun; Jun 13, Queen's Official Birthday; Jul 4, Constitution Day; Nov 14, Remembrance Day; Christmas.
Central African Republic	Jan 1; Mar 29, Anniversary of the Death of Barthelemy Boganda; Easter; May 1, May Day; May 12, Ascension; Whitsun; Jun 30, National Day of Prayer; Aug 13, Independence Day; Aug 15, Assumption; Nov 1, All Saints; Dec 1, National Day; Christmas.
Chad	Jan 1; Ramadan; Easter; May 1, Labour Day; Whitsun; May 25, OUA Foundation Day; Aug 11, Independence Day; Aug 15, Assumption; Aug 19, Prophet's Birthday; Nov 1, All Saints; Nov 28, Proclamation of the Republic; Christmas; plus all Muslim festivals which vary year to year.
Chile	Jan 1; Easter; May 1, Labour Day; May 21, Battle of Iquique Navy Day; May 30, Corpus Christi; Jun 29, St Peter and St Paul; Aug 15, Assumption; Sep 18, Independence Day; Sep 19, Army Day; Oct 12, Columbus Day; Nov 1, All Saints; Dec, Immaculate Conception; Christmas.
China	Jan/Feb, Chinese New Year; Mar 8, International Women's Day; May 1, Labour Day; May 4, Chinese Youth Day; Jun 1, International Children's Day; Jul 1, Founding of the Communist Party of China; Aug 1, Army Day; Sep 9, Teacher's Day; Oct 1-2, National Days.
Colombia	Jan1; Jan 6, Epiphany; Mar 19 St Joseph's Day; Easter; May 1, Labour Day; May 12, Ascension Day; Jun 2, Corpus Christi; June 29, Sts Peter and Paul; July 20, Independence Day; Aug 7, Battle of Boyaca; Aug 15, Assumption; Oct 12, Discovery of America; Nov 1, All Saints Day; Nov 11, Independence of Cartagena; Dec 8, Immaculate Conception; Christmas.
Congo	Jan 1; Easter; May 1, Labour Day; Aug 15, Independence Day; Christmas.
Costa Rica	Jan 1; Mar 19, St. Joseph's Day; Easter; Apr 11, Anniversary of the Battle of Rivas; May 1, Labour Day; Jun 2, Corpus Christi; June 29, Sts Peter & Paul; July 25, Anniversary of the Annexation of Guanacaste Province; Aug 2, Our Lady of Angels; Aug 15, Assumption; Sept 15, Independence Day; Oct 12, Columbus Day; Dec 8, Immaculate Conception; Christmas - New Year, Holy Week.

Côte d'Ivoire	Jan 1; Ramadan; Easter; May 1, Labour Day; May 12, Ascension Day; Whit Monday; Aug 15, Assumption; Nov 1, All Saints Day; Dec 7, Independence Day; Christmas; plus all Muslim holidays which vary year to year.
Cuba	Jan 1, Liberation Day; May 1, Labour Day; Jul 25-27 Anniversary of the 1953 Revolution; Oct 10, Wars of Independence Day.
Cyprus	Jan 1; Epiphany; Mar 6, Green Monday; Mar 25, Greek National Day; Apr 1,Greek-Cypriot National Day; Easter; Jun 20, Festival of the Flood; Aug 15, Assumption; Oct 1, Independence Day; Oct 28, Greek National Day; Christmas.
Czech Republic	Jan 1; Easter; May 1, Labour Day; Jul 5, Day of the Apostles St Cyril and St Methodius; Jul 6, Anniversary of the Martydom of Jan Hus; Oct 28, Independence Day; Christmas.
Denmark	Jan 1; Easter; Apr 29 General Prayer Day; May 12, Ascension Day; Whit Monday; June 5, Constitution Day; Christmas.
Djibouti	Jan 1; Ramadan; May 1, Workers Day; Jun 10, Islamic New Year; Jun 27, Independence Day; Aug 19, Prophet's Birthday; Christmas; plus all Muslim holidays which vary year to year.
Dominica	Jan 1; Feb, Carnival; Easter; May 1, May Day; 1st Monday in Aug; Nov 3, National Day; Nov 4, Community Service Day; Christmas.
Dominican Republic	Jan 1; Jan 6, Epiphany; Jan 21, Our Lady of Altagracia; Jan 26, Duarte; Feb 27, Independence Day; Easter; May 1, Labour Day; Jun 2, Corpus Christi; Aug 16, Restoration Day; Sept 24, Our Lady of Las Mercedes; Oct 12, Columbus Day; Nov 1, All Saints; Christmas.
Ecuador	Jan 1; Feb, Carnival; Easter; May 1, Labour Day; May 24, Battle of Pichincha; Jul 24, Birthday of Simon Bolivar; Aug 10, Independence of Quito; Oct 9, Anniversary of the Independence of Guayaquil; Oct 12, Discovery of America; Nov 1, All Saints; Nov 2, All Soul's Day; Nov 3, Independence of Cuenca; Dec 6, Foundation of Quito; Christmas.
Egypt	Jan ; Ramadan; Jun 10, Islamic New Year; Jun 18, Evacuation Day; Jun 23, Revolution Day; Aug 19, Prophet's Birthday; Oct 6, Armed Forces Day; Oct 24, Popular Resistance Day; Dec 23, Victory Day; Dec 30, Ascension of the Prophet; plus all Muslim festival which vary year to year.
El Salvador	Jan 1; Easter; May 1, Labour Day; Jun 2, Corpus Christi; Aug 1-6approx, San Salvador Festival; Sept 15, Independence Day; Oct 12, Discovery of America; Nov 2, All Souls' Day; Nov 5, First Call for Independence; Christmas.
Equatorial Guinea	Jan 1; Mar 5, Independence Day; Easter; May 1, Labour Day; May 25, OAU Day; Dec 10, Human Rights Day; Christmas.
Eritrea	Jan 1; Jan, Timket; Ramadan; May 24, Liberation Day; Jun 20, Martyrs Day; Aug 19, Prophet's Birthday; Sep 1, Start of the Armed Struggle; plus all Muslim Holidays that vary year to year.
Estonia	Jan 1; Feb 24, Independence Day; Easter; May 1, Labour Day; Jun 23, Victory Day; Jun 24, Midsummer Day; Christmas.
Ethiopia	Ethiopia still uses the Julian Calendar; Jan 7, Christmas; Jan 19, Epiphany; Ramadan; Mar 2, Battle of Adowa Day; Apr 6, Victory Day; Easter; Aug 19, Prophet's Birthday; Sep, New Years Day; Sep 27, Feast of the True Cross; plus all Muslim festivals that very year to year.

Falkland Islands	Jan 1; Easter; Apr 21, HM Queen's Birthday; Jun 14, Liberation Day; Aug 14, Falkland Day; Oct 5; Dec 8, Anniversary of the Battle of the Falkland Islands; Christmas.
Fiji	Jan 1; Easter; May 30, Ratu Sir Lala Sukuna Day; Jun 13, Queen's official Birthday; Oct 9, Independence Day; Nov 3, Diwali; Christmas; plus Hindu and Muslim festivals which vary year to year.
Finland	Jan 1; Jan 6, Epiphany; Easter; May 1; May 12, Ascension; Whitsun; June 24, Midsummer's Day; Nov 5, All Saint's Day 3; Dec 6, Independence Day; Christmas.
France	Jan 1; Easter; May 1, Labour Day; May 8, Liberation Day; May 12, Ascension Day; Whitsun; July 14, National day, Fall of the Bastille; Aug 15, Assumption; Nov 1, All Saints' Day; Nov 11, Remembrance Day; Christmas.
Gabon	Jan 1; Ramadan; Mar 12, Renovation Day; Easter; May 1, Labour Day; Whit Monday; Aug 17, Anniversary of Independence; Aug 19, Prophet's Birthday; Nov 1, All Saints' Day; Christmas; plus all Muslim holidays which vary year to year.
Gambia	Jan 1; Ramadan; Feb 18, Independence Day; Easter; May 1, Labour Day; Aug 15, Assumption; Aug 19, Prophet's Birthday; Christmas; plus all Muslim festival which vary year to year.
Georgia	Jan 1; Jan 7, Orthodox Christmas; Easter; May 26, Independence Day; Aug 28, St Marian's Day; Oct 14, Khetkhob; Nov 23, St George's Day.
Germany	Jan 1; Jan 6, Epiphany; Easter; May 1, Labour Day; May 12, Ascension Day; Whit Monday; Jun 2, Corpus Christi; Aug 15, Assumption; Oct 3, Day of Unity; Oct 31, Reformation Day; Nov 1, All Saint's Day; Nov 16, Day of Prayer and Repentance; Christmas.
Ghana	Jan 1; Jan 7, Fourth Republic Anniversary; Mar 6, Independence Day; Easter; May 1, Labour Day; Jul 1, Republic Day; Christmas.
Gibraltar	Jan 1; Mar 14, Commonwealth Day; Easter; May 1, May Day; last Mon in May; Jun 13, Queen's Birthday; last Mon in Aug; Sep 12, Referendum Day; Christmas.
Greece	Jan 1; Jan 6, Epiphany; Shrove Monday; Mar 25, Independence Day; Easter; May 1, Labour Day; June 20, Day of the Holy Spirit; Aug 15, Assumption; Oct 28, Ochi Day; Christmas.
Greenland	Jan 1; Easter; Apr 29, General Prayer Day; May 12, Ascension; Whit Monday; Jun 5, Constitution Day; Jun 2, National Day; Christmas.
Grenada	Jan 1; Feb 7, Independence Day; Easter; May 1, Labour Day; Whit Monday; Jun 2, Corpus Christi; Aug 1-2, Emancipation Day; Aug Carnival; Oct 25, Thanksgiving; Christmas.
Guatemala	Jan 1; Jan 6, Epiphany; Easter; May 1, Labour Day; Jun 30, Anniversary of the Revolution; Aug 15, Assumption; Sep 15, Independence Day; Oct 12, Columbus Day; Oct 20, Revolution Day; Nov 1, All Saints' Day; Christmas.
Guernsey	Jan 1; Easter; May 1, May Day; May 9, Liberation Day; last Mon in May; last Mon in Aug; Christmas.
Guinea Republic	Jan 1; Ramadan; Easter; May 1, Labour Day; Aug 19, Prophet's Birthday; Aug 27, Anniversary of the Women's Revolt; Sep 28, Referendum Day; Oct

2, Republic Day; Nov 1, All Saints' Day; Nov 22, Day of the 1970 Invasion; Christmas; plus all Muslim festivals which vary year to year.

Guinea-Bissau Jan 1; Jan 20, Death of Amilcar Cabral; Mar 2, Korite; May 1, Labour Day; May 21, Tabaski; Aug 3, Anniversary of the Killing of Pidjiguiti; Sep 24, National Day; Nov 14, Anniversary of the Movement of Readjustment; Christmas; plus all Muslim festivals that vary year to year.

Guyana Jan 1; Feb 23, Republic Anniversary; Ramadan; Easter; May 1, Labour Day; May 5, Indian Heritage Day; Jun 27, Carribean Day; Aug 1, Freedom Day; Christmas; plus all Muslim festivals that vary year to year.

Honduras Jan 1; Easter; Apr 14, Pan-American Day; May 1, Labour Day; Sep 15, Independence Day; Oct 3, Birth of General Morazan; Oct 12, Discovery of America Day; Oct 21, Armed Forces Day; Christmas.

Hong Kong The first weekday in Jan; Lunar New Year; Easter; Apr 5, Ching Ming Festival; Jun 13, the Queen's Birthday; Jun 14, Dragon Boat Festival; Aug 29, Liberation Day; Day following the Chinese Mid-Autumn Festival; Chung Yeung Festival; Christmas.

Hungary Jan 1; Mar 15, Anniversary of 1848 uprising against Austrian rule; Easter; May 1, May Day; Aug 20, Constitution Day; Oct 23, Day of Proclamation of the Republic; Christmas.

Iceland Jan 1; Easter; Apr 20, first Day of Summer; May 12, Ascension Day; Whit Monday; June 17, National Day; Christmas.

India Jan 1; Jan 26, Republic Day; Aug 15, Independence Day; Oct 2 Mahatma Gandhi's Birthday; Dec 25. Also 32 other religious (Hindu, Christian and Muslim) or special occasions which are observed either with national or regional holidays.

Indonesia Jan 1; Ramadan; Easter; May 12, Ascension Day; Jun 10, Islamic New Year Aug 17, Indonesian National Day; Aug 19 Prophet's Birthday; Christmas; plus all Muslim festivals which vary year to year.

Iran Feb 11, National Day (Fall of the Shah); Ramadan; Mar 20, Oil Nationalisation Day; Mar 21, Iranian New Year; Apr 1, Islamic Republic day; Apr 2, Revolution Day; Jun 4, Passing away of Imam Khomeini, Jun 19, Ashoura; Jul 14, Martyrdom of Iman Ali; Aug 19, Prophet's Birthday; Dec 30, Ascension of the Prophet; plus all Muslim festivals which vary year to year.

Iraq Jan 1; Jan 6, Army Day; Ramadan; May 21, Feast of the Sacrifice; Jun 10, Islamic New Year; Jun 19, Ashoura; Jul 14, Republic Day; Aug 19 Prophet's Birthday; July 17; Dec 30, Ascension of the Prophet; plus all Muslim festivals which vary year to year.

Ireland Jan 1; Mar 17, St Patrick's Day; Easter; May 1, May Day; Jun 6, Bank Holiday; First Mon in Aug; Oct 21; Christmas.

Israel All business activity ceases on Saturdays and religious holidays, the dates of which vary from one year to another. Passover, first day; Passover, last day; Apr 14, Israel Independence Day; Shavout (Feast of Weeks); Pentecost; Rosh Hashana (New Year); Yom Kippur (Day of Atonement); First Day of Tabernacles; Last Day of Tabernacles; Hanukkah.

Italy Jan 1; Jan 6, Epiphany; Easter; Apr 25, Liberation Day; May 1, Labour Day; Aug 15, Assumption; Nov 1, All Saints' Day; Nov 5, National Unity Day;

Dec 8, Immaculate Conception; Christmas.

Jamaica
Jan 1; Ash Wednesday; Easter; May 23, Labour Day; Aug 1, Independence Day; Oct 17, National Heroes' Day; Christmas.

Japan
Jan 1; Jan 16, Coming of Age Day; Feb 11, National Foundation Day; Vernal Equinox Day (variable date); Apr 29, Greenery Day; May 3, Constitution Memorial Day; May 5, Children's Day; Sept 15, Respect of the Aged Day; Autumnal Equinox Day (variable date); Oct 10, Physical Culture Day; Nov 3, Culture Day; Nov 23, Labour Thanksgiving Day; Dec 23, Birthday of the Emperor;

Jersey
Jan 1; Easter; May 1, May Day; May 9, Liberation Day; last Mon in May; last Mon in Aug; Christmas.

Jordan
Jan 15, Arbour Day; Ramadan; Mar 22, Arab League Day; May 25, Independence Day; Jun 10, Islamic New Year; Aug 11, King Hussein's Accession; Aug 19, Prophet's Birthday; Nov 14, King Hussein's Birthday; Plus all Muslim holidays which vary year to year.

Kazakhstan
Jan 1; Jan 27, Constitution Day; Mar 8, International Women's Day; May Labour Day; May 9, Victory Day; Dec 16, Republic Day; plus some Muslim holidays which vary year to year.

Kenya
Jan 1; Ramadan; Easter; May 1, Labour Day; Jun 1, Madraka Day; Oct 10, Moi Day; Oct 20, Kenyatta Day; Dec 12, Jamhuri Day; Christmas; plus some Muslim festivals which vary year to year.

Korea (South)
Jan 1; Lunar New Year; Mar 1, Independence Day; Apr 5, Arbor Day; May 5, Children's Day; May 18, Buddha's birthday; Jun 6, Memorial Day; Jul 17, Constitution Day; Aug 15, Liberation Day; Thanksgiving Day; Oct 3, National Foundation Day; Christmas.

Kuwait
Religious holidays vary from one year to another. The only fixed holidays in Kuwait are New Year's Day and Kuwait National Day (Feb 25).

Kyrgyzstan
Jan 1; Jan 7, Russian Orthodox Christmas; Lunar New Year; Mar 8, International Women's Day; May 1, Labour Day; May 5, Constitution Day; May 9, Victory Day; Jun 13, Day of Remembrance; Aug 31, Independence Day; plus some Muslim holidays which vary year to year.

Laos
Jan 1; Apr, Lao New Year; May 1, Labour Day; Dec 2, National Day.

Latvia
Jan 1; Easter; May 1, Labour Day; Jun 23, Ligo Festival; Jun 24, Midsummer Festival; Nov 18, National Day; Christmas.

Lebanon
Jan 1; Feb 9, Feast of St Marron; Ramadan; Mar 22, Arab League Anniversary; Easter; Ascension Day; Jun 10, Islamic New Year; jun 19, Ashora; Aug 15, Assumption; Aug 19 Prophet's Birthday; Nov 1, All Saints Day; Nov 22, Independence Day; Christmas; Dec 31, Evacuation Day. plus all Muslim festivals which vary year to year.

Liberia
Jan 1; Mar 12 Decoration Day; Mar 15, J.J. Robert's birthday; April 12, National Redemption Day; May 14, National Unification Day; Jul 26, Independence Day; Aug 24, National Flag Day; Thanksgiving Day;Nov 12, National Memorial Day; Nov 29, President Trubman's Birthday; Christmas.

Liechtenstein
Jan 1; Jan 6, Epiphany; Shrove Tuesday; Mar 19, St Joseph's Day; Easter; May 1, Labour Day; Ascension; Whit Monday; Jun 2; Corpus Christi; Aug

15, Assumption; Sep 8, Nativity of the Virgin Mary; Nov 1, All Saints; Dec 8, Immaculate Conception; Christmas.

Lithuania   Jan 1; Feb 16, Independence Day; Mar 11, Day of Restoration of the Lithuanian State; Easter; May 1, Mother's Day; Jun 14, Day of Mourning and Hope; Jul 6, Day of Statehood; Nov 1, All Saints' Day; Christmas.

Luxembourg   Jan 1; Easter; May 1, Labour Day; Ascension Day; Whit Monday; June 23, National Day; Aug 15, Assumption Day; Nov 1, All Saints' Day; Christmas.

Macau   Jan 1; Feb, Chinese New Year; Apr 5, Ching Ming Festival; Apr 25, Anniversary of Portuguese Revolution; Easter; May 1, Labour Day; Jun 10, Camoens Day and Portuguese Communities; Jun 13, Dragon Boat Festival; Jun 24, Feast of St. John the Baptist; Sept, Mid-Autumn Festival; Oct 1, National Day of the People's Republic of China; Oct 5, Republic Day; Oct 13 Festival of Ancestors; Nov 2, All Souls' Day; Dec 1, Restoration of Independence; Dec 8, Feast of Immaculate Conception; Dec 22, Winter Solstice; Christmas.

Madagascar   Jan 1; Mar 29, Commemoration of the 1947 Rebellion; Easter; May 1, Labour Day; May 12, Ascension; June 26, Independence Day; Nov 1, All Saint's Day; Christmas; Dec 30, Anniversary of the Republic.

Malawi   Jan 1; Mar 3, Martyr's Day; Easter; May 14, Kamuzu Day, President Banada's Birthday; Jul 6, Republic Day; Oct 17, Mother's Day; Dec 21, National Tree Planting Day; Christmas.

Malaysia   Chinese New Year; Ramadan; May 1, Labour Day; May, Vesak Day; Jun 3, King's Birthday; Aug 18, Prophet's Birthday; Aug 31, Independence Day; Christmas; plus all Muslim festivals which vary year to year.

Maldives   Jan 2, Martyr's Day; Ramadan; Jun 10, Islamic New Year; Jul 26, Independence Day; Aug 18, Prophet's Birthday; Nov 3, Victory Day; Nov 11, Republic Day; plus all Muslim festivals which vary year to year.

Mali   Jan 1; Jan 20, Armed Forces Day; Ramadan; Easter; May 1, Labour Day; May 25, Africa Day; Aug 18, Prophet's Birthday; Aug 29, Assumption; Nov 1, All Saint's; Nov 3, Baptism of the Prophet; Nov 19, Anniversary of the 1968 Coup; Christmas. Plus all Muslim festivals which vary year to year.

Malta   Jan 1; Feb 10, St Paul's Shipwreck; Mar 19, St Joseph's Day; Mar 31, Freedom Day; Easter; May 1, Worker's Day; Jun 7, Commemoration of 1919 Riot; Jun 29, Feast of St Peter and St Paul; Aug 15, Assumption;Sep 8, Feast of our Lady of Victories; Sep 21, Independence Day; Dec 8, Immaculate Conception; Dec 13, Republic Day; Christmas.

Mauritius   Jan 1; Jan 2; Feb 10, Chinese Spring Festival; Ramadan; Mar 12, Independence Day; May 1, Labour Day; Nov 1, All Saints; Christmas; plus all Muslim festivals which vary year to year.

Mexico   Jan 1; Feb 5, Constitution Day; Mar 21, Birth of Benito Jaurez; Easter; May 1, Labour Day; May 5, Anniversary of the Battle of Puebla; Sep 1, President's Annual Message; Sep 16, Independence Day; Oct 12, Discovery of America; Nov 20, Anniversary of the Mexican Revolution; Christmas.

Monaco   Jan 1; Jan 27, St Devote's Day; Easter; May 1, Labour Day; Ascension; Whit Monday; Corpus Christi; Aug 15, Assumption; Nov 1, All Saint's Day; Nov 19, Monaco National Day; Dec 8, Immaculate Conception; Christmas.

Mongolia	Jan 1; Tsagaan Sar (Lunar New Year); Mar 8, International Women's Day; Jul 11-13, National Days; Nov 26, Republic Day;
Monserrat	Jan 1; Mar 17, St Patrick's Day; Easter; May 1, Labour Day; Whit Monday; Jun 13, Queen's Official Birthday; First Mon in Aug; Nov 23, Liberation Day; Christmas
Morocco	Jan 1; Ramadan; Mar 3, Festival of the Throne; May 1, Labour Day; Jun 10, Islamic New Year; Jun 19, Ashora; Aug 19, Prophet's Birthday; Nov 6, Anniversary of the Green March; Nov 18, Independence Day; plus all Muslim festivals which vary year to year.
Myanmar	Jan 4, Independence Day; Feb 12, Union Day; Mar 2, Peasants' Day; Mar 27, Armed Forces Day; mid-Apr Thingyan Water Festival ; May 1, Worker's Day; early May, Tazaundaing Festival of Lights; Dec 1, National Day; Christmas.
Namibia	Jan 1, Mar 21, Independence Day; Easter; May 1, Worker's Day; May 4, Casinga Day; Ascension; May 25, Africa Day; Aug 26, Heroes' Day; Dec 10, Human rights Day; Christmas.
Nepal	Jan 11, National Unity Day; Jan 30, Martyr's Day; Feb 18, King's Birthday; Mar 8, Nepalese Women's Day; Apr 10, Teacher's Day; Apr 14, New Year; Nov 7, Queen's Birthday; Nov 9, Constitution Day; Dec 17, Mahendra Jayanti; Dec 28, King's Birthday; many other religious, holidays which change every year according to Lunar and other calendars. Biggest festival Dassain (Sept/Oct) when everything closes for a week.
Netherlands	Jan 1; Easter; Apr 30 Queen's Day; May 5, National Liberation Day; May 12, Ascension Day; Whit Monday; Christmas.
New Zealand	Jan 1; Easter; Apr 25, ANZAC Day; Jun 1, the Queen's Birthday; Oct 26, Labour Day; Christmas; each province has its own particular holiday.
Nicaragua	Jan 1; Easter; May 1, Labour Day; Jul 19, Liberation Day; Sep 14, Battle of San Jacinto; Sep 15, Independence Day; Christmas.
Niger	Jan 1; Ramadan; Easter; Apr 15, Anniversary of the 1974 coup; Jun 10, Islamic New Year; Aug 3, Independence Day; Aug 19, Prophet's Birthday; Dec 18, Republic Day; Christmas; plus all Muslim festivals which vary year to year.
Nigeria	Jan 1; Ramadan; Easter; May 1, May Day; Oct 1, National Day; Christmas; plus all Muslim festivals which vary year to year.
Norway	Jan 1; Easter; May 1, May Day; Ascension; May 17, National Independence day; Christmas.
Oman	Ramadan; Jun 10, Muslim New Year; Aug 18, Prophet's Birthday; Nov 18, Sultan's Birthday; plus all Muslim festivals which vary year to year.
Pakistan	Ramadan; Mar 23, Pakistan Day; Easter; May 1, Labour Day; Jun 10, Islamic New Year; Jun 19, Ashora; Aug 14, Independence Day; Sep 6, Defence of Pakistan Day; Sep 11, Anniversary of the death of Quaid-i-Azam; Nov 9, Iqbal day; Dec 25, Quaid-i-Azam's Birthday, Christmas; plus all Muslim festivals which vary year to year.
Panama	Jan 1; Jan 9, National Martyr's Day; Shrove Tuesday; Easter; May 1, Labour Day; Aug 15, Foundation of Panama City; Oct 11, Revolution Day; Nov 1, National Anthem Day; Nov 2, All Soul's Day; Nov 3, Independence from

Colombia Day; Nov 4, Flag Day; Nov 5, Independence Day; Nov 10, First Call for Independence; Nov 28, Independence from Spain; Dec 8, Mother's Day; Christmas.

Papua New Guinea   Jan 1; Easter; Jun 6, Queen's Official Birthday; Jul 23, Remembrance Day; Sep 16, Independence Day; Christmas; plus various regional festivals.

Paraguay   Jan 1; Feb 3, San Blas Patron Saint; Mar 1, Hero's Day; Easter; May 1, Labour Day; May 14 and 15, Independence Day; June 12, Chaco Peace; Corpus Christi; Aug 15, Founding of Asuncion; Aug 25, Constitution Day; Sep 29, Battle of Boqueron (Chaco War); Oct 12, Colombus Day, Nov 1, All Saints Day; Dec 8, Immaculate Conception; Christmas.

Peru   Jan 1; Easter; May 1, Labour Day; June 24, Day of the Peasant; June 29, St Peter and St. Paul; July 28/29, Independence Days; Aug 30, St. Rose of Lima; Oct 8, Battle of Angamos; Nov 1, All Saints' Day; Dec 8, Immaculate Conception; Christmas.

Philippines   Jan 1; Easter; May 1, Labour Day; May 6, Day of Valour; Jun 12, Independence Day; Nov 1, All Saints' Day; Nov 30, Bonifacio Day; Dec 25; Dec 30, Rizal Day.

Poland   Jan 1; Easter; May 1, Labour Day; May 3, Polish National Day; May 9, Victory Day; Corpus Christi; Nov 1, All Saints' Day; Nov 11, Independence Day; Christmas.

Portugal   Jan 1, Carnival; Easter; Apr 25, National Day; May 1, Labour Day; Corpus Christi; Jun 10, Portugal Day; Aug 15, Assumption; Oct 5, Republic Day; Nov 1, All Saint's Day; Dec 1, Independence Day; Dec 8, immaculate Conception; Dec 25. Carnival is also an important event in Portugal and takes place during the four days preceding Lent.

Qatar   Ramadan; Sep 3, Independence Day. Plus all Muslim festivals which vary year to year.

Romania   Jan 1; Orthodox easter; May1-2, International Labour Day; Dec 1, National Day; Christmas.

Russian Federation   Jan 1; Jan 7, Orthodox Christmas; Mar 8, International Women's Day; May 1-2, International Solidarity Day; May 9, Victory in Europe Day; Jun 12, Russian Independence Day: Nov 7, October Revolution.

Rwanda   Jan 1; Jan 28, Democracy Day; Easter; May 1, Labour Day; Whit Monday; Jul 1, Anniversary of Independence; Jul 5, National Peace and Unity Day; Aug 15, Assumption; Sep 25, Kamarampaka Day; Oct 26 Armed Forces Day; Nov 1, All Saints' Day; Christmas.

St Kitts & Nevis   Jan 1; Easter; May 4, Labour Day; Whit Monday; Jun 11, Queen's Official Birthday; first Mon in Aug; Sep 19, Independence day; Nov 14, Prince of Wales' Birthday; Christmas.

St Lucia   Jan 1; Feb Carnival; Easter; May 1, Labour Day; Whit Monday; Jun 11, Queen's Official Birthday; first Mon in Aug; Oct 3, Thanksgiving Day; Dec 13, St Lucia Day; Christmas.

St Vincent   Jan 1; Jan 22, St Vincent & The Grenadines Day; Easter; May 1, Labour Day; Whit Monday; Jul 11, Caricom Day; Carnival, first Mon in Aug; Oct 27, Independence day; Christmas.

San Marino   Jan 1, Jan 6, Epiphany; Feb 5, Liberation and St Agatha's Day; Mar 25, Anniversary of the Arengo; Apr 1, Captain-Regent Investiture; Easter; May

1, Labour Day; Corpus Christi; Jul 28, Anniversary of the fall of Fascism; Aug 15, Assumption; Sep 3, Republic Day; Nov 1, All Saints' Day; Nov 2, Commemoration of the Dead; Dec 8, Immaculate Conception; Christmas.

Saudi Arabia	Ramadan; plus all Muslim festivals which vary year to year.
Seychelles	Jan 1; Easter; May 1, Labour Day; June 5, Liberation Day; June 29, Independence Day; Corpus Christi; Aug 15, Assumption of Mary; Nov 1, All Saints' Day; Dec 8, Immaculate Conception; Christmas.
Sierra Leone	Jan 1; Ramadan; Easter; Apr 27, Independence Day; 25 Dec; plus all Muslim festivals which vary year to year.
Singapore	Jan 1; Chinese New Year; May 1, Labour Day; Vesak Day; Aug 9, National Day; Oct 29, Dec 25; plus all Muslim festivals which vary year to year.
Slovak Republic	Jan 1; Jan 6, Epiphany; Easter; May 1, Labour Day; Jul 5, Day of the Apostles St Cyril and St Methodius; Aug 29, Anniversary of the Slovak National Uprising; Sep 1, Day of Constitution of the Slovak Republic; Sep 15, Our Lady of the Seven Sorrows; Nov 1, All Saints' Day; Christmas.
Slovenia	Jan 1; Feb 8, Culture Day; Easter; Apr 27, Resistance Day; May 1, Labour Day; Jun 25, Statehood Day; Aug 15, Assumption; Oct 31, Reformation Day; Nov 1, Remembrance Day; Dec 25; Dec 26, Independence Day.
South Africa	Jan 1; Apr 4, Family Day; Apr 6, Founder's Day; Easter; May 1, Worker's Day; Ascension Day; May 31, Republic Day; Oct 10, Kruger Day; Dec 16, Day of the Vow; Dec 25; Dec 26, Day of Goodwill.
Spain	Jan 1; Jan 6; Easter; May 1, St Joseph the Workman; June 24, King Jaun Carlos' Day; July 25, St James of Compostela; Aug 15, Assumption; Oct 12, National Day; Nov 1, All Saint's; Dec 8, Immaculate Conception; Dec 25.
Sri Lanka	Jan 1; Feb 4, Independence Day; Ramadan; Easter; May 1, May Day; May 22, National Heroes' Day; Jun 30; Dec 25; plus all Muslim festivals which vary year to year.
Sudan	Jan 1, Independence Day; Ramadan; Mar 3, Unity Day; Apr 6, Uprising Day; Jun 10, Islamic New Year; Jul 1, Decentralisation Day; Aug 19, Prophet's Birthday; Dec 25, Christmas; plus all Muslim festivals which vary year to year.
Suriname	Jan 1; Ramadan; Easter; May 1, Labour Day; Jul 1, National Union Day; Nov 25, Independence Day; Dec 25, Christmas; plus all Muslim and Hindu holidays which vary year to year.
Sweden	Jan 1; Jan 6, Epiphany; Easter; May 1, Labour Day; Ascension Day; Whit Monday; Midsummer's Day; All Saints' Day; Dec 25; Dec 26.
Switzerland	Jan 1; Easter; Ascension Day; Whit Monday; Aug 1, National Day; Dec 25; Dec 26.
Syria	Jan 1; Ramadan; Mar 8, Revolution Day; Easter; Jun 10, Islamic New Year; Aug 19, Prophet's Birthday; Oct 6, Beginning of October War; Nov 16, National Day; Dec 25, Christmas; plus all Muslim holidays which vary year to year.
Taiwan	Jan 1, New Year and Founding Day; End of Jan, Chinese New Year; Mar 29, Youth Day; Apr 5, Women and Children's Day, Tomb Sweeping Day and Death of President Chiang Kai-shek; May 1, Labour Day; Jun 13, Dragon

Boat Festival; Sep 28, Teacher's Day; Oct 10, Double Tenth National Day; Oct 25, Retrocession Day; Oct 31, Birthday of Chiang Kai-shek (Veteran's Day) Nov 12, Dr Sun Yat Sen's Birthday; Dec 25, Constitution Day.

Tajikistan   Jan 1; Ramadan; Mar 21, Navrus; Sep 9, Independence Day.

Tanzania   Jan 12, Zanzibar Revolution Day; Feb 5, Chama Cha Mapinduzi Day; Ramadan; Easter; Apr 26, Union Day; May 1, International Labour Day; Jul 7, Saba Saba (Peasants's Day); Aug 19, Prophet's Birthday; Dec 9, Independence Day; Dec 25, Christmas; plus all Muslim holidays which vary year to year.

Thailand   Jan 1; Apr 12, the Songkran Festival (Buddhist New Year); May 5, Coronation Day; May 11, Royal Ploughing Ceremony; May, Visakhja Pua (Buddhist Festival); June/July, Buddhist Lent Begins; Aug 12, Queen's Birthday; Oct 23, Chulalongkorn Day; Dec 5, King's Birthday; Dec 31.

Tonga   Jan 1; Easter; Apr 25, ANZAC Day; May 4, Birthday of Crown Prince Tupouto'a; Jun 4, Independence Day; Jul 4, King's Birthday; Nov 4, Constitution Day; Dec 4 King Tupou I Day; Dec 25, Dec 26.

Trinidad and Tobago   Jan 1, Carnival; Easter, Whit Monday; Corpus Christi; Labour Day; first Monday in Aug, Discovery Day; Aug 31, Independence Day; Sept 24, Republic Day; Eid-Ul-Fitr (Muslim Festival), Divali (Hindu Festival); Dec 25; Dec 26.

Tunisia   Jan 1; Ramadan; Mar 20, Independence Day; Mar 21, Youth Day; Apr 19, Martyr's Day; May 1, Labour Day; Jun 25, Republic Day; Aug 13, Women's Day; Oct 15, Evacuation of Bizerta; Nov 7, Accession of President Ben Ali; plus all Muslim festivals which vary year to year.

Turkey   Jan 1; Apr 23, National Independence Children's Day; May 19, Youth and Sports Day; Aug 30, Victory Day (Anniversary of the Declaration of the Turkish Republic). plus all Muslim holidays which vary year to year.

Turkmenistan   Jan 1; Jan 12, Remembrance Day; Feb 19, Birthday of Turkmen President Sapurmurat Turkmenbashi; May 9, Victory Day; May 18, Day of Revival and Unity; Oct 27, Independence Day; plus all Muslim holidays which vary year to year.

Turks & Caicos   Jan 1; Mar 8, Commonwealth Day; Easter;May 30, National Hero's Day; Jun 11 HM the Queen's Birthday; Aug 1, Emancipation Day; Sep 30, National Youth Day; Oct 10, Columbus Day; Oct 24, International Human Rights Day; Dec 25; Dec 26.

Uganda   Jan 1; Easter; May 1, labour day; Jun 3, Martyr's Day; Jun 9, Hero's Day; Oct 9, Independence Day; Christmas.

Ukraine   Jan 1; Jan 7, Orthodox Christmas; Mar 8, International Women's Day; May 1, Labour Day; May 9, Victory Day; Aug 24, Independence Day.

United Arab Emirates   Jan 1; Ramadan Jun 6, Islamic New Year; Aug 6, Accession Day of HH Sheikh Zayed, President; Aug 18, Prophet's Birthday; Dec 2, National Day; plus all Muslim holidays which vary year to year.

United Kingdom   Jan 1; Easter; first and last Mon of May; last Mon in Aug; Christmas.

USA   Jan 1; Jan 17, Martin Luther King Day; Feb 21, President's Day; May 30, Memorial Day; Jul 4, Independence Day; Sep 5, Labor Day; Oct 10, Columbus Day; Nov 11, Veteran's Day; Thanksgiving; Christmas.

Uruguay	Jan 1; Jan 6; Carnival; Apr 19, Landing of the 33 Patriots; May 1, Labour Day; May 18, Battle of Las Piedras; June 19, Birth of Artigas; July 18, Constitution Day; Aug 25, Independence Day; Oct 12, Colombus Day; Nov 2, All Souls' Day; Dec 8, Blessing of the Waters; Dec 25.
Uzbekistan	Jan 1; Ramadan; Mar 8, International Women's Day; Sep 1, Independence Day; Dec 8, Constitution Day; plus all Muslim holidays which vary year to year.
Vanuatu	Jan 1; Easter; May 1, Labour Day; May 12, Ascension Day; Jul 30, Independence Day; Aug 15, Assumption; Oct 5, Constitution Day, Nov 29, Unity Day; Christmas.
Venezuela	Jan 1; Carnival; Easter; Apr 19, Declaration of Independence; May 1, Labour Day; Jun 24, Battle Of Carabobo; Jul 5, Independence Day; Jul 24, Birth of Simon Bolivar and Battle of Lago de Maracaibo; Sep 4, Civil Servant's day; Oct 12, Columbus Day; Christmas.
Virgin Islands (US)	Jan 1; Jan 6, Three Kings Day; Jan 17, Martin Luther King's Birthday; Feb 21, President's Day; Mar 31, Transfer Day; Easter; Apr, Carnival; May 30, Memorial Day; Jun 20, Organic Act Day; Jul 3, Emancipation Day; Jul 4, Independence Day; Sep 5, Labor Day; Oct 10, Columbus Day; Oct 17, Virgin Island's Thanksgiving Day; Nov 1, Liberty Day; Nov 11, Veteran's Day; Christmas.
Yemen	Jan 1; Ramadan; Mar 8, International Women's Day; May 1, Labour Day; Jun 10, Islamic New Year; Jun 13, Corrective Movement Anniversary; Jun 19, Ashoura; Aug 19, Prophet's Birthday; Oct 14, National Day; plus all Muslim holidays which vary year to year.
Yugoslavia	(Serbia and Montenegro) Jan 1; Jan 2; May 1-2, Labour Days; Jul 4, Fighter's Day; Jul 7, Serbian National Day; Jul 13, Montenegrin National Day; Nov 29-30, Republic Days.
Democratic Rep. of Congo (Zaire)	Jan 1; Jan 4, Day of the Martyr's of Independence; May 1, Labour Day; May 20, Anniversary of the Movement Populaire de la Revolution; Jun 24, Day of the Fisherman; Jun 30, Independence Day; Aug 1, Parent's Day; Oct 14, Youth Day; Oct 27, Anniversary of the name Zaire; Nov 17, Army Day; Nov 24, Anniversary of the Second Republic; Dec 25.
Zambia	Jan 1; Mar 11, Youth Day; Easter; May 1, Labour Day; May 24, African Freedom Day; Jul 5, Hero's Day; Jul 8, Unity Day; Aug 5, Farmer's Day; Oct 24, Independence Day; Dec 25; Dec 26.
Zimbabwe	Jan 1; Easter; Apr 18, Independence Day; May 1, Worker's Day; May 25, African Day; Aug 11, Hero's Day; Aug 12, Armed Forces Day; Christmas.

BUSINESS HOURS WORLD-WIDE

Afghanistan	08.00-12.00, 13.00-16.30 Sat-Wed; 08.30-13.30 Thurs.
Albania	07.00-14.00 Mon-Sat, 17.00-20.00 Mon-Tue, Apr-Sept; 07.00-14.30 Mon-Sat, 16.00-19.00 Mon-Tue, Oct-Mar.
Algeria	08.00-12.00, 14.00-17.30 Sat-Wed.
Andorra	09.00-13.00, 15.00-18.45 Mon-Fri.
Angola	07.30-12.00, 14.30-18.00 Mon-Thu; 07.30-12.03, 14.30-17.30 Fri.

Anguilla	08.00-12.00, 13.00-16.00 Mon-Fri.
Antigua and Barbuda	08.00-12.00, 13.00-16.00 Mon-Fri.
Argentina	09.00-19.00 Mon-Fri.
Aruba	08.00-17.00 Mon-Fri.
Australia	09.00-17.30 Mon-Fri.
Austria	08.00-16.00 Mon-Fri.
Bahamas	09.00-17.00 Mon-Fri.
Bahrain	07.30-12.00, 14.30-1800 Sat-Thurs.
Bangladesh	09.00-16.00 Sun-Thurs.
Barbados	08.00/08.30-16.00/16.30 Mon-Fri.
Belarus	09.00-18.00 Mon-Fri.
Belgium	08.30-17.30 Mon-Fri.
Belize	08.00-12.00, 13.00-17.00 Mon-Thurs; 08.30-12.00, 13.00 -16.45 Fri.
Benin	08.30-12.30, 15.00-18.30 Mon-Fri.
Bermuda	09.00-17.00 Mon-Fri.
Bolivia	08.00-12.00, 14.00-18.00 Mon-Fri.
Bonaire	08.00-12.00, 14.00-18.30 Mon-Fri.
Botswana	08.00-17.00 Mon-Fri, Apr-Oct; 07.30-16.30 Mon-Fri, Oct-Apr.
Brazil	09.00-18.00 Mon-Fri.
British Virgin Is	08.30-17.00 Mon-Fri.
Brunei	08.00-12.00, 13.00-17.00 Mon-Thurs; 08.00- 12.00 Sat.
Bulgaria	08.00-18.00 Mon-Sat.
Burkina Faso	08.00-12.30, 15.00-17.30 Mon-Fri.
Cambodia	07.30-12.00, 14.30-17.00 Mon-Fri.
Cameroon	08.00-12.00, 14.30-17.30 Mon-Fri.
Canada	09.00-17.00 Mon-Fri
Cayman Islands	08.30-17.00 Mon-Fri.
Central African Rep	06.30-13.30 Mon-Fri; 07.00-12.00 Sat.
Chad	07.30-14.00 Mon-Sat; 07.00-12.00 Fri
Chile	09.30-18.00 Mon-Fri; 09.00-13.00 Sat.
China	08.00-12.00, 14.00-18.00 Mon-Sat.
Colombia	08.00-12.00, 14.00-17.30 Mon-Fri.
Comoro Islands	07.30-17.30 Mon-Thurs; 07.30-11.00 Fri.
Congo	08.00-12.00, 15.00-18.00 Mon-Fri; 07.00-12.00 Sat.
Cook Islands	08.00-16.00 Mon-Fri.
Costa Rica	08.00-11.30, 13.30-17.30 Mon-Fri.
Cote d'Ivoire	07.30-12.00, 14.30-17.30 Mon-Fri; 08.00-12.00 Sat.
Croatia	08.00-16.00 Mon-Fri.
Cuba	08.30-12.30, 13.30-17.30 Mon-Fri.
Curaçao	08.00-12.00, 13.30-16.30 Mon-Fri.
Cyprus	08.00-13.00, 16.00-19.00 Mon-Fri; half-day Wed.
Czech Republic	08.00-16.00 Mon-Fri.
Denmark	09.00-17.00 Mon-Fri.
Djibouti	06.30-13.00 Sat-Thurs.
Dominica	08.00-13.00, 14.00-16.00 Mon-Fri.
Dominican Rep.	08.30-12.00, 14.00-18.00 Mon-Fri.
Ecuador	09.00-13.00, 15.00-19.00 Mon-Fri; 08.30-12.30 Sat.
Egypt	09.00- 14.00 Sat-Thurs.
El Salvador	08.00-12.30, 14.30-17.30 Mon-Fri.
Equatorial Guinea	08.00-17.00 Mon-Fri.
Eritrea	08.00-12.00, 14.00-17.00 Mon-Fri; 08.00-14.00 Sat.
Estonia	08.30-18.30 Mon-Fri.
Ethiopia	08.00-12.00, 13.00-16.00 Mon-Fri;.08.00-12.00 Sat.
Fiji	08.00-16.30 Mon-Fri.
Finland	08.00-16.15 Mon-Fri.
France	09.00-12.00, 14.00-18.00 Mon-Fri.
French Guiana	08.00-13.00, 15.00-18.00 Mon-Fri.
French Polynesia	07.30-17.00 Mon-Fri.
Gabon	07.30-12.00, 14.30-18.00 Mon-Fri.
Gambia	09.00-16.00 Mon-Thurs; 08.00-12.00 Fri, Sat.

Germany	08.00-16.00 Mon-Fri.
Ghana	08.00-12.00, 14.00-17.00 Mon-Fri.
Gibraltar	09.00-13.00, 15.00-18.00 Mon-Fri.
Greece	09.00-18.00 Mon-Fri.
Greenland	09.00-15.00 Mon-Fri.
Grenada	08.00-12.00, 13.00-16.00 Mon-Fri.
Guadeloupe	08.00-17.00 Mon-Fri; 08.00-12.00 Sat.
Guatemala	08.00-18.00 Mon-Fri; 08.00-12.00 Sat.
Guernsey	09.00-17.00 Mon-Fri.
Guinea	08.00-16.30 Mon-Thurs; 08.00-13.00 Fri.
Guinea-Bissau	08.00-16.30 Mon-Thurs; 08.00-13.00 Fri.
Guyana	08.00-12.00, 13.00-16.30 Mon-Fri.
Haiti	07.00-16.00 Mon-Fri.
Honduras	08.00-12.00, 14.00-17.00 Mon-Fri; 08.00-11.00 Sat.
Hong Kong	09.00-13.00, 14.00-17.00 Mon-Fri; 09.00-12.30 Sat.
Hungary	08.30-17.00 Mon-Fri.
Iceland	09.00-17.00 Mon-Fri.
India	09.30-17.30 Mon-Fri; 09.30-13.00 Sat.
Indonesia	07.00/09.00-15.00/17.00 Mon-Fri.
Iran	08.00-14.00 Sat-Wed; 08.00-13.00 Thurs.
Iraq	08.00-14.00 Sat-Wed; 08.00-13.00 Thurs.
Ireland	09.00-17.30 Mon-Fri.
Israel	08.00-13.00, 15.00-18.00 Sun-Thurs.
Italy	09.00-13,00, 14.00-18.00 Mon-Fri.
Jamaica	08.30-16.30/17.00 Mon-Sat.
Japan	09.00-17.00 Mon-Fri.
Jersey	09.00/09.30-17.00/17.30 Mon-Fri.
Jordan	08.00-13.00, 15.30-18.00 Sat-Thurs
Kenya	08.00-13.00, 14.00-17.00 Mon-Fri; 08.30-12.00 Sat.
Kiribati	08.00-12.30, 13.30-16.15 Mon-Fri.
Korea (South)	08.30-18.00 Mon-Fri; 09.00-13.00 Sat.
Kuwait	08.00-13.00, 16.00-20.00 Sat-Thurs, winter; 08.00-13.00, 15.00-19.00 Sat-Wed, summer.
Kyrgyzstan	09.00-17.30 Mon-Fri.
Laos	08.00-12.00, 14.00-17.00 Mon-Fri; 08.00-12.00 Sat.
Latvia	08.30-17.30 Mon-Fri.
Lebanon	08.00-13.00 Mon-Sat, summer; 08.30-12.30, 15.00-18.00 Mon-Fri, 08.30-12.30 Sat, winter.
Lesotho	08.00-13.00, 14.00-16.30 Mon-Fri; 08.00-13.00 Sat.
Liberia	08.00-12.00, 14.00-16.00 Mon-Fri.
Libya	07.00-14.00 Sat-Thurs.
Liechtenstein	08.00-12.00, 14.00-18.00 Mon-Fri.
Lithuania	09.00-13.00, 14.00-18.00 Mon-Fri
Luxembourg	08.30-17.30 Mon-Fri.
Macau	09.00-17.00 Mon-Fri; 09.00-13.00 Sat.
Macedonia	07.00/08.00-15.00/16.00 Mon-Fri.
Madagascar	07.30-17.00 Mon-Fri; 07.30-11.30 Sat.
Malawi	07.30-17.00 Mon-Fri.
Malaysia	08.30-16.30 Mon-Fri; 08.30-12.30 Sat.
Maldives	07.30-13.30 Sat-Thurs.
Mali	07.30-12.30, 13.00-16.00 Mon-Thur; 07.30-12.30, 14.30-17.30 Fri.
Malta	08.30-12.45, 14.30-17.30 Mon-Fri; 08.30-12.00 Sat.
Martinique	08.00-17.00 Mon-Fri; 08.00-12.00 Sat.
Mauritania	08.00-15.00 Sat-Wed; 08.00-13.00 Thurs.
Mauritius	09.00-16.00 Mon-Fri; 09.00-12.00 Sat.
Mexico	08.00-15.00 Mon-Fri.
Monaco	09.00-12.00, 14.00-17.00 Mon-Fri.
Mongolia	09.00-18.00 Mon-Fri; 09.00-15.00 Sat.
Montserrat	08.00-12.00, 13.00-16.00 Mon-Fri.
Morocco	08.30-18.30 Mon-Fri.

Mozambique	08.00-12.00, 14.00-17.00 Mon-Fri; 08.00-12.00 Sat.
Myanmar	09.30-16.30 Mon-Fri.
Namibia	07.30-16.30/17.00 Mon-Fri.
Nepal	10.00-17.00 Sun-Fri, summer; 10.00-16.00 Sun-Fri, winter.
Netherlands	08.30-17.00 Mon-Fri.
New Caledonia	07.30-11.30, 13.30-17.30 Mon-Fri; 07.30-11.30 Sat.
New Zealand	09.00-17.00 Mon-Fri.
Nicaragua	08.00-12.00, 14.30-17.30 Mon-Fri; 08.00-13.00 Sat.
Niger	07.30-12.30, 15.30-18.30 Mon-Sat; 07.30-12.30 Sat.
Nigeria	07.30-15.30 Mon-Fri.
Niue	07.30-15.00 Mon-Thurs; 07.30-16.00 Fri.
Norway	08.00-16.00 Mon-Fri.
Oman	08.30-13.00, 16.00-19.00 Sat-Wed; 08.00-13.00 Thur.
Pakistan	09.00-16.00 Sat-Thur.
Panama	08.00-12.00, 14.00-17.00 Mon-Fri.
Papua New Guinea	08.00-17.00 Mon-Fri.
Paraguay	08.00-12.00, 15.00-17.30/19.00 Mon-Fri; 08.00-12.00 Sat.
Peru	09.00-17.00 Mon-Fri.
Philippines	08.00-12.00, 13.00-17.00 Mon-Fri.
Poland	07.00-16.00 Mon-Fri.
Portugal	09.00-13.00, 15.00-19.00 Mon-Fri.
Puerto Rico	08.30-16.30 Mon-Fri.
Qatar	07.30-12.00, 15.00-18.00 Sat-Thurs
Reunion	08.00-12.00, 14.00-18.00 Mon-Fri.
Romania	07.00-15.30 Mon-Fri; 07.00-12.30 Sat.
Russian Federation	09.00-18.00/19.00 Mon-Fri.
Rwanda	08.00-16.00 Mon-Fri; 08.00-12.00 Sat.
Saba	08.00-12.00, 13.30-16.30 Mon-Fri.
St Eustatius	08.00-12.00, 13.30-16.30 Mon-Fri.
St Kitts & Nevis	08.00-12.00, 13.00-16.00 Mon-Sat.
St Lucia	08.00-16.00 Mon-Fri.
St Maarten	08.00-12.00, 13.30-16.30 Mon-Fri.
St Vincent and	
The Grenadines	08.00-12.00, 13.00-16.00 Mon-Fri; 08.00-12.00 Sat.
Saudi Arabia	09.00-13.00, 16.30-20.00 Sat-Thurs.
Senegal	08.00-12.00, 14.30-18.00 Mon-Fri; 08.00-12.00 Sat.
Seychelles	08.00-12.00, 13.00-16.00 Mon-Fri.
Sierra Leone	08.00-12.00, 14.00-16.45 Mon-Fri.
Singapore	09.00-17.00 Mon-Fri; 09.00-13.00 Sat.
Slovak Republic	08.00-16.00 Mon-Fri.
Slovenia	07.00-15.00 Mon-Fri.
Solomon Islands	08.00-12.00, 13.00-16.30 Mon-Fri; 07.30-12.00 Sat.
Somalia	08.00-12.30, 16.30-19.00 Sat-Thurs.
South Africa	08.30-16.30 Mon-Fri.
Spain	09.00-18.45 Mon-Fri winter; 09.00-14.00, 16.00-19.00 Mon-Fri, summer.
Sri Lanka	08.30/09.00-16.30/17.00 Mon-Fri.
Sudan	07.30-14.30 Sat-Thurs.
Suriname	07.00-15.00 Mon-Fri; 07.00-14.30 Sat.
Swaziland	08.00-13.00, 14.00-17.00 Mon-Fri; 08.00-13.00 Sat.
Sweden	09.00-17.00 Mon-Fri.
Switzerland	08.00-12.00, 14.00-17.00 Mon-Fri.
Syria	08.00-14.30 Sat-Thurs.
Taiwan	08.30-17.30 Mon-Fri; 08.30-12.30 Sat.
Tajikistan	09.00-17.00/18.00 Sat-Thurs.
Tanzania	07.30-14.30 Mon-Fri; 07.30-12.00 Sat.
Thailand	08.30-16.30 Mon-Fri.
Togo	07.30-12.00, 14.30-17.30 Mon-Fri.
Tonga	08.30-16.30 Mon-Fri; 08.00-12.00 Sat.
Trinidad and Tobago	08.00-16.00 Mon-Fri.
Tunisia	08.00-12.30, 14.30-18.00 Mon-Fri; 08.00-12.00 Sat, winter; 07.00-13.00

	Mon-Sat, summer.
Turkey	08.30-12.00-13.00-17.30 Mon-Fri.
Turks and Caicos Is.	08.00-13.00, 14.00-16.30 Mon-Fri; 08.00-12.00 Sat.
Uganda	08.00-12.30, 14.00-16.30 Mon-Fri.
Ukraine	09.00-13.00, 14.30-17.00/18.00 Mon-Fri.
United Arab Emirates	08.00-13.00, 16.00-19.00 Sat-Wed; 07.00-12.00 Thurs.
United Kingdom	09.00/09.30-17.00/17.30 Mon-Fri.
United States	09.00-17.30 Mon-Fri.
Uruguay	08.30-12.00, 14.30-18.30/19.00 Mon-Fri.
Uzbekistan	09.00-17.00 Sat-Thurs.
Vanuatu	07.30-11.30, 1330-16.30 Mon-Fri.
Venezuela	08.00-18.00 Mon-Fri (long lunch).
Vietnam	07.30-12.00, 13.00-16.30 Mon-Fri; 08.00-12.30 Sat.
Western Samoa	08.00-12.00, 13.00-16.30 Mon-Fri.
Yemen	08.00-12.30, 16.00-19.00 Mon-Wed; 08.00-11.00 Thurs.
Yugoslavia (Serbia and Montenegro)	07.00-14.30 Mon-Fri.
Zaire (DRC)	07.30-17.00 Mon-Fri; 07.30-12.00 Sat.
Zambia	08.00-13.00, 14.00-17.00 Mon-Fri.
Zimbabwe	08.00-16.30 Mon-Fri.

Note: These are only the official hours, and generally apply to the capital. There will be considerable variation according to area and the size of the business. Banking hours tend to be shorter. Further Reading: *World Travel Guide* (Columbus Press) ■

FINDING OUT MORE
Section 2

RECOMMENDED BOOK AND MAP RETAILERS

Austicks Map Shop
91 The Headrow
Leeds LS1 8EH
Tel: **01132-452326**
Best travel bookshop in Yorkshire. A large map selection including large-scale Ordnance Survey maps.

Blackwell Map & Travel Bookshop
50 Broad Street
Oxford OX1 3BU
Tel: **01865 792792**
An excellent selection of books and knowledgeable staff.

The Booksellers' Association
Minster House
272-4 Vauxhall Bridge Road
London SW1W 1BA
Tel: **0171-834 5477**
email: 100437.2261@compuserve.com
Publishes an annual directory of members detailing information on bookshops nationwide.

Books Etc.
120 Charing Cross Road
London WC2H 0JR
Tel: **0171-379 6838**

The British Cartographic Society
Hon Membership Secretary
JK Atherton
12 Elworthy Drive
Wellington
Somerset TA21 9AT
Tel: **01823-663 965**

Compendium Bookshop
234 Camden High Street
London NW1 8QS
Tel: **0171-485 8944**
A useful source of books which are difficult to obtain elsewhere.

Daunt Books
83 Marylebone High Street
London W1M 3DE
Tel: **0171-224 2295**
Large and comprehensive travel bookshop which stocks all the usual guide series as well as backlisted titles, second-hand, out of print novels, political histories and biographies. Mail order service available.

Dillons
82 Gower Street
London WC1E 6EQ
Tel: 0171-636 1577
Has a good travel section in the basement. Branches throughout the UK.

Foyles
Travel Department
Ground Floor
119 Charing Cross Road
London WC2H 0EB
Tel: **0171-437 5660**
Mail order or in person only.

The Good Book Guide
24 Seward Street
London EC1V 3PB
Tel: **0171-490 0900**
World-wide mail order service based on selection featured in the Good Book Guide catalogue.

Hatchards
187 Piccadilly
London W1V 0LE
Tel: **0171-439 9921**

Heffers
20 Trinity Street
Cambridge CB2 1TY
Tel: **01223-568400**
Very good selection of travel guides and books.

Heffers Map Shop
19 Sidney Street
Cambridge CB2 3HL
Tel: **01223-568400**
Leading map sellers for the region.

Latitude
34 The Broadway
Darkes Lane
Potters Bar
Herts EN6 2HW
Tel: **01707-663090**
Map and globe specialist which also produces a mail order catalogue.

Map Marketing
92-104 Carnwath Road
London SW6 3HW
Tel: **0171-736 0297**
Offer a range of over 400 laminated maps, framed or unframed. The range includes world maps, individual country maps and over 300 section maps of the UK.

The Map Shop
15 High Street
Upton-upon-Severn
Worcestershire WR8 OHJ
Tel: **01684-593146**
email: themapshop@btinternet.com
Agents for Ordnance Survey, large-scale maps and guides for Europe and other areas world-wide –in stock or to order. Send for free catalogue stating area of interest.

The National Map Centre
22-24 Caxton Street
London SW1H 0QU
Tel: **0171-222 2466**
Main agent for Ordnance Survey maps, and retailers for all major publishers. Also the retail outlet for cartographic printing company, Cook, Hammond & Kell Ltd.

Nomad
781 Fulham Road
London SW6 5HA
Tel: **0171-736 4000**
Basement devoted to travel guides, literature and history.

Dick Phillips
Whitehall House
Nenthead
Alston
Cumbria CA9 3PS

Tel: **01434-381440**
Specialises in books and maps of Iceland and Faroe.

Nigel Press Associates Ltd
Crockham Park
Edenbridge
Kent TN8 6SR
Tel: **01732-865023**
Offers a free service to bona fide expeditions supplying satellite images. They have a large archive covering most parts of the world.

Rallymaps of West Wellow
PO Box 11
Romsey
Hampshire S051 8XX
Tel: **01794-515444**
Mail order specialists for Ordnance Survey.

Stanfords
12-14 Long Acre
London WC2 9LP
Tel: **0171-836 1321**
and…
c/o British Airways
156 Regent Street
London W1R 5TA
Tel: **0171-434 4744**
The largest map seller in the world carrying a wide range of maps, globes, charts and atlases, including Ordnance Survey and Directorate of Overseas Surveys.

John Smith & Son Ltd
57 St Vincent Street
Glasgow G2 5TB
Tel: **0141-221 7472**
Ordnance Survey agents for western Scotland. Foreign and Michelin maps.

Trailfinders Travel Centre
194-196 Kensington High Street
London W8 7RG
Tel: **0171-938 3999**
Stocks a wide range of guides and maps as well as travel equipment.

The Travel Bookshop
13 Blenheim Crescent
London W11 2EE
Tel: **0171-229 5260**
Provide a 'complete package' for the traveller, including regional guides, histories, cookery books, relevant fiction and so on. They also stock old and new maps and topographical prints.

Waterstones
91 Deansgate
Manchester M3 2BW
Tel: **0161-832 1992**

Whitemans Bookshop
7 Orange Grove
Bath BA1 1LP
Tel: **01225 464029**
An extensive range of guide books and maps, atlases, walking guides, natural history guides and so on.

YHA Bookshops
14 Southampton Street
London WC2E 7HY
Tel: **0171-836 8541**
Books, maps and guides for backpackers, hostellers, adventure sportsmen and budget travellers.

Further reading:
***Sheppards Book Dealers in the British Isles –A* Directory of Antique and Second Hand Book Dealers** (Richard Joseph, £24)
This very useful reference work includes a section on topography and travel and will be very helpful for anyone looking for rare or out of print travel books, etc.
Also publishes guides to North America; Europe; Australia and New Zealand; India and the Orient; Japan; International Printed Map-sellers.

Books on the WEB:
www.AdventurousTraveler.com
www.amazon.com
www.bookshop.co.uk

BOOK AND MAP PUBLISHERS AND DISTRIBUTORS

AA Publishing
Norfolk House
Priestly Road
Basingstoke
Hants RG21 2EA
Tel: **01256-493581**
Guide and map publishers and distributors including the Baedeker guides.

John Bartholomew/Times
77-85 Fulham Palace Road
London W6 8JB
Tel: **0181-741 7070**
Publish tourist, road, topographic/general maps and atlases and guides.

B.T.Batsford Ltd
4 Fitzhardinge Street
London W1H 0AH
Tel: **0171-486 8484**
Guides and topographical publications.

BBC Books
80 Wood Lane
London W12 0TT
Tel: **0181-576 2000**
Publishes books related to television and radio series, and more. Also publishes language learning books and materials.

A & C Black
35 Bedford Row
London WC1R 4JH
Tel: **0171-242 0946**
Publishes the Blue Guide series.

BFP Books
Focus House
497 Green Lanes
London N13 4BP
Tel: **0181-882 3315**
Fax: 0181 886 5174
Publish The Freelance Photographer's Market Handbook

Bradt Publications
41 Nortoft Road
Chalfont St Peter
Bucks SL9 0LA
Tel: **01494-873478**
Publish a comprehensive range of travel guides aimed at the more adventurous or backpacking traveller.

Cadogan
3rd Floor
27-29 Berwick Street
London W1V 3RF
Tel: **0171-287 6555**
Publishes the Cadogan travel guide series.

Century
Random House
20 Vauxhall Bridge Road
London SW1V 2SA
Tel: **0171-973 9670**
Publishes a regular flow of travel narratives.

Chatto & Windus Ltd
Random Century House
20 Vauxhall Bridge Road
London SW1V 2SA
Tel: **0171-973 9740**
Includes archaeology and travel titles.

Cicerone Press
2 Police Square
Milnthorpe
Cumbria LA7 7PY
Tel: **01539-562069**
Publishers of books on outdoor activities including climbing and walking.

The Crowood Press
The Stable Block
Crowood Lane
Ramsbury
Marlborough
Wilts SN8 2HR
Tel: **01672-520320**
Mountaineering and climbing books.

Department of Defense and Mapping Agency
Hydrographic/Topographic Center
Washington DC 20315
USA
Publish charts of oceans and coasts of all areas of the world and pilot charts. Supply maps or photocopies of maps on request provided that the exact area is specified.

Footprint Handbooks
6 Riverside Court
Lower Bristol Road
Bath BA2 3DZ
Tel: **01225-469141**
Fax 01225 469461
email:**handbooks@footprint.cix.co.uk**
http://**www.footprint-handbooks.co.uk**
Guidebooks for the independent traveller. They cover Latin America - including the famous South American Handbook - Caribbean, India and the rest of South East Asia, Africa, Middle East and Europe.

Globe Pequot Press
PO Box 833
6 Business Park Road
Old Saybrook
CT 06475-0833 USA
Tel: **860-395 0440**
email: **info@globe-pequot.com**
http:// **www.globe-pequot.com**
Good travel-only publisher. Extensive range of books on North America.

Hippocrene Books
171 Madison Avenue
New York
NY 10016
USA
Tel: **718-454 2366**
Publishers of travel guides, international literature and dictionaries with an extensive backlist.

Hodder Headline
338 Euston Road
London NW1 3BH
Tel: **0171-873 6000**
Publish numerous mountaineering and climbing narratives as well as the Which? travel guides.

Hydrographic Department
MOD (Navy)

Admiralty Way
Taunton
Somerset TA1 2DN
Tel: **01823-337900**
Publishes world series of Admiralty Charts and hydrographic publications. Available from appointed Admiralty Chart Agencies.

Insight Guides
81 The Cut
Waterloo
London SE1 8LL
Tel: **0171-620 0008**

Institut Géographique National
170 Rue la Boétie
75008 Paris
France
Tel: **(331) 42 56 06 68**
Mail Order Sales for Individuals. Publish and sell maps of France and very many of the former French possessions.

Kummerly und Frey Ltd
Alpenstrasse 58
30-52 Zollekofen
Switzerland
Tel: **31 915 2211**
Publish charts and political, topographic, road and other maps.

Roger Lascelles
47 York Road
Brentford
Middlesex TW8 0QP
Tel: **0181-847 0935**
Guide and map publisher and distributor. Catalogue published twice a year, extensive selection.

Lonely Planet Publications
10 Barley Mow Passage
Chiswick
London W4 4PH
Tel: **0181-742 3161**
email: **lonelyplanetuk@compuserve.com**
http://**www.lonelyplanet.com/**
One of the world's largest guide book publishers. Extensive selection of off-beat destinations.

Rand McNally & Co
8255 North Central Park
Skokie
Illinois 60076
Tel: 847 329 8100
Large American publisher of maps, atlases, guides and globes.

Michelin Maps & Guides
Edward Hyde Building
38 Clarendon Road
Watford WD1 1SX

Tel: **01923-415000**
Publish excellent maps and the famous Red and Green Guides.

John Murray
50 Albermarle Street
London W1X 4BD
Tel: **0171-493 4361**
Publishes the Literary Companion series and an excellent selection of travel literature.

Moon Publications
722 Wall Street
Chico
CA 95928-9960
USA
Tel: **916-345 5473**
Publishers of the Moon Handbook series.

National Geographic Society
1145 17th Street North West
Washington DC 20036
USA
Tel: **202-857 7000**
Publish mainly topographical maps to accompany National Geographic magazine. Also sell wall, relief and archaeological maps, atlases and globes. Also magazines and books.

NOAA Distribution Branch
N/CG33
National Ocean Service
Riverdale
Maryland 20737
USA
The National Ocean Service (NOS) publishes and distributes aeronautical charts of the US. Charts of foreign areas are published by the Defense Mapping Agency Aerospace Center (DMAAC) and are sold by the NOS.

Ordnance Survey
Romsey Road
Maybush
Southampton SO16 4GU
Tel: **01703-775555**
The official mapping agency for the UK. The Overseas Surveys Directorate at the same address publishes maps of former and current British possessions.

Pallas Athene Publications
59 Linden Gardens
London W2 4HJ
Tel: **0171-229 2798**
Historical and cultural guides to European cities.

Passport Books
NTC/Contemporary Publishing
4255 West Tonky Avenue
Lincolnwood

Illinois 60646-1975 USA
Tel: **847-679 5500**

George Philip & Son Ltd
Michelin House
81 Fulham Road
London SW3 6RB
Tel: **0171-581 9393**
Publish a wide range of topographical and thematic maps, globes, atlases and charts, and some guides.

RAC Publishing
RAC House
PO Box 100
Bartlett Street, South Croydon
Surrey CR2 6XW
Tel: **0181-686 0088**
Publishers of guides, handbooks and maps for motorists and travellers in the UK and on the continent.

Reed Travel Group
Church Street
Dunstable
Beds LU5 4HB
Tel: **01582-600111**
Publishes a comprehensive range of guides geared towards the professional travel planner.

Regenbogen-Verlag
Bodmerstrasse 9
8027 Zurich
Switzerland
Tel: **1 201 3676**
Switzerland and c/o Los Amigos del Libro Casilla Postal 450 Cochabamba Bolivia. Publish books for the independent traveller.

Rough Guides
1 Mercer Street
London WC2H 9QJ
Tel: **0171-379 3329**
email: *mail@roughguides.co.uk*
http://**www.roughguides.com**

Royal Geographical Society
Publications Dept.
1 Kensington Gore
London SW7 2AR
Tel: **0171-591 3000**
email: **maps@rgs.org**
Sells maps originally published in the Geographical Journal and maps published separately by the Society. Special edition photographs are also available from the library.

Springfield Books Ltd
Norman Road Denby Dale
Huddersfield
W Yorks HD8 8TH
Tel: **01484-864955** ⇨

Publishers and distributors of maps and guides, including the Freytag & Berndt maps.

Thames and Hudson
30-34 Bloomsbury Street
London WC1B 3QP
Tel: **0171-636 5488**
Publishers of numerous illustrated, large format books on travel ranging from the academic to the exotic.

Ulysses Travel Publications
4176 St. Denis
Montréal
Quebec H2W 2M5
Canada
Tel: **514-843 9882**
Guidebooks for independent travellers. Bookstores in Montréal and Toronto.

**US Department of the Interior
Geological Survey**
Earth Science Information Center (ESIC)
507 National Center
Reston
VA 20192
USA
Tel: **703-648 5577**
Information about maps and related data for US areas.

Vacation Work Publications
9 Park End Street
Oxford OX1 1HJ
Tel: **01865-241 978**
Publishers of books for budget travellers and for anyone wanting to work or study abroad.

Wilderness Press
2440 Bancroft Way
Berkeley
CA 94704
USA
Tel: **415-843 8080**
Natural history, adventure travel guides and maps of North America. All mail order, including from abroad, to be paid in US dollars.

PERIODICALS

African Affairs
Prof. P. Woodward
Dept of Politics
University of Reading
PO Box 218
Reading, Berks
RG 6 6AA
Tel: **01734-875123**
Quarterly journal, featuring learned articles on contemporary African issues.

Australian Gourmet Traveller
Australian Consolidated Press
PO Box 4088
54 Park Street
Sydney
NSW 2000
Tel: **29-282 8000**
Consumer publication for travellers who enjoy their food.

BBC Wildlife Magazine
Broadcasting House
Whiteladies Road
Bristol BS8 2LR
Tel: **0117-9732211**
Monthly wildlife and conservation issues world-wide.

BBC On Air Magazine
BBC World Service
227 NW Bush House
The Strand
London WC2B 4PH
Tel: **0171-257 2875**
Monthly magazine with world outlook and full radio and television guide.

Bulletin Voyages
78 St. Joseph West
Montreal H2T 3A5
Canada
Tel: **514-287 9773**

Business Traveller
Compass House
22 Redan Place
London W2 4SZ
Tel: **0171-229 7799**
A monthly magazine aimed at the business traveller and featuring airfare cost-cutting information that will show quickly and clearly how to save your air travel costs.

Canadian Geographic
39 McArthur Avenue
Vanier
Ontario K1L 8L7
Canada
Tel: **613-745 4629**

Camping and Caravanning
Greenfields House
Westwood Way
Coventry CV4 8JH
Tel: **01203-694995**
Monthly journal for enthusiasts.

Camping Magazine
Link House
Dingwall Avenue
Croydon CR9 2TA
Tel: **0181-686 2559**

Monthly magazine focusing on walking and camping for the family.

Condé Nast Traveller
Vogue House
1 Hanover Square
London W1R0AD
Tel: **0171-499 9080**
or 360 Madison Avenue
New York
NY 10017
USA
Tel: **212 880 7688**

Consumer Reports Travel Letter
301 Junipero Serra Blvd
Suite 200
San Francisco
CA 94127
USA
Tel: **415-239 6001**
Comprehensive examination of major travel questions, with company-by-company, comparisons of competitive travel services. Feature length articles on places and issues.

Essentially America, Lifestyle and Travel Magazine
Phoenix Publishing and Media Ltd
18-20 Scrutton Street
London EC2 4RJ
Tel: **0171-247 0537**
Bi-monthly consumer magazine covering lifestyle and travel in the USA and Canada.

Executive Travel
Church Street
Dunstable LU5 4HB
Tel: **01582-600111**
Monthly business travel publication.

Explore
Suite 400
301-14 St N.W.
Calgary
Alberta
Canada T2N 2A1
Tel: **403-270 8890**
Quarterly colour magazine devoted to adventure travel world-wide.

The Explorers Journal
The Explorers' Club
46 East 70th St
New York
NY 10021
USA
Tel: **212-799 6473**
email: **EXJOURNAL@aol.com**
Official quarterly of The Explorers Club. Established 1904. Interdisciplinary in scope, highlights all areas of exploration work.

Flight International
Reed Business Information
Oakfield House
Perrymount Road
Haywards Heath
West Sussex RH16 3DH
Tel: **0181-402 8491**
Highly respected weekly journal covering everything to do with the aviation industry – both commercial and military.

Geographical
Unit 2, Utopia Village
7 Chalcott Street
London NW1 8LX
Tel: **0171-938 4011**
email: **geogmag@gn.apc.org**
The Royal Geographical Society's monthly magazine.

Globe
The Globetrotters Club
BCM/Roving
London WC1N 3XX
Club newsletter. Featuring articles on individual experiences, news of 'members on the move', tips, mutual-aid column for members.

Great Expeditions
PO Box 64699
Station G
Vancouver
BC V6R 4GT
Canada
Tel: **604-734 3938**
For people who want to travel and explore, offers trips, a free classified ads service, discounts on books, an information exchange, articles and travel notes.

The Great Outdoors
The Plaza Tower
East Kilbride
Glasgow G74 1LW
Tel: **01355-246444**
Monthly publication featuring walking, backpacking and countryside matters.

Holiday Which?
2 Marylebone Road
London NW1 4DX
Tel: **0171-830 6000**
Quarterly publication published by the Consumers' Association, featuring destinations world-wide.

Islands
3886 State Street
Santa Barbara
CA 93105
USA ⇨

Tel: **805-682 7177**
Glossy colour title devoted to the world's islands, large and small.

International Travel News
Martin Publications Inc
2120 28th Street
Sacramento
CA 95818
USA
Tel: **916-457 3643**
News source for the business and/or pleasure traveller who often goes abroad. Contributions mostly from readers. Free sample copy on request.

The Lady
39-40 Bedford Street
The Strand
London WC2E 9ER
Tel: **0171-379 4717**
Classified ads in this weekly publication can be a useful source for self-catering accommodation and some overseas jobs.

Lonely Planet Newsletter
Lonely Planet Publications
10 Barley Mow Passage
Chiswick
London W4 4PA
Tel: **0181-742 3161**
Quarterly newsletter giving updates on all the LP guidebooks and lots of useful tips from other travellers.

Mountain Biking UK
Beaufort Court
30 Monmouth St
Bath BA1 2AP
Tel: **01225-442244**
Monthly publication for mountain bikers.

National Geographic
National Geographic Society
17th and Main St, NW
Washington DC 20036
Tel: **202-857 7000**

National Geographic Traveller
3000 University Center
Tampa
Florida 33612
USA
Tel: **813-979 6625**
Quarterly consumer title from the National Geographic stable devoted to travel and destination reports.

Nomad
BCM-Nomad
London WC1V 6XX
Newsletter aimed at people on the move and
written by peripatetic publisher, with many readers' reports.

Official Airlines Guide (OAG)
World Timetable Centre
Church Street
Dunstable
Bedfordshire
LU5 4HB
Tel: **01582-600111**
Monthly airline timetable in pocket format, aimed at the consumer.

The Outrigger
c/o Pacific Islands Society
Tom Hughes
Alpines
Franklands Village
Haywards Heath
Sussex RH16 3RL

Outside Magazine
Chicago
IL 60610
USA
Tel: **312-222 1100**
Aimed at the active adult, it is a contemporary lifestyle magazine that features sports, fitness, photography, adventure travel and portraits of men and women adventurers.

The Railway Magazine
King's Reach Tower
Stamford Street
London SE1 9LS
Tel: **0171-261 5533**
Monthly title established in 1897.

Resident Abroad
Greystoke Place
Fetter Lane
London EC4A 1ND
Tel: **0171-405 6969**
Monthly publication for British expatriates.

Rough Notes
Rough Guides
1 Mercer Street
London WC2H 9QJ
Tel: **0171-379 3329**
The new newsletter of the Rough Guides series. Three issues a year.

The South American Explorer
South American Explorers Club
Casilla 3714
Lima 100
Peru
Official journal of the South American Explorers Club. Accounts of scientific studies, adventure, and sports activities in South America.

South East Asia Traveller
Compass Publishing
336 Smith Street
04-303 New Bridge Centre
Chinatown
Singapore 0105
Tel: **221 1111**
Glossy title geared at frequent and business travellers to the region.

Thrifty Traveler Newsletter
Traveling Free Publications Inc.
P.O. Box 8168
Clearwater
Florida 34618
USA
Tel: **813-447 4731**
Monthly newsletter for the thrifty traveller.

Time Off
Time Off Publications
60 Berwick Street
Fortitude Valley
QLD 4006
Australia
Tel: **7-252 9761**

Travel and Leisure
1120 Avenue of the Americas
New York
NY 10036
USA
Tel: **212-382 5600**

Travel Trade Gazette
Morgan Grampian Plc
30 Calderwood St
London SE18 6QH
Tel: **0181-855 7777**
Oldest weekly UK travel industry newspaper.

Traveller
WEXAS International
45-49 Brompton Road
Knightsbridge
London SW3 1DE
Tel: **0171-581 4130**
Quarterly publication established in 1970 as Expedition. Photo-features on travel, mostly outside western Europe. Letters, news, book reviews, travel photography and medical advice.

Travel Smart
40 Beechdale Road
Dobbs Ferry
NY 10522
USA
Tel: **914-693 8300**
Travel Smart newsletter for sophisticated travellers who expect honest value for their money. Also discount-cruises, super-charters, hotel,

car rentals, etc., for members.

Travltips
PO Box 580188
Flushing
NY 11358
USA
Tel: **718-939 2400**
First person accounts of freighter and passenger ship travel to all parts of the world. Bi-monthly publication includes updated listing of passenger-carrying freighters, primarily embarking in N. American ports.

Der Trotter
Deutsche Zentrale für Globetrotter e.v.
Tonsheide 4
D-24613
Aukrug
Germany
German language newsletter featuring articles and news on destinations largely outside Europe. Tips, readers' reports and advice for club members.

RECOMMENDED READING

compiled by Sarah Anderson

The following list is arranged geographically. There are now so many series of guidebooks on the market that it would be impossible to list them all. I have concentrated on some of the main series – these provide a cross-section of what is available, but a visit to a good travel bookshop would allow you to see a wider range.

I have always believed that you can get more out of travelling by reading background material and with that in mind each guide book section is followed by a selection of travel writing both in and out of print. The books with a publisher are in print at the time of going to press.

World Travel

The Action Guide to the UK (Harvill)
Anderson's Travel Companion (Scolar Press)
Daily Telegraph Guide to Working Abroad (Kogan Page)
Family Travel Handbook (Bloomsbury)
Good Health Good Travel (Hodder & Stoughton)
Have Bride will Travel – Summer (Cadogan)
Have Bride will Travel – Winter (Cadogan)
Healthy Travel: Bugs Bites & Bowels (Cadogan)
Hostelling International (International YHA)
More Women Travel (Rough Guide)
Nothing Ventured - Disabled People Travel the

World (Rough Guide)
Outward Bound First Aid Handbk (Ward Lock)
Pitstops and Pitfalls: Health Guide for Older
Travellers (Quay Books)
The SAS Survival Handbook (HarperCollins)
Stay Healthy Abroad (Health Education
Authority)
Summer Jobs Abroad (Vacation Work)
Travel By Cargo Ship (Cadogan)
Travel with Children (Lonely Planet)
Travel Writing & Photography (Traveller's
Press)
Traveller's Health - How to Stay Healthy
Abroad (OUP)
The Tropical Traveller (Penguin)
The Vegetarian Traveler (Larson)
Work Your Way Round the World (Vacation
Work)
The World's Most Dangerous Places (Fielding)
The World Weather Guide (Helicon)

World Travel Literature
Best of Granta Travel ed. Bill Buford
Oxford Book of Travel Stories ed. Patricia
Craig (OUP)
Oxford Book of Travel Verse ed. Kevin
Crossley-Holland (OUP)
The Oxford Book of Exploration ed. Robin
Hanbury-Tenison (OUP)
A Book of Traveller's Tales Eric Newby
(Picador)
A Merry Dance Round the World Eric Newby
(Picador)
Mapping Men and Empire Richard Phillips
(Routledge)
Great Journeys (BBC)

Africa

General
Africa By Road (Bradt)
Africa on a Shoestring (Lonely Planet)
A Field Guide to the Larger Mammals of Africa
(Collins)
A Field Guide to the Mammals of Africa
(Collins)

Africa General Travel Literature
A Good Man in Africa William Boyd (Penguin)

North Africa
Morocco Essential (AA)
Morocco (Blue Guide)
Morocco (Cadogan)
Morocco (Everyman)
Morocco Handbook (Footprint)
Morocco (Insight)
Morocco (Lonely Planet)
Morocco (Rough Guide)
North Africa (Lonely Planet)
Sahara Handbook (Lascelles)
Tunisia (Blue Guide)

Tunisia (Cadogan)
Tunisia Handbook (Footprint)
Tunisia (Insight)
Tunisia (Rough Guide)

North Africa Travel Literature
Impossible Journey Michael Asher
Ibn Battuta. Travels in Asia and Africa (Darf)
The Passionate Nomad Isabelle Eberhardt
(Virago)
Tangier Iain Finlayson (Flamingo)
Hideous Kinky Esther Freud (Penguin)
Morocco That Was Walter Harris (Eland)
Lords of the Atlas Gavin Maxwell
A Year in Marrakesh Peter Mayne (Eland)
A Cure for Serpents Duke of Pirajno (Eland)

Egypt
Egypt Essential (AA)
Egypt (Blue Guide)
Egypt (Cadogan)
Egypt Handbook (Footprint)
Egypt (Insight)
Egypt (Lonely Planet)
Egypt Handbook (Moon)
Penguin Guide to Ancient Egypt
Egypt (Rough Guide)
Nile (Insight)

Egypt Travel Literature
A Guide to the Antiquities of Egypt Arthur
Weigall (Bracken Books)
The Leisure of an Egyptian Official Edward
Cecil (Parkway)
A Thousand Miles Up the Nile Amelia
Edwards (Parkway)
Beyond the Pyramids Douglas Kennedy
(Abacus)

West Africa
Field Guide to the Birds of West Africa
(Collins)
Gambia & Senegal (Insight)
West Africa (Lonely Planet)
West Africa (Rough Guide)

West Africa Travel Literature
The Innocent Anthropologist Nigel Barley
(Penguin)
Wanderings in West Africa Richard Burton
(Dover)
Africa Dances Geoffrey Gorer
Journey Without Maps Graham Greene
(Penguin)
Our Grandmother's Drums Mark Hudson
(Mandarin)
Travels in West Africa Mary Kingsley
(Everyman)
Cameroon with Egbert Dervla Murphy
(Arrow)
Travels into the Interior of Africa Mungo Park

East Africa
East Africa (Lonely Planet)
East African Wildlife (Insight)
East Africa Handbook (Footprint)
Essential Kenya (AA)
Eritrea (Bradt)
Ethiopia (Bradt)
Kenya (Insight)
Kenya (Lonely Planet)
Kenya (Rough Guide)
Tanzania (Bradt)
Trekking in East Africa (Lonely Planet)
Uganda (Bradt)

East Africa Travel Literature
Out of Africa Karen Blixen (Penguin)
First Footsteps in East Africa Richard Burton (Dover)
White Mischief James Fox (Penguin)
African Nights Kuki Gallman (Penguin)
I Dreamed of Africa Kuki Gallman (Penguin)
Journey to the Jade Sea John Hillaby (Constable)
The Flame Trees of Thika Elspeth Huxley (Penguin)
The Mottled Lizard Elspeth Huxley (Penguin)
West With the Night Beryl Markham (Penguin)
A Far Country Philip Marsden
The Tree Where Man Was Born Peter Matthiessen (Harvill)
The Blue Nile and The White Nile Alan Moorehead (Penguin)
North of South Shiva V.S.Naipaul (Penguin)
The Danakil Diary Wilfred Thesiger (HarperCollins)
Waugh in Abyssinia Evelyn Waugh (Penguin)

Central & Southern Africa
Africa Central (Lonely Planet)
Botswana (Rough Guide)
Malawi (Lonely Planet)
Mozambique (Bradt)
Namibia (Insight)
Namibia Handbook (Footprint)
South Africa (Cadogan)
South Africa (Insight)
South Africa (Rough Guide)
South Africa Handbook (Footprint)
South Africa, Lesotho & Swaziland (Lonely Planet)
Southern Africa on the Wildside (Cadogan)
Zambia (Bradt)
Zimbabwe (Rough Guide)
Zimbabwe, Botswana & Namibia (Lonely Planet)
Zimbabwe & Malawi Handbook (Footprint)

Central & Southern Africa Travel Literature
Mukiwa Peter Godwin (Picador)
My Traitor's Heart Rian Malan (Vintage)

Congo Journey Redmond O'Hanlon (Hamish Hamilton)
Cry of the Kalahari Mark & Delia Owens (HarperCollins)
The Boer War Thomas Pakenham (Abacus)
Lost World of the Kalahari Laurens Van Der Post (Penguin)
Venture to the Interior Laurens Van Der Post (Penguin)
A Walk With a White Bushman Laurens Van Der Post (Penguin)

African Islands
Madagascar (Bradt)
Madagascar Wildlife (Bradt)
Mauritius (Bradt)
Zanzibar (Bradt)

African Islands Travel Literature
Muddling Through in Madagascar Dervla Murphy (Arrow)

Central America
Adventure Guide to Costa Rica (Hunter)
America - Central (Cadogan)
Belize (Bradt)
Belize (Cadogan)
Belize (Insight)
Belize Guide (Open Road)
Belize Handbook (Moon)
Central America (Lonely Planet)
Central & South America By Road (Bradt)
Costa Rica (Insight)
Costa Rica (Lonely Planet)
Costa Rica (Rough Guide)
Costa Rica Handbook (Moon)
Guatemala (Cadogan)
Guatemala, Belize & Yucatan (Lonely Planet)
Guatemala and Belize (Rough Guide)
New Key to Costa Rica (Ulysses)

Central America Travel Literature
Beyond the Mexique Bay Aldous Huxley (Granada)
Rites Victor Perera (Eland)
The Jaguar Smile Salman Rushdie (Picador)
Incidents of Travel in the Yucatan J.L.Stephens (Dover)
Time Among the Maya Ronald Wright (Abacus)

Mexico
Baja Handbook (Moon)
Baja California (Lonely Planet)
Cancun Handbook (Moon)
Central Mexico Handbook (Moon)
Essential Mexico (AA)
A Guide to the Birds of Mexico & Northern Central America (OUP)
Mexico (Blue Guide)

Mexico (Cadogan)
Mexico (Insight)
Mexico (Lonely Planet)
Mexico (Rough Guide)
Mexico & Central America Handbook
(Footprint)
Mexico Handbook (Moon)
North Mexico Handbook (Moon)
Pacific Mexico Handbook (Moon)
Yucatan Handbook (Moon)

Mexico Travel Literature
A Visit to Don Otavio Sybille Bedford (Eland)
The Conquest of New Spain B. Diaz (Penguin)
Viva Mexico Charles Flandrau (Eland)
The Lawless Roads Graham Greene (Penguin)
A Trip to the Light Fantastic Katie Hickman
(Flamingo)
Mornings in Mexico D.H.Lawrence (Penguin)

South America
Amazon Wildlife (Insight)
Argentina (Insight)
Argentina, Uruguay & Paraguay (Lonely
Planet)
Bolivia (Lonely Planet)
Brazil (Insight)
Brazil (Lonely Planet)
Brazil (Rough Guide)
Chile & Easter Island (Lonely Planet)
Chile Handbook (Footprint)
Chile (Insight)
Colombia (Lonely Planet)
Colombia, Ecuador, Galapagos (Cadogan)
Ecuador Handbook (Footprint)
Ecuador (Insight)
Ecuador & the Galapagos (Lonely Planet)
Galapagos Islands (Odyssey)
Peru (Insight)
Peru (Lonely Planet)
Peru (Rough Guide)
Peru Handbook (Footprint)
South America (Insight)
South America (Lonely Planet)
South American Handbook (Footprint)
Trekking in the Patagonian Andes (Lonely
Planet)
Venezuela (Bradt)
Venezuela (Insight)
Venezuela (Lonely Planet)

South America Travel Literature
In Patagonia Bruce Chatwin (Picador)
Brazilian Adventure Peter Fleming
The Conqest of the Incas John Hemming
(Papermac)
Red Gold John Hemming (Papermac)
The Cloud Forest Peter Matthiessen (Harvill)
Amazon Watershed George Monbiot (Abacus)
Eight Feet in the Andes Dervla Murphy
(Flamingo)

The Old Patagonian Express Paul Theroux
(Penguin)
Travels in a Thin Country Sara Wheeler

Caribbean
Bahamas (Insight)
Barbados (Insight)
Bermuda (Insight)
Bermuda (Lonely Planet)
Caribbean (Cadogan)
Caribbean - North East (Cadogan)
Caribbean - South East (Cadogan)
Caribbean (Insight)
Caribbean Handbook (Moon)
Caribbean Islands Handbook (Footprint)
Cuba (Insight)
Cuba (Lonely Planet)
Eastern Caribbean (Lonely Planet)
Jamaica (Cadogan)
Jamaica (Insight)
Jamaica (Lonely Planet)
Jamaica (Rough Guide)
Jamaica Handbook (Moon)
Puerto Rico (Insight)
Trinidad (Insight)

Caribbean Travel Literature
The Traveller's Tree Patrick Leigh Fermor
(Penguin)
Travels with My Trombone Henry Shukman
(Flamingo)
The Weather Prophet Lucretia Stewart
(Vintage)

North America
General
Native America (Insight)
Traveller's Survival Kit – USA & Canada
(Vacation Work)
USA (Rough Guide)
USA National Parks East (Insight)
USA National Parks West (Insight)
USA By Rail (Bradt)
Smithsonian Guides to Historic America

United States
Alaska (Insight)
Alaska (Lonely Planet)
Alaska Yukon Handbook (Moon)
Backpacking in Alaska (Lonely Planet)
Essential California (AA)
California (Eyewitness)
California (Rough Guide)
California & Nevada (Lonely Planet)
San Francisco (Eyewitness)
San Francisco (Rough Guide)
Essential Florida (AA)
Florida (Insight)
Florida (Lonely Planet)
Florida (Rough Guide)

Hawaii (Lonely Planet)
Hawaii (Rough Guide)
Big Island of Hawaii (Rough Guide)
Boston & Cambridge (Blue Guide)
New England (Insight)
New England (Lonely Planet)
New England (Michelin)
Boston & New England Essential Explorer (AA)
Essential New York (AA)
New York (Blue Guide)
New York (Cadogan)
New York (Everyman)
New York (Eyewitness)
New York (Michelin)
New York (Rough Guide)
New York State (Insight)
New York, New Jersey & Pennsylvania (Lonely Planet)
Pacific Northwest (Lonely Planet)
Pacific Northwest (Rough Guide)
Colorado Handbook (Moon)
Oregon Handbook (Moon)
Washington Handbook (Moon)
Rockies (Insight)
Rocky Mountain States (Lonely Planet)
Idaho Handbook (Moon)
Montana Handbook (Moon)
Nevada Handbook (Moon)
Utah Handbook Moon)
Wyoming Handbook (Moon)
Arizona Handbook (Moon)
New Mexico Handbook (Moon)
American Southwest (Insight)
Southwest (Lonely Planet)
Southwest USA (Rough Guide)
Georgia Handbook (Moon)
Texas (Insight)
Texas Handbook (Moon)
Washington DC (Rough Guide)
Washington DC & the Capital Region (Lonely Planet)

United States Travel Literature
LA Lore Stephen Brook (Picador)
New York Days, New York Nights Stephen Brook (Picador)
The Lost Continent Bill Bryson (Abacus)
The Heart of the World Nik Cohn (Vintage)
American Notes Charles Dickens (Penguin)
Blue Highways William Least Heat-Moon (Minerva)
In God's Country Douglas Kennedy (Abacus)
Great American Bus Ride Irma Kurtz (Fourth Estate)
A Turn in the South V.S. Naipaul (Penguin)
Maximum City Michael Pye (Picador)
Hunting Mr Heartbreak Jonathan Raban (Picador)
Old Glory Jonathan Raban (Picador)
Life on the Mississippi Mark Twain (Penguin)

Canada
Canada (Insight)
Canada (Lonely Planet)
Canada (Michelin)
Canada (Rough Guide)
Quebec (Michelin Green)
Alberta & NW Territories (Moon)
Atlantic Canada Handbook (Moon)
British Colombia Handbook (Moon)

Canada Travel Literature
The Oatmeal Ark Rory Maclean (HarperCollins)

Asia

Middle East
Middle East (Lonely Planet)
Arab Gulf States (Lonely Planet)
Iran (Lonely Planet)
Iran (Odyssey)
Holy Land (Everyman)
Essential Israel (AA)
Israel (Insight)
Israel (Rough Guide)
Israel & the Palestine Territories (Lonely Planet)
Jerusalem Essential Guide (AA)
Jordan (Blue Guide)
Jordan (Insight)
Jordan & Syria (Lonely Planet)
Lebanon (Bradt)
Lebanon (Lonely Planet)
Syria & Lebanon (Cadogan)
United Arab Emirates (Camerapix)
Yemen (Insight)
Yemen (Lonely Planet)
Yemen (Pallas Athene)

Middle East Travel Literature
The Road to Oxiana Robert Byron (Picador)
From the Holy Mountain William Dalrymple (HarperCollins)
Travels in Arabia Deserta Charles Doughty (Dover)
A History of the Arab Peoples Albert Hourani (Faber)
Eothen Alexander Kinglake (Picador)
Seven Pillars of Wisdom T.E. Lawrence (Penguin)
The Arabs Peter Mansfield (Penguin)
A Reed Shaken By the Wind Gavin Maxwell (Eland)
Among the Believers V.S. Naipaul (Penguin)
Arabia Jonathan Raban (Picador)
Arabian Sands Wilfred Thesiger (Penguin)
The Life of My Choice Wilfred Thesiger (Flamingo)
The Marsh Arabs Wilfred Thesiger (Penguin)
Mirror to Damascus Colin Thubron (Penguin)
Return to the Marshes Gavin Young (Penguin)

Indian Subcontinent
Bangladesh (Lonely Planet)
Bhutan (Odyssey)
Delhi, Agra & Jaipur (Odyssey)
Goa (Cadogan)
Goa (Rough Guide)
India (Cadogan)
India (Insight)
India (Lonely Planet)
India (Rough Guide)
India Handbook (Footprint)
Louise Nicholson's India Companion
(Headline)
India By Rail (Bradt)
Indian Himalaya (Lonely Planet)
South India (Cadogan)
India South (Insight)
Indian Wildlife (Insight)
Maldives (Bradt)
Nepal Baedeker (AA)
Nepal (Insight)
Nepal (Lonely Planet)
Nepal (Rough Guide)
Nepal Handbook (Moon)
Kathmandu Valley (Odyssey)
Pakistan Handbook (Footprint)
Pakistan Handbook (Moon)
Pakistan (Insight)
Pakistan (Lonely Planet)
Rajasthan (Everyman)
Rajasthan (Insight)
Rajasthan (Lonely Planet)
Seychelles (Camerapix)
Sri Lanka (Camerapix)
Sri Lanka (Insight)
Sri Lanka (Lonely Planet)
Sri Lanka & Maldives Handbook (Footprint)
Trekking in the Indian Himalaya (Lonely
Planet)
Trekking in the Nepal Himalaya (Lonely
Planet)
Western Himalaya (Insight)
Birds of India (Odyssey)

Indian Subcontinent Travel Literature
Memoirs of a Bengal Civilian John Beames
(Eland)
One Indian Summer James Cameron
(Penguin)
City of Djinns William Dalrymple (Flamingo)
Chasing the Monsoon Alexander Frater
(Penguin)
Explorers of the Western Himalaya John Keay
(John Murray)
Kim Rudyard Kipling (Penguin)
Plain Tales from the Hills Rudyard Kipling
A Goddess in the Stones Norman Lewis
(Picador)
Grandmother's Footsteps Imogen Lycett
Green (Pan)
The Snow Leopard Peter Matthiessen (Harvill)

Calcutta Geoffrey Moorhouse
India Britannica Geoffrey Moorhouse
Om Geoffrey Moorhouse (Sceptre)
To the Frontier Geoffrey Moorhouse (Sceptre)
India. A Million Mutinies Now V.S. Naipaul
(Minerva)
Travels in Nepal Charlie Pye-Smith (Penguin)
Slowly Down the Ganges Eric Newby (Picador)
Midnight's Children Salman Rushdie
(Vintage)
Travels on My Elephant Mark Shand (Penguin)
The Heart of India Mark Tully (Penguin)

South East Asia
Angkor (Odyssey)
Asia South East (Insight)
Bali (Cadogan)
Bali (Everyman)
Bali (Insight)
Bali Handbook (Moon)
Bali & Lombok (Lonely Planet)
Bali & Lombok (Rough Guide)
Bangkok Handbook (Moon)
Burma (Odyssey)
Cambodia Handbook (Footprint)
Cambodia (Lonely Planet)
Dive Sites of Thailand (New Holland)
Indonesia Handbook (Footprint)
Indonesia Handbook (Moon)
Indonesia (Insight)
Indonesia (Lonely Planet)
Java (Insight)
Java (Lonely Planet)
Laos Handbook (Footprint)
Laos (Lonely Planet)
Malaysia (Insight)
Malaysia & Singapore Handbook (Footprint)
Malaysia, Singapore & Brunei (Lonely Planet)
Malaysia, Singapore & Brunei (Rough Guide)
Myanmar Handbook (Footprint)
Myanmar (Insight)
Myanmar (Lonely Planet)
Philippines (Insight)
Philippines (Lonely Planet)
Philippines Handbook (Moon)
Phuket (Odyssey)
Singapore (Lonely Planet)
Singapore (Rough Guide)
South East Asia (Lonely Planet)
South East Asia Handbook (Moon)
Thailand Essential Explorer (AA)
Thailand (Everyman)
Thailand Handbook (Footprint)
Thailand Handbook (Moon)
Thailand (Cadogan)
Thailand (Insight)
Thailand (Lonely Planet)
Thailand (Rough Guide)
Vietnam (Bradt)
Vietnam Handbook (Footprint)
Vietnam, Laos, Cambodia Handbook (Moon)

Vietnam (Insight)
Vietnam (Lonely Planet)
Vietnam (Rough Guide)

South East Asia Travel Literature
God's Dust Ian Buruma (Vintage)
The Missionary and the Libertine Ian Buruma
(Faber)
Islands of Indonesia Violet Clifton (OUP)
The Beach Alex Garland (Viking)
Stranger in the Forest Eric Hansen (Sphere)
Indonesia John Keay (Boxtree)
A Dragon Apparent Norman Lewis (Eland)
Golden Earth Norman Lewis (Eland)
Land of Jade Bertil Lintner (Kiscadale)
Borderlines Charles Nicholl (Pan)
Into the Heart of Borneo Redmond O'Hanlon
(Penguin)
Burmese Days George Orwell (Penguin)
Dark Ruby Zoe Schramm-Evans (Pandora)
A Bright Shining Lie Neil Sheehan
River of Time Jon Swain (Minerva)
The Great Railway Bazaar Paul Theroux
(Penguin)
Malay Archipelago Alfred Russel Wallace
(OUP)
Six Years in the Malay Jungle Carveth Wells
(OUP)
In Search of Conrad Gavin Young (Penguin)

Far East
China: Essential Explorer (AA)
China (Blue Guide)
China (Insight)
China (Lonely Planet)
China (Rough Guide)
Hong Kong (Insight)
Hong Kong, Macau & Guangzhou (Lonely
Planet)
Hong Kong Handbook (Moon)
Hong Kong & Macau (Rough Guide)
Japan (Cadogan)
Japan (Insight)
Japan (Lonely Planet)
Japan Handbook (Moon)
Korea (Insight)
Korea (Lonely Planet)
South Korea Handbook (Moon)
Mongolia (Lonely Planet)
North-East Asia (Lonely Planet)
Taiwan (Insight)
Taiwan (Lonely Planet)

Far East Travel Literature
Way to Xanadu Caroline Alexander (Phoenix)
On the Narrow Road to the Deep North Basho
(Penguin)
The Japanese Chronicles Nicolas Bouvier
(Polygon)
The Roads to Sata Alan Booth (Penguin)
Wild Swans Jung Chang (HarperCollins)

The Taipans Colin Crisswell (OUP)
One's Company Peter Fleming (Penguin)
White Month's Return Guy Hart (Book Guild)
The Lady and the Monk Pico Iyer (Black
Swan)
The Japanese Joe Joseph (Penguin)
Peking Story David Kidd (Eland)
Last Disco in Outer Mongolia Nick Middleton
(Phoenix)
The Mongols David Morgan (Blackwell)
Pictures from the Water Trade John David
Morley (Abacus)
Hong Kong Jan Morris (Penguin)
Travels Through Sacred China Martin Palmer
(Thorsons)
The Inland Sea Donald Richie (Kodansha)
In Search of Genghis Khan Tim Severin
(Arrow)
Frontiers of Heaven Stanley Stewart
(Flamingo)
Riding the Iron Rooster Paul Theroux
(Penguin)
Behind the Wall Colin Thubron (Penguin)
Slow Boats to China Gavin Young (Penguin)

Central Asia
Central Asia (Cadogan)
Central Asia (Lonely Planet)
Karakoram Highway (Lonely Planet)
Silk Road (Odyssey)
Tibet (Lonely Planet)
Tibet Handbook (Footprint)
Tibet Handbook (Moon)
Uzbekistan (Odyssey)

Central Asia Travel Literature
A Mountain in Tibet Charles Allen (Abacus)
Black Sea Neal Ascherson (Vintage)
In Xanadu William Dalrymple (Flamingo)
Danziger's Travels Nick Danziger (Flamingo)
Bayonets to Lhasa Peter Fleming (OUP)
News from Tartary Peter Fleming (Abacus)
Seven Years in Tibet Heinrich Harrer (Grafton)
Foreign Devils on the Silk Road Peter Hopkirk
(OUP)
Great Game Peter Hopkirk (OUP)
Trespassers on the Roof of the World Peter
Hopkirk (OUP)
Eastern Approaches Fitzroy Maclean
(Penguin)
A Short Walk in the Hindu Kush Eric Newby
(Picador)
From Heaven Lake Vikram Seth (Phoenix)
Goodnight Mr Lenin Tiziano Terzani
The Lost Heart of Asia Colin Thubron
(Penguin)
The Heart of a Continent Francis
Younghusband (OUP)

Australasia and the Pacific

Australia Essential (AA)
Australia (Insight)
Australia (Lonely Planet)
Australia Handbook (Moon)
Australian Outback Handbook (Moon)
Australia (Rough Guide)
Bushwalking in Australia (Lonely Planet)
Bushwalking in Papua New Guinea (Lonely Planet)
Fiji (Lonely Planet)
Fiji Islands Handbook (Moon)
Great Barrier Reef (Insight)
Islands of Australia's Great Barrier Reef (Lonely Planet)
Micronesia (Lonely Planet)
Micronesia Handbook (Moon)
New Caledonia (Lonely Planet)
New South Wales & the ACT (Lonely Planet)
Northern Territory (Lonely Planet)
Outback Australia (Lonely Planet)
Papua New Guinea (Lonely Planet)
Queensland (Lonely Planet)
Raratonga and the Cook Islands (Lonely Planet)
Samoa (Lonely Planet)
Solomon Islands (Lonely Planet)
South Australia (Lonely Planet)
South Pacific Handbook (Moon)
Sydney (Eyewitness)
Tahiti & French Polynesia (Lonely Planet)
Tahiti Polynesia Handbook (Moon)
Tasmania (Lonely Planet)
Tonga (Lonely Planet)
Vanuatu (Lonely Planet)
Victoria (Lonely Planet)
Western Australia (Lonely Planet)
New Zealand (Insight)
New Zealand (Lonely Planet)
Tramping in New Zealand (Lonely Planet)
New Zealand Handbook (Moon)
New Zealand (Rough Guide)

Australasia Travel Literature
The Songlines Bruce Chatwin (Picador)
Manning Clark's History of Australia Manning Clark (Pimlico)
Tracks Robyn Davidson (Vintage)
Kon-Tiki Thor Heyerdahl (Flamingo)
The Fatal Shore Robert Hughes (Harvill)
Under the Mountain Wall Peter Matthiessen (Harvill)
Tales from the South China Seas Robert Louis Stevenson (Canongate)
The Happy Isles of Oceania Paul Theroux (Penguin)
Slow Boats Home Gavin Young (Penguin)

Europe

General
Channel Islands (Insight)
Europe (Rough Guide)
Mediterranean Europe (Lonely Planet)
Western Europe (Lonely Planet)
Waterways of Europe (Insight)

Europe General Travel Literature
Between East and West Anne Applebaum (Papermac)
Neither Here Nor There Bill Bryson (Mandarin)
Between the Woods and the Water Patrick Leigh Fermor (Penguin)
A Time of Gifts Patrick Leigh Fermor (Penguin)
On the Shores of the Mediterranean Eric Newby (Picador)
The Pillars of Hercules Paul Theroux (Penguin)
The Sign of the Cross Colm Tçibin (Vintage)

Great Britain and Ireland

Great Britain
Literary Britain & Ireland (Blue Guide)
Great Britain (Eyewitness)
Britain (Lonely Planet)
Great Britain (Michelin Green Guide)
Great Britain and Ireland (Michelin Red Guide)
Britain (Rough Guide)
England Essential (AA)
England (Blue Guide)
England (Rough Guide)
London Essential (AA)
London (Blue Guide)
Museums & Galleries of London (Blue Guide)
London (Cadogan)
London (Everyman)
London (Eyewitness)
London (Michelin Green Guide)
London (Rough Guide)
Scotland (Blue Guide)
Scotland (Cadogan)
Scotland (Insight)
Scotland (Michelin Green Guide)
Scotland (Rough Guide)
Wales (Blue Guide)
Wales (Insight)
Wales (Michelin Green Guide)
Wales (Pallas Athene)
Wales (Rough Guide)
West Country (Michelin Green Guide)
Churches & Chapels of Northern England (Blue Guide)
Charming Small Hotel Guide (Duncan Petersen)
Egon Ronay's Guide Hotels and Restaurants (Bookman)
Good Hotel Guide (Ebury)
Which? Good Bed and Breakfast Guide (Which)
Good Food Guide (Ebury)

Great Britain Travel Literature
Native Land Nigel Barley (Penguin)
Notes from a Small Island Bill Bryson (Black Swan)
On the Black Hill Bruce Chatwin (Picador)
Journey to the Hebrides Johnson & Boswell (Canongate)
Cider With Rosie Laurie Lee (Penguin)
The Matter of Wales Jan Morris (Penguin)
Coasting Jonathan Raban (Picador)
The Kingdom by the Sea Paul Theroux (Penguin)
Lark Rise to Candleford Flora Thompson (Penguin)
The Journals of James Boswell ed. John Wain (Mandarin)

Ireland
Ireland (Blue Guide)
Ireland (Cadogan)
Ireland South West (Cadogan)
Ireland (Eyewitness)
Ireland (Michelin Green Guide)
Ireland (Rough Guide)

Ireland Travel Literature
Ireland and the Irish John Ardagh (Penguin)
Walled Gardens Annabel Davis-Goff (Eland)
A Place Apart Dervla Murphy (Penguin)
Round Ireland in Low Gear Eric Newby (Picador)
The Road to Roaringwater Christopher Somerville (HarperCollins)

France

France (Blue Guide)
Michelin Regional Green Guides to France
Michelin Red Guide France
France South West (Blue Guide)
France South (Cadogan)
France SW (Cadogan)
France (Eyewitness)
France (Insight)
France (Lonely Planet)
France (Rough Guide)
Brittany Essential (AA)
Brittany (Everyman)
Brittany and Normandy (Rough Guide)
Burgundy (Blue Guide)
Corsica (Blue Guide)
Corsica (Rough Guide)
Dordogne Essential (AA)
Dordogne & Lot (Blue Guide)
Lazy Days Out in Dordogne (Cadogan)
Loire Valley (Blue Guide)
Loire Lazy Days (Cadogan)
Loire Valley (Everyman)
Loire (Eyewitness)
Normandy Essential (AA)
Paris (Cadogan)

Paris (Everyman)
Paris (Eyewitness)
Paris (Rough Guide)
France, Cote d'Azur (Cadogan)
France - Provence (Cadogan)
Provence (Everyman)
Provence (Eyewitness)
Provence (Insight)
Provence & the Cote d'Azur (Rough Guide)
Pyrenees (Rough Guide)

France Travel Literature
Granite Island Dorothy Carrington (Penguin)
Travels Through France and Italy Tobias Smollett (OUP)
Travels with a Donkey Robert Louis Stevenson (OUP)
Celestine Gillian Tindall (Minerva)
Three Rivers of France Freda White (Pavilion)

Italy and Malta

Italy
Italy Northern (Blue Guide)
Italy Southern (Blue Guide)
Italy (Cadogan)
Italy Northwest (Cadogan)
Italy South (Cadogan)
Italy (Eyewitness)
Italy (Lonely Planet)
Italy Green (Michelin)
Italia Red (Michelin)
Italy (Rough Guide)
Florence (Blue Guide)
Florence/Tuscany (Eyewitness)
Bay of Naples (Cadogan)
Naples & Pompeii (Everyman)
Rome (Blue Guide)
Rome (Cadogan)
Rome (Everyman)
Rome (Eyewitness)
Sardinia (Insight)
Sicily (Cadogan)
Sicily (Blue Guide)
Sicily (Insight)
Sicily (Rough Guide)
Tuscany (Blue Guide)
Tuscany (Cadogan)
Lazy Days Out in Tuscany (Cadogan)
Tuscany & Umbria (Rough Guide)
Umbria (Blue Guide)
Lazy Days Out in Umbria (Cadogan)
Umbria (Insight)
Venice (Blue Guide)
Venice (Everyman)
Venice & Veneto (Eyewitness)
Venice for Pleasure (Pallas Athene)
Venice (Rough Guide)

Malta
Malta Essential (AA)

Malta & Gozo (Blue Guide)
Malta & Gozo (Cadogan)

Italy Travel Literature
The Italians Luigi Barzini (Penguin)
Italian Journeys Jonathan Keates (Picador)
DH Lawrence & Italy (Penguin)
The Stones of Florence & Venice Observed
Mary McCarthy (Penguin)
Venice Jan Morris (Faber)
Italian Education Tim Parks (Minerva)
Within Tuscany Matthew Spender (Penguin)

Greece, Turkey and Cyprus

Greece
Greece Mainland Essential (AA)
Greece (Blue Guide)
Greece (Eyewitness)
Greece (Insight)
Greece (Lonely Planet)
Greece (Michelin)
Greece (Rough Guide)
Athens (Everyman)
Corfu Essential (AA)
Corfu & the Ionian Islands (Rough Guide)
Crete (Blue Guide)
Crete (Cadogan)
Crete (Everyman)
Crete (Rough Guide)
Cyclades (Cadogan)
Dodecanese (Cadogan)
Greek Islands (Cadogan)
Greek Islands (Insight)
Greek Islands (Rough Guide)
Rhodes (Rough Guide)
Rhodes & Dodecanese (Blue Guide)

Turkey
Istanbul (Blue Guide)
Istanbul (Everyman)
Turkey (Blue Guide)
Turkey (Cadogan)
Turkey Western (Cadogan)
Turkey (Rough Guide)

Cyprus
Cyprus Essential (AA)
Cyprus (Blue Guide)
Cyprus (Insight)
Cyprus (Rough Guide)

Greece, Turkey, Cyprus Travel Literature
Bitter Lemons Lawrence Durrell (Faber)
Prospero's Cell Lawrence Durrell (Faber)
Reflections on a Marine Venus Lawrence
Durrell(Faber)
Journey to Kars Philip Glazebrook (Penguin)
Ataturk Patrick Kinross (Pimlico)
Mani Patrick Leigh Fermor (Penguin)
Roumeli Patrick Leigh Fermor (Penguin)

The Colossus of Maroussi Henry Miller
(Penguin)
Portrait of a Turkish Family Irfan Orga
(Eland)
The Turkish Labyrinth James Pettifer (Viking)
A Fez of the Heart Jeremy Seal (Picador)
Journey into Cyprus Colin Thubron (Penguin)
Modern Greece C.M. Woodhouse (Faber)

Spain and Portugal

Spain
Spain (Blue Guide)
Spain (Cadogan)
Spain Northern (Cadogan)
Spain: The South (Cadogan)
Spain (Eyewitness)
Spain (Lonely Planet)
Spain (Michelin Green)
España Portugal (Michelin Red)
Spain (Rough Guide)
Trekking in Spain (Lonely Planet)
Lazy Days Out in Andalucia (Cadogan)
Seville, Andalucia (Eyewitness)
Andalucia Handbook (Footprint)
Andalucia (Rough Guide)
Barcelona (Blue Guide)
Barcelona (Rough Guide)
Catalonia (Insight)
Madrid (Blue Guide)
Mallorca & Ibiza (Insight)
Mallorca & Menorca (Rough Guide)
Pyrenees (Rough Guide)

Portugal
Portugal (Blue Guide)
Portugal (Cadogan)
Portugal (Lonely Planet)
Portugal (Michelin Green)
Portugal (Rough Guide)
Algarve Essential (AA)
Algarve (Cadogan)

Canary Islands
Baedeker's Gran Canaria (AA)
Lanzarote (Windrush)

Spain & Portugal Travel Literature
The Face of Spain Gerald Brenan (Penguin)
The Select Traveller in Portugal Ann Bridge &
Susan Lowndes
The Journal of a Voyage to Lisbon Henry
Fielding (Penguin)
Between Hopes and Memories Michael Jacobs
(Picador)
Cities of Spain David Gilmour (Pimlico)
For Whom the Bell Tolls Ernest Hemingway
(Arrow)
As I Walked Out One Midsummer Morning
Laurie Lee (Penguin)
They Went to Portugal Rose Macaulay
Spain Jan Morris (Penguin)

Roads to Santiago Cees Nooteboom (Harvill)
Homage to Catalonia George Orwell
(Penguin)
Portugal Ian Robertson (John Murray)
The Spanish Civil War Hugh Thomas -Penguin

Germany and Austria

Austria Essential (AA)
Austria (Blue Guide)
Austria (Insight)
Austria (Lonely Planet)
Austria (Michelin Green)
Bavaria & Alpine Forest (Cadogan)
Berlin (Cadogan)
Berlin & East Germany (Blue Guide)
Berlin (Rough Guide)
Deutschland (Michelin Red)
Germany Western (Blue Guide)
Germany (Cadogan)
Germany (Insight)
Germany (Michelin Green)
Germany (Rough Guide)
Vienna (Blue Guide)
Vienna (Everyman)
Vienna (Eyewitness)
Vienna (Rough Guide)

Germany & Austria Travel Literature
Germany and the Germans John Ardagh
(Penguin)
Double Eagle Stephen Brook
Vanishing Borders Michael Farr
In Europe's Name Timothy Garton Ash
(Vintage)
Danube Claudio Magris (Harvill)

Switzerland

Switzerland Essential (AA)
Switzerland (Blue Guide)
Switzerland (Insight)
Switzerland (Lonely Planet)
Walking in Switzerland (Lonely Planet)
Switzerland (Michelin Green)

Switzerland Travel Literature
Neither Here Nor There Bill Bryson (Minerva)

Belgium and Holland

Amsterdam (Blue Guide)
Amsterdam (Everyman)
Amsterdam (Eyewitness)
Amsterdam (Lonely Planet)
Amsterdam (Rough Guide)
Belgium & Luxemburg (Blue Guide)
Belgium (Insight)
Belgium (Michelin Green)
Belgium & Luxembourg (Rough Guide)
Benelux (Michelin Red)
Brussels, Bruges & Ghent (Cadogan)
Brussels (Michelin Green)

Flemish Cities (Pallas Athene)
Holland (Blue Guide)
Holland (Rough Guide)
Netherlands (Michelin Green)

Belgium & Holland Travel Literature
The Sorrow of Belgium Hugo Claus (Penguin)
The Embarrassment of Riches Simon Schama
(HarperCollins)

Scandinavia

Scandinavia (Rough Guide)
Scandinavia & Baltic Europe (Lonely Planet)
Denmark Essential (AA)
Denmark (Blue Guide)
Denmark (Insight)
Denmark (Lonely Planet)
Finland (Insight)
Finland (Lonely Planet)
Iceland, Greenland & the Faroe Islands (Lonely
Planet)
Norway (Insight)
Norway (Rough Guide)
Sweden (Blue Guide)
Sweden (Insight)
Sweden (Rough Guide)

Scandinavia & Iceland Travel Literature
Last Places Laurence Millman (Sphere)
A Short Residence in Sweden, Norway &
Denmark Mary Wollstonecroft (Penguin)
Njal's Saga (Penguin)
The Vinland Sagas

Central and Eastern Europe

Central Europe (Lonely Planet)
Eastern Europe (Lonely Planet)
Europe Eastern (Insight)
Albania (Blue Guide)
Albania (Bradt)
Baltic States & Kaliningrad (Lonely Planet)
Bulgaria (Rough Guide)
Czechoslovakia (Blue Guide)
Czech Republic Essential (AA)
Czech & Slovak Republics (Lonely Planet)
Czech & Slovak Republics (Rough Guide)
Czechoslovakia (Pallas Athene)
Hungary (Blue Guide)
Budapest (Blue Guide)
Prague (Everyman)
Prague (Rough Guide)
Poland and Ukraine (Bradt)
Poland (Insight)
Poland (Pallas Athene)
Poland (Rough Guide)
Romania (Rough Guide)
Russia, Ukraine & Belarus (Lonely Planet)
Moscow/Leningrad (Blue Guide)
Moscow & St Petersburg (Cadogan)
St Petersburg (Everyman)

St Petersburg (Rough Guide)
Warsaw (Eyewitness)
The Trans-Siberian Rail Guide (Compass Star)

Central & Eastern Europe Travel Literature
One Hot Summer in St Petersburg Duncan
Fallowell (Vintage)
Exit into History Eva Hoffman (Minerva)
St Petersburg. A Traveller's Companion
Laurence Kelly (Constable)
Stalin's Nose Rory Maclean (Flamingo)
The Bronski House Philip Marsden (Flamingo)
The Crossing Place Philip Marsden (Flamingo)
Transylvania and Beyond Dervla Murphy
(Arrow)
The Big Red Train Ride Eric Newby (Penguin)
Among the Russians Colin Thubron (Penguin)
Journey into Russia Laurens van der Post
(Penguin)

Former Yugoslavia, Slovenia and Bosnia

Slovenia (Lonely Planet)
Companion Guide Yugoslavia (Boydell &
Brewer)
Yugoslavia (Blue Guide)

Travel Literature
The Fall of Yugoslavia Misha Glenny
(Penguin)
The Impossible Country Brian Hall (Minerva)
Bosnia. A Short History Noel Malcolm
(Papermac)
Black Lamb, Grey Falcon Rebecca West
(Canongate)
White Eagles Over Serbia Lawrence Durrell
(Faber)

Polar Regions

Antarctica (Bradt)
Antarctica (Cadogan)
Antarctica (Lonely Planet)
Antarctica. A Guide to the Wild Life (Bradt)
Spitsbergen (Bradt)

Polar Regions Travel Literature
The Worst Journey in the World Apsley
Cherry-Garrard (Picador)
Mind Over Matter Ranulph Fiennes (Mandarin)
Scott and Amundsen Roland Huntford
(Weidenfeld)
North Pole, South Pole Bertrand Imbert
(Thames and Hudson)
Arctic Dreams Barry Lopez (Picador)
I May Be Some Time Francis Spufford (Faber)
Polar Dream Helen Thayer (Warner Brothers)
Terra Incognita Sara Wheeler (Cape)

FOREIGN TOURIST BOARDS IN THE UK

*Please note that if there is no Tourist Office
listed the Embassy or Consulate may be able to
provide tourist information. Some of the numbers listed here are for tourist departments
within the Embassy. Always ring in advance to
make an appointment if you need to speak to
someone in person.*

Andorra
63 Westover Road
London SW18 2RF
Tel: **0181-874 4806**
email: atbtour@candw.com.ai
http://www.candw.com.ai/~atbtour/

Anguilla
3 Epirus Road
London SW6 7UJ
Tel: **0171-937 7725**

Antigua & Barbuda
Antigua House
15 Thayer Street
London W1M 5LD
Tel: **0171-486 7073**
http://www.interknowledge.com/antigua-
barbuda/

Argentina
27 Three Kings Yard
London W1Y 1FL
Tel: **0171-318 1340**

Australia
Gemini House
10/18 Putney Hill
London SW15 6AA
Tel: **0181-780 2227**
http://www.aussie.net.au/

Austria
30 St George Street
London W1R 0AL
Tel: **0171-629 0461**
http://www.austria-info.at/

Bahamas
10 Chesterfield Street
London W1X 8AH
Tel: **0171-629 5238**
http://www.interknowledge.com/bahamas/

Barbados
263 Tottenham Court Road
London
W1P 0LA
Tel: **0171-636 9448**
http://www.barbados.org/

Belgium
29 Princes Street
London W1R 7RG
Tel: **0171-629 1988**
email: belinfo@nyxfer.blythe.org
(consumer inquiries)
http://www.visitbelgium.com/

Bermuda
1 Battersea Church Road
London SW11 3LY
Tel: **0171-771 7001**

Brazil
32 Green Street
London W1Y 4AT
Tel: **0171 499 0877**

British Virgin Islands
110 St Martin's Lane
London WC2N 4DY
Tel: **0171 240 4259**

Bulgaria
18 Princes Street
London W1R 7RE
Tel: **0171-499 6988**

Canada
62-65 Trafalgar Square
London SW1Y 5BJ
Tel: **0891-715000**
http://info.ic.gc.ca/Tourism/

Caribbean Tourism
Vigilant House
120 Wilton Road
London SW1V 1JZ
Tel: **0171-233 8382**

Cayman Islands
6 Arlington Street
London SW1A 1RE
Tel: **0171-491 7771**

China: see Russia

C.I.S: see Russia

Cyprus
213 Regent Street
London W1R 8DA
Tel: **0171-734 9822**

Czech Republic
95 Great Portland Street
London W1N 5RA
Tel: **0171 291 9920**

Denmark
55 Sloane Street
London SW1X 9SR
Tel: **0171-259 5959**
http://www.deninfo.com/index.htm

Dominica
1 Collingham Gardens
London SW5 0HW
Tel: **0171-835 1937**

Egypt
170 Piccadilly
London W1V 9DD
Tel: **0171-493 5282**
http://interoz.com/egypt/

Falkland Islands
Falkland House
14 Broadway
London SW1H 0BH
Tel: **0171-222 2542**

Finland
30-35 Pall Mall
London SW1Y 5LP
Tel: **0171-839 4048**

France
178 Piccadilly
London W1V 0AL
Tel: **0891 244 123**
email: piccadilly@mdlf.demon.co.uk

Gambia
57 Kensington Court
London W8 5DG
Tel: **0171-376 0093**

Germany
Nightingale House
65 Curzon St
London W1Y 7PE
Tel: **0891 600 100**

Ghana
13 Belgrave Square
London SW1X 8PR
Info Tel: **0181-342 8686**

Gibraltar
Arundel Great Court
179 The Strand
London WC2R 1EH
Tel: **0171-836 0777**
email: piccadilly@mdlf.demon.co.uk

Greece
4 Conduit Street
London W1R 0DJ
Tel: **0171 734 5997**
http://www.eexi.gr
email: gnto@eexi.gr

Grenada
1 Collingham Gardens
London SW5 0HW
Tel: **0171-370 5164**

Hong Kong
125 Pall Mall
London SW1Y 5EA
Tel: **0171-930 4775**
http://www.hkta.org/usa/

Iceland
172 Tottenham Court Road
London W1P 9LG
Info Tel: **0181-286 8008**

India
7 Cork Street
London W1X 2LN
Tel: **0171-437 3677**
http://www.tourindia.com/

Indonesia
3-4 Hanover Street
London W1R 9HH
Tel: 0171 493 0030

Ireland
150 New Bond Street
London W1Y 0AQ
Tel: **0171-493 3201**
http://www.ireland.travel.ie

Israel
UK House, 180 Oxford Street
London W1N 9DJ
Tel: **0171-299 1111**
http://www.infotour.co.il

Italy
1 Princes Street
London W1R 8AY
Tel: **0171-408 1254**

Jamaica
1-2 Prince Consort Road
London SW7 2BZ
Tel: **0171-224 0505**
email: JAMAICATRV@aol.com
http://www.jamaicatravel.com/

Japan
Heathcote House
20 Saville Row
London W1X 1AE
Tel: **0171-734 9638**
http://www.jnto.go.jp/

Jersey
38 Dover Street
London W1X 3RB
Tel: **0171-493 5278**
email: jtourism@itl.net
http://www.jersey.gov.uk/tourism/

Jordan
211 Regent Street
London W1R 7DD

Tel: **0171-437 9465**

Kenya
25 Brook's Mews
London W1Y 1LG
Tel: **0171-355 3144**
http://www.africanvacation.com/kenya

Korea (South)
20 St George Street
London W1R 9RE
Tel: **0171-409 2100**
http://www.knto.or.kr/

Luxembourg
122 Regent Street
London W1R 5FE
Tel: **0171-434 2800**
email: tourism@luxuk.demon.co.uk
http://www.luxuk.demon.co.uk/

Macau
1 Battersea Church Road
London SW11 3LY
Tel: **0171-771 7000**

Malawi
33 Grosvenor Street
London W1X 0DE
Tel: **0171-491 4172**

Malaysia
Malaysia House
57 Trafalgar Square
London
WC2N 5DU
Tel: **0171-930 7932**
http://www.interknowledge.com/malaysia/

Maldives
c/o Maldives Travel Ltd
3 Esher House
11 Edith Terrace
London SW10 0TH
Tel: **0171-352 2246**

Malta
36-38 Piccadilly
London W1V 0PP
Tel: **0171 292 4900**
email: office.ntom@tourism.org.mt
http://www.tourism.org.mt

Mauritius
32/33 Elvaston Place
London SW7 5NW
Tel: **0171-581 0294**
http://www.mauritius.net/

Mexico
60/61 Trafalgar Square
London
WC2N 5DS

Tel: **0171-734 1058**
http://www.mexico-travel.com/

Monaco
3/18 Chelsea Garden Market
Chelsea Harbour
London
SW10 0XE
Tel: **0171-352 9962**
**http://www.monaco.mc/monaco/guide_en.h
tml**

Monserrat
3 Epirus Road
London SW6 7UJ
Tel: **0171-233 8382**

Morocco
205 Regent Street
London W1R 7DE
Tel: **0171-437 0073**
http://www.znet.se/marocko/

Namibia
6 Chandos Street
London W1M 0LQ
Tel: **0171-636 2924**

Netherlands
P.O. Box 253
London SW1E 6NT
Tel: **0891-200 277**
email: info@nbt.nl
http://www.nbt.nl/

New Zealand
New Zealand House
Haymarket
London SW1Y 4TQ
Tel: **0171-930 1662**
http://www.nztb.org.nz/

Norway
Charles House
5-11 Lower Regent Street
London SW1Y 4LR
Tel: **0171-839 2650**
**http://www.sn.no/rl/op/og96/f/Osloguiden.h
tml**

Peru
Embassy of Peru – Tourist Section
52 Sloane Street
London SW1X 9SP
Tel: **0171-235 1917**
email: postmaster@foptur.gob.pe

Philippines
17 Albermarle Street
London W1X 4LX
Tel: **0171-499 5443**
http://www.sequel.net/RPinUS/Tourism/

Poland
1st Floor, Remo House
310-312 Regent Street,
London W1R 5AJ
Tel: **0171-580 8811**
email: pnto@dial.pipex.com
http://w3.poland.net/travelpage/

Portugal
2nd Floor
22/25a Sackville Street
London W1X 2LY
Tel: **0171-494 1441**

Romania
83a Marylebone High Street
London W1M 3DE
Tel: **0171-224 3692**
http://www.romtour.com/~tour/office

Russia
Intourist
219 Marsh Wall
Isle of Dogs
London E14 9PD
Tel: **0171-538 8600**
http://www.russia-travel.com/

Saudi Arabia
Cavendish House
18 Cavendish Square
London W1M 0AQ
Tel: **0171-629 8803**

Seychelles
Eros House
111 Baker Street
London W1M 1FE
Tel: **0171-224 1670**

Sierra Leone
33 Portland Place
London W1N 3AG
Tel: **0171-636 6483**

Singapore
Carrington House
126/130 Regent Street
London W1R 5FE
Tel: **0171-437 0033**
http://www.travel.com.sg/sog/

Slovak Republic
Cedok
49 Southwark Street
London SE1 1RU
Tel: **0891-171 266**
email: viktvl@aol.com
**http://members.aol.com/viktvl/slovakia/pag
e01.htm**

Slovenia
2 Canfield Place ⇨

London NW6 3BT
Tel: **0171-372 3767**
email: **infolink@hq.gzs.si**
http://www.gzs.si/eng/index.htm

South Africa
5/6 Alt Grove
Off St George's Road
Wimbledon
London SW19 4DZ
Tel: **0181-944 8080**

Spain
57-58 St. James's Street
London SW1A 1LD
Tel: **0171-499 0901**

Sri Lanka
Sri Lanka Centre
22 Regent Street
London SW1Y 4QD
Tel: **0171-930 2627**

St. Kitts & Nevis
10 Kensington Court
London W8 5DL
Tel: **0171-376 0881**

St. Lucia
421a Finchley Road
London NW3 6HT
Tel: **0171-431 3675**

St. Vincent & The Grenadines
10 Kensington Court
London W8 5DL
Tel: **0171-937 6570**

Sweden
11 Montague Place
London W1H 2AL
Tel: **0171-724 5868**
email: **sttc-info@swedish-tourism.org.uk**

Switzerland
Swiss Court
New Coventry Street
London W1V 8EE
Tel: **0171-734 1921**
http://www.switzerlandtourism.ch/

Tanzania
80 Borough High Street
London SE1 1LL
Tel: **0171-407 0566**

Thailand
49 Albermarle Street
London W1X 3FE
Tel: **0171-499 7679**
http://www.tat.or.th/

Trinidad & Tobago
International House
47 Chase Side
Enfield Middlesex EN2 6NB
Tel: **0800 960 057**
http://www.tidco.co.tt/

Tunisia
77A Wigmore Street
London W1H 9LJ
Tel: **0171-224-5561**
email: **info@tourismtunisia.com**
http://www.tourismtunisia.com

Turkey
170-173 Piccadilly (1st Floor)
London W1V 9DD
Tel: **0171-629 7771**
http://infoweb.magi.com/~toturcan/

Turks & Caicos
47 Chase Side
Enfield
Middlesex EN2 6HB
Tel: **0181-364 5188**
email: **mki@ttg.co.uk**

USA
P.O. Box 1EN
London W1A 1EN
Tel: **0171-495 4466**
See **http://www.mbnet.mb.ca/lucas/travel/**
for individual states

US Virgin Islands
Molasses House
Clove Hitch Quay
Plantation Wharf
London SW11 3PN
Tel: **0171-978 5262**

Zambia
2 Palace Gate
London W8 5NG
Tel: **0171-589 6343**
http://www.zamnet.zm/zamnet/zntb.html

Zimbabwe
429 The Strand
London WC2R 0QE
Tel: **0171-836 7755**

AGENCIES FOR SINGLES AND COMPANIONS

Great Company
31 Amwell Street
London EC1R 1UN
Tel: **0171-278 0328**
World-wide destinations and single room accommodation without the usual supplement.

Single Parent Travel Club
37 Sunningdale Park
Queen Victoria Road
New Tupton
Chesterfield
Derbyshire S42 6DZ
Tel: **01246-865069**
UK and some European destinations.

Solo's Holidays
54-58 High Street
Edgeware
Middx HA8 7ED
Tel: **0181-951 2800**
Holidays for singles over 30 (no married travellers allowed) in Europe, the Far East, Australasia and East Africa.

Travelmate
52 York Place
Bournemouth BH7 6JN
Tel: **01202-431520**
Introduction service for travellers.

Travel Companions
110 High Mount
Station Road
London NW4 3ST
Tel: **0181-202 8478**
Introduction service for travellers.

Travel Companions International Ltd.
Snoad Street Manor
Throwley
Faversham
Kent ME13 0JN
Tel: **01233-713976**
Introduction service based on lifestyle, similar interests and destination. ■

SPECIALIST TRAVEL
Section 3

SPECIALIST ASSOCIATIONS AND TOUR OPERATORS

Environmental

Action d'Urgence Internationale
10 Rue Felix-Aiem
75018 Paris
France
Tel: **142 64 7588**
Run training courses for people interested in helping rescue operations in times of natural disasters.

Arcturus Expeditions
PO Box 850
Gartocharn Alexandria
Dunbartonshire G83 8RL
Tel: **01389-834204**
Specialise in the Arctic's natural history, archaeology and native peoples. Also dog sledding, kayaking and skiing.

Bellerive Foundation
PO Box 3006
CH-1211
Geneva 3
Switzerland
Tel: **22-3468866**
New organisation devoted to protecting the Alps from pollution and thoughtless tourism.

Centre for the Advancement of Responsive Travel (CART)
Dr Roger Milman
70 Dry Hill Park Road
Tunbridge
Kent TN10 3BX
Educational organisation specialising in "creative cultural interchange, economic sustainability and in environmental and cultural sensitivity".

Charioteer Travel Tours
10 Agias Sofias St
Thessaloniki
Greece GR 54322
Tel: **31 28 4373**
Tailor-made birdwatching and natural history tours, 10% of profits towards conservation.

Convention of International Trade in Endangered Species of Wild Flora and Fauna (CITES)
Conservation Monitoring Centre (CMC)
219 Huntingdon Road
Cambridge CB3 0DL
Tel: **01223-277314**
Charity devoted to end the trade in rare flora and fauna.

Coral Cay Conservation Expeditions
The Ivy Works
154 Clapham Park Road
London SW4 7DE
Tel: **0171-498 6248**
Recruits qualified divers over 18 to help establish a marine park in Belize.

Discover the World Ltd
29 Nork Way
Banstead
Surrey SN7 1PB
Tel: **01697-748356**
Organises tours on behalf of the WWF and for the Whale and Dolphin Conservation Society

Discovery Initiatives
No.3, 68 Princes Square
London W2 4NY
Tel: **0171-229 9881**
email:**enquiry@discoveryinitiatives.com**
Tour operator that supplies outdoor holidays based around particular conservation projects.

Earthwatch
Belsyre Court
57 Woodstock Road
Oxford OX2 6HU
Tel: **01865-311600**
Charity which matches paying volunteers to research projects world-wide.

Ecumenical Coalition on Third World Tourism (ECTWT)
PO Box 24
Chorakhebua
Bangkok 10230
Thailand
Tel: **662 510 7287**
Church organisation concerned with monitoring tourism development and preventing exploitation.

Elefriends
Born Free Foundation
Coldharbour
Dorking
Surrey RH5 6HA
Tel: **01306-713320**
Campaign for the protection of the elephant.

English Nature
Northmister House
Northminster Road
Peterborough PE1 1UA
Tel: **01733-455 000**
Aims to raise public awareness of conservation issues and will act as a consultancy on environmental matters.

Environment Investigation Agency
15 Bowling Green Lane
London EC1R OBD
Tel: **0171 490 7040**
http://**www.pair.com/eia/**

Europa Nostra
Lange Voorhut 35
2514 EC
The Hague
Holland
Tel: **70 356 0333**
Devoted to preserving Europe's national and cultural heritage, improving the environment and encouraging high standards of town and country planning.

Europe Conservation
Col. Vilanna 6A
20143 Milano
Italy
Tel: **2-5810 3135**
Charity which runs ecological and archaeological holiday and research programmes in Europe's parks and nature reserves.

Field Studies Council
Preston Montford
Montford Bridge
Shrewsbury SY4 1HW
Tel: **01743-850674**
The council runs over 500 courses a year at its 11 centres in England and Wales.

Field Studies Council Overseas
Mrs Anne Stephens, Overseas
Expeditions Co-ordinator
Montford Bridge
Shrewsbury SY4 1HW
Tel: **01743-850164**
email: **100643.1675@CompuServe.com**
Runs environmental study courses of one to four weeks' duration in countries world-wide.

Friends of the Earth
26-28 Underwood Street
London N1 7JQ
Tel: **0171-490 1555**
Campaigning organisation promoting policies which protect the natural environment.

Green Flag International
PO Box 396
Linton
Cambridgeshire CB1 6UL
Tel: **01223-893587**
Environmental consultancy for the tourism industry and the general travelling public.

Greenpeace
Canonbury Villas
London N1 2PN
Tel: **0171-865 8100**
International environmental pressure group.

Institute of Travel and Tourism
113 Victoria Street
St Albans
Herts AL1 3TJ
Tel: **01727-854395**

Interface – North-South Travel
Moulsham Mill
Parkway
Chelmsford
Essex CM2 7PX
Tel: **01245-492882**
A travel agency which ploughs back its profits into development projects in the Third World.

The Land is Ours
Box E, 111 Madalen Road
Oxford OX4 1RQ
Tel: 01865 722 016
A land rights charity that campaign's for Britain.

Marine Conservation Society
9 Gloucester Road

Ross-on-Wye
Herefordshire HR9 5BU
Tel: **01989-566017**

Mediterranean Action Plan (MAP)
Lazriou Avenue 301
19002 Peania
Athens
Greece
Tel: **1-665 7912**
Conservation body which carries out research into the protection of the Mediterranean coastal and marine environment.

National Trust Working Holidays
33 Sheep Street
Cirencester
Gloucestershire GL7 1RQ
Tel: **01285-644 727**
Run over 400 volunteer working projects/holidays a year all over the UK.

National Trust for Scotland
5 Charlotte Square
Edinburgh EH2 4DU
Tel: **0131-243 9470**
Working holidays all over Scotland as well as a variety of cruises around the world, the profits of which go to the Islands Fund

Naturetrek
Chautara
Bighton
Nr. Alresford
Hants SO24 9RB
Tel: **01962-733051**
Birdwatching, natural history and botanical tours world-wide, donate a percentage of profits to environmental charities.

Reef and Rainforest Tours
Prospect House
Jubilee Road
Totnes
Devon TQ9 5BP
Tel: **01803-866965**
Small outfit running wildlife and diving tours to Indonesia, Papua New Guinea, Honduras, Venezuela, Peru, Belize, Ecuador and Costa Rica.

Royal Society for the Protection of Birds (RSPB)
The Lodge
Sandy
Bedfordshire SG19 2DL
Tel: **01767-8680551**

Save the Rhino International
21 Bentinck Street
London W1M 5RP
Tel: **0171-935 5880**

email: **save@rhinos.demon.co.uk**
Offer unique safaris to Namibia to see desert rhinos. Proceeds fund their protection.

Survival International
11-15 Emerald Street
London WC1N 3QL
Tel: **0171-242 1441**
Charity devoted to protecting the human rights of the world's tribal peoples.

Sustainability Limited
The People's Hall
91-97 Freston Road
London W11 4BD
Tel: **0171-243 1227**

Symbiosis Expedition Planning
113 Bolingbroke Grove
London SW11 1DA
Tel: **0171-924 5906**
email: **101456.2155@compuserve.com**
Ecologically and culturally sensitive tailor-made adventure holidays in SE Asia.

Tourism Concern
Stapleton House
277-281 Holloway Road
London N7 8HN
Tel: **0171-753 3330**
Runs regular seminars and meetings dealing with tourism development, and links interested parties concerned with tourism development.

Tourism with Insight
Hadorfer Strasse 9
D-8130 Starnberg
Germany
A consortium of organisations (including Tourism concern) promoting 'green' tourism.

Travelwatch
Suite 23, Grafton House
2-3 Golden Square, London W1R 3AD
Tel: **0171-287 3691**
Consultancy specialising in working with government and industry assesing the environmental impact of travel and tourism. Established in 1997 as a sister company to the successful oil sector environmental consultancy Rundall Blanchard Associates.

University Research Expeditions Program
University of California
Berkeley
CA 94720
Tel: **510-642 6586**
Organises a range of expeditions from Environmental studies to Art and Culture.

Whale and Dolphin Conservation Society
Alexander House ⇨

James Street West
Bath
Avon BA1 2BT
Tel: **01225-334511**

**World Conservation Union
(formerly IUCN)**
28 Rue Mauverney
CH-1196 Gland
Switzerland
Tel: **22-99 90001**
International organisation co-ordinating the work of various charities working in the field of conservation.

World Tourism Organisation
Capitan Haya 42
28020 Madrid
Spain
Tel: **1-571 0628**

World Wide Fund for Nature (WWF)
Pand House
Weyside Park
Godalming
Surrey GU7 1XR
Tel: **01483-426444**
Major international nature conservancy body which concerns itself with all aspects of the environment including the problems associated with tourism development.

Expedition

(see also Adventure & Sporting)

Arcturus Expeditions
PO Box 850
Gartocharn Alexandria
Dunbartonshire G83 8RL
Tel: **01389-830204**
Specialise in the Arctic's natural history, archaeology and native peoples. Also dog sledding, kayaking and skiing.

Alpine Club
55 Charlotte Road
London EC2A 3QT
Tel: **0171-259 5591**
Has an important reference collection of mountaineering literature, guidebooks and map. View by appointment only.

Archaeology Abroad
31-34 Gordon Square
London WC1 0PY
Tel: **0171-380 7495**
Provides information about opportunities for archaeological field work and excavations outside Britain.

Brathay Exploration Group
Brathay Hall
Ambleside
Cumbria LA22 0HP
Tel: **01539-433942**
Provides expedition and training opportunities for young people – 40 years of experience.

British Schools Exploring Society
Royal Geographic Society
1 Kensington Gore
London SW7 2AR
Tel: **0171-591 3141**
Organises major adventurous and scientific expeditions each year for 17 to 20 year olds.

Earthquest
54 Sunderland Terrace
Ulverston
Cumbria LA12
Tel: **0229 57885**
Runs world-wide research and development expeditions, volunteer leaders and support staff required.

Earthwatch
57 Woodstock Road
Oxford OX2 6HJ
Tel: **01865-311600**
Environmental charity which matches paying volunteers to scientific research projects worldwide.

Erskine Expeditions
16 Braid Farm Road
Edinburgh EH10 6LF
Tel: **0131-447 7218**
Organises adventure tours in Arctic regions including dog-sledging, mountaineering and cross-country skiing.

Expedition Advisory Centre
Royal Geographical Society
1 Kensington Gore
London SW7 2AR
Tel: **0171-591 3030**
The Expedition Advisory Centre provides an information and training service for those planning expeditions. Publishers of The Expedition Planners' Handbook and Directory.

Exploration Logistics
Rank Xerox Business Park
Mitcheldean
Gloucestershire GL17 0DD
Tel: **01594-544733**
Tailor-made support service for expeditions, with consultancy, design and purchase of equipment, survival courses and field support.

The Explorers Club
46 East 70th St

New York
NY 10021 USA
Tel: **212-628 83 83**
The Club has financed over 140 expeditions and awarded its flag to over 300 expeditions.

Foundation for Field Research
PO Box 2010
Alpine, California 92001
Sponsors research expeditions and finds volunteers to staff projects.

Iceland Information Centre
PO Box 434
Harrow
Middlesex HA1 3HY
Specialises in expeditions to Iceland and publishes useful Iceland: the Traveller's Guide.

National Geographical Society
17th and M Streets, NW
Washington DC 20036
USA
The Society's aim is to pursue and promulgate geographical knowledge and to promote research and exploration. The Society often sponsors significant expeditions.

Mountain and Wildlife Adventures
The Adventure Traveller
Compston Road
Ambleside
Cumbria LA22 9BJ
Tel: **01539-433285**
Specialises in travel and expedition advice for Scandinavia.

Dick Phillips
Whitehall House
Nenthead Alston
Cumbria CA9 3PS
Long-established specialist in travel in those parts of Iceland beyond the interests of the mainstream travel trade.

K & J Slavin Quest Ltd
Cow Pasture Farm
Louth Road
Hainton
Market Rasen LN8 6LX
Tel: **01507-313401**
Directors Ken and Julie Slavin are expedition and aid consultants offering complete support services to individual and commercial clients on projects world-wide.

Raleigh International
27 Parsons Green Lane
London SW6 4HS
Tel: **0171-371 8585**
email: **info@raleigh.org.uk**

Royal Geographical Society
1 Kensington Gore
London SW7 2AR
Tel: **0171-591 3000**
email: **eac@rgs.org**
A focal point for geographers and explorers. It directly organises and finances its own scientific expeditions and gives financial support, approval and advice to numerous expeditions each year.The RGS maintains the largest private map collection in Europe and has a large library with books and periodicals on geography, travel and exploration.

Royal Scottish Geographical Society
40 George Street
Glasgow G1 1QE
Tel: **0141-552 3330**
Also has centres all over Scotland.

Scientific Exploration Society
Expedition Base
Motcombe
Shaftesbury
Dorset
Tel: **01747-853353**
Maintains close links with commerce, industry, educational establishments, the services and other scientific and exploration organisations. The Society 'approves and supports' expeditions but rarely gives cash to any project.

Scott Polar Research Institute
Lensfield Road
Cambridge CB2 1ER
Tel: **01223-336540**
Has a specialist library concerned with all aspects of polar expeditions and research.

South American Explorers Club
Av. Portugal 146
Brena
Postal Casilla 3714
Lima 100
Peru
Tel: 1 425 0142
or
Jorge Washington 311 y L.Plaza
Postal Apartado 21-431
Quito
Ecuador
Tel/Fax: 2 225 228
or
126 Indian Creek Road
Ithaca
NY14850
Exists to promote travel and sporting aspects of exploration. Publications include The South American Explorer magazine. The Club House, with reading rooms, maps and guidebooks is at the address in Lima listed above, people may visit any time.

Trekforce
134 Buckingham Palace Road
London SW1W 9SA
Tel: **0171-824 8890**
*Mounts several expeditions each year to study
the tropical forests of Indonesia.*

University Research Expeditions Program
University of California
Berkeley
CA 94720
Tel: **510-642 6586**
*Organises a range of expeditions from
Environmental studies to Art and Culture.*

Vander-Molen Foundation
The Model Farm House
Church End
Hendon
London NW4 4JS
Tel: **0181-203 2344**
*Helps to organise expeditions especially for the
handicapped.*

World Challenge Expeditions
Walham House
Walham Grove
London SW6 1QP
Tel: **0171-386 9828**
Month-long, fee-paying projects in a variety of
locations with the emphasis on personal
development for the 16-20 year old age group.

**Young Explorers Trust (The Association of
British Youth Exploration Societies)**
The Royal Geographical Society
1 Kensington Gore
London SW7 2AR
Provides a forum within which societies and
individuals can exchange information. It does
not organise its own expeditions or make travel
bookings. The Trust is a registered charity.

Adventure and Sporting

Access Tours
5th Floor 58 Pitt St
Sydney
NSW 2070
Australia
Tel: **2-241 1128**
*Activity holidays in the former Soviet Union and
Southeast Asia.*

Adirondack Mountain Club
174 Glen St
Glens Falls
NY 12801
USA
Tel: **518-793 7737**
ADK is a non-profit membership organisation.

*Works to retain the wilderness and magic of
New York's Adirondack and Catskill parks.*

Adrift
Collingbourne House
Spencer Court
140-142 High Street
Wandsworth
London SW18 4JJ
Tel: **0181-874 4969**
email: **raft@adrift.co.uk**
Whitewater rafting holidays world-wide.

Airtrack Services Ltd
16-17 Windsor Street
Uxbridge
Middlesex
UB8 1AB
Tel: **01895-810 810**
*Organises sporting holidays around the world,
from bungy jumping in Switzerland to tickets for
the IndyCar championships in the US*

Alternative Travel Group
69-71 Banbury Road
Oxford OX2 6PE
Tel: **01865-513333**
*Walking and trekking holidays for groups and
individuals in Europe*

Appalachian Trail Conference
Box 807
Harpers Ferry
WV 25425
USA
Tel: **304 535 6331**

The American Hiking Society
1701 18th St NW
Washington DC 20009
USA

Arcturus Expeditions
PO Box 850
Gartocharn Alexandria
Dunbartonshire G83 8RL
Tel: **01389-834204**
*Specialise in the Arctic's natural history,
archaeology and native peoples. Also dog
sledding, kayaking and skiing.*

Big Mountain Tours
25 Bury Hill
Woodbridge
Suffolk IP12 1JD
Tel/Fax: **01394-385416**
Guided walking and trekking in the Pyrenees.

Bike Events
PO Box 75
Bath BA1 1BX
Tel: **01225-480130**

Blue Green Adventures
2 Priory Cottages
Parsonage Lane
Lamberhurst
Kent TN3 8DS
Tel: **01892-891071**
Adventure riding holidays (no experience needed) in South America.

British Activity Holiday Association (BAHA)
Orchard Cottage
22 Green Lane
Hersham
Walton-on-Thames KT12 5HD
Tel: **01932-252994**
email: **http://www.baha.org.uk.**
Provides information on activity holidays in the UK.

The British Association of Parachute Clubs (BAPC)
18 Talbot Lane
Leicester LE1 4LR
Tel: **01162-530318**

British Canoe Union (BCU)
Adbolton Lane
West Bridgford
Nottinghamshire NT2 5AS
Tel: **01159-821100**
Advice and information on courses, clubs, etc.

British Gliding Association
Kimberley House
Vaughan Way
Leicester LE1 4SE
Tel: **01162-531051**

British Mountaineering Council (BMC)
177-179 Burton Road
Manchester M20 2BB
Tel: **0161-445 4747**
Reference books and information on all aspects of mountaineering.

British Orienteering Federation
Riverdale
Dale Road North
Darley Dale
Matlock
Derbyshire DE4 2HX
Tel: **01629-734042**

British Parachute Association
Kimberley House
Vaughan Way
Leicester LE1 4SG
Tel: **01162-519778**

British Sub-Aqua Club
Telford's Quay
Elsmere Port

South Wirral L65 4FY
Tel: **0151-357 1951**
Diving instruction through regional branches and a diving holidays information service.

The Adventure Travel Society
6551 S. Revere Parkway, Suite 160
Englewood. CO80111, USA
Tel: **303-649 9016**
email: ats@adventuretravel.com
Web: http://www.adventuretravel.com/ats
ATS is a professional corporation dedicated to promoting natural resource sustainability, economic viability and cultural integrity through the development of tourism.

Canadian Wilderness Trips
187 College St
Toronto
Ontario M5T 1P7
Canada
Tel: **416-977 3703**
Whitewater rafting and canoeing in Northern Ontario.

Continental Divide Trail Society
PO Box 30002
Bethesda
MD 20814
USA

Coral Cay Conservation Expeditions
The Ivy Works
154 Clapham Park Road
London SW4 7DE
Tel: **0171-498 6248**
Recruits qualified divers over 18 to help establish a marine park in Belize.

Destination USA
41-45 Goswell Road
London EC1V 7EH
Tel: **0171-336 7788**
Golfing holidays world-wide.

Encounter Overland
267 Old Brompton Road
London SW5 9JA
Tel: **0171-370 6845**
World-wide adventure/overland travel, with tours lasting as long as 29 weeks.

Erna Low Consultants
9 Reece Mews
London SW7 3HE
Tel: **0171-584 2841**
Golfing and spa holidays world-wide.

Exodus Expeditions
9 Weir Road
London SW12 0LT
Tel: **0181-675 5550**

Expeditions Inc
Route 4
Box 755
Flagstaff
Arizona 86001
USA
Tel: **602-774 8176**
Kyaking and rafting tours in the Grand Canyon.

Explore Worldwide
1 Frederick Street
Aldershot
Hampshire GU11 1LQ
Tel: **01252-333031**
Adventure and walking tours around the world.

Four Corners School of Outdoor Education
East Route
Monicello
Utah 84535
USA
Tel: **801-587 2859**
Adventure activities in the Colorado Plateau from 14 years old upwards including backpacking and rafting.

Frontiers
18 Albemarle Street
London W1X 3HA
Tel: **0171-629 2044**
Hunting, shooting and fishing holidays world-wide.

Go Fishing
6 Baron's Gate
33-35 Rothchilds Road
London W4 1RX
Tel: **0181-742 3700**
Organises fishing trips to the Falklands Islands, Canada, and the USA

The Grand Touring Club
Model Farm
Rattlesden
Bury St Edmunds
Suffolk
IP30 0SY
Tel: **01449-737774**
Classic motoring rally/tours in France.

Guerba Expeditions
Wessex House
40 Station Road
Westbury BA13 3JN
Tel: **01373-826611**
Camping tours to Africa.

Gung Ho
6 Enys Road
Eastbourne
East Sussex BN21 2DH
Tel: **01323-431860**
email: **gungho@mistral.co.uk**

Adventure tours, particularly in Borneo.

Headwater Holidays
146 London Road
Northwich
Cheshire
CW9 5HH
Tel: **01606-48699**

The International Long River Canoeist Club
c/o Peter Salisbury
238 Birmingham Road, Redditch
Worcs B97 6EL
The International Long River Canoeist Club is the only United Kingdom association that can offer details of thousands of rivers around the World. Members in 26 countries ready to offer help and advice.

Journey Latin America
14-16 Devonshire Road
Chiswick
London W4 2HD
Tel: **0181-747 3108**
Large selection of South American tours to suit all pockets.

KE Adventure Travel
32 Lake Road
Keswick
Cumbria CA12 5DQ
Tel: **01768-773966**
email: **keadventure@enterprise.net**
Trekking, climbing and mountain biking holidays world-wide.

The London Underwater Centre
13 Glendower Road
London SW14 8NY
Tel: **0181-876 0735**
Scuba diving holidays world-wide for reasonably experienced divers.

Motor Safari
Pinfold Lane
Buckley
Clwyd CH7 3NS
Tel: **01244-548849**
Jeep mountain safaris, squad biking and amphibious vehicles in Wales and Cyprus.

Origins
Woodcock Travel
25-31 Wicker
Sheffield S3 8HW
Tel: **0114-272 9619**
Adventure holidays world-wide.

Outward Bound Trust
Watermillock
Nr. Penrith
Cumbria CA11 0JL
Tel: **0990-134 227**

Adventure holidays in off-beat regions of UK.

Pacific Crest Club
PO Box 1907
Santa Ana
CA 92702

Page and Moy
136-140 London Road
Leicester LE2 1EN
Tel: **0116-2552521**
Established specialist operator offering motor racing holidays to Grand Prix events world-wide, as well as golfing, music and archaeological tours.

Rafting & Sports Team Allgau
Splash House
Hauptstr. 15
88457 Kirchdord a.d.Iller
Germany
Tel: **(7354) 91 865**
Fax: (7354) 91 929
Specialises in white water rafting and Alpine sports tours in Austria, Switzerland and South Germany.

The Ramblers Association
1-5 Wandsworth Road
London SW8 2XX
Tel: **0171-582 6878**

Ramblers Holidays
PO Box 43
Church Road
Welwyn Garden City AL8 6PQ
Tel: **01707-331133**
Walking holidays throughout Europe from an offshoot of the Ramblers' Association.

Safari Drive Ltd
127 High Street
Hungerford
Berkshire RG17 0DL
Tel: **01488-681 611**
Organises self-drive safaris in Africa, also white water rafting and microlighting.

Sheerwater
PO Box 125
Victoria Falls
Zimbabwe
Canoe trips along the Zambezi.

The Sierra Club
730 Polk St
San Francisco
CA 94109
Tel: **415-776 2211**
Every sort of adventure holiday.

Ski Club of Great Britain
The White House

57/63 Church Road
London SW19 5DQ
Tel: **0181-410 2000**
Unbiased advice on resorts, travel and equipment; snow reports; club flights and special discounts are amongst the many benefits

Sobeck Expeditions Inc
Box 1089
Angels Camp
California 95222
USA
Tel: **800-777 7939**

Sporting International
13201 Northwest Freeway
Suite 800
Houston
TX 77040
USA
Tel: **713-744 5260**
They control Ker, Downey and Selby who have vast concessions for safaris in the Okavango, notably Pom Pom, Shinid Island and Mahcaba.

Tana Delta Ltd
PO Box 24988
Nairobi
Kenya
River journeys along the Tana Delta aboard the African Queen.

World Expeditions
4 Northfields Prosect
Putney Bridge Road
London SW18 1PE
Tel: **0181-870 2600**
email: **worldex@dircom.co.uk**
Australian-based adventure tour operator.

Arctic and Antarctic

Abercrombie & Kent
1520 Kensington Road
Oak Brook
IL 60521-2141
USA
Tel: **630-954-2944**
email: **info@abercrombiekent.co**
Offers several different cruises to Antarctica from Ushuaia in Argentina on Explorer, the vessel originally commissioned by Antarctic tourism pioneer Lars-Eric Linblad.

Arctic Experience
29 Nork Way
Banstead
Surrey SM7 1PB
Tel: **01737-218800**
email: **sales@arctic-discover.co.uk**
Expeditions to Greenland and other arctic

destinations.

Arcturus Expeditions
PO Box 850
Gartocharn Alexandria
Dunbartonshire G83 8RL
Tel: **01389-830204**
Specialise in the Arctic's natural history, archaeology and native peoples. Also dog sledding, kayaking and skiing.

GMMS Polar Journeys
441 Kent Street
Sydney
NSW 2000
Australia
Tel: **2 264 3366**
The only cruise company offering the chance to camp ashore in Antarctica overnight. Tours generally two weeks in length.

Travel Dynamics
132 East 70th Street
New York
NY 10021
USA
Tel: **212 517 7555**
Operating for the past 25 years with small ships taking parties on educational voyages to Antarctica for non-profit organisations.

WildWings
International House
Bank Road
Bristol
Avon BS15 2LX
Tel: **0117-984 8040**
email: **http://www.wildwings.co.uk**
Operates bird and wildlife tours to Antarctica. Expeditions are led by bird expert Dick Filby and cetacean authority Mark Carwardine. Tours range from 18-27 days.

Student - Awards & Grants

BP Conservation Programme
C/o Expeditions Officer
BirdLife International
Wellbrook Court
Girton Road
Cambridge CB3 0NA
Tel: **01223-277318**
email: **eo@birdlife.org.uk**
Is jointly administered by the International Council for Bird Preservation and the Fauna and Flora Preservation Society. Each year a total of £34,000 is given in grant funding.

Mount Everest Foundation
Hon Secretary: W. H. Ruthven
Gowrie
Cardwell Close
Warton
Preston PR4 1SH
Tel: **01772-635346**
Supports British and New Zealand expeditions only. Dates for grant application - August 31 and December 31 for the following year.

The Rolex Awards for Enterprise
The Secretariat
PO Box 178
1211 Geneva 26
Switzerland
The Rolex Awards provide financial assistance in three broad fields: Applied Sciences and Invention, Exploration and Discovery, the Environment.

Royal Geographical Society
1 Kensington Gore
London SW7 2AR
Tel: **0171-591 3030**
email: **awards@rgs.org**
Administer not only their own awards and grants but those of many other sponsors. Details and applications from the Grants Secretary at the above address. Applications to be submitted by January 31st each year. (See article on expeditionary travel, Chapter 3.)

WEXAS International
Awards administered by The Royal Geographical Society. Write for details to: The Information Officer, The Royal Geographical Society, 1, Kensington Gore, London SW7 2AR.

Winston Churchill Memorial Trust
15 Queens Gate Terrace
London SW7 5PR
Tel: **0171-581 0410**
Awards about 100 travelling Fellowships annually to enable British citizens to carry out study projects overseas in approximately ten categories of interest or occupation which are varied annually.

Young Explorers Trust
C/o Royal Geographical Society
1 Kensington Gore
London SW7 2AR
Tel: **0171-591 3030**
Gives grants to school expeditions.

Further reading:
The International Directory of Voluntary Work (Vacation Work).
Volunteer Work (Central Bureau).
Expedition Planners' Handbook (Expedition Advisory Centre).

Student - Educational and Exchange

Council on International Education Exchange (CIEE)
205 East 42nd Street
New York
NY10017
USA
Tel: **212-661 1414**

Cultural and Educational Services Abroad
Western House
Malpas
Truro TR1 1SQ
Tel: **01872-225300**
Language learning courses in Europe, Russia and Japan.

En Famille Overseas
The Old Stables
60b Maltravers Street
Arundel
W Sussex BN18 9BG
Tel: **01903-883266**
Stay as a paying guest with a French family and language courses in Paris also available.

European Community Young Worker Exchange Programme
Central Bureau for Educational Visits and Exchanges
Vocational and Education Department
10 Spring Gardens
London SW1A 2BN
Tel: **0171-389 4004**
EC nationals aged 18 to 25 with vocational experience can apply for placements lasting between three and 16 months.

Gap Activity Projects
44 Queens Road
Reading
Berkshire RG1 4BB
Tel: **01734-594914**
Provides school leavers with work experience opportunities overseas including the Soviet Union, Poland and China.

Goodwill Holidays
Manor Chambers
The Green
School Lane
Welwyn AL6 9EB
Tel: **01438-716421**
Holidays in the CIS that provide an opportunity to gain insight into the culture, society and politics

Inscape Fine Art Tours
Austins Farm

High Street
Stonesfield
Whitney
Oxon OX9 8PU
Tel: **01993-891726**
Fine-art study tours to Europe.

International Educational Opportunities
28 Canterbury Road
Lydden
Dover
Kent CT15 7ER
Tel: **01304-823631**
An educational agency arranging language courses, homestays and term stays abroad.

International Farm Experience Programme YFC Centre
National Agricultural Centre
Kenilworth
Warwickshire CV8 2LG
Offers opportunities for young agriculturist and horticulturists to further their knowledge through international exchanges.

International Association for the Exchange of Students for Technical Experience (IAESTE-UK)
10 Spring Gardens
London SW1A 2BN
Tel: **0171-389 4004**
World-wide opportunities for undergraduates to gain industrial, technical or commercial experience.

Le Touron
St Mayme de Pareyrol
24380 Vergt
France
Tel: **553-54 7907**
Offers dinner party cookery courses and wine safari weeks in France.

LSG Theme Holidays
201 Main Street
Thornton
Leicestershire LE67 1AH
Tel: **01509-231713**
Conversational French in all areas of France.

Painting School of Montmiral
Rue de la Port Neuve
81140 Castelnau de Montmiral
Tel: **63 33 1311**
Painting courses with individual tuition.

STA
Priory House
6 Wrights Lane
London W8 6TA
Tel: **0171-361 6100**
Student travel agent.

Youth for Understanding
International Exchange
3501 Newark St, NW
Washington DC 20016
USA
Tel: **202-966 6800**
Devoted to promoting world peace through high school student exchange programmes.

Voluntary

Action Health
International Voluntary Health Association
The Director
The Gate House
25 Gwydir St
Cambridge CB1 2LG
Tel: **01223-460853**
Charitable organisation which places qualified medics, nurses and physiotherapists with at least two years experience in voluntary health programmes in developing countries.

British Executive Service Overseas
164 Vauxhall Bridge Road
London SW1V 2RB
Tel: **0171-630 0644**
Consider retired applicants with lots of experience to advise projects overseas using technical and managerial skills. Short-term placements on an expenses only basis.

British Trust for Conservation Volunteers
Wallingford
Oxon
Tel: **01491-839766**
Practical conservation work and training courses for all age groups throughout England, Wales, Northern Ireland and overseas (eighteen + for overseas placements), including leadership courses.

International Health Exchange
8-10 Dryden Street
London WC2E 9NA
Tel: **0171-836 5833**
Provides details of job vacancies and training for health workers in developing countries.

Catholic Institute for International Relations
Unit 3, Canonbury Yard
190a New North Road
London N1 7BJ
Tel: **0171-354 0883**
Recruits skilled, qualified people for minimum of two year's work experience overseas.

Christians Abroad
1 Stockwell Green
London SW9 9HP
Tel: **0171-737 7811**

Places qualified workers, mainly teachers, abroad for two year minimum placements, committed Christians preferred.

Christian Outreach
1 New Street
Leamington Spa
Warwickshire CV31 1HP
Tel: **01926-315301**
Welcomes well-qualified applicants for one year minimum for overseas placements, but must have Christian commitment.

Christian Vocations
Unit 2
Holloway St West
Lower Gornal
West Midlands
DY3 2DZ
Tel: **01902-882836**
Short and long term voluntary opportunities for work overseas ranging from missionary work to engineering and farming.

Concordia (Youth Service Volunteers)
Heversham House
20-22 Boundary Road
Hove
Sussex BN3 4ET
Tel: **01273-422293**
International voluntary work camps, should be over seventeen. Accommodation provided but not expenses.

Community Service Volunteers
237 Pentonville Road
London N1 9NJ
Tel: **0171-278 6601**
Provides volunteering opportunities for people aged 16-35, helping people in need for period of 4-12 months, in the UK. Volunteers work with people with physical disabilities and learning difficulties.

Council Of Churches for Britain and Ireland
Inter Church House
35-41 Lower Marsh
London SE1 7RL
Tel: **0171-620 4444**
Part of international interdominational youth service of the Ecumenical Youth Council in Europe. Groups of young people to carry out four-week projects.

East European Partnership (EEP)
Carlton House
27a Carlton Drive
London SW15 2BS
Tel: **0181-780 2841**
Part of VSO. English teachers needed in East European countries. Special education teachers and others required for Albania.

Gap Activity Projects
44 Queens Road
Reading
Berkshire RG1 4BB
Tel: **01734-594914**
Offers school leavers seventeen + employment abroad before going to university. Apply 1st term of final year at school.

Health Projects Abroad
PO Box 24
Bakewell
Derbyshire DE45 1ZW
Tel: **01629-640051**
Volunteers, 18-28, needed with a willingness to work hard in a team for four month in Tanzania, Must raise over £2,450 for travel and project.

Health Unlimited
Prince Consort House
27-29 Albert Embankment
London SE1 7TS
Tel: **0171-582 5999**
Recruits medically qualified volunteers for one year or more to work on projects world-wide.

H.E.L.P. (Scotland)
60 The Pleasance
Edinburgh EH8 9TJ
Tel: **0131-556 9497**
Work camps run by a committee of Scottish students. Expansion planned into long term projects and to other Scottish Universities, working in E. Europe and the Third World.

International Cooperation For Development (ICD)
Unit 3
Canonbury Yard
190a New North Road
London N1 7BJ
Tel: **0171-354 0883**
Qualified, experienced agrriculturalists, technical and health people for two years in Nicaragua, Peru, Honduras, Ecuador, El salvador, Dominican Rep, Yemen, Zimbabwe and Namibia.

Involvement Volunteers
PO Box 218
Port Melbourne
Victoria 3207
Australia
Opportunities for voluntary conservation projects.

Kibbutz Representatives
1a Accommodation Road
London NW11 8ED
Tel: **0181-458 9235**
Working Holidays on Kibbutz in Israel. Must be 18-32 years. Applicants pay air fare and

insurance. Free board and small allowance.

Project 67
10 Hatton Garden
London EC1N 8AH
Tel: **0171-831 7626**
Kibbutz and Moshav voluntary work in Israel.

Project Trust
The Hebridean Centre
Bally Hough
Isle of Coll
Argyll
PA78 6TE
Tel: **01879-230444**
Opportunities for young people seventeen to nineteen years to serve in developing countries on twelve month projects. Must be in full time education at time of application. Volunteer must raise part of the costs.

Quaker International Social Projects
Friends House
173-177 Euston Road
London NW1 2BJ
Tel: **0171-387 3601**

Raleigh International
27 Parsons Green Lane
London SW6 4HZ
Tel: **0171-371 8585**
email: **info@raleigh.org.uk**
Organises challenging expeditions world-wide, based around community conservation, for young people aged 17-25, also skilled people over 25 years.

Skillshare Africa
3 Belvoir Street
Leicester LE1 6SL
Tel: **01162-541862**
Offers qualified and experienced people opportunities for working in southern Africa for a minimum of two years.

Teaching Abroad
10 Drew Street
Brixham
Devon TQ5 9JU
Tel: **01803-855 565**
Opportunities to teach English in Moldavia, Romania and Ukraine, for graduates, undergraduates and those delaying entry in to university. All year from one month to one year. Volunteers pay for accommodation and travel.

Tear Fund Gap Programme
100 Church Road
Teddington Middlesex
TW11 8QE
Tel: **0181-977 9144**
Christian organisation with strong

development programmes, needing qualified volunteers prepared to serve two to four years.

Third World First
$a East Avenue
Oxford OX4 1XW
Tel: **01865-245678**
Organises student groups in the UK.

Unias
57 Goodramgate
York YO1 2LS
Tel: **01904-647799**
Agricultural, health and engineering experts needed for 2 years in Brazil, Bolivia, Burkina Faso, Mali, West Bank and Gaza.

United Nations Volunteers (UNV)
Palais des Nations
1211 Geneva 10
Switzerland
Tel: **22 798 5850**
Qualified volunteers from all members of the UN needed with relevant experience. Normally two years but shorter humanitarian relief work also. British Passport holders enquire through VSO London.

Universities' Educational Fund for Palestinian Refugees (UNIPAL)
Volunteer Programme Organiser
12 Helen Road
Oxford OX2 0DE
Voluntary English teachers for education and caring programme in the occupied West Bank and in the Gaza Strip.

University of California Research Expeditions Programme (UREP)
Desk L University of California
Berkeley
CA 94270 USA
Tel: **415-642 6586**
Will take inexperienced volunteers on UREP expeditions world-wide. Wide variety of areas and subjects.

US Peace Corp
Washington DC 20526
USA
Tel: **202 606 3886**
Places volunteers in 62 developing countries. Volunteers with all kinds of backgrounds are accepted.

Vacation Work International
9 Park End Street
Oxford OX1 1HJ
Tel: **01865-241978**
Produces useful, regularly updated, publications on work, travel and study abroad.

Volunteers for Peace
43 Tiffany Road
Belmont
Vermont 05730
USA
Tel: **802-259 2759**
Publishes an International Work Camp Directory, featuring voluntary opportunities in work camps world-wide.

Voluntary Service Overseas
317 Putney Bridge Road
London SW15 2PN
Tel: **0181-780 2266**
Volunteers are selected from people with skills and qualifications e.g. teachers, nurses, agriculturalists, social workers, carpenters to work in the Third World.

VSO Canada
Lynn Sim
35 Centennial Boulevard
Ottawa
KIY 2H8
Recruiting Canadian experienced, qualifies, teachers and foresters for VSO.

World Council of Churches
Ecumenical Youth Action
150 Route de Ferney
PO Box 2100
1211 Geneva 2
Switzerland
Tel: **22 791 6111**
Opportunities for young volunteers aged 18 to 30 to work in international work camps contributing to local and national development in developing countries.

For further information there are many useful books available including: International Directory of Voluntary Work and Directory of Work and Study in Developing Countries (Vacation Work, 9 Park End Street, Oxford OX1 1HJ), Work Your Way Around the World (Vacation Work) and Volunteer Work (Central Bureau for Educational Visits and Exchange, 10 Spring Gardens, London, SW1A 2BN, tel: 0171-389 4004).

Expatriate

Corona Worldwide
c/o Commonwealth Institute
Kensington High Street
London W8 6NQ
Tel: **0171-610 4407**
A valuable source of information for women expatriates. Their Notes for Newcomers series gives lots of practical advice for100 countries.

Expats International
29 Lacon Road
Dulwich
London SE22 9HE
Tel: **0181-299 4986**
An association for expatriates which has a large job advertisement section in its magazine and will advise on contracts and finance.

Employment Conditions Abroad
Anchor House
15 Britten Street
London SW3 3TY
Tel: **0171-351 5000**

The Fry Group
Crescent House
Crescent Road
Worthing
West Sussex
BN11 1RN
Tel: **01903-231545**
Consultancy specialising in the financial side of moving abroad e.g. tax clearance, financial regulations, National Health Insurance contributions and investments.

World-Wide Education Service
St. George's House
14-17 Wells Street
London W1P 3FP
Tel: **0171-637 2644**
email: **office@weshome.demon.co.uk**
Provides a service for those wishing or having to teach children at home or supplement thier schooling.

Working

(see also Voluntary and Section 12 on Teaching English Abroad)

Action d'Urgence Internationale
10 Rue Felix-Aiem
75018 Paris
France
Tel: **142 64 7588**
Runs training courses for people interested in helping rescue operations in times of natural disasters. Branches in France, UK, Morocco, India, Dominican Republic and Guadeloupe.

BUNAC
16 Bowling Green Lane
London EC1R 0BD
Tel: **0171-251 3472**
Young person work/travel programmes in US, Canada, Australia and Jamaica.

Camp America
37a Queen's Gate
London SW7 5HR

Tel: **0171-581 7373**

Eurocamp Summer Jobs
Canute Court
Toft Road
Knutsford
Cheshire WA16 0NL
Tel: **01565-625522**

Kibbutz Representatives
1a Accomodation Road
London NW1 8ED
Tel: **0181-458 9235**

Keycamp Holidays
Courier Recruitment Department
92-6 Lind Road
Sutton
Surrey SM1 4PL
Tel: **0181-395 8909**

National Trust Working Holidays
33 Sheep Street
Cirencester
Gloucestershire GL7 1RQ
Tel: **01285-644 727**
Run over 400 volunteer working projects/holidays a year all over England, Wales and Northern Ireland.

National Trust for Scotland
5 Charlotte Square
Edinburgh EH2 4DU
Tel: **0131-243 9470**
Working holidays all over Scotland as well as a variety of cruises around the world, the profits of which go to the Islands Fund.

NetJobs
6695 Millcreek Drive, Unit 1
Mississauga
Ontario
Canada L5N 5R8
Tel: **905 542 9484 (x258)**
email: **info@netjob.com**
http://www.netjobs.com/
Career centre on the internet. Post career opportunities from all disciplines world-wide.

Further Reading: *Work Your Way Around the World (Vacation Work, 9 Park End Street, Oxford, tel: 01865-241978).*

Business

Many travel agencies offer leisure and business travel services but GBTA members (Guild of Business Travel Agents, tel: **0171-222 2744**) specialise in Business Travel Management. Leading members include:

Ayscough Travel
134-138 Borough High Street
London SE1 1LB
Tel: **0171-403 7433**

Britannic Travel
230 Burlington Road
New Morden
Surrey KT3 4NW
Tel: **0181-330 2701**

Carlson Wagonlit Travel
22 Bank Street
Kilmarnock KA1 1HA
Tel: **01563-527377**

Gray Dawes Travel
Dugard House
Peartree Road
Stanway
Colchester
Essex CO3 5UL
Tel: **01206-762241**

Hogg Robinson Travel
Abbey House
282 Farnborough Road
Farnborough
Hampshire GU 14 7NJ
Surrey GU21 5XD
Tel: **01252-372 2000**

The Travel Company
Marble Arch House
66/68 Seymour Street
London W1H 5AF
Tel: **0171-262 5040**

Portman Travel Ltd
15 Berners Street
London W1P 3DE
Tel: **0171-753 8127**

Ian Allan Travel Ltd
Terminal House
Shepperton
Middlesex TW17 8AS
Tel: **01932-228950**

WEXAS International
45-49 Brompton Road
London SW3 1DE
Tel: **0171-589 3315**

Luxury

Abercrombie and Kent
Sloane Square House
Holbein Place
London SW1W 8NS
Tel: **0171-730 9600**
and...

1420 Kensington Road
Suite 111
Oakbrook IL
60521
USA
Tel: **312 954 2944**
email: **info@abercrombiekent.co**
One of the most extensive tour company programmes, emphasis on luxury.

Caribbean Connections
Concorde House
Forest Street
Chester CH1 1QR
Tel: **01244-329556**

Continental Villas
52 Station Road
Petersfield
Hampshire GU32 3ES
Tel: **01243-575338**
Villas in France, West Indies, Spain, Portugal, Italy, Greece, Cyprus.

Cox and Kings Travel Ltd
St. James Court Hotel
Buckingham Gate Road
London SW1E 6AF
Tel: **0171-873 5006**

Cunard Line Ltd
South Western House
Canute Road
Southampton SO14 3NR
Tel: **01703-716 634**
52 Berkeley Street
London W1X 5FP

CV Travel
43 Cadogan Street
London SW3 2PR
Tel: **0171-581 0851**

Elegant Resorts
The Old Palace
Little St. John Street
Chester CH1 1RB
Tel: **01244-350408**
Top of the range resorts in the Caribbean.

Venice Simplon Orient Express Ltd
Sea Containers House
20 Upper Ground
London SE1 9PF
Tel: **0171-928 6000**

WEXAS International
45-49 Brompton Road
London SW3 1DE
Tel: **0171-589 3315**
Can organise all possibilities of luxury travel.

World Apart
PO Box 44209
Nairobi
Kenya
Tel: **228961**
and c/o
Flamingo Tours of East Africa
Tel: **0181-995 3505**
Luxury, traditional tented safaris.

Gay

The Damron Company
PO Box 422458
San Francisco, CA 94142
Tel: **415-255 0404**

The Ferrari Guides
PO Box 37887
Phoenix, AZ 85069
Tel: **602-863 2408**
email: **ferrari@q-net.com**
web: **http:www.rainbow-mall.com/igta**

In Touch
24 Chiswick High Road
London W4 1TE
Tel: **0181-742 7749**
Offers a range of gay holidays world-wide.

Man Around
89 Wembley Park Road
Wembley Park
Middlesex HA9 8HS
Tel: **0181-902 7177**
Gay holidays Europe and Australia.

Our World Magazine
Our World Publishing
1104 N Nova Road
#251 Daytona Beach, FL 32117
Tel: **904-441 5367**
email: **ourworldmg@aol.com**

Positive Discounts
PO Box 347
Twickenham, TW1 2SN
UK
Tel: **0181-891 2561**
email: **hello@positive-discounts.org.uk**
web: **http;///www.positive-discounts.org.uk**
Travel insurance whether or not you are HIV+.

Pride Travel
Devonshire Mansions
Devonshire Place
Brighton BN2 1QH
Tel: **01273-606656**
Trips to USA, Canada, Australia and New Zealand.

Sensations
22 Blenheim Terrace
London NW8 0EB
Tel: **0171-625 6969**
Gay holidays mainly in Europe and USA.

Spartacus International Gay Guide
Leuschnerdamm 31
Berlin 10999
Germany
Tel: **30-614 3071**

Uranian Travel
Infocus House
111 Kew Road
Richmond TW9 2PN
Tel: **0181-332 1022**
Tour operator to mainly European gay resorts.

Art, Photography, History and Archaeology

The British Institute
Piazza Strozzi 2
Florence 50123
Italy
Tel: **55-284031**
Drawing and art history holidays in Florence.

British Museum Tours
46 Bloomsbury Street
London WC1B 3QQ
Tel: **0171-323 3395**
World-wide tours.

Camera Carriers
49 Bare Avenue
Morecambe LA4 6BD
Tel: **01524-411436**
Group photography holidays world-wide.

Cricketer Holidays
4 The White House
Beacon Road
Crowborough
East Sussex TN6 1AB
Tel: **01892-664242**
Painting and drawing holidays.

Francophiles Discover France
66 Great Brockeridge
Bristol BS9 3UA
Tel: **0117-9621975**
Cultural, lighthearted study tours in France.

Galina International Battlefield Tours
711 Beverley High Road
Hull HU6 7JN
Tel: **01482-804409**
Tours of Famous European battlefields.

Hosking Tours
Pages Green House
Wetheringsett
Stowmarket
Suffolk IP14 5QA
Tel: **01728-861113**
Wildlife photographic holidays.

James Keogh Tours
138 Hanworth Road
Hounslow
TW3 1UG
Tel: **0181-570 4228**
Archaeology, art and architecture tours.

Jasmine Tours
High St
Cookham
Maidenhead
Berks SL6 9SQ
Tel: **01628-531121**
Long-haul archaeological tours.

Major and Mrs Holt's Battlefield Tours
The Golden Key Building
15 Market Street
Sandwich
Kent CT13 9DA
Tel: **01304-612248**
Battlefield tours.

Martin Randall
Andrew Brock Travel Ltd
10 Barley Mow Passage
London W4 4PH
Tel: **0181-742 3355**
Specialist in art-history and architectural tours.

Middlebrook's Battlefield Tours
48 Linden Way
Boston PE21 9DS
Tel: **01205-364555**
Guided battlefield tours in France, Belgium and Turkey.

Page and Moy
136-140 London Road
Leicester LE2 1EN
Tel: **01162-552521**
Established specialist operator offering motor racing holidays to Grand Prix events world-wide, as well as golfing, music and archaeological tours.

Photo Travellers
PO Box 58
Godalming
Surrey GU7 2SE
Tel: **01483-425448**
Escorted world-wide photography tours.

Prospect Art Tours Ltd.

454-458 Chiswick High Road
London W4 5TT
Tel: **0181-995 2151**
World-wide music and art history tours.

Special Tours Ltd
81a Elizabeth Street
London SW1W 9PG
Tel: **0171-730 2297**
Organises art history tours on behalf of the National Art Collections Fund.

Steamond International
23 Eccleston Street
London SW1W 9LX
Tel: **0171-730 8646**
Tailor made birdwatching, natural history and archaeology tours.

Swan Hellenic
77 New Oxford St
London WC1A 1PP
Tel: **0171-800 2200**
Guided archaeological and art history cruises - Greece, Turkey, Egypt, Cyprus, Italy, France, Spain, Portugal, Ireland, Scotland, Morocco, Bulgaria, Tunisia, Syria, Jordan and Israel.

Musical

Blair Travel
117 Regent's Park Road
London NW1 8UR
Tel: **0171-483 2290**
Music holidays with either of two subsidiaries Travel for the Arts and Travel with the Friends (Friends of Covent Garden).

Festival Tours International
73 Platts Lane
London NW3 7NL
Tel: **0171-431 3086**
and
15237 Sunset Boulevard
Suite 17
Pacific Palisades
CA 90272
USA
Tel: **310 454 4080**
Page and Moy
136-140 London Road
Leicester LE2 1EN
Tel: **01162-552521**
Established specialist operator offering motor racing holidays to Grand Prix events world-wide, as well as golfing, music and archaeological tours.

ACE Study Tours
Babraham
Cambridge CB2 4AP

Tel: **01223-835055**
email: **culturex@dial.pipex.com**
Offers a range of musical appreciation tours combined with expert interpretive sessions and general sightseeing.

Further Reading: Music Festivals from Bach to Blues *by Tom Clynes (Visible Ink Press Tel: Visible Ink Press USA 313 961 2242). See also web site:* ***http://www.festivalfinder.com***

Natural History and Safari

African Experience
7 Buckingham Gate
London SW1E 6JX
Tel: **0171-630 0100**
Tailor made safari itineraries throughout Africa.

Andrews Safaris
PO Box 31993
Lusaka
Zambia
Foot safaris in the Luangwa.

Andrew Brock Travel Ltd.
54 High Street East
Uppingham
Rutland LE15 9PZ
Tel: **01572-821330**
Specialist in botanical, walking and garden Travel.

Animal Watch
Granville House
London Road
Sevenoaks
Kent TN13 1DL
Tel: **01732-741612**
Wildlife tours around the world.

Art of Travel Ltd
21 The Bakehouse
Bakery Place
London SW11 1JQ
Tel: **0171-738 2038**
Tailor-made safaris.

Birdwatching Breaks
26 School Lane
Herne Bay
Kent CT6 7AL
Tel: **01227-740799**
Birdwatching holidays in Europe, Britain and North America.

Cara Spencer Safaris
75 Weydon Hill Road
Farnham
Surrey GU9 8NY

Tel: **0252-424513**

Cygnus Wildlife Holidays
57 Fore St
Kingsbridge
Devon TQ7 1PG
Tel: **01548-856178**
Birdwatching and wildlife holidays.

Charioteer Travel Tours
10 Agias Sofias St
Thessaloniki
Greece GR 54322
Tel: **31 229 230**
Tailor-made birdwatching and natural history tours of Greece, 10 per cent of profits towards conservation.

Discover the World
29 Nork Way
Banstead
Surrey SM7 1PB
Tel: **01737-218800**
email: **sales@arctic/discover.co.uk**
Whale watching, wildlife and wilderness holidays world-wide.

Explorers Tours
223 Coppermill Road
Wraysbury TW19 5NW
Tel: **01753-681999**
Astronomical tours and diving holidays..

Falklands Experience
29 Queen's Road
Weston-super-Mare
Avon BS23 2LH
Tel: **01934 622025**
Organises tours to the Falkland Islands specialise in information for philatelists.

Flamingo Tours Ltd
PO Box 44899
Nairobi
Kenya
Camel safaris in the Samburu.

The Legendary Adventure Company
18 Albemarle Street
London W1X 3HA
Tel: **0171-629 2044**
Tailor-made safaris in Africa and trekking in Nepal.

Motor Safari
Pinfold Lane
Buckley
Clwyd CH7 3NS
Tel: **01244-548849**
Jeep mountain safaris, squad biking and amphibious vehicles in Wales and Cyprus.

Naturetrek
Chautara
Bighton
Nr. Alresford
Hants SO24 9RB
Tel: **01962-733051**
Birdwatching, natural history and botanical tours world-wide, donate a percentage of profits to environmental charities.

Origins
Woodcock Travel
25-31 Wicker
Sheffield S3 8HW
Tel: **0114-272 9619**
Nature holidays world-wide.

Ornitholidays
1-3 Victoria Drive
Bognor Regis
West Sussex PO21 2PW
Tel: **01243-821230**
Established operator offering a large variety of birdwatching holidays world-wide.

Papyrus Tours
9 Rose Hill Court
Bessacarr
Doncaster DN4 5LY
Tel: **01302-530778**
Wildlife tours in East Africa.

Peregrine Holidays
41 South Parade
Summertown
Oxford OX2 7JP
Tel: **01865-511642**
Birdwatching and natural history - but also see section 6 for their equestrian holidays.

Reef and Rainforest Tours
Prospect House
Jubilee Road
Totnes
Devon TQ9 5BP
Tel: **01803-866965**
Small outfit running wildlife and diving tours to Indonesia, Papua New Guinea, Honduras, Venezuela, Peru, Belize, Ecuador and Costa Rica.

Safari Drive Ltd
127 High Street
Hungerford
Berkshire RG17 0DL
Tel: **01488-681 611**
Organises self-drive safaris in Africa, also white water rafting and microlighting.

Save the Rhino International
21 Bentinck Street
London W1M 5RP

Tel: **0171-935 5880**
email: **save@rhinos.demon.co.uk**
Offer unique safaris to Namibia to see desert rhinos, and then the proceeds of the safari go directly to protecting them.

Snail's Pace
25 Thorpe Lane
Almondbury
Huddersfield HD5 8TA
Tel: **01484-426259**
Gentle, natural history tours.

Steamond International
23 Eccleston Street
London SW1W 9LX
Tel: **0171-730 8646**
Tailor made birdwatching, natural history and archaeology tours.

Tiger Mountain Groups and Expeditions
PO Box 170
Lazimpat
Kathmandu
Nepal
Tel: **1 411 225**
email: **tiger@mtn.mos.com.np**
Himalayan treks, jungle lodges and wildlife camps.

Wildlife Worldwide
170 Selsdon Road
South Croydon
Surrey CR2 6PJ
Tel: **0181-667 9158**
email: **wildlifecompuserve.com**

Honeymoon

There are several British tour operators specialising in honeymoon travel, some of whom have world-wide portfolios and others who concentrate on just one area. Specialist honeymoon tour operators with world-wide portfolios include:

Abercrombie & Kent
Tel: 0171-730 9600
Fax: 0171-730 9376

British Airways Holidays
Tel: 01293-723181
Fax: 01293-722624

CV Travel
Tel: 0171-581 0851
Fax: 0171-584 5229

Elegant Resorts
Tel: 01244-897 888
Fax: 01244-897 880

Hayes & Jarvis
Tel: 0181-748 0088
Fax: 0181-741 0299

Kuoni
Tel: 01306-742222
Fax: 01306-744222

Silk Cut Travel
Tel: 01730-265211
Fax: 01730-268482

Sunset Travel UK Office
Tel: 0171-498 9922
Fax: 0171-978 1337)

Thomas Cook Holidays
Tel: 01733-332255
Fax: 01733-505784

Tropical Places
Tel: 01342-825123
Fax:01342-822364

Worldwide Journeys & Expeditions
Tel: 0171-381 8638
Fax: 0171-381 0836

Honeymoon tour operators for specific areas:

Caribbean Connection
Tel: 01244-341131
Fax: 01244-310255

Sandals Resorts
Tel: 0171-581 9895
Fax: 0171-823 8758

Simply Caribbean
Tel: 01423-526887
Fax: 01423-526889

Cox & Kings
Tel: 0171-873 5000
Fax: 0171-630 6038

Journey Latin America
Tel: 0181-747 8315
Fax: 0181-742 1312

Passage to South America
Tel: 0171-602 9889
Fax: 0171-602 4251
email: psauk@atlas.co.uk

Asia World
Tel: 01932-820050
Fax: 01932-820633

Art of Travel
Tel: 0171-738 2038
Fax: 0171-738 1893

Best of Morocco
Tel: 01380-828533
Fax: 01380-828630

Theobald Barber
Tel: 0171-221 0555
Fax: 0171-221 0444

World Archipelago
Tel: 0181-780 5838
Fax: 0181-780 9482
email: 100711.3161@compuserve.com

Magic of Spain/Italy/Portugal/Italian Escapades
Tel: 0181-748 4220
Fax: 0181-748 3731

Women

Amazonians
Unit 115, 31 Clerkenwell Close
London EC1R 0AT
Tel: **0171-608 3953**
Association for professional women travel writers.

Outdoor Vacations for Women over 40
PO Box 200
Groton
MA 01450
Tel: **508 448 3331**

Rainbow Travel Inc: Adventure travel for Women over 30
15033 Kelly Canyon Road
Bozeman
MT 59715
Tel: **406 587 3888**

Silvermoon Women's Bookshop
64-68 Charing Cross Road
London WC2H 0BB
Tel: **0171-836 7906**

Travel Companions
110 High Mount
Station Road
London NW4 3ST
Tel: **0181-202 8478**
Non-profit service which puts single travellers in touch with other like-minded people.

Woodswomen
25 W Diamond Lake Road
Minneapolis
MN55419
Tel: **612 822 3809**
Adventure trips for women of all ages - some include facilities for children.

Womanship
The Boathouse
410 Severn Avenue
Annapolis
MD 21403
Tel: **301 269 0784**
Sailing cruises for women of all ages, no previous experience needed.

Women's Corona Society/
Corona Worldwide
c/o Commonwealth Institute
Kensington High Street
London W8 6NQ
Tel: **0171-610 4407**
A support/advice group for expatriate women, offers briefings and advice to those about to move abroad and for those retuning to the UK.

Women's Travel Advisory Bureau
Lansdowne
High Street
Blockley
Gloucestershire GL56 9HF
Tel: **01865-310574**
Supplies information packs tailored to individuals travel plans.

Women Welcome Women
88 Easton Street
High Wycombe
Bucks HP11 1DJ
Tel: **01494-465441**
Organisation to promote international friendship by helping female travellers to stay with other members and their families.

Cyberspace

Useful travel-related web sites, correct at time of going to press, give an good idea of what is available.

Adventurous Traveller Bookstore
http://www.gorp.com/atbook.htm

AESU
http://www.aesu.com/
Discount airfare specialist.

Airlines of the Web
http://www.itn/airlines
Links to hundreds of airlines and airport information.

Air Traveller's Handbook
http://www.cis.ohiostate.edu/hypertext/faq/usenet/

Arab Net
http://www.arab.net

Asia Online
http://www.asia-online.com.sg/

Asia World
http:www.asiaworld.co.uk

Automap
http://www.microsoft.com/automap/

Bargain Holidays (EMAP)
http://www.bargainholidays.com

Bermuda Triangle
http://tigger.cc.uic.edu/~toby-g/tri.html

British Foreign Office Travel Advice
http://www.fco.gov.uk/

The Campground Directory
http://www.holipub.com/camping/director.htm

CIA World Factbook
http:www.odci.gov/cia/publications/pubs.html

Currency Converter
http:bin.gnn.com/cgi-bin/gnn/currency

Earthwatch
http://www.earthwatch.org

Expedia
http://expedia.msn.com

Festival Finder
http://www.festivalfinder.com

Flight Bookers
http://www.flightbookers.co.uk

GNN Travel
http://www.u-net.com/hotelnet/
Net directory of travel-related sites.

Hertz
http://www/hertz.com

Himalayan Explorers Club
http://www.abwam.com/himexp
Information for travellers to the Himalayas.

Hospex
http://hospex.icm.edu.pl/~hospex/
Network offering travellers the chance to either offer a fellow traveller a bed for a few nights, or find somewhere to stay whilst abroad themselves.

Hotel Net
http://www.u-net.com/hotelnet
Information about European hotels, where you can reserve a room online.

How far is it?
http://www/indo.com/distance/
Find out the distant between any two cities.

The Inn Traveller
http://www.inntraveller.com/
Directory of bed and breakfasts.

Internet Holidays
http://www.holiday.co.uk

Internet Travel Services
http://www.istc.org
Information from 28 operators including a late booking search which shows what flights are still available from the UK.

London Calling
http://www.demon.co.uk/london-calling/
listings ezine to London's atrs world.

London Club Guide
http://secure.londonmall.co.uk/londonclubguide/

London Pubs Reviewed
http://www.cs.ucl.ac.uk/misc/uk/london/pubs/index

Lonely Planet Guidebooks
http://www.lonelyplanet.com.au

MapBlast!
http://www.mapblast.com
Local maps world-wide.

MCW International Travellers Clinic
http://www.intmed.mcw.edu/ITC/Health.html

Moon City
http://www.euro.net/5thworld/mooncity/moon.html
Virtual tour of Amsterdam.

Outside Online
http://outside.starwave.com
Online version of Outside Magazine.

Paddynet
http://www.paddynet.com

Paris
http://www.paris.org/

PC Travel
http://www.pctravel.com/
Flight bookings with over 500 airlines.

Rough Guides
http://hptwired.com/rough

Round the World Travel Guide
http://www.solutions.net/rec-travel/rtw/html
Advice for long term travellers.

Route 66 Collection
http://www.kaiwan.com/~wem

Terraquest
http://www.terraquest.com
Travel magazine.

Time Out
http://www/timeout.co.uk

Tourism Offices Worldwide
http://www.mbnet.mb.ca/lucas/travel/tourism-offices.html

Traffic and Road Conditions
http://www.accutraffic.com

Travelmag
http://www.travelmag.co.uk/travelmag
The award winning magazine published sponsored by WEXAS 's Traveller magazine

Travel Weekly's list of travel agents
http://www.traveler.net/two/twpages/twagents.html

TravelWeb
http://www.travelweb.com
Hotel reservations world-wide.

Uniglobe Online
http://www.uniglobe.com

US Travel Warnings
http://www.stolaf.edu/network/travel-advisories.html

Webcrawler's Travel Adventures
http://webcrawler.com/select/trav.advent.html

WEXAS International Travel Website
http://wexas.com/travel
The Traveller's Handbook and Traveller *magazine on-line as well as excellent discounted scheduled airfairs, hotels and carhire.*

World Traveller Books and Maps
http://www.travelbookshop.com

World's Largest Subway Map
http://metro.jussieu.fr:10001

Worldwide Agency Locator
http://agencylink.sys1.com

Older Traveller

ACE Study Tours
Babraham
Cambridge CB2 4AP
Tel: **01223-835055**
email: **culturex@dial.pipex.com**
Cultural study tours throughout Europe.

Age Concern England
Astral House
1268 London Road
London SW16 4ER
Tel: **0181-679 8000**
Provides holiday fact sheets and books.

Help the Aged
16-18 St James's Walk
London EC1R 0BE
Tel: **0171-253 0253**

Saga Holidays
The Saga Building
Middelburg Square
Folkestone CT20 1AZ
Tel: **01303-857000**
Extensive range of holidays world-wide for the over 60's (companions can be over 50).

Time of Your Life
78 Capel Road
East Barnet
Herts EN4 8JF
Tel: **0181-449 4506**
Organises retirement-planning holidays.

Tripscope
The Courtyard
Evelyn Road
London W4 5JL
Tel: **0181-994 9294**
Transport information service for disabled or elderly people.

Wallace Arnold Tours
62 George Street
Croydon
Surrey CR9 1DN
Tel: **0181-688 7255**
Coach holidays on the continent.

World Expeditions
4 Northfields Prospect
Putney Bridge Road
London SW18 1PE
Tel: **0181-870 2600**
email: **worldex@dircom.co.uk**
Australian-based tour operator who offer adventure holidays for over 50s.

Further reading:
Life in the Sun:
A guide to Long-stay Holidays and Living Abroad in Retirement (Age Concern)
Good Non Retirement Guide (Kogan Page)

Diabetic

British Airways Medical Services For Travellers Abroad (BAMSTA)
51 Gower Street
London WC1E 6HJ
Tel: **0171-436 2625**

British Diabetic Association
10 Queen Anne St
London W1M 0BD
Tel: **0171-323 1531**

Health Care Abroad
DHSS Overseas Branch
Longbenton
Benton Park Road
Newcastle upon Tyne NE98 1YX
Tel: **0191-213 5000**

International Diabetes Federation
1 Rue Defacqz
1050 Brussels
Belgium
Tel: **2 538 5511**

Identification

Medic Alert Foundation
1 Bridge Wharf
156 Caledonian Road
London N1 9UU
Tel: **0171-833 3034**

Golden Key Company
1 Hare Street
Sheerness
Kent ME12 1AH
Tel: **01795- 663403**

SOS Talisman Co Ltd
21 Grays Corner
Ley Street
Ilford
Essex IG2 7RQ
Tel: **0181-554 5579**

Travel Insurance

BDA Travel Insurance
PO Box 555
Cardiff CF5 6XH
Tel: **0990-001541**

Vaccinations

BAMSTA (Head Office)
51 Gover Street

London WC1E 6HJ
Tel: **0171-436 2625**

Berkeley Street Travel Clinic
32 Berkeley Street
London W1X 5FA
Tel: **0171-629 6233**
or
70 North End Road
West Kensington
London W14 0SJ
Tel: **0171-371 6570**

Diabetes supplies

Becton-Dickinson UK Ltd
Between Towns Road
Cowley
Oxford OX4 3LY
Tel: **01865-777722**

Beyer PLC
Beyer House
Strawberry Hill
Newbury
Berkshire RG14 1JA
Tel: **01635-563000**

Boeringer Manheim UK
Bell Lane
Lewes
East Sussex BN7 1LG
Tel: **01273-480444**

Lilly Industries Ltd
Dextra Court
Chapel Hill
Basingstoke
Hampshire
RG21 5SY
Tel: **01256-473241**

Novo Nordisk Pharmaceuticals Ltd
Broadfield Park
Brighton Road
Pease Pottage
Crawley
West Sussex RH11 9RT
Tel: **01293-613555**

Gourmet

Alternative Travel Group
69-71 Banbury Road
Oxford OX2 6PE
Tel: **01865-310344**
Organise a number a special interest holidays including walking and wine tours.

Arblaster and Clarke
Clarke House

Farnham Road
West Liss
Hants GU33 6JU
Tel: **01730-895353**
email: **106144.400@compuserve.com**
World-wide wine tours.

Symbiosis Expedition Planning
113 Bolingbroke Grove
London SW11 1DA
Tel: **0171-924 5906**
email: **101456.2155@compuserve.com**
Gastronomic and cultural tours in SE Asia.

Vegetarian

The Australian Vegetarian Society
PO Box 65
2021 Paddington
email: avs@moreinfo.com.au

Canadian Natural Health Society Inc
6250 Mountain Sights
H3W 2Z3 Montreal

The European Vegetarian Union
Larensweg 26
NL 1221 CM Hilversum
Brussels
Belgium
Tel: **31-35 834 796**
Based at the offices of the Dutch Vegetarian Society, it aims to encourage better communications between the European vegetarian groups, and has a regular newsletter.

International Jewish Vegetarian Society
853/5 Finchley Road
London NW11 8LX
Tel: **0181-455 0692**
email: (London) - **bmjjhr@easynet.co.uk**
(Israel) - **ijvsjlem@netmedia.net.il**

The International Vegetarian Union (IVU)
Mr Maxwell Lee
Honorary General Secretary
King's Drive
Marple
Stockport
Cheshire SK6 6NQ
Tel: **0161-427 5850**

Honorary Regional Secretaries -

Africa
Mr Jan Beeldman
82 Darrenwood Village
First St
Darrenwood
2194 Randburg, South Africa

Australasia
Mark Berriman
AVS
PO Box 65
Paddington
NSW 2021
Australia
Tel: **2 698 4339**
email: **avs@moreinfo.com**

Middle East
Mr Mark Weintraub
8 Balfour Street
Jerusalem 92101
Israel

India and the East
Shah Jashu
114 Mittal Court
Nariman Point
Bombay 400 021
Tel: **22 285 5755/56**

USA
PO Box 9710
Washington, DC 20016
USA
Tel: **301 577 5215**
email: **dalal@kcilink.com**

Europe (UK)
John Mitchell
183 Folden Road
Great Barr
Birmingham B48 2EH
Tel: **0121-357 2772**

New Zealand Vegetarian Society Inc
Box 77-034
Auckland 3
New Zealand

North American Vegetarian Society (NAVS)
PO Box 72
Dolgeville
NY 13329
USA
email: darer@admin.njit.edu

**Vegetarian Awareness Network
(VEGANET)**
PO Box 76390
USA 20013
Tel: **202-347 8343**

**The Vegetarian Society of the United
Kingdom**
Parkdale
Dunham Road
Altrincham
Cheshire WA14 4QG
Tel: **0161-928 0793**

The Vegetarian Society of Russia
Moscow 109462
Volsky Bulwar
d39-k3-kv23
Moscow 109462
Russia
Tel: **951728633**

Food for Life
Paul Turner
10310 Oaklyn Drive
Potomac
MD 20854
USA
Tel: **301 299 4797**

Further reading:
The Vegetarian Travel Guide (The Vegetarian
Society), *a world-wide guide to vegetarian
restaurants, societies and vegetarian meals in
transit.*
The Vegetarian Traveller (Grafton), *Andrew
Sanger's excellent guide to world-wide travel
for vegetarians.*

Disabled

Access to the Skies
c/o RADAR
12 City Forum
250 City Road
London EC1V 8AF
Tel: **0171-250 3222**
*Information on airline facilities and services for
the disabled.*

ACROD
(The Australian Council for the Rehabilitation
of the Disabled)
PO Box 60
Curtin
ACT 2605
Canberra
Tel:**62 82 4333**
*Australia's national organisation for disability,
offers information for disabled travellers.*

The Across Trust
70-72 Bridge Road
East Molesey
Surrey KT8 9HF
Tel: **0181-783 1355**
*Operates large luxury fully-equipped
ambulances called 'Jumbulances' which take
severely disabled people on organised group
pilgrimages and holidays across Europe.*

Assist Travel
P.O. Box 83
Lara
Victoria 3212

Australia
Tel: **52 84 1284**
Specialist tour operator

Association of British Insurers
51 Gresham Street
London EC2V 7HQ
Tel: **0171-600 3333**
Information on travel insurance for the disabled.

Lin Berwick Trust
9 Hunter Drive
Hornchurch
Essex RM12 5TP
Tel: **01708-477582**
Holiday Accomodation for disabled people and their carers.

Barrier-Free Travel
36 Wheatley Street
North Bellingen
New South Wales 2454
Australia
Tel: **66 552733**
Offers a consultancy service for disabled travel.

BREAK
20 Hooks Hill Road
Sheringham
Norfolk NR26 8NL
Tel: **01263-823170**
Holidays in Norfolk for the physically and mentally handicapped.

British Railways Board
Liaison Manager (Disabled Passengers)
Euston House
24 Eversholt St
PO Box 100
London NW1 1DZ
Tel: **0171-928 5151**

British Red Cross
9 Grosvenor Crescent
London SW1 7ET
Tel: **0171-235 5454**
Can provide companions for disabled travellers.

British Ski Club for the Disabled
Mr H.M. Sturgess
Spring Mount
Berwick St John
Shaftesbury
Dorset SP7 0HQ
Tel: **01747-828515**

British Sports Association for the Disabled
Solecast House
13-27 Brunswick Place
London W1 6DX

Tel: **0171-490 4919**

Camping for the Disabled
20 Burton Close
Dawley
Telford
Shropshire TF4 2BX
Tel: **01743-761889**
Advice and information on camping in the UK and overseas.

Canadian Rehabilitation Council for the Disabled
45 Sheppard Avenue E
Toronto
Ontario M2N 5W9
Tel: **52 84 1284**
Gives advice and publishes 'Handi-Travel', a book of tips for the disabled traveller.

Carefree Holidays
64 Florence Road
Northampton
NN1 4NA
Tel: **01604-34301**

CPA
(Canadian Paraplegic Association)
1550 Don Mills Road
Suite 201
Don Mills
Ontario M3B 3K4
Tel: **416 391 0203**

Department of Transport Disability Unit
Great Minster House
76 Marsham St
London SW1P 4DR
Tel: **0171-271 5256**

DIAL UK
Park Lodge St Catherine's Hospital
Tickhill Road
Balby
Doncaster DN4 8QN
Tel: **01302-310123**

Disabled Drivers Association
National Headquarters
Ashwellthorpe Hall
Norwich
NR16 1EX
Tel: **01508-489449**

Disabled Drivers' Motor Club
Cottingham Way
Thrapston
Northants
NN14 4PL
Tel: **01832-734724**

Disabled Kiwi Tours (NZ) Ltd
East Coast Highway

P.O. Box 550
Opotiki
New Zealand
Tel: **7 315 7867**
Personalised tours of NZ for the disabled.

Disabled Living Foundation
380-384 Harrow Road
London W9 2HU
Tel: **0171-289 6111**

Disabled Motorists Federation
Unit 2a
Atcham Estate
Upton Magna
Shrewsbury
SY4 4UG
Tel: **01743-761889**

Disabled Persons Assembly
P.O. Box 10-138
The Terrace
Wellington
New Zealand
Tel: **4 472 2626**
National organisation for the disabled.

Disaway Trust
2 Charles Road
Merton Park
London SW19 3BD
Tel: **0181-543 3431**
Holidays for groups overseas and in the UK.

Going Down
46 Hill Drive
Hove
Sussex
BN3 6QL
Tel: **01273-566616**
Arranges diving expeditions for people with disabilities.

Health Services Information Centre
Jewish Rehabilitation Hospital
3205 Place Alton Goldbloom
Chomedey
Laval
Quebec H7V 1R2
Canada
Tel: **514 688 9550**
Has over 800 access guides and extensive information on travel within Canada.

Help the Handicapped Holiday Fund
147a Camden Road
Tunbridge Wells
Kent TN1 2RA
Tel: **01892-547474**
Free holidays for the physically disabled.

Holiday Care Service
2nd Floor, Imperial Buildings
Victoria Road
Horley
Surrey RH6 7PZ
Tel: **01293-774535**
Travel advice and information. Also has a service called 'Holiday Helpers' which matches volunteer helpers with elderly or disabled travellers.

Holidays for the Disabled
c/o Miss Linda Browning
9 Shapton Close
Holbury
Southampton SO45 1QY
Tel: **01703-892413**
Organises one annual holiday abroad for disabled people aged 30-60.

John Grooms Association for Disabled People
50 Scrutton Street
London EC2A 4PH
Tel: **0171-452 2145**
This charity has launched Grooms Holidays, which specialises in holidays for the disabled.

Joint Committee on Mobility for Disabled People
Tim Shapley OBE
9 Moss Close
Pinner
Middlesex HA5 3AY

Jubilee Sailing Trust
Jubilee Yard
Merlin Quay
Hazel Road
Woolston
Southampton
SO19 7GB
Tel: **01703-449138**
Offers the opportunity of working as a crew member on the tall ship, the 'Lord Nelson'.

London Regional Transport
Unit for Disabled Passengers
172 Buckingham Palace Road
London SW1W 9TN
Tel: **0171-918 3312**

MAVIS (Mobility Advice and Vehicle Information Service)
O Wing
MacAdam Avenue
Old Wokingham Road
Crowthorne
Berks RG45 6 XD
Tel: **01344-661000**

Mobility International USA
P.O. Box 3551
Eugene
Oregon 97403
USA
Tel: **541 343 1284**
International club offering travel and educational exchanges for the disabled, annual membership $35.

Mobility International
228 Borough High St
London SE1 1JX
Tel: **0171-403 5688**
Exists to encourage the integration of handicapped people with the non-handicapped. Mobility International News *is published three times a year.*

New Zealand CCS
P.O. Box 6349
Te Aro
Wellington
New Zealand
Tel: **4 384 5677**
Agency providing services to help disabled travellers

Physically Handicapped and Able Bodied

(PHAB)
Summit House
Wandle Road
Croydon CRO 1DF
Tel: **0181-667 9443**
Holidays for all ages and abilities.

Project Phoenix Trust
68 Rochfords
Coffee Hall
Milton Keynes MK6 5DJ
Tel: **01908-678038**
A non-profit organisation running visits overseas. These tours involve a lot of activity and are probably best suited to energetic and strong disabled people.

RADAR Royal Association for Disability and Rehabilitation
Unit 12 City Forum
250 City Road
London EC1V 8AF
Tel: **0171-250 3222**
A registered charity devoted to helping and promoting the rights of the disabled. RADAR finds suitable accommodation and facilities for holidays for the disabled. Publish a wealth of useful reference literature.

Rehabilitation Inter USA
25 East 21 Street
4th Floor

New York
NY 10010
USA
Tel: **212 420 1500**
email: **rehabintl@aol.com**
Disability society with information on disabled travel in North America.

Society for the Advancement of Travel for the Handicapped (SATH)
347 Fifth Avenue
Suite 610
New York NY 10016
USA
Tel: **212 447 7284**
email: **sathtravel@aol.com**
Non-profit educational forum for the exchange of knowledge and the gaining of new skills to facilitate travel for the handicapped, the elderly and the retired. SATH publishes 'The United States Welcomes Handicapped Visitors'.

TRIPSCOPE
The Courtyard
Evelyn Road
London W4 5JL
Tel: **0181-994 9294**
or:
Tripscope-South West
Pamwell House
160 Pennywell Road
Bristol
BS5 0TX
Tel: **0117-941 4094**
A registered charity, they provide reliable transport advice and information for local or international journeys.

Uphill Ski Club of Great Britain
12 Park Crescent
London W1N 4EQ
Tel: **0171-636 1989**
Organises wintersports for disabled people.

The Wheel Resort
39-51 Broken Head Road
Byron Bay
NSW 2481
Australia
Tel:**66 85 6139**
Luxury cabins designed for disabled travellers and owned by wheelchair users.

Winged Fellowship Trust
Angel House
20-32 Pentonville Road
London N1 9XD
Tel: **0171-833 2594**
UK and overseas holidays for severely disabled adults.

Young Disabled on Holiday
c/o Miss R Girdlestone
33 Longfield Avenue
Heald Green
Cheadele
Cheshire
SK8 3NN
Organises holidays for 18-35 year olds, in Britain and overseas with the emphasis on activities and entertainment.

Further reading:
Nothing Ventured (Harrap Columbus), distributed in Canada by Penguin Books and in US by Viking Penguin and called *Able to Travel, personal accounts of journeys world-wide by disabled travellers, plus advice, and detailed listings of useful contacts for every aspect of travel for the disabled.*

RECOMMENDED TRAVEL AGENTS

National Agency Chains

The following major companies offer national coverage and a broad range of travel service including discounts on package holidays, plus flight bookings, currency and traveller's cheques.

American Express
6 Haymarket
London SW1Y 4BS
Tel: **0171-930 4411**

Going Places
7 Haymarket
London SW1Y 4BT
Tel: **0171-930 2411**
Owned by Airtours Plc.

Lunn Poly
116 High Holborn
London WC1V 6RD
Tel: **0171-831 2991**
Part of Thomson Travel Group.

A T Mays
Moffat House
Nineyard Street
Saltcoats
Ayrshire
KA21 5EF
Tel: **01294-462199**

Thomas Cook
45 Berkeley Street

London W1A 1EB
Tel: **0171-499 4000**

Local Independent Agents

Local travel agents will offer a broader range of specialist tour operator brochures and a more personalised service, based on local experience. These local agents, too numerous to list individually should be ABTA members but are also more likely to offer a range of AITO brochures (Association of Independent Tour Operators).

Tailor-made Travel

National newspapers offer a good source of specialist agencies,often concentrating on a specific destination such as America or Australia. To ensure full financial protection, ensure that they offer ABTA, IATA and ATOL cover.
Respected names include:

Blair Travel & Leisure Ltd
117 Regent's Park Road
London NW1 8UR
Tel: **0171-483 2297**
Including art tours.

Bridge the World
47 Chalk Farm Road
Camden Town
London NW1 8AN
Tel: **0171-911 0900**
Long haul.

Trailfinders
42/50 Earls Court Road
London W8 6EJ
Tel: **0171-937 5400**
Australasia and world-wide.

Travelbag
12 High Street
Alton
Hampshire GU34 1BN
Tel: **01420-541441**
Australia .

WEXAS International
45-49 Brompton Road
London SW3 1DE
Tel: **0171-589 3315**
email: **mship@wexas.com**
http://wexas.com/travel
Australasia, Far East, America and world-wide. ■

GETTING THERE BY AIR
Section 4

AIR TRANSPORT ASSOCIATIONS

Air Transport Services (Freight)
Unit A, Golden Crescent Industrial Estate
Golden Crescent
Hayes, Middlesex. UB3 1AQ
Tel: **0181-813 5544**

Aircharter Brokers (ABA)
4 London Wall Buildings
Blomfield Street
London EC2M 5NT
Tel: **0171-638 3522**

Airport Council International (ACI)
PO Box 16
CH-1215 Geneva 15-Airport
Geneva, Switzerland
Tel: **(22) 798 4141**

Association of European Airlines
Avenue Louise 350
Bte 4, 1050 Brussels
Belgium
Tel: **(322) 648 4017**

Aviation Training Association
125 London Road
High Wycombe
Bucks HP11 1BT
Tel: **01494 445262**

Air Transport Users Council (AUC)
5th Floor, Kingsway House
103 Kingsway
London WC2 6QX
Tel: **0171-242 3882**
Fax: 0171-831 4132

British Air Line Pilots Association (BALPA)
81 New Road
Harlington, Hayes
Middlesex UB3 5BG

Tel: **0181-476 4000**

British Airports Authority (BAA)
Public Affairs Department
Heathrow Airport Ltd.
234 Bath Road, Harlington
Hayes, Middlesex, UB3 5AP
Tel: **0181-759 4321**
and...
Public Affairs Department
Gatwick Airport Ltd
Gatwick
West Sussex RH6 0NP
Tel: **01293-505000**

British Air Transport Association (BATA)
5/6 Pall Mall East
London SW1Y 5BA
Tel: **0171-930 5746**

British Helicopter Advisory Board (BHAB)
Building C2, West Entrance
Fairoaks Airport, Chobham
Surrey GU24 8HX
Tel: **01276-856100**
Fax: 01276-856126

Civil Aviation Authority
CAA House
45-59 Kingsway
London WC2B 6TE
Tel: **0171-379 7311**

Commonwealth Air Transport Council (CATC)
Room S5/05A
2 Marsham St
London SW1P 3EB
Tel: **0171-276 5436**

European Civil Aviation Organisation⇨
(ECAO)
3 bis Villa Emile Bergerat
9220-Neuilly sur Seine
France
Fax: **1-46 24 18 18**

European Regional Airlines Organisation
(ERA)
The Baker Suite
Fairoaks Airport, Chobham
Surrey GU24 8HX
Tel: **01276-856495**

Federation Aeronautique International
155 Avenue de Wagram
Paris 75017
France
Tel: **1-44 29 92 00**

Flight Safety Committee
Aviation House
South Area
Gatwick Airport
West Sussex RH6 0YR
Tel: **0173- 60664**

Foreign Airlines Association
4 Summerhays
Cobham
Surrey KT11 2HQ
Tel: **01932-63639**

Guild of Air Pilots and Air Navigators
(GAPAN)
Cobham House
291 Grays Inn Road
London WC1X 8QF
Tel: **0171-837 3323**

International Federation of Airline Pilots
Associations (IFALPA)
Interpilot House
Gogmore Lane
Chertsey, Surrey KT16 9AP
Tel: **01932-571711**

Institute of Air Transport (ITA)
103 rue La Boetie
75008 Paris
France
Tel: **(1) 43 593868**

International Air Carrier Association
(IACA)
Abelag Building
PO Box 36
Brussels National Airport
B-1930 Zaventum 2
Belgium
Tel: **720 5880**

International Air Transport Association
POB 672
CH-1215 Geneva 15 Airport
Geneva
Switzerland
Tel: **022-799 2525**

International Airline Passengers Association
PO Box 380
Croyden
Surrey CR9 2ZQ
Tel: **0181-681 6555**

Royal Aeronautical Society
4 Hamilton Place
London W1V 0BQ
Tel: **0171-499 3515**

AIRLINE HEAD
OFFICES WORLD-WIDE

ACES (Aerolineas Centrales de Colombia)
Calle 49, No 50-21
Edificio del Cafe
Piso 34,
PO Box 6503
Colombia
Tel: **456 053**

Adria Airways
6100 Ljublijana
Republic of Slovenia
Tel: **(61) 313 366**
Fax: 38 61 323 356

Aer Lingus
PO Box 180
Dublin Airport
Dublin
Republic of Ireland
Tel: **370011**
Fax: 420801

Aeroflot-Russian International Airlines
Leningradski Prospekt 37
Moscow 125167
Russian Federation
Tel: **155 54 94**

Aerolinas Argentinas
Paseo Colon 185
1063 Buenos Aires
Argentina
Tel: **308 551**
Fax: 331 0356

Aeromexico
Paseo de la Reforma 445
Col. Cuauhtemoc
Mexico City 06500
Mexico Tel: **286 4422**

Air Afrique
01 BP 3927
Abidjan 01
Cote d'Ivoire
Tel: **20 30 00**
Fax: 20 30 08

Air Algerie
1 Place Maurice Audin
Algiers
Algeria
Tel: **(63) 92 34/5/6**

Air Botswana
Cycle Mart Building
Lobatse Road
PO Box 92
Gaborone
Botswana
Tel: **52812**
Fax: 374802

Air Caledonie International
8 rue Frederic Surleau
BP 3736
Nourmea, New Caledonia
Tel: **283333**
Fax:(687) 272772

Air Canada
PO Box 1400
Postal Station Saint-Laurent
Montreal, Quebec
Canada H4Y 1H4
Tel: **(514) 422 5000**
Fax: (514) 879 7990

Air China
Capital International Airport
Beijing 100621
P.R. China
Tel: **(1) 456 3220**
Fax: (1)456 3348

Air France
45 Rue de Paris
F-95747 Roissy CDG Cedex
France
Tel: **43 23 81 81**
Fax: 43239711

Air Gabon
B.P 2206
Libreville, Gabon
Tel: **73 21 97**

Air India
218 Backbay Reclamation
Nariman Point
Bombay 400 021
India
Tel: **(22) 202 4142**
Fax: (22) 202 4897

Air Jamaica
72-76 Harbour St
Kingston, Jamaica
West Indies
Tel: **922-3460**
Fax: 922-0107

AirLanca
37 York Street
Colombo 01
Sri Lanka
Tel: **(1) 735555**
Fax: (1) 735122

Air Liberte SA
3 rue du Pont des Halles
F-94656 Rungis Cedex
France
Tel: **149 792300**
Fax: 146 872883

Air Madagascar
31 Avenue de l'Independance
Antananarivo
101 Madagascar
Tel: **(2) 44222**
Fax: (2) 44674

Air Malawi
PO Box 84
Blantyre
Rep. of Malawi
Tel: **620 811**
Fax: 620 042

Air Maldives
26 Ameeru Ahmed Magu
Male, Rep. of Maldives
Tel: **322438**
Fax: 325056

Air Malta
Head Office
Luqu, Malta
Tel: **824330**
Fax: 673241

Air Namibia
PO Box 731
Windhoek
Namibia 9000
Tel:**(61) 223019**
Fax: (61) 221916

Air New Zealand
Private Bag 92007
Level 21 Quay Tower
29 Customs Street West
Auckland
New Zealand
Tel: **(9) 3662400**
Fax: (9) 366 2667

Air Niugini
ANG House
Jacksons Airport
PO Box 7186
Boroko, Papua New Guinea
Tel: **273200**
Fax: 273482

Air Pacific
Private Mail Bag
Nadi Airport
Fiji Islands
Tel: **720777**
Fax: 720686

Air Rwanda
BP 808
Kigali
Rwanda
Tel: **75492**
Fax: 72462

Air Seychelles
PO Box 386
Seychelles International
Airport
Mahe, Seychelles
Tel: **225300**
Fax: 225159

Air Tahiti
PO Box 314
Boulevard Pomare
Papeete
Tahiti, French Polynesia
Tel: **86400**
Fax: 864069

Air Tanzania
ATC House, City Drive
PO Box 543
Dar-es-Salaam
United Republic of Tanzania
Tel: **(51) 38300**
Fax: (51) 46545

Air UK
Stansted House
Stansted Airport, Stansted
Essex CH24 1QT
United Kingdom
Tel: **(01279) 680146**
Fax:(01279) 680012

Air Ukraine
14 Prospect Peremogy
252135 Kiev
Ukraine
Tel: **(044) 2262567**
Fax: (044) 2168235

Air Vanuatu
Lolam House, Kumul
Highway
PO Box 248
Port Vila, Vanuatu
Tel: 23838
Fax: 23250

Air Zimbabwe
PO Box API
Harare Airport
Zimbabwe
Tel:(4) **575 111**
Fax:(4) 575 068

Alaska Airlines
P.O. Box 68900
Seattle, Washington 98168
USA
Tel: **(206) 433 3200**
Fax: (206) 433 3366

Albanian Airlines
Pruga Kongresi 1 Permetit
202
Tirana
Albania

Alitalia
Viale Alessendro Marchetti
111
Roma1-00148
Italy
Tel: (6) **65621**
Fax: (6) 65624733

All Nippon Airways
Kasumigaseki Building
3-2-5 Kasumigaseki
Chiyoda-ku
Tokyo 100
Japan
Tel:(03) **580 4711**
Fax:(03) 592 3039

Aloha Airlines
371 Aokea St
PO Box 30028
Honolulu International
Airport
Hawaii 96820
USA
Tel: **(808) 836 4210**
Fax: (808) 833 3671

**Alymeda – Democratic
Yemen Airlines**
PO Box 6006
Khormaksar Civil Airport
Aden
Yemen
Tel: **52267**

American Airlines Inc
PO Box 619616
Dallas/Fort Worth Airport
Texas 75261-9616
USA
Tel: **(817) 967 1234**
Fax: (817) 967 4318

Ansett Australia
501 Swanston St
Melbourne
Victoria 3000
Australia
Tel: **(3) 9668 1211**
Fax: (3) 9668 1114

Ansett New Zealand
110 Tuam Street,
Christchurch
PO Box 14-139
Christchurch Airport
New Zealand
Tel: **(9) 309 6235**
Fax: (9) 309 6434

Ariana Afghan Airlines
Ansari Watt
P.O. Box 76,Kabul
Afghanistan
Tel: **25541 /45, 26541/45**

Armenian Airlines
Airport Zvartnots,
375042 Yerevan
Armenia
Tel: **(2) 225 447**
Fax: (2) 151 393

Austrian Airlines
PO Box 50
Fontanastrasse 1
A-1107 Vienna
Austria
Tel: **(1) 1766**
Fax: (1) 68 55 05

AVIANCA
Av Eldorado No 93-30
Bogota
Colombia
Tel: **(1) 413 9511**
Fax: (1) 269 9131

AVIATECA S.A.
Avenida Hincapie
Aeropuerto La Aurora
Guatemala City
Guatemala
Tel: **(2) 318261**
Fax: (2) 317412

Bahamas Air
Po Box N-4881

Nassau
Bahamas
Tel:**(809) 327-8451**
Fax: (809) 327 7408

Balkan-Bulgarian Airlines
Sofia Airport
1540 Sofia
Bulgaria
Tel: **(2) 661690**
Fax: (2) 723496

Biman Bangladesh Airlines
Biman Bangladesh Building
100 Mitijheel
Dhaka 1000
Bangladesh
Tel: **(2) 240151**
Fax: (2) 863005

**Braathens Safe Air
Transport**
Oksenoy veien 3
PO Box 55
N-1330 Oslo Aiport
Norway
Tel: **67597000**
Fax: 67591309

British Airways
P.O. Box 10
Heathrow Airport
Hounslow
Middlesex TW6 2JA
Tel: **0181-759 5511**
Fax: 0181-562 9930

British Midland
Donington Hall
Castle Donington
Derby DE7 2SB
Tel: **01332 854000**
Fax: 01332 854662

**BWIA International
Trinidad & Tobago
Airways**
E and M Hangar Compound
Piarco
Trinidad
Tel: **664 4871**

Cameroon Airlines
BP 4092
3 Avenue General de Gaulle
Douala
United Republic of Cameroon
Tel: **42 25 25**
Fax: 42 24 87

Canadian Airlines International
Suite 2800
700 2nd St SW
Calgary
Alberta T2P 2W2
Canada
Tel: **(403) 294 2000**
Fax: (403) 294 2066

Cathay Pacific Airways
Swire House
9 Connaught Road
Central, Hong Kong
Tel: **2745 5000**
Fax: 28 10 65 63

Cayman Airways
PO Box
1101 George Town
Grand Cayman
British West Indies
Tel:**(94 9) 8200**
Fax: (949) 7607

China Eastern Airlines
Honggiao International
Airport
Shanghai, 200335
Tel: **(21) 255 88 99**
Fax: (21) 255 60 39

China Southern Airlines
Baiyun International Airport
Guanzhou City
Guangdong Province 51045
Tel: **(20) 667 89 01**
Fax: (20) 664 46 23

CityJet
The Mezzanine, Terminal
Building
Dublin Airport
Co. Dublin , Ireland
Tel: **(1) 844 5588**
Fax: (1) 704 4753

Commercial Airways
PO Box 7015
1622 Bonaero Park, Transvaal
South Africa
Tel: **(11) 921 01 11**
Fax: (11) 973 39 13

Compagnie Aerienne Corse Mediterranee
Aeroport de Campo dell'Oro
BP 505, F-20186 Ajaccio
Cedex
France
Tel: **95 29 05 00**
Fax: 95 29 05 05

Continental Airlines
PO Box 4607
Houston
Texas 77210-4607
USA
Tel: **(713) 834 5000**
Fax: (713) 639 3087

Croatia Airlines
Savska Cesta 41
41000 Zagreb
Croatia
Tel: **(41) 61 31 11**
Fax: (41) 53 04 75

Crossair
PO Box 1903
CH-8058 Zurich Airport
Switzerland
Tel: **(61) 325 25 25**
Fax: (61) 325 32 67

Cubana
Calle 23 No 64
Havana, Cuba
Tel: **(7) 36 775**
Fax: (7) 36 190

Continental Airlines
2929 Allen Parkway
Houston
Texas 77019
USA
Tel: **713 630 5000**

Cyprus Airways
21 Alkeou Street
PO Box 1903
Nicosia, Cyprus
Tel: **(2) 443 054**
Fax: (2) 443 167

Czech Airlines
Revolucni 1, 11000 Praha 1
Czech Republic
Tel: **(2) 316 89 21**
Fax: (2) 316 27 74

Delta Airlines
1030 Delta Blvd
Atlanta, Georgia 30320
USA
Tel: **(404) 715 2600**
Fax: (404) 767 8499

EasyJet
Easyland, London Luton
Airport
Luton LU2 9LS
Tel: **(01582) 44 55 66**
Fax: (01582) 44 33 55

Ecuatoriana
Box 505 Colon y Reina
Victoria
Quito
Ecuador
Tel: **(2) 563 003**
Fax: (2) 563 931

Egyptair
Cairo International Airport
Cairo, Egypt
Tel: **(2) 390 24 44**
Fax: (2) 39 15 57

El Al – Israel Airlines
PO Box 41
Ben-Gurion Airport
Tel Aviv 70100
Israel
Tel: **(3) 971 6111**
Fax: (3) 971 1442

Emirates
PO Box 686
Dubai
United Arab Emirates
Tel: **(4) 82 2511**
Fax: (4) 82 2357

Estonian Air
2 Lennujaama Street
Tallinn EE0011
Estonia
Tel: **(6) 401 101**
Fax: (6) 312 740

Ethiopian Airlines
PO Box 1755
Bole Airport
Addis Ababa, Ethiopia
Tel: **(1) 61 22 22**
Fax: (1) 61b14 74

Eurowings Luftverkehrs
Flughafenstrasse 21
D-44319 Dortmund
Germany
Tel: **(911) 36 560**
Fax: (911) 365 203

Finnair
Mannerheimintie 102
00250 Helsinki
Finland
Tel: **(0) 81881**
Fax: (0) 818 8736

Gambia Airways
68/69 Wellington Street
Banjul
The Gambia
Tel: **220 27778**
Fax: 220 29339

Garuda Indonesia
Jalan Merdeka Selatan No 13
Jakarta 10110
Indonesia
Tel: **3801901**
Fax: (21) 363595

GB Airways
Ian Stewart Centre
Beehive Ringroad
Gatwick Airport
West Sussex
RH6 OPB
Tel: **01293-664228**
Fax: 01293 664218

Ghana Airways
PO Box 1636
Ghana Airways House
White Avenue
Accra, Ghana
Tel: **(21) 773321**
Fax: (21) 777675

Gulf Air
PO Box 138
Manama
Bahrain
Tel: **322 200**
Fax: 330 466

Guyana Airways
32 Main Str
PO Box 102
Georgetown
Guyana
Tel: **59490**

Hawaiian Airlines
Honolulu International
Airport
PO Box 30008
Hawaii 96813
USA
Tel: **(808) 537 5100**
Fax: (808) 525 6719

Iberia
130 Calle Velazquez
E-28006 Madrid
Spain
Tel: **(1) 587 8787**
Fax: (1) 587 7193

Icelandair
Reykjavik Airport
IS-101 Reykjavik
Iceland
Tel: **(354) 5050 300**
Fax: (354) 5690 391

Indian Airlines
Airlines House

113 Gurdwara Rakabganj
Road
Parliament St
New Delhi 110001
India
Tel: **(11) 388951**
Fax: (11) 381730

Iran Air
Iran Air Building
Mehrabad Airport, PO
Box13185-775
Tehran, Iran
Tel: **(21) 882 9080**
Fax: (21) 600 32 48

Istanbul Airlines
Incirli Cad 50/4,
34740 Barkikroy
Istanbul, Turkey
Tel: (212) **509 2121**
Fax: (212) 593 6035

Japan Airlines – JAL
Daini Tekko Building
1-8-2 Marunouchi
Chiyoda-ku, Tokyo 100
Japan
Tel: **(03) 284 2831**
Fax: (03) 284 2719

Jersey European Airways
Exeter Airport
Exeter, Devon EX5 2BD
UK
Tel: **01392 366 669**
Fax:01392 366 151

Kenya Airways
PO Box 19002
Nairobi, Kenya
Tel: **(254) 2 823000**

KLM Royal Dutch Airlines
PO Box 7700
NL-1117 ZL Schiphol Airport
Amsterdam, The Netherlands
Tel: **(0120) 6499123**
Fax: (0120) 6488391

Korean Air
41-3 Seosomun-Dong
Jung-Gu
Seoul, Rep. of Korea
Tel: **(2) 7517 114**
Fax: (2) 751 7522

Kuwait Airways
PO Box 394
Kuwait International Airport
1304 Safat, Kuwait
Tel: **434 5555/6666/7777**
Fax: 431 9912

Laker Airways
LAN, Chile SA
Estado 10, Piso 8~Casilla
147-D
Santiago, Chile
Tel: **(2) 394 411**
Fax: (34) 359 7714

Lao Aviation
BP Box 119
2 Rue Pan Kham
Vientiane
Lao People's Democratic
Republic
Tel: **2094**

**LAPSA (Lineas Aereas
Paraguayas)**
Avenida Peru 456
Ascuncion, Paraguay
Tel: **(21) 491 041**
Fax: (21) 496 484

Lauda Air
P.O. Box 56
A-1300 Vienna Airport
Vienna, Austria
Tel: (1) **7 1110 2081/2/3/4**
Fax: (1) 7 1110 3157

Lesotho Airways
Leabua Jonathan Airport
PO Box 861
Maseru 100, Lesotho
Tel: **22483**
Fax: 310126

Lithuanian Airlines
8 Radunes
Vilnius Airport
Vilnius 2023, Lithuania
Tel: (2) **63 01 16**
Fax: (2) 22 68 28

LOT - Polish Airlines
65/79 Jerozolmskie Av
00-697 Warsaw
Poland
Tel: **(22) 630 50 07**
Fax: (22) 630 55 03

**Lufthansa – German
Airlines**
Von-Gablenz-Strasse 2-6
D-5000 Koln 21
Germany
Tel: **(221) 8260**
Fax: (221) 826 3818

Luxair
Aeroport de Luxembourg
L-2987 Luxembourg

Tel: **4798 2311**
Fax: 43 24 82

Maersk Air
Copenhagen Airport South
DK-2791, Dragoer
Denmark
Tel: (45) **32 31 44 44**
Fax: (45) 32 31 44 90

Malaysia Airlines
33rd Floor
Bangunan MAS
Jalan Sultan Ismail 50250
Kuala Lumpur
Malaysia
Tel: **261 0555**
Fax:(6) 37 746 2581

Manx Airlines
Isley of Man Ranoldsway
Airport
Ballasalla, Isle of Man
UK
Tel: **(01624) 826000**
Fax: (01624) 826031

Malev – Hungarian Airlines
Roosevelt Ter 2
Budapest, Hungary H-1051
Tel: (1) **266 9033**
Fax: (1) 266 2685

MEA (Middle East Airlines)
P.O. Box 206
Beirut, Lebanon
Tel:**(01) 316316**
Fax: (01) 8711 754104

Mexican
Xola No 535
Piso 30
Col del Valle, PO Box 12-813
Mexico City 03100, Mexico
Tel: **(5)325 0909/227 0260**
Fax: (5)543 4587

Mount Cook Airlines
PO Box 4644
Christchurch
New Zealand
Tel: (3) **348 2099**
Fax: (3) 348 8159

Nigeria Airways
Airways House
Murtala Muhammed Airport
PO Box 136, Lagos
Nigeria
Tel: **900476**

Northwest Airlines Inc
Minneapolis/St Paul

International Airport
St Paul, Minnesota 55111
USA
Tel: **(612) 726 2111**

Olympic Airways
96 Syngrou Avenue
Athens 11741, Greece
Tel: **929 2111**
Fax: (1) 926 7156

PIA- Pakistan International Airlines
PIA Building
Karachi Airport, Pakistan
Tel: **412011**
Fax: (9221) 727727

Philippine Airlines
PO Box 954 Manila
Philippines
Tel: **818 0111**
Fax: (13) 818 3298

Qantas Airways
Qantas International Centre
GPO Box 489
Sydney, NSW 2001
Australia
Tel: **(2) 691 3636**

Royal Air Maroc
Anfa Airport
Casablanca
Morocco
Tel: **36 16 20**
Fax: 36 05 20

Royal Brunei Airlines
PO Box 737
Bandar Seri Begawan
Brunei Darussalam 2085
Tel: **240500**

Royal Jordanian Airlines
Housing Bank Commercial
Centre, Queen Noor Street
P.O. Box 302
Amman, Jordan
Tel: (6) **607300**
Fax: (6) 672 527

Royal Nepal Airlines
RNAC Building
Kanti Path, Kathmandu
Nepal
Tel: **214511**

Royal Swazi Airways
Matsapha Airport
PO Box 939, Manzini,
Swaziland
Tel: **53151** / Fax: 84420

Ryanair
Dublin Airport
Dublin
Rep of Ireland
Tel: **(01) 844 4400**
Fax: (01) 844 4402

SABENA
Ave. E Mounierlaan 2
B-1200 Brussels
Belgium
Tel: (02)**723 23 23**

SAS – Scandinavian Airlines
Frosundaviks Alle 1
S-161 87 Stockholm
Sweden
Tel: (08) **797 0000**

Saudi
P.O. Box 167
Jeddah 21231
Saudi Arabia
Tel: **686 000**
Fax: 686 4589

Sempati Air
JLN Medan Merdeka Timur
No 7
PO Box 2068, Jakarta
Indonesia
Tel: **348 760/343 323**
Fax: (21) 367743

Sierra National Airlines
25 Putney Street
Freetown, Sierra Leone
Tel: **(22) 2026/075**
Fax: (22)2026

Singapore Airlines
Airline House
25 Airline Road
Singapore 1781
Tel: **542 3333**
Fax: 545 5749

Solomon Airlines
PO Box 23
Honiara, Solomon Islands
Tel: **20031**

SAA – South African Airways
Airways Towers
PO Box 7778
Johannesburg 2000
Transvaal, South Africa
Tel: **(011)28 1728**
Fax: (011)773 8988

Sudan Airways
PO Box 253
Khartoum
Sudan
Tel: **41766**

Suriname Airways
Coppenamelaan 136
PO Box 2029, Pararibo
Republic of Suriname
Tel: **73939**

Swissair
Zurich Airport
Zurich
Switzerland CH-8058
Tel: **812 1212**
Fax: 810 8046

Syrian Arab Airlines
PO Box 417
Damascus
Syria
Tel: **22343**

TAAG - Angola Airlines
Rua de Missao 123
PO Box 79, Luanda
Angola
Tel: **336510**

Taca International Airlines
Edificio Caribe 2 Piso
San Salvador, El Salvador
Central America
Tel: **232244**

TAP Air Portugal
Aeroporto (Apartado 5194)
P-1704 Lisboa Codex
Portugal
Tel: (1) **841 5000**

TAROM (Romanian Air Transport)
Otopeni Airport
Soseaua Bucharest - Ploesti
KM 16.5
Romania
Tel: **333137**

Thai Airways International
89 Vibhavadi Rangsit Road
Bangkok 10900
Thailand
Tel: **513 0121**

Transavia Airlines
P.O. Box 7777
NL-1118 ZM Schiphol-Centraal
The Netherlands

Tel: **(020) 6046318**
Fax: (020) 484637

Transbrasil–Linhas Aeras
Aeroporto de Congohas
Hangar
Sao Paulo, Brazil
Tel: **240 7411**

TWA – Trans World Airlines
One City Centre
515 N 6th St
St. Louis, Missouri 63101
USA
Tel: **(314) 589 7544**

Tunis Air
Boulevard du 7 Novembre
Tunis Carthage 2035
Tunisia
Tel: **700 100**
Fax: 700 008

Turkish Airlines
Ataturk Hava Limani
Yesilkoy, Istanbul
Turkey
Tel: **(0212) 663 6300**
Fax: (0212)663 4744

Ukraine International Airlines
Prospekt Pobedy 14,
252135 Kiev
Ukraine
Tel: **(044) 216 6758**
Fax: (044) 216 7994

United Airlines
PO Box 66100
O'Hare International Airport
Chicago
Illinois 60666
USA
Tel: **(847) 700 4000**

VARIG – Brazilian Airlines
365 Avenida Almirante
Sylvio de Noronha
Edificio Varig
Rio de Janeiro GB 20021-010
Brasil
Tel: **292 6600**
Fax: (55) 21 240 6859

VIASA – Venezolana Internacional de Aviación
Torre Viasa
Avenida Sur 25
Plaza Morelos, Caracas 105
Venezuela
Tel: **572 9522**

Virgin Atlantic Airways
Ashdown House
High Street, Crawley
West Sussex RH10 1DQ
Tel: **01293 562345**
Fax: 01293 561721

Yemenia – Yemen Airways
PO Box 1183
Sana'a, Republic of Yemen
Tel: **232389**
Fax: 252991

AIRLINE OFFICES IN THE UK

Aer Lingus
83 Staines Road
Hounslow, Middx PW3 3JB
Tel: **0181-569 4646**
Fax: 0181-569 6264

Aeroflot
70 Piccadilly
London W1V 9HH
Tel: **0171-355 2233**
Fax: 0171-493 1852

Aerolineas Argentinas
54 Conduit Street
London W1R 9FD
Tel: **0171-494 1001**
Fax: 0171-494 1002

Air Afrique
86 Hatton Gds
London EC1 N8QQ
Tel: **0171-430 0284**
Fax: 0171-430 0508

Air Algerie
10 Baker Street
London W1M 1DA
Tel: **0171-487 5709**
Fax: 0171-935 1715

Air Botswana
177/178 Tottenham Ct. Road
London W1P 9LF
Tel: **0171-757 2737**
Fax: 0171-757 2277

Air Burundi c/o Air France

Air Canada
7/8 Conduit Street
London W1R 9TG
Tel: **0990 247226**
Fax: 0171- 465 0095

Air China
41 Grosvenor Gardens
London SW1W OBP
Tel: **0171- 630 0919**
Fax: 0171-630 7792

Air France
Colet Court, 100 Hamersmith
Road, London W6 7JP
Tel: **0181-759 2311**
Fax: 0181-750 4391

Air Gabon
19 Colonnade Walk
151 Buckingham Palace Road
London SW1W 9SH
Tel: **0171 931 9225**
Fax: 0171 931 9232

Air India
Air India Building
Mathisen Way, Cornbrook
Slough SL3 OHF
Tel: **0181-745 1000**
Fax: 0181-745 1059

Air Inter c/o Air France

Air Lanka
22 Regent Street
London SW1Y 0QD
Tel: **0171-930 2099**
Fax: 0171 930 5626

Air Malawi c/o British
Airways

Air Malta
314/316 Upper Richmond
Road, Putney
London SW15 6TV
Tel: **0181- 785 3199**
Fax: 0181-785 5164

Air Mauritius
49 Conduit Street
London W1R 9FB
Tel: **0171-434 4375**
Fax: 0171-439 4101

Air Namibia
Beaumont House
Lambton Road
London SW20 OLW
Tel: **0181 -944 6181**
Fax: 0181- 944 7199

Air New Zealand
Elsinore House
77 Fulham Palace Road
London W6 8JA
Tel: **0181-846 9595**
Fax: 0181-741 4645

Air Seychelles
Suite 6, Kelvin House
Kelvin Way, Crawley
West Sussex RH10 2SE
Tel: **01293 542101**
Fax: 01293 562353

Air UK
Stansted House
Stansted Airport
Essex CM24 1AE
Tel: **01279 660 400**
Fax: 01279 660 330

Air Zimbabwe
Colette House
52-55 Piccadilly
London W1V 9AA
Tel: **0171-491 0009**
Fax: 0171-355 3326

Alitalia
205 Holland Park Avenue
London W11 4XB
Tel: **0171-602 7111**
Fax: 0171-602 5584

All Nippon Airways
ANA House
6/8 Old Bond Street
London W1X 3TA
Tel: **0171-355 1155**
Fax: 0171-915 3399

American Airlines
23/59 Staines Road
Hounslow
Middlesex TW3 3HE
Tel: **0181-572 5555**
Fax: 0181-572 8646

Ansett Australia
20 Savile Row
London W1X 2AN
Tel: **0171-494 2141**
Fax: 0171-734 4333

Arian Afghan Airlines
169 Piccadilly
London W1V 9D
Tel: **0171-493 1411**
Fax: 0171-629 1611

Austrian Airlines
5th Floor, 10 Wardour Street
London W1V 4BQ
Tel: **0171-434 7350**
Fax: 0171-434 7219

Avianca
Ocean House
Hazelwick Avenue
3 Bridges, Crawley

West Sussex, RH10 1NP
Tel: **01293-553 747**
Fax: 01293-553 321

AVIATECA
Ocean House
Hazelwick Avenue
Three Bridges, Crawley
Surrey RH10 1NP
Tel: **01293-553330**
Fax: 01293 553321

**BWIA International
Trinidad & Tobago**
Lampton Road
Hounslow
Middlesex TW3 1HY
Tel:**0181-577 1100**
Fax: 0181-577 6658

Bahamasair
79 Dean Street
London W1V 5AB
Tel: **0171-437 8766**
Fax: 0171-734 6460

Balkan Bulgarian
322 Regent Street
London W1R 5AB
Tel: **0171-637 7637**
Fax: 0171-637 2481

Biman Bangladesh
17 Conduit Street
London W1R 9DD
Tel: **0171-629 0252**
Fax: 0171-629 0736

British Airways
PO Box 10
London-Heathrow Airport
Hounslow
Middlesex TW6 2JA
Tel: **0181-897 4000**
and...
156 Regent Street
London W1R 5TA
Tel: **0171-434 4700**
Fax: 0171-434 4636

British Midland
Donington Hall
Castle Donington
Derby DE7 2SB
Tel: **01332-854000**
Fax: 01332-854662

Cameroon Airlines
17 Clifford Street
London W1X 1RG
Tel: **0171-734 7676**
Fax: 0171-439 3349

Canadian Airlines
15 Berkley Street
London W1X 5AE
Tel: **0345-616767**
Fax: 0181-814 4330

Cathay Pacific
7 Apple Tree Yard
Duke of York Street
London SW1Y 6LD
Tel: **0171-747 7000**
Fax: 0171-925 0445

Cayman Airways
Trevor House
100 Brompton Road
London SW3 1EX
Tel: **0171-491 7771**
Fax: 0171-584 4463

China Airlines
5th Floor, Nuffield House
41-46 Piccadilly
London W1V 9AJ
Tel: **0171-434 0707**
Fax: 0171-439 4888

Conti-Flug
612 Kingston Road
London SW20 8DN
Tel: **01293-568885**
Fax: 01293-512229

Continental Airlines
Beulah Court
Albert Road, Horley
Surrey RH6 7HZ
Tel: **01293-776464**
Fax: 01293-773726

Croatian Airlines
162-168 Regents Street
London W1R 5TB
Tel: **0171-306 3138**
Fax: 0171-306 3166

Cubana
49 Conduit Street
London W1R 9FB
Tel: **0171-734 1165**
Fax:0171-437 0681

Cyprus Airlines
29-31 Hampstead Road
Euston Centre
London NW1 3JA
Tel: **0171-388 5411**
Fax: 0171-388 9237

Czechoslovak Airlines
72 Margaret Street
London W1N 7HA
Tel: **0171-255 1898**

Fax: 0171-323 1633

Delta Airlines
Victoria Place,Unit 19
Buckingham Palace Road,
London SW1
Tel: **0800-414767**
Fax: 0181-601 6037

Dragonair c/o Cathay Pacific

Egyptair
296 Regent Street
London W1R 6PH
Tel: **0171-580 5477**
Fax: 0171-637 4328

El Al Israel Airlines
180 Oxford Street
United Kingdom House
London W1N OEL
Tel: **0171-957 4100**
Fax: 0171-957 4299

Emirates
1st Floor, 95 Cromwell Road
Gloucester Park,
London SW7 4DL
Tel: **0171-808 0808**
Fax: 0171-808 0080

Ethiopian Airlines
Foxglove House
166 Piccadilly
London W1V 9DE
Tel: **0171-491 9119**
Fax: 0171-491 1892

Faucett-The First Airline of Peru
41 Boltro Road
Haywards Heath
West Sussex RH16 1BJ
Tel: **01444 414 116**
Fax: 0171-839 5379

Finnair
14 Clifford Street
London W1X 1RD
Tel: **0171-408 1222**
Fax: 0171-629 7289

GB Airways
Ian Stewart Centre
Beehive Ring Road
Gatwick Airport
Surrey RH6 0PB
Tel: **01293-664239**
Fax: 01293-664218

Garuda Indonesia
35 Duke Street
London W1M 5DF

Tel: **0171-486 3011**
Fax: 0171-224 3971

Ghana Airways
3 Princes Street
London W1R 7RA
Tel: **0171-499 0201**
Fax: 0171-491 1504

Gulf Air
10 Albermarle Street
London W1X 3HE
Tel: **0171-408 1717**
Fax: 0171-629 3989

Iberia Airlines
Venture House
29 Glasshouse Street
London W1R 5RG
Tel: **0171-413 1201**
Fax: 0171-413 1264

Icelandair
172 Tottenham Court Road
London W1P 9LG
Tel: **0171-388 5599**
Fax: 0171-387 5711

Iran Air
73 Piccadilly
London W1V 0QX
Tel: **0171-409 0971**
Fax: 0171-408 1360

Japan Airlines
5 Hanover Court
Hanover Square
London W1R 0DR
Tel: **0171-408 1000**
Fax: 0171-499 1071

JAT – Yugoslav
37 Maddox Street
London W1R 1AQ
Tel: **0171-629 2007**
Fax:0171- 493 8092

Jersey European Airways
Exeter Airport
Exeter EX5 2BD
Tel: **0990 676676**
Fax: 01392 366151

Kenya Airways
16 Conduit Street
London W1R 9TD
Tel: **0171-409 0277**
Fax: 0171-4992973

KLM
8 Hanover Street
London W1R 9HF
Tel: **0990 750 900**

Fax: 0181-750 9990

Korean Airlines
66-68 Piccadilly
London SW1Y 4RF
Tel: **0800 413000**
Fax: 0171-495 1616

Kuwait Airlines
16-20 Baker Street
London W1M 2AD
Tel: **0171-412 0006**
Fax: 0171-412 0008

LAB (Lloyd Aereo Boliviano)
41 Boltro Road
Haywards Heath
West Sussex RH16 1BJ
Tel: **01444-413 366**
Fax: 0171-930 1878

LAN Chile
150 Buckingham Palace Road
London SW1W 9TR
Tel: **0171-730 2128**
Fax: 0171-730 1180

LIAT c/o British Airways

LOT – Polish
313 Regent Street
London W1R 7PE
Tel: **0171-580 5037**
Fax: 0171-323 0774

Lufthansa
Lufthansa House
10 Old Bond Street
London W1X 4EN
Tel: **0345-737747**
Fax: 0181-750 3545

Luxair
Room 2003, Terminal 2
London-Heathrow Airport
Hounslow
Middlesex TW6 1HL
Tel: **0181-745 4254**
Fax: 0181-759 7974

Malaysia Airlines
247-249 Cromwell Rd
London SW5 9GA
Tel: **0171-341 2020**
Fax: 0171-341 2022

Malev Hungarian
10 Vigo Street
London W1X 1AJ
Tel: **0171-439 0577**
Fax: 0171-734 8116

Mexicana
215 Chalk Farm Road
London NW1 8AF
Tel: **0171-284 2550**
Fax: 0181-267 2004

Middle East Airlines
45 Albermarle Street
London W1X 3FE
Tel: **0171-493 6321**
Fax: 0171-629 4163

Nigeria Airways
11-12 Conduit Street
London W1R 0NX
Tel: **0171-493 9726**
Fax: 0171-491 9644

Northwest Airlines
Northwest House
Tinsley Lane North
Crawley
West Sussex RH10 2TP
Tel: **01293-565454**
Fax: 01293-574537

Olympic Airways
11 Conduit Street
London W1R 0LP
Tel: **0171-409 3400**
Fax: 0171-493 0563

PIA
1-5 King Street
London W6 9HR
Tel: **0181-741 8066**
Fax: 0181-741 9376

Philippine Airlines
1 Denderden Street
Hanover Square
London W1R 9AH
Tel: **0171-499 9446**
Fax: 0171-629 6096

Qantas
395/403 King Street
London W6 9NJ
Tel: **0181-846 0466**
Fax: 0181-748 8551
and...
182 Strand
London WC2
Tel: **0800-477767**

Royal Air Maroc
205 Regent Street
London W1R 7DE
Tel: **0171-439 4361**
Fax: 0171-734 6183

Royal Brunei Airlines
49 Cromwell Road

London W1R 7DD
Tel: **0171-584 6660**
Fax: 0171-581 9279

Royal Jordanian
32 Brook Street
London W1 Y1AG
Tel: **0171-878 6300**
Fax: 0171-629 4068

Royal Nepal Airlines
13 New Burlington St
London W1X 1FF
Tel: **0171-494 0974**
Fax: 0171-494 1767

Ryanair
Stansted Airport
Stansted
Essex CM24 1QW
Tel: **0541-569 569**
Fax: (31) 609 7801

South African Airways
61 Conduit Street
London W1R ONE
Tel: **0171-312 5000**
Fax: 0171-312 5009

SAS - Scandanavian
52 Conduit Street
London W1R 0AY
Tel: **0171-734 4020**
Fax: 0171-465 0537

Sabena
Gemini House
10-18 Putney Hill
London SW15 6AA
Tel: **0181-780 1444**
Fax: 0181-780 1502

Saudi Arabia Airlines
508 Chiswick High Road
London W4 5RG
Tel: **0181-995 7777**
Fax: 0181-995 3803

Singapore Airlines
580-586 Chiswick High Road
London W4 5RB
Tel: **0181-747 0007**
Fax: 0181-563 6753

Sudan Airways
32 Rutland Gate
London SW7 1PG
Tel: **0171-584 2400**
Fax: 0171-225 3561

Swissair
Swiss Centre
10 Wardour Street ⇨

London W1V 4BJ
Tel: **0171-434 7300**
Fax: 0171-439 7375

TAP – Air Portugal
Gillingham House
38-44 Gillingham Street
London SW1V 1JW
Tel: **0171-828 0262**
Fax: 0171-931 0805

Tarom-Romanian Airlines
27 New Cavendish Street
London W1M 7RL
Tel: **0171-224 3693**
Fax: 0171-487 2913

Thai Airways International
41 Albermarle Street
London W1X 3FE
Tel: **0171-499 9113**
Fax: 0171-4091463

TWA
Central House
Lampton Road
Hounslow
Middlesex TW3 1TW
Tel: **0181-814 0707**
Fax: 0181-754 2791

Turkish Airlines
11/12 Hanover Street
London W1R 9HF
Tel: **0171-499 9249**
Fax: 0171-495 2441

United Airlines
United House
Southern Perimeter Road
London Heathrow Airport
Hounslow TW6 3LP
Tel: **0181-990 9988**
Fax: 0181-750 9634

Varig Brazilian
St. George House
61 Conduit Street
London W1R OHG
Tel: **0171-287 3131**
Fax: 0171-478 2199

VIASA
c/o Iberia Airlines

Virgin Atlantic
The Office
Crawley Business Quarter
Manor Royal, Crawley
West Sussex RH10 2NU
Tel: **01293-562 345**
Fax: 0171-561 721

Yemenia
52 Stratton Street
London W1X 5FF
Tel: **0171-491 7186**
Fax: 0171-355 3062

AIRLINE TWO-LETTER CODES

The codes listed below are often used in timetables, brochures and tickets to identify airlines.

A

AA	American Airlines
AC	Air Canada
AE	Mandarin Airlines
AF	Air France
AH	Air Algerie
AI	Air India
AJ	Air Belgium
AM	AERO MEXICO
AN	Ansett Australia
AO	AVIACO
AQ	Aloha Airlines
AR	Aerolineas Argentinas
AS	Alaska Airlines
AT	Royal Air Maroc
AV	AVIANCA
AY	Finnair
AZ	Alitalia

B

BA	British Airways
BD	British Midland
BG	Biman Bangladesh Airlines
BI	Royal Brunei Airlines
BL	Pacific Airlines
BO	Bouraq Indonesia Airlines
BP	Air Botswana
BR	EVA Airways
BU	Braathens SAFE
BV	Sun Air
BW	BWIA International Trinidad & Tobago Airways

C

CA	Air China
CF	Compania de Aviacion Faucett
CI	China Airlines
CM	COPA Compania Panamena
CO	Continental Airlines
CP	Canadian Airlines
CU	CUBANA
CW	Air Marshall Islands
CX	Cathay Pacific
CY	Cyprus Airways
CZ	China Southern Airlines

D

DL	Delta Airlines
DM	Maersk Air
DO	Dominicana
DS	Air Senegal
DT	TAAG-Angolan Airlines

E

EF	Far Eastern Air Transport
EG	Japan Asia Airways
EH	SAETA
EI	Aer Lingus
EL	Air Nippon
EM	Empire Airlines
ET	Ethiopian Airlines
EU	ECUATORIANA
EW	Eurowings

F

FG	Ariana Afghan Airlines
FI	Icelandair
FJ	Air Pacific
FQ	Air Aruba
FR	Ryanair

G

GA	Garuda Indonesia
GE	Trans Asia Airways
GF	Gulf Air
GH	Ghana Airways
GN	Air Gabon
GU	AVIATECA
GV	Riga Airlines

GY	Guyana Airways

H

HA	Hawaiian Airlines
HM	Air Seychelles
HP	America West Airlines
HV	Transavia Airlines
HY	Uzbekistan Airlines

I

IB	IBERIA
IC	Indian Airlines
IE	Solomon Airlines
IJ	TAT European Airlines
IL	Istanbul Airlines
IP	Airlines of Tasmania
IR	Iran Air
IV	Fujian Airlines
IY	Yemen Airways
IZ	Arkia Israeli Airlines

J

JE	Manx Airlines
JL	Japan Airlines
JM	Air Jamaica
JP	Adria Airways
JR	Aero California
JY	Jersey European Airways

K

KA	Dragonair
KB	Druk-Air
KE	Korean Air
KI	Air Atlantique
KL	KLM
KM	Air Malta
KQ	Kenya Airways
KU	Kuwait Airways
KV	Eastern Air
KX	Cayman Airways

L

LA	LAN Chile
LB	Lloyd Aereo Boliviano
LG	Luxair
LH	Lufthansa
LI	LIAT
LO	LOT Polish Airlines

LR	LACSA
LX	Crossair
LY	El Al Israel Airlines
LZ	Balkan

M

MA	MALEV
MD	Air Madagascar
ME	Middle East Airlines
MK	Air Mauritius
MO	Calm Air International
MR	Air Mauritanie
MS	Egyptair
MW	Maya Airways
MX	Mexicana

N

NF	Air Vanuatu
NG	Lauda Air
NH	All Nippon Airways
NN	Cardinal Airlines
NW	Northwest Airlines
NZ	Air New Zealand

O

OA	Olympic Airways
OK	Czechoslovak Airlines
ON	Air Nauru
OS	Austrian Airlines
OU	Croatia Airlines
OV	Estonian Air

P

PB	Air Burundi
PC	Air Fiji
PG	Bangkok Airways
PH	Polynesian Airlines
PK	Pakistan International Airlines
PL	AeroPeru
PR	Philippine Airlines
PS	Ukraine International Airways
PX	Air Niugini
PY	Surinam Airways
PZ	LAPSA

Q

QF	Qantas Airways
QL	Air Lesotho
QM	Air Malawi
QU	Uganda Airlines
QV	Lao Aviation
QW	Turks and Caicos National Airline

R

RA	Royal Nepal Airline
RB	Syrian Arab Airlines
RG	VARIG
RJ	Royal Jordanian
RK	Air Afrique
RO	TAROM
RR	Royal Air Force
RY	Air Rwanda

S

SA	South African Airways
SD	Sudan Airways
SF	Shanghai Airlines
SH	Air Toulouse
SK	SAS
SN	Sabena
SO	Sunshine Airlines
SQ	Singapore Airlines
SR	Swissair
SU	Aeroflot
SV	Saudia
SW	Air Namibia
SZ	China Southwest

T

TA	Taca International Airlines
TC	Air Tanzania
TE	Lithuanian Airlines
TG	Thai Airways International
TK	Turkish Airlines
TM	Linhas Aereas de Mocambique
TP	TAP Air Portugal
TQ	Transwede
TR	Transbrasil Linhas Aereas
TS	Samoa Aviation
TT	Airline Lithuania
TU	Tunis Air
TW	TWA - Trans

	World Airlines

U

UA	United Airlines
UB	Myanmar Airways
UK	Air UK
UL	Air Lanka
UM	Air Zimbabwe
UP	Bahamasair
UY	Cameroon Airlines

V

VA	VIASA
VE	AVENSA
VJ	Royal Air Cambodge
VN	Vietnam Airlines
VO	Tyrolean Airways
VP	VASP
VR	Transportes Aereos de Cabo Verde
VS	Virgin Atlantic
VT	Air Tahiti
VU	Air Ivoire

W

WM	Windward Islands Airways International
WN	Southwest Airlines
WT	Nigeria Airways
WY	Oman Air

Y

YT	Skywest Airlines

Z

ZB	Monarch Airlines
ZQ	Ansett New Zealand

AIRPORT/CITY CODES

A

AAK	Aranuka, Kiribati
ABJ	Abidjan, Ivory Coast
ABT	Al-Baha, Saudi Arabia
ABZ	Aberdeen, UK
ACA	Acapulco, Mexico
ACC	Accra, Ghana
ACE	Lanzarote, Canary Islands
ACY	Atlantic City International, USA
ADA	Adana, Turkey
ADD	Addis Ababa, Ethiopia
ADE	Aden, Rep of Yemen
ADL	Adelaide, Australia
AEP	Buenos Aires Airport, Argentina
AGA	Agadir, Morocco
AGP	Malaga, Spain
AGR	Agra, India
AIY	Atlantic City, NJ, USA
AJA	Ajaccio, Corsica
AKL	Auckland, New Zealand
AKS	Auki, Solomon Islands
ALA	Almaty, Kazakhstan
ALB	Albany, NY USA
ALC	Alicante, Spain
ALG	Algiers Algeria
ALP	Aleppo, Syria
ALY	Alexandria, Egypt
AMM	Amman, Jordan
AMS	Amsterdam, Netherlands
ANC	Anchorage, Alaska, USA
ANK	Ankara, Turkey
ANR	Antwerp, Belgium
ANU	Antigua, Leeward Islands
APW	Apia, Samoa
AQJ	Aqaba, Jordan
ARN	Stockholm Arlanda Apt, Sweden
ASB	Ashkhabad, Turkmenistan
ASM	Asmara, Eritrea
ASP	Alice Springs, NT, Australia
ASU	Asuncion, Paraguay
ASW	Aswan, Egypt
ATH	Athens, Greece
ATL	Atlanta, GA, USA
AUA	Aruba, Neth. Antilles
AUH	Abu Dhabi, UAE
AVN	Avignon, France
AXA	Anguilla, Leeward Islands
AYT	Antalya, Turkey

B

BAH	Bahrain
BAK	Baku, Azerbijan
BBQ	Barbuda, Leeward Islands
BBR	Basse-Terre, Guadeloupe
BBU	Bucharest Banfasa Apt, Romania
BCN	Barcelona, Spain
BDA	Bermuda Kindley Field, Bermuda
BEL	Belem, PA Brazil
BER	Berlin West, Germany
BEY	Beirut, Lebanon
BFN	Bloemfontein, South Africa
BFS	Belfast, UK
BGF	Bangui, Central African Rep.
BGI	Barbados
BGO	Bergen, Norway
BHX	Birmingham, UK
BIM	Bimini, Bahamas
BIO	Bilbao, Spain
BJL	Banjul, Gambia
BJM	Bujumbua, Burundi
BJS	Beijing, P R China
BKK	Bangkok, Thailand
BKO	Bamako, Mali
BLQ	Bologna, Italy
BLZ	Blantyre, Malawi
BNA	Nashville, TN, USA
BNE	Brisbane, QL Australia
BNJ	Bonn, Germany
BOB	Bora Bora, Society Islands
BOD	Bordeaux, France
BOG	Bogota, Colombia
BOM	Bombay, India
BON	Bonaire, Netherland

	Antilles
BOS	Boston, MA USA
BRE	Bremen,Germany
BRN	Berne,
	Switzerland
BRU	Brussels,
	Belgium
BSB	Brasilia, Brazil
BSL	Basle,
	Switzerland
BTH	Batu Besar,
	Indonesia
BTS	Bratislava,
	Slovakia
BUD	Budapest,
	Hungary
BUE	Buenos Aires,
	Argentina
BUH	Bucharest,
	Romania
BUQ	Bulawayo,
	Zimbabwe
BWI	Baltimore, MD,
	USA
BWN	Bandar Seri
	Begawan, Brunei
BXO	Bissau, Guinea-
	Bissau
BZE	Belize City
BZV	Brazzaville,
	Congo

C

CAI	Cairo, Egypt
CAP	Cap Haitien, Haiti
CAS	Casablanca,
	Morocco
CAY	Cayenne, French
	Guiana
CBR	Canberra, ACT,
	Australia
CCS	Caracas,
	Venzuela
CCU	Calcutta, India
CDG	Paris Charles de
	Gaulle, France
CEB	Cebu, Phillipines
CFU	Corfu, Greece
CGH	Sao Paulo
	Congonhas Apt.,
	Brazil
CGK	Jakarta Airport,
	Indonesia
CGN	Cologne,
	Germany
CGP	Chittagong,
	Bangladesh
CHC	Christchurch,
	New Zealand
CHI	Chicago, IL USA

CIA	Rome Ciampino
	Apt, Italy
CJU	Cheju, Rep.Korea
CKY	Conakry, Guinea
CLE	Cleveland, OH,
	USA
CLT	Charlotte, NC,
	USA
CMB	Colombo, Sri
	Lanka
CNS	Cairns, QL,
	Australia
CNX	Chang Mai,
	Thailand
COO	Cotonou, Benin
COS	Colorado
	Springs, CO,
	USA
CPH	Copenhagen,
	Denmark
CPT	Cape Town,
	South Africa
CUE	Cuenca, Ecuador
CUN	Cancun, Mexico
CUR	Curacao, Neth.
	Antilles
CVG	Cincinnati, OH,
	USA
CYB	Cayman Brac,
	Cayman Islands

D

DAC	Dhaka,
	Bangladesh
DAD	Da Nang,
	Vietnam
DAL	Dallas, Fort
	Worth, TX , USA
DAM	Damascus, Syria
DAR	Dar es Salaam,
	Tanzania
DBV	Dubrovnik,
	Croatia
DCF	Dominica Airport
DEL	Delhi, India
DEN	Denver, CO,
	USA
DFW	Dallas/Fort
	Worth, TX USA
DHA	Dhahran, Saudi
	Arabia
DKR	Dakar, Senegal
DLA	Douala,
	Cameroon
DME	Moscow
	Domodedovo Apt., Russia
DOH	Doha, Qatar
DOM	Dominica
DPS	Denpasar Bali,
	Indonesia

DRS	Dresden,
	Germany
DRW	Darwin, NT, Aus.
DTT	Detroit, MI, USA
DUB	Dublin, Ireland
DUR	Durban, South
	Africa
DUS	Dusseldorf,
	Germany
DXB	Dubai, UAE
DYU	Dushanbe,
	Tajikistan

E

EBB	Entebbe,
	Kampala, Uganda
EDI	Edinburgh, UK
EIS	Beef Island,
	British Virgin
	Islands
EMA	East Midlands
	Airport, UK
ERS	Windhoek Eros
	A/port, Namibia
ESB	Ankara
	International Apt,
	Turkey
ETH	Eilat, Israel
EWR	New York
	Newark Apt., NJ,
	USA
EZE	Ministro
	Pistarini, Buenos
	Aires Apt, Brazil

F

FAE	Faroe Islands,
	Denmark
FAI	Fairbanks, AK,
	USA
FAO	Faro, Portugal
FBU	Oslo Int A/port,
	Norway
FCO	Rome, Leonardo
	da Vinci Apt,
	Italy
FDF	Fort de France
	A/port,
	Martinique
FEZ	Fez, Morocco
FIH	Kinshasa, Zaire
FKI	Kisangani, Zaire
FLL	Fort Lauderdale,
	FL, USA
FLR	Florence, Italy
FMY	Fort Myers,
	Florida, USA
FNA	Freetown, Sierra
	Leone

FNC	Funchal, Madeira Islands	HNL	Apt, Japan Honolulu Int Apt, HI USA	KUL	Kuala Lumpur, Malaysia
FNJ	Pyongyang, North Korea	HOU	Houston, TX	KWI	Kuwait
FPO	Freeport, Bahamas	HRE	Harare, Zimbabwe		

L

LAD	Luanda, Angola
LAS	Las Vegas, NY USA
LAX	Los Angeles, CA USA
LBV	Libreville, Gabon
LCA	Larnaca, Cyprus
LCY	London City Airport, UK
LED	St Petersburg, Russia
LFW	Lome, Togo
LGA	New York La Guardia Apt, NY
LGW	London, Gatwick Apt. UK
LHE	Lahore, Pakistan
LHR	London, UK - Heathrow Apt...
LIM	Lima, Peru
LIN	Milan Int A/port, Itlay
LIS	Lisbon, Portugal
LJU	Ljubljana, Slovenia
LON	London, UK
LOS	Lagos, Nigeria
LPB	La Paz, Bolivia
LTN	London, UK - Luton Int.
LUN	Lusaka, Zambia
LUX	Luxembourg
LXA	Lhasa, Tibet, China
LXR	Luxor, Egypt
LYS	Lyon, France

FRA Frankfurt Int Apt, Germany
FUK Fukuoka, Japan

G

GBE	Gaborone, Botswana
GCI	Guernsey, UK
GCM	Grand Cayman, Cayman Islands
GDN	Gdansk, Poland
GDT	Grand Turk, Turks and Caicos
GEN	Oslo Gardermoen Apt, Norway
GEO	Georgetown, Guyana
GGT	George Town, Bahamas
GIB	Gibraltar
GIG	Rio de Janeiro Int Apt., Brazil
GLA	Glasgow, UK
GND	Grenada, Windward Islands
GOT	Gottenburg, Sweden
GUA	Guatemala City, Guatemala
GUM	Guam
GVA	Geneva, Switzerland
GYE	Guayaquil, Ecuador

I

IAD	Washington Dulles Int Apt., DC
IAH	Houston Int Apt., TX USA
IBZ	Ibiza, Spain
IEV	Kiev, Ukraine
IND	Indianapolis, IN, USA
INN	Innsbruck, Austria
INU	Nauru Island
IOM	Isle of Man, UK
ISB	Islamabad, Pakistan
IST	Istanbul, Turkey
IUE	Niue

J

JAX	Jacksonville, FL, USA
JED	Jeddah, Saudi Arabia
JER	Jersey, UK
JFK	New York John F. Kennedy Apt, NY USA
JIB	Djibouti
JKT	Jakarta, Indonesia
JNB	Johannesburg, South Africa
JOG	Yogyakarta, Indonesia
JRS	Jerusalem, Israel

H

HAJ	Hanover, Germany
HAK	Haikou, PR China
HAM	Hamburg, Germany
HAN	Hanoi, Vietnam
HAV	Havana, Cuba
HEL	Helsinki, Finland
HIR	Honiara, Solomon Islands
HKG	Hong Kong Int Apt, Hong Kong
HKT	Phuket, Thailand
HLP	Jakarta Airport, Indonesia
HND	Tokyo Haneda

K

KAN	Kano, Nigeria
KBL	Kabul, Afghanistan
KEF	Reykjavik Keflavik Apt., Iceland
KGL	Kigali, Rwanda
KHH	Kaohsiung, Taiwan
KHI	Karachi, Pakistan
KIN	Kingston, Jamaica
KRT	Khartoum, Sudan
KTM	Kathmandu, Nepal

M

MAA	Madras, India
MAD	Madrid, Spain
MAH	Menorca, Spain
MAN	Manchester, UK
MAO	Manaus, Brazil
MAR	Maracaibo, Venezuela
MBA	Mombasa, Kenya
MBJ	Montego Bay, Jamaica
MCM	Monte Carlo, Monaco
MCT	Muscat, Oman
MDL	Mandalay, Myanmar
MED	Medina, Saudi Arabia

MEL	Melbourne, Australia
MEM	Memphis, TN,
MEX	Mexico City, Mexico
MGA	Managua, Nicaragua
MGQ	Mogadishu, Somalia
MIA	Miami, FL USA
MIL	Milan, Italy
MKC	Kansas City, MO, USA
MKE	Milwaukee, WI, USA
MLA	Malta
MLE	Male, Maldives
MLW	Monrovia, Liberia
MNI	Montserrat, Leeward Islands
MNL	Manila, Philippines
MOW	Moscow, Russia
MPM	Maputo, Mozambique
MRS	Marseille, France
MRU	Mauritius
MSP	Minneapolis, MN, USA
MSQ	Minsk, Belarus
MST	Maastricht, Netherlands
MSU	Maseru, Lesotho
MUC	Munich, Germany
MVD	Montevideo, Uruguay

N

NAN	Nadi Airport, Fiji
NAP	Naples, Itlay
NAS	Nassau, Bahamas
NBO	Nairobi, Kenya
NCE	Nice, France
NCL	Newcastle, UK
NIM	Niamey, Niger
NKC	Nouakchott, Mauritania
NOU	Noumea, New Caledonia
NRT	Tokyo Narita Apt., Japan
NSN	Nelson, New Zealand
NUE	Nuremberg, Germany
NYC	New York, NY USA

O

OKA	Okinawa, Naha Airport, Japan
OKA	Oklahoma, OK, USA
OOL	Gold Coast, QL, Australia
OPO	Porto, Portugal
ORD	Chicago O'Hare Int Apt., IL USA
ORL	Orlando, FL, USA
ORY	Paris Orly Apt., France
OSA	Osaka, Japan
OSL	Oslo, Norway
OTP	Bucharest Int A/Port, Romania
OUA	Ouagadougou, Burkina Faso

P

PAC	Panama City Paitilla Apt., Panama
PAP	Port au Prince, Haiti
PAR	Paris, France
PBM	Paramaribo, Suriname
PDX	Portland, OR, USA
PEK	Beijing Capital Apt., China
PEN	Penang Int Apt., Malaysia
PER	Perth, WA, Australia
PHL	Philadelphia, PA, USA
PHX	Pheonix, AZ, USA
PIT	Pittsburg, PA, USA
PLZ	Port Elizabeth, South Africa
PMI	Palma de Mallorca, Spain
PNH	Phnom-Penh, Cambodia
PNI	Pohnpei Int, Micronesia
POM	Port Moresby, Papua New Guinea
POS	Port of Spain, Trinidad and Tobago
PPG	Pago Pago, American Samoa
PPT	Papeete, Tahiti
PRG	Prague, Czech Republic
PTP	Pointe-a-Pitre, Guadeloupe
PTY	Panama City, Panama

R

RAI	Praia, Cape Verde
RAK	Marrakesh, Morocco
RAR	Rarotonga, Cook Islands
RBA	Rabat, Morocco
REK	Reyjavik, Iceland
RGN	Yangon, Myanmar
RIO	Rio de Janeiro, Brazil
RIX	Riga, Latvia
ROC	Rochester, NY, USA
ROM	Rome, Italy
RTM	Rotterdam, Netherlands
RUH	Riyadh, Saudi Arabia
RUN	St Denis, Reunion

S

SAH	Sanaa, Republic of Yemen
SAL	San Salvador, El Salvador
SAN	San Diego, CA, USA
SAO	Sao Paulo, Brazil
SAT	San Antonio, TX, USA
SCL	Santiago, Chile
SDQ	Santo Domingo, Dominican Rep.
SDV	Tel Aviv Sde - Dov Int Apt., Israel
SEA	Seattle, WA,USA
SEL	Seoul, Republic of Korea
SEZ	Mahe Island, Seychelles
SFO	San Francisco, CA USA
SGN	Ho Chi Minh City, Vietnam
SHA	Shanghai, China
SHJ	Sharjah, UAE

SID	Sal Amilcar Int A/port, Cape Verde
SIN	Singapore
SJO	San Jose, Costa Rica
SJU	San Juan, Puerto Rico
SKB	St. Kitts, Leeward Islands
SKP	Skopje, Macedonia
SLC	Salt Lake City, UT, USA
SLU	St Lucia
SNN	Shannon, Ireland
SOF	Sofia, Bulgaria
SRZ	Santa Cruz, Bolivia
STL	St Louis, MO USA
STN	London Stansted Apt., UK
STO	Stockholm, Sweden
STR	Stuttgart, Germany
SVO	Moscow Sheretyevo Apt., Russia
SXB	Strasbourg, France
SXF	Berlin A/Port, Germany
SXM	Saint Maarten, Netherland Antilles
SXR	Srinagar, India
SYD	Sydney, Australia
SZG	Salzburg, Austria

T

TAB	Tobago, Trinidad & Tobago
TAS	Tashkent, Uzbekistan
TCI	Tenerife, Canary Islands
THF	Berlin Tempelhof Apt., Germany
THR	Tehran, Iran
TIP	Tripoli, Libya
TLL	Tallinn, Estonia
TLS	Toulouse, France
TLV	Tel Aviv Israel
TNG	Tangier, Morocco
TNR	Antananarivo, Madagascar
TPE	Taipei, Taiwan
TRN	Turin, Itlay

TSR	Timisoara, Romania
TUN	Tunis, Tunisia
TXL	Tegel Berlin Apt, Germany
TYO	Tokyo, Japan
TZA	Belize City Municipal Apt., Belize

U

UIO	Quito, Ecuador
UVF	Saint Lucia, Int Apt..

V

VCE	Venice, Italy
VIE	Vienna, Austria
VNO	Vilnius, Lithuania
VTE	Vientiane, Laos

W

WAS	Washington, DC USA
WAW	Warsaw, Poland
WDH	Windhoek, Namibia
WLG	Wellington, New Zealand

X

XCH	Christmas Island

Y

YAP	Yap, Caroline Islands
YAO	Yaounde, Cameroon
YEA	Edmonton, AL, Canada
YEG	Edmonton Int A/Port, AL, Canada
YHZ	Halifax, NS, Canada
YMQ	Montreal, Quebec, Canada
YMX	Montreal Int A/port, Canada
YOW	Ottawa Ontario, Canada
YQB	Quebec City, QU, Canada
YTO	Toronto, OT, Canada
YTZ	Toronto Island A/Port, Canada

YUL	Montreal Dorval Int A/port Canada
YVR	Vancouver, BC, Canada
YWG	Winnipeg, MN, Canada
YYC	Calgary, AL, Canada
YYJ	Victoria, BC, Canada
YYZ	Toronto Int A/Port, OT, Canada

Z

ZAG	Zagreb, Croatia
ZRH	Zurich, Switzerland

MAJOR AIRPORTS WORLD-WIDE

Country	City	Airport Name	Distance from town Miles	kms	Telephone No
Argentina	Buenos Aires	Ministro Pistarini	31.5	51	(54)1480 0217
Australia	Adelaide	International	3.7	6	(618) 8380 9211
	Brisbane	International	8	13	(617) 3406 3000
	Cairns	International	5	8	(617) 7052 3888
	Canberra	Canberra	5.5	9	(616) 209 3333
	Darwin	International	8	13	(618) 8920 1811
	Hobart	Hobart	10	16	(613) 6248 5279
	Melbourne	International	13	21	(613) 9339 1600
	Perth	International	6	10	(619) 478 8888
	Sydney	Kingsford Smith	5	8	(612) 9667 9893
Austria	Innsbruck	Flughafen	3.5	5.5	(43) 512 225250
	Salzburg	Salzburg WA Mozart	2.5	4	(43) 662 85800
	Vienna	International	11	18	(43) 170070
Bahamas	Nassau	International	10	16	(1809) 327 7281
Bahrain	Manama	International	4	6.5	(973) 321 000
Bangladesh	Dhaka	Zia International	11	20	(880) 289 48704
Barbados	Bridgetown	Grantley Adams Int.	6.8	11	(1246) 428 7101
Belarus	Minsk	Minsk 2 International	27	40	(375) 172 791838
Belgium	Antwerp	International	2	3	(323) 218 1211
	Brussels	National	8	13	(322) 753 4200
Belize	Belize City	PSW Goldson Int.	10	16	(501) 25 2045
Benin	Cotonou	Cadjehoun	3	5	(229) 30 1413
Bermuda	Hamilton	International	10	16	(1441) 293 2470
Bhutan	Paro	Paro	3	5	(975) 29140
Bolivia	La Paz	John F. Kennedy Int.	9	14.5	(591) 2810320
Botswana	Gaborone	Sir Seretse Khama Int.	9	15	(267) 351191
Brazil	Brasilia	International	7	11	(55) 61365 1941
	Rio de Janeiro	International	13	21	(55) 21398 4208
	Sao Paulo	Guarulhos Int.	16	25	55 11-945 2200
Brunei Darussalam	Brunei	Bandar Seri Begawan	7	11	(673) 2330 483
Bulgaria	Sofia	International	6	10	(359) 2661 616
Burundi	Bujumbura	International	7	11	(257) 22 3707
Cameroon	Douala	Douala	6	10	(237) 42 2775
Canada	Calgary	International	5	8	(1403) 735 1200
	Edmonton	International	17	28	(1403) 890 8382
	Montreal	Dorval Int.	15	25	(1514) 476 3010
	Montreal	Mirabel Int.	33	53	(1514) 476 3010
	Ottawa	Macdonald-Cartier Int.	8	15	(1613) 998 3151
	Toronto	Lester B Pearson Int.	17	27	(1905) 676 3506
	Vancouver	International	9	15	(1604) 276 6101
	Winnipeg	International	6	10	(1204) 983 8403
Cape Verde	Ilha do Sal	Sal Amilcar Cabral Int.	1.1	1.8	(238) 4111 35
Cayman Islands	Grand Cayman	Owen Roberts Int.	1.5	2.4	(949) 4528
Chile	Santiago	Comodoro Arturo Merino Benitez	13	21	(562) 601 9001
China	Beijing	Capital	16	26	(8610) 456 4201
	Shanghai	Hongqiao	7.5	12	(8621) 253 6530
Colombia	Bogotá	El Dorado Int.	7.5	12	(571) 413 9500
Comoros	Moroni	Int. Prince Said Ibrahim	15.5	25	(269) 731593
Congo	Brazzaville	Maya Maya	2	4	(242) 810 996
Cook Islands	Rarotonga	International	2	3	(682) 25890
Côte d'Ivoire	Abidjan	Port Bouet	10	16	(225) 270771
Croatia	Dubrovnik	Dubrovnik	13	22	(385) 20773233

Country	City	Airport Name	Distance from town Miles	kms	Telephone No
Croatia	Zagreb	Zagreb	10	16	(385) 1456 2222
Cuba	Havana	José Marti Int.	11	18	(53) 707701/8
Cyprus	Larnaca	International	5	8	(357) 4630 700
Cyprus	Paphos	Internaional	8	13	(357) 6422833
Czech Republic	Prague	Ruzyné	11	17	(422) 360 922
Denmark	Billund	Billund	1.2	2	(45) 76 50 5050
	Copenhagen	International	5	8	(45) 32 31 3231
Djibouti	Djibouti City	International	3	5	(253) 340101
Dominica	Dominica	Cane Field	3	5.2	(1809) 44 91990
Ecuador	Quito	Mariscal Sucre	5	8	(59) 593 244 0082
Egypt	Cairo	International	14	22	(202) 2914 4255
El Savador	San Savador	International	38.5	62	(503) 339 9455
Eritrea	Asmara	International	3.7	6	(291) 181822
Estonia	Tallinn	Tallinn	2.5	4	(372) 638 8888
Ethiopia	Addis Ababa	Bole	5	8	(251) 180455
Fiji	Nadi	International	5	8	(679) 790 325
Finland	Helsinki	Vantaa	12	19	(358) 60001
	Turku	Turku	4.5	7	(358) 0271 4601
France	Bordeaux	Bordeaux	7	12	(335) 56 345000
	Lyons	Satolas	15.5	25	(334) 72 227221
	Marseille	Provence	19	30	(334) 42 14 14 14
	Nice	Côte d'Azur	4	6	(334) 93 21 30 12
	Paris	Charles de Gaulle	14	23	(331) 48 62 22 80
	Paris	Orly	9	14	(331) 49 75 15 15
	Strasbourg	International	7	12	(338) 86 46 767
French Guiana	Cayenne	Rochambeau	9	15	(594) 29 97 00
French Polynesia	Papeete	Faaa	4	6	(689) 86 60 61
Gabon	Libreville	Libreville	7	12	(241) 73 62 44
Gambia	Banjul	Yundum International	15	24	(220) 47 27 30
Germany	Berlin	Schonefeld	12	19	(49) 30 60910
	Berlin	Tegel	5	8	(49) 30 41011
	Cologne	Cologne/Bonn-Konrad Adenauer	9	14	(49) 2203 400
	Düsseldorf	Rhein-Ruhr	5	8	(49) 211 4210
	Frankfurt	Frankfurt	5.5	9	(49) 69 69 01
	Hamburg	Hamburg	5.5	9	(49) 40 50750
	Hanover	Hanover	7	11	(49) 51 19 770
	Munich	Flughafen Munchen	18	28.5	(49) 89 97 500
	Stuttgart	Echterdingen	9	14	(49) 711 948 3375
Ghana	Accra	Kotoka	6	9	(233) 776 171
Greece	Athens	Athinai	9	14	(301) 9699111
Grenada	St. George's	Greanda Point	8	11	(1809) 44 4555
Guatemala	Guatemala City	La Aurora	4	6	(502) 23 22 841
Hong Kong	Hong Kong	Kai Tak International	3	5	(852) 2769 7531
Hungary	Budapest	Ferihegy	10	16	(361) 157 6000
Iceland	Reykjavik	Keflavik	32	51	(354) 450 6000
India	Bombay	International	18	29	(91) 22 6116660
	Calcutta	International	8	13	(91) 33 552 9977
	Delhi	Indira Gandhi Int.	15	22	(91) 11 545 2011
Indonesia	Jakarta	Soekarno-Hatta	12	20	(62) 21 5505048
Iran	Tehran	Mehrabad	3	5	(98) 21 91021
Ireland	Cork	Cork	5	8	(353) 21 313131
	Dublin	Dublin	5	8	(353) 1844 4900
Israel	Tel Aviv	Ben Gurion Int.	9	14	(972) 397 10111
Italy	Milan	Linate	6	10	(392) 2810 6306
	Naples	Capodichino	4	6	(398) 1789 626

Country	City	Airport Name	Distance from town Miles	kms	Telephone No
	Rome	Leonardo da Vinci	16	26	(396) 6595 6350
	Venice	Marco Polo	8	13	(394) 12606 111
Jamaica	Kingston	Norman Manley Int.	11	17	(1809) 924 8452/6
Japan	Osaka	International	10	16	(81) 52 0568 28111
	Tokyo	Narita	40	65	(81) 476 34 5037
Jordan	Amman	Queen Alia Int.	20	32	(962) 85 2000
Kazakstan	Almaty	Almaty	9.5	15	(7) 57 1 300
Kenya	Mombasa	Moi International	8	13	(254) 11 433211
	Nairobi	Jomo Kenyatta Int.	8	13	(254) 2 822111
Korea	Seoul	Kimpo International	10	17	(822) 660 2234
Kuwait	Kuwait	International	10	16	(965) 4335599
Kyrgyzstan	Manas	Bishkek	19	30	(7) 3312 31 38 50
Latvia	Riga	International	4.5	8	(371) 720 7009
Lebanon	Beirut	International	10	16	(961) 1629 0141
Lesotho	Maseru	Moshoeshoe 1 Int.	11	18	(266) 350 777
Liberia	Monrovia	Roberts International	36	60	(231) 721031
Lithuania	Vilnius	International	3.5	6	(370) 226 2702
Luxembourg	Luxembourg	Findel	3	5	(352) 4798 1
Macau	Macau	International	3.7	6	(853) 785448
Malaysia	Kuala Lumpur	Sultan Abdul Aziz Shah	14	22	(603) 746 1833
Malta	Valletta	International	3	5	(356) 24 9600
Mexico	Acapulco	Juan N Alvarez	16	26	(52) 748 44741
	Mexico City	International	8	13	(525) 571 3600
Mongolia	Ulaanbaatar	Buyant-Ukhaa	9	15	(976) 1 379 986
Morocco	Casablanca	Mohammed V	19	30	(212) 33 90 40
Mozambique	Maputo	International	1.8	3	(258)1 465351
Namibia	Windhoek	International	25	40	(264) 626 351
Nepal	Katmandu	Tribhuvan Int.	4	6.4	(977) 147 1933
Netherlands	Amsterdam	Schiphol	9	14	(31) 06 350 34050
New Caledonia	Noumea	La Tontouta	23	37	(687) 35 25 00
New Zealand	Auckland	International	14	22	(64) 9 275 0789
	Christchurch	International	6	10	(64) 3 585 029
	Wellington	International	5	8	(64) 43 85 5100
Nigeria	Lagos	Murtala Muhammed	13	22	(234) 1 90 11707
Norway	Oslo	Fornebu	5	8	(47) 67 59 33 40
Oman	Muscat	Seeb	25	40	(968) 519 210
Pakistan	Karachi	Quaid-e-Azam Int.	10	15	(92) 21 457 91444
	Islamabad	International	5	8	(92) 51 590256
P.N.G.	Port Moresby	Jacksons Int.	7	11	(675) 273 320
Peru	Lima	Jorge Chavez Int.	10	16	(51) 14 529 570
Philippines	Manila	Ninoy Aquino Int.	7	12	(63) 2 832 1961
Poland	Krakow	International	9	14	(48) 12 11 19 55
	Warsaw	Okecie	6	10	(48) 2 650 30 00
Portugal	Lisbon	Lisbon	4.5	7	(351) 1 8481101
Puerto Rico	San Juan	Luis Munoz Marin Int.	9	14	(1787) 791 4670
Qatar	Doha	Doha	5	8	(974) 351 550
Romania	Bucharest	Otopeni Int.	10.5	17	(7) 812 1043 450
Russia	Moscow	Sheremetyevo Int.	18	29	(7) 095 578 5540
	St Petersburg	Pulkovo	10.5	17	7-812 1043456
Rwanda	Kigali	Gregoire Kayibanda	7	12	(250) 85400
Saudi Arabia	Dhahran	International	8	13	(966) 386 40817
	Jeddah	King Abdulaziz Int.	11	18	(966) 26854212
	Riyadh	King Khaled Int.	22	35	(966) 1 2211000
Singapore	Singapore	Changi	12	20	(65)-5456222
South Africa	Johannesburg	Jan Smuts	15	24	(27) 11 921 6911
	Cape Town	International	14	22	(27) 21 934 0444

Country	City	Airport Name	Distance from town Miles	kms	Telephone No
Spain	Barcelona	Barcelona	8	13	(34) 3 298 38 38
	Madrid	Barajas	8	13	(34) 1 393 60 00
Sri Lanka	Colombo	Bandaranayake Int.	20	32	(94) 01 252 861
Sweden	Stockholm	Arlanda	25	40	(46) 8 797 8600
Switzerland	Basle	Mulhouse	5	8	(41) 61 325 31 11
	Berne	Belp	5.5	9	(41) 31 960 21 11
	Geneva	International	3	5	(41) 22 717 7111
	Zurich	Zurich	7	11	(41) 1816 2211
Syria	Damascus	International	18	29	(963) 11 430405
Taiwan	Taipei	Chaing Kai Shek Int.	25	40	(886) 3 398 2001
Tanzania	Dar Es Salaam	International	9	15	(255) 84 4211
Thailand	Bangkok	International	13.6	22	(66) 2 5351515
Tunisia	Ankara	Esenboga	22	35	(90) 4 3980 329
	Istanbul	Atatürk Int.	15	24	(90) 1212 6636262
Uganda	Kampala	Entebbe Int.	22	35	(256) 42 205 16
Ukraine	Kiev	Borispol Int.	21	34	(380) 44 296 72 44
UAE	Abu Dhabi	International	21	35	(971) 2 757500
	Dubai	International	3	5	(971) 4 245555
UK	Aberdeen	Aberdeen	7	11	(44) 1224 722331
	Belfast	International	18	29	(44) 1849 422888
	Birmingham	International	8	13	(44) 121 767 5511
	Bristol	Bristol	7	11	(44) 1275 474444
	Cardiff	International	12	19.2	(44) 1446 711111
	Derby	East Midlands	12	19	(44) 1332 852852
	Edinburgh	Edinburgh	7	11	(44) 131 333 1000
	Glasgow	International	9	14	(44) 141 887 1111
	Liverpool	Liverpool	7	11	(44) 151 486 8877
	London	London City	6	10	(44) 171 474 5555
		Gatwick	28	46	(44) 1293 535353
		Heathrow	15	24	(44) 181 759 4321
	Luton	Luton	32	51	(44) 1582 405100
	Stansted	Stansted	34	50	(44) 1279 680 500
	Manchester	Manchester	10	16	(44) 161 489 3000
	Newcastle	Newcastle	5	8	(44) 191-286 0966
	Norwich	Norwich	4	6.4	(44) 1603 411 923
	Darlington	Teeside Int.	6	10	(44) 1325 332811
USA	Atlanta	Hartsfield Atlanta Int.	10	16	(1) 404 209 1700
	Baltimore	Washington Int.	30	48	(1) 410 859 7111
	Boston	Logan Int.	4	6	(1) 617 561 1800
	Chicago	O'Hare International	14	22.5	(1) 312 686 2200
	Cincinnati	Northern Kentucky Int.	12	20	(1) 606 767 3151
	Cleveland	Hopkins International	12	19	(1) 216 265 6000
	Dallas	Fort Worth Int.	15	24	(1) 214 574 3197
	Denver	International	23	38	(1) 303 342 2300
	Detroit	Metropolitan	20	32	(1) 313 942 3694
	Honolulu	International	6	10	(1) 808 836 6444
	Houston	Intercontinental	20	32	(1)281 230 3100
	Kansas City	International	20	32	(1) 816 243 5237
	Las Vegas	McCarran Int.	9	14	(1) 702 261 5211
	Los Angeles	International	15	27	(1) 310 646 5252
	Miami	International	7	11	(1) 305 876 7862
	Minneapolis	International	11	17	(1) 612 726 5555
	New Orleans	International	10	16	(1) 504 464 0831
	New York	JF K Int.	14	22	(1) 718 244 4444
		La Guardia	8	13	(1) 718 533 3400
	Newark	International	2	3	(1) 201 9616000

Country	City	Airport Name	Distance from town		Telephone No
			Miles	kms	
	Orlando	International	10	16	(1) 407-825 2055
	Philadelphia	International	8	13	(1) 215 937 5499
	Pheonix	Sky Harbour Int.	4	6	(1) 602 273 3321
	Pittsburg	International	16	26	(1) 412 472 3500
	Portland	International	9	14.5	(1) 503 335 1151
	St Louis	Lambert Int.	13	21	(1) 314 426 8000
	San Diego	International	2	3	(1) 619 686 8050
	San Francisco	International	15	25	(1) 415 876 2217
	Seattle	Tacoma Int.	14	22	(1) 206 431 4444
	Washington DC	Dulles Int.	26	43	(1) 703 572 2700
		National	4	7	(1) 703 417 8000
Venezuela	Caracas	Simon Bolivar	13	22	(58) 2821 00
Yemen	Sana'a	International	8	13	(967) 2 250819
Yugoslavia	Belgrade	Belgrade	12	19	(381) 11 601166
Zaire	Kinshasa	N'Djili	15	25	(243) 12 23570
Zambia	Lusaka	International	16	26	(260) 1 271044
Zimbabwe	Harare	Harare	7	12	(263) 4 575 164

Further reading:
Guide to International Travel (OAG)
The International Air Travel Handbook (ABC)
BAA Flight Guide (BAA)
ABC Air Travel Atlas (ABC)
ABC World Airways Guide – Part 1 & 2 (ABC)

AIRPORT/DEPARTURE TAXES

The taxes listed below are those paid locally and do not include those pre-paid before departure. Please note taxes can and do change, and although the information below was correct at the time of going to press it is advisable to check with your travel agent.

Albania	USD 10
Algeria	None
American Samoa	None
Angola	None
Anguilla	XCD 26.50
Antigua & Barbuda	USD 25 for nationals
	USD 30 for others
Argentina	USD 13 (international)
Aruba	None
Australia	None
Austria	None
Bahamas	BSD15
Bahrain	BHD 3
Bangladesh	None
Barbados	BBD 25
Belgium	None
Belize	BZD 22.50
Benin	None
Bermuda	BMD 20
Bolivia	USD 20
Botswana	None
Brazil	None
British Virgin Islands	USD 5
Brunei	BND 5 to Malaysia and Singapore
	BND 12 to all other destinations
Bulgaria	None
Burkina Faso	None
Burundi	None
Cambodia	USD 8
Cameroon	XAF 500 (domestic)
	XAF 10,000 (int.)
Canada	None
Cape Verde	None
Cayman Islands	KYD 8
Chile	USD 18
China	CNY50 (domestic)
	CNY90 (international)
Colombia	USD 20
	USD 19 (exit tax)
Comoro Islands	None
Congo	None
Cook Islands	NZD 25;
	NZ$10 (Children)
Cote d'Ivoire	XOF 800 (Africa)
	XOF 5,000 (elsewhere)
Croatia	None
Cuba	USD 15
Cyprus	None
Czech Republic	None
Denmark	None
Djibouti	None
Dominica	USD 10
	XCD 5 (security tax)
Ecuador	USD 1.50 (domestic)
	USD 25 (international)
Egypt	None
El Salvador	USD 22
Eritrea	ETB 60 (int. nationals)
	ETB 13 (nationals)
	USD 12 (all others)
Estonia	None
Ethiopia	US$10
Falkland Islands	None
Fiji	FJD10
Finland	None
France	None
French Guiana	None
French Polynesia	None
Gabon	None
Gambia	GMD 150 (int.)
Georgia	None
Germany	None
Ghana	GHC 500 (domestic)
	GHC 22,000 (int.)
Gibraltar	None
Greece	None
Grenada	XCD25 (international)
Guatemala	GTQ 50
Haiti	USD 15
Honduras	USD 10
Hong Kong	HKD 150
Hungary	None
Iceland	Noner
India	INR150 (sub continent)
	INR300 (long-haul)
Indonesia	IDR11,000 (dom)
	INR25,000 (int.)
Iran	None
Ireland	None
Israel	None
Italy	None
Jamaica	JMD500
Japan	JPY2000
Jordan	JOD10
Kenya	USD20 (international)
	KES100 (domestic)
Korea (south)	KRW9000
Kuwait	KD2
Lao (PDR)	US$5
Latvia	None
Lebanon	None
Lesotho	LSL20
Liberia	US$20
Lithuania	None
Luxembourg	None
Macau	MOP130 (int.)
Madagascar	MGF33000
Malawi	US$20

Malaysia	MYR3 (domestic)
	MYR20 (international)
Maldives	USD10
Mali	CFA Fr2500 (Africa)
	CFA FR (elsewhere)
Malta	None
Martinque	None
Mauritania	MRO 220 (Africa)
	MRO 560 (outside
	Africa)
Mauritius	MUR100
Mexico	None
Micronesia	USD5
Monaco	None
Mongolia	None
Montserrat	USD8
Morocco	None
Mozambique	USD20 (international)
	USD5 (domestic)
Myanmar	USD6
Namibia	None
Nauru	AUD10
Nepal	NPR50 (subcontinent)
	NPR500 (elsewhere)
Netherlands	None
Netherlands Antilles	ANG10 (domestic)
	ANG22.50 (int.)
New Caledonia	None
New Zealand	NZD20
Nicaragua	USD18
Niger	None
Nigeria	USD35
Niue	NZD20
Norway	None
Oman	OMR3
Pakistan	PKR40 (domestic)
	PKR400-800 (int.)
Panama	PAB20
Papua New Guinea	PGK15
Paraguay	USD18
Peru	USD25
Philippines	PHP50 (domestic)
	PHP500 (international)
Poland	None
Portugal	None
Puerto Rico	None
Qatar	QAR20
Reunion	None
Romania	None
Russian Federation	None
Rwanda	USD5 (domestic)
	USD20 (international)
St. Kitts & Nevis	XCD20 (international)
St. Lucia	XCD27
St. Vincent	
& the Grenadines	XCD20
Samoa	WST20
Sao Tomé e Principe	USD20
Saudi Arabia	None
Senegal	None
Seychelles	SCR100

Sierra Leone	SLL10 (domestic)
	SLL20 (international)
Singapore	None
Slovakia	None
Slovenia	None
Solomon Islands	SBD40
Somalia	US$20
South Africa	None
Spain	None
Sri Lanka	LKR500
Sudan	SDP600 (domestic)
	SDP2500 (int.)
Suriname	USD10
Swaziland	SZL20
Sweden	None
Switzerland	None
Syria	SYP200
Taiwan (Rep of China)	TWD300
Tanzania	None
Thailand	THB250
Togo	None
Tonga	TOP15
Trinidad & Tobago	TTD75
Tunisia	TND45
Turkey	None
Turks & Caicos	USD15
Tuvalu	AUD20
Uganda	USD20
Ukraine	None
United Arab Emirates	None
UK	None
United States	None
Uruguay	USD6
Vanuatu	VUV250 (domestic)
	VUV2000 (int.)
Venezuela	USD15 (domestic)
	VEB1300
Vietnam	USD5
Yemen	USD10
Yugoslavia	YUM20 (domestic)
	YUM70 (international)
Zaire	None
Zambia	USD20 (international)
	ZMK3000 (domestic)
Zimbabwe	USD20

Transit passengers, children and diplomats are often exempted or charged a reduced rate.

AIRPASSES

Airpasses are essentially concessionary airfares offered by airlines for visitors to a particular country or region. When a journey requires a number of flights within a particular country or region, the airpass is likely to be an attractive option, particularly if flights will be long-distance.

In most cases an airpass must be booked before departure from the country of origin, as it will not be available from the destinations themselves. A minimum number of flights (or 'coupons' as they are usually referred to) have to be pre-purchased. These are typically a minimum of three flights and up to a maximum of ten. It is also worth remembering that the airpasses are only valid for a specified number of days.

Airpasses can offer excellent value for money (when your itinerary includes the minimum number of flights) as they permit a greater degree of flexibility than most concessionary or discounted fares. Usually you can change the dates of travel (and in some cases the route) at little or no extra cost, whereas most other cheap or discounted airfares incur either penalties or do not allow changes.

Most IATA travel agents can sell airpasses as long as they are an accredited agent for the required airline; WEXAS International is able to offer airpasses on a wide range of airlines, and have additional 'Members only' discounts on certain types of airpasses.

However, in the past few years, now that airlines are offering fairs that include multiple stopovers as part of the main or international ticket, airpass sales have been dwindling, especially to North America. WEXAS International, or any good travel agent, will be able to advise which is the most suitable type of ticket for your particular journey.

While many of the airlines offer airpasses, no two are exactly the same. Below we have listed a selection of the most regular routes to some key destinations:

Africa

South African Airlines

Africa Explorer Pass requires a minimum purchase of four coupons and a maximum of eight. Validity from three days to one month. Prices vary according to the sectors flown and some destinations outside South Africa are included in the pass, which should be booked in conjunction with an international ticket either to or from South Africa.

Latin America

Aerolineas Argentinas (AR)

Visit Argentina Pass allows a minimum of four coupons for US$500 to a maximum of eight with additional coupons costing US$120 each. One stopover allowed per city. Valid for 30 days. International flights must be be with AR.

Mercosur Airpass links 36 Agentine cities with those of Brazil, Uruguay and Paraguay, valid on the services of AR and eight other carriers. Fares are based on the number of kilometres travelled with a maximum of two stops per country. Valid for 30 days.

Varig (RG)

Available in conjunction with international travel on the same airline, *Brazilian Airpass* costs from US$490 for up to five sectors to a maximum of nine from US$940. One stopover per city is allowed and the maximum validity is 21 days.

LAN Chile (LA)

Six separate airpasses are available for routes within Chile from US$300 excluding Easter Island. Validity of 21 days.

Mexico (MX/AM)

MexiPass, from US$120, is in conjunction with a return transatlantic ticket and valid for 90 days on Mexicana and AREOMEXICO Services. Coupons start at US$60 with a minimum of two.

North and America and the Carribean

American Airlines

Visit USA Pass from £259, a minimum of three coupons from £239 to a maximum of ten from £689. Maximum of two stopovers at any one city and valid for 60 days.

In conjunction with transatlantic travel on American Airlines, Virgin or British Airways.

America West Airlines

Tristate Pass from £112 covers the states of California, Nevada and Arizona with prices starting at £112 for two coupons up to £44 for twelve. Available for six months with one stopover at any one point.

Canadian Airlines International

Go Canadian Travel Pass from CAD$454 has a minimum of three coupons to a maximum of eight for CAD$754. Valid on all routes within Canada and mainland USA, except Hawaii. Minimum stay seven days, with a maximum of two stopovers per city and 60 days validity.

Delta Airlines
Discover America from US$359, has a minimum of three coupons and a maximum of ten for CAD$999. It covers mainland USA and Delta Services between USA and Canada with add-ons to Hawaii, Mexico and the Carribean available. Transatlantic flights need to be with Delta Airlines or any US carrier. Valid for 60 days from first flight.

United Airlines
US Airpass from £240 has a minimum of three coupons to a maximum of eight from £440, in conjunction with the international sector on United Airlines, British Airways or Virgin. For transatlantic travel on any carriers three coupons from US449 to a maximum of eight coupons from US$739. Valid on all routes in mainland US and some Canadian, Mexican and Alaskan destinations. To include Hawaii a supplement from £55 a coupon can be made.

Pacific/Asia/Australia

Air New Zealand
Explore New Zealand Airpass from NZ$480,a minimum of three coupons, to a maximum of eight at NZ$1280. Valid up to one year and with any scheduled airline on international flights.

Ansett Airlines
G'Day Pass from £176, available with any international airline to Australia and New Zealand. Fares from £176 (single zone) to £230 (multi-zone) for two coupons with additional coupons from £88/£115 respectively. Up to a maximum of eight coupons per visit to Australia or New Zealand.

Garuda Indonesia
Visit Indonesia Airpass from US$300 covers domestic routes with one stopover permitted per city on Garuda or selected Merpati Nusantera services. Minimum purchase of three coupons for $300, five coupons for US$500 with additional coupons at US$110 to a maximum of ten coupons. The period of validity increases with the number of coupons booked - from five to 60 days. International flights must be booked with Garuda or British Airways flight to Indonesia.

Indian Airlines
Discover India Pass US$500, unlimited travel valid on Indian Airlines network in India with one stopover at each point. 21 days validity.

Qantas (QF)
Boomerang Pass from £160, for travellers to Australia, New Zealand or Fijii on any airline. The region is divided into four zones across Australia, New Zealand and selected islands of the South West Pacific. Prices start at £88 (single zone) or £115 (multi-zone), with a minimum of two coupons to a maximum of ten.

Thai Airways (GA)
Discover Thailand Pass from US$259 for a minimum of four coupons to a maximum of eight with additional sectors at $70 each. The first sector must be prebooked and international travel can be with any airline. Valid for 60 days on domestic network. ■

GETTING THERE BY ROAD
Section 5

MOTORING ORGANISATIONS WORLD-WIDE

Algeria

Touring Club d'Algérie
30 Rue Hassen Benamane
BP 18 Les Vergers
Birkhadem, Alger
Tel: **213-254 1313**

Andorra

Automobil Club d'Andorra
13 rue Babot Camp
Andorra La Vella
Tel: **376-820890**

Argentina

Touring Club Argentino
Esmeralda 605, 3er piso
C.P. 1007
Buenos Aires
Tel: **1-322 7994**

Australia

Australian Automobile Association
212 Northbourne Avenue
Canberra ACT 2601
Tel: **6-247 7311**

National Roads & Motorists Association
NRMA House
151 Clarence St
Sydney NSW 2000
Tel: **2-260 92 22**

RAC of Australia
89 Macquarie St
Sydney NSW 2000
Tel: **2-233 2355**

Austria

Österreichischer Automobil-Motorad-und Touring Club
Schubertring 1-3
1010 Vienna
Tel: **1-711 99-0**

Bangladesh

Automobile Association of Bangladesh
3/B Outer Circular Road
Dhaka 17
Tel: **2-230782 / 831492**

Belarus

The Byelorusian Club of General Assistance and Automobile Service
Romanovskaya Sloboda Str.24
Minsk 220004
Tel: **172-231 055 / 230 893 / 236 320**

Belgium

Touring Club Royal de Belgique
Rue de la Loi 44/Wetstraat 44
1040 Brussels
Tel: **2-233 2211**

Bolivia

Automóvil Club Boliviano
Avenida 6 de Agosto 2993
San Jorge
Castilla 602
La Paz
Tel: **2-351 667 / 432 136 / 432 135**

Bosnia Herzegovina

Bosanskohercegovacki Auto Moto Klub
Gajev Trg 4/1 ⇨

71000 Sarajevo
Tel: 71-668 950 / 664 374

Brazil

Automovel Club do Brasil
Rua do Passeio 90 Lapa
20021 Rio de Janeiro
Tel: **021 297 4455**

Bulgaria

Union des Automobilistes Bulgares
BP 257
Sofia 1090
Tel: **2-86151**

Canada

Canadian Automobile Association
1145 Hunt Club Road, Suite 200
Ottawa
Ontario, K1V 0Y3
Tel: **613-247 0117**

Chile

Automóvil Club de Chile
Av. Vitacura
Santiago 30
Tel: **2-212 5702**

China

China Touring Automobile and Ship Association
No. 94 Nan Heng West Street
Xuan Wu, Beijing 100 053
Tel: **10-352 8410**

Colombia

Touring y Automóvil Club de Colombia
Diagonal 187 No. 41-85
Centro Comercial Plaza Norte
Santafe de Bogota DC
Tel: **1-678 4484**

Costa Rica

Automóvil Club de Costa Rica
Calle 2 Avenidas 7 y 9
San José, Costa Rica
Tel: **256 6557**

Cote D'Ivoire

Federation Ivorienne du Sport Automobile et des Engines Assimilees (FISA)
BP 3883
Abidjan 01
Tel: **32 29 78**

Croatia

Hrvatski Autoklub

Draskoviceva 25
10000 Zagreb
Tel: **1-455 4433**

Cyprus

Cyprus Automobile Association
12 Chrysanthou Mylonas St
Nicosia 2014
Tel: **2-31 32 33**

Czech Republic

Ustrední Automotoklub CR
Na Rybnícku 16
120 76 Prague 2
Tel: **2-24 21 04 12**

Denmark

Forenede Danske Motorejere
Firskovvej 32
P O Box 500
2800 Lyngby
Tel: **45-27 07 07**

Ecuador

Touring y Automóvil Club del Ecuador
Eloy Alfaro 218 y Berlin
PO Box 17-21 0087
Quito
Tel: **2-562 254 / 229 021 / 229 024**

Egypt

Automobile et Touring Club d'Egypte
10 rue Kasr el Nil
Cairo
Tel: **2-574 3176 / 574 33 55 / 574 34 18**

Estonia

Eesti Autoklubi
Ravala 9 I kor./fl.
EE0001 Tallinn
Tel: **2-6317 280 / 6317 289**

El Salvador

Automovil Club de El Salvador
la Calle Poniente 930
Entre 15 y 17 Av. Notre
San Salvador
Tel: **228950**

Finland

Autoliitto Automobile and Touring Club of Finland
PO Box 35
00551 Helsinki
Tel: **9-774 761**

France

Automobile Club National
5 Rue Auber
75009 Paris
Tel: **1-44 51 53 99**

Germany

Allgemeiner Deutscher Automobil-Club e.V.
Am Westpark 8
81373 Munich 70
Tel: **89-76 760**

Ghana

The Automobile Association of Ghana
Fanum House
Labadi Road
Ring Road East
Accra
Tel: **77 42 29 / 77 59 93**

Greece

Automobile and Touring Club of Grece
2 Messogion St
115 27 Athens
Tel: **1-774 88 800**

Holy See

Conseil Pontifical pour la Pastorale des Migrants et des Personnes en Deplacement
Palace Saint-Calixle
Vatican City 00120
Tel: **6-698 87131**

Hong Kong

Hong Kong Automobile Association
405 Houston Centre
63 Mody Road
Tsimshatsui East
Kowloon
Hong Kong
Tel: **273 52 73**

Hungary

Magyar Autóklub
Rómer Floris u 4/a
1024 Budapest
Tel: **1-212 2938 / 212 51 36**

Iceland

Felag Islenzkra Bifreidaeigenda
Borgartun 33
105 Reykjavik
Tel: **562 99 99**

India

Federation of Indian Automobile
Associations
76 Veer Nariman Road
Bombay 400 020
Tel: **22-204 1085 / 204 7032 / 204 1293**

Indonesia

Ikatan Motor Indonesia
Tennis Stadium
Right Wing Senayan
Jakarta 10270
Tel: **21-571 2032 / 571 2033**

Iran

Touring and Automobile Club of the Islamic Republic of Iran
Avenue Khorramshahr
Avenue Nobakht No.12
15338 Tehran
Tel: **1-8741190 - 93**

Iraq

Iraq Automobile and Touring Association
P O Box 6172
Al-Mansour
Baghdad
Tel: **1-537 5862**

Ireland

The Automobile Association Ireland Ltd
23 Rock Hill
Blackrock
Co Dublin
Tel: **1-283 3555**

Israel

Automobile and Touring Club of Israel
Memsi House
20 Harakevet Street
65117 Tel Aviv
Tel: **3-564 1122 / 564 1122**

Italy

Automobile Club d'Italia
Via Marsala 8
00815 Rome
Tel: **6-49 981**

Jamaica

The Jamaica Automobile Association
41 Half Way Tree Road
Kingston 5
Tel: **809-929 1200 / 929 1201**

Japan

Japan Automobile Federation
3-5-8 Shibakoen ⇨

Minato-Ku
Tokyo 105
Tel: **3-3436 2811**

Jordan
Royal Automobile Club of Jordan
Wadi Seer Cross Roads
8th Circle
Amman
Tel: **6-81 52 61**

Kazakhstan
Automotorsport Federation of the Rep. Kazakhstan
101 Strelkovaja Brigada st., 4
463000 Aktubinsk
Tel: **313-2 57 72 26 / 55 24 33**

Kenya
Automobile Association of Kenya
AA Nyaku House
Hurlingham
Nairobi
Tel: **2-72 03 82**

Korea
Korea Automobile Association 1
592-4 Shinsa-dong
Kangnam-gu
Seoul
Tel: **515 2131**

Kuwait
The Automobile Association of Kuwait and the Gulf
Airport Road
P O Box 2100 Safat
Khaldiyah 72300
Tel: **483 24 06 / 483 23 88**

Latvia
Auto-moto Society of Latvia
16b Raunas
1039 Riga
Tel: **2-56 62 22**

Lebanon
Automobile et Touring Club du Liban
Avenue Sami Solh - Imm Kalot
Beirut
Tel: **1-39 06 45 / 39 06 46**

Libya
Automobile and Touring Club of Libya
Sayedy Street
PO Box 3566
Tripoli
Tel: **21-360 59 86 / 360 59 87 / 360 58 02**

Liechtenstein
Automobile Club des Furstentums Liechtenstein
Schwefelstr 33
9490 Vaduz
Tel: **075 2 60 66**

Lithuania
Lietuvos Automobilininku Sajunga
Lvovo 9
2005 Vilnius
Tel: **2-72 12 73 / 72 21 86**

Luxembourg
Automobile Club du Grand-Duché de Luxembourg
Route de Longwy 54
8007 Bertrange
Tel: **45 00 45**

Macedonia
Auto Moto Sojuz na Makedonija
Ivo Ribar Lola 51
PO Box 180
91000 Skoipje
Tel: **91-226 825 / 226 827 / 223 706**

Malaysia
The Automobile Association of Malaysia
No 25 Jalan Yap Kwan Seng
50450 Kuala Lumpur
Tel: **3-262 57 77**

Malta
Touring Club Malta
Philcyn House
Ursuline Sisters St
G'Mangia
Tel: **24 16 65 / 32 03 49**

Mexico
Asociación Mexicana Automovilística
PO Box 24-486
Orizaba No. 7
06700 Mexico D F
Tel: **5-208 8329 / 207 2054**

Morocco
Touring Club du Maroc
3 Avenue F. A. R.
Casablanca
Tel: **20 30 64 / 26 52 31 / 27 92 88**

Namibia
Automobile Association of Namibia
Carl List House

15 Independence Avenue
Peter Müller St
9000 Windhoek
Tel: **61-22 42 01**

Nepal

Automobile Association of Nepal
Traffic Police
Ramshah Path, Opp. Sinhdwar
Kathmandu
Tel: **1 10 93 / 56 62**

Netherlands

**Koninklijke Nederlandse Toeristenbond
ANWB**
Wassenaarseweg 220
2596 The Hague
Tel: **70-314 7147**

New Zealand

The New Zealand Automobile Association
Level 17, AA Centre
99 Albert Street
Auckland 1
Tel: **9-377 4660**

Nigeria

Automobile Club of Nigeria
48 Adegbola Street
Anifowoshe
Lagos
Tel: **960514**

Norway

Norges Automobil-Forbund
PO Box 494 Sentrum
0105 Oslo 1
Tel: **22 34 14 00**

Oman

Oman Automobile Association
PO Box 776
Muttrah 114
Tel: **510 239**

Pakistan

The Automobile Association of Pakistan
155 Chenab Block
Allama Iqbal Town
Lahore 54570
Tel: **42-44 53 20 / 44 25 94**

Papua New Guinea

**Automobile Association of Papua New
Guinea**
GPO Box 5999
Boroko

Tel: **25-63 25**

Paraguay

Touring y Automóvil Club Paraguayo
25 de Mayo y Brasil
Asuncion
Tel: **21-212102**

Peru

Touring y Automóvil Club del Perú
PO Box 2219
Av. César Vallejo 699, Lince
Lima 100
Tel: **1-221 2432 / 422 4934 / 221 3164**

Philippines

Philippine Motor Association
683 Aurora Boulevard
Quezon City
Manila
Tel: **2-723 0808 / 726 0191 / 724 8181**

Poland

Polski Zwiazek Motorway
ul Kazimierzowska 66
02-518 Warsaw
Tel: **22-49 93 61 / 49 41 38**

Portugal

Automóvel Club de Portugal
Rua Rosa Araujo 24
1250 Lisbon
Tel: **1-356 39 31 / 357 79 55**

Qatar

Qatar Automobile and Touring Club
PO Box 18
Doha
Tel: **41 32 65**

Romania

Automobil Clubul Roman
Str. Tache Ionescu 27, Sector 1
70154 Bucarest 22
Tel: **1-615 5510 / 659 3910**

Russian Federation

Intourist
13 Mokhoraya Street
103009 Moscow
Tel: **7095-292 2260**

Saudi Arabia

Saudi Automobile and Touring Association
PO Box 51880
Riyadh 11553
Tel: **1-465 3215 / 463 0722**

Senegal

Automobile Club du Sénégal
12, Bd Djily Mbaye (Ex-Pinet Laprade)
Face à la Grande Poste
Dakar
Tel: **23 10 25**

Singapore

The Automobile Association of Singapore
AA Centre
336 River Valley Road 03-00
238366 Singapore
Tel: **737 2444**

Slovak Republic

Ústredny AutomotoklubSlovenskej Republiky
Wolkrova 4
851 01 Bratislava
Tel: **7-81 09 09 / 81 09 11**

Slovenia

Auto-moto zve za Slovenije
Dunajska 128
1001 Ljubljana
Tel: **61-168 1111**

South Africa

AA House
PO Box 596
Johannesburg 2000
Tel: **11-799 1000**

Spain

Real Automóvil Club de España
Jose Abascal 10
28003 Madrid
Tel: **1-447 3200 / 446 05 38**

Sri Lanka

Automobile Association of Ceylon
40 Sir M M M Mawatha
Colombo 3
Tel: **1-42 15 28 / 42 15 29 / 44 60 74**

Sweden

Motormännens Riksförbund
Sveavägen 159
Stockholm 104 35
Tel: **8-690 38 00**

Switzerland

Automobile Club de Suisse
9 rue Pierre-Fatio
Case postale 3900
Geneva
Tel: **22-737 1212**

Syria

Automobile et Touring Club de Syrie
Rue Zouhair ibn abi Salma
Imm. B. Obeji - 2ème étage
Aleppo
Tel: **21-24 72 72**

Tanzania

The Automobile Association of Tanzania
PO Box 3004
2309/50 Maktaba Street
Dar Es Salaam
Tel: **51-2 1965 / 2 7727**

Thailand

Royal Automobile Association of Thailand
151 Rachadapisek Road
Bang Khen
Bangkok 10900
Tel: **2-511 2230 / 511 2231**

Trinidad & Tobago

Trinidad & Tobago Automobile Association
41 Woodford St
Newtown
Port-of-Spain
Tel: **809-622 7194 / 628 9047**

Tunisia

Touring Club de Tunisie
15 rue d'Allemagne
Tunis
Tel: **1-24 31 82 / 24 31 14**

Turkey

Türkiye Turing Ve Otomobil Kurumu
1. Oto Sanayi Sitesi Yani
4 Levent
Istanbul - TR
Tel: **212-282 81 40**

Ukraine

Fédération Automobile d'Ukraine
290000 Lviv
P/b 10697
Tel: **322-27 21 12 / 75 50 68**

United Arab Emirates

Automobile and Touring Club for United Arab Emirates
Al Nasr St
PO Box 27487
Abu Dhabi
Tel: **2-21 21 75**

UK

The Automobile Association
Norfolk House
Priestley Road
Basingstoke
Hants RG24 9NY
Tel: **0990-448866**

The Royal Automobile Club
89 Pall Mall
London SW1Y 5HS
Tel: **0171-930 2345**

USA

American Automobile Association
1000 AAA Drive
Heathrow
Florida 32746-5063
Tel: **407-444 7000**

American Automobile Touring Alliance
188 The Embarcadero
San Francisco
CA 94105
Tel: **415-777 40 00**

Uruguay

Centro Automovilistica del Uruguay
Boulevard Artigas 1773, esq Dante
Montevideo
Tel: **2-48 61 31 / 48 20 91 / 41 25 28**

Venezuela

Touring y Automóvil Club de Venezuela
Aptdo 68.102
Attamira 1062-A
Caracas
Tel: **2-781 9743**

Yemen

Yemen Club for Touring and Automobile
PO Box 19406
San'a
Tel: **1-268751 / 268752**

Yugoslavia

Auto-Moto Savez Jugoslavije
Ruxveltova 18
11000 Belgrade
Tel: **11-40 16 99**

Zaire (Dem. Rep of Congo)

Federation Automobile du Zaire
Av. des Inflammables 25
Kingabwa
Kinshasa

Zimbabwe

Automobile Association of Zimbabwe
57 Samora Michel Avenue
C1 Harare
Tel: **4-75 27 79**

MAJOR CAR RENTAL COMPANIES

Australia

Avis Rent-a-Car
327 Pacific Highway
North Sydney
NSW 2060
Tel: **02-439 3733**
and...
46 Hill St
Perth
WA 6000
Tel: **325 7677**

Budget Rent-a-Car
21 Bedford Street
North Melbourne
Victoria 3051
Tel: **61-3320 6222**

Hertz Rent-a-Car
39 Milligan St
Perth
WA 6000
Tel: **093-217 7777**

Canada

Avis Rent-a-Car
624 Princess Street
(Princess + Nelson Street)
Kingston
Ontario
Tel: **613-549 2847**

Budget Rent-a-Car
185 The West Mall
Suite 900
Etobicoke
Ontario M9C 5L5
Tel: **1-416-622 3366**

Hertz Rent-a-Car
1073 Drummond Street
Montreal
Quebec
Tel: **514 938 1717**

France

Europcar International
65 Avenue Edouard Vaillant
92100 Boulogne
Billancourt
Paris
Tel: **1-4910 5454**

UK

Alamo Rent A Car
Alamo House
Stockley Close
Stockley Road
West Drayton
Middlesex UB7 9BA
Tel: **0800-272 200** (toll free)

Avis Rent-a-Car
Avis House
Park Road
Bracknell, Berks
RG12 2EW
Tel: **01344-426644**

Budget Rent-a-Car International Inc
41 Marlowes
Hemel Hempstead
Herts HP1 1XJ
Tel: **0800-181181**
One of the top three car and van rental companies in the world.

Europcar Interrent
Interrent House
Aldenham Road
Watford WD2 2LX
Tel: **0345-222525**

Hertz Rent-a-Car
Radnor House
1272 London Road
Norbury
London SW16 4XW
Tel: **0990-996699**
The world's largest vehicle rental and leasing company.

Euro-Dollar Rent-a-Car
3 Warwick Place
Uxbridge
Middx UB8 1PE
Tel: **0990-365365**

USA

Alamo Rent a Car
Detroit Depot
287 Lucas Drive
Detroit
Michigan
Tel: **313-941 8420**

Avis Rent-a-Car
217 East 43rd Street
(between 2nd + 3rd Avenue)
New York City
Tel: **212-593 8378**

Budget Rent-a-Car
200 North Michigan Avenue
Chicago
Ill 60601
Tel: **312-913 9301**

Dollar Rent-a-Car Systems Inc
World Headquarters
6141 W. Century Blvd
PO Box 45048
Los Angeles
CA 900045
Tel: **213-776 8100**

Hertz Rent-a-Car Headquarters
10401 North Pennysylvania Avenue
Oklahoma City
Tel: **405 721 6440**

INTERNATIONAL VEHICLE LICENCE PLATES

A	*Austria*
AL	*Albania*
AND	*Andorra*
AUS	*Australia*
B	*Belgium*
BDS	*Barbados*
BG	*Bulgaria*
BH	*Belize*
BR	*Brazil*
BRN	*Bahrain*
BRU	*Brunei*
BS	*Bahamas*
C	*Cuba*
CDN	*Canada*
CH	*Switzerland*
CI	*Côte d'Ivoire*
CL	*Sri Lanka*
CO	*Colombia*
CR	*Costa Rica*
CZ	*Czech Republic*
CY	*Cyprus*
D	*Germany*
DK	*Denmark*
DOM	*Dominican Republic*
DY	*Benin*
DZ	*Algeria*
E	*Spain*
EAK	*Kenya*
EAT	*Tanzania*

EAU	*Uganda*
EAZ	*Zanzibar*
EC	*Ecuador*
EIR	*Ireland*
ET	*Egypt*
F	*France*
FJI	*Fiji*
FK	*Slovak Republic*
FL	*Liechtenstein*
FLO	*Slovenia*
G	*Gabon*
GB	*United Kingdom*
GBA	*Alderney*
GBG	*Guernsey*
GBJ	*Jersey*
GBM	*Isle of Man*
GBZ	*Gibraltar*
GH	*Ghana*
GLA	*Guatemala*
GR	*Greece*
GUY	*Guyana*
H	*Hungary*
HK	*Hong Kong*
HKJ	*Jordan*
HR	*Croatia*
I	*Italy*
IL	*Israel*
IND	*India*
IR	*Iran*
IRQ	*Iraq*
IS	*Iceland*
J	*Japan*
JA	*Jamaica*
K	*Cambodia*
K	*Myanmar*
L	*Luxembourg*
LAO	*Laos*
LAR	*Libya*
LB	*Liberia*
LS	*Lesotho*
M	*Malta*
MA	*Morocco*
MAL	*Malaysia*
MC	*Monaco*
MEX	*Mexico*
MS	*Mauritius*
MW	*Malawi*
N	*Norway*
NA	*Netherlands Antilles*
NIC	*Nicaragua*
NIG	*Niger*
NL	*Netherlands*
NZ	*New Zealand*
P	*Portugal*
PA	*Panama*
PAK	*Pakistan*
PE	*Peru*
PI	*Philippines*
PL	*Poland*
PY	*Paraguay*
R	*Romania*

RA	*Argentina*
RB	*Botswana*
RC	*Taiwan*
RCA	*Central African Republic*
RCB	*Congo*
RCH	*Chile*
RH	*Haiti*
RI	*Indonesia*
RIM	*Mauritania*
RL	*Lebanon*
RM	*Madagascar*
RMM	*Mali*
RNR	*Zambia*
ROK	*Korea*
RSM	*San Marino*
RSR	*Zimbabwe*
RU	*Burundi*
RUS	*Russian Federation*
RWA	*Rwanda*
S	*Sweden*
SD	*Swaziland*
SDV	*Vatican City*
SF	*Finland*
SGP	*Singapore*
SME	*Suriname*
SN	*Senegal*
SY	*Seychelles*
SYR	*Syria*
T	*Thailand*
TG	*Togo*
TN	*Tunisia*
TR	*Turkey*
TT	*Trinidad & Tobago*
U	*Uruguay*
UA	*Ukraine*
USA	*USA*
VN	*Vietnam*
WAG	*Gambia*
WAL	*Sierra Leone*
WAN	*Nigeria*
WD	*Dominica*
WG	*Grenada*
WL	*St. Lucia*
WS	*Western Samoa*
WV	*St. Vincent*
YU	*Yugoslavia*
YV	*Venezuela*
Z	*Zambia*
ZA	*South Africa*
ZR	*Zaire*
ZRE	*Yemen*

VEHICLE SHIPMENT

Car ferry operators from the UK

Belgian Maritime Transport Authority
Premier House
10 Greycoat Place
London SW1P 1SB
Tel: **0171-233 0365**

Condor Ferries
Condor House
Newharbour Road
Poole
Dorset BH15 4AJ
Tel: **01305-761551**

Brittany Ferries
Millbay
Plymouth PL1 3EW
Tel: **0990-360360**

Caledonia MacBrayne
The Ferry Terminal
Gourock PA19 1QP
Tel: **01475-650100**

Scandinavian Seaways
Scandinavia House
Parkeston Quay
Harwich
Essex CO12 4QG
Tel: **01255-240240**

Fred Olsen Lines
Whitehouse Road
Ipswich
Suffolk IP1 5LL
Tel: **01473-292200**

Hoverspeed Ltd
International Hoverport
Marine Parade
Dover
Kent CT17 9TG
Tel: **01304-240241**

Irish Ferries
2/4 Merrion Row
Dublin 2
Ireland
Tel: **1-661 0511**

Isles of Scilly Steamship Co.
Quay Street
Penzance
Cornwall TR18 4QX
Tel: **0345-105555**

Colorline
International Ferry Terminal
Royal Quays
North Shields
Tyne & Wear
NE29 6EE
Tel: **0191-296 1313**

Norfolk Line
Norfolk House
The Dock
Felixstowe
Suffolk IP11 8UY
Tel: **01394-673676**

P&O North Sea Ferries
King George Dock
Hedon Road
Hull HU9 5QA
Tel: **01482-377177**

Orkney Ferries
Shore Street
Kirkwall
Orkney KW15 1LG
Tel: **01856-872044**

P&O European Ferries
Channel House
Channel View Road
Dover Kent CT17 9TJ
Tel: **01304-203388**

P&O Ferries (Orkney & Shetland Services)
PO Box 5
Jamiesons Quay
Aberdeen AB9 8DL
Tel: **01224-572615**

Holyman Sally Ferries
Argyle Centre
York Street
Ramsgate
Kent CT11 9DS
Tel: **0990-595522**

Sealink Stena Line
Charter House
Park Street
Ashford
Kent TN24 8EX
Tel: **01233-647047**

Shannon Ferries
Killimer
Kilrush
Co Clare
Ireland
Tel: **65-53124**

Viking Line
c/o Finman Travel

87-89 Church Street
Leigh
Greater Manchester WN7 1AZ
Tel: **01942-262662**

Western Ferries
Hunters Quay
Dunoon
Argyll PA23 8HJ
Tel: **01369-704452**

Other helpful organisations

Michael Gibbons Freight
21 Berth, Tilbury Freeport
Tilbury Docks
RM18 7JT
Tel: **01375-843461**
*One of the biggest shipment companies, with
offices world-wide. Both the AA and the RAC
refer their members to this company.*

Verband Der Automobilindustrie e.V (VDA)
Westendstrasse 61
6000 Frankfurt am Main 1
Germany
Tel: **69 75 70-0**

**Motor Vehicle Manufacturers' Association
of the United States**
7430 Second Avenue
Suite 300
Detroit
Michigan 48202 USA
Tel: **313-872 4311**

Federal Chamber of Automotive Industries
10 Rudd St
Canberra City ACT
2601 Canberra
Australia
Tel: **6-247 3811**

Further reading:

ABC Passenger Shipping Guide (Reed Travel
Group)

DRIVING REQUIREMENTS WORLD-WIDE

For further information, contact the appropriate embassy, consulate or motoring organisation. For insurance details see Chapter 9.

International Driving Permit = IDP, CPD = *Carnet de Passages en Douanes*.

Country	Vehicle Import Requirements	Driving Permits	Fuel Availability
Afghanistan	Prior authorisation from Ministry of Commerce in Kabul	IDP	Unclear
Albania	Borders closed to tourist traffic	IDP	Expensive and scarce
Algeria	CPD may be required Customs document issued on entry — valid for three months	IDP	Good. Spares are difficult to find
Andorra	None	Yes, all licences	Good
Antigua	None	Driver's permit obtained at police station by showing national licence	Good
Argentina	Written undertaking to export or CPD	IDP	Good
Australia	CPD	All accepted but IDP preferred	Good
Bahamas	For under 6 months, redeemable bond must be paid	IDP British licence	Spares rare
Bahrain	—	IDP	Good
Bangladesh	CPD	IDP or national licence	Unclear
Barbados	—	Licences recognised if presented to police and BD$10 fee paid	Good
Belgium	None	National licences	Good
Belize	—	Licences recognised for 3 months	Good
Benin	—	IDP	OK
Bermuda	—	Visitors not permitted to drive a motor vehicle	Good
Bolivia	—	IDP	Unclear
Botswana	CPD.	Local licence after 6 months All licences recognised	Good
Brazil	—	IDP required National licence valid for 6 months if certified	No fuel sold on Saturday, Sunday or after 8pm every day
British Virgin Islands	—	BVI temporary licence issued on presentation of foreign licence	
Country	*Vehicle Import*	*Driving Permits*	*Fuel Availability*

	Requirements		
Brunei	—	Local licence required on presentation of foreign licence	Good
Bulgaria	None	Foreign licences recognised for short periods, otherwise IDP	Good
Burkina Faso	Acquit-a-caution	Certain licences recognised, otherwise IDP	Unclear
Cameroon	Written undertaking	IDP	Scarce
Canada	Free entry but deposit may be required	IDP accepted, national licence valid for 3 months	Good
Cayman Islands	—	IDP	Good
Central African Rep	CPD	IDP	Scarce
Chad	CPD	IDP	Expensive
Chile	CPD	IDP	Diesel only on Pan Am Highway
China	No foreign vehicles allowed except trade vehicle		Unclear
CIS		IDP or national licence with authorised translation	Scarce
Colombia	CPD	National licence accepted, accompanied by local licence	Good
Congo	CPD	IDP	Good
Costa Rica	Written undertaking to re-export	National licences accepted	Good
Côte d'Ivoire	CPD	IDP	OK
Croatia		National licence or IDP	
Cuba	—	National licences accepted for 6 months	Good
Cyprus	Written undertaking to export vehicle	National licence accepted for 1 year	Good
Czech Republic	Must be entered on passport	National licence accepted	Filling stations often closed in evening
Denmark	None	National licence accepted	Good
Dominican Republic	—	National licence accepted	Good
Ecuador	CPD	IDP	Good
Egypt	CPD through Alexandria only	IDP National licence accepted	Good
El Salvador	Written undertaking to export	National licence of IDP	
Ethiopia	Deposit of customs duty	Temporary Ethiopian licence should be obtained on arrival	Unclear
Fiji	—	National licence accepted	Good
Finland	None	National licence accepted	Good
France	None	National licence accepted	Good

Country	Vehicle Import Requirements	Driving Permits	Fuel Availability
Gabon	CPD	National licence	Unclear
Gambia	Advance permission from Controller of Customs and Excise	National licence accepted for short visit	Good
Germany	None	Certain licences accepted, otherwise IDP required	Good
Ghana	CPD	Commonwealth country licence accepted for 90 days. IDP recommended	Unclear
Gibraltar	None	National licence accepted	Good
Greece	Non EEC visitors issued with vehicle-free entry card	Certain licences recognised otherwise IDP	Good
Grenada	—	National licence accepted and local licence	Good
Guinea	Visas not issued for tourist purposes	IDP	OK
Guyana	Deposit of duty	Certain licences recognised, otherwise IDP	OK
Haiti	—	IDP	OK
Honduras	—	National licence	OK
Hong Kong	Import declaration required	National licence –after 12 months must apply for HK driving licence	Good
Hungary	None. Registration number entered on documents at border	IDP	Good
Iceland	None. Diesel vehicles must pay weight tax for each week in Iceland	Certain licences accepted otherwise licence/IDP presented to police for temporary licence	Good
India	CPD. Duty is around 300%. Virtually impossible to get Carnet Indemnity Insurance	To get a local licence, 5yr licence costs RS20/ you must do an oral test. Certain licences recognised, otherwise IDP	Good
Indonesia	Border closed to tourist vehicles	IDP	Good
Iran	CPD. You usually have to be escorted and pay for it	IDP	OK
Iraq	CPD (validity 3 months)	IDP	Unclear
Ireland	None	National licence	Good
Israel	None	National licence recognised but IDP preferred	Good
Italy	None	Certain licences accepted or accompanied by translation or ID	Good. Concessionary petrol coupons available

Country	Vehicle Import Requirements	Driving Permits	Fuel Availability
Jamaica	CPD or deposit of duty	Certain licences accepted otherwise IDP	Good
Japan	CPD. Tax has to be paid–customs clearance. And will need modifying to conform to standard. *NB* Not advised to take car	IDP. Local will be given after sight and co-ordination tests.	Good
Jordan	CPD	IDP Visitor not allowed to drive vehicles with normal Jordanian reg. plates	Good
Kenya	CPD	National licence. IDP required to drive for up to 90 days Kenyan registered vehicle	OK
Korea (South)	—	IDP	Good
Kuwait	CPD	IDP. National licence accepted if accompanied by local temporary licence	Unclear
Laos	Borders closed	National licence accepted but IDP preferred	OK
Lebanon	CPD	National licence must be validated	Unclear
Leeward Islands	—	All licences accepted if presented to police on arrival for temporary three month licence	OK
Lesotho	CPD	National licence if in English/translated	Unclear
Liberia	Deposit of duty	National licence accepted if presented to police on arrival for temporary 30-day licence	Unclear
Libya	CPD	National licence good for three months	Good
Luxembourg	None	National licence accepted	Good
Macau	Cannot bring cars in	IDP (except UK drivers)	Good
Madagascar	Advance permission and local guarantee	National licence accepted	Unclear
Malawi	Written undertaking	Certain licences recognised otherwise IDP	Good
Malaysia	CPD	Certain licences accepted otherwise IDP	Good
Malta	Temporary import permit issued on entry. Valid for 3 months	National licence	Petrol stations closed on Sundays
Mauritania	CPD	National licence accepted for limited period or IDP	Unclear
Mauritius	CPD	National licence accepted if endorsed by police	Good
Mexico	Temporary importation of vehicle noted on Tourist Card or Visa	National licences or IDP	Good

Country	Vehicle Import Requirements	Driving Permits	Fuel Availability
Mongolia	Borders closed	IDP	OK
Morocco	Temporary importation form is issued at border	National licence is accepted for 3 months. IDP required to hire car	Good
Myanmar	No entry overland allowed	IDP presented to police for issue of visitor's driving licence	OK
Nepal	CPD	IDP accepted for 15 days then local licence required. Certain licences recognised, otherwise IDP	Good
Netherlands		National licence	Good
New Zealand		Certain national licences otherwise IDP	Good
Nicaragua	Written undertaking to export vehicle	National licence/IDP valid 1 month for vehicle registered abroad then local licence	OK
Niger	CPD	IDP	OK
Nigeria	Temporary importation document issued at border	IDP	Good
Norway	None	National licence or IDP	Good
Oman	No	National licence valid seven days then local licence issued, valid 3 months	Good
Pakistan	CPD	IDP	OK
Panama	Proof of ownership	National licence accepted	Good
Papua New Guinea	—	National licence accepted	Unclear
Paraguay	CPD	National licence or IDP	Good
Peru	CPD	IDP	OK
Philippines	CPD	IDP with national licence	Good
Poland	None	Certain licences recognised otherwise IDP	Good
Portugal	None	National licence or IDP	Good
Qatar	CPD	National licence accepted if accompanied by local	Good
Romania	None	National licence or IDP	Unclear
Rwanda	—	IDP	Unclear
Saudi Arabia	Carnets are not valid	Women are not permitted to drive. Local licence essential for longer stays	Good
Senegal	CPD	IDP	Good
Seychelles	—	National licence accepted	Good
Sierra Leone	CPD	IDP	Unclear
Singapore	CPD	IDP	Good
Solomon Islands	—	National licence accepted	Good
Slovak Republic		National licence	
Slovenia	None	National licence	
South Africa	CPD	IDP	Good

Country	Vehicle Import Requirements	Driving Permits	Fuel Availability
Spain	None	IDP or translating of national licence	Good
Sri Lanka	CPD	National licence accepted if accompanied by temporary driving licence available on arrival	Good
Sudan	CPD	International licence OK for six months. National licence accepted if presented to police	Unclear
Swaziland	CPD	English-text licences accepted or IDP	Good
Sweden	None	National licence accepted	Good
Switzerland	None	National licence accepted	Good
Syria	CPD	IDP	Good
Tahiti	—	National licence accepted	Good
Tanzania	CPD	Temporary licence on presentation of national licence to police or IDP which must be endorsed	Unclear
Thailand	Deposit of duty	IDP	Good
Togo	Entry by land: written undertaking. Entry by sea: bank guarantee and advance authorization	IDP	Unclear
Tonga	—	Local licence required, issued by police dept, need an international or national licence and T$8	Good
Trinidad & Tobago	CPD. Left-hand drive cars restricted	Most national licences accepted if accompanied by an English translation where necessary for 90 days	Good
Tunisia	Written undertaking	National licence	Good
Turkey	None – vehicle details entered on passport	National licences in English or French, accepted for temporarily imported vehicles, otherwise IDP	Good
Turks & Caicos	—	Local licence required	Good
Uganda	Deposit of duty	National licence accepted for 90 days or IDP	OK
United Kingdom		National licence accepted	Good
United Arab Emirates	CPD recommended	National licences must be presented to Traffic Dept. with letters from sponsor	Good
US Virgin Islands	No	National licence	Good
USA	None	National licence or IDP	Good
Uruguay	CPD	National licence accepted if presented to authorities	Good
Vanuatu	—	National licence accepted	Good
Venezuela	CPD	IDP	Good

Country	Vehicle Import Requirements	Driving Permits	Fuel Availability
Vietnam	Borders closed	IDP	OK
Yemen	—	IDP	OK
Zaire (DRC)	CPD	IDP	—
Zambia	None –guaranteed written undertaking	IDP	OK
Zimbabwe	None –guaranteed written undertaking or CPD	IDP	Good

Note:

1. The requirements given here are the minimum accepted by each country. In some countries, visitors are recommended to carry an IDP in addition to a national licence.

2. Many countries will let you take in a car for a brief tourist visit without a carnet and without paying duty, but this should not be relied upon.

3. Generally, a motor vehicle may be temporarily imported into a European country from between 6 and 12 months, without formality.

Information supplied by the RAC.

METRIC CONVERSIONS

Tyre pressures

lbs per sq in	kg per sq cm	Atmosphere	Kilo Pascals (kPa)
14	0.98	0.95	96.6
16	1.12	1.08	110.4
18	1.26	1.22	124.2
20	1.40	1.36	138.0
22	1.54	1.49	151.8
24	1.68	1.63	165.6
26	1.83	1.76	179.4
28	1.96	1.90	193.2
30	2.10	2.04	207.0
32	2.24	2.16	220.8
36	2.52	2.44	248.4
40	2.80	2.72	276.0
50	3.50	3.40	345.0
55	3.85	3.74	379.5
60	4.20	4.08	414.0
65	4.55	4.42	448.5

Litre to gallon conversion

To convert:	Multiply by
Gallons to Litres	4.546
Litres to Gallons	0.22

Measures of capacity

2 pints =	1 quart =	1.136 Litres
4 quarts =	1 gallon =	4.546 Litres
	5 gallons =	22.73 Litres

Distances

1 yard=	0.91 metres
100 yards=	91 metres
1 mile=	1.6 kilometres

To convert:
Miles to kilometres divide by 5 then multiply by 8
Kilometres to miles divide by 8 then multiply by 5

VEHICLES: PURCHASE, HIRE & CONVERSION

Allied Self-Drive Rental
Allierd House
17 Crawford St
London W1H 1PF
Tel: **0171-224 2257**
Specialists in Audi and Volkswagen rentals.

Brownchurch (Land Rovers) Ltd
Hare Row, off Cambridge Heath Road
London E2 9BY
Tel: **0181-556 0011**
Specialist safari preparation for Land Rovers, Range Rovers and Discovery: roof racks, light guards, bush bars, jerry can holders, suspension and over-drive modifications, winches, sand ladders, high-lift jacks, oil cooler kits etc. Cover all Land Rover needs for trips anywhere, including the fitting of jerry cans and holders, sand ladders, sump and light guards, crash bars, winches, water purifying plants, roof-racks (custom-made if necessary), overdrive units. They also supply new vehicles and offer a maintenance and spares service for Land, Range Rovers and Discovery.

Cross Country Vehicles Ltd
Hailey
Witney
Oxon OX8 5UF
Tel: **01993-776622**
Sell and convert vehicles, prepare them for safari use. Range Rover and Land Rover specialists – new and used vehicles and any other 4WD vehicle too. They offer service, special preparation, conversion parts (new and reconditioned). Parts and preparation quotes by return.

Dunsfold Land Rovers Ltd
Alfold Road
Dunsfold
Godalming
Surrey GU8 4NP
Tel: **01483-200567**
Offers free travel advice to those contemplating overland travel: comprehensive stores, rebuilding to owner's specifications.

Land Rover Ltd
Direct Sales Department
Lode Lane
Solihull
West Midlands B92 8NW
Tel: **0121-722 2424**
Manufacturers of Land Rovers and Range Rovers. Purchase must be through authorised dealers.

Sanderson Ford
Ashton Old Road
Ardwick
Manchester M12 6JD
Tel: **0161-272 6000**
Deal in Mevaride 4WD vehicles.

MOTORIST'S CHECK–LIST
by Jack Jackson

If you are an experienced off–road motorist and vehicle camper, you are, without doubt, the best person to decide exactly what you need to do and take for your trip. Even so, extensive experience doesn't guarantee perfect recall and everyone might find it useful to jog their memories by consulting other people's lists.

These lists do assume some experience — without some mechanical expertise, for example, an immaculately stocked tool-box is of limited use. It is also assumed that the motorist in question will spend at least some time driving off–road, most probably in a four-wheel drive vehicle.

Vehicle spares and tools

Petrol Engines
3 fan belts (plus power steering pump belts and air conditioning pump belts if fitted)
1 complete set of gaskets
4 oil filters (change every 5000 km)
2 tubes of Silicone RTV gasket compound
1 complete set of radiator hoses
2 metres of spare heater hose
2 metres of spare fuel pipe hose
0.5 metres of spare distributor vacuum pipe hose
2 exhaust valves
1 inlet valve
1 complete valve spring
Fine and coarse valve grinding paste and valve grinding tool
1 valve spring compressor
1 fuel pump repair kit (if electric type, take a complete spare pump)
1 water pump repair kit
1 carburettor overhaul kit
2 sets of sparking plugs
1 timing light or 12 volt bulb and holder with leads
3 sets of contact breaker points (preferably with hard fibre cam follower, because plastic types wear down quickly and close up the gap in the heat)
2 distributor rotor arms
1 distributor condenser

1 distributor cap
1 sparking plug spanner
1 set of high tension leads (older, wire type)
1 ignition coil
Slip ring and brushes for alternator or a complete spare alternator.
2 cans of spray type ignition sealant, for dusty and wet conditions
2 spare air intake filters, if you do not have the oil–bath type

Extras for diesel engines

Delete sparking plugs, contact breaker points, distributor, vacuum pipe hose, rotor arms, distributor cap and condenser, high tension leads, coil, and carburettor overhaul from the above list and substitute:
1 spare set of injectors, plus cleaning kit
1 complete set of high pressure injector pipes
1 set injector copper sealing washers plus steel sealing washers where these are used
1 set injector return pipe washers
1 metre of plastic fuel pipe, plus spare nuts and ferrules
A second in–line fuel filter
4 fuel filter elements
3 spare heater plugs, if fitted

Brakes and clutch

2 wheel cylinder kits (one right and one left)
1 flexible brake hose
1 brake bleeding kit
1 brake, master cylinder seals kit
1 clutch, master cylinder seals kit
1 clutch, slave cylinder kit (or a complete unit for Land Rover series III or 110). (It is important to keep all these kits away from heat)
1 clutch centre plate
If you have an automatic gearbox, make sure you have plenty of the special fluid for this, a spare starter motor and a spare battery, kept charged.
If you have power steering, carry the correct fluid and spare hoses.
Some Land Rovers have automatic gearbox fluid in a manual gearbox.

General spares

2 warning triangles (compulsory in most countries)
1 good workshop manual (not the car handbook)
1 good torch and a fluorescent light with leads to work it from vehicle battery, plus spare bulbs and tubes
1 extra tyre in addition to that on the spare wheel. (Only the spare wheel and tyre will be necessary if two identical vehicles are travelling together.)
3 extra inner tubes (6 in areas of Acacia thorns)

1 large inner tube repair kit
1 set of tyre levers and 1 kg sledge hammer for tyres
5 spare inner tube valve cores and 2 valve core tools
4 inner tube valve dust caps (metal type)
1 Schrader tyre pump, which fits into sparking plug socket threads. Or a 12 volt electric compressor, which is the only system available if you have a diesel engine
Plenty of good quality engine oil
2 litres of distilled water or 1 bottle of water de–ionizing crystals
12-volt soldering iron and solder
Hand drill and drills
16 metres of nylon or terylene rope, strong enough to upright an overturned vehicle
1 good jack and wheel brace (if hydraulic, carry spare fluid)
1 (at least) metal fuel can, e.g. a jerry can
1 grease gun and a tin of multi–purpose grease
5 litres of correct differential and gearbox oil
1 large fire extinguisher suitable for petrol and electrical fires
1 reel of self–vulcanizing rubber tape, for leaking hoses
1 pair heavy-duty electric jump leads at least 3 metres long
10 push fit electrical connectors (of type to suit vehicle)
2 universal joints for prop shafts
0.5 litre can of brake and clutch fluid
1 small can of general light oil for hinges, etc
1 large can WD40
1 starting handle, if available
2 complete sets of keys, kept in different places
1 small Isopon or fibre glass kit for repairing fuel tank and body holes
2 kits of general adhesive eg. Bostik or Araldite Rapid
1 tin of hand cleaner (washing up liquid will do in an emergency)
Spare fuses and bulbs for all lights, including those on the dash panel, the red charging light bulb is often part of the charging circuit
1 radiator cap
Antifreeze —if route passes through cold areas
Spare windscreen wipers for use on return journey (keep away from heat)
Inner and outer-wheel bearings

A good tool kit containing:

Wire brush to clean dirty threads
Socket set
Torque wrench
Ring and open-ended spanners
Hacksaw and spare blades
Large and small flat and round files
Selection of spare nuts, bolts and washers, of type and thread/s to fit vehicle 30cm Stillson

pipe wrench
1 box spanner for large wheel-bearing lock nuts
Hammer
Large and small cold chisels, for large and stubborn nuts
Self–grip wrench, e.g. Mole type
Broad and thin nosed pliers
Circlip pliers
Insulating tape
3 metres electrical wire (vehicle type, not mains)
1 set of feeler gauges
Small adjustable wrench
Tube of gasket cement, e.g. Red Hermetite
Tube Loctite thread sealant
Large and small slot head and Phillips head screwdrivers
Accurate tyre pressure gauge
Hardwood or steel plate, to support the jack on soft ground

Extras for off–road use

2 sand ladders per vehicle (4 if vehicle travels alone)
3 wheel bearing hub oil seals
1 rear gearbox oil seal
1 rear differential oil seal
1 rear spring main leaf, complete with bushes
1 front spring main leaf, complete with bushes
4 spare spring bushes
4 spring centre bolts
1 set (=4) of spring shackle plates
1 set (=4) of spring shackle pins
2 rear axle 'U' bolts
1 front axle 'U' bolt.
If instead of leaf springs you have coil springs, carry one spare plus 2 mountings and 4 bushes
1 set of shock absorber mounting rubbers
2 spare engine mounting rubbers
1 spare gearbox mounting rubber
2 door hinge pins
1 screw jack (to use it on its side when changing springs and/or bushes)
2 metres of strong chain plus bolts to fix it, for splinting broken chassis axle or spring parts
Snow chains if you expect a lot of mud or snow
5cm paint brush, to dust off the engine, so that you can work on it
Large groundsheet for lying on when working under the vehicle or repairing tyres, so as to prevent sand from getting between the inner tube and the tyre
1 high lift jack
2 long-handled shovels for digging out
2 steering ball joints
2 spare padlocks
Radiator stop leak, compound (dry porridge or raw egg will do in an emergency)

Specific to Series IIA Land Rovers

1 set rear axle half shafts (heavy duty)

Specific to Series III Land Rovers

1 complete gear change lever, if you have welded bush type (or replace with groove and rubber ring type)
4 nylon bonnet hinge inserts (or 2 home–made aluminium ones)
2 windscreen outer hinge bolts (No 346984)
2 windscreen inner tie bolts
2 rear differential drain plugs
1 set big end nuts
1 rear axle drive plate (Salisbury)

Specific to Land Rover Turbo Diesel and Tdi Engines

2 spare glass fibre main timing belts, stored flat and in a cool place
3 pushrods
3 brass cam followers
2 air filter paper elements

Maintenance check before departure

1. Change oil and renew all oil and fuel filters
2. Clean air filter and change oil bath or air filter element
3. Lubricate drive shafts, winch, speedometer cable
4. Lubricate all locks with dry graphite
5. Adjust and lubricate all door hinges
6. Inspect undercarriage for fluid leaks, loose bolts, etc.
7. Rotate all tyres, inspecting for cuts and wear
8. Check and adjust brakes
9. Check adjustment of carburettor or injection pump
10. Check fan belts and accessory belts
11. Check sparking plugs. Clean and re–gap if necessary (replace as necessary). If diesel, clean or replace injectors.
12. Check ignition timing
13. Check and top up: front and rear differentials, swivel–pin housings, transmission, transfer case, overdrive, power steering pump, and air conditioning pump (if applicable), steering box, battery, brake and clutch fluid, cooling system
14. Check that there are no rattles
15. Inspect radiator and heater hoses
16. Check breather vents on both axles, gearbox and fuel filler cap
17. Check all lights and direction indicators
18. Check wheel balance and steering alignment (always do this with new wheels and/or tyres)
19. Check battery clamps and all electrical wiring for faulty insulation ■

GETTING THERE BY OTHER MEANS
Section 6

CYCLING ASSOCIATIONS AND HOLIDAY OPERATORS

Apex Cycles
40-42 Clapham High Street
London SW4 7UR
Tel: **0171-622 1334**
Large retailer of bikes and equipment with a number of branches nationwide.

Back Road Bicycle Touring
1516 5th Street
Suite M23
Berkeley
California 94710
Tel: **510-527 1555**

Bents Bicycle Tours
The Priory
High Street
Redbourne
Hertfordshire AL3 7LZ
Tel: **01568-780800**
World-wide cycling tours in Bavaria and the Black Forest.

Bicycle Africa
4887 Columbia Drive S
Seattle
Washington 98108-1919
USA
Tel: **202-682 9314**
Cycle tours through Africa lasting 2 to 4 weeks.

Bicycle Australia
PO Box K499
Haymarket
NSW 2000
Australia
Tel: **46-272 186**

Bicycle Association of New Zealand
PO Box 2454

Wellington
New Zealand
Tel: *Wellington* **4 472 3733**
      Auckland **9 357 35 50**

Bike Events Ltd
82 Walcot Street
Bath Avon BA1 5BD
Tel: **01225-310859**
Organizes a range of activities from day events to touring holidays in Britain and world-wide. Also produces a magazine, BE Magazine.

British Cycling Federation
National Cycling Centre
Stuart St
Manchester
M11 4DQ
Tel: **0161-230 2301**
The national association of cycle-racing clubs, offering an information service for members.

USA Cycling Federation
1 Olympic Plaza
Colorado Springs
CO 80909-577
Tel: **719-578 4581**

Canadian Cycling Association
1600 James Naismith Drive
Gloucester
Ontario K1B 5N4, Canada
Tel: **416-781 4717**

Cyclists' Touring Club (CTC)
69 Meadrow
Godalming
Surrey GU7 3HS
Tel: **01483-417217**
Britain's oldest and largest national associa-

tion for all types of cyclists, with a touring information service. Also offers insurance, magazine, and organised cycling holidays.

Covent Garden Cycles
2 Nottingham Court
Covent Garden
London WC2H 9AY
Tel: **0171-836 1752**

League of American Wheelmen
190 West Ostend Street
Suite 120
Baltimore
MD 21230
USA
Tel: **301 944 3399**

London to Paris Bike Ride
Sports Pro International Ltd
26A The Terrace
Riverside
Barnes
London SW13
Fax: **0181-392 1539**
Fax the organisers, Sports Pro, by mid-April for an application form.

Susie Madron's Cycling for Softies
2-4 Birch Polygon
Rusholme
Manchester M14 5HX
Tel: **0161-248 8282**
Tours of rural France and Italy, equipment provided, accommodation in 2 and 3 star hotels.

United States Cycling Federation
1750 East Boulder St
Colorado Springs
CO 80909
Tel: **719-578 4581**

HITCHHIKING ASSOCIATIONS

Allostop
The collective name for the associations Allauto, Provoya and Stop-Voyages. Allostop puts you in contact with drivers with a view to sharing petrol costs. Enrol sufficiently in advance. A small sum of between £15 and £20 (which constitutes an annual subscription fee and which cannot be refunded) allows you to an unlimited number of journeys in a year starting from the date of enrolment. If you wish to make only one journey, the subscription is less.

The main offices in France are:

Maison des Langue et des Voyages
1 Place du Marichal Juin
35043 Rennes
Tel: **2-99 30 93 93**

Autostop
190 Avenue du Pere Soulas
34004 Montpelier
Tel: **4-67 04 36 66**

C.R.I.J.
17 Rue de Metz
31000 Toulouse
Tel: **5-61 21 20 20**

Autopass
21 Rue Patou
59800 Lille
Tel: **3-20 14 31 96**

Voyage au Fil
28 Rue du Calvaire
44000 Nantes
Tel: **40-89 04 85**

Allostop
8 Rue Rochambeau
Paris
Tel: **1-53 20 42 42** (Rides out of Paris)
Tel: **4-53 20 42 43** (Rides to Paris)
email: **allostop@ecritel.fr.**
Open from 9.00 hrs to 19.30 hrs on Monday to Friday and from 9.00 hrs to 13.00 hrs and 14.00 hrs to 18.00 hrs on Saturday.

In GERMANY:
Mitfahrzentrale
Lammerstrasse 4,
8 Munich 2
Tel: **89-19440**
Autostop agency in Germany, offices in Hamburg, Frankfurt, Berlin. £7 fee will put you in touch with drivers going your way on expenses basis.

In DENMARK:
Kor-Med-Centralen
Vestesbroagade
1620 Kopenhagen
Tel: **1-23 24 40**

In SPAIN:
Barnastop
Calle San Ramon 29.
08001 Barcelona
Tel: **4-43 06 32**

Iberstop
Called elvira 85
18018 Granada
Tel: **958-29 29 20**

Viage Facil
Apartada 336 Enrique Granados 17
17310 Lloret del Mar
Tel: **972-36 57 37 or 36 83 01**

Iberstop
Calle Maria 13-2
29013 Malaga
Tel: **525-45 84**

Dedo Express
Pozo Amarillo 26-1. 37002 Salamanca
Tel: **923-26 72 88**

Iberstop
Calle Marco Sancho 24
41000 Sevilla
Tel **954-38 82 80**

In CANADA:
Allostop
4317 Rue Saint Denis
Montreal H2J 2K9
Quebec
Tel: **514-985 30 32**

Allostop
467 Rue Saint-Jean,
61R Quebec
Auebec
Tel: **418-522 34 30**

Allostop
238 Rue Dalhousie
Ottawa KIN 7EZX Ontario
Tel: **613-562 82 48**

Allostop
185 Rue Alexandre
Sherbrooke
JIH 4S8 Quebec
Tel: **819-821 36 37**

In SWITZERLAND:
Allostop
Mitfahrzentrale
Ankerstr. 16
3006 Berne
Tel: **031-44 707**

In the CZECH REPUBLIC:
Auto Tip Cestovni Cerntala
Lipova 12 Prague 2 120 00
Tel: **2-2043 83**

Gomez Travel Agency
Mrs Vera Rybova
Malatova 7 150 00 Prague 5
Tel: **2-53 52 48**

Similar Organisations:

In AUSTRIA:
Mitfahrzentrale
Brixener str. 3
Innsbruck
Tel: **512-57 23 43**

Mitfahrzentrale
Kapuzinerstrasse 14A4020 Linz
Tel: **732-28 27 20**

Mitfahrzentrale
Daungasse la. 1080 Vienna
Tel: **22-42 72 74**

In HOLLAND:
International Lift Center
Oudezijds Achterburgwal 169
1012DH Amsterdam
Tel: **20-6 224 342**

UK:
Freewheelers
25 Low Friar Street
Newcastle-Upon-Tyne NE15UE
Tel: **0191-222 00 90**

Taxi-stop
The Allostop card can be used for Taxi-stop in Belgium. Taxi-stop offices are:

Infor-Jeunes
27 Rue du Marche-aux-Herbes
100 Brussels
Tel: **223-2231**

Taxi-stop
51 Onderbergen
9000 Gent
Tel: **91-23 23 10**

Taxi-stop
21 Place de l'Universite
1348 Louvain la Neuve
Tel: **10-45 14 14**

Polorbis
Department of Tourism
Ul. Marszalkowska 142
PL-00-061- Warsaw
Poland
Tel: **22-273673**
Poland has an official hitchhiking scheme run by Polorbis. Drivers get points for helping you. Ask before going.

CARGO & FREIGHTER TRAVEL

Shipping Companies:

Bank Line
Dexter House
2 Royal Mint Court
London EC3N 4XX
Tel: **0171-265 0808**
Fax: 0171-481 4784
Itineraries include round-the-world through the Pacific islands.

Blue Star Line
20 Queen Elizabeth Street
London SE1 2LS
Tel: **0171-407 2345**
Fax: 0171-407 4636
Cargo/Passenger services from Great Britain to Canada (West Coast) and the USA.

Compagnie Général Maritime
22 quai Galliéni
92158 Suresnes
France
Tel: **01-49 24 24 73**
Fax: 01-47 42 04 53
The famous banana boats sailing between France and French West Indies.

Egon Olendorff
PO Box 2135
Funfhausen 1
D-2400 Lübeck 1
Germany
Tel: **0451-15000**
Fax: 0451-73522
Famous company for its tramp ships, sailing on irregular routes all over the world.

Grimaldi
Via Marchese Campodisola 13
80133 Naples
Italy
Tel: **081-496111**
Fax: 081-551 7716

N.S.B.
Violenstrasse 22
D-28195 Bremen
Germany
Tel: **0421-32 16 68**
Fax: 0421-32 40 89
Big German company with itineraries world-wide, including round-the-world.

Polish Ocean Lines
Gdynia America Lines
238 City Road
London EC1V 2QL
Tel: **0171-251 3389**
Fax: 0171-250 3625
Very interesting routes at interesting prices.

St. Helena Shipping Co. Ltd
The Shipyard
Porthleven
Helston
Cornwall TR13 9JA
Tel: **01326-563434**
Fax: 01326-564347
From Great Britain to the Canary Islands, St. Helena, Ascension Island, South Africa.

Agencies:

Frachtschiff Touristick
Exhöft 12
24404 Massholm
Germany
Tel: **0-4642 6068**
Fax: 0-4642 6767
Created by a long-time sea captain, proposes a wide range of very original routes.

Freighter World Cruises
180 South Lake Avenue 335
Pasadena
CA 91101, USA
Tel: **818-449 3106**
Fax: 818-449 95 73
Created in 1977, publishes a fortnightly report with pictures.

Gill's Travel
23 Heol-Y-Deri
Rhiwbina
Cardiff CF4 6YF
Tel: **01222-693808**

Hamburg Sud Reiseagentur
Ost-West Strasse 59-61
20457 Hamburg
Germany
Tel: **040-3705155**
Fax: 040-37052420

Mer et Voyages
3 rue Tronchet
75008 Paris
France
Tel: **01-44 51 01 68**
Fax: 01-40 07 12 72

The Strand Cruise Centre
Charing Cross Shopping Concourse
The Strand
London WC2N 4HZ
Tel: **0171-836 6363**
For advice on voyages on passenger-carrying cargo ships around the world.

Trav'l Tips
Dpt. V5
PO Box 218
Flushing
NY 11358, USA
Tel: **800-872 8584**

Further Reading: Travel by Cargo Ship by Hugo Verlomme (Cadogan Guides)

CRUISES

Carnival Cruise Lines (also Star Lauro Lines)
Alton House
177 High Holborn
London WC1V 7AA
Tel: **0171-240 3336**
Cargo/Passenger services – Mediterranean to the Caribbean, Central America and back. Also South America.

Carnival Cruises Lines, Inc
Carnival Place 3655 NW 87 Avenue
Miami
Florida, USA
Tel: **305-471 5777**

The Cruise Advisory Service
35 Blue Boar Row
Salisbury
Wiltshire SP1 1DA
Tel: **01722-335505**
General advice on cruising holidays worldwide.

The Cruise People
88 York Street
London W1H 1DP
Tel: **0171-723 2450**
email: **cruise@dial.pipex.com**

CTC Lines
1-3 Regent St
London SW1Y 4NN
Tel: **0171-930 5833**
World-wide cruises.

Cunard Line Ltd
South Western House
Canute Road
Southampton SO9 1ZA
Tel: **01703-634166**

Cunard Line Ltd
55 Fifth Avenue
New York
NY 10017
Tel: **212-880 7500**

ESCOA Cruises
45 Colston Street
Bristol BS1 5AX
UK
Tel: **0117-927 2273**
Specialist in small ship, unusual cruises worldwide.

Holland America Line
300 Elliott Avenue
West Seattle
WA 98119, USA
Tel: **206-281 3535**
Cruises.

Windjammer Barefoot Cruises
PO Box 120
Miami Beach
FL 33119, USA
Cruises.

TRAVEL BY RAIL

Foreign railway reps. in the UK

Amtrack (American)
41-45 Goswell Road
London EC1V 7EH
Tel: **0171-253 9009**

Australia
c/o Longhaul Leisure Rail
PO Box 113
Peterborough PE1 8HY
Tel: **01733-335599**

Austrian Federal Railways
30 St George St
London W1R 0AL
Tel: **0171-629 0461**

Belgian National Railways
Premier House
10 Greycoat Place
London SW1P 1SB
Tel: **0171-233 0360**

Rail Canada
c/o Longhaul Leisure Rail
PO Box 113
Peterborough PE1 8HY
Tel: **01733-335599**

Danish State Railways
c/o Scandinavian Seaways
Scandinavia House
Parkeston Quay
Harwich, Essex CO12 4QG
Tel: **01255-241234**

Finnish State Railways
Finlandia Travel Agency
227 Regent Street
London W1R 7DP
Tel: **0171-409 7334**
Package rail tours in Finland.

French Railways (SNCF)
179 Piccadilly
London W1V 0BA
Tel: **0171-633 0111**

German Rail
Suite 4
The Sanctuary
23 Oakhill Grove
Surbiton
Surrey KY6 6DU
Tel: **0181-390 8833**

India Rail
c/o S D Enterprises Ltd
103 Wembley Park Drive
Wembley
HA9 8HG
Tel: **0181-903 3411**

Ireland – Coras Iompair Eirann
185 London Road
Croydon
Surrey CR0 2RJ
Tel: **0181-6860994**

Italian State Railways
3/5 Lansdowne Road
Croydon
Surrey CR9 1LL
Tel: **0181-686 0677**

Japan Railways Group
20 Saville Row
London W1X 1AE
Tel: **0171-734 9638**

Luxembourg National Railways
122 Regent Street
London W1R 5FE
Tel: **0171-434 2800**

New Zealand Railways Corporation
c/o Longhaul Leisure Rail
PO Box 113
Peterborough PE1 8HY
Tel: **01733-335599**

Norwegian State Railways
c/o European Rail
London SW1Y 5DA
Tel: **0171-387 0444**

Polish State Railways
310-312 Regent Street
London SW1R 5HA Tel: **0171-580 8811**

Portuguese Railways
c/o Portuguese Trade & Tourism Office
2nd floor, 22-25a Sackville Street
London W1X 2LY
Tel: **0171-494 1441**

South Africa (Sartravel)
Regency House
1/4 Warwick Street
London W1R 5WA
Tel: **0171-287 1133**

Spanish National Railways
c/o Spanish National Tourist Office
57-8 St James' Street
London SW1Y 5DA
Tel: **0171-499 0901**

Swedish State Railways
c/o Norwegian State Railways
21-24 Cockspur St
London SW1Y 5DA
Tel: **0171-387 0444**

Swiss Federal Railways
Swiss Centre
Swiss Court
London W1V 8EE
Tel: **0171-734 4577**

USA - see Amtrak

Specialist rail tour operators

Abercrombie & Kent
Sloane Square House
Holbein Place
London SW1W 8NS
Tel: **0171-730 9600**
Rail tours France, Germany, Spain and Switzerland.

Cox & Kings Travel
Gordon House
10 Greencoat Place
London SW1P 1PH
Tel: **0171-873 5006**
Palace on Wheels tour through Rajasthan and the Andaluce Express

Explorers Tours
223 Coppermill Road
Wraysbury TW19 5NW
Tel: **01753-681999**
Rail tours of the USA.

International Rail Centre
Victoria Centre
London SW1V 1JY
Tel: **0990-848848**

Intourist Moscow
Intourist House

219 Marsh Wall
London E14 9PD
Tel: **0171-538 5902**
Trans-Siberian Express.

Longhaul Leisure Rail
PO Box 113
Peterborough PE1 8HY
Tel: **01733-335599**

Railroad Enthusiast Tours
PO Box 1997
Portoloa
California 96122
Tel: **916-836 1745**
Trains unlimited tours.

TEFS Railway Tours Limited
77 Frederick St
Loughborough LE11 3TL
Tel: **01509-262745**
Specialist rail holidays.

Trains Unlimited
PO Box 1997
Portola
California 96122
USA
Tel: 916-836 1745
and
c/o GW Travel Limited
6 Old Market Place
Altrincham
Cheshire WA14 4NP
Tel: **0161-928 9410**

Venice Simplon Orient-Express
Sea Containers House
20 Upper Ground
London SE1 9PF
Tel: **0171-620 0003**

Further reading:
International Timetable (Thomas Cook)
Overseas Timetable (Thomas Cook)
ABC Rail Guide (Reed Travel Group), UK and
Europe.
Eurail Guide (Houghton Mifflin Co. NY, USA)

LOW COST RAIL PASSES WORLD-WIDE

Below is listed a selection of the numerous travel passes available on rail networks world-wide. The passes listed are valid for the whole national system unless otherwise stated.
N.B. : (1) all prices are for 2nd class tickets
(2) validity is unlimited unless otherwise stated
(3) summertime-only or limited availability tickets (e.g. from Campus Travel) not included

(4) extra persons travelling and supplements not included
(5) **IR** = Inter-Rail Card
IR+ = Inter-Rail 26+
FP = Freedom Pass / Euro Domino

Europe

[1] Inter-Rail
(a) must be under 26 yrs when start using ticket
(b) must have been resident in Europe for more than 6 months
(c) includes 24-hour helpline; legal assistance; discounts in hotels, cafes etc. around Europe
(d) divided into 7 zones: see article in Chapter 7
(e) 1 zone ticket: £179/ 15 days
   any 2 zones: £209 for 1 month
   any 3 zones: £299 for 1 month
   all zones: £249 for 1 month

[2] Inter-Rail 26+
(a) must be over 26 yrs
(b) same as Inter-Rail, but NOT valid in: Belgium, France, Great Britain, Italy, Macedonia, Morocco, Portugal, Spain, Switzerland
(c) 15 days or 1 month unlimited travel: £215 or £275

[3] Freedom Pass (Euro Domino)
(a) 3, 5 or 10 days unlimited travel within 1 month
(b) Tickets available: Adult 1st Class; Adult 2nd Class; Under 26; Child
(c) Prices vary according to country
(d) includes some local supplements
(e) passport required
(f) valid in all European countries except: Albania, Bosnia-Herzegovina, and ex-Soviet republics

[4] Eurail Passes : available to US citizens, these allow a variety of discount fares and different types of pan-European rail travel.

Please note as well as general passes to Europe, passes to individual countries are also available, please see under country heading.

Argentina

Argenpass: 30-90 day unlimited 1st class travel
Youth Pass: -25% for under 30s
Senior Pass: -25% for men 60+; women 55+
Student Pass: -25%
(only obtainable within Argentina)

Australia

Austrailpass: valid: 14, 21, 30 days
Austrail Flexi-Pass: valid: 8 days ⇨

(only obtainable outside Australia - operated on state-by-state- basis)

Austria

Puzzle: valid: 10 days. Max use: 4 days choose from 4 regions. Cost: ATS1090
Puzzle Junior: Puzzle but for under 26's
cost: ATS660
IR & IR+
FP

National Rail Pass: Available for one month and valid on all Austrian railways

Environmental Ticket: Purchase a half-fare pass and pay half fares for all train travel for one year. Also available are Environmental Tickets for pensioners

Belgium

B-Tourrail: valid: 1 month. Max use 5 days cost:BEF 2060
Reductie Kaart: valid: 1 month. 50% off all fares
Cost: BEF590
Nettreinkaart: valid: 1 week cost: BEF 2180
Benelux-Tourrail: valid: 1 month max use: 5 days (N + L) cost: BEF4400
IR
FP

Canada

Canrailpass: valid: 12 days Cost: CAN$535 (hi-season) CAN$365 (lo-season)
Youth: same as Canrail. Under 24's cost: CAN$482 (hi-season) CAN$329 (lo-season)
Senior: 60+ Cost: same as Youth
Alaska Pass: valid: 8-30 day. Alaska & B.C. only, + buses. Cost: CAN$499-879
(must be obtained outside Canada)

Czech Republic

Kilometricka banka 2000: max 2000 kms travel. Cost: CZK740
Kilometricka banka 5000: max 5000 kms travel. Cost: CZK1790
IR & IR+
FP

Denmark

Danmarkskort: valid 1 month cost: DKK2800
Scanrail
IR & IR+
FP

Finland

Finnrail Pass: valid:1 month Max use: 3 - 10 days Cost: FIM540 - 995
Scanrail
IR & IR+
FP

Germany

DB Railcard: allows buying unlimited 50% 2nd class tickets. Cost: GBP104 / DEM220
IR & IR+
FP

Greece

Tourism Card: valid: 10, 20, 30 days. Unlimited 2nd class travel. Cost: GRD14150-28320
IR & IR+
FP

Hungary

Turistaberlet: valid 7/10 days.
Cost: HUF6820-9820
IR & IR+
FP

India

Indrail Pass : permits travel on all trains
Child Indrail: 50% fares
(purchase inside or outside India: only with £ or $ in India)

Ireland

Irish Explorer: valid: 15days Max use: 5 days (2nd class only). Cost: IRP60
Irish Explorer Rail & Bus: valid: 15 days Max use: 8 days. Cost: IRP90
Irish Rover: valid: 15 days Max use 5 days 2nd class only. Cost: IRP 75
Emerald Card: valid: 15/30 days Max use 8/15 days 2nd class only + bus. Cost: IRP105-180
IR & IR+
FP

Italy

Italy Railcard: valid: 8-30 days. Cost: GBP110-190 (available from Wasteels)
Biglietto Chilometrico: valid: 2 months Max use: 20 journeys to max 2000kms. Cost: GBP88 / ITL200,000
IR
FP

Japan

Japan Rail Pass: must be obtained outside Japan

Luxembourg

Ticket Reseau: valid: 1 day until 8:00 next day. Cost: LUF160
Benelux-Tourrail
IR & IR+
FP

Malaysia

Malayan Railway Pass: valid: 10-30 days

The Netherlands

Eurodomino Plus: valid: 3-10 days (buses, trams & metros) cost: NLG107-295
Benelux-Tourrail: NOT obtainable in Netherlands
IR & IR+
FP includes rail, bus, metro & tram)

New Zealand

New Zealand Travelpass: unlimited travel on train, coach & ferry

Norway

NIR Weelky Tourist Ticket: (1) valid:7-14 days. Cost: NOK1010-1365
(2) valid 1 month Max use 3 days NOK720 (all prices increase 25% in summer)
Scanrail
IR & IR+
FP

Pakistan

concessions for tourists on presentaion of a certificate issued by railways
50% off for students

Poland

Polrail Pass: valid: 8 days - 1 month cost: adult: GBP32-84, <26: GBP23-41 (available from Wasteels)
IR & IR+
FP

Portugal

Bilhete Turisticos: valid 7-21 days. Cost: ESC17,500-40,000
IR & FP

Singapore

The Malaysian-Singapore Rail Pass
Covers Singapore, Malaysia and Thailand and lasts for 10 days.

Slovakia

Kilometrica banka: valid: 6 months Max use: 2000 kms of travel. Cost: GBP19.50
IR & IR+
FP

Slovenia

Slovenia Rail: valid: 10-30 days. Cost: SIT7830-15660 (SIT220 = GBP1 approx)
IR
FP

Sweden

Sweden Rail Pass: valid: 7-30 days Max use: 3-14days. Cost: GBP95-174
Scanrail
IR & IR+
FP

Switzerland

Swiss Pass: valid: 4 days - 1 month (includes public transport in 35 towns).
Cost: GBP110-220
Swiss Flexi Pass: valid: 15 days Max use: 3 days (includes public transport in 35 towns) cost GBP110
Swiss Half-Fare: valid: 1 month 50% off unlimited number of full card fare tickets
cost: GBP47
IR
FP

UK

Britexpress Card: gives 30% off over 30 consecutive days
Tourist Trail Pass: Unlimited travel for periods from 5-30 days

USA

National Rail Pass: valid: 15-30 days. Cost: $355-440 (peak season) / $245-350(off-peak)
Regional passes: East, Northeast, West , Far West valid: 15 or 30 days

EQUESTRIAN ASSOCIATIONS AND TOUR OPERATORS

The American Horseshows Association Inc
220 East 42nd Street
Suite 409
New York
NY10017
Tel: **212-972 2472**

Arctic Experience
29 Nork Way
Banstead SM7 1PB
Tel: **01737-362321**
Riding in Iceland.

Association Nationale de Tourisme Equestre Hippotour
Rue du Moulin 12
B-1331 Rosieres
Belgium
Tel: **2653 24 87**
Organises riding holidays in Belgium. Also Morocco, Mali and Senegal.

Aventura Ltd
42 Greenlands Road
Staines
Middlesex TW18 4LR
Tel: **01784-459018**
Riding holidays in Southern Spain.

The British Horse Society
The British Equestrian Centre
Stoneleigh Park
Kenilworth
Warwickshire CV8 2LR
Tel: **01203-696697**

Boojum Expeditions
2625 Garnet Avenue
San Diego
California 92109
USA
Tel: **619-581 3301**
Riding tours of China, Tibet and Inner Mongolia.

Canadian Equestrian Federation
1600 James Naismith Drive
Gloucester
Ontario K1B 5N4
Tel: **613-748 5632**

The New Zealand Equestrian Federation
PO Box 47
Hastings
Hawks Bay
Tel: **6470 850 85**

Equitour/ Peregrine Holidays
40/41 South Parade
Summertown
Oxford OX2 7JP
Tel: **01865-511642**
Equestrian holidays world-wide.

The Equestrian Federation of Australia Inc
52 Kensington Road
Rose Park
South Australia 5067
Tel: **618 311 8411**

Explore Worldwide Ltd
1 Frederick St
Aldershot
Hants GU11 1LQ
Tel: **01252-344161**
Many of their tours include pony trekking.

Inntravel
Hovingham
York YO6 4JZ
Tel: **01653-628862**
Holidays in France and Spain.

International Horse Travel Association
12 Rue du Moulin
1331 Rosieres
Belgium
Tel: **32-2652 1010**
Equestrian holidays world-wide.

Pyrenee Trail Rides
Cas Martina
Farrera Del Pallars
Llavorsi
Lerida
Spain
Tel: **34-73 630029**

Sobek Expeditions Inc
Box 1089
Angels Camp
California 95222
USA
Tel: **800-777 7939**
Riding tours in the Canadian Rockies.

Steamond International
23 Eccleston Street
London SW1W 9LX
Tel: **0171-730 8646**
Riding tours in Argentina, also polo playing.

SAILING ASSOCIATIONS AND HOLIDAY OPERATORS

Australian Yachting Federation
Locked Bag 806
Post Office
Milsons Point
New South Wales 2060
Australia
Tel: **2 9922 4333**

British Marine Industries Federation
Mead Lake Place
Thorpe Lea Road
Egham
Surrey TW20 8HE
Tel: **01784-473377**
Body representing sailing holiday companies, offers Boatline, a holiday information service.

Canadian Yachting Association
1600 James Naismith Drive
Gloucester
Ontario K1B 5N4
Canada
Tel: **613-748 5687**

Centro Velico Capera
Corso Italia 10
Milana 20122
Italy
Tel: **289-010826**
Sailing courses and cruising near Sardinia, minimum age 17.

Chichester Sailing Centre
Chichester Marina
Sussex PO20 7EL
Tel: **01243-512557**
Holidays for beginners and experienced sailors, with facilities for the physically, visually and mentally handicapped.

Crestar Yachts Ltd
Colette Court
125-126 Sloane St
London SW1X 9AU
Tel: **0171-730 9962**
Luxury charters in Europe, the South Pacific and the Caribbean, complete with crew.

National Federation of Sea Schools
Saddlestones
Fletchwood Lane
Totton
Southampton SO40 7DZ
Tel: **01703-869956**
Full details of sail training nationwide and affil-

iated to the International Sailing Schools Association.

Ocean Youth Club
South St
Gosport
Hampshire PO12 1EP
Tel: **01705-528421**
Adventure sailing holidays for young people.

New Zealand Yachting Federation
PO Box 90900
Mail Centre
Auckland 1
New Zealand
Tel: **649-303 2360**

Royal Yachting Association (RYA)
Royal Yachting Association House
Romsey Road
Eastleigh
Hants SO5 4YA
Tel: **01703-629962**

United States Yachting Racing Union
PO Box 209
Newport
Rhode Island 02840
USA
Tel: **401-849 5200**

Yacht Charter Association
c/o D. R. Howard
60 Silverdale
New Milton
Hants BH25 7DE
Listing of approved members available.

Further reading:
Adventure Holidays (Vacation Work)

WALKING ASSOCIATIONS

Long Distance Walkers Association
Geoff Saunders
117 Higher Lane
Rainford
St Helens
Merseyside WA11 8BQ
Tel: **01744-882 638**

Ramblers Association
1-5 Wandsworth Road
London SW8 2XX
Tel: **0171-582 6878**
Publish the Ramblers Yearbook and Accomodation Guide. ⇨

For tour operators, please see *Adventure and Sporting* in Section 3.

Further Reading: *Hiking Trails, Western United States* and *Hiking Trails, Eastern United States* (McFarland & Company, Inc.)

MICROLIGHTING ASSOCIATIONS

British Microlight Aircraft Association
Bullring
Deddington
Banbury
Oxon OX15 0TT
Tel: **01869-338888**

United States Ultralight Association
USUA
PO Box 667
Frederick MD21705
Tel: **301 695 9100**

European Air Sports
The Secretary
Royal Belgium Aeroclub
1 rue Montoyre
Boite 12
1040 Brussells
Tel: **2 511 7947**

MOUNTAINEERING ASSOCIATIONS

Alpine Club
55 Charlotte Road
London EC2A 3QT
Tel: **0171-613 0755**

British Mountaineering Council
177-179 Burton Road
Manchester
M20 2BB
Tel: **0161-445 4747**

Mount Everest Foundation
Gowrie
Cardwell Close
Preston
Lancashire PR4 1SH
Tel: **01772-635346**

Mountain Medicine Data Centre
Department of Neurological Sciences
St Bartholomew's Hospital
38 Little Britain
London EC1A 7BE
Tel: **0171-601 8888** ■

GREAT JOURNEYS OVERLAND
Section 7

OVERLAND OPERATORS AND ASSOCIATED CLUBS

AAT Kings Tours
2nd Floor William House
14 Worple Road
Wimbledon SW19 4DD
Tel: **0181-879 7322**
Four wheel drive safaris in the Australian Outback.

Acacia Expeditions Ltd
5 Walm Lane
London NW2 5SJ
Tel: **0181-451 3877**
Camping safaris in Africa.

The Adventure Travel Centre
131-135 Earls Court Road
London SW5 9RH
Tel: **0171-370 4555**
Agency for all the most overland companies.

Adventure Center
1311 63rd Street
Duite 200
Emmeryville
California 94608
Tel: **510-654 1879**

The Africa Travel Centre
4 Medway Court
Leigh St
London WC1H 9QX
Tel: **0171-387 1211**
Offers a consultancy service to overland travellers.

American Adventures Inc
6762a Centinela Avenue
Colver City
California 90230
Tel: **310-390 7495**
Tel: **800 864 0335** (Toll Free)

American Adventures Inc
45 High Street
Tunbridge Wells
Kent TN1 1XL
Tel: **01892-511894**
Tours in the USA, Canada and Mexico.

American Pioneers
PO Box 229
Westlea
Swindon
Wiltshire SN5 7HJ
Tel: **01793-881882**
Camping tours in Venezuela, Mexico, Canada and the US.

Bridge the World
1 Ferdinand Street
London NW1 8ES
Tel: **0171-911 0900**
Travel agency stocking most of the overland companies brochures.

Dragoman Adventure Travel
Camp Green
Kenton Road
Debenham
Suffolk IP14 6LA
Tel: **01728-861133**
Overland trips in Asia, South Africa and South America.

Encounter Overland
267 Old Brompton Road
London SW5 9JA
Tel: **0171-370 6845**
Founded over 30 years ago, they now operate 45 different expeditions ranging from ten days to 32 weeks throughout Asia, Africa, Central and South America.

Exodus Expeditions
9 Weir Road
Balham
London SW12 OLT
Tel: **0181-675 5550**
Transcontinental expeditions lasting between two and 26 weeks.

Explore Worldwide Ltd
1 Frederick St
Aldershot GU11 1LQ
Tel: **01252-344161**
Wide variety of tours (4-wheel drive, camel, riverboat) overland in 50 countries world-wide.

The Globetrotters Club
BCM/Roving
London WC1N 3XX
An informal association of travellers from all over the world, linked by an interest in low cost travel and the desire to study the cultures of other lands. Members share their experiences and knowledge. The club concentrates on attracting 'non-tourist' members with a genuine empathy for the people in other lands.

Guerba Expeditions
Wessex House
40 Station Road
Westbury BA13 3JN
Tel: **01373-826611**
Camping safaris tours from one to 27 weeks in Africa.

Journey Latin America Ltd
14-16 Devonshire Road
Chiswick
London W4 2HD
Tel: **0181-747 8315**
Experts in South American travel, guided tours using local transport.

Mountain Travel Inc
6420 Fairmount Avenue
El Cerrito
CA 94530
Tel: **510-527 8100**
Overland through Patagonia.

Overland Latin America
13 Dormer Place
Leamington Spa
Warwickshire CV32 5AA
Tel: **01926-33222**

Sundowners Travel Centre
151 Dorcas Street
South Melbourne
Victoria 3205
Australia
Tel: **03-690 2499**

Sun Travel Ltd
407 Great South Road
Penrose
Auckland
New Zealand
Tel: **9-525 3074**

Top Deck Travel
131-135 Earls Court Road
London SW5 9RH
Tel: **0171-244 8641**
London to Kathmandu via Africa, and a variety of escorted tours in Southeast Asia.

Trailfinders
194 Kensington High Street
London W8 7RG
Tel: **0171-938 3939**
Travel agency which can organise some trips with some overlanding companies.

Trek America
4 Waterperry Court
Middleton Road
Banbury
Oxon OX16 8QG
Tel: **01295-256777**
North American adventure camping and trekking tours.

WEXAS International
45-49 Brompton Road
London SW3 1DE
Tel: **0171-589 3315**
email: **mship@wexas.com**
A travel club, which can offer advice and book overlanding trips for its members. ■

GOVERNMENT REPRESENTATIVES WORLD-WIDE

Canadian Reps. Abroad

AUSTRALIA
Commonwealth Avenue
Canberra
ACT 2600
Tel: **6 273 3844**
Fax: 6 273 3285

AUSTRIA
Laurenzerberg 2
A-1010 Vienna
Tel: **1 531 38 3000**
Fax: 1 531 38 3321

BAHAMAS
PO Box SS-6371
Nassau
Tel: **809 362 5193**
Fax: 809 393 1305

BELGIUM
2 Avenue de Tervuren
B-1040 Brussels
Tel: **2 741 0611**
Fax: 2 741 0619

BRAZIL
Avenida das Naçoes Lote 16
Brasilia 70410-900
Tel: **61 321 2171**
Fax: 61 321 4529

CHILE
Ahumada 11, Piso 10
Casilla 427
Santiago
Tel: **2 696 2256/7/8/9**
Fax: 2 696 2424

CHINA
19 Dong Zhi Men Wai Street
Chao Yang District
Beijing 100600
Tel: **10 532 3536**
Fax: 10 532 4311

COSTA RICA
La Sabana Executive
Business Centre,
Building No. 5, 3rd Floor
San Jose
Tel: **506 296 4149**
Fax: 506 296 4270

CROATIA
Hotel Esplanade
Mihanoviceva 1
41000 Zagreb
Tel: **1 477 905**
Fax: 1 477 913

CUBA
Calle 30
No. 518 Esquina a7a
Miramar
Havana
Tel: **7 33 25 16**
Fax: 7 33 20 44

DENMARK
Kr Bernikowsgade 1
DK-1105 Copenhagen K
Tel: **33 12 22 99**
Fax: 33 14 05 85

EGYPT
6 Mohamed Fahmi El Sayed
Street
Garden City
Cairo
Tel: **2 354 3110**
Fax: 2 356 3548

ESTONIA
Toom Kooli 13, 2nd Floor
0100 Tallinn
Tel: **631 3570**
Fax: 631 3573

FRANCE
35 Avenue Montaigne
F-75008 Paris
Tel: **1 44 43 29 00**
Fax: 1 44 43 29 99

GAMBON
PO Box 4037
Libreville
Tel: 74 34 64 / 74 34 65
Fax: 74 34 66

GERMANY
Godesberger Allee 119
53175 Bonn
Tel: **228 812 4001**
Fax: 228 812 3459

GREECE
4 Ioannou Ghennadiou Street
GR-11521 Athens
Tel: **1 725 4011**
Fax: 1 725 3994

GREENLAND
PO Box 1012
3900 Nuuk
Tel: **28888**
Fax: 27288

GUATEMALA
PO Box 400
Guatemala City
Tel: **2 33 61 04**
Fax: 2 33 61 89

GUINEA
Corniche Sud
PO Box 99
Conakry
Tel: **412 23 95 / 41 44 48**
Fax: 41 42 36

GUYANA
PO Box 10880
Georgetown
Tel: **2 72081**
Fax: 2 58380

HAITI
PO Box 826
Port-au-Prince
Tel: **23 23 58**
Fax: 23 87 20

HONDURAS
PO Box 3552
Tegulcigalpa
Tel: **31 45 45 / 31 45 51**
Fax: 31 57 93

HONG KONG
GPO Box 11142
Hong Kong
Tel: **2 2810 4321**
Fax: 2 2810 6736

HUNGARY
Budakeszi ut 32
H-1121 Budapest
Tel: **1 275 1200**
Fax: 1 275 1210

ICELAND
Suöurlandsbraut 10
108 Reykjavik
Tel: **5 68 0820**
Fax: 5 68 0899

INDIA
7/8 Shantipath
Chanakapuri
New Delhi 110021
Tel: **11 687 6500**
Fax: 11 687 6579 / 687 0031

INDONESIA
PO Box 8324/JKS.MP
Jakarta 12084
Tel: **21 525 0709**
Fax: 21 571 2251

IRAN
PO Box 11365-4647
Tehran
Tel: **21 873 2623**
Fax: 21 873 3202

IRELAND
66 St Stephens Green
Dublin 2
Tel: **1 478 1988**
Fax: 1 478 1285

ISRAEL
PO Box 6410
Tel Aviv 61063
Tel: **3 527 2929**
Fax: 3 527 2333

ITALY
Via G de Rossi 27
1-00161 Rome
Tel: **6 44 59 81**
Fax: 6 445 98912 / 445 98760

JAMAICA
PO Box 1500
Kingston 10
Tel: **809 926 1500**
Fax: 809 926 1702

JAPAN
3-38 Akasaka 7-chome
Minato-ku
Tokyo 107
Tel: **3 3408 2101**
Fax: 3 3479 5320

JORDAN
PO Box 815403
Amman
Tel: **6 666 124**
Fax: 6 689 227

KAZAKHSTAN
157 Prospekt Abaya
6th Floor
480009 Almaty
Tel: **3272 50 93 81**
Fax: 3272 50 93 80

KENYA
PO Box 30481
Nairobi
Tel: **2 21 48 04**
Fax: 2 22 69 87

KOREA
CPO Box 6299
Seoul 100-662
Tel: **2 753 2605/06/07/08**
Fax: 2 755 0686

KUWAIT
PO Box 25281
Safat 13113
Kuwait City
Tel: **256 3025**
Fax: 256 4167

LATVIA
Doma Iaukums 4
4th Floor
Riga LV-1977

Tel: **783 0141 / 782 1161**
Fax: 783 0140

LITHUANIA
Didzioji 8-5
2001 Vilnius
Tel: **2 220 898**
Fax: 2 220 884

LUXEMBOURG
PO Box 1443
Luxembourg
Tel: **40 24 20**
Fax: 402455 (x 600)

MALAYSIA
PO Box 10990
50732 Kuala Lumpur
Tel: **3 261 2000 / 261 2031**
Fax: 3 261 3428

MEXICO
Calle Schiller No 529
Colonia Polanco
11560 Mexico DF
Tel: **5 724 7900**
Fax: 5 724 7980

MOROCCO
PO Box 709
Agdal-Rabat
Tel: **7 67 28 80**
Fax: 7 67 21 87

MOZAMBIQUE
PO Box 1578
Maputo
Tel: **1 492 623**
Fax: 1 492 667

NEPAL
PO Box 4574
Kathmandu
Tel: **1 415 193 / 389 / 391**
Fax: 1 410 422

THE NETHERLANDS
PO Box 30820
250 GV
The Hague
Tel: **70 361 4111**
Fax: 70 356 1111

NEW ZEALAND
PO Box 12-049
Thorndon
Wellington
Tel: **4 473 9577**
Fax: 4 471 2082

NICARAGUA
PO Box 514
Managua
Tel: **2 28 75 74 / 2 28 13 04**
Fax: 2 28 48 21

NIGER
PO Box 362
Niamey
Tel: **75 36 86 / 7**
Fax: 75 31 07

NIGERIA
PO Box 54506
Ikoyi Station
Lagos
Tel: **1 262 2512 / 262 2513**
Fax: 1 262 2517

NORWAY
Oscar's Gate 20
0244 Oslo
Tel: **22 46 69 55**
Fax: 22 69 34 67

PAKISTAN
GPO Box 1042
Islamabad
Tel: **51 21 11 01 / 21 11 07**
Fax: 51 21 15 40

PANAMA
PO Box 3658
Balboa
Tel: **64 70 14**
Fax: 23 54 70

PARAGUAY
PO Box 883
Asunción
Tel: **21 22 95 05 / 49 17 30**
Fax: 44 95 06

PERU
Calle Libertad 130
Miraflores
Lima
Tel: **444 4015 / 444 4688**
Fax: 444 4347

PHILIPPINES (THE)
9th & 11th Floors
Allied Bank Centre
6754 Ayala Avenue
Makati
Metro Manilla
Tel: **2 810 8861**
Fax: 2 810 8839

POLAND
Ulica Matejki 1/5
00-481 Warsaw
Tel: **22 29 80 51 / 29 80 54**
Fax: 22 29 64 57

PORTUGAL
Avenida da Liberdade 144/56
Piso 4
P-1200 Lisbon
Tel: **1 347 4892**
Fax: 1 347 6466

PUERTO RICO
Dealt with by Canadian
Consulate in Atlanta at:
One CNN Centre
South Tower
Suite 400
Atlanta
Georgia 30303-2705
Tel: **404 577 6810 / 577 6812**
Fax: 404 524 5046

QUATAR
See **Kuwait**

ROMANIA
36 Nicolae Iorga
71118 Bucharest
Tel: **1 222 9845**
Fax: 1 312 0366

RUSSIA
23 Starokonyushenny Perelok
Moscow
Tel: **095 956 6666**
Fax: 095 241 9043

RWANDA
Parcel 1534
Akagera Street
Kigali
Tel: **73210 / 73278 / 73787**
Fax: 72719

SAUDI ARABIA
PO Box 94321
Riyadh 11693
Tel: **1 488 2288**
Fax: 1 488 1997

SENEGAL
45 Avenue de la République
Dakar
Tel: 23 92 90
Fax: **23 87 49**

SINGAPORE
IBM Towers
14th and 15th Floors
80 Anson Road
Singapore 0207
Tel: **225 63663**
Fax: 225 2450

SLOVAKIA
c/o Blaha & Erben & Novak
& Werner
Advokatska Kancelaria
Stefanikova 47
811 04 Bratislava
Tel: **7 3610 220**
Fax: 7 36 1220

SOUTH AFRICA
PO Box 26006
Arcadia 0007

Tel: **12 342 6923**
Fax: 12 342 3837

SPAIN
Calle Nunez de Balboa 35
Edificio Goya
E-28001 Madrid
Tel: **431 4300**
Fax: 431 2367

SWEDEN
Tegelbacken 4
PO Box 16129
S-10323 Stockholm
Tel: **8 453 3000**
Fax: 8 24 24 91

SWITZERLAND
Kirchenfeldstr 88
CH-3005 Bern
Tel: **31-446381**
Fax: 31-447315

SYRIA
PO Box 3394
Damascus
Tel: **11 2236 851 / 2236 892**
Fax: 11 2228 034

TAIWAN
Canadian Trade Office
13th Floor
365 Fu Husing North Road
Taipei
Tel: **2 713 7268**
Fax 2 712 7244

TANZANIA
38 Mirabo Street
Dar-es-Salaam
Tel: **514 6000 / 1/2/3/4**
Fax: 514 6005/9/7

THAILAND
Boonmitr Building
11th Floor
138 Silom Road
Bangkok 10500
Tel: **2 237 4125**
Fax: 2 236 6463

TRINIDAD & TOBAGO
Huggins Building
72 South Quay
Port of Spain
Tel: **809 623 7254**
Fax: 809 624 4016

TUNISIA
3 Rue du Sénégal
Place d'Afrique
Tunis
Tel: **1 798 004 / 796 577**
Fax: 1 792 371

TURKEY
Nenehatun Caddesi No. 75
Gaziosmanpasa 06700
Ankara
Tel: **312 436 1275**
Fax: 312 446 4437

TURKMENISTAN
See **Kazakhstan**

UKRAINE
31 Yaroslaviv Val Street
Kiev 252034
Tel: **044 212 2112 / 212 0212**
Fax: 044 225 1305 / 212 2339

UNITED KINGDOM
MacDonald House
1 Grosvenor Square
London W1X 0AB
Tel: **0171 258 6600**
Fax: 0171 258 6533

UNITED STATES
501 Pennsylvania Avenue
North West
Washington
DC 20001
Tel: **202 682 1740**
Fax: 202 682 7726

VENEZUELA
Edificio Torre Europa
7th Floor
Av. Francisco de Miranda
Caracas
Tel: **2 951 6166**
Fax: 2 951 4950

VIETNAM
31 Hong Vuong Street
Hanoi
Tel: **4 23 55 00**
Fax: 4 23 53 33

YUGOSLAVIA(FRSM)
Kneza Milosa 75
11000 Belgrade
Tel: **11 64 46 66**
Fax: 11 64 14 80

ZAMBIA
5199 United Nations Avenue
Lusaka
Tel: **1 25 08 33**
Fax: 1 25 41 76

ZIMBABWE
45 Baines Avenue
Harare
Tel: **4 73 38 81**
Fax: 4 73 29 17

UK Reps. Abroad

ALBANIA
Rrugo Vso Pasha 7/1
1st Floor
Tirana
Tel: 42 34973
Fax: 42 34975

ALGERIA
Residence Cassiopée
Batiment B
7 Chemin des Glycines
16000 Alger-Gare
Algiers
Tel: 2 622 411
Fax: 2 692 410

ANGOLA
PO Box 1244
Rua Diogo Cão 4
Luanda
Tel: 2 392 991 / 334 582/3
Fax: 2 333 331

ANTIGUA AND BARBUDA
Box 483
11 Old Parnham Road
St. Johns
Antigua
Tel: 462 0008/9
Fax: 462 2806

ARGENTINA
Dr. Luis Agote 2412/52
Casilla de Correo
1425 Buenos Aires
Tel: 1 803 7070/71
Fax: 1 803 1731

ARMENIA
28 Charents Street
Yerevan
Tel: 2 151 842
Fax: 2 151 807

AUSTRALIA
Commonwealth Avenue
Yarralumla
Canberra ACT 2600
Tel: 6 270 6666
Fax: 6 273 3236

AUSTRIA
Jaurèsgasse 12
A-1030 Vienna
Tel: 1 713 1575
Fax: 1 715 7824

AZERBAIJAN
2 Ismir Street
370065 Baku
Tel: 12 985 558
Fax: 12 922 739

BAHAMAS
PO Box N-7516
3rd Floor, Bitco Building
East Stret
Nassau
Tel: 325 7471/2/3/4
Fax: 323 3871

BAHRAIN
PO Box 114
21 Government Avenue
Manama
306 Bahrain
Tel: 534404
Fax: 531273

BANGLADESH
PO Box 6079
United Nations Road
Baridhara
Dhaka 1212
Tel: 2 882 705
Fax: 2 883 437

BARBADOS
Lower Collymore Rock
PO Box 676
St Michael
Tel: 436 6694
Fax: 436 5398/426 7916

BELARUS
Karl Marx 37
220030 Minsk
Tel: 172 292 303
Fax: 172 292 306

BELGIUM
85 Rue d'Arlon
1040 Brussels
Tel: 2 287 6211
Fax 2 287 6360

BELIZE
PO Box 91
Embassy Square
Belmopan
Tel: 8 22146/7
Fax: 8 22761

BENIN
See **Nigeria**

BOLIVIA
Avenida Arce 2732
Casilla 694
La Paz
Tel: 2 357 424
Fax: 2 391 063

BOSNIA-HERZEGOVINA
8 Tine Ujavica
71000 Sarajevo
Tel: 71 444 429
Fax: 71 666 131

BOTSWANA
Private Bag 0023
Gabarone
Tel: 352 841/2/3
Fax: 356 105

BRAZIL
Setor de Embaixadas Sul
Quadra 801, Loto 8
Conjunto K
70408 900 Brasilia
Tel: 61 225 2710/223 5357
Fax: 61 225 1777

BRUNEI
PO Box 2197
3rd Floor Hong Kong and
Shanghai Bank Chambers
Jalan Pemancha
Bandar Seri
Begawan 2085
Tel: 2 222 231/226 001
Fax: 2 226 002

BULGARIA
38 Vassili Levski Boulevard
Sofia 1000
Tel: 2 988 5361
Fax 2 988 5362

BURKINA FASO
01 BP 2581
Abidjan 01
Côte d'Ivoire
Tel: 225 226 850
Fax: 225 223 221

CAMBODIA
29 Street 75
Phnom Penh
Tel: 23 42 71 24
Fax: 32 42 71 25

CAMEROON
Avenue Winston Churchill
BP 547 Yaoundé
Tel: 220 545/200796
Fax: 220 148

CANADA
80 Elgin Street
Ottawa KIP 5K7
Tel: 613 237 1530
Fax: 613 237 7980

CHILE
Cassila 72D
Av. el Bosque Norte 0125
Santiago 9
Tel: 2 231 3737
Fax: 2 231 9771

CHINA
11 Guang Hua Lu
Jian Guo Men Wai
Bejing 100600

Tel: **6 6532 1961/5**
Telex: 6 6532 1937

COLUMBIA
Apdo Aéro 4508
Torre Propaganda Sancho
Calle 98
No 9-03, Piso 4
Santa Fé de Bogota
Tel: **1 218 5111**
Fax: 1 218 2460

CONGO
See **Zaïre**

COSTA RICA
Apartado 815, 11th Floor
Edificio Centro Colón
1007 San José
Tel: **221 5566**
Fax: 233 9938

CÔTE D'IVOIRE
01 BP 2581, 3rd Floor
Immeuble 'Les Harmonies'
Angle blvd Carde et ave Dr
Jamot
Plateau
Abidjan
Tel: **226 850/1/2 / 328 209**
Fax: 223 221

CROATIA
Valaska 121
10000 Zagreb
Tel: **1 455 5310**
Fax: 1 455 1685

CUBA
Calle 34
7th Avenue
Miramar
Havana
Tel: **7 331 771**
Fax: 7 338 104

CYPRUS
PO Box1978
Alexander Pallis Street
Nicosia
Tel: 2 **473 131/7**
Fax: 2 367 198

CZECH REPUBLIC
Thunovská 14
CS-11800 Prague 1
Tel: 2 **24 51 04 39**
Fax: 2 24 51 13 14

DENMARK
36-40 Kastelsvej
DK-2100 Copenhagen Ø
Tel: **35 26 46 00**
Fax: 31 38 10 12

DOMINICAN REPUBLIC
Edificio Corominas Pepin
Av. 27 de Febrero 233
Santo Domingo
Tel: **472 7111**
Fax: 472 7574

ECUADOR
Casilla 314
Calle González Suárez 111
Quito
Tel: **2 560 669/670/1**
Fax: 2 560 730

EGYPT
7 Sharia Ahmed Ragheb
Garden City
Cairo
Tel: **2 354 0850**
Fax: 2 354 0859

EL SALVADOR
PO Box 1591
4828 Paeso General Escalón
San Salvador
Tel: **298 1763**
Fax: 298 3328

ERITREA
British Consulate
PO Box 5584
Asmara
Tel: **4 120 145**
Fax: 4 120 104

ESTONIA
Kentmanni 20
0001 Tallinn
Tel: **313 353/313 461/2**
Fax: 313 354

ETHIOPIA
PO Box 858
Fikre Mariam Abatechan
Street
Addis Ababa
Tel: **1 612 354**
Fax: 1 610 588

FIJI
Victoria House
47 Gladstone Road
Suva
Tel: **311033**
Fax: 301406

FINLAND
Itänien Puistotie 17
00140 Helsinki
Tel: **9 22 86 51 00**
Fax: 9 22 86 52 62

FRANCE
35 Rue du Faubourg St
Honoré
75383 Paris

Cedex 08
Tel: **1 44 51 31 00**
Fax: 1 44 51 32 34

GAMBON
See Cameroon

GAMBIA
48 Atlantic Road
Fajara
Banjul
Tel: **495 133/4**
Fax: 496 134

GEORGIA
Metekhi Palace Hotel
380003 Tbilisi
Tel: **32 955 497**

GERMANY
Friedrich-Elert-Allée 77
53113 Bonn
Tel: **228 91670**
Fax: 228 916 7331/916 7200

GHANA
PO Box 296
Osu Link
Off Gamel Abdul Nasser Av.
Accra
Tel: **21 221 665/669 585**
Fax: 21 664 652

GREECE
Odos Ploutarchou 1
106 75 Athens
Tel: 1 **723 6211**
Fax: 1 724 1872

GRENADA
14 Church Street
St George's
Grenada
Tel: **440 3222, 440 3536**
Fax: 440 4939

GUADELOUPE
See Barbados

GUATEMALA
7th Floor, Edificio Centro
Financer
Tower 2
7a Av. 5-10
Zona 4
Guatemala City
Tel: **502 332 601/2/4**
Fax: 502 3341904

GUYANA
44 Main Street
Georgetown
Tel: 2 **65881/4**
Fax: 2 53555/50671

HONDURAS
Apartado Postal 290
Edificio Palmira, 3rd Floor
Colonia Palmira
Tegucigalpa
Tel: **325 429/320 612/8**
Fax: 325 480

HONG KONG
9th Floor
Bank of America Tower
12 Harcourt Road
Hong Kong
Tel: **5230176**
Fax: 854 2870

HUNGARY
Harmincad Utca 6
H-1051 Budapest
Tel: **1 266 2888/266 1430**
Fax: 1 266 0907

ICELAND
Laufásvegur 49
121 Reykjavik
Tel: **511 5883/4**
Fax: 552 7940

INDIA
Shanti Path
Chanakyapuri
New Delhi 110021
Tel: 11 **687 2161**
Fax: 11 687 2882

INDONESIA
Jalan M H Thamrin 75
Jakarta 10310
Tel: **21 330904**
Fax: 21 321824

IRAN
PO Box 11365-4474
143 Ferdowsi Avenue
Tehran 11344
Tel: 21 **675 011**
Fax: 21 678 021

IRAQ
See **Jordan**

IRELAND
33 Merrion Road
Dublin 4
Tel: 1 205 3700
Fax: 1 205 3885

ISRAEL
192 Rechov Hayarkon
Tel Aviv 63405
Tel: 3 524 9171/8
Fax: 3 524 3313

ITALY
Via XX Settembre 80A
1-00187 Rome

Tel: **6 482 5551**
Fax: 6 487 3324

JAMAICA
28 Trafalgar Road
Kingston 10
Tel: **926 9050**
Fax: 929 7869

JAPAN
No 1 Ichiban-cho
Chiyoda-ku
Tokyo 102
Tel: 3 **32 65 55 11**
Fax: 3 52 75 31 64

JORDAN
PO Box 87
Abdoun
Amman
Tel: **6 823 100**
Fax: 6 813759

KAZAKHSTAN
173 Furmanov Street
Almaty 480110
Tel: **3272 506 192**
Fax: 3272 506 260

KENYA
PO Box 30465
Bruce House
Standard Street
Nairobi
Tel: **2 335 944**
Fax: 2 333 196

KOREA
4 Chung-dong
Chung-ku
Seoul 100
Tel: 2 735 7341/3
Fax: 2 733 8368

KUWAIT
Arabian Gulf Street
PO Box 2
13001 Safat
Tel: **240 3334/5/6**
Fax: 240 7395

LAOS
See **Thailand**

LATVIA
Alunana iela 5
LV-1510
Riga
Tel: **733 8126**
Fax: 733 8132

LEBANON
Rabieh, Rue 8
Beirut
Tel: **1 405 070/403 640**
Fax: 1 402 032

LESOTHO
PO Box 521
Maseru 100
Tel: **313 961**
Fax: 310 120

LIBERIA
See **Côte d'Ivoire**

LIBYA
C/o Italian Embassy
PO Box 4206
Sharia Uahran 1
Tripoli
Tel: 21 333 1191

MALAWI
PO Box 30042
Lingadzi House
Lilongwe 3
Tel: **782 400**
Telex: 782 657

MALAYSIA
185 Jalan Ampang
PO Box 11030
50732
Kuala Lumpur
Tel: 3 **248 2122/7122**
Fax: 3 244 7766/9692

MALTA
PO Box 506
7 St Anne Street
Floriana
Valletta VLT 15
Tel: **233 134**
Fax: 242 001

MAURITANIA
See **Morocco**

MAURITIUS
Les Cascades Building
Edith Cavel Street
Port Louis
Mauritius
Tel: **211 1361**
Fax: 211 1369

MEXICO
Rio Lerma 71
Col Cuauhtémoc
06500 Mexico City
Tel: **5 207 2089**
Fax: 5 207 7672

MONGOLIA
PO Box 703
30 Enkh Taivny Gudamzh
Ulan Bator 13
Tel: **1 358 133**
Fax: 1 358 036

MOROCCO
17 Boulevard de la Tour
Hassan

Rabat
Tel: **7 720 905/6 / 731 403/4**
Fax: 7 704 531

MOZAMBIQUE
CP55 Avenida Vladimir I
Lénine 310
Maputo
Tel: **1 420 111/2/5/6/7**
Fax: 1 421 666

MYANMAR
PO Box 638
80 Strand Road
Yangon
Tel: **1 295 300**
Fax: 1 289 566

NAMIBIA
PO Box 22202
116 Robert Mugabe Avenue
Windhoek
Tel: **61 223 022**
Fax: 61 228 895

NEPAL
PO Box 106
Lainchaur
Kathmandu
Tel: **1 410 583**
Fax: 1 411 789

NETHERLANDS
Lange Voorhout 10
2514 ED
The Hague
Tel: **70 364 5800 / 427 0427**
Fax: 70 427 0345

NEW ZEALAND
PO Box 1812
44 Hill Street
Wellington 1
Tel: **4 472 6049**
Fax: 4 473 4982

NICARAGUA
Apartado A-169
El Reparto 'Los Robles'
Primera Etapa
Entrada principal de la
Carretera a Masaya
4a Casa da Mano Derecha
Managua
Tel: **2 780 014/780 887/674 050**
Fax: 2 784 085

NIGERIA
11 Eleke Crescent
Victoria Island
Lagos
Tel: **1 261 9531**
Fax: 1 261 4021

NORWAY
Thomas Heftyesgate 8
0244 Oslo
Tel: 22 **552 400**
Fax: 22 551 041

OMAN
PO Box 300
113 Muscat
Tel: 693 077
Fax: 693 087

PAKISTAN
PO Box 1122
Diplomatic Enclave
Ramna 5
Islamabad
Tel: **51 822 131/5**
Fax: 823439

PANAMA
Apartado 889
4th Floor
Torre Banco Suizo
Calle 51
Marbella
Panamá 1
Tel: **269 0866**
Fax: 223 0730

PAPUA NEW GUINEA
PO Box 212
Kiroki Street
Waigani
Tel: **202 745 3680**
Fax: 202 745 3679

PARAGUAY
Casilla 404
Calle Presidente Franco 706
Asunción
Tel: **21 444 472 / 449 146**
Fax: 21 446 385

PERU
PO Box 854
Natalio Sanchez 125
Plaza Washington
Lima 1
Tel: **1 433 4783**
Fax: 1 433 4735

PHILIPPINES
LV Locsin Building
6752 Ayala Avenue
Makati
Metro Manila 1226
Tel: 2 **816 7116 / 816 7348/9**
Fax: 2 819 7206

POLAND
Aleja Róz No 1
PL 00-556
Warsaw
Tel: **22 628 1001/2/3/4/5**
Fax: 22 621 7161

PORTUGAL
33 Rua de São Bernado
1200 Lisbon
Tel: **1 392 4000/4160**
Fax: 1 392 4185

QATAR
PO Box 3
Doha
Tel: **421 991**
Fax: 438 692

ROMANIA
24 Strada Jule Michelet
70154 Bucharest
Tel: **1 312 0303/7**
Fax: 1 312 0229

RUSSIA
Sofiskaya Naberezhnaya 14
Moscow 72
Tel: **095 956 7200**
Fax: 095 956 7420 / 956 7440

RWANDA
BP 576
Parcelle 1071
Kimihurura
Kigali
Tel: **84098 / 85771 / 85773**
Fax: 82044

SAINT LUCIA
PO Box 227
Derek Walcott Square
Castries
Tel: **452 2484**
Fax: 453 1543

SAINT VINCENT
PO Box 132
Kingstown
Tel: **457 1701/2**
Fax: 456 2750

SAUDI ARABIA
PO Box 94351
Riyadh 11693
Tel: **1 488 0077**
Fax: 1 488 2373

SENEGAL
BP 6025
20 Rue du Docteur Guillet
Dakar
Tel: **237 392**
Fax: 232 766

SEYCHELLES
PO Box 161
Victoria House
3rd Floor
Victoria
Mahé
Tel: **225 225 / 225 356**
Fax: 225 127

SIERRA LEONE
6 Spur Road
Wilberforce
Freetown
Tel: **22 223 961/5**
Fax: 22 228 169

SINGAPORE
Tanglin Road
Singapore 247919
Tel: **473 9333**
Fax: 475 9706

SLOVAK REPUBLIC
35 Grösslingova
81109 Bratislava
Tel: **7 364 420**
Fax: 7 3364 396

SLOVENIA
4th Floor
Trg Republike 3
1000 Ljubiana
Tel: **61 125 7191**
Fax: 61 125 0174

SOLOMON ISLANDS
PO Box 676
Telekom House|
Mendana Avenue
Honiara
Tel: **21705/6**
Fax: 21549

SOMALIA
PO Box 1036
Hassan Geedi Abtow 7/8
Mogadishu
Tel: **1 202 88/9**
Telex: 3617

SOUTH AFRICA
255 Hill Street
Arcadia
Pretoria
Tel: **12 433 121**
Fax:12 433 207

SPAIN
Calle de Fernando el Santo 16
28004 Madrid
Tel: **1 319 0200**
Fax: 1 319 0423

SRI LANKA
PO Box 1433
190 Galle Road
Kollupitiya
Colombo 3
Tel: **1 437 336**
Fax: 1 430 308

SUDAN
PO Box 801
Off Sharia Al Baladiya
Khartoum East

Tel: **11 770 769 / 780 856**
Telex: 22189

SWAZILAND
Allister Miller Street
Mbabane
Tel: **42581**
Fax: 42585

SWEDEN
Skarpogatan 6-8
115 27 Stockholm
Tel: **8 671 9000**
Fax: 8 662 9989

SWITZERLAND
Thunstrasse 50
3005 Berne 15
Tel: **31 352 5021/6**
Fax: 31 352 0583

SYRIA
PO Box 37
Quater Malki
11 rue Mohammad Kurd Ali
Immeuble Kotob
Damascus
Tel: **11 3712 561/2/3**
Fax: 11 373 1600

TAJIKISTAN
See Uzbekistan

TANZANIA
PO Box 9200
Hifadhi House
Samora Avenue
Dar es Salaam
Tel: **51 117 660**
Fax: 51 112 951

THAILAND
1031 Ploechit Road
Bangkok 10330
Tel: **2 253 0191/9**
Fax: 2 255 8619

TONGA
PO Box 56
Vuna Raod
Nuku'alofa
Tel: **21020/1**
Fax: 24109

TRINIDAD AND TOBAGO
PO Box 778
19 St. Clair Avenue
St. Clair
Port of Spain
Tel: **622 2748**
Fax: 622 4555

TUNISIA
5 Place de la Victoire
Tunis
Tel: **1 431 444**
Fax: 1 354 877

TURKEY
Sehit Ersan Caddesi 46/A
Cankaya
Ankara
Tel: **312 468 6230**
Fax: 312 468 3214

UGANDA
10/12 Parliament Avenue
PO Box 7070
Kampala
Tel: **41 257 054/9**
Fax: 41 257 304

UKRAINE
vul. Desyatinna 9
252025 Kiev
Tel: **44 462 0011/2**
Fax: 44 462 0013

**UNITED ARAB EMI-
RATES**
PO Box 248
Abu Dhabi
Tel: **2 326 600 / 321 364**
Fax: 2 341 774

UNITED STATES
3100 Massachusetts Avenue
NW Washington DC 20008
Tel: 202 **462 1340**
Fax: 202 588 7850 / 7892

URAGUAY
PO Box 16024
Calle Marco Bruto 1073
11300 Montevideo
Tel: **2 623 630**
Fax: 2 627 815

UZBEKISTAN
67 Gogolya Street
Tashkent
Tel: **3712 345 652 / 406 288**
Fax: 873 406 549

VENEZUELA
Apartado 1246
Edificio Torre Las Mercedes
3rd Floor
Avenida la Estancia
Chuao
Caracas 1060
Tel: **2 993 4111**
Fax: 2 993 9989

VIETNAM
16 Pho Ly Thuong Kiet
Hanoi
Tel: **4 825 2349**
Fax: 4 826 5762

YEMEN
PO Box 1287
129 Haddah Road
Sana'a

Tel: **1 264 081**
Fax: 1 263 059

**THE FORMER REPUB-
LIC OF YUGOSLAVIA
(SERBIA AND MON-
TENEGRO)**
Generala Zdanova 46
11000 Belgrade
Tel: **11 235 1434 / 235 1465**
Fax: 11 659 651

ZAÏRE (DRC)
BP 8049
Av. des 3Z
Kinshasa-1
Tel: **12 33775 / 33130 / 33453**

ZAMBIA
PO Box 50050
Independence Avenue
Ridgeway
Lusaka
Tel: **1 251 133**
Fax: 1 253 798

ZIMBABWE
PO Box 4490
Corner House
Samara Machel
Avenue/Leopold Takawira
Street
Harare
Tel: **4 793 781**
Fax: 4 728 380

USA Reps. Abroad

AFGHANISTAN
Embassy currently closed, see
Pakistan.

ALBANIA
PO Box 100
Rruga Labinoti 103
Tirana
Tel: **42 32875 / 33520**
Fax: 42 32222

ALGERIA
4 Chemin Cheikh Bachir El
Ibrahimi
Algiers
Tel: **2 691255/186/854**
Fax: 2 693979

ANGOLA
Caixa Postal 6484
32 Rua Houari Boumedienne
Luanda
Tel: **2 346 418 / 345 481**
Fax: 2 396 924

ARGENTINA
Unit 4334
4300 Colombia
1425 Buenos Aires
Tel: **1 774 7611/777 4533/4**
Fax: 1 775 4205 / 777 0197

ARMENIA
18 Marshall Baghramian
Street
Yerevan 375019
Tel: **2 151 144/551**
Fax: 2 151 550

AUSTRALIA
Moonah Place
Canberra ACT 2600
Tel: **6 270 5000**
Fax: 6 270 5970

AUSTRIA
Boltzmanngasse 16
A-1090
Vienna
Tel: **1 31339**
Fax: 1 310 0682

AZERBAIJAN
Prospect Azadlyg 83
Baku
Tel: **12 980 335/6/7**
Fax: 12 983 755

BAHAMAS
Mosmar Building
Queen Street
Nassau
(PO Box N-8197)
Tel: **322 1181**
Fax: 328-7838

BAHRAIN
Building No. 979
Road No. 3119
Block/Area 331
Zinj
Manama
(PO Box 26431)
Tel: **273 300**
Fax: 272 594

BANGLADESH
PO Box 323
Diplomatic Enclave
Madani Avenue
Baridhara Model Town
Dhaka 1212
Tel: **2 884 700**
Fax: 2 883 744

BARBADOS
PO Box 302
Canadian Imperial Bank of
Commerce Building
Broad Street
Bridgetown

Tel: **436-4950**
Fax: 429-5246

BELARUS
Starlovilenskaya 46
220002
Minsk
Tel: **172 315 000**
Fax: 172 347 853

BELGIUM
27 Boulevard du Regent
B-1000 Brussels
Tel: **2 508 2111**
Fax: 2 511 2725

BELIZE
PO Box 286
Gabourel Lane and Hutson
Street
Belize City
Tel: **2 77161**
Fax: 2 35321

BENIN
BP 2012
Rue Caporal Anani Bernard
Cotonou
Tel: **301 792**
Fax: 301 974

BERMUDA
PO Box HM 325
16 Middle Road
Devonshire DX 03
Hamilton
Tel: **441 295 1342**
Fax: 441 295 1592

BOLIVIA
Avenida Arce 2780
Casilla 425
La Paz
Tel: **2 430 251**
Fax: 2 433 900

BOSNIA-HERZEGOVINA
Ali Pashina 43
Sarajevo
Tel: **71 659 743 / 445 700**
Fax: 71 659 722

BOTSWANA
PO Box 90
Gaborone
Tel: **353 982**
Fax: 356 947

BRAZIL
Avenida das Nações
Lote 3, Unit 3500
70403-900 Brasilia
Tel: **61 321 7272**
Fax: 61 225 9136

BRUNEI
3rd Floor Teck Guan Plaza
Jalan Sultan
Bandar Seri Begawan 2085
Tel: **2 229 670**
Fax: 2 225 293

BULGARIA
Boulevard A Stamboliski 1
Sofia
Tel: 2 **884 801**
Fax: 2 801 977

BURKINA FASO
01 BP 35
rue Raoul Folereau
Ougadougou 01
Tel: **306 723/5 / 312 660/707**
Fax: 312 368

BURUNDI
BP 1720
Ave des Etats-Unis
Bujumbura
Tel: **2 23454**
Fax: 2 22926

CAMBODIA
27 EO Street 240
Phnom Phen
Tel: **23 426436/8**
Fax: 23 426437

CAMEROON
BP 817
Rue Nachtigal
Yaoundé
Tel: **234 014**
Fax: 230 753

CANADA
100 Wellington Street
Ottawa ON K1P 5TI
Tel: **613 238 5335**
Fax: 613 238 8750

CAPE VERDE
CP 201
Rua Abilio Macedo 81
Praia
São Tiago
Tel: **615 616**
Fax: 611 355

CENTRAL AFRICAN REPUBLIC
BP 924
Avenue David Dacko
Bangui
Tel: **610 200**
Fax: 614 494

CHAD
BP 413 Avenue Félix Eboué
N'Djaména

Tel: **519 233**
Fax: 515 654 / 523 372

CHILE
Avenida Andrés Bello 2800
Las Condes
Santiago
Tel: **2 232 2600**
Fax: 2 330 3710

CHINA
Xiu Shui Bei Jie 3
Beijing 100600
Tel: **6 6532 3831**
Fax: 6 6532 3178

COLOMBIA
Apdo Aéreo 3831
Calle 22D-bis
No 47-51
Santa Fe de Bogotá
Tel: **1 315 0811**
Fax: 1 315 2197

CONGO
BP 1015
Avenue Amílcar Cabral
Brazzaville
Tel: **81 832 070**
Fax: 81 836 338

COSTA RICA
PO Box 920-1200
Pavas
San José
Tel: **220 3939**
Fax: 220 2305

CÔTE D'IVOIRE
01 BP 1712
5 Rue Jesse Owens
Abidjan
Tel: **210 979**
Fax: 223 259

CROATIA
Andrije Herbranga 2
10000 Zagreb
Tel: **1 455 5500**
Fax: 1 455 8585

CUBA
US Interests Section
Swiss Embassy
Calzada entre Calle L y M
Vedado
Havana
Tel: **7 333 967**
Fax: 7 333 869

CYPRUS
PO Box 4536
Metochiou and Ploutarchou
Street
Engomi
Nicosia

Tel: **2 476 100**
Fax: 2 465 944

CZECH REPUBLIC
Trziste15
11801 Prague 1
Tel: **2 24 51 08 47**
Fax: 2 24 51 10 01

DENMARK
Dag Hammarskjølds Allé 24
2100 Copenhagen Ø
Tel: **31 42 31 44**
Fax: 35 43 02 23

DJIBOUTI
BP 185
Villa Plateau du Serpent
Boulevard Maréchal Joffre
Djibouti
Tel: **353 995**
Fax: 353 940

DOMINICAN REPUBLIC
Unit 5500
Calle César Nicholás Pensón
& Calle Leopoldo Navarro
Santo Domingo, DN
Tel: **541 8000**
Fax: 686 7437

ECUADOR
Avenida 12 Octobre y Patria
120
Quito
Tel: **2 562 890 / 561 749**
Fax: 2 502 052

EGYPT
North Gate 8
Sharia Kamal ed-Din
Garden City
Cairo
Tel: **2 355 7371**
Fax: 2 357 3200

EL SALVADOR
Santa Elena Sur Blvd
Antiguo Cuscatlán
San Salvador
Tel: **278 4444**
Fax: 278 6011

EQUATORIAL GUINEA
See **Cameroon**

ERITREA
PO Box 211
Asmara
Tel: **4 123 410**
Fax: 4 117 584

ESTONIA
Kentmanni 20
EE-0001 Tallinn
Tel: **6 312 021/4**
Fax: 6 312 025

ETHIOPIA
PO Box 1014
Entoto Street
Addis Ababa
Tel: **1 550 666**
Fax: 1 551 094

FIJI
PO Box 218
31 Loftus Street
Suva
Tel: **314 466**
Fax: 300 081

FINLAND
Itäinen Puistotie 14B
00140 Helsinki
Tel: **9 171 931**
Fax: 9 652 057

FRANCE
2 Avenue Gabriel
75008 Paris Cedex 08
Tel: **1 43 12 22 22**
Fax: 1 42 66 83 97

GABON
BP 4000
Boulevard de la Mer
Libreville
Tel: **762 003/4 / 743 492**
Fax: 745 507

THE GAMBIA
PO Box 19
Kairaba Avenue
Fajara
Banjul
Tel: **392 856/858**
Fax: 392 475

GEORGIA
25 Ulitsa Atoneli
380026 Tblissi
Tel: 32 989 967
Fax: 32 933 759

GERMANY
Deichmanns Aue 29
53170 Bonn
Tel: **288 3391**
Fax: 288 339 2663

GHANA
Ring Road East
PO Box 194
Accra
Tel: **21 775 347/8**
Fax: 21 776 008

GREECE
91 Leoforos Vasilissis
Sophias Blvd
106 60 Athens
Tel: **1 721 2951/8401**
Fax: 1 645 6282

GRENADA
PO Box 54
Point Salines
St. George's
Tel: **444 1173/8**
Fax: 444 4820

GUATEMALA
7-01 Avenida de la Reforma
Zona 10
Guatemala City
Tel: **502 331 1541**
Fax: 502 331 8885

GUINEA REPUBLIC
BP 603
2nd Blvd and 9th Avenue
Conakry
Tel: **441 520/3**
Fax: 441 522

GUINEA-BISSAU
Bairro de Penha
CP 297
Codex 1067
Bissau
Tel: **252 273/6**
Fax: 252 282

GUYANA
PO Box 10507
100 Young and Duke Streets
Kingston
Georgetown
Tel: **2 54900 / 579 6027**
Fax: 2 58497

HAITI
Harry Truman Boulevard 5
BP 1761
Port-au-Prince
Tel: **220 200 / 220 354**
Fax: 231641

HONDURAS
Avenido La Paz
Apdo 26-C
Tegucigalpa
Tel: **323 120**
Fax: 320 027

HONG KONG
26 Garden Road
Hong Kong
Tel: **25 23 90 11**
Fax: 28 45 15 98

HUNGARY
Unit 1320
Szabadság tér 12
1054 Budapest
Tel: **1 267 4400**
Fax: 1 269 9326 / 9337

ICELAND
PO Box 40
Laufásvegur 21
PSC 1003
101 Reykjavik
Tel: **562 9100**
Fax: 562 9139

INDIA
Shanti Path
Chanakyapuri
New Delhi 110021
Tel: **11 688 9033**
Fax: 11 687 2028

INDONESIA
5 Jalan Merdeka Selatan 5
Jakarta
Tel: **21 360 360**
Fax: 21 386 2259

IRAQ
C/o Polish Embassy
PO Box 2051
30 Zuqaq 13
Mahalla 931
Hay Babel
Baghdad
Tel: **1 719 0297**
Fax: 1 719 0227

IRELAND
42 Elgin Road
Ballsbridge
Dublin 4
Tel: **1 668 7122**
Fax: 1 294 2952

ISRAEL
71 Hayarkon Street
Tel Aviv 63903
Tel: **3 519 7575**
Fax: 3 517 3227

ITALY
Via Veneto 119/A
100187 Rome
Tel: **6 46741**
Fax: 6 488 2672

JAMAICA
Jamaica Mutual Life Center
2 Oxford Road
3rd Floor
Kingston 5
Tel: **929 4850/9**
Fax: 935 6019

JAPAN
1-10-5 Akasaka 1-chome
Minato-ku
Tokyo 107
Tel: **3 32 24 50 00**
Fax: 3 35 05 18 62

JORDAN
PO Box 354
Jabel
Amman 11118
Tel: **6 820 101**
Fax: 6 820 121

KAZAKHSTAN
99 Furmanova Street
Almaty 480012
Tel: **3272 633 639**
Fax: 3272 632 942

KENYA
PO Box 30137
Unit 64100
Moi/Haile Selassie Avenue
Nairobi
Tel: **2 334 141/7**
Fax: 2 340 838

REPUBLIC OF KOREA
Unit 15550
82 Sejong-Ro
Chongno-ku
Seoul 96205-0001
Tel: **2 397 4114**
Fax: 2 738 8845

KUWAIT
PO Box 77
Arabian Gulf Street
13001 SAFAT
Kuwait City
Tel: **242 4151**
Fax: 244 2855

KYRGYZSTAN
Erkindik Prospeckt 66
720002 Bishkek
Tel: **3312 222 920**
Fax: 3312 223 551

LAOS
BP 114
Rue Bartholonie
Vientiane
Tel: **21 212 581**
Fax: 21 212 584

LATVIA
Raina Bulvaris 7
LV-1510 Riga
Tel: **721 0005**
Fax: 728 0047

LEBANON
Aoucar
Beruit
Tel: **1 417 774/402 200 /403 300**
Fax: 1 407 112

LESOTHO
PO Box 333
Maseru 100

Tel: **312 666**
Fax: 310 116

LIBERIA
PO Box 10-0098
111 United Nations Drive
Mamba Point
Monrovia
Tel: **226 370**
Fax: 226 148

LITHUANIA
Akmenu 76
2600 Vilnius
Tel: **2 223 031 / 222 737**
Fax: 2 222 779

LUXEMBOURG
22 Blvd. Emmanuel Servais
L-2535
Luxembourg Ville
Tel: **460 123**
Fax: 461 401

MACEDONIA
Blvd. Ilinden bb
91000 Skopje
Tel: **91 116 180**
Fax: 91 117 103

MADAGASCAR
BP 620
Antsahvola
101 Antananarivo
Tel: **2 21257 / 20089 / 20718**
Fax: 2 34539

MALAWI
PO Box 30016
Area 40, Flat 18
Lilongwe 3
Tel: **783 166**
Fax: 780 471

MALAYSIA
PO Box 10035
376 Jalan Tun Razak
50400 Kuala Lumpur
Tel: **3 248 9011**
Fax: 3 243 5207

MALDIVES
See **Sri Lanka**

MALI
BP 34
Rue de Rochester NY et Rue
Mohamed VI
Bamako
Tel: **225 470**
Fax: 223 712

MALTA
PO Box 535
3rd Floor
Development House
St. Anne Street

Floriana
Valletta
Tel: **235 960**
Fax: 243 229

MARSHALL ISLANDS
PO Box 1379
Majuro 96960
Tel: **692 4011**
Fax: 692 4012

MAURITANIA
BP222
Nouakchott
Tel: **52660/3**
Fax: 51592

MAURITIUS
4th Floor
Rogers House
President J.F. Kennedy Av.
Port Louis
Tel: **208 2347**
Fax: 208 9534

MEXICO
Paseo de la Reforma 305
Colonia Cuauhtémoc
06500 Mexico DF
Tel: **5 211 0042**
Fax: 5 511 9980

MOLDOVA
103 Strada Alexi Mateevich
Chisinãu
Tel: **2 233 772 / 237 345**
Fax: 2 232 494

MONGOLIA
See **China**

MOROCCO
BP 003
2 Ave. de Marrakech
Rabat
Tel: **7 762 265**
Fax: 7 765 661

MOZAMBIQUE
BP783
Avenida Kenneth Kaunda 193
Maputo
Tel: **1 490 071 / 490 723**
Fax: 1 490 114

MYANMAR
PO Box 521
581 Merchant Street
Yangon
Tel: **1 282 055 / 282 181**
Fax: 1 280 409

NAMIBIA
Private Bag 12029
14 Lossen Street
Windhoek

Tel: **61 221 601**
Fax: 61 229 792

NEPAL
Pani Pokhari
Kathmandu
Tel: **1 411 179**
Fax: 1 419 963

NETHERLANDS
Lange Voorhout 102
2514 EJ, The Hague
Tel: **70 310 9209**
Fax: 70 361 4688

NEW ZEALAND
PO Box 1190
29 Fitzherbert Terrace
Thorndon
Wellington
Tel: 4 **472 2068**
Fax: 4 472 3537 / 471 2380

NICARAGUA
Apartado A-169
Km. 4.5 Carretera Sur.
Managua
Tel: 2 **666 010 / 015/8**
Fax: 2 666 046

NIGER
BP 11201
Rue Des Ambassades
Niamey
Tel: **722 661/2/3/4**
Fax: 733 167

NIGERIA
PO Box 554
2 Eleke Crescent
Victoria Island
Lagos
Tel: 1 **261 0097/0050**
Fax: 1 261 0257

NORWAY
Drammensveien 18
0244 Oslo 2
Tel: **22 448 550**
Fax: 22 430 777

OMAN
PO Box 202
Madinat Qaboos
115 Muscat
Tel: **698 989**
Fax: 699 771

PAKISTAN
PO Box 1048, Unit 62200
Diplomatic Enclave
Ramna 5
Islamabad
Tel: **51 826 161**
Fax: 51 821 193

PANAMA
Apartado 6959
Avenida Balboa
Entre Calle 37 y 38
Panamá 5
Rep. de Panama
Tel: **227 1777**
Fax: 227 1964

PAPUA NEW GUINEA
PO Box 1492
Douglas Street
Port Moresby
Tel: **321 1455**
Fax: 321 3423

PARAGUAY
Casilla Postal 402
1776 Mariscal López Avenue
Asunción
Tel: **21 213 715**
Fax: 21 213 728

PERU
PO Box 1995
Avenida Encalada cuadra 17
Lima 33
Tel: 1 **221 1202**
Fax: 1 221 3543

PHILIPPINES
1201 Roxas Blvd
Metro Manila
Tel: 2 **521 7116**
Fax: 2 522 4361

POLAND
Aleje Ujazdowskie 29/31
00-540 Warsaw
Tel: **22 628 3041**
Fax: 22 628 8298

PORTUGAL
Avenida das Forças Armadas
1600 Lisbon
Tel: 1 **727 3300**
Fax: 1 726 9109

QATAR
PO Box 2399
149 Ali Bin Ahmed Street
Farig Bin
Omran
Doha
Tel: **864 701/2/3**
Fax: 861 669

ROMANIA
Strada Tudor Arghezi 7-9
Sector 2
Bucharest
Tel: **613 789 5345**
Fax: 613 789 4365

RUSSIA
Novinskiy Bulvar 19/23
Moscow
Tel: **095 252 2451-9**
Fax: 095 956 4261

RWANDA
BP 28
Blvd. de la Révolution
Kigali
Tel: **75601-3**
Fax: 72128

ST. LUCIA
See **Barbados**

SAUDI ARABIA
PO Box 94309
Collector Road M
Riyadh Diplomatic Quarter
Tel: 1 **488 3800**
Fax: 1 488 3278

SENEGAL
BP 49
Avenue Jean XXII
Dakar
Tel: **234 296**
Fax: 222 991

SEYCHELLES
PO Box 251
Victoria House
Victoria
Mahé
Tel: **225 256**
Fax: 225 189

SIERRA LEONE
Corner of Walpole and Siaka
Stevens Streets
Freetown
Tel: **22 226 481/5 / 226 155**
Fax: 22 225 471

SINGAPORE
30 Hill Street
Singapore 179360
Tel: **338 0251**
Fax: 338 4550

SLOVAK REPUBLIC
4 Hviezdoslavovo námestie
811 02 Bratislava
Tel: **7 533 0861**
Fax: 7 361 085

SLOVENIA
Prazakova 4
1000 Ljubljana
Tel: **61 301 427/472/485**
Fax: 61 301 401

SOUTH AFRICA
PO Box 9536
877 Pretorius Street
Pretoria 0001 ⇨

Tel: **12 342 1048**
Fax: 12 342 2299

SPAIN
Serrano 75
28006 Madrid
Tel: 1 **587 2200 / 577 4000**
Fax: 1 587 2303

SRI LANKA
PO Box 106
210 Galle Road
Colombo 3
Tel: **1 448 007**
Fax: 1 437 345

SUDAN
PO Box 699
Khartoum
Tel: **11 774 700**
Fax: 11 774 137

SURINAME
PO Box 1821
Dr. Sophie Redmondstraat
129
Paramaribo
Tel: **472 900 / 476 459**
Fax: 410 025 / 410 972

SWAZILAND
PO Box 199
Central Bank Building
Warner Street
Mbabane
Tel: **46441**
Fax: 46446

SWEDEN
Strandvägen 101
115 89 Stockholm
Tel: **8 783 5300**
Fax: 8 661 1964

SWITZERLAND
Jubiläeumstrasse 93
3005 Bern
Tel: **31 357 7011**
Fax: 31 357 7344

SYRIA
PO Box 29
Abou Roumaneh
Rue al Mansur 2
Damascus
Tel: **11 333 0788 / 333 2814**
Fax: 11 224 7938

TAIWAN
Suite 7, Lane134
Hsin Yi Road
Sec 3
Taipei
Tel: **2 709 2000**
Fax: 2 702 7675

TAJIKISTAN
4th Floor
Octyabrskaya Hotel
Prospekt Rudaki 105a
Dushanbe 734001
Tel: **3772 210 356**
Fax: 3772 210 362

TANZANIA
PO Box 9123
36 Laibon Road
Dar Es Salaam
Tel: **51 666 010/5**
Fax: 51 666 701

THAILAND
95 Wireless Road
Bangkok 10330
Tel: **2 205 4000**
Fax: 2 205 2990

TOGO
BP 852
Rue Pelletier Caventou & Rue
Vauban
Lomé
Tel: **217 717 / 212 991-4**
Fax: 217 952

TRINIDAD & TOBAGO
PO Box 752
15 Queen's Park West
Port-of-Spain
Tel: **622 6371-6**
Fax: 628 5464

TUNISIA
144 Avenue de la Liberté
Belvédère
1002 Tunis
Tel: **1 782 566**
Fax: 1 789 719

TURKEY
PO Box 5000
110 Atatürk Buluvari
Kavaklidere
Ankara
Tel: **312 468 6110**
Fax: 312 467 0019 / 468 6131

TURKMENISTAN
Pushkin Street 9
Ashgabat 744000
Tel: **1 244 4994**
Fax: 1 251 1305

UGANDA
PO Box 7007
Kampala
Tel: **41 259 792/3/5**
Fax: 41 259 794

UKRAINE
vul. Yuri Kotsyubinsky 10
252053 Kyiv 53

Tel: **44 244 7344**
Fax: 44 244 7350

**UNITED ARAB
EMIRATES**
PO Box 4009
Al-Sudan Street
Abu Dhabi
Tel: **2 436 691**
Fax: 2 434 771

UNITED KINGDOM
24 Grosvenor Square
London W1 1AE
Tel: **0171 499 9000**
Fax: 0171 409 1637

URUGUAY
PO Box 464
Avadie Santos 808
Montevideo
Tel: **2 236 061 / 487 777**
Fax: 2 488 611

UZBEKISTAN
82 Chilanzarskaya Street
Tashkent 700115
Tel: **3712 771 407**
Fax: 3712 406 335

VENEZUELA
Suite F
Street Suapre
Colinas de Valle Arriba
Caracas
Tel: **2 977 2011**
Fax: 2 977 0843

VIETNAM
PO Box 400
7 Lang Ha Road
Ba Dinh District
Hanoi
Tel: **4 843 1500**
Fax: 4 835 0484

WESTERN SAMOA
PO Box 3430
5th Floor, Beach Road
Apia
Tel: **21631**
Fax: 22030

YEMEN
PO Box 2234
Dhahr Himyar Zone
Sheraton Hotel District
Sana'a
Tel: **1 238 843/853**
Fax: 1 251 563

**YUGOSLAVIA (SERBIA
& MONTENEGRO)**
Kneza Milosa 50
11000 Belgrade
Tel: 11 **645 655 / 646 481 /**

644 053
Fax: 11 645 221

ZAÏRE (DRC)
BP 697, Unit 31550
310 Avenue des Aviateurs
Kinshasa
Tel: **12 21532-5**
Fax: 88 43805

ZAMBIA
PO Box 31617
Corner Independence and
United Nations Avenues
Lusaka
Tel: **1 250 955 / 252 230**
Fax: 1 252 225

ZIMBABWE
PO Box 3340
172 Herbert Chitapo Avenue
Harare
Tel: **4 794 521**
Fax: 4 796 488

FOREIGN GOVERNMENT REPS. OVERSEAS

In Canada

ALGERIA
435 Daly Avenue
Ottowa K1N 6H3
Tel: **613 789 8505 / 232 5823**
Fax: 613 789 1406

ANTIGUA
Antigua Dept. of Tourism and
Trade
Suite 304
60 St. Clair Avenue East
Toronto
ON M4T 1N5
Tel: **416 961 3143**

ARGENTINA
90 Sparks Street
Suite 620
Ottawa
ON K1P 5B4
Tel: **613 236 2351/4**
Fax: 613 235 2659

AUSTRALIA
Suite 710
50 O'Connor Street
Ottawa

ON K1P 6L2
Tel: **613 236 0841**

AUSTRIA
445 Wilbrod Street
Ottawa
ON K1N 6M7
Tel: **613 789 1444**
Fax: 613 789 3413

BAHRAIN
1869 René Lévesque Blvd
West
Montréal
Québec H3H 1R4
Tel: **514 931 7444**
Fax: 514 931 5988

BANGLADESH
Suite 302
275 Bank Street
Ottawa
ON K2P 2L6
Tel: **613 236 0138/9**
Fax: 613 567 3213

BARBADOS
Suite 600
130 Albert Street
Ottawa
ON K1P 5G4
Tel: **613 236-9517/8**
Fax: 613 230 4362

BELGIUM
4th Floor, 80 Elgin Street
Ottawa
ON K1P 1B7
Tel: **613 236 7267**
Fax: 613 236 7882

BENIN
58 Glebe Avenue
Ottawa
ON K1S 2C3
Tel: **613 233 4429**
Fax: 613 233 8952

BOLIVIA
Suite 504
130 Albert Street
Ottawa
ON K1P 5G4
Tel: **613 236 5730**
Fax: 613 236 8237

BRAZIL
450 Wilbrod Street
Ottawa
ON K1N 6M8
Tel: **613 237 1090**
Fax: 613 237 6144

BULGARIA
325 Stewart Street
Ottawa

ON K1N 6K5
Tel: **613 789 3215**
Fax: 613 7893524

BURKINA FASO
48 Range Road
Ottawa
ON K1N 8J4
Tel: **613 238 4796**
Fax: 613 238 3812

BURUNDI
50 Kaymar Drive
Rothwell Heights
Gloucester
ON K1J 7C7
Tel: **613 741 8828**
Fax: 613 741 2424

CAMEROON
170 Clemow Avenue
Ottawa
ON K1S 2B4
Tel: **613 236 1522**
Fax: 613 236 3885

CENTRAL AFRICAN REPUBLIC
500 Place d'Armes
Suite 1703
Montréal
H2Y 2W2
Tel: **514 849 8381**
Fax: 514 849 8383

CHILE
151 Slater Street
Suite 605
Ottawa
ON K1P 5H3
Tel: **613 235 4402 / 235 9940**
Fax: 613 235 1176

CHINA
515 St. Patrick's Street
Ottawa
ON K1N 5H3
Tel: **613 789 3434 / 789 3511**
Fax: 613 789 1911

COLOMBIA
Suite 1002
360 Albert Street
Ottawa
ON K1R 7X7
Tel: **613 230 3760**
Fax: 613 230 4416

COSTA RICA
Suite 208, 135 York Street
Ottawa
ON K1N 5T4
Tel: **613 562 2855**
Fax: 613 562 2582

CÔTE d'IVOIRE
9 Marlborough Avenue
Ottawa
ON K1N 8E6
Tel: **613 236 9919**
Fax: 613 563 8287

CROATIA
Suite 1700, 130 Albert Street
Ottawa
ON K1P 5G4
Tel: **613 230 7351**
Fax: 613 230 7388

CUBA
388 Main Street
Ottawa
ON K1S 1E3
Tel: **613 563 0141**
Fax: 613 563 0068

CZECH REPUBLIC
541 Sussex Drive
Ottawa
ON K1N 6Z6
Tel: **613 562 3875**
Fax: 613 562 3878

DENMARK
Suite 450, 47 Clarence Street
Ottawa
ON K1N 9K1
Tel: **613 562 1811 / 562 1805**
Fax: 613 562 1812

DOMINICAN REPUBLIC
Suite 241, 1055 St Mathieu
Central Tower
Montréal
Québec H3H 2S3
Tel: **514 933 9008**
Fax: 514 933 2070

ECUADOR
Suite 1311, 50 O'Connor
Street
Ottawa
ON K1P 6L2
Tel: **613 563 8206**
Fax: 613 563 5776

EGYPT
454 Laurier Avenue East
Ottawa
ON K1N 6R3
Tel: **613 234 4931 / 4935**
Fax: 613 234 9347

EL SALVADOR
209 Kent Street
Ottawa
ON K2P 1Z8
Tel: **613 238 2939**
Fax: 613 238 6940

ETHIOPIA
Suite 210, 151 Slater Street
Ottawa
ON K1P 5H3
Tel: **613 235 6637**
Fax: 613 235 4638

FINLAND
Suite 850, 55 Metcalfe Street
Ottawa
ON K1P 6L5
Tel: **613 236 2389**
Fax: 613 238 1474

FRANCE
42 Sussex Drive
Ottawa
ON K1M 2C9
Tel: **613 789 1795**
Fax: 613 562 3704

GABON
BP 368
4 Range Road
Ottawa
ON K1N 8J3
Tel: **613 232 5301/2**
Fax: 613 232 6916

GAMBIA
Suite 300, 101 Yorkville
Avenue
Toronto
M5R 1C1
Tel: **416 923 2935**
Fax: 416 923 2526

GERMANY
PO Box 379, Postal Station A
1 Waverley Street
Ottawa
ON K2P 0H8
Tel: **613 232 1101-5**
Fax: 613 594 9330

GHANA
1 Clernow Avenue
Ottawa
ON K1S 2A9
Tel: **613 236 0871-3**
Fax: 613 236 0874

GREECE
76-80 MacLaren Street
Ottawa ON K2P 0K6
Tel: **613 238 6271**
Fax: 613 238 5676

GRENADA
Suite 920
439 University Avenue
Toronto
ON M5G 1Y8
Tel: **416 595 1343**
Fax: 416 595 8278

GUATEMALA
Suite 1010, 130 Albert Street
Ottawa
ON K1P 5G4
Tel: **613 233 7237**
Fax: 613 233 7188

GUINEA
483 Wilbrod Street
Ottawa
ON K1N 6N1
Tel: **613 789 8444**
Fax: 613 789 7560

GUYANA
151 Slater Street
Suite 309, Burnside Building
Ottawa
ON K1P 5H3
Tel: **613 235 7240**
Fax: 613 235 1447

HAITI
112 Rue Kent Street
Suite 205
Place de Ville
Tower B
Ottawa
ON K1P 5P2
Tel: **613 238 1628/9**
Fax: 613 238 2986

HONDURAS
Suite 908
151 Slater Street
Ottawa
ON K1P 5H3
Tel: **613 233 8900**
Fax: 613 232 0193

HUNGARY
299 Waverley Street
Ottawa
ON K2P 0V9
Tel: **613 230 2717**
Fax: 613 230 7560

ICELAND
485 Broadview Avenue
Ottawa
ON KT8 2L2
Tel: **613 724 5982**
Fax: 613 724 1209

INDIA
10 Springfield Road
Ottawa
ON K1M 1C9
Tel: **613 744 3751/2/3**
Fax: 613 744 0913

INDONESIA
55 Parkville Avenue
Ottawa
ON K1Y 1E5

Tel: **613 724 1100**
Fax: 613 724 1105 / 4959

IRAN
245 Metcalfe Street
Ottawa
ON K2P 2K2
Tel: **613 235 4726 / 233 4726**
Fax: 613 232 5712

IRAQ
See **Jordan**

IRELAND
170 Metcalfe Street
Ottawa
ON K2P 6L2
Tel: **613 233 6381**
Fax: 613 233 5835

ISRAEL
50 O'Connor Street
Suite 1005
Ottawa
ON K1P 6L2
Tel: **613 567 6450**
Fax: 613 237 8865

ITALY
275 Slater Street
Ottawa
ON K1P 5H9
Tel: **613- 232-2401**

JAMAICA
275 Slater Street
21st Floor
Ottawa
ON K1P 5H9
Tel: **613 233 2401/2/3**
Fax: 613 233 1484

JAMAICA
Suite 800, 275 Slater Street
Ottawa
ON K1P 5H9
Tel: **613 233 9311**
Fax: 613 233 0611

JAPAN
255 Sussex Drive
Ottawa
ON K1N 9E6
Tel: **613 241 8541**
Fax: 613 241 7415

JORDAN
100 Bronson Avenue
Suite 701
Ottawa
ON K1N 6R4
Tel: **613 238 8090**
Fax: 613 232 3341

KENYA
415 Laurier Avenue East
Ottawa

ON K1N 6R4
Tel: **613 563 1773-6**
Fax: 613 233 6509

REPUBLIC OF KOREA
5th Floor, 151 Slater Street
Ottawa
ON K1P 5H3
Tel: **613 232 1715**
Fax: 613 232 0928

KUWAIT
Suite 410, 360 Albert Street
Ottawa
ON K1R 7X7
Tel: **613 780 9999**
Fax: 613 780 9905

LATVIA
Suite 208, 112 Kent Street
Tower B, Place de Ville
Ottawa
ON K1P 5P2
Tel: **613 238 6868**
Fax: 613 238 7044

LEBANON
640 Lyon Street
Ottawa
ON K1S 3Z5
Tel: **613 236 5825**
Fax: 613 232 1609

LIBERIA
Suite 1720, 1080 Beaver Hall
Hill
Montréal
Québec
H2Z 1S8
Tel: **514 871 4741**
Fax: 514 397 0816

LITHUANIA
Suite 502, 235 Yorkland Blvd
Willowdale
ON M2J 4Y8
Tel: **416 494 8313**
Fax: 416 494 4382

MADAGASCAR
649 Blair Road
Gloucester
Ottawa
ON K1J 7M4
Tel: **613 744 7995**
Fax: 613 744 2530

MALAWI
7 Clemow Avenue
Ottawa
ON K1S 2A9
Tel: **613 236 8931**
Fax: 613 236 1054

MALAYSIA
60 Bolteler Street
Ottawa
ON K1N 8Y7
Tel: **613 241 5182**
Fax: 613 241 5214

MALI
50 Goulburn Avenue
Ottawa
ON K1N 8C8
Tel: **613 232 1501 / 232 3264**
Fax: 613 232 7429

MALTA
PO Box 186, Station C
St. John's
Newfoundland
Tel: **709 722 744**
Fax: 709 722 3208

MAURITANIA
249 McLeod Street
Ottawa
ON K2P 1AJ
Tel: **613 237 3283-5**
Fax: 613 237 3287

MEXICO
Suite 1500, 45 O'Connor
Street
Ottawa
ON K1P 1A4
Tel: **613 233 8988**
Fax: 613 235 9123

MONACO
Suite 1500
1155 Sherbrooke West
Montréal
Québec
H3A 2W1
Tel: **514 849 0589**
Fax: 514 631 2771

MOROCCO
38 Range Road
Ottawa
ON K1N 8J4
Tel: **613 236 7391/2/3**
Fax: 613 236 6164

MYANMAR
Suite 902
The Sandringham Appts.
85 Range Road
Ottawa
ON K1N 8J6
Tel: **613 232 6434/5**
Fax: 613 232 6435

NEPAL
2 Shepherd Avenue East
Suite 1700
North York, Toronto
M2N 5Y7 ⇨

Tel: **416 224 2555**
Fax: 416 224 9070

NETHERLANDS
Suite 2020, 2350 Albert Street
Ottawa
ON K1R 1A4
Tel: **613 237 5030**
Fax: 613 237 6471

NEW ZEALAND
99 Bank Street
Suite 727
Ottawa
ON K1P 6G4
Tel: **613 238 5991**
Fax: 613 238 5707

NICARAGUA
Suite 407
130 Alberts Street
Ottawa
ON K1P 5G4
Tel: **613 234 9361/2**
Fax: 613 238 7666

NIGER
38 Avenue Blackburn
Ottawa
ON K1N 8A2
Tel: **613 232 4291/2/3**
Fax: 613 230 9080

NIGERIA
295 Metcalfe Street
Ottawa
ON K2P 1R9
Tel: **613 236 0521**
Fax: 613 236 0529

NORWAY
90 Sparks Street
Suite 532, Royal Bank Centre
Ottawa
ON K1P 5B4
Tel: **613 238 6571**
Fax: 613 238 2765

**ORGANISATION OF
EASTERN CARIBBEAN
STATES**
Suite 1610, Tower B
112 Kent Street
Ottawa
ON K1P 5P2
Tel: **613 236 8952**
Fax: 613 236 3042

PAKISTAN
151 Slater Street
Suite 608, Burnside Building
Ottawa
ON K1P 5H3
Tel: **613 238 7881**
Fax: 613 238 7296

PANAMA
Suite 300, 130 Albert Street
Ottawa
ON K1P 5G4
Tel: **613 236 7177**
Fax: 613 236 5775

PARAGUAY
151 Slater Street
Suite 401
Ottawa
ON K1P 5H3
Tel: **613 567 1283**
Fax: 613 567 1679

PERU
Suite 1901
130 Albert Street
Ottawa
ON K1P 5G4
Tel: **613 288 1777**
Fax: 613 232 3062

PHILIPPINES
130 Albert Street
Suite 606
Ottawa
ON K1P 5G4
Tel: **613 233 1121/3**
Fax: 613 233 4165

POLAND
1500 Pine Avenue West
Montréal
H3G 1B4
Tel: **514 937 9481**
Fax: 514 937 7272

PORTUGAL
645 Island Park Drive
Ottawa
ON K1Y 0B8
Tel: **613 729 0883 / 729 2922**
Fax: 613 729 4236

ROMANIA
655 Rideau Street
Ottawa
ON K1N 6A3
Tel: **613 789 5345**
Fax: 613 789 4365

RUSSIA
285 Charlotte Street
Ottawa
ON K1N 8L5
Tel: **613 235 4341**
Fax: 613 236 6342

RWANDA
121 Sherwood Drive
Ottawa
ON K1Y 3V1
Tel: **613 722 7921**
Fax: 613 729 3291

SAUDI ARABIA
99 Bank Street
Suite 901
Ottawa
ON K1P 6B9
Tel: **613 237 4100-3**
Fax: 613 237 7350

SENEGAL
57 Marlborough Avenue
Ottawa
ON K1N 8E8
Tel: **613 238 6392**
Fax: 613 238 2695

SINGAPORE
Suite 1305
999 West Hastings Street
Vancouver
BC V6C 2W2
Tel: **604 669 5115**
Fax: 604 669 5153

SLOVAK REPUBLIC
50 Rideau Terrace
Ottawa
ON K1M 2A1
Tel: **613 749 2496**
Fax: 613 749 4989

SLOVENIA
Suite 2101
150 Metcalfe Street
Ottawa
ON K2P 1P1
Tel: **613 565 5781/2**
Fax: 613 565 5783

SOUTH AFRICA
15 Sussex Drive
Ottawa
ON K1M 6E2
Tel: **613 744 0330**
Fax: 613 741 1639

SPAIN
74 Stanley Avenue
Ottawa
ON K1R 7S8
Tel: **613 747 2252**
Fax: 613 744 1224

SRI LANKA
Suite 1204
333 Laurier Avenue West
Ottawa
ON K1P 1C1
Tel: **613 233 8440**
Fax: 613 238 8448

SUDAN
Suite 507
85 Range Road
Ottawa
ON K1N 8J6

Tel: **613 235 4000**
Fax: 613 2356880

SWEDEN
Mercury Court
377 Dalhousie Street
Ottawa
ON K1N 9N8
Tel: **613 241 8553**
Fax: 613 241 2277

SWITZERLAND
5 Marlborough Avenue
Ottawa
ON K1N 8E6
Tel: **613 235 1837**
Fax: 613 563 1394

TAIWAN
Taipei Economic and Cultural
Office
Suite 1202, 151 Yonge Street
Toronto
ON M5C 2W7
Tel: **416 369 9030**
Fax: 416 369 1473

TANZANIA
50 Range Road
Ottawa
ON K1N 8J4
Tel: **613 232 1509**
Fax: 613 232 5184

THAILAND
180 Island Park Drive
Ottawa
ON K1Y 0A2
Tel: **613 722 4444**
Fax: 613 722 6624

TOGO
12 Range Road
Ottawa
ON K1N 8J3
Tel: **613 238 5916/7**
Fax: 613 235 6425

TRINIDAD & TOBAGO
75 Albert Street
Suite 508
Ottawa
ON K1P 5E7
Tel: **613 232 2418/9**
Fax: 613 232 4349

TUNISIA
515 O'Connor Street
Ottawa
ON K1S 3P8
Tel: **613 237 0330/2**
Fax: 613 237 7939

TURKEY
197 Wurtemburg Street
Ottawa

ON K1N 8LN
Tel: **613 789 4044/ 789 3440**
Fax: 613789 3442

UGANDA
231 Cobourg Street
Ottawa
ON K1N 8J2
Tel: **613 789 7797**
Fax: 613 789 8909

UKRAINE
331 Metcalfe Street
Ottawa
ON K2P 1S3
Tel: **613 230 2961**
Fax: 613 230 2400

UNITED KINGDOM
80 Elgin Street
Ottawa
ON K1P 5K7
Tel: **613 237 1530**
Fax: 613 237 7980

UNITED STATES
PO Box 866
100 Wellington Street
Station B
Ottawa
ON K1P 5T1
Tel: **613 238 5335**
Fax: 613 238 8750

URUGUAY
130 Albert Street
Suite 1905
Ottawa
ON K1P 5G4
Tel: **613 234 2727**
Fax: 613 233 4670

VENEZUELA
32 Range Road
Ottawa
ON K1N 8J4
Tel: **613 235 5151**
Fax: 613 235 3205

VIETNAM
226 MacLaren Street
Ottawa
ON K2P 0L6
Tel: **613 236 0772**
Fax: 613 236 2704

YEMEN
Suite 110
350 Sparks Street
Ottawa
ON K1R 7S8
Tel: **613 232 8525**
Fax: 613 232 8276

**YUGOSLAVIA (SERBIA
& MONTENEGRO)**
17 Blackburn Avenue
Ottawa
ON K1N 8A2
Tel: **613 233 6289**
Fax: 613 233 7850

ZAÏRE (DRC)
18 Range Road
Ottawa
ON K1N 8J3
Tel: **613 565 8245**
Fax: 613 685 0189

ZIMBABWE
322 Somerset Street West
Ottawa
ON K2P 0J9
Tel: **613 237 4388**
Fax: 613 563 8269

In the UK

Consulates are closed on English Public Holidays and on the national holidays observed in their own countries. Where there is no embassy in the UK, the nearest available has been listed.

AFGHANISTAN
31 Prince's Gate
London SW7 1QQ
Tel: **0171 589 8891**
Fax: 0171 581 3452

ALBANIA
4th Floor
38 Grosvenor Gardens
London SW1W 0EB
Tel: **0171 730 5709**
Fax: 0171 730 5747

ALGERIA
54 Holland Park
London W11 3RS
Tel: **0171 221 7800**
Fax: 0171 221 0448

ANGOLA
98 Park Lane
London W1Y 3TA
Tel: **0171 495 1752**
Fax: 0171 495 1635

ANTIGUA
15 Thayer Street
London W1M 5LD
Tel: **0171 486 7073/4/5**
Fax: 0171 486 9970

ARGENTINA
53 Hans Place
London SW1
Tel: **0171 589 3104**
Fax: 0171 589 3106

ARMENIA
25a Cheniston Gardens
London W8 6TG
Tel: **0171 938 5435**
Fax: 0171 938 2595

AUSTRALIA
Australia House
The Strand
London WC2B 4LU
Tel: **0171 379 4334**
Fax: 0171 240 5333

AUSTRIA
18 Belgrave Mews West
London SW1X 8HU
Tel: **0171 235 3731**
Fax: 0171 344 0292

AZERBAIJAN
4 Kensington Court
London W8 5DL
Tel: **0171 938 5482**
Fax: 0171 937 1783

BAHAMAS
10 Chesterfield Street
London W1X 8AH
Tel: **0171 408 4488**
Fax: 0171 499 9937

BAHRAIN
98 Gloucester Road
London SW7
Tel: **0171 370 5132**
Fax: 0171 835 1814

BANGLADESH
28 Queen's Gate
London SW7 5JA
Tel: **0171 584 0081**
Fax: 0171 225 2130

BARBADOS
1 Great Russell Street
London WC1B 3NH
Tel: **0171 631 4975**
Fax: 0171 323 6872

BELARUS
6 Kensington Court
London W8 5DL
Tel: **0171 937 3288**
Fax: 0171 361 0005

BELGIUM
103-5 Eaton Square
London SW1W 9AB
Tel: **0171 470 3700**
Fax: 0171 259 6213

BELIZE
22 Harcourt House
19 Cavendish Square
London W1M 9AD
Tel: **0171 499 9728**
Fax: 0171 491 4139

BENIN
Dolphin House
16 The Broadway
Stanmore
Middlesex
Tel: **0181 954 8800**
Fax: 0181 954 8844

BOLIVIA
106 Eaton Square
London SW1W 9AD
Tel: **0171 235 4248 / 235 2257**
Fax: 0171 235 1286

BOSNIA-HERZEGOVINA
320 Regent Street
London W1R 5AB
Tel: **0171 225 3758**
Fax: 0171 225 3760

BOTSWANA
6 Stratford Place
London W1N 9AE
Tel: **0171 499 0031**
Fax: 0171 495 8595

BRAZIL
32 Green Street
London W1Y 4AT
Tel: **0171 499 0877**
Fax: 0171 493 5105

BRUNEI
49 Cromwell Road
London SW7 2ED
Tel: **0171 581 0521**
Fax: 0171 235 9717

BULGARIA
186-8 Queen's Gate
London SW7 3HL
Tel: **0171 584 9400/9433**
Fax: 0171 584 4948

BURKINA FASO
5 Cinnamon Row
Plantation Wharf
London SW11 3TW
Tel: **0171 738 1800**
Fax: 0171 738 2820

BURUNDI
46 Square Marie Louise
1040 Brussels
Belgium
Tel: **2 230 4535**
Fax: 2 230 7883

CAMEROON
84 Holland Park
London W11 3SB
Tel: **0171 727 0771**
Fax: 0171 792 9353

CANADA
MacDonald House
1 Grosvenor Square
London W1X 0AA
Tel: **0171 258 6600**
Fax: 0171 258 6333

CHAD
65 Rue des Belles Feuilles
75116 Paris
Tel: **1 45 53 36 75**
Fax: 1 45 53 16 09

CHILE
12 Devonshire Street
London W1N 2DS
Tel: **0171 580 6392**
Fax: 0171 436 5204

CHINA
49-51 Portland Place
London W1N 3AH
Tel: **0171 636 9375**
Fax: 0171 636 2981

COLOMBIA
Flat 3a Hans Crescent
London SW1X 0LN
Tel: **0171 589 9177**
Fax: 0171 589 1829

CONGO
Alliance House
12 Caxton Street
London SW1H 0QS
Tel: **0171 222 7575**
Fax: 0171 233 2087

COSTA RICA
Flat 1, 14 Lancaster Gate
London W2 3LH
Tel: **0171 706 8844**
Fax: 0171 706 8655

CÔTE d'IVOIRE
2 Upper Belgrave Street
London SW1X 8BJ
Tel: **0171 235 6991**
Fax: 0171 259 5320

CROATIA
21 Conway Street
London W1P 5HL
Tel: **0171 387 1144**
Fax: 0171 387 3276

CUBA
167 High Holborn
London WC1V 6PA
Tel: **0171 240 2488**
Fax: 0171 836 2602

CYPRUS
93 Park Street
London W1Y 4ET
Tel: **0171 499 8272**
Fax: 0171 491 0691

CZECH REPUBLIC
26-30 Kensington Palace
Gardens
London W8 4QY
Tel: **0171 243 1115**
Fax: 0171 727 9654

DENMARK
55 Sloane Street
London SW1X 9SR
Tel: **0171 333 0200**
Fax: 0171 333 0271

DJIBOUTI
26 Rue Emile-Menier
75116 Paris
France
Tel: **01 47 27 49 22**
Fax: 01 45 53 50 53

DOMINICA
1 Collingham Gardens
London SW5 0HW
Tel: **0171 370 5194**
Fax: 0171 373 8743

DOMINICAN REPUBLIC
6 Queens Mansions
Brook Green
London W6 7EB
Tel: **0171 602 1885**
Fax: 0171 602 1885

ECUADOR
Flat 3b, 3 Hans Crescent
London SW1X 0LS
Tel: **0171 584 1367**
Fax: 0171 823 9701

EGYPT
26 South Street
London W1Y 6DD
Tel: **0171 499 2401**
Fax: 0171 355 3568

EL SALVADOR
Tennyson House
159 Great Portland Street
London W1N 5FD
Tel: **0171 436 8282**
Fax: 0171 436 8181

ERITREA
96 White Lion Street
London N1 9PF
Tel: **0171 713 0096**
Fax: 0171 713 0161

ESTONIA
16 Hyde Park Gate
London SW7 5DG

Tel: **0171 589 3428**
Fax: 0171 589 3430

ETHIOPIA
17 Princes Gate
London SW7 1PZ
Tel: **0171 589 7212**
Fax: 0171 589 7212

FIJI
34 Hyde Park Gate
London SW7 5DN
Tel: **0171 584 3661**
Fax: 0171 584 2838

FINLAND
38 Chesham Place
London SW1X 8HW
Tel: **0171 235 9531**
Fax: 0171 235 3680

FRANCE
58 Knightsbridge
SW1X 7JT
Tel: **0171 201 1000**
Fax: 0171 201 1004

GABON
27 Elvaston Placet
London SW7 5NL
Tel: **0171 823 9986**
Fax: 0171 584 0047

THE GAMBIA
57 Kensington Court
London W8 5DG
Tel: **0171 937 6316-8**
Fax: 0171 937 9095

GEORGIA
45 Avonmore Road
London W14 8RT
Tel/Fax: **0171 603 5325**

GERMANY
23 Belgrave Square
1 Chesham Place
London SW1X 8PZ
Tel: **0171 824 1300**
Fax: 0171 824 1435

GHANA
104 Highgate Hill
London N6 5HE
Tel: **0181 342 8686**
Fax: 0181 342 8566/70

GREECE
1A Holland Park
London W11 3TP
Tel: **0171 229 3850**
Fax: 0171 229 7221

GRENADA
1 Collingham Gardens
London SW5 0HW

Tel: **0171 373 7809**
Fax: 0171 370 7040

GUATEMALA
13 Fawcett Street
London SW10 9HN
Tel: **0171 351 3042**
Fax: 0171 376 5708

GUINEA REPUBLIC
51 rue de la Faisanderie
75016, Paris
Tel: **1 47 04 81 48**
Fax: 1 47 04 57 65

GUINEA-BISSAU
8 Palace Gate
London W8 5NF
Tel: **0171 589 5253**
Fax: 0171 589 9590

GUYANA
3 Palace Court
London W2 4LP
Tel: **0171 229 7684**
Fax: 0171 727 9809

HAITI
10 rue Theobule Ribot
16017 Paris
Tel: **1 47 63 47 78**
Fax: 1 42 27 02 05

HONDURAS
115 Gloucester Place
London W1H 3PJ
Tel: **0171 486 4880**
Fax: 0171 486 4550

HONG KONG
Hong Kong Tourist
Association
125 Pall Mall, 5th Floor
London SW1Y 5EA
Tel: **0171 930 4775**
Fax: 0171 930 4777

HUNGARY
35 Eaton Place
London SW1X 8BY
Tel: **0171 235 4048**
Fax: 0171 823 1348

ICELAND
1 Eaton Terrace
London SW1W 8EY
Tel: **0171 730 5131/2**
Fax: 0171 730 1683

INDIA
India House
Aldwych
London WC2B 4NA
Tel: **0171 836 8484**
Fax: 0171 836 4331

INDONESIA
38 Grosvenor Square
London W1X 9AD
Tel: **0171 499 7661**
Fax: 0171 491 4993

IRAN
16 Prince's Gate
London SW7 1PT
Tel: **0171 225 3000**
Fax: 0171 589 4440

IRAQ
21 Queen's Gate
London SW7 5JG
Tel: **0171 584 7141**
Fax: 0171 584 7716

IRELAND
17 Grosvenor Place
London SW1X 7HR
Tel: **0171 235 2171**
Fax: 0171 245 6961

ISRAEL
2 Palace Green
London W8 4QB
Tel: **0171 937 9500**
Fax: 0171 957 9555

ITALY
14 Three Kings Yard
London W1Y 2EH
Tel: **0171 312 2200**
Fax: 0171 312 2230

JAMAICA
1-2 Prince Consort Road
London SW7 2BZ
Tel: **0171 823 9911**
Fax: 0171 589 5154

JAPAN
101-104 Piccadilly
London W1V 9FN
Tel: **0171 465 6500**
Fax: 0171 491 9348

JORDAN
6 Upper Phillimore Gardens
London W8 7HB
Tel: **0171 937 3685**
Fax: 0171 937 8795

KAZAKHSTAN
4th Floor, 114a Cromwell Rd
London SW7 4ES
Tel: **0171 244 0011/244 6572**
Fax: 0171 244 0129

KENYA
45 Portland Place
London W1N 4AS
Tel: **0171 636 2371/5**
Fax: 0171 323 6717

SOUTH KOREA
4 Palace Gate
London W8 5NF
Tel: **0171 581 0247 / 581 3330**

KUWAIT
2 Albert Gate
Knightsbridge
London SW1X 7JU
Tel: **0171 590 3400**
Fax: 0171 259 5042

LAOS
74 Avenue Raymond-
Poincare
75116 Paris
France
Tel: **1 45 53 02 98**
Fax: 1 47 27 57 89

LATVIA
45 Nottingham Place
London W1M 3FE
Tel: **0171 312 0040**
Fax: 0171 312 0042

LEBANON
21 Kensington Palace
Gardens
London W8 4QM
Tel: **0171 229 7265**
Fax: 0171 243 1699

LESOTHO
7 Chesham Place
London SW1 8HN
Tel: **0171 235 5686**
Fax: 0171 235 5023

LIBERIA
2 Pembridge Place
London W2 4XB
Tel: **0171 221 1036**

LIBYA
See **Saudi Arabia**

LITHUANIA
84 Gloucester Place
London W1H 3HN
Tel: **0171 486 6401/2**
Fax: 0171 4868 4603

LUXEMBOURG
27 Wilton Crescent
London SW1X 8SD
Tel: **0171 235 6961**
Fax: 0171 235 9734

MACAU
see **Portugal**

MACEDONIA
10 Harcourt House
19a Cavendish Square
London W1M 9AD

Tel: **0171 499 5152**
Fax: 0171 499 2864

MADAGASCAR
16 Lanark Mansions
Pennard Road
London W12 8DT
Tel: **0181 746 0133**
Fax: 0181 746 0134

MALAWI
33 Grosvenor Street
London W1X 0DE
Tel: **0171 491 4172/7**
Fax: 0171 491 9916

MALAYSIA
45 Belgrave Square
London SW1X 8QT
Tel: **0171 235 8033**
Fax: 0171 235 5161

MALI
487 Avenue Molière
B-1050 Brussels
Tel: **2 345 7432**
Fax: 2 344 5700

MALTA
Malta House
36-38 Piccadilly
London W1V 0PP
Tel: **0171 292 4800**
Fax: 0171 734 1832

MAURITANIA
140 Bow Common Lane
London E3 4BH
Tel: **0181 980 4382**
Fax: 0181 980 2232

MAURITIUS
32 Elvaston Place
London SW7 5NW
Tel: **0171 581 0294**
Fax: 0171 823 8437

MEXICO
8 Halkin Street
London SW1X 7DW
Tel: **0171 235 6393**
Fax: 0171 235 5480

MONACO
4 Cromwell Place
London SW7 2JE
Tel: **0171 225 2679**
Fax: 0171 581 8161

MONGOLIA
7 Kensington Court
London W8 5DL
Tel: **0171 937 0150**
Fax: 0171 937 1117

MOROCCO
49 Queen's Gate Gardens
London SW7 5NE
Tel: **0171 581 5001/4**
Fax: 0171 225 3862

MOZAMBIQUE
21 Fitzroy Square
London W1P 5HJ
Tel: **0171 383 3800**
Fax: 0171 383 3801

MYANMAR
19A Charles Street
London W1X 8ER
Tel: **0171 499 8841**
Fax: 0171 629 4169

NAMIBIA
6 Chandos Street
London W1M 0LQ
Tel: **0171 636 6244**
Fax: 0171 637 5694

NEPAL
12A Kensington Palace
Gardens
London W8 4QU
Tel: **0171 229 1594**
Fax: 0171 792 9861

NETHERLANDS
38 Hyde Park Gate
London SW7 5DP
Tel: **0171 590 3200**
Fax: 0171 581 3458

NEW ZEALAND
New Zealand House
80 Haymarket
London SW1Y 4TQ
Tel: **0171 930 8422**
Fax: 0171 839 4580

NICARAGUA
2nd Floor
36 Upper Brook Street
London W1Y 1PE
Tel: **0171 409 2536**
Fax: 0171 409 2593

NIGER
154 Rue de Longchamp
75116 Paris
France
Tel: **1 45 04 80 60**
Fax: 1 45 04 62 26

NIGERIA
9 Northumberland Avenue
London WC2N 5BX
Tel: **0171 839 1244**
Fax: 0171 839 8746

NORWAY
25 Belgrave Square
London SW1X 8QD

Tel: **0171 235 7151**
Fax: 0171 245 6993

OMAN
167 Queen's Gate
London SW7 5HE
Tel: **0171 255 0001**
Fax: 0171 5898 2505

PAKISTAN
35-6 Lowndes Square
London SW1X 9JN
Tel: **0171 235 2044**

PANAMA
48 Park Street
London W1Y 3PD
Tel: **0171 493 4646**
Fax: 0171 493 4333

PAPUA NEW GUINEA
14 Waterloo Place
London SW1R 4AR
Tel: **0171 930 0922**
Fax: 0171 930 0828

PARAGUAY
Braemar Lodge
Cornwall Gardens
London SW7 4AQ
Tel: **0171 937 1253**
Fax: 0171 937 5687

PERU
52 Sloane Street
London SW1X 9SP
Tel: **0171 235 1917**
Fax: 0171 235 4463

PHILIPPINES
9a Palace Green
London W1V 9LE
Tel: **0171 937 1600**
Fax: 0171 937 2925

POLAND
47 Portland Place
London W1N 3AG
Tel: **0171 580 4324/9**
Fax: 0171 323 4018

PORTUGAL
62 Brompton Road
London SW3 1BJ
Tel: **0171 581 8722**
Fax: 0171 581 3085

QATAR
1 South Audley Street
London W1Y 5DQ
Tel: **0171 493 2200**
Fax: 0171 493 2819

ROMANIA
4 Palace Green
London W8 4QD

Tel: **0171 937 9666/8**
Fax: 0171 937 8069

RUSSIA
13 Kensington Palace
Gardens
London W8 4QX
Tel: **0171 229 3628**
Fax: 0171 229 3215

RWANDA
58-59 Trafalgar Square
London WC2N 5 DX
Tel: **0171 930 2570**
Fax: 0171 930 2572

SAUDI ARABIA
30 Charles Street
London W1X 8LP
Tel: **0171 917 3000**
Fax: 0171 917 3255

SENEGAL
Norway House
21-24 Cockspur Street
London SW1Y 5BN
Tel: **0171 930 7606**
Fax: 0171 937 7607

SEYCHELLES
2nd Floor, Eros House
Baker Street
London W1M 1FE
Tel: **0171 224 1660**
Fax: 0171 487 5756

SIERRA LEONE
33 Portland Place
London W1N 3AG
Tel: **0171 636 6483/6**
Fax: 0171 323 3159

SINGAPORE
2 Wilton Crescent
London SW1X 8SA
Tel: **0171 235 8315**
Fax: 0171 245 6583

SLOVAK REPUBLIC
25 Kensington Palace
Gardens
London W8 4QY
Tel: **0171 243 0803**
Fax: 0171 727 5824

SLOVENIA
Suite 1 Cavendish Court
11-15 Wigmore Street
London W1H 9LA
Tel: **0171 495 7775**
Fax: 0171 495 7776

SOUTH AFRICA
Trafalgar Square
London WC2N 5DP
Tel: **0171 930 4488**
Fax: 0171 451 7284

SPAIN
24 Belgrave Square
London SW1X 8QA
Tel: **0171 235 5555**
Fax: 0171 259 5392

SRI LANKA
13 Hyde Park Gardens
London W2 2LU
Tel: **0171 262 1841**
Fax: 0171 262 7970

SUDAN
3 Cleveland Row
London SW1A 1DD
Tel: **0171 839 8080**
Fax: 0171 839 7560

SWAZILAND
20 Buckingham Gate
London SW1E 6LB
Tel: **0171 630 6611**
Fax: 0171 630 6564

SWEDEN
11 Montagu Place
London W1H 2AL
Tel: **0171 917 6400**
Fax: 0171 724 4174

SWITZERLAND
16-18 Montagu Place
London W1H 2BQ
Tel: **0171 723 0701**
Fax: 0171 724 7001

SYRIA
8 Belgrave Square
London SW1X 8PH
Tel: **0171 245 9012**
Fax: 0171 235 4621

TAIWAN
50 Grosvenor Gardens
London SW1W 0EB
Tel: **0171 396 9152**
Fax: 0171 396 9145

TANZANIA
43 Hertford Street
London W1Y 7TF
Tel: **0171 499 8951**
Fax: 0171 491 9321

THAILAND
29 Queen's Gate (Ground
Floor), London SW7 5JB
Tel: **0171 584 5421/2384**
Fax: 0171 581 0122

TOGO
rue Alfred Roll 8
75017, Paris
Tel: **1 43 80 12 13**
Fax: 1 43 80 90 71

TONGA
36 Molyneux Street
London W1H 6AB
Tel: **0171 724 5828**
Fax: 0171 723 9074

TRINIDAD & TOBAGO
42 Belgrave Square
London SW1X 8NT
Tel: **0171 245 9351**
Fax: 0171 823 1065

TUNISIA
29 Prince's Gate
London SW7 1QG
Tel: **0171 584 8117**
Fax: 0171 225 2884

TURKEY
43 Belgrave Square
London SW1X 8AP
Tel: **0171 393 0202**
Fax: 0171 393 0066

UGANDA
58-9 Trafalgar Square
London WC2N 5DX
Tel: **0171 839 5783**
Fax: 0171 839 8925

UKRAINE
78 Kensington Park Road
London W11 2PL
Tel: **0171 727 6312**
Fax: 0171 729 1708

**UNITED ARAB
EMIRATES**
30 Prince's Gate
London SW7 1PT
Tel: **0171-581 1281**
Fax: 0171 581 9616

UNITED STATES
24-31 Grosvenor Square
London W1A 1AE
Tel: **0171 499 9000**

URUGUAY
2nd Floor
140 Brompton Road
London SW3 1HY
Tel: **0171 584 8192**
Fax: 0171 581 9585

VENEZUELA
1 Cromwell Road
London SW7 2HW
Tel: **0171 584 4206/7**
Fax: 0171 589 8887

VIETNAM
12-14 Victoria Road
London W8 5RD
Tel: **0171 937 1912**
Fax: 0171 937 6108

YEMEN
57 Cromwell Road
London SW7 2ED
Tel: **0171 584 6607**
Fax: 0171 589 3350

**YUGOSLAVIA (SERBIA
& MONTENEGRO)**
5-7 Lexham Gardens
London W8 5JJ
Tel: **0171 370 6105**
Fax: 0171 370 3838

ZAÏRE (DRC)
26 Chesham Place
London SW1X 8HH
Tel: **0171 235 6137**
Fax: 0171 235 9048

ZAMBIA
2 Palace Gate
London W8 5NG
Tel: **0171 589 6655**

ZIMBABWE
429 Strand
London WC2R 0SA
Tel: **0171 836 7755**
Fax: 0171 379 1167

In the USA

AFGHANISTAN
2341 Wyoming Avenue
NW, Washington DC 20008
Tel: **202 234 3770/1**
Fax: 202 328 3516

ALBANIA
Suite 1000, 1511 K Street
NW, Washington, DC 20005
Tel: **202 233 4942**
Fax: 202 628 7342

ALGERIA
2118 Kalorama Road
NW, Washington DC 20008
Tel: **202 265 2800**
Fax: 202 667 2174

ANGOLA
Suite 760
1050 Connecticut Avenue
NW, Washington, DC 20036
Tel: **202 785 1156**
Fax: 202 785 1258

ARGENTINA
1600 New Hampshire Avenue
NW, Washington DC 20009
Tel: **202 939 6400-3**
Fax: 202 332 3171

ARMENIA
2225 R Street
NW, Washington, DC 20008

Tel: **202 319 1976**
Fax: 202 319 2982

AUSTRALIA
1601 Massachusetts Avenue
NW, Washington DC 20036
Tel: **202 797 3000**
Fax: 202 797 3168

AUSTRIA
3524 International Court
NW, Washington DC 20008-3035
Tel: **202 895 6700**
Fax: 202 895 6750

AZERBAIJAN
Suite 700
927 15th Street
NW, Washington DC 20038-8790
Tel: **202 842 0001**
Fax: 202 842 0004

BAHAMAS
2220 Massachussettes Av.
NW, Washington DC 20008
Tel: **202 319 2660**
Fax: 202 319 2668

BAHRAIN
3502 International Drive
NW, Washington DC 20008
Tel: **202 342 0741/2**
Fax: 202 362 2192

BANGLADESH
2201 Wisconsin Avenue
NW, Washington DC 20007
Tel: **202 342 8372/6**
Fax: 202 333 4971

BARBADOS
2144 Wyoming Avenue
NW, Washington DC 20008
Tel: **202 939 9200/1/2**
Fax: 202 939 332 7467

BELARUS
1619 New Hampshire Avenue
NW, Washington DC 20009
Tel: **202 986 1604**
Fax: 202 986 1805

BELGIUM
3330 Garfield Street
NW, Washington DC 20008
Tel: **202 333 6900**
Fax: 202 333 3079

BELIZE
2535 Massachusetts Avenue
NW Washington DC 20008
Tel: **202 332 9636**
Fax: 202 332 6888

BENIN
2737 Cathedral Avenue
Washington DC 20008
Tel: **202 232 6656/7/8**
Fax: 202 265 1996

BOLIVIA
3014 Massachusetts Avenue
NW, Washington DC 20008-2603
Tel: **202 483-4410/1/2**
Fax: 202 328 3712

BOSNIA-HERZEGOVINA
Suite 760, 1707 L Street
NW Washington DC 20036
Tel: **202 833 3612/3**
Fax: 202 833 2061

BOTSWANA
Suite 7M,
3400 International Drive
NW, Washington DC 20008
Tel: **202 244-4990/1**
Fax: 202 244 4164

BRAZIL
3006 Massachusetts Avenue
NW, Washington DC 20008
Tel: **202 745 2700**
Fax: 202 745 2827

BRUNEI
Suite 300, 3rd Floor
2600 Virginia Avenue
NW, Washington DC 20037
Tel: **202 342 0159**
Fax 202 342 0158

BULGARIA
1621 22nd Street
NW, Washington DC 20008
Tel: **202 387 7969**
Fax: 202 234 7973

BURKINA FASO
2340 Massachusetts Avenue
NW, Washington DC 20008
Tel: **202 332 5577**
Fax: 202 332 6895

BURUNDI
Suite 212, 2233 Wisconsin Avenue
NW, Washington DC 20007
Tel: **202 342 2574**
Fax: 202 342 2578

CAMBODIA
4500 16th Street
NW, Washington DC 20011
Tel: **202 726 7742**
Fax: 202 726 8381

CAMEROON
2349 Massachusetts Avenue
NW, Washington DC 20008

Tel: **202 265 8790/4**
Fax: 202 387 3826

CANADA
501 Pennsylvania Avenue
Washington DC 20001
Tel: **202 682 1740**
Fax:202 682 1740

CAPE VERDE
3415 Massachusetts Avenue
NW, Washington DC 20007
Tel: **202 965 6820**
Fax: 202 965 1207

CENTRAL AFRICAN REPUBLIC
1618 22nd Street
NW, Washington DC 20008
Tel: **202 462 4009**
Fax: 202 265 1937

CHAD
2002 R. Street
NW Washington DC 20009
Tel: **202 462 4009**
Fax: 202 265 1937

CHILE
1732 Massachusetts Avenue
NW, Washington DC 20036
Tel: **202 785 1746**
Fax: 202 887 5579

CHINA
2300 Connecticut Avenue
NW, Washington DC 20008
Tel: **202 328 2500**
Fax: 202 232 7855

COLOMBIA
2118 Leroy Place
NW, Washington DC 20008
Tel: **202 387 8338**
Fax: 202 797 2714

CONGO
4891 Colorado Avenue
NW, Washington DC 20011
Tel: **202 7260825**
Fax: 202 726 1860

COSTA RICA
2114 S Street
NW, Washington DC 20008
Tel: **202 234 2945**
Fax: 202 265 4795

CÔTE d'IVOIRE
2424 Massachusetts Avenue
NW, Washington DC 20008
Tel: **202 797 0300**
Fax: 202 462 9444

CROATIA
2342 Massachusettes Avenue
NW, Washington DC 20008

Tel: **202 588 5899**
Fax: 202 588 8936

CUBAN INTERESTS
2630 & 2639 16th Street
NW, Washington DC 20009
Tel: **202 797 8518**

CYPRUS
2211 R Street
NW, Washington DC 20008
Tel: **202 462 5772**
Fax: 202 483 6710

CZECH REPUBLIC
3900 Spring of Freedom St.
NW, Washington DC 20008
Tel: **202 274 9100**
Fax: 202 966 8540

DENMARK
3200 White Haven Street
NW, Washington DC 20008
Tel: **202 234 4300**
Fax: 202 328 1470

DJIBOUTI
Suite 515, 1156 15th Street
NW, Washington DC 20005
Tel: **202 331 0270**
Fax: 202 331 0302

DOMINICAN REPUBLIC
1715 22nd Street
NW, Washington DC 20008
Tel: **202 332 6280**
Fax: 202 265 8057

ECUADOR
2535 15th Street
NW, Washington DC 20009
Tel: **202 234 7200**
Fax: 202 667 3482

EGYPT
3521 International Court
NW, Washington DC 20008
Tel: **202 232 5400**
Fax: 202 244 4319

EL SALVADOR
2308 California Street
NW, Washington DC 20008
Tel: **202 265 9671**
Fax: 202 234 3824

EQUATORIAL GUINEA
Suite 405, 1511 K Street
NW Washington DC 20005
Tel: **202 393 0525**
Fax: 202 393 0348

ERITREA
1780 New Hampshire Avenue
NW, Washington DC
Tel: **202 319 1991**
Fax: 202 319 1304

ESTONIA
2131 Massachusettes Avenue
NW, Washington DC 20008
Tel: **202 588 0101**
Fax: 202 588 0108

ETHIOPIA
2134 Kalorama Road
NW, Washington DC 20008
Tel: **202 234 2281/2**
Fax: 202 328 7950

FIJI
2233 Wisconsin Avenue
NW, Washington DC 20007
Tel: **202 337 8320**
Fax: 202 337 1996

FINLAND
3301 Massachusettes Avenue
NW, Washington DC 20008
Tel: **202 398 5800**
Fax: 202 298 6030

FRANCE
4101 Reservoir Road
NW, Washington DC 20007
Tel: **202 944 6000**
Fax: 202 944 6072

GABON
2034 20th Street
NW, Washington DC 20009
Tel: **202 797 1000**
Fax: 202 332 0668

GAMBIA
1155 15th Street
NW, Washington DC 20005
Tel: **202 785 1399**
Fax: 202 785 1430

GEORGIA
Suite 4242, 1511 K Street
NW, Washington DC 20005
Tel: **202 393 5959**
Fax: 202 393 6060

GERMANY
4645 Reservoir Road
NW, Washington DC 20007-
1998
Tel: **202 298 4000**
Fax: 202 298 4249

GHANA
3512 International Drive
NW, Washington DC 20008
Tel: **202 686 4520**
Fax: 202 686 4527

GREECE
2221 Massachusetts Avenue
NW, Washington DC 20008
Tel: **202 939 5800**
Fax: 202 939 5824

GRENADA
1701 New Hampshire Avenue
NW, Washington DC 20009
Tel: **202 265 2561**
Fax: 202 265 2468

GUATEMALA
2220 R Street
NW, Washington DC 20008
Tel: **202 745 4952-4**
Fax: 202 745 1908

GUINEA REPUBLIC
2112 Leroy Place
NW, Washington DC 20008
Tel: **202 483 9420**
Fax: 202 483 8688

GUINEA-BISSAU
Mezzanine Suite
918 16th Street
NW, Washington DC 20006
Tel: **202 872 4222**
Fax: 202 872 4226

GUYANA
2490 Tracy Place
NW, Washington DC 20008
Tel: **202 265 6900/01**
Fax: 202 323 1297

HAITI
2311 Massachusetts Avenue
NW, Washington DC 20008
Tel: **202 322 4090/2**
Fax: 202 745 7215

HONDURAS
3007 Tilden Street 4M
NW, Washington DC 20008
Tel: **202 966 7702**
Fax: 202 966 9751

HUNGARY
3910 Shoemaker Street
NW, Washington DC 20008
Tel: **202 362 6730**
Fax: 202 966 8135

ICELAND
Suite 1200, 1156 15th Street
NW, Washington DC 20005
Tel: **202 265 6653-5**
Fax: 202 265 6656

INDIA
2107 Massachusetts Avenue
NW, Washington DC 20008
Tel: **202 939 7000**
Fax: 202 265 4351

INDONESIA
2020 Massachusetts Avenue
NW, Washington DC 20036
Tel: **202 775 5200**
Fax: 202 775 5365

IRAQ INTERESTS
C/o Embassy of Algeria
1801 Peter Street
NW, Washington DC 20008
Tel: **202 483 7500**
Fax: 202 462 5066

IRELAND
2234 Massachusetts Avenue
NW, Washington DC 20008
Tel: **202 462 3939**
Fax: 202 232 5993

ISRAEL
3514 International Drive
NW, Washington DC 20008
Tel: **202 364 5500**
Fax: 202 364 5610

ITALY
1601 Fuller Street
NW, Washington DC 20009
Tel: **202 328 5500**
Fax: 202 483 2187

JAMAICA
1520 New Hampshire Avenue
NW, Washington DC 20036
Tel: **202 452 0660**
Fax: 202 452 0081

JAPAN
2520 Massachusetts Avenue
NW, Washington DC 20008
Tel: **202 939 6700**
Fax: 202 328 2187

JORDAN
3504 International Drive
NW, Washington DC 20008
Tel: **202 966 2664**
Fax: 202 966 3110

KAZAKHSTAN
3421 Massachusetts Avenue
NW, Washington DC 20008
Tel: **202 333 4504/7**
Fax: 202 333 4509

KENYA
2249 R Street
NW, Washington DC 20008
Tel: **202 387 6101**
Fax: 202 462 3829

SOUTH KOREA
2450 Massachusetts Avenue
NW, Washington DC 20008
Tel: **202 939 5600**
Fax: 202 797 0595

KUWAIT
2940 Tilden Street
NW, Washington DC 20008
Tel: **202 966 0702**
Fax: 202 966 0517

KYRGYZSTAN
1732 Wisconsin Avenue
NW, Washington DC 20007
Tel: **202 338 5141**
Fax: 202 338 5139

LAOS
2222 S Street
NW, Washington DC 20008
Tel: **202 332 6416**
Fax: 202 332 4923

LATVIA
4325 17th Street
NW, Washington DC 20011
Tel: **202 726 8213/4**
Fax: 202 726 6785

LEBANON
2560 28th Street
NW, Washington DC 20008
Tel: **202 939 6300**
Fax: 202 939 6324

LESOTHO
2511 Massachusetts Avenue
NW, Washington DC 20008
Tel: **202 797 5533/4/5/6**
Fax: 202 234 6815

LIBERIA
5201 16th Street
Washington DC 20011
Tel: **202 723 0437**
Fax: 202 723 0436

LITHUANIA
2622 16th Street
NW, Washington DC 20009
Tel: **202 234 5860**
Fax: 202 328 0466

LUXEMBOURG
2200 Massachusetts Avenue
NW, Washington DC 20008
Tel: **202 265 4171/2**
Fax: 202 328 8270

MACAU
2125 Kalorama Road
NW, Washington DC 20008
Tel: **202 328 8610**
Fax: 202 462 3726

MACEDONIA
Suite 210, 3050 K Street
NW, Washington 20007
Tel: **202 337 3063**
Fax: 202 337 3093

MADAGASCAR
2374 Massachusetts Avenue
NW, Washington DC 20008
Tel: **202 265 5525/6**
Fax: 202 483 7603

MALAWI
2408 Massachusetts Avenue
NW, Washington DC 20008
Tel: **202 797 1007**
Fax: 202 265 0976

MALAYSIA
2401 Massachusetts Avenue
NW, Washington DC 20008
Tel: **202 328 2700**
Fax: 202 483 7661

MALI
2130 R Street
NW, Washington DC 20008
Tel: **202 332 2249**
Fax: 202 332 6603

MALTA
2017 Connecticut Avenue
NW, Washington DC 20008
Tel: **202 462 3611/2**
Fax: 202 387 5470

MAURITANIA
2129 Leroy Place
NW, Washington DC 20008
Tel: **202 232 5700**
Fax: 202 319 2623

MAURITIUS
Suite 441
4301 Connecticut Avenue
NW, Washington DC 20008
Tel: **202 244 1491**
Fax: 202 966 0983

MEXICO
2827 16th Street
NW, Washington DC 20006
Tel: **202 736 1000**
Fax: 202 797 8458

MOLDOVA
1511 K Street
Suite 329
NW, Washington DC 20005
Fax: **202 667 1130**

MONGOLIA
2833 M Street
NW, Washington DC 20007
Tel: **202 333 7117**
Fax: 202 298 9227

MOROCCO
1601 21st Street
NW, Washington DC 20009
Tel: **202 462 7979/82**
Fax: 202 265 0161

MOZAMBIQUE
Suite 570, 1990 M Street
NW, Washington DC 20036
Tel: **202 293 7146**
Fax: 202 835 0245

MYANMAR
2300 S Street
NW, Washington DC 20008
Tel: **202 332 9044/5**
Fax: 202 332 9046

NAMIBIA
1605 New Hampshire Avenue
NW, Washington DC 20009
Tel: **202 986 0540**
Fax: 202 986 0540

NEPAL
2131 Leroy Place
NW, Washington DC 20008
Tel: **202 667 4550**
Fax: 202 667 5534

NETHERLANDS
4200 Linnean Avenue
NW, Washington DC 20008
Tel: **202 244 5300**
Fax: 202362 3430

NEW ZEALAND
37 Observatory Circle
NW, Washington DC 20008
Tel: **202 328 4800**
Fax: 202 667 5227

NICARAGUA
1627 New Hampshire Avenue
NW, Washington DC 20009
Tel: **202 939 6570**
Fax: 202 939 6545

NIGER
2204 R Street
NW, Washington DC 20008
Tel: **202 483 4224**
Fax: 202 483 3169

NIGERIA
1333 16th Street
NW, Washington DC 20036
Tel: **202 986 8400**
Fax: 202 775 1385

NORWAY
2720 34th Street
NW, Washington DC 20008
Tel: **202 333 6000**
Fax: 202 337 0870

OMAN
2535 Belmont Road
NW, Washington DC 20008
Tel: **202 387 1980/2**
Fax: 202 745 4933

PAKISTAN
2315 Massachusetts Avenue
NW, Washington DC 20008
Tel: **202 939 6200**
Fax: 202 387 0484

PANAMA
2862 McGill Terrace
NW, Washington DC 20008
Tel: **202 483 1407**
Fax: 202 483 8413

PAPUA NEW GUINEA
3rd Floor
1615 New Hampshire Avenue
NW, Washington DC 20009
Tel: **202 745 3680**
Fax: 202 745 3679

PARAGUAY
2400 Massachusetts Avenue
NW, Washington DC 20008
Tel: **202 483 6960/1/2**
Fax: 202 234 4508

PERU
1700 Massachusetts Avenue
NW, Washington DC 20036
Tel: **202 833 9868/9**
Fax: 202 659 8124

PHILIPPINES
1600 Massachusetts Avenue
NW, Washington DC 20036
Tel: **202 467 9300**
Fax: 202 328 7614

POLAND
2640 16th Street
NW, Washington DC 20009
Tel: **202 234 3800/1/2**
Fax: 202 328 6271

PORTUGAL
2125 Kalorama Road
NW, Washington DC 20008
Tel: **202 328 8610**
Fax: 202 462 3726

QATAR
4200 Wisconsin Avenue
NW, Washington DC 20016
Tel: **202 274 1600**
Fax: 202 237 0061

ROMANIA
1607 23rd Street
NW, Washington DC 20008
Tel: **202 332 4848**
Fax: 202 232 4748

RUSSIA
2650 Wisconsin Avenue
NW, Washington 20007
Tel: **202 298 5700**
Fax: 202 298 5735

RWANDA
1714 New Hampshire Avenue
NW, Washington DC 20009
Tel: **202 232 2882**
Fax: 202 232 4544

ST. KITTS & NEVIS
3216 New Mexico Avenue
NW, Washington DC 20016
Tel: **202 686 2636**
Fax: 202 686 5740

SAINT LUCIA
3216 New Mexico Avenue
NW, Washington DC 20016
Tel: **202 364 6792**
Fax: 202 364 6723

ST. VINCENT & THE GRENADINES
3216 New Mexico Avenue
NW, Washington DC 20016
Tel: **202 364 6730**
Fax: 202 364 6736

SAUDI ARABIA
601 New Hampshire Avenue
NW, Washington DC 20037
Tel: **202 342 3800**
Fax: 202 337 4084

SENEGAL
2112 Wyoming Avenue
NW, Washington DC 20008
Tel: **202 234 0540/1**
Fax: 202 332 6315

SEYCHELLES
Suite 253E, 40 Street 24A
New York
NY 10016
Tel: **212 687 9766/7**
Fax: 212 922 9177

SIERRA LEONE
1701 19th Street
NW, Washington DC 20009
Tel: **202 939 9261**
Fax: 202 483 1793

SINGAPORE
3501 International Place
NW, Washington DC 20008
Tel: **202 265 7915**
Fax: 202 537 3100

SLOVAK REPUBLIC
Suite 250, 220 Wisconsin Avenue
NW, Washington DC 20007
Tel: **202 965 5160/5**
Fax: 202 965 5166

SLOVENIA
1525 New Hampshire Avenue
NW, Washington DC 20036
Tel: **202 667 5363**
Fax: 202 667 4563

SOMALIA
600 New Hampshire Avenue
NW, Washington DC 20037
Tel: **202 342 1575**

SOUTH AFRICA
3051 Massachusetts Avenue
NW, Washington DC 20008
Tel: **202 232 4400**
Fax: 202 265 1607

SPAIN
2375 Pennsylvania Avenue
NW, Washington DC 20037
Tel: **202 452 0100**
Fax: 202 728 2302

SRI LANKA
2148 Wyoming Avenue
NW, Washington DC 20008
Tel: **202 483 4025**
Fax: 202 232 7181

SUDAN
2210 Massachusetts Avenue
NW, Washington DC 20008
Tel: **202 338 8565/6/7**
Fax: 202 667 2406

SURINAME
Suite 108, Van Ness Centre
4301 Connecticut Avenue
NW, Washington DC 20008
Tel: **202 244 7488**
Fax: 202 244 5878

SWAZILAND
Suite 3M, 3400 International
Drive
NW, Washington DC 20008
Tel: **202 362 6683**
Fax: 202 244 8059

SWEDEN
1501 M Street
NW, Washington DC 20005
Tel: **202 467 2600**
Fax: 202 467 2699

SWITZERLAND
2900 Cathedral Avenue
NW, Washington DC 20008
Tel: **202 745 7900**
Fax: 202 387 2564

SYRIA
2215 Wyoming Avenue
NW, Washington DC 20008
Tel: **202 232 6313**
Fax: 202 234 9548

TANZANIA
2139 R Street
NW, Washington DC 20008
Tel: **202 939 6125**
Fax: 202 797 7408

THAILAND
1024 Kalorama Road,
Suite 401
NW, Washington DC 20008

Tel: **202 483 7200**
Fax: 202 944 3611

TOGO
2208 Massachusetts Avenue
NW, Washington DC 20008
Tel: **202 234 4212**
Fax: 202 232 3190

TRINIDAD & TOBAGO
1708 Massachusetts Avenue
NW, Washington DC 20036
Tel: **202 467 6490**
Fax: 202 682 7272

TUNISIA
1515 Massachusetts Avenue
NW, Washington DC 20005
Tel: **202 862 1850**
Fax: 202 862 1858

TURKEY
1714 Massachusettes Avenue
NW, Washington DC 20036
Tel: **202 659 8200**
Fax: 202 659 0744

TURKMENISTAN
2207 Massachusettes Avenue
NW, Washington DC 20008
Tel: **202 588 1500**
Fax: 202 588 0697

UGANDA
5911 16th Street
NW, Washington DC 20011
Tel: **202 726 7100**
Fax: 202 726 1727

UKRAINE
3350 M Street
NW, Washington DC 20007
Tel: **202 757 3884**
Fax: 202 333 0817

**UNITED ARAB
EMIRATES**
Suite 600
3000 K Street
NW, Washington DC 20037
Tel: **202 338 6500**
Fax: 202 337 7029

UNITED KINGDOM
3100 Massachusetts Avenue
NW, Washington DC 20008
Tel: **202 462 1340**
Fax: 202 588 7889

URUGUAY
1918 F Street
NW, Washington DC 20006
Tel: **202 331 1313/6**
Fax: 202 331 8142

UZBEKISTAN
1746 Massachusettes Avenue
NW, Washington DC 20036
Tel: **202 887 5300**
Fax: 202 293 6804

VENEZUELA
1099 30th Street
NW, Washington DC 20007
Tel: **202 342 2214**
Fax: 202 342 6820

VIETNAM
Suite 501, 1233 20th Street
NW, Washington DC 20036
Tel: **202 861 0737**
Fax: 202 861 0917

WESTERN SAMOA
820 Second Street
#800D
New York
NY 10017
Tel: **212 599 6196**
Fax: 212 599 0797

YEMEN
Suite 705
2600 Virginia Avenue
NW, Washington DC 20037
Tel: **202 965 4760/1**
Fax: 202 337 2017

YUGOSLAVIA
2410 California Street
NW, Washington DC 20008
Tel: **202 462 6566**
Fax: 202 462 2508

ZAÏRE (DRC)
1800 New Hampshire Avenue
NW, Washington DC 20009
Tel: **202 234 7690/1**
Fax: 202 686 3631

ZAMBIA
2419 Massachusetts Avenue
NW, Washington DC 20008
Tel: **202 265 9711/9**
Fax: 202 332 0826

ZIMBABWE
1608 New Hampshire Avenue
NW, Washington DC 20009
Tel: **202 3332 7100**
Fax: 202 438 9326

CURRENCY RESTRICTIONS

Many countries impose restrictions on the import or export of local and foreign currency. Often these take the form of ceilings, normally reasonably generous, so that the traveller should rarely be aware of their existence. However, it is worth checking every country you intend to visit.
The following is a list of currency regulations which may impinge on the traveller.

KEY
U - Unlimited import or export of local or foreign currency.
P - Prohibited import or export of local or foreign currency.
D - Foreign currency may be imported but must be **D**eclared.
E - Foreign currency may be exported up to an **E**qual amount imported.
C - Check with relevant embassy.

Country	LOCAL CURRENCY		FOREIGN CURRENCY	
	IMPORT	**EXPORT**	**IMPORT**	**EXPORT**
Afghanistan	AF500	AF500	U	U
Albania	P	P	D	E
Algeria	DZD50	DZD50	D	C
Angola	AOR15,000	P	D	=AOR5000
Anguilla	UD	UD	UD	UD
Antigua & Barb.	UD	UD	UD	UD
Argentina	U	U	U	U
Armenia	P	P	UD	UD
Aruba	U	U	U	U
Australia	>A$5,000 or equivalent must be declared on import or export.			
Austria	U	ASch100,000	U	U
Azerbaijan	P	P	UD	E
Bahamas	U	B$70	U	U
Bahrain	U	U	U	U
Bangladesh	100Tk	100Tk	UD	E
Barbados	UD	E	U	U
Belarus	P	P	UD	E
Belgium	U	U	U	U
Belize	Bz$100	Bz$100	UD	UD
Benin	UD	E	UD	UD
Bermuda	U	Bda$250	UD	E

| Country | LOCAL CURRENCY | | FOREIGN CURRENCY | |
	IMPORT	EXPORT	IMPORT	EXPORT
Bhutan	U	U	UD	U
Bolivia	UD	UD	UD	UD
Bosnia-Herzegov.	C	C	C	C
Botswana	U	BWP50	U	U
Brazil	U	U	UD	E
British Virgin Is.	UD	E	UD	E
Brunei	U	Br$1000	UD	UD
Bulgaria	P	P	UD	E
Burkina Faso	U	U	U	U
Burundi	Bufr2000	Bufr2000	UD	E
Cambodia	P	P	UD	E
Cameroon	UD	CFAfr20,000	UD	U
Canada	UD	UD	UD	UD
Cape Verde	P	P	UD	E
Cayman Islands	U	U	U	U
Central African Republic	U	CFAfr75,000	UD	UD
Chad	UD	E	UD	E
Chile	U	U	U	E
China	U	P	UD	Unused foreign currency may be exported.
Colombia	U	U	UD	E
Congo	U	CFAfr25,000	UD	E
Costa Rica	U	U	U	U
Côte d'Ivoire	U	CFAfr10,000	UD	E
Croatia	K2000	K2000	U	U
Cuba	P	P	UD	C
Cyprus	U	U	UD	UD
Czech Republic	U	U	U	U
Denmark	UD	UD	UD	UD

Country	LOCAL CURRENCY		FOREIGN CURRENCY	
	IMPORT	EXPORT	IMPORT	EXPORT
Dominica	UD	E	UD	E
Dominican Rep.	P	P	UD	E
Ecuador	U	U	U	U
Egypt	£E100	P	UD	E
El Salvador	U	U	UD	E
Equatorial Guinea	U	CFAfr3,000	U	U
Eritrea	UD	UD	UD	UD
Estonia	UD	UD	UD	UD
Ethiopia	Birr100	Birr100	UD	UD
Fiji	U	F$500	U	=F£500
Finland	U	U	U	U
France	U	U	U	U
Gabon	U	CFAfr200,000	UD	E
Gambia	C	C	C	C
Georgia	P	P	UD	E
Germany	U	U	U	U
Ghana	c3000	c3000	UD	E
Gibraltar	U	U	U	U
Greece	Dr100,000	Dr40,000	UD	E
Grenada	U	U	U	U
Guatemala	U	U	U	U
Guinea Rep.	P	P	UD	E
Guinea-Bissau	P	P	UD	E
Guyana	C	C	UD	UD
Haiti	U	U	U	U
Honduras	U	U	US$D	US$E
Hong Kong	U	U	U	U
Hungary	U	U	UD	E
Iceland	U	U	UD	E

Country	LOCAL CURRENCY		FOREIGN CURRENCY	
	IMPORT	EXPORT	IMPORT	EXPORT
India	P	P	UD	E
Indonesia	Rp50,000	Rp50,000	U	U
Iran	IR200,000	IR200,000	UD	UD
Iraq	ID25	ID5	UD	UD
Ireland	U	IR£150	UD	E
Israel	U	C	U	C
Italy	L20,000,000	L20,000,000	=L20,000,000	=L20,000,000 - C
Jamaica	UD	UD	UD	UD
Japan	U	Y5,000,000	U	U
Jordan	UD	JD300	UD	E
Kazakstan	P	P	UD	E
Kenya	P	P	UD	E
North Korea	P	P	UD	UD
South Korea	C	W500,000	UD	E
Kuwait	U	U	U	U
Kyrgyzstan	P	P	UD	E
Latvia	U	U	U	U
Lebanon	U	U	U	U
Lesotho	UC	UC	UC	UC
Liberia	U	U	U	U
Libya	P	P	UD	E
Lithuania	UD	E	UD	E
Luxembourg	U	U	U	U
Macau	U	U	U	U
Macedonia	U	U	U	U
Madagascar	Mgfr500	P	UD	E
Malawi	K200	K200	UD	E
Malaysia	U	U	U	U
Maldives	U	U	U	U

Country	LOCAL CURRENCY		FOREIGN CURRENCY	
	IMPORT	EXPORT	IMPORT	EXPORT
Mali	U	U	UD	E
Malta	Lm50	Lm25	UD	E
Mauritania	P	P	UD	E
Mauritius	U	U	UD	E
Mexico	peso5,000	peso5,000	UD	E
Moldova	P	P	UD	E
Mongolia	P	P	UD	E
Montserrat	UD	E	UD	E (1.75% Levy)
Morocco	P	P	U	U
Mozambique	P	P	UD	E
Myanmar	P	P	UD	C keep declaration certificate safe.
Namibia	NAD500	NAD500	UD	E
Nepal	P	P	Only 10% of foreign currency converted to local can be converted back on departure.	
Netherlands	U	U	U	U
New Zealand	U	U	U	U
Nicaragua	U	U	U	U
Niger	U	CFAfr25,000	U	U
Nigeria	N100	N100	UD	E
Niue	U	U	U	U (C for New Zealand currency)
Norway	NKr25,000	NKr25,000	UD	E
Oman	U	U	U	U
Pakistan	PRs100	PRs100	U	U
Panama	U	U	U	U
Papua New G.	U	C	U	C
Paraguay	U	U	U	U
Peru	U	U	UD	E
Philippines	P5000	P5000	U	U
Poland	P	P	UD	E

Country	LOCAL CURRENCY		FOREIGN CURRENCY	
	IMPORT	EXPORT	IMPORT	EXPORT
Portugal	U	Esc100,000	U	=Esc1,000,000 C
Qatar	U	U	U	U
Romania	P	P	UD	E
Russian Fed.	P	P	UD	E
Rwanda	Frw5000	Frw5000	UD	E
St Kitts & N.	U	U	UD	E
St. Lucia	UD	E	UD	E
St Vincent & G.	UD	E	UD	E
São Tomé & P.	UD	UD	UD	UD
Saudi Arabia	U	U	U	U
Senegal	UD	CFAfr20,000	UD	EC
Seychelles	U	SRs100	U	U
Sierra Leone	Le50,000	Le50,000	UD	C
Singapore	U	U	U	U
Slovak Republic	P	P	U	U
Slovenia	SIT300,000	SIT300,000	UD	E
Solomon Is.	U	SI$250	UD	E
Somalia	SoSh200	SoSh200	UDC	E
South Africa	R500	R500	UD	E
Spain	UD	UD	UD	UD
Sri Lanka	SLRs1000	SLRs1000	UDC	E
Sudan	P	P	UD	UD
Suriname	SG100	SG100	UDC	UDC
Swaziland	U	U	U	U
Sweden	U	U	U	U
Switzerland	U	U	U	U
Syria	U	P	UD	E/US$5000
Taiwan	NT$40,000	NT$40,000	UD	E/US$5000
Tajikistan	P	C	UD	E

Country	LOCAL CURRENCY		FOREIGN CURRENCY	
	IMPORT	EXPORT	IMPORT	EXPORT
Tanzania	P	P	UD	E/Tsh4000
Thailand	UD	Bt50,000	UD	U
Togo	CFAfr1,000,000	CFAfr25,000	UD	E
Trinidad & T.	U	TT$200	UD	E
Tunisia	P	P	UD	E
Turkey	UC	=US$5000	UC	E/US$5000
Turkmenistan	P	P	UD	E
Uganda	U	U	UD	E
Ukraine	C	C	C	C
United Arab E.	U	U	U	U
UK	U	U	U	U
USA	U	U	U	U Must declare anything over US$10,000 or equivalent
Uruguay	U	U	U	U
Uzbekistan	P	P	UD	E
Venezuela	U	U	U	U
Vietnam	P	P	UD	UD
Western Samoa	U	P	UD	E
Yemen	P	P	UD	UD
The Former Rep. of Yugoslavia	30N.Din	30N.Din	UD	E
Zaïre	P	P	UD	E
Zambia	K100	K100	UD	E
Zimbabwe	Z$500	Z$500	UDC	EC

WORKING RESTRICTIONS WORLD-WIDE

Afghanistan	No work visas at present
Algeria	Only possible if with a company that has a govt. contract. Need a work permit if staying more than 3 months and must produce diplomas.
Andorra	There is an annual allocation of work permits that must be applied for personally in Andorra - after the applicant has secured a position.
Antigua & Barbuda	Work permits required. You can only work if locals cannot perform the function. Must arrange the permit in advance.
Argentina	Need a work permit.
Australia	Must have a work permit - not easy to get hold of.
Austria	Work permits are required for all types of employment, but are never issued for part-time employment.
Bahamas	Need a work permit, but no expatriate may be offered employment in a post for which a suitably qualified Bahamian is available. You may not apply once in the country. Rigidly enforced.
Bahrain	Employer must get permit in Bahrain and send it to the employee to be stamped by the embassy in his or her own country. Difficult to get renewed.
Bangladesh	Can work for up to three months without a permit.
Barbados	Work permits are issued to employers not employees - you must apply for a job before hand.
Belgium	The Belgian employer must apply for the permit.
Belize	Work permit required. Must have job offer for which there are no suitable nationals. Apply to Ministry of Labour, Belmopan.
Bhutan	Can work by government invitation only.
Bermuda	Must have a job and work permit before entering.
Benin	Need to have a contract with a company of the Benin Government before applying.
Bolivia	Only residents in Bolivia are allowed employment.
Botswana	Need work permit. No rigid restrictions and there are usually jobs available.
Brazil	Working visas are only issued on the presentation of a work contract, duly certified by the Brazilian Ministry of Labour.
British Virgin Islands	Work permit required.
Brunei	Work permit required in all cases. Must be proposed by a registered Brunei company and have trade qualifications and experience above those available locally.
Bulgaria	It is not possible to get a work permit.
Cameroon	You need a work permit, which can be obtained in the Cameroon.
Canada	Work permit required. Must apply from outside the country. Will not be granted if there is a permanent resident or qualified Canadian for the job.
Cayman Islands	You must satisfy the Cayman Protection Board that no local can do the job to get a work permit. Contact the Dept. of Immigration. Permits for 1-5 years usually granted to professionals.
Chile	Must have a contract with a company before applying.
China	No work unless either a teacher or technician when one works under contract.
Cocos (Keeling Islands)	All non-locals work for the Australian Govt. No casual work available.
Colombia	Work visa needed. Normally for 2 years at a time. Renewable. Only granted for work no national can do.

Cook Islands	Apply to New Zealand High Commission for temporary residence permit. Not normally given unless you have special skills not available locally.
Costa Rica	Need a signed contract with employer and 'resident' status to be able to work.
Côte d'Ivoire	You are not allowed to work here unless sent by a private company which will arrange your permit for you.
Cuba	It is not possible to work here.
Cyprus	Work permit needed - must be obtained by employer. Usually granted for one year but can be renewed. Can be prosecuted and deported for working without one.
Czech Republic	Permission to work involves a complicated procedure - enquire at embassy before you go.
Denmark	Nationals of EC countries do not need permits. Others do, but they are not being issued at present.
Djibouti	Not much work available.
Dominica	Need work permit obtained from country of origin.
Dominican Republic	Work permit required.
Eastern Caribbean	Work permit offered only if a national cannot do the job.
Ecuador	Work permit required. Available only if being brought in by an Ecuadorean company for professional reasons (i.e. training, or for your specialist skills). Must register permit on arrival.
El Salvador	Work permit can be obtained for technical or specialized work. Employer must apply.
Ethiopia	Employer must apply on your behalf to Ministry of Labour and Social Affairs. Casual work forbidden.
Falkland Islands	Employer must apply for work permit.
Fiji	Need a work permit before entering Fiji. Rarely given.
Finland	Work permit required.
France	Nationals of EC countries do not need work permits. Others do.
Gabon	Work permit required.
Gambia	Work permit required.
Germany	Nationals of EC countries do not need permits. Others do, but they are only issued once work has been found.
Ghana	Work permit required.
Gibraltar	All foreign nationals except the British need work permits.
Greece	Need a permit issued by the Greek Ministry of Labour. Yearly, renewable. Employer should also apply.
Grenada	Work permit needed.
Guadeloupe	EC nationals don't need work permits; others do.
Guyana	Work permit needed.
Haiti	First need to get a Permit de Séjour, then your employers must apply for a work permit for you.
Hong Kong	You need a work permit if working in the private sector but not if working for the Hong Kong Government or a UK citizen.
Hungary	Work permit needed. Only granted if you are immigrating permanently. Apply to Foreign Nationals Office, Budapest Police HQ.
Iceland	Need a work permit prior to arrival - prospective employer should apply and prove no suitable Icelander is available. Permits renewable yearly.
India	No permit is needed, but you cannot take the money earned out.

Indonesia	Apply for the work permit through Foreign Affairs Dept. and the Dept. of Manpower. Getting more difficult and impossible for casual work. Must have a skill not available locally.
Ireland	Not required by EC citizens, but needed by all others.
Iran	Work permit required.
Iraq	Work permit may be arranged by foreign companies working in Iraq. Otherwise it is impossible.
Israel	Apply to the embassy in your home country with letter from your potential employer.
Italy	Nationals of EC countries may work without permits. All others need them.
Jamaica	Work permit required.
Japan	Long-term commercial business visa is needed if working for your own company in Japan. Others require work permits. Can do part-time casual work on a study visa.
Jordan	You can only get work through a local company or a foreign company's local offices.
Kenya	Prospective employer in Kenya must obtain a permit for you before you arrive. Heavy fines/deportation for working without a permit.
South Korea	Need a work permit from the Korean embassy in your normal country of residence.
Kuwait	Need a contract from Kuwait before the permit will be issued. No casual work. Can get 2 year contracts for specialist jobs.
Lesotho	Employer must apply and prove no local is suitable. Permits for 2 years but renewable.
Liberia	Work permit required. Must go to Ministry of Labour and Immigration and Labour. Permits valid for one year but can be renewed.
Liechtenstein	Very rare to be granted a permit.
Luxembourg	EC citizens may work without a permit. All other nationals require one.
Macao	Work permit
Madagascar	Not required if working for a cultural institution such as the American School. Most expats working for the govt. More difficult for individuals.
Malawi	Work permit required
Malaysia	Work permit required. You need a sponsor in Malaysia who agrees to assure your maintenance and repatriation.
Malta	Permits only issued for specialized skills not found on the island.
Mauritius	Work permit required. Must provide good reasons and only available if no local can do the job. Permits usually for one or two years, renewable. Fee payable.
Mexico	No work allowed unless you are specifically requested by a Mexican company.
Morocco	Work permit required. Employer must apply. Permit included with residence certificate.
Myanmar	Government approval required.
Nepal	Work permits required. Complex process - usually only possible for aid/embassy staff, govt. projects and airlines.
Netherlands	EC citizens do not need work permits. All other nationalities do.
New Zealand	All nationalities except Australian need a work permit.
Nigeria	Work permit compulsory for all foreigners. Employers are given a yearly quota. Two years, renewable. Some expat wives can get part-time `unofficial' work.

Norway	Work permit required.
Oman	Work permit required. Need a sponsor - either an Omani company or Omani national. Two years' renewable permits for specific employment. Casual labour not allowed.
Panama	Permit required. Apply in Panama.
Papua New Guinea	Permit required - usually for a 3 year contract - obtained before arrival. Must be sponsored by an employer. Casual work not allowed.
Paraguay	No permit needed.
Peru	Arrange everything in Peru.
Philippines	Permit required. Only if you already have a job. Employer should apply.
Poland	Foreigners cannot work in Poland.
Portugal	Work permit required.
Qatar	Must have sponsorship and resident's status. Work permit must be obtained by employer.
American Samoa	Severe restrictions. Immigration approval is necessary first, and this is only granted for special needs and skills that cannot be satisfied locally.
Saudi Arabia	Must obtain job and residence permit before arrival. Formalities horribly complicated, so leave it to your employer.
Senegal	Work permits can be obtained in Dakar with great difficulty for working with international or private organizations. Impossible for semi-private or official companies.
Seychelles	Apply for a Gainful Occupation Permit. Permit granted only if the job cannot be filled locally and for the duration of the contract. Difficult and expensive to get without political connections.
Sierra Leone	Required even for casual labour. Apply to Principal Immigration Officer, who is secretary of the Business Immigration Quota Committee.
Singapore	All non-residents require work permit. Apply to Ministry of Labour and Dept. of Immigration.
South Africa	Not allowed to accept employment without special permission from the Director General, Internal Affairs.
Spain	Permit needed to work legally.
Sri Lanka	Cannot work without Government approval which is rarely given. 1 year permits occasionally granted for specific projects.
St. Kitts & Nevis	Permits required but will only be granted when no national is available. Apply to Ministry of Home Affairs
Sudan	Permits required. Available for aid workers etc. but more difficult for others.
Swaziland	Work permit required.
Sweden	Work permit required.
Switzerland	Work permit required. Employer must apply. Permit renewable annually.
Syria	Work permits required, but whether you'll get one depends on who you'd be working for.
Tahiti	Work permit difficult to obtain. Employer must apply and ensure the employee's return to his country of origin.
Tanzania	Work permit required. Employer must apply on your behalf. If you haven't got a job, write to the ministry concerned with your field to offer your services.
Tibet	Generally no foreigners allowed to work, but a few teachers are being given one year contracts for Lhasa.
Togo	Work permit required.

Tonga	Work permit required. Length of permit depends on individual circumstances.
Trinidad & Tobago	Work permit required. Employer must apply.
Tunisia	Work permit required. Need a job contract before applying to the Ministry of Social Affairs. Only for those skills unobtainable in the country.
Turkey	Working visa required. Minimal restrictions but must apply through prospective employer
Turks and Caicos	Work permit required.
Uganda	Work permits required - restricted and difficult to obtain. Normally granted for a maximum of 3 years for those with skills lacking in Uganda.
United Arab Emirates	Work permit needed. No casual work and permit must be obtained before arrival. Permit normally for 2/3 years dependent on job/nationality. Must be sponsored by a UAE-based company or individual.
United Kingdom	Commonwealth nationals aged 17 to 27 can work for two years on a holiday visa. All others (apart from EC) need a work permit.
US Virgin Islands	Work permit required.
United States	Work permit (Green Card) required for permanent jobs. Difficult to obtain. Some types of work allowed under exchange or temporary workers' visas.
Uruguay	Work permit needed.
Vanuatu	Work permit required. Given to people in positions which locals can't fill for 1 year.
Zambia	Work permit must be arranged by your employer before you enter. Will only be given for skills not obtainable locally.
Zimbabwe	Apply for a work permit through your prospective employer. Maximum stay as an expat usually 3 years. ∎

A PLACE TO STAY
Section 9

CAMPING ASSOCIATIONS

Austrian Camping Club
Schubertring 1-3
Mandistrasse 28
D-80802 Munich
Tel: **89-38 01 42**

Camping and Caravanning Club – Belgium
F.F.3C.B
rue des Chats 104
B-1082 Brussels
Tel: **2-465 98 80**

Camping Club of Brazil
Rua Senador Dantas 75-29 andar
BR-20037-900
Rio de Janeiro
Tel: **21-210 3171**

Canadian Camping Association
1810 Avenue Road
#2 Toronto ON M5M 3Z2
Canada
Tel: **416-781 4717**

Dansk Camping Union – Denmark
Gammei Kongevej 74D
DK1850 Frederiksberg C
Tel: **31-21 06 04**

Finnish Travel Association
PO Box 778
00101 Helsinki 10
Tel: **0-170 868**

French Federation of Camping and Caravaning
78 rue de Rivoli
F-75004 Paris
France
Tel: **1-42 72 84 08**

Camping and Caravanverband der DDR
Helmut Koch Lichtenberger Str.27
DDR-1020
Berlin
Germany

Camping and Caravanning Club – G.B.
Green Fields House
Westwood Way
Coventry CV4 8JH
Tel: **01203-694995**

The Caravan Club
East Grinstead House
East Grinstead
West Sussex RH19 1UA
Tel: **01342-326 944**

Campers Association of Northern Greece
16 Tsimiski Street
546 24 Thessaloniki
Tel: **31-286897**

Camping and Caravanning Club – Hungary
Kalvin ter 9
1091 Budapest
Tel: **21-852 59**

The Israel Camping Club
Mr. Baruch Preiss
PO Box 13029
61130 Tel Aviv
Tel: **3-647 88 23**

Italian Fed. of Camping and Caravanning
Via Vittorio Emanuel 11
50041 Calenzano, FI
Tel: **55-88 23 91**

Japan Autocamping Federation
5F Yotsuya Takagi Building
2-9 Yotsuya ⇨

Shinkjuku-Ku
Tokyo
Tel: **33-357 2851**

Netherlands Camping Reservation Service
Het Kolkije 4
NL-7606 CA Almelo
Netherlands
Tel: **5490-18767**

Camp and Cabin Association – New Zealand
4A Kanawa Street
Waikanae
New Zealand

Federazione Italiana del Campeggio e del Caravannia
PO Box 23
Via V Emanuelle 11
1-50041 Florence
Italy
Tel: **55-882391**

Norwegian Caravan Club
Solheimveien 18
1473 Skarer
Tel: **67-97 49 20**

Casagrande Camping Club – Paraguay
Calle 23 de Octubre #278 – Recoleta
Asuncion
Tel: **21-663 730**

Polish Federation of Camping and Caravanning
ul. Grochowska 331
03-838 Warsaw
Tel: **22-27 24 08**

Portugese Camping and Caravanning Club
Av. Colonel Eduardo Galhardo #24 D
1170 Lisbon
Tel: **1-812 6890**

Camping and Caravanning Federation – Slovak Republic
Junacka ul Nr. 6
832 80 Bratislava
Tel: **7-27 90 228**

International Camping Federation – Spain
Edificion Espana
Grupo 4 Pl.11
E-28013 Madrid
Spain
Tel: **1-242 1089**

Camping and Caravanning Club – Turkey
Bastekar Sokak 62/12
Kavaklidere 06680
Ankara
Tel: **312-426 1132**

Campgrounds of America
PO Box 30558
Billings MT 59114
USA
Tel: **406-248 7444**

Motor Camping America
PO Box 127
8189 Valleyview Road
Custer
WA 98240
USA

National Campground Owners Association
11706 Bowman Green
Reston
VA 22090
USA
Tel: **703-471 0143**

SELF-CATERING HOLIDAYS

American Dream Holidays
1/7 Station Chambers
High St North
London E6 1JE
Tel: **0181-470 1181**
Villas and apartments in Hawaii and Florida.

Austravel
44 Colcton Street
Bristol BS1 5AX
Tel: **0272 277425**
Apartments in Australia and New Zealand.

Brittany Ferries
Millbay Docks
Plymouth
Devon PL1 3EW
Tel: **01705-751708**
Brittany, the Dordogne.

Interhomes
383 Richmond Road
Twickenham
Middlesex TW1 2EF
Tel: **0181-891 1294**
Apartments, chalets, villas all over Europe.

Lakes and Mountains
The Red House
Garstons Close
Titchfield
Fareham PO14 4EW
Tel: **01329-844405**
Alpine village homes.

Landmark Trust
Shotterbroke

Maidenhead
Berkshire SL6 3SW
Tel: **01628-825920**

National Trust Holiday Cottages
PO Box 536
Melksham
SN12 8SX
Tel: **01225-791199**

P & O European Ferries
Channel House
Channel View Road
Dover
Kent CT17 9TJ
Tel: **01304-863000**

Scanmeridian
28b High Street
Hampstead
London NW3 1QA
Tel: **0171-431 5393**
Traditional Scandinavian summer houses.

Stena Line
Charter House
Park Street
Ashford
Kent TN24 8EX
Tel: **01233-647033**
Cote d'Azur, Brittany, the Dordogne, the Loire, Costa Brava.

Simply Caribbean
3 Victoria Avenue
Harrogate HG1 1EQ
Tel: **01423-526887**
Apartments in Bermuda.

MAIN HOTEL CHAIN RESERVATION NUMBERS

The headquarters address, telephone and fax numbers are then followed by reservation numbers around the world, which are generally toll-free.

Best Western
6201 N 24th Parkway
Phoenix AZ 85016
Tel: **602-780 6000** Fax: **602-780 6099**
Australia **800-131 779**
New Zealand **0800 800 567**
USA **800-528 1234**
UK **0800-393 130**

Choice Hotels International
10750 Columbia Pike
Silver Spring MD 20901
Tel: **301-593 5600** Fax: **301-681 7478**
USA **800-4.CHOICE**
UK **0800-444444**
New Zealand **0800 808 228**

Concorde Hotels
83 Blvd Exelmans
Paris 75016
Tel: **1-40 71 21 21** Fax: **1-40 71 21 31**
USA **800-888 4747**
UK **0800-181 591**
Australia **2-247 83 80**

Forte Hotels Inc.
Forte House
Gate House Road
Aylesbury, Buckinghamshire, UK.
UK **0800-404040**
USA **800-578 7878**
Australia **008-222440**

Four Seasons Hotels
1165 Leslie Street
Don Mills ON M3C 2K8, Canada
Tel: **416-449 1750** Fax: **416-441 4374**
USA **800-332 3442**
UK **0800-526648**
Australia **008-24 2907**

Golden Tulip International
2 Kew Bridge Road
Brentford TW8 0JF, UK
UK **0800-951000**
USA **800-344 1212**

Hilton International
One Wall Street Ct, 10th Floor
New York, NY 10005-3302
Tel: **212-820 1700** Fax: **212-809 7595**
USA **800 HILTONS**
UK **0345-581595**
Australia **800-222255**

Holiday Inns International
3 Ravinia Dr, Ste 2000
Atlanta GA30346-2149
Tel: **404-604 2000** Fax: **404-604 2782**
USA **800 HOLIDAY**
UK **0800-897121**
Australia **800-221066**

Hyatt Hotels Worldwide
The Madison Plaza
200 W Madison Street
Chicago IL 60606
Tel: **312-750 1234**
USA **800-233 1234**
UK **0345 581 666**
Australia **2-13 1234**

Inter-Continental
PO Box 4590
Stanford CT 06907
Tel: **203-351 8250** Fax: **203-351 8222**
USA **800-327 0200**
UK **0345-581444**
Australia **2-232 1199**

Inter-Europe Hotels
Ebenaustrasse 10
PO Box 279
Lucerne CH-6048, Switzerland
Tel: **41-430 3636** Fax: **41-430 3668**
USA **800-221 6509**
UK **0800-136234**
Australia **3-329 8844**

Leading Hotels of the World
747 Third Avenue
New York, NY 10017
Tel: **212-838 3110** Fax: **212-758 7367**
USA **800-223 6800**
UK **0800 181 123**
Australia **800-222033**

Mandarin Oriental
281 Gloucester Road
PO Box 30632
Causeway Bay, Hong Kong
Tel: **2895-9282**
USA **800-526 6566**
UK **0800-962667**
Australia **800-653328**

Marriott Hotels and Resorts
1 Marriot Drive
Washington DC 20058
Tel: **301-380 9000** Fax: **301-897 5045**
USA **800-228 9290**
UK **0800-221222**
Australia **800-251259**

Meridien Hotels
171 Blvd Haussmann
Paris, 75008 France
Tel: **1-40 68 34 20** Fax: **1-40 68 34 22**
USA **800-543 4300**
UK **0171-439 1244**
Australia **2-235 1311**

New Otani Co
4-1 Kioi-cho, Chiyoda-ku
Tokyo, Japan
Tel: **3-3265 1111** Fax: **3-3221 2619**
USA **800-421 8795**
UK **0171-584 6666**

Nikko Hotels International
Nichirei Higashiginza Bldg, 10th Floor
6- 19- 20 Tsukiji, Chuo-Ku,
Tokyo 104, Japan
Tel: **3-3248 4321** Fax: **3-3248 3020**

USA **800-645 5687**
UK **0800-282502**

Oberoi Hotels International
7 Sham Nath Marg
Delhi 110 054, India
USA **800-6.OBEROI**
UK **0181-788 2070**
Australia **2-274 6061**

Preferred Hotels and Resorts Worldwide
311 S Wacker Drive #1900
Chicago IL 60606
Tel: **312-913 0400** Fax: **312-913 0444**
USA **800-323 7500**
UK **0800-893391**
Australia **2-247 6537**

Radisson Hospitality Worldwide
Carlson Parkway
PO Box 59159
Minneapolis MN 55459
USA **800-333 3333**
UK **0800-374411**
Australia **800-333333**

Ramada International Hotels and Resorts
17/F1 New World Tower II
16-18 Queen's Road Central
Hong Kong
Tel: **2526 2233** Fax: **2877 5699**
USA **800-854 7854**
UK **01293-824124**
Australia **3-699 2122**

Regent International Hotels
New World Centre, 15th Floor
Salisbury Road, Kowloon
Hong Kong
Tel: **2366 3361** Fax: **2721 4400**
USA **800-545 4000**
UK **0800-282245**
Australia **1800-022800**

SRS Hotels Steigenberger Reservation Service
Lyonerstr 40
Frankfurt am Main D60258, Germany
USA **800-223 5652**
UK **800-898852**
Australia **008-553549**

ITT Sheraton Group
60 State Street
Boston MA 02109
Tel: **617-367 3600** Fax: **617-367 5676**
USA **800-325 3535**
Australia **1800-073535**

Southern Pacific Hotel Corporation
504 Pacific Highway, Level 9
St Leonards NSW 2065, Australia

USA **800-835 7742**
UK **0345 581666**
Australia **2-9935 8300**

Supernational Hotels
Suite 1 Grasmere
The Butlers Wharf Building
36 Shad Thames, London, SE1 2YE, UK
Tel: **0171-357 0770** Fax: **0171-357 0699**
UK **0500-303030**
USA **800-843 3311**

Utell
Utell House, 2 Kew Bridge Road
Brentford, TW8 0JF, UK
Tel: **0181-995 7881** Fax: **0181-995 2474**
USA **800-44.UTELL**
UK **0800-660066**
Australia **008-22 1176**

Further reading:
Official Hotel Guide (3 volumes) – Published
annually by Reed Travel Group

HOSTELLING ASSOCIATIONS

Virtually every single country in the world has
an Hostel Association or at least an Associate
Organization. For further contact addresses the
International Youth Hostel Federation annually
publishes the Hostelling International Book (2
Volumes £7 each).

UK

Scottish Youth Hostel Association
7 Glebe Crescent
Stirling FK8 2JA
Tel: **01786-891400**

Youth Hostel Association
Trevelyan House
8 St Stephens Hill
St Albans
Herts AL1 2DY
Tel: **01727-855215**

Youth Hostel Association of Northern Ireland
22-32 Donegal Road
Belfast BT12 5JN
Tel: **01232-324733**

USA

American Youth Hostels Inc
National Offices
PO Box 37613
Washington DC 20013-7613, USA
Tel: **202-783 6161**

TIMESHARE AND HOME EXCHANGE ORGANISATIONS

The Timeshare Council
23 Buckingham Gate
London SW1E 6LB
Tel: **0171-821 8845**
*Gives free advice to members, and makes a
small charge for affiliation where owners
belong to non-member resorts.*

Homelink International
Linfield House
Gorse Hill Road
Virginia Water
Surrey GU25 4AS
Tel: **01344-842642**

International Home Exchange
DAT/TRAVEL
Level 2
17 Sydney Road
Manly NSW 2095
Australia
Tel: **8-232 2022**

International Home Exchange
PO Box 38615
11 Peach Parade
Ellerslie
New Zealand
Tel: **9-522 2933**

Intervac
3 Orchard Court
North Wraxall
Chippenham
Wilts SN14 7AD
Tel: **01225-892208**
email: **intervac-gb@msn.com**

Vacation Exchange Club
PO Box 820
Haleiwa, HI 96712, USA
Tel: **800 638 3841**
*The longest-established home exchange agency
in the United States, publishes two directories
each year.*

West World Holiday Exchange
1707 Platt Crescent
North Vancouver
BC VJ7 1X9, Canada
Tel: **604-987 3262**

Worldwide Home Exchange Club
50 Hans Crescent
London SW1X 0NA
Tel: **0171-823 9937** ∎

A BASIC GUIDE TO HEALTH
Section 10

VACCINATION CENTRES AND INFORMATION

In the UK, most vaccinations can be given by the traveller's own doctor. Yellow fever vaccine can be given by some general practitioners or this and unusual vaccinations can be obtained from clinics run by the Public Health Department in most large towns or cities and from the centres listed below, unless otherwise indicated. Most vaccines for travel will have to be paid for by the traveller. Consult your own doctor before ringing any of the hospital-based clinics (unless they have an 0839 or 0891 number, however you will be charged for making these calls).

Vaccination requirements are listed under each country in the Geographical Section in Section 1 of the Directory. Please note these are only guidelines as inoculations can change with new outbreaks of diseases, so please check with your own doctor or with a travel clinic as far in advance as you can.

British Airways Travel Clinics
Tel: **01276-685 040** *for your nearest travel clinic, 25 clinics nationwide.*

British Airways Immunization Centre
156 Regent Street
London W1
Tel: **0171-439 9584**
Open Monday-Friday 9am-4.30pm and Saturday 10.00am - 4.00pm. No appointment necessary.

British Airways' Victoria Clinic
Victoria Plaza
Victoria Station
London SW1
Tel: **0171-233 6661**
Open 8.15am-11.30am; 12.30pm-3.45pm Also at: North Terminal, Gatwick Airport. Open all day, evenings and weekends for emergencies.

Centers for Disease Control Traveler's Health section
Tel: **404-332 4559**
Based in Atlanta, they run a 24-hour automated system giving advice by region and on special problems such as malaria, food, water precautions and advice for pregnant travellers.

Central Public Health Laboratory
61 Colindale Avenue
Colindale
London NW9 5HT
Tel: **0181-200 4400**
Provides advice and supplies of rabies vaccines and supplies of gammaglobulin to general practitioners for immunization against hepatitis A.

Convenience Care Centers
Suite 100
10301 East Darvey
Armani
CA 91733
USA
Undertakes all necessary vaccinations.

Department of Health
Public Enquires Office
Richmond House
79 Whitehall
London SW1A 2NS
Tel: **0171-210 4850**
Also publish a free booklet Health Advice for Travellers. *Call Tel 0800-555777 to order.*

Department of Infectious Diseases and Tropical Medicine
Birmingham Heartlands Hospital
Bordesley Green East
Birmingham B9 5SS
Tel: **0121 766 6611**
Pre-travel telephone advice and expertise in investigation and treatment of tropical illness.

**Department of Infectious Diseases &
Tropical Medicine**
North Manchester General Hospital
Delaunays Road
Manchester M8 5AB
Tel: **0161-795 4567**

**Department of Infectious Diseases and
Tropical
Medicine/Travel Information**
Ruchill Hospital
Glasgow G20 9NB
Tel: **0141-946 7120**
*Together with Communicable Disease
(Scotland) Unit, provides telephone advice for
general practitioners and other doctors and
maintains 'Travax', a computerized database
on travel medicine that may be accessed
remotely by modem. Pre- and post-travel clinics
and limited travel health supplies.
Enquiries/referrals to clinics are best initiated
by your general practitioner.*

Health Control Unit
Terminal 3 Arrivals
Heathrow Airport
Hounslow
Middlesex TW6 1NB
Tel: **0181-745 7209**
*Can give at any time up-to-date information on
compulsory and recommended immunizations
for different countries.*

Hospital for Tropical Diseases
4 St. Pancras Way
London NW1 0PE
Tel: **0171-637 6099**(Travel clinic)
*Comprehensive range of pre–travel immuniza-
tions and advice, and post–travel check-ups in
travel clinic and large travel shop. Pre-recorded healthline gives country-specific health hazards — you will be asked to dial the
international dialling code of the relevant country, so have it ready. Centre for investigation
and treatment of tropical illness.*

**International Association for Medical
Assistance to Travelers**
417 Center Street
Lewiston
NY 14092
Tel: **716 754 4883**
http://www.sentex.net/~iamat
*Non-profit organisation dedicated to the gath-
ering and dissemination of health and sanitary
information world-wide. Publish a directory of
English speaking medical centres world-wide
and many leaflets on world climates, immunization, malaria and other health risks world-wide.*
also at
40 Regal Road
Guelph, Ontario

N1K 1B5
Canada
Tel: **519 836 0102**

Liverpool School of Tropical Medicine
Pembroke Place
Liverpool L3 5QA
Tel: **0151-708 9393** (pre-recorded pre-travel
advice and medical queries) or **0891 172111**
(travel clinic) 50p per minute
Fax: **0151-708 8733**
**Web:
http://www.liv.ac.uk/lstm/travelmed.html.**
*Regular immunization and post-travel clinics
and limited range of travellers' health supplies.
International centre of expertise and research
on venoms and snake bites, and investigation
and management of tropical diseases.*

Malaria Reference Laboratory
Tel: **0171-636 7921/8636**
Advice on malaria prophylaxis and prevention.

**Biting Insects and How to Avoid Getting
Bitten Advice Line**
Tel: **0891-600 270**
Calls cost 50p per minute.

MASTA
London School of Hygiene and Tropical
Medicine
Keppel Street
London WC1E 7BR
Tel: **0171-631 4408**
Health Brief: **0891 224 100**
*Markets a wide range of products. For detailed
advice on all health requirements for your
intended destination(s), ring the Health Brief
line; calls typically take 3-4 minutes and follow-
ing this your health brief arrives by first class
post (covered by the cost of the call).*

Ross Institute Malaria Advisory Service
London School of Hygiene & Tropical
Medicine
Keppel Street
London WC1E 7HT
Tel: **0171-636 7921**
24-hour taped advice.

Travellers Healthline
Tel: **0891-224 100**
*This is a regularly updated advice line (with
inter-active technology) for travellers seeking
information about vaccinations etc.*

**UDS Department of Health and Human
Services**
Public Health Service
Centers for Disease Control,
Center for Prevention Service
Division of Quarantine

101 Marietta Street, Rm 1515
Atlanta
GA 30323
Tel: **404-331 2442**

West London Designated Vaccination Centre
53 Great Cumberland Place
London W1H 7HL
Tel: **0171-262 6456**
Open 8.45am-5pm Mon-Fri, no appointment necessary.

Additional helpful medical organisations

Department of Social Security
Overseas Branch
Newcastle upon Tyne NE 98 1YX
or
Department of Health and Social Services
Overseas Branch
8-14 Callender Street
Belfast BT1 5DP
For residents of Northern Ireland
Freefone **0800 555 777** for supplies of leaflets
For advice on eligibility for health care abroad (Freefone). The selected vaccination requirements for all countries are updated on Prestel. Does not provide immunizations, etc.

National AIDS Helpline
Tel: **0800 567 123**
24-hour free helpline providing advice on all aspects of HIV infection.

Terence Higgins Trust
Tel: **0171-242 1010**
Hours: 12.00-22.00 daily
Confidential phoneline for detailed information about travel restrictions, insurance, etc. for HIV positive individuals.

EMERGENCY MEDICAL TRAVEL KIT SUPPLIERS

Homeway Ltd
Fighting Cocks
West Amesbury
Salisbury
Wilts SP4 7BH
Tel: **01980-626361**
Provides a Travel with Care package and also sells sterile medical packs.

Dr Jones and Partners
Charlotte Keel Health Centre

Seymour Road
Easton
Bristol BS5 0UA
Tel: **0117 951 2244**
Travel medical kits.

Medical Advisory Services for Travellers (Masta)
London School of Hygiene & Tropical Medicine
Keppel Street
London WC1
Tel: **0171-631 4408**
MASTA has helped to design the 'Travel-Well' personal water purifiers. It removes particulate matter, bacteria, protozoa and viruses from contaminated water. The Trekker Travel Well costs £24.95 and the Pocket Travel Well £9.95. They also sell Sterile Medical Equipment Packs and Emergency Dental Packs.

Nomad
3-4 Wellington Terrace
Turnpike Lane
Hornsey
London N8 0PX
Tel: **0181-889 7014**
or
4 Potters Road
New Barnet
Hertfordshire
EN5 5HW
Tel: **0181-441 7208**
Full medical centre, immunisation and pharmacy. Wide range of not only medical equipment, but also clothing and mosquito nets. Mail order.

Oasis
High Street
Stoke Ferry
King's Lynn
Norfolk
PE33 9SP
Tel: **01366-500466**
Not only sells mosquito nets, but will also send a free malaria advice sheet, also can provide sterile medical kits.

Safety and First Aid (SAFA)
59 Hill Street
Liverpool L8 5SB
Tel: **0151-708 0397**
As well as general medical kits also provide Aids and Hepatitis B prevention kits.

MAJOR HOSPITALS WORLD-WIDE

This list is not comprehensive, but is intended as an initial guide, listing one important hospital in capital cities world-wide.

Albania - ABC Clinic (British Clinic), Rruga Ludovik Shllaku, Tirana, Tel: **42-27707 / 29752**
Algeria - Hospital Mustapha, Place du 1er Mai, Algiers, Tel: **2-67 33 33**
Andorra - Hospital Nostra Senyora de Meritxell, 13 Av Fiter I Rossell, Escalades-Engordany, Tel: **871 000**
Anguilla - Princess Alexandra Hospital, Stoney Ground, Anguilla BW1, Tel: **809-497 2552**
Antigua & Barbuda - , Holberton Hospital, Queen Elizabeth Highway, St. John's, Tel: **462 0251/4**
Argentina - Hospital general de Agudos, Cerviño 3356, Buenos Aires, Tel: **1-801 0027 / 801 0412**
Armenia - Republican Clinical Hospital, 6 Margarian Street, Achapniak, Yerevan, Tel: **2-34 50 83**
Australia :
(NSW) - Royal Prince Albert Hospital, Missenden Road, Camerdown 2050,Sydney, Tel: **2-516 6111**
(Northern Territory) - Royal Darwin Hospital, Rocklands Drive, Casuarina, Tel: **89-228 888**
(Queensland) - Royal Brisbane Hospital, Herston Road, Herston, Brisbane, Tel: **7-3253 8111/8222**
(South Australia) - Royal Adelaide Hospital, North Terrace, Adelaide, Tel: **8-223 0230**
(Tasmania) - Royal Hobart Hospital, Liverpool Street, Hobart, Tel: **2-388 308**
(Victoria) - Central Welling ton Health Service, Guthridge Parade, Sale 3850, Tel: **51-44 41 11**
(Western Australia) - Poyal Perth Hospital, Welling ton Street, Perth WA6000, Tel: **9-224 2244**
Austria - Allgemeines Krankenhaus, 18-20 Waehringer Guertal, Vienna A-1090, Tel: **1-402 0660**
Azerbaijan - Semashko Clinical Hospital No. 1, 1M Kasimova Street, Baku, Tel: **12-95 49 04**
Bahamas - Princess Margaret Hospital, Shirley Street and Elizabeth Avenue, Nassaum Tel: **322 2861**
Bahrain - International Hospital of Bahrain, PO Box 1084, Manama, Tel: **591 666**
Bangladesh - Dhaka Medical College Hospital, Tel: **2-31 82 02**
Barbados - Queen Elizabeth Hospital, Martindales Road, St. Michael, Tel: **436 6450**
Belarus - Minsk clinic No. 10, 73 Uborevich Street, Minsk, Tel: **172-419 811**
Belgium - Clinique Univeritaire St Luc, Avenue Hippocrate 10, Brussels 1200, Tel: **2-555 3111**
Belize - Karl Heusner Memorial Hospital, Princess Margaret Drive, Belize City, Tel: **2-31548**
Benin - Centre Hospitalier Départemental de l'Ouémé, Porto Novo, Tel: **21 32 29**
Bermuda - King Edward VII Memorial Hospital, Hamilton HM DX, Tel: **236 2345**
Bhutan - Jigme Dorji Wamgchuk National Referral Hospital, Thimphu, Tel: **2-22496/7**
Bolivia - Hospital General, Avenida Saavedra 2245, La Paz, Tel: **2-367 711**
Botswana - Princess Marina Hospital, Gaborone, Tel: **353 221**
Brazil - Hospital de Base do Distrito Federal, Area Especial SMHS, Brasilia, Tel: **61-325 5050**
Brunei - Raja Isteri Pengiran Anak Saleha Hospital (RIPAS), Bandar Seri Begawan, Tel: **2-242424**
Bulgaria - Medical University Hospital "Sveta Anna", Sofia, Tel: **2-75 51 24**
Burkina Faso - Clinique Notre Dame de la Paix, BP5666, Tanghin secteur 24, Ouagadougou, Tel: **36 26 40**
Burundi - Clinique Prince Louis Rwagasore, Bujumbura, **Tel: 2-223 881/2**
Cambodia - European Medical Clinic, 195a Norodom Blvd, Phnom Penh, Tel: **23-91200**
Cameroon - Centre Médico-Social (Coopération Française), Yaoundé, Tel: **22/23-230 139**
Central African Republic - Hôpital de l'Amitie, Ave de l'Independance, Bangui, Tel: **615 700**
Chad - Hôpital Central N'Djaména Capitol, BP77, Tel: **515 309 / 515 336**
Chile - Hospital Jose Joaquin Aguirre, 999 Santos Dumont, Santiago, Tel: **2-737 3031**
China - Beijing Hospital, 1 Dahua Road, Dongdan, Beijing 100730, Tel: **10-513 2266**
Colombia - San Juan de dios, carrera 10, Calle de la Sur, Santa Fe de Bogotá, Tel: **1-233 4044**
Congo - Centra Hospitalier et Universitaire de Brazzaville, BP32, Tel: **82 88 10 / 82 23 65**
Costa Rica - Hospital México, San José, Tel: **232 6122**
Côte d'Ivoire - Centre Hospitalier et Universitaire de Cocody, Tel: **44 91 00 / 44 90 38**
Croatia - KBC Zagreb, Salata 2, Tel: **1-273457**
Cuba - Civa Garcia International Clinic, Havana, Tel: **7-332 605**
Cyprus - Lefkosia General Hospital, Nicosia, Tel: **2-451 111**
Czech Republic - Nemocnice na Homolce, 2 Roentgenove, 151 19 Prague 5, Tel: **2-52921111**
Denmark - Rogshospitalet, Copenhagen Ø, DK-2100, Tel: **45-35 45 35 45**
Djibouti - Hôpital Peltier, Djibouti, Tel: **35 27 12**
Dominica - Princess Margaret Hospital, Goodwill, Roseau, Tel: **448 2231**
Dominican Republic - Hospital Dr Dario Contreras, Santo Domingo, Tel: **596 3686 / 596 7231**
Ecuador - Hospital Metropolitano, Ave Mariana Jesús y Occidental, Quito, Tel: **2-431 520 / 439 030**
Egypt - 3 Syria Street, Mohessien, Cairo, Tel: **2-3029091/5**
El Salvador - Hospital de Ninos Benjamin Bloom, 25 Av Norte Final, San Salvador, Tel: **225 4692**

Eritrea - Mekane Hiwot Hospital, Asmara, Tel: **1-127762**
Estonia - Mustamae Haigla, 19 Sutiste Tee, Tallinn EE0034, Tel: **7-428 211**
Ethiopia - Black Lion Hospital, Addis Ababa, Tel: **1-511211**
Fiji - Colonial War Memorial Hospital, Suva, Tel: **679-321 066**
Finland - Helsinki University Central Hospital, Stenbackinpratu 9, Helsinki, Tel: **0-4711**
France - Cochin Hospital, 27 rue du Faubourg St Jaques, Paris, Tel: **1-42 34 12 12**
French Guiana - Centre Hospitalier Général de Cayenne, Ave des Flamboyants, Cayenne, Tel: **39 50 50**
Gabon - Centre Hospitalier de Libreville, BP 50, Tel: **76 36 18**
Gambia - Royal Victoria Hospital, Banjul, Tel: **228 223**
Georgia - Treatment and Diagnostic Centre, 5 I Chavchavdze Ave, Tbilisi, Tel: **32-23 04 92**
Germany - Krankenhauser Klinikum Buch, 50 Wiltberghstr, Berlin 13125, Tel: **30-94010**
Ghana - Ridge Hospital, Castle Road, Accra, Tel: **21-775341**
Greece - Regional General Hospital Evangelismos, Tpsilantou 45, Athens, Tel: **1-722 0101 / 722 1501**
Grenada - General Hospital, St George's, Tel: **440 2051**
Guatemala - Hospital Centro Medico, 6a Av 3-47, Zona 10, Guatemala City, Tel: **2-323 555 / 342 157**
Guinea Republic - CHU Donka, BP 234, Conakry, Tel: **44 19 33 / 44 46 86**
Guinea-Bissau - Simão Mendes National hospital, Bissau, Tel: **212 861**
Guyana - Georgetown Hospital, New Market Street, Georgetown, Tel: **2-56900**
Haiti - Hôpital Saint Francois de Sales, rue Chareron, Port-au-Prince, Tel: **22 5033**
Hong Kong - Queen Elizabeth Hospital, 30 Gascoigne Road, Kowloon, Tel: **2958 8888**
Hungary - Szent János Kórház, 1 Diósárok Ucta, Budapest 1125, Tel: **1-156 1122 / 1410**
Iceland - Landspítalinn, v/Hringbraut, Reykjavík 101, Tel: **560 1000**
India - Appollo Hospital, Saritarihar, Delhi Maghura Road, New Delhi, Tel: **11-6925858**
Indonesia - Cipto Mangun Kusuma Hospital, Diponogoro 71, Jakarta Central, Tel: **21-566 8284**
Iran - Imam Khomeini Hospital, End of Kesharvarz Blvd, Tehran, Tel: **21-938 081**
Iraq - WHO representative Dr Habib Rejab c/o UNDP Office, PO Box 2048, Baghdad, Tel: **1-718 0875**
Ireland - Beaumont Hospital, Beaumont Road, Dublin 9, Tel: **1-837 7755**
Israel - Kiryah Hadassah, Jerusalem, Tel: **2-777111**
Italy - Ospedale Agostino Gemelli, 8 Largo Gemelli, Rome 00168, Tel: **6-30151**
Jamaica - University of West Indies, Mona, Kingston 7, Tel: **927 1620**
Japan - International Clinic, 5-9 Azabudai 1-chrome, Minato-ku, Tokyo, Tel: **3-582 2646**
Jordan - Al Basheer Hospital, Amman, Tel: **6-771111**
Kazakhstan - Adult Medical Care Diagnostic Centre, 57 Auezova Street, Almaty, Tel: **3272-42 29 79**
Kenya - Kenyatta National Hospital, Nairobi, Tel: **2-726 300**
Korea (North) - Korean Red Cross General Hospital, Pyongyang
Korea (South) - Seoul National University Hospital, 28 Yon-gon-dong, Chongno-gu, Tel: **2-760 2114**
Kuwait - Al Amiri Hospital, Safat 13041, Kuwait City, Tel: **2451442**
Kyrgystan - Rep. Clinical Hospital No 1, Togolok Moldo Street 1, Bishkek 720011, Tel: **3312-223424**
Laos - International Clinic, Fangum Road, Vientiane, Tel: **21-214 022**
Latvia - Latvian Medical Academy, 13 Pilsonu, Riga LV 1002, Tel: **2-611 198**
Lebanon - Beirut General Hospital, Tel: **1-850213/4**
Lesotho - Queen Elizabeth II Hospital, PO Box 122, Maseru, Tel: **322501**
Libya - El Khadra Hospital, Tripoli, Tel: **21-903301**
Lithuania - Vilnius University Emergency Hospital, Siltnamiu 29, Vilnius, Tel: **2-269 069/140**
Luxembourg - Clinique d'Eich, 78 rue d'Eich, Luxembourg-Ville, Tel: **43 77 71**
Macau - Hospital Kiang Wu, Rua de Kiang, Tel: **37 13 33**
Macedonia - Clinical Centre of the Rep. of Macedonia, 17 Vodnjanska Street, Skopje, **Tel: 91-114 244**
Madagascar - Hôpital Général de Befelatanana, Mahamasina, Antananarivo 101, Tel: **2-22384**
Malawi - Kamuzu Central Hospital, Lilongwe, Tel: **721 555**
Malaysia - General Hospital, Jalan Pahang, Kuala Lumpur 50586, Tel: **3-292 1044**
Maldives - Indira Gandhi Memorial Hospital, Malé, Tel: **316 647**
Mali - French Medical Centre, Bamako, Tel: **225071**
Malta - St. Luke's Hospital, Guardamangia, Tel: **241 251 / 234 101 / 247 860**
Mauritania - Centre Hospitalier National, Nouakchott, Tel: **2-52135**
Mauritius - Dr A Jeetoo Hospital, Volcy Pougnet Street, Port Louis, Tel: **2123201**
Mexico - Hospital General, Andador 5, entre Calle 12 y Calle 13, Cancún, QR, Tel: **98-842666**
Moldova - Republican Clinical Hospital, 29 Strada N Testemitanu, Chisinău, Tel: **2-72 85 85**
Mongolia - National Medical Institute, Ard Augushin Street, Tel: **1-361155**
Morocco - Clinique Agdal, 6 Place Talha, Ave Ibn Sina, Agdal, Rabat, Tel: **7-770100 / 675030**
Myanmar - AEA International Clinic, Nawarat Arcade, 257 Insein Road, Hlaing Township 11052, Yangon
Namibia - Medicity Windhoek, Heliodoor Street, Eros Park, Windhoek, Tel: **61-222687**

856

Nepal - Anandaban Hospital, Kathmandu, Tel: **1-290545**
The Netherlands - Academisch Medisch Centrum, Meibergdreef 9, Amsterdam 1105 AZ, Tel: **20-5669111**
New Zealand - Auckland Hospital, Park Road, Grafton, Tel: **9-379 7440**
Nicaragua - La Mascota, Managua, Tel: **2-289 7700**
Niger - Hôpital National de niamey, BP 238, Niamey, Tel: **72 22 53 / 72 28 55 / 72 25 21**
Nigeria - St Nicholas Hospital, 57 Campbell Street, Lagos, Tel: **1-2600070-9**
Norway - Rikshospitalet, 32 Pilestredet, Oslo 0027, Tel: **22-86 70 10**
Oman - The Royal Hospital, PO Box 1331, Muscat 111, Tel: **590491**
Pakistan - Federal Government Services Hospital, Islamabad, Tel: **51-218300 / 859511-19**
Panama - Hospital Santo Tomás, Ave 1, Panamá 1, Tel: **227 4075**
Papua New Guinea - Port Moresby General Hospital, Boroko 111, Tel: **3248200**
Paraguay - Sanatorio Migone Battilana, Eligio Ayala 1293, Asunción, Tel: **021-498200**
Peru - Hospital de Emergencia "Casimiru Ulloa", Ave Republica de Panama, Lima, Tel: **1-445 5096**
Philippines - St Luke's Medical Center, 279 E Rodriquez Senior Blvd, Manilla, Tel: **2-799661**
Poland - Centralny Szpital Kliniczny, 1A Banacha Street, Warsaw 02-097, Tel: **22-6583516**
Portugal - Hospital Santa Maria, Avenida Prof. Egas Moniz, Lisbon 1600, Tel: **1-7975171**
Puerto Rico - University District Hospital, Puerto Rico Medical Center, San Juan, Tel: **754 3700 / 754 3600**
Qatar - Hamad General Hospital, PO Box 3050, Doha, Tel: **394444**
Romania - The Emergency Hospital, 10 Sos Berceni, Sector 4, Bucharest, Tel: **1-6836895**
Russia - American Medical Center, Bldg No. 10, 2nd Tverskoy-Yamskoy Per, Moscow, Tel: **095-956 33 66**
Rwanda - CHK (Centre Hospitalier de Kigali), Ave de l'Hopital, Kigali, Tel: **75555**
Saudi Arabia - Riyadh Central Hospital, Riyadh 11196, Tel: **1-435 5555**
Senegal - Hôpital Principal, Ave Nelson Mandela, Dakar, Tel: **232 741**
Seychelles - Victoria Hospital, PO Box 52, Victoria, Mahé, Tel: **388 000**
Sierra Leone - Connaught Hospital, 1 Johnston Street, Freetown, Tel: **22-222 962**
Singapore - Singapore General Hospital, Outram Road, Singapore, Tel: **2223322**
Slovak Republic - Berer 3 Hospital, 5 Limbová, Bratislava, Tel: **7-374 503**
Slovenia - Klinicni Center Ljubljana, 7 Zaloska, Ljublijana, Tel: **61-1313113**
Solomon Islands - Central Hospital, Honiara, Tel: **23 600**
Somalia - Benadir Hospital, Mogadishu
South Africa - Entabeni Hospital, PO Box 2230, Durban 4000, Tel: **31-811344**
Spain - Hospital 12 de Octubre, Carretera de Andalucia, Madrid 4-28041, Tel: **1-469 7600 / 460 4000**
Sri Lanka - National Hospital, Columbo, Tel: **1-691111 / 698443**
Sudan - Khartoum Teaching Hospital, PO Box 102, Khartoum, Tel: **11-770208**
Suriname - Academisch Ziekenhuis, PO Box 389, Flustraat, Paramaribo, Tel: **498552**
Swaziland - Mbabane Government Hospital, PO Box 8, Mbabane, Tel: **42111**
Sweden - Karolinsko Sjukhuset, 171 76 Stockholm, Tel: **8-729 2000**
Switzerland - Inselspital, Freiburg Strasse 18, Bern 3010, Tel: **31-6322802**
Tahiti - Hôpital Mamao, Papeete, Tel: **466262**
Taiwan - Cathay General Hospital, 280 Jen Ai Road, Section 4, Taipei, Tel: **2-7082121**
Tajikistan - Karaboloev Medical Center, 59 Samoni, Dushanbe, Tel: **3772-361510**
Tanzania - Muhimbil Medical Centre. PO Box 65000, Dar es Salaam, Tel: **51-26211**
Thailand - Bangkok General Hospital, 2 Soi Soonvichai 7, Bangkok, Tel: **2-318 0066**
Togo - Centre Hospitalier Universitaire, PO Box 57, Tokoin, Lomé, Tel: **212501 / 215072 / 254739**
Trinidad & Tobago - Port of Spain General Hospital, Charlotte Street, Tel: **632 951**
Tunisia - Hôpital Charles Nicole, Blvd Bab Benat, Tunis, Tel: **1-663 000/949**
Turkey - University of Hacettepe Hospital, Hacettepe, Ankara, Tel: **312-3103545**
Turkmenistan - The Central Clinical Hospital, UI Gorgoli, Pirigova NI, Ashgabat, Tel: **3632-253243**
Uganda - Mulago Hospital, PO Box 7051, Kampala, Tel: **41-541250**
Ukraine - Ukrainian Medical Service, 16 Olzhicha Street, Kiev 86, Tel: **44-440 63 44**
United Arab Emirates - Al Jazira Hospital, PO Box 2427, Abu Dhabi, Tel: **2-214800**
Uruguay - British Hospital, 2420 Ave Italia, Montevideo, Tel: **2-471020**
Uzbekistan - International Medical Clinic, 4 Taras Shevchenko Street, Tashkent, Tel: **3712-560606**
Venezuela - Hospital Clinico Universitario, Ciudad Universitaria, Caracas, Tel: **2-6627540**
Vietnam - Bach Mai Medical Centre, Foreigner Admittance, Phuong Mai Street, Hanoi, Tel: **4-8522089**
Yemen - Al Thawra Hospital, Sana'a, Tel: **1-246972**
Yugoslavia - Klinicki Centar Beograd, 2 PAsterova, Belgrade 11000, Tel: **11-662 755 / 661 122**
Zaïre (DRC) - Zaïre American Clinic, 1054 Ave Batétéla, Kinshasa, Tel: **12-50929**
Zambia - University Teaching Hospital, Lusaka, Tel: **1-253955**
Zimbabwe - Parirenyatwa Hospital, PO Box CY 198, Causeway, Harare, Tel: **4-794411**
Further information: World Travel Health Guide (Columbus Press) ■

EQUIPPING FOR A TRIP
Section 11

EQUIPMENT SUPPLIERS

Alpine Sports
456 Strand
London WC2
Tel: **0171-839 5161**
Travel and mountaineering equipment.

Berghaus
17-19 Brindley Road
Heartburn
District 11, Washington
Tyne & Wear NE37 2SF
Tel: **0191-415 0200**
*Britain's leading suppliers of specialist packs
and clothing for hiking and climbing. Suppliers
to many expeditions.*

Blacks Camping and Leisure Ltd
8-10 Old Hall Street
Hanley
Stoke on Trent ST1 1QT
Tel: **01782-212870**
*Have lightweight, mountain and touring tents;
camp furniture, kitchen kits, stoves and lamps;
clothing and accessories and convertible
specialist and summer-weight sleeping bags.*

The Brasher Boot Company
White Cross
Lancaster, LA1 4XY
Tel: **01524-841000**

Clothtec
92 Par Green
Par, Cornwall PL24 2AG
Tel: **01726 813602**
*Manufacturers of special products that have
been supplied to expeditions all over the world.
Specialists in jungle sleeping units, mosquito
nets. Also repairs equipment. Will give advice
over the telephone to first time expeditioners.*

Cotswold Camping
42-46 Uxbridge Road
London W12 8ND
Tel: **0181 743 2976**
*Supply a wide store of outdoor equipment and
have a comprehensive range of water filtering
and purification equipment.*

Darr Expeditions Service
Theresienstrasse 66
D-8000 Munchen
Germany
Tel: **89 282 032**

Field and Trek (Equipment) Ltd
Mail Order:
3 Wates Way
Brentwood
Essex CM15 9TB
Tel: **01277-233122**
Retail:
3 Palace Street
Canterbury Kent CT1 2DY
Tel: **01227-470023**
101 Baker Street
London
Tel: **0171-224 0049**
*Illustrated catalogue with products at
discounted prices on most leading makes of
expedition equipment – tents, rucksacks, boots,
waterproof clothing, sleeping bags and
mountaineering gear.*

Laurence Corner
62/64 Hampstead Road
London NW1 2NU
Tel: **0171-813 1010**

Karrimore International Ltd.
Petre Road
Clayton-le-Moors ⇨

Accrington, Lancs, BB5 5JZ
Tel: **01254-385911**

Mountain Equipment
Peaco House
Dawson Street
Hyde
Cheshire, SK14 1RD
Tel: **0161-366 5020**

Penrith Survival Equipment
Morland
Penrith
Cumbria CA10 3AZ
Tel: **01931-714444**
Mail order retail outfit for Survival Aids

Rohan
30 Maryland Road
Tongwell
Milton Keynes MK15 8HN
Tel: **01908-618888**

*Design practical clothes for everyday wear,
with particular attention to the needs of the
serious traveller and outdoor enthusiast.*

Tenson
Plymouth House
The Square
Sawbridgeworth
Hertfordshire, CM21 5RU
Tel: **01279-600618**

**Tent and Tarpaulin Manufacturing
Company**
101-103 Brixton Hill
London SW2 1AA
Tel: **0181-674 0121**

Travelling Light
Morland House
Morland
Penrith
Cumbria
CA10 3AZ
Tel: **01931-714488**
Mail Order.

YHA Adventure Shop
14 Southampton Street
London WC2E 7HY
Tel: **0171-836 8541**

USA

Advanced Filtration Technology
2424 Bates Avenue
Concord
CA 94520
Portable water filter and Super Straw.

Banana Republic
1 Harrison Street
San Francisco
CA 94105
Tel: **415 777 0250**
Mail order travel clothing and books.

Basic Designs, Inc
1100 Stearns Drive
Sauk Rapids
Minnesota 56379
Tel: **320 252 1642**
Telex: 9103806641
*Make the H20 Sun Shower, a solar-heater
portable shower consisting of a heavy duty vinyl
bag which holds 11¹/₂ litres of water and heats
the water to between 32 and 49 C depending on
exposure and the heat of the day. The pack
measures 10 by 33cms and weighs only 340g.*

L.L. Bean Inc
Freeport
ME 04033
Tel: **207- 865 3111**
*Operates a mail order service and has a
salesroom which is open 24 hours a day, 365
days a year. Firm sells outdoor garments and
accessories, boots and other footwear, canoes,
compasses, axes, knives, binoculars,
thermometers, stoves, tents, sleeping bags,
packs and frames, skis and snowshoes,
campware, travel bags, lamps, blankets.*

The Complete Traveller
199 Madison Avenue
New York, NY 10016
Tel: **212- 679 4339**
Annual catalogue US$1.

Katadyn USA, Inc
Warehouse + Service-Center
3019 North Scottsdale Road
Scottsdale
AZ 85251
Tel: **602- 990 3131**

North by Northeast
181 Conant Street
Pawtucket
RI 02862

Parks Products
3611 Cahuenga
Hollywood
CA 90068
Tel: **213- 876 5454**
*Make voltage converters and adaptor plugs to
fit electronic/portable appliances anywhere in
the world.*

Sierra West
121 Gray Avenue
Santa Barbara
CA 93101
Tel: **805- 963 87 27**
*Sierra West is a manufacturer of high quality
rainwear, outer-wear, tents and backpacking
accessories. For further information, please
write and request a free colour catalogue.*

Survival Cards
PO Box 1805
Bloomington, IN 47402
*Supplies Survival Cards measuring 7.5 by 12.5
cms and made from plastic, which are crammed
with information, including edible plant
classification, emergency shelter construction,
first aid, Morse Code, climbing techniques and
knot tying.*

Thinsulate
6 Thermal Insulation 3M
3M Centre
Building 275-6W-01
St Paul
MN 55114
Tel: **800 328 1689**

Traveler's Checklist
335 Cornwall Bridge Road
Sharon
CT 06069
Tel: **860 364 0144**
*International mail order company sells hard-to-
find travel accessories, including electrical
devices, security, health and grooming aids,
money convertors and other travel items.*

SPECIALIST EQUIPMENT SUPPLIERS

Medical

BCB Ltd
Moorland Road
Cardiff CF2 2YL
Tel: **01222-464464**
*First Aid and medical kits to any specification.
Catalogues available.*

John Bell and Croyden
50-54 Wigmore Street
London W1H 0AU
Tel: **0171-935 5555**
*Chemists in London who specialize in making
up travel and expedition supplies.*

MASTA
c/o London School of Hygiene and Tropical
Medicine
Keppel Street (Gower Street)
London WC1E 7HT
Tel: **0171-631 4408**
*Medical advisory service. Will also provide
sterile kits of syringes, needles, etc. for those
going into areas with a high incidence of AIDS
or Hepatitis B.*

Rhone-Poulenc Rorer Ltd
Rainham Road South
Dagenham
Essex RM10 7XS
Tel: **0181-919 3060**
*May & Baker are one of the largest
pharmaceutical manufacturers in the UK. They
have several remedies for the minor everyday
accidents that occur at home or abroad.*

Tender Corp
After Bite
PO Box 290
Littleton
NH 03561
USA
Tel: **603 444 5464**
*America's leading treatment for the relief of
pain and irritation due to insect bites or stings.*

Wyeth Laboratories
PO Box 8299
Philadelphia
PA 19101
USA
Tel: **215 878 9500**
*Manufacturer of anti-venoms against
poisonous snakes of the United States. The
serum is sold in a freeze-dried condition,
making it ideally suited for expeditions (no need
for refrigeration), and in small quantities.*

Optical

Heron Optical Co
23-25 Kings Road
Brentwood
Essex CM14 4ER
Tel: **01277-222 230**
*Mail Order: 3 Wates Way Brentwood Essex
CM15 9TB Tel: 01277-233 122*
*Stock all leading makes of binoculars,
telescopes. Associate company of Field and
Trek (Equipment) Ltd.*

Viking Optical Ltd
Blythe Road
Halesworth
Suffolk IP19 8EN
Tel: **01986-875315** ⇨

Supplies Sunto compasses and binoculars, and other precisions instruments.

Olympus Optical Co (UK) Ltd
2-8 Honduras St
London EC1Y 0TX
Tel: **0171-253 2772**

Photographic

Agfa UK
27 Great West Road
Brentford
Middlesex TW8 9AX
Tel: **0181-560 2131**

British Photographic Enterprise Group
1 West Ruislip Station
Ruislip
Middlesex HA4 7DW
Tel:**01895-634515**
Association of British manufacturers of photographic, cine and audio-visual equipment.

Camera Care Systems
Vale Lane
Bedminster
Bristol BS3 5RU
Tel: **0117-9635263**
Manufacture protective casings for and distribute fine photographic equipment.

Canon UK Ltd
Brent Trading Centre
North Circular Road
Neasden
London NW10 0JF
Tel: **0181-459 1266**

Colab Ltd
Head Office
Herald Way
Coventry CV3 1BB
Tel: **01203-455 007**
UK's leading photographic processing laboratory, branches around country and mail order.

Fuji UK Ltd
Fuji Film House
125 Finchley Road
London NW3 6HY
Tel: **0171-586 5900**

Ilford UK Ltd
14 Tottenham Street
London W1
Tel: **0171-636 7890**

Jessop Photo Centre
67 New Oxford Street
London WC1A 1DG
Tel: **0171-240 6077**
Low price film, other branches around Britain.

KJP
93 Drummond St
London NW1 2HJ
Tel: **0171-380 1144**
Major suppliers for all photographic equipment and accessories, including a selection of second-hand goods.

Kodak Ltd
Kodak House
PO Box 66
Station Road
Hemel Hempstead
Herts HP1 1JU
Tel: **01442-61122**

Minolta UK Ltd
Rooksley Park
Precedent Drive
Rooksley
Milton Keynes MK13 8HF
Tel: **01908-200400**

Nikon UK Ltd.
Nikon House
380 Richmond Road
Kingston Upon Thames
Surrey KT2 5PR
Tel: **0181-541 4440**

Olympus Optical Co (UK) Ltd
2-8 Honduras St
London EC1
Tel: **0171-253 2772**

Pentax UK Ltd
Pentax House
Heron Drive
Langley
Slough SL3 8PNHA2 OLT
Tel: **01753-792792**

Photo Paste (Odeon Photo)
110 Blvd St Germain
75006
Paris, France
Tel: **1 4329 4050**
Is a photographic developing and printing service that will process photos of films sent from anywhere in the world, and send the results on anywhere. They will undertake a variety of processes; will give advice on film handling and photographic technique; will retain negatives safely until your journey is over; and charge reasonable prices for these services.

A. Saunders & Co
70 Watling Street
Radlett
Herts. WD7 7NP
Tel: **01923-858 339**
Flexible all-risks insurance policies for photographers and equipment.

TAMRAC
9240 Jordan Avenue
Chatsworth
CA 91311
USA
Tel: **818 407 9500**
Make the TeleZoom Pak (Model 517), Photo Backpack (Model 757) and a full line of instant access foam padded weatherproof cases for 35mm systems.

FREIGHT FORWARDERS

Abco Shipping Ltd.
1 Fenning Street
Off St. Thomas Street
London SE1 3QR
Tel: **0171-407-2220**

Action Shipping Ltd.
Action House
Unit 3B
Tideway Industrial Estate
87 Kirtling Street
London SW8 5BP
Tel: **0171-627 0282**

Atlasair Ltd.
UPS House
Forest Road
Feltham
Middlesex TW13 7DY
Tel: **0181-844 1122**

Claydon NCOY Ltd
Ensign House
42/44 Thomas Road
London E14 7BJ
Tel: **0171-987 8211**

Evan Cook Ltd
134 Queen's Road
London SE15 2HR
Tel: **0171-635 0224**

Jeppesen Heaton Ltd
94A Whitechapel High Street
London E1 7QY
Tel: **0171-377 9080**

Allied Pickfords Ltd.
345 Southbury Road
Enfield
Middlesex EN1 1UP
Tel: **0800 289 229**

Sealandair Transport Company
101 Stephenson Street
Canning Town
London E16 4SA
Tel: **0171-511 2288**

Further information:
British International Freight Association (BIFA)
Redfern House
Browells Lane
Feltham
Middlesex TW13 7EP
Tel: **0181-844 2266**
BIFA publishes a directory of members. ■

COMMUNICATIONS
Section 12

COUNTRY-BY-COUNTRY
GUIDE TO CONTACTING THE UK

Afghanistan
Air mail post to UK: About 7 days.
Telegrams: May be sent from Central Post Office, Kabul (closes 21.00 hours.)
Telex: Public terminal at PTT Office, Jad Ibn Sina (next to Kabul Hotel).
Telephoning the UK: International operator service, reasonably efficient; shortage of lines may cause delay.

Albania
Air mail post to UK: Up to 2 months.
Telegrams: Not available.
Telex: Only available in emergencies through Government Offices.
Telephoning the UK: The only public phones are in the Main Post Office.

Algeria
Air mail post to UK: 3-4 days.
Telegrams: May be sent from any post office (8.00-19.00). Main post office in Algiers at 5 Blvd Mohamed Khemisti offers 24 hour service.
Telex: At main post office, Algiers; also public facilities at Aurassi and Aletti Hotels.
Telephoning the UK: IDD to UK, also international operator service 24 hours, but subject to delays.

American Samoa
Air mail post to UK: Up to 2 weeks.
Telegrams: Available in main towns and hotels.
Telex: Available in main towns and hotels.
Telephoning the UK: IDD available.

Andorra
Air mail post to UK: 4-5 days.
Telegrams: Services available throughout.
Telex: Services available throughout.

Telephoning the UK: Normal code dial system.

Angola
Air mail post to UK: 5-10 days.
Telegrams: In Post Offices, fairly reliable.
Telex: In good hotels.
Telephoning the UK: IDD from Luanda, elsewhere calls have to be booked 6 hours in advance through the operator.

Anguilla
Air mail post to UK: Up to 2 weeks.
Telegrams: May be sent from Cable & Wireless, Booth, The Valley.
Telex: May be sent from Cable & Wireless, as above.
Telephoning the UK: Full IDD available.

Antigua
Air mail post to UK: 3-4 days.
Telegrams: May be sent from Cable & Wireless, High Street, St. Johns or from your hotel.
Telex: From Cable & Wireless, St. Johns.
Telephoning the UK: IDD or through hotel operator, or via Cable & Wireless.

Argentina
Air mail post to UK: About 7 days.
Telegrams: May be sent from General Post Office (Correo Central), corner of Samrieto and L N Alem.
Telex: ENTEL (state-owned telephone and telegraph company) has two booths in Buenos Aires; also from General Post Office.
Fax: Available in most hotels.
Telephoning the UK: IDD; also 24 hour international operator service. (expensive).

Armenia
Air mail post to UK: Erratic – months or never

Telegrams and Telex: Not available
Telephoning the UK: All international calls made through operator, long delays.

Aruba
Air mail post to UK: 7-10 days.
Telegrams and Telex: Available at the Telegraph and Radio Office in the Post Office Building, Oranjestad and in good hotels.
Telephoning the UK: IDD available.

Australia
Air mail post to UK: About 7 days.
Telegrams: May be sent from local Post Offices and by telephone.
Telex: Telecom operates Public Telex Bureaux at all capital city Chief Telegraph Offices and at the following Telecom country offices: Canberra, Newcastle, Dubbo, Wollongong, Ballarat, Townsville, Rickhampton, Mt Gambier, Darwin, Alice Springs, Launceston.
Fax: Available at OTC offices (Overseas Telecommunications Commission).
Telephoning the UK: IDD; also operator-connected calls.

Austria
Air mail post to UK: 3-5 days.
Telegrams: From Post Offices Mon-Fri 0800-1200, 1400-1800. Sat 0800-1000 in selected offices.) Main and station post offices in larger cities open round the clock including Saturdays, Sundays and public holidays).
Telex: From Post Offices and hotels.
Telephoning the UK: IDD, from Post Offices or international call boxes.

Azerbaijan
Air mail post to UK: Long delays, perhaps months.
Telegrams and Telex: Not available.
Telephoning the UK: Through the operator and extremely difficult.

Bahamas
Air mail post to UK: 3-5 days.
Telegrams and Telex: May be sent through BatelCo offices in Nassau and Freeport.
Fax: From the Centralised Telephone Office, East Street, Nassau.
Telephoning the UK: IDD and International operator service.

Bahrain
Air mail post to UK: 3-4 days.
Telegrams: Ordinary, letter telegrams may be sent 24 hours a day from Cable & Wireless, Mercury House, Al-Khalifa Road, Manama.
Telex: Public call offices at Cable & Wireless open 24 hours.
Fax: From Bahrain Telecom, Sh Mubarak Building on Government Avenue.

Telephoning the UK: IDD.

Bangladesh
Air mail post to UK: 3-4 days.
Telegrams: From telegraph and post offices; major hotels.
Telex: Links with almost every country in the world. Hotel Intercontinental in Dacca has a public telex service. Telex facilities also available from Chittagong, Khulna.
Telephoning the UK: Limited IDD.

Barbados
Air mail post to UK: 4-7 days.
Telegrams: via Cable & Wireless (WI) Ltd, Wildey, St. Michael.
Telex: via Cable & Wireless.
Fax: Available at large hotels.
Telephoning the UK: IDD.

Belarus
Air mail post to UK: At least 10 days.
Telegrams: From major hotels.
Telex: From major hotels, e.g. the Yubileynaya and the Planeta in Minsk.
Fax: Public fax office at ul. Opanskogo 5, Minsk and at ul. Chkalova 1, Minsk, normal office hours.
Telephoning the UK: IDD available in major cities.

Belgium
Air mail post to UK: 3-4 days.
Telegrams: In main towns, telegraph offices (usually found in the stations or close at hand) are open day and night.
Telex: Extensive facilities available throughout.
Fax: Extensive facilities.
Telephoning the UK: IDD.

Belize
Air mail post to UK: Up to 5 days.
Telegrams: Available at BTL – Belize Telecommunications LTD, public booths in Belize City and Belmopan.
Telex: As telegrams but also major hotels.
Fax: Available from BTL public booths
Telephoning the UK: IDD.

Benin
Air mail post to UK: 3-5 days
Telegram: Not available
Telex: Available in major hotels and post offices in Cotonou.
Telephoning the UK: IDD available in major towns.

Bermuda
Air mail post to UK: 5-7 days.
Telegrams: From all post offices.
Telex: Via Cable & Wireless.
Fax: Available at hotels.
Telephoning the UK: IDD.

Bhutan
Air mail post to the UK: Up to 2 weeks.
Telegrams: Not available
Telex: Available in main centres, but disruptions frequent
Telephoning the UK: Only in main centres, through the operator.

Bolivia
Air mail post to UK: About 4 days.
Telegrams: From West Coast of America Telegraph Co Ltd, main office at Edificio Electra, Calle Mercado 1150, La Paz and Sheraton Libertador, Crillon, El Dorado, Gloria. Ordinary, urgent and letter telegrams.
Telex: Public telex facilities also available at West Coast of America Telegraph offices.
Fax: Services available.
Telephoning the UK: IDD and international operator service.

Bonaire
Air mail post to UK: 4-6 days.
Telegrams and Telex: Main post office in Kralendijk.
Telephoning the UK: IDD available.

Bophuthatswana
Air mail post to UK: Up to 10 days.
Telegrams and Telex: All post offices.
Fax: Available at major hotels and conferences centres.
Telephoning the UK: IDD available.

Bosnia-Herzegovina
Air mail to the UK: Postal service badly disrupted.
Telegrams and Telex: Intermittent and uncertain.
Telephoning the UK: Extremely difficult.

Botswana
Air mail post to UK: 1-3 weeks.
Telegrams: May be sent via post office.
Telex: Via post offices.
Fax: Available in major centres.
Telephoning the UK: IDD and international operator service.

Brazil
Air mail post to UK: 4-6 days.
Telegrams: From EMBRATEL (Empresa Brasileira de Telecomunicacoes SA) offices in Rio de Janeiro and Sao Paulo.
Telex: International Telex facilities available at EMBRATEL offices.
Fax: From main post offices and major hotels.
Telephoning the UK: IDD.

British Virgin Islands
Air mail post to UK: Up to 1 week.
Telegrams and Telex: Available through Cable & Wireless offices
Fax: Available through Cable & Wireless
Telephoning the UK: IDD

Brunei
Air mail post to UK: 2-5 days.
Telegrams: Available at the Government Telecommunication Office in Bandor Seri, Begawan.
Telex: No public telex, available in some hotels.
Telephoning the UK: IDD available.

Bulgaria
Air mail post to UK: 4 days.
Telegrams: From General Post Office, 4 Gurko Street, Sofia.
Telex: Public telex available at post offices.
Fax: Available at Bulgarian Telegraph Agency.
Telephoning the UK: IDD in main cities.

Burkina Faso
Air mail post to UK: Up to 2 weeks.
Telegrams: Limited facilities.
Telex: Major hotels in Ougadougou.
Telephoning the UK: IDD available in Ougadougou.

Burundi
Air mail post to UK: 1 week.
Telegrams and Telex: From Direction des Tele-communications in Bujumbura.
Telephoning the UK: Mainly through operator, although IDD available.

Cambodia
Air mail post to UK: 4-5 days.
Telegrams and telex: Few facilities available.
Fax: Few facilities available.
Telephoning the UK: IDD has now been restored.

Cameroon
Air mail post to UK: 7 days.
Telegrams: Telegraph office does not operate at night, and messages are apt to be delayed.
Telex: Facilities are available from the main intelcom office in Yaounde and also larger hotels in Yaounde and Douala.
Fax: At intelcom offices.
Telephoning the UK: IDD and international operator service.

Canada
Air mail post to UK: 4-8 days.
Telegrams: Cannot be sent through the post offices in Canada. Telegrams or 'Telepost' messages should be phoned or delivered to CN/CP Telecommunications – address and telephone number can be found in the local telephone directory. In Newfoundland and Labrador telegrams are sent through Terra Nova Tel. ⇨

Telex: Telex facilities easily located in all major Canadian cities.
Fax: Most hotels.
Telephoning the UK: IDD

Cape Verde
Air mail post to UK: 1-2 weeks.
Telegrams: Not available.
Telex: Available in some hotels.
Telephoning the UK: IDD in main towns.

Cayman Islands
Air mail post to UK: About 5 days.
Telegrams: Public Telegraph operates daily from 07.30-18.00 hours Cayman time. Telecommunications are provided by Cable and Wireless (West Indies) Ltd.
Telex: Available at Cable & Wireless office; many hotels and apartments have their own telex.
Telephoning the UK: IDD.

Central African Republic
Air mail post to UK: 1-3 weeks.
Telegrams: Available in major post offices.
Telex: The main post office in Bangui and some major hotels.
Telephoning the UK: IDD available.

Chad
Air mail post to UK: 1 week.
Telegrams and Telex: Few facilities available
Telephoning the UK: Through the operator.

Chile
Air mail post to UK: 3-4 days.
Telegrams: From Transradio Chilena at Bandera 168, Santiago, and at Esmerelda 932, Valparaiso; ordinary and letter telegrams.
Telex: Facilities at Transradio Chilena, Bandera 168, and at ITT Communicaciones Mundiales SA, Agustinas 1054, Santiago.
Telephoning the UK: IDD.

China
Air mail post to UK: 1 week.
Telegrams: From Administration of Telecommunications at 11 Sichanganjian Street, Beijing, and at Nanking Road East 30, Shanghai, or any telegraph office. Ordinary, urgent or letter telegrams.
Telex: Telex facilities available at Administration of Telecommunications offices and major hotels.
Fax: At major hotels.
Telephoning the UK: IDD.

Colombia
Air mail post to UK: 5-7 days.
Telegrams: From any chief telegraph office in main towns. Ordinary and urgent telegrams.
Telex: International telex facilities available at hotels Tequendama and Hilton, Bogota, at Telecom (Empresa Nacional de Telecommunicaciones) offices and chief telegraph offices in main towns.
Fax: Major hotels in Bogota.
Telephoning the UK: IDD and operator service.

Comoro Islands
Air mail post to UK: 1-2 weeks.
Telegrams and Telex: Few facilities available.
Telephoning the UK: Through international operator.

Congo
Air mail post to UK: Unreliable 1-2 weeks.
Telegrams and Telex: Main post offices in the cities.
Telephoning the UK: IDD.

Cook Islands
Air mail post to UK: 1-2 weeks.
Telegrams and Telex: From the telecom office in Rarotonga.
Telephoning the UK: IDD available.

Costa Rica
Air mail post to UK: 6-10 days.
Telegrams: Facilities available at all main post offices, but not to the UK.
Telex: From Radiografica, Costariricense SA on the corner of Calle 1 and Avenida 5 in San Jose.
Telephoning the UK: IDD.

Côte d'Ivoire
Air mail post to UK: About 10 days.
Telegrams: May be sent from the post offices.
Telex: Facilities in the post offices and major hotels.
Telephoning the UK: IDD and international operator service.

Croatia
Air mail post to UK: Limited service, can take months
Telegrams and Telex: Badly disrupted.
Fax: Limited service.
Telephoning the UK: IDD available.

Cuba
Air mail post to UK: Up to 1 month.
Telegrams: Can be sent from post office in Havana and RCA offices.
Telex: Not available.
Telephoning the UK: IDD from Havana only.

Curaçao
Air mail post to UK: 4-6 days.
Telegrams and telex: Available in large hotels and main post office in Willemstad.
Telephoning the UK: IDD service.

Cyprus
Air mail post to UK: 3 days.
Telegrams: From any telegraphic office, including Electra House, Museum Street, Nicosia. 24 hour service. Ordinary and urgent telegrams.
Telex: No public telex offices, but larger hotels have telex facilities.
Fax: Available at the District Post Office.
Telephoning the UK: IDD.

Czech Republic
Air mail post to UK: About 7 days.
Telegrams: Facilities available at all main post offices.
Telex: Telex for tourists not available.
Telephoning the UK: IDD.

Denmark
Air mail post to UK: About 3 days.
Telegrams: May be sent from main post offices.
Telex: Facilities available from your hotel or main post offices in major towns.
Fax: Available at most post offices.
Telephoning the UK: IDD.

Djibouti
Air mail post to UK: About 7 days.
Telegrams: May be sent from main post offices.
Telex: Available from any post office.
Telephoning the UK: IDD. International telephone calls (by satellite) are possible 24 hrs a day.

Dominica
Air mail post to UK: About 7 days.
Telegrams: Available from All America Cables and Radio ITT, JulioVerne 21, Santo Domingo; RCA Global Communications, El Conde 203, Santo Domingo.
Telex: Facilities available from All America Cables and Radio ITT and RCA Global Communications.
Telephoning the UK: IDD and international operator service.

Ecuador
Air mail post to UK: 6-7 days.
Telegrams: From chief telegraphic office in main towns. In Quito, 24 hour service. Also from Hotel Quito and Hotel Coloìn up to 20.00 hours. Ordinary and urgent telegrams.
Telex: Public booths at Hotels Quito, Coloìn and Humboldt, Quito; Hotel Humboldt, Continental, Grand Hotel, Palace, Guayaquil; also at IETEL (Instituto Ecuatoriano de Telecommunicaciones) offices.
Telephoning the UK: IDD and international operator service; sometimes long delays.

Egypt
Air mail post to UK: Minimum 2 days.

Telegrams: From telegraph offices. Ordinary telegrams.
Telex: Public telex facilities at major hotels for guests only; other telex services in Cairo at: 19 El Alfi Street (24 hours); 26 July Street, Zamalek; 85 Abdel Khalek Sarwat Street, Attaba; El Tazaran Street, Nasr City; Transit Hall, Cairo Airport.
Telephoning the UK: IDD. International operator calls should be booked in advance.

El Salvador
Air mail post to UK: 7-10 days.
Telex: From ANTEL.
Telephoning the UK: IDD.

Equatorial Guinea
Air mail post to UK: 2 weeks.
*Telegrams and Telex:*Not available .
Telephoning the UK: IDD available, however more likely to get through via the operator.

Eritrea
Air mail post to UK: Long delays likely.
Telegrams: Not available.
Telex: From the telex office in Asmara.
Telephoning the UK: IDD but only from Asmara, Massawa and Assab.

Estonia
Air mail post to UK: 6 days.
Telegrams and Telex: Not available.
Telephoning the UK: IDD available.

Ethiopia
Air mail post to UK: 4 days.
Telegrams: From Telecommunications Authority, Adoua Square, Addis Ababa, and telegraphic offices. Ordinary, urgent and letter telegrams.
Telex: Facilities available at Telecommunications Board, Churchill Road, Addis Ababa.
Fax: In major hotels.
Telephoning the UK: IDD. Link available from Addis 15.00-20.00 East African Time.

Falkland Islands
Air mail post to UK: 4-7 days.
Telex: By satellite from Cable & Wireless
Fax: New system installed – available.
Telephoning the UK: IDD.

Fiji
Air mail post to UK: 10 days.
Telegrams: Overseas telegrams accepted at all telegraph offices. Ordinary and deferred (LT) telegrams.
Telex: International telex facilities available at Fiji International Telecommunications Ltd (FINTEL), Victoria Parade, Suva, or at major hotels. ⇨

Fax: Major hotels and the FINTEL office.
Telephoning the UK: IDD and international operator service.

Finland
Air mail post to UK: About 3 days.
Telegrams: Can be left with the nearest post office or hotel desk.
Telex: Facilities available at Post Offices. The Central Post Office, Mannerheimintie 11, Helsinki.
Fax: Major hotels and businesses.
Telephoning the UK: IDD.

France
Air mail post to UK: 2 days.
Telegrams: Facilities available throughout.
Telex: Extensive facilities available, in post offices.
Fax: Widely available.
Telephoning the UK: IDD.

French Guiana
Air mail post to UK: 2 weeks.
Telex: Facilities in Cayenne.
Fax: Widely available.
Telephoning the UK: IDD available.

French Polynesia
Air mail post to UK: 2 weeks.
Telegrams: Limited services available.
Telex: Available at the Post Office, Boulevard Pomare, Papeete, Tahiti.
Fax: At some post offices and major hotels.
Telephoning the UK: IDD available.

Gabon
Air mail post to UK: 1-2 weeks.
Telegrams and Telex: Main post office in Libreville and major hotels.
Telephoning the UK: IDD available.

Gambia
Air mail post to UK: 3 days.
Telegrams: From GAMTEL, Cameron Street, Banjul. Ordinary telegrams.
Telex: Public telex booth at Russell Street, Banjul.
Fax: At the 9 GAMTEL offices in Banjul.
Telephoning the UK: IDD and 24-hour international operator service.

Georgia
Air mail post to UK: months.
Telegrams and Telex: Not available.
Telephoning the UK: IDD in theory available, in practice almost impossible.

Germany
Air mail post to UK: 3 days.
Telegrams: May be sent from post offices.
Telex: From main post offices and hotels.

Fax: Available throughout.
Telephoning the UK: IDD.

Ghana
Air mail post to UK: Up to 2 weeks.
Telegrams: From External Tele-communications Service of Posts and Telecommunications Corporation, Extelcom House, High St, Accra, and Stewart Avenue, Kumasi. Ordinary, urgent and letter telegrams.
Telex: Public call facilities at External Telecommunication Service offices.
Telephoning the UK: IDD. Operator connected calls may be made 08.15-18.15 hours, weekdays only. Often difficult and delays sometimes of 2-3 days.

Gibraltar
Air mail post to UK: 2-6 days.
Telegrams and Telex: From Gibtel, 60 Main Street or Mount Pleasant, 25 South Barracks Road.
Fax: Available in some hotels.
Telephoning the UK: IDD.

Greece
Air mail post to UK: 4-5 days.
Telegrams: May be sent from OYE (Telecommunications Centre).
Telex: Facilities available from OTE.
Telephoning the UK: IDD.

Greenland
Air mail post to UK: 4-5 days.
Telegrams: All towns have a telegraph station.
Telephoning the UK: IDD available.

Grenada
Air mail post to UK: 10 days
Telegrams and Telex: Available from International Cable & Wireless (West Indies) Ltd.
Fax: Cable & Wireless in St Georges.
Telephoning the UK: IDD.

Guadeloupe
Air mail post to UK: 1 week.
Telex: Available in Point-a-Pitre.
Telephoning the UK: IDD.

Guam
Air mail post to UK: Up to 2 weeks.
Fax: In major hotels.
Telephoning the UK: Only in Agana.

Guatemala
Air mail post to UK: 6-12 days.
Telegrams: only available locally.
Telex: Available in Guatemala City.
Fax: In some major hotels in the city.
Telephoning the UK: IDD available.

Guinea Republic
Air mail post to UK: Up to 2 weeks.
Telex: Available at the Hotel de
L'Indepépéndence and Grand Hotel de L'Unité
Telephoning the UK: IDD.

Guinea-Bissau
Air mail post to UK: Up to 2 weeks.
Telex: Available at the main post office in
Bissau.
Telephoning the UK: IDD available.

Guyana
Air mail post to UK: 7-10 days.
Telegrams: Can be sent 24 hours a day from
Bank of Guyana Bldg, Avenue of the Republic
and Church Street, Georgetown. Ordinary and
night letter telegrams.
Telex: Public call offices at the Bank of Guyana
Building.
Fax: As Telegrams.
Telephoning the UK: IDD and international
operator service at all times.

Haiti
Air mail post to UK: 1 week.
Telex: At main hotels and office of TELECO.
Telephoning the UK: IDD.

Honduras
Air mail post to UK: Up to 1 week.
Telegrams and Telex: Available at
HONDUTEL.
Fax: At HONDUTEL.
Telephoning the UK: IDD.

Hong Kong
Air mail post to UK: 3-5 days.
Telegrams: From telegraphic offices. Ordinary,
letter and social telegrams.
Telex: Public telex facilities available at
Mercury House, 3 Connaught Road, Central,
Hong Kong Island, and at Ocean Terminal,
Kowloon and from Kai Tak Airport.
Fax: From BureauFax.
Telephoning the UK: IDD and 24-hour
international operator service.

Hungary
Air mail post to UK: About 4 days.
Telegrams: May be sent from hotel desks.
Telex: At major hotels and main post office in
Budapest.
Telephoning the UK: IDD.

Iceland
Air mail post to UK: All items automatically
sent by air – 7-10 days.
Telegrams: From Chief Telegraphic Office,
Reykjavik.
Telex: From post offices.
Fax: At the telephone headquarters in

Austurvoil Square and hotels.
Telephoning the UK: IDD and international
operator services 24 hours a day.

India
Air mail post to UK: 6-7 days.
Telegrams: From any telegraphic office.
Express, letter and urgent.
Telex: International telex facilities available
24 hours a day at large hotels, and at
telegraph/telex offices in major cities.
Fax: At Overseas Communications Service in
major cities.
Telephoning the UK: IDD and international
operator service.

Indonesia
Air mail post to UK: 7-10 days.
Telegrams: From any telegraphic office. In
Jakarta, facilities available 24 hours a day.
Telex: Public telex facilities operated from
Directorate General for Posts and
Communications, Medan Merdeka Selatan 12
(24 hours); also in some major hotels; and at the
chief telegraphic offices in Semarang;
Jogjakarta, Surabaya and Denpasar.
Telephoning the UK: IDD and international
operator service 24 hours, seven days a week.

Iran
Air mail post to UK: 2-3 weeks.
Telegrams: Must be dispatched from Chief
Telegraph Office, Meidane Sepah, Tehran,
which is open all night. Ordinary, letter and
urgent telegrams.
Telex: Public facilities at Chief Telegraph
Office and some some hotels.
Telephoning the UK: IDD and international
operator service.

Iraq
Air mail post to UK: 5-10 days.
Telegrams: Telegraph office attached to central
post office in Rashid Street, Baghdad, also at
Basrah, Kerkuk and Musul.
Telex: Facilities available at the PTT in Rashid
Street, Baghdad, and at a number of hotels.
Telephoning the UK: IDD

Ireland
Air mail post to UK: 2-3 days.
Telex: Main post offices and hotels.
Fax: Many hotels.
Telephoning the UK: IDD.

Israel
Air mail post to UK: 4-7 days.
Telegrams: From telegraphic offices. Ordinary.
Telex: Facilities available to guests in most de
luxe hotels in Jerusalem and Tel Aviv. Public
telex booths at 23 Rehov Yafo, Jerusalem; 7
Rehov Mikve Yisrael, Tel Aviv. ⇨

*Fax:*4 and 5 star hotels.
Telephoning the UK: IDD 19.00-07.00 weekdays; 15.00-07.00 Sunday at cheaper rate.

Italy
Air mail post to UK: 1 week.
Telegrams: Italcable available over the phone.
Telex: Main Post Offices.
*Fax:*Some hotels.
Telephoning the UK: IDD.

Jamaica
Air mail post to UK: About 10-14 days.
Telegrams: Telegram service available from any post office (inland).
Telex: Telex service available from Jamaica International Telecommunication Ltd, Jamintel Centre, 15 North Street, Kingston.
*Fax:*As Telex.
Telephoning the UK: IDD.

Japan
Air mail post to UK: 4-6 days.
Telegrams: May be sent from the main hotels, from offices of Kokusai Denshin Denwa Co Ltd and from Nippon Denshin Denwa Kosha and from larger post offices in major cities. Ordinary, letter and express telegrams.
Telex: Telex booths are available at main post offices and main offices of Kokusai Denshin Denwa Co Ltd and Nippon Denshin Denwa Kosha.
Fax: Major hotels and KDD offices.
Telephoning the UK: IDD.

Jordan
Air mail post to UK: About 5 days.
Telegrams: Overseas service reasonably good. May be sent from the Central Telegraph Office; Post Office, 1st Circle, Jebel Amman; or any post office.
Telex: Public telex facilities are available at the Central Telegraph Office and in a number of hotels.
Fax: Most hotels.
Telephoning the UK: IDD.

Kazakhstan
Air mail post to UK: 2-3 weeks.
Telex: At main hotels.
Telephoning the UK: Telephone offices are next to the post offices or at the Hotel Otar.

Kenya
Air mail post to UK: 3-4 days.
Telegrams: Overseas telegrams can be sent from all post and telegraphic offices. Nairobi GPO open 24 hrs. Ordinary, letter and urgent telegrams.
Telex: Facilities available at Nairobi GPO. New Stanley and Hilton Hotels have facilities for their guests, otherwise no public call booths.

*Fax:*Main Post Office in Nairobi and the Kenyatta International Conference Centre.
Telephoning the UK: IDD and operator service.

Kiribati
Air mail post to UK: Up to 2 weeks.
Telegrams: Possible but delays.
Telex: Available at Telecom offices.
Fax: At Telecom offices.
*Telephoning the UK:*IDD in Tarawa or through operator.

Korea
Air mail post to UK: 7-10 days.
Telegrams: May be sent by dialling 115 and delivering message in English or by visiting a telegraph office of the Korea International Telecommunications Office (KIT) near Capitol Building and delivering message in written English.
Telex: Telex facilities available in main hotels; also from the Post Office in Seoul and office of Korea International Telecommunications Services.
Fax: At major hotels.
Telephoning the UK: IDD.

Kuwait
Air mail post to UK: 5 days.
Telegrams: Telegrams sent from Chief Telegraph Office 6 hours after being handed in at the Post Office.
Telex: Facilities available at main hotels or from main Post Office (24 hours).
Fax: Several hotels.
Telephoning the UK: IDD.

Kyrgyzstan
Air mail post to UK: 2 weeks – 2 months.
Telegrams: Post offices in large towns.
Telex: In main hotels for residents only.
*Telephoning the UK:*Through the operator, can have delays.

Laos
Air mail post to UK: Months.
Telephoning the UK: Limited, – links to Bangkok, where messages can be passed on.

Latvia
Air mail post to UK: 6 days.
Telegrams: From public phones.
Telex: Main post office in Riga, Brivibas Bulvaris 21.
Fax: Same as telex.
Telephoning the UK: IDD.

Lebanon
Air mail post to UK: 4-6 days.
Telex: Contact the Embassy in emergency.
Telephoning the UK: IDD.

Lesotho
Air mail post to UK: 1 week.
Telegrams and Telex: Limited, in the main post office only.
Telephoning the UK: IDD available in Maseru.

Liberia
Air mail post to UK: 7-10 days.
Telegrams: Facilities provided by the Liberian Telecommunications Corporation and French Cables, Monrovia.
Telex: Services provided by the Liberian Telecommunications Corporation.
Telephoning the UK: IDD.

Libya
Air mail post to UK: 2 weeks but can be subject to censorship.
Telex: At the larger hotels.
Telephoning the UK: IDD.

Lithuania
Air mail post to UK: 6 days.
Fax: Services in Vilnius, at the Telegraph Centre, Universteto 14 and at the Hotel Lietuva, Ukmerges 20 and at the Comilet Office, Architeku 146.
Telephoning the UK: IDD.

Luxembourg
Air mail post to UK: About 3 days.
Telegrams: Telegram facilities available at the Main Post Office in Luxembourg City; Bureau de Postes, 8a Avenue Monterey (open 07.00 20.45 Mon Sat); Luxembourg Railways Station Main Post Office, 9 Place de la Gare (open 24 hours, 7 days a week).
Telex: Facilities available from post offices named above. Also Luxembourg Airports Post Office, inside main airport terminal, 1st floor.
Fax: At the main post office.
Telephoning the UK: IDD.

Macau
Air mail post to UK: About 3 days.
Telegrams: May be sent from hotels and from General Post Office in Leal Senado Square.
Telex: Facilities from the General Post Office.
Fax: Several hotels.
Telephoning the UK: Most hotels have direct dial telephones but otherwise through operators or from the General Post Office.

Macedonia
Air mail post to UK: 10 days.
Telegrams and Telex: At the main post office in Skopje.
Telephoning the UK: IDD available.

Madagascar
Air mail post to UK: 7-10 days.

Telegrams: PTT in Antananarivo.
Telex: At PTT and Colbert and Hilton Hotels
Telephoning the UK: IDD in major towns.

Malawi
Air mail post to UK: 10 days.
Telegrams: Main post office.
Telex: Bureaux in Blantyre and Zomba.
Fax: Same as telex.
Telephoning the UK: IDD available.

Malaysia
Air mail post to UK: 4-7 days.
Telegrams: May be sent by 'phone 24 hours a day by dialling 104, or at any Telegraph office and most post offices. Ordinary, urgent letter and greetings telegrams.
Telex: Public facilities available 24 hours at Telegraph Office, Djalan Raja Chulan, Kuala Lumpur, and most hotels.
Fax: Main post offices.
Telephoning the UK: IDD.

Maldives
Air mail post to UK: Up to 1 week.
Telegrams: Telecommunications service in Malé.
Telex: Available at Dhiraagu and other resorts.
Fax: Services in Malé.
Telephoning the UK: IDD available.

Mali
Air mail post to UK: 2 weeks.
Telex: Central telex office in Bamako and main hotels.
Telephoning the UK: Limited IDD service.

Malta
Air mail post to UK: 3 days.
Telegrams: From Telemalta offices and most hotels.
Telex: Facilities from Telemalta and most hotels.
Fax: Through Telemalta.
Telephoning the UK: IDD.

Martinique
Air mail post to UK: 1 week.
Telex: Available in some hotels.
Telephoning the UK: IDD available.

Mauritania
Air mail post to UK: 2 weeks at least.
Telex: Available in Nouakchott and Nouadhibou.
Telephoning the UK: Limited IDD available.

Mauritius
Air mail post to UK: 5-7 days.
Telegrams and Telex: From the Mauritius: Telecommunications Service at Cassis and Port Louis. Also available at the Overseas Telecoms

Services Ltd, Rogers House, President John F Kennedy Street, Port Louis.
Fax: Most hotels.
Telephoning the UK: IDD is available.

Mexico
Air mail post to UK: About 7 days.
Telegrams: Telegraphic system maintained by Telegrafos Nacionales, and telegrams to be handed in to their offices. In Mexico City the main office for international telegrams is at Balderas y Coloìn, Mexico 1 DF.
Telex: International telex facilities available at a number of locations in Mexico City; hotels reluctant to despatch messages for guests but willing to receive them.
Fax: Major hotels.
Telephoning the UK: IDD.

Moldova
Air mail post to UK: 6-8 weeks.
Telephoning the UK: IDD in major towns.

Monaco
Air mail post to UK: 2-3 days.
Telegrams and Telex: Available at hotels and post offices.
Fax: Some major hotels.
Telephoning the UK: IDD.

Mongolia
Air mail post to UK: Up to 2 weeks.
Telex: Limited facilities in Ulan Bator.
Telephoning the UK: Must be booked through the operator.

Montserrat
Air mail post to UK: 1 week.
Telegrams and Telex: Cable & Wireless in Plymouth.
Telephoning the UK: IDD.

Morocco
Air mail post to UK: At least 5 days.
Telegrams: From all telegraph offices. Ordinary and urgent telegrams.
Telex: International telex facilities available at Hotels Hilton and Tour Hassan, Rabat; Hotels El Manour and Marhaba, Casablanca.
Fax: Major 4 and 5 star hotels.
Telephoning the UK: IDD. Calls may be made at any time, but delays might be experienced. also from major hotels.
Telephoning the UK: IDD.

Mozambique
Air mail post to UK: 7-10 days.
Telex: Services in Maputo and Beira.
Telephoning the UK: IDD in main towns.

Myanmar
Air mail post to UK: 1-2 weeks.
Telegrams: From Central Office on Maha Bandoola Street, and also Post Office and Telecommunications Corporation in Yangon.
Telex: At some main hotels form businessmen.
Telephoning the UK: IDD in main cities.

Namibia
Air mail post to UK: 4-7 days.
Telegrams and Telex: Good facilities in every town.
Telex: Good facilities available in every town.
Fax: Available in some hotels.
Telephoning the UK: IDD available.

Naura
Air mail post to UK: 1 week.
Telegrams and Telex: Available through the Naura Government Communications Office.
Telephoning the UK: Through operator.

Nepal
Air mail post to UK: 4-10 days.
Telegrams: Telecommunication Office, Tripureshwar, Kathmandu.
Telex: International telex facilities available at large hotels and Telecommunication Office, Kathmandu.
Fax: Available through some travel agents and 4 and 5 star hotels.
Telephoning the UK: IDD from Kathmandu. International operator service in other towns.

The Netherlands
Air mail post to UK: 4-5 days.
Telegrams: At all post offices.
Telex: Main hotels and conference centres.
Fax: Widely available.
Telephoning the UK: Full IDD service available.

Netherland Antilles
Air mail post to UK: 1 week.
Telegrams and Telex: Through Lands Radio Dienst and All American Cables.
Telephoning the UK: IDD, through the operator is very expensive.

New Caledonia
Air mail post to UK: 1 week.
Telegrams and Telex: Through the Central Office at rue Eugène Porcheron, Nouméa.
Telephoning the UK: IDD.

New Zealand
Air mail post to UK: About 7 days.
Telegrams: From all post offices 09.00 17.00 hours, and telephoned through at any time. Ordinary, letter and urgent telegrams.
Telex: All major hotels, banks, government offices and some commercial practices have telex facilities.
Fax: Many hotels.

Telephoning the UK: IDD.

Nicaragua
Air mail post to UK: 1 week.
Telegrams and Telex: Facilities in Managua.
Telephoning the UK: IDD.

Niger
Air mail post to UK: Up to 2 weeks.
Telegrams: From Chief Telegraph Office, Niamey, and at all other telegraph offices. Ordinary, urgent, and letter telegrams.
Telex: Public facilities available at Chief Telegraph Office, Niamey.
Telephoning the UK: IDD. Good quality, direct telephone line to Paris from Niamey, which links with UK. Service available 08.30, 12.30, 15.30 and18.00 hours daily in Niamey. Calls should be made by asking exchange for L'Inter Radio.

Nigeria
Air mail post to UK: Unreliable – up to 3 weeks.
Telegrams and Telex: Through the Nigerian Telecommunications Ltd (NITEL) in all major cities.
Telephoning the UK: IDD.

Niue
Air mail post to UK: Up to 2 weeks.
Telegrams and Telex:: Available at the Telecommunications Department, Central Reservations Building, Alofi, which is open 24 hours a day.
Telephoning the UK: IDD.

Norway
Air mail post to UK: 2-4 days
Telegrams: Via the telephone.
Telex: Televerket's, Teledirektoratet, Universitetgt 2, Oslo.
Fax: Major hotels.
Telephoning the UK: IDD.

Oman
Air mail post to UK: 1 week – 10 days.
Telegrams: May be sent from post offices.
Telex: Facilities available from post offices.
Fax: At the GTO (Post Office).
Telephoning the UK: IDD.

Pakistan
Air mail post to UK: 5-10 days.
Telegrams: Post offices, telegraph offices and hotels. The Central Telegraph Office, 1.1 Chundrigar Road, Karachi, provides 24 hours service.
Telex: The Central Telegraph Office provides telex facilities 24 hrs.
Telephoning the UK: IDD. International operator service.

Panama
Air mail post to UK: 5-10 days.
Telegrams: In main post office in the main towns.
Telex: In Panama City and major hotels.
Fax: Main post offices and major hotels.
Telephoning the UK: IDD.

Papua New Guinea
Air mail post to UK: 7-10 days.
Telegrams: In the main centres.
Telex: Some hotels have telex machines.
Fax: Through companies and government offices.
Telephoning the UK: IDD.

Paraguay
Air mail post to UK: 5-7 days.
Telegrams: May be sent from post offices, banks, and hotels, through Antelco (Administración Nacional de Telecommicaciones.)
Telex: Facilities available from post offices, banks and hotels.
Telephoning the UK: IDD or via operator.

Peru
Air mail post to UK: About 10 days.
Telegrams: From ENTEL PERU telegraph offices. Ordinary and night telegrams.
Telex: Telex machines with international connections installed at Hotels Bolivar, Crillon and Sheraton in Lima.
Fax: Some hotels.
Telephoning the UK: IDD or international operator service at all times.

Philippines
Air mail post to UK: 10 days, often more.
Telegrams: From Eastern Telecommunications Philippines Inc. offices. Ordinary and urgent telegrams.
Telex: Public telex booths operated by Eastern Telecommunications Philippines Inc, Globe Mackay Cable and Radio Corporation, and RCA Communications Inc.
*Fax:*3 to 5 star hotels.
Telephoning the UK: IDD or international operator service 24 hrs a day.

Poland
Air mail post to UK: 4 days.
Telegrams: Most post offices and by 'phone.
Telex: At Foreign Trade Enterprises and Urzad Pocztowy, Warsaw and Orbis hotels.
Telephoning the UK: IDD.

Portugal
Air mail post to UK: About 3 days.
Telegrams: Facilities available from all post offices.
Telex: From post offices and the Public Telex

Office, Praca D Luis 30-1, Lisbon which is open
09.00-18.00 Monday to Friday.
*Fax:*Fax bureaux in main towns.
Telephoning the UK: IDD.

Puerto Rico
Air mail post to UK: Up to a week.
Telex: In main hotels in the capital.
Telephoning the UK: IDD.

Qatar
Air mail post to UK: Up to a week.
Telegrams: For telegraph service dial 130.
Telex: Facilities available from Qatar National
Telephone Service (QNTS) and the Cable &
Wireless office in Doha.
Fax: Major hotels.
Telephoning the UK: IDD.

Réunion
Air mail post to UK: 2-3 weeks.
Telegrams and Telex: Available only in St
Denis.
Telephoning the UK: IDD.

Romania
Air mail post to UK: Up to 2 weeks.
Telegrams: At post offices and night telegrams
can be sent in Bucharest.
Telex: Large hotels.
Fax: In large hotels.
Telephoning the UK: Through the operator.

Russian Federation
Air mail post to UK: 10 days.
Telegrams: From hotels.
Telex: In an emergency through the
Commercial Department at the British
Embassy, Kutuzovsky Prospekt 7/4, 12148
Moscow.
Telephoning the UK: IDD from Moscow, St
Petersburg and Novgorod, elsewhere through
the operator.

Rwanda
Air mail post to UK: 2-3 weeks.
Telegrams and Telex: In Kigali and main hotels
Telephoning the UK: Through the operator.

St Kitts and Nevis
Air mail post to UK: 5-7 days.
Telegrams: Through SKANTEL, Canyon
Street, Basseterre and Main Street,
Charlestown.
Fax: Available at SKANTEL.
Telephoning the UK: IDD.

St Lucia
Air mail post to UK: 1 week.
Telegrams: Through Cable & Wireless,
Casteries.
Telex: Public telex booth at Cable & Wireless.

Fax: Cable and Wireless.
Telephoning the UK: IDD.

St Vincent and the Grenadines
Air mail post to UK: Up to 2 weeks.
Telex: Limited to main hotels.
Fax: From most hotels.
Telephoning the UK: IDD.

Sâo Tomé e Principe
Air mail post to UK: 2-3 weeks.
Telex: Main hotel in Sâo Tomé.
Telephoning the UK: Limited IDD – through
operator.

Saudi Arabia
Air mail post to UK: Up to 1 week.
Telegrams: From all post offices.
Telex: From major hotels.
Fax: Major hotels.
Telephoning the UK: IDD.

Senegal
Air mail post to UK: 7-10 days.
Telegrams and Telex: Available at most major
post offices.
Fax: SONATEL has a fax machine.
Telephoning the UK: IDD.

Seychelles
Air mail post to UK: Up to 1 week.
Telegrams and Telex: SEYTELS/Cable &
Wireless Ltd, Francis Rachel Street, Victoria,
Mahé.
Fax: Same as telegrams.
Telephoning the UK: Through the operator.

Sierra Leone
Air mail post to UK: 5 days.
Telegrams: From Mercury House, 7 Wallace
Johnson Street, Freetown. Ordinary, urgent and
letter telegrams.
Telex: Facilities available at Mercury House.
Telephoning the UK: IDD or international
operator calls between 11.00 and midnight local
time any day of the week.

Singapore
Air mail post to UK: Usually 5 days, but can
take 10-14 days.
Telegrams: From telegraph offices. Ordinary,
urgent, letter and social telegrams.
Telex: Public telex facilities available at Central
Telegraph Office, 35 Robinson Road and the
Comcentre near Orchard Road.
Telephoning the UK: IDD; operator service 24
hours.

Slovak Republic
Air mail post to UK: 4-6 days.
Telegrams and Telex: Main hotels and
Kollárkska 12, Bratislava.

Telephoning the UK: Special kiosks for International calls – IDD.

Slovenia
Air mail post to UK: 10-14 days.
Telegrams and Telex: Limited.
Fax: Available.
Telephoning the UK: IDD.

Solomon Islands
Air mail post to UK: 7 days.
Telegrams and Telex: At Solomon Telekom.
Fax: At the Solomon Telekom office in Honiara.
Telephoning the UK: IDD.

Somalia
Air mail post to UK: Up to 2 weeks, long at the time of writing due to the civil war.
Telex: Main post office in Mogadishu and Hotel Juba.
Telephoning the UK: IDD.

South Africa
Air mail post to UK: 3-7 days.
Telegrams: Telegraph service available in every town, however small.
Telex: Public call facilities available in Cape Town, Durban, Johannesburg and Pretoria post offices. Most hotels and offices have telex.
Fax: Main hotels.
Telephoning the UK: IDD available from all centres.

Spain
Air mail post to UK: 4-5 days.
Telegrams: May be sent from main post offices.
Telex: Facilities from main post offices.
Fax: Most 4 and 5 star hotels.
Telephoning the UK: IDD.

Sri Lanka
Air mail post to UK: 4-7 days.
Telegrams: From all post offices. Ordinary, letter and urgent telegrams.
Telex: Public telex booth at OTS Building, Duke Street, Colombo.
Fax: General post office in Colombo.
Telephoning the UK: IDD and international operator service 24 hours.

Sudan
Air mail post to UK: Up to a week.
Telegrams: The Central Telegraph Office, Gamma Avenue, Khartoum.
Telex: Main post offices.
Telephoning the UK: Through the operator.

Suriname
Air mail post to UK: At least a month.
Telegrams and Telex: At the Government Telegraph Office, Gravenstraat 33, Paramaribo
Telephoning the UK: IDD.

Swaziland
Air mail post to UK: About 10 days.
Telegrams: May be sent from most post offices.
Telex: Facilities from most post offices.
Fax: Some hotels.
Telephoning the UK: IDD.

Sweden
Air mail post to UK: 3-4 days.
Telegrams: Telephone the telegrams in by dialling 0021 or send by post.
Telex: Public Telexes not available.
Telephoning the UK: IDD.

Switzerland
Air mail post to UK: 2-4 days.
Telegrams: May be sent from post offices and hotels.
Telex: Some hotels have telex facilities.
Fax: At telegraph offices, post offices and major hotels.
Telephoning the UK: IDD.

Syrian Republic
Air mail post to UK: Up to a week.
Telegrams: Telegraph office in Damascus.
Telex: From main hotels.
Telephoning the UK: IDD.

Taiwan
Air mail post to UK: Up to 10 days.
Telegrams: ITA offices, 28 Hangchow South Road, Section 1, Taipei.
Telex: Major hotels and ITA.
Fax: ITA.
Telephoning the UK: IDD.

Tahiti
Telegrams: Facilities can be found at the Office des Postes et Telecommunications, Boulevard Pomare, Papeete.
Telex: Services from the Office des Postes et Telecommunications.
Telephoning the UK: IDD or dial 19 for international operator service.

Tajikistan
Air mail post to UK: 2-4 weeks.
Telegrams: Limited facilities.
Telex: Major hotels in Dushanbe.
Telephoning the UK: From International telephone offices only, usually adjoining the main post office in a town.

Tanzania
Air mail post to UK: About 7 days.
Telegrams: From post office. Ordinary, urgent, letter and greetings telegrams.
Telex: Public telex at post office in Mkwepu Street, Dar Es Salaam,and in some hotels.
Telephoning the UK: IDD or international operator service 24 hours.

Thailand

Air mail post to UK: 5 days.
Telegrams: From GPO Building, New Road, Bangkok, or any telegraph office. Ordinary, urgent, letter telegrams.
Telex: Public call office facilities at the GPO, New Road, Bangkok.
Fax: Facilities widely available.
Telephoning the UK: IDD or international operator service, by contacting Long Distance Telephone Office behind GPO in New Road (tel: 32054 or 37056).

Togo

Air mail post to UK: Up to 2 weeks.
Telegrams: Main post offices.
Telephoning the UK: IDD.

Tonga

Air Mail post to UK: 10 days.
Telegrams: Via Cable & Wireless, Salote Rd. Tel: 21 499.
Telex: Via Cable & Wireless. Private booths available.
Telephoning the UK: IDD or dial 913 for International Operator.

Trinidad and Tobago

Air mail post to UK: About 10 days.
Telegrams: Via Trinidad and Tobago External Telecommunications Company Ltd (Textel) located at 1 Edward Street, Port of Spain, Trinidad.
Telex: Textel provide a telex agency service for the receipt of telex messages on behalf of customers who do not have their own installations.
Telephoning the UK: IDD.

Tunisia

Air mail post to UK: About 5 days.
Telegrams: From Central Post Office in Rue Charles de Gaulle, Tunis (24 hrs), and other telegraph offices.
Telex: At the Telecommunications Centre, 29 Jamal Abdelnassel, Tunis.
Telephoning the UK: IDD and international operator service 24 hours a day.

Turkey

Air mail post to UK: 3 days.
Telegrams: From telegraph and post offices. Ordinary and urgent telegrams.
Telex: Public call office at main post office, Ulus, Ankara and at main post office, Telegraf Gisesi, Sirkeci, Istanbul (24 hrs).
Fax: At some hotels.
Telephoning the UK: IDD or international operator service.

Turkmenistan

Air mail post to UK: 2-4 weeks.

Telegrams: At some post offices.
Telex: Major hotels.
Telephoning the UK: Booked through the international operator.

Turks and Caicos Islands

Air mail to UK: 5-10 days.
Telegrams: Via Cable & Wireless.
Telex: Via Cable & Wireless.
Fax: Available.
Telephoning the UK: IDD or through operator.

Tuvalu

Air mail post to UK: 5-10 days.
Telegrams: Via the post office in Funafuti.
Telex: Telecommunications centre in Funafuti.
Fax: Same as telex.
Telephoning the UK: IDD.

Uganda

Air mail post to UK: 2 weeks.
Telex: Postal and Telecommunications Office. in Kampala.
Telephoning the UK: Through the operator.

Ukraine

Air mail post to UK: 2-3 weeks.
Telegrams and Telex: From central post offices in main towns.
Fax: Some offices and hotels.
Telephoning the UK: Limited IDD.

United Arab Emirates

Air mail post to UK: 5 days.
Telegrams: Phone and send telegrams from ETISALAT offices in each town.
Fax: ETISALAT offices.
Telephoning the UK: IDD.

USA

Air mail post to UK: 5-6 days but varies. More from West Coast.
Telegrams: From all post and telegraph offices. Full and night letter telegrams.
Telex: Western Union international telex facilities throughout the USA.
Fax: Widely available.
Telephoning the UK: IDD.

Uruguay

Air mail post to UK: About 7 days.
Telegrams: Public booths in main banking and commercial offices.
Telex: Facilities in main banking and commercial offices.
Telephoning the UK: IDD or via the operator.

Uzbekistan

Air mail post to UK: 4 weeks.
Telegrams: Limited.
Telex: Main hotels.
Fax: Major hotels for residents only.

Telephoning the UK: Through operator as IDD is limited.

Vanuatu
Air mail post to UK: 7 days.
Telegrams and Telex: Central post office in Port Vila.
Fax: Some hotels.
Telephoning the UK: Through operator.

Venezuela
Air mail post to UK: 4-7 days.
Telegrams: Usual telegram services from public telegraph offices, ordinary, and night letter telegrams.
Telex: Public telex facilities provided by CANTV.
Fax: Large hotels.
Telephoning the UK: IDD.

Virgin Islands
Air mail post to UK: 5-10 days.
Telegrams: Via Cable & Wireless.
Telex: Via Cable & Wireless.
Telephoning the UK: IDD or through operator.

Western Samoa
Air mail post to UK: 3 weeks.
Telegrams: Telegraph desk at the post office.
Telephoning the UK: Through the operator.

Yemen
Air mail post to UK: 4-5 days.
Telegrams: From any telegraph office. Ordinary, urgent and letter telegrams.
Telex: Telex booths at Cable & Wireless offices in Sana'a, Hodeida and Taiz.
Telephoning the UK: IDD or operator service. Telephone link available 08.00 – 20.30 local time.

Yugoslavia (Serbia and Montenegro)
Air mail post to UK: Disrupted, normally 4-5 days.
Telegrams: Facilities at post offices.
Telex: Via post offices.
Telephoning the UK: IDD.

Zaïre (DRC)
Air mail post to UK: 4-10 days.
Telegrams: From Chief Telegraph Offices. Ordinary and urgent telegrams.
Telex: Facilities only available at Kinshasa and Lubumbashi Chief Telegraph Offices; also at Intercontinental Hotel.
Telephoning the UK: IDD or international operator service.

Zambia
Air mail post to UK: 5-7 days.
Telegrams: From telegraph offices. Urgent will be accepted at Lusaka Central Telegraph

Offices up to 21.00 hrs Mon – Sat.
Telex: Public telex facilities at Lusaka GPO; also main hotels.
Telephoning the UK: IDD or international operator service.

Zimbabwe
Air mail post to UK: About 5-7 days.
Telegrams: Facilities found in all major cities and tourist centres.
Telex: From all major cities and tourist centres.
Telephoning the UK: IDD or operator service.

Note: Although most countries now have some form of IDD connection, this is often only operative in major centres and even this can involve lengthy delays in some cases. Be warned.

INTERNATIONAL DIRECT DIALLING

Countries in alphabetical order to which international direct dialling is available. Country codes are the same from anywhere in the world.

Country	Country Code	Time Difference (based on GMT)
Afghanistan	93	(+4)
Albania	355	(+1)
Algeria	213	(+1)
Andorra	33 628	(+1)
Angola	244	(+1)
Anguilla	1 809	(-4)
Antigua	1 809	(-4)
Antilles	559	(_4)
Argentina	54	(-3)
Aruba	2 978	(-4)
Ascension	247	GMT
Australia	61	(+8-10)
Austria	43	(+1)
Azores	351	(-1)
Bahamas	1 809	(-5)
Bahrain	973	(+3)
Bangladesh	880	(+6)
Barbados	1 809	(-4)
Belgium	32	(+1)

Belize	501	(-6)	*Estonia*	7	(+3)
Benin	229	(+1)	*Ethiopia*	251	(+3)
Bermuda	1 809	(-4)	*Falkland Islands*	500	(-4)
Bhutan	975	(+6)	*Faroe Islands*	298	GMT
Bolivia	591	(-4)	*Fiji*	679	(+12)
Bosnia-Hercegovina	38	(+1)	*Finland*	358	(+2)
Botswana	267	(+2)	*France*	33	(+1)
Brazil	55	(-2-5)	*French Guiana*	594	(-4)
Brunei	673	(+8)	*French Polynesia*	689	(-10)
Bulgaria	359	(+2)	*Gabon*	241	(+1)
Burkina Faso	226	(GMT)	*Gambia*	220	GMT
Burundi	257	(+2)	*Germany*	49	(+1)
Cambodia	855	(+7)	*Ghana*	233	GMT
Cameroon	237	(+1)	*Gibraltar*	350	(+1)
Canada	1	(-3½-9)	*Greece*	30	(+2)
Canary Islands	34	GMT	*Greenland*	299	(-3)
Cape Verde Islands	238	(-1)	*Grenada*	1 809	(-4)
Cayman Islands	1 809	(-5)	*Guadeloupe*	590	(-4)
Central African Republic	236	(+1)	*Guam*	671	(+10)
Chad	235	(+1)	*Guatemala*	502	(-6)
Chile	56	(-4)	*Guinea*	224	GMT
China	86	(+8)	*Guinea -Bissau*	245	GMT
Christmas Island	6724	(+7)	*Guyana*	592	(-3)
Cocos Island	6722	(+6½)	*Haiti*	509	(-5)
Colombia	57	(-5)	*Honduras*	504	(-6)
CIS	7	(+3-+10)	*Hong Kong*	852	(+8)
Comoros	269	(+3)	*Hungary*	36	(+1)
Congo	242	(+1)	*Iceland*	354	GMT
Cook Islands	682	(-10½)	*India*	91	(+5½)
Costa Rica	506	(-6)	*Indonesia*	62	(+7-9)
Côte d'Ivoire	225	GMT	*Iran*	98	(+3½)
Cuba	53	(-5)	*Iraq*	964	(+3)
Cyprus	357	(+2)	*Ireland*	353	GMT
Czech Republic	42	(+1)	*Israel*	972	(+2)
Denmark	45	(+1)	*Italy*	39	(+1)
Djibouti	253	(+3)	*Jamaica*	1 809	(-5)
Dominica	1 809	(-4)	*Japan*	81	(+9)
Dominican Rep	1 809	(-5)	*Jordan*	962	(+2)
Ecuador	593	(-5)	*Kenya*	254	(+3)
Egypt	20	(+2)	*Kiribati*	686	GMT
El Salvador	503	(-6)	*Korea (North)*	850	(+9)
Equatorial Guinea	240	(+1)	*Korea (South)*	82	(+9)
Eritrea	291	(+3)	*Kuwait*	965	(+3)
			Laos	856	(+7)

Latvia	7	(+3)	*Pakistan*	92	(+5)
Lebanon	961	(+2)	*Palau*	6 809	(+9)
Lesotho	266	(+2)	*Panama*	507	(-5)
Liberia	231	GMT	*Papua New Guinea*	675	(+10)
Libya	218	(+1)	*Paraguay*	595	(-3)
Liechtenstein	41 75	(+1)	*Peru*	51	(-5)
Lithuania	7	(+3)	*Philippines*	63	(+8)
Luxembourg	352	(+1)	*Poland*	48	(+1)
Macau	853	(+8)	*Portugal*	351	GMT
Madagascar	261	(+3)	*Puerto Rico*	1 809	(-4)
Madeira	351 91	GMT	*Qatar*	974	(+3)
Malawi	265	(+2)	*Reunion*	262	(+4)
Malaysia	60	(+8)	*Romania*	40	(+2)
Maldives	960	(+5)	*Russian Federation*	7	(+3-+12)
Malta	356	(+1)	*Rwanda*	250	(+2)
Mali	233	GMT	*St Kitts & Nevis*	1 809	(-4)
Marshall Islands	692	(+12)	*St Lucia*	1 809	(-4)
Martinique	596	(-4)	*St Pierre* *& Miquelon*	508	(-3)
Mauritania	222	GMT			
Mauritius	230	(+4)	*St Vincent* *& Grenadines*	1 809	(-4)
Mayotte	269	(+3)			
Mexico	52	(-6-8)	*American Samoa*	684	(-11)
Micronesia	691	(+10-+11)	*Western Samoa*	685	(-11)
Monaco	33 93	(+1)	*San Marino*	39 541	(+1)
Mongolia	976	(+8)	*Sâo Tomé e Principe*	23912	GMT
Montserrat	1 809	(-4)	*Saudi Arabia*	966	(+3)
Morocco	212	GMT	*Senegal*	221	GMT
Mozambique	258	(+2)	*Seychelles*	248	(+4)
Myanmar	95	(+6½)	*Sierra Leone*	232	GMT
Namibia	264	(+2)	*Singapore*	65	(+8)
Nauru	674	(+13)	*Slovak Republic*	42	(+1)
Nepal	977	(+5½)	*Slovenia*	38	(+1)
Netherlands	31	(+1)	*Solomon Islands*	677	(-11)
Neth. Antilles	599	(-4)	*Somalia*	252	(+3)
New Caledonia	687	(+11)	*South Africa*	27	(+2)
New Zealand	64	(+12)	*Spain*	34	(+1)
Nicaragua	505	(-6)	*Sri Lanka*	94	(+5½)
Niger	227	(+1)	*Sudan*	249	(+2)
Nigeria	234	(+1)	*Suriname*	597	(-3)
Niue	683	(-11)	*Swaziland*	268	(+2)
Norfolk Island	672 3	(+11½)	*Sweden*	46	(+1)
Northern Marianas	670	(+10)	*Switzerland*	41	(+1)
Norway	47	(+1)	*Syria*	963	(+2)
Oman	968	(+4)	*Taiwan*	886	(+8)
			Tanzania	255	(+3)

Thailand	66	(+7)
Togo	228	GMT
Tonga	676	(+13)
Trinidad & Tobago	1 809	(-4)
Tunisia	216	(+1)
Turkey	90	(+2)
Turks and Caicos	1 809	(-5)
Tuvalu	688	(+12)
Uganda	256	(+3)
UAE	971	(+4)
Uruguay	598	(-3)
USA	1	(-5-11)
Vanuatu	678	(+11)
Venezuela	58	(-5)
Vietnam	84	(+7)
Virgin Islands	1 809	(-4)
Yemen	967	(+3)
Yugoslavia (Serbia + Montenegro)	38	(+1)
Zaire	243	(+1/2)
Zambia	260	(+2)
Zimbabwe	263	(+2)

Charge bands, standard and cheap rates

These vary world-wide due to time differences. For further information on charge bands dialling from UK, please see the front of any telephone directory. IDD cheap rate, available to most countries from the UK, is from 8pm to 8am Monday to Friday, all day Saturday and Sunday. For charge bands and standard rates elsewhere contact the local operator.

Note: New countries are constantly being added to the international network. If you would prefer to dial direct and the number is not listed here, ask the operator for an update.

TRAVEL SERVICES

There are numerous American Express representatives world-wide and travellers can use them as *post restante* addresses (letters and telegrams only, no parcels). You may also cash and purchase your American Express travellers' cheques or buy foreign currency. Call in advance to arrange for post to be held. The representatives listed below will be able to tell you where your nearest office is.

Albania – Tirana, Tel: **42-27908**
Algeria – Alger, Tel: **2-631067/68**
Argentina – Buenos Aires, Tel: **1-312 0900**
Australia – Canberra, Tel: **6-247 2333**
Austria – Vienna, Tel: **222-51540**
Bahamas – Nassau, Tel: **322-2931**
Bahrain – Manama, Tel: **254081**
Bangladesh – Dacca, Tel: **2-86 3741 / 4875**
Barbados – Bridgetown, Tel: **431-2423**
Belgium – Brussels, Tel: **2-6762727**
Belize – Belize City, Tel: **2-77185 / 77364**
Bermuda – Hamilton, Tel: **295-4545**
Bhutan – Thimpu, Tel: **22592 / 23586**
Bolivia – La Paz, Tel: **2-360616 / 341201**
Botswana – Garborone, Tel: **31-352021**
Brazil – Brasilia, Tel: **61-225 2686**
Brunei – Bandar Seri Begawan, Tel: **2-228225**
Bulgaria – Sofia, Tel: **2-872567 . 808889**
Burma – Yangon, Tel: **1-75361**
Cambodia – Phnom Penh, Tel: **23-26648**
Cameroon – Douala, Tel: **421184**
Canada – Ottawa, Tel: **613-820 8222**
Chile – Santiago, Tel: **2-230 1000**
China – Beijing, Tel: **1-505 2888**
Colombia – Bogota, Tel: **1-218 7923**
Congo – Brazzaville, Tel: **833957 / 830723**
Costa Rica – San Jose, Tel: **223-3644**
Côte d'Ivoire – Abidjan, Tel: **242352**
Croatia – Zagreb, Tel: **1-427623 / 427633**
Cyprus – Nicosia, Tel: **2-443777**
Czech Republic – Prague, Tel: **2-24227786**
Denmark – Copenhagen, Tel: **33122301**
Djibouti – Djibouti, Tel: **352351**
Dominica – Roseau, Tel: **448-2181**
Dominican Rep. – St. Domingo, Tel: **5633233**
Ecuador -Quito, Tel: **2-560 488**
Egypt – Cairo, Tel: **2-670895**
El Salvador – San Salvador, Tel: **79-3844**
Estonia – Tallinn, Tel: **6-313313 / 313318**
Ethiopia – Addis Ababa, Tel: **1-514838**
Fiji Islands – Suva, Tel: **302333**
Finland – Helsinki, Tel: **0-638788**
France – Paris, Tel: **1-47237215**
Gabon – Libreville, Tel: **241-762787**
Gambia – Banjul, Tel: **92259 / 92505**
Germany – Berlin, Tel: **30-8845880**
Ghana – Accra, Tel: **21-664456**
Greece – Athens, Tel: **1-3244976**
Grenada – St. George's, Tel: **440-2945**
Guadeloupe – Pointe-à-Pitre, Tel: **268-610**
Guatemala – Guatemala City, Tel: **2-311311**
Haiti – Port-au-Prince, Tel: **22-5900 / 23-5900**
Honduras – San Pedro Sula, Tel: **523400**
Hong Kong – Hong Kong, Tel: **27327327**
Hungary – Budapest, Tel: **1-2668680**
Iceland – Reykjavik, Tel: **1-5699300**
India – New Delhi, Tel: **11-332 4119**
Indonesia – Jakarta, Tel: **21-5216238**
Ireland – Dublin, Tel: **1-6772874**
Israel – Tel Aviv, Tel: **3-5242211 / 5248050**
Italy – Rome, Tel: **3-67641**

Jamaica – Kingston, Tel: **929-3077**
Japan – Tokyo, Tel: **3-3214 0280**
Jordan – Amman, Tel: **6-607014**
Kenya – Nairobi, Tel: **2-334722**
South Korea – Seoul, Tel: **2-398 0114**
Kuwait – Safat, Tel: **4843988**
Laos – Vientiane, Tel: **21-213833 / 215920**
Latvia – Riga, Tel: **8820020**
Lebanon – Beirut, Tel: **1-867424 / 641493**
Lesotho – Maseru, Tel: **312554**
Lithuania – Vilnius, Tel: **2-724156**
Luxembourg – Luxembourg, Tel: **228555**
Macau – Macau, Tel: **707007**
Macedonia – Skopje, Tel: **91-230064**
Madagascar – Antananarivo, Tel: **4192 / 2104**
Malawi – Lilongwe, Tel: **784144 / 783521**
Malaysia – Kuala Lumpur, Tel: **3-2486700**
Maldives – Male, Tel: **323 116**
Mali – Bamako, Tel: **224435**
Malta – Valletta, Tel: **232141**
Martinique – Fort de France, Tel: **71-5555**
Mexico – Mexico City, Tel: **5-2801101**
Monaco – Monte Carlo, Tel: **93-257445**
Morocco – Marrakesh, Tel: **4-433022**
Namibia – Windhoek, Tel: **37946**
Nepal – Kathmandu, Tel: **1-227635**
Netherlands – Amsterdam, Tel: **20-5207777**
New Guinea – Port Moresby, Tel: **22 0725**
New Zealand – Wellington, Tel: **4-473 7766**
Nicaragua – Managua, Tel: **2-664050**
Nigeria – Lagos, Tel: **1-263456**
Norway – Oslo, Tel: **2-286 1300**
Oman – Muscat, Tel: **677739**
Pakistan – Islamabad, Tel: **51-212425**
Panama – Panama, Tel: **642444**
Paraguay – Asunçion, Tel: **21-490111**
Peru – Lima, Tel: **14-276624**
Philippines – Manila, Tel: **2-509601**
Poland – Warsaw, Tel: **2-630 6952/3**
Portugal – Lisbon, Tel: **1-3155885**
Qatar – Doha, Tel: **422411 / 417348**
Romania – Bucharest, Tel: **1-3123969**
Russian Federation – Moscow, Tel: **95-9000**
Saudi Arabia – Riyadh, Tel: **1-4648810**
Senegal – Dakar, Tel: **234040**
Seychelles – Victoria, Tel: **322414**
Sierra Leone – Freetown, Tel: **22-24423**
Singapore – Singapore, Tel: **2355789**
Slovak Republic – Bratislava, Tel: **7-335536**
Slovenia – Ljubljana, Tel: **61-222741**
South Africa – Pretoria, Tel: **12-3222620**
Spain – Madrid, Tel: **1-322 5418**
Sri Lanka – Colombo, Tel: **1-329881 / 329563**
Sudan – Khartoum, Tel: **72262 / 71598**
Suriname – Paramaribo, Tel: **477148 / 474448**
Swaziland – Mbabane, Tel: **42298 / 42101**
Sweden – Stockholm, Tel: **8-6795200**
Switzerland – Geneva, Tel: **22-7317600**
Syria – Damascus, Tel: **11-2217813**
Tahiti – Papeete, Tel: **427526**
Taiwan – Taipei, Tel: **7-228 7200**

Tanzania – Dar es Salaam, Tel: **51-29125**
Thailand – Bangkok, Tel: **2-2165759**
Togo – Lome, Tel: **216916 / 212611**
Trinidad & Tobago – P/Spain, Tel: **6251636**
Tunisia – Tunis, Tel: **347015**
Turkey – Ankara, Tel: **41-467334 / 4677335**
Uganda – Kampala, Tel: **41-236767**
UAE – Abu Dhabi, Tel: **2-212100**
UK – London, Tel: **171-5846182**
Uruguay – Montevideo, Tel: **2-920829**
Venezuala – Caracas, Tel: **2-950 1011**
Yemen – Sanaa,, Tel: **2-272432 / 271803**
Zambia – Lusaka, Tel: **22-8605 / 224960**
Zimbabwe – Harare, Tel: **4-703421 / 708441**

WORLD SERVICE FREQUENCIES

Frequencies are given in kiloHertz and a choice is given as they vary depending on the time of day

Afghanistan	17790; 15575; 15310; 11955; 9740; 9580; 5975; 5965; 1413
Albania	17640; 15070; 12095; 9410; 6180
Algeria	17705; 15070; 12095; 9410; 7325; 6195
Angola	21660; 17790; 15400; 9600; 6005;
Argentina	17790; 15260; 15190; 11750; 9915; 7325
Australia	17830; 11955; 11695; 9740; 9640; 7110; 6110
Austria	15575; 15070; 12095; 9410; 6195
Azores	17705; 15400; 15070; 12095; 9410
Bangladesh	17790; 15310; 11955; 11750; 9740; 7160; 5975; 5965; 792
Belgium	15575; 12095; 9410; 6195; 648; 198
Bolivia	17840; 15260; 15220; 9915; 9640; 9590; 7325
Borneo	17830; 15360; 11955; 9740; 6195; 3915
Bosnia-Herzegovina	15070; 12095; 9410; 6195
Botswana	21660; 21470; 17885; 17880; 15420; 15400; 11940; 6190; 3255
Brazil	17790; 15260; 15190; 11750; 9915; 7325
Brunei	17830; 15360; 11955; 9740; 6195; 3915
Bulgaria	17640; 15070; 12095; 9410; 6180
Burundi	21470; 17885; 15575; 15420; 9630; 6135; 6005
Cambodia	17830; 17790; 15360; 11955; 11750; 9740; 9570; 6195; 3915
Cameroon	21660; 17880; 17790; 15400; 9600; 6005
Canada	17840; 15260; 15220; 11820; 9740; 9640; 9590; 9515; 7325; 6175; 5975
Canary Islands	17705; 15400; 15070; 12095; 9410
Caribbean	17840; 15220; 9915; 7325; 6195; 5975; 930
Cent. America	17840; 15220; 9915; 9640; 9590; 7325; 5975
Central African Rep	21660; 17880; 17790; 15400; 9600; 6005
Chad	21660; 17880; 17790; 15400; 9600; 6005
Chile	17790; 15260; 15190; 11750; 9915; 7325
China	21715; 17830; 17790; 15360; 15280; 9740; 9570; 7180; 6195
CIS	17640; 15070; 12095; 9410; 6195
Colombia	17840; 15260; 15220; 9915; 9640; 9590; 7325
Congo	21660; 17880; 17790; 15400; 9600; 6005
Czech Republic	15575; 15070; 12095; 9410; 6195; 1296
Denmark	12095; 9410; 6195; 198
Djibouti	21470; 17885; 15420; 11730; 9630; 6135; 6005
Ecuador	17840; 15260; 15220; 9915; 9640; 9590; 7325
Egypt	17640; 15575; 15070; 12095; 9410; 7325; 1323; 639
Eritrea	21470; 17885; 15420; 11730; 9630; 6135; 6005
Estonia	15070; 12095; 9410; 6195
Ethiopia	21470; 17885; 15420; 11730; 9630; 6135; 6005
Falkland Islands	17790; 15260; 15190; 11750; 9915; 7325
France	15070; 12095; 9410; 7325; 6195; 648; 198
Gabon	21660; 17880; 17790; 15400; 9600; 6005
Germany (NE)	15575; 15070; 12095; 9410; 6195; 1296
Germany (NW)	15575; 12095; 9410; 6195; 648; 198
Germany (S)	15575; 15070; 12095; 9410; 6195
Gibraltar	17705; 15070; 12095; 9410; 7325; 6195
Greece	17640; 15070; 12095; 9410; 6180; 1323
India (W)	17790; 15575; 156310; 11955; 11750; 9580; 7160; 5965; 1413
India (E)	17790; 15310; 11955; 11750; 9740; 7160; 5975; 5965; 792
Indonesia	17830; 15360; 11955; 9740; 6195; 3915

Iran	15575; 15070; 12095; 11955; 11760; 9740; 7235; 7160; 1413
Ireland	15575; 12095; 9410; 6195; 648; 198
Israel	1323; 639
Italy	17640; 15575; 15070; 12095; 9410; 6195
Japan	21715; 17830; 15280; 11955; 11820; 9740; 7180
Jordan	1323; 639
Kenya	21470; 17885; 15575; 15420; 9630; 6135; 6005
Korea	21715; 17830; 15280; 11955; 11820; 9740; 7180
Laos	17830; 17790; 15360; 11955; 11750; 9740; 9570; 6195; 3915
Latvia	17640; 15070; 12095; 9410; 6195
Lebanon	1323; 720
Lesotho	21660; 21470; 17885; 17880; 15420; 15400; 11940; 6190; 3255
Libya	17640; 15575; 15070; 12095; 9410; 7325
Lithuania	17640; 15070; 12095; 9410; 6195
Luxembourg	15575; 12095; 9410; 6195; 648; 198
Macedonia	17640; 15070; 12095; 9410; 6180
Madagascar	21470; 17885; 15575; 15420; 9630; 6135; 6005
Malawi	21660; 21470; 17885; 17880; 15420; 15400; 11940; 6190; 3225
Malaysia	17830; 15360; 11955; 9740; 6195; 3915
Maldives	17790; 15310; 11955; 11750; 9740; 7160; 5975; 5965; 792
Malta	17640; 15575; 15070; 12095; 9410
Mauritius	21470; 17885; 15575; 15420; 9630; 6135; 6005
Mexico	17840; 15220; 9915; 9640; 9590; 7325; 5975
Middle East	15575; 15070; 12095; 11760; 9410; 7160; 1413
Mongolia	21715; 17830; 17790; 15360; 15280; 9740; 9570; 7180; 6195
Morocco	17705; 15070; 12095; 9410; 7325; 6195
Mozambique	21660; 21470; 17885; 17880; 15420; 15400; 11940; 6190; 3225
Myanmar	17830; 17790; 15360; 11955; 11750; 9740; 9570; 6195; 3915
Namibia	21660; 17790; 15400; 9600; 6005; 1197
Nepal	17790; 15310; 11955; 11750; 9740; 7160; 5975; 5965; 792
Netherlands	15575; 12095; 9410; 6195; 648; 198
Norway	12095; 9410; 6195; 198
Pacific Islands	17830; 11955; 11695; 9740; 9640; 7110; 6110
Pakistan	17790; 15575; 15310; 11955; 9740; 9580; 5975; 5965; 1413
Papua New Guinea	17830; 11955; 11695; 9740; 7110; 6110
Paraguay	17790; 15260; 15190; 11750; 9915; 7325
Peru	17840; 15260; 15220; 9915; 9640; 9590; 7325
Philippines	21715; 17830; 15360; 11955; 9740; 6195
Poland	15575; 15070; 12095; 9410; 6195; 1296
Portugal	17705; 15070; 12095; 9410; 7325; 6195
Romania	17640; 15070; 12095; 9410; 6180
Rwanda	21470; 17885; 15575; 15420; 9630; 6135; 6005
Serbia	17640; 15070; 12095; 9410; 6180
Slovak Republic	15575; 15070; 12095; 9410; 6195; 1296
Somalia	21470; 17885; 15420; 11730; 9630; 6135; 6005
South Africa	21660; 21470; 17885; 17880; 15420; 15400; 11940; 6190; 3255; 1197
Spain	17705; 15070; 12095; 9410; 7325; 6195
Sri Lanka	17790; 15310; 11955; 11750; 9740; 7160; 5975; 5965; 792
Sudan	17640; 15575; 15070; 12095; 9410; 7325
Swaziland	21660; 21470; 17885; 17880; 15420; 15400; 11940; 6190; 3255
Switzerland	15575; 15070; 12095; 9410; 6195
Syria	1323; 720
Tanzania	21470; 17885; 15575; 15420; 9630; 6135; 6005
Thailand	17830; 17790; 15360; 11955; 11750; 9740; 9570; 6195; 3915

Tunisia	17705; 15070; 12095; 9410; 7325; 6195
Turkey	17640; 15070; 12095; 9410; 6180
Uganda	21470; 17885; 15575; 15420; 9630; 6135; 6005
UK	15575; 12095; 9410; 6195; 648; 198
Uruguay	17790; 15260; 15190; 11750; 9915; 7325
USA	17840; 15260; 15220; 11820; 9740 9640; 9590; 9515; 7325; 6175; 5975
Vietnam	17830; 17790; 15360; 11955; 11750; 9740; 9570; 6195; 3915
West Africa	17790; 17705; 15400; 15105; 15070; 9600; 9410; 6005
Zaïre (DRC) (E)	21470; 17885; 15575; 15420; 9630; 9135; 6005
Zaïre (DRC) (W)	21660; 17880; 17790; 15400; 9600; 6005
Zambia	21660; 21470; 17885; 17880; 15420; 15400; 11940; 6190; 3255
Zimbabwe	21660; 21470; 17885; 17880; 15420; 15400; 11940; 6190; 3255

*For further information the BBC publish a monthly magazine called **On Air** Magazine which lists not only current frequencies, which change every six months or so, but also the World Service Radio and Television listings, and is available in some shops and airports or by subscription. Call **0171-257 2211** (Answerphone). Current subscription £18 ($30) per year. For up to date frequency information, write to: Audience Relations, BBC World Service, Bush House, Strand, London, WC2B 4PH, United Kingdom.*

ENGLISH LANGUAGE NEWSPAPERS

This is a selection of newspapers found in a selection of countries.

Afghanistan
The Kabul Times – daily

Antigua & Barbuda
Nation's Voice – twice a month
Worker's Voice – once a week
The Sentinel – once a week
Outlet – once a week

Argentina
Buenos Aires Herald – weekly
The Review of the River Plate (on financial matters)

Armenia
Yerevan News – weekly

Australia
The Australian – daily
The Australian Financial Review – daily

Austria
The Vienna Reporter

Bahamas
Nassau Guardian – daily
Nassau Tribune – daily
Freeport News - daily

Bahrain
Gulf Daily News – daily

Bangladesh
Bangladesh Observer – daily
Bangladesh Times – daily
News Nation – daily
Holiday – weekly

Bangladesh Today – weekly
Tide – weekly

Barbados
The Barbados Advocate – daily
The Nation – Mon-Fri

Belgium
The Bulletin

Belize
The Belize Times – weekly
Belize Today – weekly
Reporter – weekly
Amandala – weekly
Government Gazette – weekly
The People's Pulse – weekly

Bermuda
Royal Gazette – daily
Mid Ocean News – Fri
Bermuda Sun – Fri

Bhutan
Kuensel – weekly

Botswana
Botswana Daily News – daily
The Reporter – weekly
The Midweek Sun – weekly
Botswana Guardian – Fri

Brazil
The Brazil Herald – only in Rio

British Virgin Islands
The BVI Beacon – weekly
The Island Sun – weekly

Brunei
Brunei Bulletin – daily

Bulgaria
Sofia News – weekly
Bulgaria – monthly

Cambodia
The Phnom Penh Post – daily
Cambodia Times – weekly
Cambodian Daily

Cameroon
Cameroon Tribune – twice weekly in English
Cameroon Post
Cameroon Times
The Herald

Canada
The Globe and Mail – only national daily

Cayman Islands
Caymanian Compass – Mon – Fri
The New Caymanian – weekly

China
China Daily
The People's Daily
The Guangming Daily
Beijing Review – weekly

Cook Islands
Cook Islands News – daily

Costa Rica
Tico Times – weekly
Costa Rica Today – weekly

Cuba
Gramma International - weekly

Curaçao
The Guardian – daily

Cyprus
Cyprus Mail – daily
Cyprus Weekly – weekly

Czech Republic
The Prague Post – weekly

Domincan Republic
Santo Domingo News – weekly
Dominican News – monthly

Egypt
Egyptian Gazette – daily
The Middle East Observer – weekly

Eritrea
Hadas Eritrea – twice weekly

Estonia
The Baltic Times – weekly

Ethiopia
The Ethiopian Herald – daily

Falkland Islands
Penguin News – weekly
Teaberry Express – weekly

Fiji
Fiji Times – daily
Daily Post – daily

Gambia
The Gambia Weekly
The Gambian Times
The Nation
The Gambia Onwards

Georgia
Georgian Times – weekly

Ghana
The Ghanaian Times – daily
Daily Graphic – daily
The Pioneer
The Mirror
The Weekly Spectator

Greece
Athens News – daily
Athens Daily Post – daily

Grenada
The Grenadian Voice – weekly
Grenada Today
The Informer

Guam
The Pacific Daily News

Guatemala
Guatemala Weekly
Central America Report

Guyana
Guyana Chronical – daily
The Mirror
The New Nation – daily

Honduras
Honduras This Week – weekly

Hong Kong
South China Morning Post – daily & Sunday
Asian Wall Street Journal – daily
Hong Kong Standard – daily & Sunday
Eastern Express – daily

Hungary
Daily News
Budapest Business Journal
Budapest Week
The Budapest Sun
The Hungarian Economy
The Hungarian Observer
The Hungarian Quarterly

Iceland
The Iceland Reporter

India
The Times of India – daily
The Hindustan Times – daily
Indian Express – daily
The Statesman – daily
The Economic Times
The Hindu
The Deccan Herald

Indonesia
The Indonesian Times – daily
Indonesian Observer – daily
The Jakarta Post – daily
The Bali Post
The World-wide News

Iran
Teheran Times – daily

Iraq
Baghdad Observer - daily

Ireland (Republic of)
The Irish Times – daily
Evening Herald – daily
Irish Independent – daily

Israel
Jerusalem Post – daily
Jerusalem Post International Edition – weekly

Italy
Daily American – daily

Jamaica
The Daily Gleaner – daily
The Jamaica Herald – daily
The Daily Star – daily

Japan
The Asahi Evening News – daily
The Daily Yomiuri – daily
The Japan Times – daily
Mainichi Daily News – daily

Jordan
Jordan Times – daily
The Star – weekly

Kenya
The Standard – daily
Daily *Nation* – daily
Kenya Times – daily

Korea (north)
Pyongyang Times – weekly

Korea (south)
Korea Herald – daily excl. Mon
Korea Times – daily excl. Mon

Kuwait
The Arab Times – daily
Kuwait Times – daily

Kyrgyzstan
Kyrgyzstan Chronicle – weekly

Laos
Vietiane Times – daily

Latvia
The Baltic Observer – weekly

Lesotho
Lesotho Today – daily
The Survivor
The Mirror

Liberia
The Daily Observer -daily
The New Times- daily
The SundayExpress – weekly
The Inquirer – daily

Lithuania
Lithuanian News – weekly
Lithuanian Weekly – weekly
The Baltic Observer – weekly

Luxembourg
The Luxembourg News

Macau
The South China Morning Post – daily
The Standard – daily
Macau Express

Madagascar
Madagscar Tribune – daily

Malawi
The Daily Times
The Malawi News – weekly
The Independent – twice weekly
Nation
New Express

Malaysia
Business Times – daily
New Straits Times – daily
Malay Mail – daily
Sunday Mail – weekly
The Star – daily
The Sun – daily

Malta
The Times of Malta – daily
The Malta Independent – daily
Business Weekly

Mexico
Mexico City Times – daily

Mongolia
Mongol Messenger
Business Time

Myanmar
The New Light of Myanmar

Namibia
The Windhoek Advertiser – daily
The Namibian – daily
New Era – weekly
The Observer – weekly

Nepal
The Rising Nepal – daily
The Commoner – daily
The Motherland – daily
The Independent – weekly

New Zealand
New Zealand Herald – daily
The Press – daily
Evening Post – daily

Nigeria
Daily Sketch
Daily Times
Daily Star
Sunday Concord
Sunday Chronicle
New Nigerian – *daily*
Nigerian Herald – daily
Nigerian Tribune – daily
The Observer – daily

Oman
Oman Daily Observer – daily
Times of Oman – weekly

Pakistan
The Financial Post – daily
The Leader – daily
The Pakistan Observer – daily
The Star – daily
The Nation – d aily
The News – daily
The Business Recorder

Papua New Guinea
Papua New Guinea Post Courier – daily

Peru
Lima Times – monthly

Philippines
Manila Times – daily
Manila Bulletin – daily
Philippine Daily Inquirer – daily
Philippine Star – daily
Philippine Daily Globe

Poland
The Warsaw Voice – weekly

Portugal
Anglo-Portuguese News – weekly
The News (Algarve) – weekly

Puerto Rico
The San Juan Star – daily

Qatar
Gulf Times – daily

Russian Federation
Moscow Times – daily
Moscow News – weekly
St. Petersburg Times – daily

Saudi Arabia
Arab News – daily
Saudi Gazette – daily

Seychelles
The Seychelles Nation – daily
Seychelles Weekend Nation – weekly
The People – monthly
Seychelles Review – monthly

Sierra Leone
The Daily Mail – daily
The New Shaft
The New Citizen

Singapore
The Business Times – daily
The New Paper – daily
Straits Times – 7 days

Slovak Republic
The Slovak Spectator – twice weekly
Slovak Foreign Trade – monthly

Slovenia
Slovenian Business Report
Slovenia Weekly
Ars Vivendi

South Africa
Business Day
Cape Times
The Argus
Mail and Guardian
The Star
Natal Mercury

Spain
Iberian Daily Sun

Sri Lanka
Daily News – daily
The Island – daily
The Times – daily

Swaziland
Times of Swaziland – daily
Swazi Observer – daily

Syria
Syria Times – daily

Tahiti
The Tahiti Beach Press – weekly

Taiwan
China News – daily
China Post – daily
Free China Journal – daily

Tanzania
Daily News
Sunday News
Business Times
The Express
Family Mirror
The Guardian

Thailand
Bangkok Post – daily
The Nation – daily

Tonga
The Times of Tonga – weekly
Tonga Chronicle – weekly

Trinidad and Tobago
Trinidad and Tobago Express – daily
Trinidad Guardian – daily

Tunisia
Tunisia News – weekly

Turkey
Turkish Daily News

Uganda
The People – daily
The Monitor – daily
The Star – daily
New Vision – daily
The Citizen – daily
Financial Times – daily

United Arab Emirates
Gulf News – daily
Khaleej Times – daily
Emirate News – daily

Venezuela
The Dial Journal – daily

Vietnam
Saigon Times – daily
The Vietnam Economic Times
Vietnam Today
Vietnam News
Vietnam Courier

Zambia
The Times of Zambia – daily
The Zambia Daily Mail – daily
Sunday Times
Sunday Mail
The Chronicle
The Post

Zimbabwe
The Herald – daily
The Chronicle – daily
The Financial Gazette – daily

LEARNING A LANGUAGE

CILT
20 Bedfordbury
London WC2 4LD
Tel: **0171-379 5101**
The Centre for Information on Language Teaching and Research, which is sponsored by the Department of Education and Science, offers information and guidance on language learning/teaching.

The Institute of Linguists
24a Highbury Grove
London N5 2DQ
Tel: **0171-359 7445**

Training Access Points (TAPS):
Government interest in promoting training and vocational skills has prompted the establishment of TAPS across the country. As the name suggests, TAPS identify where training – including but not exclusively language training – is available from providers in the public and private sectors. Any local Civic Library or Chamber of Commerce should be able to put you in contact with the local office/reference point. Alternatively your local TAPS office should be in Yellow Pages (see Training Agency/Training Enterprise: TEAD)

Services:

Accelerated Learning Systems Ltd
50 Aylesbury Road
Aston Clinton
Aylesbury
Buckinghamshire HP22 5AH
Tel: **01296-631177**
They offer a variety of self-disciplined open learning language training packages using audio cassettes and suggestopaedia.

The Berlitz Schools of Language Ltd
9-13 Grosvenor Street
London W1A 3BZ
Tel: **0171-915 0909**
Berlitz offers a range of language learning materials and courses ranging from low budget, pocket books.

BBC Enterprises
Woodlands
80 Wood Lane
London W12 0TT
The BBC offers a range of language learning materials and courses including videos, audio cassettes and books. Prices range from the GET BY series (e.g. GET BY in Spanish) from £10 to the more expensive video language courses.

Linguaphone
124-126 Brompton Road
London SW3 1JD
Tel: **0171-589 2422**
This company, although most noteworthy for language training courses, has an affiliated school, the Regent School, Tel: 0171-637 8041.

Richard Lewis Communications plc
Riversdown House
Warnford
Nr. Southampton
Hampshire SO32 3LH
Tel: **01962-771111**
RLC specialises in tailor-made course, including the residential, for the corporate market administered from centres at home and abroad.

The French Institute
14 Cromwell Place
London SW7 2JR
Tel: **0171-581 2701**

The Goethe Institute
50 Prince's Gate
Exhibition Road
London SW7 2PH
Tel: **0171-411 3451**

The Spanish Institute
22 Manchester Square
London WM1 5AP
Tel: **0171-935 1518**

ENGLISH TEACHING RECRUITMENT ORGANISATIONS

This is a list of the headquarters of several international language schools. They will be able to send you lists of their branches world-wide.

ARELS
(Association of Recognised English Language Services)
2 Pontypool Place
London SE1 8QF
Tel: **0171-242 3136**
An organization of English Language Schools in UK inspected and accredited by the British Council. Publishes an annual guide listing member schools.

The Bell Language Schools
The Personnel Department
Hillscross
Red Cross Lane
Cambridge CB2 2QX
Tel: **01223-246644**
Only hires those with experience.

Bénédict Schools
PO Box 270
1000 Lausanne 9
Switzerland
Tel: **21 323 66 55**
Over 80 language schools world-wide. Hires TEFL qualified teachers.

Berlitz UK
9-13 Grosvenor Street
London W1A 3BZ
Tel: **0171-915 0909**
330 schools world-wide. Teachers trained in the "Berlitz Method".

The British Council Overseas Appointment Services
Medlock Street
Manchester M15 4AA
Tel: **0161-957 7383**

Central Bureau for Educational Visits and Exchanges
Seymour Mews
London W1H 9PE
Tel: **0171-486 5101**
Organises exchange programmes for qualified teachers and language assistant placements.

CfBT Education Services
1 The Chambers
East Street
Reading
Berks, RG1 4JD
Tel: **0118-952 3900**
TEFL qualifed recruitment world-wide.

Christians Abroad
1 Stockwelll green
Lonodn SW9 9HP
Tel: **0171-737 7811**

Connect Teaching Recruitment Services
Kirkdale House
Kirkdale Road
London E11 1HP
Tel: **0181-988 7002**
Recruit supply teachers for places all over Britain.

ELS Language Centers
International Division
5761 Buckingham Parkway
Culver City, CA 90230-6583
USA
Tel: **310-642 0988**
90 schools world-wide. TEFL qualified applicants only.

English Worldwide
The Italian Building
Dockhead
London SE1 2BS
Tel: **0171-252 1402**
Recruits TEFL qualified teachers only to placements in Europe, Middle East, Far East and Latin America.

ILC International Language Centres
White Rock
Hastings
East Sussex TN43 1JY
Tel: **01424-720109**

inlingua Teacher Training and Recruitment
Rodney Lodge
Rodney Road
Cheltenham
Glos GL50 1JF
Tel: **01242-253171**
Has 270 language schools world-wide. Recruits 100 teachers annually for its schools – mainly

those in Russia, Germany, France and Singapore.

Japanese Exchange Teaching Programme (JET)
The Council for International Exchange
33 Seymour Place
London W1H 6AT
Tel: **0171-224 8896**

Wall Street Institute International
Torre Mapfre
Marina 16-18
08005 Barcelona
Spain
Tel: **3-225 4555**
164 language schools in Europe and South America

Worldwide Education Service
Canada House
272 Field End Road
Eastcote
Middlesex, HA4 9NA
Tel: **0181-866 4400**
Recruits qualified teachers for posts mainly in Britain, but internationally as well.

TEFL CENTRES

The British Council
Central Management of Direct Teaching
10 Spring Gardens
London SW1A 2BN
Tel: **0171-389 4931**
Publishes a comprehensive list of centres world-wide that offer a Certificate in English Language Teaching to Adults (CELTA).

Australia
Australian Centre for Languages
420 Liverpool Road
South Strathfield
Sydney NSW 2136
Australia
Tel: **612 742 5277**

Canada
Languages Studies Toronto
20 Eglington Avenue East
Suite 300
Toronto, Ontario M4P 1A9
Tel: **1416 488 2200**

New Zealand
Capital Language Academy
PO Box 1100
Wellington 6000
New Zealand
Tel: **644 472 7557**
email: **100245.13@compuserve.com.nz**

UK
Cambridge RSA (CELTA Certificate)
University of Cambridge Exam. Service
Syndicate Buildings
1 Hills Road
Cambridge CB1 2EU
Tel: **01223-553789**

Trinity College London (TESOL Certificate)
16 Park Crescent
London W1N 4Ap
Tel: **0171-323 2328**

USA
The Centre for English Studies
International House New York
330 Seventh Avenue
New York 10001
USA
Tel: **212 629 7300**

English International San Francisco
655 Sutter Street (Suite 500)
San Francisco
CA 94108
USA
Tel: **415 749 5633**

Further Reading:

EL Gazette
EL Publications
Dilke House
1 Malet Street
London WC1E 7JA
Tel: **0171-255 1970**

ELT Guide also published by EL Publications (see above).

Jobs in Japan
Teaching English Abroad
Teaching English in Asia
All published by Vacation Work
9 Park End Street
Oxford
Tel: **01865-241978**

Vacant TEFL posts are advertised in *The Guardian* (Tuesdays), *Times Educational Supplement* (Fridays) and *Overseas Jobs Express* (1st and 15th of each month). ■

WHEN THINGS GO WRONG
Section 13

RED CROSS AND RED CRESCENT SOCIETIES WORLD-WIDE

Afghanistan
Puli Harlan
Kabul
Tel: **32357 / 32211 / 34288**

Albania
Rruga 'Muhammet Gjollesha'
Sheshi 'Karl Topia'
Tirana
Tel: **42-25855 / 22037**

Algeria
15bis
Boulevard Mohammed V
Algiers
Tel: **2645727 / 2645728 / 2610741**

Andorra
Prat de la Creu 30
Andorra La Vella
Tel: **825225**

Angola
Rua 1. Congresso no. 21
Luanda
Tel: **2-336543 / 333991**

Antigua and Barbuda
Red Cross House
Old Parham Road
St John's
Antigua W.I.
Tel: **809-4620800**

Argentina
Hipolito Yrigoyen 2068
1089 Buenos Aires
Tel: **1-9511391 / 9511854 / 9512389**

Armenia
Antarain str. 188

Yerevan 375019
Tel: **2-560630 / 583630 / 564881**

Australia
National Office
206 Clarendon Street
East Melbourne
Victoria 3002
Tel: **3-94185200**

Austria
Wiedner Hauptstrasse 32
Vienna 4
Tel: **1-58900-0**

Azerbaijan
Prospekt Azerbaijan 19
Baku
Tel: **12-931912 / 938481 / 936346**

Bahamas
PO Box N.8331
Nassau
Tel: **809-3284415 / 3237370/71/72/73**

Bahrain
PO Box 882
Manama
Tel: **973-293171**

Bangladesh
National Headquarters
684-686 Bara Maghbazar
Dhaka - 1217
GPO Box 579
Tel: **2-407908/406902/400188/400189/402540**

Barbados
Red Cross House
Jemmotts Lane, Bridgetown
Tel: **809-4262052**

Belarus
25 Karl Marx Str.
220030 Minsk
Tel: **17-2272620**

Belgium
Ch. de Vleurgat 98
1050 Bruxelles
Tel: **2-6454411**

Belize
1 Gabourel Lane
Belize City
Tel: **2-73319**

Benin
BP No.1
Porto Novo
Tel: **229-212886**

Bolivia
Avenida Simon Bolivar 1515
La Paz
Tel: **2-340948 / 326568 / 376874**

Botswana
135 Independence Avenue
Gaborone
Tel: **352465 / 312353**

Brazil
Praça Cruz Vermelha 10
20230-130 Rio de Janeiro RJ
Tel: **21-2323223 / 2326325 / 2426537**

Brunei
P.O. Box 3065
Bandar Seri Begawan 1920
Tel: **2-339774**

Bulgaria
61 Dondukov Boulevard
1527 Sofia
Tel: **2-441443 / 441444 / 441445**

Burkina Faso
01 B.P. 4404
Ougadougou
Tel: **300877**

Burundi
Comite National
18 Av de la Croix-Rouge
Bujumbura
Tel: **223159 / 223576**

Cambodia
17 Vithei de la Croix-Rouge Cambodgienne
Phnom-Penh

Cameroon
Rue Henri-Dunant
Yaounde
Tel: **224177**

Canada
1800 Alta Vista Drive
Ottawa
Ontario K1G 4J5
Tel: **613-739 3000**

Cape Verde
Rua Andrada Corvo
Praia
Tel: **611701 / 614169 / 611621**

Central African Republic
Avenue Koudoukou Km 5
Bangui
Tel: **612223**

Chad
BP 449
N'djamena
Tel: **515218 / 513434**

Chile
Avenida Santa Maria No. 150
Providencia
Santiago de Chile
Tel: **2-7771448**

China
53 Ganmian Hutong
100010 Beijing
Tel: **10-5124447**

Colombia
Avenida 68 No.66-31
Santafé de Bogotá D.C
Tel: **1-2506611 /2319445 / 2259775**

Congo
Place de la Paix
Brazzaville
Tel: **824410**

Costa Rica
Calle 14
Avenida 8
San Jose 1000
Tel: **2337033 / 2553761 / 2553759**

Côte d'Ivoire
P.O. Box 1244
Abidjan 01
Tel: **321335**

Croatia
Ulica Crvenog kriza 14, 10000 Zagreb
Tel: **1-415 458/467**

Cuba
Calle Calzada No. 51 Vedado
Cuidad Habana
C.P 10400
Tel: **7-326005**

Cyprus
'Z' Compound
Off Prodromos Street
Nicosia
Tel: **2-446956/7**

Czech Republic
Thunovska 18
CZ-118 04 Prague 1
Tel: **2-24510347**

Denmark
Blegdamsvej 27
2100 Kobenhavn O
Tel: **31-381444**

Djibouti
B P 8
Djibouti
Tel: **352451 / 353552**

Dominica
National Headquarters
Federation Drive
Goodwill
Tel: **809-488280**

Dominican Republic
Calle Juan E. Dunant No. 51
Ens. Miraflores
Santo Domingo
Tel: **809-6823793 / 6897344**

Ecuador
Av. Colombia y Elizalde Esq
Quito
Tel: **2-582485 / 514587**

Egypt
29 El Galaa Street
Cairo
Tel: **2-5750558 / 5750397**

El Salvador
17 C Pte y Av. Henri Dunant
San Salvador
Tel: **2227749 / 227743**

Equatorial Guinea
Alcalde Albilio Balboa 92
Malabo
Tel: **9-3701**

Eritrea
Red Cross Society of Eritrea

P.O. Box 575
Asmara
Tel: **1-120922**

Estonia
Lai Street 17
EE0001 Tallinn
Tel: **6411643**

Ethiopia
Ras Desta Damtew Avenue
Addis Ababa
Tel: **1-449364 / 159074**

Fiji
22 Gorrie Street
Suva
Tel: **314133 / 314138**

Finland
Tehtaankatu 1 a.
00141 Helsinki 14115
Tel: **9-12931**

France
1 Place Henri-Dunant
F-75384 Paris
Cedex 08
Tel: **1-44431100**

Gabon
B.P. 2271
Libreville
Tel: **753175**

Gambia
Kanifing
Banjul
Tel: **392405 / 393179 / 392347**

Georgia
15 Krilov St.
Tbilisi
Tel: **32-953826 / 953304**

Germany
Friedrich-Ebert-Allee 71
D-53113
Bonn
Tel: **228-5411**

Ghana
National Headquarters
Ministries Annex Block A3
Off Liberia Road Extension
Accra
Tel: 21-662298

Greece
Rue Lycavittou 1, Athens 106 72
Tel: **1-3646005 / 3628648 / 3615606 / 3621681**

Grenada
Upper Lucas Street
St. George's
Tel: **809-4401483**

Guatemala
3a Calle 8-40
Zona 1
Guatemala, C.A.
Tel: **2-532026 / 532027 / 532028 / 26518**

Guinea
B.P. 376
Conakry
Tel: **443825**

Guinea-Bissau
Avenida Unidade Africana 12
Bissau
Tel: **212405**

Guyana
PO Box 10524
Eve Leary
Georgetown
Tel: **2-65174**

Haiti
1 rue Eden
Bicentenaire
Port-au-Prince
Tel: **225553 / 225554 / 231035**

Honduras
7a Calle
entre la. y. 2a Avenidas
Comayaguela D C
Tel: **378876 / 374628 / 378654 / 372240**

Hungary
Arany Janos utca 31
1051 Budapest V
Tel: **1-1313950 / 1317711**

Iceland
Raudararstigur 18
105 Reykjavik
Tel: **5626722**

India
Red Cross Building
1 Red Cross Road
New Delhi 110001
Tel: **11-3716441/2/3**

Indonesia
J1 Jenderal Datot Subroto Kav. 96
Jakarta 12790
Tel: **21-7992325**

Iran
Ostad Nejatolahi Ave.
Tehran
Tel: **21-8849077 / 8849078**

Iraq
Al-Mansour
Baghdad
Tel: **1-8862191 / 5343922**

Ireland
16 Merrion Square
Dublin 2
Tel: **1-6765679 / 6765686 / 6765135/6/7**

Italy
12 Via Toscana
I - 00187 Rome
Tel: **6-47591**

Jamaica
Central Village
Spanish Town
St. Catherine
Tel: **809-98478602**

Japan
1-3 Shiba-Daimon
1-Chome
Minato-Ku
Tokyo - 105
Tel: **3-34381311**

Jordan
Madaba Street
Amman
Tel: **6-773141 / 773142 / 773687**

Kazakhstan
Kunaev st. 86
480100 Almaty
Tel: **3272-616291 / 610058**

Kenya
Nairobi South 'C'
(Belle Vue), off Mombasa Road
Nairobi
Tel: **2-503781 / 503789 / 503816**

Korea (North)
Ryonhwa 1
Central District
Pyongyang
Tel: **2-850218111 / 850218222**

Korea (South)
32-3ka Namsan dong
Choong-Ku
Seoul 100-043
Tel: **2-7559301**

Kuwait
Al-Jahra St.
Shuweek
Tel: **4839114 / 4815478 / 4814793 / 481805/06**

Kyrgyzstan
10 prospekt Erkindik
720000 Bishkek
Tel: **3312-222414 / 222411**

Laos
Avenue Sethathirath
Vientiane
Tel: **21-216610 / 222398 / 212036**

Latvia
1 Skolas Street
Riga
LV-1350
Tel: **7-310902**

Lebanon
Rue Spears
Beirut
Tel: **1-865561 / 372801/2/3/4**

Lesotho
23 Mabile Road
Maseru 100
Tel: **313911**

Liberia
National Headquarters
107 Lynch Street
1000 Monrovia 20
Tel: **225172**

Libya
PO Box 541
Benghazi
Tel: **61-9095827 / 9099420**

Liechtenstein
Heiligkreuz 25
FL-9490 Vaduz
Tel: **75-2322294**

Lithuania
Gedimino ave 3a
2600 Vilnius
Tel: **2-611914 / 628947**

Luxembourg
Parc de la Ville
L - 2014 Luxembourg
Tel: **450202-1**

Macedonia
No 13 Bul. Koco Racin
91000 Skopje
Tel: **91-114355**

Madagascar
Maison de la Croix-Rouge Malgache
1 Rue Patrice Lumumba
Antananarivo
Tel: **2-22111**

Malawi
Red Cross House
(along Presidential Way)
Lilongwe
Tel: **732877 / 732878**

Malaysia
JKR 32 Jalan Nipah
off Jalan Ampang
55000 Kuala Lumpur
Tel: **3-4578122 /236/348/159/227**

Mali
Route Koulikoro
Bamako
Tel: **224569**

Mauritania
BP 344
Avenue Gamal Abdel Nasser
Nouakchott
Tel: **2-51249**

Mexico
Calle Luis Vives 200
Colonia Polanco
Mexico, D.F. 11510
Tel: **5-3951111 / 5800070 / 3950606 / 5575270**

Moldova
67a Strada Gheorge Asachi
277028 Chisinau
Tel: **2-729700**

Mongolia
Central Post Office
Post Box 537
Ulaanbaatar
Tel: **1-320635**

Morocco
Palais Mokri
Takaddoum
Rabat
Tel: **7-650898 / 651495**

Mozambique
Avanida 24 de Julho, 641
Maputo
Tel: **1-430045/46**

Myanmar (Burma)
Red Cross Building
42 Strand Road, Yangon
Tel: **1-296552 / 295238 / 295214 / 295133**

Namibia
Red Cross House
100 Robert Mugabe Avenue
Windhoek
Tel: **61-235226 / 235216 / 235346 / 235348**

Nepal
Red Cross Marg
Kalimati
Kathmandu
Tel: **1-270761 / 270650 / 270167 / 278719**

Netherlands
Leeghwaterplein 27
2521 CV The Hague
Tel: **70-4455666 / 4455755**

New Zealand
Red Cross House
14 Hill Street
Wellington 1
Tel: **4-4723750**

Nicaragua
Reparto Belmonte
Carretera Sur
Mangua
Tel: **2-652082 / 652084**

Niger
BP 11386
Niamey
Tel: **733037**

Nigeria
11 Eko Akete Close
off St. Gregory's Road
South West Ikoyi
Lagos
Tel: **1-2695188 / 2695189**

Norway
Hausmannsgate 7
0133 Oslo
Tel: **22054000**

Pakistan
National Headquarters
Sector H-8
Islamabad
Tel: **51-854885 / 856420**

Panama
Calle 'E', No.11'50
Panama
Tel: **2283014 / 2282786 / 2280692**

Papua New Guinea
Taurama Road
Port Moresby, Boroko
Tel: **3258577 / 3258759**

Paraguay
Brasil 216 esq.
Jose Berges
Asunçion
Tel: **21-22797 / 208199 / 205496**

Peru
Av. Camino del Inca y Nazarenas
Urb. Las Gardenias - Surco
Lima
Tel: **14-4489431 / 4482005 / 4481653**

Philippines
Bonifacio Drive
Port Area
Manila 2803
Tel: **2-5278384**

Poland
Mokotowska 14
00-561 Warsaw
Tel: **22-6285201-7**

Portugal
Jardim 9 de Abril
1 a 5
1293 Lisbon Codex
Tel: **1-605571 / 605650 / 605490 / 3962127**

Qatar
PO Box 5449
Embassy Road
Doha
Tel: **435111**

Romania
Strada Biserica Amzei 29
Sector 1
Bucarest
Tel: **1-6593385 / 6506233 / 6503813 / 3124026**

Russian Federation
Tcheryomushkinski Proezd 5
117036 Moscow
Tel: **095-1266770 / 1261403**

Rwanda
BP 425
Kigali
Tel: **73302 / 74402 / 75088**

Saudi Arabia
General Headquarters
Riyadh 11129
Tel: **1-4067956**

Senegal
Boulevard. Franklin-Roosevelt
Dakar
Tel: **233992**

Seychelles
Mahe
Tel: **322122**

Sierra Leone
6 Liverpool Street
Freetown
Tel: **22-222384**

Singapore
Red Cross House
15 Penang Lane
Singapore 0923
Tel: **65-3373587 / 3360269**

Slovakia
Grosslingova 24
814 46 Bratislava
Tel : **7-325305**

Slovenia
Mirje 19
61000 Ljubljana
Tel: **61-1261200**

Somalia
c/o ICRC Box 73226
Nairobi, Kenya
Tel: Mogadishu **871** or **873-1312646**

South Africa
25 Erlswold Way
Saxonwold
Johannesburg 2196
Tel: **11-6461384 / 4861313/4**

Spain
Rafael Villa
s/n (Vuelta Gines Navarro)
28023 El Plantio
Madrid
Tel: **1-3354444 / 3354545**

Sri Lanka
106 Dharmapala Mawatha
Colombo 7
Tel: **1-691095 / 699935**

Sudan
PO Box 235
Khartoum
Tel: **11-772011**

Suriname
Gravenberchstraat 2
Paramaribo
Tel: 498410

Swaziland
National Heradquarters
104 Johnstone Street

Mbabane
Tel: **42532**

Sweden
Oesthammarsgatan 70
Stockholm
Tel: **8-6655600**

Switzerland
Rainmattstrasse 10
3001 Berne
Tel: **31-3877111**

Syria
Al Malek Aladel Street
Damascus
Tel: **11-4429662**

Tajikistan
120 Umari Khayyom Str.
724017, Dushanbe
Tel: **3772-240374**

Tanzania
Upanga Road
Dar es Salaam
Tel: **51-30643 / 31883 / 24564/5**

Thailand
Paribatra Building
Central Bureau
1873 Rama IV Road
Bangkok 10330
Tel: **2-2564037 / 2564038**

Togo
51 rue Boko Soga
Amoutive
Lome
Tel: **212110**

Tonga
PO Box 456
Nuku'Alofa
South West Pacific
Tel: **21360 / 21670**

Trinidad and Tobago
Lot 7A
Fitz Blackman Drive
Wrightson Road
Port of Spain
West Trinidad
Tel: **809-6278215 / 6278128**

Tunisia
19 Rue d'Angleterre
Tunis 1000
Tel: **1-240630 / 245572**

Turkey
Genel Baskanligi
Karanfil Sokak No. 7
06650 Kizilay
Ankara
Tel: **312-4317680**

Turkmenistan
48 A. Novoi str.
744000 Ashgabat
Tel: **3632-295512**

Uganda
Plot 97
Buganda Road
Kampala
Tel: **41-258701/2**

Ukraine
30 ulitsa Pushkinskaya
252004 Kiev
Tel: **44-225015 / 2250334**

United Arab Emirates
PO Box 3324
Abu Dhabi
Tel: **2-6615000**

United Kingdom
9 Grosvenor Crescent
London SW1X 7EJ
Tel: **0171-235 5454**

United States
17th and D. Streets NW
Washington DC 20006
Tel: **202-7286600 / 2066156**

Uruguay
Avenida 8 de Octubre 2990
11600 Montevideo
Tel: **2-802112**

Uzbekistan
33 Yusuf Hos Hojib St.
700031 Tashkent
Tel: **3712-563741**

Vanuatu
PO Box 618
Port Vila
Tel: **22599**

Venezuela
Avenida Andres Bello 4
Caracas 1010
Tel: **2-5714380 / 5712143 / 5715435**

Vietnam
68 Rue Ba-Trieu, Hanoi
Tel: **8-262315 / 264868 / 266283/4**

Western Samoa
PO Box 1616
Apia
Tel: **23686**

Yemen
Head Office
Building No. 10
26 September Street
Sanaa
Tel: **1-283131 / 283132**

Former Yugoslavia (Serbia & Montenegro)
Simina 19
11000 Belgrade
Tel: **11-623564**

Zaïre (Democratic Rep. of Congo)
41 Avenue. de la Justice
Zone de la Gombe
Kinshasa I
Tel: **12-34897**

Zambia
2837 Los Angeles Boulevard
Longacres
Lusaka
Tel: **1-250607 / 254798**

Zimbabwe
Red Cross House
98 Cameron Street
Harare
Tel: **4-775416 / 773912 / 775418**

International Association for Medical Assistance to Travellers (IAMAT)
417 Center Street
Lewiston
NY 14092
Tel: **716-754 4883**
*This organisation publishes a wealth of useful medical information for travellers including a World Immunization chart, World Malaria Risk chart, World Schistosomaisis Risk chart and a directory of **English speaking doctors** worldwide. Membership is free, but the organisation is funded by members' donations.* ∎

TRAVEL WRITING, FILM AND PHOTOGRAPHY
Section 14

TRAVEL/FEATURES EDITORS

National Newspapers

Daily/Sunday Express
Ludgate House
245 Blackfriars Road
London SE1 9UX
Tel: **0171-928 8000**
Jeremy Gates

Daily Mail
Northcliffe House
2 Derry St
London W8 5TT
Tel: **0171-938 6000**
Cathy Wood

Daily Mirror
1 Canada Square
Canary Wharf
London E14 5AP
Tel: **0171-510 3000**
Sarah Whitfield-King

Daily Record
Anderston Quay
Glasgow
G3 8DA
Tel: **0141-248 7000**
Alan Rennie

Daily Sport
19 Great Ancoats Street
Manchester
M60 4BT
Tel: **0161-236 4466**
Tony Hoare

Daily Star
Ludgate House
245 Blackfriars Road
London SE1 9UX
Tel: **0171-928 8000**
Brian O'Hanlon

Daily/Sunday Telegraph
1 Canada Square
Canary Wharf
London E14 5AP
Tel: **0171-538 5000**
Gill Charlton

The European
Orbit House
5 New Fetter Lane
London EC4A 1AP
Tel: **0171-418 7777**
Cleo Mitchell

Financial Times
1 Southwark Bridge
London SE1 9HL
Tel: **0171-873 3000**
Jill James

The Guardian
119 Farringdon Road
London EC1R 3ER
Tel: **0171-278 2332**
Jeannette Page

The Herald (Glasgow)
195 Albion Street
Glasgow
G1 1QP
Tel: **0141-552 6255**
Harry Reid

The Independent/Independent on Sunday
40 City Road
London EC1Y 2DB
Tel: **0171-345 2000**
Simon Calder / Jeremy Atiyah

Mail on Sunday
Northcliffe House
2 Derry St
London W8 5TT
Tel: **0171-938 6000**
Frank Barrett

The Observer
Chelsea Bridge House
Queenstown Road
London SW8 4NN
Tel: **0171-278 2332**
Desmond Balmer

The Scotsman
20 North Bridge
Edinburgh
EH1 1YT
Tel: **0131-225 2468**
Alastair MaKay

The Sun
1 Virginia Street
London E1 9XP
Tel: **0171-782 4000**
Katie Wood

The Sunday Times
1 Pennington St
London E1 9XN
Tel: **0171-782 5000**
Christine Walker

The Times
1 Pennington Street
London E1 9XN
Tel: **0171-782 5000**
Brian MacArthur

Magazines

Arena
Wagadon Ltd.
Pine St
London EC1R OJL
Tel: **0171-689 9999**
Natasha Marsh

Business Traveller
Compass House
22 Redan Place
London W2 4SZ
Tel: **0171-229 7799**
Gillian Upton

Camping and Caravanning
Greenfields Hose
Westwood Way
Coventry
CV4 8JH
Tel: **01203-694995**
Peter Frost

Camping Magazine
Garnet Dickinson Publishing
Eastwood Works
Fitzwilliam Road
Rotherham
S65 1JU
Tel: **01709-364 721**
John Lloyd

Climber and Hill Walker
The Plaza Tower
East Kilbride
Glasgow G74 1LW
Tel: **01355-246444**
Tom Prentice

Conde Nast Traveller
Vogue House
1 Hanover Square
London W1R 0AD
Tel: **0171-499 9080**
Sarah Miller

Cosmopolitan
National Magazine Co Ltd
72 Broadwick St
London W1V 2BP
Tel: **0171-439 7144**
Linda Wood

Country Living
National Magazine House
72 Broadwick St
London W1V 2BP
Tel: **0171-439 5000**
Henrietta Holder

Dazed & Confused
112 Old St
London EC1V 9BD
Tel: **0171-336 0766**
Jefferson Hack

EatSoup
IPC Magazines
Kings Reach Tower
Stamford St
London SE1 9LS
Tel: **0171-261 5000**
David Lancaster

Elle
189 Shaftesbury Avenue
London WC2H 8JG
Tel: **0171-437 9011**
Susan Ward Davies

Esquire
National Magazine House
72 Broadwick St
London W1V 2BP
Tel: **0171-439 5000**

Joanne Glasbey

Executive Travel
Church Street
Dunstable LU5 4HB
Tel: **01582-600111**
Mike Toynbee

FHM
Mappin House
4 Winsley St
London W1N 7AR
Tel: **0171-436 1515**
Ben Raworth

Geographical
47c Kensington Court
London S8 5DA
Tel: **0171-938 4022**
Fiona McWilliam

The Great Outdoors
The Plaza Tower
East Kilbride
Glasgow G74 1LW
Tel: **01355-246444**
Cameron McNeish

GQ
Vogue House
1 Hanover Square
London W1R OAD
Tel: **0171-499 9080**
Philip Watson

GQ Active
Vogue House
1 Hanover Square
London W1R OAD
Tel: **0171-499 9080**
Simon Mills, Simon Tiffin

Harpers and Queen
National Magazine House
72 Broadwick St
London W1V 2BP
Tel: **0171-439 5000**
Catherine Fairweather

House and Garden
Vogue House
1 Hanover Square
London W1R 0AD
Tel: **0171-499 9080**
Pammy Goodman

Loaded
IPC Magazines
Kings Reach Tower
Stamford St
London SE1 9LS
Tel: **0171-261 5000**
David Bennum

Marie Claire
2 Hatfields
London SE1 9PG
Tel: **0171-261 5240**
David Wickers

Practical Photography
Apex House
Oundle Road
Peterborough
Cambs PE2 9NP
Tel: **01733-898100**
Martin Moore

Saga Magazine
The Saga Building
Middleburg Square
Folkestone
Kent CT20 1BR
Tel: **01303-711526**
Paul Bach

The Tatler
Vogue House
1 Hanover Square
London W1R 0AD
Tel: **0171-499 9080**
Victoria Mather

Traveller
WEXAS International
45-49 Brompton Road
Knightsbridge SW3 1DE
Tel: **0171-589 3315**
Miranda Haines

Vogue
Vogue House
Hanover Square
London W1R 0AD
Tel: **0171-499 9080**
Rebecca Willis

Wanderlust
P.O. Box 1832
Windsor
Berks SL4 6YP
Tel: **01753-620474**
Lyn Hughes

Wallpaper*
Brettenham House
1 Lancaster Place
London WC2 E7TL
Tel: **0171-322 1177**
Helen Pipin

Further reading:
The Writer's Handbook (Macmillan/PEN)
Writers' & Artists' Yearbook (Black)
Pimms United Kingdom Media Directory
(PIMS)

ASSOCIATIONS FOR WRITERS AND PHOTOGRAPHERS

The Association of Authors' Agents
c/o 503-504 The Chambers
Chelsea Harbour
Lots Road
London SW10 0XF
Tel: **0171-344 1000**

Association of Photographic Laboratories
Peel Place
50 Carver Street
Hockley
Birmingham B1 3AS
Tel: **0121-212 0299**

Book Trust
Book House
45 East Hill
Wandsworth
London SW18 2QZ
Tel: **0181-870 9055**

British Amateur Press Association
Michaelmas
Cimarron Close
South Woodham Ferrers
Essex CM3 5PB
Tel: **01245-324059**

British Association of Picture Libraries and Agencies (BAPLA)
18 Vine Hill
London EC1R 5DX
Tel: **0171-713 1780**

The British Council
10 Spring Gardens
London SW1A 2BN
Tel: **0171-930 8466**

British Guild of Travel Writers
The Secretary
John Harrison
90 Corryngway
London W53HA
Tel: **0181-998 2223**
email: **bgtw@compuserve.com**
http://rworld.comperserve.com/homepages/

British Institute of Professional Photography
Fox Talbot House
Amwell End
Ware
Herts SG12 9HN
Tel: **01920-464011**

Bureau of Freelance Photographers (BFP)
Focus House
497 Green Lanes
London N13 4BP
Tel: **0181-882 3315**

Foreign Press Association in London
11 Carlton House Terrace
London SW1Y 5AJ
Tel: **0171-930 0445**

General Practitioner Writers Association
Mr Wilfred Hopkins
633 Liverpool Road
SOUTHPORT PR8 3NG
Tel & Fax: **01704-577 839**
email: **GPWA@lepress.demon.co.uk**

The Institute of Journalists
Unit 2
Dock Offices
Surrey Quays Road
London SE16 2XL
Tel: **0171-252 1187**

Master Photographers Association
Halmark
2 Beaumont Street
Darlington
Co Durham DL1 5SZ
Tel: **01325-356555**

National Union of Journalists
314-320 Gray's Inn Road
London WC1X 8DP
Tel: **0171-278 7916**

Press Council
1 Salisbury Square
London EC4Y 8AE
Tel: **0171-353 1248**

The Royal Photographic Society
The Octagon
Milsom St
Bath BA1 1DN
Tel: **01225-462841**

The Society of Authors
84 Drayton Gardens
London SW10 9SB
Tel: **0171-373 6642**

Society of Women Writers and Journalists
110 Whitehall Road
London E4 6DW
Tel: **0181-529 0856**

The Writers' Guild of Great Britain
430 Edgware Road
London W2 1EH
Tel: **0171-723 8074** ■

AND FINALLY...
Section 15

CUSTOMS REGULATIONS

Australia

Each passenger over the age of 18 is entitled to the following duty free admissions:
250 cigarettes
or
250 grams cigars
or
250 grams tobacco
plus
1 litre of alcoholic liquor (including wine and beer)
plus
Other goods to the value of A$400 (A$200 if under 18).

General Items:

Gifts, souvenirs, household articles unused or less than 12 months old are duty free to a value of A$200. Goods to the value of a further A$160 are duty-payable at 20 per cent.
You may also take in: Items of the type normally carried on your person or in your personal baggage including jewellery or toilet requisites, but not electrical items.
Binoculars
Portable typewriters
Exposed film
Photographic cameras
Personal sporting requisites
Bicycles and motorcycles
Clothing (excepting fur apparel, unless it is valued at A$150 or less or you have owned and worn it for 12 months or more).

In order to qualify for duty-free status, goods should be for your personal use, and not have been bought on behalf of someone else, and should have travelled with you.

Prohibited Articles:

Non-prescribed drugs. Firearms and weapons.

Wildlife – there is a strict control of all wildlife and wildlife products in and out of Australia. Travellers should be warned that articles of apparel, accessories, ornaments, trophies, etc., made from endangered species of fauna will be seized if imported into Australia. This includes animals such as alligators and crocodiles, elephants, rhinoceros, snakes, lizards, turtles, zebra, and the large cats.

Domestic pets – you cannot bring in cats or dogs, except from the United Kingdom and Ireland, Papua New Guinea, Fiji, New Zealand, Hawaii and Norfolk Island. The animals must have been resident in one of these approved countries for at least six months. A permit is required in all cases.

Other goods – most meat and meat products, dairy produce, plants and plant produce.

Canada

Visitors may bring in duty free all items of personal baggage including clothing, jewellery, etc. Sporting equipment, radios, television sets, musical instruments, typewriters, cameras, are all included in this category.

Alcoholic Beverages:

The age limit is 18 in some provinces, and 19 in others, and should be checked before travelling.
1.1 litres (40 oz) of liquor or wine
or
24 x 336ml (12oz cans or bottles) of beer, or its equivalent of 8.2 litres (28fl oz).

A further 9 litres (two gallons) of alcoholic beverages may be imported (except to Prince Edward Island and the Northwest Territories) on payment of duty.

Tobacco:
Persons over 18 years of age may bring in:
200 cigarettes
50 cigars
400g of manufactured tobacco
400g tobacco sticks

Gifts:
Gifts may be imported duty free to a value of C$60 per gift.

Prohibited and Restricted Goods:
Animals – any pet or bird requires a Canadian import permit and a veterinary certificate of health from its country of origin. Domestic dogs and cats may be imported only from rabies-free countries without quarantine or vaccination if: they are shipped directly from the country, and they are accompanied by a vet's certificate, and that the country has been rabies-free for the six months prior to the animal's departure.

Endangered species – restrictions on the movement of endangered species stretch also to products made from them. A permit is required for many skins, trophies, etc., as well as live animals.

Foods – meat and meat products are only allowed in if canned and sterile; or commercially cooked and prepared; and the total weight accompanying the traveller does not exceed 10kg per person.

Processed cheese and cooked eggs are the only permissible dairy products.

Food, in general, can be imported duty free provided the amount is only sufficient for two days' personal use by the importer.

Plants – it is forbidden to import plants or plant produce without permission under the Plant Quarantine Act.

Firearms – hand guns are not allowed entry to Canada. Firearms are restricted to those with a legitimate sporting or recreational use. A permit is not required for long guns.

All explosives, ammunitions, pyrotechnic devices, etc., except the following, are forbidden entry to Canada: sporting and competitive ammunition for personal use; distress and life-saving devices such as flares.

New Zealand

Personal effects will be allowed to enter duty free, provided they are your own property, are intended for your own use, and are not imported for commercial purposes. Items such as clothing, footwear, articles of adornment, watches, brushes and toilet requisites can be included here. Jewellery can be included, but not unmounted precious or semi-precious stones, and fur apparel purchased overseas can only be included if you have owned and worn it for more than 12 months.

Tobacco:
Passengers over 17 years of age are allowed the following:
200 cigarettes **or**
250 grams of tobacco **or**
50 cigars **or**
A mixture of all three, weighing not more than 250 grams.

Alcohol:
Passengers over 17 years of age are allowed the following:4.5 litres of wine (this is the equivalent to six 750ml bottles)
and
one bottle containing not more than 1.125litres of spirits or liqueur.

All passengers are given a general concession on goods up to a combined value of NZ$700. Persons travelling together may not combine their allowances. Children may claim their allowances provided the goods are their own property and of a type a child would reasonably expect to own.

Visitors to New Zealand are also permitted to bring in such items as a camera, a pair of binoculars, a portable radio and camping equipment, on condition that the goods leave the country with them.

Prohibited or Restricted Items
Drugs – the import of drugs is strictly forbidden and incurs heavy penalties. Should they be necessary for your health, carry a letter of authorization and carry the medication in its original, clearly marked bottle.

Firearms – the importation of any weapon is strictly controlled and requires a Police permit. Flick knives, sword sticks, knuckle dusters, and other such weapons are prohibited.

Flora and Fauna – the entry of domestic dogs and cats is governed by the Agricultural Quarantine Service to whom you should apply for further details. The following goods must be declared:-
food of any kind
plants or parts of plants (dead or alive).
animals (dead or alive) and animal products.
equipment used with animals.
equipment such as camping gear, golf clubs and used bicycles.

United Kingdom

The following are legal limits, per adult, for goods brought into the UK duty and tax free, from outside the EU:

Tobacco:
200 cigarettes **or**
100 cigarillos **or**
50 cigars **or**
250g of tobacco.

Alcoholic Drinks:
1 litre of alcoholic drinks over 22% vol **or**
2 litres of fortified or sparkling wine or other liqueurs.**plus**
2 litres of still table wine.

Perfume:
50g perfume **and** 250ml toilet water.

Other goods:
£145 worth.

GOODS OBTAINED IN THE EC

Duty Free
Duty-free shops can sell you goods for each journey only up to the levels listed above. Eg. if flying from London to Paris for the weekend you can buy 200 cigarettes on the outward bound flight and 200 on your return.

Duty and Tax paid
Provided they are for your personal use there is no further tax to be paid on goods you have obtained duty and tax paid in the European Community.
Personal use includes gifts, but if you are receiving any payment in return for buying alcohol and tobacco (such as help with travelling expenses) the transaction will be dutiable and you should contact HM Customs and Excise to arrange to pay the duty due.
European Community law sets out guide levels and if you bring more than the amounts in the guide levels you must be able to show that the goods are for your personal use.
The guide levels are:

Tobacco:
800 cigarettes
400 cigarillos
200 cigars
1 kg of smoking tobacco.

Alcoholic Drinks:
10 litres of spirits
20 litres intermediate products (such as port and sherry)
90 litres of wine (of which not more than 60 litres sparkling)
110 litres of beer.

There are special schemes for private purchases of motor vehicles, boats and planes contact HM Customs and Excise for details

Notes:
1. Persons under 17 are not entitled to tobacco and drinks allowances.
2. If you are visiting the UK for less than six months, you are also entitled to bring in all personal effects (except those mentioned above) which you intend to take with you when you leave (except for prohibited or restricted goods).

The following goods are restricted or prohibited if travelling to the UK directly from another EC country:

Drugs
Firearms
Certain weapons, eg flick knives
Explosives
Obscene material
Indecent and obscene material featuring children
Unlicensed mammals susceptible to rabies, eg cats, dogs and mice.
Please note this is not a complete list, but covers the main restrictions.

If you are travelling to the UK from a country outside the EC:
All of the above, plus amongst others:
Radio transmitters (e.g. CB) capable of operating on certain frequencies.
Counterfeit and fake goods e.g. watches, garments, CDs and other audio equipment, and goods with false origin markings.
Improperly cooked meat and poultry.
Plants, parts thereof and plant produce.
Most animals and birds – alive or dead; certain articles derived from animals including ivory, fur skins, reptile leather goods.
Any live mammal – unless a British import licence has previously been issued.
Goods over 50 years old, including photographs valued at £2,000 or more, clothing, footwear, textiles and portraits of British Heritage Personages valued at £6,000 or more, firearms, arms and armour valued at £20,000 or more, oil and tempera paintings valued at £119,000 or more and all other goods valued at £39,600 or more, require an export licence issued by the Department of National Heritage before they can be exported.

United States

Everyone entering the United States will be asked to fill in a Customs declaration listing everything except clothes, jewellery, toilet articles, etc., owned by you and intended for your own use. The exceptions are duty free. If jewellery worth $300 or more is sold within three years, duty must then be paid or the article will become subject to seizure.

Alcoholic Drinks:
Adult non-residents can bring in not more than 1 litre of any form of alcohol.

If you are only in transit, you are permitted up to 4 litres of alcohol, as long as it accompanies you out of the country. Liquor-filled candy and absinthe are prohibited goods.

Tobacco:
200 cigarettes **or**
50 cigars **or**
2kg tobacco.

Perfume:
Reasonable quantity.

Gift Exemption:
A non-resident may take in goods valued at up to $100 for use as gifts, provided he/she is to remain in the country for at least 72 hours. This allowance may only be claimed once every 6 months.

Notes:
Antiques are free of duty if produced 100 years prior to the date of entry.

A person emigrating may bring in professional equipment duty free.

If in transit, you may take dutiable goods worth up to $200 through the United States without payment.

Prohibited Items:
Lottery tickets, narcotics and dangerous drugs, obscene publications, seditious and treasonable materials, hazardous articles (e.g. fireworks, dangerous toys, toxic or poisonous substances), products made by convicts or forced labour, switchblade knives, pirate copies of copyright books. Leather items from Haiti.

Firearms and ammunition intended for lawful hunting or sporting purposes are admissible, provided you take the firearms and unfired ammunition with you out of the country.

Cultural objects, such as ethnic artwork, will be allowed in only if accompanied by a valid export certificate from their country of origin.

Bakery items, all cured cheeses, professionally canned foods are permitted. Most plants, or plant products are prohibited or require an import permit. The importation of meat or meat products is dependent on the animal disease condition in the country of origin.

A traveller requiring medicines containing habit-forming drugs or narcotics should always carry a doctor's letter or prescription; make sure that all medicines are properly identified; and do not carry more than might normally be used by one person.

Cats and dogs must be free of diseases communicable to man. Vaccination against rabies is not required for dogs and cats arriving from rabies-free countries. There are controls and prohibitions on all livestock, and anyone wishing to import any should apply to the US Customs for further information.

Vehicles:

All countries will let you bring in a vehicle, whether car, camper van or yacht, without paying duty, either on presentation of a carnet de passages or on an assurance that you will not sell the vehicle for a certain length of time.

You may have to have the vehicle steam-cleaned to help prevent the spread of diseases in the soil.

CUSTOMS OFFICES

Australia

The Regional Director of Customs
GPO Box 8
Sydney
NSW 2001
Tel: **2- 9213 2000**

The Regional Director of Customs
GPO Box 2809AA
Melbourne
Victoria 3001
Tel: **3-9244 8000**

The Regional Director of Customs
GPO Box 1464
Brisbane
Queensland 4001
Tel: **7- 3835 3444**

The Regional Director of Customs
PO Box 396
Freemantle
WA 6160
Tel: **9-430 1444**

The Regional Director of Customs
GPO Box 148B
Hobart
Tasmania 7001
Tel: **3-6230 1201**

The Regional Director of Customs
GPO Box 210
Darwin
NT 0801
Tel: **8-8946 9999**

The Regional Director of Customs
PO Box 50
Port Adelaide
South Australia 5015
Tel: **8-8447 9211**

Australian Quarantine and Inspection Service
Edmund Barton Building
Broughton Street
Barton
Australian Capital Territory
Tel: **6-272 5455**

Canada

Revenue Canada
Customs and Excise
Public Relations Branch
Ottawa
Ontario
Canada K1A 015
Tel: **613- 593 6220**

Canada Customs
2 St André St
Quebec
Quebec G1K 7P6
Tel: **418- 694 4445**

400 Carre Youville
Montreal
Quebec H2Y 3N4
Tel: **514- 283 2953**

360 Coventry Road
Ottawa
Ontario K1K 2C6
Tel:**613- 993 0534** 8.00am to 4.30pm
    613- 998 3326 after 4.30pm and weekends

Manulife Centre, 10th Floor
55 Bloor St
West Toronto
Ontario M5W 1A3
Tel:**416- 966 8022** 8.00am to 4.30pm
    416- 676 3643 evenings and weekends

Federal Building
269 Main St
Winnipeg
Manitoba R3C 1B3
Tel: **204- 949 6004**

204 Towne Square
1919 Rose St
Regina
Saskatchewan S3P 3P1
Tel: **306-359 6212**

220 4th Avenue SE, Ste 720
PO Box 2970
Calgary Alberta T2P 2M7
Tel: **403-231 4610**

1001 West Pender Street
Vancouver
British Columbia
V6E 2M8
Tel: **604- 666 1545/6**

New Zealand

PO Box 29
Auckland
Tel: **09-773-520**

PO Box 73003
Auckland Int. Airport
Tel: **09-275-9059**

PO Box 2098
Christchurch
Tel: **03-796-660**

Private Bag
Dunedin
Tel: **03-4779-251**

PO Box 840
Invercargill
Tel: **03-2187-329**

PO Box 440
Napier
Tel: **06-8355-799**

PO Box 66
Nelson
Tel: **054-81-484**

PO Box 136
New Plymouth
Tel: **067-85-721**

PO Box 5014
Mt Maunganui
Tauranga
Tel: **075-759-699**

PO Box 64
Timaru
Tel: **03-6889-317**

PO Box 11746
Wellington
Tel: **04-736-099**

PO Box 873
Whangarei
Tel: **089-482-400**

United Kingdom

For notices and forms contact any Customs and Excise Office. Addresses are shown in local telephone directories or write to:

H.M. Customs and Excise
New King's Beam House
22 Upper Ground
London SE1 9PJ
Tel: **0171-620 1313**

Live Animals:
Ministry of Agriculture, Fisheries and Food
Animal Health Division
Hook Rise South
Tolworth
Surrey KT6 7WF
Tel: **0181-330 4411**

Endangered Species:
Department of the Environment
Endangered Species Branch (Global Wildlife)
Rm 814, Tollgate House
Houlton St
Bristol BS2 9DJ
Tel: **0117-987 8032 / 8467**

Plant Health:
Ministry of Agriculture, Fisheries and Food
Plant Health Division
Room 304, Foss House
King's Pool
1/2 Peasholme Green
York
TO1 2PX
Tel: **01904-455188**

Meat and Poultry:
Ministry of Agriculture, Fisheries and Food
Meat Hygiene Department
Hook Rise South
Tolworth
Surbiton
Surrey KT6 7NF
Tel: **0181-330 4411**

USA

US Customs Service
PO Box 17423
Washington DC
20041 USA
*For detailed information and suggestions write to above address. **Customs Hints for Visitors, and Importing a Car,** available on request.*

United States Embassy
Grosvenor Square
London W1A 2JB
For complaints and suggestions write to above address. On request:
Customs Hints for Returning US Residents – Know Before You Go.

Further information:
The Customs Co-operation Council
Rue L'Industrie 26-38
B1040 Brussels
Belgium
Tel: **322-514 3372**

CONSUMER ADVICE AND COMPLAINTS

Association of British Travel Agents (ABTA)
55 Newman Street, London W1P 4AH
Tel: **0171-637 2444**
Professional body of the British travel industry, with a bond to protect travellers against financial collapse.

Air Transport Users Committee
103 Kingsway, London WC2B 6QX
Tel: **0171-242 3882**
Small committee, funded by CAA, but acting independently, to investigate complaints.

Civil Aviation Authority
CAA House, 45 Kingsway, London WC2B 6TE
Tel: **0171-379 7311**
Overall controller of the British airline industry.

DUTY FREE ALLOWANCES WORLD-WIDE

Afghanistan	Reasonable quantity of tobacco products. Any amount of perfume. No alcohol.
Albania	Reasonable quantity of tobacco products. Alcohol and perfume for personal use.
Algeria	200 cigarettes or 50 cigars or 250g tobacco. 1 bottle spirits. 2 bottles wine. All valuables must be declared on arrival.
Andorra	No restrictions.
Angola	Reasonable amount tobacco products. 3 different bottles alcohol. Reasonable quantity perfume in opened bottles.
Anguilla	200 cigarettes or 50 cigars or 225g tobacco. 1 quart wine or spirits.
Antigua & Barbuda	200 cigarettes or 100 cigarillos or 50 cigars or 250g tobacco. 1 litre wine or spirits. 6oz perfume.
Argentina	400 cigarettes or 50 cigars. 2 litres alcohol. 5kg foodstuffs. Goods to value of US$300. Residents returning from stay of less than 1 year in Bolivia, Brazil, Chile, Paraguay or Uruguay – no restrictions.
Armenia	400 cigarettes or 100 cigars or 500g tobacco. 2 litres alcohol. Reasonable quantity perfume for personal use. Other goods to value US$5000 for personal use.
Aruba	200 cigarettes or 50 cigars or 250g tobacco. 2 litres alcohol. 250ml perfume. Gifts to value AFl 100.
Australia	See Customs Regulations at beginning of the section.
Austria	**Travellers from EU countries with duty paid goods:** 800 cigarettes and 400 cigarillos and 200 cigars and 1kg tobacco. 90 litres wine. 10 litres spirits. 20 litres fortified wine or vermouth. 110 litres beer. **Travellers from non-EU countries:** 200 cigarettes or 100 cigarillos or 50 cigars or 250g tobacco. 2 litres wine. 1 litre spirits. 1 bottle eau de cologne. 60ml perfume. Gifts to value of ASch 300.
Azerbaijan	1000 cigarettes or 100g tobacco products. 1.5 litres spirits. 2 litres wine. Reasonable quantity perfume for personal use. Goods to value of US$10,000.
Bahamas	200 cigarettes or 100 cigarillos or 50 cigars or 454g tobacco. 1 litre spirits. 50g perfume. Goods to value of £36.
Bahrain	200 cigarettes. 50 cigars. 250g tobacco. 1 litre alcohol. 6 bottles beer (non-muslims only) 8oz perfume. Other good to value of US$667.
Bangladesh	200 cigarettes or 50 cigars or 225g tobacco. 2 bottles alcohol. Reasonable amount perfume. Goods to value Tk500.
Barbados	200 cigarettes or 250g tobacco. 0.75 litre spirits and 0.75 litre wine. 50g perfume. Goods to value of Bd$100.
Belarus	1000 cigarettes or 1000g tobacco products. 2 litres alcohol. Reasonable quantity perfume for personal use. Goods to value US$10,000.
Belgium	**Travellers from EU countries with duty paid goods:** 800 cigarettes and 400 cigarillos and 200 cigars and 1kg tobacco. 90 litres wine. 10 litres spirits. 20 litres fortified wine or vermouth. 110 litres beer. **Travellers from non-EU countries:** 200 cigarettes or 50 cigars or 250g tobacco. 2 litres wine. 1 litre spirits. 8 litres Luxembourg wines. 50g perfume. 250ml toilet water. Goods to value BFr2000.
Belize	200 cigarettes or 225g tobacco. 568ml alcohol. 1 bottle perfume.
Benin	200 cigarettes or 25 cigars or 100 cigarillos or 250g tobacco. 1 bottle spirits. 500ml eau de toilet. 250ml perfume.
Bermuda	200 cigarettes. 50 cigars. 454g tobacco. 1.137 litres alcohol.
Bhutan	200 cigarettes or 50 cigars or 250g tobacco. 1 litre spirits. 250ml toilet water.
Bolivia	200 cigarettes. 50 cigars. 450g tobacco. 1 opened bottle alcohol.
Botswana	200 cigarettes or 100 cigarillos or 50 cigars or 250g tobacco. 2 litres wine. 1 litre spirits. 60ml perfume. 250ml toilet water. Goods to value £136.
Brazil	400 cigarettes. 250g tobacco. 25 cigars. 2 litres alcohol. Goods to value US$500.
British Virgin Islands	200 cigarettes or 50 cigars or 230g tobacco. 1 litre alcohol.

Brunei	200 cigarettes or 250g tobacco. 60ml perfume. 250ml toilet water. 2 bottles alcohol and 12 cans beer.
Bulgaria	200 cigarettes or 50 cigars or 250g tobacco. 1 litre spirits. 2 litres wine. 100g perfume.
Burkina Faso	200 cigarettes or 25 cigars or 100 cigarillos or 250g tobacco. 1 litre spirits. 1 litre wine. 500ml toilet water. 250ml perfume.
Burundi	1000 cigarettes or 1 kg tobacco. 1 litre alcohol. Reasonable quantity perfume
Cambodia	200 cigarettes or equivalent in cigars/tobacco. 1 bottle spirits. Reasonable quantity perfume.
Cameroon	400 cigarettes or 50 cigars or 5 pk. tobacco. 1 bottle alcohol. 1 bottle perfume
Canada	See Customs Regulations at beginning of section.
Cayman Islands	200 cigarettes or 50 cigars or 225g tobacco. 1 litre spirits or 4 litres wine.
Central African Rep.	1000 cigarettes or cigarillos or 250 cigars or 2kg tobacco. 5 bottles alcohol. 5 bottles perfume.
Chad	400 cigarettes or 125 cigars or 500g tobacco. 3 bottles wine. 1 bottle spirits.
Chile	400 cigarettes. 500g tobacco. 50 large cigars or 50 small cigars. 2.5 litres alcohol. Reasonable quantity perfume.
China	400 cigarettes (600 for stays over 6 months). 2 litres alcohol. Reasonable quantity perfume.
Colombia	200 cigarettes. 50 cigars. 500g tobacco. 2 bottles alcohol. Reasonable quantity perfume.
Congo	200 cigarettes or 1 box cigars or tobacco. 1 bottle alcohol. Reasonable quantity perfume.
Cook Islands	200 cigarettes or 50 cigars or 250g tobacco. 2 litres spirits or wine or 4.5 litres beer. Goods to value NZ$250.
Costa Rica	500g tobacco products. 3 litres alcohol. Reasonable quantity perfume.
Côte d'Ivoire	200 cigarettes or 25 cigars or 250g tobacco or 100 cigarillos. 1 bottle wine. 1 bottle spirits. 500ml toilet water. 250ml perfume.
Croatia	200 cigarettes or 50 cigars or 250g tobacco. 3 litres wine. 1 litre spirits. 250cl eau de cologne. 1 bottle perfume.
Cuba	400 cigarettes or 50 cigars or 250g tobacco. 3 litres alcohol. Good to value US$100 and 10kg medicines.
Cyprus	200 cigarettes or 50 cigars or 250g tobacco. 1 litre spirits. 750cl wine. 300ml perfume. Good to value C£50.
Czech Republic	200 cigarettes or equivalent. 1 litre spirits. 2 litres wine. 500ml perfume. Goods to value Kc1000 for non-residents.
Denmark	**Travellers from EU country with duty paid goods from EU country:** 300 cigarettes or 150 cigarillos or 75 cigars or 400g tobacco. 1.5 litres spirits or 20 litres sparkling wine. 90 litres table wine. Beer no limit. **Travellers from non-EU countries with goods purchased outside an EU country:** 200 cigarettes or 1000 cigarillos or 50 cigars or 250g tobacco. 500g coffee. 100g tea. 1 litre spirits. 2 litres wine. 50g perfume. 250ml toilet water
Djibouti	As for France.
Dominica	200 cigarettes or equivalent. 2 litres alcohol.
Dominican Republic	200 cigarettes or 1 box cigars. 1 bottle alcohol to the value US$5. 2 bottles perfume.
Ecuador	200 cigarettes or 50 cigars or 200g tobacco. 1 litre alcohol. Reasonable amount perfume.
Egypt	200 cigarettes or 25 cigars or 200g tobacco. 1 litre alcohol. Reasonable amount perfume. 1 litre eau de cologne. Goods to value E£500.
El Salvador	200 cigarettes or 50 cigars. 2 litres alcohol. Reasonable amount perfume. Goods to value US$500.
Equatorial Guinea	200 cigarettes or 50 cigars or 250g tobacco. 1 litre wine. Reasonable amount perfume.
Eritrea	A reasonable number of items for personal use.
Estonia	200 cigarettes or 20 cigars or 250g tobacco. 1 litre spirits. 1 litre wine. 10 litres beer.
Ethiopia	100 cigarettes or 50 cigars or 225g tobacco. 1 litre alcohol. 2 bottles perfume. Goods to value Birr10.
Falkland Islands	A reasonable amount of tobacco and alcohol.

Fiji	500 cigarettes or 500g tobacco. 2 litres spirits or 4 litres wine/beer. Goods to value F$400
Finland	300 cigarettes or 400g tobacco. 200 cigarette papers. 1 litre spirits or 3 litres aperitifs. 15 litres beer. 5 litres of alcohol under 22% vol.
France	**Travellers from EU countries with duty paid goods:** 800 cigarettes and 400 cigarillos and 200 cigars and 1kg tobacco. 90 litres wine. 10 litres spirits. 20 litres fortified wine or vermouth. 110 litres beer.
	Travellers from non-EU countries: 200 cigarettes or 100 cigarillos or 50 cigars or 250g tobacco. 2 litres wine. 1 litre spirits. 50g perfume. 250ml toilet water. Goods to value FFr1200.
French Guyana	As for France
Gabon	200 cigarettes or 50 cigars or 250g tobacco. 2 litres alcohol. 50g perfume. Goods to value CFAfr5000.
The Gambia	200 cigarettes or 50 cigars or 250g tobacco. 1 litre spirits. 1 litre wine. Goods to value D1000.
Georgia	250 cigarettes 05 250g tobacco. 1 litre spirits. 2 litres wine. Reasonable quantity perfume.
Germany	**Travellers from EU countries with duty paid goods:** 800 cigarettes and 400 cigarillos and 200 cigars and 1kg tobacco. 90 litres wine. 10 litres spirits. 20 litres fortified wine or vermouth. 110 litres beer.
	Travellers from non-EU countries: 200 cigarettes or 100 cigarillos or 50 cigars or 250g tobacco. 2 litres wine. 1 litre spirits >22% or 2 litres <22%. 50g perfume or 250ml toilet water. Goods to value ECU175.
Ghana	400 cigarettes or 100 cigars or 454g tobacco. 0.75 litre wine. 227ml perfume
Gibraltar	200 cigarettes or 10 cigarillos or 50 cigars pr 250g tobacco. 2 litres fortified wine or 1 litre spirits or 2 litres wine. 50g perfume and 250ml toilet water. Goods to value Gib£32.
Greece	**Travellers from EU countries with duty paid goods:** 800 cigarettes and 400 cigarillos and 200 cigars and 1kg tobacco. 90 litres wine. 10 litres spirits. 20 litres fortified wine or vermouth. 110 litres beer.
	Travellers from non-EU countries or from EU countries with goods bought duty free: 200 cigarettes or 50 cigars or 100 cigarillos or 250g tobacco. 1 litre alcohol >22% or 2 litres wine. 50g perfume. 250ml toilet water. 500g coffee. 100g tea. Goods to value Dr25,000.
Greenland	200 cigarettes or 250g tobacco and 200 cigarette papers. 1 litre spirits or 2 litres fortified wine. 2 litres wine.
Grenada	200 cigarettes or 50 cigars or 225g tobacco. 1 litre alcohol.
Guadeloupe	As for France.
Guam	As for USA.
Guatemala	80 cigarettes or 99g tobacco. 1.5 litres alcohol. 2 bottles perfume.
Guinea Republic	1000 cigarettes or 250 cigars or 1kg tobacco. 1 bottle alcohol. Reasonable quantity perfume.
Guinea-Bissau	2.5 litres alcohol. Reasonable quantity tobacco. Reasonable quantity perfume
Guyana	200 cigarettes or 50 cigars or 225g tobacco. 570ml spirits. Reasonable quantity perfume.
Haiti	200 cigarettes or 50 cigars or 1kg tobacco. 1 litre spirits. Small quantity perfume for personal use.
Honduras	200 cigarettes or 100 cigars or 454g tobacco. 2 bottles alcohol. Reasonable quantity perfume. Goods to value US$1000.
Hong Kong	200 cigarettes or 50 cigars or 250g tobacco. 1 litre alcohol.
Hungary	200 cigarettes or 50 cigars or 250g tobacco. 1 litre spirits. 2 litres wine. 250ml perfume. Goods to value Ft3000.
Iceland	200 cigarettes or 250g tobacco. 1 litre spirits or 1 litre wine. 6 litres beer.
India	200 cigarettes or 50 cigars or 250g tobacco. 1 litre alcohol. 250ml toilet water. Goods to value Rs600.
Indonesia	200 cigarettes or 50 cigars or 100g tobacco. 2 litres alcohol (opened). Reasonable quantity perfume. Goods to value US$100.
Iran	200 cigarettes or equivalent. Perfume for personal use. Goods on which import duty does not exceed US$80.
Iraq	200 cigarettes or 50 cigars or 250g tobacco. 1 litre alcohol. 500ml perfume.

Iraq cont'd	Goods to value ID100 (less value of above items).
Ireland	**Travellers from EU countries with duty paid goods:** 800 cigarettes and 400 cigarillos and 200 cigars and 1kg tobacco. 10 litres spirits. 20 litres fortified wine or vermouth. 25 litres wine. 50 litres beer.
	Goods originating outside EU or duty free goods: 200 cigarettes or 100 cigarillos or 50 cigars or 250g tobacco. 1 litre spirits or 2 litres other alcohol <22%. 2 litres wine. 50g perfume. 250ml toilet water. Goods to value IR£142.
Israel	250 cigarettes or 250g tobacco. 1 litre spirits. 2 litres wine. 250ml eau de cologne or perfume. Goods to value US$125.
Italy	**Travellers from EU countries with duty paid goods:** 800 cigarettes and 400 cigarillos and 200 cigars and 1kg tobacco. 90 litres wine. 10 litres spirits. 20 litres fortified wine or vermouth. 110 litres beer.
	Travellers from non-EU countries or from EU countries with goods bought duty free: 200 cigarettes or 50 cigars or 100 cigarillos or 250g tobacco. 1 litre alcohol >22% or 2 litres wine. 50g perfume. 250ml toilet water. 500g coffee. 100g tea.
Jamaica	200 cigarettes or 50 cigars or 250g tobacco. 1 litre spirits. 2 litres wine. 340ml toilet water. 150g perfume.
Japan	400 cigarettes or 100 cigars or 500g tobacco. 3 bottles spirits. 57ml perfume. Goods to value Y200,000.
Jordan	200 cigarettes or 25 cigars or 200g tobacco. 1 bottle alcohol. Reasonable quantity perfume. Goods to value JD50/US$150.
Kazakhstan	400 cigarettes or 100 cigars or 500g tobacco. 2 litres alcohol. Reasonable quantity perfume. Goods to value US$5000 for personal use.
Kenya	200 cigarettes or 50 cigars or 225g tobacco. 1 bottle alcohol. 568ml perfume.
Korea (North)	Reasonable quantity tobacco and alcohol.
Korea (South)	200 cigarettes or 50 cigars or 250g tobacco. 1 litre alcohol. 2oz perfume. Goods to value W300,000.
Kuwait	500 cigarettes or 907g tobacco. No alcohol.
Kyrgyzstan	400 cigarettes or 100 cigars or 500g tobacco. 1 litre spirits. 2 litres wine. Reasonable quantity perfume. Goods to value US$5000 for personal use.
Laos	500 cigarettes or 100 cigars or 500g tobacco. 1 bottle spirits. 2 bottles wine. Reasonable quantity perfume.
Latvia	200 cigarettes or 20 cigars or 200g tobacco. 1 litre alcohol. Ls15 of food. Ls300 of new duty free goods. Ls225 other goods.
Lebanon	200 cigarettes or 200g cigars or 200g tobacco. (Jun 1 – Oct 31: 500 cigarettes or 500g tobacco). 1 litre alcohol. 60g perfume.
Lesotho	400 cigarettes. 50 cigars. 250g tobacco. 1 bottle alcohol. Reasonable quantity perfume.
Liberia	200 cigarettes or 25 cigars or 250g tobacco. 1 litre alcohol. 100g perfume. Goods to value US$125.
Libya	200 cigarettes or 250g tobacco or 25 cigars. Reasonable quantity perfume.
Liechtenstein	As for Switzerland.
Lithuania	200 cigarettes or 50 cigars or 250g tobacco. 1 litre spirits or 2 litres wine. Reasonable quantity perfume.
Luxembourg	**Travellers from EU countries with duty paid goods:** 800 cigarettes and 400 cigarillos and 200 cigars and 1kg tobacco. 90 litres wine. 10 litres spirits. 20 litres fortified wine or vermouth. 110 litres beer.
	Travellers from non-EU countries or from EU countries with goods bought duty free: 200 cigarettes or 50 cigars or 100 cigarillos or 250g tobacco. 1 litre alcohol >22% or 4 litres wine. 50g perfume. 250ml toilet water. Goods to value Luxfr1000.
Macau	Reasonable quantity of tobacco, alcohol and perfume for personal use.
Macedonia	1 box cigarettes. 1 bottle alcohol. Goods to value Den60.
Madagascar	500 cigarettes or 25 cigars or 500g tobacco. 1 bottle alcohol.
Malawi	200 cigarettes or 250g tobacco. 1 litre spirits. 1 litre wine or 1 litre beer. 50g perfume. 250ml toilet water.
Malaysia	200 cigarettes or 50 cigars or 225g tobacco. 1 litre alcohol. Perfume to value M$200. Goods to value M$200.
Maldives	Reasonable quantity tobacco and other goods.

Mali	1000 cigarettes or 250 cigars or 2kg tobacco. 2 bottles alcohol. Reasonable quantity perfume.
Malta	200 cigarettes or 50 cigars or 250g tobacco. 1 litre spirits. 1 litre wine. 10ml perfume. 125ml toilet water. Goods to value Lm50.
Martinique	As for France.
Mauritania	200 cigarettes or 25 cigars or 450g tobacco. 50g perfume.
Mauritius	250g tobacco. 1 litre spirits. 2 litres wine or beer. 100ml perfume. 250ml toilet water.
Mexico	400 cigarettes or 50 cigars or 250g tobacco. 3 litres wine or spirits. Reasonable quantity perfume. 1 still camera. 1 portable film/video camera. 12 unexposed rolls of film/video cassettes for each camera. Goods to value of US$300.
Mongolia	200 cigarettes. 2 litres alcohol. Reasonable quantity perfume.
Montserrat	200 cigarettes or 50 cigars. 1.14 litres alcohol. 168g perfume. Goods to value EC$250.
Morocco	200 cigarettes or 50 cigars or 250g tobacco. 1 litre spirits. 1 litre wine. 50g perfume.
Mozambique	200 cigarettes or 250g tobacco. 500ml spirits. Reasonable quantity perfume.
Myanmar	400 cigarettes or 100 cigars or 250g tobacco. 1.136 litres alcohol. 500ml perfume.
Namibia	400 cigarettes or 50 cigars or 250g tobacco. 1 litre spirits. 2 litres wine. 50ml perfume. 250ml toilet water. Goods to value NAD50,000 including above.
Nepal	200 cigarettes or 50 cigars. 1 litre alcohol or 12 cans beer. Reasonable quantity perfume.
Netherlands (The)	**Travellers from EU countries with duty paid goods:** 800 cigarettes and 400 cigarillos and 200 cigars and 1kg tobacco. 90 litres wine. 10 litres spirits. 20 litres fortified wine or vermouth. 110 litres beer. **Travellers from non-EU countries or from EU countries with goods bought duty free**: 200 cigarettes or 50 cigars or 100 cigarillos or 250g tobacco. 1 litre alcohol >22% or 2 litres fortified wine. 2 litres wine. 60g perfume. 250ml toilet water. Goods to value G125.
New Caledonia	200 cigarettes or 50 cigars or 250g tobacco. 1 bottle alcohol. Reasonable quantity perfume.
New Zealand	See Customs Regulations at beginning of section.
Nicaragua	200 cigarettes of 500g tobacco. 3 litres alcohol. 1 bottle perfume.
Niger	200 cigarettes or 100 cigarillos or 25 cigars or 250g tobacco. 1 litre spirits. 1 litre wine. 250ml perfume. 500ml toilet water.
Nigeria	200 cigarettes or 50 cigars or 200g tobacco. 1 litre spirits. 1 litre wine. Small quantity perfume. Goods to value N300.
Norway	**Residents of European countries:** 200 cigarettes or 250g tobacco. 200 cigarette papers. 1 litre spirits and 1 litre wine or 2 litres wine and 2 litres beer. Goods to value NKr1200. **Residents of non-European countries:** 400 cigarettes or 500g tobacco. 200 cigarette papers. 1 litre spirits and 1 litre wine or 2 litres wine and 2 litres beer. Goods to value NKr1200.
Oman	Reasonable quantity tobacco. 227ml perfume.
Palau	200 cigarettes or 454g tobacco. 2 litres alcohol.
Pakistan	200 cigarettes or 50 cigars or 500g tobacco. 250ml perfume. Still and/or video camera with film.
Panama	500 cigarettes or 50 cigars or 500g tobacco. 3 bottles alcohol. Perfume for personal use.
Papua New Guinea	200 cigarettes or 50 cigars or 250g tobacco. 1 litre alcohol. Reasonable quantity perfume. Goods to value Kina200.
Paraguay	Reasonable quantity tobacco, alcohol and perfume for personal use.
Peru	400 cigarettes or 50 cigars or 500g tobacco. 2 litres alcohol. Reasonable quantity perfume.
Philippines	400 cigarettes or 50 cigars or 250g tobacco. 2 litres alcohol.
Poland	250 cigarettes or 50 cigars or 250g tobacco. 0.235 litre white vodka/pure alcohol or 0.5 litre spirits or 2 litres wine.
Portugal	**Travellers from EU countries with duty paid goods:** 800 cigarettes and 400 cigarillos and 200 cigars and 1kg tobacco. 90 litres wine. 10 litres spirits.

Portugal cont'd	20 litres fortified wine or vermouth. 110 litres beer. **Travellers from non-EU countries or from EU countries with goods bought duty free:** 200 cigarettes or 50 cigars or 100 cigarillos or 250g tobacco. 1 litre alcohol >22% or 2 litres fortified wine. 2 litres wine. 60g perfume. 250ml toilet water. Goods to value Esc7500.
Puerto Rico	As for USA.
Qatar	454g tobacco. Perfume to value QR1000. No Alcohol.
Romania	200 cigarettes or 200g tobacco. 1 litre spirits. 4 litres wine/beer. Goods to value Lei200.
Russian Federation	1000 cigarettes, cigars or grams of tobacco. 2 litres alcohol Reasonable quantity perfume. Goods to value US$1000.
Rwanda	200 cigarettes or 50 cigars or 454g tobacco. 2 bottles alcohol. Reasonable quantity perfume.
St Kitts & Nevis	200 cigarettes or 509 cigars or 225g tobacco. 1.136 litres alcohol. 170ml perfume.
St Lucia	200 cigarettes or 250g tobacco. 1 litre alcohol.
St Vincent & The Grenadines	200 cigarettes or 50 cigars or 225g tobacco. 1.136 litres alcohol.
São Tomé e Príncipe	Reasonable quantity of tobacco. Alcohol and perfume in opened bottles.
Saudi Arabia	600 cigarettes or 100 cigars or 500g tobacco. Perfume for personal use. No alcohol.
Senegal	200 cigarettes or 50 cigars or 250g tobacco. Reasonable quantity perfume. Goods to value CFAfr5000.
Seychelles	200 cigarettes or 50 cigars or 250g tobacco. 2 litres alcohol. 200ml perfume. Goods to value SRs1000.
Sierra Leone	200 cigarettes or 225g tobacco. 1.136 litres alcohol. 1.136 litres perfume.
Singapore	1 litre spirits. 1 litre wine. 1 litre beer. Food items to value S$50. No chewing gum.
Slovak Republic	200 cigarettes or 100 cigarillos or 50 cigars or 250g tobacco. 1 litre spirits. 2 litres wine. 50g perfume or 250ml toilet water. Goods to value Sk3000.
Slovenia	200 cigarettes or 50 cigars or 250g tobacco. 1 litre spirits. 2 litres wine. 50ml perfume. 250ml toilet water. Goods to value US$100.
Solomon Islands	200 cigarettes or 250g cigars or 225g tobacco. 2 litres alcohol. Goods to value SI$40.
Somalia	400 cigarettes or 40 cigars or 400g tobacco. 1 bottle alcohol. Reasonable quantity perfume.
South Africa	400 cigarettes. 50 cigars. 250g tobacco. 1 litre spirits. 2 litres wine. 50ml perfume. 250ml toilet water. Goods to value R500.
Spain	**Travellers from EU countries with duty paid goods:** 800 cigarettes and 400 cigarillos and 200 cigars and 1kg tobacco. 90 litres wine. 10 litres spirits. 20 litres fortified wine or vermouth. 110 litres beer. **Travellers from non-EU countries or from EU countries with goods bought duty free:** 200 cigarettes or 50 cigars or 100 cigarillos or 250g tobacco. 1 litre alcohol >22% or 2 litres fortified wine. 2 litres wine. 50g perfume. 250ml toilet water. Goods to value Pta5000.
Sri Lanka	200 cigarettes or 50 cigars or 375g tobacco. 1.5 litres spirits. 2 bottles wine. Small quantity or 250ml toilet water.
Sudan	200 cigarettes or 50 cigars or 225g tobacco. Reasonable quantity perfume. No alcohol.
Suriname	400 cigarettes or 100 cigars or 200 cigarillos or 500g tobacco. 2 litres spirits. 4 litres wine. 50g perfume. 1 litre toilet water. 8 rolls of unexposed film. 60m unexposed cine film. 100m unrecorded tape. Goods to value of SG40.
Swaziland	400 cigarettes. 50 cigars. 250g tobacco. 1 bottle alcohol. 50ml perfume . 250ml toilet water. Goods to value E200.
Sweden	**Non-EU residents:** 200 cigarettes or 100 cigarillos or 50 cigars or 250g tobacco. 1 litre spirits or 2 litres wine. 15 litres beer. **EU residents:** 300 cigarettes or 150 cigarillos or 75 cigars or 400g tobacco. 1 litre spirits or 3 litres fortified wine. 5 litres wine. 15 litres beer.
Switzerland	**Non-EU residents:** 40-0 cigarettes or 100 cigars or 500g tobacco. 2 litres alcohol (<15%). 1 litre alcohol (>15%). Goods to value SFr100.

Syria	200 cigarettes or 25 cigars or 250g tobacco or 50 cigarillos. 0.570 litre spirits 500ml lotion. 500ml eau de cologne.
Tahiti	200 cigarettes or 50 cigars or 100 cigarillos or 200g tobacco. 2 litres spirits >22% vol. 2 litres wine. 50g perfume. 250ml toilet water.. Goods to value CFPFranc5000.
Taiwan	200 cigarettes or 25 cigars or 454g tobacco. 1 bottle alcohol. Goods to value NT$20,000 for personal use.
Tajikistan	400 cigarettes or 100 cigars or 500g tobacco. 2 litres alcohol. Reasonable quantity perfume. Goods to value US$5000.
Tanzania	200 cigarettes or 50 cigars or 250g tobacco. 1 litre alcohol. 250ml perfume.
Thailand	200 cigarettes or 250g cigars/tobacco. 1 litre alcohol. 1 still camera and 5 rolls film. 1 movie camera with 3 rolls of 8 or 16mm film.
Togo	100 cigarettes or 50 cigars or 100 cigarillos or 100g tobacco. 1 bottle spirits. 1 bottle wine. 250ml perfume. 500ml toilet water.
Trinidad & Tobago	200 cigarettes or 50 cigars or 250g tobacco. 1.5 litres alcohol. Goods to value TT$1200.
Tunisia	400 cigarettes or 100 cigars or 500g tobacco. 1 litre spirits >25% vol. 2 litres alcohol<25% vol. 250ml perfume. 1 litre toilet water. 2 cameras and 20 rolls film. 1 video camera and 20 cassettes. 1 radio cassette player. Goods to value TD100.
Turkey	200 cigarettes or 50 cigars or 200g tobacco and 200 cigarette papers or 50g chewing tobacco or 200g pipe tobacco or 200g snuff. 5 litre alcohol. Reasonable amounts or tea and coffee. 5 bottle perfume. Goods to value DM500.
Turkmenistan	Subject to change.
Uganda	200 cigarettes or 25g tobacco. 1 bottle alcohol. 268ml perfume.
Ukraine	200g tobacco. 1 litre spirits. 2 litres wine. Goods to value US$1400.
United Arab Emirates	2000 cigarettes or 400 cigars or 2kg tobacco. 2 litres spirits. 2 litres wine. Reasonable amount perfume for personal use.
United Kingdom	See Customs Regulations at beginning of section.
USA	See Customs Regulations at beginning of section.
Uruguay	**Travellers from Argentina, Bolivia, Brazil, Chile or Paraguay:** 200 cigarettes or 25 cigars or 250g tobacco. 1 litre alcohol. 2kg foodstuffs. **All others:** 400 cigarettes or 50 cigars or 500g tobacco. 2 litres alcohol. 5 kg foodstuffs.
Uzbekistan	400 cigarettes or 100 cigars or 500g tobacco. 2 litres alcohol. Reasonable quantity perfume. Goods to value US$10,000.
Venezuela	200 cigarettes. 25 cigars. 2 litres alcohol. 4 small bottles perfume.
Vietnam	200 cigarettes or 50 cigars or 250g tobacco. 1 bottle alcohol. Reasonable quantity perfume.
Yemen	200 cigarettes or 50 cigars or 225g tobacco. 2.2 litres alcohol. 568ml perfume.
Yugoslavia	200 cigarettes or 50 cigars or 250g tobacco. 1 litre alcohol. Reasonable quantity perfume. 250ml toilet water.
Zaire (DRC)	100 cigarettes or 50 cigars or equivalent tobacco. 1 bottle alcohol. Reasonable quantity perfume.
Zambia	400 cigarettes or 500g tobacco. 1.5 litres spirits. 2.5 litres wine. 2.5 litres beer. 1oz perfume. US$150.
Zimbabwe	Inclusive of tobacco and perfume, goods to value Z$2000. 5 litres alcohol. No honey.

WORLD-WIDE VOLTAGE GUIDE

In general, all references to 110V apply to the range from 100V to 160V. References to 220V apply to the range from 200V to 260V. Where 110/220V is indicated, voltage varies within country, depending on location.

An adaptor kit may be necessary to provide prongs of various types that will fit into outlets which do not accept plugs from the traveller's own country. A converter is also necessary where the voltage differs from that of the traveller's electrical appliances. Plugging an electrical appliance manufactured to 110V into a 220V outlet without using a converter may destroy the appliance and blow fuses elsewhere in the building. A special adaptor will probably be necessary for electronic items such as computers. Check with the manufacturer. Plugging straight in could wipe the memory.

Afghanistan	220V
Algeria	110/220V
Angola	220V
Anguilla	220V
Antigua	110/220V
Argentina	220V
Aruba	110V
Australia	220V
Austria	220V
Azores	110/220V
Bahamas	110/220V
Bahrain	220V
Bangladesh	220V
Barbados	110/220V
Belgium	110/220V
Belize	110/220V
Benin	220V
Bermuda	110/220V
Bhutan	220V
Bolivia	110/220V
Bonaire	110/220V
Botswana	220V
Brazil	110/220V Y
British Virgin Is	110/220V
Bulgaria	110/220V
Burkina Faso	220V
Burundi	220V
Cambodia	110/220V
Cameroon	110/220V
Canada	110/220V
Canary Islands	110/220V
Cayman Islands	110V
Central African Rep	220V
Chad	220V
Channel Islands	220V*
Chile	220V Y
China	220V
Colombia	110V

Costa Rica	110/220V
Côte d'Ivoire	220V
Cuba	110V
Curacao	110V
Cyprus	220V Y
Czech Republic	110/220V
Denmark	220V
Dominica	220V
Dominican Rep	110/220V
Ecuador	110/220V
Egypt	110/220V
El Salvador	110V
Ethiopia	110/220V
Fiji	220V
Finland	220V
France	110/220V
French Guiana	110/220V
Gabon	220V
Gambia	220V
Germany	110/220V
Ghana	220V
Gibraltar	220V
Greece	110/220V
Greenland	220V
Grenada	220V
Grenadines	220V
Guadeloupe	110/220V
Guatemala	110/220V
Guinea	220V
Guyana	110/220V
Haiti	110/220V
Honduras	110/220V
Hong Kong	220V*
Hungary	220V
Iceland	220V
India	220V Y
Indonesia	110/220V
Iran	220V
Iraq	220V
Ireland	220V
Isle of Man	220V
Israel	220V
Italy	110/220V
Jamaica	110/220V
Japan	110V
Jordan	220V
Kenya	220V
South Korea	220V
Kuwait	220V
Laos	110/220V
Lebanon	110/220V
Lesotho	220V
Liberia	110/220V
Libya	110/220V
Liechtenstein	220V
Luxembourg	110/220V
Macao	110/220V

Madagascar	220V
Madeira	220V Y
Majorca	110V
Malawi	220V
Malaysia	110/220V
Mali	110/220V
Malta	220V
Martinique	110/220V
Mauritania	220V
Mexico	110/220V
Monaco	110/220V
Montserrat	220V
Morocco	110/220V
Mozambique	220V
Myanmar	220V
Nepal	220V
Netherlands	110/220V
Nevis	220V
New Caledonia	220V
New Zealand	220V
Nicaragua	110/220V
Niger	220V
Nigeria	220V*
Norway	220V
Oman	220V
Pakistan	220V
Panama	110V
Papua New Guinea	220V
Paraguay	220V Y
Peru	220
Philippines	110/220V
Portugal	110/220V
Portugal	110V
Qatar	220V
Romania	110/220V
Russia	110/220V
Rwanda	220V
St. Barthèlemy	220V
St. Eustatius	110/220V
St. Kitts	220V
St. Maarten	110/220V
St. Vincent	220V
Saudi Arabia	110/220V
Senegal	110V
Seychelles	220V
Sierra Leone	220V
Singapore	110/220V*
Slovakia	110/220V
Somalia	110/220V
South Africa	220V
Spain	110/220V
Sri Lanka	220V
Sudan	220V
Suriname	110/220V
Swaziland	220V
Sweden	110/220V Y
Switzerland	110/220V
Syria	110/220V
Tahiti	110/220V
Taiwan	110/220V
Tanzania	220V

Togo	110/220V
Tonga	220V
Trinidad and Tobago	110/220V
Tunisia	110/220V
Turkey	110/220V
Turks & Caicos	110V
Uganda	220V
Uruguay	220V
UAE	220V
United Kingdom	220V*
USA	110V
US Virgin Islands	110V
Vanuatu	220V
Venezuela	110/220V
Vietnam	110/220V
North Yemen	220V
South Yemen	220V
The Former Yugoslavia	220V
Zaire (DRC)	220V
Zambia	220V
Zimbabwe	220V*

Denotes countries in which plugs with 3 square pins are used (in whole or part).

Y Countries using DC in certain areas. ∎

NOTES ON CONTRIBUTORS

Benedict Allen is an explorer and broadcaster. He made a BBC Video *Diary Raiders of the Lost Lake* in the Peruvian Amazon, presented *Mombasa to the Mountains of the Moon*, part of the More Great Train Journeys series for the BBC, and filmed a six part BBC series *The Skeleton Coast*, recording his journey with three camels through the Namib Desert.

Clive Anderson has presented many comedy TV programmes including the hugely successful *Whose Line Is It Anyway?* and has had his own comedy chat show both on Channel 4 and BBC1. He has also presented many travel documentary programmes including the series *Our Man In...* and one of the *BBC's Great Railway Journeys of the World* when he travelled in China and Hong Kong. He is a barrister by profession.

Sarah Anderson having travelled widely, founded the Travel Bookshop in London in 1979. She is author of *Anderson's Travel Companion* and now combines travelling with writing and painting.

Jeremy Atiyah is Travel Editor of *The Independent on Sunday* and co-author of the *Rough Guide to China.*

Nicholas Barnard specializes in writing on the tribal and folk arts, his books include: *Living with Kilims, Living with Decorative Textiles, Living with Folk Art and Traditional Indian Textiles,* published by Thames & Hudson, and *Indian Arts and Crafts,* published by Conran Octopus.

John Batchelor is a Fellow of the Royal Geographical Society. He has travelled extensively in Africa, with his wife Julie Batchelor who is a teacher, and they have co-authored several books, including *The Congo.*

Dr Nick Beeching is Senior Lecturer in Infectious Diseases at the Liverpool School of Tropical Medicine, and a Consultant at the Regional Infectious Disease Unit at Fazakerly Hospital in Liverpool. He and his young family have travelled widely, and he has worked in India, Australia, New Zealand and the Middle East.

Simon Beeching is Managing Director of WEXAS International and co-founder of the environmental consultancy *Travelwatch.* He has an MA in Modern Languages from Jesus College, Oxford and studied Business Administration at INSEAD in France. He is a fellow of the Institute of Travel and Tourism and of the Royal Geographical Society.

Prof. David Bellamy is one of the world's leading environmentalists. Campaigning for the preservation of areas of special interest throughout the world, from Tasmania to the Lake District, he has written countless books, made numerous television programmes and also set up his own charity, The Conservation Foundation.

Col John Blashford-Snell is founder of Operations Drake and Raleigh, and leader of countless expeditions world-wide.

Dominic Boland is past editor of *Practical Photography, British Photographic Industry News,* and *Professional Photographer* magazines and has written, lectured and broadcast extensively in the UK on photography and video. As a travel photographer, recent assignments have included Mexico, the West Indies and the Canary Islands.

Chris Bonington, the eminent mountaineer, was the first to climb the Southwest face of Everest in 1975.

Lt. Col Peter Boxhall is an explorer, writer and Arabist. He has worked in the Arab world for many years, including posts as PA to the Mayor of Jeddah, and Director of Save the Children Fund in Jeddah. He writes for many publications, and has led a number of expeditions.

Matthew Brace is a freelance travel journalist specialising in environmentally aware tourism.

Hilary Bradt divides her time between leading trips in South America, East Africa and Madagascar, and writing and publishing guide books for independent travellers.

Cathy Braithwaite has worked for the Saga Group, which specialises in travel for the elderly.

Caroline Brandenburger was the editor of *Traveller* magazine between 1991-1996. She has also written several books including *Establishment Wives* and *Around the World in 80 Ways* and previously edited *The Traveller's Handbook*.

Roger Bray was Travel Editor of *The Evening Standard* and is now a freelance writer.

Greg Brookes has, since 1963, interspersed periods of full-time study with teaching in Europe and Africa where he is widely travelled.

Tania Brown has a degree in Linguistics from Lancaster University. She speaks fluent German, French and Spanish and worked for two years as an administrator before resigning to join Keith Kimber on a trip round the world. They left in 1983, and were last reported in Cyprus in 1991.

Warren Burton joined Encounter Overland in 1980, having travelled extensively in Asia, Middle East, Europe and North America. He spent four years leading expeditions throughout Asia, Africa and South America, before taking on his present position as the company's Operation Manager.

Tony Bush is editor of *Export Times*, the international trade and finance magazine, and also author of the *Business Travel Planner* (Oyez).

Roland Butler is the marketing assistant and cataloguer at Stanford's travel bookshop in London. He has two years experience of travel literature.

Gill Cairns is a freelance writer and associated with the London Buddhist Centre.

Simon Calder is Travel Editor for *The Independent*. Author of *Hitch-hikers Manual* — Britain and Europe – a manual for hitch-hikers, plus several guides in the Travellers Survival Kit series.

John Carlton is a keen walker and backpacker. An active member of the YHA for over 36 years, he has worked in the travel trade for the same period. He has visited most countries in Western and Eastern Europe, Morocco, Canada and the USA.

Roy Carter writes on corporate security and risk management for the international business and professional press. He has lectured on related subjects at Loughborough University. He is a former Head of Consultancy for an international group of security companies.

Roger Chapman, MBE, FRGS, was commissioned into the Green Howards after completing a Geography degree at Oxford and a spell at Sandhurst. He has been involved in many expeditions — down the Blue Nile and Zaire Rivers, to Central and South America, to East Greenland with the British Schools Exploration Society, and to Papua New Guinea with Operation Drake, to name a few.

David Churchill writes regularly on business travel for *The Times* and *The Sunday Times*.

Nicholas Crane has cycled in 29 countries. His charity fund-raising trips Bicycles up Kilimanjaro and Journey to the Centre of the Earth were undertaken with cousin Richard Crane for Intermediate Technology. He has worked for Afghan Aid in the Hindu Kush mountains, and written and co-written seven books. He also made the TV journey *Atlas Biker* for Central TV and National Geographic Films. He works as a journalist, contributing regularly to *The Sunday Times* and *The Daily Telegraph* newspapers and is President of the Globetrotters Club. He recently walked the length of Europe.

Ingrid Cranfield edited three earlier editions of this book. A freelance writer and broadcaster, she is a Fellow of the Royal Geographical Society.

Jill Crawshaw is a travel expert, writer and broadcaster. She has won the Travel Writer of the Year award three times and is a regular columnist for *The Times*.

Quentin Crewe is a writer (author of many books, most recently *A World Guide to Food*), traveller, sometime restaurateur. He has been in a wheelchair since boyhood.

Sheila Critchley is a Canadian journalist now based in London, and has run an airline in-flight magazine.

Dr. Richard Dawood is the author of *How to Stay Healthy Abroad* (OUP). A leading expert on travel health, he contributes a regular column to *Traveller* magazine and is Health Editor of the American magazine *Condé Nast Traveler*.

René Dee was a regular soldier in the Intelligence Corps, serving in Singapore and Malaysia. In 1967, after leaving the army, he travelled overland to India and Nepal, and then led a series of trips to Morocco, specialising in treks by camel and mule.

Christina Dodwell is an inveterate traveller, horsewoman, writer, and microlight pilot. She has written a number of books, most recently *Beyond Siberia*, published by Hodder & Stoughton .

John Douglas, author and photographer, is a former Army officer who has travelled solo and with expeditions through Asia, Africa and the Arctic. He is the author of *Creative Techniques in Travel Photography*, and a director of Geoslides Photo Library.

Doris Dow became a single expatriate in Central Africa, married, and spent 24 years there before returning to the UK. By profession a secretary and teacher, she is actively involved with the Women's Corona Society in London.

Peter Drake has led or been a member of 26 expeditions visiting 55 countries. He was a member of the British Mountaineering Council Training Committee, chairman of the Expedition Advisory Centre at the Royal Geographical Society and Chairman of the Expedition and Training Committee of the Young Explorers Trust.

Col. Andrew Duncan retired from the International Institute for Strategic Studies in 1995. He now works as a Defence Analyst and Commentator.

Tim Ellerby is the Operations Manager of Stanfords, the world's largest map and travel bookshop.

Sir Ranulph Fiennes Bt. was commissioned into the Royal Scots Greys in 1963, and attached to the 22 SAS Regiment in 1966. He has led several major expeditions, including the Transglobe Expedition which lasted three years. Author of ten books, he has been awarded the Founders Medal of the Royal Geographical Society and the Polar Medal with Bar from the Queen.

Michael Furnell has been involved with property journalism for many years; he edited *Homefinder* magazine, and in 1963 founded *Homes Overseas*, the monthly specialist periodical for people wishing to buy homes abroad. He is the author of *Living and Retiring Abroad*.

Adrian Furnham is a lecturer in psychology at London University. He holds degrees from the Universities of London, Strathclyde, and Oxford, and is particularly interested in applied and medical psychology. He is the co-author with Prof. F. Bochner of *Culture Shock: Psychological Consequences of Geographic Movement* (Methuen).

Jon Gardey grew up in California, and has lived in Alaska, Switzerland and England. He is a writer, traveller, and film-maker.

Sarah Gorman trained as a journalist on provincial newspapers before moving to Hong Kong where she worked as News Editor of the Education Desk on the Hong Kong Standard. She has travelled widely and edited *Traveller* magazine between 1989 and 1991. She now lives in New York, where she works as a travel writer.

Jan and Rupert Grey have undertaken many journeys to the remoter parts of the world, both before and after having children. They travelled through the interior of Borneo with their two eldest children, and wrote a number of articles about their experiences.

Susan Griffith is a Canadian based in England who writes books for working travellers such as *Work Your Way Around the World* and *Teaching English Abroad.*

Susan Grossman is a former travel editor of *The Telegraph Magazine*, a presenter of the BBC *Food and Drink* Programme, and now editor of BUPAS's *Upbeat* magazine, and *The Best of Britain Guide* (Redwood).

Miranda Haines is editor of *Traveller* magazine and the 8th edition of *The Traveller's Handbook*. Previously she worked for the *International Herald Tribune* in Paris for two years before becoming a freelance journalist in London, specialising in travel and business journalism.

Robin Hanbury-Tenison, OBE, is a well-known explorer, author and broadcaster who has taken part in many major expeditions in South America, Africa and the Far East. He is also founder and President of Survival International, the organisation that seeks to prevent the extinction of the world's remaining tribal groups.

Diana Hanks of the Timeshare Council, has worked in consumer relations for many years, particularly in the field of tourism.

Nick Hanna is a freelance journalist and has been travelling in the tropics intermittently for the past twelve years. His features and photographs have appeared in *The Sunday Times*, *The Guardian* and *Harpers & Queen* amongst many others. Author of the *BMW Tropical Beach Handbook* (Fourth Estate), and *The Greenpeace Book of Coral Reefs*.

Sir David Hannay was a diplomat for 36 years. He served in Tehran, Kabul, Brussels, Washington and New York and has travelled widely elsewhere. He retired in 1995 after spells as Britain's Ambassador to the European Union and the United Nations.

Bryan Hanson is an executive member of the Globetrotters Club and former editor of the club magazine, and has travelled extensively.

Richard Harrington is a widely travelled freelance travel writer.

Lucy Hone is a freelance travel writer specialising in up-market travel and is author of *The Good Honeymoon Guide* (Trailblazer).

Ian Irvine is a registered insurance broker, specialising in insurance for adventure and overland travellers.

Jack Jackson is an experienced expedition leader and overland traveller, explorer, mountaineer, author, photographer, lecturer and diver. He is co-author with Ellen Crampton of *The Asian Highway* (Angus and Robertson) and author of *The Four Wheel Drive Book* (Gentry).

Dr. Jay Kettle-Williams BA, M Litt, FIL, is National Marketing Executive for Richard Lewis Communications, responsible for the Foreign Language Division. He is also Editor of *The Linguist*, the journal of the Institute of Linguists.

Keith Kimber has a degree in Electronics from Southampton University and worked for four years as an electronics engineer before resigning his job and selling everything to travel at the age of 25, with Tania Brown, on a 500cc Honda motorbike.

Robin Knox-Johnston, CBE, RD, was the first man to sail single-handed non-stop around the world in 1968-9, completing the journey in 313 days. He was World Class II Multihull Champion in 1985, and is author of many books on sailing. More recently he set the world record for sailing round the world in a catamaran. He is the author of numerous books on sailing, including *History of Yachting* 1990.

Samantha Lee is a freelance journalist and writer, based in London and Scotland.

David Learmount joined the Royal Naval College, Dartmouth, from school in 1965, was briefly an airline steward with British Airways where he learned to fly in his time off, and then joined the RAF for ten years where he worked as a transport pilot and a flying instructor. He has worked at Flight International for eleven years where he is Air Transport Editor, and is an expert in flight safety.

Tony Leonard is a freelance writer and a regular contributor to *Gay Times*.

Colin McElduff is a Fellow of the Royal Geographical Society, the Royal Anthropological Institute and the Society of Antiquaries (Scotland). In India, Burma and Africa, during the war, he later joined the Colonial Police Service, serving in Malaya, Cyprus, Nigeria and Borneo. In 1965 he returned to the UK and worked for the Royal Automobile Club. He is now retired.

Julian McIntosh lived in Africa for several years, and has travelled extensively. His overland experiences prompted him to set up his own specialist tropical equipment firm.

Stephen McLelland is editor of *Telecommunications Magazine*.

Alex McWhirter has worked in the travel business since he left school, and is now Travel Editor of *Business Traveller* magazine. He has travelled widely in North America, Australia, Europe, the Middle East and Far East.

Paul Melly writes on foreign news, business and travel, for *Export Times*, *The Guardian*, *Africa Analysis* and *The Scotsman* amongst others.

George Monbiot is a writer, broadcaster and campaigner for the environment and threatened tribal peoples. The author of the *Poisoned Arrows, Amazon Watershed* and *No Man's Land*, all published by Macmillan. He is a Visiting Fellow of Green College, Oxford.

Dervla Murphy is a committed independent traveller, and author of many highly successful travel books including *The Road to Coorg*, *Cameroon with Egbert* and *The Ukimwi Road*.

Carey Ogilvie is an experienced traveller, most recently in Kamchatka. She also drove a Fire Engine from Cape North in Norway to Cape Agulhas in South Africa to raise money for the Samaritans. She is co-author of *Around the World in 80 Ways*, published by WEXAS.

Michael Palin established his reputation with *Monty Python's Flying Circus* and has made several films including *A Private Function* and *American Friends*. He also gave an award winning performance for his portrayal of Ken in *A Fish Called Wanda*. Latterly, he has become more well known as a traveller and is the author of two travel books that recount his expeditions; *Around the World in 80 Days* and *Pole to Pole*. He has also made two films for the BBC's *Great Railway Journeys* series.

Chris Parrott has lived in France, Singapore, Spain and Brazil, as well as travelling extensively in Europe, the Middle East and the Americas. He is now a director of Journey Latin America.

Tony Pearson has made a serious academic study of outdoor equipment. He worked for several years at Field and Trek Ltd, and is now a freelance consultant to the outdoor equipment trade.

Tony Peisley is a freelance journalist specialising in the cruise industry. He is also a regular contributor for the TV programme *Wish You Were Here*.

Robin Perlstein is a Registered Dietician who has worked at the British Diabetic Association, where she was Assistant in the Diabetes Care Department and was involved in writing and giving advice in many areas relating to diabetes.

Christopher Portway has been a freelance travel writer for nearly twenty years, is the author of several books and recently, aged 70, cycled from the Baltic to the Black Sea.

Paul Pratt has been a ship's radio officer in the British Merchant Navy and an electronics engineer in Britain and Scandinavia. His interest in motorcycles began with cross-country sporting trials and he now claims the longest continuous journey in motorcycle history which, between 1966 and 1979, took him through 48 countries, a distance of nearly 165,000km. His book of the trip is called *World Understanding on Two Wheels*.

Philip Ray has been a journalist for the whole of his career, specialising in writing about the airline and travel businesses for the past 21 years. He was Deputy Editor of *Travel News*, the weekly UK travel trade newspaper, until he switched to freelance writing and market research consultancy.

Kent Redding is from Texas, but after travelling through Europe, the Middle East and Africa, now works in London as a journalist.

Annie Redmile has been a journalist specialising in aviation subjects for over twenty years.

David Richardson is a freelance journalist specialising in the travel industry.

John Rose was the Principal at the Customs Directorate Division E Branch 4, HM Customs and Excise.

Martin Rosser is a freelance writer and self-professed vagabond. His writing and travelling have taken him to Africa, Australia and Europe.

Andrew Sanger, journalist and editor, is a frequent contributor to the travel pages of several national newspapers and magazines, among them *The Guardian, The Daily and Sunday Telegraph*, and the *Sunday Express*. He has written a number of popular guidebooks, including *The Vegetarian Traveller* (Grafton).

Dave Saunders is a freelance journalist in the photographic press, having edited a number of magazines and written and illustrated several books.

Douglas Schatz is Director and General Manager of Stanfords, the world's largest map and travel bookshop.

Gilbert Schwartz, a teacher and veteran traveller, spent over a year researching and compiling his book *The Climate Advisor* (Climate Guide Publications, New York) which has had several printings.

Chris Scott has biked in the Sahara and West Africa several times, describing his trips in *Desert Travels* (Travellers Bookshop). He also contributes to Rough Guides and has recently produced an overlanding guide for motorcyclists: *The Adventure Motorbiking Handbook* (Compass Star).

Melissa Shales edited *Traveller* magazine for five years and since 1987 has worked as a freelance travel writer and editor. Widely travelled in Africa and Europe, she is a Fellow of the Royal Geographical Society and a member of the British Guild of Travel Writers. She is also the editor of two previous editions of this book.

Anne Sharpley now deceased, was a journalist and travel writer, and won awards as Woman Journalist of the Year, and Descriptive Writer of the Year.

David Shenkin is the Higher Executive Officer at the Customs Directorate 4D, HM Customs.

Ted Simon rode a Triumph 500cc motorcycle round the world, between 1973 and 1977. He travelled extensively in America, Latin America, Australia and Asia, and his book on the journey is *Jupiter's Travels* (Hamish Hamilton).

Anthony Smith is a zoologist by training, and a writer, broadcaster and presenter of television programmes, including the *Wilderness* series on BBC Television. His first expedition was to Iran with an Oxford University team in 1950. Since then he has ridden the length of Africa on a motorcycle, written an account of the Royal Geographical Society/Royal Society Mato Grosso Expedition of 1967, and built and flown hydrogen-filled balloons and airships. He was co-founder of the British Balloon and Airship Club, and involved with the RGS Expeditions Committee.

Richard Snailham read Modern History at Oxford and was a teacher until 1965, when he became a Senior Lecturer at the Royal Military Academy, Sandhurst. He has been on expeditions to the Middle East, Africa, Asia and South America. He is a co-founder of the Scientific Exploration Society, author of several books, and is actively involved with the Young Explorer's Trust and Operation Raleigh.

Daniel Start led the Lorentz '95 conservation expedition to Irian Jaya, Indonesian New Guinea. The group, together with the consultants from WWF and Unesco were kidnapped and held hostage for four months by the Free Papua Movement in 1996. He is the author of *The Open Cage* (Harper Collins), an account of his experiences as a hostage.

Harry Stevens is a businessman running his own engineering and electronics company, which often takes him abroad.

Keith Strickland is a civil servant, and an expert on train travel. He is author of the *Steam Railways Around the World* (Alan Sutton Publishing).

Dr. Mike Stroud specializes in the effect of physical extremes on the body and is attached to the Army Personnel Research Establishment at Farnborough. He recently made Polar history with Sir Ranulph Fiennes by completing the longest unsupported journey in the Antarctic.

Mike Thexton is a chartered accountant whose life took an unexpected turn in 1986 when he was trapped on a hi-jacked aeroplane.

Max Thorowgood is a barrister and a veteran inter-rail traveller.

Sarah Thorowgood is a freelance editor and armchair traveller.

Sir Crispin Tickell GCMG, KCVO, is Warden of Green College, Oxford; Chancellor of the University of Kent at Canterbury; Chairman of the Climate Institute of Washington, DC; Director of the Green College Centre for Environmental Policy and Understanding Initiative. Sir Crispin was a member of the Diplomatic Service and is author of *Climatic Change and World Affairs* (1977 and 1986), and *Mary Anning of Lyme Regis* (1996). His interests are wide-ranging and include business and charities. More personally he cherishes mountains, pre-Colombian art and palaeo-history.

Edwina Townsend has worked in the travel trade for twenty years and is now the Customer Relations Officer at WEXAS International.

Isabella Tree is travel correspondent on *The Evening Standard*, and is currently writing a book about her travels in Papua New Guinea.

Clive Tully is an expert and well-known writer on outdoor clothing and equipment. His work regularly appears in walking magazines and national newspapers.

Hugo Verlomme author of *Travel by Cargo Ship* (Cadogan), is a French journalist and writer and has written several books, fiction and non-fiction, around the sea.

Myfanwy Vickers is a traveller, writer and radio producer.

Paul Vickers is a designer and freelance journalist based in Paris.

Paul Wade is a freelance travel writer and broadcaster for publications and radio stations in the UK and USA. Despite searching out regional dishes wherever he goes, he is still reasonably slim.

Debbie Warne is the Sales Support Manager for WEXAS International and has eleven years experience of negotiating airline fares.

Steve Watkins is a photo-journalist specialising in adventure travel.

Steve Weinman was editor of *BBC Worldwide Magazine*, the magazine of the World Service.

Stafford Whiteaker is author of *The Good Retreat Guide* (Rider Books).

Ralph Whitmarsh is Head of the Passport and Visa Section at Thomas Cook in London.

Arnie Wilson is skiing correspondent of *The Financial Times*, and author of *Tears in the Snow*, an account of his record-breaking 365 consecutive days on skis with Lucy Dicker in 1994.

Nigel Winser is Deputy Director of the Royal Geographical Society and has been responsible for a number of RGS expeditions.

Shane Winser is Information Officer of the Royal Geographical Society and its Expedition Advisory Centre. She studied Zoology and Information Science at London University, before helping her husband to organise scientific expeditions to Sarawak, Pakistan, Kenya and Oman. She writes a regular column, Frontiers, for *Geographical* Magazine.

Pat Yale is an associate lecturer in travel and tourism at a further education college in Bristol, and a freelance travel writer. She is the author of *The Budget Travel Handbook* and *From Tourist Attractions to Heritage Tourism*. She has travelled extensively through Europe, Africa, Asia and Central America, frequently alone, and always on a shoestring. ■

MAP OF THE WORLD

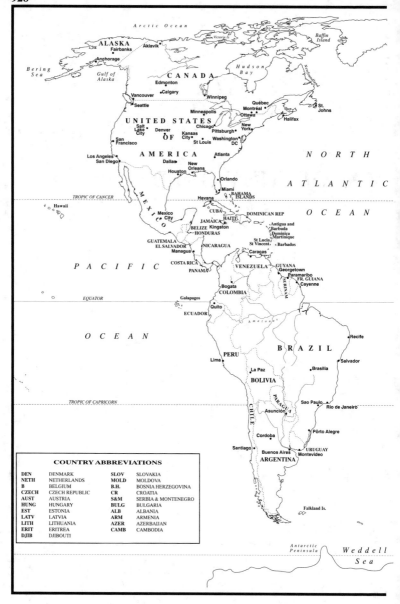

COUNTRY ABBREVIATIONS

DEN	DENMARK	**SLOV**	SLOVAKIA
NETH	NETHERLANDS	**MOLD**	MOLDOVA
B	BELGIUM	**B.H.**	BOSNIA HERZEGOVINA
CZECH	CZECH REPUBLIC	**CR**	CROATIA
AUST	AUSTRIA	**S&M**	SERBIA & MONTENEGRO
HUNG	HUNGARY	**BULG**	BULGARIA
EST	ESTONIA	**ALB**	ALBANIA
LATV	LATVIA	**ARM**	ARMENIA
LITH	LITHUANIA	**AZER**	AZERBAIJAN
ERIT	ERITREA	**CAMB**	CAMBODIA
DJIB	DJIBOUTI		

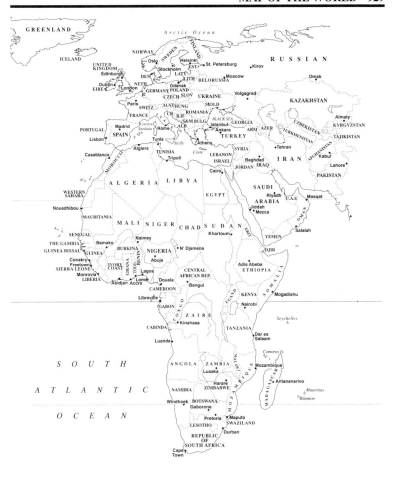

F E D E R A T I O N   Yakutsk

Bering
Sea

Omsk

Irkutsk

KAZAKHSTAN

Ulaanbaatar

MONGOLIA

Vladivostok

Almaty

KYRGYZSTAN

N.KOREA

JAPAN

UZBEKISTAN

Beijing

Pyongyang

TURKMENISTAN

TAJIKISTAN

Seoul

C H I N A

S.KOREA

Tokyo

AFGHANISTAN

Kabul

Shanghai

Lahore

T I B E T

PAKISTAN

Khatmandu

P A C I F I C

Delhi

NEPAL

Dacca

Masqat

T'ai-pei

I N D I A

Hanoi

O C E A N

OMAN

MYANMAR

Hong
Kong

Bombay

LAOS

Salalah

Yangdon

THAILAND

VIETNAM

Bangkok

PHILIPPINES

Manila

CAMB.

Ho Chi Minh

SRI
LANKA

Nicobar Is.

Colombo

M A L A Y S I A

Maldives

Kuala
Lumpur

Singapore

BORNEO

I N D I A N

SUMATRA

Jakarta

NEW
GUINEA

SOLOMON
ISLANDS

BALI

O C E A N

JAVA

TIMOR

PAPUA

Pt Moresby

Darwin

Mauritius

Réunion

Alice
Springs

NEW
CALIDONIA

A U S T R A L I A

Brisbane

Kalgoorlie

Perth

Sydney

Auckland

Canberra

NEW
ZEALAND

Melbourne

TASMANIA

Wellington

Hobart

Christchurch

INDEX

934

940

NOTES

FREE TRIAL OFFER
to the UK's leading travel club for independent travellers.

WEXAS, the publisher of The Traveller's Handbook, is the UK's leading travel club. With over 35,000 members world-wide, WEXAS offers you substantial money-saving travel benefits — see how you can save your subscription many times over:

- Scheduled airfares world-wide at reduced rates to and from London and other UK airports
- Global hotel discount programme with savings up to 68%
- Reductions on standard car rental rates up to 30%
- Discoverers' holidays to over 60 countries world-wide
- Customised Round-the-World itineraries
- Year-round travel insurance for only £75 (1997 price)
- Discounted airport car parking
- FREE International SOS Assistance
- London Hotel Supersavers programme
- Update newsletter on fares and tours every quarter
- FREE subscription to *Traveller,* the prestigious colour magazine
- Exclusive brochures detailing WEXAS services
- Membership Card with unique ID numbers providing access to hotel and car rental discounts world-wide
- Discounts on local tours and sightseeing world-wide
- Telephone reservations service on members-only numbers
- Commission FREE travellers' cheques services and foreign currency
- Health information and discounts at BA Travel Clinics

SAVE 50%

As a reader of The Traveller's Handbook you will also receive a discount of 50% on your first year's WEXAS membership if you complete the enquiry coupon provided.

*COMPLETE THE INSERTED CARD AND **POST TODAY** FOR FULL DETAILS OF MEMBERSHIP AND FREE TRIAL OFFER*

Please send me, by return and without obligation, your **FREE** brochure **(Postage FREE if mailed in UK)**

NAME(Mr/Mrs/Ms)_____

ADDRESS_____

_____

The UK's Premier Travel Club　　　　　　　　　　N152